Classical Mythology

IMAGES AND INSIGHTS

Second Edition

Stephen L. Harris
Gloria Platzner
California State University, Sacramento

MAYFIELD PUBLISHING COMPANY

Mountain View, California

London • Toronto

Library of Congress Cataloging-in-Publication Data

Harris, Stephen L.
    Classical mythology : images and insights /
Stephen L. Harris, Gloria Platzner.—2nd ed.
        p.   cm.
    Includes bibliographical references and index.
    ISBN 1-55934-826-7
    1. Mythology, Classical.   I. Platzner, Gloria.
    II. Title.
    BL722.H38   1997
    292.1'3—dc21   97-5388
                                                CIP

Manufactured in the United States of America
10   9   8   7   6   5   4   3   2

Mayfield Publishing Company
1280 Villa Street
Mountain View, CA 94041

Sponsoring editor, Kenneth King; production editor,
Julianna Scott Fein; manuscript editor, Margaret Moore;
design and art manager, Jean Mailander; text designer,
Donna Davis; cover designer, Linda Robertson; cover
image, Museo Gregoriano Profano/Vatican Museums/
Art Resource; illustrator, Joan Carol; photo editor, Brian
Pecko; manufacturing manager, Randy Hurst. The text
was set in 10/12 Garamond by G & S Typesetters, Inc.,
and printed on acid-free 45# Chromatone Matte by Banta
Book Group.

Acknowledgments and copyrights continue at the back of
the book on pages 992–993, which constitute an exten-
sion of the copyright page.

Preface

New to This Edition

The second edition of *Classical Mythology: Images and Insights* has been extensively revised to make readers' exploration of Greek and Roman myths easier and more enjoyable. Besides adding color photos of both ancient and modern art works depicting gods and heroes, we have included more of Ovid's tales of love, loss, and change, inserted pronunciation guides for all major terms and characters, and reorganized several chapters.

The new edition offers expanded coverage of the historical background of Greek myth, including its affinity with ancient Near Eastern narratives such as the Gilgamesh epic, fuller discussions of Hesiod, Homer, and the principal Olympian deities, as well as a more unified approach to the wine god Dionysus, his relation to Greek drama, and the concept of the tragic hero. Euripides's powerful drama of the irrational, the *Bacchants,* is now integrated into the section on the Dionysian theater (Chapter 13).

Our portrait of the primal Great Goddess—a controversial deity whom many anthropologists believe dominated prehistoric European religion—appears earlier in the second edition, juxtaposing her legacy with the rise of Olympian Zeus and Hesiod's myth of the first woman, Pandora, whom the poet associates with humanity's decline from a primordial Golden Age. Both the hero and his nemesis, Death and the Underworld, receive expanded coverage, including the incorporation of Plato's "Myth of Er" into the discussion of Hades's subterranean realm (Chapter 9). Every part of the book has been revised to make connections between different myths and their continuing relevance to human experience clearer and more accessible.

In addition to a generally chronological survey of the art and literature embodying Greco-Roman mythology, this textbook includes individual chapters on several of classical myth's most influential concepts and divinities. Besides presenting the Goddess culture, with its natural cycle of life, death, and rebirth, the new edition offers further examination of the hero's self-defeating quest for eternal fame, including additional accounts of heroic descents to Hades's kingdom. The sections on Apollo and Dionysus, the two sons of Zeus who represent the polar opposites of reason and passion inherent in both humans and gods, have also been revised to emphasize further the paradox and contrarieties that Greek myth expresses.

Because the Roman use of mythology differs significantly from the Greek, it is treated separately in Part 4. In "The World of Roman Myth," we examine the Roman tendency to adapt older Greek traditions to accommodate pragmatic national and political needs (Chapter 18). The contrasts between Aeneas (a paradigm of the ideal Roman citizen-soldier who sacrifices personal happiness to serve an empire he will not live to see) and Homer's Achilles (a glamorous but self-absorbed hero who fights only for his individual glory) help to illustrate qualitative differences between Greek and Roman values reflected in myth.

The final chapter surveys modern works of art and literature that reveal the continuing vitality of Greco-Roman mythology in our own time. Classical gods and heroes, although transformed by inevitable changes in time and culture, not only survive but flourish in the creative imagination of today's poets, painters, sculptors, playwrights, composers, and filmmakers. The discussion of modern artists has been updated to include additional art forms, such as dance (illustrated in photographs) and recent poetry, such as a newly published mythological text by the Irish poet Eavan Boland. The entire epic sweep of myth's evolution from its ancient Near Eastern roots to its contemporary flowering in America and Europe is thus encompassed in this single illustrated volume.

A Combination of Analysis and Readings

Classical Mythology remains the only one-volume introduction to Greek and Roman myth that combines the critical analysis of myth with generous selections of primary sources, many presented in their entirety. In this text, students encounter Zeus and Athene, Heracles and Medea—along with a vivid array of other divinities, heroes, and heroines—via the same path traversed by the Greeks themselves—the epic poems of Homer and Hesiod and the plays of Aeschylus, Sophocles, and Euripides.

Besides lengthy excerpts from Hesiod's *Theogony;* Homer's *Iliad* and *Odyssey;* the Homeric Hymns to Demeter, Apollo, and Dionysus; Virgil's *Aeneid;* and Ovid's *Metamorphoses*—all in modern translations—this book presents the full texts of eight tragedies: Aeschylus's *Prometheus Bound* and the three-part *Oresteia;* Sophocles's two Oedipus plays; and Euripides's *Medea* and the *Bacchants.* (Only the *Libation-Bearers,* because of copyright restrictions, is partly incomplete.)

Complementing the literary sources of Greek and Roman myth are more than 200 photographs of classical works of art depicting mythic characters and themes. *Classical Mythology* provides not only the poets' re-creation of their culture's traditions but also the painters' and sculptors' equally important insights into their mythical heritage. While reading Aeschylus's *Oresteia,* students can also study how Athenian vase painters, contemporaries of the playwright, responded to the drama's harrowing scenes of murder and revenge (Chapter 15). The adventures of Odysseus similarly inspired artistic renditions of the hero's struggles against gods and monsters (Chapter 12).

Pedagogical Features

To help students undertake their first systematic study of mythology, this book features several pedagogical devices. Each chapter begins with a "Key Themes" section that summarizes the main points discussed. All major names and concepts appear first in **boldface,** are given a pronunciation guide, and are concisely defined in an extensive glossary at the end of the book. The pronunciation guides also appear in the glossary. (Although translators employ a variety of transliterations of Greek and Latin names, we generally use the standard anglicized spelling provided by the *Oxford Companion to Classical Literature*.)

Besides providing a critical analysis of the particular myth under consideration, each chapter features "Questions for Discussion and Review" and a list of "Recommended Reading" referring students to the most accessible resources for further study. To give students the most recent information on important scholarly publications about individual topics, we have updated the chapter-by-chapter bibliography that appears at the back of the book—an essential aid for preparing oral reports or writing papers on classical myth.

Many of the maps, graphs, and illustrations include captions offering mini-essays on a particular god, hero, or other mythological subject, providing an informative counterpoint to the textual material. Finally, *Classical Mythology* has an extensive index, making it easy for students to look up individual names, terms, and topics. We have made every effort to revise this textbook to make it as "reader friendly" as possible and hope that these features will enhance students' enjoyment of ancient myths and their enduring relevance to our common human experience.

For instructors using the second edition, the publisher has issued a revised instructor's manual that includes numerous sample test questions and answers, detailed outlines of material covered in each chapter, informational boxes, and suggestions for teaching.

Acknowledgments

The authors are grateful to colleagues who used the first edition of *Classical Mythology* and offered extremely helpful suggestions to make the second edition even more effective. We wish particularly to thank Richard E. Clairmont, University of New Hampshire; Lisa Rengo George, Skidmore College; Patricia Marshall, University of Richmond; Betty Rose Nagle, Indiana University; Katherine Payant, Northern Michigan University; Louis Roberts, SUNY, Albany; Robert Sanborn, McHenry Co. College; Carl P. E. Springer, Illinois State University; Christina Stough, California State University, Long Beach; Elizabeth Wheeler, Nassau Community College; and J. E. Ziolkowski, George Washington University.

The authors also gratefully acknowledge the expert guidance provided by the project's original editor, Jim Bull, and his successor, Ken King. We also thank Julianna Scott Fein, the production editor, and Margaret Moore, who copyedited the manuscript.

Contents

PART THREE   The World of Classical Tragedy   421

PART FOUR The World of Roman Myth 779

PART FIVE The Western World's Transformations of Myth   911

PART ONE

The Universality of Myth

Introduction to the Nature of Myth

KEY THEMES

Like all world mythologies, Greek myths originated with anonymous story-tellers of the remote past and were transmitted orally for innumerable generations, a fluid process that produced many variations in stories about gods and heroes. Strongly influenced by the older traditions of ancient Egypt and Mesopotamia (modern Iraq), Greek myths apparently assumed their distinctive character during the Mycenaean period (about 1600–1100 B.C.). The oldest surviving Greek myths appear in the narrative poetry of Homer and Hesiod (eighth century B.C.) and the Homeric Hymns, *although some of the best known were preserved (and transformed) by the classical Athenian dramatists (fifth century B.C.). Distinguished by their humanism, anthropomorphism, and literary sophistication, Greek myths were later further modified by Roman authors, who typically adapted them for their own political and didactic purposes.*

Almost twenty-five hundred years ago, the people of Athens built a new marble temple to honor **Athene** [uh-THEE-nuh], the goddess of wisdom after whom their city was named. Dedicated to Athene Parthenos (the virgin), the Parthenon (Figure 1-1) was designed to house a colossal statue of Athene by the sculptor Phidias. Phidias also decorated the temple's two pediments (triangular gables under its peaked roof) with sculptures representing key scenes from Athene's myth.

The east pediment, over the Parthenon's main entrance, depicted one of the crucial moments in Greek mythology—the birth of Athene from **Zeus,** king of the gods. A modern reconstruction of this scene pictures an enthroned Zeus contemplating the daughter who has just sprung, clutching a warrior's spear and shield, from his head

FIGURE 1-1   A Reconstruction of the Parthenon and Associated Structures on the Acropolis. A conviction that the goddess Athene presided over and defended their city inspired the Athenians of the mid-fifth century B.C. to create an extraordinary work of classical architecture, the temple dedicated to Athene Parthenos (the virgin).

(Figure 1-2). Pictured behind Athene is an unlikely midwife, the god of fire and metalcraft, **Hephaestus** [he-FES-tuhs], who recoils from the ax blow he has boldly delivered to split Zeus's skull. Seated to Zeus's right is his wife **Hera,** who keenly observes her husband's latest display of power, his usurpation of the female's reproductive function.

In this version of Phidias's sculpture (based partly on a bas-relief shown in Figure 1-3), the entire family of Olympian gods—all brothers, sisters, wives, children, or mistresses of Zeus—has gathered to witness a typically mythical paradox. The god who upholds universal law has violated the natural order: the divine **patriarch** (the "father" or founder of a family, tribe, or clan) demonstrates that a male can give birth without the participation of a mother. Zeus, who has recently overthrown his own father and an older generation of gods, the Titans, to assume control of the universe, now proves that he has the will and capacity to reverse age-old processes and amaze even the gods.

Myth also credits Zeus with giving birth to a second child, his son **Dionysus** [dye-oh-NYE-suhs], god of wine and intoxication. In Figure 1-4, a Greek vase painter shows the infant Dionysus emerging from his father's thigh. In contrast to Athene, who is literally Zeus's brainchild, a manifestation of divine wisdom and the civilized intellect, Dionysus represents the expression of natural amoral impulses. Born not from Zeus's head but his "thigh," he is a god who combines sensuality and joy with savage aggression (chapters 8 and 13).

Whereas most of Zeus's innumerable children, both mortal and divine, are born in the ordinary way, these two images of Athene and Dionysus say much about Greek myth's presentation of the gods' complex, often contradictory natures. That a single deity can produce, by himself, two such different offspring—a virgin goddess whose

FIGURE 1-2   The Birth of Athene. In this modern reconstruction of the Parthenon's east pediment, the central figures of Zeus and Athene confront each other immediately after Athene, bearing a warrior's spear and shield, has burst from her father's head. The entire Olympian family of Zeus has gathered to witness the prodigy, including his disapproving wife Hera, who sits holding a royal scepter, indicating her position as queen of heaven. Partly visible behind Athene's shield is the figure of Hephaestus, god of fire and the forge, who has just split Zeus's skull with his ax and now appears torn between his satisfaction at having struck Zeus and his fear of Zeus's displeasure. The scene is rife with family resentments: Hera is outraged by her husband's preemption of her maternal function. According to Hesiod, she, without male aid, gave birth to Hephaestus, who is entirely her son and who typically takes his mother's part in her endless quarrels with Zeus. To the viewer's right is the seated figure of Zeus's powerful brother Poseidon, god of sea and earthquakes. At the extreme right, Apollo appears with his lyre, a musical instrument symbolizing his patronage of music, harmony, and the creative intellect. (*Acropolis Museum, Athens.*)

FIGURE 1-3   A drawing of the Madrid Puteal. This circular bas-relief, thought to depict the scene of Athene's birth that Phidias created for the Parthenon's east pediment, shows a recoiling Hephaestus behind Zeus's throne and Athene being crowned by the winged figure of Nike (Victory). As defender of the polis (city-state), Athene is also goddess of military victory through intelligent planning and strategy. Note that Zeus and Athene meet each other's gaze at the same eye level. The king of the universe is entranced by the daughter he has just produced—a brilliant image of the divine consciousness. For the Athenians, Zeus's unique relationship to Athene enhanced their prestige: the chief god's firstborn child was also their special protector and patron. (*Archaeological Museum, Madrid.*)

FIGURE 1-4 The Birth of Dionysus. The painting on this crater (large wine vessel) shows the infant Dionysus, god of wine and intoxication, emerging from Zeus's thigh and surrounded by figures representing participants in the ecstatic Dionysian cult (Chapter 8). Myth's insistence that both Athene's cool rationality and Dionysus's passionate sensuality derive from the same father-god conveys the Greek belief that both disciplined intellect and unrestrained emotion are part of the natural order and therefore equally divine. (*Museo Archeologico Nazionale, Taranto.*)

cool ingenuity and military cunning protect the Greek **polis** (city-state) and a bisexual god whose irrational passion can reduce civilized society to total disorder—suggests myth's power to integrate polar opposites. Among its many other functions, myth confronts and defines tensions such as those between Athene's hard-edged rationality and Dionysus's indulgent, potentially destructive emotionalism, recognizing that these seeming opposites express the contrarieties and conflicts inherent in existence. Both deities are necessary aspects of a cosmic whole encompassed in the Greek concept of divinity.

Characteristics of Myth

The Importance of the Supernatural

Although many myths focus on mortal heroes, such as the strongman Heracles or the overconfident Oedipus, supernatural beings are almost invariably present, even when operating invisibly behind the scenes. Greek myth shares with religion a conviction that the **cosmos** (world order) has a spiritual as well as a physical dimension and that human beings somehow participate in both spheres. The gods of myth, like those of most world religions, serve to inject meaning and purpose into a universe that can overwhelm the human mind with its painful complexities. To the Greeks, gods such as Zeus and Athene represent principles of equity, cosmic harmony, and wisdom, qualities that many contemporary faiths still honor as divine.

Myth and Dream Symbols

As universal as dreaming, mythmaking characterizes every known people and culture throughout the world. From prehistoric India and aboriginal Australia to Africa and

FIGURE 1-5   A Reconstruction of Phidias's Athene Parthenos. The Parthenon was built to house a cult statue of Athene that the sculptor Phidias created in ivory and gold. Approximately thirty-seven feet high, Phidias's rendition of Zeus's most formidable child, an embodiment of intellect and martial prowess, dominates the temple's lavish marble interior.

Polynesia, myths express the common experience of all humanity. Like the most vivid dreams, myths also have an intriguing connection with external reality. As dreams may combine elements from everyday life—familiar objects, routines, or persons— with fantastic actions in which the dreamer flies over mountaintops or is pursued by grotesque monsters, so myths create a fluid environment in which ordinary life expands to include extraordinary figures and actions that transcend the limits of nature.

Although nothing seems impossible in the mythic realm, even the most ostensibly illogical events are subtly grounded in the values, attitudes, and expectations that govern the society producing the myths. Athene's leaping forth, fully armed, from Zeus's head violates our sense of reality, but it makes good sense symbolically. In asserting that Zeus produced Athene from his own being, Greek myth issues a powerful statement about the supreme value of wisdom and its close relationship to divinity. Athenian artists like Phidias capitalized on this myth to promote their city's unique connection with the highest gods (Figure 1-5). As Athene is Zeus's favored offspring, so the city she protects enjoys a special relationship with the king of heaven. The dreamlike image of pure thought from the mind of god taking visible shape as Athens's supernatural patron also suggests myth's intimate connection with human social and political institutions. (See Chapter 3 for a fuller discussion of Athene's birth.)

Myth as Oral Tradition

As products of the creative imagination reacting to the material and psychological forces that shape human life, myths may have arisen almost as soon as language acquired sufficient flexibility to articulate them. No one knows exactly when or where the process of mythmaking originated, but it probably began in many widely separated regions of Africa, Asia, and Europe tens of thousands of years ago. Spectacular cave paintings of wild animals and hunting scenes discovered in France and elsewhere date from the late Pleistocene epoch (Ice Age) and may be the visual counterpart of tales spun by Paleolithic (Old Stone Age) storytellers.

The word *myth,* taken from the Greek *mythos,* literally means "utterance," or "something one says." **Myth** is commonly expressed as a story involving gods and/or heroes. Although some people today may equate myth with falsehood, modern scholars use the term more respectfully. Myth has a truth of its own that transcends mere fact. Conveying realities that cannot be verified empirically, ancient tales typically articulate a culture's worldview, including its understanding of life's goals and the dangers attending them.

In origin, myth was essentially an oral phenomenon, a product of the storyteller's art that was transmitted by word of mouth from generation to generation before being written down. In the process of oral transmission, myths became extremely fluid and open to spontaneous change at every retelling. As a result, most myths survive in several different, even contradictory, versions.

In ancient Greece, these differences were reinforced by the physical isolation of Greek city-states. Because many Greek settlements were separated by steep mountain ranges or inhospitable coastlines, each polis tended to develop its own variation of popular myths, commonly attaching them to tales about gods who honored their particular city, as Athene championed Athens, or to local heroes whose exploits enhanced the polis's reputation. Leading families of a given polis typically compiled genealogies linking them to famous leaders of the distant past, thus boosting their local prestige while perpetuating the ancestral hero's story. Citizens could point out to visitors the site where heroes such as Heracles, Orestes, or Oedipus had slain monsters, had died, or were buried. Whereas some tales remained of purely local interest, many others, spread abroad by sailors, merchants, and itinerant poets, eventually became part of the national heritage. Stories of gods serving similar functions and heroes performing similar feats commonly merged, with figures like Heracles gradually incorporating the stories of innumerable strongmen. Only by slow degrees were Heracles's labors fixed at twelve—a popular number in Greek mythology as well as in the Judeo-Christian Bible—and only over long periods of time were the identities, attributes, and number of the Greeks' principal gods (the twelve Olympians) also agreed upon. The form in which Greek myth comes to us is thus the end result of a long evolutionary process.

The Literary Character of Greek Myth

By the time that Greek myths were first incorporated into the poems of Homer and Hesiod during the eighth century B.C., they had been repeatedly modified and transformed by centuries of extemporaneous transmission. We do not know when Homer's *Iliad* and *Odyssey,* which had been composed orally, were first committed to writing; however, it was probably no later than the sixth century B.C. Because Greek poets typically took their people's traditional tales about gods and heroes as their principal subject matter, most of Greek myth survives in works of literature. In his discussion of Greek poetry, the philosopher Aristotle (384–322 B.C.) gives myth (*mythos*) a precise meaning, using it to denote the plot (the careful structuring of incidents) in a literary work. Literary myths typically involve conflict between major characters (such as that between Achilles and Agamemnon in the *Iliad*), which rises to a decisive crisis or climax and which is then finally resolved through some kind of accommodation or reconciliation.

In addition to the epic form, represented by Homer's *Iliad* and *Odyssey,* Greek authors invented or perfected other literary categories that made myth their chief topic. Writing in imitation of Homer, several (generally) anonymous poets later composed a series of hymns praising the twelve Olympians. Known collectively as the *Homeric Hymns,* they preserve important myths about the mother goddess Demeter, her daughter Persephone, the volatile Dionysus, and Apollo, god of healing and prophecy.

Next to the narrative poetry of Homer and Hesiod, our single most valuable source of Greek myth is the tragic drama, an art form that the Athenian playwrights brought to its fullest development during the fifth century B.C. The tragedies of Aeschylus, Sophocles, and Euripides and some comedies of Aristophanes borrow extensively from the older epic tradition, which the authors freely revise to express their individual understanding of myth's relevance to their own day.

In this text, we approach Greek myth in roughly chronological order, beginning in Part 2 with the earliest narrative traditions. This section opens with Hesiod's account of the world's origins, surveys the major gods, goddesses, and heroes, and concludes with Homer's epic poems about the Trojan War. In Part 3, we leap ahead several hundred years to the fifth century B.C. to examine myths transformed into dramatic works for the Athenian stage. Although the epic and dramatic forms contain the most memorable expressions of Greek myth, some lyric poetry, such as that by Sappho, Xenophanes, and Pindar, preserves numerous but brief references to mythological subjects. Of the Greek narrative poets after Homer, only Apollonius of Rhodes, in his *Argonautica,* has left a full account of an entire myth, the story of Jason's quest for the Golden Fleece.

Interestingly, the most comprehensive collection of Greek myths is not a literary composition by Homer or Sophocles, but a prosaic anthology of stories misnamed the *Library of Apollodorus.* Although this compendium of traditional tales is attributed to Apollodorus of Athens (c. 140 B.C.), scholars believe that it was actually compiled by an unknown hand two or three centuries later. The *Library* may have been composed as a sourcebook to aid Greek schoolchildren in learning their mythic heritage. Despite its lack of artistic flair, the *Library* is exceptionally valuable: arranging the myths in a generally chronological sequence, it begins with a creation story that largely parallels Hesiod's *Theogony* and narrates a wide range of heroic adventures, including those of such diverse figures as Bellerophon, Perseus, and Heracles. The *Library* closes with the Greek siege of Troy, traditionally regarded as the final great event in Greece's mythic past. As an epilogue to the Homeric legacy, the writer adds fascinating details about the aftermath of the Trojan War, recounting the death of Odysseus, the last of myth's great heroes.

Although the *Library* was probably written in the late first or early second century A.D., approximately thirteen hundred years after the traditional date of the Greek assault on Troy, this compendium is believed to contain versions of some myths that are much older than the time of their written composition. Unlike the poets, who were interested in reshaping the myths for their own artistic purposes, the *Library's* unknown author was chiefly interested in preserving them unchanged for posterity.

Pausanias, who wrote a *Guide to Greece* late in the second century A.D., was similarly concerned with recording ancient traditions. Devoting fourteen years to traveling throughout Greece, Pausanias describes what he personally saw and heard about the history, religious practices, and mythology of such important city-states as Athens, Thebes, and Sparta, as well as sacred institutions such as Apollo's Oracle at Delphi (Chapter 7). His detailed report provides insight into the varying beliefs, rites, and customs prevailing in different parts of late classical Greece.

At a slightly earlier date, the Greek historian and biographer Plutarch (c. A.D. 46– c. 120), best known for his *Parallel Lives* of eminent Greek and Roman leaders, recorded a number of local myths, particularly those of his native province Boeotia and nearby Delphi, where he served as a priest of Apollo. Plutarch explores some popular beliefs not usually addressed by the great poets in his "On the Cessation of Oracles," which contains a discussion of demons (*daimones*), invisible beings intermediate between gods and men.

Sagas and Folklore

Collections of narratives about a particular city or family, such as the many interconnected tales about Troy, Thebes, or Argos and their ruling dynasties, are called **sagas.** Greek dramatists, such as Aeschylus and Euripides, expanded the Trojan saga by composing numerous plays about the postwar adventures of both Greeks and Trojans, particularly the children of Agamemnon. Whereas legends and sagas typically recount the exploits of a military aristocracy (a Greek term referring to government by the "best people"), **folktales** relate the doings of more humble persons. In contrast to myths, which feature major gods of sky and earth, folktales, such as stories about greedy Midas and his golden touch, deal with the lesser figures of popular imagination, such as witches, elves, or fairies. **Folklore,** as the word implies, concerns the experiences of common folk and does not ordinarily include myth's characteristic preoccupation with the human spirit struggling against the limits of its own mortality. Some literary works based on myth, notably the *Odyssey,* also contain elements of folklore—giants, sorceresses, magic spells, and assorted monsters—as do tales of dragon-slaying heroes like Perseus. Some scholars, however, argue that attempts to differentiate between myth and other categories of traditional tales are misleading and that all nonhistorical Greek narratives should be classed as myths.

The Historical Origins of Greek Mythology

For the ancient Greeks, myth took the role of prehistory, providing traditions about their supposed ancestors in the extremely remote past. In the Greek view, the mythic past included everything from the world's beginnings to the aftermath of the Trojan War. Having few historical facts about this distant period, Greek storytellers typically regarded it as an almost magical era, qualitatively different from their own mundane time. It was an epoch in which gods communed more openly with human beings, appearing unexpectedly in their midsts and, frequently, making love to mortal women who then produced sons or daughters so outstandingly strong or beautiful that only a deity could have been their parent. After the last of the great heroes perished, however, the gods withdrew permanently to Mount Olympus, thereafter communicating with mortals only through dreams, visions, or oracles delivered at prophetic shrines such as Delphi. Most commonly, the gods remained silent or produced highly ambiguous "signs" of their intentions in the flight of birds, the rustling of leaves on a sacred oak, or the entrails of a sacrificial animal.

Myth's relation to history is as ambiguous and hotly debated among scholars as the most cryptic utterances of the Delphic Oracle. Some archaeologists believe that certain events—such as the siege and fall of Troy—no matter how embellished by the poets, have a basis in historical fact. During the nineteenth century, the amateur archaeologist Heinrich Schliemann excavated the traditional site of Troy, near the modern village of Hissarlik in northwestern Turkey. He discovered that the site contained the ruins of a series of Bronze Age cities, each built atop the rubble of its predecessor. Schliemann concluded that the ruin labeled Troy VII-A was the citadel Homer described in the *Iliad.* Some archaeologists argued that Troy VII-A was too puny to fit the Homeric description; however, recent surveys of the site indicate that the city destroyed about 1250–1200 B.C. was much larger and more impressively fortified than previously supposed. (Archaeologists' dating of Troy's fall is remarkably close to the traditional date, equivalent to 1184 B.C., that Greek scholars of Alexandria assigned to the event; see Figure 1-6.)

Schliemann also excavated the site of **Mycenae** [mye-SEE-nee], a late Bronze Age city over which Agamemnon, leader of the Greek forces against Troy, was said to have ruled. Schliemann discovered that Homer was correct in describing Mycenae as "rich in gold," for its royal tombs contained superbly crafted metalwork, including a gold death mask that may have belonged to one of Agamemnon's ancestors (Figure 1-7). If further investigations provide evidence that prehistoric Greeks did indeed capture Troy, the famous war may prove to be legendary rather than purely mythic. The term **legend** is commonly used to denote a tradition that has some nucleus of historical truth, as opposed to an account that is entirely fictional.

Ancient Near Eastern Sources of Greek Myth

Herodotus, a Greek historian of the fifth century B.C., reports that when a race of giants attacked Zeus and the other Olympians, the gods disguised themselves in animal form and fled to Egypt (*Histories,* Book 2). Aware that the ancient Egyptians pictured their gods as having the heads of birds, reptiles, or mammals—Horus ap-

Major Periods of Ancient Greek History

APPROXIMATE DATE	HISTORICAL EPOCH
c. 3000 B.C.	Beginnings of Minoan culture on Crete
c. 2200–1450	Middle Minoan palace culture on Crete
c. 2100	Probable arrival of Mycenaean Greeks in Greece
1600–1200	Development of Mycenaean palace culture in Greece, initially dependent on Cretan models
1450	Mycenaeans take over Minoan Knossos on Crete

Between 1250 and 1150 B.C., there was a breakdown of settled conditions in the eastern Mediterranean and Asia Minor.

c. 1220 B.C.	Destruction of Troy VII-A, the probable event that inspired traditions of the Trojan War and which may represent the last major enterprise of the Mycenaean Greeks
1200–1125 B.C.	Widespread destruction of Mycenaean sites in Greece; Mycenae falls c. 1150 B.C.
1100–1000	Invasion of Dorian Greeks (in myth, the return of the sons of Heracles); beginning of DARK AGES
1050–950	Migration of mainland Greeks to Aegean Islands and coast of Asia Minor; iron tools in use after 1050; period of crude geometric pottery
750–700	Age of Homer and Hesiod; production of epic poems

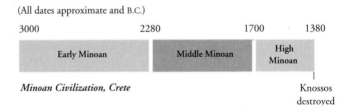

(All dates approximate and B.C.)

3000	2280	1700	1380
Early Minoan	Middle Minoan	High Minoan	

Minoan Civilization, Crete

Knossos destroyed

FIGURE 1-6   Minoan and Mycenaean Timelines. Although most Greek myths apparently originated during the Mycenaean period (c. 1600–1100 B.C.), some derive from the earlier Minoan culture on Crete. The last great events of Greek mythology concern the war against Troy and the homecomings of heroes such as Agamemnon, king of Mycenae, and Odys-

APPROXIMATE DATE	HISTORICAL EPOCH
	ARCHAIC AGE
600 B.C.	Renaissance in Ionia (Asia Minor); birth of primitive science and philosophy in Miletus
546	Pisistratus establishes tyranny at Athens
534	First tragedy competition held at Athens
510	Expulsion of Hippias from Athens; establishment of world's first democracy
490–479	PERSIAN WARS: Marathon (490); Salamis (480); Plataea and Mycale (479)
	CLASSICAL AGE (Golden Age of Pericles at Athens)
431–404 B.C.	Peloponnesian Wars between Athens and Sparta
406	Deaths of Euripides and Sophocles
338	Philip II of Macedonia conquers Athens and Thebes; end of Greek independence
336–323	Conquests of Alexander the Great, son of Philip II
	HELLENISTIC PERIOD
323 B.C.	Successors of Alexander rule eastern Mediterranean world and Near East
146	Rome conquers Greece: Corinth is destroyed and Macedonia becomes a Roman province

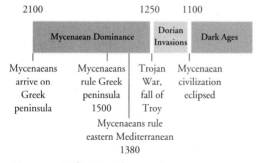

Mycenaean Civilization, Peloponnesus

seus, king of Ithaca (c. 1250–1200 B.C.). During the Dorian invasions, or infiltrations of the Greek peninsula, the Mycenaean urban centers were destroyed, plunging Greece into the Dark Ages.

FIGURE 1-7   Mycenaean Gold Death Mask. When the pioneer archaeologist H. Schliemann excavated the circular shaft graves at Mycenae, he found royal entombments that had miraculously escaped the
plundering of ancient grave robbers. Although Schliemann thought that
he had "looked upon the face of Agamemnon" when he discovered this
remarkable gold mask, he had actually found a funerary artifact belonging to one of Agamemnon's regal ancestors. (*National Museum, Athens.*)

pears as a falcon, Anubis as a jackal (Figure 1-8), and Hathor as a cow—Herodotus
presumes that the Greek deities, metamorphosed into divine beasts, could mingle
with their Egyptian counterparts safely unobserved. Herodotus's statement that the
Olympians temporarily took up residence in northeast Africa also reflects the Greeks'
view that their ideas about the gods were influenced by the older civilizations of the
ancient Near East, particularly Egypt and Mesopotamia.

Mesopotamia—the "land between the rivers"—is the name the Greeks assigned
to a region at the head of the Persian Gulf in what is now southern Iraq. In this flat,
swampy area near the mouths of the Tigris and Euphrates Rivers, the world's first
urban civilization was born. Shortly after 3500 B.C., a people called the Sumerians
founded the earliest cities, such as Ur, the native city of the biblical patriarch Abra-
ham, and Uruk, home to Gilgamesh, the first hero of Western myth. A remarkably
innovative group, the Sumerians produced a series of inventions that ranged from the
wheel, to the first law codes, to the art of writing.

FIGURE 1-8   Anubis, the Jackal-Headed God. Egyptians and other ancient Near Eastern peoples commonly depicted their gods in animal form. In this scene of posthumous judgment from a papyrus Book of the Dead, the jackal-headed god Anubis weighs the heart of an Egyptian princess against the figure of truth. Osiris, who was first a mortal king before becoming god of the Underworld, sits enthroned at the right. His sister-wife, Isis, stands behind the princess at the left. (*Metropolitan Museum of Art, New York. Rogers Fund.*)

The Invention of Writing

About 3200 B.C., the Sumerians devised a system of wedge-shaped symbols, known as **cuneiform** [kue-NEE-uh-form], which they used to record business transactions on clay tablets. When dried or baked, these inscribed tablets proved almost indestructible, surviving to the present in the tens of thousands. Although most cuneiform writing dealt with such matters as tax lists, inventories, or magical formulas, some tablets preserve ancient tales of gods and heroes that foreshadow themes and concepts that later appear in Greek myth.

Almost a millennium after the Sumerian invention of writing, Mesopotamia was invaded by a Semitic people known as the Akkadians. Assimilating the sophisticated Sumerian culture, including its cuneiform script, which they adapted to transcribe their own language, the Akkadians eventually established one of the ancient world's greatest cities, Babylon. Sumero-Akkadian beliefs about the world's origin, structure, and divine rulers proved to be enormously influential, shaping widely disseminated traditions about creation, a prehistoric global flood, and the dynamic interplay between gods and human beings. One version of these Mesopotamian myths about universal origins, transformed by Israelite monotheism, appears in the biblical Book of Genesis; another form of Sumero-Akkadian lore, reshaped by Greek poets, appears in such works as Hesiod's *Theogony,* an account of how the cosmos began (Chapter 3).

FIGURE 1-9   The Sumerians built the world's first skyscrapers, towers of sunbaked bricks known as ziggurats. In this artist's reconstruction of the ancient ziggurat at Ur, the chapel to Nanna, god of the moon, crowns the temple structure. These artificial mountains served as conduits connecting the human and divine realms, their ceremonial staircases providing the means by which gods descended to earth and mortals ascended to commune with them. (*The British Museum.*)

Mesopotamian Influences

Mesopotamian influence is particularly evident in four areas of the Greek mythological worldview, including beliefs about (1) the shape and structure of the universe; (2) the genealogical descent of the gods and their intergenerational conflicts; (3) the character and goals of the mythic hero; and, as a corollary of the heroic quest, (4) the growth of a pervasive tension between human aspiration for god-like immortality and the severe limits death imposes on human achievement. In the universe postulated by both Mesopotamian and Greek myth, human beings are permanently barred from the divine enjoyment of everlasting life, a condition that threatens to rob individual lives of real meaning (compare chapters 9 and 10).

When Greeks such as Herodotus visited Babylon or other Mesopotamian cities, they were commonly struck by the towering, multitiered structures that dominated the urban skyline. The most distinctive form of Sumero-Babylonian architecture, the **ziggurat** [ZIG-oo-rat] was a massive edifice of glazed brick crowned by a small chapel at the top, a shrine believed to house the individual deity to whom the building was dedicated. With broad staircases connecting its several levels, the ziggurat was, like the spire of a Christian cathedral, a visible link symbolically connecting humans on earth with invisible divinities inhabiting the sky (Figure 1-9).

Both biblical and Greek traditions echo aspects of the ziggurat's mythic function. In Genesis's Tower of Babel story, ambitious humans impiously erect a lofty tower by which they plan to invade heaven, only to have their misguided project overthrown

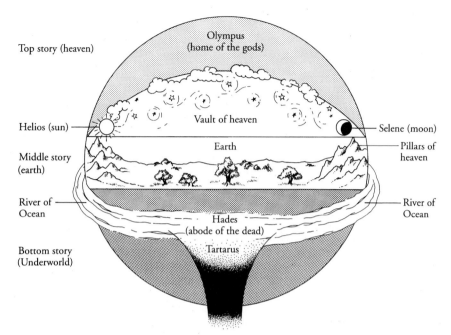

FIGURE 1-10   The "Three-Story Universe." Following ancient traditions from the Near East, Greek mythographers conceived of the earth as a massive disc surrounded by a watery waste, the circular River of Ocean. The physical heavens arched overhead like an inverted bowl, the edges of which were supported by mountainous pillars—or held up by Atlas, the mightiest Titan. The Olympian gods lived somewhere above the clouds. Beneath the earth lay the eternally dark kingdom of Hades, a vast subterranean cavern housing the dead. Tartarus, a deep pit beneath Hades's main level, served as a prison for fallen Titans and the souls of notorious sinners.

by God. In the Greek version of this myth, the giants Ephialtes and Otus try to enter the divine realm by piling one huge mountain on top of another—Pelion upon Ossa and Ossa upon Olympus—until Zeus destroys them. In another Genesis narrative, the patriarch Jacob dreams of a colossal "ladder" by which supernatural figures ascend to or descend from heaven. Historians believe that Jacob's dream more accurately pictures the ziggurat's purpose: rather than a means for humans to trespass into the gods' territory, the ziggurat served as an artificial mountain by which divine beings could visit earth and human beings could rise partway to meet them. A sacred place at which earth and heaven, the material and the spiritual, intersected, the ziggurat had a role resembling that of the Greek holy mountain of Parnassus, a sanctuary where Apollo revealed the gods' will to human questioners (Chapter 7).

The ziggurat, whose foundations lie beneath the earth's surface and whose pyramidal shape points toward heaven, is also a paradigm of the vertically structured universe. Like their Mesopotamian predecessors, the Greeks believed that we inhabit a vertical, three-story world (Figure 1-10). The top level, infinitely beyond human reach, is an invisible heaven where deathless gods enjoy a carefree existence, maintaining their eternal youth by dining on ambrosia and drinking nectar. Although called

Mount **Olympus** after the highest peak in Thessaly, this realm is usually envisioned as a celestial paradise vaguely located somewhere above the clouds. The Olympian gods may descend to earth by way of Mount Olympus, but their actual home occupies a loftier dimension (chapters 2 and 3).

The Olympian gods' bliss contrasts sharply with the harshness of life in the middle story—earth—where Fate assigns mortals an uneven mixture of joy and pain that inevitably ends in death. The cosmic basement is the kingdom of **Hades** [HAY-deez], named for Zeus's brother who reigns over the Underworld. A dank subterranean cavern, Hades's realm permanently houses all the dead, who exist only as disembodied shades flitting aimlessly in perpetual darkness. Pitiless Hades allows no one, except for a very few heroes, to escape from his gloomy dominion, effectively banishing all hope from the afterlife (Chapter 9).

Myths of Marduk and Zeus

Besides inheriting the concept of a three-tier cosmos, the Greeks adopted the Mesopotamian belief in a diverse **pantheon**—a religion's collective body of recognized gods—consisting of both male and female divinities, most of whom were associated with either the sky and weather or the Underworld and fertility. In addition, the Greeks inherited a tradition that the gods who ruled their world were not eternal, but were the younger descendants of primordial deities who had been displaced or overthrown. Both the Greek Zeus and the Babylonian **Marduk** were young male sky gods, forces of air and storm, who seized power by battling and defeating an older generation of divine beings. Anticipating Hesiod's poem of divine origins, the Babylonian creation account, the ***Enuma Elish,*** pictures a sequential evolution of deities who engage in violent conflict. In the *Enuma Elish,* the young Marduk—whom the Greeks readily identified with Zeus—slays Tiamat, the primordial dragon of chaos, just as in the *Theogony* Zeus kills Typhoeus, a reptilian monster of destruction.

Gilgamesh, the Western World's First Hero

As Zeus and Marduk prove their superior strength—and right to rule—by defeating terrifying embodiments of disorder, so the mythic hero demonstrates his value by fighting and killing monsters, threats to the human community. In the oldest surviving hero myth, the Sumero-Babylonian ***Epic of Gilgamesh,*** the title character battles such formidable opponents as the fire-breathing Humbaba and the voracious Bull of Heaven. In personal qualities, actions, and motivation, Gilgamesh establishes a pattern or model of the hero that appears throughout world myth. His story falls into two parts: in the first, which anticipates elements of Homer's *Iliad,* he takes the role of warrior, defending his city, Uruk, against destructive adversaries. Like the *Iliad*'s chief character, Achilles, Gilgamesh has a divine mother, the goddess Ninsun, from whom he presumably inherits his god-like strength and ambition. As in the case of Achilles, Gilgamesh is deeply bonded to a beloved friend and companion in heroic deeds, Enkidu, whose death marks the major turning point in his career.

The second part of the Gilgamesh myth, the hero's long journey in search of immortality, foreshadows Odysseus's heroic quest in the *Odyssey.* Like Odysseus, Gilgamesh has drawn the wrath of an angry deity: for rejecting the sexual advances of

Ishtar, goddess of love, fertility, and war, he is condemned to lose Enkidu, the event that sparks his departure from Uruk to find Utnapishtim, a distant ancestor who was the only man to survive a global flood and the sole mortal upon whom the gods bestowed immortality. Gilgamesh's perilous travels across the "waters of death," through a mythic terrain inhabited by grotesque creatures such as the scorpion men, to a faraway paradise where Utnapishtim lives, manifest some of the same fantastic strangeness that later surfaces in Homer's account of Odysseus's voyage. From Utnapishtim, Gilgamesh learns of the great prehistoric flood that the gods sent to drown all humanity, and which his ancestor survived by building an ark and taking pairs of animals and birds aboard. One version of the Mesopotamian flood story appears in the biblical Book of Genesis; the Greek account is preserved in the tale of Deucalion, the Hellenic counterpart of Noah and Utnapishtim (Chapter 6). After Utnapishtim tells him where to find the mysterious plant that restores youth and which a serpent then steals, Gilgamesh returns to Uruk, at last accepting the limits of human mortality.

Aspects of Gilgamesh's story resonate in the adventures of numerous Greek heroes. These motifs include the hero's divine parentage, royal status, personal courage, phenomenal strength, martial skill, insatiable ambition to accomplish extraordinary deeds, conflict with a divine adversary, pursuit of a quest for immortality, and a confrontation with death, typically in the guise of a visit to the Underworld. In many cases, the hero's tale will also take a circular form, his travels among unknown and dangerous domains being followed by a return to his place of origin, a pattern sometimes referred to as the "myth of the eternal return."

The Mycenaean Origins of Distinctively Greek Myth

Many significant elements of Greek myth derive from Near Eastern sources—and beyond that to remote and unrecoverable oral traditions extending far back into the Paleolithic era. Historians generally agree, however, that Greek myth began to assume its distinctive qualities during the mid-to-late Bronze Age, between about 1600 and 1100 B.C. In this period, mainland Greece was fragmented into numerous small kingdoms, characterized by heavily fortified hilltop citadels (Figure 1-11). This proto-Greek civilization is called **Mycenaean** [mye-see-NEE-uhn], named for the city Mycenae, which then politically dominated much of the Peloponnesian Peninsula. The art and architecture of Mycenaean cities (which included Tiryns, Pylos, and Sparta) were strongly influenced by contact with a remarkably creative older civilization, the **Minoan** [mih-NOH-an] civilization, which had developed on the island of Crete before about 2000 B.C. Named for **Minos** [MYE-nohs], king of Knossos—Crete's largest palace complex—the Minoan civilization attained a high level of material and artistic sophistication. Its sprawling palaces featured such amenities as beautifully painted frescoes, columned halls, and flushing toilets—a combination of domestic elegance and convenience not matched again until the age of imperial Rome (Figure 1-12). (For an overview of the Greek world, see Figure 1-13.)

A few Greek myths apparently go back to Minoan times, including the story of **Theseus** [THEE-see-uhs], a prince of Athens who found his way through the Labyrinth of King Minos's palace to slay the **Minotaur** [MIN-oh-tahr], a monster half-human and half-bull that resulted from Minos's wife's mating with a sacred bull.

FIGURE 1-11 The Lion Gate at Mycenae (c. 1300 B.C.). Unlike the Minoan palace complexes, Mycenaean cities were heavily fortified against attack. Originally, the carved lions—nine feet high—atop the huge stone slabs composing the city's main entryway probably had heads of bronze. After the collapse of Mycenaean civilization (about 1150 B.C.), later generations referred to such massive defensive walls as *cyclopean,* believing that only a race of giants, the Cyclopes, could have built them.

FIGURE 1-12 Ladies of the Minoan Court at Knossos. The beauty and elegance characterizing aristocratic life at the Minoan royal palaces are evident in this fresco from Knossos. A vast multistory structure extending over many acres, the Knossos palace was excavated by Sir Arthur Evans in the early twentieth century. (*Archaeological Museum Heraklion, Crete.*)

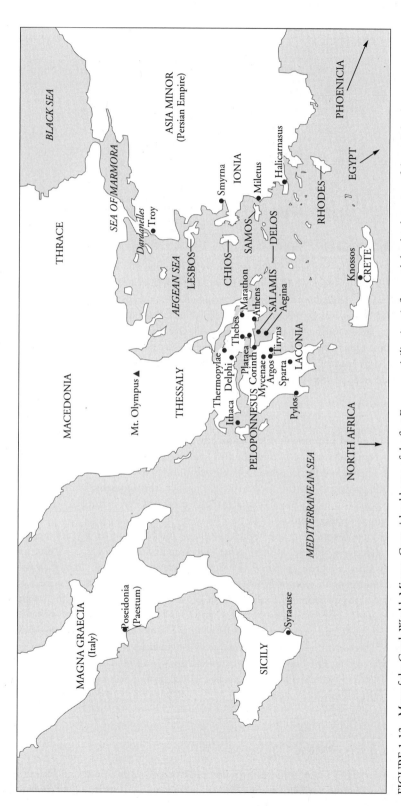

FIGURE 1-13 Map of the Greek World. Minoan Crete, island home of the first European civilization, influenced the development of the mainland Mycenaean culture, the earliest proto-Greek culture. Note the locations of Mycenae, Sparta, and Troy, cities that figure prominently in Greek myth.

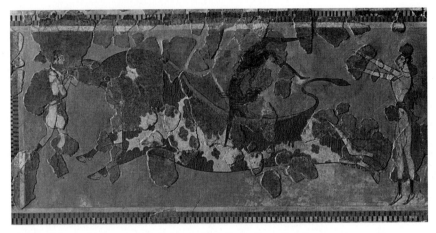

FIGURE 1-14   The Minoan Bull Dance. This fresco from the Minoan palace at Knossos shows both young women (white figures) and a young man (brown figure) participating in an apparently death-defying ritual involving a Cretan bull. Such rites may have given rise to the myth of the flesh-devouring Minotaur, half-man, half-bull. Bull horns carved in stone formed a dominant architectural motif at Knossos, suggesting that, for the Minoans, the bull represented a divine force. In Greek myth, Poseidon, god of the sea (over which the Minoans ruled), is represented by a bull. Poseidon is also the cause of earthquakes, which sporadically devastated Crete and other parts of the Aegean region. (*Archaeological Museum, Heraklion, Crete.*)

(The bull figured prominently in Minoan myth, architecture, and even sports; see Figure 1-14). Most of the famous myths, such as those involving the tragic royal family of Thebes and the Greeks' Trojan expedition, all reflect a civilization and way of life that vanished shortly after 1100 B.C., when the **Dorians,** a fierce Greek-speaking people from the north, swept through most of Greece, bringing the Mycenaean civilization to an end.

Rather than assimilating the higher culture of the Minoans or Mycenaeans, the Dorians effectively obliterated these proto-Greek civilizations, plunging Greece into the **Dark Ages,** a regressive period that lasted for several hundred years. Following the Dorian onslaught, refugees from Mycenaean cities fled east across the Aegean Sea and settled along the coast of Ionia, in what is now western Turkey. As the prosperity and material culture of these Greek settlements gradually improved—primarily through sea trade and commerce with older Near Eastern centers of culture—a distinctively Greek civilization began to emerge in Ionian cities such as Miletus, Smyrna, and Halicarnassus. The first important signs of this Greek renaissance were the epic poems of Homer, which effectively reshaped a vital part of the mythic legacy inherited from the distant Mycenaean past.

Distinctive Qualities of Greek Myth

Greek myth shares many qualities with the traditions of other cultures, including an emphasis on heroic conflict, warfare, sexual aggression, and other acts of violence.

Dealing with murder, rape, incest, treachery, and family strife, many Greek myths are uncompromisingly grim, even savage in their unflinching insistence on the inevitability of human suffering and death. Despite their images of noble heroes defeating evil adversaries, they do not include many happy endings.

Humanism

In the hands of the greatest poets, Greek myths were reinterpreted in ways that could transcend their almost brutal subjects. Homer, the lyric poets, and the Athenian dramatists of the fifth century B.C. refashioned the mythic heritage, giving it a typically Greek orientation toward humanistic values.

In addition to its literary sophistication, Greek myth is distinguished by its emphases on humanism, individualism, and competitiveness. In contrast to many other mythologies of antiquity, the majority of Greek myths ultimately focused on human heroes, a fact the Greeks themselves noted. Gods are important in most heroic tales, but their presence is typically intermittent and their influence indirect: it is the heroes' personal struggles and suffering that occupy the foreground. Greek myth consistently expresses an anthropocentric (human-centered) cosmos. A worldview that places human consciousness squarely at the center of the universe, **humanism** asserts the intrinsic worth, dignity, and creative potential of the individual human being. "Man is the measure of all things," declared the fifth-century philosopher Protagoras, and it is human perceptions—guided by logic and moral principle—that define the nature of reality. The human element is so essential to the Greek perspective that Hesiod's *Theogony* contains no reference to man's creation, perhaps because the poet could not conceive of a world without men (although he easily imagined one without women).

Given their emphasis on humanity's unique value, it is not surprising that Greek artists and writers portrayed their gods as very much like themselves, only larger, more powerful, and immune to sickness or death. This **anthropomorphism** (ascribing human form to supernatural beings) characterizes Greek art and literature from its earliest inception through the end of classical antiquity in the fifth century A.D. Although some Greek writers, such as Herodotus, believed that the prehistoric Greeks borrowed their beliefs about the gods from ancient Egypt (*Histories*, Book 2), Greek artists depicted their gods very differently from Egyptian prototypes. Whereas Egyptian artists represented their deities in animal or reptilian shapes (a practice known as **theriomorphism** [thir-ee-oh-MOR-fizm]), Greek painters and sculptors rendered the gods as idealized human beings, perfect in form and resplendent in beauty (Figure 1-15). Because they resemble humans not only physically but also psychologically, the Greek gods typically behave like flawed mortals, their lusts and competitiveness showing more of human fallibility than of divine perfection.

Individualism and Competitiveness

Classical myth typically expresses a distinctively Greek emphasis on competitiveness and individual achievement. The Homeric heroes strive to surpass their peers, to attain the foremost place—as judged by an admiring public—as the bravest, strongest, most skilled, and most eloquent of their leaders. The Homeric warrior prefers public duels with individual opponents of equal social rank rather than mass assaults

FIGURE 1-15   Bronze Statue of Zeus (or Poseidon) (c. 460 B.C.). This larger-than-life bronze probably represents the king of the gods about to hurl a lightning bolt at some offending mortal. An awesome embodiment of nature's power revealed in electrical storms, Zeus is a sky god who also represents the Greek conviction that the universe is based on principles of justice and cosmic harmony. When human crimes upset the world's moral balance, Zeus punishes the guilty to restore the natural order, a view expressed in Homer's *Odyssey* and other works of Greek myth. (*National Museum, Athens.*)

on the enemy, for only in solo confrontations with another aristocratic fighter can he effectively demonstrate his incomparable superiority.

Achilles's military career demonstrates both the glory and the cost of unrestrained **individualism:** he recognizes no equals and adamantly refuses to cooperate with his fellow Greeks after Agamemnon confiscates his captive slave girl, the trophy of his valor in battle, thus calling into question his uniquely heroic status. When Hector, Troy's leading defender, slays Achilles's beloved Patroclus, Achilles insists on avenging his friend by meeting the Trojan prince alone in hand-to-hand combat (Chapter 11).

The most celebrated example of Greek competition, the Olympic Games (founded, according to tradition, in 776 B.C.), perpetuated the heroic ideal of a single competitor triumphing over all rivals. Awarding only a first prize, the Olympic judges acknowledged no second- or third-best entrants: all runners-up were losers, typically condemned to public jeers and other humiliations. The winning athlete and the mythic hero—Achilles, Odysseus, Oedipus, Medea—share a common destiny: they stand alone, willing to risk virtually everything in accomplishing feats that will distinguish them qualitatively from all lesser mortals. As the myths never tire of saying, this obsessive quest for preeminence is a noble goal, but it invariably exacts a terrible cost.

The world of Greek myth thus reflects the tensions and perplexities of Greek society. The gods possess everything the Greek male desires or admires—eternal youth, unblemished good looks, honor, reputation, irresistible power, and the uninhibited assertion of individual selfhood. For all their superiority to mortals, however, the gods are also driven by the same kind of competitive ambition and jealous regard for their prerogatives that destroy the mental peace of human leaders. Worshiping divine beings who were largely projections of their own ideal (and fallible) selves, the Greeks created myths in which the gods are almost as fascinated by human activities as their mortal subjects were intrigued by the gods.

Roman Mythology

Although classical mythology is essentially Greek myth, the Romans also contributed extensively to the field. Ovid, a leading Roman poet during the reign of Augustus (27 B.C.–A.D. 14), created the single most important collection of Greco-Roman tales—the *Metamorphoses of the Gods.* Ovid's stories about gods and heroes changing their physical forms, undergoing a metamorphosis, were designed to suit Roman tastes, however, and differ considerably in tone and style from most Greek myths. The Romans borrowed most of their myths from Greek sources, but they typically revised and transformed them to highlight distinctively Roman social and political concerns. Because Roman poets such as Ovid and Virgil, author of the *Aeneid,* produced their work at a much later historical period than the Greeks, and for a much different audience, Roman mythology is discussed in a separate section (Part 4, chapters 18–20). Some readers may find it instructive to compare the Greek creation myth in Hesiod's *Theogony* (Chapter 3) with the later, much more sophisticated account in Ovid's *Metamorphoses* (Chapter 20), recognizing that Ovid wrote approximately 750 years after Hesiod and inhabited an entirely different thought world.

Questions for Discussion and Review

1. According to Greek myth, what is unusual about the births of Athene (goddess of wisdom) and Dionysus (god of wine and emotional freedom)? Why do you suppose that many ancient traditions tell of events that are literally impossible? Can you see any symbolic meaning in having Zeus, king of the gods, personally give birth to two such different divine children?

2. Suggest some possible definitions for the term *mythos.* What role does oral storytelling play in the origin and development of myth? Why do Greek myths survive in so many different versions?

3. Discuss the literary character of much Greek myth. In what sense does the philosopher Aristotle use *mythos?* What are the major written sources of classical myth?

4. Describe the influence of Mesopotamian, Minoan, and Mycenaean civilization in the historical development of Greek myth.

5. Discuss the distinctive qualities of Greek mythology, including its literary character and emphasis on competitive action. Define the concepts of *humanism, anthropomorphism,* and *individualism* as they relate to Greek myth.

Recommended Reading

Carpenter, T. H. *Art and Myth in Ancient Greece.* London: Thames and Hudson, 1991. A profusely illustrated handbook.

Dalley, Stephanie. *Myths from Mesopotamia: Creation, the Flood, Gilgamesh and Others.* New York: Oxford University Press, 1989. Fresh translations of Near Eastern myths.

Gantz, Timothy. *Early Greek Myth: A Guide to Literary and Artistic Sources.* Baltimore: Johns Hopkins UP, 1993. Gantz has compiled the only one-volume compendium of Greek myth, giving the ancient textual or artistic source for each myth.

Grimal, Pierre. *The Dictionary of Classical Mythology.* Trans. A. R. Maxwell-Hyslop. Oxford: Basil Blackwell, 1986. A comprehensive resource for all major figures in Greco-Roman myth.

Hornblower, Simon, and Antony Spawforth, eds. *The Oxford Classical Dictionary.* 3rd ed. New York: Oxford UP, 1996. An authoritative reference work on the classical world.

Howatson, M. C., ed. *The Oxford Companion to Classical Literature.* 2nd ed. New York: Oxford UP, 1989. An invaluable reference to both historical writers and mythological characters.

2

Ways of Interpreting Myth

KEY THEMES

Despite a few skeptics, the Greeks generally regarded their myths as plausible accounts of their distant past. By contrast, modern scholars try to define the precise nature and purpose of myth, advancing numerous theories to explain its origin and functions. Some theorists argue that myths are largely prescientific responses to the external world of nature or social institutions and that they were designed to (1) give meaning to traditional practices, such as initiation rites, (2) explain the causes of natural phenomena, or (3) retroactively justify social conventions whose actual origins had been forgotten. Other theorists believe that myth is a spontaneous product of the human mind, operating to express typically unconscious fears or desires, chart the difficulties of psychological maturation, or mediate the contrarieties of existence.

In late July the Athenians held an annual festival, the Panathenaea, commemorating their goddess's birth. Every fourth year, at the Great Panathenaea, the celebrations were particularly elaborate, featuring poetic recitations, horse races, athletic games, and musical contests. The festival climaxed in a solemn procession of Athens's leading citizens, allies, and visiting dignitaries across the agora (marketplace) and up the steep hill of the Acropolis to Athene's temple. Phidias made this procession the subject of the Parthenon frieze, a long band of low-relief sculptures running horizontally along the top of the walls inside the temple's exterior colonnade (Figure 2-1).

The east frieze depicts a panorama of Athene's chief worshipers, including those especially honored with carrying out the main purpose of the procession—a group of young Athenian women carrying the peplos (an elaborately embroidered robe to be placed on the goddess's oldest statue; Figure 2-2). Like the Parthenon itself, the peplos was decorated with mythical motifs highlighting Athene's triumphs, in this case, her defeat of the Giants who dared to attack Olympus. Other architectural sculptures of the Parthenon represent similar victories of civilization over savagery: a

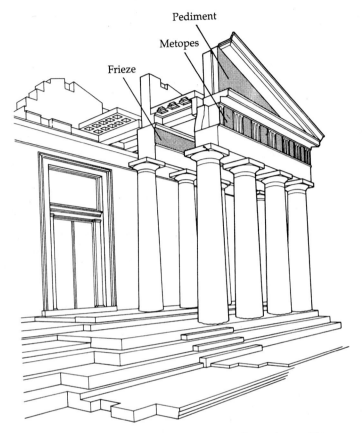

Pediment

Metopes

Frieze

FIGURE 2-1   The Location of the Sculptures on the Parthenon. This cross section of Athene's temple shows the positions of the pediment sculptures, the frieze featuring scenes from the Panathenaea procession, and the metopes (architectural panels decorated with bas-reliefs).

band of Lapiths, mountain tribesmen in Thessaly, overcome centaurs (male figures whose bestial natures are indicated by their horselike anatomy from the waist down; Figure 2-3). In another scene, heroes battle the Amazons (female warriors who invaded prehistoric Attica, the territory governed by Athens), further emphasizing Athene's role in protecting civilized values.

In contrast to scenes depicting violent conflict on earth, the east frieze of the Parthenon presents the gods—invisible participants in the Panathenaea—as infinitely calm and relaxed. Having demonstrated their ability to vanquish all opposition, they exhibit the serenity born of supreme confidence. The seated Apollo, god of health, mental discipline, and artistic creativity, leans casually toward his uncle Poseidon to exchange a private word; his twin sister Artemis, patron of wildlife and the hunt, modestly adjusts the body-clinging folds of her diaphanous gown (Figure 2-4). In another Olympian group, even fierce Ares, god of war and bloodshed, exhibits total repose. His hands grasp the knee of a crossed leg while he shares a

FIGURE 2-2 Young Women Carrying the Peplos. In this scene based on the Panathenaea procession, aristocratic Athenian women carry the peplos, a sacred garment—lavishly embroidered with pictorial episodes from the goddess's myth—to clothe Athene's oldest cult statue on the Acropolis. (*British Museum, London.*)

FIGURE 2-3 A Centaur and a Lapith in Hand-to-Hand Combat. In this Parthenon metope, agents representing barbarism (the half-animal centaur) and civilization (the unarmed human warrior) battle for dominance. As defender of the civilized values of the polis, Athene champions the forces of rational order against savagery. (*British Museum, London.*)

FIGURE 2-4   Olympian Gods, East Frieze of the Parthenon. A visible symbol of Athens's
triumph over barbarian invaders (the Persians, who invaded Greece in 490 and 480–479
B.C.), the Parthenon (constructed c. 447–438 B.C.) embodies principles of cosmic order, a
mythic theme reinforced by picturing the highest gods as present in Athene's sanctuary.
Apollo, god of rational order, turns toward his uncle Poseidon, lord of the sea. Apollo's twin
sister, Artemis, patron of women and wildlife, is at the right. (*Acropolis Museum, Athens.*)

conversation with his aunt Demeter, mighty goddess of earth's fertility, and his two
half-brothers, Hermes and Dionysus (Figure 2-5). Although probably already slightly
drunk (Dionysus's raised hand may originally have held a beaker of wine), the god of
unbridled freedom—whose frenzy can elicit either joy or terror—is mellow. Dionysus's right arm casually embraces the shoulders of Hermes, the trickster god of thieves,
gamblers, and businessmen—and Zeus's trusted messenger.

The Olympian gods are assembled to observe the Panathenaean games, savor the
fragrance of burnt animal sacrifices, and offer favored humans the comfort of their
presence and protection. Like all the Parthenon sculptures and friezes—and those
decorating other sanctuaries throughout the Greek world—Phidias's scenes evoking
the mythic past and suggesting the continuing patronage of divine beings illustrate
the close connection between myth and Greek society. The rituals of the Panathenaea, as well as the art and architecture of the Parthenon, serve multiple religious,
social, and political purposes: Athene's preeminence among the gods and her special
link to Athens are consciously exploited to affirm the Athenians' identity as a divinely
favored people and to validate both their distinctive customs and their right militarily
to dominate less powerful Greek states.

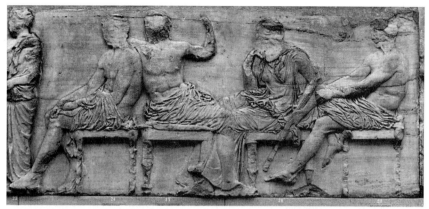

(a)

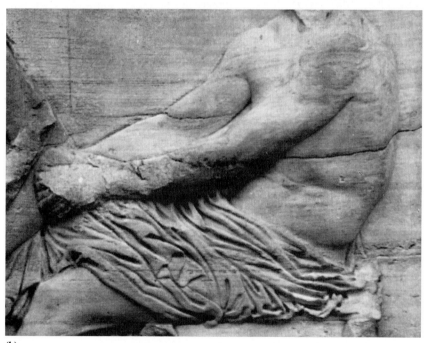

(b)

FIGURE 2-5   A Gathering of the Olympian Family, East Frieze of the Parthenon. (a) Although their faces have been obliterated, this seated quartet of gods still exhibits a divine grace and repose. With his arm raised, the wine-god Dionysus leans confidentially against his half-brother Hermes (left), god of boundaries, travelers, tricksters, gamblers, and thieves. Zeus's sister Demeter, great goddess of earth's fertility, turns an interested gaze on the tipsy Dionysus. Ares, god of violent aggression and bloodshed, appears on the right. (b) In this close-up of Ares, the war god manifests an uncharacteristic serenity. Phidias's study of strength in a pose of total relaxation emphasizes the god's latent power. (*British Museum, London.*)

Ancient Ways of Viewing Myth

Although myth substituted for ancient history and theology in popular Greek imagination, it is important to realize that even the most revered writings, the Homeric epics, did not have the binding authority of scripture. Homer provided examples of noble action, and he was widely quoted as an arbiter of proper behavior. But the *Iliad* and *Odyssey* were not viewed as repositories of divinely revealed truth, as are the Judeo-Christian Bible and the Islamic Qur'an (Koran). Nor did Greek society have a hereditary priesthood charged with preserving and enforcing the revealed will of a single omnipotent God. Instead of promoting dogmatic conformity, the Greeks tended to be flexible and inclusive in their religious ideas, commonly regarding foreign deities as analogous to their own. Assuming that the same gods, in different guises, appeared in different cultures, Greek travelers such as the historian Herodotus had little trouble recognizing the Babylonian Marduk as the equivalent of Zeus or the Egyptian Osiris as another version of Dionysus, the dying and rising god.

Most Greeks seem to have accepted their myths uncritically, as tales that provided a generally reliable account of the world's origins, the nature of divinity, and the way things were in the extremely distant past. After the sixth century B.C., a new emphasis on logical analysis and scientific observation—the Greek philosophical movement—introduced some skepticism, but the majority of Greek writers rarely questioned myth's intrinsic credibility. With few exceptions, Greek authors used the tools of philosophical reasoning only to correct or rationalize certain aspects of Greek myth. In his play the *Bacchants* (the *Bacchae*), Euripides has the mythical prophet Tiresias explain the correct understanding of Dionysus's birth from the thigh of Zeus: the popular misconception that Zeus literally carried Dionysus in his thigh after saving the embryo from a fire consuming the child's mother, Semele, results from a careless confusion of similar words. Zeus did not stitch the unborn Dionysus into his thigh (in Greek, *meron*); instead, Tiresias says, he rescued the child from Hera's jealous wrath by hiding him away and making, out of bright air, a replica of the infant's body, giving this false image to Hera as a hostage (*homeron;* Figure 2-6).

Euripides's ingenious use of wordplay to explain the "impossible" elements in myth is paralleled by the ancient practice of interpreting myth as allegory. A complex narrative in which all components—persons, places, actions—function as symbols of something else, an **allegory** operates through metaphor and figurative language. In *The Uses of Greek Mythology,* Ken Dowden cites several ancient writers to illustrate the ways in which Greeks typically interpreted myth. Dowden (40–41) cites a late-classical commentator on the *Iliad* who, quoting one Theagenes of Rhegion (c. 525 B.C.), states that when Homer tells of gods fighting each other (behavior that classical thinkers deemed unsuitable to divinity), he is really creating allegories about natural processes in which the elements of primitive science—the hot, dry, wet, cold—are in endless conflict. The gods are thus symbols of natural phenomena, with celestial fire represented by Apollo or Helios, water by Poseidon or Troy's river god Scamander, the moon by Artemis, and the air by Hera. In Theagenes's view, the gods can also signify human qualities or dispositions: Aphrodite is desire; Ares, insanity; and Athene, intelligence.

The philosopher Anaxagoras similarly avoided taking a literal view of myths that, at face value, seemed to present the gods behaving badly. In the old tradition, Hermes steals Apollo's cattle; Zeus rapes the virgin Io; Ares seduces Hephaestus's wife, Aphro-

FIGURE 2-6   The Birth of Dionysus from the Thigh of Zeus. In this bas-relief, the new-born Dionysus emerges from his father's lap and reaches out to Hermes, who prepares to wrap the infant in swaddling clothes. Whereas a few educated Greeks, such as the playwright Euripides and the philosopher Plato, tried to rationalize myth to make it seem more plausible, none seem to have questioned its fundamental relation to supposedly historical events in the distant past. Viewing myth as a purely imaginary creation—perhaps invented to express insights about physical nature, social institutions, or human psychology—is a modern, post-Enlightenment development. (*Vatican Museums, Rome.*)

dite; and Hera persecutes her husband's innocent (although commonly illegitimate) children. The list of divine misdemeanors is almost endless. Adopting Theagenes's allegorical method to resolve the problem, Anaxagoras contended that Homeric myth was actually meant to expose the evil results of unethical conduct and to promote virtue.

As early as the sixth century B.C., Xenophanes of Colophon had objected to Homer on moral grounds, lamenting the poet's depiction of the gods' committing theft and adultery, as well as their collective penchant for conspiracy and deceit. Aware that gods mirror the virtues and defects of a society's human inhabitants, Xenophanes called attention to the Greeks' tendency to fashion gods in their own image.

1
Man made his gods, and furnished them
with his own body, voice and garments.

2
If a horse or lion or a slow ox
had agile hands for paint and sculpture,
the horse would make his god a horse,
the ox would sculpt an ox.

3
Our gods have flat noses and black skins
say the Ethiopians. The Thracians say
our gods have red hair and hazel eyes. (*Barnstone* 131)

Some Greek philosophers, notably the Athenian Socrates (c. 469–399 B.C.) and his disciple Plato (427–347 B.C.), were particularly offended by the poor moral example the Olympians set, objecting to such tales as Uranus's castration by his son Cronus, the father of Zeus, or to those about Zeus's innumerable adulteries. Insisting that the gods must be viewed as entirely good and free of human passions, Plato banned Homeric myth from his ideal republic. Despite his aversion to unworthy traditions, however, Plato himself freely revised selected myths to illustrate his vision of an invisible spirit realm that parallels our material world (Chapter 9).

Eventually, some Greek thinkers viewed the gods as merely different aspects or attributes of a single unknowable Deity, essentially agreeing with Xenophanes's assertion that

There is one God—supreme among gods and men—
who is like mortals in neither body nor mind. (*Barnstone* 130)

In addition to skeptics who criticized the traditional gods' lack of ethical standards, another Greek writer questioned the truth of the gods' historical existence. About two generations after Plato, Euhemerus of Messene composed a fictional travel story, *Sacred Scripture* (*Hiera anagraphē*, c. 300 B.C.), in which he described visiting an island, Panchaia, in the Indian Ocean. According to Euhemerus's startling account, he found written evidence that the Greek gods were originally mortal, ancient kings whose people had posthumously deified them. Known today as *Euhemerism*, this theory made a strong impact on some critical thinkers in the Hellenistic world, where successors of Alexander the Great were claiming divine honors, a practice later adopted by some of the Roman emperors.

Some Modern Interpretations of Myth

Despite Euhemerus's shocking assertion, however, or an occasional philosopher's rejection of its more brutal aspects, myth generally kept its hold on Greco-Roman society until the Roman government's legitimization of Christianity as the official state religion in the fourth century A.D. Denounced by the Christian Church as being opposed to the true faith, classical mythology was largely devalued in Western culture during the Middle Ages. Although medieval theologians commonly identified Greek deities with demons, the rebirth of classical learning during the European Renaissance reintroduced myth to the world of art, literature, and scholarship. The development of modern scientific methodology during the Enlightenment (seventeenth century A.D.), with its emphasis on reason, objectivity, classification, and analysis, eventually inspired a renewed scholarly interest in myth. During the last two centuries, scholars have applied techniques from a variety of academic disciplines—including anthropology, cultural history, psychology, sociology, and religious studies—to studying myth and interpreting its significance.

Mythology has two general meanings. First, it can be defined as a set or system of myths, such as the vast collection of Greek and Roman tales known as classical mythology. It also refers to a methodological analysis of myths, particularly their form, purpose, and function. In trying to isolate some theme or principle that all myths have in common, scholars have produced numerous theories that claim to provide *the* correct key for understanding the precise nature of myth. Although no one theory or definition of myth has yet won universal acceptance, scholarly attempts to break myths down into their component parts and discover some unifying element behind their almost infinite variety have greatly increased our knowledge of what myths are and what they are not. Most scholarly theories fit into one of two broad categories: those that assume an external basis, such as a reaction to physical nature, for the creation of myth; and those that see mythmaking as spontaneous and internal, an instinctive expression of the human mind.

Externalist Theories: Myth as a Product of Environment

The "externalists" typically view myth as a prescientific attempt to explain natural phenomena or to provide justifications for social, religious, or political customs or institutions. These theories generally view myth as a quasi-rational response to the physical or social environment.

Nature Myths One of the first modern efforts to fashion a comprehensive theory of myth was in fact anticipated by Theagenes's argument that mythical characters and actions are really disguised representations of natural processes. The **nature myth** theory holds that myth is essentially a reaction to the awe-inspiring power of physical nature, particularly those phenomena that directly affect human life: the continuing cycles of day and night, sunshine and darkness, summer and winter, heat and cold, fair weather and storm, rainfall and drought, plant life and death.

Even casual readers will immediately recognize that many Greek tales personify (give human traits to) solar, atmospheric, meteorological, or other natural processes. Zeus, who gathers storm clouds, detonates thunder, and hurls lightning bolts, is clearly a **personification** of meteorological forces. His brother Poseidon is lord of the sea and earthquakes, a volatile manifestation of natural energy that makes both sea and land violently roll and pitch, with potentially disastrous consequences for mortals.

Some of the older gods, whom the Greeks believed preceded the Olympians in time, are directly identified with astronomical objects or functions. The Titan **Hyperion** [hye-PEER-ee-uhn] (or his son **Helios** [HEE-lee-ohs]) is the sun, and **Selene** [se-LEE-nee] is the moon that typically rises as the sun sets—a cycle depicted at the corners of the Parthenon's east pediment to frame the central scene of Athene's birth (see Figures 3-1 and 3-2). **Eos** [EE-ohs], whom Homer calls "rosy-fingered" and whom the Romans named **Aurora** [ah-ROR-uh], personifies the dawn. A few myths about Apollo, who in later traditions assumes Hyperion's duties as the sun god, illustrate solar movement, signified by Apollo's fiery chariot making its daily journey across the sky.

Scholars advocating the nature myth theory—such as the nineteenth-century philologist F. Max Müller (1823–1900), whose work helped popularize the concept—rigorously applied their view to the entire range of myth. If a particular myth's relation to natural phenomena was not immediately obvious, it was interpreted allegorically to make it fit the theory. According to Müller and others of his school, the Greeks used mythic figures and events to symbolize the tensions, oppositions, and seasonal changes in nature, such as the anxiety-producing alternation of flood and aridity that so profoundly affected the human activities of sowing, growing, and harvesting and upon which the human community depended to survive.

Interpreting all myths as ingeniously disguised representations of natural phenomena, the nature theory fails to account for the full content of most myths. Zeus is undeniably a weather god, but he is also the champion of justice, hospitality, and legitimate kingship; defining him only as a personification of atmospheric turbulence explains none of his higher ethical functions. Artemis is commonly identified with the moon, but that does not explain her role as patron of childbirth and guardian of wildlife. Nor does regarding Dionysus, god of the vine, as merely an embodiment of the vegetative life cycle adequately explain his role as liberator of the human psyche.

Myth and Ritual A more persistent and influential theory associates myth exclusively with **ritual,** a religious or quasi-religious ceremony in which a prescribed series of actions—accompanied by the repetition of traditional phrases—are scrupulously observed. At the annual festival of Dionysus in Athens, a ritual parade included representations of the god's mythic birth and death, as well as traditional songs and dances out of which Athenian tragedy is said to have developed. According to the ritualist view, promoted by several leading scholars of Cambridge University during the late nineteenth and early twentieth centuries, myths are the byproduct of such ritual enactments as those performed at Dionysian celebrations. They are stories invented to explain ceremonies whose real origins have long been forgotten. In his multivolume compendium of European myth, the *Golden Bough* (1890–1915), the English anthropologist Sir James Frazer (1854–1941) provided numerous examples from European folk rituals to illustrate the close bond between myth and ancient rites, particularly those that evoked plant, animal, and human fertility. Robert Graves, an English poet and critic, among others, maintained that myths derive from mimes, dances, and other performances given at public festivals. The Cambridge school, which included such distinguished critics as Jane Harrison and Gilbert Murray, argued that even supposedly sophisticated Greek myths were based on primitive, irrational customs. Stories of Heracles's famous labors and his later ascension to heaven were alleged to derive from oral recitations made at his purported tomb. Widespread as this view became, most contemporary scholars do not believe that ritual is the exclusive, or even the principal, source of myth. Ritual theorists, moreover, do not explain why rituals develop in the first place.

The Charter Theory The **charter** theory developed from direct observations of a preliterate people in the active process of making myth serve practical or social purposes. Stranded on the Trobriand Islands near New Guinea during the first world war, the Polish anthropologist Bronislaw Malinowski (1884–1942) noted that the Trobrianders used myth to validate existing communal institutions, beliefs, and practices. These "charter" myths are narratives that supply the rationale for some ritual or custom; they serve to justify the practice of a particular initiation rite or other ceremony and promote its regular repetition, presumably to help maintain stability and communal order.

A few Greek myths seem to function as charters, justifying some debatable social or religious observance. In his poem of origins, the *Theogony,* Hesiod provides a foundation story to support the Greek habit of offering their gods only the least desirable parts of sacrificial animals. Like the biblical Hebrews and other ancient peoples, the Greeks shared a communal meal with their divine protectors, eating cooked meat and burning the residue, which wafted its way to heaven as a column of smoke. According to Hesiod, when the newly empowered Olympian gods met with primitive men (women had not yet been created) at Mekone "to settle accounts," the cunning Titan Prometheus slew a sacrificial ox, dividing its carcass into two unequal portions. Concealing the meat and hide beneath an unappetizing stomach, he tricked Zeus, king of the gods, into accepting as the gods' share a pile of inedible bones covered with fat. Hesiod's story operates as a charter, a validation of the ancient practice of offering the gods only the least desirable parts of a sacrificial animal, the bones and fat, while human participants ate the tastier portions. Although Hesiod's Zeus severely punishes the human race on whose behalf Prometheus has acted, this subversive myth confirms, in typically Greek fashion, humanity's right to enjoy even that which the gods might wish to claim. While explaining the "how" or "what" of ritual sacrifice, applying the charter theory to this myth fails to account for the important "why"—the distinctive favoring of human welfare over divine prerogative.

Myth and Etiology The etiological method sees myths as attempts to explain the cause or origin of things. From the Greek word for cause (*aition*), **etiology** encompasses two schools of thought. The first regards myth as primitive science, the product of naive minds trying to give plausible causes of the present structure and operation of the natural world. Hesiod, for example, devotes part of his *Theogony* to narrating the origins of earth, sky, air, day, night, ocean, mountains, and other aspects of physical nature.

A more comprehensive etiological approach emphasizes the broadly explanatory purpose of myth. More than prescientific attempts to account for the natural or social environment, myths can also give theological or metaphysical interpretations of the human condition. Hesiod's *Theogony* and *Works and Days* explain why humanity's possession of fire, which Zeus had wished to retain as an exclusively divine prerogative, led to a tragic alienation between men and gods. Hesiod links the forbidden fire motif to the creation of the first woman, Pandora, whom the gods mold from clay as a "lovely evil" to plague mankind. As Hesiod's poetry demonstrates, etiological myths can be richly diverse, ranging from narratives of cosmic evolution and divine-human conflict to the human male's highly ambivalent attitude toward women.

Although numerous myths serve an etiological purpose, many heroic tales ordinarily classified as myth have little to do with etiology. Most of Heracles's labors, Jason's quest for the Golden Fleece, Medea's vengeance on her faithless husband, Oedipus's tragic fall, and Theseus's slaying of the Minotaur are not concerned with explaining world origins or social institutions.

Internalist Theories: Myth as a Product of the Mind

Whereas the nature, ritual, charter, and etiological theorists view myths as essentially interpretations of the external world, a second major school of thought sees them as spontaneous expressions of the human mind. A study of the human *psyche* (the Greek word meaning "soul," or "center of consciousness"), **psychology** proposes an intimate link between myth and several mental processes.

Freudian Theory and Myth Sigmund Freud (1856–1939) emphasized the importance of the subconscious in determining behavior and belief. He also formulated the practice of psychoanalysis, a method of therapeutic analysis based on a theory that abnormal mental states result from the repression of desires that the conscious mind rejects but which persist in the unconscious. In his *Interpretation of Dreams*, Freud argues that dreams, which typically resemble myths in their imagery and narrative form, are fundamentally the fulfillment of wishes that the waking mind suppresses or denies. Freed of mundane restraints, the dreamer can fly like Icarus (Figure 2-7), descend into Hades like Orpheus searching for his dead Eurydice, or battle dragons like Perseus and Apollo. Freud believed that mythic and dream figures often assume fantastic shapes because they are disguised versions of drives or wishes that are unacceptable to the conscious intellect. The work of dreams, Freud suggests, is to relieve anxiety and release psychic tension by transforming forbidden impulses into symbols that protect the mind from recognizing its own antisocial tendencies.

According to Freudian theory, "dream-work" accomplishes its purgative task by condensing and rearranging ordinary events of daily life, rendering them in images that both express and conceal subconscious desire. Dreams also achieve their protective purpose by transferring emotions to a sphere or activity very different from that which they occupy in the dreamer's daylight experience. This process, which Freud called *displacement,* helps give dreams their bewildering or disorienting effect.

Like dreams, myths permit one to violate taboos with impunity: parental or other authority figures commonly appear as one secretly *feels* them to be. Thus, hostility toward the mother transforms her into the man-devouring Sphinx or the snake-haired Gorgon Medusa, whose gaze emasculates men and turns them into crumbling stone. Oedipus can defeat the Sphinx (an image of the evil mother) by answering her riddle and then go on to commit incest with (and thus destroy) the mother who had once abandoned him for wild animals to eat (see Chapter 16). Beheading Medusa, Perseus can kill what he hates in maternal power, psychologically freeing himself to rescue Andromeda, the future mother of his children.

Freud divided the mind into three basic components—which his English translators have named the *id,* the *ego,* and the *superego*—that in some ways mirror Greek myth's tripartite universe. Corresponding to the murky Underworld, where souls hunger for the blood of life (*Odyssey,* Book 11), the id houses biological drives and appetites that fuel the emotions of fear and desire, the primal source of psychic and sexual energy. A subconscious reservoir of amoral impulses, the id contains the *libido,* a term derived from the Latin word for "lust," or "desire." The psyche's daylight world is the ego (literally, "I"), the conscious self, the sense of individual personhood. The top level of the psychic structure is the superego, the individual ego's awareness of the taboos and ethical standards that society imposes to maintain public order. Driven by the id and inhibited by the externally imprinted values of the superego (including beliefs about gods and divine law), the self must mediate between instinctual desire and societal prohibitions.

Freud drew his most celebrated example of mythic wish fulfillment that violates societal taboos from the story of Oedipus, a king of Thebes who kills his father and marries his mother. According to Freud's theory of infantile sexuality, the male child passionately desires exclusive possession of his mother, whom he regards as the source of all nurturing pleasure. To claim the mother entirely, he must eliminate his male parent, whom he instinctively recognizes as the chief rival for his mother's affection. Upon growing older and discovering that both his incestuous feelings toward his mother and hostility toward his father are unacceptable, the boy experiences guilt and gradually banishes such forbidden wishes from his conscious mind.

FIGURE 2-7 Bas-relief of Daedalus and Icarus. Daedalus, prototype of the artist-inventor, makes wings of feathers and wax for his son Icarus. Ignoring his father's warning not to fly too high, Icarus rashly approaches too near the sun, causing the wax holding his wings together to melt and precipitating his lethal fall into the sea. A cautionary tale about humans foolishly trespassing into the gods' realm, the Icarus myth is also an example of human wish fulfillment in which an adventuresome youth soars through the heavens like Zeus's eagle—and of the inevitable consequences when religious or societal laws are broken. (*Villa Albani, Rome.*)

In Sophocles's *Oedipus the King,* the hero literally acts out the Oedipal drive, and his doom graphically illustrates the high price society exacts for this error. Oedipus's wife, Jocasta (when not yet aware that she is also his mother), explicitly connects incestuous desire and dream fulfillment but dismisses the anxiety it provokes (see Chapter 16).

Because Greek plays typically dramatize conflicts between members of a single family, Freudian insights into the domestic psychodrama may offer helpful starting points in understanding many tragic myths. Some of Freud's disciples have noted that the myth of Electra, heroine of three separate Greek tragedies, is psychologically analogous to that of Oedipus. Idolizing the memory of her dead father, Agamemnon, Electra jealously plots to murder her mother, Clytemnestra (Chapter 15).

In *The Glory of Hera,* Philip Slater applies some Freudian principles to illustrate the connection between Greek family life and the harrowing battles between family members in Greek myth. Slater points out that Greek boys were raised in an exclusively female environment during their early years and then abruptly transferred to an all-male society of school, gymnasium, and military camp, where they were inculcated with the attitudes of a patriarchal worldview. It seems credible that Greek mothers must have entertained decidedly mixed feelings about their sons, taking pride in their achievements yet simultaneously resenting their free enjoyment of opportunities denied to women. That youths who had first been acculturated by their mothers subsequently acquired a socially approved masculine contempt for all things feminine must have created considerable bitterness for Greek women.

Although the concept is highly controversial, some feminist critics propose that the anxiety about female hostility contained in some Greek myths has its roots in the distant past (see Chapter 4). As early as Homer's *Odyssey,* Agamemnon rails at his wife's treachery, a theme extensively developed in Aeschylus's *Oresteia* (Chapter 15). Outstanding even in myth's portrait gallery of cruel and dangerous mothers, the Aeschylean Clytemnestra is not only a conniving adulteress but an unnatural mother, abusing her helpless daughter and eager to kill her son Orestes. Aeschylus also identifies this monster-mother with the Furies, creatures addicted to torture and castration of the male. In Euripides's play the *Hippolytus,* Phaedra develops an incestuous passion for her stepson and, when rejected, successfully contrives to destroy him. Two of Euripides's mothers, Agave and Medea, actually murder their sons, the former ripping her son's body to pieces (chapters 13 and 17).

Jung's Archetypal Myths   Although Freudian analysis yields important clues to the excessive behavior of a few mythic characters, some modern critics find the work of one of Freud's leading protégés (and later rival), the Swiss analytical psychologist Carl Jung (1875–1961), even more instructive. After studying thousands of myths from cultures all over the globe, Jung was struck by their similarity to dreams in which the same major figures kept reappearing. It did not matter whether the myth—or dreamer—was Italian, Japanese, African, American, or Indonesian; figures of the great mother, stern paternal judge, threatening stranger, clever trickster, or benign guide were consistently present. One would expect that basic human emotions such as fear, desire, and greed would dominate both dreams and myths, but Jung also found that particular situations and actions—journeys, encounters with frightening monsters, struggles with unidentified assailants—were universal. Jung identified these recurring mythic characters, situations, and events as archetypes.

An **archetype** is the primal form or original pattern of which all other things of the same kind are representatives or copies. In Western cultures, for example, paintings of Mary holding the infant Jesus convey an archetypal image of the mother figure, providing an ideal model of maternal tenderness. The Christian Madonna and child, in turn, are a relatively late manifestation of ancient images found throughout the world, from Egyptian art that depicts Isis nursing a newborn Horus to Greek murals that show a tearful Demeter searching for her lost daughter, Persephone. A fundamental aspect of human existence, the imprint of a maternal image undoubtedly characterized the human psyche from its prehistoric beginnings.

The Greek gods and/or heroes commonly represent archetypal characteristics or personalities, serving as paradigms for a whole class or category of human types: Zeus, the powerful father whose least frown may evoke terror; Prometheus, the heroic rebel who defies unjust authority; Hera, the strong wife who upholds the institution of matrimony that effects her own subordination; Artemis, the female free spirit who roams wild, disdaining social restraints; Hermes, the epitome of swift mobility who delights in deceiving lesser intellects; Athene, the master planner and strategist who outwits the opposition; Aphrodite, patron of love and desire who revels in the passions she arouses (see chapters 5 and 6).

Because the same basic facts shape all human consciousness, major life events are also archetypal, including birth, sexual maturation, struggles with parents or other authority figures, fraternal rivalry, mating, competition for power, and the onset of sickness and death. Myth, therefore, typically involves archetypal actions suggesting transitions from one stage of being to another: the gods' struggle to overthrow parental control and assert their individual egos on a cosmic scale (Chapter 3); the hero's battle against evil monsters or an arduous journey of discovery into strange and dangerous territory, commonly including a journey to the Underworld (chapters 10–12).

The myth of Icarus combines a form of Freudian wish fulfillment with an archetypal situation in which the human desire to experience near-absolute freedom overpowers even the instinct of self-preservation. **Icarus** [IK-uh-ruhs] is the son of an Athenian craftsman, **Daedalus** [DEE-duh-luhs], prototype of the artist and inventor, who designs the labyrinth, the vast maze beneath the Knossos palace in which King Minos houses the flesh-eating Minotaur. When Minos refuses to permit the invaluable Daedalus to leave Crete, Daedalus makes wings of feathers and wax so that he and Icarus can escape from Minoan captivity. Aware of the perils of humans unnaturally behaving like birds, Daedalus warns his son not to fly too low lest his wings become waterlogged or too high lest the sun's heat melt the wax holding his wings together. Suddenly given the dizzying freedom from earthly constraints, Icarus soars heavenward, trespassing boundaries between mortal and immortal spheres. Approaching too near the sun, Icarus finds that his artificial wings disintegrate, plunging him to his death in the Aegean Sea, a part of which was later named the Icarian Sea after him. When granted the opportunity to break barriers that ordinarily separate humanity from the gods, Icarus, an image of human nature, cannot resist exploring the unknown and forbidden. His adventurous impulse, and its fatal consequences, are as inevitable as Pandora's opening the jar of woes (see Chapter 6).

Archetypal figures, events, and situations seem to pervade the minds of every ethnic group, whether belonging to a literate technological society or to a preliterate hunting-and-gathering community (Figure 2-8). For Jung these archetypes spring from the collective unconscious, a term he used to denote the mental images, cognitive patterns, symbols, innate memories, and intrinsic assumptions that all members of a given culture—or the entire human race—hold in common. According to Jungian theory, the collective unconscious spawns virtually all creative activity, including dreams, religious visions, and mythologies. Living in the late twentieth century, we can still relate intimately to myths of birth, testing, conflict, death, and rebirth that originated thousands of years ago because our unconscious minds have inherited these mythic archetypes from our remotest ancestors.

Jung further postulated that the human unconscious also houses archetypal images of both the male and female principles. The **anima,** an internal expression of archetypal feminine wisdom and creativity, inhabits the minds of men as well as women. Correspondingly, the **animus,** which embodies essential masculine qualities, is present in both male and female psyches. Because the anima and animus are also partly determined by feelings derived from an individual's direct experience of other men or women, these indwelling images can include negative perceptions of masculinity or femininity. A distorted anima can produce an internalized view of woman as dangerous or destructive (a Medusa or Fury). Similarly, a woman may perceive the male primarily as a potential rapist or tyrant, the way Zeus's brother Hades appears to

FIGURE 2-8   A Female Archetype: Aphrodite. A personification of erotic desire and sensual pleasure, Aphrodite, as shown in this statue from Cyrene, North Africa, first century B.C., was said to have been born from the sea, whose murky, unfathomable depths hide forms of life that are commonly so grotesque as to seem unimaginable. The tradition of her sea origin (see Chapter 3) hints at the love goddess's connection with the human psyche's amoral unconscious and instinctual appetites. The tradition in which she is the daughter of Zeus and Dione (a Titan goddess), however, serves to place Aphrodite's rampant sexuality within the framework of cosmic order: as Zeus's child, natural lust must be subject to religious and social restraints. (*National Museum of Terme, Rome.*)

Persephone when he abducts the young woman and imprisons her in the Underworld (Chapter 4). In the healthy psyche, however, anima and animus achieve a whole and harmonious relationship with each other, as they do in the reunion of Odysseus and his wife, Penelope (Chapter 12).

In addition, the mind contains a sinister force that Jung called the **shadow,** a composite of unacknowledged negative elements—unconscious fear, hatred, envy, or unsatisfied desire—within the human personality. As we shall discover, numerous myths about the Greco-Roman gods and heroes present a Jungian tension between a character's conscious intentions and an unacknowledged shadow self—repressed or undervalued aspects of the personality—that commonly functions counterproductively or self-destructively. Despite his victory over the Titans, Zeus is internally subverted by lust and a tyrannical egocentrism, as is Heracles by deadly outbursts of uncontrolled rage. Both god and hero ultimately triumph, but only after overcoming or assimilating some morally ambiguous aspect of their own natures.

Many contemporary interpreters of myth have been influenced by Freud or Jung, including Joseph Campbell, who has written numerous books applying Jungian insights to world myths. In such works as *The Masks of God* and *The Hero with a Thou-*

sand Faces, Campbell explores the archetypal hero's adventures, particularly his tests of courage, honor, and self-knowledge. The hero's rite of passage typically features a cyclical process involving a necessary separation from his original environment: a journey in which he encounters frightening, even supernatural forces; an initiation into hitherto unknown regions, roles, or relationships; and an eventual return to his point of departure. These rites of passage represent the hero's stages of psychological development and maturation: by meeting challenges and surmounting obstacles, such heroes as Odysseus, Perseus, and Heracles fulfill their innate potential and grow into true selfhood, a process Jung called *individuation.*

Other important writers giving psychological analyses of myth include Ernst Cassirer, Mircea Eliade, and Victor Turner. Cassirer argues that myth is no less than the mind's spontaneous creation of an emotionally satisfying cosmos that it imposes upon the external world. Myths satisfy because, like religion, they project symbolic meaning upon the natural and human environment, imparting a significance otherwise absent in objective reality. In *Myth and Reality* and *The Sacred and the Profane,* Eliade, a philosopher and historian of religion, presents world myths as sacred tales emanating from a singularly creative era of prehistory.

While Eliade emphasizes myth's relationship to a vanished epoch of unique holiness, Turner argues that myths serve a combined psychological and social purpose in the present, promoting liminal, or threshold, experiences. Whereas the charter approach sees myths associated with rituals operating primarily to justify or validate the ritual itself, Turner sees myth and ritual linked by their psychological function, helping to ease people through life's difficult transitions. Thus, stories involving certain rituals help individuals cope with various crises or changes in social position, including rites of passage for boys initiated into warrior status, for girls into marriageable womanhood, or for adults into roles of community leadership.

Structuralism and Myth   Most psychological theorists regard myths as a natural expression of the psyche—one that functions therapeutically to purge unacceptable desire, provide creative energy, reconcile individuals to their environment, and attribute moral order and meaning to the universe. **Structuralism** further refines this concept, viewing myth as a reflection of the mind's binary organization. Structuralists, such as the Belgian anthropologist Claude Lévi-Strauss (1908–), observe that human beings tend to see the world as a reflection of their own physical and cerebral structure. Equipped with two eyes, legs, arms, and hands and—most important—a brain divided into two hemispheres, we automatically project a binary significance onto experience, typically dividing everything into polar opposites: right/left, light/dark, pleasure/pain, beautiful/ugly, good/evil, cooked/raw, civilized/savage. In Lévi-Strauss's view, myth deals with the perception and reconciliation of these opposites, which may be rendered as conflicts between natural order and human lawlessness, instinctual desire and social prohibition, or the divine will and human ambition. The many tensions inherent in the human predicament, such as the dichotomy between individual need and communal obligation, are the inspiration of myth, which is created to resolve or mitigate these contradictory forces.

Jean-Pierre Vernant and Pierre Vidal-Naquet, contemporary French classical scholars who employ a modified structuralism in their studies of Greek myth, have produced some intriguing reinterpretations. In *Myth and Tragedy in Ancient Greece,* Vernant and Vidal-Naquet emphasize the contradictions and confusions of reality that characterize the Greek tragic drama. Vernant's *Myth and Society in Ancient Greece* focuses on the alien quality of Greek culture, with its primeval traditions of ceremonial hunting, blood sacrifice, slavery, ritualized warfare, and religious ecstasy. Avoiding a literalist application of Lévi-Strauss's binary mode, Vernant provides an insightful critique of structuralism that emphasizes the ambiguity, complexity, and mercurial nature of myth.

Helpful as it can be in highlighting the oppositions and conflicts inherent in many myths, some scholars question structuralism's overly neat binary approach, pointing out that not all myths present a quantitative division of opposites or even a formal linear development. In the story of Odysseus and Penelope, for instance, the two partners evince a complementary rather than conflicted relationship.

Narratology   Some aspects of structuralism were anticipated in the work of the Russian folklorist Vladimir Propp. In his seminal *Morphology of the Folktale* (1928), Propp identified seven "spheres of action" and thirty-one "functions" that he believed were intrinsic to traditional tales. In analyzing a narrative's sequence of events, Propp emphasized that the action follows a distinctive pattern, giving traditional stories a recognizably similar structure. **Narratology,** the study of narrative structure, assumes that virtually all tales exhibit a common language in the form of universal patterns that control the order of events. In many Greek myths, for example, the hero's adventures conform to a predictable order: born from the union of a divine being with a mortal, the hero typically combines god-like ambition with human vulnerability; he leaves home on a quest in which he confronts and defeats supernatural adversaries, passes difficult or perilous tests of courage and intelligence, and narrowly escapes death. His tasks may involve retrieving treasure from a guardian dragon and/or rescuing an endangered princess; his rewards commonly include winning the princess in marriage, gaining riches, and/or receiving a crown. Thus, Odysseus sails from Ithaca to Troy where he proves his mettle as a warrior; embarks on a long voyage home beset by ogres and lethal temptresses, all of which obstacles he overcomes; battles rivals successfully to demonstrate his right to claim the princess (in this case his wife, Penelope); and reclaims his property and kingship. Rarely is this sequence reversed: ordinarily the hero does not first win a bride, find a treasure, and mount a throne, and only afterward wrestle a hydra, kill a Medusa, or descend to the Underworld.

Whereas the mythic narrative commonly observes the sequence of quest, challenge, struggle, victory, and reward, the order is far from universal. The tragic hero in particular may face his greatest threats and obstacles *after* he has already attained wife, kingship, and fame. By cleverly and courageously solving the riddle of the Sphinx, Oedipus acquires a royal wife, crown, and reputation, only to lose it all in a fatal quest for his true identity (Chapter 16). The "last acts" in the careers of such heroes as Agamemnon, Jason, and Heracles manifest this postreward reversal, which characteristically involves making a fatally flawed decision concerning their marital relationships.

Because myth takes the form of narrative—the sequential arrangement of action and its consequences over time—it expresses a linear and irrevocable movement in its characters' lives, a progression in which time's arrow flies in only one direction—toward death. As the ultimate shaping influence on the contours of even the greatest heroic endeavor, Greek myth's unrelenting emphasis on human mortality—the chief factor that distinguishes heroes from gods—gives most heroic tales a final vertical twist. The graph of a hero's life typically features a linear upward motion as he climbs fame's pinnacle by performing immortal deeds, but it takes an abrupt right-angle downward turn at his career's end. In contrast to much folklore, Greek myth never concludes with a pronouncement that the tale's principal couple "lived happily ever after." Eschewing such optimism, Greek mythology routinely insists on narrating the manner and circumstances of the hero's death. Besides describing in detail the slaughter of military leaders who perish at Troy or in other wars, the narratives, with extraordinary consistency, encompass the demise of those who survive conflicts as well. From Heracles to Jason and Agamemnon to Odysseus, virtually no hero exits his myth still alive; in most stories, the vertical descent to Hades's realm is made explicit. As if to assure us of this universal morbidity, many tales include a visit to the Underworld, where the shades of dead heroes are interviewed, providing unimpeachable evidence that all personal narratives end at a state in which no further action is possible. (In rare cases, a mortal son of Zeus, such as Heracles, undergoes posthumous deification and joins the gods in heaven, thus transcending the linear confines of his story by entering a supranatural dimension; see Chapter 10.)

The Autonomy of Myth

Myth has a vitality and inner logic of its own that baffle attempts to make it conform to any given theory. Some modern efforts to reduce its diversities to fit a single monolithic interpretation recall the myth of Procrustes, a notorious thief and extortionist who kidnapped travelers and tied them to an iron bed. If a victim was too tall and his legs extended over the foot of the bed, they were chopped off. If the victim was too short, he was forcibly stretched out to fit the iron frame. To avoid the Procrustean excess, this book tries not to force every myth discussed into one theoretical mold. The authors believe that several different methods provide valid approaches to particular myths, including some etiological, Freudian, Jungian, and structuralist techniques. Recent work of feminist critics has also aided in our understanding of myths, providing a new awareness of important factors previously overlooked in traditional criticism. Rather than a formal school, the feminist approach may utilize a variety of methodologies to explore the roles myths assign to the intricate interplay of male and female characters.

Certain myths seem to invite a distinctive mode of interpretation: Aeschylus's presentation of Orestes's dilemma dramatizes a conflict and final resolution of opposites, suggesting a structuralist approach—while still allowing for other approaches, such as a Freudian analysis of Orestes's tangled family relationships (see Chapter 15). In the Orestes plays, Aeschylus's characters seem to act out a dialectic between the id (amoral instinct), the ego (individual will), and the superego (divine law). By contrast, the *Odyssey*'s hero appears to undergo a process of individuation in which he learns and matures through contact with and the assimilation of archetypal principles of feminine wisdom, inviting a Jungian interpretation. At the same time, Homer's narrative may represent the hero's adventures as a complex series of initiations or rites of passage (see Chapter 12). Several elements in Hesiod's creation story, such as the origin of earth's topographical features, have an etiological component; yet other events in the *Theogony,* such as the miraculous births of Athene and Aphrodite, exhibit a wide range of functions on which the nature, charter, etiological, and a variety of psychologically based theories can all shed light. In some cases, myths are presented theory-free, with an emphasis on the historical circumstances of their development. Readers, of course, will apply whichever means of interpretation they find more effective in illuminating a given myth's relevance to their own life experience.

Questions for Discussion and Review

1. How did most Greeks apparently interpret their myths? What was the ancient Greek belief about myth's relation to history? In what ways could a city-state, such as Athens, employ myth to bolster its prestige or political authority?

2. Some nineteenth-century scholars regarded mythmaking as a quasi-scientific attempt to interpret the natural world and/or the human social environment. Describe the nature, ritual, charter, and etiological theories about the origin or purpose of myth.

3. Some scholars believe that mythmaking is an innate—and spontaneous—function of the human mind. Explain some psychologically based theories of myth, particularly the claims that Freud and Jung make about the operations of the human psyche. Define the terms *id, ego, superego, libido, dream-work, displacement, collective unconscious, anima, animus, archetype, shadow,* and *individuation.*

4. If human beings tend automatically to perceive the world in terms of tensions between opposites, how can myth function to mediate these assumed contrarieties? Describe the structuralist position.

Works Cited

Dowden, Ken. *The Uses of Greek Mythology.* London: Routledge, 1992.

Recommended Reading*

Burkert, Walter. *Structure and History in Greek Mythology.* Berkeley, CA: U of California P, 1979. An influential study.

Eisner, Robert. *The Road to Daulis: Psychoanalysis, Psychology, and Classical Mythology.* New York: Syracuse UP, 1987.

Jung, Carl G. *Psyche and Symbol: A Selection from the Writings of C. G. Jung.* Trans. V. S. de Laszlo. Princeton: Princeton UP, 1991.

Kirk, G. S. *The Nature of Greek Myths.* New York: Penguin, 1974. A review of the principal critical theories about the purpose and function of Greek mythology.

Segal, Robert A., ed. *Literary Criticism and Myth.* NY: Garland Publishing, Inc., 1996. 6 volumes. This multi-volume set includes critical essays by leading exponents of all the major schools of myth theory.

Slater, Philip E. *The Glory of Hera: Greek Mythology and the Greek Family.* Princeton: Princeton UP, 1968. A lucid Freudian analysis of the principal myths.

---

*A more complete list of references on theories of myth appears in the bibliography for Chapter 2 at the back of this book.

PART TWO

⤬

The Mythic World
of Gods, Goddesses,
and Heroes

CHAPTER

3

In the Beginning:
Hesiod's *Theogony*

KEY THEMES

In ancient Greek thought, the universe is a cosmos—a world order that evolved from Chaos, the primal Chasm or Void. Chaos and Gaea (the earth) are the sources of all that exists, including seas, mountains, monsters, and gods. Celebrating the rise of Zeus to cosmic rulership, Hesiod's The-ogony traces the gods' descent from Gaea and her son, Uranus (the sky), who mate to produce the Titans, a race of giant deities led by Cronus. On Gaea's advice, Cronus emasculates his father, Uranus, separating sky from earth, and seizes control of the cosmos. Cronus, in turn, is overthrown by his youngest son, Zeus, who defeats the Titans in battle, imprisons them in Tartarus, and establishes his Olympian sovereignty.

Some Greek scientists such as Aristarchus of Samos (c. 320 B.C.) correctly postulated that the earth is a globe, suspended in space, that orbits around the sun. Long before classical astronomers produced theories based on mathematical calculations, however, Greek poets such as Hesiod (about 750 B.C.) promoted a mythic conception of the universe, based partly on ancient Near Eastern models and partly on commonsensical observations of their physical environment. The world structure reflected in Hesiod's *Theogony,* the Greeks' oldest and most influential account of how all things began, is that which a careful observer might infer after taking a look around. When viewed from a hilltop affording a 360-degree panorama of the surrounding terrain, the earth's surface appears to extend an equal distance in all directions, forming a generally circular boundary. From this perspective, the sky resembles a huge bowl or dome that, from its highest point overhead, seems to curve evenly downward to the most distant horizon.

The sun, rising in the East, appears to trace an arc across the sky before sinking into darkness in the West, typically to be followed by the moon's ascent. In addition,

FIGURE 3-1   Detail, East Pediment of the Parthenon. The Olympians assembled to witness Athene's miraculous birth were framed by personifications of sun and moon. In this modern reconstruction of the extreme left corner of the pediment appear the heads of celestial horses drawing the chariot of the rising sun (Helios). The reclining figure of Dionysus, awakening from sleep, faces Helios's fiery steeds. The Parthenon sculptures thus picture the gods inhabiting an invisible region above the solar and lunar orbits, a demonstration of their superior power and status. (*Acropolis Museum, Athens.*)

one may assume that Olympus, dwelling place of the immortal gods, lies somewhere above heaven's vault. This picture, in fact, is precisely the structure used to frame the scene of Athene's birth on the Parthenon's east pediment. In the extreme lower-left corner, horses pulling Helios's chariot rear their heads, heralding the sunrise (Figure 3-1); in the right-hand corner, Selene pilots the moon's descending car. The family of gods gathered on Olympus presumably stands above the solar and lunar orbits (Figure 3-2).

The earthly stage, where celestial beings manipulate the human drama, is thus a relatively flat disc, except where high mountains like Olympus seem to touch the sky. Earth's circular surface is surrounded by ocean, not an open sea like the Atlantic, but an immeasurable river coiled around the central landmass. Far below ground lies Hades's kingdom, the subterranean destination of all mortals (see Figure 1-10).

Hesiod's *Theogony* as Cosmogony and Cosmology

The Greeks called this arrangement of heaven, earth, and Underworld a **cosmos,** an orderly, harmonious universe. The subject of Hesiod's *Theogony* is both a **cosmogony** (*cosmos* + *gonos* ["offspring"]), an account of the universe's origination, and a **cosmology,** a metaphysical statement about the universe's nature and purpose. As its title implies, the *Theogony* (*theos* ["god"] + *gonos*) is primarily a religious work, a vision of the gods' birth, offspring, and genealogical descent.

Readers familiar with the biblical creation account may find Hesiod's version of how all things began somewhat alien. Unlike the Genesis account, which describes a single God bringing heaven and earth into existence by the power of his word alone, the *Theogony,* commonly translated "birth of the gods," presents a world spontane-

FIGURE 3-2   Detail, East Pediment of the Parthenon. The moon (Selene) is shown descending below the horizon in the extreme right corner of the pediment. The Titan goddesses Dione (who is not usually included among the Olympian family) and her languishing daughter, Aphrodite, look toward the declining moon. Inhabiting the uppermost level of the three-story universe, the Olympians live high above the astronomical phenomena of physical nature. (*Acropolis Museum, Athens.*)

ously evolving, moving swiftly from primal emptiness to a universe teeming with life. Instead of biblical monotheism (belief in one God), Hesiod assumes a polytheistic universe, one populated by almost innumerable divine beings.

Hesiod's starting point is **Chaos,** literally the yawning Chasm or Void that early on somehow came into being—it did not necessarily exist from eternity. Hesiod's understanding of Chaos contrasts with that in Ovid's *Metamorphoses,* where it is defined as anarchic dark matter that preceded the formation of the cosmos (Chapter 20). For Hesiod, **Gaea** [JEE-uh]. (*Gaia*), who is both the earth and the primordial mother, is also a primal entity. Gaea springs independently into existence, along with **Tartarus** [TAHR-tahr-uhs], the subterranean abyss that will later house monsters and fallen gods, and **Eros** [AIR-ohs], the driving force of procreative love. Although Chaos and Gaea, as well as some male deities, occasionally give birth without a mate, Eros's presence ensures that life will multiply chiefly through sexual reproduction. Like later Greek scientists and philosophers, Hesiod shows a keen interest in organizing and classifying material, in this poem delineating the genealogies and familial relationships of three generations of gods.

The Poet and His Inspiration

Intergenerational conflict among the gods is one of Hesiod's main themes, but he also wishes to show that conflict permeates every level of the cosmos, especially family life and economic competition on earth. Introducing an autobiographical subtheme, Hesiod states that his father, unable to prosper as a sea trader in Ionia, migrated west to Boeotia on the Greek mainland (see Figure 3-3), where Hesiod was born to a life of poverty and hard work. Hesiod's poetry bristles with complaints about the slights

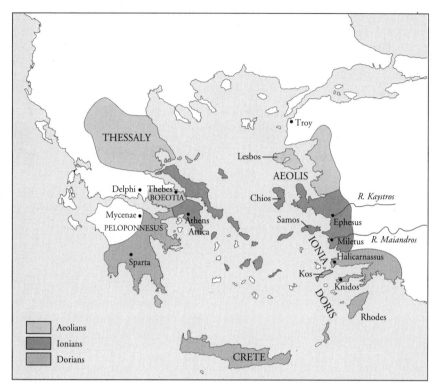

FIGURE 3-3   Map of Greece and the Aegean. Hesiod's father hailed from Ionia, the strip of Greek settlements along the west coast of Asia Minor (modern Turkey). Active in trade with older cultures in Egypt, Mesopotamia, and Phoenicia, the Ionian Greeks probably assimilated many ancient Near Eastern myths, which they adapted and integrated with local traditions. Hesiod, a native of rural Boeotia, reshaped some of these older tales in his account of the gods' origins, the *Theogony.*

and injustice he and other small landholders had to endure. According to Hesiod, his difficulties were compounded by the dishonesty and greed of his brother Perses, whom he accuses of bribing corrupt magistrates to award him an unfairly large por-tion of their father's modest estate. Much of Hesiod's second major poem, *Works and Days,* is aimed at correcting Perses's misbehavior, which stripped the poet of his right-ful heritage and means of livelihood.

The Muses

The most intriguing of Hesiod's allusions to his personal experience is that describ-ing the origin of his poetic inspiration, which he says derives from an encounter on Mount Helicon with the **Muses** (Figure 3-4), the nine daughters of Zeus and **Mnemosyne** [nee-MAHS-ih-nee], a personification of memory. Hailed as the source of artistic and intellectual creativity, the Muses become Hesiod's unseen companions,

FIGURE 3-4   The Nine Muses. Each of the nine daughters of Zeus and Mnemosyne (memory) eventually became associated with a particular field of creativity (see the box on p. 54), but in Hesiod's day they were seen collectively as the inspirers of all fine arts and skills. (The manual crafts, such as metallurgy, were under the direction of Hephaestus; Athene was the patron of weavers, spinners, and potters.) (*Discovered near Ostia, Italy, this bas-relief is now in the Capitoline Museum, Rome.*)

a spiritual link to Zeus and the divine authority that validates his poem. In typically blunt style, Hesiod has the Muses contrast the ignorance of his backwater environment with their divine omniscience:

"Listen, you country bumpkins, you swag-bellied yahoos,*
we know how to tell many lies that pass for truth,
and we know, when we wish, to tell the truth itself."
So spoke Zeus's daughters, masters of word-craft,
and from a laurel in full bloom they plucked a branch,
and gave it to me as a staff, and then breathed into me
divine song, that I might spread the fame of past and future,
and commanded me to hymn the race of the deathless gods,
but always begin and end my song with them.

Hesiod receives the laurel branch, sacred to Apollo, patron of the Muses, to authenticate his revelation of the gods' origins. (We presume that the Muses are prepared to "tell the truth" in this case.) Although little more than a thousand lines long, one-fifteenth the length of the *Iliad,* Hesiod's *Theogony* is an enormously ambitious effort: an attempt to unfold the history of the universe from its inception to the poet's own day. Honoring the goddesses' request, Hesiod begins each major segment of the poem with an invocation of the Muse, asking Mnemosyne's daughters to inspire him with creative success. Note that it is the Muses in their *Olympian* guise (line 60) who inspire the poet to sing of the highest gods, transforming his song into a hymn exalting Zeus.

---

*Yahoos—the term Jonathan Swift uses in *Gulliver's Travels* to denote a race of brutes that has the form and vices of humans.

The Nine Daughters of Zeus and Mnemosyne

The source of all poetic, artistic, and intellectual inspiration, the Muses embody the Greek conviction that music—the most sublime expression of cosmic harmony—is a primary and integral part of the universe. Although Hesiod names the nine daughters of Zeus and Mnemosyne, it was only later that each Muse acquired a particular creative function. Their distinctive spheres of activity are:

1. Calliope—epic poetry
2. Clio—history
3. Polyhymnia—mime
4. Melpomone—tragedy
5. Thalia—comedy
6. Erato—lyric choral poetry
7. Euterpe—the flute
8. Terpsichore—light verse and dance
9. Urania—astronomy

The Origins of the Gods

Hesiod devotes considerable space to recounting the origins of innumerable deities who, in surviving myths, play relatively small roles, such as the children of Night (Nyx) or Nereus, a primeval water god. These long genealogical catalogues do not obscure his main purpose, however, which is to trace the divine succession that culminates in Zeus, whose reign is the ultimate goal of cosmic evolution. (Note that genealogical lists are omitted between lines 242 and 243 in the edition of the *Theogony* excerpted at the end of this chapter.)

The Rise of Zeus

As Figure 3-5 indicates, Zeus is the grandson of the primal couple Gaea and her firstborn son, Uranus (Ouranos), a personification of the "starry sky," whom she produced without a father. The incestuous union of Gaea and **Uranus** [OOR-a-nuhs] results in the race of **Titans,** gigantic beings led by **Cronus** [KROH-nuhs] (Kronos), who mates with his sister **Rhea** [REE-uh] to produce Zeus and his older siblings, the future Olympians.

The Birth of Aphrodite

Of the scores of births catalogued in the *Theogony,* two—those of Aphrodite and Athene—most strikingly represent the contradictory themes that Hesiod weaves into his account. **Aphrodite** [af-roh-DYE-tee], the embodiment of love, beauty, and sexual desire, is the result of a grotesquely violent act—the castration of Uranus by his son Cronus. Gaea, who deeply resents Uranus for his refusal to allow her the relief of giving birth to the many children painfully confined in her subterranean womb, initiates the events leading to her husband's dethronement and Aphrodite's miraculous appearance. Following his mother's instructions and using the adamantine sickle she had fashioned for the purpose, Cronus, the most "crafty" of the Titans, ambushes his parents during copulation and severs his father's genitals, which he throws into the sea.

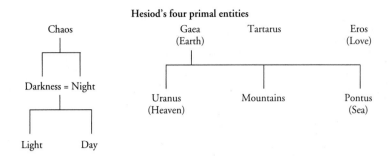

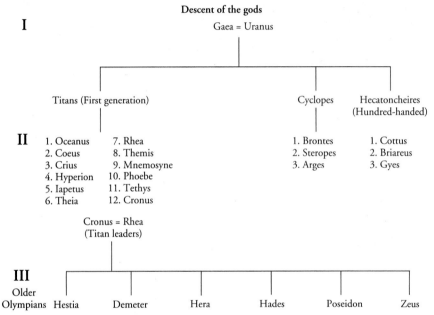

FIGURE 3-5   Genealogy of the Gods. According to Hesiod, all things that exist, including both gods and geographic figures like mountains, rivers, and seas, owe their being to the four primordial entities—Chaos, Gaea, Tartarus, and Eros. There is a direct line of divine descent from the first parents, Gaea and Uranus, to the second generation of gods, the Titans, to the third (reigning) generation of deities—the Olympians, headed by Zeus.

This act, which permanently separates earth and sky, has a strangely paradoxical effect: drops of phallic blood touching the earth generate both giants and the Furies (Erinyes), dreaded female spirits who punish criminals guilty of slaying their kin. The sea foam that collects around Uranus's severed phallus is transformed into "golden" Aphrodite, the most beguilingly feminine of all goddesses yet born without a female parent (Figure 3-6). In the *Theogony*, Aphrodite's origin clearly testifies to her function as patron of masculine sexual pleasure. (Homer more conventionally makes her the daughter of Zeus and Dione, a minor goddess sometimes listed among the children of Gaea and Uranus.)

FIGURE 3-6   Aphrodite Rising from the Sea. In Hesiod's version of her origin, the love goddess has no mother and is born from the sea foam surrounding the severed genitals of Uranus, the primal sky god. She rises from a watery element as if to demonstrate that a conscious awareness of human sexuality as a divine force is born from the universal unconscious. (*National Museum of Terme, Rome.*)

Aphrodite rising from the sea, accompanied by figures of Eros and Desire—and the vengeful Furies rising from blood-clotted earth—reveal the paradoxical aspects of Uranus's mutilation. Cronus's action leads the world another step closer to Zeus's inevitable reign, of which the love goddess will be a radiant ornament (Figure 3-7); however, it is also a savage betrayal of a kinsman that brings the spirits of hatred and revenge into being. Resulting from an act that combines sexual passion and violence, Aphrodite's birth expresses a characteristic Greek ambivalence about sexual love: although promising beauty and joy, it can also inspire acts of violent aggression. Aphrodite's appearance before Zeus or any other Olympians are born also implies the love goddess's primacy, both in time and in universal significance.

Consistent with his treacherous brutality, Cronus attempts to avoid Uranus's fate by devouring his own children, all of Zeus's older brothers and sisters (Figure 3-10), thereby imitating his father's life-denying policy and ensuring that any offspring who might escape his cannibalism—as Zeus does—will repeat his rebellion. With the exception of Prometheus, whose name means "forethought," the Titans are not known for their intelligence.

The Separation of Earth and Sky

Cronus's overthrow of Uranus embodies several basic mythological themes. In many world traditions, an early stage of creation is the enforced separation of earth and sky,

FIGURE 3-7 Aphrodite Crouching. Pictured as if drying her hair after a bath (or after her emergence from earth's primordial sea), Aphrodite embodies a graceful charm that captivates even the gods. Judged the most beautiful of divinities (see Chapter 11), she and her companion (or son) Eros (god of love) inspire and manipulate every being in the universe, from Zeus to ordinary mortals. (*Rhodes Museum.*)

a division necessary to achieve an inhabitable cosmos. In Egyptian tradition, which reverses the sexes of the two primal entities, the goddess Nut (Sky) is separated from her brother Geb (Earth) because their original embrace was so tight that their divine children had no room in which to be born. Accordingly, their father, Shu, god of the air, parted the incestuous couple, elevating Nut so that she arched her body far above Geb and thereby allowing the gods Isis, Osiris, Nephthys, and Seth to emerge into the atmosphere. Another Egyptian theme appearing in Hesiod's account is that of parent devouring child: it was said that Nut not only swallowed the sun every night, but that in the morning she ate her own offspring, the stars, which, of course, were reborn every evening after sunset.

Rather than serving as a model or justification for sons in primitive societies to seize power from their aged fathers, the Uranus-Cronus conflict echoes a convention of ancient cosmogony. The creative process demands that sky be removed from earth in order for life to develop. As in the Egyptian tale, Hesiod's account makes it clear that new gods cannot appear until their divine parents are permanently riven. Representing the dark night sky, studded with brilliant stars, Uranus remains in the distant background to be consulted occasionally, as when Rhea asks for his and Gaea's

The Origins of Sexual Attraction: Aristophanes's Speech in Plato's *Symposium*

Although Hesiod's *Theogony* does not include an account of humanity's creation, it emphasizes the crucial role of Eros (Love), the divine power that expresses itself through human sexual desire. In Hesiod's view, Eros is the procreative force responsible for populating the universe, generating both gods and heroes. About three and a half centuries after Hesiod's day, the Athenian philosopher Plato (427–347 B.C.) made the nature and purpose of Eros the subject of one of his most important dialogues, the *Symposium* (Figure 3-8). The fictional re-creation of a drinking party attended by some of Athens's most famous citizens, including Socrates, Agathon, Alcibiades, and the comic playwright Aristophanes, the *Symposium* contains numerous references to different myths about Eros's origin and purpose. Aristophanes, a fictive character whom Plato bases on the historical author of erotic comedies, offers an etiological myth to explain both the universality of sexual attraction and the reason for its diverse manifestations.

In the beginning, Aristophanes states, there were not merely two sexes—male and female—but three, the third being androgynous, composed of both male and female characteristics. The male sex derived from the sun, the female from the earth, and the androgynous from the moon, which the ancients believed to partake of both sun and earth. Originally, human beings were twice the person they are now: round in shape, each had two heads facing in opposite directions and two sets

FIGURE 3-8   A Greek Symposium. An all-male drinking party, the symposium provided educated Greeks with a time-honored forum for discussing ideas, such as the nature of Love (Eros) that Plato makes the subject of his famous dialogue. In Plato's *Symposium*, the comic playwright Aristophanes proposes a creation myth that explains the origin and purpose of both heterosexual and homosexual love. (*British Museum, London.*)

FIGURE 3-9   Scene from a Typical Symposium. A youth plays the diaulos (a kind of double oboe) for an older man who seems to forget the wine cup in his hand as he listens raptly. According to Aristophanes's story, Love (Eros) is the force that drives all people to seek out and commingle with the person who represents the part of their original nature that was lost when Zeus bifurcated the primal human beings. (*Louvre, Paris.*)

of arms and legs. These double creatures could go either forward or backward without turning around. They could also use their eight limbs to turn cartwheels, rolling along at high speeds wherever they wished to go.

Strong and confident—their circular form indicating their completeness—these primordial humans were also intensely ambitious. Like the giants Ephialtes and Otus, sons of Poseidon, who attempted to invade the heavens, the early human race dared to challenge the gods with a direct attack. Zeus, who did not want to obliterate them with lightning as he had the giants, decided instead to weaken humanity by splitting each person in two. As soon as Zeus bisected an individual, Apollo turned the creature's head around to face the side that had been cut, drawing skin over it "like a pouch with drawstrings" and tying the skin together in a knot on the abdomen, thus giving humans a navel.

With their ambition punished and their power diminished, human beings ceased rivaling the gods and began to devote their energies to seeking the half of their original person that had been lost. The androgynes, who had resembled the biblical Adam before the female Eve was separated from his body, sought their other half in members of the opposite sex, forming heterosexual combinations. Those who had been all male naturally endeavored to reunite with members of the same sex, while formerly all-female beings longed to restore their basic nature by coupling with other women.

Human sexual attraction, Aristophanes declares, is inspired by a profound need to recapture the wholeness of personality that existed before Zeus bifurcated us (Figure 3-9). The playwright then conjures up the spirit of Hephaestus, the ingenious god of metalcraft, who offers to fuse together those lovers who desire total union with their beloved, melding the artificially divided two into one. By thus uniting humanity's fragmented nature, Eros enables lovers to regain the lost paradise of spiritual and physical completeness.

FIGURE 3-10   Cronus Devouring One of His Children. Goya's famous painting (c. 1819–1823) of Cronus's cannibalistic attempt to prevent a son from replacing him as universal sovereign emphasizes the fierce savagery of Zeus's Titan predecessors. In Hesiod's view of an evolving universe, Zeus's success in overthrowing Cronus represents the triumph of civilized justice over primitive brutality. (*Prado Museum, Madrid.*)

help, but heaven's extreme remoteness means that sky plays little role in subsequent events, an impotence symbolized by Uranus's emasculation.

The tale of a primal deity whose body, like that of Uranus, suffers mutilation and then is used as building material to form part of the physical universe, is common in global mythology. In the *Enuma Elish,* Marduk cuts Tiamat's body into two sections, fashioning the sky with the upper half of her corpse and the earth with the lower half. In Scandinavian myth, the Norse creator gods slay Ymir, a huge frost giant, and make the earth from his body, the oceans from his blood, and the dome of heaven from his skull. Chinese myth offers a parallel account: a primordial deity, Pangu, exhausts himself performing the essential function of holding up the sky so that it will not fall and crush the earth, in effect sacrificing his life so that the cosmos can exist. In death, Pangu provides his body as the substance out of which the visible world is created.

The theme of primordial sacrifice, often taking the form of **sparagmos** [spuh-RAHG-mohs]—the ritual tearing apart of a sacrificial victim, divine or human—plays a significant role in Greek myth, not only in Hesiod's *Theogony* but also in narratives about Dionysus and mortal heroes (Chapter 13). These, and many analogous creation stories from around the world, imply that the universe did not come into being without pain and loss, including the sacrificial suffering of divine beings. A god who, like Uranus, withdraws from the earthly scene or disappears altogether after his creative function is completed, is called a *deus otiosus.* This shadowy figure, who can be defined as a god "at leisure" or "out of work," is familiar in the mythology of Africa, Mesoamerica, and ancient Canaan.

Some feminist scholars see in the myths of Uranus's mutilation a remnant of ancient matriarchal rites in which the primal goddess's consort was ritually killed (and perhaps eaten) to ensure fertility of flock and field, as well as the human community. Etiologically, the episode suggests the mysterious psychological affinity between love and hate, explains the enforced division of masculine and feminine principles in the cosmos, and offers a reason why "starry sky" (Uranus) is so remote and seemingly irrelevant to human affairs. The myth is also a classic illustration of the Freudian domestic psychodrama, a father-son rivalry in which the mother sides with her ambitious male child to subvert the dominance of a tyrannical husband.

The Birth of Athene

Hesiod's tale of Athene's birth also lends itself to a variety of interpretations. After Zeus, again with Mother Gaea's help, has succeeded in conquering the Titans and imprisoning most of them in Tartarus, he sets about populating the universe in his own image. Although he creates neither heaven nor earth, he becomes "father of gods and men" by mating with almost every available female, human or divine.

The first of Zeus's seven successive wives is **Metis** [MEE-tis], a personification of the Greek word meaning "thought," or "cunning," a concept about which the Greeks had mixed feelings, particularly when it involved female astuteness. When Gaea and Uranus warn Zeus that he too may have a son strong enough to depose him, Zeus reacts in a way that echoes Cronus's cannibalism but significantly differs from it: he swallows Metis, already pregnant with their child. Whereas Cronus could ingest but not absorb his children, Zeus successfully incorporates Metis into himself, controlling female cunning by internalizing it as part of his character. By assimilating Metis, Zeus is able personally to give birth to his first child, **Athene,** a potent manifestation of her father's creative intelligence (Figure 3-11; see also figures 1-2 and 1-3).

Like most myths, the story of Athene's birth can be understood from a variety of perspectives. Viewed as a nature myth, the tale of Athene's origin is largely a recognition that human thought takes place in the brain. In its etiological function, the myth describes a shift from matriarchal to patriarchal values: thought and cunning, formerly independent as an autonomous female, are now, embodied in Zeus's daughter, subordinated to male rule. Athene's perpetual virginity means that her father will always be the decisive force in her life and that his influence will never be challenged by an overly ambitious son-in-law. Operating as a charter, the myth validates both patriarchy and the institution of marriage in which the husband has total control of his wife, even to the point of taking over her identity.

In terms of Jungian psychology, Athene's birth from a male represents the archetypal union of the animus and the anima. As an example of psychoanalysis, it expresses the male fear of the castrating female: Zeus swallows Metis to prevent her from dominating him or producing a rival who will usurp his masculine power. In a Freudian sense, Zeus reenacts an Oedipal fear of and competition with the father, imitating Cronus's method of preventing future rivalry by imprisoning all potential threats within his own body and then transforming feminine intelligence into a daughter under his control.

Zeus's assimilation of Metis also illustrates the god's progression from a merely successful warrior to a mature ruler who understands the value of taking pragmatic Metis as his internal voice and the wise-counseling Athene as his favored confidante.

FIGURE 3-11   Archaic Vase Painting of the Birth of Athene. This crude but vigorous painting effectively illustrates Hesiod's tradition of Athene's birth from the head of Zeus (compare
a much later version in Figure 1-2). Athene emerges from Zeus's skull thrusting a shield before her as Hephaestus gazes in amazement at the result of his ax blow. (*British Museum,
London.*)

By this act Zeus moves to a higher stage of development, a *liminal* experience that
marks his advance beyond the mental limitations of his Titan predecessors. Finally,
viewed from a binary or structuralist perspective, the myth expresses the benefit to
humanity of reconciling its natural, instinctual, physical component (Zeus, who wins
his throne largely through unreflecting strength) with its higher potential centered in
the rational intellect (Metis). The creative union of this body-mind dichotomy produces Athene, whose harmonizing consciousness must acknowledge and encompass
both material and spiritual aspects of life.

Goddess of Victory   The fact that Athene is born wearing a soldier's armor and
accompanied by a figure of Nike (Victory) (see Figure 1-3) suggests that Zeus will
use his intellect in successfully defending his newly acquired power. For Athene is
not only the epitome of wisdom, she is also the goddess of victory in war, the ingenious strategist who outmaneuvers all opponents. As defender of the Greek polis, she
teaches the rational arts of logical argument and persuasion, replacing civil strife with
disciplined cooperation (see Chapter 15, the *Eumenides*).

   Zeus will need to co-opt all of Athene's qualities because, as the Prometheus myth
makes clear, only the acquisition of wisdom—and all the divine attributes that go
with it—will protect him from falling as ignominiously as his predecessors. Although
he will never again face enemies as formidable as those he defeats early in his reign,
Zeus contains in his own patriarchal character the seeds of his potential undoing (see
Chapter 14, *Prometheus Bound*). Even in his own household, Zeus encounters spo-
radic opposition, particularly from his sister-wife **Hera,** a goddess of marriage and
domesticity, who may have been worshiped independently before the imposition of
patriarchal religion reduced her to the status of Zeus's consort (Figure 3-12).

FIGURE 3-12   The Marriage of Zeus and Hera. In this bas-relief (fifth century B.C.), Hera unveils herself to her new husband. The posture of the divine couple suggests the ambiguity of their relationship: while extending his arm as if to control his wife's movements, Zeus is also mesmerized by Hera's beauty. Although myth affirms the pair's sexual compatibility, their union is marred by his obsessive infidelities and her unforgiving jealousy. (*National Museum, Palermo.*)

Hera and Hephaestus

Hera's rivalry with her husband, whose policies she regularly sabotages, appears at the outset of their relationship and pervades virtually all of the myths about her. Hesiod asserts that as soon as Hera sees Zeus giving birth to Athene, she counters, without any male assistance, by producing a son who is entirely hers, **Hephaestus.** (Because myth typically operates without regard for chronological sequence, the Parthenon sculptures of Athene's birth can show Hephaestus as already present on Olympus.) As Athene, Zeus's favorite child, consistently supports her father, so Hephaestus is his mother's devoted son, repeatedly taking Hera's side in his parents' many quarrels. In some versions of the myth, Hephaestus, the only imperfect Olympian, is born lame; in others, he becomes a cripple after Zeus hurls him down to earth for conspiring with Hera once too often. Although the myths of Olympian familial strife partly

FIGURE 3-13   Vase Painting of Zeus Battling Typhoeus (Typhon). After defeating the Titans, Zeus faces an even greater challenge to his sovereignty, the reptilian monster Typhoeus, child of Gaea and Tartarus. Typhoeus, shown here with only one head, is a Greek version of the Mesopotamian dragon of chaos and represents Gaea's final attempt to circumvent undisputed male rule of the universe. Originally, this serpent may have been a guardian of the earth goddess, which later myth reinterpreted as a destructive threat to Zeus's patriarchal regime. This close-up of Typhoeus shows that the monster's lower torso ends in serpentine coils and that his scaly wings extend to blot out the sun. Although Zeus defeats him with overpowering thunderbolts in Hesiod's account, other myths indicate that Zeus almost suffers defeat from the dragon's attack. (*Antikensammlungen, Munich.*)

replay the deadly mother-son-father triangle of Gaea, Cronus, and Uranus, Zeus's superior wisdom and his improved technological resources, his arsenal of thunderbolts, allow him to master the competitive dynamics of family life and thus maintain his throne. (For a variant tradition about Hephaestus's relationship to his mother, see the description of Hera in Chapter 5.)

Gaea and Typhoeus

Although Hesiod passionately supports a patriarchal society, in heaven as on earth, he seldom underestimates the crucial role of the feminine principle in cosmic history. Gaea, instrumental in every change in divine leadership, ultimately confirms Zeus's right to rule, but not before she has subjected him to his supreme test. Having contrived Uranus's downfall and tricked Cronus into vomiting up his children so that they can assist in Zeus's campaign against the Titans, she now presents Zeus with his most formidable opponent, the monster **Typhoeus** [tye-FEE-uhs], a Greek version of the ancient Near Eastern dragon of chaos (Figure 3-13). Gaea's "youngest child," Typhoeus, in some traditions called Typhon, is deliberately created by his mother's mating with Tartarus, the abysmal spawning ground of demonic forces. With his hundred reptilian heads, fiery breath, and fierce, predatory shrieks, Typhoeus, who aspires to rule both gods and men, represents a frightening alternative to Zeus's benevolent despotism.

Some commentators note that Typhoeus, whom Hesiod depicts as an incarnation of cosmic evil, may be a distorted picture of the guardian serpent that was once associated with the worship of a prehistoric goddess, before she was dethroned by male sky gods (see Chapter 4). Other scholars suggest that Hesiod's description of the conflagration that ravages earth during Zeus's war with Typhoeus expresses not only a patriarchal assault on Gaea but also a faint memory of some distant geological catastrophe, such as devastating prehistoric eruptions of Mount Etna or Thera (Santorini).

Hesiod pictures Zeus defeating Typhoeus by merely summoning the full might with which he had vanquished the Titans, but later traditions emphasize the great difficulty Zeus had in subduing this embodiment of universal disorder. According to Apollodorus, the cunning monster severs the tendons of Zeus's hands and feet and hides them, rendering the god impotent (a variation of Uranus's emasculation) until Zeus's clever son Hermes restores them to his father. In an elaboration from the fifth century A.D., Typhoeus steals Zeus's thunder and lightning, as well as his tendons, making the outcome of this battle between good and evil even more uncertain.

Although Gaea's last strategy to prevent Zeus's complete triumph fails, her ambivalent attitude toward the king of the gods lives on in Hera: according to some versions of the tale, Hera herself gives birth to Zeus's would-be nemesis Typhoeus (see Chapter 7, *Hymn to Pythian Apollo*), source of the violently destructive winds that sink ships and ravage crops. One tradition states that Zeus finally defeated Typhoeus by burying him beneath Mount Etna, Europe's largest and most active volcano. This etiological myth explains Etna's fiery outbursts as Typhoeus's convulsive struggles to escape from his underground prison.

Hesiod's Worldview

As noted in Chapter 1, Hesiod's view of world origins strikingly resembles that of ancient Mesopotamia. Both the *Enuma Elish* and the *Theogony* assume that several generations of elder gods successively ruled the universe before a young, male sky deity waged war against his ancestors to achieve supremacy. In both the Mesopotamian and the Greek traditions, violent conflict characterizes the creative process: sky and earth, once conjoined, are wrenched apart; the gods are fatally divided by intergenerational rivalry; in a climactic battle, Marduk slays the dragon-like Tiamat just as Zeus defeats the chaotic monster Typhoeus. Both Marduk and Zeus prove their right to rule the universe through their superior strength and martial skill, and both gods are able to retain their power by shrewd policies. After conquering their opponents, they wisely assign spheres of influence to other gods, establishing an orderly administration based on cooperation and the judicious delegation of shared authority.

Besides parallels to the *Enuma Elish*, the *Theogony* contains motifs from other ancient Near Eastern sources, such as the Hurrian-Hittite *Kingship in Heaven* and the *Song of Ullikummi*. The account in which the usurping god Kumarbi bites off and swallows Anu's genitals, for example, anticipates the castration of Uranus. In both the Greek and Near Eastern versions, as the defeated god, Anu or Uranus, withdraws

Greek and Anglicized Spellings of Characters' Names in the *Theogony*

Because different translators adopt differing transliterations of Greek names, the names of characters in Greek myth and literature are spelled in a variety of ways. Whereas this text uses an Anglicized spelling, the version of Hesiod's *Theogony* included here adopts a spelling approximating the pronunciation of the original Greek. The following list provides a brief sampling of both forms of the names. (For a more complete list of variant spellings of gods' names, see Chapter 5, p. 123; a similar list of characters' names in the *Iliad* appears in Chapter 11, p. 266.)

Atropos (Atropus)	Moirai (Moirae, the Fates)
Gaia (Gaea)	Okeanos (Oceanus)
Helikon (Helicon)	Olympos (Olympus)
Hephaistos (Hephaestus)	Ouranos (Uranus)
Herakles (Heracles, Hercules)	Phoibus Apollon (Phoebus Apollo)
Kerberos (Cerberus)	Pontos (Pontus)
Klotho (Clotho)	Rheia (Rhea)
Kronos (Cronus)	Tartaros (Tartarus)
Kyklopes (Cyclopes)	

upward to the distant heavens, his severed genitals produce new divinities. Hesiod and his fellow Greeks probably absorbed these Near Eastern myths piecemeal, picking up narrative fragments from sailors, merchants, and other travelers who plied the trade routes between Mesopotamia and the eastern Mediterranean. The Phoenicians, a seafaring people from whom the Greeks borrowed the alphabet, were perhaps the chief mediators in transmitting the Near East's cultural legacy to Greece.

In his attempt to synthesize ancient Near Eastern and native Greek traditions into an orderly account of the Greek gods' complex ancestry, functions, and kinships, Hesiod pictured a universe that is inherently contradictory. The primal Void (Chaos) is the unlikely source of an exuberant proliferation of life that culminates in Zeus's joyous begetting of both mortal heroes and deathless gods, figures who will dominate the mythic environment. Each stage of cosmic development, however, is marked by acts of appalling violence—mutilation, cannibalism, treachery, or war—illustrations of strife's power to trigger conflict on both the divine and human levels. Yet while celebrating the chief Olympian's ultimate triumph as the "bringer of good," Hesiod is deeply pessimistic about the human scene. He envisions a deteriorating world in which Zeus's reign inaugurates a progressive social and moral decline that imposes poverty and suffering on most of the god's human subjects (Chapter 6).

THEOGONY[1]

Hesiod

I begin my song with the Helikonian Muses;
they have made Helikon, the great god-haunted mountain, their domain;
their soft feet move in the dance that rings
the violet-dark spring and the altar of mighty Zeus.
They bathe their lithe bodies in the water of Permessos
or of Hippokrene or of god-haunted Olmeios.
On Helikon's peak they join hands in lovely dances
and their pounding feet awaken desire.
From there they set out and, veiled in mist,
glide through the night and raise enchanting voices   10
to exalt aegis-bearing Zeus and queenly Hera,
the Lady of Argo who walks in golden sandals;
gray-eyed Athena, daughter of aegis-bearing Zeus,
and Phoibos Apollon and arrow-shooting Artemis.
They exalt Poseidon, holder and shaker of the earth,
stately Themis and Aphrodite of the fluttering eyelids,
and gold-wreathed Hebe and fair Dione.
And then they turn their song to Eos, Helios, and bright Selene,
to Leto, Iapetos, and sinuous-minded Kronos,
to Gaia, great Okeanos, and black Night,   20
and to the holy race of the other deathless gods.
It was they who taught Hesiod beautiful song
as he tended his sheep at the foothills of god-haunted Helikon.
Here are the words the daughters of aegis-bearing Zeus,
the Muses of Olympos, first spoke to me.
"Listen, you country bumpkins, you swag-bellied yahoos,
we know how to tell many lies that pass for truth,
and we know, when we wish, to tell the truth itself."
So spoke Zeus's daughters, masters of word-craft,
and from a laurel in full bloom they plucked a branch,   30
and gave it to me as a staff, and then breathed into me
divine song, that I might spread the fame of past and future,
and commanded me to hymn the race of the deathless gods,
but always begin and end my song with them.
Yet, trees and rocks are not my theme. Let me sing on!
Ah, my heart, begin with the Muses who hymn father Zeus
and in the realm of Olympos gladden his great heart;
with sweet voices they speak of things that are
and things that were and will be, and with effortless smoothness
the song flows from their mouths. The halls of father Zeus   40

1. Translation by Apostolos N. Athanassakis.

the thunderer shine with glee and ring, filled with voices
lily-soft and heavenly, and the peaks of snowy Olympos
and the dwellings of the gods resound. With their divine voices
they first sing the glory of the sublime race of the gods
from the beginning, the children born to Gaia and vast Ouranos
and of their offspring, the gods who give blessings.
Then they sing of Zeus, father of gods and men—
they begin and end their song with him
and tell of how he surpasses the other gods in rank and might.
And then again the Olympian Muses and daughters of aegis-bearing Zeus   50
hymn the races of men and of the brawny Giants,
and thrill the heart of Zeus in the realm of Olympos.
Mnemosyne, mistress of the Eleutherian hills,
lay with father Zeus and in Pieria gave birth to the Muses
who soothe men's troubles and make them forget their sorrows.
Zeus the counselor, far from the other immortals, leaped
into her sacred bed and lay with her for nine nights.
And when, as the seasons turned, the months waned,
many many days passed and a year was completed,
she gave birth to nine daughters of harmonious mind,   60
carefree maidens whose hearts yearn for song;
this was close beneath the highest peak of snowy Olympos,
the very place of their splendid dances and gracious homes.
The Graces and Desire dwell near them and take part
in their feasts. Lovely are their voices when they sing
and extol for the whole world the laws
and wise customs of all the immortals.
Then they went to Olympos, delighting in their beautiful voices
and their heavenly song; the black earth all about resounded
with hymns, and a harmonious tempo arose as they pounded their feet   70
and advanced toward their father, the king of the sky
who holds the thunderbolt that roars and flames.
He subdued his father, Kronos, by might and for the gods
made a fair settlement and gave each his domain.
All this was sung by the Olympian Muses,
great Zeus's nine daughters whose names are
Kleio, Euterpe, Thaleia, Melpomene,
Terpsichore, Erato, Polyhymnia, Ourania
and Kalliope, preeminent by far,
the singers' pride in the company of august kings.   80
And if the daughters of great Zeus honor a king
cherished by Zeus and look upon him when he is born,
they pour on his tongue sweet dew
and make the words that flow from his mouth honey-sweet,
and all the people look up to him as with straight justice
he gives his verdict and with unerring firmness
and wisdom brings some great strife to a swift end.
This is why kings are prudent, and when in the assembly

injustice is done, wrongs are righted
by the kings with ease and gentle persuasion.   90
When such a king comes to the assembly he stands out;
yes, he is revered like a god and treated with cheerful respect.
Such is the holy gift the Muses gave men.
The singers and lyre players of this earth
are descended from the Muses and far-shooting Apollon,
but kings are from the line of Zeus. Blessed is the man
whom the Muses love; sweet song flows from his mouth.
A man may have some fresh grief over which to mourn,
and sorrow may have left him no more tears, but if a singer,
a servant of the Muses, sings the glories of ancient men   100
and hymns the blessed gods who dwell on Olympos,
the heavy-hearted man soon shakes off his dark mood, and forgetfulness
soothes his grief, for this gift of the gods diverts his mind.
Hail, daughters of Zeus! Grant me the gift of lovely song!
Sing the glories of the holy gods to whom death never comes,
the gods born of Gaia and starry Ouranos,
and of those whom dark Night bore, or briny Pontos fostered.
Speak first of how the gods and the earth came into being
and of how the rivers, the boundless sea with its raging swell,
the glittering stars, and the wide sky above were created.   110
Tell of the gods born of them, the givers of blessings,
how they divided wealth, and each was given his realm,
and how they first gained possession of many-folded Olympos.
Tell me, O Muses who dwell on Olympos, and observe proper order
for each thing as it first came into being.
Chaos was born first and after her came Gaia
the broad-breasted, the firm seat of all
the immortals who hold the peaks of snowy Olympos,
and the misty Tartaros in the depths of broad-pathed earth
and Eros, the fairest of the deathless gods;   120
he unstrings the limbs and subdues both mind
and sensible thought in the breasts of all gods and all men.
Chaos gave birth to Erebos and black Night;
then Erebos mated with Night and made her pregnant
and she in turn gave birth to Ether and Day.
Gaia now first gave birth to starry Ouranos,
her match in size, to encompass all of her,
and be the firm seat of all the blessed gods.
She gave birth to the tall mountains, enchanting haunts
of the divine nymphs who dwell in the woodlands;   130
and then she bore Pontos, the barren sea with its raging swell.
All these she bore without mating in sweet love. But then
she did couple with Ouranos to bear deep-eddying Okeanos,
Koios and Kreios, Hyperion and Iapetos,
Theia and Rheia, Themis and Mnemosyne,
as well as gold-wreathed Phoibe and lovely Tethys.

Kronos, the sinuous-minded, was her last-born,
a most fearful child who hated his mighty father.
Then she bore the Kyklopes, haughty in their might,
Brontes, Steropes, and Arges of the strong spirit,   140
who made and gave to Zeus the crushing thunder.
In all other respects they were like gods,
but they had one eye in the middle of their foreheads;
their name was Kyklopes because of this single
round eye that leered from their foreheads,
and inventive skill and strength and power were in their deeds.
Gaia and Ouranos had three other sons, so great
and mighty that their names are best left unspoken,
Kottos, Briareos, and Gyges, brazen sons all three.
From each one's shoulders a hundred invincible arms   150
sprang forth, and from each other's shoulders atop the sturdy trunk
there grew no fewer than fifty heads;
and there was matchless strength in their hulking frames.
All these awesome children born of Ouranos and Gaia
hated their own father from the day they were born,
for as soon as each one came from the womb,
Ouranos, with joy in his wicked work, hid it
in Gaia's womb and did not let it return to the light.
Huge Gaia groaned within herself
and in her distress she devised a crafty and evil scheme.   160
With great haste she produced gray iron
and made a huge sickle and showed it to her children;
then, her heart filled with grief, she rallied them with these words:
"Yours is a reckless father; obey me, if you will,
that we may all punish your father's outrageous deed,
for he was first to plot shameful actions."
So she spoke, and fear gripped them all; not one of them
uttered a sound. Then great, sinuous-minded Kronos
without delay spoke to his prudent mother:
"Mother, this deed I promise you will be done,   170
since I loathe my dread-named father.
It was he who first plotted shameful actions."
So he spoke, and the heart of giant Earth was cheered.
She made him sit in ambush and placed in his hands
a sharp-toothed sickle and confided in him her entire scheme.
Ouranos came dragging with him the night, longing for Gaia's love,
and he embraced her and lay stretched out upon her.
Then his son reached out from his hiding place and seized him
with his left hand, while with his right he grasped
the huge, long, and sharp-toothed sickle and swiftly hacked off   180
his father's genitals and tossed them behind him—
and they were not flung from his hand in vain.
Gaia took in all the bloody drops that spattered off,
and as the seasons of the year turned round

she bore the potent Furies and the Giants, immense,
dazzling in their armor, holding long spears in their hands,
and then she bore the Ash Tree Nymphs of the boundless earth.
As soon as Kronos had lopped off his genitals with the sickle
he tossed them from the land into the stormy sea.
And as they were carried by the sea a long time, all around them   190
white foam rose from the god's flesh, and in this foam a maiden
was nurtured. First she came close to god-haunted Kythera
and from there she went on to reach sea-girt Cyprus.
There this majestic and fair goddess came out, and soft grass
grew all around her soft feet. Both gods and men
call her Aphrodite, foam-born goddess, and fair-wreathed Kythereia;
Aphrodite because she grew out of *aphros,* foam that is,
and Kythereia because she touched land at Kythera.
She is called Kyprogenes, because she was born
in sea-girt Cyprus, and Philommedes, fond of a man's genitals,   200
because to them she owed her birth. Fair Himeros and Eros
became her companions when she was born and when she joined the gods.
And here is the power she has had from the start
and her share in the lives of men and deathless gods:
from her come young girls' whispers and smiles and deception
and honey-sweet love and its joyful pleasures.
But the great father Ouranos railed at his own children
and gave them the nickname Titans, Overreachers,
because he said they had, with reckless power, overreached him
to do a monstrous thing that would be avenged some day.   210
Night gave birth to hideous Moros and black Ker
and then to Death and Sleep and to the brood of Dreams.
After them dark Night, having lain with no one,
gave birth to Momos and painful Oizys
and to the Hesperides, who live beyond renowned Okeanos
and keep the golden apples and the fruit-bearing trees.
She also bore the ruthless Keres and the Moirai,
Klotho, Lachesis, and Atropos, who when men are born
give them their share of things good and bad.
They watch for the transgressions of men and gods,   220
and the dreadful anger of these goddesses never abates
until wrongdoers are punished with harshness.
Baneful Night bore Nemesis, too, a woe for mortals,
and after her Deception and the Passion of lovers
and destructive Old Age and capricious Strife.
Then loathsome Strife bore Ponos, the bringer of pains,
Oblivion and Famine and the tearful Sorrows,
the Clashes and the Battles and the Manslaughters,
and Quarrels and the Lies and Argument and Counter-Argument,
Lawlessness and Ruin whose ways are all alike,   230
and Oath, who, more than any other, brings pains on mortals
who of their own accord swear false oaths.

Pontos sired truthful Nereus, his oldest son,
who tells no lies; they call him the old man
because he is honest and gentle and never forgetful
of right, but ever mindful of just and genial thought.
Then Pontos lay with Gaia and sired great Thaumas,
Phorkys the overbearing, and fair-cheeked Keto,
and Eurybie, who in her breast has a heart of iron.
To Nereus and Doris of the lovely hair,   240
the daughter of Okeanos, the stream surrounding the earth,
a host of godly daughters was born in the barren sea:

. . . .

[Cronus and Rhea produce the Olympians.]

Rhea succumbed to Kronos's love and bore him illustrious children,
Hestia and Demeter and Hera, who walks in golden sandals,
imperious Hades, whose heart knows no mercy
in his subterranean dwelling, and the rumbling Earthshaker,
and Zeus the counselor and father of gods and men,
Zeus under whose thunder the wide earth quivers.
But majestic Kronos kept on swallowing each child
as it moved from the holy womb toward the knees;   250
his purpose was to prevent any other child of the Sky Dwellers
from holding the kingly office among immortals.
He had learned from Gaia and starry Ouranos
that he, despite his power, was fated
to be subdued by his own son, a victim of his own schemes.
Therefore, he kept no blind watch, but ever wary
he gulped down his own children to Rhea's endless grief.
But as she was about to bear Zeus, father of gods
and men, she begged her own parents,
Gaia, that is, and starry Ouranos,   260
to contrive such a plan that the birth of her dear child
would go unnoticed and her father's Erinys would take revenge
for the children swallowed by majestic, sinuous-minded Kronos.
And they listened to their dear daughter and granted her wish
and let her know what fate had in store
for King Kronos and his bold-spirited son.
And so they sent her to Lyktos, in the rich land of Crete,
just as she was about to bear the last of her children,
great Zeus, whom huge Gaia would take into her care
on broad Crete, to nourish and foster with tender love.   270
She carried him swiftly in the darkness of night, and Lyktos was
the first place she reached; she took him in her arms
and hid him inside the god-haunted earth in a cave
lodged deep within a sheer cliff of densely wooded Mount Aigaion.
But to the great Lord Kronos, king of the older gods,
she handed a huge stone wrapped in swaddling clothes.
He took it in his hands and stuffed it into his belly—

the great fool! It never crossed his mind that the stone
was given in place of his son thus saved to become
carefree and invincible, destined to crush him by might of hand,   280
drive him out of his rule, and become king of the immortals.
The lord's strength and splendid limbs grew swiftly
and, as the year followed its revolving course,
sinuous-minded Kronos was deceived by Gaia's
cunning suggestions to disgorge his own offspring—
overpowered also by the craft and brawn of his own son.
The stone last swallowed was first to come out,
and Zeus set it up on the broad-pathed earth,
at sacred Pytho, under the rocky folds of Parnassos,
forever to be a marvel and a portent for mortal men.   290
He freed from their wretched bonds his father's brothers,
[Brontes and Steropes and Arges of the bold spirit,]
whom Ouranos, their father, had thrown into chains;
they did not forget the favors he had done them,
and they gave him the thunder and the smoky thunderbolt
and lightning, all of which had lain hidden in the earth.
Trusting in these, he ruled over mortals and immortals.
Iapetos took as his wife the fair-ankled Klymene,
daughter of Okeanos, and shared her bed,
and she bore him Atlas, a son of invincible spirit,   300
and Menoitios of the towering pride, and Prometheus,
whose mind was labyrinthine and swift, and foolish Epimetheus,
who from the start brought harm to men who toil for bread;
he was first to accept the virgin woman fashioned by far-seeing Zeus,
who with flaming thunderbolt struck Menoitios
and cast him into murky Erebos
for his folly and reckless flaunting of manliness.
By harsh necessity, Atlas supports the broad sky
on his head and unwearying arms,
at the earth's limits, near the clear-voiced Hesperides,   310
for this is the doom decreed for him by Zeus the counselor.
With shackles and inescapable fetters Zeus riveted Prometheus
on a pillar—Prometheus of the labyrinthine mind;
and he sent a long-winged eagle to swoop on him
and devour the god's liver; but what the long-winged bird ate
in the course of each day grew back and was restored to its full size.
But Herakles, the mighty son of fair-ankled Alkmene,
slew the eagle, drove the evil scourge away
from the son of Iapetos and freed him from his sorry plight,
and did all this obeying the will of Olympian Zeus,   320
who rules on high, to make the glory of Herakles, child of Thebes,
greater than before over the earth that nurtures many.
Zeus so respected these things and honored his illustrious son
that he quelled the wrath he had nursed against Prometheus,
who had opposed the counsels of Kronos's mighty son.

When the gods and mortal men were settling their accounts
at Mekone, Prometheus cheerfully took a great ox,
carved it up, and set it before Zeus to trick his mind.
He placed meat, entrails, and fat within a hide
and covered them with the ox's tripe,   330
but with guile he arranged the white bones of the ox,
covered them with glistening fat, and laid them down as an offer.
Then indeed the father of gods and men said to him:
"Son of Iapetos, you outshine all other kings,
but, friend, you have divided with self-serving zeal."
These were the sarcastic words of Zeus, whose counsels never perish,
but Prometheus was a skillful crook and he smiled faintly,
all the while mindful of his cunning scheme,
and said: "Sublime Zeus, highest among the everlasting gods,
choose of the two portions whichever your heart desires."   340
He spoke with guileful intent, and Zeus, whose counsels never perish,
knew the guile and took note of it; so he pondered evils in his mind
for mortal men, evils he meant to bring on them.
With both hands he took up the white fat,
and spiteful anger rushed through his mind and heart
when he saw the white bones of the ox laid out in deceit.
From that time on the tribes of mortal men on earth
have burned the white bones for the gods on smoky altars.
Then Zeus the cloud-gatherer angrily said:
"Son of Iapetos, no one matches your resourceful wits,   350
but, friend, your mind is clinging stubbornly to guile."
So Zeus, whose counsels never perish, spoke in anger
and thereafter never forgot that he had been beguiled
and never gave to ash trees the power of unwearying fire
for the good of men who live on this earth,
but the noble son of Iapetos deceived him again
and within a hollowed fennel stalk stole the far-flashing
unwearying fire. This stung the depths of Zeus's mind,
Zeus who roars on high, and filled his heart with anger,
when he saw among mortal men the far-seen flash of fire;   360
so straightway because of the stolen fire he contrived an evil for men.
The famous lame smith took clay and, through Zeus's counsels,
gave it the shape of a modest maiden.
Athena, the gray-eyed goddess, clothed her and decked her out
with a flashy garment and then with her hands
she hung over her head a fine draping veil, a marvel to behold;
Pallas Athena crowned her head with lovely wreaths
of fresh flowers that had just bloomed in the green meadows.
The famous lame smith placed on her head a crown of gold
fashioned by the skill of his own hands   370
to please the heart of Zeus the father.
It was a wondrous thing with many intricate designs
of all the dreaded beasts nurtured by land and sea.

Such grace he breathed into the many marvels therein
that they seemed endowed with life and voice.
Once he had finished—not something good but a mixture of good
and bad—he took the maiden before gods and men,
and she delighted in the finery given her by gray-eyed Athena,
daughter of a mighty father. Immortal gods and mortal men
were amazed when they saw this tempting snare   380
from which men cannot escape. From her comes the fair sex;
yes, wicked womenfolk are her descendants.
They live among mortal men as a nagging burden
and are no good sharers of abject want, but only of wealth.
Men are like swarms of bees clinging to cave roofs
to feed drones that contribute only to malicious deeds;
the bees themselves all day long until sundown
are busy carrying and storing the white wax,
but the drones stay inside in their roofed hives
and cram their bellies full of what others harvest.   390
So, too, Zeus who roars on high made women
to be an evil for mortal men, helpmates in deeds of harshness.
And he bestowed another gift, evil in place of good:
whoever does not wish to marry, fleeing the malice of women,
reaches harsh old age with no one to care for him;
then even if he is well-provided,
he dies at the end only to have his livelihood shared
by distant kin. And even the man who does marry
and has a wife of sound and prudent mind
spends his life ever trying to balance   400
the bad and the good in her. But he who marries into a foul brood
lives plagued by unabating trouble in his heart
and in his mind, and there is no cure for his plight.
So there is no way to deceive or hide from the mind of Zeus,
for not even noble Prometheus, son of Iapetos,
escaped the heavy wrath of Zeus, but, despite his many skills,
succumbed to force and was bound in mighty chains.
First father Ouranos nursed anger in his heart
against Briareos, Kottos, and Gyges, and bound them in chains
and then settled them under the earth of the wide paths,   410
awed at their size, their shape, and their towering vigor.
There they stayed and suffered great pains,
sitting at the utmost limits of the boundless earth,
their hearts stung by endless grief and mourning.
But the son of Kronos and the other immortal gods
born of the love of Kronos and lovely-haired Rhea
brought them into the light again, following Gaia's instructions,
for she kept on reminding them that in alliance
with those three they would win victory and dazzling glory.
The divine Titan and the gods Kronos sired   420
struggled for a long time against one another

and did fierce battle, heartsore with strife,
the noble Titans from the peak of lofty Othrys,
and the gods born of Kronos and lovely-haired Rhea
—the very gods who give blessings—from Olympos.
With heavy hearts, they did battle against one another
and fought incessantly for ten full years;
their strife was harsh and there was no end and no resolution
for either side, and the outcome was indecisive.
But when Zeus gave the three gods what strengthens the body,   430
the very nectar and ambrosia of the gods,
and they drank nectar and ate exquisite ambrosia,
then the spirit rose bold in the hearts of all,
and Zeus, the father of gods and men, spoke and said:
"Listen to me, noble sons of Ouranos and Gaia,
for I wish to speak out what spirit and heart command.
So far the divine Titans and the gods Kronos sired
have fought against one another every day
and far too long for victory and power.
Now in this bitter battle give the Titans proof   440
of the unyielding strength in your invincible arms.
Remember our noble friendship and the pains you suffered
until, through plans we conceived, you came up to the light again
out of cruel chains and murky darkness."
So he spoke, and blameless Kottos gave this answer:
"Lord Zeus, you speak of things that are not unknown,
for we know full well that your mind is sharp
and that you defined the gods against dread disaster.
O Lord and son of Kronos it is through plans
conceived by you that we, sore from unexpected pains,   450
came back up again out of cruel chains and murky darkness.
For this, with unbending mind and shrewd resolve,
we shall battle the Titans with might and main,
to defend your power in the savage clash."
So he spoke, and the gods, givers of blessings,
heard and acclaimed his words. Then more than ever before
they yearned for war and they fought a fierce battle
on that day, all of them, both male and female:
the divine Titans and the gods Kronos sired,
and those whom Zeus from Erebos brought up into the light,   460
the dread and mighty ones, whose strength was matchless.
From each one's shoulders a hundred arms sprang forth
and from each one's shoulders and sturdy trunk
there grew no fewer than fifty heads.
They pitted themselves against the Titans in relentless battle,
with huge boulders in their stout hands.
The Titans, for their part, strengthened their ranks
and both sides eagerly gave proof of mettle and might of hand.
The deep and boundless sea resounded all around,

the earth boomed and the wide sky above shook   470
and groaned while lofty Olympos heaved from its foundation
in the whirl of missiles flung by the immortals. A heavy din
and the ear-splitting sound of feet in merciless pursuit
and of hefty missiles reached gloomy Tartaros.
They hurled whining missiles at one another
and the rousing shouts when both sides clashed
with deafening clamor reached the starry heavens.
Zeus could no longer hold back his fighting spirit,
which straightway surged to fill his heart
and showed all his strength, as from the sky and from Olympos   480
he advanced with steady pace amid flashes of lightning
and from his stout hand let fly thunderbolts
that crashed and spewed forth a stream of sacred flames.
The life-giving earth burned and resounded all over
and the vast forest groaned, consumed by fire.
The whole earth and Ocean's streams seethed,
and so did the barren sea; then the heated vapor engulfed
the earth-born Titans and towering flames licked the bright sky.
For all the Titans' might, the blazing flash
of thunderbolt and lightning blinded their eyes.   490
Wondrous conflagration spread through Chaos, and to eyes and ears
it seemed as though what they saw and heard
was the collision of the Earth and the wide Sky above.
For so vast a crash could only arise
if earth collapsed under collapsing sky;
such was the uproar of the battling gods.
The winds churned quaking land, dust, and thunder,
lightning, too, and glowing thunderbolts, great Zeus's weapons,
and they swept the noise and clamor into the midst
of the warring hosts. Unbearable din hovered above   500
the horrid fray. Both sides gave proof of strength,
and then the scales of the conflict tipped; before, each side charged
against the other and fought a grisly and stubborn battle.
But now Kottos and Briareos and war-hungry Gyges
in the front lines stirred up bitter battle
and from their stout hands hurled three hundred boulders
in thick-falling volleys that threw a mantle of darkness
over the Titans. And though the Titans' spirit was bold,
they were vanquished and then hurled beneath the earth
of the wide paths and bound with racking chains,   510
as deep down below the earth as the sky is high above it;
so deep down into the gloomy Tartaros they were cast.
A bronze anvil falling from the sky would travel
nine days and nights to reach the earth on the tenth day
and a bronze anvil falling from the earth would need
nine days and nights to reach Tartaros on the tenth day.
Tartaros is fenced with bronze and round its gullet

drifts night in triple array, while above it grow
the roots of the earth and of the barren sea.
There, by the decree of Zeus the cloud-gatherer,   520
the divine Titans have been hidden in the misty gloom
in a rank realm at the utmost limits of giant earth.
There is no escape for them; Poseidon built gates of bronze,
and a wall runs all around on every side.
There dwell Gyges, Briareos, and high-mettled Kottos,
ever the trusted guards of aegis-bearing Zeus.
There, in proper order, lie the sources and the limits
of the black earth and of mist-wrapt Tartaros,
of the barren sea, too, and of the starry sky—
grim and dank and loathed even by the gods—   530
this chasm is so great that, once past the gates,
one does not reach the bottom in a full year's course,
but is tossed about by stormy gales;
even the gods shudder at this eerie place.
There also stands the gloomy house of Night;
ghastly clouds shroud it in darkness.
Before it Atlas stands erect and on his head
and unwearying arms firmly supports the broad sky,
where Night and Day cross a bronze threshold
and then come close and greet each other.   540
When the one descends the other shrinks away,
and the house is never host to both of them,
but always one of the two is out and away from it
and roams over the earth, while the other inside it
awaits the appointed time for its own journey.
The one brings to mortals the light that sees all,
while the other, the harmful Night, veiled in dusky fog,
carries in her arms Sleep, Death's own brother.
There, too, dwell the children of black Night,
Sleep and Death, the awesome gods who are never seen   550
by the rays of the blazing sun when it rises
on the sky, or moves on its downward path.
Of these, the one wanders over land and broad-backed sea,
ever at peace and ever gentle to mortals,
but the other, a ghoul even the gods detest,
has a heart of iron and feelings hard as bronze,
and no man gripped by him can free himself again.
There, too, stand the echoing halls of Hades,
whose sway is great, and of awesome Persephone.
A hideous and ruthless hound guards the place   560
skilled in an evil trick: wagging his tail
and wriggling his ears he fawns on those who enter,
but he does not let them out again;
instead, he lies in wait and devours those he catches
outside the gates of sovereign Hades and of awesome Persephone.

There dwells a goddess loathed by the gods,
dreadful Styx, eldest daughter of Ocean, whose stream
flows back on itself; she dwells apart from the gods
in a stately palace roofed by lofty rocks and ringed
by silver pillars that tower into the sky.   570
Seldom does fleet-footed Iris, the daughter of Thaumas,
roam on the broad-backed sea to bring her a message
when strife and quarrel arise among the immortals
and when one of the Olympian dwellers lies.
Then Zeus sends Iris far away to fetch in a golden jar
the legendary cold water by which the gods swear great oaths,
water that tumbles down from a steep and soaring rock.
This water flows through the black night
from a sacred river, far below the earth of the wide paths.
It is a branch of Ocean allotted one tenth of the water;   580
the other nine parts wind round the earth and the broad-backed sea
and, silver-swirled, cascade into the briny deep,
but this one branch—this bane for the gods—runs off a cliff.
If any one of the gods who hold the peaks of snowy Olympos
pours a libation of this water and then swears a false oath,
he lies breathless for no less than a full year's course;
and he cannot come close to ambrosia and nectar
for nourishment, but no longer able to speak or breathe
lies in bed, wrapped in the shroud of evil coma.
And when the illness is over at the long year's end,   590
another, even harsher, trial is in store for him.
For nine years he is an outcast to the eternal gods
and does not mingle with them at council or feast
for nine full years, but on the tenth he joins again
the meetings of the gods whose homes are on Olympos.
Such is the oath the gods made of the primeval and immortal
water of Styx that gushes through a rugged place.
There, in proper order, lie the sources and the limits
of black earth and of mist-wrapped Tartaros,
of the barren sea, too, and of the starry sky,   600
and they are grim and dank and loathed even by the gods.
There stand the gates of marble and the threshold of bronze,
unshakable and self-grown from the roots that reach
deep into the ground. In front of these gates, away from all the gods
dwell the Titans, on the other side of murky Chaos.
But the renowned allies of Zeus, whose thunder echoes
through the sky, have their houses at Ocean's foundations.
These are Kottos and Gyges, and noble Briareos;
to him the deep-rumbling Shaker of the Earth gave Kymopoleia,
his own daughter, and thus made Briareos his son-in-law.   610
When Zeus drove the Titans out of the sky
giant Gaia bore her youngest child, Typhoeus;
goaded by Aphrodite, she lay in love with Tartaros.

The arms of Typhoeus were made for deeds of might,
his legs never wearied, and on his shoulders were
a hundred snake heads, such as fierce dragons have,
and from them licking black tongues darted forth.
And the eyes on all the monstrous heads flashed
from under the brows and cast glances of burning fire;
from all the ghastly heads voices were heard,   620
weird voices of all kinds. Sometimes they uttered words
that the gods understood, and then again
they bellowed like bulls, proud and fierce
beyond restraint, or they roared like brazen-hearted lions
or—wondrous to hear—their voices sounded like a whelp's bark,
or a strident hiss that echoed through the lofty mountains.
An irreversible deed would have been done that day,
and Typhoeus would have become lord over gods and men,
had not the father of gods and men kept sharp-eyed watch.
He hurled a mighty bolt and its ear-splitting crash   630
reverberated grimly through the earth and the wide sky above,
through the sea, the streams of Ocean, and through the underworld.
And when the lord moved, massive Olympos shook
and the earth groaned under his indestructible feet,
and the heat of the duel engulfed the violet-dark sea,
heat from Zeus's lightning and thunder, from hurricanes
and from the fire that raged as thunderbolts struck the monster.
The whole earth, the sea, and the sky seethed;
a dread quake arose in the wake of the immortals' charge
and heaving waves rolled up against the shores;   640
then Hades, lord of the wasted shades below,
and the Titans under Tartaros and around Kronos
shuddered at the unending din and grisly clash.
But now Zeus's strength surged and he grasped his weapons,
thunder and lightning and glowing thunderbolt,
and, lunging from Olympos, he set fire
to all of the hellish monster's gruesome heads.
Then, when Zeus's blows had whipped him to submission,
Typhoeus collapsed, crippled, on the groaning giant earth;
and the flame from the thunder-smitten lord   650
leaped along the dark and rocky woodlands
of the mountain, and the infernal blast of the flames
set much of the giant earth on fire until it melted
like tin that has been heated by craftsmen
over a well-pierced crucible, or like that strongest metal,
iron, which in mountain woodlands the scorching fire tames
and the craft of Hephaistos melts inside the divine earth.
So melted the earth from the flash of the burning fire,
and Zeus in terrible anger cast Typhoeus into broad Tartaros.
From Typhoeus come the violent and damp winds,   660
but not Notos, Boreas, and bright Zephyros,

who are descended from the gods, a great boon to mortals.
But other fitful blasts blow over the sea to bring harm.
They swoop down on the face of the misty sea,
a raging and wicked gale, a great scourge to mortals;
they blow in all directions, and they scatter ships
and wipe out the sailors, and men who run into such winds
in the open sea have no way to fend off havoc.
They fill the flowering and boundless earth
with harmful and whirling clouds of dust   670
and sweep away the lovely works of earth-born men.
But when the gods achieved their toilsome feat
and by brute force stripped the Titans of their claim to honor,
then, through Gaia's advice, they unflaggingly urged
Olympian Zeus, whose thunder is heard far and wide, to rule
over the gods, and he divided titles and power justly.
Zeus, king of the gods, took as his first wife Metis,
a mate wiser than all gods and mortal men.
But when she was about to bear gray-eyed Athena,
then through the schemes of Gaia and starry Ouranos,   680
he deceived the mind of Metis with guile
and coaxing words, and lodged her in his belly.
Such was their advice, so that of the immortals
none other than Zeus would hold kingly sway.
It was fated that Metis would bear keen-minded children,
first a gray-eyed daughter, Tritogeneia,
who in strength and wisdom would be her father's match,
and then a male child, high-mettled
and destined to rule over gods and men.
But Zeus lodged her in his belly before she did all this,   690
that she might advise him in matters good and bad.
His second wife was radiant Themis; she bore the Seasons,
Lawfulness and Justice and blooming Peace,
who watch over the works of mortal men,
and also the Fates, to whom wise Zeus allotted high honors.
These are Klotho, Lachesis, and Atropos,
and they give mortals their share of good and evil.
Then Eurynome, Ocean's fair daughter,
bore to Zeus the three Graces, all fair-cheeked,
Aglaia, Euphrosyne, and shapely Thalia;   700
their alluring eyes glance from under their brows,
and from their eyelids drips desire that unstrings the limbs.
After Zeus slept with Demeter who nurtures many,
she bore white-armed Persephone, whom Aidoneus
snatched away from her mother with the consent of wise Zeus.
Then he fell in love with Mnemosyne the lovely-haired,
who gave birth to the gold-filleted Muses,
lovers, all nine, of feasts and of enchanting song.
Leto lay in love with aegis-bearing Zeus

and gave birth to Apollon and arrow-shooting Artemis, 710
children comelier than all the other sky-dwellers.
Last of all, Zeus made Hera his buxom bride,
and she lay in love with the king of gods and men
and bore Hebe and Ares and Eileithyia.
Then from his head he himself bore gray-eyed Athena,
weariless leader of armies, dreaded and mighty goddess,
who stirs men to battle and is thrilled by the clash of arms.
Hera wrangled with her husband and because of anger,
untouched by him, she bore glorious Hephaistos
who surpasses all the other gods in craftsmanship. 720
From the union of rumbling Poseidon and Amphitrite
came the great Triton, whose might is far-flung,
an awesome god dwelling in a golden house that lies
at the sea's bottom, near his cherished mother and lordly father.
Now to shield-shattering Ares Kythereia bore the dreaded twins
Fear and Panic who with Ares, sacker of cities,
force men to flee in disorder from the thick array of battle.
Harmonia, too, the wife of bold Kadmos, was her daughter.
Maia, daughter of Atlas, shared the sacred bed of Zeus
and gave birth to Hermes, renowned herald of the gods. 730
Semele, daughter of Kadmos, yielded to Zeus's lust,
and she, a mere mortal, is now the divine mother
of the dazzling and deathless god in whom many exult.
Alkmene gave birth to invincible Herakles
after she had lain in love with Zeus the cloud gatherer.
And Hephaistos, the lame smith of wide renown,
took as his buxom bride Aglaia, the youngest of the Graces.
Golden-haired Dionysos took blond Ariadne,
daughter of Minos, to be his buxom bride,
and then Zeus made her ageless and immortal. 740
Herakles, mighty son of fair-ankled Alkmene,
accomplished his grim labors and took Hebe,
daughter of great Zeus and gold-sandaled Hera,
to be his noble spouse on snowy Olympos.
Blessed is he! His exploits all finished,
he is now among the gods, griefless and ageless forever.

. . . .

Questions for Discussion and Review

1. Describe the structure of the mythic cosmos. Define *cosmogony* and *cosmology*.

2. At what point in cosmic history does Hesiod begin his account of world origins? Define the primordial entities of Chaos, Gaea, Eros, and Tartarus. What is Hesiod's major purpose in composing the *Theogony?* Why do you suppose that he makes Zeus a third-generation god? What are the implications of a universe ruled by a god who is neither its creator nor eternal?

3. What role do the Muses play in the poetry of myth?

4. Discuss the unusual births of Aphrodite and Athene. What are the paradoxes involved in the love goddess's birth from an act of sexual mutilation and violence? How is Zeus able to give birth to Athene, and why does she issue from her father's head? Which theories of myth are useful in interpreting these births?

5. Discuss Zeus's battles with the Titans and with Typhoeus. What role does Gaea play in each change of divine administration? Why does she side with sons who overthrow their fathers? Why does she create Zeus's most formidable opponent?

6. Why does myth attribute at least seven principal wives to Zeus? What significance do you give to the fact that most of his early children are personifications of abstract qualities? Why does Zeus feel compelled to mate with so many females, both divine and human, making him the "father of gods and men"? Why does he wait until after he has defeated all his enemies before embarking on his amorous exploits?

Recommended Reading

Athanassakis, Apostolos N., ed. and trans. *Hesiod: Theogony, Works and Days, Shield.* Baltimore: Johns Hopkins UP, 1983. Contains many helpful interpretive notes.

Caldwell, Richard S., ed. and trans. *Hesiod's Theogony.* Cambridge, MA: Focus Classical Library, 1987. Offers an elaborate Freudian analysis of Hesiod's version of world origins.

Penglase, Charles. *Greek Myths and Mesopotamia: Parallels and Influence in the Homeric Hymns and Hesiod.* New York: Routledge, 1994.

West, M. L., ed. and trans. *Theogony and Works and Days.* New York: Oxford UP, 1988. Prose translation of the Hesiodic poems, with extensive notes.

The Great Goddess and the Goddesses: The Divine Woman in Greek Mythology

KEY THEMES

The Great Goddess of early Europe shares with her nearly universal counterparts three functions: she is the source of the complete cycle that encompasses life, death, and rebirth—both literal and spiritual. Once the secrets of agriculture are mastered, she is associated with earth. As patriarchal systems overseen by male sky gods replace the older matriarchal ones, the Great Goddess is typically divided, and her three aspects are parceled out among separate goddesses who are subordinated to the male gods. In Greek mythology, the primordial goddess is Gaea, whose functions under the Olympian system are most completely syncretized in the figure of Demeter. Her importance is emphatically revealed in the Eleusinian Mysteries performed in her honor. The individual functions of the Great Goddess, divided and redefined in their relation to men, are variously assimilated into such figures as Hera, Athene, Aphrodite, Artemis, and Hecate.

The Great Goddess

Long before there were gods, there was the Goddess (or the **Great Goddess,** as she is sometimes called, to distinguish this singular, primordial figure from later goddesses who incorporated some of her functions)—a powerful, creative force who, by parthenogenesis (conception without sex), gave birth to the universe. Although discussions of classical myths have, through the ages, emphasized the male gods, recent

FIGURE 4-1   Venus of Willendorf. Stone Age figures of the Great Goddess typically depicted her as pregnant and with enlarged breasts, illustrating her role as creator and sustainer of life. This small (4 3/4″) limestone sculpture, found in Austria and dating from approximately 30,000–25,000 B.C., is characteristic of Stone Age goddess figures. (*Museum of Natural History, Austria.*)

feminist scholars, both male and female, have revealed a new understanding (widely accepted but still the subject of occasional controversy) of the significance of the female goddess. The extensive research of modern archaeologists has demonstrated that from the Paleolithic (Old Stone Age) through the Bronze Age in Europe, images of the Great Goddess abound, yet few images of warriors or heroes dating before the Bronze Age have been found. Long before the invention of agriculture in the Neolithic (New Stone Age) period, the Great Goddess prevailed and was worshiped for her capacity to create and sustain life (Figure 4-1).

The Universality of the Great Goddess

The Great Goddess occurs in myth systems from all over the world: Gaea and Demeter in Greek myths, Ceres and Terra Mater in Roman myths, Isis in Egyptian myths, Inanna in Sumerian myths, Ishtar in Babylonian myths, Nerthus in Norse myths, and many others. The earliest images depict her with enlarged breasts and

FIGURE 4-2   Artemis of Ephesus. Although she was a virgin
goddess, Artemis, like most Greek
goddesses, retained the association
with childbirth and nurturing derived from the ancient Great Goddess. In this alabaster and bronze
sculpture (a Roman copy of a
Greek original, c. 500 B.C.), her
power to nourish is manifested
in her multiple breasts. (Some
scholars have suggested that the
"breasts" are actually the testicles
of sacrificed bulls.) The representations of many varieties of beasts
and insects with which she is covered emphasize Artemis's power as
a sustainer of animal as well as human life. (*National
Museum, Naples.*)

abdomen; she is often shown as pregnant, or sometimes in the act of giving birth,
symbolizing her power to create and nourish (Figure 4-2).

The Three Functions of the Great Goddess

In these early images, the Great Goddess was not associated with love or sex. Before
human beings understood the male role in procreation, the female ability to create
life from within herself seemed magical. The Great Goddess was typically associated
with three functions—as the source of life, of death, and of transfiguration or rebirth.
Her triple nature is repeated in the patterns of heaven–earth–Underworld and

FIGURE 4-3 Atargatis, or Dea Syria. One of the many deities imported by the Romans as they enlarged their empire by conquest, this Syrian goddess is another variant of the almost universal Great Goddess. She is shown in this bronze sculpture with two of her most important symbols: the serpent and the tree. Both the serpent (which can penetrate the secrets of the Underworld and also renew itself by shedding its skin) and the tree (which bears fruit annually after a period of dormancy) symbolize the Goddess's power of rebirth or renewal, typically combined on this figure. The snake surrounds the goddess as it would the trunk of a tree so that her body, embraced by the serpent, figuratively becomes the Tree of Life. As in figures 4-4 and 4-5, the serpent is depicted as a beautiful and benevolent creature. (*National Museum of Terme, Rome.*)

maiden–mother–old woman. Uniting opposites within herself, the Great Goddess encompasses both light and darkness, both upper and lower worlds, embracing the totality of the cycle of birth, death, and renewal in all its aspects—the terrifying along with the beneficent. Later, after humans understood the life cycle of plants and learned to plant, grow, and harvest food, she was also identified as the grain goddess or earth goddess—responsible for the rising, dying, and rebirth of vegetation—who now added these functions to the primal one of maintaining the eternal cycle of life, death, and regeneration.

Symbols of the Great Goddess

Although the guises in which the Goddess appears in myths throughout the world vary, certain key images remain constant, suggesting that these are recurring symbols of an archetypal female principle shared by human beings in all times and cultures.

Among the key symbols, perhaps the most prominent is the serpent (figures 4-3, 4-4, 4-5). Crawling underground as well as on the surface, the snake is privy to the

FIGURE 4-4   Snake Goddess from Knossos. The Minoans, whose civilization, centered on Crete, preceded and influenced the Greeks', also worshiped snake goddesses. In this unfortunately damaged figure, the goddess, whose bared breasts reflect her nurturing function, is wearing a skirt with serpentine designs and holds aloft serpents, traditional symbols of the Goddess's mysteries—her knowledge of the secrets of life, death, and regeneration. (*Heraklion Museum, Knossos.*)

mysteries of the Underworld, to the magic that transforms seeds into plants, and to the secrets of life, death, and rebirth. Because it sheds its skin each spring after a period of hibernation, the snake also symbolizes immortality, visually embodying the continuity of the eternal cycle. To emphasize that connection, the snake is sometimes depicted with its tail in its mouth. A related symbol is the tree (or its variants, the pillar or column)—the Tree of Life, or the World Tree, with its roots in the Underworld and its branches in the heavens, often depicted with the serpent twined around its trunk (Figure 4-6).

The Goddess is also associated with the moon, whose cycles of waxing and waning

FIGURE 4-5   Ceremony in Honor of Lares. The Lares were guardian spirits of the household, who had their counterparts in the guardian spirits of the State—Jupiter (the Roman Zeus), Juno (the Roman Hera), and, of course, Ceres, the Roman version of the grain goddess Demeter. In the top panel of this fresco from Pompeii, offerings are made to the Lares; in the bottom panel, as grain sprouts in abundance, the serpents appear to accept the offerings. (*National Museum, Naples.*)

approximate the menstrual cycle, while the swelling of the moon from the crescent of the new moon to its full state suggests the swelling of the womb in pregnancy so that the worldwide connection of the moon with women's fertility is not surprising. Moreover, the moon then disappears from view for several nights and is "reborn" to begin the lunar cycle anew, a pattern reflected in the many myths depicting the lunar goddess who mourns for a lover or child who dies or descends to the Underworld, or who descends herself and then returns to the upper world or arranges for the return/rebirth of the child or lover. The lunar cycle, recapitulating the cycle of life, death, and rebirth, creates a link between the physical and spiritual realms of existence. Some mythographers even speculate that the impulse of human beings to engage in mythmaking is initially inspired by their imaginative response to the lunar cycle.

Visible as light against the dark sky, the moon also unites contradictory elements, unlike the sun, whose blinding light obliterates darkness. Other symbols include various forms of the vessel (water jar, vase, pot, oven, chest, chalice, grail), which depict the body of the Great Goddess and were often decorated with breasts and abdomen.

FIGURE 4-6   Heracles in the Garden of the Hesperides. The Greek hero Heracles engages
in several battles with serpents. To the male hero, unlike the goddesses (see figures 4-3 through
4-5), the serpent is a threat, and he must kill it (as Heracles does in some versions of this
myth) or seduce its female guardians before he can acquire the Golden Apples of Immortality.
It is notable that the hero—typically not satisfied with rebirth through children, through
spiritual renewal in this life, or through the hope of resurrection in the hereafter—wants his
immortality literally and is willing to risk the potentially fatal encounter with the serpent to
obtain it. In this Athenian vase painting (fifth century B.C.), Heracles rests after his journey to
the land of the setting sun, where the Greek version of the Tree of Life grows, guarded, of
course, by a serpent. In this painting, Heracles has apparently charmed the Hesperides (the
nymphs who guard the Golden Apples that grow on that tree) into giving one to the hero.
(*British Museum, London.*)

As vessel, her body becomes the womb of creation, container of the waters of life.
Thus a descent to the Underworld becomes a return to the womb of the Great Goddess, the source of all, a journey sometimes archetypally identified as a descent into
the unconscious. As some scholars have noted, in many locations in Europe and Asia
Minor, from the Paleolithic era to a civilization as sophisticated as that of the Minoans on Crete, shrines to the Great Goddess were located in caves.

Other common goddess symbols include birds (whose flight links earth and sky),
the sow (an image of fecundity), and the cow (the source of nourishment, sustainer
of life, whose horns recapitulate the shape of the crescent moon). In the earliest figures, the body of the Goddess is often inscribed with lozenge shapes, frequently with
a dot inside, representing the seed in the field.

Division of the Great Goddess

Eventually, the three aspects of the Great Goddess are divided into separate figures, each of which represents one aspect of her totality. In Greek mythology, some scholars speculate that this division may in part reflect the invasion of Europe by martial Indo-European cultures with their weapon-bearing gods whose symbols are linear and phallic—spears, swords, thunderbolts, and other weapons. Some evidence suggests that the relationship between the Goddess and male deities may have been perceived as cooperative. For example, the Cretan cave-shrines dedicated to the Goddess contain representations of the horns of a bull-god. But eventually, the Great Goddess is divided, absorbed, and subordinated into forms not threatening to the sky gods. Thus the Goddess's triple aspects as maiden–mother–old woman are redefined from the patriarchal perspective—in their relation to men—as virgin–wife–mistress/whore and embodied in separate figures such as Athene, Hera, and Aphrodite.

The reign of patriarchy gives rise to a new archetype, the hero. In contrast to the feminine archetype, the masculine model of experience, focused on the singular achievements of a unique individual, is linear, not cyclical, making death terrible and final. Thus the hero, whose primary role is to escape mortality and achieve personal transcendence, becomes necessary. From this new perspective, the feminine archetype is a threat that must be counteracted. The association of the sun with the male deities typically creates a system of dualism, depicting the universe as an arena of combat between opposing forces: the sky gods of light and the sun are portrayed as "good," whereas the forces of darkness, including the Underworld functions of the Great Goddess, are termed "evil." Thus the snake becomes a dragon, with whom gods and heroes alike must do battle.

Gaea

In Greek myths, the original, parthenogenetic goddess is named Gaea, one of the components of the primordial universe. She includes all levels of the cosmos within herself, mediating between the upper and lower worlds, between light and darkness, and between life and death. It is she who is the source of the physical universe, including the sky, personified as the god Uranus.

As with many creation myths, the story of Gaea's creation describes a process of separation and differentiation. Stirred from stillness into motion, Gaea separates the male components out of herself and gives birth to the many forms of life that inhabit our world. Those many and varied life forms must then struggle to preserve their separate uniqueness, in competition with all other life forms. Life is the condition of *agon,* struggle, tension, unfulfilled desire. But that very tension produces a contradictory urge—the desire to return to the condition of undifferentiated wholeness. Borrowing the names of the Greek gods, Freud portrayed this contradictory state as tension between Eros, the life force, and Thanatos (after the Greek god of death)—the return to the peace of the womb that is the death wish. In the Greek creation myth, however, it is Eros himself who ignites the desire that brings the universe as we know it into being, but also Eros whose universal amorous influence drives male and female gods toward reconnecting with their opposites.

The tension between these two opposing impulses—male and female—is reflected in worldwide myths in a variety of ways—as an expanding and contracting universe undergoing repeated cycles of creation and destruction, as gods or heroes who desire erotic reunion with the feminine force while pursuing ego-preserving or power-enhancing goals often at the expense of the females and children in their lives, or as heroes who strive to attain the immortal condition of the male sky gods only to find that they must descend to the (feminine) underworld in order to make the attempt. When Gaea creates the universe out of her wholeness, life happens, in all its glorious complexity, and with it the tensions between feminine and masculine, earth and sky, goddess and god, parent and child.

At the second stage of the Greek creation myth, as if acknowledging this tension, Gaea takes a step in the direction of compromising with the masculine principle by acknowledging the male role in conception. According to Hesiod, she mates with Uranus and gives birth to offspring that include both deities (the Titans) and monsters (the Cyclopes and the Hundred-Handed) whom Uranus imprisons in the Underworld—the womb of the goddess—thus preventing the usurpation of his own powers by undoing hers, reversing the birth process.

Gaea and Her Consort

Though Uranus now nominally reigns as king of the gods, it is clearly Gaea who retains her functions as the source of life and death, conspiring with her children to overthrow Uranus by castrating him while he is making love to her, his desire for erotic reunion with the goddess undermining his impulses toward the augmentation of his own separate powers. (In later myths and related rituals, it is often the case that the male god or consort, sometimes in the form of an animal such as a horned bull, must undergo sparagmos, a ritual in which he must be dismembered—and commonly eaten raw—to ensure the renewal of life.) Gaea's bonds are clearly with her children, and her commitment is to the continuity of the cycle, whereas Uranus, whose interest is in the acquisition and maintenance of his personal power, sees his potentially violent children as personal threats and imprisons them. Although from the masculine perspective this scene of primal violence might reflect the sons' Oedipal envy of their father, from the feminine point of view it perpetuates the power of the goddess, dispensing with the male after his biological function as provider of semen is fulfilled. The pattern of domination of the violent male by the goddess who bonds with her children is continued in the relationship of Rhea and Cronus, who in turn are overthrown by Zeus.

Subordination of the Great Goddess

Zeus's last battle, after his successful war with his father and the rest of the Titans, is with the dragon Typhoeus (see Chapter 3), a belated, patriarchal revision of the World Serpent who incorporates the feminine archetype. Under Zeus's Olympian regime, the patriarchal gods are in firm control. Gaea largely evaporates from view, her triple functions most often syncretized with Demeter or divided into separate functions, each reinterpreted from the male perspective. The Great Goddess in her

FIGURE 4-7 The Gorgon. As long as death is perceived as part of the ongoing cycle of life, death, and rebirth, the Goddess's serpent is portrayed as a beneficent creature. Once the patriarchal perspective takes hold, however, death becomes the final blow to the hero's ego, and the Goddess's Underworld functions come to seem terrifying. The once beautiful serpent is now transformed into the hero's perpetual enemy, the dragon. The Goddess herself, in her death-related functions, is similarly transformed. The Greek Gorgons, three women with snakes for hair, were called Sthenno, Euryale, and Medusa (whose eyes turned men to stone). In this marble relief from the temple of Artemis at Corfu (sixth century B.C.), we see a Gorgon, whose bulging eyes, protruding tongue, and hair of snakes, along with her belt of entwined snakes, render her a truly hideous figure. (*Museum of Corfu.*)

chthonic [THOH-nik], death-wielding aspect is transformed by the patriarchal system into a hideous old hag, such as the **Gorgon** (Figure 4-7), or into a witch, such as Hecate. Often associated with images including the spider, the web, the net, and the noose, the terrifying old woman is depicted as imprisoning the free male or paralyzing him in place by turning him to stone, symbolically repressing the unconscious forces the feminine archetype invokes. The other aspects of the Great Goddess (maid, mother) are reinvoked in forms clearly subordinate to Zeus: Athene, whose divine wisdom is now reborn out of the mind of Zeus; Hera, whose protection of the institution of marriage supports the patriarchal social structure; and Aphrodite, in whom the creative cosmic energy of Eros is reduced to the spirit of sexual pursuit and gratification. But despite the official subordination of the feminine, the fear of the castrating goddess remains.

The god of war himself, Ares, so glorious on the battlefield, is more easily humiliated in the bedroom. Ares is outwitted by the love goddess's nonathletic husband, Hephaestus, who captures the lovers in a compromising position in bed, as Homer recounts the tale. Driven by his love for Aphrodite into a situation no opposing warrior could ever hope to bring about, Ares is literally trapped in the invisible but binding web of sexual desires and jealousies. Similarly, human warrior-heroes such as Heracles, Jason, and others who model themselves on Ares will continue to be undone whenever they enter the world of the feminine (see Chapter 10).

The Great Goddess Divided

Although reconciled under patriarchal rule with the reign of the male gods, the other Olympian goddesses, individually, retain some of the Great Goddess's characteristics and symbols. Three of her aspects are reconstituted as virgin (Athene), wife (Hera), and lover (Aphrodite), while her chthonian aspects (Hecate and Artemis) are treated separately.

Athene

Athene retains the role of the Great Goddess as a source of wisdom; further, despite her condition as virgin goddess, she is also invoked during childbirth. Descended, like Hera, from the Cretan snake goddess, she continues to bear the serpent of the Goddess behind her shield and the Gorgon's head on its front. Her other symbols, the owl and other birds, are likewise associated with the Goddess. Portrayed as the inventor of the domestic arts of pottery and weaving, Athene is thus symbolically associated with the Goddess as vessel and as spinner of fate.

Born from the head of Zeus, Athene appears fully grown and, as goddess of defensive war, fully armed with masculine weapons (see Chapter 3). Guided by wisdom enforced with strength, she helps all the important heroes as they defend their families and cities. Thus Athene combines the strength and aggression of the male archetype with the commitment to family and the domestic bonds of the female: she bears the shield of the god but keeps the serpent of the goddess in reserve behind it (Figure 4-8). As portrayed in the myth of her birth, the divine Intellect must incorporate the female archetype in order to carry out its tasks.

Hera

The most powerful of the Olympian goddesses, Hera is the only one to retain the creative power of parthenogenesis originally possessed by Gaea, albeit with somewhat diminished effectiveness, since she produces by that method only the ungainly Hephaestus. Possibly descended from the Cretan snake goddess (see Figure 4-4), Hera is said to renew her virginity every spring as naturally as a serpent sheds its skin. She retains the Great Goddess's features as patron of childbirth—a function doubled in her daughter Eileithyia, also a childbirth goddess—and her portrayal as "cow-eyed" connects her with the Great Goddess as Queen of Heaven, sustainer of life as she is creator, whose breasts give the milk that forms the Milky Way (see Chapter 5).

Hera is interpreted under the patriarchy as the goddess of marriage. Thus she is subject to a double standard of judging sexual behavior. She remains, as expected, sexually loyal to Zeus, while he constantly betrays her with other females, as well as males, both divine and human. According to some mythographers, his first extramarital affair was with Io, a priestess of Hera. Zeus turns Io into a heifer to protect her from the anger of Hera. (In some variants, it is Hera who turns Io into a cow to prevent her rape by Zeus, who then comes to Io in the form of a white bull.) When all ruses and preventions fail, Hera is furious and sends a gadfly to torment the heifer, pursuing her all the way to Egypt, where she is credited with spreading the worship of Demeter. Some versions even conflate Io with the Egyptian goddess Isis, who is often portrayed as the traditional "horned goddess." Although in this tale Hera and

FIGURE 4-8 Athene Parthenos. This Roman copy of the original gold, wood, and ivory statue of Athene from her temple in Athens, the Parthenon (438 B.C.), is thirty-seven feet high, including the pedestal. The sculptor, Phidias, conveys Athene's dignity and stature among the gods. In her role as warrior, defender of cities, she carries the goddess Victory in one hand and holds her shield in the other. But she also wears the Gorgon's head, symbol of the terrifying death-giving function of the Great Goddess, while the serpent, symbol of the ancient Goddess's mysteries, lies coiled behind her shield. (*National Museum, Athens.*)

Io are rivals, some scholars see Io as a variant of Hera, who is also a cow goddess—a white cow married to Zeus in the form of a white bull.

Hera's power, manifest in her ability to metamorphose her rivals into animals, is also revealed in her ability to drive heroes like Heracles insane (see Chapter 10). But despite her power, she is portrayed under Zeus's patriarchal regime as the stereotype of the nagging, jealous wife. The tension between Hera's continuation of some powers of the creator goddess and her subordination under Zeus's rule is similar to the ambiguous status of another cow goddess, the Egyptian goddess Nut (or Hathor, another Egyptian cow goddess whose stories are often conflated with those of Nut). The sun god, Amon-Ra, in his form as a bull, descends into the womb of the goddess, sails all night through her belly, and is born again each morning as a golden calf, the

FIGURE 4-9 Zeus and Hera. This bas-relief shows Zeus on his throne clasping the arm of his wife, Hera. His gesture is somewhat ambivalent, suggesting both affection and control. As queen of the gods, she is a power-ful figure in her own right, but she is neverthe-less subordinate to her husband. (*Archaeological Museum, Palermo.*)

bull calf of the sun, who then grows into a powerful bull, only to repeat the journey each night. The cow goddess who, in earlier myths, sacrificed the bull god to ensure renewal is now depicted as his mother. The goddess is clearly essential to give birth (and rebirth) to the god. But the calf she bears each morning rules her world, and she is subordinated.

Hera exists in a similarly complex relationship with Zeus. As Zeus's wife, Hera reinforces marriage as a social institution, in effect chartering her own subordination. After an early attempt at rebellion—a failed conspiracy, with Poseidon, to overthrow Zeus—Hera settles down into an uneasy but permanent relationship with her hus-band, reserving her anger for his many children conceived by other females divine and human. At the same time, her marriage transforms Zeus from an expendable source of conception (as were Uranus and Cronus) to a god of family love who, unlike his predecessors, maintains positive relationships with his children and whose reign is thus comparatively stable (Figure 4-9).

Aphrodite

Originally an Asiatic goddess, as Herodotus claims, or more precisely, related to vari-ous Near Eastern goddesses such as the Syrian Goddess, the Sumerian goddess Inanna (or her Babylonian equivalent, Ishtar), the Canaanite Astarte, or even the Egyptian Isis, Aphrodite shares many characteristics with these deities, including her connec-tion to the sea—the "waters of life"—and her unusual birth: the Syrian Goddess, for example, emerges from an egg which has fallen into the Euphrates River and is pushed to shore by fish; Aphrodite herself, according to Hesiod, is born from the foam surrounding the severed genitals of Uranus, which Cronus tossed into the sea. Floating to shore on a clam shell, Aphrodite emerges from the sea as the last out-

FIGURE 4-10   Aphrodite of Cnidos. This Roman copy of Praxiteles's sculpture (original c. 350–330 B.C.) depicts Aphrodite, traditionally shown unclothed as she is here. She is sensuous but detached, beautiful but unself-conscious. Her gaze turns inward in reflective repose, suggesting a combination of feminine beauty with mature self-awareness. (*Vatican Museums, Rome.*)

pouring of the primeval gods' creative energies. Initially a powerful embodiment of Eros, the prime creative force of the universe, and its life-principle, Aphrodite was a powerful deity to whom all creation—human and divine—was subject (Figure 4-10).

Under the auspices of the patriarchy, however, such a powerful force embodied in a female must have aroused some anxiety, for we find two conflicting perceptions of

Aphrodite manifested even within Hesiod's *Theogony:* on the one hand, in the form of the male figure Eros (later portrayed as Aphrodite's son), love is the mysterious force that literally makes the world go round and to which the gods themselves succumb; on the other, Aphrodite is a silly, flirtatious girl, an appropriate companion to her lover, the athletic but not terribly bright Ares, god of war. As with her birth, her connection to the war god is perhaps a vestige of the dual role as goddess of love and war of the Near Eastern goddesses from which she derives. An alternative version of her birth mentioned by Homer describes Aphrodite as a daughter of Zeus and Dione, more firmly subordinating her in the Olympian hierarchy.

Perhaps reflecting her connection with the temple prostitutes who would serve in the shrines of the Near Eastern love goddesses, Aphrodite is variously redefined as a flirt who seduces men for the fun of it, as a mistress or lover, or as a whore. Consequently, she remains alluring, but her power is drastically diminished: in a world in which marriage is sanctified, she has no legitimate social place. (The Romans later went even further, reducing Aphrodite's force to the pranks of a mischievous boy, **Amor** [ah-MOHR], or **Cupid,** whose arrows cause nothing but trouble, although even the Romans acknowledged her importance by claiming her counterpart, Venus, as ancestor of Julius Caesar.) Aphrodite's own marriage, to the lame and singularly unattractive, though highly intelligent, Hephaestus, is a failure: she cheats on him with humans and gods alike. Nevertheless, when her husband catches her in bed with the embarrassed Ares, it is Hephaestus himself who suffers the ultimate sexual humiliation, for he clearly cannot satisfy her needs. The goddess herself remains sublimely impervious to such tricks: unlike human wives, Aphrodite has the sexual freedom that, in ancient Greek society, only men possessed.

Aphrodite interacts with humans as well as gods, often with far-reaching and sometimes devastating consequences. She persuades Eros to make Medea fall in love with Jason, for example, enabling Jason to win the Golden Fleece and setting in motion both the successful return of the Argonauts (Chapter 10) and the ensuing tragedies in Jason's family (Chapter 17). And it is Aphrodite's promise—of the love of the most beautiful woman in the world—to Prince Paris of Troy that sparks the conflagration of the Trojan War (Chapter 11). That promise is made in exchange for the gift of a Golden Apple of Immortality from the Tree of Life belonging to Gaea, once again connecting Aphrodite to the primal goddess herself.

Dangerous enough when offering gifts, when she is angry at humans, as she is at Hippolytus (son of King Theseus of Athens), Aphrodite can be deadly. Because Hippolytus has spurned her, vowing to live a celibate life, she causes his stepmother, Phaedra, to become infatuated with him. When Hippolytus rejects Phaedra, she is enraged and lies about him to Theseus, claiming that Hippolytus raped her. The hapless young man, pursued by his enraged father, becomes entangled in the reins of his horses and is dragged to his death, ensnared by the very goddess he had spurned.

Aphrodite's own affairs with humans are likewise ill fated: as Ares is not always victorious in war, so Aphrodite is sometimes unlucky in love. Her affair with the Trojan Anchises, for example, is brought about by Zeus, in a reversal of roles, to give Aphrodite a taste of her own medicine and to get, perhaps, some small revenge for her effects on the gods in general and on Zeus in particular. When she and Anchises prove psychologically incompatible, Aphrodite returns to Olympus, leaving Anchises to raise their son, Aeneas, who, when Troy falls, will have to leave, in succession, his wife, his homeland, and his lover (Chapter 19).

Aphrodite's affair with Adonis, her most famous human lover, is also a source of grief for both. When the Queen of Cyprus boasts that her daughter, Smyrna, is more beautiful than Aphrodite, the goddess gets her revenge by causing Smyrna to seduce and be impregnated by her own father, whom she had gotten drunk. When the father realizes what has happened, he tries to kill his daughter, whom Aphrodite turns into a myrrh tree to save her. When her father splits the tree open with his sword, the beautiful child Adonis emerges. Aphrodite then saves the child by concealing him in a chest, which she gives to Persephone to hide until he grows up. However, Persephone, too, falls in love with the boy and refuses to relinquish him. Just as in the story of Demeter and Persephone, a compromise is worked out: Adonis is to spend part of each year in the Underworld with Persephone and part in the upper world with Aphrodite. Tricking Persephone, Aphrodite causes Adonis to remain with her in the upper world beyond his allotted time, thus arousing the jealousy of her divine lover, Ares. When Adonis is out hunting, Ares disguises himself as a boar and kills Adonis, whose blood penetrates the Underworld. Transformed by the power of Aphrodite's love into the blood-red anemone, Adonis emerges again as the flower each spring. Like his Near Eastern counterparts, Tammuz and Osiris, Adonis becomes the subject of a popular cult.

Indeed, many details of the Aphrodite-Adonis tale underline the link between Aphrodite and her Near Eastern sources, allowing us a glimpse of the powers of the Great Goddess that still are sustained beneath the surface of the charming but superficial nymph into which Aphrodite had ostensibly been changed. But not even Zeus can entirely negate the power of Aphrodite, and the residue of the Great Goddess keeps surfacing. Like the Babylonian myth of Ishtar and Tammuz, the tale of Aphrodite and Adonis incorporates the descent to the Underworld and the return to the upper world, in defiance of the Underworld goddess; like the Egyptian myth of Isis and Osiris, it incorporates the entombing of the male in a tree, his subsequent release when the tree is split, and his resurrection. In all these tales, the transformational role of the ancient Goddess—the giver of life, death, and rebirth—is brought about through the power of love that, dimmed but not obliterated, radiates still from the embrace of Aphrodite.

Artemis

It is the huntress **Artemis** [AR-te-mis]—one of the most beautiful of the goddesses (Figure 4-11), but also "the dangerous one"—who inherits the chthonic aspect of the Great Goddess. Her symbol is the moon, and she is associated with the chthonic goddess Hecate. Self-sufficient and not dependent on men (who must nevertheless appeal to her as patron of the hunt), Artemis has powers that threaten the male hegemony, and she is portrayed as terrifying, even deadly, to men who find themselves attracted to her beauty. Actaeon, for example, a cousin of Dionysus, was turned into a stag and torn apart by his own hounds for spying on Artemis as she was bathing, another variant on the sparagmos theme (Figure 4-12). (Some writers suggest that Actaeon is a variant of the Horned God, a bull-god, consort of the goddess, who, in many cultures that practiced such rituals, was mutilated by women wearing dog masks.) The "Lady of the Beasts" who spends much of her time in the fields and woods, Artemis is associated with the power of instinct, of nature, or of unconscious drives often represented in animal form in dreams (Figure 4-13). She is the guardian

FIGURE 4-11   Artemis of Gabii.
Unlike Aphrodite, Artemis was traditionally shown clothed. In this copy
of a sculpture from the fifth century
B.C., Artemis, in her loose-fitting
hunter's garb and sandals, is about to
pluck an arrow from her quiver. Her
lithe, graceful form and delicate features convey her much-admired
beauty, but her short hair and tunic
reflect her scorn of feminine fashion
or erotic pursuits. Perhaps eyeing her
quarry, her alert, intent gaze suggests
her keen intelligence. (*Louvre, Paris.*)

FIGURE 4-12   Artemis and Actaeon. This vase painting depicts
Artemis, goddess of the hunt, as she
takes aim at Actaeon, for seeing her
bathing. As punishment, Artemis is
about to turn Actaeon into a stag. As Actaeon kneels before her, we see his hounds
already attacking the fallen hunter. (*James
Fund and by special contributions. Courtesy,
Museum of Fine Arts, Boston.*)

FIGURE 4-13   Artemis. In this stone sculpture from Italy (c. 500 B.C.), Artemis is shown with a pair of lions. A deity of woods and fields, Artemis not only is a hunter; she also has the capacity to tame and communicate with wild beasts, who flock to her. (*British Museum, London.*)

of women's mysteries and perpetuates the creative function of the primeval Goddess: despite her virginity, she is invoked, like Athene, in childbirth. Like Athene, too, she wields men's weapons and upholds an image of freedom which human women must have envied. Bearing the same weapon as her twin brother, Apollo, Artemis is the only goddess who cannot effectively be subordinated to Zeus.

Hecate

In the *Theogony,* Hesiod attributes to **Hecate** [HEK-uh-tee] the powers of all the gods and considers her the deity most honored by Zeus. She has power associated with both earth and sea and can offer as her gifts fertility of the soil, victory in contests or war, and wealth through fishing, farming, and animal breeding. She is associated with Demeter, both because she helped Demeter in her search for Persephone and because of their shared fertility functions.

Because of her Underworld connection, Hecate is gradually stripped of her positive associations with wealth and plenty and is identified exclusively with fearful associations. These include night, unlucky places such as crossroads, the moon (a symbol shared with her younger associate Artemis), and witchcraft and sorcery. Under patriarchal auspices, the dread goddess—perceived in youth as the beguiling but deadly femme fatale—in old age becomes a witch. Thus, in addition to her connection with the often-fatal Artemis, Hecate joins the ranks of the Gorgons, the Graiae, the Furies, and other loathsome and fearful inheritors of the death-giving functions of the Great Goddess.

Demeter

The most complex of the goddess figures to survive the shift to patriarchy, Demeter embodies—albeit in somewhat domesticated form—all the functions of the Great

FIGURE 4-14   Demeter and Kore. In this stone relief from Eleusis (fifth century B.C.), Demeter is seated, holding her corn-tipped scepter and stalks of grain. She talks with her daughter Persephone (Kore, also known as the Maiden), who holds an agricultural implement. Not only their functions as grain goddesses but also the close bonds between mother and daughter are implied in this bas-relief. (*Eleusis Museum.*)

Goddess except the capacity for parthenogenesis: Zeus is the father of **Persephone** [per-SEF-oh-nee], also known as **Kore** [KOHR-ee], or the Maiden (Figure 4-14). The story of Persephone—her abduction by Hades, her rape by and marriage to the Underworld god, and her reunion with her mother—operates on several levels of meaning (Figure 4-15).

As a nature myth, the story of Persephone represents the seed, planted under the ground (the trip to the Underworld), watered by the rain (Zeus's intervention), and sprouting in the spring as grain, whose mature form is represented by Demeter. As an etiological myth, the story explains why we have seasons. As a charter myth, the story establishes the basis for several rituals, from the Eleusinian Mysteries and the Thesmophoria (festival honoring Demeter) to the common practice by farmers' wives of setting an extra place at the table in honor of Demeter.

FIGURE 4-15 Persephone and Hades. In this vase painting, the King and Queen of the Underworld are depicted in a pleasant domestic scene. Hades holds the cornucopia, or Horn of Plenty, suggesting the fertility aspects of these chthonian deities, as well as Persephone's adaptation to her adult role. (*British Museum, London.*)

The Rituals in Honor of Demeter

The two most important rituals in honor of Demeter reflect the two major functions of the goddess: as source of the cycle of life, death, and transfiguration, she inspires the Greater and Lesser Eleusinian Mysteries; as Grain Goddess, the protector of agricultural fertility, she is honored in the Thesmophoria.

The Eleusinian Mysteries The **Eleusinian** [el-oo-SIN-ee-uhn] **Mysteries** were celebrated in the town of Eleusis (where Demeter rested in her wanderings in search of Persephone) and in the nearby city of Athens. Large numbers of men and women, led by officially approved priests, participated in the annual nine-day event each September and October. As in all mystery religions, participating in the emotionally intense ritual was restricted to initiates who were forbidden to reveal the secret rites. As a result, little is known about the rites performed in the temple at Eleusis itself.

Such evidence as exists suggests that the Lesser Mysteries were celebrated earlier in the year in preparation for the Greater Mysteries. The rituals involved fasting, the wearing of costumes, and ritual purification in the sea, with the participants carrying sacrificial pigs. Processions—possibly symbolic of Persephone's trip to the Underworld or of Demeter's search for her daughter—would take place along the Sacred Way between Athens and the Temple of Demeter at Eleusis. During the procession, bawdy jokes and obscene gestures would apparently be exchanged, enhancing the fertility component of the rituals. Within the temple, participants would partake of a sacred drink of barley and water. Prayers would be recited and sacred objects revealed. Some scholars believe that among the sacred objects revealed during the mystery was a single seed of grain. The rite may have included dramatic elements, possibly some form of enactment of a **hieros gamos** [HYE-rohs GAHM-ohs] (sacred marriage), presumably between Zeus and Demeter or Kore, which would produce a sacred child. The climax of the ritual was undoubtedly the final **epiphany** of the goddess, when her direct communion with or manifestation to the worshipers would take place. Participating in the ritual, according to the *Homeric Hymn to Demeter,* enabled the soul to experience, in a direct and emotional way, the connection between death, life, and rebirth—to achieve spiritual renewal in the moment and to look forward confidently to "joy" after death, thus ensuring spiritual, and possibly literal, rebirth and immortality.

Demeter and Dionysus   The ritual itself may have gradually incorporated elements from the worship of Dionysus, a male counterpart of Demeter and Persephone. Indeed, Demeter's gift of bread, like Dionysus's wine, is a sacred symbol of transformation. Certainly, the dramatic elements—the procession and costumes, the ritualized jesting, and possibly the reenactment of some events in the myth—were analogous to the plays performed during the Dionysian festival (see Chapter 13). Dionysus shares with Demeter and Persephone not only some vaguely feminine attributes (the long, flowing garments and hair, for example), but also the reconciliation of polarities—the cyclical process of life, death, and rebirth and the terror and joy of the Bacchic ritual.

   When Dionysus's mother, **Semele** [SEM-uh-lee], was unable to sustain the epiphany of Zeus in his true form as lightning—the Divine Fire itself—she was burned to death in the flame. For a mere mortal, naked divinity—the godhead seen face-to-face—is destructive. In the Mysteries of Demeter, as in those for Dionysus, the ritual provides a mediated form of ecstatic communion with the deity, perhaps less electrifying than Semele's direct confrontation, but more appropriate to the human worshiper, who can thus experience the love of god and live to tell the tale.

The Thesmophoria

Unlike the Eleusinian Mysteries, which were open to initiates of both sexes, the **Thesmophoria** [thes-moh-FOHR-ee-uh], a sowing ritual, was practiced by women only. This ritual involved placing the bodies of sacrificed pigs (symbols of the Great Goddess) into gullies filled with snakes, along with pine cones and cakes baked in phallic shapes. After three days, properly purified women would be lowered into the pit, reenacting Persephone's descent to Hades, to retrieve the material, which would then be mixed with the seeds for next year's crop to ensure plant, animal, and human fertility.

The Psychological Components of the Demeter Myth

The Mediation of Contraries As described in the *Homeric Hymn to Demeter,* it is Zeus who arranges for the marriage of Persephone, negotiating the compromise between Hades and Demeter that will allow Persephone to remain for part of the year in the Underworld with her husband and for the other part back on earth with her mother. The myth thus mediates between the self-sufficient Great Goddess and the patriarchy, as well as between life and death. The Greeks referred to the souls of the dead, whose bodies were often buried in clay jars, as those who "rest in the womb of the Goddess." Clay pots with corn seeds were often kept near the hearth to ensure the renewal of life in the spring.

The myth also reconciles the Great Goddess with the patriarchy through the institution of marriage, itself a union of contraries. Presented as legalized rape, since it is ultimately justified by Zeus, Persephone's marriage brings about her symbolic death and descent to the Underworld. But it also is the occasion for understanding the women's mysteries and the cycle of existence. Unlike the heroes' descent to the Underworld, which was the climax of a literally death-defying quest for personal immortality (see Chapter 10), Persephone's descent results in marriage with Hades. Their marriage achieves a reconciliation of life and death, portrayed as part of a continuing cycle that includes her annual rebirth as she returns to the upper world to be reunited with Demeter.

The Feminine Archetype As an embodiment of the feminine archetype, Demeter manifests the threefold nature of the Goddess as mother (creator), as grain goddess (source of sustenance), and as goddess of the mysteries (the link in the process of life, death, and renewal, and the source of spiritual rebirth or transformation). The Demeter myth also repeats the motif of the triple functions in the figures of the mother (Demeter), the maiden (Persephone), and the older woman (Hecate, who helps Demeter locate her missing daughter). Even the role of Persephone as Kore, the Maiden, is tripled, her virginity appearing in the three aspects of the goddesses who accompany her to the fields: Athene, who personifies self-sufficient reason; Artemis, who shuns men; and Persephone herself, who is innocent because she is inexperienced.

Demeter and Female Values Beyond sharing the functions and symbols of the archetypal female, the myth of Demeter explores feminine values. As contemporary psychologists have perceived, the myth upholds a model of self-fulfillment at odds with the independent, autonomous path that the masculine archetype—the hero—personifies. The linear male archetype requires that the hero, a unique individual, separate himself from others—and from his father in particular—and go out to contend with powerful forces alone. In fact, the characteristic hostility between father and son in the archetypal male experience, as exemplified in the myths of Uranus and Cronus, requires the son to define himself by literally or symbolically killing or emasculating his father. In contrast, the female archetype exemplifies the importance of the continuity of the generations, especially the bond between mother and daughter, who must be reunited if life is to continue.

The hero, furthermore, achieves his quest by spurning his sexual attraction to women as a "temptation" that would weaken his drive toward immortality. The female, on the other hand, experiences renewal by accepting her sexuality, which allows her to achieve the desired bond with her children: in giving birth, Demeter becomes, in effect, her daughter; in growing up, Persephone becomes the woman. Like many women since, who grow up and possibly have children of their own only to discover that they share unanticipated links with their mothers ("I'm turning into my own mother!" is a frequent observation), Persephone returns from the Underworld transformed into another version of Demeter, thus joining the endless pattern of such renewals. This ultimate identification of mother and daughter is reflected in the fact that they were referred to collectively as *The Two Goddesses* and that in many of the rituals their roles were interchangeable.

Agriculture and the Source of Civilization

The myth goes one step further and presents the female principle as the source of civilization itself via the invention of agriculture. Demeter, having agreed to renew her task as grain goddess, teaches the secrets of life to **Triptolemus** [trip-TOHL-e-muhs] (Figure 4-16), whose name means "thrice-plowed field" (which may refer to a field ready for planting and/or to Demeter's having sex with him three times) and who is sometimes identified as the *Holy Child* of the Eleusinian rite. Demeter gives him a plow and grain seed, instructing him to share the secrets of planting with the rest of the human race. What modern anthropologists call the *agricultural revolution* derives from this insight, allowing humans to settle into permanent locations while they plant, tend their crops, and await the harvest. It is from these early villages that complex cultures, stable and enduring in time, will develop.

Demeter thus presents a rather different perspective on the source of civilization from the equivalent male myth, the story of Prometheus and the theft of fire (see Chapter 6). Giving fire—the divine spark—to men, Prometheus sets them free. Men are no longer dependent on Zeus's lightning and are now able to create both civilization and the technology, including weapons, upon which a more aggressive model of civilization will be built. Prometheus's gift creates antagonism between men and gods, reinforcing a model of hostility and separation, whereas the feminine myth emphasizes bonding and reconciliation, among the gods as well as between gods and humans.

The Demeter Myth and Female Psychology

Besides expressing the feminine archetype, the Demeter myth also explores the psychology of the individual female as she goes through the life cycle from girlhood to old age, passing from virgin to lover to mother and eventually to the wisdom of age that is partly represented in the myth by Hecate, a lunar goddess whose capacity for vision is not obliterated by darkness. In the *Homeric Hymn to Demeter,* although she cannot literally see what has occurred, Hecate knows a rape when she hears one and acts, in defiance of Zeus, to help reunite mother and daughter. The last stage of the life cycle is also expressed by Demeter herself as, searching for her daughter, she goes about disguised as an old woman.

The myth addresses the emotional experiences of both mother and daughter as they pass through the stages in the life of a woman. The mother must watch as her child is wrenched from her by the patriarchal institution of marriage and must struggle to restore the bond afterward, albeit under different auspices. The daughter

FIGURE 4-16   Demeter, Triptolemus, and Kore. In this marble relief from Eleusis (fifth century B.C.), Demeter (holding the scepter)
and her daughter Kore confide the secrets of agriculture to Triptolemus and instruct him to spread the knowledge to the rest of humankind. Humans are thus both blessed by the goddesses and initiated
into their mysteries. (*National Museum, Athens.*)

must discard her former home and identity and subordinate herself to a male who
now determines her functions as well as the conditions under which she must live.
But the change involves gains as well as losses: the mother, relinquishing her protective bond to her child, gains a new friendship, on equal terms, with a now mature
woman like herself; the daughter, losing the comforting protection of a parent, gains
at least relative independence, and new understanding of herself as an adult woman.

The innocent but ignorant Persephone, abducted by Hades, undergoes her first
sexual experience: eating the pomegranate, a symbol of sexual knowledge like the fruit
eaten by Eve in the Book of Genesis, Persephone has passed on to another stage of
feminine experience and cannot go back to the upper world or return to her previous
condition of naive virginity. (Another interpretation identifies the pomegranate, with

its red juice, as an emblem of the onset of menstruation, with the descent into the Underworld a reflection of a common taboo, practiced in many patriarchal societies, requiring the isolation of the female during the menstrual period.) The result, for Persephone as for Eve, is her first consciousness of herself as a woman and her initiation into the mysteries of the life cycle. Like Eve, she has eaten from the Tree of Knowledge (the Tree of Life) and is ready to emerge as an adult woman. No longer dependent entirely either on mother or husband, no longer exclusively either somebody's child or somebody's wife, she is ready to relate to both on her own terms. Persephone's new powers reflect her new state—once a naive girl, she has become Queen of the Underworld. Hades also is changed by her presence. Not only has the power of Eros been extended to his dread Kingdom, thus embracing all three levels of the universe, but Hades himself has been transformed from sexual predator to spouse. Albeit under patriarchal auspices, the Underworld is thereby reclaimed, and the complete cycle encompassed by the Goddess is restored.

The *Homeric Hymn to Demeter*

Most of the "Homeric" hymns, a collection of poems by mostly unknown authors in honor of various deities in the Greek pantheon, were probably composed in the eighth to seventh centuries B.C. (A few may have been composed much later, in the Hellenistic period, between the fourth and second centuries B.C.) Varying in length from a few short lines to full-length narratives, these poems were used at festivals as a prologue to the reciting of longer poems or to musical performances and were traditionally attributed to Homer, a doubtful attribution already questioned by Hellenistic readers. The *Homeric Hymn to Demeter,* the longest of the group, probably dates from the seventh century B.C. and is one of our major sources of information about the rituals performed at Eleusis.

The *Homeric Hymn to Demeter* tells the story of the abduction of Persephone by Hades and describes Demeter's search for her and their eventual reunification. It also describes some of the mystery rites for Demeter celebrated at Eleusis, where Demeter is given refuge during her wanderings in search of her daughter. Unlike other versions of the myth, the *Hymn* does not mention Demeter's gift of agriculture to Triptolemus—the residents of Eleusis described in the poem seem already to engage in plowing—but stresses instead the goddess's promise of rebirth to her worshipers: the cult is presented as an alternative to the literal immortality that Demeter offers to Demophon, child of the king and queen of Eleusis. When his terrified mother interrupts the process of placing him in the Divine Fire, Demeter reveals her true identity to the queen and insists that a cult be started in her honor. The myth thus simultaneously charters the mystery and establishes its functions: as a way of achieving communion with Demeter and as a way of ensuring an alternative to the literal immortality that is too terrifying and too destructive a transformation for humans to undergo.

HOMERIC HYMN TO DEMETER[1]
Author unknown

I begin my song of the holy goddess, fair-haired Demeter, and of her slim-ankled daughter whom Aidoneus snatched away; and Zeus the loud-crashing, the wide-voiced one, granted it. She was playing with the deep-bosomed daughters of Ocean, away from Demeter of the golden weapon and glorious fruit, and she was gathering flowers throughout the luxuriant meadow—roses, saffron, violets, iris, hyacinth, and a narcissus which was a trap planted for the blossoming maiden by Earth (Gaia) in accord with Zeus's plans, a favor to Hades the receiver of many guests; it was radiantly wonderful, inspiring awe in all who saw it, whether immortal god or mortal man; a hundred stems grew from its root; and the whole wide heaven above, the whole earth, and the salt surge of the sea smiled for joy at its fragrance. The girl was charmed by it, and reached out both hands to pluck the pretty plaything—suddenly, the earth split open wide along the plain and from it the lord host of many, Kronos's son of many names, darted out on his immortal horses. He grabbed her, resisting and screaming, and took her away in his golden chariot. She lifted her voice in a cry, calling upon father Zeus, the almighty and good. But no one, god or mortal, heard her voice, not even the glorious-fruited olive trees, except the childish daughter of Perses, Hecate of the glistening veil, who—from her cave—heard, and so did Lord Helios the glorious son of Hyperion, as the maiden calling upon father Zeus, though he was sitting, removed from the other gods, in his much-besought temple, receiving fine sacrifices from mortal men.

Her, all unwilling, with the approval of Zeus, he took away on his immortal horses, Kronos's son of many names, brother of her father, designator of many, host of many. As long as the goddess could see the earth and the starry sky, the flowing, fish-filled sea and the rays of the sun, she still had hope that her holy mother and the race of the immortal gods would see her, and there was still much hope in her heart in spite of her distress. . . . The peaks of the mountains and the depths of the sea echoed back the immortal voice, and her blessed mother heard her. Then sharp grief seized the mother's heart; she tore the head-dress upon her ambrosial hair, and threw her dark veil down from both her shoulders; and like a bird she darted over land and sea, searching. None of the gods or of mortal men would give her a true report, nor would any of the birds come to her as a true messenger.

For nine days then lady Deo wandered the earth, holding blazing torches in her hands; in her grief she touched neither ambrosia nor the sweetness of nectar, nor did she bathe her body with water. But when the tenth day dawned Hecate, bearing light in her hands, encountered her and spoke to her this message: "Lady Demeter, bringer of seasons and glorious gifts, who of the gods of heaven or of mortal men has taken Persephone and pained your own heart? I heard her

1. Translation by David G. Rice and John E. Stambaugh.

109

voice, but did not see who it was. I am telling you everything promptly, and accurately."

So spoke Hecate. The daughter of fair-haired Rhea did not answer a word, but she immediately darted off with her, holding blazing torches in her hands, and they came to Helios, the viewer of gods and men. They stood before his horses and the divine goddess said, "Helios, as a god, respect me, as a goddess, if ever in word or deed I have warmed your heart. The maiden whom I bore— sweetest blossom—beautiful—I heard her voice, sobbing, as if she were being raped, but I did not see her. But you survey from the bright heaven all the earth and the sea with your rays; tell me accurately whether you have seen who of gods or mortal men has forced her and taken her away, all unwillingly, in my absence."

So she spoke, and the son of Hyperion answered her: "Lady Demeter, daugh-   5
ter of fair-haired Rhea, you will know all: I have great respect for you and pity you in your grief for your slim-ankled child: none of the immortals is responsible except Zeus the cloud-gatherer, who has granted to Hades his own brother that she be called his tender wife; and he has taken her, screaming a loud cry, away on his horses down into the misty darkness. So, goddess, stop your loud lament; you should not rashly hold on to this boundless anger; Aidoneus, the designator of many, is after all not an unsuitable son-in-law for you, since you have the same mother and father; and his honor he gained when at the beginning a division into three parts was made; and he dwells with those over whom the lot made him king." When he had said this he called to his horses, and at his command they bore the swift chariot like broad-winged birds.

Then grief still more horrible and oppressive came upon her heart, and in anger at Zeus, shrouded in clouds, she deserted the gatherings of the gods and went far from Olympus to the cities and farms of men and for a long time disguised her appearance. No man, no woman who saw her recognized her, until she arrived at the home of clever Keleos, who was the king of fragrant Eleusis at the time. At the spring Parthenion where the citizens draw water in the shade of a towering olive tree she sat by the side of the road in the guise of an old woman, one who is beyond the age of childbearing and the gifts of Aphrodite who bears the garland of love, one who might be a nurse of royal children or governess of important households. The daughters of Keleos of Eleusis saw her as they came to draw water and carry it in bronze vessels to their father's house. There were four of them, like goddesses in youthful bloom—Kallidike, Klesidike, lovely Demo, and Kallithoe, the eldest of them all. They did not recognize her, for gods are hard for mortals to see. They approached her and said, "Old woman, who are you? Why have you kept away from the city and not approached the settlement? There in the dusky houses there are women as old as you and younger, who would treat you kindly in word and deed."

So they spoke, and the goddess mistress said in answer, "Dear children, daughters of womanly mothers, be of good cheer, and I will tell you, for it is right to tell you the truth. The name my lady mother gave to me is Doso. I have just come across the sea from Crete, forced by pirate men who abducted me against my will. They brought their swift ship to shore at Thorikos, and a crowd of women came on board from the land and they all prepared their dinner by the ship's stern-cables. But my heart had no desire for a pleasant supper; instead I got up secretly and escaped those arrogant overlords across the dark countryside, so that they might not enjoy any profit from selling me. I wandered about until I arrived here; but I do not know what land it is nor which people dwell here. May all the gods who dwell on Olympus grant you vigorous husbands and all the progeny they want; but pity me, maidens; dear children, help me come propitiously to some home of a man and a woman where I may provide the services of an aged woman for them: I could hold their infant child in my arms and nurse it well, I could keep house, make the master's bed in the inmost chamber, and instruct the women in their tasks."

So said the goddess, and the maiden Kallidike, most beautiful of Keleos's daughters, answered her, "Mother, we humans endure the gifts of the gods, even under grievous compulsion, for they are much mightier. I will explain it all to you clearly, and tell you the men who hold the power of authority here, and who stand out in the government and direct the defense of the city with their counsels and decisions. There are Triptolemos the clever, Dioklos, Polyxeinos, Eumolpos the blameless, Dolichos, and our father the manly one. Their wives manage everything in their households, and not one of them would dishonor you at first sight by making you depart from their houses. They will receive you, for you are godlike. If you wish, wait here while we go to our father's house and tell Metaneira our deep-belted mother all these things, and see whether she bids you come to our house and not search for another's. A favorite son, born to her late, is being nursed in the strongly built palace; she prayed much for him, and rejoiced in him. If you would nurse him and he would reach adolescence, any woman would envy the sight of you, for she (viz. Metaneira) would give you so great a reward for nursing him."

So she spoke, and she nodded her head, and then they filled their shining jugs with water and carried them proudly. Soon they reached their father's great house, and quickly told their mother what they had seen and heard. She told them to go quickly and bid her come, at a vast wage. As deer or heifers frolic across the meadow eating to their heart's content, so they darted along the road down the gulley, holding up the folds of their lovely gowns, and their hair streamed along their shoulders like saffron blossoms. They reached the spot near the road where they had left the glorious goddess, and they led her to their father's house. She, grieved at heart, walked behind them with her head veiled, and the dark robe trailed along around the slender feet of the goddess.

Soon they reached the house of Zeus-descended Keleos, and went through   10 the portico to the place where their lady mother was sitting beside a column of the carefully made chamber, holding her new baby in her lap. The girls ran to her, but Demeter trod upon the threshold, and her head reached the roof-beam, and she filled the doorway with a divine radiance. At this awe, reverence, and pale fear seized the woman. She rose from her chair and urged her to be seated, but Demeter the bringer of seasons and glorious gifts did not wish to be seated on the gleaming chair, but silently cast down her beautiful eyes and waited until Iambe understood and set a jointed stool out for her, and threw a shining white fleece upon it. She sat down, holding her veil in front with her hands. For a long time she sat there on the stool sorrowfully, without speaking; and made no contact with anyone in word or gesture. Without smiling, without touching food or drink she sat, consumed with yearning for her daughter, until Iambe understood and made plenty of jokes and jests and made the holy Lady smile with kindly heart, and ever afterward she continues to delight her spirit. Then Metaneira filled a cup of sweet wine and offered it to her, but she refused it, for she said it was not right for her to drink red wine. Instead she asked her to give her barley groats and water mixed with crusted pennyroyal to drink. She made the compound, the *kykeon,* as she commanded, and offered it to the goddess. Deo the greatly revered accepted it for the sake of the ceremony. . . . Fair-belted Metaneira began with these words, "Be of good cheer, woman; I do not expect that you are sprung from base stock, but from good; dignity and grace are manifest in your eyes, like those of kings, stewards of the right. But we humans endure the gifts of the gods, even under grievous compulsion, for a yoke lies upon our neck. But now that you have come here, all that is mine shall be yours. Nurse this child for me, whom the immortals have given me, late-born and unexpected, but much prayed for. If you would nurse him and he would reach adolescence, any woman would envy the sight of you, for I would give you so great a reward for nursing him."

Then Demeter of the fair crown said to her, "May you also be of good cheer, woman, and may the gods grant you all good things; I willingly accept the child, as you bid me. I will nurse him, and I do not expect that he will be injured by nurse's incompetence, supernatural attacks, nor magical cuttings, for I know an antidote more mighty than the woodcutter, and I know a fine preventative against malignant attacks."

When she had said this she received him with her immortal hands in her fragrant lap, and the mother's heart rejoiced. So she nursed the glorious son of clever Keleos, Demophon, whom fair-belted Metaneira bore, and he grew like a god, eating no food, being suckled on no milk, for Demeter would [feed and] anoint him with ambrosia, like the progeny of a god, and she breathed sweetly on him and held him in her lap. At night she would hide him like a fire-brand within the might of the flame, without his parents' knowledge. It made them wonder greatly how he was so precocious, and why his appearance was like the gods'. She would have even made him ageless and deathless, if it had not been that fair-belted Metaneira foolishly kept watch one night and watched her from her fragrant bed-chamber. She screamed and struck both her thighs in fear for her child and in a frenzy of mindlessness. Wailing, she said, "My child Demophon, the stranger woman is hiding you in the blazing fire, and is making grief and bitter sorrow for me."

So she spoke, lamenting, and the divine goddess heard her. Demeter of the beautiful crown was amazed at her; with her immortal hands she put from her the dear child whom Metaneira had borne, all unexpected, in the palace, and threw him at her feet, drawing him out of the fire, terribly angry at heart, and at the same time she said to fair-belted Metaneira, "Humans are short-sighted, stupid, ignorant of the share of good or evil which is coming to them. You by your foolishness have hurt him beyond curing. Let my witness be the oath of the gods sworn by the intractable water of Styx, that I would have made your son deathless and ageless all his days, and given him imperishable honor. But now it is not possible to ward off death and destruction. Still he will have imperishable honor forever, since he stood on my knees and slept in my arms; in due season, as the years pass around, the children of the Eleusinians will conduct in his

honor war (games) and the terrible battle-cry with each other for ever and ever.
I am Demeter, the Venerable, ready as the greatest boon and joy for immortals
and mortals. So now let the whole people build me a great temple, and an altar
beneath it, below the city and the towering wall, above Kallirhoe on the ridge
which juts forth. I myself will establish rites so that henceforth you may celebrate
them purely and propitiate my mind."

With these words the goddess altered size and form and sloughed off old age;
beauty wafted about her. A lovely fresh smell radiated from her lovely gown and
the radiance from the skin of the immortal goddess shone afar. Her blonde hair
flowed down over her shoulders, and the sturdy house was filled with light like a
flash of lightning. She went out through the palace. As for the other, her knees
gave way, and for a long time she was speechless. She did not even remember the
child, her favorite, to pick him up from the floor. His sisters heard his piteous
crying, and they leapt down from their well-covered beds. Then one of them
took the child in her hands and put him in her lap, one kindled a fire, and
another hurried on gentle feet to rouse her mother out of the fragrant chamber.
Crowding around they washed him, covering him with love as he squirmed; his
heart was not comforted, however, for less skillful nurses and nurse maids were
holding him now.

All night long the women, quaking with fear, propitiated the glorious god-   15
dess. As soon as dawn appeared they gave a full report to wide-ruling Keleos, as
Demeter of the beautiful garlands commanded. He summoned the people from
their many boundaries and ordered them to build an elaborate temple to fair-
haired Demeter and an altar on the ridge which juts forth. They obeyed him
straightway, and hearkened to him as he spoke, and started to build as he commanded. And it grew at the dispensation of the divinity. When they finished and
ceased from their toil, each person went back to his home. Blonde Demeter
stayed there, seated far from all the blessed gods, wasting with grief for her deep-
belted daughter.

She made the most terrible, most oppressive year for men upon the nourishing land, and the earth sent up no seed, as fair-garlanded Demeter hid it. Cattle
drew the many curved plows in vain over the fields, and much white barley seed
fell useless on the earth. By now she would have destroyed the entire race of men
by grievous famine, and deprived those who dwell on Olympus of the glorious
honor of offerings and sacrifices, if Zeus had not taken notice and taken counsel
with his mind. First he roused gold-winged Iris to summon fair-haired Demeter,
of the very desirable beauty. So he spoke, and she obeyed Zeus wrapped in
clouds, the son of Kronos. She rushed down the middle and arrived at the citadel
of fragrant Eleusis. In the temple she found Demeter dark-clad, and addressed
her with winged words. "Demeter, father Zeus who understands imperishable
things summons you to come among the race of the immortal gods. So come,
and let my message from Zeus not be fruitless."

So she spoke in supplication, but her heart was not persuaded. Therefore the
Father sent out the blessed, ever-living gods one after another, and they went in
turn and implored her, and offered her many fine gifts and whatever honors she
might choose among the immortal gods. None, however, was able to persuade
the heart and mind of the angry goddess. She rejected their speeches firmly, and

claimed that she would never set foot upon fragrant Olympus, nor allow any fruit to grow on the earth, until she saw with her eyes the beautiful face of her daughter.

When Zeus the loud-crashing, the wide-voiced one, heard this, he sent Hermes the slayer of Argos with his golden wand to Erebos, to use smooth words on Hades and lead pure Persephone out of the misty darkness into the light to join the deities, in order that her mother might see her with her eyes and turn from her anger. Hermes obeyed, and eagerly rushed down under the recesses of the earth, leaving the seat of Olympus. He found the Lord inside his house, seated on couches with his modest and very unwilling wife, yearning for her mother. . . .

The mighty slayer of Argos came near and said, "Dark-haired Hades, ruler of the departed, Father Zeus has ordered me to lead glorious Persephone out of Erebos to join them, in order that her mother might see her with her eyes and cease from her anger and terrible wrath, since she is contriving a tremendous deed, to destroy the fragile race of earth-born men, hiding the seed under the earth and obliterating the honors of the immortals. Her anger is terrible, she has no contact with the gods, but sits apart inside her fragrant temple, holding the rocky citadel of Eleusis."

So he spoke, and Aidoneus the lord of the underworld smiled with his brows, 20 and did not disobey the injunctions of Zeus the king. Promptly he gave the command to diligent Persephone: "Go, Persephone, to your dark-clad mother, and keep gentle the strength and heart in your breast. Do not be despondent to excess beyond all others. I shall not be an inappropriate husband for you among the immortals; I am a brother of Father Zeus. Being there, you will rule over all that lives and moves, enjoying the greatest honors among the immortals. And there shall be punishment forever on those who act unjustly and who do not propitiate your might with sacrifices, performing the pious acts and offering appropriate gifts."

So he spoke, and Persephone the discreet was glad, and swiftly leapt up for joy. But he gave her a honey-sweet pomegranate seed to eat, having secretly passed it around (himself?), so that she might not stay forever there by modest dark-clad Demeter. Aidoneus, designator of many, harnessed the immortal horses in front of the golden chariot, and she stepped on the chariot; beside her the mighty slayer of Argos took the reins and a whip in his hands and drove out of the palace. The pair of horses flew willingly. They finished the long journey quickly. Neither sea nor rivers nor grassy glens nor mountain peaks held back the rush of the immortal horses; they went above them, and cut through the high air. He drove them where Demeter of the fair crown waited in front of her fragrant temple, and he stopped them there. Seeing them, she darted up like a maenad in the woods on a thick-shaded mountain. . . .

(Demeter asked Persephone if she had eaten anything in the underworld. If not,) "you will come up and dwell with me and Zeus of the dark clouds and be honored by all the immortals. But if you have tasted anything, then you shall go back down and dwell there for the third part of the season, and for the other two, here with me and the other immortals. Whenever the earth blossoms with all the sweet-smelling flowers of spring, then you will come back up from the misty darkness, a great wonder to gods and to mortal men. But what trick did the powerful host of many use to deceive you?"

Persephone, the exceedingly beautiful, gave her this response: "I will tell you, Mother, everything accurately. When the swift slayer of Argos came to me from Father Zeus and the others in heaven with the message to come out of Erebos, so that seeing me with your eyes you might cease from your anger and terrible wrath, I leapt up for joy. But he secretly insinuated a pomegranate seed, honey-sweet food, and though I was unwilling, he compelled me by force to taste it. How he snatched me away through the clever plan of Zeus and carried me off, down into the recesses of the earth, I will tell you and I will go through it all as you ask. We were all there in the lovely meadow—Leukippe, Phaino, Elektre (Electra), Ianthe, Melite, Iache, Rhodeia, Kallirhoe, Melobosis, Tyche, Okyrhoe of the flowering face, Chryseis, Ianeira, Akaste, Admete, Rhodope, Plouto, charming Kalypso, Styx, Ouranie, lovely Galaxaure, Pallas the inciter of battles, Artemis the shooter of arrows—playing and picking the lovely flowers, a profusion of gentle saffron blossoms, iris, hyacinth, rose buds, and lilies, a marvel to see, and narcissus, which the broad land grew like saffron. Full of joy, I was picking them, but the earth under me moved, and the powerful Lord, the host of many, leapt out. And he took me under the earth on his golden chariot, against my will, and I screamed loudly with my voice. Grieved though I am, I am telling you the whole truth."

Then with minds in concord they spent the whole day warming their hearts and minds, showering much love on each other, and her mind found respite from its griefs, as they gave and received joys from each other. And there came near them Hecate of the glistening veil, and she also showered much love on the daughter of holy Demeter, and ever since she has been her attendant and lady-in-waiting.

Zeus the loud-crashing, the wide-voiced one, sent fair-haired Rhea as a messenger to them, to bring dark-gowned Demeter among the race of the gods; he promised to give her whatever honors she might choose among the immortal gods. He granted that her daughter should spend the third portion of the year in its cycle down in the misty darkness, but the other two with her mother and the other immortals.

So he spoke, and the goddess obeyed the biddings of Zeus. Promptly she darted along the peaks of Olympus, and came to the Rarian plain, the life-bringing udder of plough-land formerly, but at that time not life-bringing at all, as it stood all barren and leafless. The white barley was concealed according to the plans of fair-ankled Demeter, but at this time it was about to grow shaggy with waves of grain as it became spring. In the field the rich furrows were to be loaded with the grain, and they were to be bound in sheaves. Here she first alighted from the boundless aether, and they saw each other gladly, and rejoiced in their hearts.

Rhea of the glistening veil said to her, "Come here, child. Zeus the loud-crashing, the wide-voiced one, summons you to come among the race of the immortal gods, and he has promised to give whatever honors you might choose among the immortal gods. He has granted that your daughter will spend the third portion of the year in its cycle down in the misty darkness, but the other

25

two with you and the other immortals. So has he promised, and nodded his head in affirmation. Go, now, my child, and obey; do not be obdurately angry at Zeus of the dark clouds but give prompt increase to the fruit, bringer of life to men."

So she spoke, and Demeter of the fair crown obeyed. Promptly she sent up fruit on the rich-soiled fields, and the whole broad land was loaded with leaves and flowers. She went to the royal stewards of the right and to Triptolemos, Diokles the driver of horses, mighty Eumolpos, and Keleos the leader of the people. She showed the tendance of the holy things and explicated the rites to them all, to Triptolemos, to Polyxeinos, and to Diokles—sacred rites, which it is forbidden to transgress, to inquire into, or to speak about, for great reverence of the gods constrains their voice. Blessed of earthbound men is he who has seen these things, but he who dies without fulfilling the holy things, and he who is without a share of them, has no claim ever on such blessings, even when departed down to the moldy darkness.

When the divine goddess had ordained all this, she went to Olympus among the assembly of the other gods. And there they dwell, sacred and reverent, with Zeus who revels in thunder. Greatly blessed of earthbound men is he whom they propitiously love: to him they promptly send to the hearth of his great house Ploutos (Wealth), who gives abundance to mortal men.

Now, ye that hold the people of fragrant Eleusis, and sea-girt Paros and rocky 30 Antron, Lady mistress Deo, bringer of seasons and glorious gifts, thou myself and Persephone, the exceedingly beautiful, do ye bestow a heartwarming livelihood in exchange for my song. Now I shall recall thee and also another song.

Questions for Discussion and Review

1. What are the three functions of the Goddess, and why are they important? Explain why and how her three functions are divided among the various Olympian goddesses.

2. One of the Great Goddess's primary symbols is the serpent. What aspects of the Goddess's power are symbolized by the serpent? Explain why the perception of the snake as depicted in the myths changes from a beautiful and beneficent creature into a terrifying monster or dragon. How does that change reflect the transformation from matriarchal to patriarchal systems?

3. What roles and qualities do Demeter and Persephone share with Dionysus? How are they different? Discuss the similarities and differences in the rites celebrating these deities. How might the gender of each of these deities help explain the differences?

4. In the *Homeric Hymn to Demeter,* why does Demeter go to Eleusis? Why does she want to make the child Demophon immortal? How does the apparent inability of gods and humans to understand each other contribute to her failure? In what ways does the Eleusinian ritual she demands to compensate for the insult to her divinity assist her worshipers in communicating with the goddess?

5. What is the gift of Triptolemus to humankind? Explain the relevance of this myth to the development of agricultural communities. How does understanding the growth processes of plants aid humans in understanding their own lives? Explain how living in agricultural villages would affect the lives of people who had previously lived as

hunters of animals and gatherers of grain. What would that change contribute to the development of civilization?

Recommended Reading

Baring, Anne, and Jules Cashford. *The Myth of the Goddess: Evolution of an Image.* London: Penguin, 1993. A study of the images of the goddess from the Paleolithic to the modern age, tracing the loss of the goddess myth and the relationship between masculine and feminine principles in contemporary culture.

Gadon, Elinor W. *The Once and Future Goddess: A Symbol for Our Times.* San Francisco: Harper & Row, 1989. A comparative study of goddess culture over vast regions from Europe and Asia Minor to the Near East, as well as over millennia from the Paleolithic era to the Middle Ages in Europe and into our own time.

Gimbutas, Marija. *The Language of the Goddess.* NY: Harper, 1989. A profusely illustrated work documenting the artifacts that are evidence for widespread worship of the Great Goddess in Old Europe and analyzing the major symbols in which the attributes of the Great Goddess are expressed.

Mylonas, George E. *Eleusis and the Eleusinian Mysteries.* Princeton: Princeton UP, 1961. The standard study of the ancient rituals in honor of Demeter.

Neumann, Erich. *The Great Mother: An Analysis of the Archetype.* Trans. Ralph Manheim. 1963. Princeton: Princeton UP, 1991. A discussion of the major functions and implications of the Great Goddess in myths throughout the world.

The Olympian Family of Zeus

KEY THEMES

Originally conceived as amoral forces—embodiments of natural processes and/or instinctual drives—the Greek gods eventually evolved into idealized images of humanity. Transformed by the poets to reflect Greek society's concept of aristocratic leadership, the Olympians typically enforce exacting standards of justice in earthly society, while enjoying the option to behave capriciously when manipulating human lives.

In comparing the antiquity of Egypt with the youthfulness of Greek civilization, Herodotus states that the Greeks did not know much about their gods "until the day before yesterday" (Book 2, Section 55). It was only a few centuries before his day (about 450 B.C.), Herodotus says, that Homer and Hesiod first defined the gods' individual characters, appearance, and functions. So effective were the poets' verbal portraits of Zeus and his divine family, however, that they permanently fixed the Greeks' concept of divinity.

In Book 15 of the *Iliad,* Homer states that Zeus and his two brothers, after defeating the Titans, cast lots to divide the world among themselves. Zeus receives the sky, Poseidon the sea, and Hades the Underworld as their respective domains, but the three agree to share jurisdiction of the earth, assuming equal freedom to intervene in human affairs.

The Older Olympians

Although the Greeks accepted the existence of many other deities, the number of high gods who administered the world from Mount Olympus was limited to twelve. In the generally recognized Olympian pantheon, the twelve are bound tightly to-

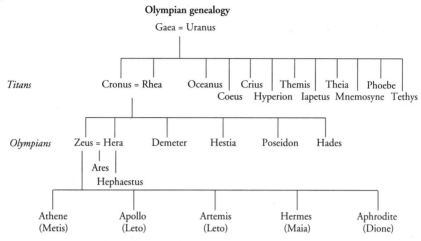

FIGURE 5-1   Genealogy of Zeus's Olympian Family. The Greek pantheon consists exclusively of close family members, all of whom are descendants of the original divine parents, Gaea and Uranus. The older Olympians, Zeus and his siblings, are offspring of the Titans Cronus and Rhea, while the younger are children of Zeus by various wives or, in the case of Hephaestus, of Hera. The names of Zeus's wives are enclosed in parentheses beneath the names of their divine offspring.

gether in a family relationship: every Olympian is a brother, or a sister, or a child of Zeus (Figure 5-1). As Hesiod reported in the *Theogony,* however, some of the Olympians, such as Aphrodite, were once thought to have appeared long before Zeus was born. As generations of mythographers, including Homer, emphasized the supremacy of Zeus, some gods that had once enjoyed an existence independent of the chief Olympian were inevitably subordinated to him. Historically, the figures of Aphrodite, Artemis, and Hermes are perhaps as old as or older than Zeus; nonetheless, in the increasingly patriarchal religion of Mycenae and archaic Greece, they became his children and therefore were under his jurisdiction.

As Homer and Hesiod had established the character and functions of the Olympians, during the archaic and classical periods Greek artists defined their physical appearance. The older generation of Zeus and his siblings, the six children of Cronus and Rhea, were depicted as physically mature, an unchanging perfection of middle age. Although retaining the superb musculature of the athlete, Zeus and his brothers have the full beards and thick, flowing locks that proclaim their patriarchal status and their membership in the age group that typically governs society. Zeus's sisters, Hera, Demeter, and Hestia, are similarly portrayed as majestic, with the ample proportions of feminine maturity. The following brief sketches review the gods' salient qualities and summarize some of their characteristic myths. More complete stories about the gods and heroes appear in the narrative poems and plays anthologized in this text. The gods' Latin names, which may be more familiar to many readers, are included in parentheses after the Greek name.

FIGURE 5-2   Zeus Holding Thunderbolt. Poised to hurl a thunderbolt, Zeus is pictured as a bearded patriarch. The epitome of masculine dignity, the King of Heaven has conquered all rivals, including his father and Gaea's chaotic serpent Typhoeus. His is the power that keeps the universe in moral equilibrium. (*Vatican Museums, Rome.*)

Zeus (Jupiter, Jove)

The closest that Greek religion came to conceptualizing a supreme being, **Zeus** is the awe-inspiring King of Heaven, the champion of justice, sworn oaths, and lawful order (Figure 5-2). He is also the only Greek deity about whose name, which dates back to Mycenaean times, most scholars agree. Of Indo-European origin, *Zeus* denotes the luminous daylight sky. The name corresponds to that of the sky god of ancient India, *Dyaus pitar,* and is the same as that of Jupiter (*Diespiter,* "God [Zeus] the father"), head of the Roman pantheon. The same root appears in the Latin *deus* ("god"), *dies* ("day"), and the Greek *eudia* ("fair weather"), indicating Zeus's association with the bright air of day. In Homer's famous phrase, Zeus is also "the cloud-gatherer," the force that generates storms and incinerates opponents with thunderbolts.

The most ethically developed Olympian, Zeus represents the ultimate court of appeal to whose judgments both men and gods must submit. Unlike the Judeo-

Christian or Islamic God, however, Zeus is not omniscient or all-powerful. His relation to Fate, the irresistible power of Necessity that directs the flow of history, is ambiguous. In many myths, Fate is a force superior to the gods; in the Homeric poems, Zeus almost always refrains from even contemplating a change in the heroes' individual destinies. For a fleeting moment he is tempted to save from an early death his mortal son Sarpedon, an exceptionally brave and noble warrior who fought against the Greeks in the Trojan War. When confronted with Hera's scorn and the unpredictable consequences of interfering with destiny, however, Zeus reluctantly agrees not to intervene on Sarpedon's behalf. In some myths it is difficult to determine whether Zeus accedes to the dictates of Fate because he does not wish to upset cosmic order or whether Zeus cannot change the basic operation of a universe he did not create.

Hesiod, for whom Zeus is ultimate power, implies the god's independence of Fate by making him the father of the **Moirae**, the three sisters who spin and weave the patterns controlling mortal lives. By the same mother, Themis (whose name means "the right" or "established custom"), Zeus also sires Lawfulness (Eunomia), Justice (Dike), and Peace (Eirene), indicating that Zeus is the force that keeps the cosmos, including his household of fractious, egocentric deities, operating in relative harmony.

Because Zeus is a compendium of amoral nature, symbolized by the thunderbolt, and a projection of Greek patriarchal leadership, his character is correspondingly paradoxical. Warring against his imperial dignity as king, husband, father, and judge is Zeus's apparently uncontrollable sexual appetite, which compels him to pursue virtually every attractive person—mortal or immortal, male or female—within his considerable reach (Figure 5-3). In the *Theogony,* Hesiod validates this aspect of Zeus's character by highlighting the cosmic benefits of his divine hero's compulsive promiscuity. Zeus's extramarital affairs with goddesses, nymphs, and mortal women produce sons and daughters of extraordinary superiority! Who could object to liaisons that result in such gods as Apollo and Artemis, or heroes such as Perseus and Heracles? In cataloguing Zeus's conquests and their offspring, Hesiod informs us that the chief Olympian's sexual adventures not only enrich the human gene pool with heroic stock, but also populate the cosmos with beings who represent the highest values of civilization. Thus Zeus begets such progeny as the Muses, who inspire all the creative arts, and other divine abstractions, including the Graces, personifications of beauty and charm, and the Seasons, guarantors of cosmic order. Without Zeus's virile generosity in siring these children, Hesiod implies, the universe would be no better than it was under the generally uncivilized Titans.

In modern astronomy, Zeus's amorous conquests have been commemorated in the sixteen moons circling our solar system's largest planet, which bears Zeus's Latin name, Jupiter. Taking their cue from classical mythology, astronomers have named each of Jupiter's satellites after one of Zeus's lovers: these include Europa, a mortal woman whom he abducted in the form of a white bull; Callisto, a nymph who was part of Artemis's virgin retinue until Zeus seduced her and she was changed into a bear; Io, a mortal virgin whom Zeus brutally raped in the form of a bull (see Chapter 15); and Ganymede, a handsome Trojan youth whom Zeus desired and, in the guise of an eagle, seized and carried off to Olympus. The only one of Zeus's lovers permanently installed in heaven, Ganymede was made cupbearer of the gods, pouring out wine at Olympian banquets.

FIGURE 5-3   Zeus and Ganymede. This terra-cotta statue depicts Zeus carrying off the Trojan boy Ganymede, whom the god will install on Olympus as his lover and cupbearer, the honored wine server at the gods' banquets. Shown striding forward in a rush to enjoy his prize, Zeus manifests the classical Greek attraction toward the physical beauty of young men. Although Hera objects passionately to her husband's liaisons with other goddesses, nymphs, or mortal women, she accepts Ganymede's presence in heaven, where the youth is identified with the zodiacal sign of Aquarius. (*Olympia Museum.*)

If future astronomers discover additional moons orbiting Jupiter, they are unlikely to run out of lovers' names to bestow upon them. By exact count, some ancient mythographers tallied no fewer than 115 different objects of Zeus's widely distributed affections.

The god's lust, which is at once the instinctual "shadow" of Zeus's ostensibly rational persona and a projection of his will to control and dominate, at times produces a comic spectacle. Myth shows heaven's love-obsessed emperor sneaking about in disguise, abandoning his divine splendor to assume the form of a bull, swan, serpent, or eagle, images of the nonhuman power he represents—all in the (usually vain) hope to escape his wife's ever-watchful eye. Although his desire can be cruelly exploitative, as it is with the unfortunate Io, many poets depict the divine king humorously, as henpecked by Hera at home and driven by an indefatigable libido abroad.

The Major Classical Gods and Goddesses

ANGLICIZED NAME	TRANSLITERATED GREEK NAME	LATIN NAME
Zeus	Zeus	Jupiter, Jove
Poseidon	Poseidon	Neptune
Hades, Pluto	Hades, Plouton	Pluto, Dis
Hera	Here	Juno
Hestia	Hestia	Vesta
Demeter	Demeter	Ceres
Athene (Athena)	Athene	Minerva
Aphrodite	Aphrodite	Venus
Hermes	Hermes	Mercury (Mercurius)
Phoebus Apollo	Phoibos Apollon	Phoebus Apollo
Artemis	Artemis	Diana
Hephaestus	Hephaistos	Vulcan (Vulcanus)
Ares	Ares	Mars
Dionysus, Bacchus	Dionysos, Bakchos	Liber
Pan	Pan	Faunus
Gaea	Gaia	Terra Mater
Uranus	Ouranos	Caelum
Cronus	Kronos	Saturn
Rhea, Cybele	Rheia, Kybele	Ops
Eros	Eros	Cupid (Cupido)
Eileithyia	Eileithyie	Lucina
Helios	Helios	Sol, Phoebus
Selene	Selene	Luna
Persephone, Cora	Persephone, Kore	Proserpina
Hebe	Hebe	Juventas

Although the myths recounting Zeus's amorous adventures may serve to uphold a double standard that permits men greater sexual freedom than women, they also remind us of the enormous variety and complexity of humanity's sexual nature. In Greek myth, Eros and Aphrodite overwhelm even the gods.

Hera (Juno)

The Queen of Heaven, **Hera** [HEE-ra] ranks highest among the Olympian goddesses (Figure 5-4). Despite her exalted status, however, myth depicts Hera as leading

FIGURE 5-4 Hera. As the goddess of marriage and marital fidelity, Hera finds herself in an unending war against her brother-husband's promiscuity. Because her function is to up-hold family values and punish those who violate them, she typically appears as an angry per-secutor of Zeus's innumerable mistresses and their children. (*Vatican Museums, Rome.*)

a frustrating and generally unhappy existence, largely because her priorities collide head-on with the will of Zeus, her husband and brother. Nor was Hera's childhood a secure and pleasant experience: along with Poseidon, Hades, Hestia, and Demeter, she was swallowed alive by her father, Cronus. Only when her mother, Rhea, be-guiled Cronus into regurgitating his children did her life begin, and then she was sent to live with foster parents, Oceanus and Tethys, while Zeus battled Cronus and his Titan allies. Although Oceanus and Tethys were also Titans, as personifications, re-spectively, of the great river that surrounds the earth and the sea's inexhaustible fe-cundity, they were essential cosmic features and hence survived the other Titans' fall. Grateful for their protection during her youth, Hera is said to have reconciled the couple after they had been divided by a bitter quarrel.

Unfortunately, Hera is less successful—and apparently much less diplomatic—in mediating differences in her own marriage to Zeus. Although she is the patron of weddings, wives, marriage, and family life, Hera rarely shares her husband's viewpoint and tries to subvert his plans whenever possible. In a famous incident from the *Iliad* (books 14–15), Hera determines to manipulate events so that the Greeks will thor-oughly trounce the Trojans, whom she fervently hates (see Chapter 11). Accordingly, she borrows Aphrodite's erotically charmed girdle, wearing it to seduce her husband

and thereby distract his attention from the war. The couple make love atop lofty Mount Ida, which Zeus swathes in a thick cloud to ensure their privacy. When Zeus awakens from postcoital slumber, however, and realizes his wife's deception, he is furious, reminding Hera of the occasion on which he used his superior strength to suspend her from Olympus by her wrists, with huge iron anvils tied to her feet!

Hera also acts to spite Zeus when, in retaliation for his producing Athene without her aid, she—without *his* participation—conceives and gives birth to Hephaestus. The only Olympian goddess who retains the Great Goddess's parthenogenetic ability, Hera pays for her attempt to upstage Zeus's patriarchal self-sufficiency. In some versions of the myth, Hephaestus is born crippled, the only physically imperfect Olympian, and in disgust Hera throws the newborn out of heaven. Landing on the volcanic island of Lemnos, where the inhabitants care for him, Hephaestus later avenges himself and his unaffectionate mother by designing and sending Hera a golden throne. Once seated on the throne, Hera is a prisoner: Hephaestus had contrived a golden chain that automatically wrapped about the throne's occupant, holding her immobile. Only when Dionysus seeks him out, gets him drunk, and leads him back to Olympus does Hephaestus reluctantly consent to release his mother.

Despite her role as celestial wife, Hera is not a maternal figure and Greek artists never picture her, as the Egyptians portrayed Isis, as a tender mother holding her child. In some accounts, the only child that she and Zeus produce is Ares, the ill-tempered war god, who is a fitting symbol of his parents' contentious union. In others, the royal couple also have **Eileithyia** [ye-lye-THYE-ya], a minor deity of childbirth, and **Hebe** [HEE-bee], a personification of blooming youth whom Zeus later replaces with Ganymede as the Olympians' cupbearer.

Interestingly, myth depicts none of the Olympian goddesses as prolific mothers who bear many children: Hestia, Athene, and Artemis remain virgins, and Demeter, for all her maternal devotion to Persephone, produces only two or three children. Even Aphrodite, the personification of sexuality and fertility, has few offspring. Although some myths make Eros (Cupid) her son by Ares, in Hesiod's *Theogony* Eros is a primal god who existed long before Aphrodite's birth.

In perhaps a majority of her myths, Hera appears as a jealous and vindictive wife: unable to punish her straying husband directly, she ferociously persecutes his mistresses and their illegitimate children. Outraged at Zeus's infidelities, which she regards as insults to her dignity, Hera tries to kill the infant Heracles (Hercules) and, failing that, imposes on the adult hero a series of grueling labors. She also attempts to prevent Leto, pregnant with Apollo and Artemis, from giving birth and arranges to have Semele, then carrying Dionysus, burned alive (Chapter 8). Hera's lack of sisterly feeling, even for innocent victims of Zeus's lust, and her unforgiving persecution of the noble Aeneas led Virgil, Rome's greatest poet, to ask, "is vindictiveness an attribute of the celestial mind?"

While acknowledging that Homeric and other myths emphasize Hera's unattractive qualities, it is important to remember that her behavior may embody a reaction to the patriarchal usurpation of the Great Goddess's rights and privileges. Zeus's imperious refusal to be faithful to Olympus's highest goddess serves to assert the male god's complete independence of the divine female. At the same time, Hera's cosmic importance is voiced in a myth about the newborn Heracles. In this tale, Hermes finds Hera asleep and stealthily places the infant Heracles at the goddess's breast. When the baby begins to nurse, however, Hera awakens, thrusting Zeus's son aside

FIGURE 5-5   Poseidon and Amphitrite. In this mosaic from the Villa Stabiae (Pompeii) depicting Poseidon—with his wife, Amphitrite—driving a chariot triumphantly over the waves, the sea god is surrounded by symbols of his marine domain, including the ships of fishermen who depend upon his good will to survive. The trident Poseidon holds in his left hand is the three-pronged instrument he uses to stir the sea to destructive fury during storms. Note the nimbi, or halos, encircling the couple's heads, a symbol of divinity later borrowed by Christian artists. (*Louvre, Paris.*)

before he can absorb the milk of immortality. But it is too late: a powerful jet of Hera's milk streams across the night sky, igniting thousands of brilliant stars. Visible every clear night, the Milky Way bears silent tribute to heaven's troubled queen, forming a display more impressive than the endless circling of Jupiter's lonely moons.

Poseidon (Neptune)

As Zeus compels obedience with his thunderbolts, so **Poseidon** [poh-SYE-duhn] uses the trident, a huge three-pronged spear with which he generates monstrous sea waves to crush the ships of any who offend him (Figure 5-5). Like the restless element over which he rules, Poseidon is volatile, unpredictable, and quick to rage. Any sailor venturing into his realm must propitiate the god with acceptable sacrifices if he hopes to reach his destination safely. In the *Odyssey,* Poseidon represents the brutal power of nature against which the hero must pit his human intelligence in order to survive. Homer also suggests an important component of Poseidon's character through his son Polyphemus, an uncouth Cyclops who devours his guests and refuses to observe any code of civilized behavior.

Although master of the sea, Poseidon is also associated with land animals such as bulls and horses—images of masculine virility. When the earth rumbles and shakes,

FIGURE 5-6 Demeter. An important aspect of the ancient Great Goddess, Demeter represents the fertility of earth's soil and hence the grain harvest upon which the entire human community depends for survival. In this monumental statue, the seated goddess stares ahead unseeingly, blinded by grief for her daughter, Persephone, whom Zeus and Hades have secretly conspired to take from her. The myth of Demeter's agonized search for the abducted girl—hidden deep in Hades's underground realm—and Persephone's role in nature's annual cycle of death and regeneration represent one of the most important religious traditions of Greek civilization (see Chapter 4). (*British Museum, London.*)

it is the effect of Poseidon in the form of a colossal bull, bellowing and pawing the ground. As the invisible earthshaker, he was worshiped from Mycenaean times on as lord of earthquakes, a personification of seismic energy.

As an embodiment of natural violence and the begetter of monstrous offspring, Poseidon is a particularly dangerous god. If offended, he is merciless even to his worshipers; when the Phaeacians, once favorites of the sea's ruler, provide Odysseus with safe conduct back to Ithaca, he angrily turns their returning ship to stone and shatters their peace by convulsing the earth, elevating a mountain range to surround their city (*Odyssey,* Book 13). It is not surprising that, when mortals first began to organize themselves in cities, many were reluctant to choose Poseidon as their presiding deity. The list of gods who successfully competed against Poseidon to become the divine patrons of cities throughout Greece is impressively long. In competition for Corinth, Poseidon lost to Helios (the Sun); for Aegina, he lost to Zeus; for Troezen and Athens, to Athene; for Argos, to Hera; for Delphi, to Apollo; and for Naxos, to Dionysus. Although widely recognized as a natural force that must be placated, Poseidon's surly temperament earned him a poor showing in mythic popularity contests.

Demeter (Ceres)

A manifestation of the Great Goddess, **Demeter** [de-MEE-ter] represents the life-giving power of earth's fertile soil (Figure 5-6). Like Hera, she is a sister of Zeus by whom the chief Olympian incestuously sires a divine child, his rape effectively subordinating the goddess to patriarchal rule. Although her principal myth—Hades's abduction of Persephone (see Chapter 4)—emphasizes her maternal love for a single child, other tales illustrate additional aspects of the Demeter tradition. According to one episode introduced into the story of Demeter's search for Persephone, Poseidon attempted to seduce his grieving sister. When Demeter tried to escape his unwelcome attentions by transforming herself into a mare, the sea god nonetheless completed his rape, fathering a horse called Arion and a mysterious daughter, named "the Mistress."

Iasion, the son of Zeus and Electra, a daughter of the Titan Atlas, fell passionately in love with Demeter. One version of the myth suggests that she did not return his affection and that Iasion, in retaliation, tried to harm her, for which Zeus killed him with a thunderbolt. According to Hesiod's *Theogony*, Demeter reciprocated Iasion's love and lay with the hero in a thrice-plowed field, their union resulting in a son, Plutus. In this chthonic myth, Iasion is the male consort of a fertility goddess to whom Demeter gives seeds of wheat, making him an adjunct of her function as the producer of grain. Greek art typically pictures their son **Plutus** [PLOO-tuhs], a personification of wealth, as a young man carrying a horn of plenty.

Hades (Pluto, Dis)

Even gloomier than the irascible Poseidon, **Hades** [HAY-deez] is "Zeus of the Underworld," a chthonic (earth-related) figure who represents the darker, more sinister aspects of divinity, a polar opposite of Zeus's sunlit vitality. Although Hades is neither evil nor the cause of death, he is dreaded for his association with the hopeless dead, over whom he rules jointly with Persephone, his queen. Wearing a cap of invisibility, Hades may be present without being seen. For the ancient Greeks, the invisible god was virtually ubiquitous; one could not know when, figuratively, Hades's subterranean realm would suddenly open, drawing the living into a chasm of perpetual darkness.

Hades rarely appears in the upper world and figures prominently in only one major myth, the story of Persephone's abduction (the *Homeric Hymn to Demeter*, Chapter 4). Also called **Pluto** [PLOO-toh] (*Plouton*, the "wealth-giver") because gems and mineral riches are found under the earth, Hades has a grim and pitiless personality, his implacability reflecting the harsh quality of natural law that condemns all living things to death. (Hades's subterranean kingdom, which played a major role in the Greek imagination, is described in Chapter 9.)

Hestia (Vesta)

Zeus's unmarried sister **Hestia** [HES-tee-uh] is the only Olympian for whom no myths were created. An immortal virgin devoted exclusively to guarding the Olympian hearth and its life-sustaining fire, she represents the unmoving, fixed center of family life, both human and divine. A symbol of unchanging permanence, she never leaves her assigned place and hence neither acts nor becomes involved in others' actions, a role that precludes her having any life story of her own. In Greek myth, her opposite is Hermes, who roams freely throughout the universe, an embodiment of divine force and movement. Hestia's colorless passivity, though essential to her identification with the domestic hearth, ultimately resulted in her being demoted from Olympus, to be replaced by the energetic Dionysus.

In Roman myth, Hestia was known as **Vesta** [VES-tuh] and figured more prominently in the civic cult as keeper of the sacred flame that symbolized Rome's essential
life force. The Vestal Virgins, famous for remaining strictly celibate while performing
their holy duties, were well-born women who maintained Vesta's eternal flame in a
temple near the Roman forum. Tradition decreed that any Vestal priestess who broke
her oath of celibacy was to be buried alive. Released from their vows only at their
fortieth birthday, the Vestals' peculiar circumstance gave birth to the adage that "life
begins at forty."

The Younger Olympians

Zeus is the only Olympian deity whose children are major gods in their own right.
Of the seven younger Olympians, only two are Hera's.

Athene (Minerva)

Like her half-brothers Hermes and Apollo, **Athene** is a complex deity whose many
attributes and functions encompass contradictory elements. Although born without
a mother, she takes a keen interest in women's activities, particularly the domestic
arts of spinning and weaving. Athene is also the patron of pottery-making and other
crafts; with Hephaestus, god of smiths and metalworkers, she shares the patronage of
virtually all civilized, productive skills. Associated closely with the city of Athens,
which bears her name, Athene has a particularly warm relationship with its citizens.
At the beginning of Athens's history, she successfully competed against her uncle
Poseidon for the city's allegiance. To win the contest, Poseidon offered Athens's citizens the dubious gift of a saltwater spring; the practical Athene easily demonstrated
her greater usefulness as a divine patron by donating the domestic olive tree, whose
fruit and oil became one of Athens's chief exports.

These beneficent qualities, however, are only part of Athene's character. When she
sprang from Zeus's head, she appeared fully armed with a warrior's helmet, shield,
and spear. Although not a deity of war as such, she is a powerful fighter and defender
of the Greek city-state (Figure 5-7). In crucial battles during the Persian invasion of
Greece, she was said to have been invisibly present supporting the Greek side, inspiring Athenian soldiers to otherwise impossible acts of courage and valor. Protector of
civilized values, especially order and justice, Athene typically wins battles through
forethought and strategy, cleverly outmaneuvering enemies. In this role she customarily wears Zeus's special insignia, the **aegis** [EE-jis], a goatskin shield or short cloak,
decorated with a terrifying Gorgon's head and a fringe of snakes (Figure 5-8). Once
aroused, Athene can be pitiless: her hostility toward Paris and his fellow Trojans is
unrelenting (Chapter 11); and she refuses to spare from death a single man among
Penelope's one hundred unwanted suitors (Chapter 12).

Implacable toward those who offend her, Athene cruelly punishes Arachne, a
young woman who foolishly challenges Athene to a contest of weaving skills, changing the impertinent mortal into a spider. In Sophocles's play *Ajax,* she is positively
fiendish, driving into madness a noble warrior who tries to win Achilles's armor from
her favorite, Odysseus. By contrast, Athene graciously befriends selected heroes, such
as Odysseus and Heracles, who mirror her attributes of intelligence and resourceful-

FIGURE 5-7 The Mourning Athene. In this fifth-century B.C. bas-relief, a helmeted Athene leans on her spear while apparently reading an inscription listing the names of men who died defending her beloved Athens. Athenian myth consistently identified the goddess with their city's welfare. (*Acropolis Museum, Athens.*)

ness. Devoted to the Athenians, she helps to establish their first law courts, encouraging a democratic jury system that tempers justice with mercy (the *Eumenides,* Chapter 15). In peace, she promotes the political art of persuasion, urging her people to cooperate for the common good.

Embodying the kind of pragmatic wisdom involved in clever planning and winning strategies, Athene is typically self-disciplined, even austere. Two myths, however, present the armor-clad virgin in surprisingly erotic situations. On one occasion, a burst of vanity embroils her in a beauty competition with Hera and Aphrodite; her bitter resentment at losing to the love goddess helps to seal Troy's doom, for the goddess of victory in war supports the Greek side. In a myth about Athens's origins, the mythographer ingeniously creates a tale in which Athene could remain perpetually virginal yet, in a sense, indirectly become the mother of one of the city's earliest rulers. While visiting Hephaestus's forge to order new weapons, Athene unexpectedly found herself fending off the lame god's passionate advances. During the struggle, Hephaestus ejaculated on Athene's thigh. Perhaps because Hephaestus's attempted rape was both clumsy and unsuccessful, Athene behaves with remarkable coolness:

FIGURE 5-8 Athene Holding a Spear. In this statue, the warrior goddess wears the aegis of Zeus—a breastplate decorated with a fringe of coiled snakes. A picture of Medusa, whose gaze turned men to stone, appears at the center of the aegis. (*Archeological Museum, Naples.*)

she neither recriminates nor plots revenge. Instead, she calmly takes a wool cloth, wipes the semen from her thigh, and tosses the wet rag out of heaven.

Because a god's seed always bears fruit, when the enseminated wool fell on mother earth, a child, Ericthonius, was born. Accepting responsibility for the baby, Athene placed Ericthonius in a basket and entrusted him to the daughters of Cecrops, the mythical first king of Athens. Against Athene's instructions, the young women looked into the basket and were driven insane by the sight: either Ericthonius had the lower body of a serpent, a characteristic of earth's offspring, or he was guarded by frightening snakes. Athene then took Ericthonius to her sacred precincts atop the Athenian Acropolis, where he grew up to become Athens's king. Under Athene's guidance, Ericthonius was said to have invented the first four-horse chariot and established the **Panathenaea,** the annual festival held in the goddess's honor. Other myths ascribe these accomplishments to **Erechtheus** [e-REK-thee-uhs], another prehistoric ruler who is variously identified as the son or grandson of Erichthonius. The Erechtheum, a small temple famous for its porch roof supported by statues of young maidens, still stands on the Athenian Acropolis.

Apollo

The sole Olympian whose name remains the same in Roman myth, **Apollo** (Apollon) is the son of Zeus and Leto, daughter of the Titans Coeus and Phoebe. A god of multiple functions, he is primarily the giver of rational harmony—both mental and physical—and a seer of future events. As communicator of the gods' will to humanity, he establishes his main sanctuary at Delphi on Mount Parnassus, where his virgin priestess—known as the *Pythia,* or *Pythoness*—issues cryptic pronouncements whose ambiguities are described as "oracular." The Delphic Oracle became the most respected and widely consulted institution of prophecy in the Greco-Roman world (Chapter 7).

Often cited as the most typically Greek of all gods, Apollo is called *Phoebus*—the radiant, or shining, one, an embodiment of intellectual and spiritual enlightenment. In late myths, he assumes the duties of Hyperion (or Helios) and is identified with the sun. Apollo shares with his half-brother Hermes the patronage of rustic shepherds, flocks, and fields, but he is preeminently a symbol of sophisticated creativity, indicated by his role as protector of the Muses. The **lyre** (a small stringed instrument used to accompany poets' songs) represents his artistic function.

Embodying a typically Greek paradox, Apollo is the great Archer King whose arrows can inflict sickness, decimating whole armies or cities with plague, but he is also the bestower of the healing arts through his son **Asclepius** [as-CLEE-pee-uhs], the first physician. Apollo's characteristic use of the arrow as his chosen weapon well expresses the god's cool detachment. Unlike Ares or even Athene, he does not wield a sword at close quarters, but chooses instead to work his effects at a great distance (Figure 5-9).

The model of civilized self-discipline, he is nonetheless capable of savage cruelty, as when he flays alive Marsyas, who claimed that he could play the flute more beautifully than the god. A satyr—an embodiment of carnality—Marsyas is Apollo's opposite, unthinking instinct stripped away by the keen edge of intellect.

Artemis (Diana)

Artemis [AR-te-mis], Apollo's twin sister, was born first and immediately acted as midwife for the birth of her younger sibling. Although patron of midwifery and childbirth, a function she shares with Hera and Eileithyia, Artemis is a virgin who jealously guards her privacy. When the hunter Actaeon inadvertently sees her bathing, she changes him into a stag that is immediately torn to pieces by his dogs.

Like her twin brother, Artemis embodies contradictory functions: she is both protector of wild animals and patron of the hunt dedicated to their slaughter. She also resembles Apollo by carrying a quiver of arrows, with which she can inflict the pains of childbirth—or even cause death. A famous vase painting shows Apollo and Artemis shooting down the children of Niobe, who naively boasts that she is Leto's superior because she has so many more sons and daughters (Figure 5-10). Guardian of women's groups, such as the Amazons, Artemis is frequently identified with the moon, an astronomical symbol of the feminine psyche.

Greek colonists of Asia Minor associated Artemis with older fertility goddesses of the Near East, depicting her as either multibreasted or covered with fruitlike symbols of fecundity (see Figure 4-2). The largest Greco-Roman temple, one of the seven wonders of the ancient world, was erected to Artemis (Diana) at Ephesus.

(a)

(b)

FIGURE 5-9   Apollo. This sculpture (c. 460 B.C., from the west pediment of the Temple of Zeus at Olympia) shows Apollo extending his arm to compel peace between warring centaurs and Lapiths. (a) The sculptor's rendition of Apollo's serene and eternally youthful countenance expresses the Greek belief in the gods' freedom from distorting human emotion. Although the god appears here to intervene in a fierce battle, he remains unaffected by the surrounding turmoil. (b) The "archer-king," Apollo is a god who works "from afar." Rather than engage an enemy directly in hand-to-hand combat as Ares does on the Trojan battlefield, he employs a weapon that allows him to fight from a great distance, shooting invisible arrows that afflict mortals with plague—or that heal them. Aloof and detached, Apollo is nonetheless Zeus's chosen channel of prophecy, the giver of divine oracles that reveal the gods' will to humanity (see Chapter 7). (*Olympia Museum.*)

FIGURE 5-10   Artemis and Apollo. In this vase painting, the twins Artemis and Apollo aim their lethal arrows at the children of Niobe. A daughter of Tantalus who has fourteen children (the number varies in different traditions), Niobe boasts that she is superior to Leto, who had only two children. At Leto's request to avenge her honor, Apollo and Artemis then slay all but two of Niobe's sons and daughters. Consumed with grief, Niobe dissolves in tears, becoming a rock from which a spring flows. (*Louvre, Paris.*)

Hermes (Mercury)

Hermes [HER-meez], the son of Zeus and Maia, a daughter of the Titan Atlas, has even more attributes and spheres of influence than Apollo, but his primary function is to serve as Zeus's personal messenger, traveling swiftly over vast distances of land and sea to carry out his father's orders. As the Olympian who represents the opposite of Hestia's intractable fixity, Hermes personifies ceaseless movement, a quality that enables him to explore every level of myth's three-tier universe, effortlessly crossing the boundaries between heaven, earth, and the Underworld.

Boundaries, whether mundane property lines separating one peasant's farm from another, or the invisible barriers dividing earthly existence from the afterlife, provide the key to Hermes's nature. In prehistoric times, he was commonly represented by a

FIGURE 5-11 Herm from Siphnos. In contrast to Praxiteles's elegant statue of Hermes, this rustic Herm is a simple
square column topped with a bearded head and an erect phallus carved in front. Similar Hermae were placed at street corners, gateways, entrances of private houses, and along country
roads, where they elicited reverence from and offered divine
protection to travelers. This crude representation suggests
Hermes's historic origins as a deity who guarded property
boundaries, fields, flocks, and shepherds. (The erect phallus
averted the evil eye and promised good luck to passersby.)
(*National Museum, Athens.*)

heap of stones marking the boundary between fields where shepherds tended their
sheep. In later periods, he is depicted as a quadrangular pillar crowned with the head
of a bearded man and sporting an erect phallus, a condition thought potent enough
to avert the evil eye. In classical times, these **ithyphallic** figures, the Hermae, appeared everywhere throughout Athens as well as other parts of Greece, guarding gates
and doorways, the literal starting point of journeys (Figure 5-11). The most celebrated portrait of the god, however, is the sculptor Praxiteles's statue of Hermes holding the infant Dionysus (Figure 5-12), in which, like his brother Apollo, he appears
as a lithe, clean-shaven athlete.

Emphasizing his attribute of extreme mobility, Greek vase painters typically portray Hermes wearing winged sandals and a broad-brimmed traveler's hat. He is also
shown holding the caduceus, a rod entwined by two serpents and topped by a pair of
wings, emblematic of both Hermes's rapid movement and his role as Zeus's personal
messenger and herald. A symbol of the physician's healing art, the caduceus was a gift
of Apollo and is also carried by Apollo's son Asclepius.

In obeying Zeus's commands, Hermes sometimes travels uncomfortably long distances—as he does when crossing a vast expanse of featureless sea to visit the nymph

FIGURE 5-12 Hermes Holding the Infant Dionysus. Praxiteles's famous statue (c. 350–340 B.C.) of Zeus's divine messenger features a contrast between the god's sinuously muscular body and the almost tender expression on Hermes's face as he gazes at his half-brother, newly born from Zeus's thigh. Although Hermes commonly appears as a bearded older male figure wearing a traveler's broad-brimmed hat and winged sandals, later Greek artists commonly present the god as a youthful athlete. (*Olympia Museum.*)

Calypso on her remote island and to whom he complains about the tedious nature of his trip (Chapter 12). He is also compelled to visit even more uninviting destinations when, as *Hermes Psychopompos,* he routinely guides souls of the recently dead on their final journey, to cheerless Hades. Associated not only with unknown paths to the mysterious netherworld, but also with sleep, dreams, magic, and fortunetelling, Hermes was sometimes perceived as a doorway to mysticism and occult knowledge. By the fourth century A.D., when Greco-Roman society was crumbling, Hermes became identified with the Egyptian Thoth, a god of arcane wisdom, and was known as *Hermes Trismegistus* ("thrice greatest").

Hermes's adult versatility was foreshadowed by his precosity as an infant: immediately after his birth, Hermes leapt out of his cradle and traveled to Thessaly, where he stole a herd of cattle from Apollo, apparently to prove that he was clever enough to get away with it. When Zeus orders his thieving son to return the animals, Hermes successfully persuades Apollo to let him keep them in exchange for his latest invention, a lyre he had fashioned out of a tortoise shell.

After equipping Apollo with his most characteristic emblem, the ingenious Hermes also invented the syrinx, or panpipes, which Apollo similarly appropriated, giving his brother the caduceus in exchange. Besides their mutual interest in musical instruments, the two brothers shared a rare skill in clairvoyance. In one tradition, Apollo taught Hermes how to discern the future by using small pebbles.

Given the large number of diverse activities over which Hermes presides, it is not surprising that he serves as patron for innumerable professions. Connected with virtually every action or trade that involves movement, Hermes is the special guardian of travelers, merchants, inventors, vagabonds, highwaymen, thieves, and gamblers. One of the supreme tricksters of world myth, he is usually several steps ahead of unwary gods or mortals who cross his devious path.

Hephaestus (Vulcan)

The tradition that **Hephaestus** is entirely Hera's creation (although other tales make Zeus the father) indicates the close bond between mother and son. As she is the upholder of domesticity, Hephaestus is the house builder, the supremely gifted craftsman who singlehandedly erects the gods' palatial dwelling on Olympus. God of fire and the forge, he manufactures Zeus's thunderbolts, fashions golden armor for Achilles, and creates the first woman, Pandora, from clay (Chapter 6).

The marriage of the sooty, clumsy, lame god of the workshop with the elegantly beautiful Aphrodite is a classic example of marital mismatching that inevitably leads to infidelity. Homer states that when Hephaestus discovers his wife's adultery with Ares, he devises an invisible net to trap the guilty pair together in bed. Instead of offering sympathy to the wronged husband, however, Apollo and Hermes confess that they would be glad to exchange positions with Ares, provoking gales of "Olympian laughter."

The Romans believed that the god of fire and molten metal located his forge under the Mediterranean island of Vulcano, from which the modern term *volcano* derives.

Aphrodite (Venus)

A personification of human sexuality, **Aphrodite** has little trouble convincing Paris, a Trojan prince, to select her as the most beautiful of all goddesses. The conflicting traditions about her birth, taken together, suggest that she is both a focus of male sexual desire (Hesiod) and a divine being who belongs among the Olympians (Homer). In Homer's version, she is the child of Zeus and Dione, a daughter of either Uranus and Gaea or the Titans Oceanus and Tethys.

The only goddess whom Greek artists (after the fourth century B.C.) depict fully nude, Aphrodite is the perfection of femininity (see Figure 4-10). In Euripides's tragedy *Hippolytus,* Aphrodite destroys the title character, a son of Theseus, for denying her divinity and presuming to live free of love's power, an affront to the intrinsic nature of the universe.

Eros (Cupid)

Either one of the oldest gods (Hesiod) or Aphrodite's son by Ares (Homer), **Eros** is a masculine aspect of the love goddess who projects arrows of fierce desire into the

FIGURE 5-13   Aphrodite and Ares. Although married to Hephaestus, god
of the forge, Aphrodite takes Ares as her favored lover. In this wall painting
from Pompeii, the artist celebrates the union of the gods of love and war, illustrating the affinity between sexual desire and martial aggressiveness. Eros,
the winged boy appearing on the upper left, is in some myths the son of Ares
and Aphrodite, explaining the mixture of calculating detachment and passionate assertiveness in his character. He is shown placing an arrow in his bow,
about to hurl the invisible dart of erotic obsession into the breast of some god
or mortal. (*National Museum, Naples.*)

hearts of both gods and mortals (Figure 5-13). Although not one of the official twelve
Olympians, he flits about Olympus as familiarly as he does on earth. The Greeks
regarded Eros as an adolescent youth, but the Romans pictured him as a chubby
infant (Cupid) and identified his mother as Venus, an Italian goddess of gardens and
flowers.

Ares (Mars)

Ares [AR-eez], the son of Zeus and Hera, is god of war in its most savage guise. A
personification of combativeness and bloodthirsty frenzy, he represents the undisciplined aspects of masculine aggression, as well as a telling symbol of his parents' strife-

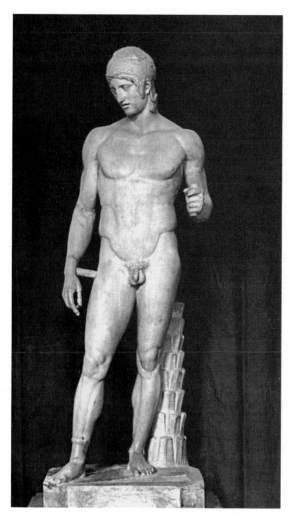

FIGURE 5-14 Ares. This Roman copy of a Greek original (c. 420–400 B.C.) depicts Ares in a moment of uncharacteristic repose; the god embodying humanity's irrational impulse to commit violence stands lost in contemplation. Although the Greeks were almost continuously at war, they rarely worshiped Ares, whom Zeus labeled "the most hated of the gods" for his hot temper and eagerness to physically dominate or kill. Later identified with an Italian god of agriculture and war, Ares became the Roman Mars. (*Louvre, Paris.*)

torn marriage (Figure 5-14). Whereas Athene achieves military victory through intelligence and planning, Ares mindlessly revels in violence and cruelty, causing Zeus to label him "the most hated of all the gods." Although the Greeks were almost continually at war, usually with fellow Greeks, they showed Ares scant respect. By contrast, the Romans, who associated Ares with Mars—their local god of agriculture and military conquest—regarded him as the divine father of Romulus, their city's founder, and patron of their far-flung empire.

Dionysus (Bacchus, Bromius, Liber)

The sole major deity in the Greek pantheon who is born human and must die to achieve immortality is **Dionysus,** god of wine, intoxication, and creative ecstasy (see Chapter 8 for his principal myths). Because his worship gave birth to an entirely new

FIGURE 5-15 Head of Pan. A god of
wild nature, Pan combines the qualities
of humans and beasts. He has the cloven
hooves, horns, and hairy shanks of a goat,
along with the head and torso of a human
being, a visible image of the tension existing
between the animal and the divine in the
human psyche. In some myths, he is the son
of Hermes, a god of goatherds, shepherds,
gamblers, thieves, liars, traders, and other
persons on the margins of civilized society.
Although sometimes gentle, he can exhibit
the cruel savagery of external nature on the
rampage, inspiring sudden terror in persons
traveling through woods or other isolated
places. An embodiment of uninhibited male
sexuality, Pan often shows up in the Dionysian retinue (see Chapter 8). (*J. Paul Getty
Museum.*)

art form—the drama—that became the primary vehicle of myth during the fifth
century B.C., this important aspect of the Dionysian cult is treated in a separate chapter. (See Chapter 13 for Dionysus's patronage of tragedy and comedy.)

When the latecomer Dionysus was added to the Olympian pantheon, the mytho-
logically undeveloped Hestia was demoted to make room for him, thus keeping the
traditional number of Olympians at twelve. Whereas the Olympians hold sway over
the universe at large, a host of minor deities preside over geographically limited areas,
specific activities, or particular landforms: lovely naiads (female nature spirits) inhabit
springs, rivers, and lakes; dryads are the indwelling spirits of trees; and oreads live in
mountainous terrain. **Pan,** who has a human torso and arms but the legs, ears, and
horns of a goat, is a personification of all natural wild things (Figure 5-15). His name,
derived from the root *pa(s),* means "guardian of flocks," designating his function as
the god responsible for the fertility of shepherds and flocks. Like nature itself, Pan
creates both beauty and terror: with the seven-reed syrinx (panpipe), he produces
enchanting music; he also is the source of unreasoning fear (panic) that can unexpectedly freeze the human heart. With his horns, hairy shanks, cloven hooves, and
lustful energy, Pan becomes in postclassical times a model for the physical shape of
the Christian devil.

A brilliant mosaic of nobility, splendor, and amoral passion, the Greek gods mirror the values and contrarieties of the patriarchal society that created them. Although
a few Greek thinkers, such as Plato, dismissed some myths about the Olympians as
ethically irresponsible (Chapter 2), most Greek and Roman writers delighted in
elaborating upon the psychological affinity that linked human beings to their gods.
Picturing a class of beings who achieve virtually every human wish, myth simultaneously emphasizes the mysterious but painfully real gulf of mortality that forever separates the human world from the divine.

Questions for Discussion and Review

1. In what specific ways does Zeus's family resemble figures or types in a human family? What is Zeus's relationship to his brothers, sisters, and children?

2. What are the distinctive qualities of the older Olympian generation? Do you see any differences in the particular qualities or functions of the younger Olympians? Why are Apollo and Artemis twins? Why does Hera favor Hephaestus and Zeus favor Athene?

3. How do the gods personally represent the distinctive characteristics of Greek myth, including its emphases on anthropomorphism, individualism, competitiveness, and anthropocentric views of the universe? Do you think the nature myth theories or psychological theories better explain the attributes and functions of Olympus's divine inhabitants?

Recommended Reading

Athanassakis, Apostolos N., ed. and trans. *The Homeric Hymns.* Baltimore: Johns Hopkins UP, 1976. Includes interpretive notes about the major deities.

Burkert, Walter. *Greek Religion.* Trans. John Raffan. Cambridge, MA: Harvard UP, 1985. A standard reference.

Grimal, Pierre. *The Dictionary of Classical Mythology.* Trans. A. R. Maxwell-Hyslop. Oxford: Basil Blackwell, 1986. Provides essential information about the principal gods of Greece and Rome.

Hornblower, Simon and Anthony Spawforth, eds. *The Oxford Classical Dictionary.* 3rd ed. New York: Oxford UP, 1996. Contains excellent brief essays on each of the Greco-Roman gods.

Kerenyi, Carl. *The Gods of the Greeks.* London: Thames and Hudson, 1951. A valuable scholarly work.

The World in Decline: Alienation of the Human and Divine

KEY THEMES

The Greek cosmos is both hierarchal and patriarchal, a system ruled by an aristocratic class of divine beings who, like human political leaders, relegate their mortal inferiors to the powerlessness of penury and hardship. In Hesiod's cosmology, male aspirations to be like the gods in the enjoyment of perfect autonomy, freedom from labor, and extreme longevity are compromised by the presence and demands of women, who subvert masculine values of order, independence, and dominion. In the Works and Days, *a primal Golden Age ends with the creation of Pandora, the gods' means of punishing men for accepting the Promethean gift of fire. Alienated from the gods, humanity's condition decays rapidly, each stage of devolution represented by a metal of inferior value to the one preceding it. Ages of gold, silver, bronze (and an interpolated Age of Heroes) culminate in the Age of Iron (the age during which Hesiod lived), characterized by injustice and strife.*

The dual themes of dynamic change and unending conflict that pervade Hesiod's creation account also dominate his view of human history. In his second major poem, the *Works and Days,* which describes humanity's steady decline from an original Golden Age, Hesiod praises Zeus for imposing lawful order on a previously chaotic universe, while lamenting the undeniable fact that people are now much worse off than they were under Cronus's rule. Deterioration in human society, Hesiod says, is a consequence of Zeus's personal quarrel with

FIGURE 6-1 Zeus and His Eagle. Perceived as both majestic and cruel, the eagle was both "king of the air" and a merciless predator that swept down on helpless prey, tearing it to pieces with razor-sharp talons. In the Prometheus myth, the eagle is Zeus's "winged hound" that symbolizes both the god's mastery of the atmosphere and his cruelty to the Titan who attempted to deceive him, as illustrated on this archaic cup. (*Louvre, Paris.*)

Prometheus [proh-MEE-thee-uhs], the supremely cunning Titan who maneuvered Zeus into accepting the inferior part of animal sacrifices (see Chapter 2).

Humanity's Alienation from the Gods: Prometheus, Fire, and Pandora

Already smarting from Prometheus's deception, Zeus reacts with violent anger when the Titan steals fire from heaven to bestow upon humankind, giving mortals a potential dominion over nature. Heaven's new king vindictively chains Prometheus to a mountain crag, where each dawn an eagle, Zeus's "winged hound," arrives to rip open his body and feast on his liver. Because he is immortal, Prometheus's entrails grow back each night, only to be devoured again the next day (Figure 6-1). The rebellious Titan's forbidden gift to humanity is a celestial flame that ignites the spark of civilization and further narrows the gap between gods and men. Indeed, Hesiod

FIGURE 6-2 Pandora as a Mannequin. In this vase painting, the newly fashioned Pandora receives attractive gifts from the gods (including Athene, left), who have designed her to sabotage humanity, weakening the race for having received Prometheus's gift of fire. The presence of Ares with his spear and shield (right) hints that the appearance of woman on earth will elicit many a battle between the sexes. (*British Museum, London.*)

emphasizes the close kinship between "men and gods," affirming that they share a "common descent." In the beginning, he states, men "lived like gods," mingling freely with the Olympians at their earthly banquets. To counteract the unlimited benefits of Promethean fire, Zeus determines to present mankind with another novelty, "a gift of evil" that will make their lives miserable—the first female mortal, **Pandora** (Figure 6-2). After Pandora's appearance, which marks an irreversible turning point in human destiny, the high gods distance themselves from mortals, permanently withdrawing to Olympus.

In giving etiological myth a religious interpretation that explains humanity's alienation from divinity, Hesiod emphasizes an interconnection between food, sacrifice, fire, cooking, and woman. Man's last banquet with the gods signals the end of an era because the introduction of fire to cook raw meat breaks human ties to nature. The guilt incurred in killing a fellow creature, the sacrificial ox, is compounded by (unnaturally) cooking and eating it. By contrast, Zeus's eagle, which belongs to nature and is also a symbol of the god, eats raw flesh, Prometheus's liver. The myth's division of animal sacrifice into two disparate elements adds a further ambiguity: whereas the gods inhale only the intangible scent of burnt meat, men, as physical beings, must consume its corruptible flesh to survive. Pandora, who arrives on the scene too late to dine with gods but who, presumably, will preside over the civilized art of cooking, introduces yet another force dividing men from gods, the human race's unresolved tension between male and female.

Humanity's Decline: Pandora and Eve

Despite significant differences, the two most influential forces in shaping the modern Western consciousness—the Greek and Judeo-Christian traditions—agree in regarding women as the catalyst of humanity's historical decline. In both the Greek and biblical worldviews, the cosmos is run by and for a male principle of divinity that is regarded as simultaneously the source and justification of a patriarchal society on earth. In the biblical and Hesiodic cosmologies alike, a previously all-male world order crumbles into chaos almost immediately after the first female is created.

Hesiod, whose personal distrust of women everywhere colors his account, wrote two significantly different versions of Pandora's creation. In the *Theogony,* where Pandora is not named, Hesiod implies that only two gods, Hephaestus and Athene, were responsible for manufacturing this "tempting snare." In the *Works and Days,* a whole array of divine beings contribute specific qualities to fashion a complex creature of irresistible beauty who also functions, paradoxically, as Zeus's "evil" curse on mankind. After Hephaestus molds Pandora of "earth and water," giving her the face of a goddess, and Athene imbues her with domestic skills, a procession of divinities, including Aphrodite, the Graces, the Seasons, and eloquent Persuasion, equip her with attributes ranging from sexual allure to luxurious tastes, "a scourge for toiling men." Finally, Hermes endows Pandora with "the mind of a bitch and a thievish nature." A trickster figure like Prometheus, Hermes is Zeus's instrument in giving men the feminine counterpart of the inferior animal sacrifice that Prometheus had led Zeus to accept at Mekone. Like the inedible bones and hide covered with an attractive pelt that Zeus selected as his part of the divine-human arrangement, Pandora is alluring on the outside but is worthless within, an economic parasite who will subvert the advantages of Promethean fire. She is Zeus's trump card in outwitting even his trickiest opponents.

In the *Works and Days,* Hesiod's picture of many deities lavishing diverse gifts on Pandora provides the context for his interpretation of her name, which he says means "All-Gifted." Many scholars believe, however, that Hesiod either inherited or created a revised version of an older myth in which Pandora was originally an earth goddess called "Giver of All." Instead of portraying her as an active embodiment of the Great Goddess's generosity (Chapter 4), Hesiod makes her the passive recipient of Olympian patriarchal largesse. Other versions of the Pandora myth indicate that the jar which she brings with her contained not evils but blessings. In this tradition, Zeus gives her a jarful of good things as a wedding present for her marriage to **Epimetheus** [ep-ih-MEE-thee-uhs], who is a brother of Prometheus and whose name means "Afterthought" (Figure 6-3). When she inadvertently opens the jar, all the blessings fly out and return to heaven, which accounts for the present imbalance of negative forces on earth. All these myths agree that Pandora, according to the divine purpose, catches Hope before it can escape, retaining the quality necessary to save the race from despair. Hesiod's narrative implies that, except for hope, the contents of Pandora's jar were completely undesirable—disease, grief, hardship, and suffering, all the miseries that now afflict humankind. Even hope, as some critics suggest, may be an evil: it provides the illusion that life will improve, inducing people to bear the more transitory evils.

Pandora's arrival on earth thus ends the original Golden Age, shatters the link between humanity and divinity, and plunges history into an irreversible downward

FIGURE 6-3   Epimetheus
Accepts Pandora. In this
vase painting, Hermes, in a
characteristic winged helmet, persuades the Titan
Epimetheus (Afterthought;
far left) to accept Pandora
(right). The first woman
rises from the earth, suggesting her origin as
divinely shaped clay. He-
phaestus, god of metalcraft
and other creative skills, extends a hand toward the
new creation, while a figure
of Eros flies overhead. (*Ash-
molean Museum, Oxford.*)

spiral. As the feminine agent responsible for all of our subsequent misfortunes,
Pandora serves the same mythic function as Eve in the Genesis story of Eden. According to Genesis 3, a serpent (representing the primordial Great Goddess's wisdom;
Chapter 4), persuades Eve to eat forbidden fruit, an image of earth's fecundity. The
fruit miraculously confers "knowledge of good and evil," a phrase denoting awareness
of the entire spectrum of existence, a breadth of vision hitherto the exclusive property
of divine beings. The prohibited fruit is the biblical counterpart of Promethean fire,
the enlightenment that makes civilization possible and simultaneously severs humanity's primal bond with nature (Eden).

After Eve convinces her husband to sample the fruit, the couple suddenly realize
that they are naked, that unlike animals they are unprotected and open to harm—
the first painful cut from knowledge's two-edged sword. In rapid fire, Eve learns of
her vulnerability to the pains of childbirth and social domination by her male partner,
Adam, whose name means "humankind." Forced into a recognition of their inevitable deaths, the pair are expelled from paradise, because Yahweh, the biblical Creator, does not want them to rival him further. Already possessed of divine knowledge,
they might also eat of the Tree of Life and live forever, giving humanity the two
qualities that distinguish mortals from gods—cosmic perspective and immortality.
Greek myth also associates fruit from the Tree of Life with a guardian serpent and
protective goddesses (see Figure 4-6).

The Bible and Greek myth similarly blame female curiosity (intelligence) for breaking the divine-human connection that prevailed when man existed alone with his patriarchal deity. Hesiod, like the author of Genesis, insists that the price humanity pays for knowledge—a dangerous and divine commodity associated with the serpentine feminine principle—is loss of innocence, loss of peace, and loss of paradise, a childlike environment in which no long-term threats to happiness are perceived. Like the post-Edenic world of Adam and Eve, what remains in Hesiod's experience is labor, pain, and awareness of imminent death. Despite his suspicion of women, however, even Hesiod admits that the gods' female creation is, like the male of the species, "a mixture of good and bad"—in fact, a newly minted image of the contradictory system over which Zeus presides.

When Hesiod states that Hermes endows Pandora with "lies, coaxing words, and a thievish nature," he implicitly identifies her with Zeus's first wife, Metis, the embodiment of cunning. Whereas Zeus could claim Metis's mental acuity as his own by swallowing her, the human male cannot do the same with his mate, whose ability to manipulate her husband remains an external threat to his sense of masculine autonomy. In a Jungian interpretation, the Hesiodic male's unwillingness or inability to value or nurture the potentially empowering feminine principle within (the anima) condemns him to an unremitting battle of the sexes.

Humanity's Alienation from Nature as the Price of Civilization

In the myths of Pandora and Eve, it is the action of a woman that severs humanity's primal tie to nature. Some other traditions, however, take a more positive view of woman's mythic role in helping the human psyche to distinguish itself from nature's mindlessness. In the Mesopotamian story of Gilgamesh and Enkidu, the civilizing of a savage male is used to show that human culture is necessarily—and tragically—based on alienation from natural instinct. As the Greek gods fashion Pandora to punish man's godlike control of fire, so the Mesopotamian gods create Enkidu, a wild, hairy, human animal, to provide a distraction and rival to Gilgamesh, a powerful king whose unfocused energies disrupt the state over which he rules.

Like Adam before he tasted the fruit of knowledge, Enkidu identifies totally with nature, running naked with wild beasts and freeing them from traps laid by city dwellers. Only after a "holy one"—a priestess of the love goddess Ishtar—awakens his sexuality and teaches him the arts of civilization does Enkidu lose his affinity with the natural world. When animals, his former companions, flee from him because, thanks to the woman, he now carries the scent of humanity, Enkidu is forced to become a part of city life. He joins Gilgamesh in a heroic campaign to fight the destructive aspects of nature, such as the fire monster Humbaba and the "bull of heaven," a personification of drought and earthquake.

When Gilgamesh spurns Ishtar's offer of love in favor of bonding with Enkidu, whom he loves as a second self, the outraged goddess afflicts Enkidu with a terminal sickness. On his deathbed, Enkidu bitterly curses the priestess, a temple prostitute, for having ensnared him in the net of civilization. Hearing Enkidu's dying words, the sun god Shamash wisely reminds him that his gains from acculturation—adventure, fame, and the love of Gilgamesh—far outweigh the loss of his original status as unencumbered natural man. Enkidu then pronounces a grateful blessing on the woman who initiated him into the larger possibilities of civilized awareness.

Hesiod's failure to perceive or articulate a comparable tribute to the feminine principle, though not true of all Greek writers, characterizes much of his culture. Greek mythology, like the patriarchal society it reflects, is essentially a male mythology. A few Greek heroes, such as Perseus and Odysseus, learn to value and assimilate feminine wisdom (chapters 10 and 12), but female intelligence and assertiveness, the qualities of a Clytemnestra or Medea, are typically seen as threats to male security (chapters 15 and 17).

The Two Natures of Strife

In a cosmos organized on the principles of male competition and conflict, one in which the gods constantly battle or conspire against each other, it is not surprising that Hesiod regarded human wars and violence as inescapable. He saw the entire cosmos permeated with manifestations of Strife (Eris), a personification of discord that takes two distinctive forms. Although both versions are daughters of Night, they are not equally bad: the first Strife triggers mindless aggression, driving men to slaughter each other. The second figure of Strife is milder, inspiring healthy competition and a striving after excellence that inspires people to produce their finest work, thus benefiting the entire community.

The Five Ages of Man

Age of Gold

The *Works and Days* divides human history into five distinctive periods, all but one of which (the Age of Heroes) is symbolized by a metal more valuable than that which chronologically follows it. The initial Age of Gold, synonymous with the paradise that men inhabited before woman was created, flourished when Cronus ruled the world. Hesiod includes no account of man's creation, perhaps because he regarded the primal race as autochthonous (spontaneously born from the earth). According to a variant myth Apollodorus records, Prometheus was humanity's creator, fashioning man from earth and water. Even if Hesiod knew this tradition, however, his disdain for Prometheus as a mere trickster who was justly punished for breaking Zeus's law would explain his omitting the story. (Prometheus's role as creator, however, would provide motivation for Hesiod's account of his stealing fire to give to men. In another tradition, Prometheus also warns humanity of Zeus's plan to annihilate the race in a global flood; see below).

During this Age of Gold, aboriginal men live in peace and enjoy the same freedom from toil or anxiety the gods possess. Like pure gold that never decays or rusts, humans live unblemished by old age or hardship until death takes them in the gentle guise of sleep. Even after their bodies perish, their indomitable spirits live on to walk the earth, acting as invisible protectors and helpers of later generations.

Age of Silver

Whereas Golden Age inhabitants are peaceful, all subsequent generations are perpetrators or victims of Strife's worst manifestation, bloody war. Represented by a less pure or costly metal, the Age of Silver demonstrates Hesiod's belief that each new historical epoch is inferior to the one before it and emphasizes a marked deterioration in the human condition. This second age is characterized by extreme opposites: people take a full hundred years to mature, but after leaving their "prudent mothers" (one of Hesiod's rare allusions to women's beneficent roles), they live only a short time, cut off by "reckless violence." Although enjoying a century of preparation for life, as adults they behave like fools: they are the first race the Olympians directly create, but they refuse to acknowledge or worship their creators, a defect that prompts Zeus to order their extinction. This failed experiment, which Hesiod oddly labels "blessed," does not haunt earth's surface, as do specters of the Age of Gold, but is confined beneath the earth.

Age of Bronze

Men of the third period are created by Zeus alone, reputedly from ash trees. Commonly used to make warriors' spears, ash wood is an appropriate source for Hesiod's Bronze Age soldiers "who eat no bread"—they are incapable of peaceful activities like agriculture—and mindlessly pursue violent conflict. Mirroring only one aspect of Zeus—his aggressive strength—the warriors achieve mutual extermination and posthumously sink even lower than their predecessors, into the dank pit of Hades.

Age of Heroes

The next generation, a short-lived Age of Heroes, is an exception to Hesiod's narration of inexorable decline. Described as "better and more just" than the races that precede or succeed them, these are the great heroes who fight at Troy or Thebes. Most of these soldiers, whose deeds are celebrated in the Homeric epics, manage to kill each other off in their endless wars, but some of the noblest Zeus carries away to a remote paradise where they enjoy conditions that prevailed during the vanished Golden Age. This Edenic reward, reserved exclusively for Zeus's few favorites, corresponds to Homer's Elysium (or Isles of the Blest), to which the Olympian transports his son-in-law Menelaus (see Chapter 9).

Scholars believe that Hesiod's passage about Greek heroes—to which he assigns no characteristic metal and which interrupts the otherwise consistent historical decline—was inserted into an older tradition of four regressive ages that the Greeks borrowed from ancient Near Eastern sources. The biblical Book of Daniel offers a parallel tradition in which a huge statue, composed of four different metals, symbolizes a succession of four historical empires. The idol has a head of gold, chest and arms of silver, belly and thighs of bronze, legs of iron, and feet of mixed iron and clay. Daniel's vision of historical decline, echoing Hesiod's older image of historical epochs as increasingly degenerative, has helped to keep the myth of humanity's post-Edenic devolution alive in some Judeo-Christian circles.

Age of Iron

The fifth and final epoch, in which the poet and his audience lived, is the brutal Age of Iron. The least precious and most harsh metal, it effectively symbolizes the hardness of heart that distinguishes the petty kings who economically exploit the class of impoverished small farmers and shepherds to which Hesiod belonged. The situation will only worsen, for Zeus already plans to wipe out the present generation as he had its forebears. Increasing signs of degeneracy will mark the End's approach: life will be so unbearable that even newborn infants will have gray hair. Natural affection among family members will disappear, and the normal social order will be reversed: good men will be punished and evil rewarded. Qualities, such as shame, that now hold wickedness in check, will flee in horror to Olympus, abandoning humanity to misery and grief.

Hesiod's view of history arbitrarily divided into five epochs of intensifying decline is essentially apocalyptic: he assumes not merely one end of the world—the doom rapidly overtaking the present system—but also four earlier divinely ordained mass extinctions. The gods thoroughly eradicate each successive race, allowing no survivors of one era to found the next and preventing any normal historical continuity. Human history, which flows inevitably toward the abyss, is thus a painful lesson teaching mortals that "there is no way to escape the designs of Zeus" (Figure 6-4).

Humanity's Destruction: Deucalion's Flood

One of the most common myths of a god-imposed destruction of humanity is the story of a global deluge, which first appears in Mesopotamian literature, most notably the *Atrahasis Epic* and the *Epic of Gilgamesh.* Although Hesiod does not mention it, the flood myth is an important part of the Greek tradition, which places it early in human prehistory. Like the flood account in the biblical Book of Genesis, the Greek version has striking parallels with its Mesopotamian antecedents. In the Gilgamesh story, Enlil, god of storm and wind, determines to annihilate the human race by drowning all earth's inhabitants. Ea, a god of wisdom who is generally friendly to humankind, subverts Enlil's plan by warning Utnapishtim, the Babylonian Noah, of the coming disaster. Following Ea's instructions to build an ark and stock it with all kinds of animals, Utnapishtim and his wife survive the world's return to a watery chaos. When the flood is over, Utnapishtim sends out birds to find dry land, leaves the ark grounded on a high mountain, and offers sacrifices to the gods. In the Greco-Roman flood story, which is most fully preserved in Ovid's *Metamorphoses,* Zeus brings on the deluge and Prometheus takes Ea's role, alerting his son Deucalion and Deucalion's wife, Pyrrha, to the danger and directing them to construct a boat, thus ensuring humanity's continued existence. As in his arrangement of sacrificial offerings and the gift of fire, Prometheus is successful in circumventing Zeus's intentions and benefiting humanity. According to Ovid and Apollodorus, after the flood waters recede, an oracle from Themis, the wise mother of Prometheus, commands the pair to repopulate the world by casting the bones of their mother. Recognizing the earth, Gaea, as their maternal parent, Deucalion and Pyrrha obey the oracle by tossing

FIGURE 6-4   Zeus Holding (Vanished) Thunderbolt. Although the guarantor of universal justice, Zeus paradoxically rules over an imperfect human world typified by war and aggression. Hesiod views human history as an ever-downward spiral from an original Golden Age, which ended with two crucial events: (1) the Promethean domestication of fire, source of all subsequent culture, and (2) Zeus's introduction of woman into human society, the source of all man's domestic misery. (*Vatican Museums, Rome.*)

stones over their shoulders. Rocks that Deucalion throws become men; those Pyrrha throws become women—thus explaining the source of humanity's presently flinty nature.

As Genesis makes the three sons of Noah the progenitors of all branches of the human race known to the early Bible writers, so Greek myth presents Deucalion and Pyrrha as the parents of Hellen, the eponymous ancestor (person from whom a group reputedly takes its name) of the Greeks. In Hellen's honor, the historical Greeks called themselves **Hellenes** [HEL-lee-neez] and their country **Hellas** [HEL-luhs].

Although Hesiod's poems provided the Greeks with a mythic past that serves the purpose of history—typically using ancient tales to justify retroactively the practices of Hellenic society—Hesiod leaves many important questions unanswered. The tension between Hesiod's admiration for Zeus and his awareness that the god is largely responsible for humanity's pain goes unresolved. It is left to a much more sophisticated poet, the Athenian playwright Aeschylus, to explore the issue of Zeus's ethical character and its implications for humankind (Chapter 14).

WORKS AND DAYS[1]

Hesiod

Pierian Muses, your songs bring fame and glory.
Come! Let us hear from you the praises of your father,
great Zeus, through whose will men
are exalted by the speech of others or remain unknown.
With ease he grants power, with ease he crushes the mighty
and with ease he lowers the noble and raises the lowly.
Yes, Zeus who thunders from his lofty dwelling
with ease straightens the crooked and shrivels the insolent.
Hark and see, O Zeus! Let your decrees be straight and fair!
And I will speak to Perses the naked truth: 10
There was never one kind of Strife. Indeed on this earth
two kinds exist. The one is praised by her friends,
the other found blameworthy. These two are not of one mind.
The one—so harsh—fosters evil war and the fray of battle.
No man loves this oppressive Strife, but compulsion
and divine will grant her a share of honor.
The other one is black Night's elder daughter;
and the son of Kronos, who dwells on ethereal heights,
planted her in the roots of the earth and among men.
She is much better, and she stirs even the shiftless on to work.   20
A man will long for work when he sees a man of wealth
who rushes with zeal to plow and plant
and husband his homestead. One neighbor envies another
who hastens to his riches. This Strife is good for mortals.
Then potters eye one another's success and craftsmen, too;
the beggar's envy is a beggar, the singer's a singer.
Perses, treasure this thought deep down in your heart,
do not let malicious Strife curb your zeal for work
so you can see and hear the brawls of the market place.
Not much time for brawls and gatherings can be spared   30
by the man in whose house the season's plentiful harvest,
Demeter's grain, fruit of the earth, has not been stored.
Have plenty of this and then incite brawls and strife
over another man's possessions. Lose no time! Seize
your only chance to let straight justice
—Zeus's fairest—settle this quarrel.
Our inheritance was divided; but there is so much
you grabbed and carried away as a fat bribe
for gift-devouring kings, fools who want to be judges

1. Translation by Apostolos N. Athanassakis.

in this trial; they know neither how the half is greater   40
than the whole, nor how asphodel and mallow nurture.
The gods keep livelihood hidden from men.
Otherwise a day's labor could bring a man enough
to last a whole year with no more work.
Then you could hang your oar over the smoke of your fireplace
without a thought for the work of oxen and hardy mules.
But Zeus was angered in his heart and hid the means to life
because Prometheus with his crooked schemes had cheated him.
This is why Zeus devised sorrows and troubles for men.
He hid fire. But Prometheus, noble son of Iapetos,   50
stole it back for man from Zeus, whose counsels are many.
In the hollow of a fennel stalk he slipped it away,
unnoticed by Zeus, who delights in thunder.
So the cloud-gatherer in anger said to him:
"Son of Iapetos, there is none craftier than you,
and you rejoice at tricking my wits and stealing the fire
which will be a curse to you and to the generations that follow.
The price for the stolen fire will be a gift of evil
to charm the hearts of all men as they hug their own doom."
This said, the father of gods and men roared with laughter.   60
Then he ordered widely acclaimed Hephaistos to mix earth with water
with all haste and place in them human voice
and strength. His orders were to make a face
such as goddesses have and the shape of a lovely maiden;
Athena was to teach her skills and intricate weaving,
and golden Aphrodite should pour grace round the maiden's head,
and stinging desire and limb-gnawing passion.
Then he ordered Hermes the path-breaker and slayer of Argos
to put in her the mind of a bitch and a thievish nature.
So he spoke, and they obeyed lord Zeus, son of Kronos.   70
Without delay the renowned lame god fashioned from earth,
through Zeus's will, the likeness of a shy maiden,
and Athena, the gray-eyed goddess, clothed her and decked her out.
Then the divine graces and queenly Persuasion
gave her golden necklaces to wear, and the lovely-haired Seasons
stood round her and crowned her with spring flowers.
Pallas Athena adorned her body with every kind of jewel,
and the Slayer of Argos—Hermes the guide—through the will
of Zeus whose thunder roars placed in her breast
lies, coaxing words, and a thievish nature.   80
The gods' herald then gave her voice and called this woman
Pandora because all of the gods who dwell on Olympos
gave her a gift—a scourge for toiling men.
Now when the Father finished this grand and wily scheme
he sent the glorious Slayer of Argos and swift messenger
to bring the gift of the gods to Epimetheus,
who did not heed Prometheus's warning never to accept

a gift from Olympian Zeus, but send it back,
for fear that some evil might befall mortals.
First he accepted it and then saw the evil in it. 90
Earlier, human tribes lived on this earth
without suffering and toilsome hardship
and without painful illnesses that bring death to men—
a wretched life ages men before their time—
but the woman with her hands removed the great lid of the jar
and scattered its contents, bringing grief and cares to men.
Only Hope stayed under the rim of the jar
and did not fly away from her secure stronghold,
for in compliance with the wishes of cloud-gathering Zeus
Pandora put the lid on the jar before she could come out. 100
The rest wander among men as numberless sorrows,
since earth and sea teem with miseries.
Some diseases come upon men during the day, and some
roam about and bring pains to men in the silence of night
because Zeus the counselor made them mute.
So there is no way to escape the designs of Zeus.
I will give you the pith of another story—if you wish—
with consummate skill. Treasure this thought in your heart:
Men and gods have a common descent.
At first the immortals who dwell on Olympos 110
created a golden race of mortal men.
That was when Kronos was king of the sky,
and they lived like gods, carefree in their hearts,
shielded from pain and misery. Helpless old age
did not exist, and with limbs of unsagging vigor
they enjoyed the delights of feasts, out of evil's reach.
A sleeplike death subdued them, and every good thing was theirs;
the barley-giving earth asked for no toil to bring forth
a rich and plentiful harvest. They knew no constraint
and lived in peace and abundance as lords of their lands, 120
rich in flocks and dear to the blessed gods.
But the earth covered this race,
and they became holy spirits that haunt it,
benign protectors of mortals that drive harm away
and keep a watchful eye over lawsuits and wicked deeds,
swathed in misty veils as they wander over the earth.
They are givers of wealth by kingly prerogative.
The gods of Olympos made a second race
—a much worse one—this time of silver,
unlike the golden one in thought or looks. 130
For a hundred years they were nurtured by their prudent mothers
as playful children—each a big baby in his house—
but when they grew up and reached adolescence
they lived only for a short while, plagued by the pains
of foolishness. They could not refrain from reckless violence

against one another and did not want to worship the gods
and on holy altars perform sacrifices for them,
as custom differing from place to place dictates.
In time Zeus, son of Kronos, was angered and buried them
because they denied the blessed Olympians their due honors.   140
The earth covered this race, too;
they dwell under the ground and are called blessed mortals—
they are second but, still, greatly honored.
Zeus the father made a third race of mortals,
this time of bronze, not at all like the silver one.
Fashioned from ash trees, they were dreadful and mighty
and bent on the harsh deeds of war and violence;
they ate no bread and their hearts were strong as steel.
No one could come near them, for their strength was great
and mighty arms grew from the shoulders of their sturdy bodies.   150
Bronze were their weapons, bronze their homes
and bronze was what they worked—there was no black iron then.
With their hands they worked one another's destruction
and they reached the dank home of cold Hades
nameless. Black death claimed them for all their fierceness,
and they left the bright sunlight behind them.
But when the earth covered this race, too,
Zeus, son of Kronos, made upon the nourishing land
yet another race—the fourth one—better and more just.
They were the divine race of heroes, who are called   160
demigods; they preceded us on this boundless earth.
Evil war and dreadful battle wiped them all out,
some fighting over the flocks of Oidipous
at seven-gated Thebes, in the land of Kadmos,
others over the great gulf of the sea in ships
that had sailed to Troy for the sake of lovely-haired Helen;
there death threw his dark mantle over them.
Yet others of them father Zeus, son of Kronos, settled at earth's ends,
apart from men, and gave them shelter and food.
They lived there with hearts unburdened by cares   170
in the islands of the blessed, near stormy Okeanos,
these blissful heroes for whom three times a year
the barley-giving land brings forth full grain sweet as honey.
I wish I were not counted among the fifth race of men,
but rather had died before, or been born after it.
This is the race of iron. Neither day nor night
will give them rest as they waste away with toil
and pain. Growing cares will be given them by the gods,
and their lot will be a blend of good and bad.
Zeus will destroy this race of mortals   180
when children are born gray at the temples.
Children will not resemble their fathers,
and there will be no affection between guest and host

and no love between friends or brothers as in the past.
Sons and daughters will be quick to offend their aging parents
and rebuke them and speak to them with rudeness
and cruelty, not knowing about divine retribution;
they will not even repay their parents for their keep—
these law-breakers—and they will sack one another's cities.
The man who keeps his oath, or is just and good,   190
will not be favored, but the evil-doers and scoundrels
will be honored, for might will make right and shame will vanish.
Base men will harm their betters with words
that are crooked and then swear they are fair.
And all toiling humanity will be blighted by envy,
grim and strident envy that takes its joy in the ruin of others.
Then Shame and Retribution will cover their fair bodies
with white cloaks and, leaving men behind,
will go to Olympos from the broad-pathed earth
to be among the race of the immortals, while grief and pain   200
will linger among men, whom harm will find defenseless.

. . . .

Questions for Discussion and Review

1. Describe Prometheus's role in humanity's primal history. What does his gift of fire to mankind signify? Why does Zeus retaliate with the creation of Pandora? In what respects is the first woman a "lovely evil"? How does she resemble Eve in the Book of Genesis? Why do both Zeus and the biblical Yahweh try to prevent human beings from acquiring forbidden knowledge?

2. Describe Hesiod's view of the two Strifes and explain their role in the devolving history of humankind. Describe the four metallic ages and the Age of Heroes. Why does Hesiod regard human history as characterized by a downward spiral toward ultimate calamity?

3. Discuss the mythic themes of a lost Golden Age and primal fall from grace that appear in both Greek and biblical traditions. Can a Freudian or Jungian approach help explain this persistent myth?

4. What is Strife's (Eris's) function in Hesiod's concept of the world order?

5. Summarize the myth of Deucalion's flood, showing its parallels to Mesopotamian and biblical deluge stories. Why did the Greeks call their country *Hellas* and themselves *Hellenes?*

Recommended Reading

Athanassakis, Apostolos N., ed. and trans. *Hesiod: Theogony, Works and Days, Shield.* Baltimore: Johns Hopkins UP, 1983. Provides informative annotations on Hesiod's account of human history.

West, M. L., ed. and trans. *Theogony and Works and Days.* New York: Oxford UP, 1988. Includes a discussion of Hesiod's view of human history.

In Touch with the Gods:
Apollo's Oracle at Delphi

KEY THEMES

Located on the slopes of Mount Parnassus, Apollo's shrine at Delphi was widely regarded as the spiritual center of the Greek world, a place where humans could consult the god to whom Zeus had given the art of prophecy. Apollo's word (oracle) was transmitted through his virgin priestess, the Pythia, named in honor of the Python, which Apollo slew when he established his Delphic rule. A sanctuary where myth and ritual combined to affirm humanity's communion with divine powers, Delphi linked the worlds of flesh and spirit.

Two of Zeus's sons—Apollo and Dionysus—embody strikingly different aspects of the human psyche: rational intellect and instinctual sensuality. Perhaps because these two forces, and the tension between them, are so crucial in human experience, the two young gods—more than any other of Zeus's male children—inspired myths and ceremonies that profoundly influenced Greek life. The worship of Dionysus, expressing life's dangerous mutability, gave birth to the Athenian tragic drama (Chapter 13); the cult of Apollo created a practical institution that allowed human beings to communicate, albeit imperfectly, with the gods (Figure 7-1).

The Shrine at Delphi: Communing with the Gods

Whereas the living could visit Olympus or Hades only in imagination, the Greeks believed that a few sacred places on earth also provided limited access to the invisible realm of divine beings. Communicating with the gods was, however, a procedure fraught with mystery and ambiguity, for Zeus had bestowed the patronage of clairvoyance and prophecy upon Apollo, a deity known to distance himself from direct

FIGURE 7-1   Apollo. Patron of the Muses and god of rationality, health, and prophecy,
Apollo is also an eternal ephebe (a youth schooled in the strict discipline of mind and body).
An embodiment of the Greek ideal of proportion, strength, and masculine beauty, Apollo
presides over his mantic shrine at Delphi, where his priestess, the Pythia, communicates the
gods' will to human questioners. Known as the *Belvedere,* this marble statue is a Roman copy
of a Greek bronze from the Hellenistic period. (*Vatican Museums, Rome.*)

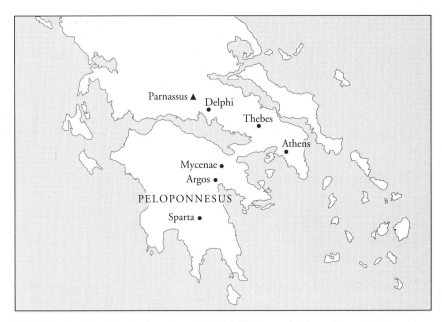

FIGURE 7-2   Map Showing Location of Delphi, Thebes, and Athens. Situated high on the wooded slopes of Mount Parnassus, Delphi's site combines the beauty of wild nature with the sophistication of classical architecture, including the ruins of Apollo's temple, an amphitheater, and a stadium where the Pythian Games were held in the god's honor.

contact with mortals. Aloof and remote, Apollo transmitted Zeus's will through a series of mediators, commonly phrasing his responses in cryptic terms more comprehensible to other gods than to the human questioners.

The prophetic shrines, the gods' words spoken there, and the persons authorized to convey and interpret a deity's typically obscure messages were all designated by the term **oracle.** One of the oldest oracles was that of Zeus at Dodona in Epirus, where the Olympian's utterances were said to issue from a sacred oak tree, perhaps via the sound of wind rustling its leaves. A few foreign oracles, particularly that of Zeus Ammon at Siwa in the Libyan desert, which was consulted by Alexander the Great, also enjoyed a high reputation among the Greeks.

By far the most popular and influential oracle, however, was that of Apollo at **Delphi** [DEL-phee], to which thousands of Greeks flocked each year to seek enlightenment from their god. Originally called **Pytho** [PYE-thoh], Delphi occupied a spur of rugged Mount Parnassus thousands of feet above the adjacent Pleistos River valley (Figure 7-2). Delphi's site combined the beauty of wild nature with the sophistication of classical architecture; these sacred precincts encompassed a large theater, a stadium where the Pythian Games were held in the god's honor, and a magnificent columned temple where the Pythia (or Pythoness), Apollo's clairvoyant priestess, gave ethical advice and issued predictions about the future that many believed were divinely inspired (Figure 7-3).

Delphi's reputation, which reached its peak between the seventh and fifth centuries B.C., was so widespread that foreign kings, as well as Greek rulers, built numerous lavishly decorated shrines along its Sacred Way. These miniature temples,

FIGURE 7-3   Artist's Reconstruction of Delphi's Magnificent Shrines. Depicted in this drawing are a colossal bronze statue of Apollo (right center), the god's chief temple (center), and a large amphitheater where thousands of people assembled to attend musical performances, poetic recitations, and dance exhibitions staged to honor the divine patron of artistic creativity.

crammed with treasure, were erected in gratitude for (or in hope of eliciting) the god's wise counsel and diplomatic intervention in settling political disputes both at home and abroad. Although some complained that the Delphic priesthood overly favored Sparta and other conservative states, Apollo's veiled oracles were generally peaceful in tone and calculated to promote a viable balance of political power and harmony among Greece's many warring factions. The facade of Apollo's temple was inscribed with maxims that urged the Greeks to practice moderation: "Nothing in Excess" and "Know Yourself"—an exhortation to remember one's human limitations and to avoid behaving as if one were a god (Figure 7-4).

Delphi's centrality in Greek religion was expressed in a belief that it stood at the exact center of earth's surface. Zeus, it was said, had released two equally swift eagles that flew in opposite directions around the globe: they met at Delphi, where an ancient carved stone, perhaps a meteor fragment, the omphalos (Figure 7-5), was kept in the temple and identified as the navel of the earth. Equating Apollo's sanctuary with the cosmic nucleus—Delphi literally means "womb"—the myth not only validated the priestly institution of prophecy, but also exalted Apollo as the essential divinity whose far-ranging intelligence unites the realms of heaven and earth.

Prehistoric Delphi

Positioned at the foot of two soaring rocky cliffs, the Phedriads, Delphi was regarded as a holy site long before Apollo's arrival there. Besides its spectacular mountainscape,

FIGURE 7-4   Apollo in His Temple at Delphi. This detail of a vase painting shows the archer king—characteristically holding the bow from which he propels his arrows of plague or healing—(invisibly) occupying his Doric temple at Delphi. The temple walls were inscribed with famous proverbs advocating self-knowledge and self-control. (*Allard Pierson Museum, Amsterdam.*)

the site was famous as a place where some persons experienced the invisible presence of divine beings willing to commune with mortals.

In Aeschylus's play the *Eumenides,* the Pythia summarizes Delphi's prehistory, noting that Apollo's rule followed that held by several ancient goddesses. After Gaea, the primordial fount of wisdom, came her equally wise daughter **Themis** [THEE-mis] (Eternal Law), who was Zeus's second wife and one of the few Titans to remain influential under Olympian jurisdiction. An aspect of the Great Goddess, Themis taught her male successor the art of prophecy, a debt Apollo acknowledged by allowing Themis's priestesses to continue officiating at a small altar within Delphi's precincts.

Apollo and the Dragon: The Transition from Earth Goddess to Sky God

As if reflecting the historical transition from chthonic powers to Olympian sky gods (Chapter 4), myths about the establishment of Apollo's worship at Delphi involve an epochal battle between female and male principles of divinity. According to the Homeric *Hymn to Pythian Apollo,* the conflict originates in Hera's anger toward Zeus for having produced Athene by himself. As granddaughter of Gaea and as the Queen of Heaven, Hera inherits the Goddess's prerogatives and feels outrage when Zeus ignores her exclusive right to bear divine children. After her attempt to duplicate Zeus's reproductive autonomy results only in the malformed Hephaestus, Hera abandons her

FIGURE 7-5   Delphic Omphalos. The social and spiritual centrality of Delphi were expressed in the myth that Apollo's sacred place of worship was literally the geographic center of the world: it is the place where Zeus's two eagles met when, departing from the same point, they flew at equal speeds around the globe. Delphi's connection with themes of birth and rebirth is suggested by its name, which means "womb," and the presence of the omphalos, a stone depicting earth's navel. Shown here is a carved replica of the "navel" stone. (*Delphi Museum.*)

husband's bed and, without male help, conceives and bears Typhon (Typhoeus), the monstrous serpent whose strength rivals that of Zeus. She entrusts Typhon's upbringing to **Python** [PYE-thuhn], a female dragon who guards the ancient sanctuary of Gaea and Themis at Delphi. According to the Delphic hymn, the monster does not challenge Zeus directly, but is associated with Python, the serpent who will threaten Zeus's noblest son, Apollo. (Compare Hesiod's account in the *Theogony*, where Gaea, not Hera, is the dragon's mother; see Chapter 3.)

Apollo's Birth

Birth stories about an infant predestined for unusual achievement, whether as a national leader or future god—such as the biblical Moses or Jesus of Nazareth—typically involve grave dangers from which the child narrowly escapes. In the case of Apollo and Artemis, Hera tries to eliminate them by preventing their birth. After Zeus impregnates their mother, **Leto** [LEE-toh], daughter of the Titans Coeus and Phoebe, Hera so terrorizes the world that no land on earth will give Leto a safe place to deliver her children. When Leto at last finds refuge on a barren floating island,

Ortygia (Island of Quails), Hera then refuses to allow Eileithyia, goddess of child-birth, to leave Olympus, causing Leto to remain in agonizing labor for nine days. Only after Athene persuades Hera to assuage her anger by giving her a gigantic gold and amber necklace does she permit Eileithyia to visit Ortygia and accomplish Leto's safe delivery. Apollo later transforms his birthplace into the island of Delos, perma-nently fixing it in the midst of the Cyclades, where it became an important religious center honoring Zeus's Olympian twins. Serving an etiological function, this tale accounts for Delos's name (meaning "brilliant") because it was here that the god of light first beheld the sun's bright rays.

Festivals and Ceremonies of Delphi

The Pythian Games

After traversing Greece and settling at Delphi, Apollo faces an immediate challenge to his new cult. Python, reputedly a child of Gaea and mentor of Typhon (embodi-ment of Hera's bitter hatred of Zeus's patriarchy), ravages the countryside, slaughter-ing sheep and humans alike. Only three days old, Apollo achieves his first victory with the bow, shooting an arrow through Python and ridding the world of a destruc-tive pest. In memory of this feat, Apollo's Delphic Oracle, a virgin prophetess empowered to speak in his name, is called the **Pythia** [PITH-ee-uh]. Further com-memorating Python's defeat, Apollo establishes the Pythian Games (Figure 7-6), which were held every fourth year and were second only to the Olympics as Greece's foremost sports competition. As befits a festival honoring the Muses' patron, the Pythian Games also emphasized performances in music, poetry, and dance.

The Stepterion: Guilt and Purification

Although Apollo must eradicate his older rival in order to found his Delphic rites, he readily acknowledges moral responsibility for having slain Python, the serpent guardian of Gaea's ancient shrine. Voluntarily exiling himself from Olympus, Apollo withdraws to the valley of Tempe, where he works as a shepherd for King Admetus. Setting the example of a god who performs slave labor to purge himself of guilt, Apollo creates a paradigm of expiation for mortals who later seek to cleanse them-selves of error (Figure 7-7). After his purification, Apollo, crowned with laurel leaves, returns to Delphi at midsummer and inaugurates the first Pythia, Herophile, who is inspired to foretell the Trojan War.

Because of Apollo's example, Delphi became a holy asylum where exiles could ritualistically rid themselves of moral pollution, as Orestes does when he is cleansed with sacrificial pig's blood, ceremonially, if not legally or ethically, absolving him from the crime of having murdered his mother (see Figure 15-10). In general, Apollo's Delphic myth helped to promote a more humane moral order in which Greek society was encouraged to abandon its ancient demands for bloody retaliation by recognizing the superiority of justice tempered with mercy—an innovation that Aeschylus cele-brates in his *Oresteia* (Chapter 15).

In classical times, every eight years the priests of Delphi reenacted Apollo's slaying of Python in a religious drama called the *Stepterion*. The rite took place on an ancient

(a)   **(b)**

FIGURE 7-6   The Charioteer. This Greek bronze of a charioteer standing in calm triumph
(a) at the moment of victory displays the classic ideal of simplicity, symmetry, and serenity—
qualities of conscious restraint associated with Apollonian balance. Victors at the Pythian
Games, held every fourth year at Delphi, were crowned with laurel wreaths cut from the valley of Tempe. This is one of the few statues to retain eyes of inlaid metal. (b) The Charioteer
once stood in a bronze chariot pulled by bronze horses. (*Delphi Museum.*)

threshing floor (the halos), where a young boy representing the infant god was guided
by priests to a hut in which the dragon lurked. After launching an arrow into the hut
and supposedly killing the hidden serpent, the boy then pantomimed Apollo's flight
to Tempe, where the god atoned for Python's death.

Consulting the Oracle

Persons wishing to ask questions of the Pythia followed a strictly regulated procedure:
applicants first washed themselves in water from the nearby Castalia Spring; paid a
fee, the size of which was determined by officiating priests; and sacrificed an animal,
usually a sheep or goat that was "perfect," in the sense that it had no visible defect.
Before the animal's throat was cut on Apollo's altar, priests doused it with cold spring
water; if the lamb shivered or trembled, the day was deemed propitious and the god
could be expected to offer a reply.

After washing in Castalia's waters, the Pythia, accompanied by priests similarly
purified, entered the temple, where she burned an offering of laurel and barley flour
in a sacred flame kept perpetually alight on Apollo's hearth. The priestess then descended into an underground chamber where she seated herself on a tripod, a high

FIGURE 7-7   Roman Copy of a Greek Apollo. This statue (original c. 450 B.C.) depicts the god as one of the athletes who competed in Delphi's Pythian Games. Embodying the principle of a healthy mind in a healthy body, Apollo presides over rites of purification that can remove guilt and restore offenders to participation in Greek society. (*Kassel Museum.*)

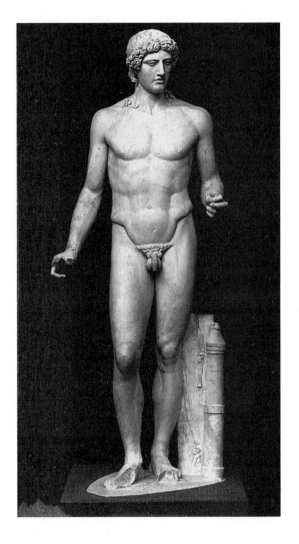

three-legged stand that normally held a bowl or cauldron used in cooking. Using the tripod as a stool (Figure 7-8), she sat preparing to receive the god's spirit. After drinking from a stream that flowed through the room and chewing bay or laurel leaves, the Pythia went into a trance during which she uttered phrases that were unintelligible to the questioner waiting in an adjoining room. A priest then wrote down her words, translating them into Greek verses, commonly using dactyl hexameters, the meter of epic poetry.

Typically couched in highly obscure terms, many of the Pythia's oracles have been preserved, chiefly in inscriptions and the histories of Herodotus. In a famous episode involving Croesus, a king of Lydia (sixth century B.C.) regarded as the world's wealthiest ruler, Herodotus reports that the king disastrously failed to cope with oracular ambiguity. Threatened by the rapidly expanding empire of his Persian neighbors under Cyrus the Great, Croesus determined to halt their expansion before it was too

FIGURE 7-8 The Pythia, Sitting Atop a Tripod in Her God's Delphic Sanctuary. Holding a laurel branch in one hand, Apollo's virgin priestess gazes intently at the contents of a
bowl she holds in her other hand, perhaps reading there an answer to the question posed by
the petitioner standing before her. At the height of its reputation, during the sixth and fifth
centuries B.C., Delphi attracted pilgrims from throughout the eastern Mediterranean world.
Sophocles's *Oedipus Rex* was written, in part, to demonstrate the inescapable truth of Apollo's
oracles (Chapter 16). (*Staatliche Museen, Berlin.*)

late. Before taking action, he sought the Oracle's advice and was told that if he crossed
the Persian border, a great nation would fall. Thinking that Persia's imperialist aspirations were doomed, Croesus boldly attacked Cyrus, only to have his capital city,
Sardis, captured by Persian troops and his kingdom incorporated into the Persian
Empire. After narrowly escaping being burned alive—Herodotus states that Apollo
sent a storm that quenched the flames—Croesus indignantly asked the Delphic
priestess how she could have so misled him. The Pythia's reply was mild: if Croesus
did not understand the first oracle, he should have made a second inquiry.

During the two Persian invasions of Greece (490 and 480–479 B.C.), the Delphic
Oracle at first seemed to favor submitting to the hitherto undefeated Persian armies,
perhaps to avoid the severe reprisals that the invaders would inflict after overcoming
Greek resistance. When at last the Oracle reluctantly conceded that the Greeks could
place their trust in "the wooden wall," Themistocles, Athens's resourceful leader,

FIGURE 7-9   The Site of Delphi. Although Delphi's shrines now lie in ruin, the site retains, for many, an almost mystical attraction. Only the foundations and a few columns remain of Apollo's temple, but the pointed cypress is an evergreen reminder of one of the god's earliest loves, the youth Cyparissus.

argued that Apollo advised relying on the Greeks' warships. After the combined Greek fleet managed to sink most of the Persian armada at the Battle of Salamis, causing the Persians to withdraw, it seemed clear that Themistocles—and Apollo— was right.

Sophocles used one of the oldest myths, that of Oedipus and his doomed royal house of Thebes, to dramatize the infallibility of Apollo's Delphic pronouncements. Oedipus's career and those of his equally tragic children, Antigone, Eteocles, and Polynices—hedged about by cryptic oracles—serve to confirm that the god speaks truly through his priestess and that no one can escape fulfilling Delphi's prophecies. (See Chapter 16, Sophocles's *Oedipus Rex.*)

Despite such unqualified support as Sophocles gave in his Oedipus plays, however, Delphi's prestige rapidly declined after the fifth century B.C. With the rise of Macedonian imperialism, under King Philip and his son Alexander, Greek city-states like Attica and Boeotia (the state bordering Delphi) were absorbed into a larger political system and lost much of their confidence in divine institutions along with their autonomy. After Rome seized final control of Greece in 146 B.C., Delphi became even more a religious curiosity or cultural artifact than a source of living faith. A few Roman emperors—such as Hadrian and his friend Herodes Atticus—provided money to rebuild its stadium and restore its shrines, but even before new gods arrived from Palestine and declared Apollo's cult obsolete, the sanctuary had fallen into disuse and ruin (Figure 7-9). When Julian (A.D. 360–363), the only non-Christian emperor after Constantine, attempted to revive worship of the classical gods and sent an envoy to Delphi, it is said that an aged Pythia gave this response:

> Tell the king the fairwrought hall has fallen to the ground,
> no longer has Phoebus a hut, nor a prophetic laurel,
> nor a spring that speaks. The water of speech even is quenched.

Apollo's Loves

Although the perfection of manly beauty, Apollo was unlucky in love. The story of his first, and unrequited, passion foreshadows his characteristic record of loss and sexual frustration. When he pursues Daphne, a mountain nymph, she flees him like the plague, praying (in some traditions) to Zeus to preserve her virginity. In an instant, Daphne is changed into a bay or laurel tree, leaving her pursuer inconsolable. As a memorial of his unconsummated love, Apollo makes a crown of laurel leaves, an emblem that was later awarded to victors in the Pythian Games.

Apollo also loved a youth named Cyparissus, who in turn was devoted to a pet stag. When Cyparissus accidentally kills the stag, he resolves to die himself, grieving so intensely for his animal friend that he refuses Apollo's pleas to transfer his affection to the god. Drained by excessive weeping, he gradually loses his human form and is transformed into a cypress. Even today a scattering of cypress trees punctuates the rocky slopes of Parnassus, standing as upright, evergreen reminders of Apollo's passion.

In the god's most celebrated affair, an outstandingly handsome boy named Hyacinthus is the object of Apollo's desire. Although this time the god's affection is returned, the relationship still ends unhappily. While throwing the discus together, a favorite pastime of Greek lovers, Hyacinthus, perhaps accidentally, steps in the way of Apollo's hurtling discus, which strikes him fatally in the head. (One version of the myth states that Zephyrus, the West Wind, also loved Hyacinthus and, when rejected in Apollo's favor, jealously diverts the discus's trajectory, causing it to strike the young man.) His mind indelibly imprinted by the sight of blood streaming over Hyacinthus's white skin, Apollo transforms the boy's corpse into a flower whose white petals are marked in red, mimicking the letters *AI,* signifying the Greeks' cry of sorrow.

Although these myths of unfulfilled love provide etiologies of various plants or blossoms, symbols of the ephemerality of mortal youth and beauty, the story of Apollo and Coronis, equally unsatisfying to the god, serves a different purpose. Coronis, a princess of Thessaly, is already pregnant by Apollo when she deserts Zeus's most attractive son for a human suitor. According to one tradition, the god is informed of Coronis's humiliating infidelity with a mere mortal by a gossipy crow; in Pindar's version of the tale, the all-seeing god does not need a bird of ill omen to bring the bad news: he discerns the truth himself and sends his sister Artemis to kill Coronis for her treachery.

The unborn child is preserved, however, and given to Chiron, wisest of the centaurs, to raise. Created by the union of divinity and fallible humanity and tutored by a creature half-human, half-horse, the child Asclepius becomes one of myth's most potent symbols of human endeavor. Inheriting from his father the art of healing, Asclepius is the first physician, using his divine legacy to combat disease and cure

FIGURE 7-10   Asclepius and Suppliant. Apollo punishes wrongdoing by inflicting plague on entire communities who harbor the guilty, as he does in the *Iliad* and *Oedipus Rex,* but he also confers the benefits of medicine on humanity through his human son Asclepius, the first physician. Myth presents Asclepius as so potent a healer that he restores even the dead to life. Zeus ends this disruption of natural processes—and assertion of human skill against the limits of mortality—by killing Asclepius, an act that outrages Apollo and brings him temporarily into conflict with heaven's king. In this votive plaque, Asclepius tends to the wounded arm of a suppliant. (*Archaeological Receipts Fund (TAP), Greece.*)

mortals of their afflictions (Figure 7-10). When Asclepius becomes so skilled at practicing medicine that he learns how to revive even the dead, Zeus, alarmed at this violation of nature, kills him with a thunderbolt. Outraged at his son's undeserved fate, Apollo promptly retaliates by killing the Cyclops who had forged Zeus's lightning. Regarding Apollo's act as rebellion, Zeus contemplates, for a moment only, imprisoning the god of light in Tartarus's infernal darkness.

Closely associated with that of Apollo, the cult of Asclepius, whom tradition granted posthumous immortality, flourished throughout Greece. When pilgrims visited the rural shrine at Epidaurus, where Asclepius's most famous temple stood, they followed a peculiar ritual in which reptilian symbols of Gaea and other chthonic goddesses played a major part. (Both Apollo and Asclepian practitioners bore the caduceus, with its two serpents entwined about a staff, which some mythographers interpret as a phallic symbol and others as a representation of the Tree of Life, an image associated with the Great Goddess's powers of regeneration.) Patients seeking a cure slept overnight on the temple floor, where snakes were allowed to crawl over their bodies so that these coldblooded creatures could absorb fevers and infections. Combining Apollonian reason with sympathetic magic (a ritual acting out of what one wants to take place), the Epidaurus physicians applied their skills to replicating on individual human beings the ancient Delphic rite of cleansing and purification.

HYMN TO PYTHIAN APOLLO[1]

Cynaethus (Kynaithos) of Chios

The glorious son of Leto
goes to steep Pytho,
playing his hollow lyre,
wearing divine and perfumed clothes.
And his lyre makes a lovely sound
with its gold pick.
And then, like a thought,
he goes to Olympos
from earth, to the house of Zeus
where the other gods   10
are gathered.
And suddenly the gods
are only concerned with
the lyre and song,
and all together the Muses sing
the divine gifts of the gods,
each one answering the other
with a beautiful voice,
and the suffering of men,
what they have   20
from the immortal gods,
how they live,
mindless, helpless,
how they can't find
a cure for death
or a defense against age.

[While roaming over Greece looking for a sacred place to found his sanctuary, the young
Apollo first wishes to set up his shrine at an enchantingly cool spring that belonged to
Telphusa, its guardian nymph. *Not* wanting a powerful god at her favorite place, Telphusa persuades Apollo to settle elsewhere. After arriving at Delphi, called Pytho in this
tradition, Apollo defeats its guardian serpent, the "she-dragon" Python. He then lays the
foundations of his temple and recruits a band of sailors from Minoan Crete to serve as
his first Delphic priests.]

There lord Phoebus Apollo
decided to make his lovely temple,
and he said this:
"It's here that I'm inclined   30
to build a very beautiful temple,
an oracle for mankind,

1. Translation by Charles Boer.

where everybody will always bring
perfect sacrifices, whether they live
in the rich Peloponnesus
or in Europe, or in the islands
that are surrounded by waves,
because they will be looking for oracles.
And I will give out oracles
to all of them, accurate advice, too,   40
I'll give it to them
in my rich temple."

And when he had said this,
he started laying out the foundations,
which were wide and very long throughout.
And over these
the sons of Erginus, Trophonius
and Agamedes, who were loved
by the immortal gods,
laid out a stone base.   50
And the innumerable tribes of men
built the temple out of smooth stone,
to be the subject of song
for all time.
But near this place there was a spring
that was flowing beautifully,
and there the lord, the son of Zeus,
killed the big fat she-dragon,
with his mighty bow.
She was a wild monster   60
that worked plenty of evil
on the men of earth,
sometimes on the men themselves,
often on their sheep with their thin feet.
She meant bloody misery.
She once received from Hera,
who sits on a golden throne,
the dreaded, cruel Typhaon,
and raised him, a sorrow for mankind.
Hera had given him birth once   70
when she was mad at father Zeus,
when the son of Cronos himself
was giving birth to glorious Athena
in his head. The lady Hera
got angry then, and said this
to the gods who were assembled:
"Listen to me,
all you gods and goddesses,

how Zeus who gathers the clouds
has begun to dishonor me,   80
after he has made me
his dearly beloved wife.
Without me, he has given birth
to bright-eyed Athena,
who stands out from all the blessed gods.
But my own boy, Hephaestus,
the one I myself gave birth to,
was weak among all the gods,
and his foot was shrivelled,
why it was a disgrace to me,   90
a shame in heaven,
so I took him in my hands
and threw him out and he fell
into the deep sea.
The daughter of Nereus, Thetis,
with her silver feet,
took him and brought him up
with her sisters.
I wish she would have done us blessed gods
some other favor!   100
Well, you crafty devil,
what do you plan to do now?
How did you dare give birth,
alone, to bright-eyed Athena?
Wouldn't I have given birth for you?
At least I was called your wife
among the gods
who live in this big heaven.
Watch out now that I don't plan
some trouble for you later on: 110
yes in fact I will plan something,
that a son will be born to me
who will stand out among the immortal gods,
and it won't shame your sacred marriage
or mine. But I won't come to your bed,
I'll go far away from you
and stay with the immortal gods."
She said all this
and went away from the gods,
her heart very angry. The lady Hera,   120
with her cow-eyes, then prayed,
and struck the ground
with the flat of her hand, and said:
"Listen to me now,
Earth and wide Heaven overhead,
and you Titan gods

who live under the earth
around big Tartarus,
from whom we get both men and gods.
Listen to me now,   130
all of you, and give me a child
separate from Zeus, and yet one
who isn't any weaker than him
in strength. In fact,
make him stronger than Zeus,
just as Zeus who sees so far
is stronger than Cronos."
She cried this out
and beat the ground
with her thick hand.   140
And then Earth,
who brings us life,
was moved. And when she saw it,
she was very happy.
And she expected a fulfillment.

From that point on,
for a full year,
she didn't go once
to the bed of wise Zeus.
She didn't even sit   150
in her elaborate chair,
as she used to do,
giving him good advice.
No, she stayed in her temples,
the lady Hera, with her cow-eyes,
where many people prayed,
and she enjoyed their sacrifices.
But when the months and days
were finished, and the seasons
came and went with the turning year,   160
she bore something
that didn't resemble the gods,
or humans, at all: she bore
the dreaded, the cruel, Typhaon,
a sorrow for mankind.
Immediately the lady Hera,
with her cow-eyes, took it
and gave it to her (the she-dragon),
bringing one wicked thing to another.
And she received it.   170
And it used to do
plenty of terrible things
to the famous tribes of mankind.

Whoever encountered the she-dragon,
it was doomsday for him,
until the lord Apollo,
who works from a distance,
shot a strong arrow at her.
And she lay there,
torn with terrible pain,   180
gasping deeply, and rolling around
on the ground.
She made an incredible, wonderful noise.
She turned over again and again,
constantly, in the wood.
And then life left her,
breathing up blood.
And Phoebus Apollo boasted:
"Rot right there now,
on the ground that feeds man.   190
You won't live anymore
to be a monstrous evil to humans
who eat the fruit of the earth
that feeds so many, and
who will bring perfect sacrifices here.
Typhoeus won't save you
from hard death,
nor the infamous Chimera,
but right here the black earth
and the bright sun will rot you."   200
Phoebus said this, gloating over her,
and darkness covered her eyes.
And the sacred power of the sun
rotted her out right there,
which is why the place is called Pytho (rot),
and why they give the lord
the name of Pythian, because it was right there
that the power of the piercing sun
rotted the monster out.
And then Phoebus Apollo   210
understood in his mind
how that beautifully flowing stream
had deceived him,
and he went for Telphusa, furious,
and he got there fast.
He stood very close to her
and said this:
"Telphusa, you weren't going to deceive my mind
and keep this lovely place
just for your beautifully flowing waters   220
to go on flowing.

My fame will also come from this place,
and not just yours alone."
Apollo, who works from a distance,
said this, and pushed over a mountain top
along with a rock-slide,
and covered over her streams.
And he made an altar in a shaded grove,
very near the beautifully flowing stream.
And everybody prays to the lord there   230
by calling him Telphusian,
because he disfigured the streams
of sacred Telphusa.
Then Phoebus Apollo thought over
in his heart who the priests should be
that he would bring in
to serve him in rocky Pytho.
And while he was thinking about it,
he spotted a fast ship on the wine-sea,
in which there were many men,   240
and good men, Cretans from Minoan Cnossos,
who make sacrifices to the lord
and announce the laws
of Phoebus Apollo with his gold sword,
whatever he says, answering
from his laurel tree in the valley of Parnassus.
They were sailing
in their black ship, for business
and profit, to sandy Pylos,
to the men of Pylos.   250
But it was Phoebus Apollo
who met them. He jumped into the sea,
like a dolphin, and onto their fast ship,
and he lay there,
a big, frightening monster.
And none of these men thought about it
in their hearts, enough to understand,
and they wanted to throw the dolphin off.
But he kept rocking the black ship
all over, and he rattled the black ship's beams.   260
So they sat back, scared and silent,
in their ship. And they didn't let go
the cables in their hollow black ship,
and they didn't let out the sail
of their dark-prowed ship, but
they kept sailing, as they had before
with the ship fastened with ox-rope.
And a fierce south wind
beat their fast ship from behind.

And first they passed by Malea,   270
and down the Laconian coast
until they came to that city
that is garlanded by the sea,
Taenarum, the land of the Sun,
who makes men happy.
Here the sheep of Lord Sun,
with their thick fleece,
are always eating,
and live in a joyful land.
Here the men wanted to land   280
their ship, and go ashore,
and think over the great wonder
and see with their eyes
if the monster would stay on the deck
of their hollow ship,
or whether it would jump back
into the salt sea that's so full of fish.
But their well-built ship
did not obey the rudders,
it kept on going   290
along the rich coast of Peloponnesus,
and lord Apollo, who works from a distance,
guided it easily with his breath.
It plied its way and came to Arena,
and to lovely Argyphia, and to Thryon,
the ford of the Alpheus, and to Aepy,
well situated, and to sandy Pylos,
to the men of Pylos. But it went on,
past Cruni and Chalcis,
past Dyme and marvellous Elis,   300
where the Epei are in power.
And while it was heading for Pherae,
rejoicing in the breeze of Zeus,
the steep mountain of Ithaca
appeared to them beneath the clouds,
and Dulichium and Same
and the woodland Zacynthus.
But when they had passed
the entire Peloponnesus, towards Crisa,
that enormous gulf appeared to them   310
which closes off the rich Peloponnesus.
A great west wind came up, clear,
by order of Zeus, blowing furiously
out of the sky, so that the ship
would cease, as soon as possible,
its journey over the salt sea.
And that's when they started sailing back

towards dawn and the sun.
The lord Apollo, son of Zeus,
led them. They reached Crisa,   320
which you see from a distance,
vine country, and harbor.
Their sea-going ship went aground here
on the sands.

Then the lord Apollo,
who works from a distance,
jumped from the ship,
like a star at mid-day.
Sparks flew off him all over,
and their light reached the sky.   330
He entered his shrine,
past the tripods,
which were very valuable,
and he made a fire,
revealing his arrows,
and the brightness filled all of Crisa.
And the wives and daughters
of the Crisans, beautifully dressed,
howled at this blast of Phoebus,
for he put great fear in each of them.   340
And then he leaped out,
like a thought, to speed to the ship again,
in the shape of a man
who is quick and strong,
an adolescent, his wide shoulders
covered with his hair.
He spoke to the men
and said winged words:
"Strangers, who are you?
Where do you come from,   350
sailing the waterways?
Was it for business
or do you wander recklessly
over the sea, like pirates
who roam around
risking their lives
as they do evil to strangers?
Why do you stand around like this,
grieving, why don't you go ashore,
why don't you put away the gear   360
of your black ship—which is the custom
among men who eat bread,
whenever they come from the sea
to land, in their black ships,

weary with work.
A desire for sweet food
usually seizes their minds right away."
He said this
and put courage in their breasts,
and the leader of the Cretans   370
answered him back and said:
"Stranger, even though you are not like
ordinary men, neither in your size or shape,
but like the immortal gods,
good health to you and hello,
and may the gods give you
good fortune.
Tell me honestly,
so that I may be sure,
what country is this?   380
what land? what people live here?
We were thinking of somewhere else
when we went sailing
over the great deep sea
to Pylos, from Crete,
which is where we boast our origin.
And now we've come on our ship here,
not at all willingly,
and we want to return,
we want another route, other paths.   390
One of the immortal gods
brought us here against our will."
Then Apollo, who works from a distance,
answered them:
"Strangers, you who once lived before this
around the very wooded Cnossos,
you will not be going back again
to the city you love,
or to your beautiful houses,
or to your dear wives. Instead,   400
you will take care of my rich temple
that is honored by many men.
I am the son of Zeus. I am Apollo.
I brought you here
over the great deep sea.
I intended no evil for you.
Instead, you will take care of my rich temple
that is so honored by all men.
You will get to know
the plans of the gods,   410
and by their will
you will forever be honored,

on and on through every single day.
But come on, do what I say right now.
First, lower the sails
and set the cables free,
and then pull the fast ship
up on land. Take out your stuff,
and everything in the balanced ship,
and make an altar on the beach of the sea.   420
Light a fire on it
and offer up white barley
and then stand around the altar
and pray. And since it was as a dolphin
that I first jumped on to your fast ship
in the misty sea, pray to me
as Delphinus. And the altar itself
will be called Delphinus,
as well as All-seeing, forever.
And then eat dinner   430
by your fast black ship
and pour an offering to the blessed gods
who live on Olympos.
And after you've satisfied your desire
for delicious food, come with me
and sing 'Io Paean,' 'Hail Healer,'
until you get to the place
where you will take care of my rich temple."

Apollo said this.
And the men heard him very well,   440
and they obeyed him.
First the men lowered the sail,
and set free the cables,
and lowered the mast with the forestays
on the mast-hold. And then the men
went up on the beach of the sea.
They dragged the fast ship
onto land out of the sea, up on the sand,
and they put big props under it.
And they made an altar   450
on the beach of the sea,
and lit a fire, and made an offering
of white barley, and they prayed,
standing around the altar,
as he told them to.
And then they had dinner
next to their fast black ship
and poured an offering to the blessed gods
who live on Olympos.

And when they had satisfied their desire   460
for food and drink, they started to go.
The lord Apollo, the son of Zeus,
led them, holding a lyre in his hands,
playing it beautifully,
walking high and nicely.
And the Cretans followed him, dancing,
to Pytho, and they sang 'Io Paean'
just like the paean-singers of Crete,
and like those men in whose breasts
the divine Muse has put   470
beautifully sounding song.
Not tired at all in their feet,
they approached the ridge, and then,
right away, they reached Parnassus
and that lovely place where they were to live
honored by many men.
He led them, and showed them
his sacred shrine and his rich temple.
But their spirit was moved
in their dear breasts,   480
and the leader of the Cretans asked him:
"O lord, you brought us here
far from our loved ones
and our fatherland, because
it seemed good in your heart,
how are we to live now?
We have to ask you that.
This place isn't any good for vineyards
and it isn't very desirable for pasture,
to live here very well,   490
and to serve mankind."

And then Apollo, the son of Zeus,
smiled on them, and said:
"What foolish people you are,
what wretches, that in your hearts
you want trouble, and painful work,
and distress. Now I'm going to tell you something,
something pleasing, and put it in your heads:
Even if each one of you,
with a knife in your hand,   500
were to kill sheep constantly,
there would still remain
an endless supply, all in fact
that the famous tribes of mankind
bring here for me.
So guard my temple,

and welcome the tribes of mankind
who gather here, and tell them
most important of all,
what my will is.   510
And maintain justice in your hearts.
But if any of you is disobedient,
or careless, or contemptuous,
or if there are any idle words
or incidents or arrogance,
which is, after all, the custom
among human beings, then other men
will become your masters,
and they will subdue you with force
forever. Now everything has been said.   520
Guard it in your hearts."
And so, farewell,
son of Zeus and Leto.
But I will remember you
in other hymns.

Questions for Discussion and Review

1. Apollo is commonly described as the quintessential Greek deity. What characteristics distinguish him from other Olympians?

2. Describe the prophetic institution at Delphi, including its physical setting, mythic traditions (including the story of Apollo's unusual birth and Hera's wrath), and religious function in classical Greek society. Why is the Pythia always a woman? How is her prophetic office connected with female deities who reigned at Delphi before Apollo's arrival?

3. How are the themes of guilt and purification involved in Apollo's myth as well as later human rituals at Delphi?

4. Discuss Apollo's generally unsatisfying love affairs. Why does myth present the most physically and intellectually gifted young male Olympian as almost invariably suffering erotic rejection or loss?

5. Connect the myth of Asclepius with that of his father.

Recommended Reading

Boer, Charles, trans. *The Homeric Hymns.* Rev. ed. Dallas: Spring Publications, 1979.

Calasso, Roberto. *The Marriage of Cadmus and Harmony.* New York: Knopf, 1993. Includes perceptive commentary on the Greek concept of Apollo and his affinity with Dionysus.

Eisner, Robert. *The Road to Daulis: Psychoanalysis, Psychology, and Classical Mythology.* Syracuse: Syracuse UP, 1987. Contains insightful Freudian analysis of Apollo and his various love affairs.

Petrakos, Basil. *Delphi.* N.p.: Clio Editions, 1977. A well-illustrated study of Delphi's history and archaeology.

8

Dionysus: Rooted in Earth and Ecstasy

KEY THEMES

If Apollo represents the conscious mind subject to rational control, Dionysus, the "twice-born" son of Zeus and Semele, embodies both the human subconscious and the instinctual life force that animates nature. As god of the vine and bestower of intoxication, he shatters conventional restraints and permits human beings to act out extremes of emotion and behavior. Some later Greek poets and mystics linked Dionysus's cult with that of Orpheus, emphasizing the god's connections with the Underworld and spiritual regeneration.

Dionysus and Apollo: Contrasts and Connections

Greek tradition held that each year Apollo left his sanctuary at Delphi to live with the Hyperboreans, a mythical tribe inhabiting the extreme North, a harsh region ruled by Boreas (North Wind). During Apollo's seasonal absence, **Dionysus** reigned in Delphi for the three winter months. A more radical change in divine patronage is difficult to imagine: Apollo, symbol of moderation and mental balance, is replaced by an irrational power that liberates human beings to explore their potential for emotional and behavioral extremes (Figure 8-1). In the absence of rational control, the subconscious, with all its amoral energy, is allowed to flourish.

Despite their fundamental differences, however, Apollo and Dionysus share some important qualities. As sons of Zeus by different mothers, the two half-brothers manifest their father's indomitable will to power, as well as his creative drive. Born under difficult, even bizarre circumstances, both gods spend their early youth recruiting new worshipers, establishing their respective cults, and winning general recognition of their divinity. Although Apollo is identified with disciplined intellect and Dionysus with spontaneous emotion, both are associated with the phenomenon of *ecstasy*, a term meaning "to stand outside oneself," to abandon rational control and surrender oneself to an overwhelming emotion. Overcome by his spirit, Apollo's

FIGURE 8-1   Dionysus Pictured as an Ephebe. The multiple, even paradoxical qualities of Dionysus are clearly rendered in this bas-relief from Herculaneum, a Greco-Roman city buried by an eruption of Mount Vesuvius in A.D. 79. Shown as a youthful athlete in a moment of relaxation, the god extends his right hand to refill a firmly gripped wine cup while he loosely holds the phallic thyrsus (a pinecone-tipped shaft) in his left hand. The apparent serenity of the scene is undercut by the presence of a snarling panther lying beneath Dionysus's chair. An unpredictable compendium of sensuous pleasure and latent savagery, the god encompasses the opposing forces of beneficence and violence characteristic of both human nature and the natural cycle of life and death. (*National Museum, Naples.*)

priestess, the Pythia, falls into a trance and speaks in tongues, a religious behavior known as *glossolalia*. When possessed by Dionysus, his followers similarly change their normal conduct, breaking into wild dances and experiencing a rapturous sense of union with their god.

This affinity between seeming opposites suggests an underlying unity between these two sons of Zeus. Does Apollo, supposedly gone to visit the Hyperboreans, in fact reappear wearing the joyous mask of his half-brother? Does the god of conscious thought, for a fourth of the year, allow himself the freedom to throw off rules and prohibitions and abandon himself to the subconscious mind's demands for unrestrained pleasure? If the same god exchanges the Apollonian laurel crown for one of Dionysian ivy, he reveals that Apollo and Dionysus are in fact two equally important aspects of the human psyche, which, like the Delphic administration, alternates between conscious self-discipline and emotional self-abandonment. In strikingly different ways, both gods transcend the limits of flesh to link humanity with divinity.

The two Greek gods most closely identified with artistic creativity, Apollo and Dionysus both inspire poetry, song, and dance. Their musical styles, however, are strongly opposed: Apollo's golden lyre, with its limpid melodies, evokes feelings of harmony and serenity. The timbrel (a small hand drum resembling a modern tambourine), which Dionysus invents, is beaten to furious, erratic rhythms that express the wine god's passionate, impulsive nature (Figure 8-2). While Apollo's worshipers sing the paean, an elegantly lyrical hymn of praise, Dionysus's followers perform the **dithyramb** [DITH-ram], a cacophonous choral dance from which, according to Aristotle, the tragic drama evolved.

The Dionysian Myth

Historical Origins

Although some myths present Dionysus as a god foreign to Greek culture, his name appears in ancient Mycenaean inscriptions composed about 1250 B.C., indicating that his cult was indigenous to Greece. The god's name seems to include "Zeus" as its first element, but scholarly attempts to interpret Dionysus as meaning "son of Zeus" have not been widely accepted. Because the infant Dionysus was, for a time, raised by nymphs living on Mount Nysa (location unknown), some historians suggest that the name may mean "Zeus of Nysa."

Dionysus is commonly identified with other male fertility gods of the ancient Near East, including the Mesopotamian and Syrian Tammuz (Dumuzi), whose name means "proper son," the true offspring of divinity; the Near Eastern Adonis (a Semitic term meaning "lord," or "master"); and the Egyptian Osiris, who is dismembered by his jealous brother Set, reassembled by his devoted sister-wife Isis, and subsequently resurrected as ruler of the Land of the Dead. All of these youthful figures have similar stories: they undergo a violent death—typically by being torn asunder—descend into the Underworld, and are ultimately reborn as immortal beings.

Myths about Dionysus's entrance into Greece reflect the Greeks' deep ambivalence about this troubling god who provides freedom from everyday reality at the same time that he stimulates potentially antisocial conduct. The most common tradition presents him as both native born and the proselytizer of a strange foreign cult. In Euripides's play the *Bacchants* (the title refers to female devotees of **Bacchus**

FIGURE 8-2 Dionysus Riding on a Panther. In this mosaic from Delos, birthplace of
Apollo and Artemis, a sullen and heavy-eyed Dionysus carries a thyrsus (pinecone-tipped
shaft) and a timbrel (a small drumlike instrument beaten to hypnotic rhythms). Music, song,
and dance were important in the cults of both Apollo and Dionysus, but the wine god's followers typically gave impassioned performances of a wild, ecstatic nature—a stark contrast to
the limpid melodies of Apollo's lyre. In this rendition, the panther is even larger than the god,
an indication of the untamed and dangerous animal power inherent in Dionysian impulses.

[BAHK-kuhs], another name for Dionysus), the god returns to Thebes, site of his
initial birth, from Asia Minor, where he has recruited a throng of enthusiastic female
worshipers (Figure 8-3). Suspicious of its "un-Greek" excesses, the Theban King
Pentheus (Dionysus's own cousin) bans the new religion and imprisons the god (disguised as a gentle youth), who then exacts a savage vengeance on the entire city (see
Chapter 13, the *Bacchants*).

Dionysus's Double Birth

As she tried to prevent Leto from delivering Apollo and Artemis, Hera also does her
best to keep Dionysus from being born. Determined to thwart Zeus's efforts to populate Olympus with children who are not her offspring, Hera appears as a harmless old

FIGURE 8-3   Dancing Maenad. This cup painting shows a maenad, a nymph or woman possessed by Dionysus's spirit, carrying a thyrsus and the body of a small panther. Unlike the formal Olympian religion, the cult of Dionysus allowed the expression of extreme emotion. Caught up in the spirit of frenzied music and dance, the worshiper could experience ecstasy, a joyous feeling in which the celebrant temporarily escaped the limitations of self and experienced a sense of union with the divine. Confined to narrow roles in most Greek society, women could enjoy an orgiastic liberation at various Dionysian festivals. (*Museum Antiker Kleinkunst, Munich.*)

lady to **Semele** (a daughter of Cadmus, king of Thebes), whom Zeus has seduced, and convinces the naive princess that the mysterious lover who visits her under cover of darkness is actually an ogre. Following Hera's instructions, Semele makes her paramour—Zeus in human form—promise to grant whatever she asks: she then demands that her lover appear as he really is. Despite Zeus's attempts to dissuade her, Semele insists he keep his vow, compelling Zeus to reveal his essential force, a blaze of lightning that incinerates the young woman. From her flaming corpse, Zeus snatches the embryo of Dionysus, which he places in his thigh until the child is fully formed. After several months, as if to spite Hera again (she never forgives Athene's motherless entrance into the world), from his own body Zeus gives birth to Dionysus (Figure 8-4), who is thus a god twice-born.

Unlike Athene, who springs from Zeus's brain, Dionysus issues from his father's thigh, a male fertility god who represents the life force energizing plants, animals, and human beings. In Dylan Thomas's phrase, he is "the force that through the green fuse drives the flower." Dionysus's nature is extremely varied and complex, but among other things he is god of the vine, a deity representing the growth, death, and rebirth of vegetation. A masculine counterpart of Persephone, whose presence stimulates earth to produce grain and whose absence brings winter's sterility, Dionysus symbolizes the annual vegetative cycle. His chief gift to humanity is the fruit of the

FIGURE 8-4   The Birth of Dionysus. Surrounded by figures associated with his ecstatic cult, the infant Dionysus emerges from his father's thigh. The second (and last) of Zeus's children to be born from their father's body, Dionysus represents the ever-changing natural world and the instinctual component of the human psyche, a counterbalance to Athene's conscious intellect. As their respective birth myths suggest, Athene and Dionysus demonstrate that reason and irrationality spring from the same powerful source. (*Museo Archeologico Nazionale, Taranto.*)

vine—wine that gladdens the hearts of all, from peasant laborers toiling in vineyards to carefree gods feasting on Olympus.

Like the paradoxical god himself, Dionysus's intoxicating gift wields a double-edged sword: wine can temporarily ease anxiety and heighten the capacity for pleasure, but its effects can also induce severe mental disorientation, followed by debilitating illness. As one of the world's first mood-altering beverages, wine triggers the rapid changes in personality and behavior that typify Dionysus's protean character (Figure 8-5). As a god of fluids—wine, blood, sap, and semen—he undergoes sudden transformations of mood and physical shape, appearing one moment as a seductive adolescent offering a brimming chalice of wine and the next as a savage bull ready to gore any offender. Greek vase painters, who decorated wine vats, mixing bowls, and drinking cups with scenes from Dionysian myth, commonly showed the god as a handsome youth casually lounging in a chariot bedecked with vine branches and ivy and drawn by panthers or leopards—feline predators ready to tear flesh at the slightest provocation.

Dionysus's Youth and Foreign Travels

Myths about Dionysus's early career are many and diverse. Although the following summary draws on a wide variety of sources originating at different periods of Greek history, two main themes consistently dominate the disparate narratives: the god represents strange foreign customs, and he repeatedly confronts opponents hostile to him and his religion. His first enemy is his father's wife. Showing the same malice that motivated her persecution of Leto and Heracles, Hera pursues the infant Dio-

FIGURE 8-5 Dionysus and His Alter Ego. The only major Olympian born from the union of Zeus with a mortal woman, Dionysus is also the only deity who undergoes sparagmos (the physical tearing asunder of a young male) and re- birth, an aspect of his myth that links him with the mysteries of the natural life cycle. In this vase painting, a bearded Dionysus, draped in leopard skins, contem- plates the slim figure of a youth holding the wine god's identifying emblems: a wine cup and a vine bearing grapes. In beholding his youthful image, a renewal of self symbolized by the flourishing vine, the mature Dionysus com- prehends both psychological and physical transformation, the strange process by which nature recreates life. In the Orphic reli- gion, Dionysus's descent to and return from the Underworld fore- shadows the human soul's quest for immortality. (*Museo Archeolo- gico Nazionale, Ferrara.*)

nysus, punishing all who try to help Semele's son. After Hermes takes the child to Semele's sister, Ino (Figure 8-6), who disguises him as a girl, Hera falls upon Diony- sus's protectors, driving both Ino and her husband, King Athamas, mad. This time Zeus transports Dionysus far from Greece, changing his son into a young goat and hiding him on Mount Nysa, where nymphs tenderly care for the child.

Dionysus's discovery of wine, his chief contribution to humanity, also involves his initiation into the mysteries of love and death. The young god's first lover is Ampelus, a youth who is gored to death by an enraged bull. When he discovers Ampelus's bloodied corpse lying in the dust, Dionysus, who has never known sorrow before, weeps unashamedly. Watered by divine tears, Ampelus's body shoots forth a vine that bears ruddy fruit, its color reflecting the boy's rosy complexion. Just as Apollo's grief transformed Hyacinthus into a fragrant symbol of perishable beauty, so Dionysus recreates Ampelus as a plant whose grape clusters, properly fermented, induce in partakers the same intoxicating joy that his first love gave to the wine god. Demeter's

FIGURE 8-6   Ino and the Infant Dionysus. When Hera attempts to destroy the newly born Dionysus, Zeus places his child in the care of Ino, a sister of Dionysus's mother, Semele. Hera punishes Ino and her husband, Athamas, by driving them mad, causing Ino to throw herself into the sea, where she is transformed into the nymph Leucothea. In this bucolic scene, Ino gives the child a drink from the Horn of Plenty while sheep graze peacefully and a boy satyr plays the syrinx (a multireed instrument invented by Pan or, in some accounts, by his father, Hermes). Even as a baby, Dionysus's presence causes a huge vine—inhabited by nesting birds, the Great Goddess's serpent, and other symbols of the life force—to spring up and shelter him. (*Lateran Museum, Rome.*)

bread and Athene's olive were necessary for existence, but Dionysus's beverage surpassed other divine gifts in liberating the human spirit.

The first person to whom Dionysus teaches the art of making wine is Icarius, an old gardener who hospitably receives the god when he appears as a human stranger. Obedient to the god's command, Icarius then travels around the countryside, supplying wine to the thirsty and instructing farmers in viniculture. When some shepherds overindulge and think that they have been poisoned, they murder Icarius, who is dressed in the skin of a goat he had killed earlier for eating his grapevines. According to one tradition, it was then that men first danced around a slain goat, a performance that allegedly developed into the choral "goat song" of tragedy (Chapter 13).

Observing Dionysus's vulnerability after his loss of Ampelus, Hera seizes the opportunity to afflict him with insanity, compelling him to wander crazily through Egypt, Syria, and Asia Minor. (The inexperienced god's erratic behavior may also have resulted from an overfondness for his own inebriating invention.)

Eventually regaining his sanity, Dionysus continues to roam the earth, acquiring some attributes of foreign deities and punishing those who fail to honor him. When in Phrygia (a region in modern Turkey), Dionysus is initiated into the orgiastic rites of **Cybele** [SIB-e-lee], an eastern fertility goddess whom the Greeks commonly identified with Rhea, mother of the Olympians. Dionysus next travels to Thrace, where King Lycurgus foolishly attempts to imprison him. After striking the king with madness and his entire country with sterility, Dionysus orders Lycurgus tied to four horses, which then bolt in four different directions, ripping the king's body to shreds.

The *Hymn to Dionysus* relates one of the wine god's last adventures, his kidnapping by Tyrrhenian pirates and the miraculous growth of vines and ivy that suddenly overwhelms the abductors' ship (Figure 8-7). For their offense, the sailors are changed into dolphins (which explains why these sea mammals are friendly to human beings). The abrupt transformation of Dionysus from a gentle youth into a ravening lion is typical of the god's terrifying changeability, a theme that Euripides emphasizes in the *Bacchants* (Chapter 13).

The Dionysian Retinue

While invading India, which he subdues partly by magic and partly by armed force, Dionysus attracts a host of rustic demigods to his train. His retinue includes throngs of **satyrs** [SAY-terz] and **silens** [sih-LEENZ], wild creatures combining the features of bearded men with aspects of the horse, such as pointed ears and a tail. By the fourth century B.C., artists gave satyrs a more goatlike appearance, apparently modeling them on images of Pan, generally human above the waist but having the shape of a goat below. The animal most closely associated with Dionysus's revels, the goat is not only the god's preferred sacrificial offering but also the form in which Dionysus customarily appears to his followers.

Called fauns by the Romans, satyrs are famous for their sexual prowess, which artists typically emphasize by depicting them with exaggeratedly large (and fully erect) penises. Symbols of unrestrained male libido, they are unabashedly lecherous, spending much of their time drinking wine and/or pursuing wood nymphs or other young men (figures 8-8 and 8-9). Whereas satyrs are generally youthful, the similarly human-animal hybrids known as silens are usually pictured as old men whose bestial

FIGURE 8-7   Dionysus Transforms the Ship's Mast into a Vine. In the last myth ascribed to Dionysus, the god, traveling disguised as a gentle youth, is kidnapped by pirates and held for ransom. When the sailors fail to recognize his divinity, the god changes them into dolphins and causes a massive vine, bearing huge clusters of grapes, to grow over the renegades' ship. Dionysus's divinity is thus revealed in natural phenomena—the vine sprouting miraculously in an unnatural environment. (*Museum Antiker Kleinkunst, Munich.*)

appearance and antic behavior belie their inner wisdom. By about the sixth century B.C., writers and artists amalgamate the concepts of satyrs and silens, using the terms interchangeably to denote virtually identical members of Dionysus's sacred band.

Possessed by the god's frenzied spirit, many women also join the retinue: these Bacchants (also called *Bacchae*) reveal their oneness with nature by dressing in tiger or fawn skins and bedecking themselves with vine leaves and ivy (Figure 8-10). **Maenads** [MEE-nadz], literally "mad women," were inspired with Dionysian mania to leave their cities and gather by night in rugged mountainscapes, where, through ritual singing and dancing, they achieved religious ecstacy (Figure 8-11).

(a)

FIGURE 8-8   A Drunken Satyr.
(a) This marble study (known as the *Barberini Faun*) of a reclining satyr sleeping off his hangover suggests the combination of sensuality and strength characteristic of members of Dionysus's retinue. Although many Greek vase paintings depict satyrs as having the form of a goat from the waist down, others show them as largely human except for possessing overlarge heads and horse tails. (b) The satyr's face, with its full lips, heavy brows, and hornlike locks of hair, also indicates his bestial traits. These hybrid creatures, generally indifferent to everything except the satisfaction of their appetites, personify the human sex drive uninhibited by civilized restraints.

(b)

FIGURE 8-9 Pan Pursuing a Young Goatherd. In this vase painting (c. 480 B.C.), a lustful Pan (depicted with a goat's head, beard, and horns) chases a young goatherd. A prominently ithyphallic statue of Hermes (right) sets the tone for this erotic scene. (*James Fund and by special contributions. Courtesy, Museum of Fine Arts, Boston.*)

FIGURE 8-10 Hephaestus, Bacchante, and Satyr. After reconciling with Hera—who threw him out of heaven—Hephaestus returns to Olympus in a Dionysian procession. Fortified by Dionysus's gift of intoxication and clutching a beaker of wine, Hephaestus carefully looks down to avoid a misstep as he follows an ecstatic Bacchante and a piping satyr. (*Louvre, Paris.*)

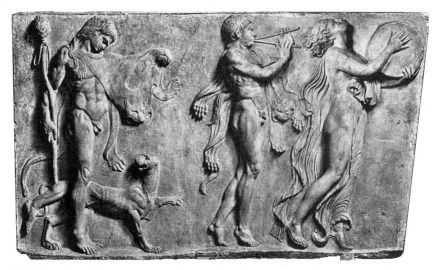

FIGURE 8-11   Dionysus, Pan, and a Maenad. In this bas-relief, a cavorting maenad beating a timbrel leads a musical procession typical of Dionysian celebrations. She is followed by the nature god Pan—wearing a panther skin and playing pipes—and an inebriated Dionysus, who walks carefully, gazing down with fond affinity at his ubiquitous panther. (*National Museum, Naples.*)

Dionysus Zagreus

Beginning in the sixth century B.C., some Greek writers forged an association between the myth of Dionysus and that of Orpheus, the poet who had descended into the Underworld to bring back his deceased wife, Eurydice (Chapter 9). An esoteric tradition known as *Orphism,* allegedly based on Orpheus's secret teachings, promoted a variation of the Dionysian myth that offered a different version of his double birth and that linked the wine god more closely with the regenerative powers of the Underworld. According to Orphic teaching, Dionysus is originally the son of Zeus and Persephone. Zeus plans to enthrone his divine son, who combines his celestial power with chthonic wisdom, as king of the universe. The ever-jealous Hera, however, induces the Titans to kill Dionysus by tearing him to pieces and devouring him. Acting for her father, Athene manages to save the child's heart, which she gives to Zeus, who swallows it (as he had Metis) and then impregnates Semele. The son of Zeus and Persephone, reformed in Semele's womb, is reborn as **Dionysus Zagreus** [ZAG-re-uhs].

Zeus punishes the Titans by striking them with lightning, carbonizing the giant cannibals who dared to kill the son of god. Orphic religion taught that the human race sprang from the Titans' ashes, which accounted for humanity's dual nature (Figure 8-12): human beings were rebels against the gods, but they also contained elements of the divine, the flesh of Zeus's son that the Titans had consumed. Although imbued with evil impulses (the Titan heritage), humanity was also infused with a spark of divinity (Dionysus's body).

Because they housed a "god within," humans could be awakened to their divine potential. Through ritual purification and a communal meal of wine and flesh—

FIGURE 8-12   Aphrodite, Eros, and Pan. This statue group shows Pan, a personification of untamed nature, attempting to seduce Aphrodite, goddess of love. Eros, the power of sexual attraction, attempts to facilitate their union. (*National Museum, Athens.*)

Dionysus's symbolic blood and body—initiates could, in the next world, eventually share their god's eternal life. The material body (soma), meanwhile, was simply the soul's prison (sema); death was merely the freeing of the soul to attain its spiritual home, the realm of the gods (see Chapter 9, Plato's "Myth of Er").

Dionysus's Descent into Hades

A more earthy account linking Dionysus with the afterlife involves his descent into Hades's realm to find Semele and install her on Mount Olympus. Dionysus, who does not know the way to the Underworld, searches for an entrance near Lake Lerna, a supposedly bottomless body of water. When he asks directions from a young man named Prosymnus (or Polymnus), the youth agrees to reveal the path if Dionysus will have sex with him on his return. After ascending from the nether regions, Dionysus finds that Prosymnus has died during his absence. Resolved to keep his promise,

(a)

(b)

(c)

FIGURE 8-13   Dionysian Initiation Ceremonies. These Roman wall paintings from the Villa of the Mysteries in Pompeii (c. 60–40 B.C.) depict a series of rituals performed during the initiation of candidates into the Dionysian Mysteries. (a) Women Initiates. Confined largely to the home, many Greek and Roman women apparently found in Bacchic rites a means of emotional release. (b) In this scene a young novice, who has probably just undergone a ritual whipping, lays her head on the lap of an older woman who offers comfort. (c) Figures from the Dionysian retinue, one holding a theatrical mask associated with Bacchus, act out preparatory rituals of initiation into the wine god's cult. (d) A woman is about to uncover the god's sacred genitalia, a climactic element illustrating the mysterious integration of sex, ecstasy, suffering, and spiritual rebirth that Dionysus represents. (*National Archaeological Museum, Athens.*)

(d)

however, Dionysus fashions a stick into an appropriately phallic shape, plants it on Prosymnus's grave, and performs the desired sexual act.

Athens's annual festival honoring the god, the Great Dionysia, featured an elaborate procession in which participants carried a statue of Dionysus and replicas of his sacred phallus (symbol of divine virility). The secret rituals through which worshipers were initiated into the Dionysian cult also included a climactic unveiling of an oversized model of the god's penis.

Erotic and fertility motifs in the Dionysian cult persisted well into Roman times. Wall paintings in the famous Villa of the Mysteries near Pompeii (buried by an eruption of Mount Vesuvius in A.D. 79) depict a variety of scenes from the Dionysian initiation ceremonies (Figure 8-13).

Providing a warmer emotional climate than that offered by the distant Olympians, the Dionysian Mysteries were extremely popular throughout Greece and Italy. Although Rome's senate banned the Bacchanalia in 186 B.C., the wine god's rites continued to be observed well into the Christian era.

The religion ascribed to Orpheus mediated between the orgiastic passion of Dionysus and the austere control of Apollo, suggesting the essential unity of these ostensibly antithetical deities. Promoting a balance between emotion and intellect, as well as strict personal ethics and thoughtful preparation for the next life, Orphism anticipated many of the doctrines of Christianity. It is not surprising that early Christian artists commonly used the figure of Orpheus—or even Dionysus—to depict their incarnation of the dying and rising god.

HYMN TO DIONYSUS[1]

Author unknown

What I remember now
is Dionysus, son of
glorious Semele, how he appeared
by the sand of an empty sea,
how it was far out, on a promontory, how
he was like a young man,
an adolescent.

     His dark hair
was beautiful, it
blew all around him, and   10
over his shoulders, the strong
shoulders, he held a purple cloak.

     Suddenly,
pirates appeared, Tyrrhenians,
they came on the sea wine
sturdily in their ship
and they came fast.
A wicked fate drove them on.

     They saw him,
they nodded to each other,   20
they leaped out
and grabbed him,
they pulled him
into their boat
jumping for joy!

They thought he was
the son of
one of
Zeus's favorite kings:
they wanted to tie him up   30
hard.

    The ropes wouldn't hold.
     Willow ropes,

---

1. Translation by Charles Boer.

they fell right off him, off
arms and legs.
        He smiled at them,
motionless,
in his dark eyes.

        The helmsman saw this,
he immediately cried out,   40
he screamed out to his men:
        "You fools!
        What powerful god is this
        whom you've seized,
        whom you've tied up?
        Not even our ship,
        sturdy as it is,
        not even our ship
        can carry him.
        Either this is Zeus,   50
        or it's Apollo, the silver-bow,
        or else it's Poseidon!
        He doesn't look like
        a human person,
        he's like the gods
        who live on Olympus.
        Come on!
        Let's unload him, right now,
        let's put him
        on the dark land.   60
        Don't tie his hands
        or he'll be angry, he'll
        draw terrible winds to us,
        he'll bring us a big storm!"
        That's what he said.

The captain, however,
in a bitter voice,
roared back:
        "You fool,
        look at the wind!   70
        Grab the ropes,
        draw the sail.
        We men
        will take care of him.
        I think
        he'll make it to Egypt,
        or Cyprus,
        or to the Hyperboreans,
        or even further.

In the end   80
he'll tell
who his friends are,
and his relatives,
and his possessions.
A god sent him to us."
       He said this,
then he fixed the mast
and the sail of the ship.
And the wind began to blow
into the sail. And then   90
they stretched the rigging.
    Suddenly,
wonderful things
appeared to them.
       First of all,
wine broke out, babbling,
bubbling over their speedy black ship,
it was sweet, it was fragrant,
its odor was divine.
Every sailor who saw it   100
was terrified.
       Suddenly,
a vine sprang up,
on each side,
to the very top of the sail.
And grapes, all over,
clung to it.
And a dark ivy
coiled the mast,
it blossomed with flowers   110
and yielded
pleasing fruit.
       Suddenly,
all the oar-locks
became garlands.
When they saw this
they cried to the helmsman
then and there
to steer their ship
to land.   120
       But
the god became a lion,
an awful lion
high up on the ship,
and he roared at them
terribly.

And then,
in their midst,
he put a bear,
a bear with a furry neck,   130
and it made gestures.
It threatened,
and the lion,
on the high deck,
scowled down.
      Everybody
fled to the stern,
they panicked, they ran
to the helmsman, because
the head of the helmsman was cool.   140
      But
the lion, suddenly,
leaped up, it seized
the captain!
They all wanted to escape
such a doom
when they saw it.
They all jumped ship
into the sea, they jumped
into the divine sea.   150
They became dolphins.
      As for the helmsman,
he was saved:
the god pitied him,
he made him very rich,
and told him this:
   "Courage, divine Hecator,
   I like you.
   I am Dionysus
   the ear-splitter.   160
   My mother,
   Cadmaean Semele,
   had me
   when she slept with Zeus."

      Farewell,
son of Semele,
who had such a beautiful face.
Without you,
the way to compose a sweet song
is forgotten.   170

Questions for Discussion and Review

1. Describe both the similarities and differences between Apollo and Dionysus. In what areas do their attributes overlap?

2. Summarize the story of Dionysus's double birth. Why does myth present this particular god as being twice-born, first from Semele's womb and then from the body of Zeus? How is this double birth thematically related to the Orphic myth that describes the death and rebirth of Dionysus (as Zagreus)?

3. Why do many myths present this god of wine, intoxication, and sensuality as "un-Greek"? Why does myth picture him traveling among foreign nations and afflicted with madness? What does his retinue of satyrs, panthers, maenads, and goats say about Dionysus's connection with both external and human nature?

4. Specify the Orphic variations in Dionysus's myth. How is his ecstatic cult linked to that of Orpheus and Orphism? What do these two figures have in common with each other—or with Apollo?

Recommended Reading

Boer, Charles, trans. *The Homeric Hymns.* Rev. ed. Dallas: Spring Publications, 1979.

Burkert, Walter. *Ancient Mystery Cults.* Cambridge: Harvard UP, 1987. Discusses cults of Dionysus and Orpheus.

Calasso, Roberto. *The Marriage of Cadmus and Harmony.* New York: Knopf, 1993. Includes perceptive commentary on the Greek concept of Apollo and his affinity with Dionysus.

Dodds, E. R. *The Greeks and the Irrational.* Berkeley: U of California, 1951. A standard work on the power of unreason in Greek culture.

Kerenyi, C. *Dionysos: Archetypal Image of Indestructible Life.* Trans. Ralph Manheim. Princeton UP, 1976. A lavishly illustrated study of the wine god.

Land of No Return: The Gloomy Kingdom of Hades

KEY THEMES

Hades and Persephone, King and Queen of the Underworld, rule over a gloomy realm inhabited by fearful monsters and shades of the dead. In the Homeric epics, Hades's subterranean domain is located far to the west, beyond the River of Ocean that encircles the earth's central landmass. The Odyssey pictures Hades's realm, eternally dark and cheerless, as the permanent prison of all dead souls; only a few of Zeus's favorites are sent to the Isles of the Blest (also called Elysium), an earthlike paradise. As Greek concepts of individual responsibility developed over time, however, many poets and philosophers argued that a person's behavior in this life determined one's fate after death. After the sixth century B.C., the old Homeric view of Hades's realm was typically modified to accommodate all righteous souls in Elysium, with the wicked atoning for their crimes in Tartarus. In the "Myth of Er," Plato (c. 427–347 B.C.) employs Orphic teachings symbolically to show the human soul's postmortem experience in a mythic realm populated by Homeric figures and the Fates (Moirae). Plato's contributions to myths about the afterlife form an indispensable link between the Homeric view of Hades (Odyssey, Book 11) and that pictured, seven centuries later, in Virgil's Aeneid (Book 6), which incorporates many Platonic ideas and themes.

The Homeric View of the Afterlife

The Greeks expressed their desire for perpetual youth, beauty, and everlasting life in myths about the gods. By contrast, myths about their heroes revealed a painful awareness of the limits that death imposes on all human striving. The Greek hero's passion to seize every opportunity for fame and individual achievement springs largely from his certainty that every quality he values—strength, good looks, even divine favor—will inevitably be taken from him. The tension between life's unrealized possibilities and the prospect of imminent oblivion in Hades's kingdom casts a chilling shadow across the mythic landscape.

In the *Odyssey,* Homer emphasizes the extreme dread with which his heroes regard the Underworld. When Circe, a wise enchantress, informs Odysseus that he must travel into Hades's realm, in effect, to die before his time, the hero feels his heart shatter within him (*Odyssey,* books 9 and 11). Far from being an escape from earthly woes into a higher realm of light and beauty, death signified only one thing: permanent imprisonment in a dark world utterly devoid of joy, purpose, or hope. In journeying to Hades's realm, Odysseus is forced to confront both the fact of his own mortality and the unspeakable bleakness of the soul's vague and unsatisfying half-life in the netherworld. The ghost of Achilles, once the Greeks' most vital and enviable hero, hastens to assure Odysseus that he would rather be a poor man's living slave than king of all the dead.

Writing in the sixth century B.C., the lyric poet Anacreon contemplated his own fear of death with similar pessimism:

> for the lightless chasm of death is dreadful
> and the descent appalling: once cast down into [Hades], there is no return.
>   (Barnstone 127)

The Homeric picture of Hades, which gave the Greeks their oldest and most influential view of the afterlife, underscores both the finality of death and the impossibility of any satisfying contact between the living and the dead. Illustrating the unbridgeable gap between the two, Homer describes Odysseus reaching out to embrace the shade (disembodied spirit) of his mother, Anticleia, only to find that he can no more grasp her shadowy form than his hands can hold a puff of smoke. Death, personified as **Thanatos** [THAN-a-tohs], severs even the closest ties of kinship and affection.

While depriving the soul of substance, death simultaneously impairs memory, reason, and will. The throng of souls that gather near Odysseus are witless, gibbering specters until they are allowed to drink sacrificial blood, which temporarily restores their mental faculties and ability to speak. Following Circe's instructions, Odysseus performs an elaborate chthonic ritual intended to summon the dead and briefly establish communication with them. The long trench he digs functions as both a symbolic grave and a boundary separating the realms of life and death, a frontier that neither the living nor the dead may cross. Into the trench Odysseus pours a mixed libation (ceremonial drink offering) representing the earth's bounty, such as honey, grain, and wine, as well as the blood of black rams, animals peculiarly sacred to Hades. A belief that blood is the essence of life was widespread in the ancient world. As the Book of Leviticus declares, "The life of the soul [living creature] is in the blood." Dead souls hunger for it.

The first soul whom Odysseus encounters is that of Elpenor, one of his men who had recently been killed by falling off Circe's roof (see Figure 12-8). Elpenor begs Odysseus to give him proper burial, without which no soul can find peace. So important was the Greek conviction that funeral ceremonies were indispensable in securing posthumous rest, that Oedipus's daughter Antigone will risk her life to perform final rites for her brother Polyneices (Chapter 16). This obligation to the dead also spurs Priam, king of Troy, to brave Achilles's wrath to retrieve the body of his son Hector (Chapter 11).

The Location and Geography of Hades's Realm

In Homer's account, Odysseus reaches Hades by sailing westward across the River of Ocean, earth's far boundary where sky's vault touches the ground and the sun sinks into darkness (Chapter 3). Odysseus's journey to the land of the dead, traversing a foggy, desolate waste, roughly parallels that of Gilgamesh to the faraway island retreat of the Sumerian king's immortal ancestor Utnapishtim. The Homeric concept of the afterlife, in fact, strikingly resembles older Mesopotamian beliefs about the Underworld: the ghost of Enkidu informs his friend Gilgamesh that departed souls mourn forever in a mildew- and worm-infested dungeon.

The Hebrew Bible (Old Testament) paints a similarly grim picture: all the dead, both good and bad, are permanently housed in an underground region called *Sheol,* a Hebrew counterpart of the Homeric Hades. Reduced to impotent shadows or wraiths (called *repaim*), the dead languish in mindless inactivity. As if he were paraphrasing Achilles's pessimism, the author of Ecclesiastes argues that it is better to be "a live dog" than a "dead lion," "because in *Sheol* [Hades], for which you are bound, there is neither doing nor thinking, neither understanding nor wisdom" (Eccles. 9:5, 10).

Over the centuries, numerous poets contributed to myths about Hades, providing more detailed aspects of its topography. Five great subterranean rivers were said to encompass or flow through the Underworld: the **Styx** (Abhorent) is Hades's principal stream, personified by a river goddess, a daughter of Ocean, who sided with Zeus in his battle with the Titans. As a result, Zeus honored her by decreeing that an oath invoking the Styx was inviolable, even by the gods. The **Acheron** [AK-e-rahn] (Distress), like the Styx, is commonly represented as Hades's official boundary across which all souls pass on the way to their allotted places below.

Cocytus [koh-SYE-tuhs] (Lament), variously defined as a branch of the Acheron or Styx, and **Phlegethon** or Pyriphlegethon (Fire Flaming) are the two other rivers Greek myth placed in Hades. In Plato's "Myth of Er," a mystical vision of the afterlife that concludes his *Republic,* the philosopher adds a "river of unmindfulness" that runs through a plain named Lethe. Roman poets later made **Lethe** [LEE-thee] (Oblivion) the name of Hades's fifth river. Drinking Lethe's waters caused souls about to be reincarnated in new bodies to forget their past lives and sufferings (Chapter 19, Virgil's *Aeneid*). The Christian poet Dante borrowed the four Greek rivers to intersect his *Inferno* and relocated Lethe atop the Mount of Purgatory so that purified souls could drink its waters to erase all memory of sin before ascending to heaven.

Elysium

In the *Odyssey,* Homer briefly refers to **Elysium** [e-LIZ-ih-uhm], a garden of earthly delights located far to the west at the extreme edge of the world, an Eden to which Zeus sends a very few of his particular favorites. Homer cites Menelaus as one of the isles' future inhabitants, not because Agamemnon's brother is virtuous, but because he is married to Helen, the beautiful daughter that Zeus, in the shape of a swan, had

FIGURE 9-1   Hades and Persephone. This vase painting shows Hades and Persephone, King and Queen of the Underworld, in a pose typical of Greek domestic life, as if they were an ordinary couple. The implications of Hades's extending a bowl toward his wife, as if inviting her to partake, are paradoxical: because Demeter's inexperienced daughter accepted hospitality—in the form of pomegranate seeds (the symbol of marriage)—from Hades, she was forced to remain in his gloomy kingdom for part of each year (see Chapter 4). Hades's bowl, however, is also a cornucopia (or Horn of Plenty), a symbol of riches—gold and gems—excavated from his subterranean realm. While dreaded as lord of the dead, Hades was also honored as Pluto, god of wealth. (*British Museum, London.*)

sired by Leda. This mythic paradise, which was later also known as the **Elysian Fields,** echoes the Mesopotamian myth of Dilmun, an Edenic island where some heroic souls could posthumously continue to enjoy life's sensual pleasures.

Residents of Hades's Domain

Hades, also called *Aidoneus,* the invisible or unseen one, represents the universality of death's hold on humanity. His queen, Persephone, whom the *Homeric Hymn to Demeter* originally associates with flowers and other emblems of youthful beauty (Chapter 4), comes to share her husband's pitilessness (Figure 9-1). Enforcing death's utter finality, the couple permits no one (except a few heroes) to escape Hades's confines. The rare myths in which the two rulers allow a shade to return to earth, as when the poet Orpheus persuades them to release his beloved wife, Eurydice, only serve to highlight the bitter inevitability of loss.

Besides reflecting the natural law condemning all that lives to perish, the kingdom of Hades also encompasses childlike fears of monsters and other bogeymen that lurk

FIGURE 9-2 Charon. As depicted in this vase painting, Charon is the mythical figure symbolizing the soul's transition from life to death. Described as hideous and frightening, he is the sole means of transporting the newly dead across the Styx or Acheron, subterranean rivers marking the boundaries of the Underworld. Reluctantly, he ferries a few bold heroes, such as Heracles and Aeneas, across waters separating the worlds of light and darkness. (*National Museum, Athens.*)

in the dark. **Cerberus** [SER-ber-uhs], the hound of hell, is a three-headed (or fifty-headed) dog with a mane (or tail) of snakes who guards the Underworld's entrance. The **Furies** (Erinyes), generated from the blood of Uranus's castration, have their home here, as does, in later myth, **Eurynomos** [oo-RIH-noh-mohs], a demonic figure associated with death and decay. Even more images of pain and terror appear in the nightmare abyss of Tartarus (see below).

In contrast to Homer, who represented the dead as being admitted directly to the Plain of Asphodel (a dreary region dotted with funereal plants related to the iris family), later mythographers emphasized the soul's symbolic crossing of Hades's watery frontier. **Charon** [KA-rohn], a hideous creature whose job is to ferry souls across the Styx or Acheron (Figure 9-2), demands a monetary fee for his services. (Because souls unable to pay were not allowed to cross over, the Greeks had a custom of burying the dead with coins in their hands or mouths.)

Less frightening in appearance, but equally intimidating to the newly dead, are

FIGURE 9-3   A Warrior's Departing Soul. This vase painting (c. 510 B.C.) shows the three figures traditionally associated with the soul's transference from earthly life to the Underworld. The winged figures Thanatos (Death) and Hypnos (Sleep) carry the body of Sarpedon, a hero of the *Iliad*. Hermes, in his role of Psychopompos (Guide of Souls), appears in the center. (*Metropolitan Museum of Art, New York.*)

the figures of Minos, a legendary ruler of Minoan Crete, and his brother **Rhadamanthus.** Renowned for their justice, after their deaths they are appointed judges in the netherworld. Plato adds a third judge, Aeacus, a son of Zeus famous for his piety. As originally conceived, these magistrates function primarily to assign souls their respective positions in Hades's domain or to arbitrate their futile quarrels. In later times, when writers began to distinguish between the respective fates of good and evil persons, Minos and Rhadamanthus determined whether a soul enjoyed the bliss of Elysium or the agony of Tartarus.

Thanatos's (Death's) twin brother **Hypnos** (Sleep) also inhabits the Underworld. A fatherless child of Night, he is commonly depicted as a winged youth who pours soporific liquid from a horn or gently touches the weary with a branch. Generally regarded as friendly toward humans, Hypnos appears in Greek funerary art as a kindly figure helping to carry souls of the recently dead to the next world (Figure 9-3). His son **Morpheus,** the god of dreams, often visits sleepers in human shape, sometimes conveying messages from the dead.

Although not a resident of Hades, Hermes is associated with the Underworld because of his role as Psychopompos, the guide of souls to their final abode (Fig-

(a)   (b)

FIGURE 9-4   Charon, Hermes, and the Soul of a Woman. In this vase painting, the artist
depicts Hermes (Psychopompos), guide of the recently dead, conducting the soul of a young
woman (a) to Charon's boat (b). Because the ancient Greeks believed that Charon demanded
a fee for his services, corpses were commonly buried or cremated with a coin in their mouths.
Shades (disembodied spirits) without the necessary payment—or those whose bodies had not
been properly buried—were denied passage, preventing them from finding peace in the netherworld. According to one tradition, when Charon refused to transport someone, the person's
ghost was condemned to wander disconsolately for a hundred years before it found rest. (*Staatliche Antikensammlungen, Munich.*)

ure 9-4). An embodiment of fluid movement, Hermes easily crosses the boundaries
separating the living and the dead. Escorting both newly deceased souls and a few
living heroes on their visits to Hades's kingdom, Hermes became known as a repositor
of occult secrets, a source of arcane knowledge about the afterlife.

Tartarus

In Hesiod's *Theogony,* Tartarus is both an elemental deity by whom Gaea conceives
Typhoeus (Typhon) and an amorphous cosmic cellar in which the fallen Titans are
chained in oppressive darkness. Described as lying as far beneath Hades as Olympus
is above the earth, Tartarus is an almost bottomless pit of anguish and despair, a
divine torture chamber foreshadowing popular Christian notions of hell.

Notorious Sinners

During his visit to the Underworld, Odysseus witnesses the sufferings inflicted on three archetypal criminals: Tityus, Tantalus, and Sisyphus, all of whom post-Homeric tradition incarcerated in Tartarus. A giant son of Gaea, Tityus attempted to rape Leto, the mother of Apollo and Artemis. For this sacrilege, he is punished by being spread-eagled on the ground and having two vultures continually feed on his liver (then believed to be the locus of sexual passion). His punishment, identical to that of Prometheus, is also an emasculation, a stripping of power and virility from one who impiously tried to compete with Zeus.

Odysseus also sees **Tantalus,** a son of Zeus who became king of Lydia, afflicted with intolerable hunger and thirst. Although standing in a pool of water, he is unable to slake his thirst because every time he lowers his head to drink, the water level recedes. Similarly, when he reaches toward the fruit growing above his head, the branches move just beyond his grasp. Experiencing insatiable desire that is eternally unsatisfied, Tantalus lends his name to the English verb *tantalize* (to tease or frustrate by appearing to promise something that is never given).

Myth gives several different accounts of Tantalus's crime. In one version, Tantalus, living at the dawn of time when humans dined with gods, abused Olympian hospitality by stealing ambrosia and giving it to undeserving mortals. In another account, Tantalus irresponsibly divulged secrets gleaned from divine tabletalk. In the most common variant, Tantalus is said to have tested divine omniscience by serving the gods the flesh of his son **Pelops** [PEE-lahps]. Only Demeter, distracted by her grief for Persephone, ate part of Pelops's body (his shoulder), which Zeus replaced with gleaming ivory when he restored the boy to life. In this version of the myth, Tantalus, for his sin of cannibalism, must suffer from a ravenous appetite that is never satisfied, making him a prime example of the gods' retributive justice.

Odysseus also sees **Sisyphus** [SIS-ih-fuhs] (reputed founder of the city of Corinth), who is forced to roll a huge stone uphill, only to have it roll back again, so that he must endlessly repeat a painfully strenuous and meaningless act (Figure 9-5). Like Tityus and Tantalus, Sisyphus was a trickster who tried to dupe or outwit the gods. When Sisyphus was alive, he betrayed Zeus by revealing one of his seductions, provoking the Olympian to send Thanatos (Death) to haul him off to Hades. Sisyphus, however, succeeded in overpowering Thanatos and chaining him so that mortals ceased to die. After Ares released Thanatos, Sisyphus was dragged into the Underworld, but not before he instructed his wife not to bury his body but to leave it in the street. His powers of deception undiminished, Sisyphus next persuaded Hades and Persephone to permit him to return to earth to punish his negligent wife. As soon as he arrived aboveground, Sisyphus refused to return, frustrating death by living to a ripe old age. The gods of course have the last laugh, ingeniously devising a torment that mocks his ephemeral victory over Thanatos.

A fourth notorious sinner, **Ixion** dared to assault Hera, as if to take Zeus's place in heaven. For his arrogance, Ixion is bound to a fiery wheel, which rolls perpetually through the air (Figure 9-6). Whereas these four are prototypes of human error, in later myth, the ordinary inhabitant of Tartarus is a human soul, sent thence to be purged of the qualities that spawned evil deeds or, in some extreme cases, to endure eternal punishment.

FIGURE 9-5   Sisyphus in Tartarus. In book 11 of the *Odyssey*, Homer describes the post-mortem torments of a few souls who have directly offended the gods. The reputed founder of Corinth, Sisyphus was notorious for his cunning, which included a successful plot to outwit Death and live to a ripe old age. When he finally dies, the gods condemn him to roll a huge boulder uphill, only to have it roll down again just before it reaches the top. This exercise in obsessive futility painfully illustrates the gods' treatment of those who attempt to thwart natural law: human ingenuity can no more forestall death than a falling boulder can escape the force of gravity. (*Vatican Museums, Rome.*)

Descents into the Underworld

In Greco-Roman myth, only a tiny handful of the most esteemed heroes succeed in reaching—and returning alive from—the House of Hades. In virtually every case, tales of a descent into the netherworld (katabasis) form one episode in a long chain of events involving the hero's learning to overcome fear and endure pain. Odysseus and Heracles are both famous for undergoing trials that severely test their courage and resourcefulness. Confronting the ultimate challenge—death's negation of all human achievement—not only places the hero's life in perspective, but also enables him to experience symbolic annihilation and rebirth. Odysseus and Aeneas (a Trojan prince), in particular, emerge from Hades's realm with a renewed sense of purpose that allows them either to reclaim a patrimony (Odysseus) or to found a new homeland (Aeneas), thus successfully completing their predestined lifework.

A hero's worthiness to face death without being destroyed is typically linked to the presence of an Olympian protector: Athene's intelligence supports Heracles and Odysseus, while Aphrodite (Venus) inspires her son Aeneas to negotiate the chthonic perils of Hades. Love (Eros) is also the force that motivates Orpheus, the first musi-

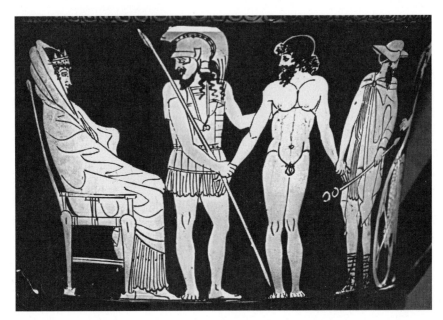

FIGURE 9-6   Hera Condemning Ixion. Like Sisyphus, Ixion was a trickster who presumed to acquire prerogatives reserved only for the gods. After Ixion tried to rape Hera—thereby taking over Zeus's place—he was affixed to an iron wheel that whirled aimlessly through the dark abyss, an image of human impotence when pitted against divine power. (*British Museum, London.*)

cian and poet, to rescue his dead wife, Eurydice, from Hades's prison. It is also a form of love that drives Dionysus, then still mortal, to retrieve his mother, Semele, from Hades (Chapter 8).

The Descent of Heracles

Odysseus's last conversation in the Underworld is with Heracles, the strongest, bravest, and longest-suffering of all Greek heroes. Although hailing Odysseus as a fellow hero, Heracles pointedly reminds him that in life he (Heracles) had already accomplished a much more difficult descent. The last of Heracles's Twelve Labors requires him to kidnap Cerberus (Figure 9-7) and exhibit the hellhound to his cowardly master, Eurystheus. Like Odysseus, before his journey, Heracles sought the guidance of an earth-goddess figure and was initiated into the Mysteries of Demeter at Eleusis, where he was taught the means of safely traversing Death's kingdom (see Chapter 10).

   Although most traditions state categorically that no Olympian ever sets foot in Hades, in the Heracles myth both Athene and Hermes (Victorious Wisdom and Safe Travel) act as his guides. As Psychopompos (Guide of Souls), Hermes normally withdraws to Olympus immediately after depositing souls at Hades's portals. According to Apollodorus, however, on this occasion he remains at Heracles's side, reminding him that monsters he encounters, such as the Gorgon Medusa, are shadows cast by his own fears. With divinely inspired courage, Heracles dares to face Hades (Pluto)

FIGURE 9-7 Heracles
Capturing Cerberus. As
his last and most chal-
lenging labor, Heracles
descends into the Under-
world to subdue Cerberus,
the savage three-headed
hound that guards the en-
trance to Hades. By bringing Cerberus into the
upper world, Heracles at-
tains the extreme limits of
heroism, braving the terrors
of death and demonstrating
that human courage and
intelligence—when sup-
ported by the gods (Athene
and Hermes act as his
guides)—may accomplish
the impossible. Heracles's
successful quest, carried out
with divine aid and ap-
proval, contrasts strongly
with the prideful ambitions
of Sisyphus, Ixion, and
Tantalus. (*Louvre, Paris.*)

himself, winning the implacable god's permission to take Cerberus—on the condition that he use none of his usual weapons.

Heracles not only performs unprecedented feats of strength, such as capturing
Cerberus with his bare hands, but also exercises his equally notable compassion to
free several heroes from Hades's prison. Besides rescuing Theseus (see below), he
releases Apollo's son, Asclepius, allowing the master physician's healing influence
again to benefit humanity at such shrines as Epidaurus.

Although he escapes Hades with Cerberus in tow, Heracles must obey universal
law in returning there after his death. As Homer observes, however, Heracles differs
from all other Underworld inhabitants: his image remains below, but his real self,
or soul, ascends to join his father and other gods on Mount Olympus. Homer does
not pursue the implications of Heracles's dual nature, his paradoxical sharing of
both human death and Olympian immortality. By placing Heracles's appearance last
in Odysseus's Underworld experience, however, Homer indirectly anticipates later
philosophic speculations about humanity's duality, its division into a perishable body
and deathless spirit, views that shape later hopes of Elysium.

The Descent of Theseus

Theseus, a legendary king of Athens who supposedly lived in Minoan times, is the rare example of a hero who dared to enter Hades's kingdom from unworthy motives—and with disastrous consequences. The Athenian hero, whose father was Poseidon, was the devoted friend of **Pirithous** [pye-RITH-oh-uhs], a mortal son of Zeus. Because they were both the offspring of gods, they decided that only daughters of Zeus would make acceptable wives. After abducting Helen from Sparta and finding that she was too young to marry, Theseus and Pirithous descended into Hades's realm for the purpose of kidnaping Persephone. While in the Underworld searching for its queen, the heroes accepted an invitation to dine with Hades, who lived up to his reputation as a host who makes all visitors permanently welcome. Seated at the banquet, they found that they were immobilized in their chairs, unable to rise. Not until Heracles arrived in the netherworld was Theseus released, and then he lost part of his buttocks when Heracles literally tore him from his seat, a crude surgery that reputedly accounted for the prevalence of slim hips among later Athenian youths. Theseus's tragedy is that he returned to life without the person he loved best: the gods denied Pirithous permission to leave, imprisoning him forever in the chair of oblivion. Like Gilgamesh and Achilles, Theseus suffered deprivation of his alter ego, condemned to exist without a beloved companion whose presence had alone given meaning to heroic adventure.

The Descent of Orpheus

The descent myth that has had the most enduring influence—commemorated for millennia in Western art, religion, and philosophy—is that of **Orpheus** [OR-fee-uhs], who entered Hades's realm to retrieve his adored wife, **Eurydice** [oo-RIH-dih-see], who had died of a poisonous snakebite. A mortal figure who combines elements of rational Apollo and ecstatic Dionysus, Orpheus is the archetypal creative artist, expressing powerful emotion in poetry of irresistible beauty. When Orpheus performs on his lyre, given him by Apollo, the entire world is captivated by his song: gods, mortals, wild animals, and even stones respond joyously (Figure 9-8). In the still darkness of death's lair, Orpheus's music charms Hades's fiercest monsters, including Cerberus and the Furies, who quietly let him pass. Singing of his love for Eurydice, Orpheus reduces Hades and Persephone to tears, winning their permission to take back his wife—provided he does not look at or speak to her until after they have emerged into the world of light.

Orpheus's fatal error is as inevitable as Adam's tasting the forbidden fruit or Pandora's opening the jar of woes. His loss of Eurydice is final (Figure 9-9) and poignantly illustrates the Greeks' realistic assessment of such romantic notions as Love (Eros) having the power to overcome Death (Thanatos).

Although Orpheus is primarily identified with Apollo's lucidity and musicality, his story after losing Eurydice parallels events in Dionysus's myth, including a violent death by sparagmos and eventual deification. According to one tradition, after discovering how cruelly the universe fails to honor or protect married love, Orpheus renounces women and devotes himself to winning the young men of Thrace, who flock to hear him play (see Figure 13-7). Furious at Orpheus's neglect, some Thracian women followers of Dionysus attack the poet, tearing him apart and scattering his

FIGURE 9-8 Orpheus Charming Wild Beasts with His Singing. A personification of musical skill, Orpheus was the world's most effective, if not first, poet. Accompanying his singing on the lyre, he charmed the gods, reduced wild animals to peaceful contemplation (as shown in this Roman mosaic), and even persuaded Hades and Persephone to release his beloved Eurydice from the confines of death. Orpheus's ability to create beauty and tame animal instincts, as well as his descent into the Underworld, made him the subject of a religious cult, Orphism, that initiated converts into the rites and purifications necessary to achieve happiness in the afterlife. (*National Museum, Palermo.*)

body parts over the earth. Even when severed from his body and cast into the sea, however, the poet's head remains fully alive and—still singing—washes ashore on the island of Lesbos. While Apollo preserves the miraculously vital head from harm and Dionysus punishes his murderous followers by turning them into oak trees, the gods agree to validate Orpheus's incomparable musicianship by transforming his lyre into the constellation Lyra and granting his soul immortality in Elysium.

Because he had penetrated the mysteries of the Underworld and overcome its terrors, Orpheus was regarded as a source of esoteric knowledge about the afterlife. A whole body of poems and hymns, known as the Orphic literature, was (falsely) ascribed to him, including mythological texts about the world's origins and about Dionysus's rebirth after the Titans had dismembered and eaten him (Chapter 8). Orphic poetry not only influenced Dionysian mystery cults but also promised initiates help after death, offering magic spells, secret passwords, and ritual practices that enabled newly deceased souls to find safe passage through Hades's dangerous paths. Persons initiated into these mysteries were sometimes buried with gold leaves inscribed with the formulae necessary to answer correctly when brought before an underworld tribunal over which Persephone, queen of the nether region, presided.

Most modern scholars believe that **Orphism** was less a formal religion than a highly diverse set of occult beliefs and practices based on Orphic literature. In Orphic teaching, humankind, formed from the ashes of Titans who had murdered and consumed the young Dionysus, bore a collective guilt for this primal crime, a contamination that had to be cleansed through ritual purification. Paralleling the doctrines of the philosopher Pythagoras (sixth century B.C.), Orphism fostered a belief in metempsychosis—that the soul underwent a series of rebirths in new bodies, pursuing a quest for spiritual cleansing that would eventually permit its escape from the wheel of reincarnation. In this view, the netherworld became a place of ultimate regeneration.

FIGURE 9-9   Hermes, Eurydice, and Orpheus. This bas-relief captures the moment at which Orpheus, having won Hades's permission to bring his beloved wife, Eurydice, back to the living world, breaks the prohibition not to look back at her until they have safely reached earth's sunlit surface. Hermes immediately appears to reclaim the veiled Eurydice, whose right arm he grasps. The most creative of all musicians, whose art even the gods admire, fails to overcome the iron grip of death. Orpheus does, however, benefit others by the arcane knowledge he acquires of the afterlife, establishing a mystery cult whose rituals purify the soul and prepare it for a safe journey to Elysium. (*Louvre, Paris.*)

Evolving Ideas about the Afterlife

For all its gloom, even the Homeric Underworld depicts the soul as too important to suffer extinction at death, granting it a tenuous survival and some retention of individual identity. This view of Hades pictures it as a Freudian or Jungian dreamlike state in which disembodied souls, like sleepers caught in a nightmare, experience a paralysis that renders them unable to control their actions or environment. Souls float helplessly amid flickering shadows, insubstantial as clouds that dissolve and re-form without purpose or volition. For Homer, death is being trapped in a murky dreamland where the rational will loses all ability to make choices or influence events.

Greek ideas about the afterlife, however, changed significantly over time. In Book 11 of Homer's *Odyssey,* except for some notorious sinners, all of the dead are housed indiscriminately in a dank cave, with no hope of seeing light again. By contrast, in Book 6 of Virgil's *Aeneid,* written approximately seven hundred years later, souls are assigned qualitatively different fates, with the virtuous enjoying a splendidly illuminated paradise and the wicked unspeakable torment. During the centuries between Homer and Virgil, Greek philosophers such as Pythagoras, Socrates, and Plato transformed beliefs about the spirit world, the nature of the human soul, and the ethical purpose of life.

Plato's "Myth of Er"

Probably the most important single influence on evolving Greek views of the afterlife was the Athenian philosopher Plato (427–347 B.C.; Figure 9-10). In dialogues such as the *Phaedo* and the *Phaedrus,* Plato argued that the human soul originates in heaven but descends to earth as a kind of fall from grace, where it is trapped in a corruptible physical body. The human being is consequently a duality composed of an invisible immortal soul and a material body tied to the natural processes of change and death. In the "Myth of Er," a mystical narrative that concludes the *Republic,* Plato offers his most complete picture of what happens to the soul after death releases it from the body. An extended parable of eschatological justice, the myth draws heavily on Orphic doctrines involving purification and regeneration. Er, who narrates the tale, is a soldier who is seemingly killed in battle and for ten days lies in a comatose state during which his soul leaves his body and journeys to a spiritual realm where the recently dead gather for judgment. In Er's near-death experience, which strikingly resembles similar reports published in this century, he witnesses the mysterious process of reincarnation in which souls choose their new lives on earth. After spending their allotted time, either in heaven or a place of torment, souls reassemble at the plain or meadow where fates are decided. Some persons who have experienced a thousand years of bliss in heaven choose unwisely because they had been virtuous merely from habit, not from philosophic conviction. Others, having painfully learned the value of righteousness from having endured a millennium of punishment for previous misdeeds, select a worthy new life. Mythic characters appear to illustrate some principles that determine individual choices: Orpheus, disgusted with human love, decides to become a swan. Odysseus, weary of laboring for distinction, chooses to return as an ordinary obscure person. In Plato's universe, the gods, symbols of

FIGURE 9-10 Plato. One of the world's most influential thinkers, Plato used myths from the Orphic tradition to provide symbols for his vision of the soul's fate after death. Plato's "Myth of Er"—which includes an account of the soul's reincarnation in new bodies to continue a necessary process of learning and purification—provided a view of human destiny that Virgil adopted in the *Aeneid* (see Chapter 19).

perfect virtue, are not responsible for human folly or wickedness or the suffering it brings: each soul freely adopts its own destiny.

Plato's contribution to myths about the netherworld forms an indispensable link connecting the Homeric view of Hades and the more sophisticated picture given in Virgil's *Aeneid.* Virgil (70–19 B.C.) follows Plato not only in assuming an essential polarity in human nature—the body/soul dichotomy—but also in portraying an afterlife in which souls are spiritually cleansed before returning to earth in new bodies. Combining mystical and ethical values, Virgil paints a complex Hades that is compartmentalized into contrasting regions such as Elysium and Tartarus, each representing a positive or negative aspect of the human psyche (Chapter 19). (Compare Odysseus's journey to Hades's kingdom in Chapter 12, pp. 394–405, and Aeneas's descent to the Underworld in Chapter 19, pp. 848–860.)

Christianity, which inherited many of its concepts from Greco-Roman tradition, also contributed to the mythic theme of descent into the Underworld. According to the New Testament, after his crucifixion, Jesus of Nazareth descended into Tartarus, preaching to spirits imprisoned in its darkness (1 Peter 3:19, 2 Peter 2:4). From these brief passages, a belief developed that Jesus entered the netherworld on Good Friday to rescue the souls of righteous persons who had died before he ascended and opened the way to heaven. In medieval theology, this doctrine was known as the *harrowing of hell.*

Color Plate 1 Sandro Botticelli, *Birth of Venus*, c. 1480. Botticelli's graceful and modest Venus (the Roman name for Aphrodite) floats serenely on her shell, gently propelled by the Zephyrs, embodiments of the west wind, whose breezes waft her toward the shore, and attended by one of the Hours (holding a robe to cloak the goddess as soon as she arrives) who presides over her birth. The painting may have been inspired by written accounts of a lost work from ancient Greece, the Aphrodite Anadyomene (Aphrodite Rising from the Sea) by Apelles, an artist at the court of Alexander the Great. Apelles's picture, in turn, ultimately derives from Hesiod's description of the love goddesses's origin in the *Theogony* (see Chapter 3). (*Uffizi, Florence.*)

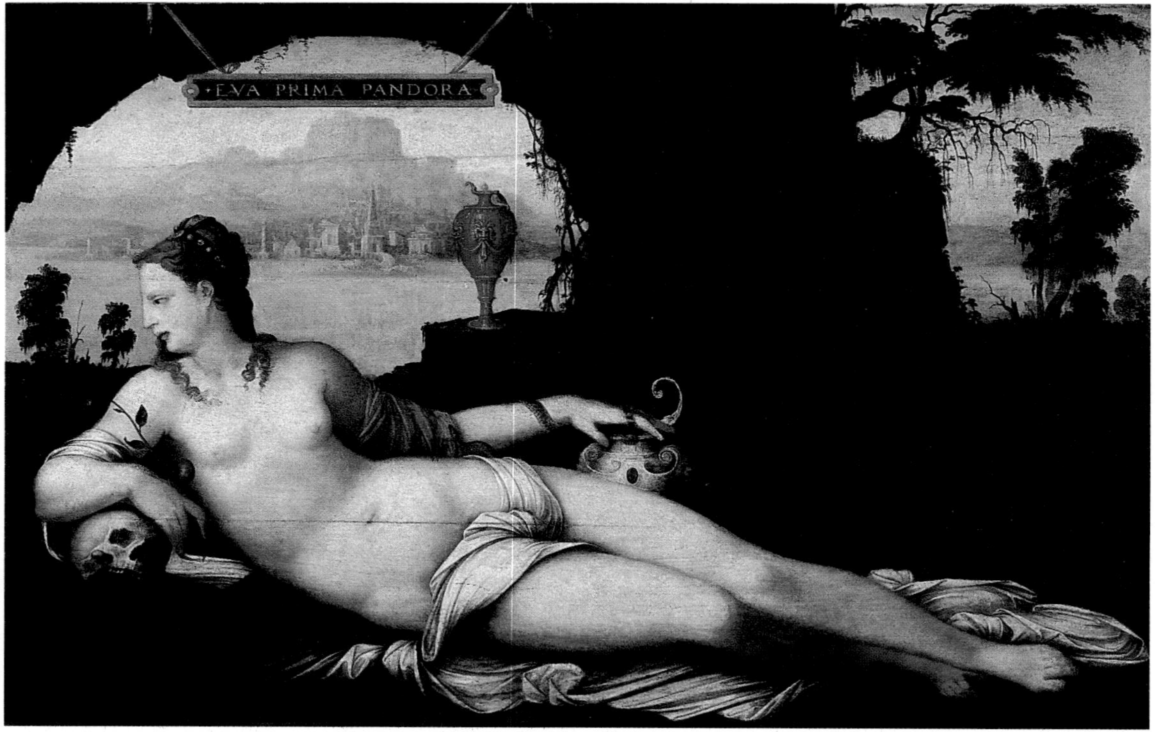

Color Plate 2 Jean Cousin the Elder, *Eva Prima Pandora*, 1538. Cousin's painting explicitly identifies the biblical first woman, Eve, whose eating of forbidden fruit causes humanity's Fall from grace, with "the first Pandora," the primal human female whom the Greek gods created to plague mankind and bring the paradisal Golden Age to an end. With one hand on her jar (containing both blessings and woes), and the other on a skull (grim symbol of human mortality), she contemplates the paradox of her creation: all life's gifts (and potential evils) that belong to the material world reside in her jar; their release will introduce the bewildering mixture of pain and pleasure, strife and death, that Hesiod says have characterized human existence ever since woman's initial appearance on earth (see Chapter 6). (*Louvre, Paris.*)

Color Plate 3 Jacopo Tintoretto, *The Origin of the Milky Way*. The Venetian painter Tintoretto (1518–1594) here captures a crucial moment in Greek myth, one involving both the perennial power struggle between Zeus (Jupiter) and Hera (Juno) and a cosmic phenomenon, the birth of a new galaxy. Set in Hera's celestial boudoir, this scene depicts the startled Queen of Heaven leaping from her bed just as Zeus's messenger Hermes (Mercury) (top right) places the infant Heracles (Hercules) at the sleeping goddess's breast, causing her milk to jet skyward, igniting a fountain of sparkling stars (see Chapter 5). Hera's angry rejection of Zeus's illegitimate child, born to a human mother, Alcmene, thwarts her husband's attempt to render Heracles immortal by absorbing divine nourishment from his wife and condemns the hero to a life of hardship and pain (see Chapter 10). Hera's sacred bird, the watchful peacock, occupies the lower right corner, while Zeus is symbolically present in the form of his eagle with a thunderbolt in its claws. (*National Gallery, London.*)

Color Plate 4 Thomas Hart Benton, *Persephone*, 1938. In this updating of the ancient myth of Persephone's abduction by Hades, an American painter depicts Demeter's virgin daughter as an innocently voluptuous (and vulnerable) figure in a rural midwestern setting, unconsciously inciting the lust of the Underworld's ruler, here shown as a lecherous voyeur about to intrude on the young woman's serenity. The transformation of an as-yet unawakened maiden associated with nature's gentle flowering into Hades's wife and grim queen of the netherworld is about to begin. (*The Nelson-Atkins Museum of Art, Kansas City, Missouri. Purchase acquired through the Yellow Freight Foundation Art Acquisition Fund and the generosity of Mrs. Herbert O. Peet, Richard J. Stern, the Doris Jones Stein Foundation, the Jacob L. and Ella C. Loose Foundation, Mr. and Mrs. Richard M. Levin, and Mr. and Mrs. Marvin Rich. © 1997 T. H. Benton and R. P. Benton Testamentary Trusts/Licensed by VAGA, New York, NY.*)

Color Plate 5   Jean-Auguste-Dominique Ingres, *Jupiter and Thetis,* 1811. Ingres's neoclassical painting employs the heroic themes characteristic of the Roman revival popular during the Napoleanic era in France. A rather stern and upright Jupiter stares straight ahead,
maintaining his composure, though seemingly annoyed by Thetis's request that he assist
Achilles in that hero's defiance of Agamemnon. Jupiter's determination to see his ultimate
commitment to order prevail is suggested by the god's angry-looking eagle at the right, balanced by the figure of Juno (Hera) at the left. Jupiter's foot, extended slightly over the base
of the throne, rests over a bas-relief depicting the battle of gods and giants, as if, having once
established order, he must now put his foot down and do so again. The pyramidal form of
the composition, with its apex at Jupiter's head, reinforces the painting's insistence on Jupiter
as the enforcer of cosmic order. (*Musée Granet, Palais de Malte, Aix-en-Provence, France.*)

Color Plate 6 Peter Paul Rubens, *The Judgment of Paris*, c. 1633–1635. Unlike his earlier version of the same subject, in which Rubens placed the victorious Venus at the center, this painting shows a young Paris gazing admiringly at Venus (the middle of the three goddesses), who returns his look as he extends the apple. But while Minerva (Athene) on the left and Juno (Hera) on the right look on in apparent detachment, their bodies curve away from the enraptured shepherd. In typical Baroque counterpoint to this seemingly calm scene complete with grazing sheep, it is Juno who, despite losing the contest, occupies the physical center of the canvas. Juno's peacock makes menacing gestures at Paris's sleeping dog, while the curve of the peacock's tail begins a visual sweep upward through the light clouds between the trees where we find Allecto, the Fury, watching the action below in anticipation of the disastrous consequences of Paris's choice. That motif is echoed in the war helmet temporarily laid aside by Minerva, along with her shield, which bears the contorted face of the Gorgon Medusa. (*National Gallery, London.*)

Color Plate 7   Perseus Frees Andromeda. In this wall painting from the House of the
Dioscuri in Pompeii, the hero Perseus, son of Zeus and the mortal Danae, releases
Andromeda, a princess of Ethiopia, from the rock where she had been chained as a sacri-
fice to a ravenous sea monster (lower right). In his hand, Perseus carries the head of the
Gorgon Medusa that he uses to petrify his opponents and a scimitar given him by the god
Hermes, who has also loaned the hero his winged footwear. According to variants of this
myth, Perseus was also temporarily given a cap of invisibility by Hades, a mirror by
Athene (so that he could avoid looking directly at Medusa and thereby escape being
turned to stone), and a special bag by the nymphs in which to keep the severed head.
Favored by the gods, the hero thus temporarily acquired divine attributes while battling
against injustice or other evils. (*Museo Archeologico Nazionale, Naples.*)

Color Plate 8   Attic Red Figure Crater from Orvieto, c. 450 B.C. Except for the figures of Athene, wearing a warrior's helmet and carrying a spear (left), and Heracles, wearing a lion skin and holding a club (center), easily identifiable by their characteristic insignia or apparel, scholars disagree on the identities of the other figures. Although commonly described as a scene depicting the Argonauts who accompanied Jason on his quest for the Golden Fleece, the painting may in fact represent Heracles's decent into the Underworld. If so, the two seated heroes are Theseus and his friend Pirithous, who had rashly invaded Hades's realm to abduct Persephone as a wife for Pirithous (see Chapter 9). (*Louvre, Paris.*)

MYTH OF ER

(from the *Republic*)

Plato

[Several other dialogues (*Gorgias, Phaedo, Phaedrus*) describe the fate of the soul before birth and after death in the poetical imagery of myth, since no certain knowledge is attainable, but Plato believed that the indestructible soul must reap the consequences of its deeds, good or bad. Unlike Dante, he leaves the scenery and topography of the other world fluid and vague. Probably some details are borrowed from dramatic representations or *tableaux vivants* shown to initiates in Orphic and other Mysteries.[1] Features common to Plato's myths and to Empedocles' religious poem, Pindar's *Dirges,* Orphic amulets found in graves, and Virgil's sixth *Aeneid* point to a common source, which may have been an Orphic apocalypse, a *Descent of Orpheus to Hades.* They include the divine origin of the soul; its fall to be incarnated in a cycle of births as a penalty for former sins; the guardian genius; the judgment after death; the torments of the unjust and the happiness of the just in the millennial intervals between incarnations; the hope of final deliverance for the purified; and certain topographical features: the Meadow (probably adapted from the Homeric Meadow of Asphodel); the two Ways to right and left; the waters of Lethe (or of Unmindfulness . . .) and of Memory.]

Such then, I [Socrates] went on, are the prizes, rewards, and gifts that the just man may expect at the hands of gods and men in his life-time, in addition to those other blessings which come simply from being just.

Yes, the rewards are splendid and sure. [Glaucon replies.]

These, however, are as nothing, in number or in greatness, when compared with the recompense awaiting the just and the unjust after death. This must now be told, in order that each may be paid in full what the argument shows to be his due.

Go on; there are not many things I [Glaucon] would sooner hear about.

My story will not be like Odysseus' tale to Alcinous;[2] but its hero was a valiant   5
man. Er, the son of Armenius, a native of Pamphylia, who was killed in battle. When the dead were taken up for burial ten days later, his body alone was found undecayed. They carried him home, and two days afterwards were going to bury him, when he came to life again as he lay on the funeral pyre. He then told what he had seen in the other world.

He said that, when the soul had left his body, he journeyed with many others

---

1. Gilbert Murray, 'The Conception of Another Life,' *Edin. Rev.,* 1914, reprinted in *Stoic, Christian and Humanist,* 1940. A learned and sober account of Orphism will be found in W. K. C. Guthrie's *Orpheus and Greek Religion,* 1935. Dieterich's *Nekyia* contains a study of the eschatological myths. (Greek mystery religions commonly involved an initiation into the secrets of the afterlife. See Walter Burkert, *Ancient Mystery Cults,* Harvard University Press, 1987.)

2. Odysseus' recital of his adventures to Alcinous, King of Phaeacia, fills four books of the *Odyssey,* including Odysseus' voyage to the realm of the dead, which Plato would reject as a misleading picture of the after-life. It became proverbial for a long story.

until they came to a marvellous place, where there were two openings side by side in the earth, and opposite them two others in the sky above. Between them sat Judges,[3] who, after each sentence given, bade the just take the way to the right upwards through the sky, first binding on them in front tokens signifying the judgement passed upon them. The unjust were commanded to take the downward road to the left, and these bore evidence of all their deeds fastened on their backs. When Er himself drew near, they told him that he was to carry tidings of the other world to mankind, and he must now listen and observe all that went on in that place. Accordingly he saw the souls which had been judged departing by one of the openings in the sky and one of those in the earth; while at the other two openings souls were coming up out of the earth travel-stained and dusty, or down from the sky clean and bright. Each company, as if they had come on a long journey, seemed glad to turn aside into the Meadow, where they encamped like pilgrims at a festival. Greetings passed between acquaintances, and as either party questioned the other of what had befallen them, some wept as they sorrowfully recounted all that they had seen and suffered on their journey under the earth, which had lasted a thousand years;[4] while others spoke of the joys of heaven and sights of inconceivable beauty. There was much, Glaucon, that would take too long to tell; but the sum, he said, was this. For every wrong done to any man sinners had in due course paid the penalty ten times over, that is to say, once in each hundred years, such being the span of human life, in order that the punishment for every offence might be tenfold. Thus, all who have been guilty of bringing many to death or slavery by betraying their country or their comrades in arms, or have taken part in any other iniquity, suffer tenfold torments for each crime; while deeds of kindness and a just and sinless life are rewarded in the same measure. Concerning infants who die at birth or live but a short time he had more to say, not worthy of mention.[5]

The wages earned by honouring the gods and parents, or by dishonouring them and by doing murder, were even greater. He was standing by when one spirit asked another, 'Where is Ardiaeus the Great?' This Ardiaeus had been despot in some city of Pamphylia just a thousand years before, and, among many other wicked deeds, he was said to have killed his old father and his elder brother. The answer was: 'He has not come back hither, nor will he ever come. This was one of the terrible sights we saw. When our sufferings were ended and we were near the mouth, ready to pass upwards, suddenly we saw Ardiaeus and others with him. Most of them were despots, but there were some private persons who had been great sinners. They thought that at last they were going to mount upwards, but the mouth would not admit them; it bellowed whenever one whose wickedness was incurable or who had not paid the penalty in full tried to

---

3. In the myth of the Judgement of the Dead in the *Gorgias*, 523 E, Minos, Rhadamanthys, and Aeacus give judgement 'in the Meadow at the parting of the two ways, one to the Islands of the Blest, the other to Tartarus.'

4. This figure, probably taken from some Orphic or Pythagorean source, is repeated by Virgil, *Aeneid* vi. 748.

5. This suggests that a limbo for infants was a feature of the Orphic apocalypse. It appears in *Aeneid* vi. 426 ff., discussed by Cumont, *After-Life in Roman Paganism,* 128 ff.

go up.[6] Then certain fierce and fiery-looking men, who stood by and knew what the sound meant, seized some and carried them away; but Ardiaeus and others they bound hand and foot and neck and flinging them down flayed them. They dragged them along the wayside, carding their flesh like wool with thorns and telling all who passed by why this was done to them and that they were being taken to be cast into Tartarus. We had gone through many terrors of every sort, but none so great as the fear each man felt lest the sound should come as he went up; and when it was not heard, his joy was great.' Such were the judgements and penalties, and the blessings received were in corresponding measure.

Now when each company had spent seven days in the Meadow, on the eighth they had to rise up and journey on. And on the fourth day afterwards they came to a place whence they could see a straight shaft of light, like a pillar, stretching from above throughout heaven and earth, more like the rainbow than anything else, but brighter and purer. To this they came after a day's journey, and there, at the middle of the light, they saw stretching from heaven the extremities of its chains; for this light binds the heavens, holding together all the revolving firmament, like the undergirths of a ship of war.[7] . . .

The Spindle turned on the knees of Necessity. Upon each of its circles stood a Siren, who was carried round with its movement, uttering a single sound on one note, so that all the eight made up the concords of a single scale.[8] Round about, at equal distances, were seated, each on a throne, the three daughters of Necessity, the Fates, robed in white with garlands on their heads, Lachesis, Clotho, and Atropos, chanting to the Sirens' music, Lachesis of things past, Clotho of the present, and Atropos of things to come. And from time to time Clotho lays her right hand on the outer rim of the Spindle and helps to turn it, while Atropos turns the inner circles likewise with her left, and Lachesis with either hand takes hold of inner and outer alternately.

The souls, as soon as they came, were required to go before Lachesis. An Interpreter first marshalled them in order; and then, having taken from the lap of Lachesis a number of lots and samples of lives, he mounted on a high platform and said:

'The word of Lachesis, maiden daughter of Necessity. Souls of a day, here shall begin a new round of earthly life, to end in death. No guardian spirit will

---

6. So in Virgil, *Georgic* iv. 493, a roar is heard when Orpheus, returning from Hades with Eurydice, looks back, and Eurydice vanishes.

7. Undergirths were ropes or braces used, either as fixtures or as temporary expedients, to strengthen a ship's hull, Acts xxvii. 17: 'they used helps, undergirding the ship.' It is disputed whether the bond holding the universe together is simply the straight axial shaft or a circular band of light, suggested by the Milky Way, girdling the heaven of Fixed Stars.

8. Aristotle, *de caelo* ii. 9: 'It seems to some thinkers [Pythagoreans] that bodies so great must inevitably produce a sound by their movement: even bodies on the earth do so . . . and as for the sun and the moon, and the stars, so many in number and enormous in size, all moving at a tremendous speed, it is incredible that they should fail to produce a noise of surpassing loudness. Taking this as their hypothesis, and also that the speeds of the stars, judged by their distances, are in the ratios of the musical consonances, they affirm that the sound of the stars as they revolve is concordant. To meet the difficulty that none of us is aware of this sound, they account for it by saying that the sound is with us right from birth and has thus no contrasting silence to show it up; for voice and silence are perceived by contrast with each other, and so all mankind is undergoing an experience like that of a coppersmith, who becomes by long habit indifferent to the din around him' (trans. W. K. C. Guthrie). Aristotle refutes this theory.

cast lots for you,[9] but you shall choose your own destiny. Let him to whom the first lot falls choose first a life to which he will be bound of necessity. But Virtue owns no master: as a man honours or dishonours her, so shall he have more of her or less. The blame is his who chooses; Heaven is blameless.'[10]

With these words the Interpreter scattered the lots among them all. Each took up the lot which fell at his feet and showed what number he had drawn; only Er himself was forbidden to take one. Then the Interpreter laid on the ground before them the sample lives, many more than the persons there. They were of every sort: lives of all living creatures, as well as of all conditions of men. Among them were lives of despots, some continuing in power to the end, others ruined in mid course and ending in poverty, exile, or beggary. There were lives of men renowned for beauty of form and for strength and prowess, or for distinguished birth and ancestry; also lives of unknown men; and of women likewise. All these qualities were variously combined with one another and with wealth or poverty, health or sickness, or intermediate conditions; but in none of these lives was there anything to determine the condition of the soul, because the soul must needs change its character according as it chooses one life or another.

Here, it seems, my dear Glaucon, a man's whole fortunes are at stake. On this account each one of us should lay aside all other learning, to study only how he may discover one who can give him the knowledge enabling him to distinguish the good life from the evil, and always and everywhere to choose the best within his reach, taking into account all these qualities we have mentioned and how, separately or in combination, they affect the goodness of life. Thus he will seek to understand what is the effect, for good or evil, of beauty combined with wealth or with poverty and with this or that condition of the soul, or of any combination of high or low birth, public or private station, strength or weakness, quickness of wit or slowness, and any other qualities of mind, native or acquired; until, as the outcome of all these calculations, he is able to choose between the worse and the better life with reference to the constitution of the soul, calling a life worse or better according as it leads to the soul becoming more unjust or more just. All else he will leave out of account; for, as we have seen, this is the supreme choice for a man, both while he lives and after death. Accordingly, when he goes into the house of death he should hold this faith like adamant, that there too he may not be dazzled by wealth and such-like evils, or fling himself into the life of a despot or other evil-doer, to work irremediable harm and suffer yet worse things himself, but may know how to choose always the middle course that avoids both extremes, not only in this life, so far as he may, but in every future existence; for there lies the greatest happiness for man.

To return to the report of the messenger from the other world. The Interpreter then said: 'Even for the last comer, if he choose with discretion, there is left in store a life with which, if he will live strenuously, he may be content and

---

9. The idea that the *daemon* (guardian spirit, genius, personified destiny) has an individual allotted to it as its portion appears in Lysias, *Epitaphius* 78, Theocritus iv. 40, and Plato's *Phaedo* (myth) 107 D.

10. These last words 'became a kind of rallying-cry among the champions of the freedom of the will in the early Christian era' (Adam). They are inscribed on a bust of Plato of the first century B.C. found at Tibur.

not unhappy. Let not the first be heedless in his choice, nor the last be disheartened.'

After these words, he who had drawn the first lot at once seized upon the most absolute despotism he could find. In his thoughtless greed he was not careful to examine the life he chose at every point, and he did not see the many evils it contained and that he was fated to devour his own children; but when he had time to look more closely, he began to beat his breast and bewail his choice, forgetting the warning proclaimed by the Interpreter; for he laid the blame on fortune, the decrees of the gods, anything rather than himself. He was one of those who had come down from heaven, having spent his former life in a well-ordered commonwealth and become virtuous from habit without pursuing wisdom. It might indeed be said that not the least part of those who were caught in this way were of the company which had come from heaven, because they were not disciplined by suffering; whereas most of those who had come up out of the earth, having suffered themselves and seen others suffer, were not hasty in making their choice. For this reason, and also because of the chance of the lot, most of the souls changed from a good life to an evil, or from an evil life to a good. Yet, if upon every return to earthly life a man seeks wisdom with his whole heart, and if the lot so fall that he is not among the last to choose, then this report gives good hope that he will not only be happy here, but will journey to the other world and back again hither, not by the rough road underground, but by the smooth path through the heavens.

It was indeed, said Er, a sight worth seeing, how the souls severally chose their lives—a sight to move pity and laughter and astonishment; for the choice was mostly governed by the habits of their former life. He saw one soul choosing the life of a swan; this had once been the soul of Orpheus, which so hated all womankind because of his death at their hands that it would not consent to be born of woman.[11] And he saw the soul of Thamyras[12] take the life of a nightingale, and a swan choose to be changed into a man, and other musical creatures do the same. The soul which drew the twentieth lot took a lion's life; this had been Ajax, the son of Telamon, who shrank from being born as a man, remembering the judgement concerning the arms of Achilles.[13] After him came the soul of Agamemnon,[14] who also hated mankind because of his sufferings and took in exchange the life of an eagle. Atalanta's[15] soul drew a lot about half-way through. She took the life of an athlete, which she could not pass over when she saw the great honours he would win. After her he saw the soul of Epeius,[16] son of Pano-

11. Orpheus was torn in pieces by the Maenads, the women-worshipers of Dionysus.

12. Another singer, who was deprived of sight and of the gift of song for challenging the Muses to a contest.

13. After Achilles' death a contest between Ajax and Odysseus for his arms ended in the defeat and suicide of Ajax. The first mention is in *Odyssey* xi. 543, where the soul of Ajax, summoned from Hades, will not speak to Odysseus.

14. The conqueror of Troy, murdered by his wife Clytemnestra on his return home.

15. Atalanta's suitors had to race with her for her hand and were killed if defeated. Milanion won by dropping three golden apples given him by Aphrodite, which Atalanta paused to pick up.

16. Maker of the wooden horse in which the Greek chieftains entered Troy.

peus, passing into the form of a craftswoman; and far off, among the last, the buffoon Thersites' soul clothing itself in the body of an ape. It so happened that the last choice of all fell to the soul of Odysseus, whose ambition was so abated by memory of his former labours that he went about for a long time looking for a life of quiet obscurity. When at last he found it lying somewhere neglected by all the rest, he chose it gladly, saying that he would have done the same if his lot had come first. Other souls in like manner passed from beasts into men and into one another, the unjust changing into the wild creatures, the just into the tame, in every sort of combination.

Now when all the souls had chosen their lives, they went in the order of their lots to Lachesis; and she gave each into the charge of the guardian genius he had chosen, to escort him through life and fulfil his choice. The genius led the soul first to Clotho, under her hand as it turned the whirling Spindle, thus ratifying the portion which the man had chosen when his lot was cast. And, after touching her, he led it next to the spinning of Atropos, thus making the thread of destiny irreversible. Thence, without looking back, he passed under the throne of Necessity. And when he and all the rest had passed beyond the throne, they journeyed together to the Plain of Lethe through terrible stifling heat; for the plain is bare of trees and of all plants that grow on the earth. When evening came, they encamped beside the River of Unmindfulness, whose water no vessel can hold. All are required to drink a certain measure of this water, and some have not the wisdom to save them from drinking more. Every man as he drinks forgets everything. When they had fallen asleep, at midnight there was thunder and an earthquake, and in a moment they were carried up, this way and that, to their birth, like shooting stars. Er himself was not allowed to drink of the water. How and by what means he came back to the body he knew not; but suddenly he opened his eyes and found himself lying on the funeral pyre at dawn.

And so, Glaucon, the tale was saved from perishing; and if we will listen, it may save us, and all will be well when we cross the river of Lethe. Also we shall not defile our souls; but, if you will believe with me that the soul is immortal and able to endure all good and ill, we shall keep always to the upward way and in all things pursue justice with the help of wisdom. Then we shall be at peace with Heaven and with ourselves, both during our sojourn here and when, like victors in the Games collecting gifts from their friends, we receive the prize of justice; and so, not here only, but in the journey of a thousand years of which I have told you, we shall fare well.

Questions for Discussion and Review

1. Why does the universal fact of death cast a sinister shadow over the efforts of Greek heroes to perform unequaled actions and achieve undying fame?

2. Describe the Homeric picture of Hades's realm (see *Odyssey,* Book 11). Where is the netherworld located, and what are its chief geographic features? Who or what dwells there?

3. Discuss the differences between Elysium and Tartarus and the posthumous state of their respective inhabitants.

4. For what reasons do certain Greek heroes descend into the Underworld? What rites of passage characterize their journeys into and from the land of Death?

5. Compare the Homeric Hades with the afterworld postulated by Plato in the "Myth of Er" and Virgil in the *Aeneid* (Chapter 19). In what ways do ideas about Hades's realm evolve over time?

Works Cited

Barnstone, Willis, trans. *Greek Lyric Poetry.* Rev. ed. New York: Bantam, 1967.

Recommended Reading

Bremmer, Jan. *The Early Greek Concept of the Soul.* Princeton: Princeton UP, 1983.

Burkert, Walter. *Ancient Mystery Cults.* Cambridge, MA: Harvard UP, 1987.

Burkert, Walter. *Greek Religion.* Trans. John Raffan. Cambridge: Harvard UP, 1985. A scholarly analysis of Greek religious beliefs, including concepts of the afterlife.

Homer. "Book 11." *Odyssey of Homer.* Trans. Allen Mandelbaum. New York: Bantam, 1990. Odysseus's visit to Hades's realm presents the oldest Greek view of the condition of the dead.

Plato. "Phaedo." *The Last Days of Socrates.* Rev. ed. Trans. Hugh Tredennick. New York: Penguin, 1969. Plato's account of Socrates's death includes the philosopher's argument for the soul's posthumous survival.

Plato. *The Republic of Plato.* Trans. F. M. Cornford. Oxford: Oxford UP, 1941. Plato's vision of the ideal state culminates in the "Myth of Er."

Vermeule, Emily. *Aspects of Death in Early Greek Art and Poetry.* Berkeley: U of California P, 1979.

West, Martin L. *The Orphic Poems.* New York: Oxford UP, 1983. Examines surviving Orphic texts.

CHAPTER

1O

The Hero: Man Divided against Himself

KEY THEMES

The heroes of Greek myths—from Perseus and Heracles to Achilles—share certain characteristics: a divine parent or ancestor, enormous strength, courage and skill, the performance of "impossible" feats, an encounter with chthonic powers (often a literal trip to the Underworld), and a quest for immortality. For the early heroes, that quest often ends in their achieving some form of divine status, whereas later heroes have to settle for a reputation that endures, though they themselves cannot. Each hero, however, also has his own unique characteristics. Perseus, possibly the earliest of the heroes, is unusual in his positive relationships with women, both divine and human; other heroes, like Heracles, Theseus, and Jason, experience difficulties in their dealings with women. In all the heroes after Perseus, we see an inner division, men pulled in two directions: toward the fulfillment of their godlike capacity to excel, on the one hand, and toward the expression of their instinctive savagery or violence, on the other. This inner division is expressed symbolically in creatures such as the centaur, half-man, half-horse. In other figures, like Icarus and Phaethon, the flight of the hero toward immortality is commented on from a didactic point of view, to teach a lesson on the dangers of excessive ambition.

The Heroic Pattern

The adventures of the Greek heroes, like those of heroes everywhere, typically follow a traditional pattern. The hero is often born in an unusual (or unnatural) fashion and, as an infant, faces terrible danger which, of course, he survives. He often demonstrates prodigious powers, even in childhood. On reaching adulthood, he craves adventure and, seeking to test his own powers, embarks on a quest or series of quests:

The Heroic Pattern: Archetypal Events

Anthropologists, folklorists, and other scholars have surveyed traditions about the hero figure in representative cultures of the world and have compiled lists of characteristics that typify the hero's life. The following list is adapted from one published by the folklorist and mythographer Lord Raglan.

1. The hero's mother is a royal virgin.
2. His father is a king.
3. The circumstances of his conception and birth are unusual, and
4. He is reputed to be the son of a god.
5. At birth an attempt is made, often by his father or maternal grandfather, to kill him, but
6. He is spirited away, and
7. Reared by foster-parents in a far country.
8. On reaching manhood he returns or goes to his future kingdom.
9. He often makes a journey to the Underworld, or the shades of the dead may visit him.
10. After a victory over the king and/or a giant, dragon, or wild beast,
11. He marries a princess, often the daughter of his predecessor, and
12. Becomes king.
13. Eventually he loses favor with the gods and/or his subjects, and
14. He meets a mysterious death.
15. His children do not succeed him.
16. His body is not buried, but
17. He has one or more holy sepulchres.

Other mythographers find different patterns. Joseph Campbell describes the heroic pattern as a "monomyth":

1. The hero is separated from his familiar surroundings and goes on a journey alone.
2. He undergoes a mysterious initiation, during which he grapples with supernatural powers and gains a new understanding of himself in relation to his community and to the gods.
3. He returns to share the new vision with his fellows.

a journey of discovery during which he will learn about himself, his society, and his universe.

In the course of that quest he is eventually isolated from his fellow human beings and, all alone, must do battle with nightmarish creatures or monsters, usually including some in serpent or dragon form—all variants of the serpents of the ancient goddess. Ultimately, he must confront the divine or cosmic powers themselves. His journey often culminates in a trip to the Underworld, from which he returns, bringing a new awareness of himself, his own limits, and his relationship to the forces that govern the universe.

The hero's trip to the Underworld has been variously interpreted as a descent into the "womb" of the Earth-goddess, connecting the masculine ego of the hero with the feminine principle, or with the unconscious, or with the life of the instincts. Thus rejoining the *animus* with the *anima*, the hero's psyche can be made whole. Additionally, by connecting with both upper and lower worlds, the hero participates in the cycle of life, death, and rebirth that the goddess religions once provided. In the competitive, linear world of the sky gods, the hero, being merely mortal, is at a serious disadvantage: the hero's quest to defy death, to achieve literal immortality, is doomed. But in descending to the Underworld, the hero recognizes the necessity of experiencing the whole cycle, however terrifying. Ascending once more to the upper world, he achieves spiritual rebirth. Unlike Dionysus, the "twice-born" god who descends into human incarnation in the womb of a human mother and is born again out of his divine parent, the human hero descends into the womb of the goddess and reclaims his spiritual life, which is his link to the divine world.

The Hero as Redeemer

The hero as a figure emerges in myths as humans enter the fallen world, the world of time, of decay and death. In Hesiod's account of the Ages of Man, the Age of Heroes follows immediately upon the Bronze and Silver ages, and the implicit function of the hero is to redeem humanity, a process begun by Prometheus's defiance of Zeus. Prometheus's gifts to humankind of sacrifice and fire serve to reconnect this fallen world to the world of the gods, at least symbolically, by providing both the means to cook our food (and thus to obliterate the obvious signs of our penchant for violence—that, like animals, we kill to eat) and the means to create technology (to use fire to forge weapons, for example). The hero's function, too, is redemptive: by his half-divine nature, his glorious deeds, and his relentless pursuit of immortality, the hero uplifts humanity from its dismal condition and reminds us of our godlike potential.

Nevertheless, he remains half-human and must therefore die. For the hero, the final burden of his humanity is the necessity of confronting his own mortality. In the polarities of the hero's experiences, nature and culture and the human and divine converge to produce a being who is contradictory in his very essence.

Protesting this condition, the ancient Sumerian hero **Gilgamesh** protested to the sun god, "If this quest is not to be achieved, why did you create in me the irresistible urge to attempt it?" The hero of Greek mythology, from Heracles to Achilles and Odysseus, is similarly trapped by his very nature into undertaking and usually achieving the impossible—paradoxically pursuing death in order to achieve immortality, a potentially tragic endeavor.

The Isolation of the Hero

At the same time, the more successful he is at reconnecting humanity, by example or imaginatively, with the divine realm, the more the hero constitutes, by his very nature, a potential threat or rivalry to the gods. It is no accident that heroes are typically objects of enmity of one deity or another.

The divided nature of the hero also creates a psychological dilemma. In his linear drive to burst through the tantalizingly transparent ceiling of mortality, the hero figure is isolated by his own uniqueness: no one understands his compulsion toward excess. Culminating the process of individuation begun at creation, the hero is the ultimate unique individual. And yet he craves human companionship and love. For the ancient Sumerian hero Gilgamesh, the gods provided a companion, Enkidu, to ease his loneliness. But even Enkidu, while sharing Gilgamesh's enormous courage and skill, fails to understand his friend's determination to do combat with Humbaba, the terrifying deity of the forest. For Gilgamesh, the mere fact of mortality is enough to fuel the compulsion to achieve something extraordinary—or die trying.

The ultimate isolation of the hero figure is even more emphatic in his relationship with women. For such a hero, essentially a warrior, the female is at best a distraction and at worst a threat. The bonds of love, domestic contentment, and/or sexual indulgence are destructive to the heroic task. To succeed in his quest—to fulfill his godlike aspirations—the hero must eschew the banal comforts of ordinary life that would bind him to the earth to which his body will eventually be returned. Thus the hero must reject, tame, or even kill the women in his life, lest he be tamed (and thus psychologically destroyed) or killed by them. The enmity of Hera, goddess of marriage, likewise reflects this essential antagonism.

The Hero and Society

In his role as protector of society, the hero is also a divided being. Charged with defending civilization from rampaging beasts or monsters or human enemies who would destroy it and return us to the savage condition from which we have only barely emerged, the hero has unique gifts that allow him to excel at protecting human societies from threats to personal, economic, or cultural survival. In addition, by his exploits and travels, he adds to our body of knowledge, both geographic and historical: Gilgamesh, for example, brings back knowledge of the world before the flood, recovering the prehistory of Uruk and recording it for future generations.

The product, furthermore, of a newly urbanized civilization, the hero, whose explicit, "official" job is protecting his city, represents an emergent civilization's self-consciousness, both of its pride in its own glorious achievements (the *Epic of Gilgamesh*, for example, opens with an extended praise of the awesome walls, temples, and gardens of Gilgamesh's city, Uruk) and of its incipient awareness that the gains of civilization, however amazing, are dependent on human beings' willingness to commit themselves to maintaining that civilization. But human beings are all too capable of backsliding into savagery and losing all they have gained. It is the hero who bears the load of that responsibility for protecting his civilization, often on behalf of (or as substitute for) the kings who organize the armies or appoint the tasks. Paradoxically, the hero's great warrior skills, his potential for violence, and his often rash, impulsive nature put civilization at risk: when we first meet Gilgamesh, he's causing havoc in Uruk, raping the women and distracting the men from their work. Similarly, the heroes in Hesiod's Bronze Age are so violent that they destroy each other, and the men of the Age of Heroes, whose exploits are recounted in the myths, constitute a second attempt at redemption.

The Hero as Centaur: Image of the Divided Self

Though required for his skill and willingness to serve in times of war or other threat, the hero becomes, in times of peace, a danger to the civilization he is charged with protecting. Further, by encouraging and rewarding his capacity for violence when it serves our needs, and then complaining about our inability to control him when he continues to act in the same fashion once the immediate threat is resolved, we create conflicting sets of demands that result in an inner division in the hero's own nature. In that inner division, the hero resembles the **centaur**—a literally divided creature.

Combining a human head and upper torso with a horse's rear end, the centaurs—beings with a capacity for intelligence, knowledge, and wisdom, but possessing voracious appetites and aggressive instincts—embody the best and worst of human potentialities, brains and brawn inextricably joined.

Two stories about centaurs exemplify their inherent contradictions. In their usual manifestation, the centaurs embody animal nature, raw and unrestrained. They are said to eat raw food and are unable to control themselves when drinking wine: invited to the wedding of a Lapith princess, the centaurs characteristically get drunk and attempt to carry off and rape the Lapith women. A horrible battle follows in which King Pirithous and his guests, including Heracles, finally drive the centaurs away.

In contrast, the leader of the centaurs, Chiron, is temperate and wise—indeed, a great teacher of both gods and men, instructing Asclepius, for example, in the art of medicine. Unlike the other centaurs, Chiron embodies all that culture and civilization have to offer. His reward is to be shot with a poisoned arrow by Heracles—in one of that hero's irrational (and ironically centaur-like) moments—as Chiron is attempting to stop the centaurs' rampage at the Lapith wedding. In agony but unable to die, Chiron generously offers to trade places with Prometheus, releasing the latter from the rock (see Chapter 14). Chiron, like Perseus, is finally transformed into a constellation, Centaurus, while the centaur-like Heracles will ultimately be elevated to divine status.

The Early Hero: Perseus

Perseus is one of the earliest of the Greek heroes. Although he shares some of the traits later seen in Heracles and has some similar adventures, Perseus is nonetheless distinguished by some important differences. While other heroes often have difficulties in their encounters with women, whether humans or goddesses, Perseus performs all of his exploits either with the aid of or on behalf of women and maintains mutually supportive relationships with them throughout his career. Perhaps because he is less estranged from the feminine powers, Perseus does not journey to the Underworld.

Perseus's Early Life

Perseus's mother, **Danae** [DA-na-ee], had been imprisoned in a bronze tower by her father, Acrisius, king of Argos. He wanted to keep her from all men in order to protect his rulership by preventing the fulfillment of a prophecy that a son of Danae would kill him. But Zeus, who is attracted to her beauty, comes to her in a shower of gold, releasing once again the procreative power that Acrisius had attempted to restrain. The child conceived by this miraculous intervention is, like most of the heroes who follow, half-divine. Unlike their sometimes ambivalent response to later heroes, the gods seem to identify closely with Perseus. When Perseus is born, Acrisius puts his daughter and grandson to sea in a chest, an archetypal symbol of both coffin and womb, connecting Perseus to the cycle of life, death, and rebirth that is the traditional province of the Great Goddess. From the very beginning of the myth of Perseus, the opposing powers of male and female, human and divine, are more closely reconciled than they will be again in later hero myths.

Danae and the child are protected by Zeus and, instead of drowning, they float safely to shore on the island of Seriphus, where they are taken in by the fisherman Dictys and where Perseus is raised. But further danger threatens. Dictys's brother, King Polydectes, desires Danae. She refuses him, and Perseus protects her, offering to bring Polydectes instead any gift of his choice. The shrewd king demands the head of **Medusa,** one of the three Gorgons, knowing that the attempt would be fatal, thus ridding himself of Perseus and giving himself free access to Danae. Perseus, of course, does not hesitate to volunteer for impossible missions, possessing, by virtue of his divine parentage, the courage and skill to succeed.

Perseus and the Gorgon

The gods, however, are concerned that, being half-human, Perseus lacks powers sufficient to the formidable task he faces. Athene therefore steps in to help, warning Perseus of the difficulties he will encounter and telling him to visit the sisters of the Gorgon, the **Graiae** [GRYE-eye]—old, gray hags from birth, with one eye and one tooth to share between them. Snatching the eye, Perseus forces them to reveal the location of the nymphs who possess magical weapons: a pouch, a pair of winged sandals (possibly Hermes's) that will enable him to fly, and a cap of invisibility, which may have belonged to Hades. Hermes also gives him a sickle of adamant, an unbreakable stone. Finally, Perseus also takes his polished bronze shield (in some versions a mirror), possibly a gift from Athene.

The terrifying, deadly aspects of the Great Goddess are portrayed in the Graiae and the Gorgons, whose powers are tamed by the hero in a striking inversion of Gaea's plan for the castration of Uranus by a sickle; here, however, it is the power of the female that is nullified. (In fact, for Freudian psychologists, decapitation is an unconscious image of castration; thus the fear of Medusa represents the male fear of castration.) However, while destroying the terrifying chthonic powers of the female, Perseus does not reject feminine powers altogether: his weapons—a pouch, a mirror, a pair of sandals, and a cap—are more "feminine" and less aggressive than those of typical heroes (we cannot imagine, for example, Heracles or Achilles needing to be invisible to his enemies) and depend for their efficacy on magic, rather than on the strength and intelligence, however great, of the hero himself. Even his sickle, an agricultural tool, is reminiscent not only of Gaea's arranged castration of Uranus, but also of Demeter's gift of agriculture to humankind.

Further, borrowing divine powers for the purposes of his quest, Perseus literally assumes, at least temporarily, powers like flight and invisibility that humans may dream of but are otherwise reserved for the gods. He thus becomes, in effect, a demigod, foreshadowing his final stellar transformation and reconciling the human and the divine more completely than later heroes were ever to accomplish.

FIGURE 10-1 Perseus Slaying Medusa. This limestone relief from the Temple at Selinus (550–540 B.C.) depicts Perseus cutting off the head of the Gorgon Medusa. Athene looks on as Pegasus, the winged horse, springs from Medusa's neck. Perseus will later give the head to Athene, thus effectively transferring this terrifying aspect of the Great Goddess's powers to the representative of the wisdom of Zeus. (*National Museum, Palermo.*)

Arriving at the Gorgons' cave, Perseus finds the petrified statues of men who had looked in the face of the horrible creatures with gold wings and hair of snakes. Waiting until the Gorgons are asleep, Perseus dons his cap of invisibility. But even though they cannot see him, he is still in danger: if he, too, looks into Medusa's face, he will be turned to stone. As clever as he is brave, Perseus enters the cave backward, looking into his shield (mirror) so he won't have to look directly into the terrible face. When he cuts off Medusa's head, a winged horse—**Pegasus**—springs from her neck (Figure 10-1). Placing the head in his pouch, Perseus flies off and escapes.

Medusa herself is a complex figure. Her wings and hair of snakes are symbols inherited from the Great Goddess (the Egyptian goddess Isis, for example, was often depicted as a winged goddess), linking the upper and lower worlds in a single figure. Variously described as inhabiting a region near the limits of the ocean, or the Garden of the Hesperides, she maintains her connection to the primal Goddess of the Tree (or the Waters) of Life. Like Artemis, Medusa is a guardian of the women's mysteries, of the secrets of the Great Goddess whose chthonic aspects she has come to represent. When Perseus avoids looking at Medusa directly, wisely viewing her reflected image rather than her face, he is astutely avoiding the fate of Actaeon or other males who spy on those mysteries.

Medusa's connection to the upper world of the heavens, where the sky gods now rule, is also evident in her connection with the sacred horses who pull the chariot of the sun, an image common to many myth systems. According to one story about Medusa, she makes love to (or is raped by) Poseidon, who comes to her in the form of a horse; in other versions of that story, she takes the form either of a mare or of a woman from the waist up, with a mare's lower half. The products of this union are Chrysaor, a human warrior, and Pegasus, the winged horse, who will fly across the heavens pulling the chariot of Zeus that bears his thunderbolt, a variant of the sun-chariot. Medusa is thus closely connected to the upper world as well as to the Underworld, as was the primal Goddess herself. As the mother of the sacred horse of the sky god, she asserts her powers as a creator figure whose realm includes the light as well as the darkness.

Other Adventures

On the way home, Perseus comes to the Garden of the Hesperides (as Heracles will later) where Atlas, afraid that Perseus will steal the Golden Apples, offends the hero, who turns Atlas into a mountain of stone by using the Gorgon's head.

Taking the long way home (as will both Heracles and Theseus), Perseus stops in Ethiopia, where he sees the Princess **Andromeda** chained to a rock, at the mercy of a sea monster. Her mother, Cassiopeia, it seems, had boasted of being more beautiful than the sea nymphs, and Poseidon sent the sea monster to punish the Ethiopians. Adromeda's father, King Cepheus, was told that only the sacrifice of his daughter would rid the kingdom of the monster.

Perseus offers to rescue Andromeda in exchange for her hand in marriage. Her parents, despite her previous betrothal to Phineus, agree, and Perseus kills the monster. He is then attacked by Phineus and his allies and wins the battle by removing the Gorgon's head from the sack (while he himself looks the other way), turning his opponents to stone. Perseus and Andromeda have a son, Perses, who becomes king of Ethiopia (and was said to be the ancestor of the Persians).

Perseus's Return

Perseus's story, much of which is recounted in Apollodorus's *Library*, embodies the complete cycle of the heroic rite of passage—departure, testing, triumph, and return. Returning home at last, now with Andromeda, Perseus finds his mother still pursued by Polydectes. Perseus uses the Gorgon's head once again to turn Polydectes and his followers to stone. Perseus then returns his magical weapons to Hermes, who restores them to the nymphs. No longer a demigod, Perseus nevertheless brings with him a gift—the Gorgon's head—which he gives to Athene. The powers of the Great Goddess are now assimilated by Athene—who personifies the wisdom of Zeus—as she puts the Gorgon's head, with its power to bind men by turning them to stone (possibly an image of impotence), behind her masculine weapon of war, her shield.

We may be witnessing in Perseus the emergence of the hero figure as he is differentiated from the various aspects of the goddess figure at an early stage in the shift from a matriarchal to a patriarchal system. Unlike the later, more exclusively "masculine" heroes, whose power depends on separating themselves from women (except, of course, for Odysseus; see Chapter 12), Perseus derives his power directly from the females, who give him magical weapons. His heroic acts are performed not in isolation, in pursuit of immortality or reputation, but in defense of women: to save his mother from rape or Andromeda from a sea monster. Finally, while the later heroes typically have difficulty settling down into peaceful, domestic lives, Perseus does exactly that, insisting on marrying Andromeda, bringing her back to his mother, and becoming the progenitor of a large and successful family.

Perseus as King

Following his return home, Perseus visits his grandfather, Acrisius, hoping to be reconciled. But at the funeral games for a friend, Perseus throws a discus that goes off course and accidentally hits his grandfather, killing him and thus fulfilling the prophecy that a son of Danae would kill Acrisius. Reluctant to assume his grandfather's throne at Argos after the accident, Perseus trades cities with his cousin Megapenthes, now king of Tiryns. Perseus had earlier petrified Megapenthes's father, Proetus, for attacking his own brother, Acrisius (who was Perseus's grandfather), and usurping his throne. Perseus thus becomes ruler of Tiryns and, eventually, Mycenae.

According to one variant, Megapenthes eventually kills Perseus to avenge his father. But most versions describe Perseus as living a long and happy life with Andromeda, who bears him one daughter and five more sons, establishing a political dynasty that rules in Argos for several generations and whose descendants include both Heracles and Eurystheus, who will assign Heracles to his labors.

The Death of Perseus

One of the earliest functions of the Perseus myth may have been etiological: the myth explains the origin of several constellations. At their deaths, Athene transforms Perseus and Andromeda into constellations (as did Poseidon upon the deaths of Cassiopeia and Cepheus). More important, the hero here fulfills, in the most literal way, the quest for immortality that underlies the heroic myth. Thus, without having to incur the enmity of the gods, Perseus completes the cycle through his heavenly rebirth and acquires the fully divine status—the reunification of the divided self, half-human, half-divine—that later heroes will risk death to achieve.

But the reconciliation is not to last. Rarely afterward will male and female, human and god, coexist so harmoniously in a single being. The seeds of the new, more exclusively patriarchal hero figure have been planted. Out of the severed neck of Medusa springs the winged horse Pegasus, whose famous rider, **Bellerophon** [bel-LER-oh-fahn], will be a new kind of hero who will take the reins from Athene, displace the Goddess from the saddle, and attempt to leap the barriers to the heavens themselves, thus spurning the feminine powers while provoking the gods' hostility—a hero, in other words, much like Heracles.

The Archetypal Hero: Heracles

It is **Heracles** [HER-a-kleez] who sets the model for Greek mythological heroes—extraordinary men who often combine the courage and strength of the gods with the bestial instincts of centaurs. The son of Zeus and a mortal woman—**Alcmene**—Heracles inherits a divided nature, half-human, half-divine; Zeus was said to have extended the night for three days in order to conceive such a son. Yet the two halves never come together for Heracles as they did for Perseus. As befits the son of a god, Heracles is unnaturally brave, strong, and clever, possessed of the spark of the divine fire that always seems, somehow, excessive when embodied in merely human form. Of course, as a hero must, he protects and preserves civilized society with these gifts and enlarges the limits of human knowledge. Bound by his human inheritance, however, he is also capable of animal-like behavior, committing acts sometimes ridiculous, sometimes irrational, and extremely violent. It is thus no accident that few heroes are as closely associated with the centaur as is Heracles, the dual components of his nature as abruptly juxtaposed as they are in the mismatched halves of that bifurcated creature. A being thus divided against himself, Heracles embodies the quintessential heroic predicament: how to fulfill the demands of the godlike desires for knowledge and achievement that drive him while bound to a mortal body that can neither fly nor turn invisible and which will surely die.

The Life of Heracles

Like most heroes, Heracles is threatened even as an infant. Ever-jealous of Zeus's infidelities, Hera hates Heracles from his birth. In fact, the hero's name, which means "Glory of Hera," may reflect the fact that every attempt of Hera's to destroy Heracles instead enhances his heroic status. According to one myth, Zeus tries to subvert her antagonism by tricking her into nursing the infant while she sleeps. When she awakes and discovers the child, she angrily pulls him from her breast, spilling the milk that becomes the Milky Way. Furious, she tries to get rid of him, sending a serpent into his cradle, thus reenacting his father's own battle with the serpent of the goddess, Typhoeus. The prodigious infant of course strangles the serpent. But though Heracles continues to foil Hera's attempts to destroy him, he cannot foil his own nature.

His early exploits reveal the ambiguity of Heracles's heroism. Turning his prowess to beneficial use, he kills a marauding lion that had been devouring the flocks of King Thespius. He also sleeps with the king's fifty daughters, either on fifty successive nights or all on one night. Extraordinary service, extraordinary appetites—these are, from the first, combined in Heracles.

One of the most popular of Greek heroes, Heracles has many stories told about his life, our sources for which include Apollodorus, Apollonius of Rhodes's *Argonautica*, Homer, and numerous others. These stories cover not just the famous Twelve Labors, but a whole range of tales that run the gamut from the serious to the comic, from the grotesque to the tragic. For instance, in his role as civic hero, Heracles helps many kings—leading armies, defeating enemies, and building and defending cities. He is also credited with founding the Olympic Games. He doesn't always play by the rules, though: in one account, he cuts off the noses and ears of an enemy's ambassadors and sends them back with the body parts hung around their necks. His innate

The Labors of Heracles

1. **Killing the Nemean lion,** whose hide was impervious to weapons. Heracles squeezes the lion to death with his bare hands and uses its own claws to skin it. Thenceforth, he wears its pelt as a cloak. He also fashions his famous club at this time to substitute for his trademark bow.

2. **Killing the Hydra,** a many-headed water snake whose heads would immediately grow back when severed. To prevent the heads from regenerating, Heracles arranges for a friend to sear the necks with a torch as each head is severed. Heracles then applies its poisonous gall to his arrows. (Eurystheus refused to count this labor because Heracles had had help.)

3. **Capturing the Cerynitian hind,** a golden-horned deer sacred to Artemis. To capture the deer, Heracles has to pursue it for a year. In some versions, he has to travel to the mythical North, the land of the Hyperboreans, to find it. (Note: the sequence of the third and fourth labors is sometimes reversed.)

4. **Capturing the Erymanthian boar,** which he has to pursue into territory occupied by the centaurs. While he is there, his host, the centaur Pholus, opens a barrel of wine, thereby attracting the other centaurs, who attack Heracles. Heracles drives them off, but in the process he accidentally wounds his host and the centaur Chiron with poisoned arrows.

5. **Cleaning the Augean stables,** for which Heracles demands a promise of payment from King Augeas. He accomplishes this unpleasant task by diverting the course of a river (or two) to wash through the barn. Because Augeas refuses to pay him, Heracles later returns with an army. (Eurystheus refused to count this labor, too, since Heracles had demanded payment.)

6. **Removing the Stymphalian birds,** whose droppings were creating a public nuisance in an Arcadian town. (According to some versions, they also ate hu-

brutality sometimes erupts into his private life as well. Married to **Megara** [ME-ga-ra] as a reward for his services to her father, Heracles settles down into domestic life. The couple has several children, and the hero appears to be happy. One night, however, in a fit of uncontrollable rage—perhaps sent by the still-angry Hera—he kills his wife and children, a tragic event dramatized in Euripides's play *Heracles*. Perhaps the heroic strength and drive and energy that define his heroic identity could not brook a life of mere domestic contentment. A savior in times of threat or war, the hero becomes a menace in time of peace: trained to use his strength to kill and to glory in his violent victories, how does a hero control the violence or repress the glorying ego when he leaves the battlefield and returns to civilized life?

The Twelve Labors and Other Stories

As expiation for his crime of domestic violence, Heracles is forced to perform Twelve Labors (some versions mention only ten) for King Eurystheus, each one designed man flesh.) Heracles drives away these birds by using brass rattles to frighten them off and by shooting many of them as they fly away.

7. **Capturing the Cretan bull,** the bovine parent of the Minotaur. Bringing it back, Heracles releases it near Marathon. (Theseus has to recapture it later.)

8. **Capturing the Thracian horses,** property of King Diomedes. To tame the horses, which ate human flesh, Heracles feeds their owner to them. While the guest of King Admetus, Heracles rescues Admetus's wife, Alcestis, from death—actually wrestling with Death (Thanatos) in the process.

9. **Bringing back the girdle (belt) of Hippolyte,** the Amazon queen. Hippolyte gives the girdle to Heracles willingly, which angers Hera, who persuades the other Amazons that Heracles was actually kidnapping Hippolyte. When they attack Heracles's ship, he kills the queen, believing she has lied to him, and keeps the belt.

10. **Bringing back the cattle of Geryon,** the three-headed giant sometimes identified as the herdsman of the dead. On this trip, the hero sets up the Pillars of Heracles at the western entrance to the Mediterranean.

11. **Bringing back the Golden Apples of the Hesperides,** apples of immortality that grow on the Tree of Life in the garden in the mythical West, where the sun sets. According to some versions, the Titan Atlas gets the apples while Heracles holds up the sky in his place.

12. **Capturing Cerberus** (the three-headed, or fifty-headed, hound of Hades). In order to accomplish this task, Heracles is first initiated into the Eleusinian Mysteries to learn how to safely traverse the kingdom of Hades. In some versions, he shoots Hades himself, wounding him in the process.

(probably at the instigation of Hera) to destroy him. Typical of the pattern of the heroic quest, Heracles's first labors are physical. Using his enormous strength and intelligence, Heracles kills the Hydra (a many-headed water snake whose heads would immediately regrow if cut off) by cleverly instructing a friend to use a torch to sear the neck of each head as the hero severs it. He also captures the Arcadian boar (also called the *Erymanthian boar,* after Mount Erymanthus, where he captures it) and the Cretan bull and tames the man-eating Thracian horses.

But even the very first of the labors reveals the savage core at the heart of the heroic task. Killing the ravaging lion of Nemea whose skin was impervious to human weapons, Heracles uses brute force by squeezing it to death with his bare hands (Figure 10-2). Required to bring back its skin as proof of the deed, Heracles demonstrates his cleverness by using its own claws to skin the lion. From this time forward, Heracles wears the lion skin as a cloak, as if he himself has become the marauding beast. Further manifesting his animal nature and suggesting his regression to a precivilized state, Heracles shapes his famous club at this point, substituting this primitive

FIGURE 10-2   Heracles's First Labor: Battling with the Nemean Lion. An illustration of the hero's amazing strength, this vase painting shows the hero strangling with his bare hands the lion whose skin is impenetrable to human weapons. After cleverly skinning it with its own claws, he wears its pelt as a cloak, a symbol of the savage element of the hero's nature. (*University of Pennsylvania Museum, Philadelphia.*)

weapon for the more conventional and equally famous bow that had been his trademark (figures 10-3 and 10-4).

Many stories depict the hero's animal-like qualities, describing him as unusually hairy and prone to bouts of excessive drunkenness, often in connection with centaurs. During one such episode, he shoots the good centaur, **Chiron** [KYE-rahn], by mistake, the strong right arm going into action before the brain is engaged: like many heroes after him, Heracles's instinct is to shoot first, ask questions later. In other stories, he is depicted comically, the object of sometimes coarse jokes. On one such occasion, he captures two enemy soldiers and slings them from a pole over his shoulders. Faced with a close-up view of the hero's hairy rear end, the two soldiers begin to laugh. Finding their laughter momentarily amusing, Heracles releases them!

On the positive side, several of the labors present the hero in his civic function as preserver of society and civilized life—killing the Stymphalian birds who were plaguing one town, for example, or cleaning out the Augean stables by diverting two rivers through the barn. Another task involved bringing back the belt of the Amazon

FIGURE 10-3   Heracles Shooting Bow. This statue (c. 490–
475 B.C.) from the Temple of Aphaia at Aegina portrays Heracles in
the act of shooting his famous bow and wearing the armor of a conventional Greek warrior. The stable posture, calm expression, and
firmly outstretched arm suggest rationality, self-control, and supreme
self-confidence. (*Glyptothek, Munich.*)

Queen Hippolyte: perhaps she yielded to him, or perhaps he killed her for it; either
way, he "tamed" a formidable female opponent.

   In the most incredible group of labors, Heracles fulfills the hero's most significant
function—to extend the parameters of human experience, to embody the scope of
the human imagination stretched to its limits, and to retrieve the power and knowledge otherwise limited to the gods. Heracles undertakes, literally, to extend the
boundaries of the known world by traveling to the ends of the earth, to the unknown
reaches of the North in pursuit of the Golden Hind (Figure 10-5) and to the Garden
of the **Hesperides** [hes-PER-ih-deez] in the mythical West to obtain the Goddess's
Golden Apples of Immortality.

   In all the hero's quests, Heracles calls upon his divine gifts to commit death-
defying acts, but, tainted by his human inheritance, he must finally confront the most
formidable obstacle of all: his own death. Twice, Heracles voyages to the Underworld,
undertaking the archetypal rite of passage that all heroes must fulfill in this most
urgent of human quests—the need to find a loophole to escape the ultimate trap of

FIGURE 10-4   Heracles with
Club. This Roman copy, known
as the *Hercules Farnese,* of a statue
by Lysippus (original from the
late fourth century B.C.) shows
Heracles, in contrast to the traditional hero of Figure 10-3, to be
larger, hairier, and more muscular
than the earlier version. The increased brawn, along with the
grim expression, adds to the savage image conveyed by the huge,
rather primitive-looking club with
the lion skin, complete with
claws, draped over it: in this
image, the warrior hero has
been transformed into a brute.
(*National Museum, Naples.*)

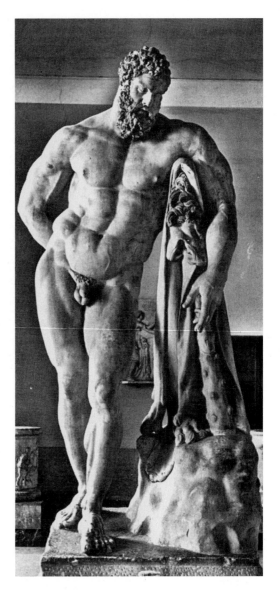

mortality. On separate trips to the Underworld, Heracles brings back the cattle of the
giant Geryon (who may be the herdsman of the dead) and also brings up Cerberus,
the three-headed hound of Hades, shooting the god Hades, King of the Underworld,
in the process. Having thus gone to the Land of the Dead and been reborn twice—
having taken on Death himself, and won—Heracles transcends the limits of the human condition, achieving literally what most heroes can achieve only through the
consolation of an immortal reputation. Heracles, like most hero figures, thus mediates the most extreme of contradictions—not only those of nature and culture, but
those of life and death as well.

FIGURE 10-5 Heracles's Third Labor: Pursuing the Cerynitian Hind. The two conflicting aspects of the hero illustrated in figures 10-3 and 10-4 are captured in this vase painting: as the daring explorer, Heracles pursues the mythical Golden Hind into the unknown North and brings back its golden antlers; as a creature of brute force, he wears the lion skin and, relinquishing his weapons (here held for him by two goddesses, possibly Athene and Artemis), he pulls off the antlers with his bare hands. (*British Museum, London.*)

The Death of Heracles

There are innumerable stories about Heracles apart from the labors, among them the voyage with Jason and the Argonauts—another mythic anachronism: Jason and the Argonauts do not appear until several generations after Heracles's death. During that voyage, the tables are turned on Heracles. Like many Greek heroes, he has an intimate and even erotic relationship with a young friend, Hylas, who disappears on shore, apparently abducted by a water nymph who falls in love with him. (Freudian theorists see the water nymph—the pool maiden who lures men to their deaths—as an expression of the fear of the female genitals, like the Gorgon's head.) Heracles's search for him proves fruitless, and he is eventually forced to sail on without him. The many sides of the hero are summed up in the story of Heracles's death. Having remarried, this time to **Deianeira** [dee-ya-NYE-ra], the sister of a friend, Heracles is still unable to rest contentedly at home. Eventually, tired of his unremitting pursuit of both erotic and heroic adventures, Deianeira sets out in pursuit of Heracles, determined to bring him home. Unable to cross a river in her path, she accepts a ride from a

FIGURE 10-6   Heracles and Nessus. In his last heroic exploit,
Heracles grabs Nessus by the hair and puts his foot on the creature's
back, as the lying centaur offers one last gesture of supplication. This
vase painting (c. 620 B.C.) is one of many illustrations of Heracles's
associations with the creatures whose physically divided natures reflect his own inner divisions—part god, part brute. Nessus's part in
the death of Heracles reflects the destructive potential of the conflicting drives at work in the warrior hero. (*National Museum, Athens.*)

centaur, **Nessus,** who ferries her halfway across and then tries to rape her. Fortunately,
Heracles comes along just in time, shoots the centaur, and rescues his wife (Figure
10-6). The dying Nessus offers Deianeira a way to ensure Heracles's commitment to
her: he tells her to collect Heracles's blood and semen in a vial and to smear it on his
shirt. As dramatized in Sophocles's *Women of Trachis,* when Heracles dons the shirt,
the mixture eats through his flesh and, destroyed by Deianeira's attempt to domesticate him, Heracles dies.

Heracles was said to have no grave. According to some versions of the myth, his
soul goes to the Underworld, while only his reputation endures; other versions, however, portray Heracles as raised up by the gods from his funeral pyre to be a god on
Olympus, where he is reconciled to Hera and married to her daughter **Hebe,** who
may be a surrogate for the goddess herself, fulfilling at last the quest for immortality
that is central to the heroic endeavor. As Hera's son-in-law, Heracles is formally reconciled with the feminine powers, and Hera and "The Glory" that is now truly hers
are rejoined. Homer, combining both versions in the *Odyssey* (Book 11), describes
Heracles's human part remaining as a shade in Hades, while his divine self takes up

residence with the gods. The hero remains divided in death as he was in life, as complex as human nature itself.

With this final transfiguration, the ongoing conflict between the masculine hero and the feminine principle is at last transcended. The hero can safely participate in this *hieros gamos,* or sacred marriage between the hero and the goddess: since she is no longer an obstacle to his pursuit of immortality, he will not feel compelled to abandon her. Nor will he need to use violence or risk death to pursue the same goal. Thus the inherent contradictions in the hero's nature are at last resolved: in death, if not in life, the beast and the god are reconciled.

Other Heroes: Theseus and Jason

Other heroes share many of the characteristics exemplified by the myths of Heracles: the divine parentage or ancestry, the amazing feats and pursuit of impossible quests, the problems with the women in their lives, and, finally, despite devoting their lives to heroic achievement, oddly nonheroic deaths. In addition, as the role of the hero and that of king or ruler converge, the lives of the heroes increasingly involve political problems as well.

Theseus

The hero Theseus follows (sometimes quite literally) in the footsteps of Heracles. His mother is Aethra, daughter of King Pittheus of Troezen; his father's identity is somewhat ambiguous, since his mother slept with **Aegeus** [EE-jee-uhs] (king of Athens) and the sea god Poseidon on the same night. As a sign and test for his son, Aegeus leaves a sword and a pair of sandals under a heavy stone. Lifting the stone, the prodigious child Theseus asserts simultaneously his political and divine inheritance.

Early Adventures Rivaling Heracles in the number of tales told about him (variously recounted by Plutarch, Apollodorus, and others), Theseus is also similar to Heracles in the specific adventures he encounters. Setting out for Athens, the young Theseus rids the road of various threats to travelers: a robber who beat his victims with a bronze club (reminiscent of Heracles's club), which Theseus takes; another who tied his victims to a pair of pine trees bent to the ground, which, when released, would tear them in two; another who pushed his victims over a cliff to be eaten by a giant sea turtle; and another who wrestled all passersby to death. Like Heracles, Theseus kills a menacing wild boar. He also punishes Procrustes on the same iron bed used by the brigand to torture his victims. (See Figure 10-7 for an illustration of Theseus's various deeds.)

Some of Theseus's adventures were actually identical to those of Heracles. Theseus, sent by his father (who was prompted in turn by his dangerous current wife, Medea) to capture the same Cretan bull once captured by Heracles, brings it back successfully. And, despite yet another anachronism, Heracles and Theseus, several generations removed from each other, even share adventures. Theseus joins Heracles on the voyage of the Argonauts and on his expedition against the Amazons. With Heracles, he is present at the Lapith wedding when the centaurs attack and helps drive them off. And, of course, Heracles rescues Theseus when he is trapped in the Underworld (see Chapter 9).

FIGURE 10-7   The Deeds of Theseus. Surrounding the central illustration in which Theseus kills the Minotaur, this vase painting depicts (clockwise from the top) the encounter with Corynetes, whose bronze club Theseus keeps after defeating this savage threat to travelers; the defeat of Procrustes, on whose bed unwary travelers were either stretched or cut off at the ankles if they did not fit; the battle with Sceiron, who robbed travelers after pretending to wash their feet and then threw them off a cliff to be devoured by a giant turtle; the capture of the Cretan bull, which Theseus brings back alive; the defeat of Sinis, who would kill travelers by tying them to one or two bent-over pine trees that he would then release, either catapulting them to their deaths or tearing them in two; and the defeat of the wild boar (or sow) whose father was Typhon. (*British Museum, London.*)

The Labyrinth   Theseus's most famous exploit is his adventure on Crete. By order of King Minos of Crete, the Athenians were forced to send a tribute of seven men and seven women every nine years to be devoured by the Minotaur, the hybrid offspring of Minos's wife, **Pasiphae** [pah-SIF-a-ee], and the Cretan bull. Hoping to free Athens from this threat, Theseus volunteers to go along as one of the seven men. Before Theseus departs, his father asks him to change his ship's black sail to a white one in the event of his successful return.

FIGURE 10-8 Theseus and the Minotaur. As shown in this vase painting, Theseus takes his sword to the Minotaur, here depicted with a human body but a bull's tail and head. As with Heracles and the centaurs, the multiple associations of the hero with beasts (especially divided creatures like the Minotaur, half-man, half-bull) suggest the battle with the beast within: the savage drives normally repressed within the labyrinth of the unconscious that the life of the warrior hero forces to the surface. (*British Museum, London.*)

Attracted to the hero, Minos's daughter **Ariadne** [ar-ih-AD-nee] procures the help of **Daedalus** to tell Theseus how to kill the Minotaur and escape (via an unrolled ball of string) from the labyrinth where the Minotaur is kept (Figure 10-8). Theseus, of course, succeeds and returns to Athens but forgets to change sails. His father, seeing the ship approaching with black sails, believes his son has died and commits suicide by jumping from a cliff (or from the walls of Athens).

From the historical perspective, this myth may reflect a shift in the center of power in the Mediterranean from Crete to the mainland, thus ending the condition of the Greek coastal city-states as tributaries of the Cretan empire. Enormous Cretan palaces, such as the one at Knossos, with its endless rooms and corridors, could easily have given rise to legends of a "labyrinth" in its basement. From the mythic perspective, we can also see in this story the persistence of the Cretan snake-goddess, herself the source of many of the Greek goddesses, part of whose worship was carried out in the Cretan Bull Dance painted on palace walls and numerous vases excavated at Knossos. Such ceremonies often involved the ritual mating of the goddess in her cow form with the bull-god, who would then be sacrificed, perhaps in place of the king, to ensure the renewal of fertility. The intercourse between Queen Pasiphae, in her cow costume, and the bull, may be the narrative form of that ritual. Similarly, Theseus's entry into the center of the labyrinth, following the string that Ariadne offers (acting here in the role of priestess of the Goddess), suggests a retracing of the umbilical link to the womb where the mysteries of the Goddess are hidden, followed by the rebirth into the upper world. And his killing of the bull and the subsequent destruction of the labyrinth may, some scholars suggest, reflect the shift from the ancient Cretan goddess religion to the patriarchal system that supplanted it in Greece.

Theseus's Women   Women are involved in many of Theseus's adventures, as they are in those of Heracles, but none of the relationships ends happily. For example, Theseus sails from Crete with Ariadne but abandons her on the way home on the island of Naxos, where (according to variant myths) she is killed by Artemis, or marries the god Dionysus, or commits suicide, grieving for the loss of Theseus.

Theseus also seduces and/or defeats the Amazon Queen Hippolyte (or her sister Antiope), whose forces then invade Athens but are in turn defeated. This relationship produces a son, **Hippolytus** [hip-PAHL-ih-tuhs], who comes to cause Theseus great distress. Having married **Phaedra** [FE-drah], the sister of Ariadne, Theseus leaves her with Hippolytus while he goes to Troezen. As dramatized in Euripides's play *Hippolytus,* Phaedra falls in love with the young man, but he refuses her advances, having taken a vow of celibacy in honor of the goddess Artemis. Furious at being rejected, Phaedra tells Theseus that Hippolytus raped her and then kills herself. Theseus calls on Poseidon to kill his son, and the god obligingly sends a bull from the sea to terrify Hippolytus's chariot horses, who bolt, overturning the chariot. Trapped in the reins, Hippolytus is dragged to his death. Artemis then tells Theseus that Hippolytus was innocent and that Aphrodite, angry at the boy's exclusive devotion to Artemis, is responsible for the catastrophe. In some oblique way, of course, Theseus's own unpredictable erotic urges are to blame: it was he, after all, who, driven by his lust, abandoned Ariadne for Phaedra and then, like Heracles, went off on other adventures, leaving Phaedra, in turn, alone.

The myths tell of many marriages of Theseus, but, like Heracles, he engages in no meaningful or lasting relationships. In yet another example of sexual misadventures, Theseus and his friend Pirithous kidnap Helen, as a child, in order to fulfill their ambition to marry a daughter of Zeus himself, something Heracles achieved only after death. The audacious pair then fix upon a scheme to bring Persephone up from the Underworld for Pirithous. Both are bound by Hades to iron chairs for eternity, but only Pirithous remains in the Underworld. Theseus is rescued from the Underworld by Heracles; however, his relationship with the feminine powers remains destructive. The hero can no more domesticate the divine than the human women in his life can domesticate the hero.

Political Problems   Theseus's kidnapping of Helen brings down the wrath of the Spartans, who attack Athens and rescue her in Theseus's absence and establish a rival, Menestheus, on the throne. This is not the first time Theseus has had to protect his rule against usurpers. Earlier, Medea had played on his father's rivalry with his uncle Pallas, brother to Aegeus, who, with his fifty sons, kept trying to take over rulership of Athens. When Medea persuaded Aegeus to send Theseus to capture the Cretan bull, it was with the hope that he wouldn't return so that her own sons could succeed to the throne. This failing, she tried to poison Theseus, but Aegeus fortunately recognized the sword his son wore and foiled her plan. Pallas and his sons repeatedly rebel, and eventually Theseus kills them, but he has to go into exile to Troezen as a result.

Despite the political threats, Theseus manages to unify Athens, to form a central government, and to form alliances with surrounding towns, thus establishing Athens's dominance over Attica, just as Perseus had established his own dominions. The myth of Theseus and the Minotaur also has political overtones. Some scholars see in that myth a reflection of the historical shift of political power in the Aegean from Crete to the mainland at the end of the Minoan Era, with the labyrinth reflecting the relatively provincial mainlanders' response to the enormous Cretan palaces, such as the one archaeologists have excavated at Knossos, with its 1,400 rooms and corridors occupying many levels.

The Death of Theseus   Theseus's death may also have resulted from political rivalries. Going to Scyrus to get allies to help him evict the usurper Menestheus, Theseus either falls or is pushed off a cliff, recapitulating the death of his own father. Like Heracles's death, however, Theseus's less than glorious death is followed by a transfiguration to divine status. Honored by the Athenians—who believed the spirit of Theseus watched over their city, aiding them in the war against the Persians and even appearing at the Battle of Marathon—Theseus was worshiped as a god.

Jason

The most equivocal of the heroes, Jason shares the heroic traits of Heracles and Theseus—the divine ancestry, the search for glory, the performing of impossible tasks—but in a somewhat diminished (if not ironic) and oddly eclectic form so that, although we have a single extended source for most of the details, it almost seems as if the myth of Jason were constructed from scraps of the myths of other heroes.

The son of Aeson of Iolcos, Jason is the grandson of Aeolus, who may be the wind god or a human with the same name. Aeson's brother, **Pelias** [PEE-lih-uhs], usurped the throne of Iolcos; thus, when Jason is born, his parents have him raised in secret by the centaur Chiron. Like Theseus, he is raised away from his father's domain and has his rightful political role usurped by his uncle. Also reminiscent of Theseus's myth, a sandal is one of the signs Jason displays on his return. Pelias had been told by an oracle that a man descended from Aeson and wearing one sandal would kill him: on the trip to Iolcos, Jason loses one sandal while helping Hera, disguised as an old woman, cross a river. Thus, according to one account, when Jason returns to Iolcos lacking one sandal, Pelias recognizes him instantly and determines to get rid of him.

The Golden Fleece   To dispose of Jason, Pelias sends him to get the Golden Fleece. This is an impossible mission since the fleece is located in the distant land of Colchis, ruled by King Aeetes, who has a reputation for treating guests abominably. To gain glory, Jason, like Perseus and Theseus, accepts this challenge and sets about organizing an expedition—one of the most famous in Greek mythology—of **Argonauts** (sailors on the ship the *Argo,* commissioned for this purpose). All the heroes—whether of Jason's generation or not, including Heracles, Orpheus, and, in some versions, Theseus, share the quest (Figure 10-9). After a long series of adventures during which they do battle with human rivals and monsters, propitiate the Phrygian

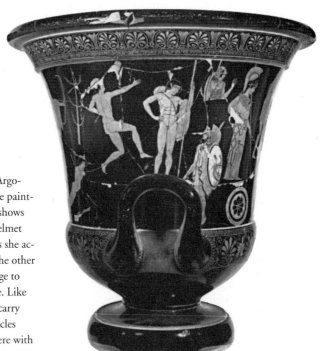

FIGURE 10-9 The Argonauts with Athene. The painting on this large bowl shows Athene, wearing her helmet and carrying a spear, as she accompanies Jason and the other Argonauts on the voyage to gain the Golden Fleece. Like Athene, the heroes all carry spears, except for Heracles (center, top), shown here with his club. (*Louvre, Paris.*)

mother-goddess Cybele, and avoid, with Athene's help, being crushed by the Clashing Rocks, they arrive at Colchis.

Hera, meanwhile, has a vested interest in the quest: having been insulted by Pelias, who worships the other gods but scorns Hera, she wants Pelias dead and believes that no one but **Medea** [me-DEE-a] can accomplish that. Thus she wants Jason to bring Medea back with him. Athene also supports the operation, and Aphrodite assists by causing Medea to fall in love with Jason on his arrival.

Just as Ariadne helped Theseus, Medea helps Jason get the Golden Fleece, but with a difference. Before Aeetes will give Jason the fleece, he orders the hero to perform another impossible feat: he must yoke a fire-breathing bull, plow a field, and sow it with dragon's teeth, left over, apparently, from the founding of Thebes by **Cadmus.** Just as in the Theban myth, Jason must kill the armed men who germinate from these teeth. Protected by a drug that Medea gives him, which he applies to himself and his weapons, Jason performs the task, only to find that Aeetes reneges on his promise and plans to attack the Argonauts.

Jason must therefore steal the fleece and escape in secret. But unlike Theseus, who killed the Minotaur, Jason doesn't actually fight the serpent or dragon guarding the tree on which the Golden Fleece is hung; rather, Medea, trusting Jason's promise to marry her, casts a spell to put the creature to sleep so that Jason can safely remove the object of his quest. To prevent pursuit by Aeetes, Medea kills and dismembers the corpse of her younger brother, tossing the pieces in the sea so that her father will be obliged to stop and retrieve them in order to give his son a proper burial. Not even the savage Heracles, cutting off the ears and noses of his enemy's ambassadors, could match such gratuitous violence.

The Role of Hecate   As Perseus was aided by Athene, so Jason continues to be helped by Medea. But again, although both Athene and Hera continue to support the Argonauts' mission, the contrasts are significant: Perseus attacks the Gorgons, the terrifying aspect of the primordial Goddess, and delivers up their power to the Olympian goddess Athene; Jason, on the other hand, propitiates the chthonic powers, performing rituals in honor of **Hecate** [HEK-uh-tee] (some of whose powers Medea also shares) both before and after his trials. It is the power of Hecate that allows him both to obtain the fleece and to escape afterward. And whereas heroes like Theseus and Heracles descend to the Underworld to subdue the power of Hades and defy mortality, Jason enters only the barbaric region of Colchis, portrayed in the myths as a remote and savage place where witchcraft and sorcery flourish and where, rather than defy the chthonic powers, he succumbs to them.

From this point on, the acts that Jason allows Medea to perform on his behalf become more appalling, while Jason himself behaves increasingly less like a hero and more like a self-serving coward who uses women as a means to gain his objectives. Ultimately, his quest for glory yields to a crass desire for wealth and status. Meanwhile, the Olympians who supported the Argonauts' voyage disappear from view. In the absence of the gods, the tension between the human and the divine that sustained, however tragically, the heroic endeavor likewise disappears. The heroic quest for victory over time—for the power of immortality—degenerates into a quest for power in merely human and thus venial terms.

Jason's Return   When Jason returns with the Golden Fleece, his uncle Pelias—who has in the meantime killed Jason's father and thus prompted his mother's suicide—is still on the throne. Medea, however, trading on her reputation as a sorceress, convinces Pelias's daughters that their aging father will be rejuvenated if they kill him, dismember the corpse, and cook it. They perform Medea's prescribed ritual, but of course without the desired result.

Having thus succeeded to the throne of Iolcos by this somewhat questionable method, Jason forfeits the trust of its people, and he and Medea are forced to leave. Whereas other heroes typically have strong regional associations—Perseus and Heracles with Mycenae and Tiryns, for example, and Theseus with Athens—Jason, already abandoned by the gods, becomes a man without a country. Emigrating to Corinth, he and Medea set up residence and have two children. But Jason is not content and, as dramatized in Euripides's *Medea* (see Chapter 17), decides to fulfill his ambitions for power by abandoning Medea and marrying the princess of Corinth, daughter of King Creon, an ironic inversion of the typical heroic achievement of status in spite of or even in defiance of marriage. He also demands custody of the children, claiming that he can support them better being married to the princess than he can as Medea's common-law husband.

Medea   Refusing to yield, Medea poisons the princess and King Creon and (at least in Euripides's version) kills the children. She then escapes in a dragon-powered chariot to Athens, where she has been promised asylum by King Aegeus in return for her promise to cure his infertility. (The child thus conceived, when Aegeus stops off briefly in Troezen and makes love to Aethra as he is returning to Athens, turns out to be none other than Theseus, who, in the typically timeless world of intersecting myths, had already accompanied Jason on his voyage to Colchis!)

In her role as the source of fertility, as in her continuing connection with dragons— the dragon that guards the Golden Fleece and the winged dragon that pulls the chariot given to her as a gift by her grandfather, Helios—Medea carries out the creative and transformative functions of the primordial Goddess. But as was true of Medusa, with whom Medea shares a link with the serpents/dragons and the sun-chariot, these powerful symbols are now reinterpreted, as was the role of Medea's divine counterpart, Hecate, in a more perverse and terrifying fashion as evidence of her witchcraft. Nevertheless, Medea drives the chariot of the sun, and unlike Phaethon, whose attempt to drive the sun vehicle ended in a fatal crash, Medea has no difficulty. The powers she commands are so awesome, no wonder Jason is no match for her! If the sky gods and the heroes who emulate them have succeeded in decapitating the ancient goddess, driving her underground and transforming her into the witch or sorceress, then in figures like Medea the goddess has her revenge.

The Death of Jason   Jason's death is the most inglorious of all of the heroes'. Bereft of friends and family as he sits, dejected, under the prow of his rotting ship, Jason is killed when a beam falls off and hits him on the head. Jason is not elevated—as are Theseus, Perseus, and Heracles—to the status of divinity or made into the object of a cult. With Jason, in death as in the latter part of his life, the hero figure has reached a new low.

The Upper Limits of Human Ambition: Phaethon

The Greeks were fascinated by heroes in the excessive Heracleian mold—indeed, they admired no hero more than Achilles, who shares many of the earlier heroes' qualities. But a society that came to value the Apollonian way of self-knowledge and moderation could hardly maintain that such heroes were appropriate role models. If myths about Heracleian heroes emphasize the transcendent elements of the fractionalized hero—half-human, half-divine—other myths, providing an alternative perspective on the heroic impulse, reminded the Greeks of the necessary limits on human ambition. The myths of Icarus and Phaethon, young men who defy those limits, reinforce the need to be aware of one's human limitations and to exercise self-control. But no one makes songs to the memories of those who walk the middle way: the Golden Mean is not the road that heroes travel.

When Clymene tells her son **Phaethon** [FEE-e-thahn] that he is actually the son of Helios, the sun god, the young man travels to the god's palace and requests proof of his divine paternity. Helios (or Apollo, in Ovid's later retelling in the *Metamorphoses*) promises to grant any wish that his son might have. Admiring the glorious chariot of the sun that his father drives, Phaethon asks to drive it himself for one day. Although he knows that the chariot is beyond the boy's powers, Helios is bound by his promise and reluctantly yields.

Phaethon is eager to test the power of the marvelous vehicle and starts off with great exuberance, but, as his father predicted, he loses control of the horses. They veer off course, first bolting up into the heavens, where they leave a visual reminder of the havoc Phaethon causes, the great scar of the Milky Way; then, careening down, they set the earth on fire from the intense heat of the sun. To save the earth from destruction, Zeus is forced to kill Phaethon with a lightning bolt. Once again, overconfidence and the desire to take on tasks better suited to the gods prove deadly. We mortals need to be reminded: half-divine is simply not enough.

Questions for Discussion and Review

1. In what ways is Perseus similar to Heracles and Theseus? In what ways is he different? Discuss the ways in which their semidivine natures influence their adventures, their relationships with women, and their political affairs, as well as their status after death.

2. For the heroes of Greek myths, the ultimate adventure is going to the Underworld and coming back alive. Why do Heracles and Theseus go to the Underworld? How does the quest help them achieve the immortality they desire?

3. The standard pattern of the rite of passage includes the hero's separation from his normal environment; his initiation or encounter with supernatural forces; and his return, bearing some new understanding to share with the members of his community. Choose a significant example from the adventures of Perseus, Heracles, and Theseus, and explain how each follows this pattern. In each case, what new understanding does the hero achieve?

4. Does Jason also undergo a rite of passage? Explain what elements of Jason's adventures fit the archetypal pattern of separation and initiation. Does Jason also return with any new insight or understanding? Explain your position.

5. Using Theseus or Heracles as an example, explain how the heroic version of the trip to the Underworld is similar to that of Persephone, who undergoes a rite of passage of her own. Explain the similarities and differences between the separation, initiation, and return of the male, as modeled in the myths of the heroes, and that of the female, as exemplified by the myth of Persephone's abduction and eventual return.

Recommended Reading

Campbell, Joseph. *The Hero With a Thousand Faces.* 1949. Cleveland: World, 1970. A study of the rite of passage of the archetypal hero as he goes through the stages of his quest: from the separation from his familiar environment, to the confrontation with the forces of the supernatural world, to his return, bearing new wisdom to share with his fellow citizens.

Dumezil, Georges. *The Stakes of the Warrior.* Trans. David Weeks. 1968. Berkeley: U of California P, 1983. Sets Heracles in the context of similar Indo-European warrior heroes who are torn between demonic and civilizing divine patrons and who thus become both monstrous themselves and slayers of monsters.

Segal, Robert A., Introduction. *In Quest of the Hero.* Ed. Robert A. Segal. Princeton: Princeton UP, 1990. Contains essays on the heroic pattern by the Freudian Otto Rank, by Lord Raglan, of the ritual school of mythographers, and by the folklorist Alan Dundes.

Heroes at War:
The Troy Saga

KEY THEMES

At the wedding of Peleus and Thetis, the uninvited goddess of discord, Eris, tosses a golden apple. When three goddesses fight over it, Zeus throws it off Mount Olympus. It is found by Paris, prince of Troy, who gives it to the goddess Aphrodite in return for her promise, the love of the most beautiful woman in the world. That woman is Helen, wife of Menelaus. When she runs off to Troy with Paris, the Greeks and Trojans go to war. After a ten-year siege, Troy is destroyed by Odysseus's trick of the Trojan Horse. In the Iliad, Homer tells of a quarrel between the general Agamemnon and the hero Achilles in the Greek camp in the ninth year of the war.

The Decision of Paris

The story of the judgment (or decision) of Paris is seminal to the study of Greek mythology, not only because it is the seed from which so many myths arise, but also because it is a paradigm of the complex world in which those myths reside. The story involves a minor sea goddess, **Thetis,** and a mortal man, **Peleus,** who are about to wed. Zeus, it seems, has heard a prophecy, perhaps revealed by Prometheus in exchange for his freedom, that a child of his, possibly by Thetis, will one day usurp his throne. To prevent such a threat, Zeus marries off Thetis, to whom he is sexually attracted, to a human prince, guaranteeing that any child of hers will be half-human and thus no threat to his divinity. Or perhaps Zeus is simply punishing her, as one variant account suggests, for refusing, out of loyalty to Hera, who raised her, to yield to his sexual advances; or perhaps (a third variant) he is rewarding Peleus for his uncommon valor.

Zeus invites to the wedding all the gods and goddesses except one—**Eris,** the goddess of strife, or discord. Naturally, she arrives uninvited and tosses at the assembled guests a golden apple bearing the inscription "For the fairest."

Three goddesses—Hera, Athene, and Aphrodite—quarrel over the apple. Determined to preserve harmony, Zeus throws the apple down off Mount Olympus. It lands in a field outside Troy, where **Paris,** son of King Priam of Troy, is tending sheep. Picking up the apple, Paris is startled by the sudden appearance of the three goddesses, each of whom asks for it, offering him a gift in exchange. Hera, queen of the gods, offers power over all of Asia Minor, but Paris will one day inherit his father's power, so he turns her down. Athene offers wisdom but, like many young men, Paris is sure that he already possesses all the wisdom he needs. Aphrodite offers the love of the most beautiful woman in the world, and, to a young man whose only company is a flock of sheep, she clearly wins the prize (Figure 11-1). The goddesses, one exultant, the other two enraged, disappear—perhaps it was a dream. Paris goes back to his sheep.

Shortly thereafter, King Priam calls for his son, now old enough to assume some political responsibilities, and sends him on his first diplomatic mission—to the home of **Menelaus** [men-e-LAY-uhs], king of Sparta. Or perhaps, prompted by Aphrodite, he chooses on his own to go. Menelaus's wife, **Helen,** is the most beautiful woman in the world because of her half-divine parentage. She is the daughter of a mortal woman, Leda, and Zeus, who appeared to Leda (who would not betray her husband, Tyndareus, with another man) in the form of a great white swan. In another variant, Paris already knows of Helen's beauty and goes to Sparta intending to kidnap her.

While Paris is a guest in Menelaus's home, Menelaus leaves for a brief trip of his own. Left alone with Helen, Paris seduces her. Or perhaps he abducts her, along with some of Menelaus's treasure, and returns to Troy. When, despite official protests, Paris refuses to return Helen, Priam feels honor-bound to defend his son, though it means war with Menelaus. The latter, however, has many powerful allies: when Tyndareus, Helen's supposed father, was ready to marry her off, he summoned all the heroes— the princes of noble families—as potential suitors. Before announcing his choice, Tyndareus made them all swear to support Helen's husband should he ever call upon their aid. Thus begins the Trojan War—ten years of death and chaos, consequences of a bad choice.

The Implications of the Story

Among the most popular bodies of material in Greek mythology, the stories that make up the saga of Troy are retold in numerous variations by many writers. Among the most important narrative sources for the pre- and post-*Iliad* materials are Apollodorus's *Library,* Ovid's *Metamorphoses,* and various works by unknown writers, often fragments, collectively referred to as the "Epic Cycle" (among them the *Cypria* and the *Little Iliad*), as well as Hyginus's *Fabulae.* Examples of the many dramatic sources include plays by Aeschylus (the *Oresteia*), Euripides (*Iphigenia at Aulis; Iphigenia Among the Taurians; Orestes; Trojan Women*), and Sophocles (*Aias; Philoctetes*). The alternative versions of parts of the story of the judgment of Paris and the endless sequels—including the sacrifice of Agamemnon's daughter Iphigenia, the destruction of Troy, the death of Achilles, the murder of Agamemnon and Orestes's revenge, the wanderings of Odysseus, as well as many other tales—reflect the multiform and open-ended nature of Greek myths. Such a complex network of overlapping but often contradictory tales inevitably prompts us to ask where the saga of Troy truly

FIGURE 11-1   Casali Altar, The Judgment of Paris. This Roman bas-relief shows Paris (seated, top right) negotiating with the three goddesses—Athene (left), Hera (center), and Aphrodite (right, shown partially disrobed)—while Hermes holds the golden apple which he has delivered to the Trojan prince. (*Vatican Museums, Rome.*)

begins: is it with Paris's judgment, with Zeus's rape of Leda (as the modern Irish poet Yeats asserts—see Chapter 21), or with the genesis of a universe that, as Hesiod describes it in the *Theogony,* emerges out of chaos at its inception? The beginning and end of the story of the decision of Paris are obscured in the mysteries of the creation and destruction of the universe itself.

The Timelessness of Myth

The myths occur in a timeless world, or at least they refuse to submit to the tests of human chronology and logic. Consider, for example, **Achilles** [a-KIL-leez], the child born of the marriage of Peleus and Thetis. Goddesses, like human females, apparently carry their offspring for nine months. Presumably, then, Achilles is born within a year of the marriage. If, meanwhile, Paris's embassy to Menelaus begins several months after the incident of the apple and lasts even a year, and even if it takes, as the myths attest, a year for the Greeks to assemble their troops and another for the armada to set sail for Troy, then Achilles would have been two years old when the war began and twelve when it ended. According to some variants, Helen and Paris spent a ten-year honeymoon on Crete before returning to Troy, but even that interval would have made Achilles twelve years old at the start of the war—still too young for the experiences attributed to him. Before the war starts, Achilles is already the Greeks' most renowned hero and was one of the suitors for Helen's hand before her marriage to Menelaus. And before the war is over, Achilles's son, Neoptolemus, is old enough to join the battle and become a hero in his own right! No reasonable computation can make sense of these numbers in terms of human time. We may ask the questions, but the myth, in its own timeless realm, refuses to address them.

Conflict in Society and the Cosmos

On a social level, Zeus, god of family love and of guest-host relationships, sanctifies values that preserve the sacred institution of marriage, harmony within families, and civilized modes of social and political exchange that maintain order. This larger cosmic perspective is reflected in political terms in the emerging concept of the Greeks as a nation, witnessed in the *Iliad,* as scholars have noted, in the collective names by which the Greeks refer to themselves: Hellenes, Danaans, Argives, **Achaeans.** Paris, making off with Menelaus's wife while a guest in the Spartan king's home, violates these god-ordained relationships. But personal and familial loyalty are also important under the older kinship system, in which the clan is the source of security, values, and justice. When Priam, believing that honor and family love oblige him to stand behind his son's bad judgment, refuses to abide by the larger social norms, adhering instead to loyalty to the clan, the two systems clash. In a world already in transition, the crisis forces these two systems into open conflict, releasing the aggressions that all such social systems usually manage to keep in check. The veneer of civilized life is stripped away, and the world is plunged into war.

It is not just social structures that can change. The cosmos itself in which the myth occurs is dynamic: although Zeus's regime appears stable, there are recurrent hints, however obscure, that it will not be eternal. Change is given in the nature of things, and not even the immortal gods rule forever. The powers of the gods in this cosmos, furthermore, are limited. Zeus is in command but not in control of the universe. He cannot by fiat decree Discord nonexistent: evil exists, and Zeus, like the rest of us, must cope with it. The disharmony in the human world, moreover, is both consequence and reflection of the disharmony in a cosmos at war with itself. The Trojan War, like the war between the Titans and the Olympians, reflects an ambiguous and contradictory universe in which, as Hesiod pointed out, a mixture of good and evil is the best one can hope for.

The Human and the Divine

The myth of the decision of Paris also depicts, in terms characteristic of Greek mythology, the conjunction of the human and the divine. So closely connected are the two—the gods so like humans, the humans so godlike—that marriage is possible between them. But such marriages are fraught with difficulties: although they remain amicable, Peleus and Thetis soon separate—they may love each other, but they fail to understand each other. Thetis, attempting to erase the father's human taint from her child, dips Achilles in the divine fire (or water), holding him by the heel. For all her efforts, though, she cannot erase his paternal inheritance: "Achilles's heel" *is* the human condition. Meanwhile, Peleus, terrified that Thetis's efforts will destroy his son, attempts unsuccessfully to stop her. They are clearly incompatible and must carry on their lives on separate planes.

The gods, furthermore, lack the power either to control human nature or to compel human fate: Thetis can neither make Achilles immortal nor prevent him from going to Troy. Thus, within the limits of mortality, human beings have the freedom to act: just as Paris freely chooses to give the apple to Aphrodite, so Achilles freely chooses to go to Troy; and both must accept responsibility for their fates. Indeed, Paris, dangling an apple over the heads of three goddesses, already has, in a way perhaps even he does not understand, more power than Hera can offer him.

The myth of the decision of Paris offers us a universe of infinite, though ambiguous, options; it offers human beings the freedom to choose, but no guarantees or clear-cut guides. Paris chooses love, sacrificing power and wisdom: could he have chosen better? Would raw power, unguided by wisdom or love, have been a better choice? Or an abstract wisdom, untempered by love and lacking the power to act? Choosing love, Paris defines himself, as do Achilles and Hector when they choose to fight (and die) for glory. Each lives the life and death he has chosen. For all its trappings of prophecies and oracles, Greek mythology depicts in the story of the decision of Paris a world of human freedom and moral responsibility, where every choice is fraught with awe and terror and every life contains the possibilities at once for transcendence and for tragedy.

The Trojan Cycle Continues: Events Preceding the *Iliad*

The Gathering of the Troops

When Menelaus calls up his allies, the most powerful Greek princes and their troops, led by Menelaus's brother, Agamemnon, begin gathering at the port of Aulis. Only two, **Odysseus** [oh-DIS-ee-uhs] and Achilles, fail to appear.

Odysseus had married Helen's cousin Penelope, who recently gave birth to their son, Telemachus. Devoted to his family, Odysseus is reluctant to leave them when the call to arms comes. When Agamemnon's ambassadors arrive, Odysseus pretends to be insane, but when they test him by placing the baby in front of the plow he is driving, Odysseus immediately acts to save his son, thus revealing the pretense. Once committed to the war effort, however, Odysseus becomes the most loyal officer and the prime strategist and morale builder of the Greek troops.

Odysseus's first assignment is to locate and recruit the missing Achilles. In a desperate attempt to protect her son from the prophecy that he would die young if he participated in the Trojan War, Thetis insisted that he hide on the island of Scyros, disguised as a girl. Disguising himself in turn as a merchant, Odysseus travels to Scyros and displays before the local women an assortment of beautiful garments and one suit of armor. While the women examine the dresses, Achilles's attention is immediately drawn to the armor. Thus found out, Achilles comes willingly.

The Events at Aulis

With the armada assembled at Aulis, the goddess Artemis, perhaps angered by Agamemnon's boast that his skill at hunting exceeded hers, causes the winds to die down, thus preventing the ships from embarking for Troy. When he appeals to the gods for some clue as to how to proceed, Agamemnon is informed by the prophet Calchas that he must sacrifice his daughter Iphigenia (see Chapter 15). Only then do the ships set sail. The war on Troy, intended to save a family, begins by destroying one, and the effort is tainted from the start.

The War Begins

While the Greeks have been gathering their troops and awaiting the invasion, the Trojans have been gathering allies of their own. When the Greeks, after taking some outlying cities, land on the beaches at Troy, they find a highly fortified city whose walls are impregnable and whose many allies prevent the Greeks from creating a total blockade. The river Scamander also runs through the city, providing its water supply. A well-defended city whose lifelines of food and water are secure can wait out even the longest siege, and thus the Trojans are in no immediate danger. If they choose to stay inside the walls, they are safe; if they choose to come out and fight, they have a safe retreat nearby. The Greeks, meanwhile, in a temporary encampment far from home, are at a strategic and psychological disadvantage.

For nine years, the Greek troops remain camped on the beaches. Battles are fought, men are killed, prisoners are taken and kept or ransomed, but the war itself remains stalemated, the Trojans unable to drive the Greeks from their shores, the Greeks unable to breach the walls and take the city. The level of frustration is high on both sides. It is at this point that Homer picks up the story in his epic poem the *Iliad.*

The Homeric Epics

The Question of Authorship

The *Iliad* and the *Odyssey* are traditionally attributed to Homer, a poet about whom we know virtually nothing beyond the speculation that he may have lived on an island off the coast of Asia Minor between 800 and 700 B.C. Legends depicting Homer as blind may have been extrapolated from his portrayal of the blind bard, Demodocus, in the *Odyssey.* But since Homer also describes a sighted bard in the same epic, we must infer the possibility of embellishment by Homer's admirers, placing him in the tradition of the blind prophet of the myths, Tiresias, who, undistracted by surface appearances, sees moral truths, just as the poet must.

Both poems exhibit what scholars agree are signs of oral composition: fixed epithets and adjectives ("wily Odysseus," "swift-footed Achilles"), set speeches made by one character and repeated verbatim by another, and genealogies of characters, weapons, and even animals. Both poems also share qualities of style and, to a lesser extent, structure. Thus some scholars believe that one poet composed both works. The poems' perspectives, however—on the characteristics of the gods, the role of women, the value of the heroic life, and the nature of the universe itself—differ radically. Did a single poet change his mind about many important issues? We have clear evidence from more recent times of poets who have done so. Or were these poems composed by one poet and later modified by different hands who wrote them down? Were they composed by different poets and possibly later recorded by the same editor? We have, to date, no verifiable answers to these questions. Although the multiple-authorship theory is the most common one among modern scholars, for ease of reference, this text will henceforth cite Homer as the author of both texts.

The Literary Transformations: Myth into Epic

Both poems make extensive use of inherited mythic materials. But neither is merely a retelling of traditional stories. Literary devices such as the use of dialogue and of an omniscient narrator (the all-knowing author who can reveal what his characters, human or divine, are thinking and can comment on the tale directly) allow the poet to impose his own perspective on the myths.

Further, the author has shaped the received material into a specific literary form, the epic. Choosing to write in the epic genre (or literary type) itself constitutes an interpretation of the myths. The epic entails what were undoubtedly, by Homer's time, already formal conventions: the proem (the opening passages establishing the author's central concerns), the semidivinity of the hero, and the hero's descent into the Underworld. The choice of the epic form—traditionally, for the Greeks, the highest of the genres—also establishes the author's conviction of the seriousness and grandeur of his subject. A long narrative poem celebrating the achievements of a culture and the deeds of a hero who protects it, the epic is itself an expression of pride in one's civilization.

Epics transform their mythic sources in other ways as well. In contrast to the timeless world of myth, the epic is rooted in human time. In the *Iliad,* for example, the poet keeps reminding his audience of the passage of time: time taken out for the cremation of corpses; time remembered in the genealogies; time compared (as the aged Nestor does, recalling the days of his youth, when heroes were *really* spectacular). In the *Odyssey,* time is even more prominent: ten years for the war, followed by ten years of wandering; the growth of Telemachus; the aging of Penelope and Odysseus. Even his dog, Argos, a pup when Odysseus left, reminds us, as he wags his tail one last time in joy at Odysseus's return before expiring, of the inexorable drive toward death that lends such urgency to human experience.

Besides using (and, indeed, expanding) the possibilities of the epic form, Homer also selected and transformed the available mythic material to reflect his own thematic perspectives. Thus, while the traditional myth presents a narrative that is itself simple but open-ended, the literary work presents a more complicated but closed narrative with a defined beginning, middle, and end.

Homer also uses epic similes (extended comparisons) to ground his works in the soil of real human experience, despite the presence of the gods and the quasi-supernatural adventures of the heroes. He thus allows us to imagine the more remote actions in terms of the more familiar. Thus, although we have surely never seen a monster like Scylla reach down, pluck a man off a ship, and eat him, we have probably seen a man fishing from a rock who casts his line and plucks a fish from the water, a more common experience to which Homer, in a simile in the *Odyssey,* compares the more fantastic one. Similarly, although we are not half-divine and may not understand what it feels like to possess the heroes' superhuman powers, we can surely understand how using a tool extends the power of the human hand; thus Paris, in a simile, compares Hector's prowess to a sharpened ax-edge which extends the powers of the hero.

Other literary devices, some of which Homer probably invented (the cliff-hanger and the interrupted flashback), also help shape the material. Consider, for example, the startling juxtaposition in the great chase scene in the *Iliad.* Achilles chases Hector three times around the walls of Troy before he finally catches and kills his rival. But in the midst of the scene, Homer interrupts the chase for an extended description of how, on that spot in the days before the war, women used to do the laundry. What better way to remind the audience of the values that, in their preoccupation with personal glory and impending death, both heroes have forgotten: what both sides in the war are ostensibly fighting for is the right to carry on their prosaic domestic lives, the right to keep their families and their daily rituals intact, the right to do the laundry in peace.

The *Iliad*

Omitting all mention of the Promethean prophecy, the decision of Paris and the divine quarrel that precedes the war, and the failed attempt of Thetis to immortalize her son, Homer centers the *Iliad* squarely in the human world. Unlike the *Odyssey,* which opens on Mount Olympus with the gods in council, the *Iliad* begins in the Greek encampment. The gods do not appear until the priest Chryses, offended at Agamemnon's refusal to ransom his daughter, calls upon Apollo to intervene. Nor does the poet choose to chronicle the war itself: neither the sacrifice of Iphigenia nor the death of Achilles nor the sacking of Troy is ever mentioned. Beginning instead with a single event in the ninth year of the long-stalemated war, Homer chooses to focus entirely on the quarrel between Achilles and Agamemnon and its consequences in order to explore some central questions that must occur in a society in which kings are warriors and warriors are heroes. What does it mean to be a hero? How valid is the code of honor by which heroes live? What are the hero's potentials and limits? How far can a hero go in pursuing his goals without either offending the gods or alienating himself from the human community? How does a hero commit violent acts to defend his civilization without destroying what he is fighting for? And, finally, how can a hero create a meaningful life for himself in the face of certain death?

The Hero's Nature

The heroes we meet in the *Iliad* are, like Heracles, divided souls. Gifted with enormous energy and the drive to use it, they take an aggressive stance toward experience, whether in the characteristic "shoot first, ask questions later" attitude or in the irresistible impulse always to "go forward," to attack their problems or their enemies head-on. Hector can no more sit contentedly inside the walls of Troy and simply outwait the Greeks—however logical a strategy that might be—than Achilles can fulfill himself by sulking in his tent or staying safely at home. Each can fulfill his gifts, his inner nature, only in being what he is. As Paris is a born lover whose gifts are the blessing of Aphrodite, so Achilles and Hector are, by nature, warriors. But to fulfill their needs as godlike warriors, they must violate their social needs as human beings.

The Hero's Two Fates Achilles is presented with not one but two fates: to die gloriously at Troy or to live anonymously at home. The choices confronting him, however, are at best ambiguous: for individuals such as Achilles and Hector, to choose inaction is to suffer the death of the soul that occurs when one's identity is shattered; to choose action, on the other hand, is to choose to die, sooner or later, in battle. Doomed whether he goes or stays, such an individual is confronted by the same tragic paradox that beset Heracles: to escape the mortality that is the inevitable lot of humanity, the hero strives to make his name immortal by pursuing glory. But in order to choose death with honor, he must of course choose death. Each, however, makes the choice in full awareness of the consequences. Propelled by the enormous heroic energy that consumes as it inspires them, both Hector and Achilles arrive at the same moment of recognition and make the same decision: "Let it come." For the epic hero, as for the hero of the later tragedies, the readiness is all.

The Hero's Reputation

The *Iliad* describes a world in which the glory of a hero is not merely the consequence of divine gifts. Rather, his reputation must be publicly confirmed. Unique by virtue of his skills, the hero nevertheless must depend on the community to confer heroic status, signified through rank, rewards, prizes, songs, and stories. It is all too easy, then, to confuse the outward signs of heroism with the intrinsic merit and the amazing deeds that earned them. Both Agamemnon and Achilles confuse the rank of general and the status of hero with the outward signs of respect from their troops or peers. Forgetting that a general needs his troops, Agamemnon neglects his responsibilities to his men, thinks of his own need for "prizes" sufficient for his rank, and suffers by losing men and battles. Forgetting that even heroes need the bonds of human society, Achilles, humiliated by having his "prize" publicly removed, withdraws from the field and suffers by losing his beloved friend **Patroclus** [pa-TROH-kluhs] (Figure 11-2).

Achilles and Hector   Enraged by grief, Achilles forgets his human limits and imagines that he can stand up to a raging river god, commit vile atrocities against the dead, and scorn the need to eat. Only when he is at last reconciled with Priam, whose son, **Hector,** Achilles has killed and whose corpse Achilles refuses to release (Figure 11-3), does he belatedly recognize that the demands of the belly signify communion with the gods (as men pray and sacrifice some of each meal), the limits of the merely human body, and, as men feast together, the bonds that unite human beings into a community. Only then does Achilles emerge from the shell of egocentricity and begin to say *we* instead of *I*.

Hector exhibits similar confusion. Determined to protect his family and honor, he confuses honor with blind loyalty and fights in what he knows is a bad cause. He, too, knows that the inevitable consequence will be the destruction of the very city for which he sacrifices himself.

Diomedes   Among these exalted but tragic heroes, one figure emerges as a more moderate alternative—**Diomedes** [dye-oh-MEE-deez] "of the loud war cry." Formidable in battle, willing and able to take on and defeat even the gods themselves, he nevertheless knows when to stop. He is able to accept limits, whether required by the rules of courtesy (he will not, for example, fight Glaucus, the Trojan descendant of a guest-friend of Diomedes's own grandfather) or by direct orders from the gods (urged on by Athene, Diomedes wounds both Aphrodite and Ares, but when Apollo tells him not to attack any more gods, he obeys). Although he possesses the courage and the skills of the hero, he is not driven to meet experience head-on in defiance of the consequences. He is, furthermore, as persuasive in the assembly as he is effective on the battlefield. No one will ever make songs about Diomedes. Nevertheless, he pos-

FIGURE 11-2   The Armour of Achilles. In this vase painting (c. 460 B.C.), Thetis embraces her son, who is still grieving for the death of Patroclus. Athene is present, on the left, to lend her support to the re-arming of the despondent hero. His new shield is held by two Nereids, one of whom, herself saddened by the spectacle of Achilles's grief, covers her own face. (*British Museum, London.*)

sesses the kind of balance that the Greeks later came to admire. (Much later, by the fifth century B.C., the qualities exhibited by Diomedes—the equal development of mind and body, the rational way of self-knowledge and self-control—would become the ideals of classical Greek culture.)

Odysseus   The most gifted speaker among the Greeks, Odysseus is able to use his characteristic diplomacy and common sense to his advantage, persuading the Greeks not to retreat to the ships, for example, stepping into the gap when Agamemnon's leadership momentarily falters, and preserving discipline and morale. But although we get to see him in action as a great soldier (rescuing the corpse of Patroclus, for example, along with his usual companion, Ajax), his most noteworthy activities are his intelligence operations, such as sneaking into Troy in disguise, for example, or wreaking havoc at night in the Trojan encampment. His willingness to use disguise and deception, of course, eventually allows the Greeks to win (via the stratagem of the Trojan Horse, a clever ruse which Homer does not include in the *Iliad*). Indeed, the Greeks valued his services, but heroes do not sneak about in disguise or under cover of darkness. Behaving as if the aim is to win the war and get home instead of to display one's heroic prowess in a game, Odysseus is a somewhat ambiguous hero (see Chapter 12).

The Gods

If the human world is confused, the realm of the Olympians is equally disordered. Divided among themselves, the gods nag, quarrel, lie, deceive, and, of course, take sides—Hera, Poseidon, and Athene favor the Greeks, while Apollo, Artemis, and Aphrodite favor the Trojans. Ares, the two-faced god of war, simply enjoys the sport

FIGURE 11-3   Priam Pleading with Achilles for the Body of Hector. In this vase painting, the bearded Priam, leaning on his staff, appeals to Achilles, shown here reclining under his famous helmet and shield, for the return of his son Hector's corpse, here stretched under Achilles's chair. Rejecting the gifts offered by Priam's followers, Achilles turns his face from the old man. (*Kunsthistorisches Museum, Vienna.*)

and fights on both sides. Zeus himself, although temporarily yielding to Thetis's request to support Achilles in his quarrel with Agamemnon, is relatively neutral, having worshipers and favorite heroes on both sides and even a son, Sarpedon, among the Trojans. He would prefer a peaceful compromise or at least an agreement by the other gods not to intervene. But he is unable to arrange the former or to prevent the latter.

The Gods' Intervention in Human Affairs   The gods intervene in human affairs in a variety of ways. They affect the action indirectly by cheering on the men to acts of courage, by sending dreams that inspire fear or affect morale, and by bringing up clouds of darkness to cover retreats or to interrupt battles. More directly, they also intervene by assuming human disguise and getting down on the battlefield, where they block the path of arrows or actually fight, both as aggressors (as when Apollo knocks the wind out of Patroclus, setting him up to be killed) and as targets (as when both Ares and Aphrodite are wounded by Diomedes). Unlike the human combatants, however, the gods bleed **ichor** [IH-kor] instead of blood and cannot really be hurt—being immortal, they need only to retreat to Olympus, where a balm applied by Hephaestus instantly cures all wounds. The gods of the *Iliad* may appear superficially human in their behavior, but the crucial distinction remains: gods simply do not die. For the gods, then, the war is like a game in which they cheer on their favorite teams and players and occasionally spill over onto the playing field. Ultimately, the fate of individual humans can be of little real consequence to them.

Greek and Anglicized Spellings of Characters' Names in the *Iliad*

Because different translators adopt differing English transliterations of Greek names, the names of characters in Greek literature are spelled in a variety of ways. Whereas this text uses an Anglicized spelling, the translation of the *Iliad* included here adopts a spelling approximating the pronunciation of the original Greek. The following list provides a sampling of both versions of the names. (For a similar list of variant spellings of gods' names, see Chapter 5, p. 123.)

Aias (Ajax)	Hektor (Hector)
Aineias (Aeneas)	Kalkhas (Calchas)
Akhaians (Achaeans)	Khryseis (Chryseis)
Akhilleus (Achilles)	Klytaimnestra (Clytemnestra)
Glaukos (Glaucus)	Menelaos (Menelaus)
Hekabe (Hecuba)	Patroklos (Patroclus)

The Powers and Limits of the Gods The gods of the *Iliad* are not omnipotent: they preside over but do not absolutely control the universe. Zeus, for example, "father of gods and men," is unable to force the Olympians to comply with his wishes. And although he may rattle their wine cups with his thunderbolts or threaten to dangle recalcitrant deities from a chain off Mount Olympus, he is in fact apparently unwilling or unable to do so—nor could he without abrogating his role as a god who (unlike his father and grandfather) rules by persuasion, not violence.

Nor can the gods control human behavior: despite his own preference for a negotiated solution, Zeus cannot force the warring parties to make peace or compel Achilles to return to Priam Hector's body, which he drags for eleven days past the tomb of Patroclus to avenge his friend's death at Hector's hands (Figure 11-4). The gods do, however, reinforce the values of courtesy and the guest-host relationship applicable to humans and gods alike. Thus Zeus, who owes a debt of gratitude to Thetis, obliges her by assenting to her request that he help Achilles. And Apollo, who was a guest-friend at the wedding of Peleus and Thetis, cannot now violate that bond by stealing Hector's corpse from their son Achilles. On similar grounds, it is clear to all, even to the Trojans themselves, that the Trojans must eventually lose the war for having violated the sanctity of the bonds between guest and host, as well as the sacred institution of marriage. At the moment when Paris, a guest in Menelaus's home, seduced and ran off with his wife and treasure, he doomed the city of Troy.

For the humans, the acknowledgment of obligations to the gods includes piety, especially the expression of their gratitude to the gods. Apollo, for instance, brings down the plague in the Greek camp in answer to the prayers of the pious Trojan priest Chryses. This divine-human connection is also made through rituals, especially various forms of sacrifice and communion, from pouring off some wine to share with the gods at each meal to sacrificing an entire animal; such rituals are symbolic expressions of the human dependence on the gods for their physical and spiritual well-being. But although the gods react firmly to punish violations of these universal

FIGURE 11-4   Achilles Dragging the Body of Hector Past the Tomb of Patroclus. In this vase painting (early fifth century B.C.), Achilles is shown dragging Hector's corpse, which he has lashed to his chariot, past Patroclus's tomb to avenge the death of his departed friend. In attempting to mutilate the body, Achilles violates the gods' requirement that the dead be respected and given proper burial. (*Metropolitan Museum of Art, New York.*)

values, they do not necessarily reward piety in corresponding fashion: Hector, admired by the gods, especially Apollo, as a pious man, is nevertheless abandoned to his fate when he confronts Achilles. Not even Apollo can enable Hector to defeat a better fighter than himself. The gods may regret the death of Hector, but they do not prevent it. Unlike the morally neat and essentially "comic" world of the *Odyssey,* where the good are eventually rewarded and the wicked struck by lightning bolts, the *Iliad* depicts a more unpredictable and thus potentially tragic world.

Human Destiny

It is not the gods, furthermore, who dictate human destiny. Rather, human beings determine their own fate, the inevitable consequences of their own freely chosen acts. The essential freedom of individuals is signified in the *Iliad* by three recurring motifs: the dual destinies, the image of the scales, and the two urns.

The dual destinies of humans are best symbolized by the alternative fates of Achilles, who is destined to live a long but unremarkable life *if* he chooses to stay at home or a short but glorious life *if* he chooses to fight at Troy. Thus his fate is not predetermined but conditional: when he makes his choice, the consequences follow. And that choice, to be meaningful, must transcend external coercion of any kind, whether divine or human, and derive instead from a sense of his own integrity. His truly heroic nature is fulfilled not merely by the use of his special gifts but, more important, by his acceptance of moral responsibility for his own fate.

On the gods' part, the sense of alternative destinies—of a universe of freedom and possibilities—is reflected in the image of the scales in which Zeus weighs the fate of humans. Each time, Zeus suspends the scales by the midpoint and reads what they reveal. Although on one level the image concretizes the act of divine judgment, it also suggests that Zeus does not determine which pan rises up or which sinks down any more than holding up a thermometer determines the temperature of the air.

The implications of a world in which humans are free to choose among complex possibilities are perhaps most concretely stated by Achilles himself, when he describes the two urns from which Zeus doles out gifts: like Pandora's jar, the urns contain both blessings and curses, pleasures and pains, good news and bad news. Unfortunate individuals, Achilles explains, experience nothing but suffering; fortunate individuals experience great joy along with the suffering. He cites his father, Peleus, as an example: heroic, wealthy, married to a goddess, and father to a son he can be proud of, Peleus is blessed beyond the hopes of most men. But he will also have to confront his son's early death and to grow old and die alone. Only the gods live happily forever; mixed blessings are the best a human being can hope for.

The Heroic Code

Homer's portrayal of the code by which the heroes live is equally ambivalent. On the positive side, we are compelled to admire the hero's strength, courage, and skill, his intensity and drive, and his willingness to risk all; on the negative side, we watch in dismay as his excess strength and zeal lead to uncontrolled violence and his need to fight drives out good sense and moral values. On the positive side, we admire the hero's dedication, his loyalty to his friends, family, and society, and his commitment to keep promises. Achilles fights in a cause not his own, for a promise made, and the depth of his friendship for Patroclus is a model of devotion. On the negative side, we witness emotional and behavioral excesses as heroic commitments turn into misdirected loyalty, such as Priam's in defending his son, right or wrong, or Hector's in fighting for what he admits is a bad cause, or Achilles's in stubbornly persisting in his attempts to mutilate Hector's corpse.

The heroic code calls for high ideals—respect among equals, courtesy, and playing by the rules on the field and off. But it also encourages a corollary contempt for inferiors. Odysseus, for example, trying to keep the demoralized troops from departing, speaks respectfully to his fellow officers but insults the ordinary soldiers.

The Heroic Combat   Similarly, we share the hero's pride as he glories in victory; we likewise watch as that pride gives way to vain egotism, to gloating over the fallen. And we are always reminded that victory for one hero necessitates death for another. The ideal model of heroic combat is the single combat between two heroes who respect each other's reputation, skill, and family; who fight face-to-face according to the rules of warfare; whose encounter, like a game, is monitored by a referee; who keep the armor but respect the corpse if they win; and who part friends if they fight to a draw.

The point of such a combat (for example, the match between Hector and Ajax) is not to defeat an enemy but to enhance one's heroic reputation. To the gods, war is a game. When war is presented as a challenge match between two heroic contenders, human beings, too, can easily idealize warfare as a glorious game, an opportunity for the heroes to exhibit their godlike skills. But, as many readers have noted, it is a zero-sum game in which there are ultimately no winners. And the illusion of the game is all too easily shattered, giving way to savagery, as Achilles captures and beheads twelve anonymous Trojans in vengeance for Patroclus's death.

Worse, in the heat of battle, the game, with its dream of glory, turns into a nightmare, and we are forced to watch in extreme close-up as brains spatter or guts spill out onto the ground. The climactic encounter between Achilles and Hector takes place on a quasi-surreal plane where there are no rules, no umpires, and no escape. The gods may, at their discretion, turn their attention from the war to their dinner, as Hephaestus suggests. Hector, chased by the relentless Achilles around and around the walls of Troy, is trapped in a nightmare from which he will never awaken.

The Role of Women

If the heroes are trapped in a nightmare, it is at least one of their own choosing. Modern readers will recognize that the real victims in the masculine world of the epics are the women. Legally the property of their husbands or fathers, the women are used freely as loot—the booty of war—or given as prizes in athletic games (in fact, their value was equated to that of draft animals: Achilles, for example, offers as a prize one woman good at crafts, valued at four oxen!). Several centuries later, the playwright Euripides will follow up the stories of the women in such plays as *Trojan Women* and *Hecuba;* but no one in the Homeric epics asks how a Chryseis or a Briseis feels about being captured to service the sexual needs of Agamemnon or Achilles.

But those women who are not literally slaves are also trapped, whether they remain within the body of the family or free themselves from its confines. Helen, for instance, the cause of it all, left her husband and family to follow her lover, only to find herself surrounded by hostile Trojans, her only refuge a lover who is reluctant to fight for her and for whom she has come to feel contempt. Nor do we find any instances of Menelaus's expressing any love for Helen. His highly ornamental property has been taken, his pride offended; it is not Helen herself that Menelaus wants, for all her beauty. And Agamemnon openly expresses contempt for his own wife, Clytemnestra. With the singular exception of Odysseus, the Greek heroes, for all that they are fighting to restore family love, express little love for their own wives. The family bonds they feel are exclusively patriarchal, the ties between fathers and sons.

In contrast to Helen, both Hector's mother, **Hecuba** [HEK-oo-ba], and his wife, **Andromache** [an-DROM-a-kee], remain entirely devoted to their families. Indeed, the household of Hector, Andromache, and the child, Astyanax, is presented as a model family—husband and wife utterly devoted to each other and openly affectionate with the child, their love so embracing that it even encompasses the horses, whom they name and pamper as family pets. It is ironic that we see the Greeks, ostensibly the pro-family side in this war, living in a military camp, having abandoned their own families to fight for the reunion of Menelaus's family, while the Trojans, responsible for the breakup of Menelaus's family, are portrayed as ideal models of family love. But, despite the mutual love of Hector and Andromache, she is nevertheless trapped in a society where her needs and perceptions are not taken as seriously as those of the warriors.

The traditional female role in the heroic myths is, of course, that of the temptress who tries to distract the hero from his quest, enticing him to indulge himself in the rewards and comforts of everyday life—food, sex, children, wealth. The Babylonian goddess of love and war, Ishtar, tempts Gilgamesh by attempting to seduce him, offering herself (as Calypso will later do to Odysseus) as his bride. He spurns her offer, pointing out that she has turned her previous lovers into animals (as Circe will do to Odysseus's crew—see Chapter 12). For the hero, to yield to such temptations is to cut himself off from expressing those heroic qualities that lift him out of the mundane world and allow him to fulfill his godlike potential. In the *Iliad* it is Aphrodite, the goddess of love, who plays that role (along with her human counterpart, Helen), although her function as a war goddess, clear in the "judgment of Paris" myth, is attenuated in the epic, where golden apples play no part and where she is portrayed as an incompetent warrior. Nevertheless, her spirit prevails in Paris, who is more at home in the bedroom than on the battlefield; and even Achilles himself withdraws from battle in a quarrel over a woman.

Similarly, the Sumerian / Babylonian wine goddess Siduri tempts Gilgamesh with prosaic creature comforts, attempting to persuade him to abort his journey to the Underworld. The *Iliad*'s counterpart to Siduri is Andromache herself, who also tempts Hector with the comforts of domestic life. Andromache thus has a dual role in the epic: from the conventional heroic perspective, as "temptress," she attempts to dissuade Hector from going into battle, an offer he of course dismisses, sending her back to her "woman's" pursuits, child care and weaving; from another perspective, as manifestation of the wise goddess, she counsels commitment to the family and to achieving continuity through one's children.

Not compelled by nature or training into fitting the heroic mold, Andromache is free to see the truth that no one else in the epic, apart from the narrator, will acknowledge: Hector's compulsion to fight is strategically unnecessary and, worse, destructive to the very family that Hector is fighting to save. She tells him as much—the price of his glory is her enslavement: she and the child will be taken as slaves by the Greeks. Stay inside the walls, she advises, or at least don't go beyond the nearby fig tree, which could thus literally be a "Tree of Life," reminding us of the archetypal symbol of the feminine principle.

Compelled both by their nature and by social conditioning, Hector and Achilles cannot acknowledge the feminine aspect of their own natures, their anima. Hector acknowledges the validity of Andromache's argument but, being a hero, cannot act on it: he *must* go forward. Achilles, too, rejects the protective urges of his mother and ends up bringing about the death of his best friend, Patroclus, who, assuming Achilles's identity along with his armor, becomes an alter ego whose death prefigures Achilles's own. This exclusively masculine heroic code is destructive to families, destructive to peace, destructive to civilization itself, which requires the stability of affection and commitment and the peace in which to nurture the relationships of domestic life. But the social code of the Bronze Age, as depicted in the *Iliad,* reinforced traditional heroic attitudes. To stay at home was associated with the feminine principle: grown men fought; women, children, and impotent old men stayed at home. Paris, who prefers making love to making war, is accused by Hector of skulking at home "like a woman."

Holding up the heroic code for us to view from a variety of often conflicting perspectives, the *Iliad* asks questions but does not offer answers. By showing us Andromache's perspective and reminding us of it in the brief reflection on domestic life when he pauses to reflect on doing the laundry in the midst of the chase scene, Homer comments ironically on the limits of the heroic model. The hero so narrowly defined cannot achieve wholeness. Such partial consciousness is self-destructive, not just to the body but to the personality as well. And it is the women who are given the last word, as they lament the death of Hector.

But for all these brief glimpses of the role of women, Homer's focus in the *Iliad* remains largely, if somewhat ambivalently, on the hero. The feminine principle will have to lie in waiting until, in the *Odyssey,* a new kind of hero will emerge to effect the reconciliation of opposites, the integration of the divided self. Achilles's phallic instrument of destruction, his Pelian ash, was presumably once a tree, the symbol of the Feminine. Odysseus will later carve the olive tree (symbol of Athene) not into a spear but into a marriage bed, leaving it still rooted in the earth, the primordial mother—the phallus and the Tree of Life rejoined.

The Conclusion of the *Iliad*

The epic ends with the funeral of Hector—a celebration of the life of a heroic individual, a ritual that affirms, even in the face of death, the value of life. Although the saga of Troy is carried on in the myths through the eventual death of Achilles and the defeat of the Trojans, in the epic, the renewed commitment of Achilles and the death of Hector make the fate of both Achilles and Troy inevitable; rather than describing them, Homer chooses for his climactic point the moment of reconciliation—of the hero and his society, of honor and integrity, of life and death.

The Rite of Passage In many myths, the hero's rite of passage is literal—he goes on a journey, often to the Underworld, and returns with new knowledge, as did Gilgamesh, Heracles, Odysseus, and Aeneas. Perhaps more like the heroes of the later tragedies, Achilles's journey has been to the hell within; his isolation is psychological rather than physical: he does not have to travel to the Underworld because it comes to him, literally, in the form of Patroclus's shade (his ghost or spirit) and the corpses he heaps up—in perverse tribute to his friend—in his camp, which quickly takes on an atmosphere of the Underworld. It also comes to him psychologically as he undergoes the experiences of separation and alienation, descends into the depths of grief and rage, and does battle with the gods themselves. Returning with new insight into the ambiguous nature of human experience and the limits of mortality, he is at last reconciled with the community of his fellow human beings. The ego-driven hero with the hair-trigger temper of the opening chapters, obsessed with honor defined externally as public reputation, has yielded, albeit after great loss, to a more mature, more compassionate, more self-controlled Achilles who will be a hero because his own integrity, not merely his public image, requires it. Later playwrights and philosophers from Aeschylus to Socrates would argue that human beings "must suffer to be wise." If that is the case, Achilles has earned—and paid for—his wisdom.

The Trojan Cycle Completed

Although the *Iliad* ends with the funeral of Hector, the myths continue the story to the end of the war and beyond. One of the many related stories tells of Penthesilea, the Amazon queen who disguises herself in a man's armor and fights with incredible skill until she is killed by Achilles himself. Removing her armor, he finds to his amazement that she is a woman.

The Death of Achilles

Achilles himself is eventually killed at the gates of Troy by an arrow in the heel, shot, according to some versions, by Paris, who was hiding behind the city walls. Other versions credit Apollo with the fatal shot or describe Apollo as guiding Paris's hand.

Achilles's corpse and armor are rescued by Odysseus and Ajax; Achilles's ashes are buried in a golden urn together with the ashes of Patroclus, and a huge mound is erected as a memorial, but the rescuers can't agree on which of them is to receive the armor. They present their cases in speeches before the assembly, and Odysseus, always a masterful speaker, is awarded the honor. Ajax, furious at being thus humiliated, goes mad. In a fit of insanity much like Heracles's, he attacks the Greek leaders in their sleep, only to have Athene turn his rage on the horses and cattle instead. When he returns to his senses and realizes what he has done, he commits suicide.

Still the war goes on. The Greeks are told of prophecies that several tasks must be accomplished before they can defeat Troy. For example, they must bring Neoptolemus, Achilles's son, to join the battle: he does so and becomes a hero in his own right. They must bring the Palladium, a statue of Athene, from the city of Troy; Odysseus, once again operating as the Greeks' major intelligence agent, sneaks into Troy disguised as a beggar to accomplish the theft. Further, the Greeks must bring the bow of Heracles from the island of Lemnos, where they had abandoned Philoctetes (the owner of the bow) because of a snakebite he'd suffered, which caused an agonizing wound that smelled so foul the troops could not bear to be near him.

The Trojan Horse

When all the assigned tasks are accomplished but the walls of Troy are still not breached, it is Odysseus who devises the trick that ends the war. He designs a hollow wooden horse in which he hides with a group of Greek officers. The prophetess **Cassandra** tries to warn the Trojans, but no one understands her warnings. A priest, **Laocoon** [lay-AHK-oh-ahn], also tries to warn them, but he is prevented by Poseidon, who sends a sea serpent to strangle him and his sons.

A soldier named Sinon is assigned to deliver the horse to the Trojans as a peace offering from the Greek armies, which pretend to be departing. Sinon claims to have been abandoned as a deserter and to be seeking asylum. The Trojans open the gates and bring the hollow horse inside the city, where they begin a great victory celebration. When the Trojans are at last asleep, Odysseus and his men emerge from the horse and open the gates from the inside for the Greek forces, which have silently assembled just outside. Once inside the city, they defeat the Trojans. The men (all but Aeneas and his household) are killed, the women and children taken prisoner, and the city looted and burned. After ten years of battling for honor and glory, after all those deaths, the city of Troy falls to a clever trick. The games, the heroic battles, the sacrifices, have all proved futile: intelligence, not prowess, is the weapon that brings victory.

The Return of the Achaeans

The battle won, the Greeks divide up the loot and sail for home. But their ten-year struggle has already set in motion consequences far beyond the military victory. The myths that spin off from the war detailing the return of Agamemnon (see Chapter 15) and Odysseus (see Chapter 12) follow the problems of a postwar world struggling to return to normalcy, or to create a new kind of order.

ILIAD[1]

Homer

BOOK 1

Anger be now your song, immortal one,
Akhilleus' anger, doomed and ruinous,
that caused the Akhaians loss on bitter loss
and crowded brave souls into the undergloom,
leaving so many dead men—carrion
for dogs and birds; and the will of Zeus was done.
Begin it when the two men first contending
broke with one another—

                    the Lord Marshal
Agamémnon, Atreus' son, and Prince Akhilleus.   10

Among the gods, who brought this quarrel on?
The son of Zeus by Lêto. Agamémnon
angered him, so he made a burning wind
of plague rise in the army: rank and file
sickened and died for the ill their chief had done
in despising a man of prayer.
This priest, Khrysês, had come down to the ships
with gifts, no end of ransom for his daughter;
on a golden staff he carried the god's white bands
and sued for grace from the men of all Akhaia,   20
the two Atreidai most of all:

                       "O captains
Meneláos and Agamémnon, and you other
Akhaians under arms!
The gods who hold Olympos, may they grant you
plunder of Priam's town and a fair wind home,
but let me have my daughter back for ransom
as you revere Apollo, son of Zeus!"

Then all the soldiers murmured their assent:

"Behave well to the priest. And take the ransom!"   30

But Agamémnon would not. It went against his desire,
and brutally he ordered the man away:
"Let me not find you here by the long ships
loitering this time or returning later,

---

1. Translated by Robert Fitzgerald.

old man; if I do,
the staff and ribbons of the god will fail you.
Give up the girl? I swear she will grow old
at home in Argos, far from her own country,
working my loom and visiting my bed.
Leave me in peace and go, while you can, in safety."   40

So harsh he was, the old man feared and obeyed him,
in silence trailing away
by the shore of the tumbling clamorous whispering sea,
and he prayed and prayed again, as he withdrew,
to the god whom silken-braided Lêto bore:

"O hear me, master of the silver bow,
protector of Ténedos and the holy towns,
Apollo, Sminthian, if to your liking
ever in any grove I roofed a shrine
or burnt thighbones in fat upon your altar—   50
bullock or goat flesh—let my wish come true:
your arrows on the Danääns for my tears!"

Now when he heard this prayer, Phoibos Apollo
walked with storm in his heart from Olympos' crest,
quiver and bow at his back, and the bundled arrows
clanged on the sky behind as he rocked in his anger,
descending like night itself. Apart from the ships
he halted and let fly, and the bowstring slammed
as the silver bow sprang, rolling in thunder away.
Pack animals were his target first, and dogs,   60
but soldiers, too, soon felt transfixing pain
from his hard shots, and pyres burned night and day.
Nine days the arrows of the god came down
broadside upon the army. On the tenth,
Akhilleus called all ranks to assembly. Hêra,
whose arms are white as ivory, moved him to it,
as she took pity on Danääns dying.
All being mustered, all in place and quiet,
Akhilleus, fast in battle as a lion,
rose and said: 70

                    "Agamémnon, now, I take it,
the siege is broken, we are going to sail,
and even so may not leave death behind:
if war spares anyone, disease will take him . . .
We might, though, ask some priest or some diviner,
even some fellow good at dreams—for dreams
come down from Zeus as well—
why all this anger of the god Apollo?

Has he some quarrel with us for a failure
in vows or hekatombs? Would mutton burned   80
or smoking goat flesh make him lift the plague?"

Putting the question, down he sat. And Kalkhas,
Kalkhas Thestórides, came forward, wisest
by far of all who scanned the flight of birds.
He knew what was, what had been, what would be,
Kalkhas, who brought Akhaia's ships to Ilion
by the diviner's gift Apollo gave him.
Now for their benefit he said:

　　　　　　　　　　　　　"Akhilleus,
dear to Zeus, it is on me you call   90
to tell you why the Archer God is angry.
Well, I can tell you. Are you listening? Swear
by heaven that you will back me and defend me,
because I fear my answer will enrage
a man with power in Argos, one whose word
Akhaian troops obey.

　　　　　　　　　A great man in his rage is formidable
for underlings: though he may keep it down,
he cherishes the burning in his belly
until a reckoning day. Think well   100
if you will save me."

Said Akhilleus:

　　　　　　　　　　　"Courage,
Tell what you know, what you have light to know.
I swear by Apollo, the lord god to whom
you pray when you uncover truth,
never while I draw breath, while I have eyes to see,
shall any man upon this beachhead dare
lay hands on you—not one of all the army,
not Agamémnon, if it is he you mean,   110
though he is first in rank of all Akhaians."

The diviner then took heart and said:

　　　　　　　　　　　　　　"No failure
in hekatombs or vows is held against us.
It is the man of prayer whom Agamémnon
treated with contempt: he kept his daughter,
spurned his gifts: for that man's sake the Archer
visited grief upon us and will again.
Relieve the Danáäns of this plague he will not
until the girl who turns the eyes of men   120
shall be restored to her own father—freely,
with no demand for ransom—and until
we offer up a hekatomb at Khrysê.
Then only can we claim him and persuade him."

He finished and sat down. The son of Atreus,
ruler of the great plain, Agamémnon,
rose, furious. Round his heart resentment
welled, and his eyes shone out like licking fire.
Then, with a long and boding look at Kalkhas,
he growled at him:
                  "You visionary of hell,   130
never have I had fair play in your forecasts.
Calamity is all you care about, or see,
no happy portents; and you bring to pass
nothing agreeable. Here you stand again
before the army, giving it out as oracle
the Archer made them suffer because of me,
because I would not take the gifts
and let the girl Khrysêis go; I'd have her
mine, at home. Yes, if you like, I rate her   140
higher than Klytaimnestra, my own wife!
She loses nothing by comparison
in beauty or womanhood, in mind or skill.

For all of that, I am willing now to yield her
if it is best; I want the army saved
and not destroyed. You must prepare, however,
a prize of honor for me, and at once,
that I may not be left without my portion—
I, of all Argives. It is not fitting so.
While every man of you looks on, my girl   150
goes elsewhere."

Prince Akhilleus answered him:

"Lord Marshal, most insatiate of men,
how can the army make you a new gift?
Where is our store of booty? Can you see it?
Everything plundered from the towns has been
distributed; should troops turn all that in?
Just let the girl go, in the god's name, now;
we'll make it up to you, twice over, three
times over, on that day Zeus gives us leave   160
to plunder Troy behind her rings of stone."

Agamémnon answered:
                    "Not that way
will I be gulled, brave as you are, Akhilleus.
Take me in, would you? Try to get around me?
What do you really ask? That you may keep
your own winnings, I am to give up mine
and sit here wanting her? Oh, no:

the army will award a prize to me
and make sure that it measures up, or if   170
they do not, I will take a girl myself,
your own, or Aías', or Odysseus' prize!
Take her, yes, to keep. The man I visit
may choke with rage; well, let him.
But this, I say, we can decide on later.

Look to it now, we launch on the great sea
a well-found ship, and get her manned with oarsmen,
load her with sacrificial beasts and put aboard
Khrysêis in her loveliness. My deputy,
Aías, Idómeneus, or Prince Odysseus,   180
or you, Akhilleus, fearsome as you are,
will make the hekatomb and quiet the Archer."

Akhilleus frowned and looked at him, then said:

"You thick-skinned, shameless, greedy fool!
Can any Akhaian care for you, or obey you,
after this on marches or in battle?
As for myself, when I came here to fight,
I had no quarrel with Troy or Trojan spearmen:
they never stole my cattle or my horses,
never in the black farmland of Phthía   190
ravaged my crops. How many miles there are
of shadowy mountains, foaming seas, between!
No, no, we joined for you, you insolent boor,
to please you, fighting for your brother's sake
and yours, to get revenge upon the Trojans.
You overlook this, dogface, or don't care,
and now in the end you threaten to take my girl,
a prize I sweated for, and soldiers gave me!

Never have I had plunder like your own
from any Trojan stronghold battered down   200
by the Akhaians. I have seen more action
hand to hand in those assaults than you have,
but when the time for sharing comes, the greater
share is always yours. Worn out with battle
I carry off some trifle to my ships.
Well, this time I make sail for home.
Better to take now to my ships. Why linger,
cheated of winnings, to make wealth for you?"

To this the high commander made reply:

"Desért, if that's the way the wind blows. Will I   210

beg you to stay on my account? I will not.
Others will honor me, and Zeus who views
the wide world most of all.

                No officer
is hateful to my sight as you are, none
given like you to faction, as to battle—
rugged you are, I grant, by some god's favor.
Sail, then, in your ships, and lord it over
your own battalion of Myrmidons. I do not
give a curse for you, or for your anger.   220
But here is warning for you:

                   Khrysêis
being required of me by Phoibos Apollo,
she will be sent back in a ship of mine,
manned by my people. That done, I myself
will call for Brisêis at your hut, and take her,
flower of young girls that she is, your prize,
to show you here and now who is the stronger
and make the next man sick at heart—if any
think of claiming equal place with me."   230

A pain like grief weighed on the son of Pêleus,
and in his shaggy chest this way and that
the passion of his heart ran: should he draw
longsword from hip, stand off the rest, and kill
in single combat the great son of Atreus,
or hold his rage in check and give it time?
And as this tumult swayed him, as he slid
the big blade slowly from the sheath, Athêna
came to him from the sky. The white-armed goddess,
Hêra, sent her, being fond of both,   240
concerned for both men. And Athêna, stepping
up behind him, visible to no one
except Akhilleus, gripped his red-gold hair.

Startled, he made a half turn, and he knew her
upon the instant for Athêna: terribly
her grey eyes blazed at him. And speaking softly
but rapidly aside to her he said:

"What now, O daughter of the god of heaven
who bears the stormcloud, why are you here? To see
the wolfishness of Agamémnon?   250
Well, I give you my word: this time, and soon,
he pays for his behavior with his blood."

The grey-eyed goddess Athêna said to him:

"It was to check this killing rage I came
from heaven, if you will listen. Hêra sent me,
being fond of both of you, concerned for both.
Enough: break off this combat, stay your hand
upon the sword hilt. Let him have a lashing
with words, instead: tell him how things will be.
Here is my promise, and it will be kept: 260
winnings three times as rich, in due season,
you shall have in requital for his arrogance.
But hold your hand. Obey."

                              The great runner,
Akhilleus, answered:
                              "Nothing for it, goddess,
but when you two immortals speak, a man
complies, though his heart burst. Just as well.
Honor the gods' will, they may honor ours."
On this he stayed his massive hand   270
upon the silver pommel, and the blade
of his great weapon slid back in the scabbard.
The man had done her bidding. Off to Olympos,
gaining the air, she went to join the rest,
the powers of heaven in the home of Zeus.

But now the son of Pêleus turned on Agamémnon
and lashed out at him, letting his anger ride
in execration:

                              "Sack of wine,
you with your cur's eyes and your antelope heart!   280
You've never had the kidney to buckle on
armor among the troops, or make a sortie
with picked men—oh, no; that way death might lie.
Safer, by god, in the middle of the army—
is it not?—to commandeer the prize
of any man who stands up to you! Leech!
Commander of trash! If not, I swear,
you never could abuse one soldier more!

But here is what I say: my oath upon it
by this great staff: look: leaf or shoot   290
it cannot sprout again, once lopped away
from the log it left behind in the timbered hills;
it cannot flower, peeled of bark and leaves;
instead, Akhaian officers in council
take it in hand by turns, when they observe
by the will of Zeus due order in debate:

let this be what I swear by then: I swear
a day will come when every Akhaian soldier
will groan to have Akhilleus back. That day
you shall no more prevail on me than this   300
dry wood shall flourish—driven though you are,
and though a thousand men perish before
the killer, Hektor. You will eat your heart out,
raging with remorse for this dishonor
done by you to the bravest of Akhaians."
He hurled the staff, studded with golden nails,
before him on the ground. Then down he sat,
and fury filled Agamémnon, looking across at him.
But for the sake of both men Nestor arose,
the Pylians' orator, eloquent and clear;   310
argument sweeter than honey rolled from his tongue.
By now he had outlived two generations
of mortal men, his own and the one after,
in Pylos land, and still ruled in the third.
In kind reproof he said:

                     "A black day, this.
Bitter distress comes this way to Akhaia.
How happy Priam and Priam's sons would be,
and all the Trojans—wild with joy—if they
got wind of all these fighting words between you,   320
foremost in council as you are, foremost
in battle. Give me your attention. Both
are younger men than I, and in my time
men who were even greater have I known
and none of them disdained me. Men like those
I have not seen again, nor shall: Peiríthoös,
the Lord Marshal Dryas, Kaineus, Exádios,
Polyphêmos, Theseus—Aigeus' son,
a man like the immortal gods. I speak
of champions among men of earth, who fought   330
with champions, with wild things of the mountains,
great centaurs whom they broke and overpowered.
Among these men I say I had my place
when I sailed out of Pylos, my far country,
because they called for me. I fought
for my own hand among them. Not one man
alive now upon earth could stand against them.
And I repeat: they listened to my reasoning,
took my advice. Well, then, you take it too.
It is far better so.   340
                   Lord Agamémnon,
do not deprive him of the girl, renounce her.
The army had allotted her to him.

Akhilleus, for your part, do not defy
your King and Captain. No one vies in honor
with him who holds authority from Zeus.
You have more prowess, for a goddess bore you;
his power over men surpasses yours.

But, Agamémnon, let your anger cool.
I beg you to relent, knowing Akhilleus   350
a sea wall for Akhaians in the black waves of war."

Lord Agamémnon answered:

                    "All you say
is fairly said, sir, but this man's ambition,
remember, is to lead, to lord it over
everyone, hold power over everyone,
give orders to the rest of us! Well, one
will never take his orders! If the gods
who live forever made a spearman of him,
have they put insults on his lips as well?"   360

Akhilleus interrupted:

                  "What a poltroon,
how lily-livered I should be called, if I
knuckled under to all you do or say!
Give your commands to someone else, not me!
And one more thing I have to tell you: think it
over: this time, for the girl, I will not
wrangle in arms with you or anyone,
though I am robbed of what was given me;
but as for any other thing I have   370
alongside my black ship, you shall not take it
against my will. Try it. Hear this, everyone:
that instant your hot blood blackens my spear!"

They quarreled in this way, face to face, and then
broke off the assembly by the ships. Akhilleus
made his way to his squadron and his quarters,
Patróklos by his side, with his companions.

Agamémnon proceeded to launch a ship,
assigned her twenty oarsmen, loaded beasts
for sacrifice to the god, then set aboard   380
Khrysêis in her loveliness. The versatile
Odysseus took the deck, and, all oars manned,
they pulled out on the drenching ways of sea.
The troops meanwhile were ordered to police camp
and did so, throwing refuse in the water;
then to Apollo by the barren surf

they carried out full-tally hekatombs,
and the savor curled in crooked smoke toward heaven.

That was the day's work in the army.
                              Agamémnon   390
had kept his threat in mind, and now he acted,
calling Eurýbatês and Talthýbios,
his aides and criers:
                    "Go along," he said,
"both of you, to the quarters of Akhilleus
and take his charming Brisêis by the hand
to bring to me. And if he balks at giving her
I shall be there myself with men-at-arms
in force to take her—all the more gall for him."
So, ominously, he sent them on their way,   400
and they who had no stomach for it went
along the waste sea shingle toward the ships
and shelters of the Myrmidons. Not far
from his black ship and hut they found the prince
in the open, seated. And seeing these two come
was cheerless to Akhilleus. Shamefast, pale
with fear of him, they stood without a word;
but he knew what they felt and called out:
                              "Peace to you,
criers and couriers of Zeus and men!   410
Come forward. Not one thing have I against you:
Agamémnon is the man who sent you
for Brisêis. Here then, my lord Patróklos,
bring out the girl and give her to these men.
And let them both bear witness before the gods
who live in bliss, as before men who die,
including this harsh king, if ever hereafter
a need for me arises to keep the rest
from black defeat and ruin.
                              Lost in folly,   420
the man cannot think back or think ahead
how to come through a battle by the ships."
Patróklos did the bidding of his friend,
led from the hut Brisêis in her beauty
and gave her to them. Back along the ships
they took their way, and the girl went, loath to go.

Leaving his friends in haste, Akhilleus wept,
and sat apart by the grey wave, scanning the endless sea.
Often he spread his hands in prayer to his mother:

"As my life came from you, though it is brief,   430
honor at least from Zeus who storms in heaven

I call my due. He gives me precious little.
See how the lord of the great plains, Agamémnon,
humiliated me! He has my prize,
by his own whim, for himself."

                           Eyes wet with tears,
he spoke, and her ladyship his mother heard him
in green deeps where she lolled near her old father.
Gliding she rose and broke like mist from the inshore
grey sea face, to sit down softly before him,   440
her son in tears; and fondling him she said:

"Child, why do you weep? What grief is this?
Out with it, tell me, both of us should know."
Akhilleus, fast in battle as a lion,
groaned and said:
                        "Why tell you what you know?
We sailed out raiding, and we took by storm
that ancient town of Eëtíôn called Thêbê,
plundered the place, brought slaves and spoils away.
At the division, later,   450
they chose a young girl, Khrysêis, for the king.
Then Khrysês, priest of the Archer God, Apollo,
came to the beachhead we Akhaians hold,
bringing no end of ransom for his daughter;
he had the god's white bands on a golden staff
and sued for grace from the army of Akhaia,
mostly the two Atreidai, corps commanders.
All of our soldiers murmured in assent:
'Behave well to the priest. And take the ransom!'
But Agamémnon would not. It went against his desire,   460
and brutally he ordered the man away.
So the old man withdrew in grief and anger.
Apollo cared for him: he heard his prayer
and let black bolts of plague fly on the Argives.

One by one our men came down with it
and died hard as the god's shots raked the army
broadside. But our priest divined the cause
and told us what the god meant by plague.

I said, 'Appease the god!' but Agamémnon
could not contain his rage; he threatened me,   470
and what he threatened is now done—
one girl the Akhaians are embarking now
for Khrysê beach with gifts for Lord Apollo;
the other, just now, from my hut—the criers
came and took her, Briseus' girl, my prize,
given by the army.

If you can, stand by me:
go to Olympos, pray to Zeus, if ever
by word or deed you served him—
and so you did, I often heard you tell it   480
in Father's house: that time when you alone
of all the gods shielded the son of Krónos
from peril and disgrace—when other gods,
Pallas Athêna, Hêra, and Poseidon,
wished him in irons, wished to keep him bound,
you had the will to free him of that bondage,
and called up to Olympos in all haste
Aigaion, whom the gods call Briareus,
the giant with a hundred arms, more powerful
than the sea-god, his father. Down he sat   490
by the son of Krónos, glorying in that place.
For fear of him the blissful gods forbore
to manacle Zeus.
                             Remind him of these things,
cling to his knees and tell him your good pleasure
if he will take the Trojan side
and roll the Akhaians back to the water's edge,
back on the ships with slaughter! All the troops
may savor what their king has won for them,
and he may know his madness, what he lost   500
when he dishonored me, peerless among Akhaians."

Her eyes filled, and a tear fell as she answered:

"Alas, my child, why did I rear you, doomed
the day I bore you? Ah, could you only be
serene upon this beachhead through the siege,
your life runs out so soon.
Oh early death! Oh broken heart! No destiny
so cruel! And I bore you to this evil!

But what you wish I will propose
To Zeus, lord of the lightning, going up   510
myself into the snow-glare of Olympos
with hope for his consent.
                             Be quiet now
beside the long ships, keep your anger bright
against the army, quit the war.
                             Last night
Zeus made a journey to the shore of Ocean
to feast among the Sunburned, and the gods
accompanied him. In twelve days he will come
back to Olympos. Then I shall be there   520
to cross his bronze doorsill and take his knees.
I trust I'll move him."

                         Thetis left her son
still burning for the softly belted girl
whom they had wrested from him.

                         Meanwhile Odysseus
with his shipload of offerings came to Khrysê.
Entering the deep harbor there
they furled the sails and stowed them, and unbent
forestays to ease the mast down quickly aft   530
into its rest; then rowed her to a mooring.
Bow-stones were dropped, and they tied up astern,
and all stepped out into the wash and ebb,
then disembarked their cattle for the Archer,
and Khrysêis, from the deepsea ship. Odysseus,
the great tactician, led her to the altar,
putting her in her father's hands, and said:

"Khrysês, as Agamêmnon's emissary
I bring your child to you, and for Apollo
a hekatomb in the Danáäns' name.   540
We trust in this way to appease your lord,
who sent down pain and sorrow on the Argives."

So he delivered her, and the priest received her,
the child so dear to him, in joy. Then hastening
to give the god his hekatomb, they led
bullocks to crowd around the compact altar,
rinsed their hands and delved in barley baskets,
as open-armed to heaven Khrysês prayed:

"Oh hear me, master of the silver bow,
protector of Ténedos and the holy towns,   550
if while I prayed you listened once before
and honored me, and punished the Akhaians,
now let my wish come true again. But turn
your plague away this time from the Danáäns."

And this petition, too, Apollo heard.
When prayers were said and grains of barley strewn,
they held the bullocks for the knife, and flayed them,
cutting out joints and wrapping these in fat,
two layers, folded, with raw strips of flesh,
for the old man to burn on cloven faggots,   560
wetting it all with wine.
                         Around him stood
young men with five-tined forks in hand, and when
the vitals had been tasted, joints consumed,
they sliced the chines and quarters for the spits,
roasted them evenly and drew them off.

Their meal being now prepared and all work done,
they feasted to their hearts' content and made
desire for meat and drink recede again,
then young men filled their winebowls to the brim,   570
ladling drops for the god in every cup.
Propitiatory songs rose clear and strong
until day's end, to praise the god, Apollo,
as One Who Keeps the Plague Afar; and listening
the god took joy.
                                    After the sun went down
and darkness came, at last Odysseus' men
lay down to rest under the stern hawsers.

When Dawn spread out her finger tips of rose
they put to sea for the main camp of Akhaians,   580
and the Archer God sent them a following wind.
Stepping the mast they shook their canvas out,
and wind caught, bellying the sail. A foaming
dark blue wave sang backward from the bow
as the running ship made way against the sea,
until they came offshore of the encampment.
Here they put in and hauled the black ship high,
far up the sand, braced her with shoring timbers,
and then disbanded, each to his own hut.

Meanwhile unstirring and with smoldering heart,   590
the godlike athlete, son of Pêleus, Prince
Akhilleus waited by his racing ships.
He would not enter the assembly
of emulous men, nor ever go to war,
but felt his valor staling in his breast
with idleness, and missed the cries of battle.

Now when in fact twelve days had passed, the gods
who live forever turned back to Olympos,
with Zeus in power supreme among them.
                                    Thetis   600
had kept in mind her mission for her son,
and rising like a dawn mist from the sea
into a cloud she soared aloft in heaven
to high Olympos. Zeus with massive brows
she found apart, on the chief crest enthroned,
and slipping down before him, her left hand
placed on his knees and her right hand held up
to cup his chin, she made her plea to him:

"O Father Zeus, if ever amid immortals
by word or deed I served you, grant my wish   610

and see to my son's honor! Doom for him
of all men comes on quickest.
                                    Now Lord Marshal
Agamémnon has been highhanded with him,
has commandeered and holds his prize of war.
But you can make him pay for this, profound
mind of Olympos!
                          Lend the Trojans power,
until the Akhaians recompense my son
and heap new honor upon him!"   620
                                    When she finished,
the gatherer of cloud said never a word
but sat unmoving for a long time, silent.
Thetis clung to his knees, then spoke again:

"Give your infallible word, and bow your head,
or else reject me. Can you be afraid
to let me see how low in your esteem
I am of all the gods?"
                              Greatly perturbed,
Lord Zeus who masses cloud said: 630
                                    "Here is trouble.
You drive me into open war with Hêra
sooner or later:
she will be at me, scolding all day long.
Even as matters stand she never rests
from badgering me before the gods: I take
the Trojan side in battle, so she says.

Go home before you are seen. But you can trust me
to put my mind on this; I shall arrange it.
Here let me bow my head, then be content   640
to see me bound by that most solemn act
before the gods. My word is not revocable
nor ineffectual, once I nod upon it."

He bent his ponderous black brows down, and locks
ambrosial of his immortal head
swung over them, as all Olympos trembled.
After this pact they parted: misty Thetis
from glittering Olympos leapt away
into the deep sea; Zeus to his hall retired.
There all the gods rose from their seats in deference   650
before their father; not one dared
face him unmoved, but all stood up before him,
and thus he took his throne.
                                    But Hêra knew
he had new interests; she had seen

the goddess Thetis, silvery-footed daughter
of the Old One of the sea, conferring with him,
and, nagging, she inquired of Zeus Kroníon:

"Who is it this time, schemer? Who has your ear?
How fond you are of secret plans, of taking   660
decisions privately! You could not bring yourself,
could you, to favor me with any word
of your new plot?"

                          The father of gods and men
said in reply:
                      "Hêra, all my provisions
you must not itch to know.
You'll find them rigorous, consort though you are.
In all appropriate matters no one else,
no god or man, shall be advised before you.   670
But when I choose to think alone,
don't harry me about it with your questions."
The Lady Hêra answered, with wide eyes:

"Majesty, what a thing to say. I have not
'harried' you before with questions, surely;
you are quite free to tell what you will tell.
This time I dreadfully fear—I have a feeling—
Thetis, the silvery-footed daughter
of the Old One of the sea, led you astray.
Just now at daybreak, anyway, she came   680
to sit with you and take your knees; my guess is
you bowed your head for her in solemn pact
that you will see to the honor of Akhilleus—
that is, to Akhaian carnage near the ships."

Now Zeus the gatherer of cloud said:
                        "Marvelous,
you and your guesses; you are near it, too.
But there is not one thing that you can do about it,
only estrange yourself still more from me—
all the more gall for you. If what you say   690
is true, you may be sure it pleases me.
And now you just sit down, be still, obey me,
or else not all the gods upon Olympos
can help in the least when I approach your chair
to lay my inexorable hands upon you."
At this the wide-eyed Lady Hêra feared him,
and sat quite still, and bent her will to his.
Up through the hall of Zeus now all the lords
of heaven were sullen and looked askance. Hêphaistos,

master artificer, broke the silence,   700
doing a kindness to the snowy-armed
lady, his mother Hêra.

                                He began:
"Ah, what a miserable day, if you two
raise your voices over mortal creatures!
More than enough already! Must you bring
your noisy bickering among the gods?
What pleasure can we take in a fine dinner
when baser matters gain the upper hand?
To Mother my advice is—what she knows—   710
better make up to Father, or he'll start
his thundering and shake our feast to bits.
You know how he can shock us if he cares to—
out of our seats with lightning bolts!
Supreme power is his. Oh, soothe him, please,
take a soft tone, get back in his good graces.
Then he'll be benign to us again."
He lurched up as he spoke, and held a winecup
out to her, a double-handed one,
and said: 720

                    "Dear Mother, patience, hold your tongue,
no matter how upset you are. I would not
see you battered, dearest.
                                It would hurt me,
and yet I could not help you, not a bit.
The Olympian is difficult to oppose.
One other time I took your part he caught me
around one foot and flung me
into the sky from our tremendous terrace.
I soared all day! Just as the sun dropped down   730
I dropped down, too, on Lemnos—nearly dead.
The island people nursed a fallen god."

He made her smile—and the goddess, white-armed Hêra,
smiling took the winecup from his hand.
Then, dipping from the winebowl, round he went
from left to right, serving the other gods
nectar of sweet delight.
                                And quenchless laughter
broke out among the blissful gods
to see Hêphaistos wheezing down the hall.   740
So all day long until the sun went down
they spent in feasting, and the measured feast
matched well their hearts' desire.

So did the flawless harp held by Apollo
and heavenly songs in choiring antiphon
that all the Muses sang.
                              And when the shining
sun of day sank in the west, they turned
homeward each one to rest, each to that home
the bandy-legged wondrous artisan   750
Hêphaistos fashioned for them with his craft.
The lord of storm and lightning, Zeus, retired
and shut his eyes where sweet sleep ever came to him,
and at his side lay Hêra, Goddess of the Golden Chair.

BOOK 2

[Zeus sends a false dream to Agamemnon to persuade him to take the field. Pretending
that they are going to give up and return home, Agamemnon first tests the resolve of the
troops, who run for the ships. Odysseus has to persuade them to return to the assembly,
appealing to the courage of the officers and threatening the rank and file. Thersites, an
ugly and cowardly but impudent member of the troops, challenges Agamemnon verbally
in the assembly, but Odysseus threatens him into submission and beats him. Offering a
ritual sacrifice, Agamemnon prays to Zeus for victory. Zeus accepts the sacrifice but, carrying out his promise to Thetis to support Achilles in his quarrel, does not grant Agamemnon's request. The array of commanders and their respective troops on both Greek
and Trojan sides is described.]

BOOK 3

[Paris (also known as Alexandros), hanging back from battle, contrasts his gifts as a
lover with Hector's as a hero. Paris is persuaded to enter the battle and proposes a single
combat between himself and Menelaus. Aphrodite rescues him from this combat, setting
him down in his own room and sending him back to Helen, who is now regretful of the
life she has chosen and contemptuous of her lover.]

BOOK 4

[The gods in council discuss the war. Zeus expresses his esteem for both sides. He wants
peace, but Athene and Hera want to punish the Trojans, while Aphrodite wants to save
them. Despite Zeus's desire for compromise, the gods continue to get involved in the
battles. Ares urges the Trojans on; Athene encourages the Greeks.]

BOOK 5

[Athene encourages the Greek warrior Diomedes, even urging him to fight the goddess
Aphrodite:]

. . . .

As this man fled, Eurýpylos leapt after him
with drawn sword, on the run, and struck his shoulder,
cutting away one heavy arm: in blood
the arm dropped, and death surging on his eyes
took him, hard destiny.
                              So toiled the Akhaians

in that rough charge. But as for Diomêdês,
you could not tell if he were with Akhaians
or Trojans, for he coursed along the plain
most like an April torrent fed by snow,   10
a river in flood that sweeps away his bank;
no piled-up dyke will hold him, no revetment
shielding the bloom of orchard land, this river
suddenly at crest when heaven pours down
the rain of Zeus; many a yeoman's field
of beautiful grain is ravaged: even so
before Diomêdês were the crowded ranks
of Trojans broken, many as they were,
and none could hold him.
       Now when Pándaros   20
looked over at him, saw him sweep the field,
he bent his bow of horn at Diomêdês
and shot him as he charged, hitting his cuirass
in the right shoulder joint. The winging arrow
stuck, undeflected, spattering blood on bronze.
Pándaros gave a great shout:

        "Close up, Trojans!
Come on, charioteers! The Akhaian champion
is hit, hit hard; I swear my arrowshot
will bring him down soon—if indeed it was   30
Apollo who cheered me on my way from Lykia!"

Triumphantly he shouted; but his arrow
failed to bring Diomêdês down. Retiring
upon his chariot and team, he stood
and said to Sthénelos, the son of Kapanéus:

"Quick, Sthénelos, old friend, jump down
and pull this jabbing arrow from my shoulder!"

Sthénelos vaulted down and, pressed against him,
drew the slim arrow shaft clear of his wound
with spurts of blood that stained his knitted shirt.   40
And now at last Diomêdês of the warcry
prayed aloud:

       "Oh hear me, daughter of Zeus
who bears the stormcloud, tireless one, Athêna!
If ever you stood near my father and helped him
in a hot fight, befriend me now as well.
Let me destroy that man, bring me in range of him,
who hit me by surprise, and glories in it.
He swears I shall be blind to sunlight soon."

So ran his prayer, and Pallas Athêna heard him.   50
Nimbleness in the legs, sure feet and hands
she gave him, standing near him, saying swiftly:

"Courage, Diomêdês. Press the fight
against the Trojans. Fury like your father's
I've put into your heart: his never quailed—
Tydeus, master shieldsman, master of horses.
I've cleared away the mist that blurred your eyes
a moment ago, so you may see before you
clearly, and distinguish god from man.
If any god should put you to the test   60
upon this field, be sure you are not the man
to dare immortal gods in combat—none,
that is, except the goddess Aphrodítê.
If ever she should join the fight, then wound her
with your keen bronze."

                                     At this, grey-eyed Athêna
left him, and once more he made his way
into the line. If he had burned before
to fight with Trojans, now indeed blood-lust
three times as furious took hold of him.   70
Think of a lion that some shepherd wounds
but lightly as he leaps into a fold:
the man who roused his might cannot repel him
but dives into his shelter, while his flocks,
abandoned, are all driven wild; in heaps
huddled they are to lie, torn carcasses,
before the escaping lion at one bound
surmounts the palisade. So lion-like,
Diomêdês plunged on Trojans.

. . . .

[Diomedes then fights the Trojan Aeneas, Aphrodite's son. The goddess attempts to rescue him, but she is wounded in the hand by Diomedes. Apollo steps in to carry out the
rescue, and Diomedes even tries to take him on. Back on Olympus, where Aphrodite has
retreated to have her wound healed, Dione relates other instances when humans have
injured gods. Ares then enters the fray, and Athene urges Diomedes to attack him, too.
With Athene's help, Diomedes wounds the god of war himself and drives him from the
field.]

BOOK 6

[The battle continues. Diomedes encounters Glaucus, a Trojan. When they discover that
their grandfathers were guest-friends, they exchange armor in token of continued
friendship and go on to fight other members of the opposing armies instead. Returning
from the field, Hector talks with his wife, Andromache:]

. . . .
Up to the great square tower of Ilion
she took her way, because she heard our men
were spent in battle by Akhaian power.
In haste, like a madwoman, to the wall
she went, and Nurse went too, carrying the child."

At this word Hektor whirled and left his hall,
taking the same path he had come by,
along byways, walled lanes, all through the town
until he reached the Skaian Gates, whereby
before long he would issue on the field.   10
There his warmhearted lady
came to meet him, running: Andrómakhê,
whose father, Eëtíôn, once had ruled
the land under Mount Plakos, dark with forest,
at Thêbê under Plakos—lord and king
of the Kilikians. Hektor was her lord now,
head to foot in bronze; and now she joined him.
Behind her came her maid, who held the child
against her breast, a rosy baby still,
Hektoridês, the world's delight, as fresh   20
as a pure shining star. Skamándrios
his father named him; other men would say
Astýanax, "Lord of the Lower Town,"
as Hektor singlehanded guarded Troy.
How brilliantly the warrior smiled, in silence,
his eyes upon the child! Andrómakhê
rested against him, shook away a tear,
and pressed his hand in both her own, to say:

"Oh, my wild one, your bravery will be
your own undoing! No pity for our child,   30
poor little one, or me in my sad lot—
soon to be deprived of you! soon, soon
Akhaians as one man will set upon you
and cut you down! Better for me, without you,
to take cold earth for mantle. No more comfort,
no other warmth, after you meet your doom,
but heartbreak only. Father is dead, and Mother.
My father great Akhilleus killed when he
besieged and plundered Thêbê, our high town,
citadel of Kilikians. He killed him,   40
but, reverent at last in this, did not
despoil him. Body, gear, and weapons forged
so handsomely, he burned, and heaped a barrow
over the ashes. Elms were planted round
by mountain-nymphs of him who bears the stormcloud.
Then seven brothers that I had at home

in one day entered Death's dark place. Akhilleus,
prince and powerful runner, killed all seven
amid their shambling cattle and silvery sheep.
Mother, who had been queen of wooded Plakos,   50
he brought with other winnings home, and freed her,
taking no end of ransom. Artemis
the Huntress shot her in her father's house.
Father and mother—I have none but you,
nor brother, Hektor; lover none but you!
Be merciful! Stay here upon the tower!
Do not bereave your child and widow me!
Draw up your troops by the wild figtree; that way
the city lies most open, men most easily
could swarm the wall where it is low: 60
three times, at least, their best men tried it there
in company of the two called Aías, with
Idómeneus, the Atreidai, Diomêdês—
whether someone who had it from oracles
had told them, or their own hearts urged them on."

Great Hektor in his shimmering helmet answered:

"Lady, these many things beset my mind
no less than yours. But I should die of shame
before our Trojan men and noblewomen
if like a coward I avoided battle,   70
nor am I moved to. Long ago I learned
how to be brave, how to go forward always
and to contend for honor, Father's and mine.
Honor—for in my heart and soul I know
a day will come when ancient Ilion falls,
when Priam and the folk of Priam perish.
Not by the Trojans' anguish on that day
am I so overborne in mind—the pain
of Hékabê herself, or Priam king,
or of my brothers, many and valorous,   80
who will have fallen in dust before our enemies—
as by your own grief, when some armed Akhaian
takes you in tears, your free life stripped away.
Before another woman's loom in Argos
it may be you will pass, or at Messêis
or Hypereiê fountain, carrying water,
against your will—iron constraint upon you.
And seeing you in tears, a man may say:
'There is the wife of Hektor, who fought best
of Trojan horsemen when they fought at Troy.'   90
So he may say—and you will ache again
for one man who could keep you out of bondage.

Let me be hidden dark down in my grave
before I hear your cry or know you captive!"

As he said this, Hektor held out his arms
to take his baby. But the child squirmed round
on the nurse's bosom and began to wail,
terrified by his father's great war helm—
the flashing bronze, the crest with horsehair plume
tossed like a living thing at every nod.   100
His father began laughing, and his mother
laughed as well. Then from his handsome head
Hektor lifted off his helm and bent
to place it, bright with sunlight, on the ground.
When he had kissed his child and swung him high
to dandle him, he said this prayer:

                    "O Zeus
and all immortals, may this child, my son,
become like me a prince among the Trojans.
Let him be strong and brave and rule in power   110
at Ilion; then someday men will say
'This fellow is far better than his father!'
seeing him home from war, and in his arms
the bloodstained gear of some tall warrior slain—
making his mother proud."

                    After this prayer,
into his dear wife's arms he gave his baby,
whom on her fragrant breast
she held and cherished, laughing through her tears.
Hektor pitied her now. Caressing her,   120
he said:

                  "Unquiet soul, do not be too distressed
by thoughts of me. You know no man dispatches me
into the undergloom against my fate;
no mortal, either, can escape his fate,
coward or brave man, once he comes to be.
Go home, attend to your own handiwork
at loom and spindle, and command the maids
to busy themselves, too. As for the war,
that is for men, all who were born at Ilion,   130
to put their minds on—most of all for me."

He stooped now to recover his plumed helm
as she, his dear wife, drew away, her head
turned and her eyes upon him, brimming tears.
She made her way in haste then to the ordered
house of Hektor and rejoined her maids,
moving them all to weep at sight of her.

In Hektor's home they mourned him, living still
but not, they feared, again to leave the war
or be delivered from Akhaian fury.   140

Paris in the meantime had not lingered:
after he buckled his bright war-gear on
he ran through Troy, sure-footed with long strides.
Think how a stallion fed on clover and barley,
mettlesome, thundering in a stall, may snap
his picket rope and canter down a field
to bathe as he would daily in the river—
glorying in freedom! Head held high
with mane over his shoulders flying,
his dazzling work of finely jointed knees   150
takes him around the pasture haunts of horses.
That was the way the son of Priam, Paris,
ran from the height of Pergamos, his gear
ablaze like the great sun,
and laughed aloud. He sprinted on, and quickly
met his brother, who was slow to leave
the place where he had discoursed with his lady.
Aléxandros was first to speak:
                                        "Dear fellow,"
he said, "have I delayed you, kept you waiting?   160
Have I not come at the right time, as you asked?"

And Hektor in his shimmering helm replied:

"My strange brother! No man with justice in him
would underrate your handiwork in battle;
you have a powerful arm. But you give way
too easily, and lose interest, lose your will.
My heart aches in me when I hear our men,
who have such toil of battle on your account,
talk of you with contempt. Well, come along.
Someday we'll make amends for that, if ever   170
we drive the Akhaians from the land of Troy—
if ever Zeus permit us, in our hall,
to set before the gods of heaven, undying
and ever young, our winebowl of deliverance."

BOOK 7

[Hector challenges the Greeks to single combat. Ajax is selected by lot from the volunteers:]

. . . .

we have no fear of any. No man here
will drive me from the field against my will,

not by main force, not by a ruse. I hope
I was not born and bred on Sálamis
to be a dunce in battle."

                    At this the soldiers
prayed to Zeus. You might have heard one say,
his eyes on heaven:

                    "Father Zeus, from Ida
looking out for us all: greatest, most glorious: 10
let Aías win the honor of victory!
Or if you care for Hektor and are inclined
to favor him, then let both men be even
in staying power and honor!"

                    So they prayed,
while Aías made his brazen helmet snug,
fitted his shield and sword strap. He stepped out
as formidable as gigantic Arês,
wading into the ranks of men, when Zeus
drives them to battle in bloodletting fury.   20
Huge as that, the bastion of Akhaians
loomed and grinned, his face a cruel mask,
his legs moving in great strides. He shook
his long spear doubled by its pointing shadow,
and the Argives exulted. Now the Trojans
felt a painful trembling in the knees,
and even Hektor's heart thumped in his chest—
but there could be no turning back; he could not
slip again into his throng of troops;
he was the challenger. Aías came nearer,   30
carrying like a tower his body shield
of seven oxhides sheathed in bronze—a work
done for him by the leather-master Tykhios
in Hylê: Tykhios made the glittering shield
with seven skins of oxhide and an eighth
of plated bronze. Holding this bulk before him,
Aías Telamônios came on
toward Hektor and stood before him. Now he spoke,
threatening him:

                    "Before long, man to man,   40
Hektor, you'll realize that we Danáäns,
have our champions, too—I mean besides
the lionhearted breaker of men, Akhilleus.
He lies now by the beaked seagoing ships
in anger at Lord Marshal Agamémnon.
But here are those among us who can face you—
plenty of us. Fight then, if you will!"

To this, great Hektor in his shimmering helmet
answered: ·

"Son of the ancient line of Télamôn,   50
Aías, lordly over fighting men,
when you try me you try no callow boy
or woman innocent of war. I know
and know well how to fight and how to kill,
how to take blows upon the right or left
shifting my guard of tough oxide in battle,
how to charge in a din of chariots,
or hand to hand with sword or pike to use
timing and footwork in the dance of war.
Seeing the man you are, I would not trick you   60
but let you have it with a straight shot,
if luck is with me."

Rifling his spear,
he hurled it and hit Aías' wondrous shield
square on the outer and eighth plate of bronze.
The spearhead punched its way through this and through
six layers, but the seventh oxhide stopped it.
Now in his turn great Aías made his cast
and hit the round shield braced on Hektor's arm.
Piercing the bright shield, the whetted spearhead   70
cut its way into his figured cuirass,
ripping his shirt along his flank; but he
had twisted and escaped the night of death.
Now both men disengaged their spears and fell
on one another like man-eating lions
or wild boars—no tame household creatures. Hektor's
lancehead scored the tower shield—but failed
to pierce it, as the point was bent aside.
Then Aías, plunging forward, rammed his spear
into the round shield, and the point went through   80
to nick his furious adversary, making
a cut that welled dark blood below his ear.
But Hektor did not slacken, even so.
He drew away and in one powerful hand
picked from the plain a boulder lying there,
black, rough and huge, and threw it
hitting Aías' gigantic sevenfold shield
square on the boss with a great clang of bronze.
Then Aías lifted up a huger stone
and whirled, and put immeasurable force   90
behind it when he let it fly—as though
he flung a millstone—crushing Hektor's shield.
The impact caught his knees, so that he tumbled

backward behind the bashed-in shield. At once
Apollo pulled him to his feet again,
and now with drawn swords toe to toe
they would have doubled strokes on one another,
had not those messengers of Zeus and men,
the heralds, intervened—one from the Trojans,
one from the Akhaian side—for both   100
Idaíos and Talthýbios kept their heads.
They held their staves out, parting the contenders,
and that experienced man, Idaíos, said:

"Enough, lads. No more fighting. The Lord Zeus,
assembler of bright cloud, cares for you both.
Both are great spearmen, and we all know it.
But now already night is coming on,
and we do well to heed the fall of night."

Said Aías Telamônios in reply:

"Idaíos, call on Hektor to say as much.   110
He was the one who dared our champions
to duel with him. Let him take the lead.
Whatever he likes, I am at his disposition."

Hektor in his shimmering helmet answered:

"Aías, a powerful great frame you had
as a gift from god, and a clear head; of all
Akhaians you are toughest with a spear.
And this being shown, let us break off our duel,
our bloodletting, for today. We'll meet again
another time—and fight until the unseen   120
power decides between these hosts of ours,
awarding one or the other victory.
But now already night is coming on,
and we do well to heed the fall of night.
This way you'll give them festive pleasure there
beside the ships, above all to your friends,
companions at your table. As for me,
as I go through Priam's town tonight
my presence will give joy to Trojan men
and to our women, as in their trailing gowns   130
they throng the place of god with prayers for me.
Let us make one another memorable gifts,
and afterward they'll say, among Akhaians
and Trojans: 'These two fought and gave no quarter
in close combat, yet they parted friends.'"

This he said, and lifting off his broadsword,

silver-hilted, in its sheath, upon
the well-cut baldric, made a gift of it,
and Aías gave his loin-guard, sewn in purple.
Each then turned away. One went to join   140
the Akhaian troops; the other joined his Trojans,
and all were full of joy to see him come
alive, unhurt, delivered from the fury
of Aías whose great hands no man withstood.
Almost despairing of him still, they led him
into the town.

.   .   .   .   .

[The Greeks and Trojans agree to a one-day truce to bury the dead.]

BOOK 8

Dawn in her saffron robe came spreading light
on all the world, and Zeus who plays in thunder
gathered the gods on peaked Olympos' height,
then said to that assembly:

                              "Listen to me,
immortals, every one,
and let me make my mood and purpose clear.
Let no one, god or goddess, contravene
my present edict; all assent to it
that I may get this business done, and quickly.   10
If I catch sight of anyone slipping away
with a mind to assist the Danáäns or the Trojans,
he comes back blasted without ceremony,
or else he will be flung out of Olympos
into the murk of Tartaros that lies
deep down in underworld. Iron the gates are,
brazen the doorslab, and the depth from hell
as great as heaven's utmost height from earth.
You may learn then how far my power
puts all gods to shame.   20
                         Or prove it this way:
out of the zenith hang a golden line
and put your weight on it, all gods and goddesses.
You will not budge me earthward out of heaven,
cannot budge the all-highest, mighty Zeus,
no matter how you try.

                        But let my hand
once close to pull that cable—up you come,
and with you earth itself comes, and the sea.
By one end tied around Olympos' top   30
I could let all the world swing in mid-heaven!
That is how far I overwhelm you all,
both gods and men."

They were all awed and silent,
he put it with such power. After a pause,
the grey-eyed goddess Athêna said:

"O Zeus,
highest and mightiest, father of us all,
we are well aware of your omnipotence,
but all the same we mourn the Akhaian spearmen   40
if they are now to meet hard fate and die.
As you command, we shall indeed
abstain from battle—merely, now and again,
dropping a word of counsel to the Argives,
that all may not be lost through your displeasure."

The driver of cloud smiled and replied:

"Take heart,
dear child, third born of heaven. I do not speak
my full intent. With you, I would be gentle."

Up to his car he backed his bronze-shod team   50
of aerial runners, long manes blowing gold.
He adorned himself in panoply of gold,
then mounted, taking up his golden whip,
and lashed his horses onward. At full stretch
midway between the earth and starry heaven
they ran toward Ida, sparkling with cool streams,
mother of wild things, and the peak of Gárgaron
where are his holy plot and fragrant altar.
There Zeus, father of gods and men, reined in
and freed his team, diffusing cloud about them,   60
while glorying upon the crest he sat
to view the far-off scene below—Akhaian
ships and Trojan city.
At that hour
Akhaian fighting men with flowing hair
took a meal by their huts and armed themselves.
The Trojans, too, on their side, in the city,
mustered under arms—though fewer, still
resolved by dire need to fight the battle
for wives' and children's sake.   70
Now all the gates
were flung wide and the Trojan army sortied,
charioteers and foot, in a rising roar.

When the two masses met on the battle line
they ground their shields together, crossing spears,
with might of men in armor. Round shield-bosses

rang on each other in the clashing din,
and groans mingled with shouts of triumph rose
from those who died and those who killed: the field
ran rivulets of blood. While the fair day   80
waxed in heat through all the morning hours
missiles from both sank home and men went down,
until when Hêlios bestrode mid-heaven
the Father cleared his golden scales. Therein
two destinies of death's long pain he set
for Trojan horsemen and Akhaian soldiers
and held the scales up by the midpoint. Slowly
one pan sank with death's day for Akhaians.

. . . .

BOOK 9

**[Fearing for the safety of their ships, the Greeks hold a feast and, in the assembly that
follows, agree to petition Achilles to return to battle. Admitting an error of judgment,
Agamemnon itemizes a list of munificent gifts he will give to Achilles if the hero will
return. The one remaining condition is that Achilles must bow to Agamemnon. Odysseus, Ajax, and Phoenix—Achilles's old tutor—are appointed as ambassadors to Achilles, who makes a feast of his own to welcome them:]**

. . . .

And Prince Akhilleus led them in. He seated them
on easy chairs with purple coverlets,
and to Patróklos who stood near he said:

"Put out an ampler winebowl, use more wine
for stronger drink, and place a cup for each.
Here are my dearest friends beneath my roof."

Patróklos did as his companion bade him.
Meanwhile the host set down a carving block
within the fire's rays; a chine of mutton
and a fat chine of goat he placed upon it,   10
as well as savory pork chine. Automédôn
steadied the meat for him, Akhilleus carved,
then sliced it well and forked it on the spits.
Meanwhile Patróklos, like a god in firelight,
made the hearth blaze up. When the leaping flame
had ebbed and died away, he raked the coals
and in the glow extended spits of meat,
lifting these at times from the firestones
to season with pure salt. When all was done
and the roast meat apportioned into platters,   20
loaves of bread were passed round by Patróklos
in fine baskets. Akhilleus served the meat.
He took his place then opposite Odysseus,

back to the other wall, and told
Patróklos to make offering to the gods.
This he did with meat tossed in the fire,
then each man's hand went out upon the meal.
When they had put their hunger and thirst away,
Aías nodded silently to Phoinix,
but Prince Odysseus caught the nod. He filled   30
a cup of wine and lifted it to Akhilleus,

saying:
                           "Health, Akhilleus. We've no lack
of generous feasts this evening—in the lodge
of Agamémnon first, and now with you,
good fare and plentiful each time.
It is not feasting that concerns us now,
however, but a ruinous defeat.
Before our very eyes we see it coming
and are afraid. By a blade's turn, our good ships   40
are saved or lost, unless you arm your valor.
Trojans and allies are encamped tonight
in pride before our ramparts, at our sterns,
and through their army burn a thousand fires.
These men are sure they cannot now be stopped
but will get through to our good ships. Lord Zeus
flashes and thunders for them on the right,
and Hektor in his ecstasy of power
is mad for battle, confident in Zeus,
deferring to neither men nor gods. Pure frenzy   50
fills him, and he prays for the bright dawn
when he will shear our stern-post beaks away
and fire all our ships, while in the shipways
amid that holocaust he carries death
among our men, driven out by smoke. All this
I gravely fear; I fear the gods will make
good his threatenings, and our fate will be
to die here, far from the pastureland of Argos.
Rouse yourself, if even at this hour
you'll pitch in for the Akhaians and deliver them   60
from Trojan havoc. In the years to come
this day will be remembered pain for you
if you do not. No remedy, no remedy
will come to hand, once the great ill is done.
While there is time, think how to keep this evil
day from the Danáäns!
                             My dear lad,
how rightly in your case your father, Pêleus,
put it in his farewell, sending you out
from Phthía to take ship with Agamémnon!   70

'Now as to fighting power, child,' he said,
'if Hêra and Athêna wish, they'll give it.
Control your passion, though, and your proud heart,
for gentle courtesy is a better thing.
Break off insidious quarrels, and young and old,
the Argives will respect you for it more.'
That was your old father's admonition:
you have forgotten. Still, even now, abandon
heart-wounding anger. If you will relent,
Agamémnon will match this change of heart   80
with gifts. Now listen and let me list for you
what just now in his quarters he proposed:
seven new tripods, and ten bars of gold,
then twenty shining caldrons, and twelve horses,
thoroughbreds, that by their wind and legs
have won him prizes: any man who owned
what these have brought him would not lack resources,
could not be pinched for precious gold—so many
prizes have these horses carried home.
Then he will give you seven women, deft   90
in household handicraft: women of Lesbos
chosen when you yourself took Lesbos town,
as they outshone all womankind in beauty.
These he will give you, and one more, whom he
took away from you then: Briseus' daughter,
concerning whom he adds a solemn oath
never to have gone to bed or coupled with her,
as custom is, my lord, with men and women.
These are all yours at once. If the immortals
grant us the pillaging of Priam's town,   100
you may come forward when the spoils are shared
and load your ship with bars of gold and bronze.
Then you may choose among the Trojan women
twenty that are most lovely, after Helen.
And then, if we reach Argos of Akhaia,
flowing with good things of the earth, you'll be
his own adopted son, dear as Orestês,
born long ago and reared in bounteous peace.
He has three daughters now at home, Khrysóthemis,
Laódikê, and Iphiánassa.   110
You may take whom you will to be your bride
and pay no gift when you conduct her home
to your ancestral hall. He'll add a dowry
such as no man has given to his daughter.
Seven flourishing strongholds he'll give to you:
Kardamylê and Enopê and Hirê
in the wild grassland; holy Phêrai too,
and the deep meadowland of Ántheia,

Aipeia and the vineyard slope of Pêdasos,
all lying near the sea in the far west   120
of sandy Pylos. In these lands are men
who own great flocks and herds; now as your liegemen,
they will pay tithes and sumptuous honor to you,
prospering as they carry out your plans.
These are the gifts he will arrange if you
desist from anger.

                    Even if you abhor
the son of Atreus all the more bitterly,
with all his gifts, take pity on the rest,
all the old army, worn to rags in battle.   130
These will honor you as gods are honored!
And ah, for these, what glory you may win!
Think: Hektor is your man this time: being crazed
with ruinous pride, believing there's no fighter
equal to him among those that our ships
brought here by sea, he'll put himself in range!"

Akhilleus the great runner answered him:

"Son of Laërtês and the gods of old,
Odysseus, master soldier and mariner,
I owe you a straight answer, as to how   140
I see this thing, and how it is to end.
No need to sit with me like mourning doves
making your gentle noise by turns. I hate
as I hate Hell's own gate that man who hides
one thought within him while he speaks another.
What I shall say is what I see and think.
Give in to Agamémnon? I think not,
neither to him nor to the rest. I had
small thanks for fighting, fighting without truce
against hard enemies here. The portion's equal   150
whether a man hangs back or fights his best;
the same respect, or lack of it, is given
brave man and coward. One who's active dies
like the do-nothing. What least thing have I
to show for it, for harsh days undergone
and my life gambled, all these years of war?
A bird will give her fledglings every scrap
she comes by, and go hungry, foraging.
That is the case with me.
Many a sleepless night I've spent afield   160
and many a day in bloodshed, hand to hand
in battle for the wives of other men.
In sea raids I plundered a dozen towns,
eleven in expeditions overland
through Trojan country, and the treasure taken

out of them all, great heaps of handsome things,
I carried back each time to Agamémnon.
He sat tight on the beachhead, and shared out
a little treasure; most of it he kept.
He gave prizes of war to his officers;   170
the rest have theirs, not I; from me alone
of all Akhaians, he pre-empted her.
He holds my bride, dear to my heart. Aye, let him
sleep with her and enjoy her!

                                Why must Argives
fight the Trojans? Why did he raise an army
and lead it here? For Helen, was it not?
Are the Atreidai of all mortal men
the only ones who love their wives? I think not.
Every sane decent fellow loves his own   180
and cares for her, as in my heart I loved
Brisêis, though I won her by the spear.
Now, as he took my prize out of my hands,
tricked and defrauded me, he need not tempt me;
I know him, and he cannot change my mind.
Let him take thought, Odysseus, with you
and others how the ships may be defended
against incendiary attack. By god,
he has achieved imposing work without me,
a rampart piled up overnight, a ditch   190
running beyond it, broad and deep,
with stakes implanted in it! All no use!
He cannot hold against the killer's charge.
As long as I was in the battle, Hektor
never cared for a fight far from the walls;
his limit was the oak tree by the gate.
When I was alone one day he waited there,
but barely got away when I went after him.
Now it is I who do not care to fight.   200
Tomorrow at dawn when I have made offering
to Zeus and all the gods, and hauled my ships
for loading in the shallows, if you like
and if it interests you, look out and see
my ships on Hellê's waters in the offing,
oarsmen in line making the sea-foam scud!
And if the great Earthshaker gives a breeze,
the third day out I'll make it home to Phthía.
Rich possessions are there I left behind
when I was mad enough to come here; now   210
I take home gold and ruddy bronze, and women
belted luxuriously, and hoary iron,
all that came to me here. As for my prize,

he who gave her took her outrageously back.
Well, you can tell him all this to his face,
and let the other Akhaians burn
if he in his thick hide of shamelessness
picks out another man to cheat. He would not
look me in the eye, dog that he is!
I will not share one word of counsel with him,   220
nor will I act with him; he robbed me blind,
broke faith with me: he gets no second chance
to play me for a fool. Once is enough.
To hell with him, Zeus took his brains away!
His gifts I abominate, and I would give
not one dry shuck for him. I would not change,
not if he multiplied his gifts by ten,
by twenty times what he has now, and more,
no matter where they came from: if he gave
what enters through Orkhómenos' town gate   230
or Thebes of Egypt, where the treasures lie—
that city where through each of a hundred gates
two hundred men drive out in chariots.
Not if his gifts outnumbered the sea sands
or all the dust grains in the world could Agamémnon
ever appease me—not till he pays me back
full measure, pain for pain, dishonor for dishonor.
The daughter of Agamémnon, son of Atreus,
I will not take in marriage. Let her be
as beautiful as pale-gold Aphrodítê,   240
skilled as Athêna of the sea-grey eyes,
I will not have her, at any price. No, let him
find someone else, an eligible Akhaian,
kinglier than I.

                              Now if the gods
preserve me and I make it home, my father
Pêleus will select a bride for me.
In Hellas and in Phthía there are many
daughters of strong men who defend the towns.
I'll take the one I wish to be my wife.   250
There in my manhood I have longed, indeed,
to marry someone of congenial mind
and take my ease, enjoying the great estate
my father had acquired.

                              Now I think
no riches can compare with being alive,
not even those they say this well-built Ilion
stored up in peace before the Akhaians came.
Neither could all the Archer's shrine contains
at rocky Pytho, in the crypt of stone.   260
A man may come by cattle and sheep in raids;

tripods he buys, and tawny-headed horses;
but his life's breath cannot be hunted back
or be recaptured once it pass his lips.
My mother, Thetis of the silvery feet,
tells me of two possible destinies
carrying me toward death: two ways:
if on the one hand I remain to fight
around Troy town, I lose all hope of home
but gain unfading glory; on the other,   270
if I sail back to my own land my glory
fails—but a long life lies ahead for me.
To all the rest of you I say: 'Sail home:
you will not now see Ilion's last hour,'
for Zeus who views the wide world held his sheltering
hand over that city, and her troops
have taken heart.
                              Return, then, emissaries,
deliver my answer to the Akhaian peers—
it is the senior officer's privilege—   280
and let them plan some other way, and better,
to save their ships and save the Akhaian army.
This one cannot be put into effect—
their scheme this evening—while my anger holds.
Phoinix may stay and lodge the night with us,
then take ship and sail homeward at my side
tomorrow, if he wills. I'll not constrain him."

After Akhilleus finished, all were silent,
awed, for he spoke with power.
Then the old master-charioteer, Lord Phoinix,   290
answered at last, and let his tears come shining,
fearing for the Akhaian ships:

                              "Akhilleus,
if it is true you set your heart on home
and will not stir a finger to save the ships
from being engulfed by fire—all for this rage
that has swept over you—how, child, could I
be sundered from you, left behind alone?
For your sake the old master-charioteer,
Pêleus, made provision that I should come,   300
that day he gave you godspeed out of Phthía
to go with Agamémnon. Still a boy,
you knew nothing of war that levels men
to the same testing, nothing of assembly
where men become illustrious. That is why
he sent me, to instruct you in these matters,
to be a man of eloquence and action.
After all that, dear child, I should not wish

to be left here apart from you—not even
if god himself should undertake to smooth   310
my wrinkled age and make me fresh and young,
as when for the first time I left the land
of lovely women, Hellas. I went north
to avoid a feud with Father, Amyntor
Orménidês. His anger against me rose
over a fair-haired slave girl whom he fancied,
without respect for his own wife, my mother.
Mother embraced my knees and begged that I
make love to this girl, so that afterward
she might be cold to the aging man. I did it.   320
My father guessed the truth at once, and cursed me,
praying the ghostly Furies that no son
of mine should ever rest upon his knees:
a curse fulfilled by the immortals—Lord
Zeus of undergloom and cold Perséphonê.
I planned to put a sword in him, and would have,
had not some god unstrung my rage, reminding me
of country gossip and the frowns of men;
I shrank from being called a parricide
among the Akhaians. But from that time on   330
I felt no tie with home, no love for lingering
under the rooftree of a raging father.
Our household and our neighbors, it is true,
urged me to stay. They made a handsome feast
of shambling cattle butchered, and fat sheep;
young porkers by the litter, crisp with fat,
were singed and spitted in Hêphaistos' fire,
rivers of wine drunk from the old man's store.
Nine times they spent the night and slept beside me,
taking the watch by turns, leaving a fire   340
to flicker under the entrance colonnade,
and one more in the court outside my room.
But when the tenth night came, starless and black,
I cracked the tight bolt on my chamber door,
pushed out, and scaled the courtyard wall, unseen
by household men on watch or women slaves.
Then I escaped from that place, made my way
through Hellas where the dancing floors are wide,
until I came to Phthía's fertile plain,
mother of flocks, and Pêleus the king.   350
He gave me welcome, treated me with love,
as a father would an only son, his heir
to rich possessions. And he made me rich,
appointing me great numbers of retainers
on the frontier of Phthía, where I lived
as lord of Dolopês. Now, it was I
who formed your manhood, handsome as a god's,

Akhilleus: I who loved you from the heart;
for never in another's company
would you attend a feast or dine in hall—   360
never, unless I took you on my knees
and cut your meat, and held your cup of wine.
Many a time you wet my shirt, hiccuping
wine-bubbles in distress, when you were small.
Patient and laborious as a nurse
I had to be for you, bearing in mind
that never would the gods bring into being
any son of mine. Godlike Akhilleus,
you were the manchild that I made my own
to save me someday, so I thought, from misery.   370
Quell your anger, Akhilleus! You must not
be pitiless! The gods themselves relent,
and are they not still greater in bravery,
in honor and in strength? Burnt offerings,
courteous prayer, libation, smoke of sacrifice,
with all of these, men can placate the gods
when someone oversteps and errs. The truth is,
prayers are daughters of almighty Zeus—
one may imagine them lame, wrinkled things
with eyes cast down, that toil to follow after   380
passionate Folly. Folly is strong and swift,
outrunning all the prayers, and everywhere
arriving first to injure mortal men;
still they come healing after. If a man
reveres the daughters of Zeus when they come near,
he is rewarded, and his prayers are heard;
but if he spurns them and dismisses them,
they make their way to Zeus again and ask
that Folly dog that man till suffering
has taken arrogance out of him.   390
                              Relent,
be courteous to the daughters of Zeus, you too,
as courtesy sways others, and the best.
If Agamémnon had no gifts for you,
named none to follow, but inveighed against you
still in fury, then I could never say,
'Discard your anger and defend the Argives—'
never, no matter how they craved your help.
But this is not so: he will give many things
at once; he promised others; he has sent   400
his noblest men to intercede with you,
the flower of the army, and your friends,
dearest among the Argives. Will you turn
their words, their coming, into humiliation?

[Achilles having rejected their offer, the Greeks decide to continue without him.]

BOOK 10

[Odysseus and Diomedes carry out a night raid. After capturing and interrogating a Trojan soldier, they kill him and use the intelligence thus obtained to kill thirteen Trojans and steal their horses.]

BOOK 11

[The Greeks continue the battle with incredible valour. Agamemnon charges into the enemy ranks, slaughtering Trojans as he goes. Then Agamemnon, Diomedes, and Odysseus are wounded. Achilles, intensely curious about the fate of his fellow soldiers, sends his beloved friend Patroclus for news. Nestor persuades Patroclus to don his friend's armor and enter the battle disguised as Achilles. Patroclus agrees and returns to tell Achilles of the plan.]

BOOK 12

[The Trojans plan to attack the ships, led by Sarpedon (a son of Zeus) and Hector. They almost succeed, and the Greeks are beaten back around the ships. Zeus sends a portent—an eagle carrying a blood-red snake, which strikes its captor; when the eagle lets go in pain, the snake falls among the Trojan troops. A Trojan officer, Poulýdamas, interprets the omen as a warning to the Trojans to retreat from the Greek ships, but Hector refuses.]

BOOK 13

[While Zeus turns his attention elsewhere, Poseidon goes to rally the Greeks, inspiring them to fight off the Trojan attack. The gods, at "cross purposes," continue to intervene on both sides.]

BOOK 14

[The recently wounded Greek heroes return to battle. Hera adorns herself with scents and fine clothes, and deceives Aphrodite into loaning her the enchanted girdle of desire. Hera uses it to entice Zeus to make love to her, in order to distract him from the war. Afterward, Zeus falls asleep. Meanwhile, Hector is wounded.]

BOOK 15

[Zeus discovers that he has been tricked and that meanwhile Poseidon has been intervening to help the Greeks. Zeus insists that the Greeks must continue to lose until the Trojans actually reach the ships so that Achilles will send Patroclus into the battle. He predicts the death of his own son, Sarpedon, at Patroclus's hands, the death of Patroclus and the consequent return of Achilles to battle, and the death of Hector. Then, Zeus promises, he will turn the tide of war to favor the Greeks.]

BOOK 16

[The Trojans set fire to the ships. Seeing the flames, Achilles tells Patroclus that the time has come to go into combat to protect the Greeks from total destruction. Patroclus arms for battle but does not have the strength to wield Achilles's spear, the famous Pelian ash. He leads the Myrmidons, Achilles's troops, into battle, wearing his friend's highly visible armor. Seeing the famous helmet, the Trojans are terrified. Patroclus encounters Sarpedon, and Zeus is divided between his desire to protect his son and his need to allow Patroclus to kill him to protect the Greeks. Reminding him that death is the fate of all men, Hera persuades him to allow Sarpedon's death. Then Patroclus encounters Hector:]

. . . .

       And fierce
Patróklos hurled himself upon the Trojans,
in onslaughts fast as Arês, three times, wild
yells in his throat. Each time he killed nine men.
But on the fourth demonic foray, then
the end of life loomed up for you, Patróklos.
Into the combat dangerous Phoibos came
against him, but Patróklos could not see
the god, enwrapped in cloud as he came near.
He stood behind and struck with open hand   10
the man's back and broad shoulders, and the eyes
of the fighting man were dizzied by the blow.
Then Phoibos sent the captain's helmet rolling
under the horses' hooves, making the ridge
ring out, and dirtying all the horsehair plume
with blood and dust. Never in time before
had this plumed helmet been befouled with dust,
the helmet that had kept a hero's brow
unmarred, shielding Akhilleus' head. Now Zeus
bestowed it upon Hektor, let him wear it,   20
though his destruction waited. For Patróklos
felt his great spearshaft shattered in his hands,
long, tough, well-shod, and seasoned though it was;
his shield and strap fell to the ground; the Lord
Apollo, son of Zeus, broke off his cuirass.
Shock ran through him, and his good legs failed,
so that he stood agape. Then from behind
at close quarters, between the shoulder blades,
a Dardan fighter speared him: Pánthoös' son,
Euphórbos, the best Trojan of his age   30
at handling spears, in horsemanship and running:
he had brought twenty chariot fighters down
since entering combat in his chariot,
already skilled in the craft of war. This man
was first to wound you with a spear, Patróklos,
but did not bring you down. Instead, he ran back
into the mêlée, pulling from the flesh
his ashen spear, and would not face his enemy,
even disarmed, in battle. Then Patróklos,
disabled by the god's blow and the spear wound   40
moved back to save himself amid his men.

But Hektor, seeing that his brave adversary
tried to retire, hurt by the spear wound, charged
straight at him through the ranks and lunged for him
low in the flank, driving the spearhead through.
He crashed, and all Akhaian troops turned pale.
Think how a lion in his pride brings down
a tireless boar; magnificently they fight
on a mountain crest for a small gushing spring—
both in desire to drink—and by sheer power   50
the lion conquers the great panting boar:
that was the way the son of Priam, Hektor,
closed with Patróklos, son of Menoitios,
killer of many, and took his life away.
Then glorying above him he addressed him:

"Easy to guess, Patróklos, how you swore
to ravage Troy, to take the sweet daylight
of liberty from our women, and to drag them
off in ships to your own land—you fool!
Between you and those women there is Hektor's   60
war-team, thundering out to fight! My spear
has pride of place among the Trojan warriors,
keeping their evil hour at bay.
The kites will feed on you, here on this field.
Poor devil, what has that great prince, Akhilleus,
done for you? He must have told you often
as you were leaving and he stayed behind,
'Never come back to me, to the deepsea ships,
Patróklos, till you cut to rags
the bloody tunic on the chest of Hektor!'   70
That must have been the way he talked, and won
your mind to mindlessness."

. . . .

[Reminding Hector that his own death is imminent—at Prince Achilles's hands—Patroclus dies.]

BOOK 17

[Hector strips Patroclus's corpse of Achilles's armor and wears it. Zeus comments on the inevitability of Hector's death. Ajax rescues the corpse.]

BOOK 18

[Achilles mourns for Patroclus and acknowledges his responsibility for his friend's death. Vowing revenge, he determines to reenter the battle, ready to face his own death in order to destroy Hector. He vows not to bury Patroclus until he brings back the mutilated corpse of Hector and cuts the throats of twelve Trojans in tribute to his friend. But now he has no war gear. Thetis appeals to Hephaestus to forge a new shield for Achilles. Hephaestus decorates the shield with scenes from two cities in which disputes occur, one solving the dispute by formal debate, the other by war. He also provides a cuirass (breastplate), helmet, and greaves (shin armor).]

BOOK 19

[Thetis brings the new armor to Achilles and promises to preserve Patroclus's corpse from decay until Achilles has fulfilled his promise. Achilles then returns to the assembly. Agamemnon and Achilles mutually apologize for their respective folly and rage, although Agamemnon blames Zeus for "stealing his wits" and repeats his offer of gifts. Odysseus reminds the impatient Achilles that the men need to eat before fighting:]

· ·

                   Akhilleus answered:
                   "Excellency,
Lord Marshal Agamémnon, make the gifts
if you are keen to—gifts are due; or keep them.
It is for you to say. Let us recover
joy of battle soon, that's all!
No need to dither here and lose our time,
our great work still undone. When each man sees
Akhilleus in a charge, crumpling the ranks
of Trojans with his bronze-shod spear, let each   10
remember that is the way to fight his man!"
Replied Odysseus, the shrewd field commander:

"Brave as you are, and like a god in looks,
Akhilleus, do not send Akhaian soldiers
into the fight unfed! Today's mêlée
will not be brief, when rank meets rank, and heaven
breathes fighting spirit into both contenders.
No, tell all troops who are near the ships to take
roast meat and wine, for heart and staying power.
No soldier can fight hand to hand, in hunger,   20
all day long until the sun goes down!
Though in his heart he yearns for war, his legs
go slack before he knows it: thirst and famine
search him out, and his knees fail as he moves.
But that man stayed with victualing and wine
can fight his enemies all day: his heart
is bold and happy in his chest, his legs
hold out until both sides break off the battle!
Come, then, dismiss the ranks to make their breakfast.
Let the Lord Marshal Agamémnon   30
bring his gifts to the assembly ground
where all may see them; may your heart be warmed.
Then let him swear to you, before the Argives,
never to have made love to her, my lord,
as men and women by their nature do.
So may your heart be peaceable toward him!

And let him sate your hunger with rich fare
in his own shelter, that you may lack nothing
due you in justice. Afterward, Agamémnon,
you'll be more just to others, too. There is   40
no fault in a king's wish to conciliate
a man with whom he has been quick to anger!"

And the Lord Marshal Agamémnon answered:

"Glad I am to hear you, son of Laërtês,
finding the right word at the right time
for all these matters. And the oath you speak of
I'll take willingly, with all my heart,
and will not, before heaven, be forsworn.
Now let Akhilleus wait here, though the wargod
tug his arm; and all the rest of you   50
wait here assembled till the gifts have come
down from our quarters, and our peace is made.
For you, Odysseus, here is my command:
choose the finest young peers of all Akhaia
to fetch out of my ship those gifts we pledged
Akhilleus yesterday; and bring the women.
Let Talthýbios prepare for sacrifice,
in the army's name, a boar to Zeus and Hêlios."
Replied Akhilleus:

                              "Excellency, Lord Marshal,   60
another time were better for these ceremonies,
some interval in the war, and when I feel
less passion in me. Look, those men lie dead
whom Hektor killed when Zeus allowed him glory,
and yet you two propose a meal! By god,
I'd send our soldiers into action now
unfed and hungry. Have a feast, I'd say,
at sundown, when our shame has been avenged!
Before that, for my part, I will not swallow
food or drink—my dear friend being dead,   70
lying before my eyes, bled white by spear-cuts,
feet turned to his hut's door, his friends in mourning
around him. Your concerns are none of mine.
Slaughter and blood are what I crave, and groans
of anguished men!"
                              But the shrewd field commander
Odysseus answered:
                              "Akhilleus, flower and pride
of the Akhaians, you are more powerful
than I am—and a better spearman, too—   80
only in sizing matters up I'd say

I'm just as far beyond you, being older,
knowing more of the world. So bear with me.
Men quickly reach satiety with battle
in which the reaping bronze will bring to earth
big harvests, but a scanty yield, when Zeus,
war's overseer for mankind, tips the scales.
How can a fasting belly mourn our dead?
So many die, so often, every day,
when would soldiers come to an end of fasting?   90
No, we must dispose of him who dies
and keep hard hearts, and weep that day alone.
And those whom the foul war has left unhurt
will do well to remember food and drink,
so that we may again close with our enemies,
our dangerous enemies, and be tough soldiers,
hardened in mail of bronze. Let no one, now,
be held back waiting for another summons:
here is your summons! Woe to the man who lingers
beside the Argive ships! No, all together,   100
let us take up the fight against the Trojans!"

He took as escort sons of illustrious Nestor:
Phyleus' son Mégês, Thoas, and Meríonês,
and the son of Kreion, Lykomêdês, and
Melánippos, to Agamémnon's quarters.
No sooner was the work assigned than done:
they brought the seven tripods Agamémnon
promised Akhilleus, and the twenty caldrons
shining, and the horses, a full dozen;
then they conducted seven women, skilled   110
in housecraft, with Brisêis in her beauty.
Odysseus weighed ten bars of purest gold
and turned back, followed by his young Akhaians,
bearing the gifts to place in mid-assembly.

.   .   .   .

[Refusing to eat, Achilles reluctantly agrees to allow the others to do so. Achilles, meanwhile, yokes his team. Xanthus, one of his magical horses, speaks, his voice given him by
Hera to prophesy Achilles's death. Achilles already knows this but is committed to satisfying his rage against Hector, whatever the cost to himself.]

BOOKS 20 AND 21

[The armies gather again. Now Zeus gives the gods permission to get engaged in the
battle. Poseidon removes Aeneas from danger, saving him for Troy's future destiny.
Achilles moves through the Trojan army like a forest fire, killing Trojans and trampling
them in the blood and dust. In contrast to his earlier practices, he refuses to take or
ransom prisoners, instead tossing body after body into the river. He tells one victim
that, however heroic, he himself will die:]

. . . .
A morning comes or evening or high noon
when someone takes my life away in war,
a spear-cast, or an arrow from a bowstring."

At this the young man's knees failed, and his heart;
he lost his grip upon the spear
and sank down, opening his arms. Akhilleus
drew his sword and thrust between his neck
and collarbone, so the two-edged blade went in
up to the hilt. Now face down on the ground
he lay stretched out, as dark blood flowed from him,   10
soaking the earth. Akhilleus picked him up
by one foot, wheeled, and slung him in the river
to be swept off downstream. Then he exulted:

"Nose down there with fishes. In cold blood
they'll kiss your wound and nip your blood away.
Your mother cannot put you on your bed
to mourn you, but Skamánder whirling down
will bear you to the sea's broad lap,
where any fish that jumps, breaking a wave,
may dart under the dark wind-shivered water   20
to nibble white fat of Lykáôn. Trojans,
perish in this rout until you reach,
and I behind you slaughtering reach, the town!
The god-begotten river swiftly flowing
will not save you. Many a bull you've offered,
many a trim-hooved horse thrown in alive
to Xánthos' whirlpools. All the same, you'll die
in blood until I have avenged Patróklos,
paid you back for the death-wounds of Akhaians
cut down near the deep-sea-going ships   30
far from my eyes."

                              On hearing this, the river
darkened to the heart with rage. He cast
about for ways to halt prodigious Akhilleus'
feats of war and keep death from the Trojans.
Meanwhile the son of Pêleus took his spear
and bounded straight for Asteropaíos,
burning to kill this son of Pêlegôn,
whom the broad river Áxios had fathered
on Periboia, eldest of the daughters   40
of Akessámenos. Whirling, deep-running
river that he was, Áxios loved her.
And now Akhilleus made for Asteropaíos,
who came up from the stream-bed to confront him,

holding two spears. And Xánthos, in his anger
over all the young men dead, cut down
by Akhilleus pitilessly in the stream,
gave heart to this contender. As they drew near,
the great runner and prince was first to speak:

"Who are you, soldier? Where do you come from,   50
daring to challenge me? Grief comes to all
whose sons meet my anger."

                            Pêlegôn's
brave son replied:
                     "Heroic son of Pêleus,
why do you ask my birth? I am a native
of rich farmland, Paiônia; Paiônês
are the spearmen I command. Today the eleventh
dawn came up since I arrived at Ilion.
My line began, if you must know, with Áxios,   60
mover of beautiful water over land,
who fathered the great spearman, Pêlegôn,
and Pêlegôn is said to have fathered me.
But now again to battle, Lord Akhilleus."

That was his prideful answer. Then Akhilleus
lifted his Pêlian ash. His enemy,
being ambidextrous, cast both spears at once
and failed. With one he hit Akhilleus' shield
but could not pierce it, for the gold plate held,
the god's gift; with his other spear he grazed   70
the hero's right forearm. Dark blood ran out,
but, craving manflesh still, the spear passed on
and fixed itself in earth. In turn, Akhilleus,
putting his heart into the cast to bring down
Asteropaíos, rifled his ashwood spear.
He missed him, hitting the high bank of the river,
where the long shaft punched in to half its length.
The son of Pêleus, drawing sword from hip,
lunged forward on his enemy, who could not
with his big fist work the spear loose: three times   80
he tried to wrench it from the arching bank,
three times relaxed his grip, then put his weight
into a fourth attempt to break the shaft,
and bent it; but Akhilleus closed
and killed him with a sword stroke. Near the navel
he slashed his belly; all his bowels dropped out
uncoiling to the ground. He gasped, and darkness
veiled his eyes. Upon his chest Akhilleus
mounted, and then bent to strip his armor,
gloating: 90

"This way you'll rest. It is rough work
to match yourself with children of Lord Zeus,
river's offspring though you are. You claimed
descent from a broad river; well, I claim
descent from Zeus almighty. My begetter,
lord over many Myrmidons, was Pêleus,
the son of Aíakos, a son of Zeus.
Zeus being stronger than the seaward rivers,
so are his offspring than a river's get!
Here's a big river for you, flowing by,   100
if he had power to help you. There's no fighting
Zeus the son of Krónos. Akhelôïos
cannot rival him; neither can the might
of the deep Ocean stream—from whom all rivers
take their waters, and all branching seas,
all springs and deep-sunk wells. And yet he too
is terrified by the lightning flash of Zeus
and thunder, when it crashes out of heaven."

With this he pulled from the bank's overhang
his bronze-shod spear, and, having torn the life   110
out of the body, left it there, to lie
in sand, where the dark water lapped at it.
Then eels and fish attended to the body,
picking and nibbling kidney fat away.
As for Akhilleus, he ran onward, chasing
spearmen of Paiônia in their rout
along the eddying river: these had seen
their hero vanquished by the hand and blade
and power of Akhilleus. Now he slew
Thersílokhos, Mydôn, and Astýpylos,   120
Mnêsos, Thrásios, Ainios, Ophelestês,
and would have killed far more, had not the river,
cold with rage, in likeness of a man,
assumed a voice and spoken from a whirlpool:

"O Akhilleus, you are first in power
of all men, first in waywardness as well,
as gods forever take your side. If Zeus
has given you all Trojans to destroy,
destroy them elsewhere, do your execution
out on the plain! Now my blue watercourses   130
back up, filled with dead; I cannot spend
my current in the salt immortal sea,
being dammed with corpses. Yet you go on killing
wantonly. Let be, marshal of soldiers."

Akhilleus the great runner answered:

"Aye,
Skamánder, child of Zeus, as you require,
the thing shall be. But as for killing Trojans,
arrogant enemies, I take no rest
until I back them on the town and try out   140
Hektor, whether he gets the best of me
or I of him."

                              At this he hurled himself
upon the Trojans like a wild god. The deep
and swirling river then addressed Apollo:

"All wrong, bow of silver, child of Zeus!
You have not worked the will of Zeus. How often
he made you free to take the Trojan side!
You could defend them until sunset comes,
till evening darkens grainland."   150

                              As he spoke,
the great spearman Akhilleus in a flash
leapt into midstream from the arching bank.
But he, the river, surged upon the man
with all his currents in a roaring flood,
and swept up many of the dead, who jostled
in him, killed by Akhilleus. He ejected
these to landward, bellowing like a bull,
but living men he kept in his blue streams
to hide them in deep places, in backwaters.   160
Then round Akhilleus with an ominous roar
a wave mounted. It fell against his shield
and staggered him, so that he lost his footing.
Throwing his arms around a leafy elm
he clung to it; it gave way, roots and all,
and tore the bank away, and dipped its branches
in the clear currents, damming up the river
when all had fallen in. The man broke free
of swirling water, turned into the plain
and ran like wind, in fear. But the great god   170
would not be shaken off: with his dark crest
he reared behind to put the Prince Akhilleus
out of action and protect the Trojans.
Akhilleus led him by a spear-throw, running
as fast as the black eagle, called the hunter,
strongest and swiftest of all birds: like him
he flashed ahead, and on his ribs the bronze
rang out with a fierce clang. At a wide angle
he fled, and the river with tremendous din
flowed on behind. Remember how a farmer   180

opens a ditch from a dark reservoir
to water plants or garden: with his mattock
he clears away the clods that dam the stream,
and as the water runs ahead, smooth pebbles
roll before it. With a purling sound
it snakes along the channel, going downhill,
outrunning him who leads it: so the wave
sent by the river overtook Akhilleus
momently, in spite of his great speed,
as gods are stronger than men are. Each time   190
the great battlefield runner, Prince Akhilleus,
turned to make a stand—to learn if all
the immortal gods who own the sweep of heaven
chased him—every time, the rain-fed river's
crest buffeted his back, and cursing
he leapt high in the air. Across his knees
the pressure of swift water tired him,
and sand was washed away under his feet.
Lifting his eyes to heaven, Akhilleus cried:

"Father Zeus, to think that in my travail   200
not one god would save me from the river—
only that! Then I could take the worst!
None of the gods of heaven is so to blame
as my own mother, who beguiled me, lying,
saying my end would come beneath Troy's wall
from flashing arrows of Apollo. Ah,
I wish Hektor had killed me; he's their best.
Then one brave man would have brought down another.
No, I was fated to ignoble death,
whelmed in a river, like a swineherd's boy   210
caught by a winter torrent as he crosses."

Now as he spoke, Poseidon and Athêna,
taking human form, moved near and stood,
and took his hands to tell him what would calm him.
Poseidon was the speaker:

                                "Son of Pêleus,
do not be shaken overmuch or fearful,
seeing what gods we are, your two allies,
by favor of Zeus—myself and Pallas Athêna.
The river is not destined to pull you down.   220
He will fall back, and you will soon perceive it.
Meanwhile here's good counsel, if you'll take it.
Do not allow your hands to rest from war—
from war that treats all men without distinction—
till you have rolled the Trojan army back

to Ilion, every man of them who runs,
and shut them in the wall. Then when you've taken
Hektor's life, retire upon the ships.
We give you glory; it is yours to win."

. . . .

[When even Achilles's skill and rage prove inadequate before the rushing flood of the river god Scamander, the gods rush in to rescue Achilles.]

BOOK 22

[At last, Achilles and Hector meet on the battlefield:]

. . . .

The old man wrenched at his grey hair and pulled out
hanks of it in both his hands, but moved
Lord Hektor not at all. The young man's mother
wailed from the tower across, above the portal,
streaming tears, and loosening her robe
with one hand, held her breast out in the other,
saying:

                      "Hektor, my child, be moved by this,
and pity me, if ever I unbound
a quieting breast for you. Think of these things,   10
dear child; defend yourself against the killer
this side of the wall, not hand to hand.
He has no pity. If he brings you down,
I shall no longer be allowed to mourn you
laid out on your bed, dear branch in flower,
born of me! And neither will your lady,
so endowed with gifts. Far from us both,
dogs will devour you by the Argive ships."

With tears and cries the two implored their son,
and made their prayers again, but could not shake him.   20
Hektor stood firm, as huge Akhilleus neared.
The way a serpent, fed on poisonous herbs,
coiled at his lair upon a mountainside,
with all his length of hate awaits a man
and eyes him evilly: so Hektor, grim
and narrow-eyed, refused to yield. He leaned
his brilliant shield against a spur of wall
and in his brave heart bitterly reflected:

"Here I am badly caught. If I take cover,
slipping inside the gate and wall, the first   30
to accuse me for it will be Poulýdamas,
he who told me I should lead the Trojans
back to the city on that cursed night

Akhilleus joined the battle. No, I would not,
would not, wiser though it would have been.
Now troops have perished for my foolish pride,
I am ashamed to face townsmen and women.
Someone inferior to me may say:
'He kept his pride and lost his men, this Hektor!'
So it will go. Better, when that time comes,   40
that I appear as he who killed Akhilleus
man to man, or else that I went down
fighting him to the end before the city.
Suppose, though, that I lay my shield and helm
aside, and prop my spear against the wall,
and go to meet the noble Prince Akhilleus,
promising Helen, promising with her
all treasures that Aléxandros brought home
by ship to Troy—the first cause of our quarrel—
that he may give these things to the Atreidai?   50
Then I might add, apart from these, a portion
of all the secret wealth the city owns.
Yes, later I might take our counselors' oath
to hide no stores, but share and share alike
to halve all wealth our lovely city holds,
all that is here within the walls. Ah, no,
why even put the question to myself?
I must not go before him and receive
no quarter, no respect! Aye, then and there
he'll kill me, unprotected as I am,   60
my gear laid by, defenseless as a woman.
No chance, now, for charms from oak or stone
in parley with him—charms a girl and boy
might use when they enchant each other talking!
Better we duel, now at once, and see
to whom the Olympian awards the glory."
These were his shifts of mood. Now close at hand
Akhilleus like the implacable god of war
came on with blowing crest, hefting the dreaded
beam of Pêlian ash on his right shoulder.   70
Bronze light played around him, like the glare
of a great fire or the great sun rising,
and Hektor, as he watched, began to tremble.
Then he could hold his ground no more. He ran,
leaving the gate behind him, with Akhilleus
hard on his heels, sure of his own speed.
When that most lightning-like of birds, a hawk
bred on a mountain, swoops upon a dove,
the quarry dips in terror, but the hunter,
screaming, dips behind and gains upon it,   80
passionate for prey. Just so, Akhilleus

murderously cleft the air, as Hektor
ran with flashing knees along the wall.
They passed the lookout point, the wild figtree
with wind in all its leaves, then veered away
along the curving wagon road, and came
to where the double fountains well, the source
of eddying Skamánder. One hot spring
flows out, and from the water fumes arise
as though from fire burning; but the other   90
even in summer gushes chill as hail
or snow or crystal ice frozen on water.
Near these fountains are wide washing pools
of smooth-laid stone, where Trojan wives and daughters
laundered their smooth linen in the days
of peace before the Akhaians came. Past these
the two men ran, pursuer and pursued,
and he who fled was noble, he behind
a greater man by far. They ran full speed,
and not for bull's hide or a ritual beast   100
or any prize that men compete for: no,
but for the life of Hektor, tamer of horses.
Just as when chariot-teams around a course
go wheeling swiftly, for the prize is great,
a tripod or a woman, in the games
held for a dead man, so three times these two
at full speed made their course round Priam's town,
as all the gods looked on. And now the father
of gods and men turned to the rest and said:

"How sad that this beloved man is hunted   110
around the wall before my eyes! My heart
is touched for Hektor; he has burned thigh flesh
of oxen for me often, high on Ida,
at other times on the high point of Troy.
Now Prince Akhilleus with devouring stride
is pressing him around the town of Priam.
Come, gods, put your minds on it, consider
whether we may deliver him from death
or see him, noble as he is, brought down
by Pêleus' son, Akhilleus."   120

              Grey-eyed Athêna
said to him:

                          "Father of the blinding bolt,
the dark stormcloud, what words are these? The man
is mortal, and his doom fixed, long ago.
Would you release him from his painful death?
Then do so, but not all of us will praise you."

Zeus who gathers cloud replied:

"Take heart,
my dear and honored child. I am not bent   130
on my suggestion, and I would indulge you.
Act as your thought inclines, refrain no longer."

So he encouraged her in her desire,
and down she swept from ridges of Olympos.
Great Akhilleus, hard on Hektor's heels,
kept after him, the way a hound will harry
a deer's fawn he has startled from its bed
to chase through gorge and open glade, and when
the quarry goes to earth under a bush
he holds the scent and quarters till he finds it;   140
so with Hektor: he could not shake off
the great runner, Akhilleus. Every time
he tried to sprint hard for the Dardan gates
under the towers, hoping men would help him,
sending missiles down, Akhilleus loomed
to cut him off and turn him toward the plain,
as he himself ran always near the city.
As in a dream a man chasing another
cannot catch him, nor can he in flight
escape from his pursuer, so Akhilleus   150
could not by swiftness overtake him,
nor could Hektor pull away. How could he
run so long from death, had not Apollo
for the last time, the very last, come near
to give him stamina and speed?
                          Akhilleus
shook his head at the rest of the Akhaians,
allowing none to shoot or cast at Hektor—
none to forestall him, and to win the honor.
But when, for the fourth time, they reached the springs,   160
the Father poised his golden scales.
                          He placed
two shapes of death, death prone and cold, upon them,
one of Akhilleus, one of the horseman, Hektor,
and held the midpoint, pulling upward. Down
sank Hektor's fatal day, the pan went down
toward undergloom, and Phoibos Apollo left him.
Then came Athêna, grey-eyed, to the son
of Pêleus, falling in with him, and near him,
saying swiftly: 170

                          "Now at last I think
the two of us, Akhilleus loved by Zeus,

shall bring Akhaians triumph at the ships
by killing Hektor—unappeased
though he was ever in his thirst for war.
There is no way he may escape us now,
not though Apollo, lord of distances,
should suffer all indignity for him
before his father Zeus who bears the stormcloud,
rolling back and forth and begging for him.   180
Now you can halt and take your breath, while I
persuade him into combat face to face."

These were Athêna's orders. He complied,
relieved, and leaning hard upon the spearshaft
armed with its head of bronze. She left him there
and overtook Lord Hektor—but she seemed
Dêíphobos in form and resonant voice,
appearing at his shoulder, saying swiftly:

"Ai! Dear brother, how he runs, Akhilleus,
harrying you around the town of Priam!   190
Come, we'll stand and take him on."

                        To this,
great Hektor in his shimmering helm replied:

"Dêíphobos, you were the closest to me
in the old days, of all my brothers, sons
of Hékabê and Priam. Now I can say
I honor you still more
because you dared this foray for my sake,
seeing me run. The rest stay under cover."

Again the grey-eyed goddess Athêna spoke:

"Dear brother, how your father and gentle mother   200
begged and begged me to remain! So did
the soldiers round me, all undone by fear.
But in my heart I ached for you.
Now let us fight him, and fight hard.
No holding back. We'll see if this Akhilleus
conquers both, to take our armor seaward,
or if he can be brought down by your spear."

This way, by guile, Athêna led him on.
And when at last the two men faced each other,
Hektor was the first to speak. He said: 210

"I will no longer fear you as before,
son of Pêleus, though I ran from you

round Priam's town three times and could not face you.
Now my soul would have me stand and fight,
whether I kill you or am killed. So come,
we'll summon gods here as our witnesses,
none higher, arbiters of a pact: I swear
that, terrible as you are,
I'll not insult your corpse should Zeus allow me
victory in the end, your life as prize.   220
Once I have your gear, I'll give your body
back to Akhaians. Grant me, too, this grace."

But swift Akhilleus frowned at him and said:

"Hektor, I'll have no talk of pacts with you,
forever unforgiven as you are.
As between men and lions there are none,
no concord between wolves and sheep, but all
hold one another hateful through and through,
so there can be no courtesy between us,
no sworn truce, till one of us is down   230
and glutting with his blood the wargod Arês.
Summon up what skills you have. By god,
you'd better be a spearman and a fighter!
Now there is no way out. Pallas Athêna
will have the upper hand of you. The weapon
belongs to me. You'll pay the reckoning
in full for all the pain my men have borne,
who met death by your spear."

                                    He twirled and cast
his shaft with its long shadow. Splendid Hektor,   240
keeping his eyes upon the point, eluded it
by ducking at the instant of the cast,
so shaft and bronze shank passed him overhead
and punched into the earth. But unperceived
by Hektor, Pallas Athêna plucked it out
and gave it back to Akhilleus. Hektor said:

"A clean miss. Godlike as you are,
you have not yet known doom for me from Zeus.
You thought you had, by heaven. Then you turned
into a word-thrower, hoping to make me lose   250
my fighting heart and head in fear of you.
You cannot plant your spear between my shoulders
while I am running. If you have the gift,
just put it through my chest as I come forward.
Now it's for you to dodge my own. Would god
you'd give the whole shaft lodging in your body!

War for the Trojans would be eased
if you were blotted out, bane that you are."

With this he twirled his long spearshaft and cast it,
hitting his enemy mid-shield, but off   260
and away the spear rebounded. Furious
that he had lost it, made his throw for nothing,
Hektor stood bemused. He had no other.
Then he gave a great shout to Dêíphobos
to ask for a long spear. But there was no one
near him, not a soul. Now in his heart
the Trojan realized the truth and said:

"This is the end. The gods are calling deathward.
I had thought
a good soldier, Dêíphobos, was with me.   270
He is inside the walls. Athêna tricked me.
Death is near, and black, not at a distance,
not to be evaded. Long ago
this hour must have been to Zeus's liking
and to the liking of his archer son.
They have been well disposed before, but now
the appointed time's upon me. Still, I would not
die without delivering a stroke,
or die ingloriously, but in some action
memorable to men in days to come."   280

With this he drew the whetted blade that hung
upon his left flank, ponderous and long,
collecting all his might the way an eagle
narrows himself to dive through shady cloud
and strike a lamb or cowering hare: so Hektor
lanced ahead and swung his whetted blade.
Akhilleus with wild fury in his heart
pulled in upon his chest his beautiful shield—
his helmet with four burnished metal ridges
nodding above it, and the golden crest   290
Hêphaistos locked there tossing in the wind.
Conspicuous as the evening star that comes,
amid the first in heaven, at fall of night,
and stands most lovely in the west, so shone
in sunlight the fine-pointed spear
Akhilleus poised in his right hand, with deadly
aim at Hektor, at the skin where most
it lay exposed. But nearly all was covered
by the bronze gear he took from slain Patróklos,
showing only, where his collarbones   300
divided neck and shoulders, the bare throat
where the destruction of a life is quickest.

Here, then, as the Trojan charged, Akhilleus
drove his point straight through the tender neck,
but did not cut the windpipe, leaving Hektor
able to speak and to respond. He fell
aside into the dust. And Prince Akhilleus
now exulted:

"Hektor, had you thought
that you could kill Patróklos and be safe?   310
Nothing to dread from me; I was not there.
All childishness. Though distant then, Patróklos'
comrade in arms was greater far than he—
and it is I who had been left behind
that day beside the deepsea ships who now
have made your knees give way. The dogs and kites
will rip your body. His will lie in honor
when the Akhaians give him funeral."

Hektor, barely whispering, replied:

"I beg you by your soul and by your parents,   320
do not let the dogs feed on me
in your encampment by the ships. Accept
the bronze and gold my father will provide
as gifts, my father and her ladyship
my mother. Let them have my body back,
so that our men and women may accord me
decency of fire when I am dead."

Akhilleus the great runner scowled and said:

"Beg me no beggary by soul or parents,
whining dog! Would god my passion drove me   330
to slaughter you and eat you raw, you've caused
such agony to me! No man exists
who could defend you from the carrion pack—
not if they spread for me ten times your ransom,
twenty times, and promise more as well;
aye, not if Priam, son of Dárdanos,
tells them to buy you for your weight in gold!
You'll have no bed of death, nor will you be
laid out and mourned by her who gave you birth.
Dogs and birds will have you, every scrap."   340

Then at the point of death Lord Hektor said:

"I see you now for what you are. No chance
to win you over. Iron in your breast

your heart is. Think a bit, though: this may be
a thing the gods in anger hold against you
on that day when Paris and Apollo
destroy you at the Gates, great as you are."

Even as he spoke, the end came, and death hid him;
spirit from body fluttered to undergloom,
bewailing fate that made him leave his youth   350
and manhood in the world. And as he died
Akhilleus spoke again. He said:

"Die, make an end. I shall accept my own
whenever Zeus and the other gods desire."

At this he pulled his spearhead from the body,
laying it aside, and stripped
the bloodstained shield and cuirass from his shoulders.
Other Akhaians hastened round to see
Hektor's fine body and his comely face,
and no one came who did not stab the body.   360
Glancing at one another they would say:

"Now Hektor has turned vulnerable, softer
than when he put the torches to the ships!"

And he who said this would inflict a wound.
When the great master of pursuit, Akhilleus,
had the body stripped, he stood among them,
saying swiftly:

                                        "Friends, my lords and captains
of Argives, now that the gods at last have let me
bring to earth this man who wrought   370
havoc among us—more than all the rest—
come, we'll offer battle around the city,
to learn the intentions of the Trojans now.
Will they give up their strongpoint at this loss?
Can they fight on, though Hektor's dead?

. . . .

[Achilles lashes Hector's corpse through the feet to his chariot and drags the body, attempting to defile it. Horrified, Hector's parents and wife express their grief.]

BOOKS 23 AND 24

[The shade of Patroclus appeals to Achilles to ask for quick burial so his soul can find
rest in the Underworld. For eleven days Achilles mourns, each day dragging Hector's
body around the burial mound of Patroclus. But Apollo protects the corpse from disfigurement. Achilles holds funeral games in honor of Patroclus. By the twelfth day, many

of the gods want to steal Hector's body. Apollo argues that Achilles's behavior is savage and inhuman:]

. . . .
                            He yoked his team, with Hektor
tied behind, to drag him out, three times
around Patróklos' tomb. By day he rested
in his own hut, abandoning Hektor's body
to lie full-length in dust—though Lord Apollo,
pitying the man, even in death,
kept his flesh free of disfigurement.
He wrapped him in his great shield's flap of gold
to save him from laceration. But Akhilleus
in rage visited indignity on Hektor   10
day after day, and, looking on,
the blessed gods were moved. Day after day
they urged the Wayfinder to steal the body—
a thought agreeable to all but Hêra,
Poseidon, and the grey-eyed one, Athêna.
These opposed it, and held out, since Ilion
and Priam and his people had incurred
their hatred first, the day Aléxandros
made his mad choice and piqued two goddesses,
visitors in his sheepfold: he praised   20
a third, who offered ruinous lust.
Now when Dawn grew bright for the twelfth day,
Phoibos Apollo spoke among the gods:

"How heartless and how malevolent you are!
Did Hektor never make burnt offering
of bulls' thighbones to you, and unflawed goats?
Even in death you would not stir to save him
for his dear wife to see, and for his mother,
his child, his father, Priam, and his men:
they'd burn the corpse at once and give him burial.   30
Murderous Akhilleus has your willing help—
a man who shows no decency, implacable,
barbarous in his ways as a wild lion
whose power and intrepid heart
sway him to raid the flocks of men for meat.
The man has lost all mercy;
he has no shame—that gift that hinders mortals
but helps them, too. A sane one may endure
an even dearer loss: a blood brother,
a son; and yet, by heaven, having grieved   40
and passed through mourning, he will let it go.
The Fates have given patient hearts to men.
Not this one: first he took Prince Hektor's life
and now he drags the body, lashed to his car,

around the barrow of his friend, performing
something neither nobler in report
nor better in itself. Let him take care,
or, brave as he is, we gods will turn against him,
seeing him outrage the insensate earth!"

Hêra whose arms are white as ivory   50
grew angry at Apollo. She retorted:

"Lord of the silver bow, your words would be
acceptable if one had a mind to honor
Hektor and Akhilleus equally.
But Hektor suckled at a woman's breast,
Akhilleus is the first-born of a goddess—
one I nursed myself. I reared her, gave her
to Pêleus, a strong man whom the gods loved.
All of you were present at their wedding—
you too—friend of the base, forever slippery!—   60
came with your harp and dined there!"

                           Zeus the stormking
answered her:

                           "Hêra, don't lose your temper
altogether. Clearly the same high honor
cannot be due both men. And yet Lord Hektor,
of all the mortal men in Ilion,
was dearest to the gods, or was to me.
He never failed in the right gift; my altar
never lacked a feast   70
of wine poured out and smoke of sacrifice—
the share assigned as ours. We shall renounce
the theft of Hektor's body; there is no way;
there would be no eluding Akhilleus' eye,
as night and day his mother comes to him.
Will one of you now call her to my presence?
I have a solemn message to impart:
Akhilleus is to take fine gifts from Priam,
and in return give back Prince Hektor's body."

At this, Iris who runs on the rainy wind   80
with word from Zeus departed. Midway between
Samos and rocky Imbros, down she plunged
into the dark grey sea, and the brimming tide
roared over her as she sank into the depth—
as rapidly as a leaden sinker, fixed
on a lure of wild bull's horn, that glimmers down
with a fatal hook among the ravening fish.
Soon Iris came on Thetis in a cave,

surrounded by a company of Nereids
lolling there, while she bewailed the fate   90
of her magnificent son, now soon to perish
on Troy's rich earth, far from his fatherland.
Halting before her, Iris said:

                        "Come, Thetis,
Zeus of eternal forethought summons you."

Silvery-footed Thetis answered:

                        "Why?
Why does the great one call me to him now,
when I am shy of mingling with immortals,
being so heavyhearted? But I'll go.   100
Whatever he may say will have its weight."

That loveliest of goddesses now put on
a veil so black no garment could be blacker,
and swam where windswift Iris led. Before them
on either hand the ground swell fell away.
They rose to a beach, then soared into the sky
and found the viewer of the wide world, Zeus,
with all the blissful gods who live forever
around him seated. Athêna yielded place,
and Thetis sat down by her father, Zeus,   110
while Hêra handed her a cup of gold
and spoke a comforting word. When she had drunk,
Thetis held out the cup again to Hêra.
The father of gods and men began:

                        "You've come
to Olympos, Thetis, though your mind is troubled
and insatiable pain preys on your heart.
I know, I too. But let me, even so,
explain why I have called you here. Nine days
of quarreling we've had among the gods   120
concerning Hektor's body and Akhilleus.
They wish the Wayfinder to make off with it.
I, however, accord Akhilleus honor
as I now tell you—in respect for you
whose love I hope to keep hereafter. Go, now,
down to the army, tell this to your son:
the gods are sullen toward him, and I, too,
more than the rest, am angered at his madness,
holding the body by the beaked ships
and not releasing it. In fear of me   130
let him relent and give back Hektor's body!
At the same time I'll send Iris to Priam,

directing him to go down to the beachhead
and ransom his dear son. He must bring gifts
to melt Akhilleus' rage."

                              Thetis obeyed,
leaving Olympos' ridge and flashing down
to her son's hut. She found him groaning there,
inconsolable, while men-at-arms
went to and fro, making their breakfast ready—   140
having just put to the knife a fleecy sheep.
His gentle mother sat down at his side,
caressed him, and said tenderly:

                         "My child,
will you forever feed on your own heart
in grief and pain, and take no thought of sleep
or sustenance? It would be comforting
to make love with a woman. No long time
will you live on for me: Death even now
stands near you, appointed and all-powerful.   150
But be alert and listen: I am a messenger
from Zeus, who tells me the gods are sullen toward you
and he himself most angered at your madness,
holding the body by the beaked ships
and not releasing it. Give Hektor back.
Take ransom for the body."

                         Said Akhilleus:
"Let it be so. Let someone bring the ransom
and take the dead away, if the Olympian
commands this in his wisdom."   160

                         So, that morning,
in camp, amid the ships, mother and son
conversed together, and their talk was long.
Lord Zeus meanwhile sent Iris to Ilion.

"Off with you, lightfoot, leave Olympos, take
my message to the majesty of Priam
at Ilion. He is to journey down
and ransom his dear son upon the beachhead.
He shall take gifts to melt Akhilleus' rage,
and let him go alone, no soldier with him,   170
only some crier, some old man, to drive
his wagon team and guide the nimble wagon,
and afterward to carry home the body
of him that Prince Akhilleus overcame.
Let him not think of death, or suffer dread,

as I'll provide him with a wondrous guide,
the Wayfinder, to bring him across the lines
into the very presence of Akhilleus.
And he, when he sees Priam within his hut,
will neither take his life nor let another   180
enemy come near. He is no madman,
no blind brute, nor one to flout the gods,
but dutiful toward men who beg his mercy."

. . . .

**[Inspired by Zeus, Priam goes alone through enemy lines to appeal to Achilles to return
Hector's corpse for burial:]**

                                Noble sons
I fathered here, but scarce one man is left me.
Fifty I had when the Akhaians came,
nineteen out of a single belly, others
born of attendant women. Most are gone.
Raging Arês cut their knees from under them.
And he who stood alone among them all,   190
their champion, and Troy's, ten days ago
you killed him, fighting for his land, my prince,
Hektor.
                    It is for him that I have come
among these ships, to beg him back from you,
and I bring ransom without stint.
                                        Akhilleus,
be reverent toward the great gods! And take
pity on me, remember your own father.
Think me more pitiful by far, since I   200
have brought myself to do what no man else
has done before—to lift to my lips the hand
of one who killed my son."

                            Now in Akhilleus
the evocation of his father stirred
new longing, and an ache of grief. He lifted
the old man's hand and gently put him by.
Then both were overborne as they remembered:
the old king huddled at Akhilleus' feet
wept, and wept for Hektor, killer of men,   210
while great Akhilleus wept for his own father
as for Patróklos once again; and sobbing
filled the room.
                        But when Akhilleus' heart
had known the luxury of tears, and pain
within his breast and bones had passed away,
he stood then, raised the old king up, in pity
for his grey head and greybeard cheek, and spoke
in a warm rush of words:

"Ah, sad and old!   220
Trouble and pain you've borne, and bear, aplenty.
Only a great will could have brought you here
among the Akhaian ships, and here alone
before the eyes of one who stripped your sons,
your many sons, in battle. Iron must be
the heart within you. Come, then, and sit down.
We'll probe our wounds no more but let them rest,
though grief lies heavy on us. Tears heal nothing,
drying so stiff and cold. This is the way
the gods ordained the destiny of men,   230
to bear such burdens in our lives, while they
feel no affliction. At the door of Zeus
are those two urns of good and evil gifts
that he may choose for us; and one for whom
the lightning's joyous king dips in both urns
will have by turns bad luck and good. But one
to whom he sends all evil—that man goes
contemptible by the will of Zeus; ravenous
hunger drives him over the wondrous earth,
unresting, without honor from gods or men.   240
Mixed fortune came to Pêleus. Shining gifts
at the gods' hands he had from birth: felicity,
wealth overflowing, rule of the Myrmidons,
a bride immortal at his mortal side.
But then Zeus gave afflictions too—no family
of powerful sons grew up for him at home,
but one child, of all seasons and of none.
Can I stand by him in his age? Far from my country
I sit at Troy to grieve you and your children.
You, too, sir, in time past were fortunate,   250
we hear men say. From Makar's isle of Lesbos
northward, and south of Phrygia and the Straits,
no one had wealth like yours, or sons like yours.
Then gods out of the sky sent you this bitterness:
the years of siege, the battles and the losses.
Endure it, then. And do not mourn forever
for your dead son. There is no remedy.
You will not make him stand again. Rather
await some new misfortune to be suffered."

The old king in his majesty replied: 260

"Never give me a chair, my lord, while Hektor
lies in your camp uncared for. Yield him to me
now. Allow me sight of him. Accept
the many gifts I bring. May they reward you,
and may you see your home again.
You spared my life at once and let me live."

Akhilleus, the great runner, frowned and eyed him
under his brows:

                              "Do not vex me, sir," he said.   270
"I have intended, in my own good time,
to yield up Hektor to you. She who bore me,
the daughter of the Ancient of the sea,
has come with word to me from Zeus. I know
in your case, too—though you say nothing, Priam—
that some god guided you to the shipways here.
No strong man in his best days could make entry
into this camp. How could he pass the guard,
or force our gateway?
                              Therefore, *let me be.*
Sting my sore heart again, and even here,   280
under my own roof, suppliant though you are,
I may not spare you, sir, but trample on
the express command of Zeus!"

                              When he heard this,
the old man feared him and obeyed with silence.
Now like a lion at one bound Akhilleus
left the room. Close at his back the officers
Automédôn and Álkimos went out—
comrades in arms whom he esteemed the most
after the dead Patróklos. They unharnessed   290
mules and horses, led the old king's crier
to a low bench and sat him down.
Then from the polished wagon
they took the piled-up price of Hektor's body.
One khiton and two capes they left aside
as dress and shrouding for the homeward journey.
Then, calling to the women slaves, Akhilleus
ordered the body bathed and rubbed with oil—
but lifted, too, and placed apart, where Priam
could not see his son—for seeing Hektor   300
he might in his great pain give way to rage,
and fury then might rise up in Akhilleus
to slay the old king, flouting Zeus's word.
So after bathing and anointing Hektor
they drew the shirt and beautiful shrouding over him.
Then with his own hands lifting him, Akhilleus
laid him upon a couch, and with his two
companions aiding, placed him in the wagon.
Now a bitter groan burst from Akhilleus,
who stood and prayed to his own dead friend: 310

                              "Patróklos,
do not be angry with me, if somehow

even in the world of Death you learn of this—
that I released Prince Hektor to his father.
The gifts he gave were not unworthy. Aye,
and you shall have your share, this time as well."

The Prince Akhilleus turned back to his quarters.
He took again the splendid chair that stood
against the farther wall, then looked at Priam
and made his declaration: 320

                         "As you wished, sir,
the body of your son is now set free.
He lies in state. At the first sight of Dawn
you shall take charge of him yourself and see him.
Now let us think of supper. We are told
that even Niobê in her extremity
took thought for bread—though all her brood had perished,
her six young girls and six tall sons. Apollo,
making his silver longbow whip and sing,
shot the lads down, and Artemis with raining   330
arrows killed the daughters—all this after
Niobê had compared herself with Lêto,
the smooth-cheeked goddess.
                         She has borne two children,
Niobê said, How many have I borne!
But soon these two destroyed the twelve.

                         Besides,
nine days the dead lay stark, no one could bury them,
for Zeus had turned all folk of theirs to stone.
The gods made graves for them on the tenth day,   340
and then at last, being weak and spent with weeping,
Niobê thought of food. Among the rocks
of Sipylos' lonely mountainside, where nymphs
who race Akhelôïos river go to rest,
she, too, long turned to stone, somewhere broods on
the gall immortal gods gave her to drink.

Like her we'll think of supper, noble sir.
Weep for your son again when you have borne him
back to Troy; there he'll be mourned indeed."

In one swift movement now Akhilleus caught   350
and slaughtered a white lamb. His officers
flayed it, skillful in their butchering
to dress the flesh; they cut bits for the skewers,
roasted, and drew them off, done to a turn.
Automédôn dealt loaves into the baskets

on the great board; Akhilleus served the meat.
Then all their hands went out upon the supper.
When thirst and appetite were turned away,
Priam, the heir of Dárdanos, gazed long
in wonder at Akhilleus' form and scale—   360
so like the gods in aspect. And Akhilleus
in his turn gazed in wonder upon Priam,
royal in visage as in speech. Both men
in contemplation found rest for their eyes,
till the old hero, Priam, broke the silence:

"Make a bed ready for me, son of Thetis,
and let us know the luxury of sleep.
From that hour when my son died at your hands
till now, my eyelids have not closed in slumber
over my eyes, but groaning where I sat   370
I tasted pain and grief a thousandfold,
or lay down rolling in my courtyard mire.
Here for the first time I have swallowed bread
and made myself drink wine.

                                    Before, I could not."

Akhilleus ordered men and servingwomen
to make a bed outside, in the covered forecourt,
with purple rugs piled up and sheets outspread
and coverings of all fleece laid on top.
The girls went out with torches in their hands   380
and soon deftly made up a double bed.
Then Akhilleus, defiant of Agamémnon,
told his guest:

                        "Dear venerable sir,
you'll sleep outside tonight, in case an Akhaian
officer turns up, one of those men
who are forever taking counsel with me—
as well they may. If one should see you here
as the dark night runs on, he would report it
to the Lord Marshal Agamémnon. Then   390
return of the body would only be delayed.
Now tell me this, and give me a straight answer:
How many days do you require
for the funeral of Prince Hektor?—I should know
how long to wait, and hold the Akhaian army."

Old Priam in his majesty replied:

"If you would have me carry out the burial,
Akhilleus, here is the way to do me grace.

As we are penned in the town, but must bring wood
from the distant hills, the Trojans are afraid.   400
We should have mourning for nine days in hall,
then on the tenth conduct his funeral
and feast the troops and commons;
on the eleventh we should make his tomb,
and on the twelfth give battle, if we must."

Akhilleus said:

                      "As you command, old Priam,
the thing is done. I shall suspend the war
for those eleven days that you require."

He took the old man's right hand by the wrist   410
and held it, to allay his fear.

. . . .

[Achilles allows Priam eleven days for Hector's funeral rites, suspending the war until
the twelfth day. Aided by Hermes, Priam escapes with the body earlier than the time
Achilles had appointed. Helen mourns for him, as her protector among the Trojans who
revile her. The funeral rites over and the death mound completed, the Trojans hold a
feast in honor of Hector, tamer of horses.]

Questions for Discussion and Review

1. Zeus tries to disinvite Eris, the spirit of strife, or discord, from the wedding of Peleus
   and Thetis, just as he arranged Thetis's marriage to forestall the birth of a child of hers
   who might usurp his throne. When Zeus overthrew the Titans, he restored peace and
   harmony to the universe. Why, then, can he not exclude Eris, even by divine decree?

2. When Zeus tosses the golden apple off Mount Olympus, in a last-ditch attempt to
   preserve harmony, not even the gods foresee the consequences: ten years of war among
   gods and humans alike. What does this failure of foresight tell us about the limitations
   on the powers of the gods and the nature of the universe they inhabit?

3. Compare the Greeks' and Trojans' attitudes toward the family, using specific examples
   from the *Iliad*.

4. Throughout the *Iliad* scenes of feasting abound, often associated with ceremonial occasions. Explain why feasting is so important in the *Iliad*. What kinds of bonds are
   formed or confirmed through feasting?

5. Diomedes and Patroclus are both great fighters—Diomedes even takes on several gods
   in battle and wins—but neither is considered as extraordinary as Achilles. What makes
   Achilles different?

6. How are Achilles and Hector alike? How are they different? What qualities does each
   share with the archetypal hero Heracles?

7. How do the gods in the *Iliad* feel about the humans? How seriously do they take
   human affairs? Why do they get involved at all? Use specific examples to support your
   answer.

8. At the end of the *Iliad,* Troy still stands, its walls still intact. Explain why you think the city survives so long, despite Achilles's efforts.

Recommended Reading

Finley, M. I. *The World of Odysseus.* 1959. Cleveland: World, 1963. A revealing glimpse into the conditions of real life in the Mycenaean Age described in the Homeric epics.

Griffin, Jaspar. *Homer.* New York: Hill and Wang, 1980. A brief but thoughtful introduction to the Homeric epics.

Redfield, James M. *Nature and Culture in the* Iliad: *The Tragedy of Hector.* Chicago: U of Chicago P, 1975. Discusses Homer's perspective on the predicament of the hero by focusing on Achilles's often-neglected rival.

CHAPTER

12

A Different Kind of Hero: The Quest of Odysseus

KEY THEMES

The resourceful hero of Homer's Odyssey *differs significantly from the brash young warriors who besiege Troy. Whereas Achilles, Ajax, and their peers strive to win undying fame by displaying physical strength, courage, and fighting skill, Odysseus cultivates the qualities of intelligence and ingenuity that will ensure his survival in a strange and unpredictable world. In a series of encounters with powerful women and goddesses, such as Circe, Calypso, and Athene, he further develops his native cunning and hones the skills that at last enable him to defeat his wife's one hundred unwanted suitors and reunite with Penelope, his feminine counterpart, thus bringing this strand of the Troy saga to a peaceful conclusion.*

Differences between the *Iliad* and the *Odyssey*

A popular Greek tradition accounts for differences between the *Iliad* and the *Odyssey* by assuming that the war poem was written in Homer's youth, while the generally peaceful world depicted in the story of Odysseus's homecoming was a product of the poet's old age. Noting the unusually large cast of female characters who play key roles—from the goddess Athene to Odysseus's aged nurse, Eurycleia—some modern critics suggest that the author is a woman, a few adding that she left a self-portrait in the figure of **Nausicaa** [nah-SIK-ay-a], a remarkably competent princess who acts as the hero's patron at the court of her parents, King **Alcinous** [al-SIN-oh-uhs] and Queen **Arete** [a-REE-tee].

Whoever the poet(s)—the same person who wrote the *Iliad* or an entire school of nameless geniuses—the *Odyssey* is a worthy sequel to the "Song of Ilium." It contains an enormous mass of traditional material about the hero's wanderings from Troy to Ithaca, which the poet shapes into a smoothly flowing narrative that builds inexorably toward the climax of Odysseus's long-delayed reunion with his wife, Penelope.

Examining some differences between the two epics is instructive. In the *Iliad,* the action is concentrated along narrow beaches where the Greek army is bivouacked or within the besieged city of Troy. In the *Odyssey,* the world opens up to encompass the entire Mediterranean basin, with the restless hero roaming from Asia Minor to Africa to Europe, encountering previously unknown peoples and strange customs. Odysseus even leaves the material realm behind, journeying to the murky kingdom of the dead. With the possible exceptions of Virgil's *Aeneid* or Dante's *Divine Comedy,* no work of literature offers a more comprehensive tour of earth, heaven, and Hades or a more dazzling parade of the gods, monsters, sorcerers, warriors, ghosts, heroes, and villains that inhabit mythology's three-tier universe.

Homer's Structuring of the *Odyssey*

The *Iliad* immediately introduces its two leading opponents, Achilles and Agamemnon, and pursues the consequences of their quarrel in generally chronological order straight through to the end of the poem. The *Odyssey*'s structure is more complex: the hero who gives the epic its name and who imprints the narrative with his distinctive personality does not appear until Book 5. Homer devotes the first four books to describing the effects in **Ithaca** of Odysseus's nineteen-year absence and the quest that his son **Telemachus** [tee-LEM-a-kuhs] makes in search of his lost father.

Apart from flashbacks recounting the hero's earlier adventures, the action covers about six weeks: the time it takes Odysseus to leave Calypso's island (where he has spent seven years as the goddess's love slave), suffer a near-fatal shipwreck, wash ashore at the Phaeacians' hospitable kingdom, be transported to Ithaca, and plot and execute his revenge on the hundred suitors who compete to replace him as king of Ithaca by marrying his wife, **Penelope** (Figure 12-1). Although Zeus points out in Book 1 the cause of Poseidon's hostility, which delays Odysseus's homecoming by ten years, we do not learn exactly how or why the hero blinded the sea god's son **Polyphemus** until almost the middle of the epic.

To the *Odyssey*'s central section (books 8–12), in which the ingenious hero narrates his own story, Homer relegates the poem's most fantastic elements. Singing for his supper at the court of King Alcinous, Odysseus regales his audience with tales of man-eating giants, amorous nymphs, and messages from the recently dead, including Achilles and Agamemnon. From Book 13 to the poem's conclusion, Odysseus is back in the familiar world of Ithacan politics, struggling to find a way to defeat the suitors and resume his mundane duties as husband, father, and king. In these later scenes of pragmatic conflict, the supernatural is represented only by the Olympians, rational administrators of the daylight world.

Demodocus: The Blind Singer

Some ancient commentators believed that in his picture of **Demodocus** [de-MAH-dah-kuhs], the blind poet whose songs delight the Phaeacian court (Book 8), Homer created an idealized self-portrait. Although the tradition that Homer was blind may derive from Demodocus's sightlessness, few modern critics take Homer's description of the Phaeacian bard as autobiographical. Demodocus's plight, in fact, represents the conventional paradox afflicting mortal recipients of divine favor: a person whom the gods single out for special attention typically receives a bittersweet, two-edged gift. The Muse who lavishes "matchless love" upon Demodocus and inspires his incom-

FIGURE 12-1   Odysseus Slaying the Suitors. Caught unaware by the sudden revelation of Odysseus's identity (top), the drunken suitors (bottom) cower before a deadly hail of arrows flying from the hero's long bow. Although a few of the young nobles courting Penelope are far less reprehensible than Antinous, the most arrogant of the suitors, Fate marks them all for sudden death because of their communal guilt in violating hospitality and seeking to take the place of their legitimate king. (*Staatliche Museen, Berlin.*)

parable poetry also robs him of his eyes. The *Odyssey*'s author, however, certainly presents Demodocus as a supreme artist who deserves all the honor and respect that King Alcinous and his courtiers bestow upon him. Odysseus remarks that Demodocus's poetic skills are so great that either Apollo or the Muse herself must have taught the poet his art.

Homer's description of Demodocus's creative role offers an important glimpse into the creative process by which Greek minstrels fashioned the epic tradition. In the first of three poems Demodocus recites, accompanied on his harp, he celebrates "men of glory, men whose deeds were chanted in a song whose fame had reached vast heaven." The bard's function is indispensable if a hero's "glory" is to last: the accomplishments of an Achilles will be remembered only when a great poet recounts them in immortal verse. In his second poem, Demodocus moves from heroes to gods, singing of the adulterous love of Ares and Aphrodite, a theme that evokes Paris's illicit affair with Helen, the cause of the Trojan War. His third poem, recounting Odysseus's infamous ruse of the wooden horse, serves multiple purposes: besides refocusing narrative attention on Odysseus and crediting him for the long-delayed Greek victory, it skillfully advances Homer's plot. Until Demodocus sings of the Trojan Horse, Odysseus remained an anonymous stranger at the Phaeacian court; his tearful response to the minstrel's art motivates him to reveal his identity as the hero whose peerless ingenuity Demodocus had praised. When Alcinous recognizes his guest as the instrument of Troy's fall, he provides Odysseus with a Phaeacian ship that escorts the hero back to Ithaca.

A Different Kind of Hero

Whereas numerous aristocratic warriors contend for our interest in the *Iliad,* a single personality dominates the *Odyssey*. All other characters, from the doting Athene to the cannibalistic Laestrygonians, are defined exclusively by their relationship to Odysseus. Odysseus has the courage, fighting skills, and leadership abilities that characterize the epic hero, but he is defined primarily by the extraordinary intelligence that equips him to cope with unexpected and dangerous situations off the battlefield. He also differs from his colleagues at Troy in his emphasis on solving problems through cunning and strategy rather than brute force. His most famous ruse, the Trojan Horse (which Demodocus describes in Book 8), succeeds in capturing Troy when direct attacks and military brawn fail.

Greek myth customarily explains the hero's superiority by making him the descendant of a god. Although Odysseus, unlike Achilles, has two mortal parents, **Laertes** [lay-ER-teez] and **Anticleia** [an-tih-KLEE-a], non-Homeric tradition assigns him a divine ancestor in **Autolycus** [ah-TUHL-ih-kuhs], his maternal grandfather. Reputedly a son of Hermes, Autolycus embodies some of his father's less desirable attributes, including a penchant for thievery and deception, qualities some later writers, such as Sophocles, also ascribe to Odysseus. As Homer portrays him, however, Odysseus is entirely human, making his refusal when the nymph **Calypso** offers him immortality all the more significant (Book 5).

Brains versus Brawn   Distinguished by brains rather than an exceptional physique, Odysseus lacks Achilles's commanding height and good looks (Figure 12-2). He has the physical power to string a huge bow that other men cannot even bend (Book 21),

Sequence of Events in the Homeward Voyage of Odysseus

After Odysseus's ruse of the Wooden Horse results in Troy's fall (c. 1250–1200 B.C.), Odysseus and his men set sail for Ithaca.

1. Odysseus raids Ismarus, city of the Cicones in southern Thrace, where some of his men are killed.

2. A storm drives his small fleet southward, away from Ithaca.

3. He stops briefly in the Land of the Lotus-Eaters.

4. On the island of the Cyclops, Polyphemus eats six of his men and brings Poseidon's curse on Odysseus.

5. After staying a month with Aeolus, Odysseus sails within sight of Ithaca when his suspicious men open Aeolus's bag of winds, creating a gale that drives him back to the wind god's island.

6. The Laestrygonians destroy all of Odysseus's fleet except for his own ship.

7. Odysseus spends a year as Circe's lover. The wise enchantress directs his descent into the Underworld.

8. Forewarned by Circe, Odysseus hears the Sirens' songs and passes between Scylla and Charybdis.

9. Marooned on the island of Helios, Odysseus's crew eat the sun god's sacred cattle, for which Zeus sinks his ship and drowns his crewmen.

10. His ship lost, he is swept alone back through the narrow straits of Scylla and Charybdis. Odysseus is eventually cast ashore on Calypso's island, where he is detained for seven years.

11. After Hermes carries Zeus's order to Calypso, Odysseus is allowed to build a raft and sail toward home, until Poseidon destroys the hero's craft, leaving him to drown.

12. Odysseus comes ashore on the island of Scheria, the kingdom of the Phaeacians ruled by King Alcinous and Queen Arete, whose sailors transport the hero back to Ithaca.

and he competes successfully with younger athletes at Alcinous's court, but this middle-aged hero must rely on Athene to apply a divine cosmetic that makes him appear taller and handsomer whenever he needs to make a good impression. When circumstances dictate, Athene also changes Odysseus's appearance for the worse, withering his skin to make his disguise as an aged beggar more convincing. These physical transformations, repeated throughout the epic, suggest Odysseus's chameleonlike traits, his uncanny ability to take on a variety of roles, from commander and king to pauper and suppliant.

Differences between Achilles and Odysseus run more than skin deep. Whereas Achilles represents the aristocratic warrior, whose chief attributes are strength, martial skill, and courage, Odysseus manifests the less spectacular quality of prudence. The ability to exercise foresight, discretion, and rational self-control, prudence is the trait

FIGURE 12-2 Head of Odysseus. The central character of Homer's *Odyssey* differs qualitatively from the *Iliad*'s impetuous heroes. Distinguished by brain rather than brawn, the middle-aged Odysseus is a human counterpart of his divine patron Athene, using forethought and ingenuity to overcome the obstacles confronting him on his long journey back to Ithaca. In this portrait of the experience-weary Odysseus, the sculptor suggests both the physical strain caused by the hero's labors and his resolve to take on new challenges. (*Archaeological Museum, Sperlonga.*)

that most commonly (but not always) distinguishes Odysseus's behavior. Whereas Achilles's brawn and bloodlust well suit his military career, Odysseus's quick-witted caution proves crucial in negotiating the obstacles, temptations, and dangers that the gods strew, like so many land mines, along his path through the postwar world.

The *Iliad*'s warrior heroes, obsessively competing for personal glory, condemn themselves to early deaths. Sacrificing their future is a necessary price for the posthumous fame that poets, singing of their prowess in war, eventually bestow upon them. The shrewd, aging hero of the *Odyssey*, however, is not predestined to share the tragic end of Achilles and his comrades. In the epic's opening scene, set on Mount Olympus, Zeus promises Athene that her beloved Odysseus will safely reach Ithaca. Even Poseidon, who persecutes Odysseus for his mutilation of Polyphemus, cannot resist the collective will of the other Olympians.

Zeus's first words sound a theme of heavenly justice that shapes the *Odyssey*'s moral universe. Mortals, he says, blame the gods for their troubles, but in reality people bring suffering on themselves, far exceeding the lot—the mixture of good and evil apportioned to each person—that Necessity decrees. Zeus then cites the example of **Aegisthus** [ee-JIS-thuhs], who had ignored Hermes's warning not to seduce **Clytemnestra** [klye-tem-NES-tra] or murder her husband, Agamemnon. As a result, Aegisthus is slain by **Orestes** [ah-RES-teez] (the son of Agamemnon and Clytemnestra), who boldly avenges his father's death, an act of filial devotion that the gods heartily approve.

FIGURE 12-3   Head of
Zeus. In the *Odyssey,* Zeus
enforces the principles of
cosmic justice, punishing
such lawbreakers as the suitors and assuring Athene
that her protégé Odysseus
will safely regain his rights
at Ithaca. Odysseus's
marked reverence for the
gods and his resourceful-
ness and persistence ensure
that, in spite of enduring
considerable pain and suffering, he will survive innumerable hardships and
reach his goal. Unlike the
tragic vision of the *Iliad,*
where death claims even
the best and bravest, the
Odyssey presents a relatively
optimistic worldview, albeit
one shadowed by the pros-
pect of a grim afterlife in
Hades's kingdom (see
Book 11). (*Vatican Mu-
seums, Rome.*)

Zeus's remarks introduce three important issues: (1) if the suitors succeed in their plot to kill Odysseus, Telemachus will be called upon to reenact Orestes's vengeance; (2) like Aegisthus, Odysseus will cause many of his own problems; and (3) the Olympians govern the world according to a principle of retributive justice that rewards persons honoring divine law and punishes the disobedient. Cosmic balance is maintained by ensuring that every crime is paid for by an appropriate punishment. The gods also distinguish among degrees of guilt: Odysseus's men, who deliberately break a divine prohibition, forfeit their lives, whereas Odysseus, who also suffers for his mistakes, avoids directly offending Zeus and survives (Figure 12-3).

Odysseus's Error with Polyphemus   Zeus does not mention Odysseus's partial responsibility for his delayed homecoming, but the hero later confesses that at least once he violated his own standards of prudence, with disastrous results. In his encounter with the Cyclops Polyphemus, Odysseus goes beyond offending mere mortals to earn the wrath of Poseidon, lord of the sea over which he and his men must travel. Odysseus imprudently enters Polyphemus's cave, where the cannibalistic giant promptly devours several of his men. After getting the monster drunk and blinding him (Figure 12-4), Odysseus then devises a way to escape the cave by tying his companions and himself to the undersides of Polyphemus's rams (Figure 12-5). Proud

FIGURE 12-4   The Blinding of Polyphemus. In the *Odyssey*'s opening pages, Zeus warns that human beings bring greater sorrows upon themselves than Necessity decrees, a truth illustrated by the hero's behavior with the Cyclops Polyphemus. Forgetting that a military leader must always plan ahead for possible retreat, Odysseus guides his men into a fatal trap, the cannibal Cyclops's cave. Although he devises a means of blinding Polyphemus and escaping with the men the giant had not yet eaten, Odysseus compounds his errors by boasting of his cleverness to the Cyclops and revealing his hitherto concealed identity, a burst of hubris (excessive pride) that brings the curse of Poseidon on him. Because of this uncharacteristic rashness, Odysseus suffers a ten-year delay in his homecoming and the loss of his men. (*Eleusis Museum.*)

FIGURE 12-5   Escape from Polyphemus's Cave. Tying himself to the underside of a large ram, Odysseus escapes from the Cyclops's lair. Odysseus's device to save himself and his men is successful, but its effect is immediately undercut by his impulsively revealing his identity—including his name and address—to Polyphemus. (*Anonymous gift in memory of L. D. Caskey. Courtesy, Museum of Fine Arts, Boston.*)

FIGURE 12-6   Odysseus in the Land of the Laestrygonians. In this episode with the cannibalistic Laestrygonians, Odysseus demonstrates that he has learned from his earlier encounter
with Polyphemus. Whereas Odysseus thoughtlessly had led his men into the Cyclops's cave
without bothering to learn anything of his putative host's disposition, he now approaches the
unknown with caution. By anchoring his ship a safe distance offshore, Odysseus and his crew
escape the fate of the rest of his command, who imprudently moor their vessels along the
beach and are destroyed when the giant Laestrygonians smash their ships with huge boulders.
This painting, in which some of the figures are identified with their names in Greek, is part
of a colorful frieze decorating the house of a wealthy Roman on the Esquiline Hill in Rome
(c. 50–40 B.C.). (*Biblioteca Apostolica Vaticana, Rome.*)

of having blinded Polyphemus and escaped alive, Odysseus temporarily acts as if he
has lost his own vision: boasting of his cleverness, he abandons the protective alias
he has used, announcing to the infuriated Cyclops that, far from being a "no-one,"
he has a famous identity, and he proceeds to divulge both his name and address. The
Cyclops's prayer to his father, Poseidon, is immediately granted: Odysseus will suffer
an agonizing ten-year delay in reaching home, the loss of all his men, and the certainty of great trouble on arriving in Ithaca.

The Polyphemus episode throws a long shadow over Odysseus's career, eventually necessitating his journey to Hades to consult the blind prophet **Tiresias** [tih-
REE-sih-as] about the future consequences of his recklessness (Book 11). Alerted to
the self-destructive aspects of his nature—the impulsive pride that subverts his rational control—Odysseus henceforth behaves with redoubled prudence. By cautiously
anchoring his vessel a safe distance off an unfamiliar shore, he escapes the fate of his
men when the Laestrygonians destroy their eleven ships (Figure 12-6). He also learns
to accept being the "no-one" that he had merely pretended to be in the Cyclops's

FIGURE 12-7   Athene in Profile. Although slightly corroded, this bronze sculpture of Athene vividly conveys the goddess's bright-eyed intelligence. A personification of the human ability to achieve victory through effective forethought, Athene advances the careers of several heroes who are characterized by their capacity to learn through experience, including Perseus, Heracles, and Odysseus. In preparing for Odysseus's successful return to Ithaca and resumption of his kingship, Athene cleverly manipulates almost every character in the *Odyssey,* from Olympian Zeus to an Ithacan swineherd. (*National Museum, Athens.*)

cave. When shipwrecked naked on the Phaeacians' island, Odysseus is a stranger without name, country, rank, possessions, identity—or even clothing. Although he later boasts of his adventures at the Phaeacian court, he is careful to keep his true identity a secret until it is safe to disclose his name. On Athene's advice, he even reenters his own palace as a social nonentity, wearing the rags of a foreign beggar.

Athene: Wise Guide and Mentor

Odysseus's exceptionally intimate relationship with his divine patron is virtually unique in Greek myth. When the two, both in disguise, meet on the beach near Ithaca, each one delights in the other's efforts to deceive (Book 13). The phenomenon of a mortal successfully matching wits with the goddess of wisdom elicits Athene's unstinted praise: "You are by far the best of mortals in [deceitful] plans and [false] stories, and I among all the gods am famed for planning and shrewdness." The affinity between Athene and Odysseus surpasses their shared attribute of mental agility, for man and goddess both set intellect to work, manipulating others to fulfill their own private agendas (Figure 12-7). As Athene maneuvers Zeus into circumventing Poseidon's vendetta, so Odysseus artfully exploits the suitors' drunken overconfidence to arrange his revenge. As giver of victory, Athene helps Odysseus plan his strategy—the reconquest of Ithaca—but, goddesslike, she does not actively intervene during his hand-to-hand battle with the suitors until he has already demonstrated both the will and ability to win.

In her final appearance, Athene again materializes as Mentor, an old Ithacan friend

Post-Homeric Traditions about Odysseus and His Family

The *Odyssey* ends with Athene's insistence on Odysseus's making peace with the dead suitors' families, although Tiresias's earlier prophecy about the hero's eventual reconciliation with his divine enemy, Poseidon, hints at Odysseus's future adventures (not covered in the Homeric epic). A later narrative poem, the *Telegonia* (ascribed to Eugammon of Cyrene and known only from brief summaries), states that after sacrificing to Hades, Persephone, and Tiresias (denizens of the Underworld to which Odysseus's bloody revenge had consigned the suitors), Odysseus leaves Ithaca and travels to Thesprotia, where he makes his obligatory peace offering to Poseidon. While among the Thesprotians (people of mythic King Thesprotus), Odysseus becomes the lover of Callidice, queen of the region, who gives birth to their son, Polypoetes. When Callidice dies, Odysseus turns the kingdom over to the young Polypoetes and returns home to Ithaca, where he finds that Penelope has borne him a second son, Poliporthes.

In the meantime, Odysseus's son by Circe, Telegonus (not mentioned in Homer but noted in Hesiod's *Theogony*), has gone in search of his father (reenacting Telemachus's quest in the *Odyssey*). After landing in Ithaca and raiding its cattle, Telegonus is beset by Ithacan herdsmen, who are aided by their king, Odysseus. Unaware of his father's identity, Telegonus kills Odysseus with a spear tipped with the poisonous tail of a stingray, only to be overcome with remorse when he learns whom he has slain. (Tiresias's prophecy that Odysseus will not die at sea is thus given an ironic twist: the hero is killed on land by the venom of a sea creature.) Telegonus then flees to Circe's island, taking Odysseus's body, Penelope, and his half-brother Telemachus with him. After Circe makes them immortal, Telegonus marries Penelope and Telemachus marries Circe. In one variant of the tradition, Circe restores Odysseus to life and, after dispatching Penelope and Odysseus's two sons to the Isles of the Blest (see Chapter 9), Circe at last marries the hero herself.

Other post-Homeric variations of the myth focus on Penelope's fate. Apollodorus cites a tradition in which Penelope is seduced by Antinous, her most aggressive suitor, for which Odysseus sends her back to her father, Icarius, where she becomes Hermes's mistress and gives birth to the rustic god Pan. Some later poets claim that Pan, a figure of unbridled lust, was the result of an orgy in which Penelope coupled with *all* of her hundred suitors—a gratuitous slander against Homer's portrait of human fidelity.

In still another version, after slaying the suitors, Odysseus receives an oracle directing him to Epirus, where he makes love to Euippe, the daughter of his host,

of Odysseus, ordering families of the slain suitors to cease their vendetta against Ithaca's king. Her last words demand that Odysseus also control his anger, the emotion that generates the blood lust of war. As it did throughout the poem, Athene's presence—the unexpected occurrence of rational thought—points the way out of difficulty, restores order among Ithaca's warring factions, and guides mortals toward a fulfillment of the divine will.

Tyrimmas (a contrast to his restrained behavior with King Alcinous's daughter Nausicaa). When the son of this union, Euryalus, grows up, his mother sends him to Ithaca with sealed proofs of his parentage. Odysseus is not at home when Euryalus arrives. Penelope, recognizing in him the illegitimate child of a rival, later jealously persuades her husband that the youth is a threat to his life. Reverting to his earlier imprudent conduct, Odysseus impulsively kills the stranger, thus becoming guilty of his son's murder.

Some Athenian dramatists were extremely critical of Odysseus's ethical character. In his tragedy *Philoctetes,* Sophocles portrays Odysseus as an amoral example of middle-aged expediency. After receiving an oracle that only possession of Heracles's famous bow can ensure the Greeks' victory at Troy, Odysseus does not hesitate to manipulate Achilles's naive son, Neoptolemus, into inadvertently deceiving the wounded Philoctetes, whom the Greeks had previously abandoned on the island of Lemnos, persuading him to relinquish Heracles's bow.

As this cursory sampling of post-Homeric myth indicates, Greek and Roman writers delighted in spinning endless new tales about Odysseus and his diverse escapades. A quintessentially human paradox of intelligence and passion, foresight and recklessness, Odysseus continued to fascinate the European imagination long after the fall of Rome. For Dante, the supreme poet of medieval Roman Catholicism, Odysseus (Ulysses) symbolizes the pride of intellect that drives men to violate God-ordained boundaries. In Dante's *Inferno* (Canto 26; see reading in Chapter 21), the poet imagines Odysseus's last journey into realms never before explored by mortals, an impious ambition that Christendom's God punishes in hell. By contrast, in a poem written in 1842, the English poet Alfred, Lord Tennyson, depicts the aged Greek hero as embodying a modern spirit of scientific heroism, his insatiable thirst to experience new life representing the finest of human aspiration (see reading, also in Chapter 21).

Homer's successors, ancient and modern, present an enormous range of possible fates for Odysseus after his return to Ithaca. As Hesiod's evolving cosmos is a seed-bed of almost unlimited potential, so Odysseus's multifaceted character presents endless opportunities for further development. Inhabiting a timeless dimension limited only by the human imagination, he confronts an open-ended universe, simultaneously journeying through parallel worlds and creating a legion of selves acting out their individual destinies. In his infinite variety—transcending time and culture—Odysseus illustrates the boundless exuberance of the mythical hero.

Odysseus and Images of the Feminine

Circe   Almost every stage of Odysseus's voyage is marked by an encounter with a woman or a goddess, each of whom typically first challenges and then assists the hero. After escaping the Laestrygonians, Odysseus's next adventure takes place on the island of **Circe** [SIR-see], an enchantress who turns men into swine. Like the demigoddess

FIGURE 12-8   Odysseus in Hades's Kingdom. Although Circe at first appears as a threat to Odysseus's manhood, she becomes his partner and guide, wisely preparing him to avoid the dangers and pitfalls he must encounter on subsequent wanderings. A mistress of occult knowledge, she instructs Odysseus on the correct path to the Underworld and the proper rituals for safely inquiring of the dead. In this vase painting, the shade of Elpenor (left) hails his former captain (center), asking that his yet unburied corpse be interred so that his soul can find peace. That Odysseus enjoys divine protection in his risky descent to Hades's realm is indicated by the presence of Hermes (right), who escorts the recently dead to their final rest. (*William Amory Gardner Fund. Courtesy, Museum of Fine Arts, Boston.*)

Calypso, who will later hold Odysseus in thrall for seven long years, Circe is a powerful female who threatens the hero's masculine identity because she plies the art of reducing human males to the lowest common denominator, their animal natures. Exercising total control over their respective domains, she and Calypso represent isolated cultural pockets in which the feminine principle still holds sway—matriarchal islands in a vast patriarchal sea.

It is significant that the only two occasions on which the grand patriarch Zeus sends his male emissary (Hermes) to aid Odysseus occur when the hero's masculine autonomy is jeopardized by a captivating female. Hermes rushes to Odysseus's side the moment he sets foot in Circe's dangerous terrain, giving him a mythical herb, the moly plant, to counteract the effect of her magic, thus protecting him from loss of manhood.

As a wise manifestation of the ancient Goddess, Circe soon becomes Odysseus's host, lover, and guide. Once Odysseus has demonstrated his ability to resist her manipulation and the right to assert his own maleness (threatening her with his phallic sword), Circe freely accepts him as her equal partner. Functioning as an aspect of his anima (Penelope is its full expression), Circe imparts the secret knowledge of such chthonic goddesses as Gaea, Demeter, and Persephone. Circe reveals the hidden path

FIGURE 12-9 Scylla. According to tradition, Scylla was once human but was changed
into a cannibal monster by a rival in love. Described as having six heads, each with a triple
row of teeth, and having a circle of vicious dogs encompassing her waist, she lived in a cave
above a narrow strait (traditionally the Straits of Messina between Sicily and Italy), opposite
the whirlpool of Charybdis. As portrayed in this Roman bronze bowl, Scylla reaches out
to grasp and devour one of Odysseus's men while her dogs maul other victims. Circe warns
Odysseus that he must sacrifice a few of his men to Scylla in order to avoid having his entire
crew drowned in Charybdis. Thanks to Circe's wise advice, Odysseus survives both encounters with these two destructive manifestations of feminine dominance. (*British Museum,
London.*)

to the Underworld (Figure 12-8), instructing Odysseus in the sacred rituals necessary
to consult the dead and enabling him to complete the rite of passage in which he
undergoes symbolic death and rebirth (books 10–12).

Circe also teaches Odysseus how to minimize his losses from the twin manifestations of the deadly aspects of the feminine—**Scylla** [SIL-la] (Figure 12-9) and
Charybdis [ka-RIB-dis], the man-devouring monsters he must experience before his
initiation into life and kingship is complete. Perceiving Odysseus's omnivorous curiosity and need to take risks, Circe further instructs him on how to hear the Sirens'
irresistible song without falling victim to their fatal attraction (Figure 12-10). Although a threat to men dominated by their bestial appetites (such as Odysseus's
intellectually undeveloped companions), Circe exemplifies the Great Goddess's beneficence to those worthy of her help.

In the final test that qualitatively distinguishes Odysseus from his remaining men,
the hero wisely heeds Circe's warning to refrain from eating the sacred cattle of Hyperion. The men, becalmed for weeks on an inhospitable island, give in to their
physical appetites, slaughtering and feasting on the sun god's property, an impious

FIGURE 12-10   Odysseus and the Sirens. Understanding Odysseus's insatiable desire to undergo extremes of experience, wise Circe instructs him how to hear the Sirens' (creatures half-woman, half-bird) lethal song without being destroyed. As shown in this vase painting (early fifth century B.C.), his men row obliviously, their ears stopped with beeswax, while Odysseus listens to the Sirens' irresistible call, struggling against the bonds that prevent him from impulsively giving in to their fatal attraction. Stunned by her failure to lure a man to his death, one Siren self-destructs, plunging into the sea (right center). (*British Museum, London.*)

act that Zeus punishes by later incinerating their ship with his thunderbolt. Only Odysseus, wise enough to sacrifice his immediate well-being in order to win the gods' approval, survives Zeus's wrath. He is then made to endure, on Calypso's isle, **Ogygia** [oh-JIJ-ih-a], the most extended test of his patience, purpose, and manhood.

Calypso   In contrast to Circe, who coolly relinquishes her lover as soon as he asks to leave, Calypso represents a different threat to Odysseus's psyche—the demands of untrammeled female sexuality. Although it may seem that Odysseus has found paradise with a goddess who drags him to her bed every night for seven years, we must remember that the hero is no longer a young man of unlimited virility. Besides the potentially castrating effects of Calypso's dominance, Odysseus—imprisoned on an island literally in the middle of nowhere—is deprived of the normal challenges and opportunities that society affords. A Greek hero can not fulfill his destiny in total isolation from other human beings.

Calypso's outrage when Hermes brings Zeus's command—given at Athene's urging—to release Odysseus reflects a female deity's deep resentment at the Olympian autocracy. Some critics view Calypso's offer to make Odysseus immortal as the echo of a prehistoric rite in which the Goddess's male consort was sacrificed, his shed blood fertilizing the ground and enhancing Gaea's fecundity. As in the Heracles myth, a hero's immortality is attained only after death and transfiguration, a posthumous deification that Odysseus rejects.

Odysseus's refusal to disavow the burden of mortality also marks a radical departure from the hero's traditional quest for divine status. Rather than deny his mortal humanity, he embraces it, spurred partly by his loyalty to Penelope, who, unlike Calypso, will grow old and die. After his prolonged contact with the wisdom of figures like Circe, Odysseus chooses to remain fixed in the earthly life cycle that includes aging and death, the wise acceptance of natural law expressed by the Great Goddess (see Chapter 4).

In his close rapport with goddesses and his employment of their gifts, Odysseus is reminiscent of earlier heroes, such as Perseus and Heracles. Like Heracles, another of Athene's select favorites, Odysseus is associated with a bow that only he can utilize and with a perilous journey into Hades's kingdom, a parallel that Homer underscores at the climax of Book 11. Combining the best traits of Perseus and Heracles, Odysseus exceeds them in the intense solitariness of his quest: no other Greek hero is more completely alone, deals with more terrifying supernatural forces, develops a higher degree of self-reliance, or returns to his place of origin with greater insight than Odysseus. In negotiating the dangerous and complex rites of passage, few heroes can match Odysseus's versatility or success.

Penelope   During Odysseus's visit to the Underworld (Book 11), the ghost of Agamemnon, obsessed by Clytemnestra's betrayal, warns him never to trust even the best of wives. Although Odysseus ignores Agamemnon's spectral advice and confides fully in Penelope after their reunion, the implied parallel between the two kings' potential fate is cited repeatedly. The key difference in this equation is Penelope's distinctive character, which makes her far more than a conventional model of the submissive and patient wife. As intelligent, perceptive, and resourceful as her husband, she shares Odysseus's prudence and inventiveness, demonstrated by her delaying tactics with the suitors: her feigned promise to marry as soon as she finishes weaving a burial shroud for Laertes (Figure 12-11)—which she covertly unravels at night—keeps the suitors at bay for years. Penelope's ability to test men's mettle ranges from the deadly trial of skill she sets up for the suitors to a final ruse about the immovability of her marriage bed. Her use of this image—a place of sexual union secretly fashioned from the trunk of an olive tree, Athene's unique gift to the Greeks—suggests Penelope's association with peaceful fecundity, a benevolent expression of the same qualities that Circe and Calypso represent, but without the attendant danger.

As weaver, keeper of nuptial secrets, and guardian of an olive trunk symbolizing the Tree of Life, Penelope implicitly functions as a priestess of the ancient Goddess. Her characteristic task of weaving also links Penelope to the feminine aspects of Athene, who is patron of women's handicrafts and protector of the home. Despite her ostensible powerlessness when pressured by the suitors, Penelope is also in control of her destiny. Although Penelope's endurance matches that of her peripatetic husband, the excessive duration of Odysseus's absence stretches the marriage bond to its utmost limit. At the moment of Odysseus's return, she appears to have exhausted her capacity for waiting and seems ready to make an active choice for her future life.

In a Jungian interpretation, Penelope—a feminine counterpart of the "godlike Odysseus"—embodies her husband's anima, an appropriately human expression of Circe's chthonic wisdom. The couple's long-delayed reunion signifies a rejoining of

FIGURE 12-11   Telemachus and Penelope. This vase painting shows the faithful Penelope sitting mournfully at her loom, pining for the husband she has not seen for almost twenty years. Homer portrays Penelope as Odysseus's equal in prudence and cunning, for she devises a scheme of keeping her one hundred unwanted suitors waiting for years while she weaves a shroud for Laertes, her father-in-law, unraveling at night what she creates by day. Telemachus, who reaches young manhood on the eve of his father's long-delayed return, sets out on an arduous journey to gather news of Odysseus's whereabouts. Most of the epic's first four books are devoted to an account of Telemachus's travels to Pylos and Sparta, where he hears characters from the *Iliad*—old King Nestor, Menelaus, and Helen—sing Odysseus's praises. (*Museo Etrusco.*)

the heroic animus and anima, a commingling that marks the completion of their respective natures and the fulfillment of their mutual quest. In one of myth's great ironies, during the night in which this archetypal pair renew their conjugal bond, Odysseus confides to his wife that he must leave her again. The hero's fate necessitates another extended journey into unknown lands, this time to seek a reconciliation with his divine enemy, Poseidon.

FIGURE 12-12 The Warrior Athene. Authoritatively grasping her shield and spear, Athene prepares to do battle. As defender of the city-state and goddess of victory in war, Athene intervenes on Odysseus's behalf not only to defeat the suitors but also to cut short a potential civil conflict and restore peace to Ithaca. The *Odyssey* concludes with Athene's decisive action, pacifying the vengeful relatives of the slain suitors and curtly ordering Odysseus to give up his anger. Unlike Ares, who glories in the vicious frenzy of mass slaughter, Athene employs her military skills primarily to impose the benefits of peace. (*Munich Museum.*)

Homer concludes the *Odyssey* by placing his hero's reunion with Penelope in the larger context of Ithacan politics. At the beginning of Book 24, it looks as if Odysseus will have to shed more of his people's blood, for the suitors' male relatives are honor-bound to avenge the young men's deaths. Zeus and Athene, however, intervene to end the feud and reestablish civic order, a climactic reconciliation of warring opposites in which Athene, again disguised as Mentor, has the final word, bringing the long Troy saga to a peaceful close (Figure 12-12).

ODYSSEY[1]

Homer

BOOK 1

Muse, tell me of the man of many wiles,
the man who wandered many paths of exile
after he sacked Troy's sacred citadel.
He saw the cities—mapped the minds—of many;
and on the sea, his spirit suffered every
adversity—to keep his life intact,
to bring his comrades back. In that last task,
his will was firm and fast, and yet he failed:
he could not save his comrades. Fools, they foiled
themselves: they ate the oxen of the Sun,   10
the herd of Hélios Hypérion;
the lord of light requited their transgression—
he took away the day of their return.

Muse, tell us of these matters. Daughter of Zeus,
my starting point is any point you choose.

All other Greeks who had been spared the steep
descent to death had reached their homes—released
from war and waves. One man alone was left,
still longing for his home, his wife, his rest.
For the commanding nymph, the brightest goddess,   20
Calypso, held him in her hollow grottoes:
she wanted him as husband. Even when
the wheel of years drew near his destined time—
the time the gods designed for his return
to Ithaca—he still could not depend
upon fair fortune or unfailing friends.
While other gods took pity on him, one—
Poseidon—still pursued: he preyed upon
divine Odysseus until the end,
until the exile found his own dear land.   30

But now Poseidon was away—his hosts,
the Ethiopians, the most remote
of men (they live in two divided parts—
half, where the sun-god sets; half, where he starts).
Poseidon, visiting the east, received

---

1. Translation by Allen Mandelbaum.

360

the roasted thighs of bulls and sheep. The feast
delighted him. And there he sat. But all
his fellow gods were gathered in the halls
of Zeus upon Olympus; there the father
of men and gods spoke first. His mind upon   40
the versatile Aegísthus—whom the son
of Agamemnon, famed Oréstes, killed—
he shared this musing with the deathless ones:

"Men are so quick to blame the gods: they say
that we devise their misery. But they
themselves—in their depravity—design
grief greater than the griefs that fate assigns.
So did Aegísthus act when he transgressed
the boundaries that fate and reason set.
He took the lawful wife of Agamemnon;   50
and when the son of Átreus had come back,
Aegísthus murdered him—although he knew
how steep was that descent. For we'd sent Hermes,
our swiftest, our most keen-eyed emissary,
to warn against that murder and adultery:
'Oréstes will avenge his father when,
his manhood come, he claims his rightful land.'
Hermes had warned him as one warns a friend.
And yet Aegísthus' will could not be swayed.
Now, in one stroke, all that he owes is paid."   60

Athena, gray-eyed goddess, answered Zeus:
"Our father, Cronos' son, you, lord of lords,
Aegísthus died the death that he deserved.
May death like his strike all who ape his sins.
But brave Odysseus' fate does break my heart:
long since, in misery he suffers, far
from friends, upon an island in the deep—
a site just at the navel of the sea.
And there, upon that island rich in trees,
a goddess has her home: the fair-haired daughter   70
of Atlas the malevolent (who knows
the depths of every sea, for he controls
the giant column holding earth and sky
apart). Calypso, Atlas' daughter, keeps
the sad Odysseus there—although he weeps.
Her words are fond and fragrant, sweet and soft—
so she would honey him to cast far off
his Ithaca; but he would rather die
than live the life of one denied the sight
of smoke that rises from his homeland's hearths.   80
Are you, Olympus' lord, not moved by this?

Was not Odysseus your favorite
when, on the spacious plain of Troy, beside
the Argive ships, he sacrificed to you?
What turned your fondness into malice, Zeus?"

Zeus, shepherd of the clouds, replied: "My daughter,
how can the barrier of your teeth permit
such speech to cross your lips? Can I forget
godlike Odysseus, most astute of men,
whose offerings were so unstinting when   90
he sacrificed to the undying gods,
the masters of vast heaven? Rest assured.
Only Poseidon, lord whose chariot runs
beneath the earth, is furious—it was
Odysseus who deprived the grandest Cyclops,
the godlike Polyphémus, of his eye.
(Thöósa—nymph whose father, Phórcys, keeps
a close watch on the never-resting deep—
gave birth to that huge Cyclops after she
had lain in her deep sea-cave with Poseidon.)   100
And ever since his son was gouged, the god
who makes earth tremble, though he does not kill
Odysseus, will not let him end his exile.
But now we all must think of his return—
of how to bring him home again. Poseidon
will set aside his anger; certainly
he cannot have his way, for he is only
one god against us all, and we are many."

Athena, gray-eyed goddess, answered him:
"Our father, Cronos' son, you, lord of lords,   110
if now the blessed gods indeed would end
the wanderings of Odysseus, let us send
the keen-eyed Hermes to Calypso's isle,
Ogýgia. Let him there at once declare
to her, the goddess with the lovely hair,
our undeniable decree: Steadfast
Odysseus is to find his homeward path.
But I shall make my way to Ithaca
at once, to give his son the strength to summon
the long-haired Ithacans; when they assemble   120
he can denounce—and scatter—all the suitors:
they are forever slaughtering his sheep,
his shambling oxen with their curving horns.
Then off to sandy Pylos and to Sparta
I'll send him to seek tidings of his father's
return; he may yet hear some hopeful word—
and men will then commend him for his search."

That said, Athena fastened on fine sandals:
these—golden, everlasting—carried her
with swift winds over seas and endless lands.   130
The goddess took her bronze-tipped battle lance,
heavy and huge and solid; with this shaft,
she—daughter of so great a force—can smash
the ranks of warriors who've earned her wrath.
One leap—and from Olympus' peaks she reached
the land of Ithaca. She stood before
Odysseus' door, the threshold of his court.
She gripped the bronze-tipped shaft, and taking on
the likeness of a stranger, she became
lord Méntës, chieftain of the Táphians.   140
She found the braggart suitors at the gate.
Delighting in their dicing, they reclined
on hides of oxen they themselves had skinned—
with pages and attendants serving them,
some mixing wine and water in wide bowls,
while others washed the tables down with sponges
and readied them for food, and others still
stacked meat in heaps on platters—high and full.

The very first to notice Méntës' presence
was young Telémachus. He—sad, morose—   150
sat with the suitors. In his reverie,
he saw his sturdy father—would that he,
returning suddenly, might banish these
intruders from his palace and restore
the rights and rule that had been his before.
Such was the sadness of Telémachus,
alone among the suitors, till he saw
Athena; he rushed toward the outer door,
ashamed that none had gone to greet the stranger.
He drew near, clasped her right hand, even as   160
his left relieved her of the heavy lance.
And when he spoke, his words were like winged shafts:
"My greetings, stranger. Welcome to our feast.
Eat first—and then do tell us what you seek."

He led the way; Athena followed him.
Once they were in the high-roofed hall, he placed
her lance against a column at whose base
a polished rack, with slots for spears, was set;
within that rack there stood still other shafts,
the many spears that brave Odysseus left.   170
He led the stranger to a tall chair, wrought
with care; across its frame he spread rich cloth.
There he invited her to sit and rest

her feet upon a stool; and he himself
sat nearby, on another well-carved chair,
set far off from the suitors, lest his guest,
in all that brouhaha, might look askance
at feasting with such overbearing men—
and, too, because he wanted so to gather
what news he could about his distant father.   180
That they might wash their hands, a servant poured
fresh water from a lovely golden jug
into a silver basin; at their side
she placed a polished table. The old housewife
was generous: she drew on lavish stores;
to each of them she offered much and more.
The carver offered meats of every sort,
and for their wine he set out golden cups;
and these—again, again—a page filled up.

But then the suitors swaggered in; they sat,   190
in order, on low seats and high-backed chairs.
The pages poured fresh water for their hands,
and servants brought them baskets heaped with bread.
The suitors' hands reached out. The feast was theirs.

When they had had their fill of food and drink,
the feasters felt the need for chant and dance—
at banquets, these are pleasing ornaments.
A steward now consigned a handsome harp
into the hands of Phémius, who was forced,
from time to time, to entertain those lords.   200
He struck the strings, and music graced his words.

Then, as Telémachus turned toward his guest,
lest he be overheard, he held his head
close to the gray-eyed goddess—and he said:

"Dear guest, will you be vexed at what I say?
This harping and this chant delight these men,
for all these goods come easily to them:
they feed—but never need to recompense.
They feast at the expense of one whose white
bones, surely, either rot beneath the rain,   210
unburied and abandoned on the land,
or else are preyed upon by churning waves.
Yet, were Odysseus to return, were they
to see him here again, they would not pray
for gold or richer clothes—just faster feet.
But he has died by now, died wretchedly;
and nothing can console us now, not even

if some man on this earth should say my father
will yet return. The day of his homecoming
is lost: it is a day we'll never see. 220
But tell me one thing—tell me honestly:
Who are you? Of what father were you born?
Where is your city, where your family?
On what ship did you sail? Why did that crew
bring you to Ithaca? And who were they?
For surely you did not come here on foot!
And also tell me truthfully—is this
the first time you have come to Ithaca,
or have you been my father's guest before?
For many other foreigners have come 230
to visit us—like you, my father knew
the ways of many men and many lands."

Athena, gray-eyed goddess, answered him:
"My words to you are true: I'm Méntës, son
of wise Anchíalus; the Táphians,
tenacious oarsmen, are the men I rule.
Now I have landed here with ship and crew;
we cross the winedark sea toward Témesë—
all this in search of copper. What we stow
is gleaming iron, which we're set to barter. 240
Outside the city, moored in Rhēīthron's harbor,
close to the fields, beneath Mount Néion's forest,
my ship is waiting. Years ago, your father
and mine were guests and friends. (Just ask the brave
Laértës—though they say he shuns the city;
it seems that now he much prefers to grieve
far off, alone, except for one old servant.
She, when his body aches from the hard climb
he makes, from slope to slope, to tend his vines,
still carries food and drink right to his side.) 250

"Now I have come—for I had heard indeed
that he, your father, had returned. Surely
it is the gods who now obstruct his journey.
For bright Odysseus has not died upon
this earth: he is alive somewhere, delayed
upon an island set among vast waves,
held by harsh savages, against his will.
I am no augur or interpreter
of flights of birds, but now I shall foretell—
even as the immortals prompt my soul— 260
events my mind can see: Your father will
not be kept back from his dear land much longer,
though they may bind him fast in iron chains;

he is a man of many wiles, who can
contrive the way to reach his home again.
But you—do tell me now with honesty:
Are you, so tall, indeed Odysseus's son?
Your head and handsome eyes resemble his
extraordinarily; we two had met
quite often in the days before he left   270
for Troy, where others, too—the Argives' best—
sailed in their hollow ships. But since then I
have not seen him, and he has not seen me."

Telémachus' reply was keen and wise:
"Dear friend, I cannot be more frank than this.
My mother says I am his son, but none
can know for sure the seed from which he's sprung.
In any case, would I had been the son
of one so blessed that he grew old among
his own belongings. I, instead, am born—   280
or so they say—of one who surely was
the most forsaken man, the most forlorn.
Now you have had and heard my full response."

Athena, gray-eyed goddess, answered him:
"Despite misfortune now, your family
can count on future fame: Penelope
is mother of a son who is most worthy.
But tell me truthfully: What sort of feast
is this? A banquet? Or a wedding party?
This surely is no meal where each has brought   290
his share. Why did this crowd seek out your house?
These guzzlers seem to me no better than
a pack of swaggerers—too rude, too coarse.
Seeing their shameful doings, any man
of sense would feel both anger and contempt."

Telémachus' response was wise, precise:
"Dear guest, to all you ask, I now reply.
I tell you that as long as he, my father,
was in his native land, this house was rich
and great. But then the gods willed otherwise—   300
they made my father vanish: they devised
oblivion for him—much deeper than
oblivion known by any other man.
And though he's dead, my grief would be less deep
if he had fallen in the land of Troy,
among his fellow warriors, or else—
once he had wound up all the threads of war—
had died at home, among his very own.

Then all of the Achǽans would have built
a tomb for him; and, too, he would have won
much glory for his son in days to come.
Instead, the spirit-winds—the stormy Harpies—
snatched him away ingloriously: he
was banished into black obscurity.
And I am left with grief and misery.
I sigh not only over him: the gods
have given me still more calamities.
All lords with power in these isles—who rule
Dulíchium and Samos and Zacýnthus,
the wooded isle, and those who now presume
to rule in rocky Ithaca—continue
to woo my mother and consume my goods.
She'll not reject the hateful wedding or
accept it. Meanwhile all their gluttony
lays waste my house; they soon will ruin me."

Pallas Athena, now incensed, replied:
"The absent one, Odysseus, is indeed
the man whom you, unhappy son, could use:
he'd break the back of this marauding band.
Would he—returned—were now to take his stand
upon the threshold with his helmet, shield,
and pair of spears—the mighty man that I
first saw on his way back from Éphyrë,
the land of Ílus, son of Mérmerus;
along his homeward way, he stayed with us—
I saw him drinking, feasting, in our house.
(He'd sailed in his fast ship to visit Ílus,
to seek a fatal venom he could smear
on his bronze arrow-tips; but in his fear
of the undying gods' displeasure, Ílus
refused to give Odysseus that dread drug.
My father gave it to him, for he loved
your father so extraordinarily.)
For if Odysseus were to show himself
among this pack of suitors with the same
strength he showed then, they all would meet quick death
and bitter wooing. But of things like these—
whether or not your father, on returning,
will take revenge within his palace—we
know nothing; such things lie upon the knees
of gods. But for yourself, you must consider
the way in which to rid your house of suitors.
Now hear my words and think on them with care.
Tomorrow ask the lords of Ithaca
to gather here; then speak to all, and let

310

320

330

340

350

the gods be witnesses. Command the suitors
to scatter, each on his own way; and order
your mother, should she be inclined to wed,
to go back to her mighty father's house.
Let him prepare his daughter's wedding and   360
the gifts—appropriately rich—she merits.
As for yourself, the path I urge is this,
if you would listen: Find the fittest ship
and, with a crew of twenty oarsmen, seek
some word of your long-absent father—for
a mortal may have heard about him, or
your ears may chance to hear the voice that Zeus
so often uses when he brings men news.
Sail first to Pylos: question noble Nestor.
Then visit Sparta's king, blond Meneláus: 370
of all Achǽans clad in bronze, he was
the last to reach his home. If you should hear
word that your father is still alive and steers
a homeward path, then—though you are much tried—
you surely can hold out for one more year.
But if you learn that he has died, return
to your dear land and raise a mound for him;
complete a just, unstinting funeral,
then marry off your mother to some man:
you will have done all that you should—and can.   380
But then weigh carefully in mind and soul
how best to kill the suitors in your halls—
by way of open combat or of guile.
Forget the pastimes of a child: you are
a boy no longer. Or have you not heard
what fame Oréstes gained when he avenged
the murder of his father? Everyone
knows how he killed that master of deceptions,
Aegísthus, slayer of great Agamemnon.
You, too, my friend—I see you tall, robust—   390
must never flinch or falter if you want
to win the praise of men in time to come.
But now I must return to my swift ship;
this long delay may make my comrades fret.
Consider carefully—heed what I've said."

Telémachus' reply was keen and wise:
"My guest, your words come from a friendly mind—
words like a father's to a son—and I
shall not forget them. But why not extend
your stay? Although your voyage presses, bathe—   400
refresh your spirit; then, fine gift in hand,
you can with satisfaction sail away.

That gift will be a precious, handsome thing,
a keepsake such as dear friends give to friends."

Athena, gray-eyed goddess, answered him:
"Do not delay me now. I truly wish
to leave; whatever gift your heart would give—
you'll choose a handsome one, I'm sure—can be
consigned when I stop here again, on my
return, that I may bear it home. And it
will earn for you a gift of equal merit."

410

When that was said, gray-eyed Athena left,
quick as a bird. Within his heart she'd set
resolve and strength and memories more intense—
more bent upon his father—than before.
And he was pensive, marveling, aware
that he had had some god as visitor.

. . . .

BOOKS 2–4

[Aware that Telemachus has now matured sufficiently to pose a threat to their plans, the suitors conspire to get rid of him. Prompted by Athene, Telemachus leaves Ithaca to search for news of his father, traveling first to the court of old King Nestor at Pylos and then, accompanied by Nestor's son Pisistratus, visiting Sparta and hearing his father's praises sung by Menelaus and Helen. With Athene's help, Telemachus will escape the suitors' ambush and return unharmed to Ithaca.]

BOOK 5

[While Telemachus gathers testimony about his father's heroic reputation, Odysseus remains trapped on Calypso's remote island, Ogygia, where for seven years he has nightly made love to the amorous nymph and spent his empty days weeping for home. Dispatched at Athene's request, Hermes appears to order Calypso to free her reluctant lover:]

. . . .

The gods, convened in council, sat with Zeus,
the thunder lord, whose force is absolute.
To them, Athena, as she called to mind
Odysseus' many miseries, defined
the threats that lay in wait, the troubling fate
he faced as captive in Calypso's cave:

"You, father Zeus, and all of this assembly
of blessed, never-dying gods, hear me:
From this time on, no sceptered king need be
benign and kind, a man of righteous mind:
let kings be cruel and corrupt, malign—
for none among his people now recall

10

divine Odysseus, though his rule was gentle
and fatherly. And now, against his will,
Calypso keeps him captive in her grotto,
her island home, where he can only sorrow.
And he cannot return to his own land:
he has no ships at hand, no oars, no friends
to carry him across the sea's broad back.
Now, too, they mean to ambush his dear son,   20
to murder him along his homeward run;
for news of his dear father, he has gone
to sacred Pylos and bright Lacedæmon."

Zeus, shepherd of the clouds, replied: "My daughter,
how can the barrier of your teeth permit
such words to cross your lips? For surely this
delay—to keep Odysseus far away
until on his return he takes revenge
against the suitors—is the scheme you planned.
As for Telémachus, your cunning can   30
return him to his land on safe sea paths,
and you can thwart the suitors' plot, so that
those baffled men retreat with empty hands."

That said, he turned to Hermes, his dear son:
"Yes, you have served us well on many missions.
Go now, and tell the nymph with lovely hair
that this is our infallible decree:
Odysseus is to reach his home, though he
must sail alone, without the company
of gods or men. His craft will be makeshift,   40
planks bound by many thongs; in such a ship,
his crossing will be trying, tiring, yet
when twenty days have passed, that man of wiles
will reach Schería's fertile soil, the isle
of the Phaeácians, men the gods befriend.
There they will honor him with willing hearts,
as if he were a god. They will escort
Odysseus to his homeland in their ship,
with bronze and gold and clothes—so many gifts:
after the sack of Troy, had he sailed back   50
directly, with his share of spoils intact,
not even then would he have been that rich.
Such is the destined way in which he'll come
to his own land, his friends, his high-roofed home."

That said, the keen-eyed messenger was quick.
First, to his feet he fastened handsome sandals:
these, golden, everlasting, carried him

with swift winds over seas and endless land.
He took the wand that charms the eyes of men:
some, he enchants with sleep, just as he can,   60
at will, awaken others. Wand in hand,
Hermes took flight. He passed Piéria's peaks
and, from the upper air, swooped toward the waves;
then, like a bird, he skimmed—a tern that bathes
its thick wings in the brine as it hunts fish
in surge that never rests—the dread abyss.
So Hermes rode the countless troughs and crests.

At last he reached landfall, the distant isle.
He quit the violet waves. He made his way
on land and found the fair-haired nymph's deep cave.   70
She was at home. A splendid fire blazed
upon her hearth; its fragrance wafted far
across the isle—the scent of burning logs
of juniper and tender thuja boughs.
Inside that grotto, with her golden shuttle,
the nymph was weaving; moving back and forth
before her loom, she sang—her voice was graceful.
The grotto was surrounded by rich forests:
alder and poplar trees and pungent cypress.
There broad-winged birds built nests: owls, cormorants,   80
and chattering sea crows, who ply their tasks
among the waves. The grotto's entranceway
was ringed by robust vines with clustered grapes.
Pure water rose from four springs in a row,
but then, meandering, the four streams flowed
through gentle fields of violets and parsley.

Even a god who chanced to see that site
would feel the force of wonder and delight.
But when his mind had marveled at it all,
he went at once into the spacious cave.   90
Calypso, brightest goddess, seeing Hermes,
did not have any doubts: the deathless gods
can recognize each other, even when
their dwelling places lie so far apart.
Yet generous Odysseus was not there,
but where he always sat, along the shore,
sighing and weeping, grieving as he tore
his heart and watched the restless sea. Calypso
sat Hermes on a gleaming chair, then asked:

"Hermes, my honored guest—a welcome one—   100
what matter brings you here with your gold wand?
You've hardly been a frequent visitor.

Tell me the thoughts you want to share. If I
can answer your request, and my heart finds
it seemly, I shall help you willingly.
But first—a time for friendship, courtesy."

That said, the goddess showed him to a table
heaped with ambrosia, and she poured red nectar.
So Hermes ate and drank, and when his soul
had been refreshed with food, this was his answer: 110

"You ask—as goddess to a god—why I
am here, and you do not want me to lie.
Zeus ordered me to come, against my will:
who'd want to cross an endless stretch of brine?
Who'd want to find no mortals' town nearby
where men, to please a god, may sacrifice
choice hecatombs, roast thighs that so delight?
And yet there is no god that can elude
or slight the will of aegis-bearing Zeus.
He says there is a man with you, a man   120
most miserable, one of those who fought
nine years for Priam's citadel, then sacked
that stronghold in the tenth year and sailed back.
But since his men had sinned against Athena,
she sent harsh winds, harsh seas, as punishment.
Then all of his brave comrades died, but he,
impelled by wind and wave, has reached your realm.
Now Zeus would have you send him home at once:
his fate is not to die here, far from friends—
he is to see his dear ones, find again   130
his high-roofed house, return to his own land."

These were his words. The lovely goddess shuddered,
then answered Hermes with her own winged words:
"You gods are cruel and more jealous than
all others: if a goddess beds a man
and wants him—openly—as her dear husband,
then you begrudge her that. Your envy punished
rose-fingered Dawn when she embraced Oríon:
you gods, at ease, your least desire appeased,
sent down chaste Ártemis of the gold throne,   140
and she, in Delos, killed him with her shafts.
And when fair-haired Deméter dared to clasp
Iásion (they mingled, breast to breast,
upon a field where plows had worked three furrows),
Zeus did not wait too long to find that out,
to kill him with a blazing thunderbolt.
So now, you gods resent my having chosen

a mortal. But when flashing lightning sent
by Zeus had smashed his ship and sunk his men,
and there, alone along the winedark sea,   150
he clutched the keel until the waves and wind
had cast him on my coast, I welcomed him:
it's I who fed him, I who took him in—
I hoped to give him immortality,
an endless life and yet without old age.
But since there is no god who can elude
or slight the will of aegis-bearing Zeus,
let this man meet his fate on restless seas.
But there's no way that I can help him leave:
I have no ships at hand, no oars, no crew   160
to carry him across the sea's broad back.
Yet I am fully ready to advise him,
keep nothing hidden from him, so that he
may make his way back to his own land—safely."

Stout Hermes said: "However this may be,
take care to send him off at once. Beware
of Zeus's wrath, lest in the future he
become your unforgiving enemy."

Then sturdy Hermes left. And having heard
the message sent by Zeus, the bright nymph went   170
to generous Odysseus. He was seated
along the shore; his eyes were never dry,
and his sweet life was squandered as he wept
for his dear home; he now took no delight
in her: the nymph no longer pleased his sight.
By night, indeed, within Calypso's cave,
he slept with her: so side by side they lay,
the willing and unwilling. But by day,
his heart was rent by torment as he sat
along the sands or on the rocks; he watched   180
the never-resting sea and, watching, wept.
Standing beside him there, the fair nymph said:

"Unhappy man, don't stay—in tears—with me:
do not destroy your life. Most willingly
I set you free. Come now, with your bronze ax
chop down stout trunks and build a broad-beamed craft.
Let cross-planks serve as sides for those base beams,
to carry you across the fog-dark sea.
Within that hull I'll stow much bread and water
and red wine—you'll not suffer thirst or hunger—   190
and I shall clothe you and provide fair winds
to carry you unharmed to your own land,

if that is what wide heaven's gods demand—
I must give way before their powers and plans."

The patient, bright Odysseus, shuddering,
replied to what he'd heard with these winged words:
"Goddess, I know you've something else in mind—
something beyond my being free to leave—
in urging me to cross the dreadful deep,
the dismal, dour abyss, aboard a craft   200
so makeshift: even quick and agile ships,
blessed with the favoring wind of Zeus, would fail.
I shall not board these fragile planks unless
you, goddess, swear to set aside all thought
of harming me with new, pernicious plots."

He spoke. Calypso, lovely goddess, smiled.
Her hand caressed him. Her reply was this:
"You are indeed astute, not short on wits:
what cunning urged you on to this request?
I call as witnesses the spacious sky   210
and earth and waves of Styx that flow below—
the most exacting, the most awesome oath
the blessed gods can swear—that I forgo
all thought of any future harm to you.
My thoughts, my plans for you, are only such
as I myself might seek were I to be
in your own place: within my breast I keep
no heart of iron—I feel for you, your needs."

That said, the lovely goddess led. He followed
her quick footsteps. Together, man and goddess,   220
they reached the hollow grotto. There he sat
on the same chair that Hermes had just left.
Calypso set before him food and drink
of every sort that suits a mortal's needs.
Then she sat opposite the bright Odysseus.
Her handmaids offered her ambrosia and nectar.
Their fare was ready now. Their hands reached out.
And when their thirst and hunger were appeased,
the lovely goddess was the first to speak:

"Are you, Odysseus, man of many wiles,   230
Laértës' godly son, still keen to leave
straightway? Is it your native land you need,
your dear home? Though you go, I wish you well.
But if your mind were to divine the trials
that fate will have you meet before you reach
your country, you would choose to stay, to keep

this house with me—and live immortally.
This you would do despite your longing for
your wife, for whom you yearn each day. And yet
I'm sure that I am not inferior   240
to her in form or stature: it's not right
for mortal women to contend or vie
with goddesses in loveliness or height."

Odysseus, man of many wiles, replied:
"Great goddess, don't be angered over this.
I'm well aware that you are right: I, too,
know that Penelope, however wise,
cannot compete with you in grace or stature:
she is not more than mortal, whereas you
are deathless, ageless. Even so, each day   250
I hope and hunger for my house: I long
to see the day of my returning home.
If once again, upon the winedark sea,
a god attacks, I shall survive that loss:
the heart within my chest is used to patience.
I've suffered much and labored much in many
ordeals among the waves and in the wars;
to those afflictions I can add one more."
These were his words. The sun sank. Darkness came.
And they, within the hollow of the cave,   260
taking delight in love, together lay.

·   ·   ·   ·   ·   ·   ·   ·   ·   ·   ·

BOOKS 6–8

[After building a raft and leaving Calypso, Odysseus sails the open sea for seventeen
days, at last coming in sight of the island of Scheria, land of the Phaeacians. When Poseidon, returning from Ethiopia, observes his enemy approaching land, the angry god
raises a storm that destroys Odysseus's raft. Washed ashore after nearly drowning, Odysseus is befriended by Nausicaa, daughter of the Phaeacian King Alcinous and his wife
Arete, who takes him to her parents' court. Moved by the bard Demodocus's singing of
the Trojan Horse episode (a brilliant example of the hero's successful cunning), Odysseus reveals his identity and tells the Phaeacians of his fantastic adventures from the
time he left Troy until his final shipwreck.]

BOOK 9

[Odysseus narrates his narrow escape when he and his men were trapped in the cave
of Polyphemus, the cannibalistic Cyclops. He describes his ruse of getting the one-eyed
giant drunk:]

·   ·   ·   ·   ·   ·   ·   ·   ·   ·   ·

"'Cyclops, after your feast of human flesh,
do take and drain this bowl, that you may know

what kind of wine our ship had stowed. For I
was bringing this to you as a libation,
hoping that, moved by mercy, you might help
to send me home. But you are furious—
intolerably mad. And after this,
who'd visit anyone so pitiless?
Why take the way that has no law, no justice?'

"These were my words. He took the bowl. He drained it.   10
The drink delighted him. He asked for more:
'Come now, good fellow, fill it up again.
And do tell me straightway what your name is:
I'll give you, as my guest, a pleasing gift.
Surely the earth, giver of grain, provides
the Cyclops with fine wine, and rain from Zeus
does well our clustered vines. But this is better—
a wine as fragrant as ambrosia and nectar.'

"These were his words. Again I poured dark wine.
Three times I offered it and—stupidly—   20
three times he drank it down. But when it wound
its way around his wits, I said most gently:

"'Cyclops, you ask me for my noted name;
I'll tell it to you if in recompense
you keep your promise and I get that present.
My name is No-one; No-one—so I'm called
by both my mother and my father, and all
my comrades.'

            "This I said. And he replied:
'No-one, your friends come first; I'll eat you last.   30
This is the gift I give to you, my guest.'

"That said, the Cyclops reeled, his hulk collapsed;
he fell upon his back, with his thick neck
aslant; sleep, lord of all, now held him fast.
Up from his gullet, bits of human flesh
and wine were gushing: in his drunken sleep,
he'd vomited. Now it was time to thrust
the stake into heaped cinders: it grew hot.
I spurred on all my men with words of hope,
that none might flinch with fear. And when that stake   40
of olive-wood, though green, was glowing, just
about to blaze, I drew it from the flames.
My men stood round me; into us a god
breathed daring. And they clasped that pointed stake,
then drove the olive-wood into his eye.

I, reaching high, my weight thrown from above,
now whirled that stake around, as one whose bore
drills deep into the timber of a ship,
while those below him twirl it with a thong
they grasp at either end; the drill whirls round 50
and never rests. So did we twirl that hot
point in his eye; around the glowing wood,
blood flowed. And both his eyelids and his brow
were singed by fire as his eyeball burned;
his eye-roots hissed. Even as, when a smith
plunges an ax or adze into cold water,
the metal hisses as he quenches it
to give that iron strength, so did that eye
hiss round the olive stake's sharp tip. His howl
was terrifying; all the rocks rang out. 60
Fear drove us back. The stake, which he tugged out,
was fouled with blood. And—crazed—he threw it far;
and then he shouted to the other Cyclops,
who lived in nearby caves on windswept hilltops.
They heard his call and, coming from all sides,
stood near his cave and asked what was awry:

"'What struck you, Polyphémus? Why do you
disturb the godlike night and spoil our sleep?
What mortal can, against your will, drive off
your flocks or try with treachery or force 70
to kill you?'

        "Polyphémus, from the cave,
replied: 'My friends, no force can damage me;
No-one, No-one is using treachery.'

"They answered: 'If no one is harming you,
and you are all alone, it surely is
some sickness sent by Zeus; you can't elude
that kind of malady. Pray to Poseidon,
your father: he's the one to call upon.'

"That said, they left. And my heart laughed: my name, 80
a perfect snare, had trapped him. Racked by pain,
the Cyclops moaned and groped for that great stone,
then shoved it from the entranceway and sat
with hands outstretched in hope that he might catch
the men who, with the sheep, came from the cave—
he must have thought my wits were dim and slack.
But I was seeking a decisive plan,
a scheme to save both me and all my men:
I wove a web of every guile and wile,

as one will do when life's at stake—so great   90
a menace threatened us. This plot seemed best.
That cave held well-fed rams; and heavy fleece,
dark wool, enfolded those fine, robust beasts.
Now silently I took the twisted withes
of willow, those on which the Cyclops—he
whose heart was set on evil—liked to sleep.
With these I bound the sheep together, three
by three. I tied one comrade fast beneath
the belly of each middle sheep, while two
sheep—one to each side—served to guard my friend.   100
Three sheep for each of them, but I instead
picked out the largest ram. I grabbed his back
and curled beneath his belly. There I grasped
his splendid fleece; faceup, I held it tight.
So, anxiously we waited for firstlight.

"As soon as Dawn's rose fingers touched the sky,
he drove the he-goats and the rams outside
to pasture. In the fold, the unmilked dams,
their udders bursting, bleated. Although racked
by pain, their master now felt out the backs   110
of all the beasts that stood before him, but
that fool did not suspect that all my men
were hid beneath the bellies of the rams.
The last to leave the cave was my great ram,
bearing the weight of his own fleece and me—
with my thick plots. Huge Polyphémus probed
and felt about his back. And then he asked:

"'Dear ram, why are you last to leave this cave?
You never lagged behind the other sheep;
you always were the very first to leave,   120
always the first to hurry out to feed,
to pasture on the tender grass, to leap
with long strides toward the riverside, to seek
the fold with longing when the sun had set.
But now you are the last to go. I'm sure
that you are grieving for your master's eye;
a coward and his crew first dimmed my mind
with their damned wine. That done, they left me blind.
I don't think death has caught that No-one yet.
Would you could think and speak and tell me where   130
he's hiding from my fury! I would dash
his brains across this cave: to smash him so
would free me from this No-one pest, these woes.'

"That said, he sent the ram out. When we'd gone
a brief way past the cave and outer pens,

I left the belly of the ram to set
my comrades free. That done, we quickly drove
the fat sheep with long shanks until we reached
our ship; and we turned round again, again,
to see if he was after us. And though   140
our comrades welcomed our escape from death,
they wept for those of us who now were lost.
But I restrained their tears; my frown forbade
such open grief. For now we had to speed—
to board the many sheep with their rich fleece,
then sail the salty sea. They rushed aboard;
each rower manned his place along the thwarts,
and then they struck the gray sea with their oars.
But when we'd gone as far as shouting distance,
I bellowed these sharp words to Polyphémus: 150

"'Cyclops, the men you snatched with brutal force
and ate within your cave were surely not
the comrades of a coward. You have caused
much grief; and it returns to haunt you now:
you did not hesitate; hard heart, you ate
your guests within your house; therefore lord Zeus
has joined with other gods to batter you.'

"My words incensed him more. He ripped the top
of a huge peak, then hurled a chunk at us;
that mass fell just beyond our ship's dark prow.   160
The sea surged as the mass dropped; and the wash
thrust our ship backward, closer to the coast.
But grabbing a long pole, I pushed us off
and signaled with my head: I spurred my men
to fall hard on the oars, to fend against
shipwreck; and they rowed hard—they strained, they bent.
When we were twice as distant as we'd been,
I shouted to the Cyclops, though my men
on all sides curbed me with these cautious words:

"'Why must you goad that savage so? Just now,   170
the mass that monster cast into the sea
drove back our ship to shore: we thought we'd reached
our end. And if he'd heard us breathe or speak
even the slightest word, he would have hurled
one more rough rock and smashed our heads and hull.
That brute has force to spare: he can throw far.'

"These were their words. But my firm heart was not
convinced. Again my anger had to taunt:
'Cyclops, if any mortal man should ask
about the shameful blinding of your eye,   180

then tell him that the man who gouged you was
Odysseus, ravager of cities: one
who lives in Ithaca—Laértës' son.'

"I spoke. As he replied, he groaned and sighed:
'I hear again an ancient prophecy.
An augur once lived here, a man most worthy,
excelling all in seeing what would come,
a seer grown old among us: Télemus,
great son of Eurymus. What he foretold
is now fulfilled. He said that I would be   190
a victim of Odysseus: he would blind me.
But I was always watching out for one
handsome and grand, a formidable man;
instead, one small and insignificant,
a weakling, now has gouged my eye—he won
his way by overcoming me with wine.
But come, Odysseus, you'll receive the gift
I owe to you, my guest; and I'll convince
the great earth-shaker to escort your ship;
I am his son—he says he is my father.   200
He is the one to heal me, if he would:
no other can—no blessed god, no man.'

"These were his words. And I replied: 'Would I
might just as surely rob you of your life
and breath and hurl you down to Hades' house,
as I am sure that even great Poseidon
will never give you back the eye you lost.'

"These were my words. He prayed to lord Poseidon,
lifting his hands up to the starry heaven:
'Listen, Poseidon, dark-haired lord who clasps   210
the earth hard fast, if I'm indeed your son
and you declare yourself my father, then
don't let this ravager of towns, Odysseus,
Laértës' son, who lives in Ithaca,
return to his own land. But if his fate
must have him see his dear ones once again
and reach his sturdy home, his native land,
then let him struggle back—a battered man,
with all his comrades lost, and on a ship
of strangers. In his house, let him meet grief.'   220

"His prayer was done. The dark-haired god took heed.
Again the Cyclops lifted up a stone,
even more staggering than the one he'd thrown
before. He whirled it round; and when he hurled,

fierce force was in that toss. The stone fell just
behind our dark-prowed ship: it barely missed
the steering oar. And as that rough rock fell,
the sea surged high astern—but that wave helped:
its thrust drove our ship toward the island's shore.

"There, on that isle, our other sturdy ships 230
awaited us; our sighing shipmates sat,
in fear. We beached our boat along the sands,
then disembarked. Out of the hollow hull
we took the Cyclops' flocks, dividing all
in equal shares: what each received was just.
One sheep alone—my ram—was set apart;
my well-greaved crew assigned that gift to me.
Along the sands I sacrificed that ram
to Cronos' son, who gathers thunderclouds,
Zeus, lord of all; for him I roasted thighs. 240
But he did not accept that sacrifice:
instead his mind was set—he meant to wreck
all of my sturdy ships and faithful friends.

. . . .

BOOK 10

[In telling his story to the Phaeacians, Odysseus makes clear that he—unlike his men—had learned from the Cyclops episode. Thus, he explains, when his small fleet approached the unknown land of the Laestrygonians to gather needed supplies, Odysseus took the precaution of anchoring his ship a safe distance from shore. Before learning anything about the local inhabitants' treatment of strangers, however, Odysseus's crewmen unwisely moored their ships along the Laestrygonian shore:]

. . . .

"We'd reached the famous harbor. On two sides,
we saw the steep rock walls with their sheer rise;
the narrow entranceway was flanked by two
long juts of land. Within that curving cove,
my comrades moored their shapely ships close by
each other: there no wave is ever vexed,
not surging or receding—a bright calm.

"But I held back and moored outside. I tied
my cable to a rock; my black ship stood
beyond one headland's edge. And then I climbed 10
a rugged slope; I stood at that lookout;
I saw no oxen's furrows and no men—
just puffs of smoke that rose up from the land.
I chose two comrades and a third as herald,
and then I sent those shipmates out to see

what sort of men—bread eaters—held this land.
They disembarked and took a well-tried way
that wagons used for bringing wood to town
down from the mountains. Just outside the town,
they met a stalwart girl beside a spring: 20
she was the daughter of Antíphatës
the Laestrygónian. The spring where she
was drawing limpid water was Artácia—
a well that served the Laestrygónians.
My men drew near; they asked what king ruled here
and who were those he ruled. She pointed out
her father's high-roofed house. When they went in,
they found his wife; but she stood mountain-high,
and they were horrified. At once she called
for firm Antíphatës; she brought him back   30
from the assembly place. But all he planned
was sad death for my men. He did not wait:
he grabbed one of my crew and swallowed him;
the other two were able to escape—
they reached our ships. But now it was too late:
the loud alarm had sounded; from all sides
stout Laestrygónians, a countless crowd,
rushed out—and they were not like men but Giants.
The boulders that they hurled down from the cliffs
were huge—the size a man could scarcely lift.   40
The clamor from the ships was sinister,
the sound of dying men and shattered decks;
they speared my comrades, carried them like fish—
an obscene meal.

         "While they were slaughtering
my crews in the deep harbor, I drew out
the sharp blade from beside my thigh: I cut
the cables of my dark-prowed ship. I spurred
my men to hurry to their oars: their heart
and haste were needed to escape this trap;   50
the fear of death pressed all to row as one.
With luck I reached the open sea, far from
the sheer cliffs. But the other ships were lost.

"We sailed away—hearts sick and sad—set free
at last, but with our dear companions dead.
We reached Aeǽa, isle of fair-haired Círcë,
the awesome goddess with a human voice,
twin sister of the sinister Aeétës:
they both were born of Hélios—who brought
his light to men—and Pérsë, Ocean's daughter.   60
In silence we put in to shore; the harbor

seemed safe; some gracious god had been our guide.
We stayed two days, two nights—fatigued and tired.

"But when, with fair-haired Dawn, the third day came,
with spear and sharpened sword in hand I climbed
up from the ship. I reached a rise from which
I hoped to see the signs of human work
and hear the sounds of men. And as I stood
upon that lookout point, up from wide fields
and through the forest and the underbrush,   70
smoke rose: it came from Círcë's house. The sight
of that black smoke inclined my heart and mind
to seek the source. But as I thought again,
another plan seemed best: I'd first go back
to my swift ship along the shore, find food
to feed my men, and then have them explore.

"But when I had already neared my ship,
some god took pity on my loneliness:
across my path he sent a tall-horned stag.
Down from his pasture in the forest, he—   80
responding to the sun's oppressive fury—
was heading to the riverbank to drink.
When he had quit the stream, I struck his back;
and right through his mid-spine, my bronze shaft passed.
He moaned; he fell into the dust; his life
took flight. I straddled him and tugged the shaft
out from the wound, then left it on the ground
and gathered lengths of brush and willow withes
to weave a rope two arm's-lengths long, twisted
from end to end. I tied that huge beast's feet   90
and slung him round my neck, then, trudging, leaned
my weight upon the spear that I'd retrieved.
That way I brought him back to the black ship:
one hand across one shoulder never could
have carried him—that stag was so immense.
I threw him down in front of our lithe ship
and gently urged my comrades, one by one:

"'O friends, however sad, let's not descend
to Hades' hall before our destined day.
No, just as long as there is food and drink   100
in our swift ship, forget your fears of starving.'

"These were my words. My men did not delay.
They'd hid their heads with cloaks in their despair,
but now they threw those wrappings off and stared:
they saw the stag along the shore: indeed

that beast was huge. And with their eyes appeased,
they washed their hands and readied the fine feast.

. . . .

**[Odysseus continues his narration: because of the Laestrygonians' savage assault, the
fleet that Odysseus commanded after leaving Troy was reduced to a single ship, which
had put ashore on Circe's enchanted island. A powerful sorceress, Circe changed a group
of Odysseus's unwary men into swine. Forewarned by Hermes, Zeus's Olympian messenger, Odysseus first threatened Circe with his sword, forcing her to return his men
to human shape. He then became her lover, benefiting greatly from Circe's extensive
knowledge and wise advice:]**

"As soon as Dawn's rose fingers touched the sky,
I called my crew together, and I said:
'Despite your long ordeal, do hear me out: 110
my friends, we've lost all sense of where we are;
this island may lie east, it may lie west—
where sun, which brings men light, sinks to its rest
or where it's born again. Let's try at once
to see if we can find some better course.
I doubt it, for I climbed a rugged lookout:
we're on an island that is ringed about
by endless seas; so crowned, the isle lies low,
and at its center I saw curling smoke
that rose up through the forest and thick brush.'   120

"My words were done. And their dear hearts were torn,
recalling the fierce Laestrygónian,
Antíphatës, and the man-eating Cyclops.
Their groans were loud, their tears were many—yet
nothing was gained by weeping. So I split
my well-greaved men into two squads: each band
had its own chief. I headed one; the second
was led by the godlike Eurýlochus.
Within a casque of bronze we mixed our lots
to see who would go off and spy the land.   130
The choice fell on the firm Eurýlochus.
And he went off with two-and-twenty men;
both they who left and we who stayed then wept.

"Within a forest glen, they found the home
of Círcë: it was built of polished stone
and lay within a clearing. Round it roamed
the mountain wolves and lions she'd bewitched
with evil drugs. But they did not attack
my men; they circled them; their long tails wagged.
And just as dogs will fawn about their master   140
when he returns from feasts—they know that he
will offer them choice bits—just so, did these

lions and sharp-clawed wolves fawn on my men.
And yet those tough beasts terrified my friends.
They halted at the fair-haired Círcë's door;
within they heard the goddess' sweet voice sing
as she moved back and forth before her web—
imperishable, flawless, subtly-woven—
such work as only goddesses can fashion.

"Polítës, sturdy captain, the most dear   150
and trusted of my men, now told his friends:
'Someone inside is singing gracefully
as she weaves her great web. And what she sings
echoes throughout the house. Let's call to her.'

"These were his words. They did what he had asked.
She came at once. She opened her bright doors,
inviting them within; and—fools—they followed.
Eurýlochus alone did not go in;
he had foreseen some snare. She led the way
and seated them on chairs and high-backed thrones.   160
She mixed cheese, barley meal, and yellow honey
with wine from Prámnos; and she then combined
malign drugs in that dish so they'd forget
all thoughts of their own homes. When they had drunk,
she struck them with her wand, then drove them off
to pen them in her sties. They'd taken on
the bodies—bristles, snouts—and grunts of hogs,
yet kept the human minds they had before.
So they were penned, in tears; and Círcë cast
before them acorns, dogwood berries, mast—   170
food fit for swine who wallow on the ground.

"Meanwhile Eurýlochus rushed back to us
to let us know our comrades' shameful fate.
But he was speechless; though he longed for words,
his heart was struck with pain, tears filled his eyes;
nothing but lamentation filled his mind.
But when we—baffled—questioned him, at last
he told us what had happened to our friends:

"'Odysseus, we did follow your commands:
we crossed the underbrush and reached the glen.   180
We found a sheltered house with smooth stone walls.
And there, intent on her great web, a goddess
or woman could be heard distinctly singing.
My comrades called to her; she opened wide
the gleaming doors, inviting them to enter.
They, unsuspecting, trailed along. But I

held back; I felt this was a trap. They dropped
from sight together. Though I kept close watch—
I waited long—no comrade reappeared.'

"These were his words. Across my back I cast   190
my massive sword of bronze with silver studs,
and then I slung my bow; I ordered him
to lead me back along the path he'd taken.
But he, his arms about my knees, implored:

"'May you, whom Zeus has nurtured, leave me here;
don't force me to retrace my path. I know
that you will not return and not bring back
our men. With those we have let's sail away,
for we may still escape the evil day.'

"These were his words. I was compelled to say: 200
'Eurýlochus, you can stay here and eat
and drink beside the hollow black ship; I
must go, however; I cannot forgo
a task so necessary—this I owe.'

"That said, I left the sea and ship behind.
But after I had crossed the sacred glades
and was about to reach the halls of Círcë,
the connoisseur of potions, I saw Hermes,
who bears the golden wand, approaching me.
He'd taken on the likeness of a youth   210
just come of age, blessed with a young man's grace.
He clasped my hands. These were his words to me:

"'Where are you wandering still, unlucky man,
alone along these slopes and ignorant
of this strange land? Círcë has locked your friends
like swine behind the tight fence of her pens.
And have you come to free them? On your own,
be sure, you never will return; you'll stay
together with the others in her sties.
But come, I'll save you from her snares, I'll thwart   220
her plans. Now, when you enter Círcë's halls,
don't leave behind this tutelary herb.
I'll tell you all her fatal stratagems:
She'll mix a potion for you; she'll add drugs
into that drink; but even with their force,
she can't bewitch you; for the noble herb
I'll give you now will baffle all her plots.
When Círcë touches you with her long wand,
draw out the sharp sword at your thigh, and head

for her as if you meant to strike her dead.   230
Shrinking, she'll ask you then to share her bed.
And do not, then or later, turn her down,
for she will free your friends and be of help
to you, her guest. But first force her to swear
the blessed gods' great, massive oath: She must
forgo all thought of any other plots—
when you are stripped and naked, she must not
deceive you, leave you feeble, impotent.'

"When that was said, he gave his herb to me;
he plucked it from the ground and showed what sort   240
of plant it was. Its root was black; its flower
was white as milk. It's *moly* for the gods;
for mortal men, the mandrake—very hard
to pluck; but nothing holds against the gods.

"Then Hermes crossed the wooded isle and left
for steep Olympus. And I took the path
to Círcë's house—most anxious as I went.
I stopped before the fair-haired goddess' door;
I halted, called aloud; she heard my voice.
At once she opened her bright doors and then   250
invited me to follow her. I went
with troubled heart. She led me to a chair,
robust and handsome, graced with silver studs;
a footrest stood below. And she poured out
an ample drink into a golden bowl.
With her conniving mind, she mixed her drugs
within that bowl, then offered it to me.
I drank it down. But I was not bewitched.
She struck me with her long wand. Then she said:
'Now to the sty, to wallow with your friends!'   260

"At that, out from its sheath along my thigh,
I drew my sword as if to have her die.
She howled. She clasped my knees and, as she wept,
with these winged words, made her appeal to me:

"'Who are you? From what family? What city?
You drank my drugs, but you were not entranced.
No other man has ever passed that test;
for once that potion's passed their teeth, the rest
have fallen prey: you have within your chest
a heart that can defeat my sorcery.   270
You surely are the man of many wiles,
Odysseus, he whom I was warned against
by Hermes of the golden wand: he said

that you would come from Troy in a black ship.
But now put back your blade within that sheath
and let us lie together on my bed:
in loving, we'll learn trust and confidence.'

"These were her words. And this was my reply:
'Círcë, how can you ask for tenderness,
you who have turned my comrades into swine   280
and now, insidiously, try to bind
me, too—for once I'm naked on your bed,
you'll snare me, leave me weak and impotent?
I will not share your bed unless you swear
the mighty oath, o goddess—to insure
that you'll forgo all thoughts of further plots.'

"These were my words. As I had asked, she swore
at once. And after that great oath was pledged,
I then climbed onto Círcë's lovely bed.

"Meanwhile four girls were busy in the halls;   290
these maids were once dear daughters of the woods
and springs and seaward-flowing sacred streams.
Across the high-backed chairs, one handmaid first
draped linen cloth and then threw purple rugs.
The second drew up silver tables set
with golden baskets, while the third maid mixed
smooth honeyed wine in silver bowls and brought
fair golden cups. The fourth maid filled a tripod
with water and, beneath it, lit a fire;
and when it bubbled in the glowing bronze   300
caldron, she set me down inside a tub.
Over my head and shoulders she poured water—
gradually tempering its heat—
to free my limbs and soul from long fatigue.
And when that maid had bathed and, with rich oil,
had smoothed my body and about me cast
a tunic and a handsome cloak, she led
the way and sat me on a high-backed chair,
robust and handsome, graced with silver studs;
a footrest stood below. A servant brought   310
a lovely golden jug from which she poured
fresh water out into a silver bowl,
so I might wash my hands; then at my side
she placed a polished table. The old housewife
was generous; she drew on lavish stores,
inviting me to eat. But I was not
inclined to feed my frame: I sat and thought
of other things; my soul foresaw the worst.

Círcë, who saw me seated there denying
all food and filled with dark despair, drew near.   320
And, at my side, she called on these winged words:

"'Odysseus, do not sit there like some mute,
with tattered heart, not touching drink or food.
Do you suspect another trap? Forget
your fears. I swore the strongest oath there is.'

"These were her words. And this was my reply:
'Círcë, what man with justice in his mind
would think of food and drink before he freed
his comrades and could see them with his eyes?
If you indeed would have me drink and eat,   330
release my men: bring back my faithful friends.'

"These were my words. And Círcë—wand in hand—
now left the hall and, opening the pens,
drove out my men; they had the shape of fat
nine-year-old hogs. They faced her. She drew close.
Upon the flesh of each of them, she spread
another herb. At that, their bodies shed
the bristles that had grown when they'd gulped down
the deadly brew she'd offered them at first.
Now they were men again—and younger than   340
they were before, more handsome and more grand.
They knew me quickly; each man clasped my hand.
Their cries of joy were long and loud; throughout
the house a clamor rose. And Círcë, too,
was moved. Then she—the lovely goddess—urged:

"'Odysseus, man of many wiles, divine
son of Laértës, go to your swift ship
along the shore and beach it on dry land.
First store your goods and all your gear in caves,
but then return with all your faithful friends.'   350

"These were her words. My proud soul was convinced:
I hurried to the shore and my swift ship.
And there I found my faithful crew in tears.
Even as calves upon a farm are glad
when cows return from pasture, having had
their fill of grass, and come back to their stalls;
and all the calves frisk round unchecked; no pen
can hold them as they race around their dams,
lowing again, again—so did my men,
when they caught sight of me, weep tears of joy: 360
they felt as if they'd touched their native land,

their rugged Ithaca, where they were bred
and born. In tears, they uttered these winged words:

"'You, whom Zeus nurtured, have come back; for us
this joy is like the joy that would erupt
on our return to Ithaca, our home.
But tell us now the fate of all the rest.'"

"These were their words. I quietly replied:
'Come, let us beach our ship along dry land
and stow our goods and all our gear in caves.   370
Then, all of you be quick to follow me;
in Círcë's sacred halls you soon will see
your comrades eating, drinking; they can count
on never-ending stores.'

                    "My words were done.
At once they answered my commands. But one—
Eurýlochus—did try to check their course:

"'My sorry friends, where are we heading now?
Why court catastrophe in Círcë's house?
She'll turn us into lions, wolves, or hogs—   380
and we'll be forced to guard her massive halls.
So did the Cyclops catch and trap our friends—
then, too, the rash Odysseus was with them.
They, too, died through the madness of this man.'

"I heard his words. I had a mind to draw
the sharp blade sheathed beside my sturdy thigh.
I'd have sliced off his head and flung it down
upon the ground—although Eurýlochus
was kin of mine by marriage. But my men   390
drew near and checked me with these gentle words:

"'If you—one sprung from Zeus—prefer it so,
he can stay here and watch the ship. We'll go
with you: lead us to Círcë's sacred house.'

"That said, they left the ship and shore behind.
Eurýlochus came, too. He did not stay:
my rage was ominous—he was afraid.

"Meanwhile, with kindness, Círcë, in her halls,
cared for my other men: she bathed them all,
and then she smoothed their skins with gleaming oil
and wrapped them in fine tunics and soft cloaks.   400
We found them feasting on abundant stores.

But when they all had recognized each other,
their tears and wails were loud throughout the halls.
Bright Círcë, standing at my side, advised:

"'Odysseus, man of many wiles, divine
son of Laértës, do not urge more tears.
I know indeed the many miseries
you have endured upon the fish-rich sea
and how, on land, you faced fierce enemies.
But eat this food and drink this wine—and find   410
the force you had when you first left behind
your homeland, rugged Ithaca. Your minds
can only think of bitter wanderings;
you're worn and weary, without joy or ease;
you've lived too long—too much—with grinding griefs.'

"These were her words. And our proud hearts agreed.
Day after day we stayed for one whole year:
we ate much meat; the wine was honey-sweet.

"But when the months that fill a year had passed,
and seasons had revolved, and once again   420
the long days reached their end, my comrades said:

"'Wake from your trance, remember your own land,
if fate is yet to save you, if you can
still reach your high-walled house, your native isle.'

"These were their words. And my proud heart agreed.
Through all that day we sat, until sunset:
the meat was fine; the wine was honey-sweet.
But once the sun had gone and darkness won,
within the shadowed halls, my comrades slept.

"And I went off to Círcë's splendid bed.   430
I clasped her knees. She heard as I beseeched:
'Círcë, fulfill the promise made to me:
do let me leave for home. My men entreat,
and my own heart wants that. Whenever you
are out of hearing, all my men implore
again, again: they long to leave these shores.'

"The lovely goddess gave this quick reply:
'Odysseus, man of many wiles, divine
son of Laértës, do not spend more time
within my house if you will otherwise.   440
But you cannot reach home till you complete
another journey—to the house of Hades

and fierce Perséphonë. There you must seek
the soul of that blind seer, Tirésias
the Theban: he alone among the dead
preserves his wits and sober sense: this gift
Perséphonë has granted just to him,
for all the other dead are wandering shades.'

"My heart was broken as I heard her words.
Seated upon that bed, I cried: my soul   450
had lost its will to live, to see the light.
But when my need to weep and writhe was done,
these were the words with which I answered her:

"'Círcë, who'll serve as pilot on that way?
No man has ever sailed in his black ship
to Hades' halls.'

                "And her reply was quick:
'Odysseus, man of many wiles, divine
son of Laértës, there's no need to fret
about a helmsman. After you have stepped   460
the mast and spread your white sail, you can sit:
the breath of Bórëas will guide your ship.
But when you've crossed the Ocean, you will see
the shore and forests of Perséphonë—
the towering poplars and the willow trees
whose fruits fall prematurely. Beach your ship
on that flat shore which lies on the abyss
of Ocean. Make your way on foot to Hades.
In those dank halls, the Pýriphlégethon
together with a branch of Styx, Cocýtus—   470
two roaring rivers—form one course and join
the Ácheron. Just there you'll find a rock.
Draw near that spot and, as I tell you, dig
a squared-off ditch—along each side, one cubit.
Three times pour offerings around that pit
for all the dead: pour milk and honey first,
then pour sweet wine; let water be the third.
And scatter over these white barley meal.
Then give the helpless dead your fervent pledge
that, when you come to Ithaca, you'll offer   480
as sacrifice your finest barren heifer
and heap her pyre high with handsome gifts.
But to Tirésias alone pledge this:
the finest jet black ram that you possess.
And after you have called upon the famed
tribes of the dead, do sacrifice a ram
and black ewe: bend their heads toward Érebus,

but you must turn toward Ocean's streams. That done,
so many souls of men now dead will come.
For them, command your crew to flay and burn 490
the slaughtered sheep, throats slit by ruthless bronze;
and pray unto the gods, to mighty Hades
and fierce Perséphonë. Draw your sharp sword
out from the sheath that lies along your thigh:
keep close watch on the blood of sacrifice,
lest any of the helpless dead draw near
that pit before you meet Tirésias.
Soon he, the seer, leader of men, will come
to tell you what will be your path, how long
your homeward journey is to take, and how 500
you'll make your way across the fish-rich sea.'

"So Círcë said. Upon the throne of gold,
Dawn came straightway. The goddess Círcë clothed
my frame in cloak and tunic; she herself
put on a long and gleaming, gracious robe
of subtly-woven threads. She bound a belt
of gold around her waist; she veiled her head.
And I went through the house; with gentle words
I spurred my comrades, one by one. I urged:
'You've had enough sweet sleep. It's time to go. 510
Great Círcë told me all that we must know.'

"These were my words. And their proud hearts agreed.
But I was not to lead all of my men
away from Círcë's isle. One of my band,
our youngest man, Elpénor—not too brave
nor too alert—had lain alone, stretched out
along the roof of Círcë's house to find
some cooler air: he'd taken too much wine.
Then, when he heard the noise of our departure,
he jumped up suddenly, and so—forgetting 520
the long way down by ladder—off the roof
headfirst he fell. And from his spine, his neck
was broken off; his spirit went to Hades.

"But I, to those who followed me, now said:
'Though you may think that you are going home,
back to your own dear land, another road
is ours, for Círcë said we first must see
the halls of Hades and Perséphonë;
there we must meet Tirésias of Thebes.'

"My words broke their dear hearts. They sat and wept; 530
they tore their hair; but all of that lament

gained nothing for us. Still in tears, we went
back to the shore; alongside our black ship,
Círcë had tied a ram and jet black ewe,
but none of us had seen her go or come;
she passed us by so easily. How can
a man detect a god who comes and goes
if gods refuse to have their movements known?"

BOOK 11

[Odysseus's account to the Phaeacians continues: following Circe's directions, Odysseus sailed westward across the River of Ocean to the dim entrance of Hades's realm. After Odysseus performed ritual animal sacrifices evoking the forces of the Underworld, shadowy forms began to appear to drink the blood that temporarily revived them enough to communicate with the living. The first to speak was Elpenor, who requested that his body be properly buried in order for his shade to find posthumous rest:]

. . . .

And after I'd implored with vows and prayers
the tribes of those dead souls, I seized the sheep
and slit their throats above the pit; cloud-dark
blood ran. From Érebus there came a crowd
of dead souls: girls, young bachelors, and old men
much tried by grief, and tender brides still new
to sorrow. Many fighting-men came, too;
they'd died in battle, pierced by bronze-tipped spears;
and they still wore their bloodstained battle gear.
These crowded round the pit upon all sides;   10
they uttered strange outcries. I paled with fear.
At that, I spurred my men to flay and roast
the sheep we'd sacrificed, whose throats I'd cut
with ruthless bronze; and we prayed to the gods,
to Hades' force and fierce Perséphonë.
With my sharp sword again unsheathed, I watched
over the pit of sacrificial blood,
lest any of the fragile dead draw near
that blood before I met Tirésias.

"The first dead soul to come was young Elpénor,   20
my comrade: one who'd yet to find a grave
beneath the earth's wide ways; we'd left his corpse
unwept, unburied, there in Círcë's house;
we had another task—and hurried off.
The sight of him provoked my tears and pity;
and when I spoke to him, my words were winged:
'Elpénor, you on foot were faster than
my ship. How did you reach this shadowed land?'

"These were my words; this was his sad reply:
'Odysseus, man of many wiles, divine   30

son of Laértës, my undoing lay
in some god sending down my dismal fate
and in too much sweet wine. I lay stretched out
on Círcë's roof; too stupefied to think
of taking the long ladder down, I fell
headfirst, down to the ground. My neck was cracked,
split from my spine; my spirit went to Hades.
Now I beseech you in the name of those
you left behind, the absent ones: your wife
and he who reared you when you were a child,   40
your father, and Telémachus, the son
you left alone at home. I know that you,
on leaving Hades' halls, will find landfall
with your stout ship at the Aeǽan isle.
There, lord, I ask you to remember me.
Do not abandon me, unwept, unburied,
lest you provoke the anger of the gods.
Burn me and any armor that is mine,
and on the shore of the gray sea, heap high
a mound for this unhappy man. Do this   50
for me, and set upon that mound the oar
I used when I, alive, rowed with my friends.'

"And then the shade of my dead mother came:
she, Anticlēia, child of generous
Autólycus, had been alive when I
had left for holy Ílion. I wept—
that sight had touched my soul with pity—yet,
even within my grief, I did not let
my mother's spirit near the blood before
Tirésias had heard all I would ask.   60

"Theban Tirésias came next. He grasped
his golden staff. He knew me, and he said:
'Odysseus, man of many wiles, divine
son of Laértës, why have you, sad man,
abandoning the sunlight, cared to come
to see the dead and this dejected realm?
But now it's time to stand aside: leave free
the pit and sheathe your sharpened blade, that I
may taste this blood and tell you words of truth.'

"He spoke. I sheathed my silver-studded sword.   70
As soon as he had tasted that dark blood,
the prince of prophets offered me these words:

"'You, bright Odysseus, seek a honey-sweet
homecoming, but a god will make it harsh.

I do not think you can elude the lord
who makes earth tremble, for his heart has stored
much fury since you blinded his dear son.
But even so—though sadly tried—you can
return to your own home if you would check
your will and your dear comrades' once you've left   80
behind the violet sea and your stout ship
has touched Thrinácia, the island where
you'll find the grazing cattle, splendid flocks
of Hélios, who sees and hears all things.
If you leave his rich herds untouched and turn
your mind to going home, then you can still
reach Ithaca, though after grim ordeals.
And even if your solitary self
escapes, your coming home will be delayed
and sad: with all your comrades lost, you'll make   90
that journey on a ship that's not your own;
and in your house you will meet griefs, a pack
of overbearing men, who would devour
your goods; they woo your godlike wife with gifts.
But you, returned, will crush their impudence;
and when, within your halls, you've killed them all
either through guile or else in open war
with your sharp bronze, then take a shapely oar
and visit many cities till you reach
a land where men know nothing of the sea   100
and don't use salt to season what they eat;
they're ignorant of boats with purple cheeks
and shapely oars that are the wings of ships.
I give you this clear sign—it can't be missed.
When, on the road, you come upon a man
who calls the oar you carry on your back
a fan for winnowing, you can be sure:
that place is where you are to plant your oar.
That done, present Poseidon with fine gifts:
a ram, a bull, a boar that mates with sows.   110
Then, once you have returned to Ithaca,
take care to offer holy hecatombs
to the undying gods, wide heaven's lords—
to each in turn. You will not die at sea:
the death that reaches you will be serene.
You will grow old—a man of wealth and ease—
surrounded by a people rich, at peace.
All I have said will surely come to be.'

"These were his words, and this was my reply:
'Tirésias, gods wove this destiny.   120
But tell me one thing—tell me honestly.

I see the soul of my dear mother; she
sits near the pit of blood, but does not speak
to her own son, nor does she look at me.
How can I let her know that I am he?'

"These were my words; this was his quick reply:
'The answer's easy; set it in your mind.
Those whom you let approach the pit of blood
will speak the truth to you, and those dead souls
whom you refuse will surely move away.'   130

"That said, the soul of lord Tirésias,
now he had given me his prophecy,
went back to Hades' halls. But I sat still
until my mother came to drink the blood
dark as a cloud. And she knew who I was
at once; I saw her tears, heard her winged words:

"'Son, how have you, despite the mist and fog,
come here alive? The living find it hard
to reach this realm: it lies so far beyond
great rivers and dread deeps and, most of all,   140
the Ocean none can cross on foot; it takes
stout ships to face that journey. Have you come
with ship and comrades, after wandering long,
from Troy? Have you been back to Ithaca?
And have you seen your wife within your halls?'

"These were her words, and this was my reply:
'Mother, it is necessity that brought me
to Hades' house, to hear the prophecy
the spirit of Tirésias the Theban
would offer me. I've yet to near the shore   150
of dear Achǽa; I've not touched our isle.
I've wandered without joy, in deep dejection,
from that day when, behind bright Agamemnon,
I left for Ílion, where fine foals graze,
to fight against the Trojans. But I need
to hear one thing—and tell me honestly:
How did fierce death defeat you? With long sickness?
Or did the archer-goddess Ártemis,
whose arrows are more gentle, find the mark?
Tell me about my father and the son   160
I left in Ithaca. Are they still seen
as kin of one who's king? Or does another
possess my scepter now, since many say
that I will not return? Reveal to me
the mind and intent of the wife I wed.

Does she stand by my son and keep all things
just as they've always been? Or was she taken
as wife by some illustrious Achæan?'

"My honored mother answered me at once:
'Indeed steadfast, within your house she stays.   170
Her dreary nights and days are wept away.
No one's usurped your kingship; and your lands
are held in peace by your Telémachus.
As suits a guardian of justice, he
shares in his people's festive gatherings:
men want his counsel; he's a precious guest.
Your father keeps to his own farm; he never
comes down into the town. To ease his rest
he has no bed, no cloak, and no bright blankets;
he sleeps, in winter, where the servants sleep,   180
in ashes by the fire; his clothes are ragged.
But when the summer and rich autumn come,
then all about the slopes of his vineyards
lie heaps of scattered fallen leaves; and there
he lies in sorrow, tending his great grief;
over your fate he weeps. A harsh old age
has overtaken him. So, too, my fate
was sadness, and my last years bore that weight.
The expert archer-goddess' gentle shafts
did not strike me within my house; no sickness   190
mined me, the sort that often saps life's force,
that wears away the body hatefully;
it was lament for you—your gentleness
and wisdom—o my radiant Odysseus—
that robbed me of the honey-sweet of life.'

"She'd spoken. And despite my doubts, I longed
to clasp my mother's shade within my arms.
Three times—my heart kept urging me—I tried;
and three times she escaped my hands, much like
a shadow or a dream. The pain grew sharp   200
and sharper in my heart. My winged words said:

"'Dear mother, why do you shrink back when I
want so to hold you fast? Can't we embrace
and, with our arms around each other, take
our fill of this chill grief in Hades' house?
Or are you just a phantom sent to me
by great Perséphonë, that she might add
still other tears to those that I have shed?'

"That said, my honored mother answered quickly:
'Poor child, most tried of men, Perséphonë,   210

daughter of Zeus, is not deceiving you
in any way: this is the law that rules
all mortals at their death. For just as soon
as life has left the white bones, and the sinews
no longer hold together bones and flesh,
when the erupting force of blazing fire
undoes the body, then the spirit wanders:
much like a dream, it flits away and hovers,
now here, now there. But hurry back to light;
and may your mind remember my reply,   220
so that you can reveal it to your wife.'

. . . .

[The shade of Agamemnon appears:]

[T]he saddened soul of Agamemnon, son
of Átreus, came forward. And a crowd
surrounded him: within Aegísthus' halls
these men had died alongside Agamemnon.
As soon as he caught sight of me, he knew
just who I was. His moan was loud, his tears
were many; he stretched out his arms; he longed
to hold me fast, but all his force was gone;
the power of his agile limbs was lost.   230
I looked, I wept, and pity filled my heart.
And when I spoke, I offered these winged words:

"'O Agamemnon, Átreus' famed son,
how did dour death defeat so great a captain?
Was it Poseidon, hurling his harsh storms
against your ships, who finally won out?
Or did you die on land, when fighting-men
destroyed you as you raided herds and flocks
or tried to win their women and their town?'

"These were my words. This was his quick reply: 240
'Odysseus, man of many wiles, divine
son of Laértës, I was not undone
by lord Poseidon: none of his harsh storms
attacked my ships. Nor did I meet my end
on land, struck down by fighting-men. My fate
was readied by Aegísthus with the aid
of my conniving wife: inviting me
to feast within his halls, he butchered me
just as one kills an ox within a stall.
And so the death I died was mean and small: 250
around me, without let, they killed us all
as, in the house of one with power and wealth,
for wedding feasts or banquets jointly set

or revels, servants slaughter white-tusked hogs.
You surely have set eyes on many men
destroyed in single combat or the clash
of frenzied ranks, but you'd have been still more
distraught if you had seen, in that great hall,
our bodies round the wine bowl and the food
heaped high; our warm blood streamed across the floor.   260
I heard Cassandra, Priam's daughter, wail
even as—clinging to me—she was killed
by Clytemnéstra, mistress of dark guile.
Face down, along the ground, my chest pierced through,
lifting my fists, dying, I beat the earth,
and my bitch-wife moved off. She had no heart:
I left for Hades, but she did not shut
my eyes nor did she move to close my mouth.
Nothing is more obscene, more bestial, than
a woman's mind when it is all intent   270
on dregs—the filth my wife concocted when
she killed her own true husband. Coming home,
it was my children's and my servant's welcome
I'd hoped for; but that artist of corruption
heaped shame upon herself and on all women
in time to come, even the upright ones.'

"These were his words, and this was my reply:
'Long since, the bitter hate of thundering Zeus
against the sons of Átreus has used
conniving women as its instruments: 280
how many of us died through Helen's fault;
and Clytemnéstra, while you were far off,
devised her plot.'

                "These were my words—and he
was quick to answer: 'Therefore do not be
too open with your wife: do not disclose
all that you know; tell her one thing and keep
another hidden—though you'll never meet
death at the hands of your Penelope,
a prudent wife, whose heart has understanding.   290
When we set off for war, Penelope
was still a young bride: at her breast she held
an infant son, who now must sit among
the ranks of men—a happy son, for he
will see the father whom he loves come home;
and as is right, he'll hold his father close.
But I was not allowed to sate my eyes,
to see my own beloved son: my wife
denied that sight to me—she killed me first.

And I should add this warning: Don't forget 300
to moor in secret when you bring your ship
to your dear shores: no woman merits trust.
But tell me one thing—tell me honestly:
Have you heard word of where my son now lives?
Has sandy Pylos or Orchómenus
or Meneláus' Spartan plain become
my son's new home? For certainly the bright
Oréstes has not died upon the earth.'

"These were his words, and this was my reply:
'Why, Agamemnon, do you ask me that? 310
I do not know if he's alive or dead.
Words empty as the wind are best unsaid.'

"So did we two shed tears and share sad talk.
And then Achilles, Péleus' son, approached;
and with the son of Péleus came Patróclus,
flawless Antílochus, and Ajax—he
whose form and stature outdid all the Dánaans'
except for the incomparable Achilles.
The shade of Áeacus' swift-footed grandson
knew me. In tears he offered these winged words: 320

"'Odysseus, man of many wiles, divine
son of Laértës, will your spirit find
new tasks still more audacious than this quest?
How did you dare to come to Hades, home
of shades of faded men, the helpless dead?'

"These were his words, and this was my reply:
'Achilles, Péleus' son, the bravest Dánaan,
I've come to seek Tirésias, to listen
to any counsel he might have: a plan
to help me reach my rocky Ithaca. 330
I've not yet neared the coasts of the Achǽans;
I have not touched our soil. I've met sad trials.
Achilles, neither past nor future holds
a man more blessed than you. In life indeed
we Argives honored you as deity;
and now, among the dead, you are supreme.
In death you have no need to grieve, Achilles.'

"These were my words. He did not wait to answer:
'Odysseus, don't embellish death for me.
I'd rather be another's hired hand, 340
working for some poor man who owns no land
but pays his rent from what scant gains he gets,

than to rule over all whom death has crushed.
But tell me something of my worthy son:
Has he, a lord of men, gone off to war,
become a chieftain? And what have you heard
of stalwart Péleus? Does he still preserve
his place of honor with the Mýrmidons,
or is he scorned in Hellas and in Phthía
because old age has slowed his hands and feet?   350
I do not rise beneath the rays of sun
to take the form I had in Troy's broad land
when, to defend the Argives, my attacks
killed stalwart men: if I could only stand
beside my father for the briefest hour,
I'd make my force and formidable hands
the hated scourge of those whose savage acts
deprive him of due honor and respect.'

"These were his words, and this was my reply:
'Of your fine father, Péleus, I've heard nothing;   360
but of your dear son, Neoptólemus,
just as you wish, I'll tell you everything.
For I myself brought him in my lithe ship
to Scyros, where he joined the well-greaved Greeks.
And when our council met to plan attacks
against the Trojans, he was always first
to speak; in what he said, he never erred.
The only ones more subtle than your son
were godlike Nestor and myself. And when
Achǽans fought along the plain of Troy,   370
your son did not draw back into the ranks
and ruck; he thrust ahead. No one could stand
against his fury: fierce, he killed and maimed
so many—I can't tell or list the names
of every warrior that he, defending
the Argives, killed. But I will tell you this:
Your son's bronze shaft struck down Eurýpylus,
the son of Télephus—the handsomest
man I had ever seen except for Memnon,
who was the son of gods. And the Cetēians   380
who crowded round Eurýpylus were slaughtered—
all died because a woman had been bribed.
And, too, when we, the finest of the Argives,
were entering the horse Epēius built,
and it was I who led, who would decide
to shut our ambush or to open wide,
then all the other Dánaan lords and chiefs
wiped tears away, their every limb was weak;
but not once did I see your son's fair face

grow pale or see him dry his cheek. Again,   390
again, he asked to leave the horse; he gripped
his sword-hilt and his massive bronze-tipped shaft,
longing to smash the Trojans. Once we'd sacked
the towering town of Priam, he went back—
bearing his share of spoils and one fine prize—
to board his ship; he was unscathed, intact;
no sharp speartip had struck him; no close fight
had left the wounds that war so often brings—
for Árës' fury strikes haphazardly.'

"That said, across the Field of Asphodels,   400
with long strides swift Achilles' spirit left;
my tale of his son's fame had made him glad.

"The other dead souls stood in sadness, each
shade speaking to me of his griefs. Just Ajax,
the son of Télamon, stood off, apart,
still angry with me for my victory
when I, not he, beside our ships, received
the prize Achilles' mother had adjudged:
the arms and armor of her son. Would I
had never won that prize, for Ajax died   410
at his own hands because of that: earth closed
above a flawless man, one who surpassed
in feats and features all the Greeks except
for Péleus' son. I spoke with gentleness:

"'Ajax, son of great Télamon, even
in death can't you forget your bitterness
against me for the fatal arms I won?
Those arms allowed the gods to heap disaster
upon the Argives: when you fell we lost
a bulwark. We Achǽans always mourn   420
your death as we do that of Péleus' son.
And Zeus alone must bear the blame: his venom,
his hatred for the ranks of Dánaan spearmen,
decreed your doom. My lord, dismiss your wrath;
come, hear my words; do not be obstinate.'

"So did I plead. He did not answer me.
He went back into Érebus; he joined
the other dead souls. Even in his wrath,
he might have spoken to me then, or I
to him. But now the heart within my chest   430
wanted to see the shades of the other dead.

"There I saw Minos—famous son of Zeus—
who, seated, holding fast his golden scepter,

delivered judgments on the dead; they gathered,
seated or standing, at the spacious gates
of Hades; they beseeched, and he passed sentence.

"And then I saw immense Oríon, driving
across the Field of Asphodels a throng
of savage beasts, those he had killed upon
the lonely mountain slopes. Within his hands   440
he gripped a club of bronze that cannot crack.

"I saw the son of splendid Gǽa, Títyus,
stretched on the ground for some six hundred cubits.
Two vultures sat, one to each side, and tore
his liver; their beaks plunged into his bowels,
he could not ward them off; for Títyus
had violated Leto, splendid mistress
of Zeus, as she was walking through the fields
of lovely Pánopeus, heading toward Pytho.

"And I saw Tántalus in deep torment;   450
he stood upright within a pool, his chin
just touched by water. But despite his thirst,
he could not drink: as soon as that old man
bent over, seeking water, all that pool—
dried by a demon—shrank; and Tántalus
saw black earth at his feet. Above his head,
trees—leafy, high—bore fruit: from pomegranates
to pears, sweet figs, bright apples, and plump olives.
But just as soon as he reached out to touch,
winds blew that fruit up toward the shadowed clouds.   460

"And I saw Sísyphus' atrocious pain:
he tried to push a huge stone with his hands.
He'd brace his hands and feet and thrust it up
a slope, but just when he had neared the top,
its weight reversed its course; and once again
that bestial stone rolled back onto the plain.
Sweat drenched his straining limbs: again he thrust,
and dust rose from the head of Sísyphus.

"And I caught sight of mighty Héraclës
(that is to say, his shade; for he himself   470
rejoices in the feasts of deathless gods
and has as wife the lovely-ankled Hébë,
daughter of Zeus and golden-sandaled Hera).
Around him rose the tumult of the dead,
like birds that scatter everywhere in terror;
and he, like dark night, gripping his bare bow

and with an arrow on his bowstring, glared
menacingly, like one about to shoot.
Around his chest he had a giant belt
of gold embossed with horrifying things: 480
lions with massive manes, wild boars, and bears;
duels and battles, massacres and murders.
May he whose craft conceived that baldric never
devise a second one. As soon as he
returned my gaze, he knew just who I was.
And as he wept he offered these winged words:

"'Odysseus, man of many wiles, divine
son of Laértës, you are saddened by
the fate you bear, a destiny like mine
when underneath the sun I lived my life.   490
I was the son of Zeus, the son of Cronos,
and yet the trials that I endured were countless;
for I was made to serve a man by far
inferior to me: he set hard tests.
He even sent me here to fetch the hound
of Hades—he was sure there was no task
more dangerous. And yet I brought it back
from Hades' house, because I had the help
of Hermes and Athena, gray-eyed goddess.'

"His words were done. But when he had gone back,   500
I, lest still others come, stood there steadfast,
waiting for more dead heroes of the past.
And I'd have seen those warriors as I wished,
had crowds of dead souls not assembled then
with such a strange outcry that, terrified
and pale, I feared that fierce Perséphonë
might, from the halls of Hades, menace me
with Gorgon's head, that grim monstrosity.

"At that, I hurried to my ship and ordered
my comrades to embark and loose the hawsers.   510
They came on board at once and manned the thwarts.
The current took our ship on Ocean's course.
At first we rowed, but then a fair wind rose."

BOOK 12

**[Odysseus continues relating his adventures. He tells the Phaeacians of his encounter
with the enchanting** Sirens, **strange creatures whose irresistible song lures mariners to
their destruction. Following Circe's directions, Odysseus stops the ears of his men with
wax so that they cannot hear the Sirens' beautiful but deadly music and has himself
lashed to the ship's mast, allowing him to listen but preventing him from throwing
himself overboard. Next he confronts two equally lethal female monsters, Scylla, a six-**

headed giant cannibal, and Charybdis, a ship-crushing whirlpool. Forced to navigate his fragile bark through the narrow strait separating these two aspects of the devouring feminine principle, Odysseus explains that he heeded Circe's advice to lose a few of his men to Scylla rather than the entire crew to Charybdis. In this section, Odysseus also tells how the last of his fellow sailors were killed—for having disobeyed the divine command not to eat the sacred cattle of Helios, god of the sun:]

. . . .

"These were my words. My men did not delay.
Of Scylla I said nothing—after all,
we had no chance against her—lest my friends,
held fast by fear, desert their oars and cringe
down in the hold. At that point I forgot
the stern command of Círcë: I was not—
so she had said—to arm myself. Instead,
I put on my famed armor and advanced,
a long lance in each hand, to the foredeck:
from there I thought I'd first catch sight of Scylla   10
among the rocks, intent on killing us.
But though I peered and pored, my face bent toward
the misty cliff, my eyes grew weary—I
could not catch sight of her. We rowed, we wailed,
we sailed on up the strait. Along one side
lay Scylla; on the other side, divine
Charýbdis now was swallowing the brine.
And when she spewed it out again, she seethed
and swirled—a whirlpool—like a caldron set
above some holocaust; on high the spray   20
rained down upon the summits of the cliffs.
But when Charýbdis gulped the salty sea,
one saw her at the whirlpool's base, in frenzy;
her cliff roared terrifyingly; beneath
the sea, the earth's black sand lay bare; pale fear
held fast my crew; we feared the end and glued
our eyes upon Charýbdis. But just then,
Scylla seized six—the strongest—of my men;
she snatched them from the hollow ship; and when
I turned my eyes aside to seek my friends,   30
all I could see were feet and hands on high.
They called my name aloud for the last time
and shrieked in anguish. As a fisherman
who, from a jutting rock, has cast his bits
of food as bait to snare small fish, lets down
into the sea his long rod tipped with horn,
and when he's made a catch will whip it back—
writhing; so were my men whirled through the air,
writhing, against the rocks. There, at the door
to her deep cavern, Scylla swallowed them   40
as, in their horrid struggle, my dear friends

stretched out to me their hands—the saddest sight
my eyes have ever seen in all that I
have suffered in my journeys on the sea.

"Once we'd escaped the cliffs of fierce Charýbdis
and Scylla, we sped on. Soon we had reached
the sun-god's lovely island: there he kept
his broad-browed cows and well-fed flocks of sheep.
Still out at sea, I heard those bleating sheep
and heard the cattle lowing as they reached   50
their stalls. And I recalled to mind the words
of that blind seer, Tirésias of Thebes,
and of Aeǽan Círcë, who had warned me
again, again, to shun the isle of him
who brings delight to mortals, Hélios.
With an uneasy heart, I told my men:

"'Friends, though your trials are harsh, hear what I say.
I must tell you Tirésias' prophecies
and those of the Aeǽan Círcë: they
warned me repeatedly to shun the land   60
of Hélios, who brings delight to men.
She said that here disaster waits for us.
No, row our black ship back; don't near this coast.'

"They heard what I had urged. Their dear hearts broke.
Eurýlochus replied with hateful words:
'Odysseus, your demands are merciless;
no man can match your courage, and your strength
will not relent. You surely must be made
of iron if you do not let your friends—
worn-out, in need of sleep—set foot ashore,   70
where, on this seagirt land, we might once more
prepare a proper meal. You'd have us row
to nowhere through the swift night, men astray,
far from this island, on the shadowed sea.
At night malicious winds will rise—the kind
that batter ships. How can we flee the steep
descent to death if frenzied winds attack:
Notus or raging Zephyr—which, despite
the will of sovereign gods, can wreck a ship?
The night is far too dark: let us submit,   80
prepare our meal, and rest along the beach.
As soon as Dawn has come, we'll board again
and then row out and toward the open sea.'

"These were his words, and all the rest agreed.
Then I was sure that some dark god had schemed
disaster. And I countered with winged words:

"'Eurýlochus, I'm one against too many:
I am outmanned. But all of you must swear
a binding oath: If we should chance to see
a herd of cattle or a flock of sheep,   90
no one—through wanton arrogance—must kill
a single beast: you are to eat in peace
the food that we received from deathless Círcë.'

"These were my words. As I had urged, they vowed
at once; that done, we anchored our staunch ship
within a sheltered bay, close to a spring
that had fresh water for us. Once ashore,
my men had soon prepared a skillful supper.
Then, with our need for food and drink appeased,
my friends began to weep, remembering   100
their dear companions Scylla had devoured.
And sweet sleep came upon them as they wept.
We reached the night's last watch, when stars turn course;
then Zeus, the gatherer of clouds, provoked
a terrifying tempest: storm clouds wrapped
both sea and land; night hurtled down from heaven.

"As soon as Dawn's rose fingers touched the sky,
we drew our ship into a sheltered place,
a grotto at the harbor's base—a cave
with seats for nymphs and ample dancing-space.   110
My shipmates gathered round me, and I said:

"'Friends, we have food and drink in our swift ship;
then, lest we meet disaster, do not touch
the cattle. They belong to a dread god,
to Hélios, who sees and hears all things.'"

"These were my words. And their proud hearts agreed.
But then winds raged—they swept from south and east.
First, Notus, for a full month, without let;
then Eurus, too, attacked. Throughout that stretch,
with food and wine still theirs, my comrades left   120
the herds untouched; they did not wish for death.
But when we'd reached the end of all our stores,
my men were forced to prey along the shores.
Yet while they sought with curving hooks to snare
fish, birds, and anything that chance might bring—
such hunger gnawed their bellies—I instead
went inland; for I wanted most to pray
unto the gods, in hope that one of them
might offer me some stratagem. And when,
deeper inland, I'd left behind my friends   130

and found a place well shielded from the wind,
I washed my hands and called on all the gods
who hold Olympus as their home. But I
heard no reply. They cast sleep on my eyes.

"Meanwhile Eurýlochus provoked my men,
and what he offered was a fatal plan:
'Friends, though your trials are harsh, hear what I say.
All deaths are dour; the fate of men is sad;
but there's no death more miserable than
the doom starvation sends. Come, let us take   140
Hypérion's best cows and sacrifice
to the undying gods, who rule the skies.
If we reach Ithaca, our fathers' land,
there we—at once—shall build for Hélios
an altar heaped with many glowing gifts.
And if our taking of his tall-horned cows
enrages Hélios, and he would wreck
our ship and has the other gods' consent,
I'd rather have my mouth drink brine and let
the waves kill me at once than meet slow death   150
by lingering on an island wilderness.'

"So did he speak, and all the rest agreed.
At once they chose the sun-god's finest cattle:
just then, those broad-browed cows with curving horns
were grazing near the dark-prowed ship; my men
surrounded them and prayed unto the gods;
since we, on board our ship, had no white barley,
they plucked the green leaves of a tall oak tree—
over their offering, they'd scatter these.
After they'd prayed and cut the throats and flayed   160
the cows, they sliced the thighs in chunks and laid
a double layer of fat across those chunks,
then spread raw flesh on top. They had no wine
to splash across the blazing sacrifice
but, using water for libations, roasted
all of the vitals on the fire. And when
the thighs were scorched and they had tasted all
the inner parts, they set the rest on spits.

"But now sweet sleep had left my eyes, and I
walked back to the swift ship at the seaside;   170
and when my steps drew close to our trim craft,
I smelled the pungent fragrance of hot fat.
I groaned, then called upon the deathless gods:

"'You, father Zeus, and all the other blessed,
undying gods, you sent this wretchedness;

it's you who left me prey to senseless sleep;
you gulled me; I am ruined; now my men,
awaiting me, contrived this horrid plan.'

"Meanwhile Lampétië, the long-robed nymph,
had hurried off to tell lord Hélios   180
that we had killed his cows. Without delay,
before his fellow gods, he cried, enraged:

"'You, father Zeus, and all the other blessed
and deathless gods—you now must take revenge:
destroy the comrades of Laértës' son,
Odysseus; in their insolence they killed
the herds that I beheld with such delight
both when I climbed the starry sky and when
I wheeled and then returned to earth again.
If they're not made to pay a penalty   190
to match their sin, I shall descend to Hades
and shine among the dead.'

                              "In turn, Zeus said:
'Shine, Hélios, with light for the immortals;
and lighten, too, the lives of those who die
on earth, the giver of the gift of grain.
As for those sinners, I'll soon strike their ship
with blazing lightning—tearing her to bits
upon the winedark sea.'

                              "I heard all this   200
from the fair-haired Calypso after she
had heard it from the messenger Hermes.

"I reached the ship and shore and—one by one—
denounced my men. But nothing could be done—
the herds lay dead. And soon the gods sent portents:
the flayed hides crawled along the ground; the flesh
upon the spits, both roast and raw, began
to bellow; we heard sounds of lowing cows.

"My faithful comrades feasted for six days
upon the finest beasts of Hélios.   210
But when Zeus, son of Cronos, brought to us
the seventh day, no longer fury-fed,
the wind died down. We boarded quickly, stepped
our mast and spread our sail, then drove ahead—
out toward the open sea.

                              "When we had left
that isle behind and saw no other land,

only the sky and sea, the son of Cronos
set a black cloud above our hollow ship;
below us waves grew dark. By now our run   220
was doomed; the howling Zephyr fell upon
our course; a wind amok, its fury cracked
the forestays of the mast. The mast fell back;
the sail and all the rigging crashed, collapsed
into the bilge. And at the stern, the mast
hit hard the helmsman's head; it crushed his skull;
and like a diver, from the deck he plunged
headlong; his sturdy spirit left his bones.
Zeus thundered as he hurled a lightning bolt.
He hit the hull: it filled with sulfurous smoke;   230
our ship whirled round full circle. All my men
pitched overboard; like sea crows they were borne
by waves around our black-bowed craft. A god
deprived them of the day of their return.

"I paced the ship until a comber ripped
the keel and hull apart. The naked keel
was carried by the surge, which also snapped
the mast off from the hulk—but it still had
a backstay made of oxhide. This I grabbed.   240
That rope in hand, I lashed the keel and mast
together; hugging them, I then was driven
by the malicious winds. And after Zephyr
had slacked his storm's wild force, Notus at once
brought back the fear that I had known; for now
I'd have to cross Charýbdis once again.

"All through the night that wind did not relent.
The sun was rising when I spied the cliffs
of Scylla and the murderous Charýbdis,
who sucked in the salt waters of the sea;   250
she drew my mast and keel into her deeps.
But reaching up and toward the great fig tree,
I gripped it, clinging to it like a bat.
Yet I could find no foothold, could not climb
that tree, because its roots stretched far below;
nor could I ever reach its long, broad boughs—
so high, they wrapped Charýbdis in their shade.
I gripped that trunk; I would not yield until
she vomited again the mast and keel.
I waited long; at last they came. Just when
an elder who is called upon to judge   260
between the claims of young contenders, stands
and says the time for judgment's at an end
and leaves the marketplace to dine, so then—

such was the hour—Charýbdis spewed the mast
and keel. My hands and feet let go the trunk;
I fell into the water with a splash
next to the keel and mast; I mounted them;
and, with that vantage, soon my arms began
to row. The father of both gods and men
did not let Scylla's eyes spy me again.   270

"For nine days I was dragged; and on the tenth
the gods cast me upon Ogýgia's coast,
the island home of lovely-haired Calypso,
the awesome goddess with a human voice,
who took me in and tended me. But why
do I retell this now? Just yesterday,
within this hall, I told that tale to you
and to your noble wife. I do not hold
with telling over what has been well told."

.   .   .   .

BOOKS 13–23

[After the Phaeacians transport him safely home to Ithaca, Odysseus, with Athene's help, disguises himself as a wandering beggar. Having revealed his identity only to Telemachus and his faithful swineherd Eumaeus, Odysseus covertly plots his revenge on the suitors. Athene inspires Penelope to propose that she will marry the man who can string her lost husband's great bow and shoot an arrow through twelve ax heads, a feat that only the most worthy hero can accomplish. After stringing the bow, Odysseus and his few supporters exact vengeance on the suitors, slaughtering every one in the great hall. Wondering at this unexpected turn of events, Penelope is called to meet her husband for the first time in twenty years. From Book 23:]

.   .   .   .

Then Euryclēïa answered: "My dear child,
how can the barrier of your teeth permit
such speech to cross your lips? How can you say
that your Odysseus never will return
when he is in this house, at his own hearth?
You've always had an unbelieving heart.
But there's another certain sign that I
must share with you: the wound that long ago
the white-tusked boar inflicted on Odysseus.
I saw this when I washed his feet; I should   10
have told you this, but it was he himself
who laid his hand upon my mouth; he would
not let me speak—yes, he is keen, astute.
But follow me; I stake my life—if I
have tricked you, I am forfeit, I must die."

Then wise Penelope replied: "Dear nurse,
however wise one is, it still is hard

to read the counsels of the deathless gods.
But let us hurry to my son, that I
may see the slaughtered and their slaughterer."   20

That said, she left behind her upper rooms.
Her heart was still unsure: Was she to probe
her husband from afar or, drawing close,
to kiss his head and hands? She crossed the sill
of stone and took a seat within the hall,
facing Odysseus as he sat beside
the far wall in the firelight. His eyes
cast down, he leaned against a pillar, waiting
to see if, when she saw him there, his wife
would speak to him. But she sat long in silence,   30
her heart assailed by wonder; now her eyes
stared full upon his face, and once again
she failed to recognize him—he was dressed
so miserably. But Telémachus
rebuked her:

            "Mother, you are hard of heart:
why do you stay so far away from my
dear father? Were you at his side, you might
ask question after question. Yes, your heart
is stubborn—surely there's no other woman   40
who'd keep her distance from her own dear husband
who, after he has suffered many trials
in more than nineteen years away, returns
to her, in her dear land. Not even stone
is harder than the hardness your heart shows."

This was the wise Penelope's reply:
"My son, the soul within my breast is struck
with wonder; I've no words; I cannot ask;
I cannot even look him in the face.
If what I see in truth is my Odysseus   50
come home to me, we two shall certainly
know one another without questioning:
we've secret signs, unknown to all but us."

That said, the patient, bright Odysseus smiled.
He turned to his dear son with these winged words:
"Telémachus, be patient: let your mother
test me within these halls; she soon will find
the way in which I can be recognized.
Now, since I'm dressed in tattered rags and filth,
she scorns me—won't admit that I am he.   60
Meanwhile the two of us can make our plans.

Even if a slain man has left few friends
who'd seek revenge, the killer flees that land—
he's exiled from his city and his clan.
But we have killed the pillars of this town,
the noblest youths of Ithaca: I ask
that you reflect most carefully on that."

Telémachus' reply was keen and wise:
"Dear father, you yourself can see to this.
They say that you're the most astute of men—   70
no mortal can contrive more cunning plans.
We three will follow where you choose to lead;
whatever strength we have is yours to spend."

Odysseus, man of many wiles, replied:
"Then I shall tell you what seems best to me.
Once you have bathed yourselves, I'd have you dress
in tunics; let the women wear their best.
The godly singer is to take his harp
and lead us in a glad and varied dance,
so those who live nearby or those who chance   80
to pass along the road will say that we
are in the middle of a wedding feast.
Then rumors will not spread throughout the town:
no one will hear about the suitors' deaths
until we've left for our well-wooded farm.
Once we are there, we can devise a scheme—
whatever plan Olympus will concede."

His words were done. They heard, and they obeyed.
They bathed, and then they dressed; in fine array
the women gathered; and the godly singer   90
took up his hollow harp and spurred them on:
they longed for seemly dance and gracious song.
Out from the great house echoed loud the tread
of men who danced and women finely dressed.
And those who heard those sounds outside now said:

"Someone has surely wed the queen at last—
the woman whom they wanted so. That bitch
no longer guards the great house of her own
true husband, waiting—firm—for his return."

So some did say, but none knew what had passed.   100
Meanwhile Eurýnomë, the housewife, bathed
in his own halls the resolute Odysseus,
then smoothed his body down with oil and cast
a tunic round his back. That done, Athena,

the gray-eyed goddess, made him more robust
and taller, and she gave him thicker hair,
which flowed down from his head in curls and clusters
that seemed much like the hyacinth in flower.
Just as a craftsman who has learned his secrets
from both the gray-eyed goddess and Hephæstus   110
frames silver with fine gold and thus creates
a work with greater plenitude and grace,
so did the goddess now enhance the face
and head and shoulders of Odysseus.
When he came from the bath and reached the hall,
his form was like the form of the immortals.
Again he took the chair from which he'd risen,
facing his wife. He said:

                "Perplexing woman!
To you the gods who hold Olympus gave   120
a heart more obdurate than any they
have ever given other—weaker—women.
What other woman has a heart so stubborn
as to deny herself her own dear husband,
who's suffered trial on trial and, after more
than nineteen years, returns to his own shores!
Come, nurse, I need to rest; prepare a couch,
that I, though all alone, may lay me down:
within her breast she has a heart of iron."

This was the wise Penelope's reply: 130
"Wild man! I am not proud, I do not taunt,
nor am I stupefied—I know full well
how you appeared when, in your long-oared ship,
you left your Ithaca. Yes, Euryclēia,
prepare the sturdy bedstead for him now
outside the solid bridal room that he
himself constructed; carry out the bed,
and over it throw cloaks, bright blankets, fleece."

These words of hers were meant to test Odysseus.
Incensed, her husband cried to his keen wife: 140
"Woman, your words have wounded me. Who tore
my bedstead from its base? For it would take
a god—if he so pleased—to shift its place.
No man alive, however young and strong,
with mortal force alone could hope to budge
that bed without great strain, for it contains
a secret in its making. No one else
contrived that bed: I fashioned it myself.
Within our court a long-leaved olive trunk

stood stout and vigorous, just like a pillar.   150
Around that trunk I built our bridal room.
I finished it with close-set stones and laid
a sturdy roof above; I added doors
that fitted faultlessly. Then I lopped off
the olive's long-leaved limbs; and so I thinned
the trunk, up from its base; with my bronze adze,
I smoothed it down with craft and care; I made
that wood run true and straight, and it became
my bedpost. Once I'd bored it with an auger,
I, starting with that part, began to shape   160
my frame and, with that job well done, inlaid
my work with silver, ivory, and gold.
Inside the frame I stretched taut oxhide thongs;
their crimson shone. My secret sign is told.
Woman, I do not know if my bed stands
where it once stood or if by now some man
has sawed the bedstead from the trunk and set
my bed elsewhere."

        These were his words; her knees
and heart went weak; the secret signs that he   170
revealed were certain proof. She ran to greet
Odysseus, threw her arms around his neck,
and kissed his head and said:

        "Dear heart, don't rage:
Odysseus, let the wisdom you've displayed
in all else show here now. It is the gods
who destined us to sorrow; they begrudged
our staying side by side—the two of us—
enjoying youth and coming to the start
of our old age together. Do not be   180
indignant if at first I did not greet
or welcome you as I do now: the heart
within my breast has always been afraid
that there might be some stranger who would come
to trick me with his blabber; many plot
with cunning malice. Even Argive Helen,
Zeus' daughter, never would have lain in love
beside a stranger had she known that sons
of the Achæans were to wage a war
to bring her back again to her own land.   190
It surely was a god who spurred her act
of wantonness, who blinded her so that
she could not see what fate had brought to pass;
our sorrows, too, were born of her blindness.
But now you've listed clear, unerring signs
of our dear bed; no mortal's ever seen
that bed except for you and me and one

lone servant, Actor's child, the girl my father
had given me when I first journeyed here
to Ithaca—the maid who kept the doors   200
of our stout bridal chamber; and with this,
my heart, which was so stubborn, is convinced."

These were her words; they spurred his need to cry;
in tears Odysseus clasped his dear, wise wife.
And as the sight of land is welcomed by
the only shipwrecked sailors to survive
when whiplash winds and crashing combers sent
by lord Poseidon have destroyed their ship;
in flight from the gray sea, they swim toward shore,
their bodies caked with brine, and now at last   210
set foot upon the beach; their grief is past:
so at the sight of him, there was delight
in her; she twined her white arms round his neck.

And Dawn with her rose fingers would have found
those two still tearful had the gray-eyed goddess,
Athena, not devised this stratagem:
She slowed the night, delayed its journey's end;
and then she held back Dawn, whose throne is gold;
she did not let her yoke the racing foals
that carry light to men—the colts of Dawn,   220
Lampus and Pháethon. Odysseus said:

"Dear wife, we've not yet reached the end of all
our toils; in days to come, I'll face a test
so long and hard—so measureless—and yet
there is no part of it I can neglect.
So did the spirit of Tirésias
foresee; of this he told me on that day
when I went down to Hades' house to ask
about my comrades' and my journey back.
But come, wife, it is time for us to see   230
our bed, our joys, our rest, wrapped in sweet sleep."

This was the wise Penelope's reply:
"Now that the gods have brought you back again
to your own house and native land, your bed
stands fully ready any time you wish.
But since you called to mind that trial—it is
some god who made you think of that—speak out:
I'll have to hear of it at some time soon,
and now is just as good a time as then."

Odysseus, man of many wiles, replied: 240
"Strange woman! Why do you incite me so

to speak? And yet I'll tell you all I know
without disguise, though there is no delight
for you—and none for me—in hearing this
just as I heard it from Tirésias.
He said that I, with shapely oar in hand,
must visit many cities till I reach
a land where men know nothing of the sea
and don't use salt to season what they eat;
they're ignorant of boats with purple cheeks   250
and shapely oars that are the wings of ships.
He told me this clear sign, which I won't keep
from you: When on the road a man meets me
and says that what I'm carrying must be
a fan for winnowing, I can be sure:
that is the place where I must plant my oar
and offer lord Poseidon handsome gifts—
a ram, a bull, a boar that mates with sows.
Then, once I have returned to Ithaca,
I am to offer holy hecatombs   260
to the undying gods, wide heaven's lords—
to each in turn. I shall not die at sea:
the death that reaches me will be serene.
I shall grow old—a man of wealth and ease—
surrounded by a people rich, at peace.
All this, he said, will surely come to be."

The wise Penelope had this to say:
"Yet if the gods, at least in your old age,
allow you better days, you may escape
at last from trials and wars. So we can hope."   270

Such were the things they shared with one another.
Meanwhile, by bright torchlight, old Euryclēia
had joined Eurýnomë, and both were busy
wrapping the sturdy bedstead in soft blankets.
The old nurse then went back to her own room.
Eurýnomë, the keeper of their chamber,
led them across the court by firelight
and then went back again. And he and she
delighted in the sight of their old couch.

Telémachus, the cowherd, and the swineherd   280
meanwhile had stayed their feet; they danced no more;
and once they'd stopped the women, they themselves
lay down to sleep within the shadowed halls.

But when Odysseus and Penelope
had had their fill of love's delights, the joys
of talk were theirs, the telling one another
of all their trials. She told him of her grief

as she—fair woman—watched the vicious suitors,
that crowd who, in their wooing her, had butchered
so many beasts—both cattle and plump sheep—   290
as well as drawing wine beyond all measure.
Odysseus, born of Zeus, in turn rehearsed
the sorrows he'd inflicted and endured;
he spared her nothing. His dear wife felt deep
delight in listening, and no sweet sleep
touched her until his telling was complete.

His story started with his victory
against the Cíconës, and how he reached
the fertile land of men who feed on lotus.
He touched on all the malice of the Cyclops,   300
and how he'd made that monster pay his due
for having mercilessly eaten some
of his stout crew. King Áeolus came next,
the lord who welcomed him, then sent him off,
though fate denied him passage to his home:
a storm wind snatched him up, thrust him across
the fish-rich sea as he groaned heavily.
And then his tale took in Telépylus,
the city of the Laestrygónians,
who wrecked his ship and killed his well-greaved men.   310
He also told of Círcë's wiles and craft
and how, upon a ship with many oars,
he came to Hades' somber house to meet
the spirit of Tirésias of Thebes;
there he saw all his comrades and his mother,
she who had borne and reared him. Then he told
how he had heard the never-ending song
the Sirens sing; and how he reached the rocks
they call the Wanderers, and grim Charýbdis,
and Scylla, she from whom no man has yet   320
escaped intact; and how his comrades killed
the herds of Hélios—and Zeus, the lord
of thunder, struck his swift ship with a bolt
of smoking lightning; all his comrades died,
and he alone escaped death's heartless Fates.
His coming to Calypso's isle, Ogýgia,
was next: that nymph had kept him in her caves;
she wanted him as husband; tending him,
she thought to make him deathless, ever young;
but she could not convince the heart within   330
his breast. So after many trials, he came
to the Phaeácians, who, most eagerly,
paid him the honors men bestow on gods
and, after they had given him much gold
and bronze and many clothes, escorted him

back to his own dear land on their swift ship.
This was the end of what he had to tell;
now sleep assaulted him, sweet sleep that can
loosen the limbs and soothe the griefs of men.

· · · · · · · · · · · · · · · · ·

[Odysseus is successfully reunited with Penelope and resumes his role as husband, father, and master of his household, but he has yet to reestablish his role as king. Ancient
laws of blood vengeance demand that relatives of the slain suitors uphold their families'
honor by killing the young men's slayer. In Book 24, Odysseus, his aged father Laertes,
his son Telemachus, and a few loyal retainers prepare to fight the suitors' angry kinsmen, threatening to plunge Ithaca into anarchy. At this point, Athene intervenes with
Zeus, who promises to make the suitors' relatives forget their grievances and conclude
a pact to accept Odysseus as their permanent king. (Zeus also directs a lightning bolt
at the feuding Ithacans to emphasize his intention.) Commanding Odysseus to renounce his anger, Athene (still in Mentor's form) restores peace and civic order to Ithacan society.]

Questions for Discussion and Review

1. Discuss the ways in which Odysseus both resembles and differs from other heroes of
   myth, particularly Achilles and Heracles. What personal qualities enable him to overcome the obstacles or survive the dangers that beset him on his long journey home
   from Troy?

2. Describe the ethical principles operating in the universe of the *Odyssey*. Discuss the
   ethical connections between the actions of individual human beings and their subsequent experiences. How do Zeus and the other Olympians regard wrongdoing? In
   view of this cosmic ethos, how does Odysseus contribute to his own suffering? Be sure
   to consider the Polyphemus episode.

3. Discuss Athene's dominant role in the *Odyssey*. Why does she so intensely favor Odysseus, Penelope, and their family?

4. Women and goddesses play extremely important parts in Odysseus's education. Specify
   what the hero learns from Athene, Circe, Calypso, Nausicaa, the Sirens, and Penelope.
   Explain how Freudian or Jungian motifs may be operating in Odysseus's relationship
   with women, including his mother, aged nurse, and wife.

5. In Book 11, Homer suggests a link between Heracles and Odysseus. What qualities
   and experiences do the two heroes share? Why is Odysseus so solitary a figure, and
   why does he undergo so much of his testing and learning completely alone? At the end
   of the epic, how does Homer place Odysseus back in the context of human society?

Recommended Reading

Bloom, Harold, ed. *Homer's Odyssey.* New York: Chelsea House, 1988. Contains critical essays
　　on major characters and themes in the epic.
Clark, Howard. *The Art of the* Odyssey. Englewood Cliffs, NJ: Prentice-Hall, 1967.
Clay, Jenny Strauss. *The Wrath of Athene.* Princeton: Princeton UP, 1983.
Finley, John H., Jr. *Homer's Odyssey.* Cambridge: Harvard UP, 1978.
Tracy, Steve. *The Story of the* Odyssey. Princeton: Princeton UP, 1991.

PART THREE

The World of
Classical Tragedy

CHAPTER

1 3

≈≈≈

The Theater of Dionysus
and the Tragic Vision

KEY THEMES

*Athens's annual festival honoring Dionysus, the City Dionysia, gave birth
to a new art form—theatrical productions of both tragedy and comedy, the
two modes reflecting the paradoxical qualities of the wine god. Whereas
tragedy emphasizes Dionysus's frightening mutability—nature's irresistible
law of change that sparks unexpected reversals in human fortune—comedy
celebrates the beneficent life force he embodies. The great Athenian playwrights reworked ancient myths illustrating Dionysian motifs of suffering,
sacrifice, rebirth, and reintegration. In the* Bacchants *(The* Bacchae*), Euripides dramatizes the tragic myth recounting Dionysus's return to his home
city of Thebes and the terrible vengeance that the god exacts on those who
reject him.*

$\qquad$Greek myth makes its primary impact to-
day in two major literary forms: the narrative poetry of Homer and Hesiod, which
dates from the mid-eighth century B.C., and the dramatic poetry of Athenian playwrights who wrote almost three hundred years later. The nearly three centuries separating Homeric epic from the oldest surviving Greek play, the *Persians* of Aeschylus
(c. 472 B.C.), witnessed enormous changes in Greek society. In 508 B.C., Athens
instituted the world's first democratic constitution, only to have this nascent democracy threatened by two successive waves of invading Persian armies—successfully repelled at the crucial battles of Marathon (490 B.C.) and Salamis (480 B.C.)—in both
of which Aeschylus, dramatist and citizen-soldier, participated (Figure 13-1). Some
of these social and political developments, including the establishment of a jury system, are reflected in the Athenian drama's creative transformation of mythological
themes.

423

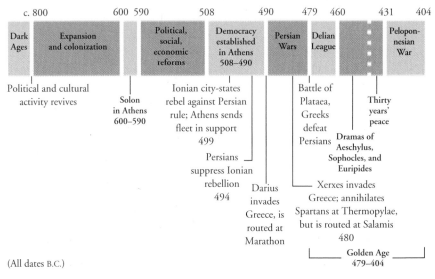

(All dates B.C.)

FIGURE 13-1   Developments in Greek History from the End of the Dark Ages to the Peloponnesian War (c. 800–404 B.C.). As this timeline indicates, Greece went through a rapid
period of development in the centuries immediately following the Dark Ages. Increased trade
and exchange of ideas with older civilizations of the Near East brought both economic and
intellectual growth as Greek city-states evolved an art and way of life that eventually gave
birth to the cultural flowering of the fifth century B.C. The leading city-states, Athens and
Sparta, united to repel two major invasions from Persia (the Persian Wars, 490 and 480–
479 B.C.), after which victory Athens, by then the world's first democracy, pursued a policy of
cultural and military imperialism. Threatened by Athenian expansion, Sparta engaged Athens
in a series of devastating conflicts (the Peloponnesian War, 431–404 B.C.), which resulted in
Athens's collapse and Sparta's exhaustion. Except for the comedies of Aristophanes, all surviving Greek plays were written between the end of the Persian Wars and the deaths of Sophocles and Euripides, just two years before Athens's surrender to Sparta in 404 B.C.

The City Dionysia and the Birth of Drama

Whereas the gods and heroes of Homer and Hesiod belonged to all Greece, helping
to define the Greek people's collective identity, it was principally in Athens that ancient myths were recast in an entirely new art form—dramatic performances in the
theater of Dionysus. Although both tragedy and comedy began in rituals honoring
Dionysus, their exact origin and earliest development are unknown. In his *Poetics,*
Aristotle (384–322 B.C.) briefly remarks that tragedy "originated with the authors of
the dithyramb" and "advanced by slow degrees" until "it found its natural form, and
there it stopped." The **dithyramb,** an ecstatic choral song celebrating the wine god's
prowess, was an integral part of an important Athenian festival dedicated to Dionysus's worship, the **City** or **Great Dionysia,** reputedly established by the Athenian
leader Pisistratus about 535–533 B.C.

Although the City Dionysia regularly featured a dithyrambic contest among Athens's ten tribes, each of which had a chorus of 50 men and another of 50 boys dancing

FIGURE 13-2   Dionysus and Satyrs Making Wine. The bearded god of wine joins satyrs (depicted here as men with pointed ears and horse tails) in a vintage revel. According to Aristotle, tragedy evolved from the dithyramb, a wild, ecstatic dance associated with such Dionysian festivals. A highly mutable deity symbolizing the ever-changing forces of physical and human nature, Dionysus is the patron of drama, both the painful reversals of tragedy and the joyous resolution of conflicts in comedy.

and singing a Dionysian hymn, only one example of the dithyramb has survived—the opening choral ode of Euripides's *Bacchants* (see pp. 447–448). Held annually in early March, the City Dionysia began with a noisy procession of citizens carrying emblems of the god's cult, including grotesque masks (representing his diverse manifestations), sacred phalluses, and an effigy of the mutilated and dismembered Dionysus (see Chapter 8). Celebrating the making of new wine (Figure 13-2), many participants generously sampled Dionysus's liquid gift, happily exploring the potentialities of intoxication. Raucous merrymaking combined with solemn ritual as celebrants offered sacrifices to the volatile deity who embodied life's irregular cycles of joy, grief, death, and rebirth. A priest of Dionysus presided over the entire five-day affair, occupying a prominent seat of honor in the front row of the theater.

When Pisistratus established a competition among playwrights as the major event of the City Dionysia, the procedure required that each contestant submit a set of three tragedies and a **satyr play,** a wild farce exploiting the comic potential of overtly sexual elements in Dionysian tradition. Each of the three different dramatic categories—tragedy, satyr plays, and comedy—staged at the City Dionysia represented a distinct aspect of Dionysus's complex nature. A jury selected by lot awarded first, second, and third places to three different sets of dramas and their accompanying satyr plays, which were publicly presented on three successive days beginning at dawn.

According to a perhaps doubtful tradition, the initial winner of the tragic competition was **Thespis,** who reportedly created the first role for an actor by separating a single performer from the traditional Dionysian chorus of singers and dancers. For the first time, an actor stood in opposition to the choral leader, engaging in dialogue that could lead to true dramatic conflict, the essence of effective theater.

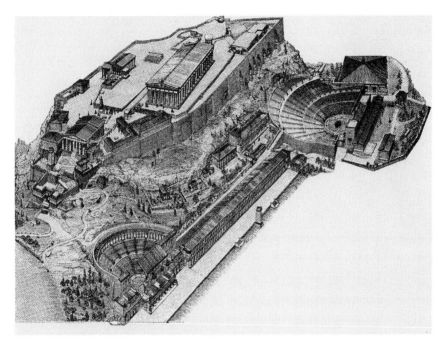

FIGURE 13-3   The Acropolis and Theater of Dionysus (upper right). The transformation
of ancient Greek myth into dramatic presentations began in Athens about 535–534 B.C. as
part of a citywide festival honoring Dionysus. At that time, the Athenian tyrant Pisistratus
established a contest among playwrights, whose tragedies were staged in an open-air amphitheater on the slopes of the Acropolis. The original theater of Dionysus, where all the plays of
Aeschylus, Sophocles, and Euripides had their premieres, was extensively reconstructed in the
fourth century B.C. The scene pictured here shows the Acropolis area, including the much
later theater of Herodes Atticus (lower left), as it appeared toward the end of the second century A.D. (*Reconstruction by Al N. Oikonomides.*)

Tragedy

The new art form that Thespis allegedly introduced, and which Aeschylus later
brought to artistic maturity, is called **tragedy,** a term combining the Greek words
tragos ("he-goat") and *oide* ("song"). The "goat song" may derive its rustic name from
the loincloths of goatskin worn by the all-male chorus. (Women were not permitted
to appear onstage, and all roles, including impersonations of Aphrodite, Clytemnestra, and Helen of Troy, were filled by men wearing masks, wigs, and long robes.)
According to another theory, "goat song" refers to the attendees' shouts and chants
performed when a goat was sacrificed on Dionysus's altar to inaugurate the dramatic
productions. Whatever the origin of its name, tragedy (*tragoidia*) rapidly became the
dominant force for reinterpreting the significance of old myths for the Athenian public. Crowds of 15,000 or more packed the theater of Dionysus—a semicircular amphitheater cut into the south flank of the Acropolis (Figure 13-3)—to witness the
latest adaptations of myth in new works of dramatic art. (Today, the theater at Epidaurus stands as the best preserved theater in Greece and is still used for the performance of classical tragedy; Figure 13-4.)

FIGURE 13-4 Theater at Epidaurus. The best preserved theater in Greece, the great amphitheater at Epidaurus is still used for performances of classical tragedy and modern opera. Although drama was an Athenian invention, the art form quickly became popular and spread throughout the Greek world, resulting in the building of theaters like this one in Greece, Sicily, Italy, and Ionia. Many Greek theaters had such good acoustics that well-trained actors could project their speeches with near-perfect clarity even to the back rows.

After witnessing his premiere tragedy, Thespis's first audience is said to have asked in disgust, "What has this to do with Dionysus?" Although Dionysus's shrine, altar, and priest were featured prominently in the theater, Thespis—like most of the playwrights who followed him—did not confine himself to staging episodes from Dionysian myth. Tragedy was firmly committed to the spirit of the wine god, with his tragic suffering, death, resurrection, and ascension to heaven, but from the beginning, Greek dramatists freely used myths about other gods and heroes as their primary subject matter. Only one surviving tragedy, Euripides's *Bacchants* (c. 406 B.C.), features Dionysus as a leading character, although he appears in some comedies, such as Aristophanes's *Frogs* (405 B.C.). The two plays offer startlingly different portraits of the wine god: Euripides presents Dionysus as an irresistible natural instinct that destroys all who oppose it, whereas Aristophanes shows the deity as a (relatively) good-natured drunk interested in restoring theatrical productions to the high standards they had before the deaths of Sophocles and Euripides in 406 B.C.

Tragedy as the Athenians knew it differed qualitatively from the solitary process of scanning a play's printed text that most readers experience today. Besides being a religious celebration that explored mysteries of life and death, dramatic presentations were communal events in which heightened emotions and sometimes shocking new insights were shared simultaneously by thousands of people. The bare bones of a tragedy's script, which is all that remains to us, cannot convey the visual and auditory spectacle of the majestic ritual—accompanied by music and dance—in which Oedipus's self-deceptions were inexorably peeled away or Medea's scheme to murder her own children moved, without a hint of divine interference, toward its unspeakable fulfillment.

Catharsis Uniting word and music to engage both intellect and emotion, Greek tragedy strives for an immediate and powerful impact on its audience. Aristotle de-

FIGURE 13-5   Maenad and Satyr. Heads thrown back in rapture, these wildly dancing figures display the effects of ecstasy—literally the standing outside of oneself, the escape from
individual self-awareness to experience a sense of unity with their god. Liberating people from
the constraints of reason and custom, Dionysian possession permitted extremes of feeling and
behavior, a freedom to express instinctual drives and appetites, appropriately represented by
the satyr, who combines bestial and human traits. The animal component of the uninhibited
psyche is also implied by the snake coiled around the maenad's left arm and by the panther
accompanying the horse-tailed satyr. Innocent of civilized taboos, the satyr unselfconsciously
pursues the satisfaction of emotional and sexual impulses, a characteristic acknowledged and
honored in the satyr plays presented after the tragic dramas. (*Metropolitan Museum of Art,
New York.*)

fined tragedy in terms of the emotional response it elicited: by arousing strong feelings of pity and fear in the spectator, tragedy is able to relieve or purge these
emotions, achieving **catharsis.** Thus tragedy's ultimate effect is not to produce de-
pression, but exhilaration, a conscious lightening of emotive burdens.

The Satyr Play

Whereas Athenian tragedy underscored the terrifying unpredictability of change that
can suddenly transform the lives of city-states and their leaders, the satyr play (which

FIGURE 13-6   Maenads Dancing. The Athenian painter Macron created this scene of joyous abandon in the first quarter of the fifth century B.C. Women dressed as maenads and carrying thyrsi dance in honor of Dionysus. One woman holds aloft an animal, possibly intended for sacrifice. The juxtaposition of joy and sacrifice in these spirit-possessed worshipers is echoed in the Dionysian drama, which pits the high aspirations of heroes against the inevitable changes in human fortunes. (*State Museum, Berlin.*)

followed a series of three tragedies) provided a welcome alternative to confronting pain. Like tragedy, satyric drama used mythical plots and characters, but it did not take them seriously. The chorus, invariably composed of Dionysus's lewdly energetic half-human satyrs (Figure 13-5), wore horses' tails and ears and sported huge artificial penises, emblems of the god's sensuality and procreativity. The satyrs' humorous antics and obscene jokes provoked audience laughter, a counterbalance to tragedy's evocation of pity and fear.

Most satyr plays have been lost. Only Euripides's *Cyclops,* a burlesque of Odysseus's encounter with the Cyclops Polyphemus (from the *Odyssey*), survives complete. Parts of Aeschylus's *Drawers of Nets* and Sophocles's *Trackers* also exist in fragmental form.

Comedy

Athens added productions of comedy to the City Dionysia in 486 B.C. and established a separate comic festival, the Lenaea, about 440 B.C. Aristotle states that comedy developed from the behavior of choral leaders who carried replicas of Dionysus's phallus in the Dionysian processions. As bands of revelers sang and danced (Figure 13-6), their leaders exchanged ribald banter with onlookers, spontaneously creating the forerunner of comic dialogue. The Greek word for comedy, *komoidia,* means "komos-singing" and is derived from the word *komos,* meaning "parade of revelers." Exploiting the humor inherent in humanity's (and the gods') diverse sexual activity, comedy offers a positive dimension to tragedy's solemn worldview. Like the satyr play, comedy promotes reconciliation of conflict and a reintegration of the disparate elements composing the Dionysian life force.

The Tragic Vision

The dramatic festival in honor of Dionysus took place in a society that saw itself as an embodiment of the spirit of Apollo, by now associated with moderation, self-control, and enlightenment through the pursuit of knowledge. The democratic constitution established in Athens in 508 B.C. was itself a model of Apollonian rationalism, with its system of checks and balances, its principle of the rule of the majority of citizens, and its use of debating and voting as the instruments of problem solving. The ancient Apollonian way, which encouraged awareness of one's human limitations, and of one's place in the social and universal order, was precisely appropriate for a democratic society.

An essentially conservative people, however, despite the remarkable political changes they had instituted, the citizens of Athens and its sister city-states in Greece retained the old mythic heroes, even while rethinking their relationship to life in an urban, democratic state. Democracy requires a well-informed citizenry capable of self-restraint and committed in principle and practice to the willingness to compromise, to abide by the will of the majority. There was clearly a gap between the old heroes, who always "go forward" and refuse to compromise, and the ideal citizen of the new city-state. The perfect expression of a feudal society where the warrior is king, the old-style "hero" no longer fits comfortably into a world where all citizens are "equal" by law.

Further, for the exceptional, "heroic" individual, Apollo's demands for self-knowledge and moderation in all things are inherently contradictory: what the tragic protagonist knows—when he or she truly acquires self-knowledge—is precisely the capacity for extremes of feeling and behavior that define the hero's extraordinary nature. The path to self-knowledge that Dionysus provides differs markedly from that of Apollo, a "binder" god who asks that we be reasonable and obey the rules. Dionysus, on the other hand, is a god of release and as such is much more in keeping with the heroic spirit.

The Dionysian drive toward self-exploration through freedom, through exuberance, through breaking down the barriers of inhibitions and prohibitions, reveals one's full range of potentialities, however irrational and even terrifying those might be. Thus the tragedies that open each Dionysian festival plunge us into the realm of the chaotic forces within the human mind, beyond the reach of the outer world of reason and moral imperatives, exploring urges—including incest, matricide or patricide, and infanticide—that violate the most basic taboos of civilized life. By bursting beyond such absolute and universal limits, however, the actions of the tragic protagonist provoke awesome and terrifying cosmic reactions. Thus tragedy makes possible—even demands—an awareness of one's connection to the incomprehensible and thus seemingly irrational mysteries of the universe. As the English poet William Blake wrote, "The road of excess leads to the palace of wisdom." Between these two divergent paths—of Dionysian freedom and Apollonian restraint, of instinct and taboo, of nature and civilization, of internal psychological needs and external social responsibilities—lies the uncharted territory that the **protagonist** (main character) of Greek tragedy must traverse.

Myth into Drama

Drama is an ideal vehicle for raising questions or exploring possibilities. In drama, there is no narrative voice, as there is in fiction (or epic), that tells us how to respond to the story, assuring us, for example, despite occasional appearances to the contrary, that Odysseus was a "wise and pious man" who therefore deserved to be rewarded by the gods. In drama, each character speaks and acts in ways that reflect only his or her personal motives or points of view. By setting various characters in motion and allowing them to state their conflicting views, the dramatist creates several different perspectives on any action that occurs and leaves them for the audience to contemplate.

Greek dramatists were not expected to create original plots for their tragedies. Rather, the tragedies were all based on inherited myths. But in transforming myths into dramatic form, the tragedies combined the intrinsic potentialities of the original myths with the heroic aspirations of the epic traditions as well as the spirit of the ritual of Dionysus during which they were performed. Further, authors often took advantage of the multiple perspectives of the dramatic medium to question accepted views, to probe conventional responses, and to explore new approaches to experience.

The Tragic Hero

Like the heroes of the epics from whom the tragic protagonists are probably at least in part descended, the tragic protagonists are noble, both in their lineage and in their character. But perhaps because the tragedies were all enacted live before the eyes of an urban audience, they updated the mythic materials and expressed the heroes' qualities in slightly more realistic, or at least accessible, ways. Thus, instead of tracing their descent from the gods, the heroes are often members of leading families; instead of performing incredible feats of physical prowess and courage in battle, they exhibit unusual moral courage and integrity. The myths that the writers of tragedy selected to dramatize, too, are often about domestic problems that involve violence: marital quarrels, sibling rivalry, incest, or the murder of wife, husband, parent, or child. And though epic heroes may descend to Hades, the hell to which the tragic heroes descend often lies within the tormented recesses of their own minds.

Like the epic heroes, the tragic heroes possess some extraordinary quality. And like their epic predecessors, it is often their unique gifts that both get them into terrible predicaments and allow them to rise above those same predicaments. It is Oedipus's determination and skill at solving riddles that is the source of his greatness; it is that very same determination and skill that bring about the confrontation with the truth that proves his own undoing. Similarly, in Sophocles's earliest play on the family of Oedipus, it is Antigone's moral commitment—her respect for the dead—that brings about both her courageous defiance and her martyrdom.

Trapped between conflicting demands, both external and internal, possessing natures whose best qualities, under duress, often prove self-destructive, the tragic heroes are doomed to suffer. And because they are important people, their suffering ripples outward, encompassing others. The role of the tragic hero, however (perhaps like that of the scapegoat in the Dionysian ritual who took on the sins of the community and was sacrificed in order to relieve the worshipers of the burden of sin), is to take the communal suffering upon himself or herself. The epic hero Achilles, by his extraordinary prowess, becomes the Greeks' point man, the major target of Trojan soldiers. So Oedipus takes the people's sorrows on himself, sending to the oracle to deal with their needs; so Orestes assumes the burden Apollo thrusts on him, of avenging the injustice of Agamemnon's murder; so Oedipus's daughter Antigone singlehandedly takes on the duty of preserving moral law in her community. Only by plumbing the depths of pain can the tragic protagonist explore the limits of human knowledge.

Like the mythic heroes, the tragic protagonists expand the parameters of human experience. But where heroes like Heracles pushed back geographic boundaries, the tragic protagonists push back psychic boundaries, bursting through the barriers of habit, convention, and comfortable illusion. "Man must suffer to be wise," says the chorus in Aeschylus's play *Agamemnon;* alternatively, as Sophocles's Tiresias (in *Oedipus Rex*) puts it, "To be wise is to suffer." The mythic and epic heroes embark on physical quests and learn through painful experience—such as losing one's best friend in battle or watching one's fellows eaten by monsters—or through direct confrontation with the ultimate suffering (death) via the descent to the Underworld. Tragedy typically turns these heroic quests inward: the tragic heroes suffer an inner torment of their own, a kind of psychological sparagmos, and the depth of their anguish is the measure of their heroism (Figure 13-7).

"Suffering is the sole origin of consciousness," wrote the Russian novelist Dostoyevsky in a statement that might aptly describe the tragic protagonist. Conversely, the inability to suffer, or to perceive or experience horror, characterizes the morally blind—for example, in Aeschylus's *Agamemnon,* even when directly presented with the truth, the chorus refuses to see it and only reiterates, like a verbal talisman, "May good prevail in the end." At the opposite end of the scale, too much suffering produces unconsciousness and, ultimately, permanent unconsciousness or death. Consciousness and the awareness of pain are the conditions of a morally responsible existence. Unwilling to face the horror of her life, Oedipus's wife, Jocasta, commits suicide. Unable to confront the tragic burden of suffering, both the chorus and Jocasta are dramatic foils (contrasts) to the tragic hero: to live on the unbearable pinnacle of agony without the merciful unconsciousness of death is Oedipus's tragic fate. Similarly, the chorus of Trojan slave women in the *Libation-Bearers* may cheer when Orestes kills Clytemnestra: they aren't the ones who have to confront the Furies and are in fact blind to their presence. While the chorus celebrates victory, it is Orestes who suffers torment.

The Tragic Universe

Such tragedies tend to depict the universe in a very particular and characteristic way. The universe is governed by divine beings whose presence, actual or implied, gives significance to the actions of the human beings whose lives the gods affect; however, the universe is anthropocentric (human centered). The gods affect human lives, but their responses to human actions are utterly unpredictable. Communication between humans and gods is not as easy as it was in the myths and epics, when the gods came down and spoke with human beings directly. In the world of the tragedies, direct, unmediated communication with the gods does occur (as in Euripides's *Bacchants*),

FIGURE 13-7   Orpheus Playing His Lyre. A mythic figure who experiences the loss, spiritual growth, and acquisition of insight through sufferings that characterize the tragic hero, Orpheus also has the tragic protagonist's ability to articulate a poetic response to the griefs he experiences. Music—in the form of instrumental playing, choral song, and dance—was an integral part of the tragic performance, as it was to Orpheus as a symbol of the creative artist. This vase painting shows Orpheus singing for the young men of Thrace, perhaps only moments before frenzied maenads are to tear him to shreds—a sparagmos he shares not only with Dionysus but also with tragic figures such as Pentheus. (*Staatliche Museen, Berlin.*)

but more rarely. Apollo and Athene do not stroll casually around the streets of downtown Athens chatting with the heroes, as they did at Troy or Ithaca. Such communication is more usually indirect—through rituals, prayers, prophecies, oracles—and thus subject to misinterpretation. The gods speak in riddles, and the humans struggle to understand in whatever ways they can, often with devastating results. But it is given in the heroes' natures that they will insist on trying, on blindly confronting the invisible limits of the cosmic order head-on, using whatever tools—reason, moral integrity, courage, persistence—are at their disposal.

The Tragic Mystery   The tragic universe, furthermore, is not morally neat: justice does not always prevail; nor can human beings count on the gods to reward virtue and punish evil. The gods' actions are often incomprehensible, and the more the heroes persist in trying to penetrate the mystery, the more they suffer. Just as the epic heroes' efforts to achieve literal immortality are doomed, so the efforts of the tragic heroes to find clarity, to assert the rational need for a moral universe, invariably fail. Even for the most gifted, well-intentioned heroes, there is no certainty.

Things unaccountably change: **peripeteia** [pair-ih-pe-TEE-uh] (reversal), as Aristotle originally pointed out, defines the tragic experience. In the world of the tragedies, questions like "why do bad things happen to good people?" have no clear-cut answers beyond a recognition of the mystery at the heart of the universe: the gods are mysterious to humans; they exist and make often impossible demands on us, but we cannot clearly ascertain or comprehend what they really want of us.

Moral Freedom   Although human beings cannot hope to understand the gods, they can at least understand the consequences of their own actions. Thus, in the ambiguous, often paradoxical world of the tragedies, the protagonist typically accepts responsibility for his or her fate, regardless of what the gods may or may not have done to bring it about. Fated or not, we must act as if we are free. In so doing, in rejecting the role of victim and defining ourselves as free moral agents, we wrench human existence out of the hands of the gods and reclaim it as our own. Through intense struggle and sacrifice, the tragic protagonist achieves a kind of moral transcendence that is both ennobling in itself and reassuring of the value of the struggle.

Often culminating in a sudden access of insight beyond the limits of ordinary sense experience, the tragic hero's experience corresponds loosely with the epiphany and consequent communion of the Dionysian ritual. As scholars have noted, the original ritual was also cathartic. The irrational drives were called up and released, allowing the worshiper to continue to function within the confines of ordinary, civilized life. So, too, in tragedy, order is restored in the world of the play: plagues and civil disruptions end; Furies are given socially useful tasks. This restoration comes, of course, at the price of enormous sacrifice. We cannot return, exactly, to our previous condition: we have looked into the abyss and will not readily forget its presence looming beneath our feet. But for the struggle to continue, the community must survive. Thus tragedy prepares the way for what follows: the release of tension in the satyr play and the confirmation and reintegration in the comedy that concludes the dramatic festival. Only in the experience of the entire dramatic cycle can Apollo and Dionysus at last be reconciled.

The *Bacchants*: Euripides's Tragic Vision

The only surviving tragedy that features Dionysus in a leading role is not only one of the last Greek dramas written but is also one of the most perplexing. Composed in 406 B.C. shortly before Euripides's death, the *Bacchants* (the *Bacchae*) dramatizes the myth of Dionysus's return to Thebes, his birthplace, where the god exacts a horrific revenge on his native city for its citizens' failure to honor his divinity. In this play, Euripides takes the Athenian theater back to its Dionysian roots, the wine god's ecstatic cult, and explores the implications of its passionate, potentially destructive nature. To many modern readers the *Bacchants* is genuinely disturbing, troublesome in part because neither of its leading characters—Dionysus nor **Pentheus** [PEN-thee-uhs], king of Thebes—may seem particularly sympathetic. The wine god appears violent and merciless, whereas Pentheus is revealed as a hollow figure, his stubborn opposition to Dionysian religion a product of his fatal inability to confront Dionysian elements in himself.

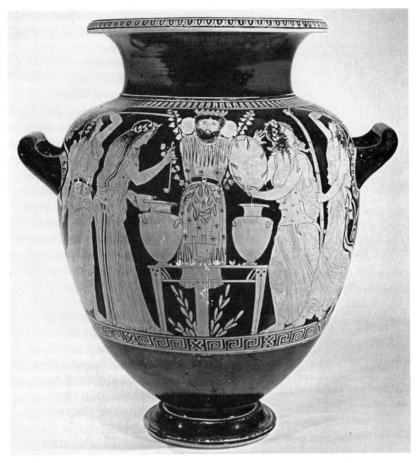

FIGURE 13-8   Dionysus and Bacchants. Surrounded by dancing maenads, two women place ivy garlands on an effigy of Dionysus. Euripides's tragedy is named after its chorus—Asian Bacchants who voluntarily worship their god. By contrast, Theban women are compelled against their will to honor Bromius (another name for Dionysus). (*National Archaeological Museum, Naples.*)

The *Bacchants* is named for its chorus, a group of foreign women passionately devoted to Dionysus, also known as **Bacchus.** These Bacchants, who have followed their god from Asia Minor to Greece, worship Dionysus voluntarily and gratefully, reveling in the emotional freedom and sense of joyous unity with nature that he imparts (Figure 13-8). Their opening song, in which the Asian Bacchants dance wildly, praising Dionysus's holy and irresistible gifts, is the only extant example of a dithyramb, the ancient choral ode associated with Dionysus's prehistoric rituals (Figure 13-9). By contrast, a group of Theban women, who do not appear on stage until near the drama's conclusion, perform the god's rites unwillingly, under divine compulsion. Driven into madness by the god's disorienting power, the Theban Bacchants, led by Pentheus's mother, **Agave** [a-GAY-vee], have abandoned their homes,

FIGURE 13-9   Dancing Maenad. As a young satyr pipes, a bare-breasted maenad dances, clad only in a scanty leopard skin. Pentheus assumes that any woman allowed the freedom to express her inner feelings during Dionysian orgies will totally abandon her civilized roles, indulging in sexual excess. (*British Museum, London.*)

husbands, and children and fled to the nearby hills of Cithaeron, where they reportedly nurse the young of wild animals and drink milk and wine that miraculously spout from the earth. The proliferation of miracles and natural signs, including an earthquake that shakes Thebes to its foundations, unmistakably denotes a divine presence at work; these unpredictable suspensions of natural law, however, serve only to stiffen Pentheus's resistance—and confirm his doom.

Pentheus

In the *Bacchants,* Euripides goes far beyond reinterpreting a cautionary myth that highlights the perils of mortals' failure to recognize or properly revere a god in their midst. Besides illustrating the dangerous folly of human insensitivity to divine visitations, the playwright also explores the tragic character flaws causing the Theban leaders' spiritual blindness. Ironically, the trait that prompts Pentheus's stubborn op-

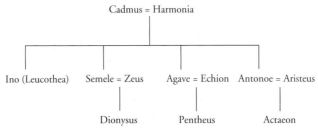

FIGURE 13-10   The Four Daughters of Cadmus. Three of the four daughters of Cadmus and Harmonia bore sons—all first cousins—who suffered sparagmos: Dionysus, son of Semele and Zeus, was dismembered by the Titans; Actaeon, son of Autonoe and Aristeus, was ripped to pieces by his hunting dogs; Pentheus, son of Agave and Echion, was torn limb from limb by a band of spirit-possessed women that included his mother. Ino also suffered a tragic fate: driven mad by Hera for sheltering the young Dionysus, she threw herself into the sea and was transformed into the sea nymph Leucothea, the "white goddess," a personification of sea spray.

position to Dionysian freedom is his lack of Apollonian self-knowledge, a defect that leads him to commit **hubris** [HYOO-bris], or excessive pride. Unable to understand himself, including the Dionysian components in his own nature, he also violates Apollo's edict against excess, foolishly pitting his human will against divine force. Contemptuously rejecting the claim that Zeus had fathered the child that his aunt Semele had mysteriously borne, Pentheus compounds his blasphemy by imprisoning Dionysus and condemning him to death.

Although Euripides emphasizes Pentheus's unacknowledged psychological affinity with Dionysus, the Athenian audience would also be aware of Pentheus's blood kinship. The inflexible Theban king and the god of intoxication are first cousins. Pentheus is the son of Agave, sister of Semele, and Echion, one of the Spartoi—men generated from the teeth of a dragon that Pentheus's grandfather **Cadmus** slew before founding the city of Thebes (Figure 13-10). According to this etiological myth, Cadmus, the son of the Phoenician King Agenor, was dispatched to search for his sister Europa after she had been abducted by Zeus. When consulting the Oracle at Delphi, he was told to found a city where a cow lay down. This led Cadmus to the site of Thebes, where he killed its guardian dragon (Figure 13-11) and sowed the dragon's teeth, from which a throng of young warriors sprang up. Most of the dragon-born crew immediately killed each other in hand-to-hand combat, but five, including Echion, were still living when Cadmus founded Thebes. Although the *Bacchants* repeatedly mentions that Cadmus passed the city's rulership to his young grandson Pentheus, tradition offers no clue to Echion's disappearance from the scene.

Born to the aunt of a god and a man derived from the primordial Goddess's serpent, Pentheus should be expected to intuit his cousin's divinity, making his adamant refusal to do so all the more puzzling. As Euripides makes clear, however, Pentheus's relentlessly hostile reaction to the young stranger, garlanded in ivy and bearing a thyrsus, who suddenly shows up to wreak havoc in Thebes springs from a deep anxiety about his own sexual identity: the young king sees in the seductive youth too much of what he fears in himself (Figure 13-12). Euripides's Dionysus appears wear-

FIGURE 13-11   Cadmus and the Serpent. Athenian playwrights seemed to delight in dramatizing the tragic errors promulgated by the rulers of Thebes, which was one of Athens's bitterest enemies at the time Euripides wrote the *Bacchants* (c. 406 B.C.). In Euripides's play, the aged Cadmus, Thebes's mythical founder, suffers both exile and loss of his humanity, condemned by Dionysus to be changed into a serpent. Cadmus's transformation is an ironic reversal of his earlier heroic act of killing a serpent (dragon) that once guarded the site of Thebes. Following Athene's advice, Cadmus sowed the dragon's teeth, out of which sprang a band of armed warriors, the Spartoi, who fought each other until only five were left. One of the survivors, Echion, married Cadmus's daughter Agave and became the father of Pentheus. In this bowl, Cadmus advances with drawn sword toward the rearing serpent. (*Louvre, Paris.*)

ing the mask of a slight, rather effeminate young man, whose long golden curls and suspicious preference for women's company Pentheus derisively mocks. But the Euripidean Pentheus also wears a mask, posing ostentatiously as a tough soldier who bravely guards his city against the kind of foreign defilement that the stranger tries to introduce. A stalwart defender of Greek masculinity, Pentheus condemns Dionysus's worshiper as his moral opposite: soft, undisciplined, vain, and ineffectual. In fact, Dionysus and Pentheus share important qualities, including sensuality, socially prohibited desires, and a will to power, but whereas these attributes are a source of strength to the god, they trigger his mortal opponent's disgrace and destruction.

Pentheus's Transformation

In the play's major reversal (peripeteia), the two leading characters' respective masks are stripped away, revealing that each is the opposite of what he had previously appeared. At the outset, Pentheus—king, soldier, and law enforcer—ostensibly has the power to humiliate and kill the stranger whose effeminacy so outrages him, making Dionysus's supposed priest a legal sacrifice to his masculine authority. Midway through the play, however, Dionysus takes charge of the action, manipulating Pen-

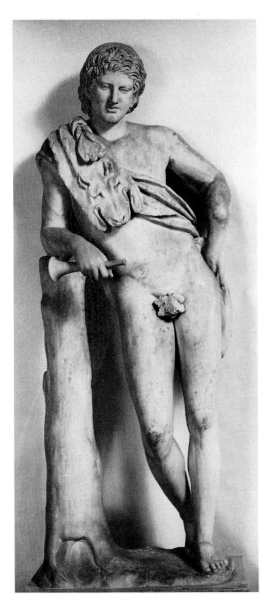

FIGURE 13-12   Resting Satyr. Satyrs, images of uninhibited male sexuality, are traditional companions of Dionysus. This Roman copy of a Greek original (c. 350–330 B.C.) combines strength and sensuality, suggesting the sexual ambivalence that so terrifies Pentheus when he is confronted with Dionysus disguised as a girlish youth. (*Vatican Museums, Rome.*)

theus into unmasking his feminine component, the androgynous traits he found so disturbing in the stranger. Every man in Euripides's audience must have cringed when the actor portraying a Greek military leader reappeared on stage outfitted in a woman's wig, gown, and flowing veil. The feminine self that Pentheus displays is not the wise anima of a mature human being, however, but the caricature of a simpering, preening female, coyly adjusting her Bacchant's regalia and flirting with the stranger. At this point Pentheus and Dionysus have changed places: the god has assumed total control, and the king who tried to execute him will become his sacrificial victim.

FIGURE 13-13   The Death of Pentheus. Refusing to accept the religious validity of Dionysian irrationality, Pentheus becomes its victim. Exhibiting irresistible strength when possessed by the god's spirit, maenads—including Pentheus's mother, Agave—prepare to dismember the young king, whom Dionysus makes them perceive as a dangerous lion. This Pompeiian fresco vividly illustrates the hallucinatory quality of religious frenzy and its potential for fanatical violence. (*National Archaeological Museum, Naples.*)

Dionysus condemns Pentheus to die, not as a brave man fighting for his city but as a transvestite voyeur torn to pieces by women on whom he had come to spy (Figure 13-13). Refusing to recognize that Dionysus embodies the instinctual passion inherent in every human psyche—and is therefore a divine power that only fools ignore—Pentheus suffers the supreme penalty for failing to know himself. Denying Bacchus the proper sacrifice owed the god, he himself becomes the ritual sacrifice, his dismemberment reenacting Dionysus's own sparagmos by the Titans (see Chapter 8). Like his cousin **Actaeon** [ak-TEE-ahn], who offended Artemis and was consequently torn to pieces by his hunting dogs (Figure 13-14), Pentheus learns too late the absolute necessity of respecting the gods' prerogatives.

FIGURE 13-14   Death of Actaeon. The young hunter Actaeon, son of Cadmus's daughter Autonoe—and therefore also a cousin of Pentheus—is torn to pieces by his fifty hunting dogs on the hills of Cithaeron outside Thebes. According to one account, he accidentally observes the nude Artemis bathing, for which intrusion the goddess incites his hounds against him. Actaeon's sparagmos foreshadows that of Pentheus. (*James Fund and by Special Contributions. Courtesy, Museum of Fine Arts, Boston.*)

As Pentheus replays the scene of Dionysian suffering, the god changes his physical shape to reflect the bestial energies previously concealed when he appeared as a languid adolescent. Manifesting his divine-animal unity, Dionysus is simultaneously a horned bull, a lion, and a luminous deity. The ethical contractions intrinsic to nature, its beauty, power, and cruelty, are sublimely combined in this frighteningly natural god.

Agave

Pentheus's nagging fear of what may result if human nature is liberated from its socially imposed restraints is abundantly justified in the manner of his death—at the hands of his own mother, Agave. Divine possession removes traditional inhibitions, allowing Agave to realize her potential in purely masculine roles, reversing the socially prescribed dichotomy between male and female. As racer, hunter, fighter, and executioner, she proves the equal of any Theban soldier. But the cost of her liberation is tragically high, paradoxically stripping Agave of her freedom of rational choice.

Although the *Bacchants* may present Agave primarily as an object lesson in the folly of resisting divine power, her plight suggests other possibilities as well. In throwing off societal prohibitions, she reveals a startling kinship with Artemis, the goddess who eschews traditionally feminine duties, such as motherhood and weaving, to pursue savage beasts in the wilderness. Like Artemis, Agave not only revels in the freedom to hunt and use weapons, but also enacts the goddess's prerogative to inflict sparagmos on any male who dares to invade her sacred privacy. As Artemis incites the mutilation and death of Actaeon, so Agave dismembers the man who spies on women's mysteries. That her victim turns out to be her son dramatizes the tragic alternatives available to women in a patriarchal society: the inner destruction of the psyche that results from oppression and lack of opportunity to achieve real fulfillment in the world of action or the outer destruction of murdering husbands or children.

As a goddess and childless (although associated with childbirth), Artemis escapes the dilemma that entangles such human figures as Agave, Medea, and Clytemnestra. As a mortal woman and a mother, however, Agave is trapped, with no avenue of escape. The tragic nature of her predicament is evident when Agave, believing that she has killed a lion with her bare hands, compares herself to Heracles—an ironic comparison that highlights the differences between their situations. Heracles, too, incurred blood guilt when, in a fit of madness, he slew his wife and children. In sharp contrast to Agave, however, Heracles was given a way to expiate his crime: he is sent on a series of quests that allow him to fulfill his heroic nature. Agave, who has staged a similarly deadly rebellion against domesticity, is permitted no redemptive action but is condemned to permanent exile.

Euripides creates one of the most powerful recognition (**anagnorisis**) scenes in all drama when he shows Agave, carrying Pentheus's severed head, struggle against a return to ordinary reality. Her desperate attempts to remain under Dionysus's spell, to avoid confronting the results of her terrible experiment with total freedom, produce one of the most painful scenes of madness ever devised for the theater.

Having been forced to experience Dionysian ecstasy and coerced into releasing a killer instinct that she loathes, Agave is in a unique position to assess the value of Bacchanalian frenzy (as depicted in figures 13-6 and 13-9). With returning sanity, she realizes that the god has violated the integrity of her personality, blinded her moral vision, robbed her of choice, and exploited her hitherto unexpected potential for aggression and impulsive violence. Agave's rationalism, which made her unable to believe that Semele's child was Zeus-begotten, resembles that of Jocasta, the unhappy wife of Oedipus, who is similarly punished for doubting that the gods personally influence human affairs (see Chapter 16). At the end of the play, Agave makes the only gesture of freedom still available to her: she rejects Dionysus and all he stands for. Tearing his ivy wreath from her hair and throwing down the thyrsus, Agave returns to her former identity, a state of being now impoverished by the loss of both her son and her country. Guilty of shedding a kinsman's blood, Agave is not allowed to join Pentheus in death: polluted, she must wander the earth to ponder and suffer the consequences of having discovered her affinity with nature's animal savagery.

Agave's decisive rejection of divine possession echoes in other myths: according to one story, the bereaved mother's scorn for Dionysus was so strong that, in exile from Thebes, she climbed a tree and lay in wait to attack him with a weapon. As the gods' human pawn, Agave resembles Cassandra, a Trojan princess who was also Apollo's prophet. Both women find that union with a god, despite its emotional gratification, is a poisonous gift that deprives them of personal autonomy and mental peace. Just as Apollo stripped Cassandra of her credibility when she repulsed his advances, so Dionysus arbitrarily deprives Agave of the civilized bonds that would keep her from acting upon the incipient violence in her soul. Driven into madness by the machinations of their divine patrons, Agave and Cassandra illustrate the paradox of religious commitment: while offering unparalleled rapture and insight, the gods punish mercilessly those who give less than complete submission. Agave's mental independence, her skepticism about Semele's conception, and Cassandra's wish to keep her body inviolate, even from Apollo, spark the wrath of the gods, who demand unconditional surrender. The opposing claims of religious devotion and Greek humanism are not easily reconciled—except in the Asian Maenads, who claim to have found grace and peace in Dionysian possession.

Tiresias

In contrast to Agave and Pentheus, Apollo's prophet Tiresias does not hesitate to accept the wine god as Zeus's legitimate son. Although aged and blind, Tiresias decks himself out in the Bacchic regalia, advising Pentheus not to resist the divine will. The only character in the play whom Dionysus does not punish, Tiresias successfully balances the unavoidable contrarieties of control and freedom.

Although Euripides does not refer to it, his audience probably would have been familiar with another myth involving Tiresias's uncanny ability to assimilate polar opposites. Having been changed from man to woman and back again, Tiresias can appreciate Dionysian mutability and androgyny (see Chapter 16). Appearing in virtually every myth associated with Thebes's ill-fated royal house, Tiresias typically offers advice that all rulers, from Cadmus and Pentheus to Oedipus and Creon, unwisely reject. He retains his prophetic powers even after death, continuing to foretell the future in Hades (see Chapter 12; *Odyssey,* Book 11).

Tiresias's accommodation of both Apollo and Dionysus, masculine control and androgynous surrender, parallels Delphi's historic accommodation of two radically different aspects of godhood. By making room for Dionysus—his temple also stood on the flanks of Mount Parnassus—the Delphic compromise between the conflicting demands of mental lucidity and sensuous abandon helped to contain (and control) incipiently dangerous human tendencies. Acknowledging its inevitability, Delphi honored the principle of irrationality by creating institutions to give it limited expression, regulating Dionysian revels to annually scheduled festivals.

Cadmus: Expediency No Substitute for Passion

Although Cadmus, the aged dragon slayer, also appears to honor the new god, his reverence is only lip service. Cadmus's advice urging Pentheus to accept Dionysus insults the god by its shallow expediency: Pentheus should at least pretend he believes that Zeus was Semele's lover, for such a rumor enhances the status of Thebes's royal house. Disdaining such lukewarm acquiescence, Dionysus condemns Cadmus to exile and eventual transformation into a serpent, reducing the former king in old age to the status of a reptile he had slain in his prime.

Dionysus's Pitiless Judgment

Like Zeus in Aeschylus's *Prometheus Bound,* the triumphant Dionysus is incapable of pity, oblivious to Agave's pain or Cadmus's despair. In Euripides's final scene, compassion for human suffering is no more part of the divine character than it is of nature, which sheds no tears for victims of earthquake, cyclone, or flood.

An aspect of nature that transcends moral judgment, Dionysus is as implacable as Hades or Persephone. In Euripides's mythic vision, sympathy and concern for others' anguish are strictly human responses to tragic loss: Agave and Cadmus can express pity for each other's suffering, but the god—impervious to everything but the brute fact of his power—cannot connect with mortals foolish enough to reject his divine reality.

Dionysus of Thebes and Jesus of Nazareth

In the *Bacchants,* Tiresias points out that Demeter and Dionysus have given humanity two indispensable gifts: grain to sustain life and wine to make life bearable. Bread and/or wine, tangible emblems of divine care for mortals, played important roles in some Greco-Roman mystery religions, where food and beverage emblematic of earth's fecundity furnished sacred dining tables at which initiates communed with their gods. Christian writers frame Jesus's public ministry with momentous feasts involving bread and wine. In John's Gospel, Jesus's first miraculous act is to change water into vintage wine at a Jewish wedding, a "sign" of his divinity that seems to mimic the wine-making magic of some Dionysian priests. In the Gospels of Mark, Matthew, and Luke (but not, strangely enough, in John), Jesus hosts a final Passover dinner with his friends at which he announces that the bread he disburses is his "body" and the wine he passes around is his "blood." The next day, Roman soldiers execute him, his wounding and crucifixion a form of sparagmos, the ritual sacrifice of God's beloved son.

The Gospels also state that partway through his career of miraculous healings and exorcisms, when large crowds flocked to have him cure their afflictions, Jesus returned to his hometown of Nazareth—only to have his former neighbors publicly doubt his supernatural abilities and reject his authority. Mark tells the story most baldly:

> Then he [Jesus] left that place, and he comes to his hometown and his disciples follow him. When the sabbath day arrived, he started teaching in the synagogue; and many who heard him were astounded and said so: "Where's he getting this?" and "What's the source of all this wisdom?" And "Who gave him the right to perform such miracles? This is the Carpenter, isn't it? Isn't he Mary's son? And who are his brothers, if not James and Judas and Simon? And who are his sisters, if not our neighbors?" And they were resentful of him.
>
> Jesus used to tell them: "No prophet goes without respect, except on his home turf and among his relatives and at home!"
>
> He was unable to perform a single miracle there, except that he did cure a few by laying hands on them, though he was always shocked at their lack of trust. (Mark 6:1–6, *Scholar's Version*)

In describing the hero's return to the scene of his early life, Mark notes that he is received without "respect" or "trust." No one in Nazareth recognizes that "Mary's son" is a figure of divine origin: the reference to Jesus as his mother's child implies illegitimacy; in Israelite tradition a male is always identified by his father's name. Defining Jesus solely by his blood relationships—mother, brothers, and sisters—the Nazarenes make it impossible for him to demonstrate his divine powers. "Shocked at their lack of trust," the one who routinely works miracles abroad among strangers was "unable to perform a single miracle there." In Luke's version of the episode, the author introduces a telling incident absent in Mark's account: the people of Nazareth not only reject Jesus's claims to supernatural gifts, they try to kill him!

> Everyone in the synagogue was filled with rage when they heard [Jesus speak]. They rose up, ran him out of town, and led him to the brow of the hill on which the town was built, intending to hurl him over it. But he slipped away through the throng and went on his way. (Luke 4:28–30, *Scholar's Version*)

Like the citizens of Thebes who refused to believe that the son of Zeus had been born among them and had now unexpectedly returned to offer spiritual liberation, the Nazarenes could not recognize Jesus as the Son of God who had come home to heal them. Unlike Dionysus, however, Jesus does not threaten to avenge his slighted divinity upon the rejecting—and insulting—townspeople.

In interpreting the significance of Jesus's life to a Greco-Roman audience, New Testament authors employed numerous parallels to Dionysian myth. Like the son of Zeus and the mortal Semele, Jesus has a divine father and a human mother; as Dionysus is spirited away to hide from Hera's wrath, so the infant Jesus is taken to Egypt to escape King Herod's murderous rage; as Dionysus performs miracles to demonstrate his divine sonship, so does Jesus; as the evil Titans inflict sparagmos on Dionysus, so the benighted Romans crucify Jesus; as Dionysus descends into Hades's realm to rescue his mother, so Jesus descends into Tartarus to preach to "spirits in prison"; as Zeus raises the slain Dionysus to immortal life in heaven, so the biblical God resurrects the glorified Jesus to sit at his right hand.

The Book of Revelation draws another analogy linking Jesus with Dionysus. Whereas Luke's Gospel preserves a tradition in which Jesus consistently shows patience and forgiveness toward people who did not value him, the author of Revelation does not hesitate to transform the historical Jesus into a cosmic being determined to execute merciless judgment on his enemies. In Revelation's visions, the nonviolent prophet from Nazareth is portrayed as a traditionally mythic avenger, a divine warrior-king whose second visit to earth is not as a sacrificial lamb but a ferocious lion, ready to slaughter the multitudes who do not accept his divinity.

> And now I saw heaven open, and a white horse appear, its rider [Christ] was called Faithful and True; he is a judge with integrity, a warrior for justice. His eyes were flames of fire, and his head was crowned with many coronets; . . . his cloak was soaked in blood. . . . From his mouth there came a sharp sword to strike the pagans with; he is the one who will rule them with an iron scepter, and tread out the wine of Almighty God's fierce anger. . . . (Revelation 19:11–16, *New English Bible*)

The myth of a deity, "despised and rejected of men," who suddenly reappears to punish unbelievers who had failed to acknowledge his supernatural status, pervades global mythology. In both tales about Dionysus and theological speculations about Jesus, the archetypal pattern of the suffering hero, posthumously deified, is clearly manifest. If the *Bacchants*'s author were to visit contemporary Western society, he would probably not be surprised to find that some elements of Bacchic tradition persist in the late twentieth century. Although significantly modified by Christian theology, in Revelation's mythic picture of Jesus's Second Coming, the story of Dionysus's catastrophic return to Thebes lives on in the Western imagination.

BACCHANTS[1]

Euripides

CHARACTERS

DIONYSUS, *also called Bacchus, Bromius, Evius*

CHORUS, *Asiatic women, devotees of Dionysus*

TIRESIAS, *the Theban prophet, old and blind*

CADMUS, *founder and formerly king of Thebes*

PENTHEUS, *king of Thebes, grandson of Cadmus*

THE STRANGER, *a missionary prophet of Dionysus*

SERVANT, *of Pentheus*

FIRST MESSENGER, *herdsman from Cithaeron*

SECOND MESSENGER, *servant of Pentheus*

AGAVE, *mother of Pentheus, daughter of Cadmus*

Guards, attendants, others

THE SCENE

The front of the royal palace at Thebes.

    The Bacchants *was written in Macedon, where Euripides spent the last years of his life (408–406 B.C.) in virtual exile. It was played in Athens after its author's death.*

[Enter DIONYSUS.*]*

Dionysus

Zeus' child has come back to the land of Thebans. I am Dionysus whom Cadmus' daughter, Semele, bore long ago by the flaming thunderbolt's midwifery. My form I have changed from divine to human, as I come now to Dirce's streams, to the water of Ismenus. Close by the palace here I mark the monument of my mother, the thunder-blasted. The ruins of her home, I see, are smouldering still; the divine fire is still alive—Hera's undying insult to my mother. All praise to Cadmus; he has made this spot holy ground, his daughter's chapel. But it was I who wreathed it in the greenery of the clustering vine.

    I come from Lydia's fields that teem with gold, and Phrygia's. I have conquered the Persians' sun-smitten steppes and the walled towns of Bactria, the wintry land of Media and Arabia the Blest. All Asia is mine, all that lies by the salt sea and possesses fair-towered cities filled with mingled Hellenes and barbarians together. This is the first city I have come to in Hellas. Everywhere else I have instituted my dances and my mysteries, that my godhead might be manifest to mortals.

    First of this Hellene land I have filled Thebes with the cries of exultant

1. Translation by Moses Hadas.

women; I have fitted the fawn-skin to their bodies and have put into their hands the militant thyrsus, entwined with ivy. For my mother's own sisters—*they* at least should have known better—said that Dionysus was no son of Zeus; that Semele had given her love to some mortal; that, schooled by Cadmus, she was fathering on Zeus her own sinful passion. That was why Zeus killed her, they vaunted aloud; because she had lied about her lover. These same sisters, therefore, I have driven in mad frenzy from their homes; they are living in the mountain, out of their minds. I have made them wear the habit of my orgies. And all the womenfolk of Thebes, every woman in the city, I have driven from home distraught, to join the daughters of Cadmus; together they sit beneath the silver firs, on the open rocks. This city must learn, whether it likes it or not, that it still wants initiation into my Bacchic rites. The cause of my mother Semele I must defend by proving to mortals that I *am* a god, borne by her to Zeus.

Now Cadmus had bestowed the kingship and its rights upon his grandson Pentheus, who opposes my worship. He thrusts me away from his offerings, and in his prayers nowhere makes mention of me. Therefore I mean to reveal myself to him and to all the Thebans as a god indeed. When I have settled things here to my satisfaction I shall direct my steps to another land and manifest myself. If the city of the Thebans becomes enraged and tries to drive the bacchants from the mountain by force of arms, I shall lead my Maenads into battle against them. That is why I have assumed this mortal form, changing myself to look like a natural man.

Ho, women that have come from Tmolus, Lydia's bulwark, my own revel band! I have brought you from among barbarians to be my companions, wherever I stay, wherever I go. Raise the native music of your Phrygian homeland, the timbrels which mother Rhea and I invented. Come to this royal palace of Pentheus, sound them loud, for the whole city to come and see. I shall go to the glens of Cithaeron where the bacchants are, and there I shall join in their dances.

[Exit DIONYSUS *before the* CHORUS *enters bearing thyrsi and timbrels.]*

Chorus

[The mark at the beginning of a line indicates a change of speaker.]

From the land of Asia I come, leaving sacred Tmolus behind me. In Bromius' honor I eagerly ply my pleasant task, my toil of ease, crying glory to the Bacchic god.

—Is any profane man in the street? Is any within? Let him withdraw. Hushed be every lip to holy silence. Ever shall I hymn Dionysus in the old, old way.

—Ah, blessed is he whom the gods love, who understands the secret rites of the gods, whose life is consecrated, whose very soul dances with holy joy. In the mountains he knows the bacchic thrill, the holy purifications; he observes the orgies of Cybele, the Great Mother; he brandishes the thyrsus on high, and crowns himself with ivy in the service of Dionysus.

—On ye bacchants, on ye bacchants; bring home Bromius the god, the son of the god, bring Dionysus from the Phrygian mountains, bring Bromius to the open squares of Hellas, spacious for dances.

—Him on a time his pregnant mother with painful travail brought forth, blasted from her womb by the flying thunderbolt of Zeus. In the stroke of the lightning she lost her own life, but straightway, in the very chamber where the mother lay, Cronian Zeus received him and concealed him in his thigh, fastening him in with golden buckles, hidden from Hera.

And when the fates had formed the babe perfect, the father brought forth the bull-horned god; and he wreathed him with the coils of serpents. That is why the Maenads catch wild serpents to twine in their hair.

—*O Thebes, Semele's nurse, crown yourself with ivy, burgeon forth, burgeon forth with verdant smilax with its bright berries. Make yourself a very bacchant with branches of oak or fir. On with the fawn-skins, dapple the hems with fleecy tufts of silvery goat's hair. Riot with the fennel-stalk, but devoutly. Soon all the land will dance—he is Bromius, whoever leads the revel-band—dance off to the mountains, to the mountains where the throng of women await, driven from loom and shuttle by the frenzy of Dionysus.*

—*O chamber of the Curetes, O holy haunts of Crete, which saw the birth of Zeus! In your caves the corybants, with helmets of triple rim, contrived this my timbrel's circle of stretched hide. For our fierce bacchic revelry they blended its note with the sweet voice of the Phrygian flute, and they placed it in the hand of Mother Rhea. To its booming the bacchants would one day utter their revel-shouts. For from the divine Mother the raving satyrs appropriated it and wedded it to the dances of the biennial festivals in which Dionysus delights.*

—*My love is in the mountains. He sinks to the ground from the racing revel-band. He wears the holy habit of fawn-skins; he hunts the goat and kills it and delights in the raw flesh. He rushes to the mountains of Phrygia, of Lydia. He is Bromius, the leader of our dance. Evoe! The ground flows with milk, flows with wine, flows with the nectar of bees. Fragrant as Syrian frankincense is the fume of the pine-torch which our bacchic leader holds aloft. Its ruddy flame shoots from the end of the fennel-stalk as he runs and dances, his delicate tresses streaming in the air, as he rouses the scattered band and shouts them to their feet. "Evoe" he cries, then loudly: "On, ye bacchants, on, bright glory of Tmolus and its golden streams, hymn Dionysus to the deep booming of the timbrels; in bacchic fashion, with Phrygian cries and call, glorify the bacchic god, while the flute, sweet-toned and holy, plays happy anthems for the wild bands trooping to the mountains, to the mountains." Then indeed the bacchant maid rejoices and gambols, light-footed, like a foal by its mother's side in the pasture.*

[*Enter* TIRESIAS.]

Tiresias

Who is at the gate? Call Cadmus from the house, Agenor's son, who left the Sidonian city and built the towers of this Theban town.

Go someone, tell him that Tiresias is seeking him. He knows himself why I have come. He knows the arrangement I have made, with a man even older than myself, to dress the thyrsus and put on skins of fawns and wreathe our heads with shoots of ivy.

[*Enter* CADMUS.]

Cadmus

Ah, my wise old friend!—I knew it was you the moment I heard your wise old voice. Here I am, all ready, in this livery of the god. For he is my own daughter's child [this Dionysus who has proved his godhead to men]; and we must do all we can to glorify his might. Where do we dance? Where do we plant our feet and toss our old, grey heads? Expound it to me, Tiresias, as one old man to another. You are the expert, I shall never weary, night or day, beating the earth with the thyrsus. In my happiness I have forgotten how old I am.

Tiresias

Then you feel as I do. I, too, feel young again. I, too, shall attempt the dance.

Cadmus

Well then, shall we get a carriage to carry us to the mountain?

Tiresias

That would not be the same tribute to the god.

Cadmus

My aged arm, then, will guide your aged feet.

Tiresias

The god will lead us there with no trouble.

Cadmus

Shall we be the only ones in the city to dance for Bacchus?

Tiresias

We alone are right. The others are wrong.

Cadmus

We delay too long. Take hold of my hand.

Tiresias

There you are, clasp hands, link yours with mine.

Cadmus

I am a mere mortal. I do not feel superior to the gods.

Tiresias

We do not rationalize about the gods. We have the traditions of our fathers, old as time itself. No argument can knock *them* down, however clever the sophistry, however keen the wit. People may say that I have no shame, at *my* age, going dancing and binding my head with ivy. Let them. The god has not specified that only the young must dance or only the old. He is pleased to receive honor from all alike. He wishes to be extolled; he does not count up a person's years.

Cadmus

Since you cannot see, Tiresias, I shall speak for you. Here is Pentheus hurrying towards the house, Echion's son, to whom I gave the rule of this land. How excited he is! What news will he tell?
[Enter PENTHEUS.*]*

Pentheus

I happened to be out of the country, but a tale of strange mischief in the city here has brought me back. Our women have left home, they tell me, in sham ecstasies. They are frisking about on the shadowy hills, honoring with dances this new-fashioned divinity, this Dionysus of theirs. In the midst of each rowdy group a brimming wine-bowl stands. Then they slink off separately to lonely corners to serve the beds of men. Of course they pretend they are priestesses, inspired priestesses; but they make more of Aphrodite than of Bacchus.

I have caught a number of them. Jailers have them safely manacled in the public prison. Those that are missing I'll chase off the mountain [—Ino and Agave, who bore me to Echion, and Autonoe, the mother of Actaeon]. I'll catch them in iron traps and put a quick stop to this immoral revelry.

They say that a stranger has arrived, a wizard, a sorcerer from Lydia, with fragrant golden curls and ruddy face and spells of love in his eyes. He spends his days and nights in the company of young women, pretending to initiate them in the bacchic mysteries. If I catch him in this house I'll stop him from beating his thyrsus and tossing his curls. I'll cut his neck from his body.

It is he that says Dionysus is a god (yet, *he* says so) and was once sewn up in the thigh of Zeus—the child that was burnt up by the flaming thunderbolt along with his mother, because she falsely named Zeus as her lover. Is it not enough to make a man hang himself in agony—this insolent effrontery, this mysterious stranger?

But look! Here's a new phenomenon. The seer Tiresias in dappled fawn-skins! And my own grandfather—how ridiculous—playing the bacchant with a fennel wand! Sir, this is not my mother's father. So old and so foolish! Please throw that ivy away. Let go that thyrsus, rid your hand of it.

This is *your* instigation, Tiresias. This is another device of yours to make money out of your bird-gazing and burnt sacrifices—introducing a *new* god to men. It is only your grey hairs that save you from sitting in chains among the bacchants for introducing these unholy rites. When the sparkle of wine finds a place at women's feasts, there is something rotten about such celebrations, I tell you.

Leader

What blasphemy! Stranger, have you no respect for the gods, no respect for Cadmus who sowed the crop of dragon's teeth? Will the son of Echion disgrace his family?

Tiresias

Give a clever man a good theme to talk on, and it is easy enough to speak well. Your tongue, indeed, runs smoothly, as if you had wit, but there is no wit in what you say. The man whose strength is his impudence, whose ability is all in his tongue, makes a bad citizen—and a stupid one.

This new divinity whom you ridicule—words cannot describe how great will be his power throughout Hellas. Mankind, young man, has two chief blessings: goddess Demeter—the earth, that is; call her whichever name you will—who sustains men with solid food, and this son of Semele, who came later and matched her gift. He invented the liquid draught of the grape and introduced it to mortals. When they get their fill of the flowing grape, it stops their grief. It gives them sleep and forgetfulness of daily sorrows. There is no other medicine for trouble. The libations we pour are the god himself making *our* peace with the gods, so that through him mankind may obtain blessings.

You sneer at the story that he was stitched inside the thigh of Zeus. I will teach you the true interpretation of that. When Zeus snatched him from the thunderbolt's flame and brought the infant god to Olympus, Hera wanted to cast him out of heaven. But Zeus contrived a counter device, as a god might. He broke off a piece of the earth-enveloping sky and gave jealous Hera an *incorporeal* Dionysus. But in time mortals got the word changed and said the child had been *incorporated* in Zeus. So they made up the story that he had been stitched inside the thigh of the god.

He is a prophetic god. Those whom his spirit fills, like people possessed, have no small prophetic power. Whenever the god enters the body in full strength, he takes possession of men and makes them tell the future. He also has taken over a part of Ares' functions. A host under arms, ay already drawn up in line, is often scattered in *panic* before raising a spear. This also is a sort of madness sent by Dionysus (and his follower *Pan*). A time will come when you will see him even on Delphi's rock, bounding over the double peak of Parnassus with his pine-torches, brandishing and tossing his bacchic wand. He shall be great throughout Hellas. Listen to *me*, Pentheus. Do not presume that mere power has influence with men. Do not be wise in your own diseased imagination. Welcome the god to the land, pour libations, wreathe your head, revel.

Not even Dionysus can compel women to be chaste. For that you must look to the women's own nature [for a chastity proof against all shocks]. Even in bacchic revels the good woman, at least, will not be corrupted.

You see, *you* take pleasure when a multitude stands at your gates and the city magnifies the name of Pentheus. He, too, I judge, takes delight in being honored. I then, and Cadmus, whom you laugh at, shall crown ourselves with ivy and dance. A hoary old pair, but dance we must. I shall not be persuaded by your logic to combat gods. You are mad, most distressingly mad. No spells can cure a disease which is itself a spell.

Leader

Old man, your words do honor to Phoebus and you are wise in honoring Bromius; he is a mighty god.

Cadmus

My boy, Tiresias has advised you well. Dwell with us, do not break with our old ways. You are flighty at the moment. Your wisdom is unwise. Even if this is no god, as you say, pretend to yourself that he is. It is a most honorable falsehood. It makes Semele seem to be the mother of a god and it will redound to the credit of our whole family.

You are familiar with the sorry fate of Actaeon. The flesh-devouring dogs that he himself had raised tore him to pieces in the fields because he boasted that he was better at the hunt than Artemis. Don't let anything like that happen to you. Come, let me crown your head with ivy. Join us in honoring the god.

Pentheus

Do not lay your hand upon me. Go play the bacchant. Do not wipe off your folly on me! This teacher of your foolishness will get what he deserves. Let someone go with all speed—go to this man's seat where he examines his birds. Heave it up with crowbars, turn it upside down. Make a general havoc of the whole place. Throw his fillets to the winds and storms. That will gall him more than anything.

Let others of you scour the city and track out this foreign epicene who has brought this strange madness upon the women and is defiling our beds. If you catch him bring him here in chains to die the death he deserves—by stoning. He will live to rue his revelry in Thebes.

[Exit PENTHEUS.*]*

Tiresias

Poor wretch, how little you know what you are saying. Now you are really mad. You did go off your head once before.

Let us go, Cadmus, and entreat the god, on this man's behalf, savage though he is, and for the city's sake, to bring no evil to pass. Come, follow me with your ivy staff. Try to hold my body up, as I do yours. It would be disgraceful for two old men to fall. However, never mind. We must serve Bacchus, son of Zeus. But beware, Cadmus, lest Pentheus bring into your house his namesake Penthos— Sorrow. That is no prophecy, but plain fact. A fool speaks folly.

[The two old men totter off.]

Chorus

Holiness, Holiness, queen of Heaven, as you turn your golden wings earthwards, do you hear these words of Pentheus? Do you hear this unholy defiance of Bromius, Semele's son, the god of lovely garlands and good cheer, the prince of the Blessed Ones? This is his realm: revelry and dancing, flute-playing and laughter and the banishing of care, whether the presence of the grape brightens the banquets of the gods, or on earth the wine bowl casts the mantle of sleep around the ivy-wreathed merrymakers.

Of unbridled lips and lawless folly the only end is disaster; but the quiet life of wisdom abides unshaken and sustains the home. For though they dwell remote in the sky, the sons of heaven regard the affairs of men. Knowledge is not wisdom. Thoughts too long make life short. If man, in his brief moment, goes after things too great for him, he may lose the joys within his reach. To my mind, that is the way of madness and perversity.

Oh that I might come to Cyprus, Aphrodite's isle, where dwell the Loves that soothe the hearts of men; to Paphos where the hundred-mouthed streams of the barbarian river bring fruits without rain. Where stands Pieria, queen of beauty, seat of the Muses, where the holy hill of Olympus stands—thither take me, Bromius, divine Bromius, leading your bacchic rout. There the Graces dwell, there dwells Desire, there it is lawful for the bacchants to celebrate their orgies.

The deity, Zeus' son, rejoices in festivals. He loves goddess Peace, who brings prosperity and cherishes youth. To rich and poor he gives in equal measure the blessed joy of wine. But he hates the man who has no taste for such things—to live a life of happy days and sweet and happy nights, in wisdom to keep his mind and heart aloof from over-busy men. Whatever the majority, the simple folk, believe and follow, that way I will accept.

*[*PENTHEUS *enters and is met by a* SERVANT, *leading attendants with the Lydian* STRANGER, *bound.]*

Servant

Pentheus, here we are. We have caught the prey you sent us to catch; our expedition was not in vain. Our quarry—here he is—is a tame creature. He did not take cover or run away. No pallor of fear chased the blood from his cheek. Of his own free will he surrendered. He even smiled as he consented to be arrested and bound. He waited for me to do my duty—he even helped me. I was touched and said to him: "Stranger, not of my will do I take you, but by the orders of Pentheus who sent me."

On the other hand, those bacchants you caught and shut up in the public jail are gone. They slipped the bonds that bound them and gambolled off to the meadows, calling upon Bromius as their god. The fetters of their feet burst asunder of their own accord, and the gates were unbarred by no human hand. This man who has come to our Thebes is full of miracles. The rest is your affair.

Pentheus
Free this man's hands. Trapped as he is, he cannot have the speed to escape me.

Well! You are quite handsome, stranger, for women's taste—and that is what brings you to Thebes. Your hair is long—apparently you never wrestle. It flows over your cheeks, full of appeal. And your complexion is so clear, studiously so. The sun never gets at it; it is in the shade you go hunting, hunting Aphrodite with your beauty. Tell me first who you are, of what race?

The Stranger
There is nothing to boast of, it is easy to tell. You have doubtless heard of flowery Tmolus.

Pentheus
I know. The circle of its hills surrounds the city of Sardis.

The Stranger
I am from there, Lydia is my country.

Pentheus
How come you to bring these rites to Hellas?

The Stranger
Dionysus initiated me, Zeus' son.

Pentheus
Is there a Zeus over there who begets new gods?

The Stranger
No, he is the same Zeus who joined in wedlock here with Semele.

Pentheus
Was it in a dream, or face to face, that he pressed you into his service?

The Stranger
He saw me and I saw him. For proof he gave me sacred rites.

Pentheus
These orgies of yours, what form do they take?

The Stranger
It is unlawful for profane mortals to know them.

Pentheus
What profit do they afford to the votaries?

The Stranger
It is not right for you to hear, but they are worth knowing.

Pentheus
You gild the tale well, to make me curious.

The Stranger
The god's orgies loathe the man who practises impiety.

Pentheus
You say you saw the god clearly. What like was he?

The Stranger
What like he pleased; it was not for me to dictate.

Pentheus
Again you side-step nimbly, and avoid the point.

The Stranger
Talk wisdom to the stupid and they will think *you* foolish.

Pentheus
And is this the first place to which you bring your god?

The Stranger
All the barbarians celebrate his rites and dances.

Pentheus
They have far less sense than Hellenes.

The Stranger
In this, at least, they have more. Customs differ.

Pentheus
These rites—do you perform them at night or by day?

The Stranger
At night, for the most part; darkness gives solemnity.

Pentheus
It betrays women and undermines their morals.

The Stranger
By day, too, shameful things may be contrived.

Pentheus
You ought to be punished for your vile sophistries.

The Stranger
And you for your coarse blasphemies against the god.

Pentheus
How bold our bacchant, a pretty fencer—with words!

The Stranger
Tell me my fate. What is the awful thing you are going to do to me?

Pentheus
First I will cut off your pretty curls.

The Stranger
I dedicate them to the god. It is for him I keep them.

Pentheus
Next hand over this thyrsus.

The Stranger
Take it from me yourself. It is Dionysus' thyrsus I carry.

Pentheus
And I will shut you up safe in prison.

The Stranger
The god himself will free me, whenever I desire.

Pentheus
Perhaps so, when you stand among your bacchants and call upon him.

The Stranger
Even now he is near and sees what I undergo.

Pentheus
Then where is he? He is not apparent to *my* eyes.

The Stranger
He is with me, but your impiety will not let you see him.

Pentheus
[to guards]
Seize him. The fellow mocks me and Thebes.

The Stranger
I give you sober warning: do not bind me, you fools.

Pentheus
But I have more authority than you. I say 'Bind.'

The Stranger
You do not know your station. You do not realize what you are doing. You forget who you are.

Pentheus
I am Pentheus, Agave's son and Echion's.

The Stranger
An apt name to be unlucky in.

Pentheus
Begone! Imprison him near the palace, in the horses' stables. Let him see glooms and darkness. Dance away *there*. These women here, whom you have brought with you, your accomplices in mischief, I shall either sell off, or keep them at the loom as my slaves. That will stop their hands from this thudding and beating of hides.

The Stranger
I shall go. I can but fulfil my destiny. But remember: Dionysus, whom you deny, will exact full payment for this outrage. When you assault me you are putting *him* in bonds.
[Exeunt PENTHEUS *and* THE STRANGER, *guarded.]*

Chorus
Daughter of Achelous, holy Dirce, blessed maiden! Once you received Zeus' babe in your fountains, when Zeus that begot him snatched him from the undying flame and placed him in his thigh and called aloud: "Come, Dithyrambus, enter this my male womb. By this name, my Bacchus, I proclaim you to Thebes, that they may so call you." And yet, blessed Dirce, you thrust me away when I hold my begarlanded revels in your land. Why do you disown me? Why do you avoid me? The time will come, I swear by the lovely clusters of Dionysus' vine, the time will come when you too shall take thought of Bromius.

[What passion, what passion.] Pentheus publishes abroad his earth-born lineage, his descent from the Dragon of old, Pentheus earth-born Echion's son. A savage monster he is; no mortal man he, but a bloody earth-born giant battling the gods. Soon he will throw chains upon me, who belongs to Bromius. Already he holds my fellow-reveller within his house, hidden away in a dark prison. Do you see these things, Dionysus, son of Zeus? Do you see your prophets amid trials and tribulations? Come, king, come down Olympus, brandishing your golden thyrsus. Quell the presumption of this bloody man.

Where, I wonder, on Nysa, the lair of wild beasts, are you holding your revels, thyrsus in hand? Or are you upon the Corycian peaks? Or perhaps you are on Olympus, embowered in thick forests, where once upon a time the music of the harp of Orpheus marshalled the trees to him, marshalled the beasts of the wildwood. You are blessed, Pieria; Evius reverences you and will come to hold his revels upon you with bacchic dances. He will cross the racing stream of Axius. He will lead his whirling maenads over Lydias, father of waters, the giver of wealth and blessing to man. Loveliest of waters are his streams, they tell me, enriching a land of noble horses.
[There is a roar of thunder. Lightning flashes over the tomb of Semele. The earth trembles. The CHORUS *dashes about shrieking. Then a voice is heard.]*

Voice
[within]
Ho, hear me, hear my voice! Ho, bacchants, Ho, bacchants!

Some of Chorus
What cry, what cry is that? Whence came the call, the bacchic call, to summon me?

Voice

[within]

Ho! Ho! Again I call. Semele's child, the son of Zeus.

Others

Ho! ho! our lord, our lord! Come to our revel rout, O Bromius, Bromius.

Voice

[within]

Shake the earth's floor, awful Earthquake.

Some of Chorus

Aha! aha! Soon the house of Pentheus will be shaken to ruins.

Others

Dionysus is in the palace! Adore him!

Others

O, we adore him!

Others

Did you mark how the stone capitals yonder on the pillars parted asunder? Bromius chants his own triumph within the halls.

Voice

[within]

Kindle the thunderbolt's lurid torch. Burn, burn down, the palace of Pentheus.

[Lightning blazes over the palace and the monument of Semele.]

Some of Chorus

Aha! aha! Look, see Semele's holy tomb. How it blazes! It is the flame the thunder-god left there long ago, the flame of Zeus' thunderbolt. Hurl to the ground your shuddering limbs, Maenads. Our king comes, the son of Zeus, confounding utterly these halls.

[Enter THE STRANGER.*]*

The Stranger

Foreign women, are you so astounded with fear that you have fallen to the ground? You have perceived, it seems, how Bacchus shook the house of Pentheus. But raise yourselves and take courage. Still your shuddering limbs.

Leader

O brightest light of our bacchant revel, how glad I am to see you. We were alone, forsaken.

The Stranger

Did you despair when they led me in and were about to hurl me into Pentheus' dark dungeons?

Leader

Despair indeed. Who was there to be my protector if any mischance were to befall you? But how did you escape from the clutches of that godless man?

The Stranger
With effortless ease I saved myself unaided.

Leader
Did he not bind your hands with chains and fetters?

The Stranger
There too I mocked him. He thought he was binding me but he never so much as laid a finger on me. He fed on fancy. In the stable where he took me to imprison me he found a bull, and he threw his nooses around its knees and the hooves of its feet. He panted furiously and dripped sweat from his body and dug his teeth into his lips. There I was, sitting nearby at my ease and looking on. At this moment Bacchus came and shook the building and kindled a fire on his mother's tomb. Seeing the glare, Pentheus thought the place was on fire and rushed back and forth ordering the servants to bring buckets of water. Every slave was busy at the task, but they had their trouble for nothing. Then he thought I had escaped. So he suspended these labors and rushed into the house with his dark sword drawn. But Bromius, as it seems to me—I give you my conjecture—created a phantom in the court. Pentheus attacked it with a rush and stabbed at the bright ether as if he were butchering me. Besides this, Bacchus brings these other afflictions on him: the prison he razed to the ground, everything lies in ruin. Most bitterly he must rue my imprisonment. Fatigue has made him drop his sword, and he lies exhausted. A mere man, he had the effrontery to join battle with a god. I slipped quietly out of the house and have come to you. I care nothing for Pentheus.

It seems to me—a boot is clattering in the house—he will soon come to the front. What will he say after this? Let him come in all his bluster; I shall bear it easily. A modest nonchalance—that is the mark of wisdom.
[Enter PENTHEUS.*]*

Pentheus
This is an outrage. The stranger has escaped, the one that was lately bound fast with chains. Ha! Here is the man! What is this? How is it you appear in front of my house? How did you come out?

The Stranger
Stay your foot! Teach your anger to walk quietly.

Pentheus
How did you escape from your chains and get out here?

The Stranger
Did I not say—or did you not hear me—that someone would free me?

Pentheus
Who? With you it is one strange saying after another.

The Stranger
He who raises the clustering vine for man.

Pentheus
[A sorry gift—to make men forget themselves.]

The Stranger
What you sneer at does him honor.

Pentheus
I will have every gate in the walls barred.

The Stranger
Why? Can gods not overleap your walls?

Pentheus
Clever you are, very clever—but not clever enough.

The Stranger
In the most important thing I am clever enough. But first hear and mark the words of this man who is coming from the mountain with some message for you. I shall await your pleasure, I shall not flee.
[Enter HERDSMAN.*]*

Herdsman
Pentheus, ruler of this Theban land, I come from Cithaeron, where . . . [the bright flakes of white snow never cease].

Pentheus
[interrupting]
What tidings do you bring in such haste?

Herdsman
I have seen the raving bacchants, who rushed barefooted from their homes in frenzy. I am here all eager to tell you and the city, king, the fearsome things they do, things surpassing wonder. Am I to speak of these events freely or abridge my story? I want you to say, O king. I am afraid of your hasty temper, so passionate, so imperious.

Pentheus
Speak on. You are quite safe from punishment on my part. To grow angry with just men is not right. The more awful your story about the bacchants, the greater the punishment I shall inflict upon this man who taught the women these arts.

Herdsman
Our herds of pasturing kine had just begun to ascend the steep to the ridge, at the hour when the sun shoots forth his rays to warm the earth. I saw three bands of women dancers; Autonoe was leader of the first choir, your mother Agave of the second, and Ino of the third. They all lay in the sleep of exhaustion. Some were reclining with their backs against branches of fir, others had flung themselves at random on the ground on leaves of oak [modestly, not, as you charge, intoxicated with the wine-bowl and the sound of the flute and hunting Cypris in the lonely forest].

Then your mother rose up in the midst of the bacchants and called upon them to bestir their limbs from sleep when she heard the lowing of the horned kine. The women then cast the heavy sleep from their eyes and sprang upright, a sight of wondrous comeliness. There were young women and old women and maids yet unmarried. First they let their hair fly loose about their shoulders and tucked up their fawn-skins, those whose fastenings had become unloosed, and girt the speckled skins about them with serpents that licked their cheek. Others held gazelles in their arms, or the untamed whelps of wolves, feeding them with white milk. These were young mothers who had left their infants behind and still had their breasts swollen with milk. Then they put on ivy wreaths and crowns of oak and flowery smilax. One took her thyrsus and struck it against a rock, and there sprang from it a dewy stream of water. Another struck her fennel wand upon the ground, and the god sent up a fountain of wine for her. Those that had a desire for the white drink scraped the earth with the tips of their fingers, and had rich store of milk. From the wands of ivy there dripped sweet streams of honey. If you had been there to see, you would have approached with prayers the god whom you now revile.

We cowherds and shepherds came together to argue and debate with one another on the fearful and wonderful things they did. One fellow who was fond of loafing about town, an experienced talker, spoke out to all and sundry: "You who dwell upon the holy terraces of the mountains, do you vote that we chase Pentheus' mother, Agave, from her bacchic revels and do our king a kindness?" He seemed to us to speak well, and so we set an ambush amidst the leafy thickets and hid ourselves. At the set time they waved the thyrsus for their revelling and all together, with one voice, invoked Bacchus, Zeus' offspring Bromius. The whole mountain cried "Bacchus" with them. The animals joined in the revelry. Everywhere there was a stirring as they raced along.

Now Agave happened to come racing by me and I jumped out and made to seize her, evacuating the ambush where I was hiding. But she raised a cry: "Ah, my fleet hounds, we are being hunted by these men! But follow me, follow with your wands in your hands for weapons."

We fled and escaped a rending at the bacchants' hands. But, with naked, unarmed, hands, the women attacked the heifers that were grazing on the grass. You could see one holding wide the legs of a well-fed calf which bellowed and bellowed. Others rent heifers apart. You could see ribs or cloven hooves tossed here and there, and pieces smeared with gore hanging from the firs, dripping blood. The wanton bulls—forgotten the menace of their levelled horns—were tripped and dragged to the ground by the hands of countless young women. Quicker were their coverings of flesh torn asunder than you could close the lids of your royal eyes. Like birds they soared off the ground in their flight as they scoured the spreading plains by the streams of Asopus which grow the fine harvests of Thebes. Like an invading army they fell upon Hysiae and Erythrae, which nestle under Cithaeron's slopes, and everywhere they wrought confusion and havoc. They pillaged homes at random. Their loot they put upon their shoulders, and though it was not tied on, it held fast; nothing fell to the dark earth, neither brass nor iron. They carried fire in their curls and it did not burn them. Some of us, angered by the depredations of the bacchants, resorted to arms. And *there* was a terrible sight to see, O king. Pointed spears drew no blood, whereas the women flung wands from their hands and wounded their assailants till they turned tail and ran. Women defeating men! There was a god with them. Then they went back whence they had started, to the fountains which the god had shot up for them. They washed off the blood, while the serpents licked clean the clots from their cheeks.

This deity then, whoever he is, O king, receive into the city. In many things he is powerful. This also they say of him, I hear, that he gave mortals the wine which ends sorrow. If *he* exists not, then neither does Cypris, nor any other joy for men at all.

[Leader]
I am fearful of speaking out freely to one who is my master, but I shall have my say: there is no god greater than Dionysus.
[Exit HERDSMAN.*]*

Pentheus
This brings it close, like a spreading fire—this bacchic menace. We are disgraced in the eyes of Hellas. There must be no delay. Go to the Electran gates; order all the hoplites and all the riders of swift horses to muster, all those who brandish targes and those whose hands twang the bow-string. We shall march against the bacchants. This is truly going too far—to be treated like this at the hands of women.

The Stranger
My words, no doubt, will fail to persuade you, Pentheus; but despite the wrong you have done me I advise you not to take up arms against a god. Keep calm. Bromius will not allow you to drive his bacchants from their hills of revelry.

Pentheus
Do not lecture me. You have escaped from bonds; keep that in mind. Or shall I call back justice upon you?

The Stranger
If I were you, I would sacrifice to him rather than rage and kick against the pricks—a man against a god.

Pentheus
I shall sacrifice indeed—these women. I shall make great and deserved slaughter in the glens of Cithaeron.

The Stranger
You will all be put to flight. And that will be a disgrace—when they with their bacchic wands turn back your brazen shields.

Pentheus
There's no dealing with this stranger we are at grips with. Both going and coming he will have his say.

The Stranger
Friend, it is still possible to mend the situation.

Pentheus
By doing what? Being a slave to my own slaves?

The Stranger
I shall bring the women here without using weapons.

Pentheus
Ah me, this is a cunning plot against me.

The Stranger
How a plot, if I want to *save* you by my devices?

Pentheus
You are in conspiracy with them, to establish your revels for all time.

The Stranger
In conspiracy indeed—that is true—but with the god.

Pentheus
[*to* SERVANTS]
Bring me my armor here.
[*To the* STRANGER]
And *you* stop your talk!

The Stranger
[*after thought*]
Ah! Would you like to see them in their gatherings upon the mountain?

Pentheus
Very much. Ay, and pay uncounted gold for the pleasure.

The Stranger
Why have you conceived so strong a desire?

Pentheus
Though it would pain me to see them drunk with wine————

The Stranger
Yet you would like to see them, pain and all.

Pentheus
Be sure I would, if I could sit quietly under the firs.

The Stranger
But they will track you out, even if you come unseen.

Pentheus
Then it shall be openly; your point is quite right.

The Stranger
Do we go then? Will you undertake the journey?

Pentheus
Lead me with all speed. I grudge you every minute.

The Stranger
Put upon your body clothes of fine linen.

Pentheus
Why so? Am I, a man, to enroll in the other sex?

The Stranger
They may kill you, if you are seen there as a man.

Pentheus
Again your point is quite right. You are something of a veteran in guile.

The Stranger
It was Dionysus taught me this lore.

Pentheus
How then shall your advice be properly carried out?

The Stranger
I shall come inside and dress you.

Pentheus
What sort of dress? A woman's? I am ashamed.

The Stranger
You are no longer eager to see the spectacle of maenads.

Pentheus
What dress will you put on my body?

The Stranger
I shall spread your hair out long over your head.

Pentheus
What is the next item in my outfit?

The Stranger
Robes that reach to the feet, and on your head a snood.

Pentheus
Is there anything else you want to add?

The Stranger
A thyrsus for your hand, and the dappled skin of a fawn.

Pentheus
I could not possibly put on a woman's dress.

The Stranger
Then you will have to fight the bacchants and cause bloodshed.

Pentheus
Right. We must first go and reconnoitre.

The Stranger

If you *will* seek evil ends, it is at least wise to eschew evil means.

Pentheus

But how can I go through the city unseen by the citizens?

The Stranger

We will go by deserted ways. I will lead you.

Pentheus

Anything is better than to have the bacchants jeer at me. Let us go inside—I shall consider what is best.

The Stranger

By all means. In any event, *I* am prepared.

Pentheus

I will come. I shall either go under arms or take your advice.
[*Exit* PENTHEUS *into palace.*]

The Stranger

Women, our fish is ready for the strike. He will go to the bacchants and there he will forfeit his life.

Dionysus, the task is now yours. You are not far off. Let us punish this man. First drive him from his wits, make him a little mad. If he is in his right mind, there is no chance of his ever consenting to put on a woman's dress. But if he is driven out of his mind he will put it on. After those truculent threats of his, I want him to become a laughing-stock to the Thebans as he is led through the city looking like a woman. I shall go and dress Pentheus in the apparel which he will take with him to Hades, slaughtered by his mother's hands. He shall come to know Dionysus, son of Zeus, who is every bit a god, terrible in power, but to mankind most gentle.
[*Exit into palace.*]

Chorus

Shall I ever again in the night-long dances plant my white foot in bacchic revelry, tossing back my head in the dewy air, like a sportive fawn rejoicing in green pastures, delivered from the terror of the chase, from the watching eyes and the well-meshed nets, from the huntsman cheering on his eager, racing pack? Sorely pressed, she flies over the river-flats, swift as a storm-wind, and rejoices in the leafy shade of forest trees, in solitudes unbroken by man.

What is wisdom? What boon from the gods is fairer among men than to hold a victorious hand over the head of one's enemies? What is fair is ever dear.

Slowly, yet surely withal, the power divine advances. It chastises those mortals who honor brutality, who in mad delusion do not give glory to the gods. The gods are cunning: they lie in wait a long march of time to trap the impious. Above the established doctrines neither knowledge nor practice should seek to go. It costs but little to believe in the power and mystery of the gods, to accept what is grounded in nature and accepted by the usage of long ages.

What is wisdom? What boon from the gods is fairer among men than to hold a victorious hand over the head of one's enemies? What is fair is ever dear.

Happy is he who has escaped the tempest at sea and found harbor. Happy is he who has risen triumphant over his toils. In one way or another one man outstrips another in the race for wealth and power. And a thousand others are cherishing a thousand hopes; some result in happiness for mortals and some fail. But I call blessed the man whose life is happy day by day.
[*The* STRANGER *enters and calls upon* PENTHEUS, *whom he has been dressing, to come out.*]

The Stranger

Pentheus! If you are so eager to pry into secret things, so bent on evil, come out in front of the house; let us see how you look dressed like a woman, a bacchic maenad, off to spy on your mother and her company.
[*Enter* PENTHEUS *in bacchic attire; he moves and speaks as if under some strange influence.*]
You *do* look like one of Cadmus' daughters.

Pentheus

I seem to see two suns, and a double Thebes, ay, two seven-gated cities. And a bull is leading me on—you seem to be a bull, with horns growing on your head. *Were* you ever an animal? Certainly you have the look of a bull.

The Stranger

The god is our escort. He was hostile before, but now he has made his peace with us. Now you see as you should.

Pentheus

What *do* I look like? Have I not the pose of Ino? Or Agave, yes, my own mother Agave?

The Stranger

When I look at you I seem to see their very selves. But here's one of your tresses out of place. It is not as I fixed it, under your snood.

Pentheus

I must have dislodged it inside, while I was tossing my locks up and down in bacchic ecstasy.

The Stranger

I will arrange it again, I am your maid. Come, hold your head up.

Pentheus

There, you dress it. I depend on you.

The Stranger

Your girdle has come undone. And the tucks of your dress are all uneven at the ankles.

Pentheus

I think so too, at least by the right foot. The rest hangs straight enough, by the left.

The Stranger

I am sure you will think me your best friend when I surprise you and show you the bacchants sober.

Pentheus

Do I hold the thyrsus in my right hand or in this one to be more like a bacchant?

The Stranger

Hold it in your right hand, and advance it when you advance your right foot. I am glad your mind is changed.

Pentheus

Do you think I could carry the crags of Cithaeron, bacchants and all, upon my shoulders?

The Stranger

You could, if you wished. The mind you had before was not sound, but now you are in a proper state.

Pentheus

Shall we take crowbars? Or shall I tear the crags up with my hands, putting a shoulder or an arm to the peaks?

The Stranger

O please! Don't destroy the shrines of the Nymphs and the haunts of Pan and his pipings.

Pentheus

Right you are. One does not overcome women by force. I shall conceal myself in the firs.

The Stranger

You will get all the concealment I think you need—creeping up to spy on the maenads.

Pentheus

Besides, I expect they won't leave their couches in the thickets, caught like birds—and loving it.

The Stranger

That is the very thing you are going to watch. Perhaps you will surprise them— if you are not surprised first yourself.

Pentheus

Take me through the middle of Thebes. I am the only man of them that would make this venture.

The Stranger

You are the only one that troubles about your city, the only one. Therefore, trials await you, fitting trials. Follow me. I shall guide you in safety; another will bring you back—

Pentheus
Yes, my mother.

The Stranger
A shining example to all.

Pentheus
It is for that I come.

The Stranger
You will be carried back—

Pentheus
You promise me luxury.

The Stranger
In your mother's hands.

Pentheus
You will make an elegant of me.

The Stranger
Elegant indeed!

Pentheus
My enterprise will earn it.

The Stranger
You are a remarkable man, remarkable indeed; and it is to a remarkable experience that you are going. You will attain renown towering to heaven. Open your arms, Agave, and you her sisters, daughters of Cadmus. I bring this bold youth to a famous contest. The victor will be I, and Bromius. The rest the event will show.
[Exit with PENTHEUS.*]*

Chorus
On, swift hounds of Madness, on to where the daughters of Cadmus hold their revels. Goad them to fury against him who masquerades in woman's attire, the maniac who spies on the maenads. His mother will see him first, as he peers from behind a smooth rock or tree-stump. She will cry out to the maenads: "Who is this sleuth who has come to the mountain, come to spy on us Thebans where we revel on the mountain? Who was the mother that bore him? Not of the blood of women is this man's birth, of some lioness, some Gorgon of Libya."

Let Justice advance in plain sight, advance sword in hand, to strike through the throat, to slaughter the godless, the lawless, the ruthless man, the earth-born son of Echion.

With ruthless temper and lawless rage he visits your orgies, Bacchus, yours and your mother's. In the madness of his heart, in the delusion of his wits, he thinks his violence can master the Invincible. But there is One ready and willing to correct his heresies—Death. To know the limits of mortality is a life without sorrow. False knowledge I do not envy; I rejoice to hunt it down. The other things, the greater

*things, are not abstruse. Ah, let my life flow quietly; let me seek the good, in purity
and piety from morn till night, honoring the gods and eschewing all unrighteous
practices.*

*Let Justice advance in plain sight, advance sword in hand, to strike through the
throat, to slaughter the godless, the lawless, the ruthless man, the earth-born son of
Echion.*

*Appear as a bull, as a many-headed dragon to the view, as a fiery glaring lion to
the sight. Up, Bacchus, with smiling face cast your noose around the hunter of the
bacchants, fallen among the deadly band of maenads.*
[*Enter* MESSENGER.]

Messenger
Ah, house once prosperous throughout Hellas, house of the old man of Sidon
who in the land of the Serpent sowed the dragon's earth-born crop, how I groan
for you! I am just a slave, but still—[good slaves are touched by their masters'
calamities.]

Leader
What is it? Have you news to tell of the bacchants?

Messenger
Pentheus is dead, the son of Echion.

Chorus
Lord Bromius, you show yourself a mighty god!

Messenger
What do you say? What was that? Do you rejoice at the misfortunes of my
master, woman?

Chorus
*An alien I am, and in barbaric strains I hail my god. No longer do I cower in fear of
chains.*

Messenger
Do you think Thebes is so wanting in men—

Chorus
It is Dionysus, Dionysus and not Thebes, who has power over me.

Messenger
I can understand; but it is not fair, women, to rejoice over afflictions past cure.

Leader
Tell me, say, what death did he die, the wicked man, the worker of wickedness?

Messenger
When we had put behind us the homesteads of this Theban land and crossed
over the streams of Asopus we came to the heights of Cithaeron, Pentheus and
I—I was attending my master—and the stranger who headed our pilgrimage.

First, we halted in a grassy glade. We kept silence, of tread and tongue alike,
in order to see without being seen. And there, across a precipitous ravine, where

the pines stood dark over the waters of a stream, the maenads were sitting, their hands busy with pleasant tasks. Some of them were wreathing afresh their worn-out wands with new tresses of ivy. Others, like colts freed from the gaudy yoke, were singing lustily their bacchic antiphons. Pentheus, poor man, did not see the crowd of women, and said: "Stranger, where we stand my eyes cannot reach these bastard maenads. If I stood at the edge and climbed a tall fir, I would get a perfect view of their wild obscenities."

Then came the miracle—I saw the stranger seize the top-most branches of a soaring fir and force it down, down, down to the black earth, till it was arched like a bow, or like an arc described by the peg-and-string in drawing the circumference of a rounded wheel. So the stranger tugged at that mountain branch with his hands, and bent it down to earth: it was no mortal deed he wrought. When he had set Pentheus on the branches of the fir, he slipped his hands along the trunk, letting it straighten again; but gently, for fear the mount should throw the rider. Aloft into the lofty air rose the sturdy fir, with my master sitting on top. And now he saw the maenads—but not so well as they saw him. They had scarcely spied him on his lofty seat, when the stranger disappeared from sight, and a voice out of the sky, I guess it was Dionysus, cried aloud: "Young women, I bring the man who has cast ridicule upon you and upon me and upon our holy rites. Take vengeance on him." Even as he spoke, he caused a mysterious pillar of fire to rise from earth to heaven.

The air was hushed, hushed were the leaves of the trees in the glen—not a cry to be heard of any creature. But the bacchants had not heard the shout distinctly. They leapt to their feet and swept the scene with their eyes. And again he exhorted them. Then the daughters of Cadmus recognized the clear command of Bacchus. They shot forth, swift as a flock of doves, speeding along on eager, straining feet, his mother Agave and her sisters and all the bacchants. Through the glen, over torrents and boulders, they leapt, maddened with the inspiration of the god. When they saw my master sitting upon the fir, they first took their stand on a towering rock opposite him and began to pelt him hard with stones. Some shot branches of fir at him, others sent their wands flying through the air. But their aim was wretched and they had no success. He sat high above their eager reach, a pitiful and helpless captive. Finally they violently rived off branches of oak and set about prying up the roots of his tree with their improvised crowbars. When they failed to achieve the end of their toils Agave spoke: "Come, stand about in a circle and take hold of the trunk. We must capture the treed beast [or he will publish the secrets of the god's dances]." Then they applied countless hands to the fir and wrenched it from the ground. Down from his lofty perch, down whirling to the earth, falls Pentheus. Many and many were his moans; for he knew his hour was near. His mother attacked him—the priestess commencing the sacrifice. He flung off his head-dress, in order that poor Agave might recognize him and not kill him. He touched her cheek and said: "I am your child, mother, Pentheus, whom you bore in Echion's house. Pity me, mother; do not, because of *my* sins, kill *your* child."

But she was foaming at the mouth and rolling distorted eyeballs, out of her right mind, possessed by Bacchus. His pleadings were of no avail. She seized the hand of his left arm and set her foot against the poor wretch's side and tore off his arm at the shoulder—not of her own strength; it was the god who made easy the work of her hands. Ino wrought havoc on the other side, rending the flesh, while Autonoe and the whole bacchic horde pressed on. All was one wild din— he groaning with the little breath that was left him, and they shrieking in triumph. One carried off an arm, another a foot, shoe and all. They stripped the flesh from his ribs with their tearing. One and all, with blood-bespattered hands, they played ball with the flesh of Pentheus.

His body lies in pieces, part under the jagged rocks, part in the green depths of the forest; no easy thing to find. His mother has his poor head. She seized it in her hands and fixed it on the top of a thyrsus. She thinks it is the head of a mountain lion that she carries through the midst of Cithaeron. She has left her sisters at the dances of the maenads and is returning within these walls gloating over her hapless prey. She is calling upon Bacchus, her "fellow-huntsman," her "comrade in the chase," her "conquering hero." Bitter for her are the fruits of victory she brings him.

I shall get out of the way of this calamity before Agave comes home. It is the loveliest thing to be virtuous and god-fearing. And I imagine it is also the *wisest* course for mortals to follow.

[Exit MESSENGER.*]*

Chorus
Let us dance to the glory of Bacchus, let us shout for the calamity of Pentheus, the spawn of the ancient serpent. He took woman's attire, he took a fair shaft of fennel: the uniform of the god—of death. And a bull showed him the way to destruction. Bacchants of Thebes, glorious is the paean you have achieved, ending in wailing and tears. It is a goodly sport to fling about one's child an arm dripping with his own blood.

Leader
But stay. I see Pentheus' mother, Agave, rushing wild-eyed towards the house. Welcome you the revel of the bacchic god.

[Enter AGAVE, *frenzied, blood-stained, with* PENTHEUS' *head on her thyrsus.]*

Agave
Bacchants of Asia————

Chorus
To what will you urge me? Oh!

Agave
I bring to our halls from the mountain a tendril newly cut. Happy was the hunting.

Chorus
I see; and I welcome you to join our revel.

Agave
Without a noose I snared it—the young whelp of a savage lion. Look and see.

Chorus
From where in the wilds?

Agave
Cithaeron———

Chorus
Cithaeron?

Agave
—Slew him.

Chorus
Who was she who smote him?

Agave
Mine was the first honor. "Happy Agave" they call me in the revel.

Chorus
And who else?

Agave
Cadmus' own—

Chorus
Cadmus' what?

Agave
His own children. They reached the prey, but after me, after me. Happy was this hunting.

Chorus

[Lacuna]

. . . .

Agave
Then share in the feast.

Chorus
What? Shall I share it? Poor woman!

Agave
The whelp is yet young; the down of his cheek is just blooming beneath his crest of delicate hair.

Chorus
By its mane it might be a beast of the field.

Agave
Bacchus, the skilful hunter, skilfully roused the maenads against this beast.

Chorus
Our king is a hunter.

Agave
Do you praise you?

Chorus
I do praise you.

Agave
Soon the Thebans———

Chorus
Yes, and your son Pentheus———

Agave
Will praise his mother for catching this quarry, this lion cub.

Chorus
Remarkable quarry!

Agave
Remarkably caught!

Chorus
Are you proud?

Agave
Overjoyed. Greatness, manifest greatness, I have achieved in this capture.

Leader
Show the townspeople, poor woman, your victory's booty, which you brought with you.

Agave
O you that dwell in this fair-towered town of the Theban land, come and see this prey, the beast which we daughters of Cadmus hunted down, not by the looped darts of the Thessalians, not with nets, but with our white arms and hands. Why then must men boast and get instruments from the armorers in vain? With our bare hands we took this animal and tore the beast's joints asunder.

Where is my old father? Let him come near. And Pentheus, my son, where is he? Let him bring a strong step-ladder and set it against the house, so that he can nail to the triglyphs this lion's head I have brought from the hunt.
[Enter CADMUS slowly with servants carrying the remains of PENTHEUS on a bier.]

Cadmus
Follow me and bring your sad burden—the corpse of Pentheus. Follow me, servants, to the house where I am taking this body. After endless wearisome searching I found it in the trackless wood, torn to pieces in the glens of Cithaeron. No two parts were in the same spot.

I had come back from among the bacchants with the old man Tiresias, and I was already within the city's walls, when some one told me of my daughter's desperate deeds. I returned again to the mountain to fetch home her child, killed by the maenads. There I saw her that once bore Actaeon to Aristaeus, Autonoe I mean, her and Ino, still frenzy-stung, poor women, in the oak forest. But Agave, they told me, was coming back here with frenzied pace. And what I heard was not untrue; for there I see her, no happy sight.

Agave

Father, the proudest boast is yours to make: you have begotten daughters by far the best in all the world—all your daughters, I say, but me above all. I have left my shuttle by the loom; I have gone to greater things, to hunting animals with my hands. I bring in my arms, as you see, this prize of my courage, to hang on your walls. Take it father, in your hands. Exult in my hunting and invite your friends to a feast. You are blessed, yes blessed, in the achievement I have wrought.

Cadmus

Ah grief beyond measure—I cannot look upon it. Murder it is that you have wrought with your wretched hands. A noble victim it is that you have laid low for the gods; and now you invite this Thebes and me to the feast! Ah me for these woes, yours first and then mine. What ruin the god, king Bromius, has dealt us; with justice indeed, but not mercy, though he is born of our house.

Agave

What a crabbed thing old age is in men, how morose of aspect! I wish my son might take after his mother's ways, and be as lucky in the chase when he goes hunting wild beasts with the young men of Thebes. But that fellow is only good for quarreling with gods. He ought to be admonished, father; and you are the one to do it. Somebody call him here into my sight, to see me in my happiness.

Cadmus

Alas, alas! If you ever realize what you have done you will grieve with a bitter grief. But if you remain to the end in your present state, your affliction will be a blessing in disguise.

Agave

What is there in this that is not right? What is there to grieve for?

Cadmus

Turn your eyes first to yonder sky.

Agave

There. Why do you tell me to look at it?

Cadmus

Is it still the same, or does it seem different to you?

Agave

It is brighter than before, more pellucid.

Cadmus

Is there the same unrest in your soul?

Agave

Unrest? I do not know. I am becoming—somehow—[sensible. The thoughts I had have gone].

Cadmus

Can you hear? Can you answer clearly?

Agave
I have forgotten what we were saying, father.

Cadmus
To whose house did you come as a bride?

Agave
You gave me to Echion—Echion of the Dragon race, they say.

Cadmus
What child was born to your husband in your house?

Agave
Pentheus, to me and his father together.

Cadmus
Whose is the face you have in your arms?

Agave
A lion's, at least those who hunted it said so.

Cadmus
Look right at it. It is small effort to see it.

Agave
Ha! What do I see? What is this I bring home in my hands?

Cadmus
Gaze at it, study it more truly.

Agave
I see a mighty grief. Ah, miserable am I!

Cadmus
It doesn't seem to you to resemble a lion?

Agave
No, it is Pentheus' head I hold, O misery!

Cadmus
Yes, bewailed by me before *you* recognized him.

Agave
Who killed him? How did he come into my hands?

Cadmus
Unhappy truth, how unseasonably you dawn!

Agave
Speak, my heart leaps in dread of what's to come.

Cadmus
You killed him, you and your sisters.

Agave

Where did he die? Was it at home? Somewhere outside?

Cadmus

Where the dogs once tore Actaeon to pieces.

Agave

Why did the unhappy creature go to Cithaeron?

Cadmus

He went to mock the god and your bacchic revels.

Agave

But we—how did we get out there?

Cadmus

You were mad, the whole city was in the frenzy of Bacchus.

Agave

Dionysus has undone us. Too late I see it.

Cadmus

Yes, for affronts put on him; you did not count him a god.

Agave

My son's dear body, father—where is it?

Cadmus

Here I bring it—retrieved with difficulty.

Agave

Is it all decently composed?
[CADMUS *is silent.*]
What part had my madness in Pentheus' fate?

Cadmus

He was like you—blaspheming against the god. So the god joined all of you in a single destruction, you and this unfortunate. The house is undone and I too; for I am without male children, and I have seen this shoot from your womb, poor woman, foully and horribly slain.
[*To the body of* PENTHEUS]
To you the house looked up; you were the stay of my halls, child. Son of my own daughter, you had the city in awe of you. No one that looked upon your presence dared outrage the old man; for you would exact due penalty. But now I shall be cast out of my house dishonored—I, the great Cadmus, who sowed the race of Thebans and harvested a most excellent crop. Ah, dearest of men— yes, even in death I shall count you with the dearest, my child—never more will you touch this chin of mine with your hand and call me "mother's father" and embrace me, child, and say: "Is anyone wronging you? Is anyone dishonoring you, old man? Is anyone annoying you and vexing your heart? Tell me, and I shall punish whoever does you wrong, father."

But now it is sorrow for me and misery for you, grief for your mother and for her sisters misery. If there is anyone who disdains the deities, let him look at the death of this man and believe in the gods.

Leader
I grieve for your sorrow, Cadmus. Your grandson has his desserts, his just desserts, but grievous for you.

Agave
Father, you see how all is changed for me————

[A long lament of Agave, a few lines of the chorus announcing the appearance of Dionysus, and the beginning of the god's speech are lost.]

. . . .

Dionysus
You will change and become a serpent; and your wife Harmonia, Ares' daughter, whom you got to wife though you were a mortal, will take a brutish form and be changed into a snake. A chariot drawn by bullocks, Zeus' oracle says, you will drive, your wife by your side, at the head of barbarians. You will sack many cities with an unnumbered host. But when they plunder the oracle of Loxias, they will receive a sorry homecoming. But Ares shall save you and Harmonia and establish your life in the land of the blessed.

These things say I, Dionysus, born of no mortal father but of Zeus. If you had learned wisdom then, when you would not, you would have been happy now, with the son of Zeus for your ally.

Cadmus
Dionysus, we beseech you, we have sinned.

Dionysus
Too late you have learned to know me. When the knowledge was wanted, you had it not.

Cadmus
We realize it. But you go too far against us.

Dionysus
Because you outraged my divinity.

Cadmus
It ill beseems gods to imitate the passions of mortals.

Dionysus
My father, Zeus, ordained these things of old.

Agave
Alas, it is decreed, old man—the misery of banishment.

Dionysus
Why then do you delay when necessity constrains?
[DIONYSUS *disappears.*]

Cadmus

Ah child, to what a fearful pass we have all come, you and your unhappy sisters, and I the sorrowful. In my old age I go to an alien land to dwell among barbarians. And there is also the prophecy—that I must lead a mingled barbarian host against Hellas. Myself a serpent, with my wife Harmonia, Ares' child, a wild and savage serpent too, I shall lead an army of spearsmen against altars and tombs of Hellas. Cadmus the Sorrowful! My sufferings will never end. Not even when I go down the chasm of Acheron river shall I have rest.

Agave

Ah, father, I shall lose you, I shall live in exile.

Cadmus

Why do you fling your arms about me, poor child—a white swan embracing its old decrepit sire?

Agave

Where then should I turn when I am cast out of my land?

Cadmus

I do not know, child; your father is small help.

Agave

Farewell, my home; farewell my native city. I leave you for misery, for exile, far from home and love.

Cadmus

Go, my child, to Aristaeus (your sister's husband); he————

Agave

I groan for you father.

Cadmus

And I for you, child; and I weep for your sisters.

Agave

In dreadful wise has king Dionysus brought this confusion upon your house.

Cadmus

Dreadful was his treatment at your hands. His name was without honor in Thebes.

Agave

Farewell, my father.

Cadmus

Farewell, my poor child. It will not be easy—if you ever do find welfare.

Agave

Take me, my guides, where I shall find my unhappy sisters, my companions in exile. Let me go where foul Cithaeron may never see me, nor my eyes see

Cithaeron, to some place where stands no memorial of the thyrsus! Let others be bacchants and care for these things.

Chorus
Many are the forms of divine intervention; many things beyond expectation do the gods fulfil. That which was expected has not been accomplished; for that which was unexpected has god found the way. Such was the end of this story.
[Exeunt.]

Questions for Discussion and Review

1. Describe Dionysus's relation to the origin of Greek tragedy. Why do you suppose that this particular god, with his passion and unpredictability, became the inspirer of Athenian drama, including tragedies, satyr plays, and comedies? Although most surviving Greek plays do not feature the wine god as a major character, why are his nature and spirit relevant to the tragic vision?

2. Discuss the similarities and differences between tragic and epic heroes. What heroic qualities do they share? In what different ways does each accept enormous challenges, descend to the Underworld, and return bearing new insights? Using examples from your readings, explain in what sense each appears to achieve success or failure.

3. Epic heroes are trapped in a paradoxical situation—to pursue immortality, they must risk death. In what sense are tragic heroes similarly caught in a paradox?

4. Peripeteia (reversal) describes the plot of a tragedy: the protagonist begins in an enviable condition, often possessing wealth, power, and prestige, and ends in an unenviable condition, suffering torment or even death. But the concept of reversal also applies to the tragic vision itself. Explain how this reversal of fortune helps bring about the protagonist's understanding of the inevitability of change, the limits of human knowledge, or the nature of the gods.

5. Why does Pentheus regard Bacchic ecstasy as a threat to civilization? Is he right in any of his objections to surrendering the rational self to the power of emotional abandonment? In presenting his version of the myth, would Euripides urge unconditional acceptance of Dionysian frenzy? Should human beings retain rational control at all times? Should one both acknowledge *and* resist instinctual passion?

6. Some critics suggest that Dionysus is ethically unacceptable because he is a cruel and vengeful god. Do you think that Euripides's tragedy provokes moral criticisms of Dionysus's character and vengeful behavior? Is Dionysus presented as a force of nature that transcends standards of human judgment? Does he represent unconscious forces in both external nature and the human psyche?

7. What do we learn from witnessing a dramatization of Dionysus's return to his home city and his punishment of close relatives who reject him? Is a prophet invariably denied honor in his hometown? (Compare the myth of the god's return with the account of Jesus's rejection by his family and former neighbors in Mark, Chapter 6, and Luke, Chapter 4.)

Recommended Reading

Baldry, H. C. *The Greek Tragic Theatre.* New York: Norton, 1971. A study of Greek tragedy, with focus on its ritual origins.

Carpenter, Thomas H., and Christopher A. Faraone, eds. *Masks of Dionysus.* Ithaca: Cornell UP, 1993. Includes discussions of Dionysian cult and drama.

Else, Gerald. *The Origin and Early Form of Greek Tragedy.* 1965. New York: Norton, 1972. Argues that tragedy develops from epic rather than ritual sources and traces its evolution from the choral leader Thespis to Aeschylus.

Kitto, H. D. F. *Greek Tragedy.* 3rd ed. New York: Barnes, 1961. A standard critical discussion of Greek drama.

Pickard-Cambridge, Arthur W. *Dithyramb, Tragedy, and Comedy.* Ed. T. B. L. Webster. 2nd ed. Oxford: Clarendon, 1962. Indispensable study of the origin and development of Greek drama.

Winkler, John J., and From I. Zeitlin, eds. *Nothing to Do with Dionysus?: Athenian Drama in Its Social Context.* Princeton: Princeton UP, 1990. Discussions place Dionysian theater in its historical and social context.

Winnington-Ingram, R. P. *Euripides and Dionysus: An Interpretation of the Bacchae.* Cambridge: n.p., 1948.

Cosmic Conflict and Evolution: Aeschylus's Transformation of the Prometheus Myth

KEY THEMES

In his dramatic revision of the Prometheus myth, the classical playwright Aeschylus transforms Hesiod's wily trickster into a heroic rebel and savior. Setting his play in the far distant past, just after Zeus has seized power from the Titans, Aeschylus presents Zeus as a despot, an embodiment of amoral power attempting to rule without justice or mercy. At this early stage of its cosmic evolution, divinity is at war with itself: divine strength (Zeus) is alienated from divine wisdom and compassion (Prometheus). Prometheus Bound, *the first in a set of three dramas, emphasizes the Titan's heroic refusal to submit to Zeus's rule; the other two plays (now lost) probably depicted Zeus's gradual realization that he needed ethical maturity for his administration to survive and his eventual reconciliation with the rebel god Prometheus.*

A Transformation of the Prometheus Myth

In his *Theogony* and *Works and Days,* Hesiod depicted Prometheus, the thief of heavenly fire, as a wily trickster whose attempts to outwit Zeus are appropriately punished. Three centuries later, an Athenian playwright transformed the crafty Titan into a tragic figure of cosmic heroism. Although he borrows his mythological subject from Hesiod, the author of *Prometheus Bound* shows a radically different attitude toward the characters of both Zeus and Prometheus. Turning Hesiod's theology on its head, the playwright changes the Titan into a champion of freedom and Zeus into a despot who rules without law, justice, or mercy.

The Question of Authorship

Although most scholars attribute *Prometheus Bound* to the tragedian Aeschylus (c. 525–456 B.C.), some critics, such as Mark Griffith, question Aeschylean authorship of the play, ascribing it to another hand, perhaps that of Euphorion, a son of Aeschylus who was also a dramatist (see Recommended Reading). Certainly *Prometheus Bound*'s highly critical portrait of Zeus differs sharply from Aeschylus's portrayal of a wise and just Zeus in the *Oresteia* (Chapter 15). Because only six (or seven) of Aeschylus's ninety plays survive, however, it is impossible to be absolutely sure that the playwright did not, for dramatic effect, vary his picture of Zeus from play to play.

The drama's unflattering picture of Zeus may have shocked its original audience, most of whom supposedly honored the Olympian, in Plato's phrase, as "the god of gods, who rules according to law." In *Prometheus Bound,* Zeus is not the benign divinity worshiped by contemporary Athenian society, but the deity as he was at the very beginning of his reign—raw power untempered by wisdom or compassion (Figure 14-1). Because he is neither omnipotent (all-powerful) nor omniscient (all-knowing), he is vulnerable to fatal error. As Hyginus, an astronomer of the second century A.D., observed: "Zeus [when tricked by Prometheus] did not act with the brains of a god, nor did he foresee everything, as befits a god."

An Evolving Universe

In this text, we take the traditional view that *Prometheus Bound* is the first part of an Aeschylean trilogy, a series of three thematically related plays intended to be performed sequentially in a single day. The other two dramas, *Prometheus Unbound* and *Prometheus the Fire-Carrier,* exist only in fragments, primarily in citations from later writers. Enough references to the lost plays remain, however, to suggest that the conflict in *Prometheus Bound* represents the painful beginning of a complex evolutionary process in which Zeus—perhaps by developing the qualities appropriate to divinity—eventually reconciles with the rebel Titan.

Although the means of their reconciliation is not specified, it is clear that Aeschylus follows a tradition in which Zeus releases Prometheus from the mountain peak on which he has been impaled. According to Hesiod's version of the myth, Zeus permits his mortal son Heracles to kill the eagle that shreds Prometheus's liver, chiefly to enhance Heracles's reputation. For Aeschylus, however, the god's change of heart is more significant: his evolving Zeus at last comes to value the Titan's superior wisdom and insight. By the end of the third play, we may assume that Zeus has not only liberated his former enemy but also sponsored his ascension to Olympus, where Prometheus is honored as the divine "fire-carrier." Making the wise Titan his heavenly companion, Zeus in effect restages his swallowing of Metis, assimilating the Promethean qualities that will equip him to rule wisely and thereby perpetuate his reign.

Prometheus and Humanity

In *Prometheus Bound,* however, Zeus's evolutionary growth has only begun: the godhead is divided, causing divine power (Zeus) to war against divine intelligence (Prometheus). The play opens with Zeus's henchmen, the unwilling Hephaestus along with the allegorical figures of Force and Violence (the qualities by which Zeus then

FIGURE 14-1   Zeus and the Eagle. In his *Prometheus Bound,* Aeschylus portrays heaven's king as a despot and his imperial eagle, which he will send to devour the rebel Titan's liver, as a cruel agent of tyranny, as shown in this Roman statue of the Olympian king. Whereas Hesiod had depicted Prometheus as a wily trickster who deserved his punishment, Aeschylus transformed the myth by making Prometheus a savior of humankind, without whose gift of celestial fire, the symbol of all art and technology, humanity could not have avoided the extinction that Zeus planned for it. (*Villa Albani, Rome.*)

FIGURE 14-2 Creation of Man. In this densely figured scene carved on a Roman sarcophagus, Prometheus (seated, slightly left of center) acts like a divine potter, fashioning from clay
the body of the first man, whose head he cradles on his lap. In a parallel to the Birth of
Athene (see Figure 1-2), the Olympians are gathered to observe humanity's creation. The
gods' combined presence, crowding about the as yet unconscious form, suggests that the new
creature will be endowed with divine qualities that each deity represents. Although Aeschylus
does not explicitly refer to this aspect of Prometheus's myth, he closely identifies the god with
humanity, for whose cause Prometheus endures Zeus's wrath. (*National Museum, Naples.*)

ruled), driving iron spikes through the Titan's flesh, immobilizing him on a barren
crag. Silent during his mutilation, Prometheus later reveals that he stole fire not
merely to defy Zeus but to rescue humanity from extinction. Zeus had planned to
allow the human race to perish in ignorance and darkness, but Prometheus, feeling
pity for helpless mortals, gave them fire and taught them the arts and skills of civilization, raising humanity from savagery to the consciousness of its potential.

Although Aeschylus does not cite the tradition making Prometheus humanity's
creator (Figure 14-2), he emphasizes the almost complete identification between the
Titan and the race for whose benefit he suffers. As the nineteenth-century English
romantic poet Percy Bysshe Shelley realized in his version of *Prometheus Unbound,*
the suffering Titan is an image of the human mind, which, despite its physical bondage to oppressive rulers, remains free in thought to explore the vast universe and
contemplate its eventual liberation.

Complexities and Functions of the Prometheus Myth

Savior and Rebel

The tension between Zeus the despot and Zeus the future promulgator of justice is
paralleled in the ambiguity of Prometheus's dual role as rebel and savior. From a
human viewpoint, the Titan is a redeemer who endures unspeakable pain for the sake
of mortals, whose continued existence he makes possible. From Zeus's perspective,
however, he is a lawbreaker whose arrogance must be punished. As a savior figure

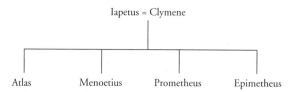

FIGURE 14-3   Genealogy of Prometheus. According to Hesiod, Prometheus is the son of the Titans Iapetus and Clymene and the brother of Atlas—whom Zeus condemns to hold up the vault of the sky—and Epimetheus (Afterthought), a dimwit who accepts Pandora on behalf of mankind. Aeschylus, however, makes Prometheus (Forethought) a son of Themis whom the playwright implicitly identifies with the earth goddess, Gaea, thus associating the rebel Titan with an aspect of earth's primal and prophetic powers. Although Prometheus had used his intelligence to help Zeus overthrow the Titans, in *Prometheus Bound,* he must use it to maintain universal absolutes of justice and freedom, principles that Zeus's despotism threatens to obliterate.

who also subverts divine authority, Prometheus reflects the Greeks' ambivalence toward a persistent individualism that can result in disrupting public order. Individual rebels, even when championing the right, can collide destructively with legitimate authority, damaging both themselves and the state. Some commentators suggest, in fact, that the play opposes two equally plausible versions of the right.

According to Hesiod, Prometheus is a second-generation Titan, the son of Iapetus and Clymene (Figure 14-3). Aeschylus, however, makes him the child of Themis, whom he implicitly identifies with Gaea, the Earth, generator of gods and primeval source of justice. As a masculine counterpart of wise-counseling Gaea, Themis, and Athene, Prometheus attracts the loyalty of Ocean's daughters, who comprise the chorus, a group of singers and dancers who comment on (and often judge) the characters and actions in a Greek play. In *Prometheus Bound,* the chorus is torn between sympathy for the hero's suffering and horror at the example of divine retribution he presents. When Prometheus refuses to submit to Zeus and thus end his pain, his obstinacy provokes the chorus to charge that he "misses the mark" of wise self-interest.

The term Aeschylus and other tragedians use to denote a character's tragic error is **hamartia,** a term drawn from archery that means "missing the mark." Although this is the same word translated as "sin" in English versions of the New Testament, it can apply to any quality or action, such as a mistake in judgment or even an excess of righteousness, that results in failure to hit the target of divine approval. From the chorus's pragmatic view, Prometheus's extreme ethical autonomy displays **hubris,** the blinding pride that typically afflicts the tragic hero (chapters 13 and 15).

At the same time, Aeschylus makes it clear that Prometheus willingly bears intolerable pain because his is the last free mind in the universe, the sole remaining consciousness that can distinguish between absolutes of good and evil (Figure 14-4). To corrupt his awareness by conforming to Zeus's demands would be to extinguish the light that he had brought to earth. In this respect, Prometheus's intellectual honesty—a virtue—is the quality that occasions his suffering.

FIGURE 14-4 Atlas and Prometheus. The brutality with which Zeus enforces his rule is vividly rendered in this archaic Spartan cup depicting two Titan brothers (c. 555 B.C.). The giant Atlas endures back-breaking pain, his shoulders bent against the weight of the heavenly vault he is condemned forever to support. Facing him while suffering even worse agony is Prometheus, whose flesh is being ripped by the beak and talons of Zeus's hungry eagle. Aeschylus's Prometheus can escape this daily repeated vivisection if he submits to Zeus's authority, an option he rejects because it means assenting to his oppressor's right to enslave bodies and control minds.

Io: A Victim of Zeus's Despotism

Two important scenes help convey Aeschylus's purpose in his startling reinterpretation of the Prometheus myth. The first introduces **Io,** a young woman driven almost insane by a stinging gadfly that Hera jealously sends to plague her. Unlike Prometheus, who has deliberately disobeyed Zeus, Io is merely an innocent victim of the despot's lust. Io's case illustrates the fate of vulnerable humanity when no law exists to restrain a despot's whim. Her appearance near the middle of the play is particularly damning to the Olympian ruler: the bully who raped her is too cowardly to protect Io from his wife's irrational fury. Both the King and Queen of Heaven are chillingly indifferent to the suffering they cause.

FIGURE 14-5   Chiron. Wisest of
the centaurs, Chiron instructs the
young Achilles in playing the lyre. A
son of Cronus and Philyra, daughter
of Ocean, Chiron belongs to the generation of Zeus. He is famous for his
kindness to human beings, helping to
bring up such heroes as Jason and Asclepius. According to Apollodorus,
when Aeschylus states that Prometheus must suffer until another god is
willing to die for him, he refers to
Chiron, who was accidentally struck
by one of Heracles's arrows, which inflicted incurable wounds. Unable to
bear unending pain, Chiron gives his
immortality to Prometheus (who in
Apollodorus's version of the myth was
apparently born mortal), thus providing a vicarious atonement for the Titan. Zeus then places Chiron in the
sky as the constellation Centaurus.
(*National Museum, Naples.*)

In the climactic episode, Hermes, portrayed as the swaggering emissary of a military junta, appears to announce the torments that Zeus will soon inflict upon Prometheus. Ocean's daughters, who had earlier begged Prometheus to give up his
resistance, now reject Hermes's advice to abandon the Titan. The chorus, which
typically voices a mediating position between the two tragic extremes of battling opponents, unanimously decides to take Prometheus's side, even if it means sharing his
punishment. Led by the chorus's example, the audience is confronted with a choice
between seemingly irresistible power and helpless principle and is asked to opt for the
latter.

The Secret: Only Prometheus Can Save Zeus

In Aeschylus's ironic vision, Prometheus's defiance of Zeus's injustice gives the Olympian an opportunity to save himself from the fate of his predecessors, Uranus and
Cronus. Prometheus alone knows the cause of Zeus's future downfall, that the Olympian's sexual energy will drive him to beget (by the sea nymph Thetis) a son strong
enough to displace him (Chapter 11). In the lost plays, Prometheus voluntarily confides this secret to Zeus, rescuing the god from destruction by his own untamed
impulses.

In his turn, as Hermes prophesies, Prometheus will benefit from the redemptive
act of a god willing to die for him. Although Aeschylus does not identify the deity
who will sacrifice himself for Prometheus, Apollodorus states that this expiatory role

is filled by the centaur Chiron (Figure 14-5). According to Apollodorus, when he is wounded by one of Heracles's poisoned arrows, Chiron suffers such exquisite agony that he is eager to die, and in perishing he somehow bestows his immortality on Prometheus. Because the Titan is already immortal, however, it is difficult to see how Chiron's vicarious sacrifice can benefit him. As Mark Griffith suggests, Hermes's prophecy may refer to either Chiron or Heracles, who not only frees Prometheus but also, as his final "labor," makes a descent into Death's realm to fetch Cerberus (chapters 8, 9, and 10).

Although Zeus finally accepts Prometheus among the Olympian immortals, one tradition states that, because he had sworn by the River Styx (a symbol of the gods' unbreakable oaths) that the Titan would never be released from his rock, Zeus forces Prometheus to wear a steel ring to which a fragment of the rock is attached. Prometheus is thus forever bound to a tangible reminder of Zeus's superior authority.

PROMETHEUS BOUND[1]

Aeschylus

CHARACTERS

FORCE, *a militaristic personification of brute strength*

VIOLENCE, *a silent personification of another aspect of Zeus's rule*

HEPHAESTUS (HEPHESTUS), *god of fire and metalcraft who serves Zeus reluctantly*

PROMETHEUS, *the rebel Titan, benefactor of humanity*

CHORUS, *daughters of Ocean, sympathetic to the Titan*

OCEAN, *a Titan son of Gaea and Uranus who submits to Zeus*

IO, *a mortal Zeus has loved, now partly cowlike in form*

HERMES, *divine messenger of Zeus*

ZEUS, *the unseen new ruler of the universe, represented by the climactic storm at the end of the play*

[PROMETHEUS° by tradition was fastened to a peak of the Caucasus.]

Force
Far have we come to this far spot of earth,
this narrow Scythian land, a desert all untrodden.
God of the forge and fire, yours the task
the Father laid upon you.
To this high-piercing, head-long rock
in adamantine chains that none can break
bind him—him here, who dared all things.
Your flaming flower he stole to give to men,
fire, the master craftsman, through whose power
all things are wrought, and for such error now   10
he must repay the gods; be taught to yield
to Zeus' lordship and to cease
from his man-loving way.

Hephestus
Force, Violence, what Zeus enjoined on you
has here an end. Your task is done.
But as for me, I am not bold to bind
a god, a kinsman, to this stormy crag.
Yet I must needs be bold.
His load is heavy who dares disobey the Father's word.
O high-souled child of Justice, the wise counselor,   20

1. Translation by Edith Hamilton.

488

against my will as against yours I nail you fast
in brazen fetters never to be loosed
to this rock peak, where no man ever comes,
where never voice or face of mortal you will see.
The shining splendor of the sun shall wither you.
Welcome to you will be the night
when with her mantle star-inwrought[2]
she hides the light of day.
And welcome then in turn the sun
to melt the frost the dawn has left behind.   30
Forever shall the intolerable present grind you down,
and he who will release you is not born.
Such fruit you reap for your man-loving way.
A god yourself, you did not dread God's anger,
but gave to mortals honor not their due,
and therefore you must guard this joyless rock—
no rest, no sleep, no moment's respite.
Groans shall your speech be, lamentation
your only words—all uselessly.
Zeus has no mind to pity. He is harsh,   40
like upstarts always.

Force
Well then, why this delay and foolish talk?
A god whom gods hate is abominable.

Hephestus
The tie of blood has a strange power,
and old acquaintance too.

Force
And so say I—but don't you think
that disobedience to the Father's words
might have still stranger power?

Hephestus
You're rough, as always. Pity is not in you.

Force
Much good is pity here. Why all this pother   50
that helps him not a whit?

Hephestus
O skill of hand now hateful to me.

Force
Why blame your skill? These troubles here
were never caused by it. That's simple truth.

---

2. Shelley's adjective is the perfect translation. Anything else would be less exact and less like Aeschylus.

Hephestus
Yet would it were another's and not mine.

Force
Trouble is everywhere except in heaven.
No one is free but Zeus.

Hephestus
I know—I've not a word to say.

Force
Come then. Make haste. On with his fetters.
What if the Father sees you lingering?   60

Hephestus
The chains are ready here if he should look.

Force
Seize his hands and master him.
Now to your hammer. Pin him to the rocks.

Hephestus
All done, and quick work too.

Force
Still harder. Tighter. Never loose your hold.
For he is good at finding a way out where there is none.

Hephestus
This arm at least he will not ever free.

Force
Buckle the other fast, and let him learn
with all his cunning he's a fool to Zeus.

Hephestus
No one but he, poor wretch, can blame my work.   70

Force
Drive stoutly now your wedge straight through his breast,
the stubborn jaw of steel that cannot break.

Hephestus
Alas, Prometheus, I grieve for your pain.

Force
You shirk your task and grieve for those Zeus hates?
Take care; you may need pity for yourself.

Hephestus
You see a sight eyes should not look upon.

Force
I see one who has got what he deserves.
But come. The girdle now around his waist.

Hephestus
What must be shall be done. No need to urge me.

Force
I will and louder too. Down with you now.   80
Make fast his legs in rings. Use all your strength.

Hephestus
Done and small trouble.

Force
Now for his feet. Drive the nails through the flesh.
The judge is stern who passes on our work.

Hephestus
Your tongue and face match well.

Force
Why, you poor weakling. Are you one to cast
a savage temper in another's face?

Hephestus
Oh, let us go. Chains hold him, hand and foot.

Force
Run riot now, you there upon the rocks.
Go steal from gods to give their goods to men—   90
to men whose life is but a little day.
What will they do to lift these woes from you?
Forethought your name means, falsely named.
Forethought you lack and need now for yourself
if you would slip through fetters wrought like these.
[Exeunt FORCE, VIOLENCE, HEPHESTUS.*]*

Prometheus
O air of heaven and swift-winged winds,
O running river waters,
O never numbered laughter of sea waves,
Earth, mother of all, Eye of the sun, all seeing,
on you I call.   100
Behold what I, a god, endure from gods.
See in what tortures I must struggle
through countless years of time.
This shame, these bonds, are put upon me
by the new ruler of the gods.
Sorrow enough in what is here and what is still to come.

It wrings groans from me.
When shall the end be, the appointed end?
And yet why ask?
All, all I knew before,   110
all that should be.
Nothing, no pang of pain
that I did not foresee.
Bear without struggle what must be.
Necessity is strong and ends our strife.
But silence is intolerable here.
So too is speech.
I am fast bound, I must endure.
I gave to mortals gifts.
I hunted out the secret source of fire.   120
I filled a reed therewith,
fire, the teacher of all arts to men,
the great way through.
These are the crimes that I must pay for,
pinned to a rock beneath the open sky.
But what is here? What comes?
What sound, what fragrance, brushed me with faint wings,
of deities or mortals or of both? [3]
Has someone found a way to this far peak
to view my agony? What else?   130
Look at me then, in chains, a god who failed,
the enemy of Zeus, whom all gods hate,
all that go in and out of Zeus' hall.
The reason is that I loved men too well.
Oh, birds are moving near me. The air murmurs
with swift and sweeping wings.
Whatever comes to me is terrible.
[Enter CHORUS. They are sea nymphs. It is clear from what follows that a winged
car brings them on to the stage.]

Leader of Chorus

Oh, be not terrified, for friends are here,
each eager to be first,
on swift wings flying to your rock.   140
I prayed my father long
before he let me come.
The rushing winds have sped me on.
A noise of ringing brass went through the sea-caves,
and for all a maiden's fears it drove me forth,
so swift, I did not put my sandals on,
but in my winged car I came to you.

---

3. This line of Keats is the exact translation.

Prometheus
To see this sight—
Daughters of fertile Tethys,
children of Ocean who forever flows   150
unresting round earth's shores,
behold me, and my bonds
that bind me fast upon the rocky height
of this cleft mountain side,
keeping my watch of pain.

A Sea Nymph
I look upon you and a mist of tears,
of grief and terror, rises as I see
your body withering upon the rocks,
in shameful fetters.
For a new helmsman steers Olympus.   160
By new laws Zeus is ruling without law.
He has put down the mighty ones of old.

Prometheus
Oh, had I been sent deep, deep into earth,
to that black boundless place where go the dead,
though cruel chains should hold me fast forever,
I should be hid from sight of gods and men.
But now I am a plaything for the winds.
My enemies exult—and I endure.

Another Nymph
What god so hard of heart to look on these things gladly?
Who, but Zeus only, would not suffer with you?   170
He is malignant always and his mind
unbending. All the sons of heaven
he drives beneath his yoke.
Nor will he make an end
until his heart is sated or until
someone, somehow, shall seize his sovereignty—
if that could be.

Prometheus
And yet—and yet—all tortured though I am,
fast fettered here,
he shall have need of me, the lord of heaven,   180
to show to him the strange design
by which he shall be stripped of throne and scepter.
But he will never win me over
with honeyed spell of soft, persuading words,
nor will I ever cower beneath his threats
to tell him what he seeks.
First he must free me from this savage prison
and pay for all my pain.

Another

Oh, you are bold. In bitter agony
you will not yield. 190
These are such words as only free men speak.
Piercing terror stings my heart.
I fear because of what has come to you.
Where are you fated to put in to shore
and find a haven from this troubled sea?
Prayers cannot move,
persuasions cannot turn,
the heart of Kronos' son.

Prometheus

I know that he is savage.
He keeps his righteousness at home. 200
But yet some time he shall be mild of mood,
when he is broken.
He will smooth his stubborn temper,
and run to meet me.
Then peace will come and love between us two.

Leader

Reveal the whole to us. Tell us your tale.
What guilt does Zeus impute
to torture you in shame and bitterness?
Teach us, if you may speak.

Prometheus

To speak is pain, but silence too is pain, 210
and everywhere is wretchedness.
When first the gods began to quarrel
and faction rose among them,
some wishing to throw Kronos out of heaven,
that Zeus, Zeus, mark you, should be lord,
others opposed, pressing the opposite,
that Zeus should never rule the gods,
then I, giving wise counsel to the Titans,
children of Earth and Heaven, could not prevail.
My way out was a shrewd one, they despised it, 220
and in their arrogant minds they thought to conquer
with ease, by their own strength.
But Justice, she who is my mother, told me—
Earth she is sometimes called,
whose form is one, whose name is many—
she told me, and not once alone,
the future, how it should be brought to pass,
that neither violence nor strength of arm
but only subtle craft could win.
I made all clear to them. 230

They scorned to look my way.
The best then left me was to stand with Zeus
in all good will, my mother with me,
and, through my counsel, the black underworld
covered, and hides within its secret depths
Kronos the aged and his host.
Such good the ruler of the gods had from me,
and with such evil he has paid me back.
There is a sickness that infects all tyrants,
they cannot trust their friends.   240
But you have asked a question I would answer:
What is my crime that I am tortured for?
Zeus had no sooner seized his father's throne
than he was giving to each god a post
and ordering his kingdom,
but mortals in their misery
he took no thought for.
His wish was they should perish
and he would then beget another race.
And there were none to cross his will save I.   250
I dared it, I saved men.
Therefore I am bowed down in torment,
grievous to suffer, pitiful to see.
I pitied mortals,
I never thought to meet with this.
Ruthlessly punished here I am
an infamy to Zeus.

Leader
Iron of heart or wrought from rock is he
who does not suffer in your misery.
Oh, that these eyes had never looked upon it.   260
I see it and my heart is wrung.

Prometheus
A friend must feel I am a thing to pity.

Leader
Did you perhaps go even further still?

Prometheus
I made men cease to live with death in sight.

Leader
What potion did you find to cure this sickness?

Prometheus
Blind hopes I caused to dwell in them.

Another Sea Nymph
Great good to men that gift.

Prometheus
To it I added the good gift of fire.

Another
And now the creatures of a day
have flaming fire?   270

Prometheus
Yes, and learn many crafts therefrom.

Leader
For deeds like these Zeus holds you guilty,
and tortures you with never ease from pain?
Is no end to your anguish set before you?

Prometheus
None other except when it pleases him.

Leader
It pleases him? What hope there? You must see
you missed your mark. I tell you this with pain
to give you pain.
But let that pass. Seek your deliverance.

Prometheus
Your feet are free.   280
Chains bind mine fast.
Advice is easy for the fortunate.
All that has come I knew full well.
Of my own will I shot the arrow that fell short,
of my own will.
Nothing do I deny.
I helped men and found trouble for myself.
I knew—and yet not all.
I did not think to waste away
hung high in air upon a lonely rock.   290
But now, I pray you, no more pity
for what I suffer here. Come, leave your car,
and learn the fate that steals upon me,
all, to the very end.
Hear me, oh, hear me. Share my pain. Remember,
trouble may wander far and wide
but it is always near.

Leader
You cry to willing ears, Prometheus.
Lightly I leave my swiftly speeding car
and the pure ways of air where go the birds.   300
I stand upon this stony ground.
I ask to hear your troubles to the end.

[Enter OCEAN *riding on a four-footed bird. The* CHORUS *draws back, and he does not see them.]*

Ocean
Well, here at last, an end to a long journey.
I've made my way to you, Prometheus.
This bird of mine is swift of wing
but I can guide him by my will,
without a bridle.
Now you must know, I'm grieved at your misfortunes.
Of course I must be, I'm your kinsman.
And that apart, there's no one I think more of.   310
And you'll find out the truth of what I'm saying.
It isn't in me to talk flattery.
Come: tell me just what must be done to help you,
and never say that you've a firmer friend
than you will find in me.

Prometheus
Oho! What's here? You? Come to see my troubles?
How did you dare to leave your ocean river,
your rock caves hollowed by the sea,
and stand upon the iron mother earth?
Was it to see what has befallen me,   320
because you grieve with me?
Then see this sight: here is the friend of Zeus,
who helped to make him master.
This twisted body is his handiwork.

Ocean
I see, Prometheus. I do wish
You'd take some good advice.
I know you're very clever,
but real self-knowledge—that you haven't got.
New fashions have come in with this new ruler.
Why can't you change your own to suit?   330
Don't talk like that—so rude and irritating.
Zeus isn't so far off but he might hear,
and what would happen then would make these troubles
seem child's play.
You're miserable. Then do control your temper
and find some remedy.
Of course you think you know all that I'm saying.
You certainly should know the harm
that blustering has brought you.
But you're not humbled yet. You won't give in.   340
You're looking for more trouble.
Just learn one thing from me:
Don't kick against the pricks.

You see he's savage—why not? He's a tyrant.
He doesn't have to hand in his accounts.
Well, now I'm going straight to try
if I can free you from this wretched business.
Do you keep still. No more of this rash talking.
Haven't you yet learned with all your wisdom
the mischief that a foolish tongue can make?   350

Prometheus
Wisdom? The praise for that is yours alone,
who shared and dared with me and yet were able
to shun all blame.
But—let be now. Give not a thought more to me.
You never would persuade him.
He is not easy to win over.
Be cautious. Keep a sharp look out,
or on your way back you may come to harm.

Ocean
You counsel others better than yourself,
to judge by what I hear and what I see.   360
But I won't let you turn me off.
I really want to serve you.
And I am proud, yes, proud to say
I know that Zeus will let you go
just as a favor done to me.

Prometheus
I thank you for the good will you would show me.
But spare your pains. Your trouble would be wasted.
The effort, if indeed you wish to make it,
could never help me.
Now you are out of harm's way. Stay there.   370
Because I am unfortunate myself
I would not wish that others too should be.
Not so. Even here the lot of Atlas, of my brother,
weighs on me. In the western country
he stands, and on his shoulders is the pillar
that holds apart the earth and sky,
a load not easy to be borne.
Pity too filled my heart when once I saw
swift Typhon overpowered.
Child of the Earth was he, who lived   380
in caves in the Cilician land,
a flaming monster with a hundred heads,
who rose up against all the gods.
Death whistled from his fearful jaws.
His eyes flashed glaring fire.
I thought he would have wrecked God's sovereignty.

But to him came the sleepless bolt of Zeus,
down from the sky, thunder with breath of flame,
and all his high boasts were struck dumb.
Into his very heart the fire burned.   390
His strength was turned to ashes.
And now he lies a useless thing,
a sprawling body, near the narrow sea-way
by Aetna, underneath the mountain's roots.
High on the peak the god of fire sits,
welding the molten iron in his forge,
whence sometimes there will burst
rivers red hot, consuming with fierce jaws
the level fields of Sicily,
lovely with fruits.   400
And that is Typhon's anger boiling up,
his darts of flame none may abide,
of fire-breathing spray,
scorched to a cinder though he is
by Zeus' bolt.
But you are no man's fool; you have no need
to learn from me. Keep yourself safe,
as you well know the way.
And I will drain my cup to the last drop,
until Zeus shall abate his insolence of rage.   410

Ocean
And yet you know the saying,
when anger reaches fever heat
wise words are a physician.

Prometheus
Not when the heart is full to bursting.
Wait for the crisis; then the balm will soothe.

Ocean
But if one were discreet as well as daring—?
You don't see danger then? Advise me.

Prometheus
I see your trouble wasted,
and you good-natured to the point of folly.

Ocean
That's a complaint I don't mind catching.   420
Let be: I'll choose to seem a fool
if I can be a loyal friend.

Prometheus
But he will lay to me all that you do.

Ocean
There you have said what needs must send me home.

Prometheus
Just so. All your lamenting over me
will not have got you then an enemy.

Ocean
Meaning—the new possessor of the throne?

Prometheus
Be on your guard. See that you do not vex him.

Ocean
Your case, Prometheus, may well teach me—

Prometheus
Off with you. Go—and keep your present mind.   430

Ocean
You urge one who is eager to be gone.
For my four-footed bird is restless
to skim with wings the level ways of air.
He'll be well pleased to rest in his home stable.
[Exit OCEAN. *The* CHORUS *now come forward.]*

Chorus
I mourn for you, Prometheus.
Desolation is upon you.
My face is wet with weeping.
Tears fall as waters which run continually.
The floods overflow me.
Terrible are the deeds of Zeus.   440
He rules by laws that are his own.
High is his spear above the others,
turned against the gods of old.
All the land now groans aloud,
mourning for the honor of the heroes of your race.
Stately were they, honored ever in the days of long ago.
Holy Asia is hard by.
Those that dwell there suffer in your trouble, great and sore.
In the Colchian land maidens live,
fearless in fight.   450
Scythia has a battle throng,
the farthest place of earth is theirs,
where marsh grass grows around Maeotis lake.
Arabia's flower is a warrior host;
high on a cliff their fortress stands,
Caucasus towers near;
men fierce as the fire, like the roar of the fire

they shout when the sharp spears clash.
All suffer with you in your trouble, great and sore.
Another Titan too, Earth mourns,   460
bound in shame and iron bonds.
I saw him, Atlas the god.
He bears on his back forever
the cruel strength of the crushing world
and the vault of the sky.
He groans beneath them.
The foaming sea-surge roars in answer,
the deep laments,
the black place of death far down in earth is moved exceedingly,
and the pure-flowing river waters grieve for him in his piteous pain.   470

Prometheus
Neither in insolence nor yet in stubbornness
have I kept silence.
It is thought that eats my heart,
seeing myself thus outraged.
Who else but I, but I myself,
gave these new gods their honors?
Enough of that. I speak to you who know.
Hear rather all that mortals suffered.
Once they were fools. I gave them power to think.
Through me they won their minds.   480
I have no blame for them. All I would tell you
is my good will and my good gifts to them.
Seeing they did not see, nor hearing hear.
Like dreams they led a random life.
They had no houses built to face the sun,
of bricks or well-wrought wood,
but like the tiny ant who has her home
in sunless crannies deep down in the earth,
they lived in caverns.
The signs that speak of winter's coming,   490
of flower-faced spring, of summer's heat
with mellowing fruits,
were all unknown to them.
From me they learned the stars that tell the seasons,
their risings and their settings hard to mark.
And number, that most excellent device,
I taught to them, and letters joined in words.
I gave to them the mother of all arts,
hard working memory.
I, too, first brought beneath the yoke   500
great beasts to serve the plow,
to toil in mortals' stead.
Up to the chariot I led the horse that loves the rein,

the glory of the rich man in his pride.
None else but I first found
the seaman's car, sail-winged, sea-driven.
Such ways to help I showed them, I who have
no wisdom now to help myself.

Leader
You suffer shame as a physician must
who cannot heal himself.   510
You who cured others now are all astray,
distraught of mind and faint of heart,
and find no medicine to soothe your sickness.

Prometheus
Listen, and you shall find more cause for wonder.
Best of all gifts I gave them was the gift of healing.
For if one fell into a malady
there was no drug to cure, no draught, or soothing ointment.
For want of these men wasted to a shadow
until I showed them how to use
the kindly herbs that keep from us disease.   520
The ways of divination I marked out for them,
and they are many; how to know
the waking vision from the idle dream;
to read the sounds hard to discern;
the signs met on the road; the flight of birds,
eagles and vultures,
those that bring good or ill luck in their kind,
their way of life, their loves and hates
and council meetings.
And of those inward parts that tell the future,   530
the smoothness and the color and fair shape
that please the gods.
And how to wrap the flesh in fat
and the long thigh bone, for the altar fire
in honor to the gods.
So did I lead them on to knowledge
of the dark and riddling art.
The fire omens, too, were dim to them
until I made them see.
Deep within the earth are hidden   540
precious things for men,
brass and iron, gold and silver.
Would any say he brought these forth to light
until I showed the way?
No one, except to make an idle boast.
All arts, all goods, have come to men from me.

Leader
Do not care now for mortals
but take thought for yourself, O evil-fated.
I have good hope that still loosed from your bonds
you shall be strong as Zeus. 550

Prometheus
Not thus—not yet—is fate's appointed end,
fate that brings all to pass.
I must be bowed by age-long pain and grief.
So only will my bonds be loosed.
All skill, all cunning, is as foolishness
before necessity.

A Sea Nymph
Who is the helmsman of necessity?

Prometheus
Fate, threefold, Retribution, unforgetting.

Another
And Zeus is not so strong?

Prometheus
He cannot shun what is foredoomed. 560

Another
And is he not foredoomed to rule forever?

Prometheus
No word of that. Ask me no further.

Another
Some solemn secret hides behind your silence.

Prometheus
Think of another theme. It is not yet
the time to speak of this.
It must be wrapped in darkness, so alone
I shall some time be saved
from shame and grief and bondage.

Chorus
Zeus orders all things.
May he never set his might against purpose of mine, 570
like a wrestler in the match.
May I ever be found where feast the holy gods,
and the oxen are slain,
where ceaselessly flows the pathway
of Ocean, my father.

May the words of my lips forever
be free from sin.
May this abide with me and not depart
like melting snow.
Long life is sweet when there is hope   580
and hope is confident.
And it is sweet when glad thoughts make the heart grow strong,
and there is joy.
But you, crushed by a thousand griefs,
I look upon you and I shudder.
You did not tremble before Zeus.
You gave your worship where you would, to men,
a gift too great for mortals,
a thankless favor.
What help for you there? What defense in those   590
whose life is but from morning unto evening?
Have you not seen?
Their little strength is feebleness,
fast bound in darkness,
like a dream.
The will of man shall never break
the harmony of God.
This I have learned beholding your destruction.
Once I spoke different words to you
from those now on my lips.   600
A song flew to me.
I stood beside your bridal bed,
I sang the wedding hymn,
glad in your marriage.
And with fair gifts persuading her,
you led to share your couch
Hesione, child of the sea.
      [Enter IO.*]*

Io

What land—what creatures here?
This, that I see—
A form storm-beaten,   610
bound to the rock.
Did you do wrong?
Is this your punishment?
You perish here.
Where am I?
Speak to a wretched wanderer.
Oh! Oh! he stings again—
the gadfly—oh, miserable!
But you must know he's not a gadfly.
He's Argus, son of Earth, the herdsman.   620
He has a thousand eyes.

I see him. Off! Keep him away!
No, he comes on.
His eyes can see all ways at once.
He's dead but no grave holds him.
He comes straight up from hell.
He is the huntsman,
and I his wretched quarry.
He drives me all along the long sea strand.
I may not stop for food or drink.   630
He has a shepherd's pipe,
a reed with beeswax joined.
Its sound is like the locust's shrilling,
a drowsy note—that will not let me sleep.
Oh, misery. Oh, misery.
Where is it leading me,
my wandering—far wandering.
What ever did I do,
how ever did I sin,
that you have yoked me to calamity,   640
O son of Kronos,
that you madden a wretched woman
driven mad by the gadfly of fear.
Oh, burn me in fire or hide me in earth
or fling me as food to the beasts of the sea.
Master, grant me my prayer.
Enough—I have been tried enough—
my wandering—long wandering.
Yet I have found no place
to leave my misery.   650
—I am a girl who speaks to you,
but horns are on my head.

Prometheus
Like one caught in an eddy, whirling round and round,
the gadfly drives you.
I know you, girl. You are Inachus' daughter.
You made the god's heart hot with love,
and Hera hates you. She it is
who drives you on this flight that never stops.

Io
How is it that you speak my father's name?
Who are you? Tell me for my misery.   660
Who are you, sufferer, that speak the truth
to one who suffers?
You know the sickness God has put upon me,
that stings and maddens me and drives me on
and wastes my life away.
I am a beast, a starving beast,

that frenzied runs with clumsy leaps and bounds,
oh, shame,
mastered by Hera's malice.
Who among the wretched   670
suffer as I do?
Give me a sign, you there.
Tell to me clearly
the pain still before me.
Is help to be found?
A medicine to cure me?
Speak, if you know.

Prometheus
I will and in plain words,
as friend should talk to friend.
—You see Prometheus, who gave mortals fire.   680

Io
You, he who succored the whole race of men?
You, that Prometheus, the daring, the enduring?
Why do you suffer here?

Prometheus
Just now I told the tale—

Io
But will you not still give to me a boon?

Prometheus
Ask what you will. I know all you would learn.

Io
Then tell me who has bound you to this rock.

Prometheus
Zeus was the mind that planned.
The hand that did the deed the god of fire.

Io
What was the wrong that you are punished for?   690

Prometheus
No more. Enough of me.

Io
But you will tell the term set to my wandering?
My misery is great. When shall it end?

Prometheus
Here not to know is best.

Io
I ask you not to hide what I must suffer.

Prometheus
I do so in no grudging spirit.

Io
Why then delay to tell me all?

Prometheus
Not through ill will. I would not terrify you.

Io
Spare me not more than I would spare myself.

Prometheus
If you constrain me I must speak. Hear then—   700

Leader
Not yet. Yield to my pleasure too.
For I would hear from her own lips
what is the deadly fate, the sickness
that is upon her. Let her say—then teach her
the trials still to come.

Prometheus
If you would please these maidens, Io—
they are your father's sisters,
and when the heart is sorrowful, to speak
to those who will let fall a tear
is time well spent.   710

Io
I do not know how to distrust you.
You shall hear all. And yet—
I am ashamed to speak,
to tell of that god-driven storm
that struck me, changed me, ruined me.
How shall I tell you who it was?
How ever to my maiden chamber
visions came by night,
persuading me with gentle words:
"Oh happy, happy girl,   720
Why are you all too long a maid
when you might marry with the highest?
The arrow of desire has pierced Zeus.
For you he is on fire.
With you it is his will to capture love.
Would you, child, fly from Zeus' bed?
Go forth to Lerna, to the meadows deep in grass.
There is a sheep-fold there,
an ox-stall, too, that holds your father's oxen—
so shall Zeus find release from his desire."

Always, each night, such dreams possessed me.
I was unhappy and at last I dared
to tell my father of these visions.
He sent to Pytho and far Dodona
man after man to ask the oracle
what he must say or do to please the gods.
But all brought answers back of shifting meaning,
hard to discern, like golden coins unmarked.
At last a clear word came. It fell upon him
like lightning from the sky. It told him   740
to thrust me from his house and from his country,
to wander to the farthest bounds of earth
like some poor dumb beast set apart
for sacrifice, whom no man will restrain.
And if my father would not, Zeus would send
his thunder-bolt with eyes of flame to end
his race, all, everyone.
He could not but obey such words
from the dark oracle. He drove me out.
He shut his doors to me—against his will   750
as against mine. Zeus had him bridled.
He drove him as he would.
Straightway I was distorted, mind and body.
A beast—with horns—look at me—
stung by a fly, who madly leaps and bounds.
And so I ran and found myself beside
the waters, sweet to drink, of Kerchneia
and Lerna's well-spring.
Beside me went the herdsman Argus,
the violent of heart, the earth-born,   760
watching my footsteps with his hundred eyes.
But death came to him, swift and unforeseen.
Plagued by a gadfly then, the scourge of God,
I am driven on from land to land.
So for what has been. But what still remains
of anguish for me, tell me.
Do not in pity soothe me with false tales.
Words strung together by a lie
are like a foul disease.

Leader
Oh, shame. Oh, tale of shame.   770
Never, oh never, would I have believed that my ears
would hear words such as these, of strange meaning.
Evil to see and evil to hear,
misery, defilement, and terror.
They pierce my heart with a two-edged sword.
A fate like that—
I shudder to look upon Io.

Prometheus
You are too ready with your tears and fears.
Wait for the end.

Leader
Speak. Tell us, for when one lies sick,   780
to face with clear eyes all the pain to come
is sweet.

Prometheus
What first you asked was granted easily,
to hear from her own lips her trials.
But for the rest, learn now the sufferings
she still must suffer, this young creature,
at Hera's hands. Child of Inachus,
keep in your heart my words, so you shall know
where the road ends. First to the sunrise,
over furrows never plowed, where wandering Scythians   790
live in huts of wattles made, raised high
on wheels smooth-rolling. Bows they have,
and they shoot far. Turn from them.
Keep to the shore washed by the moaning sea.
Off to the left live the Chalybians,
workers of iron. There be on your guard.
A rough people they, who like not strangers.
Here rolls a river called the Insolent,
true to its name. You cannot find a ford
until you reach the Caucasus itself,   800
highest of mountains. From beneath its brow
the mighty river rushes. You must cross
the summit, neighbor to the stars.
Then by the southward road, until you reach
the warring Amazons, men-haters, who one day
will found a city by the Thermodon,
where Salmydessus thrusts
a fierce jaw out into the sea that sailors hate,
stepmother of ships.
And they will bring you on your way right gladly   810
to the Cimmerian isthmus, by a shallow lake,
Maeotis, at the narrows.
Here you must cross with courage.
And men shall tell forever of your passing.
The strait shall be named for you, Bosporus,
Ford of the Cow. There leave the plains of Europe,
and enter Asia, the great Continent.
—Now does he seem to you, this ruler of the gods,
evil, to all, in all things?
A god desired a mortal—drove her forth   820
to wander thus.

A bitter lover you have found, O girl,
for all that I have told you is not yet
the prelude even.

Io
Oh, wretched, wretched.

Prometheus
You cry aloud for this? What then
when you have learned the rest?

Leader
You will not tell her of more trouble?

Prometheus
A storm-swept sea of grief and ruin.

Io
What gain to me is life? Oh, now to fling myself   830
down from this rock peak to the earth below,
and find release there from my trouble.
Better to die once than to suffer
through all the days of life.

Prometheus
Hardly would you endure my trial,
whose fate it is not ever to find death
that ends all pain. For me there is no end
until Zeus falls from power.

Io
Zeus fall from power?

Prometheus
You would rejoice, I think, to see that happen?   840

Io
How could I not, who suffer at his hands?

Prometheus
Know then that it shall surely be.

Io
But who will strip the tyrant of his scepter?

Prometheus
He will himself and his own empty mind.

Io
How? Tell me, if it is not wrong to ask.

Prometheus
He will make a marriage that will vex him.

Io
Goddess or mortal, if it may be spoken?

Prometheus
It may not be. Seek not to know.

Io
His wife shall drive him from his throne?

Prometheus
Her child shall be more than his father's match.   850

Io
And is there no way of escape for him?

Prometheus
No way indeed, unless my bonds are loosed.

Io
But who can loose them against Zeus' will?

Prometheus
A son of yours—so fate decrees.

Io
What words are these? A child of mine shall free you?

Prometheus
Ten generations first must pass and then three more.

Io
Your prophecy grows dim through generations.

Prometheus
So let it be. Seek not to know your trials.

Io
Do not hold out a boon and then withdraw it.

Prometheus
One boon of two I will bestow upon you.   860

Io
And they are? Speak. Give me the choice.

Prometheus
I give it you: the hardships still before you,
or his name who shall free me. Choose.

Leader
Of these give one to her, but give to me
a grace as well—I am not quite unworthy.
Tell her where she must wander, and to me
tell who shall free you. It is my heart's desire.

Prometheus

And to your eagerness I yield.
Hear, Io, first, of your far-driven journey.
And bear in mind my words, inscribe them   870
upon the tablets of your heart.
When you have crossed the stream that bounds
the continents, turn to the East where flame
the footsteps of the sun, and pass
along the sounding sea to Cisthene.
Here on the plain live Phorcys' children, three,
all maidens, very old, and shaped like swans,
who have one eye and one tooth to the three.
No ray of sun looks ever on that country,
nor ever moon by night. Here too their sisters dwell.   880
And they are three, the Gorgons, winged,
with hair of snakes, hateful to mortals.
Whom no man shall behold and draw again
the breath of life. They garrison that place.
And yet another evil sight, the hounds of Zeus,
who never bark, griffins with beaks like birds.
The one-eyed Arimaspi too, the riders,
who live beside a stream that flows with gold,
a way of wealth. From all these turn aside.
Far off there is a land where black men live,   890
close to the sources of the sun, whence springs
a sun-scorched river. When you reach it,
go with all care along the banks up to
the great descent, where from the mountains
the holy Nile pours forth its waters
pleasant to drink from. It will be your guide
to the Nile land, the Delta. A long exile
is fated for you and your children here.
If what I speak seems dark and hard to know,
ask me again and learn all clearly.   900
For I have time to spare and more
than I could wish.

Leader

If in your story of her fatal journey
there is yet somewhat left to tell her,
speak now. If not, give then to us
the grace we asked. You will remember.

Prometheus

The whole term of her roaming has been told.
But I will show she has not heard in vain,
and tell her what she suffered coming hither,
in proof my words are true.   910
A moving multitude of sorrows were there,

too many to recount, but at the end
you came to where the levels of Molossa
surround the lofty ridge of Dodona,
seat of God's oracle.
A wonder past belief is there, oak trees that speak.
They spoke, not darkly but in shining words,
calling you Zeus' glorious spouse.
The frenzy seized you then. You fled
along the sea-road washed by the great inlet,   920
named for God's mother. Up and down you wandered,
storm-tossed. And in the time to come that sea
shall have its name from you, Ionian,
that men shall not forget your journey.
This is my proof to you my mind can see
farther than meets the eye.
From here the tale I tell is for you all,
and of the future, leaving now the past.
There is a city, Canobus, at the land's end,
where the Nile empties, on new river soil.   930
There Zeus at last shall make you sane again,
stroking you with a hand you will not fear.
And from this touch alone you will conceive
and bear a son, a swarthy man,
whose harvest shall be reaped on many fields,
all that are washed by the wide-watered Nile.
In the fifth generation from him, fifty sisters
will fly from marriage with their near of kin,
who, hawks in close pursuit of doves, a-quiver
with passionate desire, shall find that death   940
waits for the hunters on the wedding night.
God will refuse to them the virgin bodies.
Argos will be the maidens' refuge, to their suitors
a slaughter dealt by women's hands,
bold in the watches of the night.
The wife shall kill her husband,
dipping her two-edged sword in blood.
O Cyprian goddess, thus may you come to my foes.
One girl, bound by love's spell, will change
her purpose, and she will not kill   950
the man she lay beside, but choose the name
of coward rather than be stained with blood.
In Argos she will bear a kingly child—
a story overlong if all were told.
Know this, that from that seed will spring
one glorious with the bow, bold-hearted,
and he shall set me free.
This is the oracle my mother told me,
Justice, who is of old, Earth's daughter.

But how and where would be too long a tale,   960
nor would you profit.

Io
Oh, misery. Oh, misery.
A frenzy tears me.
Madness strikes my mind.
I burn. A frantic sting—
an arrow never forged with fire.
My heart is beating at its walls in terror.
My eyes are whirling wheels.
Away. Away. A raging wind of fury
sweeps through me.   970
My tongue has lost its power.
My words are like a turbid stream,
wild waves that dash against a surging sea,
the black sea of madness.
[Exit Io.*]*

Chorus
Wise, wise was he,
who first weighed this in thought
and gave it utterance:
Marriage within one's own degree is best,
not with one whom wealth has spoiled,
nor yet with one made arrogant by birth.   980
Such as these he must not seek
who lives upon the labor of his hands.
Fate, dread deity,
may you never, oh, never behold me
sharing the bed of Zeus.
May none of the dwellers in heaven
draw near to me ever.
Terrors take hold of me
seeing her maidenhood
turning from love of man,   990
torn by Hera's hate,
driven in misery.
For me, I would not shun marriage nor fear it,
so it were with my equal.
But the love of the greater gods,
from whose eyes none can hide,
may that never be mine.
To war with a god-lover is not war,
it is despair.
For what could I do,   1000
or where could I fly
from the cunning of Zeus?

Prometheus
In very truth shall Zeus, for all his stubborn pride,
be humbled, such a marriage he will make
to cast him down from throne and power.
And he shall be no more remembered.
The curse his father put on him
shall be fulfilled.
The curse that he cursed him with as he fell
from his age-long throne. 1010
The way from such trouble no one of the gods
can show him save I.
These things I know and how they shall come to pass.
So let him sit enthroned in confidence,
trust to his crashing thunder high in air,
shake in his hands his fire-breathing dart.
Surely these shall be no defense,
but he will fall, in shame unbearable.
Even now he makes ready against himself
one who shall wrestle with him and prevail, 1020
a wonder of wonders, who will find
a flame that is swifter than lightning,
a crash to silence the thunder,
who will break into pieces the sea-god's spear,
the bane of the ocean that shakes the earth.
Before this evil Zeus shall be bowed down.
He will learn how far apart are a king and a slave.

Leader
These words of menace on your tongue
speak surely only your desire.

Prometheus
They speak that which shall surely be— 1030
and also my desire.

Leader
And we must look to see Zeus mastered?

Prometheus
Yes, and beneath a yoke more cruel than this I bear.

Leader
You have no fear to utter words like these?

Prometheus
I am immortal—and I have no fear.

Another Sea Nymph
But agony still worse he might inflict—

Prometheus
So let him do. All that must come I know.

Another
The wise bow to the inescapable.

Prometheus
Be wise then. Worship power.
Cringe before each who wields it.   1040
To me Zeus counts as less than nothing.
Let him work his will, show forth his power
for his brief day, his little moment
of lording it in heaven.
—But see. There comes a courier from Zeus,
a lackey in his new lord's livery.
Some curious news is surely on his lips.
[Enter HERMES.*]*

Hermes
You trickster there, you biter bitten,
sinner against the gods, man-lover, thief of fire,
my message is to you.   1050
The great father gives you here his orders:
Reveal this marriage that you boast of,
by which he shall be hurled from power.
And, mark you, not in riddles, each fact clearly.
—Don't make me take a double journey, Prometheus. You can see Zeus isn't
    going to be made kinder by this sort of thing.

Prometheus
Big words and insolent. They well become you,
O lackey of the gods.
Young—young—your thrones just won,
you think you live in citadels grief cannot reach.
Two dynasties I have seen fall from heaven,   1060
and I shall see the third fall fastest,
most shamefully of all.
Is it your thought to see me tremble
and crouch before your upstart gods?
Not so—not such a one am I.
Make your way back. You will not learn from me.

Hermes
Ah, so? Still stubborn? Yet this willfulness
has anchored you fast in these troubled waters.

Prometheus
And yet I would not change my lot
with yours, O lackey.   1070

Hermes
Better no doubt to be slave to a rock
than be the Father's trusted herald.

Prometheus
I must be insolent when I must speak to insolence.

Hermes
You are proud, it seems, of what has come to you.

Prometheus
I proud? May such pride be
the portion of my foes.—I count you of them.

Hermes
You blame me also for your sufferings?

Prometheus
In one word, all gods are my enemies.
They had good from me. They return me evil.

Hermes
I heard you were quite mad.   1080

Prometheus
Yes, I am mad, if to abhor such foes is madness.

Hermes
You would be insufferable, Prometheus, if you were not so wretched.

Prometheus
Alas!

Hermes
Alas? That is a word Zeus does not understand.

Prometheus
Time shall teach it him, gray time,
that teaches all things.

Hermes
It has not taught you wisdom yet.

Prometheus
No, or I had not wrangled with a slave.

Hermes
It seems that you will tell the Father nothing.

Prometheus
Paying the debt of kindness that I owe him?   1090

Hermes
You mock at me as though I were a child.

Prometheus
A child you are or what else has less sense
if you expect to learn from me.
There is no torture and no trick of skill,
there is no force, which can compel my speech,
until Zeus wills to loose these deadly bonds.
So let him hurl his blazing bolt,
and with the white wings of the snow,
with thunder and with earthquake,
confound the reeling world.   1100
None of all this will bend my will
to tell him at whose hands he needs must fall.

Hermes
I urge you, pause and think if this will help you.

Prometheus
I thought long since of all. I planned for all.

Hermes
Submit, you fool. Submit. In agony learn wisdom.

Prometheus
Go and persuade the sea wave not to break.
You will persuade me no more easily.
I am no frightened woman, terrified
at Zeus' purpose. Do you think to see me
ape women's ways, stretch out my hands   1110
to him I hate, and pray him for release?
A world apart am I from prayer for pity.

Hermes
Then all I say is said in vain.
Nothing will move you, no entreaty
soften your heart.
Like a young colt new-bridled,
you have the bit between your teeth,
and rear and fight against the rein.
But all this vehemence is feeble bombast.
A fool, bankrupt of all but obstinacy,   1120
is the poorest thing on earth.
Oh, if you will not hear me, yet consider
the storm that threatens you from which
you cannot fly, a great third wave of evil.
Thunder and flame of lightning will rend
this jagged peak. You shall be buried deep,
held by a splintered rock.

After long length of time you will return
to see the light, but Zeus' winged hound,
an eagle red with blood,   1130
shall come a guest unbidden to your banquet.
All day long he will tear to rags your body,
great rents within the flesh,
feasting in fury on the blackened liver.
Look for no ending to this agony
until a god will freely suffer for you,
will take on him your pain, and in your stead
descend to where the sun is turned to darkness,
the black depths of death.
Take thought: this is no empty boast   1140
but utter truth. Zeus does not lie.
Each word shall be fulfilled.
Pause and consider. Never think
self-will is better than wise counsel.

Leader

To us the words he speaks are not amiss.
He bids you let your self-will go and seek
good counsel. Yield.
For to the wise a failure is disgrace.

Prometheus

These tidings that the fellow shouts at me
were known to me long since.   1150
A foe to suffer at the hands of foes
is nothing shameful.
Then let the twisting flame of forked fire
be hurled upon me. Let the very air
be rent by thunder-crash.
Savage winds convulse the sky,
hurricanes shake the earth from its foundations,
the waves of the sea rise up and drown the stars,
and let me be swept down to hell,
caught in the cruel whirlpool of Necessity.   1160
He cannot kill me.

Hermes

Why, these are ravings you may hear from madmen.
His case is clear. Frenzy can go no further.
You maids who pity him, depart, be swift.
The thunder peals and it is merciless.
Would you too be struck down?

Leader

Speak other words, another counsel,
if you would win me to obey.

Now, in this place, to urge
that I should be a coward is intolerable. 1170
I choose with him to suffer what must be.
Not to stand by a friend—there is no evil
I count more hateful.
I spit it from my mouth.

Hermes
Remember well I warned you,
when you are swept away in utter ruin.
Blame then yourselves, not fate, nor ever say
that Zeus delivered you
to a hurt you had not thought to see.
With open eyes, 1180
not suddenly, not secretly,
into the net of utter ruin
whence there is no escape,
you fall by your own folly.
[Exit HERMES.*]*

Prometheus
An end to words. Deeds now.
The world is shaken.
The deep and secret way of thunder
is rent apart.
Fiery wreaths of lightning flash.
Whirlwinds toss the swirling dust. 1190
The blasts of all the winds are battling in the air,
and sky and sea are one.
On me the tempest falls.
It does not make me tremble.
O holy Mother Earth, O air and sun,
behold me. I am wronged.

Questions for Discussion and Review

1. Discuss the specific ways in which Aeschylus's depiction of Prometheus differs from Hesiod's portrait of the trickster Titan. What qualities characterize Zeus in the *Prometheus Bound?* How does Hephaestus's attitude toward the captive Titan differ from that of Force?

2. The English romantic poet Percy Bysshe Shelley regarded Prometheus as a heroic rebel fighting against the unjust authority of despotism. Do you find the Titan a fitting symbol of the human mind awakening to the distinction between political power and humanistic values of individual freedom, justice, and compassion? In Aeschylus's presentation of gods divided between force and wisdom, what hope is there for the ultimate reconciliation of these polar opposites?

3. Describe Io's function in the play. Does she increase our respect for Zeus's authority? In the final scene, why does the chorus decide to suffer with Prometheus?

4. In the lost plays of the Prometheus cycle, Zeus and the Titan were apparently reconciled. Speculate on why this mediation of opponents is necessary or desirable. Which of the two figures would have to modify his position more?

Recommended Reading

Griffith, Mark. *Aeschylus: Prometheus Bound.* New York: Cambridge UP, 1983. Offers arguments for and against Aeschylean authorship, as well as extensive commentary on the play.

Herington, C. J. *Aeschylus.* New Haven: Yale UP, 1986.

Hogan, James C. *A Commentary on the Complete Greek Tragedies—Aeschylus.* Chicago: U of Chicago P, 1984.

Thomson, George. *Aeschylus and Athens.* London: Lawrence, 1941.

Winnington-Ingram, R. P. *Studies in Aeschylus.* New York: Cambridge UP, 1983.

I 5

The House of Atreus:
Aeschylus's *Oresteia*

KEY THEMES

In three sequential plays, Aeschylus dramatizes the tragic effects of Clytem-nestra's murder of Agamemnon, king of Argos (Mycenae), and the ordeal of their son, Orestes, who is forced to avenge his father's death by killing his own mother. In the final play, which pits chthonic forces (the Furies) against the Olympian sky gods, Athene intervenes in Orestes's plight to me-diate between the ancient principles of blood vengeance and new laws of civic order.

Aeschylus's Drama of Crime and Redemption

The only surviving Greek trilogy, Aeschylus's *Oresteia* was first produced in 458 B.C., two years before the playwright's death. A sweeping reinterpretation of Homeric myth, the three plays examine the causes and consequences of Agamemnon's murder by his wife, **Clytemnestra,** and the unbearable dilemma facing their son, Orestes, who is compelled to kill his own mother in order to avenge his father's death. Al-though Aeschylus inherited his characters and dramatic situation from Homer, he turned this domestic tragedy of adultery and matricide into a cosmic event: Orestes, after whom the trilogy is named, affords the gods an opportunity to redefine the nature of justice and establish a new concept of divinity that transforms both religion and Greek society.

The playwright's major concern is the force of evolutionary change, in both the human and divine spheres, that ultimately unites contrarieties and mediates a bipolar view of existence. Incorporating a dominant theme of the Prometheus trilogy, Aes-chylus explores the implications of Greek belief that gods are not eternal and un-changing but, like human beings, are born, grow, and develop into ethical maturity only with the slow passing of time. Time eventually heals the breach between Zeus and Prometheus, ultimately merging the Titan's superior wisdom and compassion with Zeus's Olympian administration. In the *Oresteia,* Aeschylus shows the influence on human society of Zeus's moral evolution, a process that reaches its climax in the *Eumenides* when the hostile spirits of blood vengeance (the **Erinyes** [e-RIN-ih-eez], or **Furies**) are transformed into benign protectors and sources of blessing for Athene's people. By the *Eumenides's* conclusion, we realize that Agamemnon's murder and his son's revenge are primarily an opportunity for a divinely guided legal and moral revolution: acts of personal barbarism (the vendetta) are replaced by instituting courts of law that recognize and enforce the civilized values of clemency.

An Overview

In his *Poetics,* the earliest extant discussion of Greek epic and tragedy, Aristotle (384– 322 B.C.) described the well-made drama as having a single major action, without distracting subplots. He added that the time covered in the play's events should be confined to "one revolution of the sun," a 24-hour period, so that the temporal duration of events on stage generally corresponded to the audience's sense of real time. Later critics of the Renaissance and French Enlightenment interpreted Aristotle's descriptive comments as formal prescriptions for the "three unities" of time, place, and action, imposing formal restrictions that supposedly intensify a drama's tragic effect.

Conceived on a grand scale perhaps never surpassed in world theater, the *Oresteia*—written more than a century before Aristotle's *Poetics*—boldly ignores any confines of time or place. Aeschylus gave his trilogy an epic scope, covering events that span at least a decade and setting the action all over the map of Greece. The first play, the *Agamemnon,* opens in Argos (rather than nearby Mycenae, the historically correct site) shortly before Agamemnon's return home from Troy. The second play, *Choephoroe,* or *Libation-Bearers,* takes place several years later, after Orestes has grown to young manhood and has returned from exile. In the third play, the *Eumenides,* the scene shifts from the Peloponnesian Peninsula to Delphi, where Orestes, pursued by the Furies, seeks purification. For the final act, after another year has passed, Aeschylus transfers the action to Athens, where Orestes is tried before a specially convened tribunal on the **Areopagus,** the "hill of Ares," a rocky spur of the Acropolis. (See Figure 15-1 for an overview of the geographic area covered in the *Oresteia.*)

The original issues of blood vengeance and filial duty that dominate in Argos become in Athens matters of civic law and religious ethics. To signal the extreme importance that Zeus attaches to Orestes's case, divine beings miraculously appear to participate in the court proceedings: the Furies act as prosecutor, Apollo as chief witness for the defense, and Athene as judge. The *Oresteia* reaches its climax not in Orestes's acquittal and absolution but in Athene's transformation of the Furies (Erinyes) into the Kindly Ones (Eumenides), thus fulfilling Zeus's plan.

As a coda to the tragic action, Aeschylus created a satyr play based on an episode in the *Odyssey:* Menelaus's comic encounter with **Proteus,** a sea god who has the Dionysian ability to change into any form he desires. The play has been lost, but it probably involved a farcical version of the Homeric account, with Proteus metamorphosing himself successively into a lion, a serpent, a panther, a boar, a body of water, and a tree. If Aeschylus followed Homer's account, we may suppose that the play featured this sequence of incidents: after a satiric agon (the contest or struggle fea-

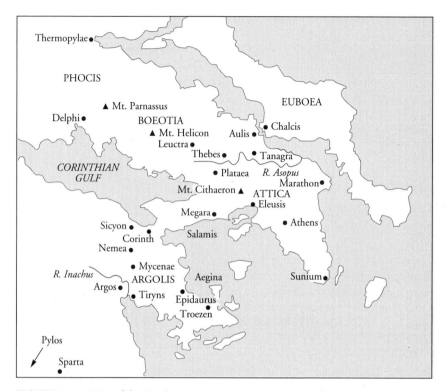

FIGURE 15-1   Map of the Northeastern Peloponnesus. The area of Greece south of the
Gulf of Corinth is called the Peloponnesus, named after Pelops, son of Tantalus. During the
Mycenaean period (c. 1600–1100 B.C.), this area was dominated by heavily fortified cities
such as Mycenae, Sparta, Tiryns, and Pylos, all of which figure prominently in Greek mythology. Although Mycenae is historically the site of Agamemnon's capital, Aeschylus transferred it to Argos, the setting of his *Agamemnon* and *Libation-Bearers.*

tured in tragedy), Menelaus at last forces Proteus to use his prophetic gifts to foretell
the Greek leader's successful return—with the now repentant Helen—to Sparta. Offering a pleasurable contrast to Agamemnon's bloody homecoming, Menelaus's adventure concludes the Dionysian tragic cycle by sexually reuniting the couple whose
marital problems helped precipitate the Trojan War. (For one of numerous versions
of Helen's reunion with Menelaus, see Figure 15-2, where the wronged husband
seems ready to take vengeance on his faithless wife, despite Helen's all-but-irresistible
allure.)

Important Elements and Themes

The Choruses   The *Oresteia*'s three very different choruses are integral parts of Aeschylus's design. The *Agamemnon* chorus is composed of Argive citizens who, even ten
years before the play opens, were too old to fight at Troy and are now reduced to the

FIGURE 15-2   Menelaus and Helen. In this vase painting, Menelaus, who has recovered Helen after the fall of Troy, threatens her with his sword. Although the *Odyssey* portrayed Helen respectfully, restoring her to Sparta with queenly rank and privileges, other Greek myths reported that Menelaus executed the woman who had betrayed him for Paris (whereas still others insisted that only a phantom Helen had eloped to Troy; see Chapter 11). Clytemnestra, who is married to Menelaus's brother, resembles her sister, Helen, in being an equally unfaithful wife, but far more deadly. (*British Museum, London.*)

status of passive onlookers. Feebly protesting Clytemnestra's take-charge attitude, they fail to perceive her homicidal intentions, even when **Cassandra,** a clairvoyant Trojan princess, explicitly describes her visions of Agamemnon's imminent death. Although physically impotent and unequal to the challenge of their queen's conspiracy, the chorus is a rich repository of traditional wisdom and religious insight. The first choral ode sounds two of Aeschylus's principal themes: that wisdom is won only through suffering and that the integrity of Zeus, the supreme god, ensures that universal moral order will ultimately prevail.

Both the second and third parts of the *Oresteia* are named after their respective choruses. The *Libation-Bearers* are captive Trojan women whom Clytemnestra orders to carry ritual drink offerings (libations) to the tomb of Agamemnon, whose ghost now troubles his widow's dreams. The enslaved women embody a typically Aeschylean paradox: although they have lost husbands, families, and homeland through

Agamemnon's conquest of Troy, they are united in honoring their slain captor and hating his arrogant queen. Their cry of triumph over the regicides' dead bodies echoes Clytemnestra's joyous shout in the *Agamemnon* when she first learns of her husband's approach and anticipates the glad cries accompanying the Eumenides' ritual procession that concludes the trilogy.

In the third play, the *Eumenides,* the chorus consists of Furies (*Erinyes*), savage spirits of vengeance whom Athene will eventually domesticate as the "Kindly Ones" (**Eumenides** [oo-MEN-ih-deez]). They first appear at the end of the *Libation-Bearers,* when, as Gorgon-like horrors, they rush on stage to seize Orestes, determined to destroy the matricide in both body and soul. In Aeschylus's vision of the gods' evolution, the Furies represent ancient chthonic (earth-oriented) powers who oppose the new ouranic (sky-god) deities of Olympus. According to Hesiod, they were generated from drops of blood falling upon Gaea from Uranus's severed genitals and are thus both earthborn and the product of castration, a primordial crime against the father. Despite their differences in appearance and function, they are half-sisters of Aphrodite, who was also created from Uranus's mutilation, and thus aspects of the Great Goddess. Commensurate with their origin, the Furies punish crimes against blood kin, especially of children against their parents. Aeschylus makes them daughters of Night (Nyx), sister of Erebus (Infernal Darkness), perhaps because this ancestry emphasizes their natural opposition to Apollo, the luminous eye of heaven.

The Curse on the House of Atreus   To illustrate his view that the gods are determined to end wanton bloodshed and cleanse even the deepest guilt, Aeschylus examines one of the most spectacularly dysfunctional families in all of Greek mythology. The royal dynasty (House) of **Atreus** [AY-tre-uhs] (Figure 15-3), father of Agamemnon and Menelaus, inherits a proclivity toward evil from a distant ancestor, Tantalus, the man who murdered and cooked his own son, serving Pelops's dismembered body to the gods to test their omniscience (Chapter 9). Although the Tantalus myth may function primarily to warn against human sacrifice—the Olympians summarily reject Tantalus's offering and condemn him to Tartarus—it anticipates the equally vile crime of Atreus himself. Atreus and his brother **Thyestes** engage in a bitter feud after the latter commits adultery with Atreus's wife, Aerope. Pretending a reconciliation, Atreus invites Thyestes to a banquet, where his unsuspecting brother dines on the flesh of his sons.

Although Aeschylus does not use it, one version of the Atreus myth emphasizes the incestuous origin of Thyestes's son Aegisthus, who avenges the wrongs done to his side of the family. After an oracle decrees that only a son conceived in incest could effect the desired revenge, Thyestes impregnates his daughter, Pelopia, who gives birth to Aegisthus. In this tradition, Aegisthus grows up to kill his uncle Atreus, become Clytemnestra's lover, and murder Agamemnon.

The Sacrifice of Iphigenia   Before leaving Argos for Troy, Agamemnon, acting on a dubious prophetic oracle, compounds the family sins by sacrificing his daughter **Iphigenia** [if-ih-je-NYE-a], Clytemnestra's favorite child (Figure 15-4). In the *Agamemnon,* the chorus implies that Argos's king slaughtered his virgin daughter because of egoism—he feared the public shame involved in disbanding his army. Other poets assigned Agamemnon different motives, some ascribing Iphigenia's murder to her father's ambition. When the unruly Greek army, assembled at the seaport of Aulis,

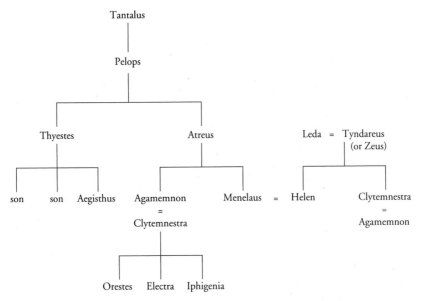

FIGURE 15-3 Genealogy of the House of Atreus. As this genealogical chart indicates, Agamemnon and his family are descended from a long line of royal criminals, including perpetrators of murder, adultery, incest, and cannibalism. In the *Oresteia,* Aeschylus takes on the issue
of whether such deeply ingrained guilt—inherited but also compounded anew in each suc-
ceeding generation—can be cleansed or its cycle of violent crime and equally heinous vengeance be brought to a peaceful end.

threatens to disperse because the gods withhold fair sailing winds, threatening to rob
Agamemnon of his major chance at glory, he exchanges his child in return for the
opportunity to sack Troy. In his *Iphigenia at Aulis,* Euripides examines the pressures
that Agamemnon's soldiers, eager to seize Troy's gold, impose on their commander,
making him the pawn of their collective greed and blood lust.

Cassandra's Prophecy When Troy falls, Agamemnon adds to his guilt by desecrat-
ing the city's holy shrines and massacring even those who seek asylum in the gods'
sanctuaries. In his treatment of the myth, Aeschylus implies Agamemnon's impiety
by showing the conqueror bringing home Cassandra, a virgin priestess of Apollo,
whom he has violated and enslaved as his concubine. A daughter of Priam and
Hecuba, Cassandra bears a heavy burden: she is a prophet who foresees the future
with frightening accuracy, but no one ever believes her. This intensely frustrating
predicament results from Cassandra's wish to protect her virginity, a symbol of her
integrity and commitment to her prophetic office, even from the god who endowed
her with clairvoyance. When Apollo attempted to seduce her, Cassandra rebuffed
him: the Delphic god could not retract his gift, but he cursed her with an undeserved
inability to make others understand her visions (Figure 15-5).

Near the end of the *Agamemnon,* as she obeys Clytemnestra's order to enter the
royal palace, where the queen will butcher her, Cassandra strips off the emblems of

FIGURE 15-4   The Sacrifice of Iphigenia. For Iphigenia's mother, Agamemnon's sin in sacrificing their daughter is unforgivable. Clytemnestra sees herself as fully justified in avenging her child by killing the murderer, who is also her husband and king, an act that perpetuates the curse on the House of Atreus. In this Roman wall painting (c. A.D. 63–79) of Iphigenia at Aulis, the port from which the Greek fleet under Agamemnon's command departed for Troy, a veiled figure hides her face in grief while in the sky above Artemis rides a stag to rescue the girl, a version of the myth absent in Aeschylus's trilogy but dramatized by Euripides (see the box on p. 606). (*National Museum, Naples.*)

Apollo's service, throwing down her prophet's veil and staff. Betrayed by her god, exploited by Agamemnon, and slaughtered by his wife, Cassandra is a victim of brutality both human and divine. Even the chorus, which is generally sympathetic to her plight, seems willfully blind to her warnings of impending disaster. In death, as in life, she is utterly alone, trapped in her solitary, unwanted vision.

FIGURE 15-5   Apollo and Cassandra. According to one tradition, Cassandra—a princess of Troy and Apollo's virgin priestess—at first consents to the god's wish to sleep with her but later refuses to make love, attempting to retain both her religious office and her independence. Although he cannot rescind his prophetic gift, the rejected Apollo takes away Cassandra's credibility so that no one will ever believe her predictions. Tormented by knowing the future but powerless to make others accept her vision, Cassandra appears in the *Agamemnon* as a demented clairvoyant, possessed by a god's spirit but unable to warn others or save herself. (*Henry Lillie Pierce Fund. Courtesy, Museum of Fine Arts, Boston.*)

The *Agamemnon*

With its long choral songs and stately pace, the *Agamemnon* moves slowly but inexorably to a powerful confrontation between Greece's victorious commander in chief and the wife who has ruled Argos in his absence. While Agamemnon remains outside the palace in his war chariot, with a procession of soldiers, captives, and booty in his

FIGURE 15-6 The Death of Agamemnon. In Aeschylus's play, Clytemnestra boasts that she kills Agamemnon with her own hands. In this vase painting (c. 470 B.C.), however, the artist follows the Homeric tradition, showing Aegisthus (with sword, at left) as the murderer of Agamemnon (center), who is caught in a netlike garment. Clytemnestra rushes in (far left), while another female figure (to the right of Agamemnon), probably the couple's daughter Electra, throws up her hands in horror. At the extreme right, another woman, perhaps Cassandra, attempts to flee. (*William Francis Warden Fund. Courtesy, Museum of Fine Arts, Boston.*)

train, Clytemnestra occupies the high ground of the ceremonial steps that she will force her husband to ascend in a way that offends the gods and marks his doom. The struggle (**agon**) between husband and wife is no contest: Clytemnestra, superior in intelligence and will, knows how to bend Agamemnon to her purpose, goading his vanity until he accepts her dare to walk up the steps she has covered with priceless carpets. Persuading Agamemnon publicly to commit hubris—a prideful act that elicits divine retribution—she manipulates him into taking upon himself an honor reserved only for gods: a conquering hero, he treads the crimson runner, a blood-red path leading to the palace interior.

Delighted that Agamemnon has escaped the dangers of war so that she can have the pleasure of killing him herself, Clytemnestra impales her husband on Aegisthus' sword, transforming his bath into a bloody sea (Figure 15-6). Carrying her gore-stained weapon as she emerges from the palace, Clytemnestra takes full credit for the regicide, for she sees herself as heaven's instrument of justice, the executioner of her daughter's killer. Acting alone, Clytemnestra strikes her husband unaided, humiliat-

FIGURE 15-7 Clytemnestra About to Kill Cassandra. Although she loathes her husband, Clytemnestra is furious when Agamemnon brings home as his concubine Cassandra, the daughter of Priam and Hecuba. At the moment depicted in this red-figured cup, Cassandra meets the fate she had earlier foreseen but been helpless to avoid. As the victim of a powerful king's lust and his wife's savage jealousy, Cassandra resembles the mythic objects of Zeus's unwanted affection, such as Io or Leda. (*National Museum, Ferrara.*)

ing him with her "woman's hand." Aegisthus, who later snarls loudly at the disapproving chorus, is little more than the queen's lapdog.

Grieving for Iphigenia as Demeter had for Persephone, Clytemnestra seems to represent matriarchal rights—the high value of the female—whose traditional prerogatives have been stolen by male usurpers. Clytemnestra, however, does not manifest feminine solidarity as such, but only so far as there exists a blood tie between females, particularly mother and a favored daughter. Even in this human bond, however, Clytemnestra is deficient. While she fixates on Iphigenia and her fate, Clytemnestra shows little affection for her younger daughter, **Electra,** of whom she would be glad to dispose. She also has no compunction about hacking Cassandra to death with an ax (Figure 15-7), although the Trojan woman is clearly an unwilling victim of male brutality. Like Hera, Clytemnestra regards her husband's mistresses not as members of an exploited sisterhood but solely as affronts to her pride, rivals she can exterminate without a qualm.

The only character who appears in all three parts of the *Oresteia*—as a murderess in the *Agamemnon,* a murder victim in the *Libation-Bearers,* and a ghost demanding revenge in the *Eumenides*—Clytemnestra is a magnificent figure whose fate raises profoundly disturbing questions about the relative value of male and female lives in Greek society. Even stronger than Medea, the only other mythic woman whose outrage against male perfidy approaches her own level of passionate hatred, Clytemnestra never wavers in her resolution or breaks down under stress. For many men in Aeschylus's audience, Clytemnestra must have epitomized the problem posed by an extraordinary female: how to deal with a woman whose wit, energy, initiative, and drive exceed that of most men. As Orestes observes after slaying his mother, such a woman cannot be trusted. Aeschylus struggles with this issue, not altogether satisfactorily to some modern critics, throughout the *Oresteia.*

The *Libation-Bearers*

Orestes, weeping alone at his father's neglected tomb, opens the *Libation-Bearers* with a brief prologue invoking Hermes, guide of the dead. Disguised as a traveling peddler because he knows that his mother would kill him in a minute to ensure her own safety, Orestes prepares to face the contradictory divine forces that push him to the brink of insanity. If he fails to obey Apollo's order to honor his father by slaying his mother, Phoebus will curse him. If he commits this most unnatural of crimes, the Furies will not only kill him but claim his soul as well.

Clytemnestra's dream that she takes a poisonous snake to her breast reflects both her unacknowledged guilt and the impending arrival of Orestes, whom she nursed but briefly before sending into exile. As Apollo's human servant, a furtive agent sent to cleanse his homeland of evil, Orestes does not hesitate to kill Aegisthus (Figure 15-8) but almost fails to complete the act that fulfills his duty to Agamemnon. At the crucial moment when Orestes seems unable to strike Clytemnestra, his companion **Pylades** [PYE-la-deez]—who dogs his friend's footsteps throughout the play but speaks only on this occasion—repeats Apollo's command: the gods give Orestes no freedom to choose. Obediently, he kills his mother (Figure 15-9) and is immediately besieged by fiends.

Aeschylus emphasizes that no one except Orestes can see the Furies. The chorus, to whom they are invisible, is baffled by Orestes's anguish, a suggestion that, in this scene, Aeschylus presents the Furies as hallucinatory, psychological projections of the mother-slayer's overpowering guilt. (In the *Eumenides,* these figures are visible not only to Orestes and the gods, but to Apollo's human priestess and, presumably, to Orestes's jurors as well.)

The *Eumenides*

Apollo's priestess, the Pythia, delivers the *Eumenides*'s prologue, a review of Delphi's history emphasizing the sanctuary's religious evolution: she reminds us that, before Apollo founded his oracle, a succession of earth goddesses presided there, including Themis and Phoebe, the "shining one," a daughter of Gaea and Uranus. The change

FIGURE 15-8 Orestes About to Kill Aegisthus. As Orestes draws back his sword to plunge it into the man who usurped his father's throne, Clytemnestra rushes in, raising an ax to defend her lover. In spite of presenting her justifications for killing Iphigenia's murderer in the *Agamemnon,* in the *Libation-Bearers,* Aeschylus reduces sympathy for Clytemnestra by showing her readiness to slaughter her own son to protect her position. This vase painting may have been produced about the time of the *Oresteia*'s first performance (458 B.C.). Whereas Greek artists commonly depicted scenes of violence, Greek dramatists always had such acts occur offstage, typically to be described later by an eyewitness or a messenger. (*William Francis Warden Fund. Courtesy, Museum of Fine Arts, Boston.*)

FIGURE 15-9   Orestes Kills Aegisthus. Although Orestes's hand is occupied driving his sword through Aegisthus, his eyes are already fixed on his next victim, his mother. Clytemnestra's attempted flight (left) will soon be cut short by her son's avenging blade. (*Kunsthistorisches Museum, Vienna.*)

from a chthonic to a ouranic cult foreshadows the play's climactic reversal: in the public arena of Orestes's trial, where gods of earth and sky contend for supremacy, the Olympians will gain universal control.

In the trial scene, binary tensions building throughout the trilogy gather in sharp focus: male is pitted against female, innovation against ancient tradition, intellect against emotion, the rule of law against individual excess, and civilization against barbarism. Presenting the world as divided between two polar opposites, Aeschylus's impassioned characters identify its most savage components with the female principle, associating the Furies with cruelty, darkness, death, and slaughter, whereas Apollo, the quintessential male figure, is seen as allied with clemency, purity, light, health, rationality, and moderation (Figure 15-10).

The characters' assault against the negative shadow of the Great Goddess reaches

FIGURE 15-10   Orestes Clinging to the Omphalos at Delphi. In this dramatic painting of a scene from the *Eumenides,* Apollo extends his right arm to banish the Furies from his sanctuary as his suppliant Orestes clutches the sacred "navel" stone, imploring the god to protect him. As the divine administrator of purification rites, Apollo cleanses Orestes of ritual guilt for having killed his mother, Clytemnestra; but only Athene's court of justice can legally absolve him of the crime and permanently deliver him from the vengeful Furies. Although she does not appear in the *Oresteia,* the figure at the right, holding a bow and accompanied by a hunting dog, may be Artemis, who shares her brother's loathing for the Furies. (*National Museum, Naples.*)

a peak when, in a burst of misogyny, Apollo claims that the mother is not a real parent but merely the "nurse" or incubator of the seed that the father deposits in her. Phoebus cites Athene as the casebook example of a father's ability to produce children without female aid, a mythic allusion that serves primarily to endorse the Athenian patriarchy: in terms of legal and social practice, only the male has genuine parental status.

Apollo's reference to Athene's motherless birth also functions symbolically to associate her, as rational consciousness and civilization, with the male principle. By contrast, the Furies—unconscious instinct and savage nature—are seen as Athene's polar opposite, a devouring feminine appetite for blood.

Although Athene does not explicitly endorse Apollo's argument, she unequivocally sides with male authority. Declaring that she cannot support the cause of a woman who kills her husband, Athene casts the deciding vote for Orestes's acquittal (Figure 15-11). (The jurors had reached a deadlock on the defendant's guilt; a vote evenly divided was equivalent to a not-guilty verdict.) Many critics have traditionally assumed that Apollo and Athene prefer mercy to strict justice and are concerned with establishing the legal principle of extenuating circumstances (in Orestes's case, the

FIGURE 15-11   Athene. Extending her
hand as if in appeal, this bronze Athene
could well represent the goddess in her
role at Orestes's trial before the Areopagus. Acting as mediator between Apollonian concern for masculine authority and
the Furies' passion to avenge matricide,
Athene uses the rhetorical arts of persuasion to tame chthonic energy and bring it
into the service of her city-state. Fulfilling the will of Zeus, the sky gods succeed
in establishing a new concept of civil justice, but the primitive fear of punishment for wrongdoing remains an integral
part of the Greek experience. Accepting
Athene's invitation to inhabit an underground grotto beneath the sunlit Acropolis, the Eumenides (Kindly Ones) remain
a potent, unseen force—ancient pro-
moters of the vendetta ironically transformed into inhibitors of future violence.
(*National Museum, Athens.*)

oracle's command) in exonerating a defendant. Aeschylus's text, however, mentions
neither compassion nor legal rationales.

Orestes's victory is necessary for Aeschylus to move on to his primary interest—
Athene's use of persuasion to change the hostile Furies into a force for human good.
Aeschylus typically cares less for formal logic or dramatic verisimilitude than for setting up conditions necessary to advance the action, a propensity he also demonstrates
in the *Libation-Bearers*. Eager to rush through the obligatory recognition scene and
join Electra and Orestes in a plot against their mother (Figure 15-12), the playwright
uses a particularly awkward (and implausible) device: Electra identifies her long-lost
brother by observing that a lock of the stranger's (Orestes's) hair and his footprints
are remarkably similar to her own, an unlikely coincidence that Euripides later mocks
in his *Electra*.

In the Prometheus trilogy, Aeschylus had portrayed divine power split between
the punishing strength of Zeus and the pain-racked compassion of Prometheus, a

FIGURE 15-12   Orestes and Electra. Athens's three greatest playwrights—Aeschylus, Sophocles, and Euripides—all dramatized the myth in which Electra and Orestes conspire to
murder their mother. In both Aeschylus's *Libation-Bearers* and Sophocles's *Electra,* the two
matricides are depicted as noble instruments of the gods' will, a heroic conception expressed
in this monumental sculpture of Agamemnon's avengers. By contrast, Euripides's *Electra* portrays Orestes as a weakling dominated by his neurotic sister, a deranged creature driven by her
thwarted desire for her dead father and sexual jealousy of her mother. (*National Museum,
Naples.*)

division that gradually evolved into the reconciliation and union of a previously bifurcated godhead. In the *Oresteia,* Aeschylus also presents two opposing aspects of divinity—the Furies and the Olympians—merging into a harmonious whole. For Aeschylus, there is no question of banishing the Furies or imprisoning them in Tartarus, as Zeus had done with the deposed Titans. (As they correctly observe, they function as single-minded detectives and executioners, in effect doing Zeus's dirty work for him.) Instead, Aeschylus uses a metaphor of the democratic process—the rhetorical art of persuasion by which political opponents can rationally settle their differences—to achieve a workable union between the divine anger that penalizes evil and the divine goodwill that heals and redeems.

Apollo, who leaves the stage immediately after the jury's verdict, cannot mediate the issues because, as god of beauty and purification, he has no common ground with the Furies, whom he sees only as filthy hags bespattered with gore from tortures and executions. Athene functions as mediator because she, like the daughters of Night, is also a female deity (although born of a male) and possesses both chthonic perception (from Metis) and ouranic wisdom (from Zeus). Her success in changing potential destroyers of the state into benign guardians fulfills the will of Zeus and unites Dionysian energy with Apollonian intelligence.

Transformed into the Eumenides (Kindly Ones), these night terrors act as a stabilizing influence in human society, inspiring a useful fear that prohibits wrongdoing—a repressive function that Athene explicitly approves—and simultaneously conferring the chthonic blessing of fertility. The Eumenides' torch-lit installation in a subterranean grotto beneath the Acropolis is an appropriate analogue to their Dionysian presence in the human subconscious, where they function as the id to Apollo's superego.

A few years after the *Oresteia's* premiere, Athene's new temple, the Parthenon, was built atop the Acropolis, a gleaming symbol of the polis's collective awareness. Standing above the Eumenides' underground chapel and beneath heaven's light, Athene's marble shrine visibly linked the dim, mysterious world of primal earth with the bright sky of Zeus.

AGAMEMNON[1]

Aeschylus

CHARACTERS

WATCHMAN

CHORUS *of old men, citizens of Argos (Mycenae)*

CLYTEMNESTRA, *queen of Argos (Mycenae)*

HERALD, *messenger of Agamemnon*

AGAMEMNON, *king of Argos (Mycenae), commander of Achaean forces at Troy*

CASSANDRA, *daughter of Priam and Hecuba*

AEGISTHUS, *son of Thyestes, lover of Clytemnestra*

CAPTAIN OF THE GUARD

The scene is the entrance to the palace of the Atreidae. Before the doors stand shrines of the gods. [A WATCHMAN *is posted on the roof.]*

Watchman

I've prayed God to release me from sentry duty
All through this long year's vigil, like a dog
Couched on the roof of Atreus, where I study
Night after night the pageantry of this vast
Concourse of stars, and moving among them like
Noblemen the constellations that bring
Summer and winter as they rise and fall.
And I am still watching for the beacon signal
All set to flash over the sea the radiant
News of the fall of Troy. So confident   10
Is a woman's spirit, whose purpose is a man's.
Every night, as I turn in to my stony bed,
Quilted with dew, not visited by dreams,
Not mine—no sleep, fear stands at my pillow
Keeping tired eyes from closing once too often;
And whenever I start to sing or hum a tune,
Mixing from music an antidote to sleep,
It always turns to mourning for the royal house,
Which is not in such good shape as it used to be
But now at last may the good news in a flash   20
Scatter the darkness and deliver us!
[The beacon flashes.]
O light of joy, whose gleam turns night to day,
O radiant signal for innumerable

---

1. Translation of the *Agamemnon, Libation-Bearers,* and *Eumenides* by George Thompson.

Dances of victory! Ho there! I call the queen,
Agamemnon's wife, to raise with all the women
Alleluias of thanksgiving through the palace
Saluting the good news, if it is true
That Troy has fallen, as this blaze portends;
Yes, and I'll dance an overture myself.
My master's dice have fallen out well, and I   30
Shall score three sixes for this nightwatching.
[A pause.]
Well, come what will, may it soon be mine to grasp
In this right hand my master's, home again!
[Another pause.]
The rest is secret. A heavy ox has trodden
Across my tongue. These walls would have tales to tell
If they had mouths. I speak only to those
Who are in the know, to others—I know nothing.
[The WATCHMAN *goes into the palace. Women's cries are heard. Enter* CHORUS OF
OLD MEN.*]*

Chorus

It is ten years since those armed prosecutors of Justice, Menelaus and Agamemnon, twin-sceptred in God-given sovranty, embarked in the thousand ships crying war, like eagles with long wings beating the air over a robbed mountain nest,
wheeling and screaming for their lost children. Yet above them some god, maybe
Apollo or Zeus, overhears the sky-dweller's cry and sends after the robber a Fury.

*[*CLYTEMNESTRA *comes out of the palace and unseen by the elders places offerings
before the shrines.]*
Just so the two kings were sent by the greater king, Zeus, for the sake of a pro-
miscuous woman to fight Paris, Greek and Trojan locked fast together in the
dusty betrothals of battle. And however it stands with them now, the end is
unalterable; no flesh, no wine can appease God's fixed indignation.

As for us, with all the able-bodied men enlisted and gone, we are left here   40
leaning our strength on a staff; for, just as in infancy, when the marrow is still
unformed, the War-god is not at his post, so it is in extreme old age, as the leaves
fall fast, we walk on three feet, like dreams in the daylight.
[They see CLYTEMNESTRA.*]*
O Queen, what news? what message sets light to the altars? All over the town
the shrines are ablaze with unguents drawn from the royal stores and the flames
shoot up into the night sky. Speak, let us hear all that may be made public, so
healing the anxieties that have gathered thick in our hearts; let the gleam of good
news scatter them.
*[*CLYTEMNESTRA *goes out to tend the other altars of the city.]*

Strength have I still to recall that sign which greeted the two kings
Taking the road, for the prowess of song is not yet spent.
I sing of two kings united in sovranty, leading
Armies to battle, who saw two eagles
Beside the palace

Wheel into sight, one black, and the other was white-tailed,
Tearing a hare with her unborn litter.
Ailinon cry, but let good conquer!

Shrewdly the priest took note and compared each eagle with each king,   50
Then spoke out and prefigured the future in these words:
"In time the Greek arms shall demolish the fortress of Priam;
Only let no jealous God, as they fasten
On Troy the slave's yoke,
Strike them in anger; for Artemis loathes the rapacious
Beagles of Zeus that have slaughtered the frail hare.
Ailinon cry, but let good conquer!
O Goddess, gentle to the tender whelp of fierce lions
As to all young life of the wild,
So now fulfil what is good in the omen and mend what is faulty.   60
And I appeal unto the Lord Apollo,
Let not the north wind hold the fleet storm-bound,
Driving them on to repay that feast with another,
Inborn builder of strife, feud that fears no man, it is still there,
Treachery keeping the house, it remembers, revenges, a child's death!"[2]
Such, as the kings left home, was the seer's revelation.
Ailinon cry, but let good conquer!

Zeus, whoe'er he be, if so it best
Please his ear to be addressed,
So shall he be named by me.   70
All things have I measured, yet
None have found save him alone,
Zeus, if a man from a heart heavy-laden
Seek to cast his cares aside.

Long since lived a ruler of the world,
Puffed with martial pride, of whom
None shall tell, his day is done;
Also, he who followed him
Met his master and is gone.
Zeus the victorious, gladly acclaim him;   80
Perfect wisdom shall be yours;

Zeus, who laid it down that man
Must in sorrow learn and through
Pain to wisdom find his way.
When deep slumber falls, remembered wrongs
Chafe the bruised heart with fresh pangs, and no
Welcome wisdom meets within.
Harsh the grace dispensed by powers immortal,
Pilots of the human soul.

2. Iphigenia.

Even so the elder prince,   90
Marshal of the thousand ships,
Rather than distrust a priest,
Torn with doubt to see his men
Harbor-locked, hunger-pinched, hard-oppressed,
Strained beyond endurance, still
Watching, waiting, where the never-tiring
Tides of Aulis ebb and flow:

And still the storm blew from mountains far north,
With moorings windswept and hungry crews pent
In rotting hulks,   100
With tackling all torn and seeping timbers,
Till Time's slow-paced, enforced inaction
Had all but stripped bare the bloom of Greek manhood.
And then was found but one
Cure to allay the tempest—never a blast so bitter—
Shrieked in a loud voice by the priest, "Artemis!" striking the Atreidae with
  dismay, each with his staff smiting the ground and weeping.

And then the king spoke, the elder, saying:
"The choice is hard—hard to disobey him,
And harder still
To kill my own child, my palace jewel,   110
With unclean hands before the altar
Myself, her own father, spill a maid's pure blood.
I have no choice but wrong.
How shall I fail my thousand ships and betray my comrades?
So shall the storm cease, and the men eager for war clamor for that virginal
  blood righteously! So pray for a happy outcome!"

And when he bowed down beneath the harness
Of cruel coercion, his spirit veering
With sudden sacrilegious change,
He gave his whole mind to evil counsel.
For man is made bold with base-contriving   120
Impetuous madness, first cause of much grief.
And so then he slew his own child
For a war to win a woman
And to speed the storm-bound fleet from the shore to battle.

She cried aloud "Father!", yet they heard not;
A girl in first flower, yet they cared not,
The lords who gave the word for war.
Her father prayed, then he bade his vassals
To seize her where swathed in folds of saffron
She lay, and lift her up like a yearling   130
With bold heart above the altar,
And her lovely lips to bridle
That they might not cry out, cursing the House of Atreus,

With gags, her voice sealed with brute force and crushed.
And then she let fall her cloak
And cast at each face a glance that dumbly craved compassion;
And like a picture she would but could not greet
Her father's guests, who at home
Had often sat when the meal was over,
The cups replenished, with all hearts enraptured   140
To hear her sing grace with clear unsullied voice for her loving father.

The end was unseen and unspeakable.
The task of priestcraft was done.
For Justice first chastens, then she presses home her lesson.
The morrow must come, its grief will soon be here,
So let us not weep today.
It shall be made known as clear as daybreak.
And so may all this at last end in good news,
For which the queen prays, the next of kin and stay of the land of Argos.
[CLYTEMNESTRA appears at the door of the palace.]
Our humble salutations to the queen!   150
Hers is our homage, while our master's throne
Stands empty. We are still longing to hear
The meaning of your sacrifice. Is it good news?

Clytemnestra
Good news! With good news may the morning rise
Out of the night—good news beyond all hope!
My news is this: The Greeks have taken Troy.

Chorus
What? No, it cannot be true! I cannot grasp it.

Clytemnestra
The Greeks hold Troy—is not that plain enough?

Chorus
Joy steals upon me and fills my eyes with tears.

Clytemnestra
Indeed, your looks betray your loyalty.   160

Chorus
What is the proof? Have you any evidence?

Clytemnestra
Of course I have, or else the Gods have cheated me.

Chorus
You have given ear to some beguiling dream.

Clytemnestra
I would not come screaming fancies out of my sleep.

Chorus

Rumors have wings—on these your heart has fed.

Clytemnestra

You mock my intelligence as though I were a girl.

Chorus

When was it? How long is it since the city fell?

Clytemnestra

In the night that gave birth to this dawning day.

Chorus

What messenger could bring the news so fast?

Clytemnestra

The God of Fire, who from Ida sent forth light   170
And beacon by beacon passed the flame to me.
From the peak of Ida first to the cliff of Hermes
On Lemnos, and from there a third great lamp
Was flashed to Athos, the pinnacle of Zeus;
Up, up it soared, luring the dancing fish
To break surface in rapture at the light;
A golden courier, like the sun, it sped
Post-haste its message to Macistus, thence
Across Euripus, till the flaming sign
Was marked by the watchers on Messapium,   180
And thence with strength renewed from piles of heath
Like moonrise over the valley of Asopus,
Relayed in glory to Cithaeron's heights,
And still flashed on, not slow the sentinels,
Leaping across the lake from peak to peak,
It passed the word to burn and burn, and flung
A comet to the promontory that stands
Over the Gulf of Saron, there it swooped
Down to the Spider's Crag above the city,
Then found its mark on the roof of this house of Atreus,   190
That beacon fathered by Ida's far-off fires.
Such were the stages of our torch relay,
And the last to run is the first to reach the goal.
That is my evidence, the testimony which
My lord has signaled to me out of Troy.

Chorus

Lady, there will be time later to thank the Gods.
Now I ask only to listen: speak on and on.

Clytemnestra

Today the Greeks have occupied Troy.
I seem to hear there a very strange street-music.
Pour oil and vinegar into one cup, you will see   200

They do not make friends. So there two tunes are heard.
Slaves now, the Trojans, brothers and aged fathers,
Prostrate, sing for their dearest the last dirge.
The others, tired out and famished after the night's looting,
Grab what meal chance provides, lodgers now
In Trojan houses, sheltered from the night frosts,
From the damp dews delivered, free to sleep
Off guard, off duty, a blissful night's repose.
Therefore, provided that they show due respect
To the altars of the plundered town and are not   210
Tempted to lay coarse hands on sanctities,
Remembering that the last lap—the voyage home—
Lies still ahead of them, then, if they should return
Guiltless before God, the curses of the bereaved
Might be placated—barring accidents.
That is my announcement—a message from my master.
May all end well, and may I reap the fruit of it!

Chorus
Lady, you have spoken with a wise man's judgment.
Now it is time to address the gods once more
After this happy outcome of our cares.   220

Thanks be to Zeus and to gracious Night, housekeeper of heaven's embroidery,
who has cast over the towers of Troy a net so fine as to leave no escape for old or
young, all caught in the snare! All praise to Zeus, who with a shaft from his
outstretched bow has at last brought down the transgressor!

"By Zeus struck down!" The truth is all clear
With each step plainly marked. He said, Be
It so, and so it was. A man denied once
That heaven pays heed to those who trample
Beneath the feet holy sanctities. He lied wickedly;
For God's wrath soon or late destroys all sinners filled
With pride, puffed up with vain presumption,
And great men's houses stocked with silver
And gold beyond measure. Far best to live   230
Free of want, without grief, rich in the gift of wisdom.
Glutted with gold, the sinner kicks
Justice out of his sight, yet
She sees him and remembers.

As sweet temptation lures him onwards
With childlike smile into the death-trap,
He cannot help himself. His curse is lit up
Against the darkness, a bright baleful light.
And just as false bronze in battle hammered turns black and shows
Its true worth, so the sinner time-tried stands condemned.   240

His hopes take wing, and still he gives chase, with foul crimes branding all his
  people.
He cries to deaf heaven, none hear his prayers.
Justice drags him down to hell as he calls for succor.
Such was the sinner Paris, who
Rendered thanks to a gracious
Host by stealing a woman.

She left behind her the ports all astir
With throngs of men under arms filing onto shipboard;
She took to Troy in lieu of dowry death.
A light foot passed through the gates and fled,   250
And then a cry of lamentation rose.
The seers, the king's prophets, muttered darkly:
"Bewail the king's house that now is desolate,
Bewail the bed marked with print of love that fled!"
Behold, in silence, without praise, without reproach,
They sit upon the ground and weep.
Beyond the wave lies their love;
Here a ghost seems to rule the palace!
Shapely the grace of statues,
Yet they can bring no comfort,   260
Eyeless, lifeless and loveless.

Delusive dream shapes that float through the night
Beguile him, bringing delight sweet but unsubstantial;
For, while the eye beholds the heart's desire,
The arms clasp empty air, and then
The fleeting vision fades and glides away
On silent wing down the paths of slumber.
The royal hearth is chilled with sorrows such as these,
And more; in each house from end to end of Greece
That sent its dearest to wage war in foreign lands   270
The stout heart is called to steel itself
In mute endurance against
Blows that strike deep into the heart's core:
Those that they sent from home they
Knew, but now they receive back
Only a heap of ashes.

The God of War holds the twin scales of strife,
Heartless gold-changer trafficking in men,
Consigning homeward from Troy a jar of dust fire-refined,
Making up the weight with grief,   280
Shapely vessels laden each
With the ashes of their kin.
They mourn and praise them saying, "He
Was practiced well in sword and spear,

And he, who fell so gallantly—
All to avenge another man's wife":
It is muttered in a whisper
And resentment spreads against each of the royal warlords.
They lie sleeping, perpetual
Owners each of a small   290
Holding far from their homeland.

The sullen rumors that pass mouth to mouth
Bring the same danger as a people's curse,
And brooding hearts wait to hear of what the night holds from sight.
Watchful are the Gods of all
Hands with slaughter stained. The black
Furies wait, and when a man
Has grown by luck, not justice, great,
With sudden turn of circumstance
He wastes away to nothing, dragged   300
Down to be food in hell for demons.
For the heights of fame are perilous.
With a jealous bolt the Lord Zeus in a flash shall blast them.
Best to pray for a tranquil
Span of life and to be
Neither victor nor vanquished.

—The news has set the whole town aflame.
Can it be true? Perhaps it is a trick.
—Only a child would let such fiery words
Kindle his hopes, then fade and flicker out.   310
—It is just like a woman
To accept good news without the evidence.
—An old wives' tale, winged with a woman's wishes,
Spreads like wildfire, then sinks and is forgotten.

We shall soon know what the beacon signifies,
Whether it is true or whether this joyful daybreak
Is only a dream sent to deceive us all.
Here comes a messenger breathless from the shore,
Wearing a garland and covered in a cloud
Of dust, which shows that he has news to tell,   320
And not in soaring rhetoric of smoke and flame,
But either he brings cause for yet greater joy,
Or else,—no, let us abjure the alternative.
Glad shone the light, as gladly breaks the day!
[Enter HERALD.*]*

Herald
O joy! Argos, I greet you, my fatherland!
Joy brings me home after ten years of war.
Many the shattered hopes, but this has held.

Now I can say that when I die my bones
Will lie at rest here in my native soil.
I greet you joyfully, I greet the Sun,   330
Zeus the All-Highest, and the Pythian King,
Bending no more against us his fatal shafts,
As he did beside Scamander—that was enough,
And now defend us, Savior Apollo; all
The Gods I greet, among them Hermes, too,
Patron of messengers, and the spirits of our dead,
Who sent their sons forth, may they now prepare
A joyful welcome for those whom war has spared.
Joy to the palace and to these images
Whose faces catch the sun, now, as of old,   340
With radiant smiles greet your sovran lord,
Agamemnon, who brings a lamp to lighten you
And all here present, after having leveled
Troy with the mattock of just-dealing Zeus,
Great son of Atreus, master and monarch, blest
Above all living men. The brigand Paris
Has lost his booty and brought down the house of Priam.

Chorus
Joy to you, Herald, welcome home again!

Herald
Let me die, having lived to see this day!

Chorus
Your yearning for your country has worn you out.   350

Herald
So much that tears spring to the eyes for joy.

Chorus
Well, those you longed for longed equally for you.

Herald
Ah yes, our loved ones longed for our safe return.

Chorus
We have had many anxieties here at home.

Herald
What do you mean? Has there been disaffection?

Chorus
Never mind now. Say nothing and cure all.

Herald
Is it possible there was trouble in our absence?

Chorus
Now, as you said yourself, it would be a joy to die.

Herald
Yes, all has ended well. Our expedition
Has been successfully concluded, even though in part   360
The issue may be found wanting. Only the Gods
Prosper in everything. If I should tell you all
That we endured on shipboard in the night watches,
Our lodging the bare benches, and even worse
Ashore beneath the walls of Troy, the rains
From heaven and the dews that seeped
Out of the soil into lice-infested blankets;
If I should tell of those winters, when the birds
Dropped dead and Ida heaped on us her snows;
Those summers, when unruffled by wind or wave   370
The sea slept breathless under the glare of noon—
But why recall that now? It is all past,
Yes, for the dead past never to stir again.
Ah, they are all gone. Why count our losses? Why
Should we vex the living with grievance for the dead?
Goodbye to all that for us who have come back!
Victory has turned the scale, and so before
This rising sun let the good news be proclaimed
And carried all over the world on wings of fame:
"These spoils were brought by the conquerors of Troy   380
And dedicated to the Gods of Greece."
And praise to our country and to Zeus the giver
And thanks be given. That is all my news.
[CLYTEMNESTRA appears at the palace door.]

Chorus
Thank God that I have lived to see this day!
This news concerns all, and most of all the queen.

Clytemnestra
I raised my alleluia hours ago,
When the first messenger lit up the night,
And people mocked me saying, "Has a beacon
Persuaded you that the Greeks have captured Troy?
Truly a woman's hopes are lighter than air."   390
But I still sacrificed, and at a hundred
Shrines throughout the town the women chanted
Their endless alleluias on and on,
Singing to sleep the sacramental flames,
And now what confirmation do I need from you?
I wait to hear all from my lord, for whom
A welcome is long ready. What day is so sweet
In a woman's life as when she opens the door

To her beloved, safe home from war? Go and tell him
That he will find, guarding his property,   400
A wife as loyal as he left her, one
Who in all these years has kept his treasuries sealed,
Unkind only to enemies, and knows no more
Of other men's company than of tempering steel.
[Exit.]

Herald
Such a protestation, even though entirely true,
Is it not unseemly on a lady's lips?

Chorus
Such is her message, as you understand,
Full of fine phrases plain to those who know.
But tell us now, what news have you of the king's
Co-regent, Menelaus? Is he too home again?   410

Herald
Lies cannot last, even though sweet to hear.

Chorus
Can you not make your news both sweet and true?

Herald
He and his ships have vanished. They are missing.

Chorus
What, was it a storm that struck the fleet at sea?

Herald
You have told a long disaster in a word.

Chorus
Has no one news whether he is alive or dead?

Herald
Only the Sun, from whom the whole earth draws life.

Chorus
Tell us about the storm. How did it fall?

Herald
A day of national rejoicing must not be marred
By any jarring tongue. A messenger who comes   420
With black looks bringing the long prayed-against
Report of total rout, which both afflicts
The state in general and in every household leaves
The inmates prostrate under the scourge of war—
With such a load upon his lips he may fitly
Sing anthems to the Furies down in hell;
But when he greets a prospering people with

News of the war's victorious end—how then
Shall I mix foul with fair and find words to tell you
Of the blow that struck us out of that angry heaven?   430
    Water and Fire, those age-old enemies,
Made common cause against the homebound fleet.
Darkness had fallen, and a northerly gale
Blew up and in a blinding thunderstorm
Our ships were tossed and buffeted hull against hull
In a wild stampede and herded out of sight;
Then, at daybreak, we saw the Aegean in blossom
With a waving crop of corpses and scattered timbers.
Our ship came through, saved by some spirit, it seems,
Who took the helm and piloted her, until   440
She slipped under the cliffs into a cove.
There, safe at last, incredulous of our luck,
We brooded all day, stunned by the night's disaster.
And so, if any of the others have survived,
They must be speaking of us as dead and gone.
May all yet end well! Though it is most to be expected
That Menelaus is in some great distress,
Yet, should some shaft of sunlight spy him out
Somewhere among the living, rescued by Zeus,
Lest the whole house should perish, there is hope   450
That he may yet come home. There you have the truth.

Chorus
Tell us who invented that
Name so deadly accurate?
Was it one who presaging
Things to come divined a word
Deftly tuned to destiny?
Helen—hell indeed she carried
To men, to ships, to a proud city, stealing
From the silk veils of her chamber, sailing seaward
With the Zephyr's breath behind her;   460
And they set forth in a thousand ships to hunt her
On the path that leaves no imprint,
Bringers of endless bloodshed.

So, as Fate decreed, in Troy,
Turning into keeners kin,
Furies, instruments of God's
Wrath, at last demanded full
Payment for the stolen wife;
And the wedding song that rang out
To greet the bride from beyond the broad Aegean   470
Was in time turned into howls of imprecation
From the countless women wailing

For the loved ones they had lost in war for her sake,
And they curse the day they gave that
Welcome to war and bloodshed.

An old story is told of an oxherd who reared at his hearth a lion-cub, a pet for
      his children,
Pampered fondly by young and old with dainty morsels begged at each meal
      from his master's table.

But Time showed him up in his true nature after his kind—a beast savaging
      sheep and oxen,
Mad for the taste of blood, and only then they knew what they had long
      nursed was a curse from heaven.

And so it seemed then there came to rest in Troy   480
A sweet-smiling calm, a clear sky, seductive,
A rare pearl set in gold and silver,
Shaft of love from a glancing eye.
She is seen now as an agent
Of death sent from Zeus, a Fury
Demanding a bloody bride-price.
[Enter CLYTEMNESTRA]

From ancient times people have believed that when
A man's wealth has come to full growth it breeds
And brings forth tares and tears in plenty.
No, I say, it is only wicked deeds   490
That increase, fruitful in evil.
The house built on justice always
Is blest with a happy offspring.

And yet the pride bred of wealth often burgeons anew
In evil times, a cloud of deep night,
Spectre of ancient crimes that still
Walks within the palace walls,
True to the dam that bore it.

But where is Justice? She lights up the smoke-darkened hut.
From mansions built by hands polluted   500
Turning to greet the pure in heart,
Proof against false praise, she guides
All to its consummation.
[Enter AGAMEMNON in a chariot followed by another chariot carrying CASSANDRA
and spoils of war.]

Agamemnon, conqueror, joy to our king! How shall my greeting neither fall
short nor shoot too high? Some men feign rejoicing or sorrow with hearts untouched; but those who can read man's nature in the book of the eyes will not

be deceived by dissembled fidelity. I declare that, when you left these shores ten years ago to recover with thousands of lives one woman, who eloped of her own free will, I deemed your judgment misguided; but now in all sincerity I salute you with joy. Toil happily ended brings pleasure at last, and in time you shall learn to distinguish the just from the unjust steward.

Agamemnon

First, it is just that I should pay my respects
To the land of Argos and her presiding Gods,
My partners in this homecoming as also
In the just penalty which I have inflicted on
The city of Troy. When the supreme court of heaven
Adjudicated on our cause, they cast   510
Their votes unanimously against her, though not
Immediately, and so on the other side
Hope hovered hesitantly before it vanished.
The fires of pillage are still burning there
Like sacrificial offerings. Her ashes
Redolent with riches breathe their last and die.
For all this it is our duty to render thanks
To the celestial powers, with whose assistance
We have exacted payment and struck down
A city for one woman, forcing our entry   520
Within the Wooden Horse, which at the setting
Of the Pleiads like a hungry lion leapt
Out and slaked its thirst in royal blood.
As to your sentiments, I take due note
And find that they accord with mine. Too few
Rejoice at a friend's good fortune. I have known
Many dissemblers swearing false allegiance.
One only, though he joined me against his will,
Once in the harness, proved himself a staunch
Support, Odysseus, be he now alive or dead.   530
All public questions and such as concern the Gods
I shall discuss in council and take steps
To make this triumph lasting; and if here or there
Some malady comes to light, appropriate
Remedies will be applied to set it right.
Meanwhile, returning to my royal palace,
My first duty is to salute the Gods
Who led me overseas and home again.
Victory attends me; may she remain with me!

Clytemnestra

Citizens of Argos, councillors and elders,   540
I shall declare without shame in your presence
My feelings for my husband. Diffidence
Dies in us all with time. I shall speak of what
I suffered here, while he was away at the war,

Sitting at home, with no man's company,
Waiting for news, listening to one
Messenger after another, each bringing worse
Disasters. If all his rumored wounds were real,
His body was in shreds, shot through and through.
If he had died—the predominant report—   550
He was a second Geryon, an outstretched giant
With three corpses and one death for each,
While I, distraught, with a knot pressing my throat,
Was rescued forcibly, to endure still more.
    And that is why our child is not present here,
As he should be, pledge of our marriage vows,
Orestes. Let me reassure you. He lives
Safe with an old friend, Strophius, who warned me
Of various dangers—your life at stake in Troy
And here a restive populace, which might perhaps   560
Be urged to kick a man when he is down.
    As for myself, the fountains of my tears
Have long ago run dry. My eyes are sore
After so many nights watching the lamp
That burnt at my bedside always for you.
If I should sleep, a gnat's faint whine would shatter
The dreams that were my only company.
    But now, all pain endured, all sorrow past,
I salute this man as the watchdog of the fold,
The stay that saves the ship, the sturdy oak   570
That holds the roof up, the longed-for only child,
The shore despaired-of sighted far out at sea.
God keep us from all harm! And now, dearest,
Dismount, but not on the bare ground! Servants,
Spread out beneath those feet that have trampled Troy
A road of royal purple, which shall lead him
By the hand of Justice into a home unhoped-for,
And there, when he has entered, our vigilant care
Shall dispose of everything as the Gods have ordained.

Agamemnon
Lady, royal consort and guardian of our home,   580
I thank you for your words of welcome, extended
To fit my lengthy absence; but due praise
Should rather come from others; and besides,
I would not have effeminate graces unman me
With barbarous salaams and beneath my feet
Purple embroideries designed for sacred use.
Honor me as a mortal, not as a god.
Heaven's greatest gift is wisdom. Count him blest
Who has brought a long life to a happy end.
I shall do as I have said, with a clear conscience.   590

Clytemnestra
Yet tell me frankly, according to your judgment.

Agamemnon
My judgment stands. Make no mistake about that.

Clytemnestra
Would you not in time of danger have vowed such an act?

Agamemnon
Yes, if the priests had recommended it.

Clytemnestra
And what would Priam have done, if he had won?

Agamemnon
Oh, he would have trod the purple without a doubt.

Clytemnestra
Then you have nothing to fear from wagging tongues.

Agamemnon
Popular censure is a potent force.

Clytemnestra
Men must risk envy in order to be admired.

Agamemnon
A contentious spirit is unseemly in a woman.   600

Clytemnestra
Well may the victor yield a victory.

Agamemnon
Do you set so much store by your victory?

Clytemnestra
Be tempted, freely vanquished, victor still!

Agamemnon
Well, if you will have it, let someone unlace
These shoes, and, as I tread the purple, may
No far-off god cast at me an envious glance
At the prodigal desecration of all this wealth!
Meanwhile, extend your welcome to this stranger.
Power tempered with gentleness wins God's favor.
No one is glad to be enslaved, and she   610
Is a princess presented to me by the army,
The choicest flower culled from a host of captives.
And now, constrained to obey you, setting foot
On the sacred purple, I pass into my home.

Clytemnestra

The sea is still there, nothing can dry it up,
Renewing out of its infinite abundance
Unfailing streams of purple and blood-red dyes.
So too this house, the Gods be praised, my lord,
Has riches inexhaustible. There is no counting
The robes *I* would have vowed to trample on,   620
Had some oracle so instructed, if by such means
I could have made good the loss of one dear soul.
So now your entry to your hearth and home
Is like a warm spell in the long winter's cold,
Or when Zeus from the virgin grape at last
Draws wine, coolness descends upon the house
(For then from the living root the new leaves raise
A welcome shelter against the burning Dog-Star)
As man made perfect moves about his home.
[Exit AGAMEMNON.*]*
Zeus, perfecter of all things, fulfil my prayers   630
And fulfil also your own purposes!
[Exit.]

Chorus

What is this delirious dread,
Ominous, oracular,
Droning through my brain with unrelenting
Beat, irrepressible prophet of evil?
Why can I not cast it out
Planting good courage firm
On my spirit's empty throne?
In time the day came
When the Greeks with anchors plunged   640
Moored the sloops of war, and troops
Thronged the sandy beach of Troy.

So today my eyes have seen
Safe at last the men come home.
Still I hear the strain of stringless music,
Dirge of the Furies, a choir uninvited
Chanting in my heart of hearts.
Mortal souls stirred by God
In tune with fate divine the shape
Of things to come; yet   650
Grant that these forebodings prove
False and bring my fears to naught.

If a man's health be advanced over the due mean,
It will trespass soon upon sickness, who stands
Next neighbor, between them a thin wall.
So does the vessel of life

Color Plate 9   Achilles with the Body of Hector, c. 560 B.C.   The painting on this Athenian water jar illustrates a dramatic scene from Book 24 of the *Iliad*. Wearing a plumed helmet and carrying a shield with a triskele, a figure composed of three legs joined together, mounts his chariot, to which he has tied the body of Hector. Achilles looks back at Hecuba and Priam, who lament this public degradation of their son's corpse. Achilles's driver stands in the chariot, holding the horses's reins as Iris, a winged figure personifying the rainbow, arrives from Olympus. Repelled by Achilles's shameful mistreatment of the fallen Trojan hero, the Olympian gods have determined that Achilles must return Hector's body to his parents for honorable burial. *(William Francis Warden Fund. Courtesy, Museum of Fine Arts, Boston.)*

Color Plate 10 Nicolas Poussin, *Bacchanalian Revel before a Term of Pan.* Whereas Apollo personifies the value of rational clarity, harmonious balance, and self-discipline, his half-brother Dionysus (also called Bacchus) represents the joyful release from care found in spontaneous emotion and unrestrained self-expression (see chapters 8 and 13). In this work of the seventeenth-century French painter Nicolas Poussin, the artist presents a surprisingly light-hearted version of the wild, ecstatic dance inspired by Dionysian possession. The garlanded statue of Pan, half-bestial god of untamed nature and instinctive sensuality, gleefully presides over the revelry, its rigid immobility contrasting with the supple and energetic movement of the human figures. In Poussin's benign vision of earthy merriment, even the potential menace of a satyr threatening to assault a young woman is belied by her smiling lack of concern about his intentions (bottom right), while a companion holding a gold vase raised to clobber the offending satyr is in turn gently restrained by the arm of a nymph standing behind her. (*National Gallery, London*).

Color Plate 11   Sandro Botticelli, *Venus and Mars*, 1485. In this Renaissance painting, fauns play with Mars's helmet and spear while the war god, exhausted after his amorous exertions, sleeps. Venus herself, calm and composed, looks on, clearly the controlling figure here, despite Mars's weapons. (*National Gallery, London.*)

Color Plate 12 Pieter Breughel, the Elder, *The Fall of Icarus*, 1555–1556. The "heroic" figure of Icarus, emblem of the aspirations of Renaissance humanism, is here shifted off to an insignificant corner. The legs of the boy, barely visible in the lower right-hand corner of the painting, hardly create a splash, while the farmer goes on plowing, the ship goes on sailing, and the shepherd doesn't even look up: Icarus is nobody special. (*Musées Royaux des Beaux-Arts, Brussels.*)

Color Plate 13   Marc Chagall, *The Fall of Icarus,* 1975. In contrast to Breughel's version of this subject (see Color Plate 12), Icarus is the central figure in Chagall's painting. With upraised wings aflame, the figure of Icarus, the largest in the painting, suggests a fallen angel who hurtles, not toward water, but toward a landscape already ablaze. The sun, depicted with menacing geometric rays, seems already darkened, as if its light as well as its heat have been transferred, via Icarus's rebellion, to the crowds of people who watch, already caught up in the tragedy about to take place. (*Private collection, St. Paul de Vence, France.*)

Color Plate 14   Diego Velázquez, *The Forge of Vulcan,* 1630. Velázquez's dramatic painting is based on the bard Demodocus's song about the illicit love affair between Aphrodite (Venus) and Ares (Mars) (*Odyssey,* Book 8). The Spanish painter depicts the precise moment at which the sun god, Helios, whose celestial perspective enables him to see everything, informs Hephaestus (Vulcan) that his wife and her paramour are then engaged in an act of adultery, bringing the god's labor to a sudden stop. The slight frame and fair skin of Helios (left), whose garlanded head radiates a solar brilliance, contrasts markedly with the darker complexions and sinuous musculature of Hephaestus and his four assistants. Although momentarily rendered immobile by the unwelcome news, the ingenious god of metalcraft soon devises a way to trap and expose the guilty lovers to public shame (see Chapter 12). *(Museo del Prado, Madrid.)*

Color Plate 15   Titian, *Venus and Adonis,* 1562. Titian shows Venus's lover, Adonis, about to leave for the hunt during which he will be killed. Characteristically, the stability of the typical Renaissance composition of geometric forms (compare figures 21-15 and 21-16) is hinted at but shattered in this painting. The legs of Venus's contorted body point out of the frame of the painting, while Adonis's spear points at another angle, and the hunting dogs strain their leashes in the opposite direction altogether, all beneath a swirling vortex of cloud formations. (*National Gallery, London.*)

Color Plate 16   Salvador Dali, *The Metamorphosis of Narcissus,* 1936–1937. Turning to classical myths just as Picasso did to express the complexities of the modern world (see Figure 21-5), Dali took as his subject the story of Narcissus, who fell in love with his own reflection in a pond and was turned into the flower that bears his name. In this painting, Dali comments on the self-destructive potential, the essentially narcissistic nature, of psychoanalysis. (Expressing his usual wit, he brought this painting to show Freud when he met the "father of psychoanalysis"!) The figure on the left stares inward at itself, its face a blank to the external world. To the right, the figure of the hand (the psychoanalyst?) that holds an egg—simultaneously the head and embryo of the self—recapitulates the figure on the left. Immobilized in stone, the egg burst forth in flower, reborn in the act of self-analysis. But it does so alone, apart from the dance of humanity that has receded to the background. The "crack" in the egg/head on the left reveals the result: the flower, too, will soon be petrified—reduced to an image, the life, like the color, has gone out of it. (*Tate Gallery, London.*)

Launched with a favoring breeze
Suddenly founder on reefs of destruction.
Caution seated at the helm
Casts a portion of the freight 660
Overboard with measured throw;
So the ship may ride the storm.
Furrows enriched each season with showers from heaven
Banish hunger from the door.
But if the red blood of a man spatters the ground, dripping and deadly,
   then who
Has the magical power to recall it?
Even the healer who knew
Spells to awaken the dead,
Zeus put an end to his necromancy.
Portions are there preordained, 670
Each supreme within its own
Province fixed eternally.
That is why my spirit groans
Brooding in fear, and no longer it hopes to unravel
Mazes of a fevered mind.
[Enter CLYTEMNESTRA.*]*

Clytemnestra
You, too, Cassandra, come inside! The merciful
Zeus gives you the privilege to take part
In our domestic sacrifice and stand
Before his altar among the other slaves there.
Put by your pride and step down. Even Heracles 680
Submitted once to slavery, and be consoled
In serving a house whose wealth has been inherited
Over so many generations. The harshest masters
Are those who have snatched their harvest out of hand.
You shall receive here what custom prescribes.

Chorus
She is speaking to you. Caught in the net, surrender.

Clytemnestra
If she knows Greek and not some barbarous language,
My mystic words shall fill the soul within her.

Chorus
You have no choice. Step down and do her will.

Clytemnestra
There is no time to waste. The victims are 690
All ready for the knife to render thanks
For this unhoped-for joy. If you wish to take part,
Make haste, but, if you lack the sense to understand,—

[To the CHORUS.*]*
Speak to her with your hands and drag her down.

Chorus
She is like a wild animal just trapped.

Clytemnestra
She is mad, the foolish girl. Her city captured,
Brought here a slave, she will be broken in.
I'll waste no words on her to demean myself.
[Exit.]

Cassandra
Oh! oh! Apollo!

Chorus
What blasphemy, to wail in Apollo's name!   700

Cassandra
Oh! oh! Apollo!

Chorus
Again she cries in grief to the god of joy!

Cassandra
Apollo, my destroyer! a second time!

Chorus
Ah, she foresees what is in store for her.
She is now a slave, and yet God's gift remains.

Cassandra
Apollo, my destroyer! What house is this?

Chorus
Do you not know where you have come, poor girl?
Then let us tell you. This is the House of Atreus.

Cassandra
Yes, for its very walls smell of iniquity,
A charnel house that drips with children's blood.   710

Chorus
How keen her scent to seize upon the trail!

Cassandra
Listen to them as they bewail the foul
Repast of roast meat for a father's mouth!

Chorus
Enough! Reveal no more! We know it all.

Cassandra

What is it plotted next? Horror unspeakable,
A hard cross for kinsfolk.
The hoped-for savior is far away.

Chorus

What does she say? This must be something new.

Cassandra

Can it be so—to bathe one who is travel-tired,
And then smiling stretch out   720
A hand followed by a stealthy hand!

Chorus

She speaks in riddles, and I cannot read them.

Cassandra

What do I see? A net!
Yes, it is she, his mate and murderess!
Cry alleluia, cry, angels of hell, rejoice,
Fat with blood, dance and sing!

Chorus

What is the Fury you have called upon?
Helpless the heart faints with the sinking sun.
Closer still draws the stroke.

Cassandra

Ah, let the bull beware!   730
It is a robe she wraps him in, and strikes!
Into the bath he slumps heavily, drowned in blood.
Such her skilled handicraft.

Chorus

It is not hard to read her meaning now.
Why does the prophet's voice never have good to tell,
Only cry woes to come?

Cassandra

Oh, pitiful destiny! Having lamented his,
Now I lament my own passion to fill the bowl.
Where have you brought me? Must I with him die?

Chorus

You sing your own dirge, like the red-brown bird   740
That pours out her grief-stricken soul,
Itys, Itys! she cries, the sad nightingale.

Cassandra

It is not so; for she, having become a bird,
Forgot her tears and sings her happy lot,
While I must face the stroke of two-edged steel.

Chorus

From whence does this cascade of harsh discords
Issue, and where will it at last be calmed?
Calamity you cry—O where must it end?

Cassandra

O wedding day, Paris accurst of all!
Scamander, whose clear waters I grew beside!   750
Now I must walk weeping by Acheron.

Chorus

Even a child could understand.
The heart breaks, as these pitiful cries
Shatter the listening soul.

Cassandra

O fall of Troy, city of Troy destroyed!
The king's rich gifts little availed her so
That she might not have been what she is now.

Chorus

What evil spirit has possessed
Your soul, strumming such music upon your lips
As on a harp in hell?   760

Cassandra

Listen! My prophecy shall glance no longer
As through a veil like a bride newly-wed,
But bursting towards the sunrise shall engulf
The whole world in calamities far greater
Than these. No more riddles, I shall instruct,
While you shall verify each step, as I
Nose out from the beginning this bloody trail.
Upon this roof—do you see them?—stands a choir—
It has been there for generations—a gallery
Of unmelodious minstrels, a merry troop   770
Of wassailers drunk with human blood, reeling
And retching in horror at a brother's outraged bed.
Well, have I missed? Am I not well-read in
Your royal family's catalogue of crime?

Chorus

You come from a far country and recite
Our ancient annals as though you had been present.

Cassandra

The Lord Apollo bestowed this gift on me.

Chorus

Was it because he had fallen in love with you?

Cassandra
I was ashamed to speak of this till now.

Chorus
Ah yes, adversity is less fastidious.   780

Cassandra
Oh, but he wrestled strenuously for my love.

Chorus
Did you come, then, to the act of getting child?

Cassandra
At first I consented, and then I cheated him.

Chorus
Already filled with his gift of prophecy?

Cassandra
Yes, I forewarned my people of their destiny.

Chorus
Did your divine lover show no displeasure?

Cassandra
Yes, the price I paid was that no one listened to me.

Chorus
Your prophecies seem credible enough to us.

Cassandra
Oh!
Again the travail of the prophetic trance
Runs riot in my soul. Do you not see them   790
There, on the roof, those apparitions—children
Murdered by their own kin, in their hands
The innards of which their father ate—oh
What a pitiable load they carry! For that crime
Revenge is plotted by the fainthearted lion,
The stay-at-home, stretched in my master's bed
(Being his slave, I must needs call him so),
Lying in wait for Troy's great conqueror.
Little he knows what that foul bitch with ears
Laid back and rolling tongue intends for him   800
With a vicious snap, her husband's murderess.
What abominable monster shall I call her—
A two-faced amphisbaene or Scylla that skulks
Among the rocks to waylay mariners,
Infernal sea-squib locked in internecine
Strife—did you not hear her alleluias
Of false rejoicing at his safe return?

Believe me or not, what must be will be, and then
You will pity me and say, She spoke the truth.

Chorus
The feast of Thyestes I recognized, and shuddered,   810
But for the rest my wits are still astray.

Cassandra
Your eyes shall see the death of Agamemnon.

Chorus
No, hush those ill-omened lips, unhappy girl!

Cassandra
There is no Apollo present, and so no cure.

Chorus
None, if you speak the truth; yet God forbid!

Cassandra
Pray God forbid, while they close in for the kill!

Chorus
What man is there who would plot so foul a crime?

Cassandra
Ah, you have altogether misunderstood.

Chorus
But how will he do it? That escapes me still.

Cassandra
And yet I can speak Greek only too well.   820

Chorus
So does Apollo, but his oracles are obscure.

Cassandra
Ah, how it burns me up! Apollo! Now
That lioness on two feet pours in the cup
My wages too, and while she whets the blade
For him promises to repay my passage money
In my own blood. Why wear these mockeries,
This staff and wreath, if I must die, then you
Shall perish first and be damned. Now we are quits!
Apollo himself has stripped me, looking upon me
A public laughingstock, who has endured   830
The name of witch, waif, beggar, castaway,
So now the god who gave me second sight
Takes back his gift and dismisses his servant,
Ready for the slaughter at a dead man's grave.
Yet we shall be avenged. Now far away,

The exile shall return, called by his father's
Unburied corpse to come and kill his mother.
Why weep at all this? Have I not seen Troy fall,
And those who conquered her are thus discharged.
I name this door the gate of Hades: now   840
I will go and knock, I will take heart to die.
I only pray that the blow may be mortal,
Closing these eyes in sleep without a struggle,
While my life blood ebbs quietly away.

Chorus
O woman, in whose wisdom is so much grief,
How, if you know the end, can you approach it
So gently, like an ox that goes to the slaughter?

Cassandra
What help would it be if I should put it off?

Chorus
Yet, while there is life there's hope—so people say.

Cassandra
For me no hope, no help. My hour has come.   850

Chorus
You face your end with a courageous heart.

Cassandra
Yes, so they console those whom life has crossed.

Chorus
Is there no comfort in an honorable death?

Cassandra
O Priam, father, and all your noble sons!
[She approaches the door, then draws back.]

Chorus
What is it? Why do you turn back, sick at heart?

Cassandra
Inside there is a stench of dripping blood.

Chorus
It is only the blood of their fireside sacrifice.

Cassandra
It is the sort of vapor that issues from a tomb.
I will go now and finish my lament
Inside the house. Enough of life! O friends!   860
I am not scared. I beg of you only this:

When the day comes for them to die, a man
For a man, woman for woman, remember me!

Chorus
Poor soul condemned to death, I pity you.

Cassandra
Yet one word more, my own dirge for myself.
I pray the Sun, on whom I now look my last,
That he may grant to my master's avengers
A fair price for the slave-girl slain at his side.
O sad mortality! when fortune smiles,
A painted image; and when trouble comes, 870
One touch of a wet sponge wipes it away.
[*Exit.*]

Chorus
And her case is even more pitiable than his.
Human prosperity never rests but always craves more, till blown up with pride it totters and falls. From the opulent mansions pointed at by all passersby none warns it away, none cries, "Let no more riches enter!" To him was granted the capture of Troy, and he has entered his home as a god, but now, if the blood of the past is on him, if he must pay with his own death for the crimes of bygone generations, then who is assured of a life without sorrow?

Agamemnon
Oh me!

Chorus
Did you hear?

Agamemnon
Oh me, again!

Chorus
It is the King. Let us take counsel!

   1 I say, raise a hue and cry!
   2 Break in at once!
   3 Yes, we must act. 880
   4 *They* spurn delay.
   5 They plot a tyranny.
   6 Must we live their slaves?
   7 Better to die.
   8 Old men, what can we do?
   9 We cannot raise the dead.
10 His death is not yet proved.
11 We are only guessing.
12 Let us break in and learn the truth!

[The doors are thrown open and CLYTEMNESTRA *is seen standing over the bodies of* AGAMEMNON *and* CASSANDRA, *which are laid out on a purple robe.]*

Clytemnestra
All that I said before to bide my time   890
Without any shame I shall now unsay. How else
Could I have plotted against an enemy
So near and seeming dear and strung the snare
So high that he could not jump it? Now the feud
On which I have pondered all these years has been
Fought out to its conclusion. Here I stand
Over my work, and it was so contrived
As to leave no loophole. With this vast dragnet
I enveloped him in purple folds, then struck
Twice, and with two groans he stretched his legs,   900
Then on his outspread body I struck a third blow,
A drink for Zeus the Deliverer of the dead.
There he lay gasping out his soul and drenched me
In these deathly dew-drops, at which I cried
In sheer delight like newly-budding corn
That tastes the first spring showers. And so,
Venerable elders, you see how the matter stands.
Rejoice, if you are so minded. I glory in it.
With bitter tears he filled the household bowl;
Now he has drained it to the dregs and gone.   910

Chorus
How can you speak so of your murdered king?

Clytemnestra
You treat me like an empty-headed woman.
Again, undaunted, to such as understand
I say—commend or censure, as you please—
It makes no difference—here is Agamemnon,
My husband, dead, the work of this right hand,
Which acted justly. There you have the truth.

Chorus
Woman, what evil brew have you devoured to take
On you a crime that cries out for a public curse?
Yours was the fatal blow, banishment shall be yours,   920
Hissed and hated of all men.

Clytemnestra
Your sentence now for me is banishment,
But what did you do then to contravene
His purpose, when, to exorcise the storms,
As though picking a ewe-lamb from his flocks,
Whose wealth of snowy fleeces never fails
To increase and multiply, he killed his own

Child, born to me in pain, my best-beloved?
Why did you not drive *him* from hearth and home?
I bid you cast at me such menaces   930
As make for mastery in equal combat
With one prepared to meet them, and if, please God,
The issue goes against you, suffering
Shall school those grey hairs in humility.

Chorus
You are possessed by some spirit of sin that stares
Out of your bloodshot eyes matching your bloody hands.
Dishonored and deserted of your kin, for this
Stroke you too shall be struck down.

Clytemnestra
Listen! By Justice, who avenged my child,
By the Fury to whom I vowed this sacrament,   940
No thought of fear shall enter through this door
So long as the hearth within is kindled by
Aegisthus, faithful to me now as always.
Low lies the man who insulted his wedded wife,
The darling of the Chryseids at Troy,
And stretched beside him this visionary seer,
Whom he fondled on shipboard, both now rewarded,
He as you see, and she swanlike has sung
Her dying ditty, his tasty side dish, for me
A rare spice to add relish to my joy.   950

Chorus
Oh, for the gift of death
To bring the long sleep that knows no waking,
Now that my lord and loyal protector
Breathes his last. For woman's sake
Long he fought overseas,
Now at home falls beneath a woman's hand.
    Helen, the folly-beguiled, having ravaged the city of Troy,
    She has set on the curse of Atreus
    A crown of blood beyond ablution.

Clytemnestra
Do not pray for death nor turn your anger against one woman as the slayer of
    thousands!   960

Chorus
Demon of blood and tears
Inbred in two women single-hearted!
Perched on the roof he stands and preens his
Sable wings, a carrion-crow.
Loud he croaks, looking down
Upon the feast spread before him here below.

Clytemnestra

Ah now you speak truth, naming the thrice-fed demon, who, glutted with blood,
   craves more, still young in his hunger.

Chorus

When will the feast be done?
Alas, it is the will of Zeus,
Who caused and brought it all to pass.   970
Nothing is here but was decreed in heaven.

Clytemnestra

It was not my doing, nor am I Agamemnon's wife, but a ghost in woman's guise,
   the shade of the banqueter whom Atreus fed.

Chorus

How is the guilt not yours?
And yet the crimes of old may well
Have had a hand, and so it drives
On, the trail of internecine murder.

Clytemnestra

What of *him?* Was the guilt not his, when he killed the child that I bore him?
   And so by the sword he has fallen.

Chorus

Alas, the mind strays. The house is falling.
A storm of blood lays the walls in ruins.
Another mortal stroke for Justice' hand   980
Will soon be sharpened.
   Oh me, who shall bury him, who sing the dirge?
   Who shall intone at the tomb of a blessed spirit
   A tribute pure in heart and truthful?

Clytemnestra

No, I'll bury him, but without mourners. By the waters of Acheron Iphigenia is
   waiting for him with a kiss.

Chorus

The charge is answered with countercharges.
The sinner must suffer: such is God's will.
The ancient curse is bringing down the house
In self-destruction.

Clytemnestra

That is the truth, and I would be content that the spirit of vengeance should
   rest, having absolved the house from its madness.   990
[Enter AEGISTHUS *with a bodyguard.]*

Aegisthus

Now I have proof that there are Gods in heaven,
As I gaze on this purple mesh in which

My enemy lies, son of a treacherous father.
His father, Atreus, monarch of this realm,
Was challenged in his sovran rights by mine,
Thyestes, his own brother, and banished him
From hearth and home. Later he returned
A suppliant and found sanctuary, indeed
A welcome; for his brother entertained him
To a feast of his own children's flesh, of which   1000
My father unsuspecting took and ate.
Then, when he knew what he had done, he fell
Back spewing out the slaughtered flesh and, kicking
The table to the floor, with a loud cry
He cursed the House of Pelops. That is the crime
For which the son lies here. And fitly too
The plot was spun by me; for as a child
I was banished with my father, until Justice
Summoned me home. Now let me die, for never
Shall I live to see another sight so sweet.   1010

Chorus
Aegisthus, if it was you who planned this murder,
Then be assured, the people will stone you for it.

Aegisthus
Such talk from the lower benches! Even in dotage
Prison can teach a salutary lesson.
Better submit, or else you shall smart for it.

Chorus
You woman, who stayed at home and wallowed in
His bed, you plotted our great commander's death!

Aegisthus
Orpheus led all in rapture after him.
Your senseless bark will be snuffed out in prison.

Chorus
You say the plot was yours, yet lacked the courage   1020
To raise a hand but left it to a woman!

Aegisthus
As his old enemy, I was suspect.
Temptation was the woman's part. But now
I'll try my hand at monarchy, and all
Who disobey me shall be put in irons
And starved of food and light till they submit.

Chorus
Oh, if Orestes yet beholds the sun,
May he come home and execute them both!

Aegisthus
Ho, my guards, come forward, you have work to do.

Captain of the Guard
Stand by, draw your swords!   1030

Chorus
We are not afraid to die.

Aegisthus
Die! We'll take you at your word.

Clytemnestra
Peace, my lord, and let no further wrong be done.
Captain, sheathe your swords. And you, old men,
Go home quietly. What has been, it had to be.
Scars enough we bear, now let us rest.

Aegisthus
Must I stand and listen to their threats?

Chorus
Men of Argos never cringed before a rogue.

Aegisthus
I shall overtake you yet—the day is near.

Chorus
Not if Orestes should come home again.   1040

Aegisthus
Vain hope, the only food of castaways.

Chorus
Gloat and grow fat, blacken justice while you dare!

Aegisthus
All this foolish talk will cost you dear.

Chorus
Flaunt your gaudy plumes and strut beside your hen!

Clytemnestra
Pay no heed to idle clamor. You and I,
Masters of the house, shall now direct it well.

LIBATION-BEARERS

Aeschylus

CHARACTERS

ORESTES, *son of Agamemnon and Clytemnestra*

CHORUS, *captive Trojan slave women who carry libations (religious drink offerings) to Agamemnon's tomb*

SERVANT

CLYTEMNESTRA, *Orestes's mother and queen of Argos*

ELECTRA, *daughter of Agamemnon and Clytemnestra who aids her brother in his revenge*

NURSE

AEGISTHUS, *Clytemnestra's lover and co-ruler of Argos*

PYLADES, *Orestes's friend*

[The *Libation-Bearers* opens several years after Agamemnon's murder when Orestes, disguised as a foreign peddler and accompanied by his friend Pylades, secretly returns to Argos (Mycenae). After revealing his identity to his sister Electra, who is also eager to avenge their father's death, Orestes arranges to lure Aegisthus and Clytemnestra into the palace, where—obeying Apollo's command—he will kill them. In the following scene, midway through the play, Orestes explains his intentions to the chorus of captive Trojan women, whose personal hatred of Clytemnestra causes them to support the royal siblings' plan to butcher their mother. Orestes tells the eager chorus exactly how he will lure Clytemnestra (the "*she*" to whom he refers in line 1) and Aegisthus to their deaths:]

. . . .

Orestes

It is soon told. First, *she* must go inside
To see that our enterprise is well concealed,
So that the couple whose cunning killed a king
Be caught by cunning, as Apollo has commanded.
Then I, with my true friend here, Pylades,
Disguised as travelers, shall approach the door
Speaking the Phocian dialect, and if no
Doorkeeper opens to us, since it is a house
Bewitched with sin, we will wait till the passersby
Take stock and say, "Where is Aegisthus? Why   10
Does he close his doors against these strangers?"—then,
Stepping across the threshold, if I find
That scoundrel seated on my father's throne,
Or if he should come to greet me, lifting up
To mine those eyes that shall soon be cast down,
Before he can ask, "Where is the stranger from?"
My steel shall strike, and so a Fury never

570

Starved shall drain a third great draught of blood.
And so to *you* I say, keep a close watch
[To ELECTRA.*]*
Inside the house, and to *you* I commend   20
[To the CHORUS.*]*
Silence in season and timeliness in speech.
The rest is for my comrade's eyes alone
To guide me in this ordeal of the sword.

Chorus
Fearful beasts bringing much
Harm to man breed on earth;
Monsters huge hid from sight lurk beneath
Smiling seas; and baleful lights sweeping through the vaulted skies
Swing suspended over all
Creatures that fly and that walk on the ground; and remember
How they rage, the stormy blasts.   30

Yet the deeds dared by man's
Forward spirit who shall tell?
Woman too, whose perverse loves contrive
Crimes of blood provoking bloodstained revenges, sin for sin.
Once a woman's lawless lust
Gains the supremacy, swiftly it brings to destruction
Wedded ties in beast and man.

Those who cannot grasp the truth, let them
Take thought touching that
Flash of torchlit treachery,   40
Which the black heart of Althaea plotted,
By whose hand the firebrand was burnt which
Dated back to the day her child
Cried as he issued from her
Womb, and measured his span of life
On to the death appointed.

No less wicked too was Scylla, whose
False heart foe-beguiled
Dared the death of dearest kin,
All for one necklace rare, wrought of fine gold,   50
A gift brought from Crete; hence in secret,
While in slumber her Nisus lay,
Ah, she shore his immortal
Locks—a pitiless heart was hers!
Hermes led him to darkness.

And since I call back to mind the wicked crimes
Of old . . . —To no purpose! *This* unhallowed, vile

Union, which the world abhors,
A wife's deceit framed against a warrior—
Have you no harsh words to censure that?   60
I praise the hearth where no fires of passion burn,
A meek heart such as graces woman.
—Of all the crimes told in tales the Lemnian
Is chief, a sin cried throughout the world with such
Horror that, if men relate
Some monstrous outrage, they call it Lemnian.
Abhorred of man, scorned of God,
Their seed is cast out for evermore;
For none respect what the Gods abominate.
Is *this* not well and justly spoken?   70

A sword of piercing steel is poised
To strike well home, which unerring Justice
Shall thrust to cleave the hearts of all
Those who trample underfoot
The sanctities
Of Zeus, to ungodly deeds inclining.

The tree of Justice shall not fall,
And Fate's strong hand forges steel to arm her.
There comes to wipe away with fresh
Blood the blood of old a son,   80
Obeying some
Inscrutable Fury's deadly purpose.
[Enter ORESTES *and* PYLADES. *They go up to the door.]*

Orestes
Ho there! Ho! I call a third time: ho!
Let Aegisthus grant us hospitality!
[A SERVANT *comes to the door.]*

Servant
All right, I hear you. Where is the stranger from?

Orestes
Announce me to your masters. I bring them news.
Go quickly, for Night's chariot draws on
The hour for travelers to seek repose.
Let someone in authority come out,
A woman, or more properly a man;   90
For we can speak more freely man to man.
*[*CLYTEMNESTRA *comes to the door, attended by* ELECTRA.*]*

Clytemnestra
Strangers, declare your wishes. Here you shall have
A welcome such as the house is noted for—

Warm baths and beds to ease the travel-tired
And the presence of an honest company;
But if you have in mind some graver matter,
That is man's business, and to men we shall impart it.

Orestes
I am a stranger from Phocis, and I have come
To Argos on an errand of my own;
But as I shod my feet to take the road,   100
A man came up to me whom I did not know—
Strophius the Phocian was his name, he said,—
"Stranger," he said to me, "if you are bound
For Argos, please inform the parents of
Orestes that their son is dead, and bring
An answer back, whether they wish to fetch
His body or leave it here duly lamented
And laid to rest an exile even in death."
That was the message. Whether I now address
One in authority and near to him   110
I do not know, but his parents should be told.

Electra
Oh, it is all over, all pitilessly destroyed!
O irresistible curse of our ancestors
So widely ranging! Even that which seemed
Safely disposed beyond the reach of harm
Has been brought down by an arrow from afar,
Leaving me desolate, stripped of all I loved.
And now Orestes—he who wisely resolved
To keep his foot outside the miry clay,
Now that one hope that might at last have purged   120
The house of wickedness, do not mark it as present.

Orestes
I could have wished, visiting such a house
On which God smiles, that happier news had made
Me known to you; for nothing brings such delight
As the gentle intercourse of host and stranger.
But I would have deemed it wrong not to fulfil
My solemn promise to those I love so dearly.

Clytemnestra
You shall be entertained as you deserve.
You are welcome notwithstanding; for, if you
Had not brought the news, others would have come.   130
Now it is time for you to be attended.
[To ELECTRA.*]*
Escort them in and wait upon their needs.
Do this, I tell you, as you shall answer for it.

Meanwhile I shall inform the master of
The house and shall consult all our friends
What should be done concerning this event.
*[*CLYTEMNESTRA, ELECTRA, ORESTES *and* PYLADES *go into the palace.]*

Chorus

How soon shall our voices be lifted in praise of Orestes? O Earth, O Tomb, now
is the time to strengthen his hand; let Hermes arise out of the darkness to look
down on the contest!
[The NURSE *comes out of the palace.]*

It seems the stranger is already making mischief.
Here is Orestes' old nurse, bathed in tears.
What is it, Cilissa? What brings you to the gates?   140

Nurse

My mistress has commanded me to bring
Aegisthus to the strangers instantly,
That he may hear their message man from man.
Before the servants she affects a sorrowful
Demeanor, yet with a lurking smile
At news that makes her happy, and he too
Will now be overjoyed. What years of grief
Are locked up in this breast, which I have borne
Within these walls—old, mixed-up memories—
And now Orestes, who was entrusted to me   150
Out of his mother's arms—my dearest care—
And what a troublesome child he was!
For sure, like a dumb animal, a senseless babe
Must needs have a nurse's wits to nourish it.
A child in swaddling clothes cannot declare
His wants, that he would eat or drink or make
Water, nor will his belly wait upon
Attendance. Nurses must have second sight,
And even so they may be deceived, and then
Must wash the linen white—such was my task   160
Tending Orestes, his father's son and heir;
And now he is dead, they tell me, and I must take
The news to him whose wickedness infects
The house, and watch how it warms his heart.

Chorus

With what equipment did she bid him come?

Nurse

Equipment? How? I do not understand you.

Chorus

Attended by his retinue, or alone?

Nurse
He is told to bring his royal bodyguard.

Chorus
Then, as you hate him, not a word about that!
Tell him to come alone, and come at once,   170
Come and fear nothing and feed his happy heart.

Nurse
Can it be that you see some good in the report?

Chorus
Who knows but Zeus may yet turn an ill wind?

Nurse
How, if our last hope, Orestes, is gone?

Chorus
A good prophet would not yet read it so.

Nurse
Have you reason to doubt that the news is true?

Chorus
Go, take your message and do as you are told.
The Gods will care for what is their concern.

Nurse
I will go. God grant that all is for the best!

Chorus
Hear us, O Father Zeus, hear our prayer!   180
Grant that those win the day who would see
Lawlessness at last dethroned!
Nothing we ask but what is just: O Zeus, defend us!
    Let the champion who has gone in
    Be upheld now in the fray. Zeus, who has made him
    Great, shall take at will a twofold recompense and threefold.

Think of that lordly sire whose untried
Colt is now yoked and all set to run!
Lay a steady, guiding hand
Upon the rein until the breathless race is over!   190

Grant that he may grasp the great
Prize the Gods have kept for him
Here—his ancient heritage.
So with vengeance fresh redeem
The full debt of those ancestral crimes.
    Let us rejoice and set a crown on the palace!
    O let it soon be revealed

Gleaming and friendly and free
Out of the veil of encircling darkness!

Hermes too shall lend a hand,   200
Named the keen and cunning one.
Much at will he can reveal.
Night he draws before the eyes
With voice veiled that none may understand.

Thus, with all done at last,
Music set to breezes fair,
Women's shrill songs of joy
Shall be heard, "All is well!"
Bringing peace to those we love.
And with stout heart, as she cries "Child!"   210
Let him cry "Father!" and kill her!

May his heart turn to stone,
Hard as Perseus', merciless!
Make the end bloody, wipe
Clean the old stain, that this
House may win deliverance!
[Enter AEGISTHUS.*]*

Aegisthus
I come in answer to the summons.
Strangers, they say, have brought unwelcome news,
Orestes' death, another wound to open
Old sores in this sad house. How shall I judge   220
Whether it is true or women's idle rumor?

Chorus
We have heard it, but go inside and ask
The strangers. Make enquiry on the spot.

Aegisthus
I want to see that messenger and ask
If he was present at the death. They shall
Not hoodwink me. My wits are wide awake.
*[*AEGISTHUS *enters the palace.]*

Chorus
Zeus, what shall I say? The moment has come, with the fate of the house on a
knife's edge. Is it to fall, or shall the son be restored to the wealth of his fathers?
That is the issue, and he faces alone two monsters—may he prove master!
[A cry is heard within.]

He is at work. Better stand clear awhile, in case
It goes against him. The issue has been decided.

[The SERVANT *comes to the door.]*

Servant
Oh, oh! My master has been murdered!   230
Oh me! A third cry for the dead! Help!
Unbolt the women's chambers! And yet even
A strong hand is too weak to help the dead.
Ho!
They must be deaf or sleeping. All my cries
Are wasted. Where is Clytemnestra? what
Is she doing? Now, it seems, her own
Head must bend beneath the axe of Justice.
*[*CLYTEMNESTRA *comes to the door.]*

Clytemnestra
What is it? What is the meaning of that shout?

Servant
It means the living are being killed by the dead.   240

Clytemnestra
Ah me, a riddle! yet I can read its meaning.
Quick, let me have a man-axe, then we shall see
Who wins, who loses. It has come to this.
*[*ORESTES *and* PYLADES *come out of the palace.]*

Orestes
I have been looking for you. He is all right.

Clytemnestra
Aegisthus, dearest love! Oh, he is dead!

Orestes
You love him? Well, then you shall share his grave,
Faithful in everything even to death.

Clytemnestra
O stay, my son! Dear child, have pity on
This bosom where in slumber long ago
Your toothless gums drew in the milk of life!   250

Orestes
Pylades, what shall I do? Shall I spare my mother?

Pylades
What then hereafter of the oracles
And solemn declarations of Apollo?
Better that men should hate you than the Gods.

Orestes
Your counsel shall prevail. Come with me. I
Shall kill you by his side. Since you preferred

Him to my father while he lived, die with him!

Clytemnestra
I brought you up—let me grow old with you!

Orestes
What, live with you, my father's murderess!

Clytemnestra
Fate had a hand, my son, in your father's end.   260

Orestes
Yes, the same fate which now decrees your own.

Clytemnestra
Have you no dread of a mother's curse, my child?

Orestes
Your child no more, because you cast me out.

Clytemnestra
No, not cast out—I sent you away to friends.

Orestes
Son of a royal father, foully sold!

Clytemnestra
What then was the payment that I took for you?

Orestes
For very shame I cannot answer that.

Clytemnestra
No, no! Remember too *his* faithlessness!

Orestes
Do not reproach him. It was for you he toiled abroad.

Clytemnestra
It is hard for a woman parted from her man.   270

Orestes
What but his labor keeps her safe at home?

Clytemnestra
So then, my son, you mean to kill your mother?

Orestes
It is not I, it is you who kill yourself.

Clytemnestra
Beware of the hell-hounds of a mother's curse!

Orestes
And how, if I spare you, escape from his?

Clytemnestra
My pleas are fruitless—warm tears at a cold tomb.

Orestes
My father's destiny has determined yours.

Clytemnestra
Ah me, I gave birth to a snake and not a son.

Orestes.
That panic-stricken nightmare was prophetic.
Wrong shall be done to you for the wrong you did.   280
[They go into the palace.]

Chorus
I mourn for them both, and yet, since the tale
Of bloodshed is now crowned in brave Orestes,
I choose to have it so, that this great house
May rise again and not perish utterly.

Upon the sons of Priam Justice in time did bring
Heavy and harsh judgment;
To Agamemnon too and to his house it came,
A double lion, double strife.
On to the goal he held his course heaven-sped,
Following well the Lord Apollo's command.   290
    Cry Alleluia, lift up in the house a song,
    Deliverance from evil and the waste of wealth,
    From rough, thorny ways.

Yes, he has come, the God who with a sly assault
Ambushes evildoers;
Deftly his hand was guided in the battle by
The child of Zeus the truly-named,
Whom it is right that mortals call Righteousness.
Deadly the blast she breathes on those that shed blood.
Just as Apollo cried out of his holy shrine,   300
So does his word advance never at fault against
The ingrown disease which in the house is lodged;
For God's will is always stronger than sin.
    On us the light has shone! Now let the fallen house
    Out of the shadows rise; for it was long enough
    The chains of evil held it down.

It shall be purified in the appointed time,
When he has cleansed the hearth of the defiling sin,

And all those who wept shall have their sorrow turned
To joy, greeting man's salvation from wrong.   310
[The doors are opened and torches lit within, revealing the bodies of AEGISTHUS *and*
CLYTEMNESTRA *laid out in purple robes on a couch, with* ORESTES *standing
over them.]*

Orestes
See here our country's double tyranny!
How stately were they sitting on their thrones,
Both pledged to slay my father and so doomed
To die themselves together—they kept their word.
See here the snare which they contrived to enmesh
My father's hands and feet—what shall I call it?
A pit for wild beasts, or a winding-sheet,
Or a cloak spread by some highwayman to catch
The passing traveler? Come, spread it out,
This skilful masterpiece, that he who is   320
Father of all creation and looks down
On the whole world, the Sun, having observed
My mother's wicked handiwork, may stand
My witness at the judgment which is to come
And certify that I put her to death
Justly—as for Aegisthus, he has paid
The penalty prescribed for adulterers;
But she, who plotted this horror for her own
Husband, to whom she bore within her womb
Children, a load of love which now has turned   330
To hate, as they have shown by their sharp fangs—
What do you think of her? If she had been
A scorpion or sea-snake, her very touch
Would rot the unbitten hand. Rather than share
House with such a monster, may the Gods
Destroy me and my children and children's children!

Chorus
With a fearful death she has paid for her foul deed, reaping the crop which she
    sowed with her own hand.

Orestes
The deed was hers, was it not? I have a witness,
This robe, that here she plunged Aegisthus' sword:
See how bloodstains have joined with time and worn   340
The dye out of the pattern! I am now present,
Now only, to praise and lament my father,
Greeting this web that wove his death and weeping
For all that has been done and suffered here,
For the whole race, and for my own fate too,
Bearing the stains of this grim victory.

Chorus

All men have been born to sorrow, which is present for some today and is stored
    up for others.

Orestes

So then, to tell you plainly—I do not know
How it will end—my wits are out of hand
Like horses that with victory in sight   350
Shy and dash wildly off the course—so I feel
Here at the heart a throbbing—but while I have
My senses, I declare that I killed my mother
In a just cause, because she killed my father,
And that I was driven to do it in obedience
To the oracle of Apollo, who proclaimed
That, if I did it, I should be cleared of guilt,
And that, if not—I will not name the penalty,
Something beyond imagination; and so,
Garlanded with these sprigs of supplication,   360
I make my way to his prophetic shrine
And the glorious light of his undying fire,
A suppliant stained with blood; for he commanded me
To seek no hearth but his; and meanwhile I
Call on my fellow-countrymen to give
In time to come their evidence, how all this
Was brought about, an outcast, leaving to
Their safekeeping, in life and death, my name.

Chorus

You must not bend your lips to such ill-omened
Talk after delivering your country and   370
With one swift stroke lopping two dragons' heads.

Orestes

Look! Do you see those women, like Gorgons,
All clothed in black, their heads and arms entwined
With writhing snakes! How can I escape?

Chorus

What imaginings are these, O father's dearest
Son? Stay and fear nothing. You have won.

Orestes

Imaginings! They are real enough to me.
Can you not see them? Hounds of a mother's curse!

Chorus

It is the blood still dripping from your hands
That confuses your wits, but it will pass.   380

Conflict and Opposition in the Myth of the House of Atreus

Before Aeschylus transformed the stories of Agamemnon and Orestes to illustrate the conflict between matriarchal and patriarchal forces in Greek society, the myth of the House of Atreus featured a more traditional competition for power between male figures. Mythic events that took place before the action of Aeschylus's *Agamemnon* typically emphasize father-son and brother-brother conflict, usually involving murder and revenge. Agamemnon's ancestor, Tantalus, kills his son, Pelops, and attempts to feed his flesh to the Olympian gods—an act that condemns him to eternal torment in Tartarus. Tantalus's descendants, Atreus and Thyestes, engage in a fraternal rivalry that culminates in Atreus's murder of Thyestes's sons and the cannibalistic banquet in which Thyestes unwittingly devours his children's flesh.

In the Homeric version of the subsequent conflict between the son of Atreus (Agamemnon) and son of Thyestes (Aegisthus), it is Aegisthus, presumably acting alone, who kills Agamemnon. In Aeschylus's tragedy, however, it is Clytemnestra who boasts that her husband is slain by her own hand, thereby setting the stage for an intense struggle involving the respective rights and authority of a strong woman pitted against a less effectual man (who is also a head of state). Aeschylus's dramatization of the struggle reaches a climax in the trial scene of the *Eumenides,* where virtually all the principal characters in the *Oresteia* are depicted as polar opposites. Aeschylus's resolution of the battle between old and new, male and female, anarchy and order utilizes the powerful image of Athene, who shares qualities with both sides of the conflict and successfully mediates between them. Aeschylus's dramatic use of ancient myth to illustrate the reconciliation of opposing forces in Greek society (and the human psyche) lends itself to a structuralist interpretation of the drama.

Orestes
O Lord Apollo! See how thick they come,
And from their eyes are oozing gouts of blood!

Chorus
You shall be purified! Apollo's touch
Shall save you and from all troubles set you free.

Orestes
You cannot see them, and yet how plain they are!
They are coming to hunt me down. Away, away!
[Exit.]

I	II
Traditions and Qualities Associated with the Feminine Principle:	Traditions and Qualities Associated with the Masculine Principle:
Clytemnestra—powerful female who avenges wrongs.	Agamemnon—rightful king and father, treacherously murdered.
Iphigenia—innocent girl sacrificed to male ambition.	Orestes—compelled by divine command to avenge his father.
The Furies—Night's daughters, spirits of blood vengeance, identified with darkness, violence, torture, bloodshed, castration, punishment, instinct, hatred, fear, irrationality, anarchy, inflexible justice, age-old tradition.	Apollo—immortal son of Zeus, identified with light, peace, spiritual insight, mental and physical health, masculine autonomy, ethical purification, moderation, restraint, rationality, stable order, clemency, divine innovation.

\   III   /

Athene—immortal daughter of Zeus who was born without a mother, identified with rationality, wisdom, courage, defense of civic order, military victory, creative skill, virginity, emotional self-sufficiency, intellectual freedom, ethical commitment, democracy, legal justice, the art of persuasion.

In the final scene of the *Eumenides,* Athene acts as mediator who reconciles the opposing claims of chthonic tradition and ouranic innovation. By the end of his three-part drama, Aeschylus has clearly demonstrated his conviction that the ancient Mycenaean legacy has evolved into a new concept of social justice that finds completion and fulfillment in the Athenian court of law. For Aeschylus and his audience, Athens—with its democracy guided by the Zeus-born embodiment of divine wisdom—is the culmination and ultimate achievement of Greek historical development.

Chorus
Good luck, and may God guide you to the end!
This is the third storm to have struck the house: first, the slaughter of children; next, the fall of the great king who had conquered Troy; and now—is it final destruction or deliverance at last? When shall the curse be laid to rest?

EUMENIDES

Aeschylus

CHARACTERS

PRIESTESS, *the prophetic oracle of Apollo at Delphi*

APOLLO, *god of healing, disease, and prophecy who purifies Orestes at Delphi*

ORESTES, *the matricide who seeks exoneration at history's first murder trial in Athens*

GHOST OF CLYTEMNESTRA, *the spirit of Orestes's murdered mother*

CHORUS, *the Furies, whom Athene (Athena) transforms into the Eumenides (Kindly Ones)*

ATHENE (ATHENA), *goddess of wisdom and protector of the city-state*

ESCORT OF WOMEN, *Athenian women who escort the Eumenides to their new shrine in Athens*

[Before the temple of Apollo at Delphi.
    Enter the PRIESTESS.]

Priestess
First among all the gods to whom this prayer
Shall be addressed is the first of prophets, Earth;
And next her daughter, Themis, who received
The oracular shrine from her; third, another
Daughter, Phoebe, who having settled here
Bestowed it as a birthday gift, together
With her own name, on Phoebus; whereupon,
Leaving his native isle of Delos and landing
In Attica, he made his way from there
Attended by the sons of Hephaestus, who tamed   10
The wilderness and built a road for him;
And here Zeus, having inspired him with his art,
Set him, the fourth of prophets, on this throne,
His own son and interpreter, Apollo.
Together with these deities I pay
Homage to Athena and to the nymphs that dwell
In the Corycian caves on the rugged slopes
Of Parnassus, where Dionysus led
His troop of frenzied Bacchants to catch and kill
King Pentheus like a mountain-hare; and so,   20
After calling on Poseidon and the springs
Of Pleistus, watering this valley, and last
On Zeus the All-Highest, who makes all things perfect,
I take my seat on the oracular throne,
Ready to be consulted. Let all Greeks

Approach by lot according to the custom
And I shall prophesy to them as God dictates.
[She enters the temple, utters a loud cry, and returns.]
O horror, horror! I have been driven back
Strengthless, speechless, a terror-struck old woman,
By such a sight as was never seen before.   30
Entering the shrine I saw at the navel-stone
In the posture of a suppliant a man
Who held an olive-branch and an unsheathed sword
In hands dripping with blood; and all round him,
Lying fast asleep, a gruesome company
Of women—yet not women—Gorgons rather;
And yet not Gorgons; them I saw once in a picture
Of the feast of Phineus: these are different.
They have no wings, and are all black, and snore,
And drops ooze from their eyes, and the rags they wear   40
Unutterably filthy. What country could
Have given such creatures birth, I cannot tell.
Apollo is the master of this house,
So let him look to it, healer, interpreter,
Himself of other houses purifier.

[The inside of the temple is revealed, as described, with APOLLO *and* HERMES *standing beside* ORESTES.*]*

Apollo
I will keep faith, at all times vigilant,
Whether at your side or far away, and never
Mild to your enemies, whom you now see
Subdued by sleep, these unloved virgins, these
Children hoary with age, whose company   50
Is shunned by God and man and beast, being born
For evil, just as the abyss from which they come
Is evil, the bottomless pit of Tartarus.
Yet you must fly before them, hotly pursued,
Past island cities and over distant seas,
Enduring all without faltering, until
You find sanctuary in Athena's citadel,
And there, embracing her primeval image, you
Shall stand trial, and after healing words
From me, who commanded you to kill your mother,   60
You shall be set free and win your salvation.

Orestes
O Lord Apollo, you have both wisdom and power,
And, since you have them, use them on my behalf!

Apollo
Remember, endure and have no fear! And you,
Hermes, go with him, guide him, guard his steps,

An outcast from mankind, yet blest of Zeus.
[Exeunt HERMES *and* ORESTES. *Enter the ghost of* CLYTEMNESTRA.*]*

Clytemnestra
Oho! asleep! What good are you to me asleep?
While I, deserted and humiliated,
Wander, a homeless ghost. I warn you that
Among the other spirits of the dead   70
(The taunt of murder does not lose its sting
In the dark world below) I am the accused
And not the accuser, with none to defend me,
Brutally slain by matricidal hands.
Look on these scars, and remember all
The wineless offerings which I laid upon
The hearth for you at many a solemn midnight—
All now forgotten, all trampled underfoot!
And *he* is gone! Light as a fawn he skipped
Out of your snare and now he laughs at you.   80
Oh hear me! I am pleading for my soul!
O goddesses of the underworld, awake!
I, Clytemnestra, call you now in dreams!

Chorus
Mu!

Clytemnestra
Ah, you may mew, but he is fled and gone.
He has protectors who are no friends of mine.

Chorus
Mu!

Clytemnestra
Still so drowsy, still so pitiless?
Orestes has escaped, the matricide!

Chorus
Oh, no!   90

Clytemnestra
Still muttering and mumbling in your sleep!
Arise, do evil! is not that your task?

Chorus
Oh, oh!

Clytemnestra
How sleep and weariness have made common cause
To disenvenom the foul dragon's rage!

Chorus
Oh, oh! where is the scent? Let us mark it down!

Clytemnestra

Yes, you may bay like an unerring hound,
But still you are giving chase only in your dreams.
What are you doing? Rise, slothful slugabeds,
Stung by the scourge of my rebukes, arise   100
And blow about his head your bloody breath,
Consume his flesh in bellifuls of fire!
Come on, renew the chase and hunt him down!
[*Exit.*]

Chorus

We have been put to shame! What has befallen us?
The game has leapt out of the snare and gone.
In slumber laid low, we let slip the prey.

Aha, son of Zeus! pilferer, pillager!
A God, to steal away the matricide!
A youth to flout powers fixed long ago!

In dream I felt beneath the heart a swift   110
Charioteer's sharp lash.
Under the ribs, under the flank
It rankles yet, red and sore,
Like the public scourger's blow.

This is the doing of the younger gods.
Dripping with death, red drops
Cover the heel, cover the head.
Behold the earth's navel-stone
Thick with heavy stains of blood!

His own prophetic cell he has himself defiled,   120
Honoring mortal claims, reckless of laws divine,
And dealing death to Fates born of old.
He injures us and yet *him* he shall never free,
Not in the depths of hell, never shall he have rest
But suffer lasting torment below.

Apollo

Out, out! Be off, and clear this holy place
Of your foul presence, or else from my golden bow
Shall spring a snake of silver and bite so deep
That from your swollen bellies you shall spew
The blood which you have sucked! Your place is where   130
Heads drop beneath the axe, eyes are gouged out,
Throats slit, and men are stoned, limbs lopped, and boys
Gelded, and a last whimper heard from spines
Spiked writhing in the dust. Such celebrations,
Which fill heaven with loathing, are your delight.

Off with you, I say, and go unshepherded,
A herd shunned with universal horror!

Chorus
O Lord Apollo, hear us in our turn!
You are not an abettor in this business.
You are the culprit. On you lies the whole guilt.   140

Apollo
Explain yourselves. How do you make that out?

Chorus
It was at your command that he killed his mother.

Apollo
I commanded him to take vengeance for his father.

Chorus
So promising the acceptance of fresh blood.

Apollo
I promised to absolve him from it here.

Chorus
Why do you insult the band that drove him here?

Apollo
This mansion is not fit for your company.

Chorus
But this is the task that has been appointed to us.

Apollo
What is this privilege that you are so proud of?

Chorus
To drive all matricides from hearth and home.   150

Apollo
And what of a woman who has killed her husband?

Chorus
That is not manslaughter within the kin.

Apollo
So then you set at naught the marriage-bond
Sealed by Zeus and Hera, and yet what tie
Is stronger, joined by Fate and watched over
By Justice, than the joy which Aphrodite
Has given to man and woman? If you let those
Who violate that covenant go unpunished,
You have no right to persecute Orestes.

Why anger here, and there passivity? 160
On this in time Athena shall pass judgment.

Chorus
We shall give chase and never let him go.

Apollo
Pursue him then, and make trouble for yourselves.

Chorus
No words of yours can circumscribe our powers.

Apollo
I would not have your powers even as a gift.

Chorus
Then take your proud stand by the throne of Zeus.
Meanwhile a mother's blood is beckoning to us,
And we must go and follow up the trail.

Apollo
And I will still safeguard the suppliant.
A wrong unheard-of in heaven and on earth 170
Would be his protest, if I should break faith.
[A year passes. Before a shrine of Athena at Athens. Enter ORESTES.*]*

Orestes
O Queen Athena, I have come here in obedience
To the Lord Apollo. Grant me sanctuary,
An outcast, yet with hands no longer sullied, for
The edge of my pollution has been worn
Off on countless paths over land and sea;
And now, in accordance with his word, present
Before your image, I entreat you to
Receive me here and pass the final judgment.

Chorus
Step where our dumb informer leads the way; 180
For as the hounds pursue a wounded fawn,
So do we dog the trail of human blood.
How far we have traveled over land and sea,
Faint and footsore but never to be shaken off!
He must be somewhere here, for I smell blood.

—Beware, I say, beware!
Look on all sides for fear he find some escape!
—Ah, here he is, desperate,
Clasping that image awaiting trial.
—It cannot be! The mother's blood 190
That he has spilt is irrecoverable.
—Ravenous lips shall feed upon his living flesh

And on his blood—a lush pasturage.
—And others shall he see in hell, who wronged
Parents, guests or gods;
For Hades is a stern inquisitor of souls,
Recording all things till the hour of judgment.

Orestes
Taught by long suffering, I have learnt at what
Times it is right to keep silence and when
To break it, and in this matter a wise   200
Instructor has charged me to speak. The stain
Of matricide has been washed out in the flow
Of swine's blood by Apollo. I could tell
Of many who have given me lodging and no
Harm has befallen them from my company;
And now with lips made pure I call upon
Athena to protect me and so join
Our peoples as allies for all time to come.
Wherever she may be, on Libyan shores
Or by the stream of Trito, where she came   210
To birth, or like a captain keeping watch
On the heights of Phlegra against some enemy,
O may she come—far off, she can still hear me—
And from my sufferings deliver me!

Chorus
Neither Apollo nor Athena can
Save your soul from perdition, a feast for fiends.
Have you no answer? Do you spurn us so,
Fattened for us, our consecrated host?

Let us dance and declare in tune with this grim music the laws which it is ours
to enforce on the life of man. It is only those that have blood on their hands who
need fear us at all, but from them without fail we exact retribution.

Mother Night, your children cry! Hear, black Night!   220
It is ours to deal by day and dark night judgment.
The young god Apollo has rescued the matricide!
    Over the blood that has been shed
    Maddening dance, melody desperate, deathly,
    Chant to bind the soul in hell,
    Spell that parches flesh to dust.

This the Fates who move the whole world through
Have assigned to us, a task for all future ages,
To keep watch on all hands that drip red with kindred blood.
    Over the blood that has been shed   230
    Maddening dance, melody desperate, deathly,
    Chant to bind the soul in hell,
    Spell that parches flesh to dust.

Such are the powers appointed us from the beginning,
None of the Gods of Olympus to eat with us, while we
Take no part in the wearing of white—no,
Other pleasures are our choice—
    Wrecking the house, hunting the man,
    Hard on his heels ever we run,
    And though his feet be swift we waste and wear him out.   240

Hence it is thanks to our zealous endeavor that from such
Offices Zeus and the Gods are exempted, and yet he
Shuns us because we are covered in blood, not
Fit to share his majesty.
    Wrecking the house, hunting the man,
    Hard on his heels ever we run,
    And though his feet be swift we waste and wear him out.

Glories of men, how bright in the day is their splendor,
Yet shall they fade in the darkness of hell,
Faced with our grisly attire and dancing   250
Feet attuned to sombre melodies.
    Nimble the feet leap in the air,
    Skip and descend down to the ground,
    Fugitive step suddenly tripped up in fatal confusion.

Caught without knowing he stumbles, his wickedness blinds him,
Such is the cloud of pollution that hangs
Over him and on his house, remembered
Many generations after him.
    Nimble the feet leap in the air,
    Skip and descend down to the ground,   260
    Fugitive step suddenly tripped up in fatal confusion.

Our task is such. With long memories
We keep constant watch on human sin.
What others spurn is what we prize,
Our heaven their hell, a region of trackless waste,
Both for the quick and dead, for blind and seeing too.

What wonder then that men bow in dread
At these commandments assigned to us
By Fate—our ancient privilege?
We are not without our own honors and dignities,   270
Though we reside in hell's unfathomable gloom.
[Enter ATHENA.*]*

Athena
I heard a distant cry, as I was standing
Beside Scamander to take possession of

The lands which the Achaean princes have
Bestowed on my people in perpetuity;
And thence I have made my way across the sea
In wingless flight; and now, as I regard
Before my shrine this very strange company,
I cannot but ask, in wonder, not in fear,
Who you may be. I address you all in common,   280
This stranger here who is seated at my image,
And you, who are not human in appearance
Nor yet divine; but rather than speak ill
Without just cause let me receive your answer.

Chorus
Daughter of Zeus, your question is soon answered.
We are the dismal daughters of dark Night,
Called Curses in the palaces of hell.

Athena
I know your names then and your parentage.

Chorus
And now let us inform you of our powers.

Athena
Yes, let me know what office you perform.   290

Chorus
We drive the matricide from hearth and home.

Athena
Where? In what place does his persecution end?

Chorus
A place where joy is something quite unknown.

Athena
Is that your hue and cry against this man?

Chorus
Yes, because he dared to kill his mother.

Athena
Was he driven to it perhaps against his will?

Chorus
What force could drive a man to matricide?

Athena
It is clear there are two parties to this case.

Chorus
We challenged him to an ordeal by oath.

Athena

You seem to seek only the semblance of justice.   300

Chorus

How so? Explain, since you are so rich in wisdom.

Athena

Do not use oaths to make the wrong prevail.

Chorus

Then try the case yourself and give your judgment.

Athena

Will you entrust the verdict to my charge?

Chorus

Yes, a worthy daughter of a worthy father.

Athena

Stranger, what is your answer? Tell us first
Your fatherland and family and what
Misfortune overtook you, and then answer
The charge against you. If you have taken your stand
Here as a suppliant with full confidence   310
In the justice of your cause, now is the time
To render on each count a clear reply.

Orestes

O Queen Athena, first let me remove one doubt.
I am not a suppliant seeking purification.
I was already cleansed before I took
This image in my arms, and I can give
Evidence of this. The manslayer is required
To keep silent until he has been anointed
With sacrificial blood. That has been done,
And I have traveled far over land and sea   320
To wear off the pollution. So, having set
Your mind at rest, let me tell you who I am.
I come from Argos, and my father's name—
For asking me that I thank you—was Agamemnon,
The great commander, with whom not long ago
You wiped out Troy. He died an evil death,
Murdered on his return by my blackhearted
Mother, who netted him in a bath of blood.
And therefore I, restored from banishment,
In retribution for my father's death,   330
I killed my mother; and yet not I alone—
Apollo too must answer for it, having
Warned me what anguish would afflict me if
I should fail to take vengeance on the guilty.
Whether it was just or not, do you decide.

Athena
This is too grave a case for mortal minds,
Nor is it right that I should judge an act
Of blood shed with such bitter consequences,
Especially since you have come to me
As one already purified, who has done no wrong   340
Against this city. But your opponents here
Are not so gentle, and, if their plea
Should be rejected, the poison dripping from
Their angry bosoms will devastate my country.
The issue is such that, whether I let them stay
Or turn them out, it is fraught with injury.
But be it so. Since it has come to this,
I will appoint judges for homicide,
A court set up in perpetuity.
Do you prepare your proofs and witnesses,   350
Then I, having selected from my people
The best, will come to pass a final judgment.
[Exit.]

Chorus
Now the world shall see the downfall of old commandments made
Long ago, if the accurst matricide should win his case.
Many a bitter blow awaits parents from their own children in the times to come.

We who had the task to watch over human life shall now
Cease to act, giving free rein to deeds of violence.
Crime shall spread from house to house like a plague, and whole cities shall be
    desolate.

Then let no man stricken cry
Out in imprecation, "Oh   360
Furies!" Thus shall fathers groan,
Thus shall mothers weep in vain,
Since the house of righteousness
Lies in ruins, overthrown.

Times there are when fear is good,
Keeping watch within the soul.
Needful too are penalties.
Who of those that have not nursed
Wholesome dread within them can
Show respect to righteousness?   370

Choose a life despot-free, yet restrained by rule of law.
God has appointed the mean as the master in all things.
Wickedness breeds pride, but from wisdom is brought forth
Happiness prayed for by all men.

So, we say, men must bow down before the shrine of Right.
Those who defy it shall fail; for the ancient commandments
Stand—to respect parents and honor the stranger.
Only the righteous shall prosper.
The man who does what is right by choice, not constraint,
Shall prosper always; the seed of just men shall never perish.   380
Not so the captain who ships a load of ill-gotten gains.
Caught in the gathering storm his proud sail shall be torn from the masthead.

He cries to deaf ears, no longer able to ride
The gale, and meanwhile his guardian spirit is close beside him
And scoffs to see him despair of ever again making port,
Dashed on the reefs of Justice, unlooked-on and unlamented.
[Enter ATHENA *with the* JUDGES, *followed by citizens of Athens.]*

Athena
Herald, give orders to hold the people back,
Then sound the trumpet and proclaim silence,
For while this new tribunal is being enrolled,
It is right that all should ponder on its laws,   390
Both the litigants here whose case is to be judged,
And my whole people for all generations.
[Enter APOLLO.*]*

Chorus
Apollo, what is there here that concerns you?
We say you have no authority in this matter.

Apollo
I come both as a witness, the accused
Having been a suppliant at my sanctuary
And purified of homicide at my hands,
And also to be tried with him, for I too
Must answer for the murder of his mother.
Open the case, and judge as you know how.   400

Athena
The case is open. You shall be first to speak.
[To the CHORUS.*]*
The prosecutors shall take precedence
And first inform us truthfully of the facts.

Chorus
Many in number, we shall be brief in speech.
We beg you to answer our questions one by one.
First, is it true that you killed your mother?

Orestes
I killed her. That is true, and not denied.

Chorus
So then the first of the three rounds is ours.

Orestes
You should not boast that you have thrown me yet.

Chorus
Next, since you killed her, you must tell us how.   410

Orestes
Yes, with a drawn sword leveled at the throat.

Chorus
Who was it who impelled or moved you to it?

Orestes
The oracle of this God who is my witness.

Chorus
The God of prophecy ordered matricide?

Orestes
Yes, and I have not repented it to this day.

Chorus
You *will* repent it, when you have been condemned.

Orestes
My father shall defend me from the grave.

Chorus
Having killed your mother, you may well trust the dead!

Orestes
She was polluted by a double crime.

Chorus
How so? Explain your meaning to the judges.   420

Orestes
She killed her husband and she killed my father.

Chorus
She died without bloodguilt, and you still live.

Orestes
Why did you not hunt her when she was alive?

Chorus
She was not bound by blood to the man she killed.

Orestes
And am I then bound by blood to my mother?

Chorus

Abandoned wretch, how did she nourish you
Within the womb? Do you repudiate
The nearest and dearest tie of motherhood?

Orestes

Apollo, give your evidence. I confess
That I did this deed as I have said.   430
Pronounce your judgment: was it justly done?

Apollo

Athena's appointed judges, I say to you,
Justly, and I, as prophet, cannot lie.
Never from my prophetic shrine have I
Said anything of city, man or woman
But what my father Zeus has commanded me.
This plea of mine must override all others,
Since it accords with our great father's will.

Chorus

Your argument is, then, that Zeus commanded you
To charge Orestes with this criminal act   440
Regardless of the bond between son and mother?

Apollo

It is not the same, to murder a great king,
A woman too to do it, and not in open
Fight like some brave Amazon, but in such
Manner as I shall now inform this court.
On his return from battle, bringing home
A balance for the greater part of good,
She welcomed him with fine words and then, while
He bathed, pavilioned him in a purple robe
And struck him down and killed him—a man and king   450
Whom the whole world had honored. Such was the crime
For which she paid. Let the judges take note.

Chorus

According to your argument Zeus gives
Precedence to the father; yet Zeus it was
Who cast into prison his own father Kronos.
Judges, take note, and ask him to explain.

Apollo

Abominable monsters, loathed by gods
And men, do you not understand that chains
Can be unfastened and prison doors unlocked?
But once the dust has drunk a dead man's blood,   460
He can never rise again—for that no remedy
Has been appointed by our almighty Father,

Although all else he can overturn at will
Without so much effort as a single breath.

Chorus
See what your plea for the defendant means.
Is this not what he did—to spill his mother's
Blood on the ground? And shall he then be allowed
To live on in his father's house? What public
Altar can he approach and where find fellowship?

Apollo
The mother is not a parent, only the nurse   470
Of the seed which the true parent, the father,
Commits to her as to a stranger to
Keep it with God's help safe from harm. And I
Have proof of this. There can be a father
Without a mother. We have a witness here,
This daughter of Olympian Zeus, who sprang
Armed from her father's head, a goddess whom
No goddess could have brought to birth. Therefore,
Out of goodwill to your country and your people
I sent this suppliant to seek refuge with you,   480
That you, Athena, may find in him and his
A faithful ally for all time to come.

Athena
Enough has now been spoken. Are you agreed
That I call on the judges to record
Their votes justly according to their conscience?

Apollo
Our quiver is empty, every arrow spent.
We wait to hear the issue of the trial.

Athena
And has my ruling your approval too?

Chorus
Sirs, you have heard the case, and now declare
Judgment according to your solemn oath.   490

Athena
Citizens of Athens, hear my declaration
At this first trial in the history of man.
This great tribunal shall remain in power
Meeting in solemn session on this hill,
Where long ago the Amazons encamped
When they made war on Theseus, and sacrificed
To Ares—hence its name. Here reverence
For law and inbred fear among my people

Shall hold their hands from evil night and day,
Only let them not tamper with the laws, 500
But keep the fountain pure and sweet to drink.
I warn you not to banish from your lives
All terror but to seek the mean between
Autocracy and anarchy; and in this way
You shall possess in ages yet unborn
An impregnable fortress of liberty
Such as no people has throughout the world.
With these words I establish this tribunal
Grave, quick to anger, incorruptible,
And always vigilant over those that sleep. 510
Let the judges now rise and cast their votes.

Chorus
We charge you to remember that we have
Great power to harm, and vote accordingly.

Apollo
I charge you to respect the oracles
Sanctioned by Zeus and see that they are fulfilled.

Chorus
By interfering in what is not your office
You have desecrated your prophetic shrine.

Apollo
Then was my Father also at fault when he
Absolved Ixion, the first murderer?

Chorus
Keep up your chatter, but, if our cause should fail, 520
We shall lay on this people a heavy hand.

Apollo
Yes, you will lose your case, and then you may
Spit out your poison, but it will do no harm.

Chorus
Insolent youth mocks venerable age.
We await the verdict, ready to let loose
Against this city our destructive rage.

Athena
The final judgment rests with me, and I
Announce that my vote shall be given to Orestes.
No mother gave me birth, and in all things
Save marriage I commend with all my heart 530
The masculine, my father's child indeed.
Therefore I cannot hold in higher esteem
A woman killed because she killed her husband.

If the votes are equal, Orestes wins.
Let the appointed officers proceed
To empty the urns and count the votes.

Orestes
O bright Apollo, how shall the judgment go?

Chorus
O black mother Night, are you watching this?

Orestes
My hour has come—the halter or the light.

Chorus
And ours—to exercise our powers or perish.   540

Apollo
Sirs, I adjure you to count carefully.
If judgment errs, great harm will come of it,
Whereas one vote may raise a fallen house.

Athena
He stands acquitted on the charge of bloodshed,
The human votes being equally divided.

Orestes
Lady Athena, my deliverer,
I was an outcast from my country, now
I can go home again and live once more
In my parental heritage, thanks to you
And to Apollo and to the third, the Savior,   550
Who governs the whole world. Before I go
I give my word to you and to your people
For all posterity that no commander
Shall lead an Argive army in war against
This city. If any should violate this pledge,
Out of the graves which shall then cover us
We would arise with adverse omens to
Obstruct and turn them back. If, however,
They keep this covenant and stand by your side,
They shall always have our blessing. And so farewell!   560
May you and your people always prevail
Against the assaults of all your enemies!
[Exit.]

Chorus
Oho, you junior gods, since you have trod under foot
The laws of old and robbed us of our powers,
We shall afflict this country
With damp contagion, bleak and barren, withering up the soil,
Mildew on bud and birth abortive. Venomous pestilence

Shall sweep your cornlands with infectious death.
To weep?—No! To work? Yes! To work ill and lay low the people!
So will the maids of Night mourn for their stolen honors. 570

Athena
Let me persuade you to forget your grief!
You are not defeated. The issue of the trial
Has been determined by an equal vote.
It was Zeus himself who plainly testified
That Orestes must not suffer for what he did.
I beg you, therefore, do not harm my country,
Blasting her crops with drops of rank decay
And biting cankers in the early buds.
Rather accept my offer to stay and live
In a cavern on this hill and there receive 580
The adoration of my citizens.

Chorus
Oho, you junior gods, etc.

Athena
No, *not* dishonored, and therefore spare my people!
I too confide in Zeus—why speak of that?—
And I alone of all the Olympian gods
Know of the keys which guard the treasury
Of heaven's thunder. But there is no need of that.
Let my persuasion serve to calm your rage.
Reside with me and share my majesty;
And when from these wide acres you enjoy 590
Year after year the harvest offerings
From couples newly-wed praying for children,
Then you will thank me for my intercession.

Chorus
How can you treat us so?
Here to dwell, ever debased, defiled!
Hear our passion, hear, black Night!
For the powers once ours, sealed long, long ago
Have by the junior gods been all snatched away.

Athena
You are my elders, and therefore I indulge
Your passion. And yet, though not so wise as you, 600
To me too Zeus has granted understanding.
If you refuse me and depart, believe me,
This country will yet prove your heart's desire,
For as the centuries pass so there will flow
Such glory to my people as will assure
To all divinities worshipped here by men
And women gathered on festive holidays

More honors than could be yours in any other
City throughout the world. And so, I beg you,
Keep from my citizens the vicious spur   610
Of internecine strife, which pricks the breast
Of manhood flown with passion as with wine!
Abroad let battle rage for every heart
That is fired with love of glory—that shall be theirs
In plenty. So this is my offer to you—
To give honor and receive it and to share
My glory in this country loved by heaven.

Chorus
How can you, etc.

Athena
I will not weary in my benedictions,
Lest it should ever be said that you, so ancient   620
In your divinity, were driven away
By me and by my mortal citizens.
No, if Persuasion's holy majesty,
The sweet enchantment of these lips divine,
Has power to move you, please, reside with me.
But, if you still refuse, then, since we have made
This offer to you, it would be wrong to lay
Your hands upon us in such bitter rage.
Again, I tell you, it is in your power to own
This land attended with the highest honors.   630

Chorus
Lady Athena, what do you offer us?

Athena
A dwelling free of sorrow. Pray accept.

Chorus
Say we accept, what privileges shall we have?

Athena
No family shall prosper without your grace.

Chorus
Will you ensure us this prerogative?

Athena
I will, and bless all those that worship you.

Chorus
And pledge that assurance for all time to come?

Athena
I need not promise what I will not perform.

Chorus

Your charms are working, and our rage subsides.

Athena

Here make your dwelling, where you shall win friends.   640

Chorus

What song then shall we chant in salutation?

Athena

A song of faultless victory—from land and sea,
From skies above let gentle breezes blow
And breathing sunshine float from shore to shore;
Let crops and cattle increase and multiply
And children grow in health and happiness,
And let the righteous prosper; for I, as one
Who tends flowers in a garden, cherish fondly
The seed that bears no sorrow. That is your part,
While I in many a battle shall strive until   650
This city stands victorious against all
Its enemies and renowned throughout the world.

Chorus

We accept; we agree to dwell with you
Here in Athens, which by grace of Zeus
Stands a fortress for the gods,
Jeweled crown of Hellas. So
With you now we join in prayer
That smiling suns and fruitful soils unite to yield
Lifelong joy, fortune fair,
Light and darkness reconciled.   660

Athena

For the good of my people I have given homes in the city to these deities, whose power is so great and so slowly appeased; and, whenever a man falls foul of them, apprehended to answer for the sins of his fathers, he shall be brought to judgment before them, and the dust shall stifle his proud boast.

Chorus

Free from blight may the early blossom deck
Budding trees, and may no parching drought
Spread across the waving fields.
Rather Pan in season grant
From the flocks and herds a full
Return from year to year, and from the rich
Store which these gods vouchsafe
May the Earth repay them well!

Athena

Guardians of my city, listen to the blessings they bring, and remember that their 670 power is great in heaven and hell, and on earth too they bring to some glad music and to some lives darkened with weeping.

Chorus
Free from sudden death that cuts
Short the prime of manhood, blest
In your daughters too, to whom
Be granted husband and home, and may the dread Fates
Keep them safe, present in every household,
Praised and magnified in every place!

Athena
Fair blessings indeed from powers that so lately were averted in anger, and I thank Zeus and the spirit of persuasion that at last there is no strife left between us, except that they vie with me in blessing my people.

Chorus
Peace to all, free from that
Root of evil, civil strife!
May they live in unity,   680
And never more may the blood of kin be let flow!
Rather may all of them bonded together
Feel and act as one in love and hate!

Athena
From these dread shapes, so quick to learn a new music, I foresee great good for my people, who, if only they repay their favors with the reverence due, shall surely establish the reign of justice in a city that will shine as a light for all mankind.
[Enter ESCORT OF WOMEN, *carrying crimson robes and torches.]*

Chorus
Joy to you all in your justly appointed riches,
Joy to all the people blest
With the Virgin's love, who stands
Next beside her Father's throne!
Wisdom man has learnt at last.
Under her protection this   690
Land enjoys the grace of Zeus.

Athena
Joy to you also, and now let me lead you in torchlight to your new dwelling place! Let solemn oblations speed you in joy to your home beneath the earth, and there imprison all harm while still letting flow your blessings!

Chorus
Joy to you, joy, yet again we pronounce our blessing.
Joy to all the citizens,
Gods and mortals both alike.
While you hold this land and pay

Homage to our residence,
You shall have no cause to blame
Chance and change in human life.

Athena

I thank you for your gracious salutations,   700
And now you shall be escorted in the light
Of torches to your subterranean dwelling,
Attended by the sacristans of my temple
Together with this company of girls
And married women and others bowed with years.
Women, let them put on these robes of crimson,
And let these blazing torches light the way,
That the goodwill of our new co-residents
Be shown in the manly prowess of your sons!
[The CHORUS *put on the crimson robes and a procession is formed led by young men
in armor, with the* CHORUS *and the escort following, and behind them the citizens
of Athens. The rest is sung as the procession moves away.]*

Chorus of the Escort

Pass on your way, O powers majestic,   710
Daughters of darkness in happy procession!
People of Athens, hush, speak fair!

Pass to the caverns of earth immemorial
There to be worshipped in honor and glory!
People of Athens, hush, speak fair!

Gracious and kindly of heart to our people,
Come with us, holy ones, hither in gladness,
Follow the lamps that illumine the way!
O sing at the end alleluia!

Peace to you, peace of a happy community,   720
People of Athens! Zeus who beholds all
Watches, himself with the Fates reconciled.
O sing at the end alleluia!

Orestes and Iphigenia

In the *Eumenides,* Orestes disappears immediately after the jury returns its verdict exonerating him, for Aeschylus is less interested in the young man's individual fate than he is in promoting Zeus's supremacy. Other poets, however, wrote extensively of Orestes's subsequent adventures, in several cases adapting the myths in a way that settles old scores involving Agamemnon and the Trojan War.

According to Euripides's play *Iphigenia in Tauris,* when Orestes asks Apollo how to rid himself of the madness that (in spite of the Furies' domestication) still plagues him, the god directs him to Tauris (in modern Turkey), where he is to find and retrieve an ancient statue of Artemis. When Orestes and Pylades (Figure 15-13) arrive in Tauris they are immediately imprisoned, for it is the local custom to sacrifice all strangers to their goddess. Brought before the high priestess of Artemis (Figure 15-14), the two captives discover that she is none other than Orestes's sister Iphigenia, whom the goddess had spirited away at the moment the priest at Aulis was about to cut her throat. Reunited, the two siblings carry off Artemis's statue and, with Pylades, attempt to escape by ship. As Thoas, king of the region, is about to capture them, Athene suddenly appears to effect their safe return to Greece, where they build a temple to Artemis in Attica.

FIGURE 15-13   Orestes and Pylades. Orestes's constant companion, Pylades is the son of Strophius, king of Phocis, and his wife, Anaxibia, sister of Agamemnon. Because he speaks only once in the *Oresteia,* his single line—to remember Apollo's command—has unique force. After accompanying Orestes on his wanderings, Pylades eventually marries his friend's sister Electra. This marble group expresses the quality of heroic friendship that characterizes their myth. (*Louvre, Paris.*)

FIGURE 15-14   Artemis. Just as her brother Apollo plays a major role in promoting Orestes's filial duty in avenging his male parent, so Artemis figures prominently in the life of Agamemnon's virgin daughter, Iphigenia. Abhorring human sacrifice, Artemis (in one version of the story) intervenes at the moment Iphigenia is about to be killed, spiriting the girl away and leaving a deer in her place. In Euripides's *Iphigenia in Tauris,* the goddess installs Iphigenia as her priestess among a barbarian tribe (the Tauri), where custom demands that all strangers be sacrificed. Artemis manipulates events so that Iphigenia, Orestes, and Pylades escape to their homeland. This Roman work, known as *Diana of Versailles* (possibly copied from a Greek original), shows the goddess in her paradoxical function as both protector of wild creatures, such as the deer she shields with her left hand, and patron of the hunt, pictured by the arrows she draws from a quiver with her right hand. (*Louvre, Paris.*)

Other episodes in the Orestes myth deal with his marriage and return to Argos. When Orestes was still an infant, Agamemnon had engaged his son to Hermione, daughter of Helen and Menelaus, but at Troy, Menelaus broke his word and married the girl instead to Neoptolemus (Pyrrhus), the only son of Achilles. After returning from Tauris, the adult Orestes visits Hermione at Sparta while Neoptolemus is at Delphi consulting the Oracle. Reenacting the elopement of Helen and Paris, Orestes abducts Hermione, taking her to Delphi, where, on her advice, he arranges Neoptolemus's death by provoking a riot in which his rival is killed. In the fates of their respective sons, the old argument between Achilles and Agamemnon dramatized in the *Iliad*'s opening scenes is at last settled to the latter's dynastic advantage.

In the final part of his mythic cycle, Orestes eventually succeeds to the throne of both Argos and Sparta, uniting the kingdoms of Agamemnon and Menelaus. When a plague devastates Sparta, the Oracle states that the epidemic will abate only when the cities of Asia Minor destroyed in the Trojan War are rebuilt. Orestes accordingly founds new colonies on the sites of the ruined cities, restoring the shrines of their respective gods and thus ameliorating the divine displeasure that had cursed the Greeks for their violations of holy places during the war. The murderous violence that had afflicted the House of Atreus for generations ends with Orestes: myth grants the son of Agamemnon and Clytemnestra a reign of seventy years and a peaceful death at age ninety.

Questions for Discussion and Review

1. Compare Aeschylus's treatment of the Agamemnon-Clytemnestra conflict with Homer's account in the *Odyssey* (books 1 and 11). What new themes or elements does Aeschylus add to the story?

2. What inspires Clytemnestra's monumental hatred of her husband? How does Aeschylus present her side of the issue? Why does Aegisthus also seek revenge on Agamemnon?

3. Define Orestes's dilemma in the *Libation-Bearers*. Do you think that Aeschylus's original audience would agree that Orestes made the right choice in obeying Apollo's command? Why does the chorus side with Orestes and Electra, and why are its members unable to see the Furies when they appear to Orestes?

4. The myth of the House of Atreus emphasizes family violence and dysfunctional relationships. Do you think that Freud's theory of the domestic psychodrama applies to the power struggles in the *Agamemnon* and *Libation-Bearers*? Describe the elements of love and hate in the relations between Agamemnon, Clytemnestra, Iphigenia, Electra, and Orestes.

5. In the *Eumenides,* Aeschylus presents ideas and traditions in fierce opposition. How would you apply the structuralist theory of interpreting myth to the religious and social divisions embodied in the Furies and Apollo? What mediating function does Athene serve in reconciling the Furies to the new Olympian order? Do the characters give the traditional feminine principle sufficient credit?

Recommended Reading

Goldhill, Simon. *Aeschylus: The* Oresteia. New York: Cambridge UP, 1992.

Tyrrell, William B., and Frieda S. Brown. *Athenian Myths and Institutions.* New York: Oxford UP, 1991. Offers a perceptive feminist analysis of the *Oresteia.*

Zak, William F. *The Polis and the Divine Order: The* Oresteia, *Sophocles, and the Defense of Democracy.* Lewisburg: Bucknell UP, 1995.

The Tragic Hero: Sophocles's *Oedipus*

KEY THEMES

One of the most popular playwrights of his age, Sophocles was a prolific writer, whose plays (seven of which survive) encompass a wide variety of tragic experiences. His three plays on the myth of Oedipus have stimulated debate among critics from Aristotle's time to the present. Oedipus Rex *(which means "Oedipus the King," the Latin title of the play called* Oedipus Tyrannus) *presents the hero in pursuit of the riddle of his identity. Oedipus, who thought he had long since escaped the fate decreed by the oracle, discovers that he has indeed killed his father and married his mother. The play is a complex study of the human psyche, with all its innermost secrets bared and its conflicting philosophical and metaphysical dimensions explored.* Oedipus at Colonus *follows the story as Oedipus, at the end of his long exile, comes to the seat of the Eumenides and fulfills the "awful destiny" as prophesied.*

The World of Sophocles

Born in approximately 496 B.C., Sophocles lived for ninety years through a remarkable century in the history of ancient Greece. The development of democracy, the rise of Athens to a position of political and cultural preeminence, the achievements of Greek artists, architects, writers, philosophers, and mathematicians all contributed to the sense of pride and the spirit of optimism that prevailed throughout what is commonly called the *classical age* of Greece.

The Athenian constitution had established what its citizens believed to be rational mechanisms for governing society, for preventing special-interest groups or individuals from gaining too much power, and for procuring justice, as Aeschylus's celebration of the jury system in his play the *Eumenides* attests. But even such careful

planning could not prevent abuses within the system or external conflicts. The Peloponnesian War between Sparta and Athens and their respective allies, which erupted
in 431 B.C., shattered many illusions, as rival political and economic factions took
advantage of the war-generated anxiety and confusion to expand their own positions
and power. Just as the myths describe people turning to their heroes to protect them
in times of crisis, so the Athenians turned to their generals, who sometimes served
them well (as did **Pericles** [PER-ik-leez]) and sometimes betrayed them (as did the
highly popular Alcibiades, who, rejected by a more conservative faction, sold out to
the Spartans). But even before these unnerving events, the rapid pace of cultural
changes led people to reexamine their traditional perspectives on human experience
and the relationship of humans to the gods. Already, confidence in a rationally ordered world was beginning to falter. In the work of playwrights like Sophocles, we
can see those questions beginning to emerge, a slightly dissonant voice running in
tense counterpoint to the upbeat public music of conventional attitudes and beliefs.
It is at just such a transitional moment—when trust in the centrality of human experience perseveres alongside a growing distrust in the commitment of the gods to
act accordingly—that tragedy of the kind we witness in the Oedipus plays becomes
especially relevant.

Sophocles: The Citizen and Writer

Sophocles himself actively participated in the life, both political and artistic, of his
time, serving in various elected offices and writing more than 125 plays, often in
competition with his older contemporary Aeschylus and younger contemporary Euripides. A highly successful playwright, he won first prize in the dramatic competition
twenty times, and after his death a hero cult was founded in his name.

Of Sophocles's many plays, only seven have survived, among them the three plays
on the family of **Oedipus** [E-dih-puhs]. Unlike Aeschylus's Oresteian trilogy, the
three plays were not written as a set and presented simultaneously—forty years separated the earliest (*Antigone*) from the last (*Oedipus at Colonus*). Nor were they written
in chronological order: *Antigone,* the first of the three to be written, is the last in the
narrative sequence, picking up the story of **Antigone**'s [an-TIG-oh-nee] defiance of
her uncle, **Creon** [KREE-on], and her subsequent martyrdom. Her story is set in the
aftermath of the civil war between Oedipus's sons, **Eteocles** [e-TEE-oh-kleez] and
Polynices [pol-ih-NYE-seez], that followed the death of Oedipus, which is depicted
in Sophocles's last play, *Oedipus at Colonus.* And not only do the plot details, charac-
terizations, and ideas and attitudes differ among the three, but also the approach to
tragedy as a mode of defining human experience changes from one play to the next.

Oedipus Rex

Perhaps no classical Greek play has stimulated as much critical discussion and debate,
beginning with the philosopher Aristotle, as has Sophocles's *Oedipus Rex.* The exact
date of *Oedipus Rex* is uncertain, but most scholars place it between 429 and 425 B.C.
Shortly earlier, in 430 B.C., plague had broken out in Athens, perhaps a result of
overcrowding and stress on the sanitation systems when people, seeking safety during

the Peloponnesian War, crowded into the city. The Athenian audience would have recognized the description of the plague in Thebes in the opening scene of the play as immediately relevant to their own contemporary experience.

Psychological Dimensions

The psychoanalyst Sigmund Freud argued that *Oedipus Rex* is relevant—to all audiences—for another reason as well. Every male child, Freud believed, unconsciously desires to kill his father and to marry his mother, being psychologically predetermined to have such desires simply because he is a human male. The Greek gods, of course, committed with impunity such acts as castrating a father or marrying a sister. For humans, however, these universally forbidden impulses must not be either openly expressed or even consciously acknowledged, and the resulting tension may give rise to a form of neurosis that Freud named, after Sophocles's protagonist, the *Oedipus complex* (see Chapter 2). Whether or not Freud's theories are universal or even valid, it is clear that Sophocles and his audience had a keen interest in human psychology.

Indeed, many Greek tragedies are concerned with the violation of universal taboos against matricide, patricide, and incest. In *Oedipus Rex,* we find such impulses addressed directly and the sources of such behavior explored. For example, **Jocasta** [joh-KAS-ta], Oedipus's wife, seems to believe that appalling urges (such as those described by Freud) are common and (also like Freud) that they are revealed in dreams. Speaking of the desire to marry one's mother, she tells Oedipus, "Many a man has dreamt as much." Even more remarkable is her insistence, centuries before Freud, on the necessity of the mechanism that Freud would later call *repression:* "Such things must be forgotten," she insists, "if life is to be endured." But although Jocasta dismisses these impulses as insignificant, Freud saw them as determinants of the human personality and compared Oedipus's detective work—tracking down the secrets of his identity—to the psychoanalytic process of ferreting out and confronting the contents of the unconscious.

In *Oedipus Rex,* two forms of the failure of knowledge—the people's indifference to the identity of their king's murderer and Oedipus's ignorance of his own identity—produce illness, whether pathology (the plague) or what in other circumstances might appear to be psychosis (Oedipus's acting out of the primal taboos). In both cases, Oedipus's discovery of the truth has a cathartic effect: the plague is presumably over, and Oedipus has completed his excruciating voyage of self-discovery and achieved at last a state of wholeness not possible while the truth about himself lay hidden.

Apollo and Fate

In both cases, it is Apollo who calls attention through his oracle to the conditions that prevail: he reveals to Oedipus the initial prophecy regarding his parents and, later, the Thebans' failure to find and punish the killer of their king. It is also Apollo, as the source of the oracle's pronouncements, who is behind the original statements about what is usually called the *fate* of King **Laius** [LAY-uhs] and of Oedipus himself.

One of the important questions the play raises is whether Apollo, in articulating the "fate" of Oedipus, is decreeing what will happen to him no matter what he does or what choices he makes, or whether, as god of prophecy, he is simply foreseeing what actually turns out to happen to Oedipus as a result of his own free choices. That is, to what degree do the gods choose Oedipus's destiny for him? To what degree is he in control of his own life? In modern terms, we might ask the same question in another way: does nature or nurture—genetic makeup or training and experience—determine an individual's behavior? Sophocles provides several clues that occur at the precise juncture of these two possible explanations of the events in Oedipus's life so that no matter how we phrase the question, the answer remains tantalizingly ambiguous. Modern readers might also note that the oracle becomes a "self-fulfilling" prophecy: the mere fact of its revelation prompts Oedipus to leave his home and family in Corinth. Going out on the road to seek his fortune elsewhere, he will eventually encounter the man who will turn out to be his biological father, thus setting in motion the whole chain of catastrophic events. As a prophetic god, to what degree is Apollo "responsible" for the consequences of the oracle's utterances?

In the play, the first and most obvious signal that Apollo interferes with events in the lives of humans is the plague that has been visited upon Thebes and its inhabitants. Punished by Apollo, god of health (and therefore of illness), for their negligence in the serious matter of regicide (the murder of a king), the people of Thebes are suffering grievously. The oracle's message, which would have been taken as seriously by the members of the Athenian audience as it was by the characters in the play, is that the plague will continue until the murderer is apprehended and exiled. And although the play does not explicitly refer to the lifting of the plague, that expectation is presumably fulfilled when Oedipus agrees to exile himself as Apollo demands.

Other components of the play also seem to support the claim that fate controls human experience—the remarkable series of coincidences, for example. The more Oedipus tries to escape the path laid out for him by the oracle, the more he is trapped into fulfilling it: the man he kills at the crossroads turns out to be his father; the city that rewards him for solving the riddle of the **Sphinx** turns out to be his birthplace; the woman to whom he is married turns out to be his mother.

Tiresias   Another figure whose presence seems to validate the oracle's authority is **Tiresias** [tih-REE-sih-as], prophet of Apollo. According to the myths, Tiresias was blinded by Hera (or possibly Athene) for seeing the goddess bathing—a view of the gods too intimate for mere mortals. He was also punished (for killing the female of a pair of copulating snakes he encountered) by being made to spend one year as a woman, after which he retained both male and female sexual characteristics. In another variant, when asked which gender enjoyed sex more, Tiresias angered Hera by replying that the woman had more pleasure. She punished him by blinding him. According to these myths, Zeus compensated him for his physical blindness by giving him the gift of inner sight, or prophetic vision. Blind to distracting surface appearances, Tiresias is also gifted with the wholeness of perspective that comes from a wider range of human experience than is available to other mortals restricted to a single gender. In the earlier epics as well as in the tragedies, Tiresias had long since become a symbol of wisdom and insight into the will of the gods. Nevertheless, the clear perception and open revelation of that will is fraught with danger to humans. The gods speak in riddles, while they themselves remain obscure and mysterious to us. Seeing a deity too close up, too clearly, in "natural," undisguised or unmediated form brought death to the Theban princess Semele, who made love to Zeus, and to her nephew Actaeon, who spied on the naked Artemis; similarly, piercing the veil that hides the nature of the deities from human perception, and having the temerity to reveal what he saw, resulted in the blinding of Tiresias, who saw more of (or into) Hera than is permitted.

The blinding of Oedipus, who likewise tries to rip the curtain off the divine mysteries, is also, from the gods' perspective, appropriate, if not inevitable: when Tiresias tells Oedipus, "To be wise is to suffer," he knows whereof he speaks. Dismissing Tiresias's warning, Oedipus, ever the rationalist, persists in his demand for clarity of vision, for a logical explanation of the mysteries of the gods. But to turn the light of human reason on the divine mysteries is to render oneself unable to see them. Thus, blinding himself to the mysteries of Dionysus, another Theban, Pentheus, was mutilated; Oedipus's self-blinding is a variant on the sparagmos theme.

Civic Responsibility   For all the ways in which fate is operative in the world of the play, Sophocles strictly circumscribes its sphere of operations. For example, the myths about Oedipus's family include references to a "curse" on the house of Labdacus, his grandfather. Such curses were presumed to be passed on from one generation to the next, until they were expiated to the gods' satisfaction. Sophocles, however, never even alludes to such a possibility, apparently excluding inherited pollution as a relevant factor in Oedipus's life.

Further, within the context of the play itself, Apollo is not initially concerned with Oedipus's violations of the primal taboos against patricide and incest. When the play opens, Oedipus has lived in Thebes for years, an honored leader, a beloved husband, a loving parent. The sin that has angered Apollo was committed not by Oedipus but by the people of Thebes.

Long regarded as being rooted in violence since its legendary founder, **Cadmus**, sowed dragon's teeth to create the city's first inhabitants, a race of armed men (see Chapter 13), Thebes had a reputation—much like that of Italy as depicted in the plays of the European Renaissance—as a place where evil reigned, where any form of corruption was possible. Thebes was, further, an enemy to Athens, having taken the side of the Persians during the Persian Wars and even fighting the Athenians directly during the Peloponnesian War. The Athenian audience would undoubtedly have been gratified to watch as, in Sophocles's portrayal, the Thebans were wrapped up in their own lives and engaged in a merely token investigation of the murder of their king while the perpetrator went unpunished. It is thus the people of Thebes—not Oedipus—who are punished by the plague. This is the message that Creon bears when he returns from the oracle: justice and civic health must be restored. Nor does Apollo speak of blinding as the desired punishment for regicide; exile (the typical sentence imposed by Athens on offenders) is the punishment Apollo requires. Oedipus's self-blinding is done by his own choice.

Oedipus's Character

Sophocles not only sets limits to the scope of fate in the play but also provides for alternative explanations of the events surrounding Oedipus's life. Although fate may provide one explanation for Oedipus's leaving Corinth to go out on the road, where he will encounter his father, Laius, Oedipus's character provides another. Laius thought he could control his destiny by taking preventive action. Thus, to prevent the prediction of his murder by his own son from being fulfilled, he had the child's ankles pierced and bound (hence the name *Oedipus,* meaning "swollen foot") and had the child exposed on a mountainside to die rather than accept responsibility for murdering his own son. How could he predict that the child would be rescued by a sympathetic shepherd and delivered to Corinth, to be adopted by the childless royal couple (Figure 16-1)? Oedipus similarly chose to leave Corinth, believing that he could prevent the oracle's fulfillment and evade the inevitable guilt. Both acts—intended to preempt the will of the gods, to avoid or change destiny—ironically help to bring it about. Thus the son's experience recapitulates the father's, both bound up in the set of innate human responses long attested to in even the most ancient of Greek myths of the creation and the generations of the gods, responses that produce rivalry and potential violence between fathers and sons.

Father and son likewise make similar behavioral choices. Fate may or may not play a role in the extraordinary circumstances that place father and son in the crossroads at the same critical moment. But the more important question is, how do individuals respond to the circumstances in which they find themselves? In the case of Laius and Oedipus, pride and anger surely determine what happens when their paths intersect. What but the massive egotism inherent in his pride in his status as king could prompt Laius to order passersby out of his way? What but pride could prompt Oedipus to refuse the request? And what but uncontrollable anger could drive Oedipus to kill an old man for what he perceives as an insult?

Oedipus may be in control of his rational decisions, but when angered, all restraints disappear, and he repeatedly lashes out at whatever targets present themselves—the old heroic impulse that prompts heroes to attack first and worry about the consequences later, as did Achilles and Hector. Thus, describing his encounter with Laius, Oedipus says, "Him I struck, for I was angry." Compelled by similar emotional responses, he lashes out at Creon, who is trying to help him, and at Tiresias, whom he himself has summoned, irrationally accusing both of crimes and conspiracies. Perhaps what Oedipus inherited from his father are not curses but personality traits.

The Importance of Riddles

Further, no oracle speaks of Oedipus's analytical intelligence—his extraordinary skill at solving riddles—or his courage in being willing even to confront the Sphinx who had killed all previous challengers. Had Oedipus been less intelligent or courageous, his marriage with the now-widowed Jocasta—his reward for saving Thebes from the ravenous creature—could not have taken place. It is one of the play's many riddles that his virtues themselves become sources of his unhappiness.

As most readers have noted, riddles are central to the play in many ways. Behind the riddles in which Tiresias speaks and the riddle of Oedipus's identity, the unraveling of which forms the plot of the play, lies the riddle of the Sphinx (Figure 16-2): what walks on four legs in the morning, two legs in the afternoon, and three legs in the evening? The answer, as Oedipus knew, to his own undoing, is "man," or, as we would now state it, human beings, who crawl on all fours in infancy, walk upright throughout most of their lives, and lean on a cane in old age. Oedipus was satisfied that he knew the answer. But although he could fill in the blank in the riddle by providing the correct word, like some kind of diabolical quiz show, and thus escape the fatal penalty, he failed to understand its significance.

FIGURE 16-1   The vase painter depicts the shepherd bringing the infant Oedipus to the childless royal couple in Corinth. The child clings to his rescuer, whose evident compassion contrasts markedly with the cruelty of Oedipus's biological parents. (*Cabinet des Modailles, Paris.*)

The riddle implies, first, that human beings are all fated at least in the sense that they are all destined to lose control even over their own bodies as they age and eventually die: independence is a brief, transitory interval between the respective inadequacies of infancy and age. The human will is free only in relative terms. During the crisis in Thebes, Oedipus believes that he is totally in charge: "I, Oedipus, whose name is known from afar." In the opening scene of the play, Oedipus comes out himself to greet the suppliants and, before the opening lines are spoken, has already taken appropriate action. He has no inkling at this stage that the illusion of control is about to be shattered or that the general human condition applies to him.

Another major implication of the riddle is that a human being is by nature a riddle—a mystery even to himself. Is it possible for human beings to truly know themselves, as Apollo commands? Oedipus may be able to follow the clues and fill in the blank surface data of his identity—his birthplace and the name of his parents— but there are depths to his own psyche that he doesn't even begin to suspect until the very last moment. Even Jocasta, who doesn't want to know, recognizes the horror before Oedipus does—that an admired and respected individual, an upright citizen and a leader of his community, conceals beneath his conscious self a shadow self that is capable of the most appalling crimes: the monster that the hero must confront is now the libidinous beast within. He is no more in control of his psyche than he will be of his body in old age.

FIGURE 16-2   Oedipus Being Questioned by the Sphinx. As depicted in this vase painting, the Sphinx (part woman, part lion, and part eagle) poses the riddle to Oedipus, who sits, looking her right in the eye, with his chin resting on his hand and his legs casually crossed. His air of bemused self-assurance suggests that he is patiently, if somewhat patronizingly, waiting for her to finish the question so that he can state aloud the answer he has already deduced. (*Vatican Museums, Rome.*)

The Male and Female Principles

The Sphinx, a winged creature with the head of a woman and the body of a lion, combines the ancient symbols of the Great Goddess, with her birds and beasts. Like all heroes, Oedipus must defeat her to fulfill his role. One modern poet, Muriel Rukeyser, suggests, in her witty revision of the myth, that Oedipus misses the point of the riddle, and thus fails to recognize his mother, because he is blind to the riddle's feminine component: saying "Man," he excludes women. The word *man* includes women, Rukeyser's Oedipus argues. "That's what you think," replies the Sphinx. While the modern poet is commenting on Oedipus's sexist language, the poem also touches on his larger failure, in the myth itself, to acknowledge the feminine principle.

In his conventional masculine-heroic identification of his integrity with the need to pursue his quest for his identity to its bitter end, regardless of the consequences,

Oedipus is determined to "go forward always," like Hector or any other hero. And like all those other heroes who follow in the footsteps of Heracles, Oedipus, who had already separated himself from the family he had in Corinth, destroys the one he acquired in Thebes: his wife/mother is dead, and no normal future for his daughters is now possible. It is not merely coincidental that, like the Sphinx who was also destroyed by Oedipus, Jocasta knew the truth long before Oedipus did but was destroyed when he "solved" the riddle and answered the question. Like many other women in Greek mythology, from Megara and Andromache to Clytemnestra and Agave, Jocasta finds that the heroic approach to experience, whether assumed by their husbands or, in a reversal of roles, by the women themselves, is destructive to women both literally and in the only two roles they are allowed: marriage and motherhood.

Unlike Heracles's quests, though, Oedipus's quest is an interior one. From the archetypal perspective, the descent into the unconscious is the descent into the womb of the mother, the exploration of the female principle which thus makes possible the recovery of the anima. The very quest that destroys Oedipus's actual mother allows him to find the mother within himself. It is only when Oedipus, having discovered the truth, accepts the mystery of his fate and of the gods' role in bringing it about and resigns himself to his condition of metaphysical blindness that he is reconciled with the feminine principle, as was Tiresias before him. It is thus appropriate that, as the myths attest, when Oedipus goes out on the road again, this time in exile, it will be one of his daughters, not one of his sons, who will guide him on his final journey.

The Metaphysical Dimensions of the Oedipus Myth

Perhaps the most important implication of Oedipus's response to the Sphinx's riddle is that he—the supreme riddler—believes that all questions have answers and that human beings can ascertain those answers by applying their wits and their logic. That there are questions that have no answers, that some mysteries are permanently insoluble, and that the cosmos of the gods may be as far beyond the reach of human reason as the human psyche is beneath it never occurs to him. Why do terrible things happen to good people who are trying to do the right thing? Why do the gods call down such a fate on individuals even before they are born? Human beings who have suffered have always asked, "why me?" and "why now?" Destiny or choice? The play poses a riddle that seems to have no definitive answer.

Once awakened from his illusion that life has a clear purpose and that he is in rational control, Oedipus comes finally to accept the mystery—that the gods are not obliged to explain themselves to human beings and that mere human logic is insufficient to explain their intentions or even to know whether they have any at all. Logic presupposes observable facts and relationships and thus can hardly be an adequate guide in a world where the blind see but the sighted do not. Oedipus, in his blindness, literalizes the condition of all tragic heroes—of all human beings—groping blindly in a world they must inhabit but cannot comprehend.

Oedipus's Triumph

Recognizing that Apollo is in some indecipherable way behind the events in his life, Sophocles's Oedipus nevertheless freely asserts his own integrity and insists on taking responsibility for his acts. His father, Laius, had exposed his son instead of simply killing him, presumably to avoid being held responsible for the child's death: when he died, it would be the gods' doing. For Oedipus, blaming the gods would be another attempt to escape. Instead, Oedipus insists, whatever Apollo might or might not have contributed to the circumstances in his life, "I did it." Paradoxically, his newfound awareness of the truth about his limits, of his essential ignorance, of the fact that he cannot ever know to what extent Apollo is responsible for his life's course, leaves him free.

From the first, Oedipus accepts his role as scapegoat—just as in the ancient ritual—taking the people's sins upon himself and ultimately redeeming them through his sacrifice and suffering. The plague is lifted; order is restored in Thebes. At the same time, he redeems himself, asserting his freedom even in the act of accepting the burdens that fate has heaped on him. Not only does he impose pain on himself in his self-blinding far more intense than anything Apollo required, but also he reaches a kind of moral transcendence. To Oedipus's infinite credit, when all the facts begin falling into place as a result of his logical investigation, he confronts the truth squarely. No longer attempting to avoid the inevitable, Oedipus now insists (as heroes must), "Let it come." In a moment of blinding insight, he recognizes the horror within. At that moment, in one of the play's many ironies, Apollo and Dionysus, control and excess, fate and freedom converge on each other.

By putting his eyes out, an ironic reversal of his previous failure to see, Oedipus confronts the reality that only the gods have seen and which is more than mortal eyes can bear. Like Tiresias, Oedipus acquires true vision, his unflinching awareness of the truth in all its complexity. He may stop the flow of sensory data, but he cannot shut off his mind. What is dredged up from the depths of his psyche cannot again be repressed. The sighted Oedipus had been blind; the blinded Oedipus becomes, like Tiresias, a seer.

In an act of supreme moral courage, when death would be the easy way out, Oedipus chooses to live with the curse of awareness, with the knowledge that is pain. As Tiresias had said, "To be wise is to suffer." Following the archetypal path of mythic heroes, Oedipus experiences total alienation from his community, descends to the death of his own inner hell, and returns. Hero and victim, subject and object of his own quest, the maimed king is transformed by his experience. Only now—when the terrible burden has been released and his fate is most completely fulfilled—is Oedipus at last truly free.

Oedipus at Colonus

It is this redeemed Oedipus that Sophocles, in his last play (produced posthumously, 401 B.C.), sets on the road to Colonus, a village on the outskirts of Athens where the playwright himself had been born. Tradition asserted that Oedipus was buried there and a shrine devoted to Oedipus, Theseus, and other ancient heroes was located on the spot. In the nearly twenty-five years between *Oedipus Rex* and *Oedipus at Colonus,* Sophocles reconsidered the myth, changing his mind about Oedipus himself as well as about some specific details in the play. For example, in *Oedipus Rex,* Oedipus was ready to go into exile immediately, though it is not clear that he actually did so; in *Oedipus at Colonus,* his exile had apparently been delayed, and his daughter Antigone, a child in the earlier play, has reached adulthood and has guided her blind father on his journey.

Meanwhile, Oedipus's sons, Eteocles and Polynices, have taken over the government of Thebes from the hands of Creon, who had been ruling as regent. But the brothers quarreled, and Polynices, now married to the daughter of the king of Argos, is leading an army against Thebes. Further complicating the situation, the oracle has revealed that victory and prosperity will be assured to whichever city earns Oedipus's goodwill while he lives and secures the right to retain his bones when he dies. Thus Oedipus's sons—who shunned their father as a defiler of civilized society during his exile and are now about to do battle with each other—want the old man back as a guarantor of their rival claims to power over Thebes.

Contemporary Relevance

The threat of war, particularly the war Oedipus predicts between Thebes and Athens, would have been immediately relevant to the Athenian audience—in fact, Thebes and Athens, on opposite sides in the Peloponnesian War, had recently fought a minor battle. Some Athenians credited their victory in that encounter to the presence of the shrine and the blessing that Oedipus had bestowed upon the city. Colonus had already been burned by the Spartans in 406 B.C. and was in ruins. The Athenians would, of course, also have responded enthusiastically to the play's praise of Athens as a city of justice and law.

Similarities and Differences between the Two Oedipus Plays

Both *Oedipus Rex* and *Oedipus at Colonus* share a thread of common contemporary references. Other components of the earlier play are also retained in *Oedipus at Colonus*. For example, Oedipus still bears the burden of being tainted by the pollution of his sins so that the inhabitants of Colonus are at first terrified of allowing him to stay. Even though several cities compete for his remains, none wants Oedipus, alive or dead, to enter the precincts of the town. Only the Eumenides, or Furies (tactfully called the "Kindly Ones"), who are themselves shunned by humans and gods alike, allow him to enter their sacred grove unharmed.

In his unremitting anger, the Oedipus in the last play is also portrayed as being like the earlier character. This time, his anger is largely directed against his son Polynices, who, like his father, refuses to back down and will pursue his intended war against Thebes despite pleas from his sister and warnings from his father.

Sophocles's final portrayal of Oedipus, however, while continuing that of *Oedipus Rex* in some respects, is also very different in others. In fact, in many ways the later play inverts the earlier. In *Oedipus Rex,* the hero insisted on his moral responsibility for his acts, whereas in *Oedipus at Colonus,* he insists on his essential innocence, blaming the gods for the sinful acts he unwittingly committed and arguing that his self-blinding was an overreaction in the heat of the moment. And whereas earlier his greatness lay in his determination to wrench his freedom from the hands of fate and shunt the gods aside, now he relishes the role of victim: here, "suffering, not doing," is his strength.

Oedipus's innocence is underscored by the approval of that favorite mythic hero Theseus and further by the thunder—the sign from Zeus—that reverberates through the play. And whereas in the earlier play Oedipus wrongly attacked the innocent Tiresias and Creon, in the last play, Creon is depicted as self-serving and tyrannical, trying to use Oedipus for his own political purposes and abusing Oedipus's daughters.

In contrast to his insistence in the earlier play on self-sufficiency, Oedipus now admits his dependent condition and confesses his loneliness. Whereas before he couldn't wait to see what fate would bring, he has now learned patience. Similarly, out of his earlier alienation, isolated in his exile and blindness, he perceives the extent of his love for his daughters, for the bonds of the human world from which he has been long exiled, just at the moment when he is about to leave the human world for good.

The Reconciliation of Opposites

Oedipus at Colonus does not merely invert the conditions of the earlier play, however; in this play, opposites are reconciled in a series of paradoxes. Thus, Oedipus is here a victim who has been patient through terrible suffering. But he is no saint—rather, he has become himself an avenger, a "Fury"—cursing his son directly (in contrast to the passive curse transferred from Laius to Oedipus in the earlier play). The victim of fate has also become its active agent. In the earlier play, too, Oedipus was the sighted man who was blind. Now, the blinded Oedipus sees: having come guided by Antigone, he now finds his own way to the "holy mystery" of his end. And, having once repudiated their interference in his life, he now achieves reconciliation with the gods through the acceptance of their will.

The Dread Goddesses

While king of Thebes, the heroic Oedipus rejected the feminine principle, defying the various avatars of the Great Goddess who is privy to the secrets of life and death—the Sphinx, who knew the secret of the riddle, "What is Man?"—and Jocasta, who knew from the very first the secrets of the human psyche and who was presented in the earlier play in the usual heroic mode: the temptress whose attempts to get the hero to abort his quest had to be rejected. Now, just as Oedipus rejects his sons, he embraces the feminine principle, abandoning the light of the intellect for the chthonic darkness of the "dread goddesses": Oedipus, who has broken all taboos, commits one final violation in entering the sacred grove of the Eumenides. But instead of destroying him, they accept him, as if, having committed all forbidden acts, Oedipus has now transcended all taboos: nothing is now forbidden to him.

Death and Transfiguration

The final paradox of the play, of course, is the apotheosis of Oedipus, as he experiences death and transfiguration, the "holy mystery," which only Theseus is permitted to witness. Having descended to the depths, Oedipus is at last not only freed but deified as well. The cursed one is now himself a dispenser of curses and blessings—the former to his son, the latter to Athens. Like the Furies, he has become one of the Kindly Ones.

Antigone

The earliest of Sophocles's plays on the family of Oedipus, *Antigone* (c. 442–441 B.C.; not included in this text) follows the story of the clan after Oedipus's death. The civil war between Oedipus's sons is over. Both brothers are dead, but Eteocles, who defended Thebes, is buried with honor, while the corpse of Polynices, who attacked Thebes, is left unburied at the orders of Creon, who now assumes the rulership.

Creon argues that the security of the state demands that traitors be punished. Offended at this act of utter impiety (proper burial of the dead being required by the gods if the soul is to find eternal rest), Antigone argues that the gods are a higher authority than the state and, defying Creon's orders, she attempts to bury the body herself.

She is arrested and, refusing to yield, accepts her martyrdom. She is condemned to be sealed up in a cave, where she will perish. Tiresias warns Creon that the gods will be angered at this unnecessary violence, and Creon eventually relents, but too late. Not only has Antigone already hanged herself, but her fiancé, Haemon (Creon's son), finding her dead, likewise kills himself. Hearing the news, Creon's wife does the same, and Creon is left a miserable and broken man presiding over a disintegrating state.

OEDIPUS REX[1]

Sophocles

CHARACTERS

OEDIPUS, *king of Thebes*

A PRIEST

CREON, *brother-in-law of Oedipus*

CHORUS *of Theban elders*

TEIRESIAS, *a prophet*

JOCASTA, *sister of Creon, wife of Oedipus*

MESSENGER

SERVANT *of Laius, father of Oedipus*

SECOND MESSENGER

(*silent*) ANTIGONE *and* ISMENE, *daughters of Oedipus*

SCENE

Before the palace of Oedipus at Thebes. In front of the large central doors, an altar; and an altar near each of the two side doors. On the altar steps are seated suppliants—old men, youths, and young boys—dressed in white tunics and cloaks, their hair bound with white fillets. They have laid on the altars olive branches wreathed with wool-fillets.

The old PRIEST OF ZEUS *stands alone facing the central doors of the palace. The doors open, and* OEDIPUS, *followed by two attendants who stand at either door, enters and looks about.*

Oedipus
O children, last born stock of ancient Cadmus,
What petitions are these you bring to me
With garlands on your suppliant olive branches?
The whole city teems with incense fumes,
Teems with prayers for healing and with groans.
Thinking it best, children, to hear all this
Not from some messenger, I came myself,
The world renowned and glorious Oedipus.
But tell me, aged priest, since you are fit
To speak before these men, how stand you here,   10
In fear or want? Tell me, as I desire
To do my all; hard hearted I would be
To feel no sympathy for such a prayer.

---

1. Translation by Albert S. Cook.

Priest

O Oedipus, ruler of my land, you see
How old we are who stand in supplication
Before your altars here, some not yet strong
For lengthy flight, some heavy with age,
Priests, as I of Zeus, and choice young men.
The rest of the tribe sits with wreathed branches,
In market places, at Pallas' two temples, 20
And at prophetic embers by the river.
The city, as you see, now shakes too greatly
And cannot raise her head out of the depths
Above the gory swell. She wastes in blight,
Blight on earth's fruitful blooms and grazing flocks,
And on the barren birth pangs of the women.
The fever god has fallen on the city,
And drives it, a most hated pestilence
Through whom the home of Cadmus is made empty.
Black Hades is enriched with wails and groans. 30
Not that we think you equal to the gods
These boys and I sit suppliant at your hearth,
But judging you first of men in the trials of life,
And in the human intercourse with spirits:—
You are the one who came to Cadmus' city
And freed us from the tribute which we paid
To the harsh-singing Sphinx. And that you did
Knowing nothing else, unschooled by us.
But people say and think it was some god
That helped you to set our life upright. 40
Now Oedipus, most powerful of all,
We all are turned here toward you, we beseech you,
Find us some strength, whether from one of the gods
You hear an omen, or know one from a man.
For the experienced I see will best
Make good plans grow from evil circumstance.
Come, best of mortal men, raise up the state.
Come, prove your fame, since now this land of ours
Calls you savior for your previous zeal.
O never let our memory of your reign 50
Be that we first stood straight and later fell,
But to security raise up this state.
With favoring omen once you gave us luck;
Be now as good again; for if henceforth
You rule as now, you will be this country's king,
Better it is to rule men than a desert,
Since nothing is either ship or fortress tower
Bare of men who together dwell within.

Oedipus

O piteous children, I am not ignorant
Of what you come desiring. Well I know   60
You are all sick, and in your sickness none
There is among you as sick as I,
For your pain comes to one man alone,
To him and to none other, but my soul
Groans for the state, for myself, and for you.
You do not wake a man who is sunk in sleep;
Know that already I have shed many tears,
And travelled many wandering roads of thought.
Well have I sought, and found one remedy;   70
And this I did: the son of Menoeceus,
Creon, my brother-in-law, I sent away
Unto Apollo's Pythian halls to find
What I might do or say to save the state.
The days are measured out that he is gone;
It troubles me how he fares. Longer than usual
He has been away, more than the fitting time.
But when he comes, then evil I shall be,
If all the god reveals I fail to do.

Priest

You speak at the right time. These men just now
Signal to me that Creon is approaching.   80

Oedipus

O Lord Apollo, grant that he may come
In saving fortune shining as in eye.

Priest

Glad news he brings, it seems, or else his head
Would not be crowned with leafy, berried bay.

Oedipus

We will soon know. He is close enough to hear.—
Prince, my kinsman, son of Menoeceus,
What oracle do you bring us from the god?

Creon

A good one. For I say that even burdens
If they chance to turn out right, will all be well.

Oedipus

Yet what is the oracle? Your present word   90
Makes me neither bold nor apprehensive.

Creon

If you wish to hear in front of this crowd
I am ready to speak, or we can go within.

Oedipus

Speak forth to all. The sorrow that I bear
Is greater for these men than for my life.

Creon

May I tell you what I heard from the god?
Lord Phoebus clearly bids us to drive out,
And not to leave uncured within this country,
A pollution we have nourished in our land.

Oedipus

With what purgation? What kind of misfortune?   100

Creon

Banish the man, or quit slaughter with slaughter
In cleansing, since this blood rains on the state.

Oedipus

Who is this man whose fate the god reveals?

Creon

Laius, my lord, was formerly the guide
Of this our land before you steered this city.

Oedipus

I know him by hearsay, but I never saw him.

Creon

Since he was slain, the god now plainly bids us
To punish his murderers, whoever they may be.

Oedipus

Where are they on the earth? How shall we find
This indiscernible track of ancient guilt?   110

Creon

In this land, said Apollo. What is sought
Can be apprehended; the unobserved escapes.

Oedipus

Did Laius fall at home on this bloody end?
Or in the fields, or in some foreign land?

Creon

As a pilgrim, the god said, he left his tribe
And once away from home, returned no more.

Oedipus

Was there no messenger, no fellow wayfarer
Who saw, from whom an inquirer might get aid?

Creon

They are all dead, save one, who fled in fear
And he knows only one thing sure to tell.   120

Oedipus

What is that? We may learn many facts from one
If we might take for hope a short beginning.

Creon

Robbers, Apollo said, met there and killed him
Not by the strength of one, but many hands.

Oedipus

How did the robber unless something from here
Was at work with silver, reach this point of daring?

Creon

These facts are all conjecture. Laius dead,
There rose in evils no avenger for him.

Oedipus

But when the king had fallen slain, what trouble
Prevented you from finding all this out?   130

Creon

The subtle-singing Sphinx made us let go
What was unclear to search at our own feet.

Oedipus

Well then, I will make this clear afresh
From the start. Phoebus was right, you were right
To take this present interest in the dead.
Justly it is you see me as your ally
Avenging alike this country and the god.
Not for the sake of some distant friends,
But for myself I will disperse this filth.
Whoever it was who killed that man   140
With the same hand may wish to do vengeance on me.
And so assisting Laius I aid myself.
But hurry quickly, children, stand up now
From the altar steps, raising these suppliant boughs.
Let someone gather Cadmus' people here
To learn that I will do all, whether at last
With Phoebus' help we are shown saved or fallen.

Priest

Come, children, let us stand. We came here
First for the sake of what this man proclaims.
Phoebus it was who sent these prophecies   150
And he will come to save us from the plague.

Chorus

Strophe A

O sweet-tongued voice of Zeus, in what spirit do you come
From Pytho rich in gold
To glorious Thebes? I am torn on the rack, dread shakes my fearful mind,
Apollo of Delos, hail!
As I stand in awe of you, what need, either new
Do you bring to the full for me, or old in the turning times of the year?
Tell me, O child of golden Hope, undying Voice!

Antistrophe A

First on you do I call, daughter of Zeus, undying Athene
And your sister who guards our land,   160
Artemis, seated upon the throne renowned of our circled Place,
And Phoebus who darts afar;
Shine forth to me, thrice warder-off of death;
If ever in time before when ruin rushed upon the state,
The flame of sorrow you drove beyond our bounds, come also now.

Strophe B

O woe! Unnumbered that I bear
The sorrows are! My whole host is sick, nor is there a sword of thought
To ward off pain. The growing fruits
Of glorious earth wax not, nor women
Withstand in childbirth shrieking pangs.   170
Life on life you may see, which, like the well-winged bird,
Faster than stubborn fire, speed
To the strand of the evening god.

Antistrophe B

Unnumbered of the city die.
Unpitied babies bearing death lie unmoaned on the ground.
Grey-haired mothers and young wives
From all sides at the altar's edge
Lift up a wail beseeching, for their mournful woes.
The prayer for healing shines blent with a grieving cry;
Wherefore, O golden daughter of Zeus,   180
Send us your succour with its beaming face.

Strophe C

Grant that fiery Ares, who now with no brazen shield
Flames round me in shouting attack
May turn his back in running flight from our land,
May be borne with fair wind
To Amphitrite's great chamber
Or to the hostile port
Of the Thracian surge.
For even if night leaves any ill undone
It is brought to pass and comes to be in the day.   190

O Zeus who bears the fire
And rule the lightning's might,
Strike him beneath your thunderbolt with death!

Antistrophe C

O lord Apollo, would that you might come and scatter forth
Untamed darts from your twirling golden bow;
Bring succour from the plague; may the flashing
Beams come of Artemis,
With which she glances through the Lycian hills.
Also on him I call whose hair is held in gold,
Who gives a name to this land,   200
Bacchus of winy face, whom maidens hail!
Draw near with your flaming Maenad band
And the aid of your gladsome torch
Against the plague, dishonoured among the gods.

Oedipus

You pray; if for what you pray you would be willing
To hear and take my words, to nurse the plague,
You may get succour and relief from evils.
A stranger to this tale I now speak forth,
A stranger to the deed, for not alone
Could I have tracked it far without some clue,   210
But now that I am enrolled a citizen
Latest among the citizens of Thebes
To all you sons of Cadmus I proclaim
Whoever of you knows at what man's hand
Laius, the son of Labdacus, met his death,
I order him to tell me all, and even
If he fears, to clear the charge and he will suffer
No injury, but leave the land unharmed.
If someone knows the murderer to be an alien
From foreign soil, let him not be silent;   220
I will give him a reward, my thanks besides.
But if you stay in silence and from fear
For self or friend thrust aside my command,
Hear now from me what I shall do for this;
I charge that none who dwell within this land
Whereof I hold the power and the throne
Give this man shelter whoever he may be,
Or speak to him, or share with him in prayer
Or sacrifice, or serve him lustral rites,
But drive him, all, out of your homes, for he   230
Is this pollution on us, as Apollo
Revealed to me just now in oracle.
I am therefore the ally of the god
And of the murdered man. And now I pray
That the murderer, whether he hides alone

Or with his partners, may, evil coward,
Wear out in luckless ills his wretched life.
I further pray, that, if at my own hearth
He dwells known to me in my own home,
I may suffer myself the curse I just now uttered.   240
And you I charge to bring all this to pass
For me, and for the god, and for our land
Which now lies fruitless, godless, and corrupt.
Even if Phoebus had not urged this affair,
Not rightly did you let it go unpurged
When one both noble and a king was murdered!
You should have sought it out. Since now I reign
Holding the power which he had held before me,
Having the selfsame wife and marriage bed—
And if his seed had not met barren fortune   250
We should be linked by offspring from one mother:
But as it was, fate leapt upon his head.
Therefore in this, as if for my own father
I fight for him, and shall attempt all
Searching to seize the hand which shed that blood,
For Labdacus' son, before him Polydorus,
And ancient Cadmus, and Agenor of old.
And those who fail to do this, I pray the gods
May give them neither harvest from their earth
Nor children from their wives, but may they be   260
Destroyed by a fate like this one, or a worse.
You other Thebans, who cherish these commands,
May Justice, the ally of a righteous cause,
And all the gods be always on your side.

Chorus
By the oath you laid on me, my king, I speak.
I killed not Laius, nor can show who killed him.
Phoebus it was who sent this question to us,
And he should answer who has done the deed.

Oedipus
Your words are just, but to compel the gods
In what they do not wish, no man can do.   270

Chorus
I would tell what seems to me our second course.

Oedipus
If there is a third, fail not to tell it too.

Chorus
Lord Teiresias I know, who sees this best
Like lord Apollo; in surveying this,
One might, my lord, find out from him most clearly.

Oedipus
Even this I did not neglect; I have done it already.
At Creon's word I twice sent messengers.
It is a wonder he has been gone so long.

Chorus
And also there are rumors, faint and old.

Oedipus
What are they? I must search out every tale.   280

Chorus
They say there were some travellers who killed him.

Oedipus
So I have heard, but no one sees a witness.

Chorus
If his mind knows a particle of fear
He will not long withstand such curse as yours.

Oedipus
He fears no speech who fears not such a deed.

Chorus
But here is the man who will convict the guilty.
Here are these men leading the divine prophet
In whom alone of men the truth is born.

Oedipus
O you who ponder all, Teiresias,
Both what is taught and what cannot be spoken,   290
What is of heaven and what trod on the earth,
Even if you are blind, you know what plague
Clings to the state, and, master, you alone
We find as her protector and her saviour.
Apollo, if the messengers have not told you,
Answered our question, that release would come
From this disease only if we make sure
Of Laius' slayers and slay them in return
Or drive them out as exiles from the land.
But you now, grudge us neither voice of birds   300
Nor any way you have of prophecy.
Save yourself and the state; save me as well.
Save everything polluted by the dead.
We are in your hands; it is the noblest task
To help a man with all your means and powers.

Teiresias
Alas! Alas! How terrible to be wise,
Where it does the seer no good. Too well I know
And have forgot this, or would not have come here.

Oedipus
What is this? How fainthearted you have come!

Teiresias
Let me go home; it is best for you to bear   310
Your burden, and I mine, if you will heed me.

Oedipus
You speak what is lawless, and hateful to the state
Which raised you, when you deprive her of your answer.

Teiresias
And I see that your speech does not proceed
In season; I shall not undergo the same.

Oedipus
Don't by the gods turn back when you are wise,
When all we suppliants lie prostrate before you.

Teiresias
And all unwise; I never shall reveal
My evils, so that I may not tell yours.

Oedipus
What do you say? You know, but will not speak?   320
Would you betray us and destroy the state?

Teiresias
I will not hurt you or me. Why in vain
Do you probe this? You will not find out from me.

Oedipus
Worst of evil men, you would enrage
A stone itself. Will you never speak,
But stay so untouched and so inconclusive?

Teiresias
You blame my anger and do not see that
With which you live in common, but upbraid me.

Oedipus
Who would not be enraged to hear these words
By which you now dishonor this our city?   330

Teiresias
Of itself this will come, though I hide it in silence.

Oedipus
Then you should tell me what it is will come.

Teiresias
I shall speak no more. If further you desire,
Rage on in wildest anger of your soul.

Oedipus

I shall omit nothing I understand
I am so angry. Know that you seem to me
Creator of the deed and worker too
In all short of the slaughter; if you were not blind,
I would say this crime was your work alone.

Teiresias

Really? Abide yourself by the decree   340
You just proclaimed, I tell you! From this day
Henceforth address neither these men nor me.
You are the godless defiler of this land.

Oedipus

You push so bold and taunting in your speech;
And how do you think to get away with this?

Teiresias

I have got away. I nurse my strength in truth.

Oedipus

Who taught you this? Not from your art you got it.

Teiresias

From you. You had me speak against my will.

Oedipus

What word? Say again, so I may better learn.

Teiresias

Didn't you get it before? Or do you bait me?   350

Oedipus

I don't remember it. Speak forth again.

Teiresias

You are the slayer whom you seek, I say.

Oedipus

Not twice you speak such bitter words unpunished.

Teiresias

Shall I speak more to make you angrier still?

Oedipus

Do what you will, your words will be in vain.

Teiresias

I say you have forgot that you are joined
With those most dear to you in deepest shame
And do not see where you are in sin.

Oedipus
Do you think you will always say such things in joy?

Teiresias
Surely, if strength abides in what is true.   360

Oedipus
It does, for all but you, this not for you
Because your ears and mind and eyes are blind.

Teiresias
Wretched you are to make such taunts, for soon
All men will cast the selfsame taunts on you.

Oedipus
You live in entire night, could do no harm
To me or any man who sees the day.

Teiresias
Not at my hands will it be your fate to fall.
Apollo suffices, whose concern it is to do this.

Oedipus
Are these devices yours, or are they Creon's?

Teiresias
Creon is not your trouble; you are yourself.   370

Oedipus
O riches, empire, skill surpassing skill
In all the numerous rivalries of life,
How great a grudge there is stored up against you
If for this kingship, which the city gave,
Their gift, not my request, into my hands—
For this, the trusted Creon, my friend from the start
Desires to creep by stealth and cast me out
Taking a seer like this, a weaver of wiles,
A crooked swindler who has got his eyes
On gain alone, but in his art is blind.   380
Come, tell us, in what clearly are you a prophet?
How is it, when the weave-songed bitch was here
You uttered no salvation for these people?
Surely the riddle then could not be solved
By some chance comer; it needed prophecy.
You did not clarify that with birds
Or knowledge from a god; but when I came,
The ignorant Oedipus, I silenced her,
Not taught by birds, but winning by my wits,
Whom you are now attempting to depose,   390
Thinking to minister near Creon's throne.

I think that to your woe you and that plotter
Will purge the land, and if you were not old
Punishment would teach you what you plot.

Chorus
It seems to us, O Oedipus our king,
Both this man's words and yours were said in anger.
Such is not our need, but to find out
How best we shall discharge Apollo's orders.

Teiresias
Even if you are king, the right to answer
Should be free to all; of that I too am king.   400
I live not as your slave, but as Apollo's.
And not with Creon's wards shall I be counted.
I say, since you have taunted even my blindness,
You have eyes, but see not where in evil you are
Nor where you dwell, nor whom you are living with.
Do you know from whom you spring? And you forget
You are an enemy to your own kin
Both those beneath and those above the earth.
Your mother's and father's curse, with double goad
And dreaded foot shall drive you from this land.   410
You who now see straight shall then be blind,
And there shall be no harbour for your cry
With which all Mount Cithaeron soon shall ring,
When you have learned the wedding where you sailed
At home, into no port, by voyage fair.
A throng of other ills you do not know
Shall equal you to yourself and to your children.
Throw mud on this, on Creon, on my voice—
Yet there shall never be a mortal man
Eradicated more wretchedly than you.   420

Oedipus
Shall these unbearable words be heard from him?
Go to perdition! Hurry! Off, away,
Turn back again and from this house depart.

Teiresias
If you had not called me, I should not have come.

Oedipus
I did not know that you would speak such folly
Or I would not soon have brought you to my house.

Teiresias
And such a fool I am, as it seems to you.
But to the parents who bore you I seem wise.

Oedipus
What parents? Wait! What mortals gave me birth?

Teiresias
This day shall be your birth and your destruction. 430

Oedipus
All things you say in riddles and unclear.

Teiresias
Are you not he who best can search this out?

Oedipus
Mock, if you wish, the skill that made me great.

Teiresias
This is the very fortune that destroyed you.

Oedipus
Well, if I saved the city, I do not care.

Teiresias
I am going now. You, boy, be my guide.

Oedipus
Yes, let him guide you. Here you are in the way.
When you are gone you will give no more trouble.

Teiresias
I go when I have said what I came to say
Without fear of your frown; you cannot destroy me. 440
I say, the very man whom you long seek
With threats and announcements about Laius' murder—
This man is here. He seems an alien stranger,
But soon he shall be revealed of Theban birth,
Nor at this circumstance shall he be pleased.
He shall be blind who sees, shall be a beggar
Who now is rich, shall make his way abroad
Feeling the ground before him with a staff.
He shall be revealed at once as brother
And father to his own children, husband and son 450
To his mother, his father's kin and murderer.
Go in and ponder that. If I am wrong
Say then that I know nothing of prophecy.

Chorus

Strophe A
Who is the man the Delphic rock said with oracular voice
Unspeakable crimes performed with his gory hands?
It is time for him now to speed

His foot in flight, more strong
Than horses swift as the storm.
For girt in arms upon him springs
With fire and lightning, Zeus' son   460
And behind him, terrible,
Come the unerring Fates.

Antistrophe A

From snowy Parnassus just now the word flashed clear
To track the obscure man by every way,
For he wanders under the wild
Forest, and into caves
And cliff rocks, like a bull,
Reft on his way, with care on care
Trying to shun the prophecy
Come from the earth's mid-navel,   470
But about him flutters the ever living doom.

Strophe B

Terrible, terrible things the wise bird-augur stirs.
I neither approve nor deny, at a loss for what to say,
I flutter in hopes and fears, see neither here nor ahead;
For what strife has lain
On Labdacus' sons or Polybus' that I have found ever before
Or now, whereby I may run for the sons of Labdacus
Is sure proof against Oedipus' public fame
As avenger for dark death?

Antistrophe B

Zeus and Apollo surely understand and know   480
The affairs of mortal men, but that a mortal seer
Knows more than I, there is no proof. Though a man
May surpass a man in knowledge,
Never shall I agree, till I see the word true, when men blame Oedipus,
For there came upon him once clear the winged maiden
And wise he was seen, by sure test sweet for the state.
So never shall my mind judge him evil guilt.

Creon

Men of our city, I have heard dread words
That Oedipus our king accuses me.
I am here indignant. If in the present troubles   490
He thinks that he has suffered at my hands
One word or deed tending to injury
I do not crave the long-spanned age of life
To bear this rumor, for it is no simple wrong
The damage of this accusation brings me;
It brings the greatest, if I am called a traitor
To you and my friends, a traitor to the state.

Chorus
Come now, for this reproach perhaps was forced
By anger, rather than considered thought.

Creon
And was the idea voiced that my advice   500
Persuaded the prophet to give false accounts?

Chorus
Such was said. I know not to what intent.

Creon
Was this accusation laid against me
From straightforward eyes and straightforward mind?

Chorus
I do not know. I see not what my masters do;
But here he is now, coming from the house.

Oedipus
How dare you come here? Do you own a face
So bold that you can come before my house
When you are clearly the murderer of this man
And manifestly pirate of my throne?   510
Come, say before the gods, did you see in me
A coward or a fool, that you plotted this?
Or did you think I would not see your wiles
Creeping upon me, or knowing, would not ward off?
Surely your machination is absurd
Without a crowd of friends to hunt a throne
Which is captured only by wealth and many men.

Creon
Do you know what you do? Hear answer to your charges
On the other side. Judge only what you know.

Oedipus
Your speech is clever, but I learn it ill   520
Since I have found you harsh and grievous toward me.

Creon
This very matter hear me first explain.

Oedipus
Tell me not this one thing: you are not false.

Creon
If you think stubbornness a good possession
Apart from judgment, you do not think right.

Oedipus
If you think you can do a kinsman evil
Without the penalty, you have no sense.

Creon
I agree with you. What you have said is just.
Tell me what you say you have suffered from me.

Oedipus
Did you, or did you not, advise my need   530
Was summoning that prophet person here?

Creon
And still is. I hold still the same opinion.

Oedipus
How long a time now has it been since Laius—

Creon
Performed what deed? I do not understand.

Oedipus
—Disappeared to his ruin at deadly hands.

Creon
Far in the past the count of years would run.

Oedipus
Was this same seer at that time practising?

Creon
As wise as now, and equally respected.

Oedipus
At that time did he ever mention me?

Creon
Never when I stood near enough to hear.   540

Oedipus
But did you not make inquiry of the murder?

Creon
We did, of course, and got no information.

Oedipus
How is it that this seer did not utter this then?

Creon
When I don't know, as now, I would keep still.

Oedipus
This much you know full well, and so should speak:—

Creon
What is that? If I know, I will not refuse.

Oedipus
This: If he had not first conferred with you
He never would have said that I killed Laius.

Creon
If he says this, you know yourself, I think;
I learn as much from you as you from me.   550

Oedipus
Learn then: I never shall be found a slayer.

Creon
What then, are you the husband of my sister?

Oedipus
What you have asked is plain beyond denial.

Creon
Do you rule this land with her in equal sway?

Oedipus
All she desires she obtains from me.

Creon
Am I with you two not an equal third?

Oedipus
In just that do you prove a treacherous friend.

Creon
No, if, like me, you reason with yourself.
Consider this fact first: would any man
Choose, do you think, to have his rule in fear   560
Rather than doze unharmed with the same power?
For my part I have never been desirous
Of being king instead of acting king.
Nor any other man has, wise and prudent.
For now I obtain all from you without fear.
If I were king, I would do much unwilling.
How then could kingship sweeter be for me
Than rule and power devoid of any pain?
I am not yet so much deceived to want
Goods besides those I profitably enjoy.   570
Now I am hailed and gladdened by all men.
Now those who want from you speak out to me,
Since all their chances' outcome dwells therein.
How then would I relinquish what I have
To get those gains? My mind runs not so bad.
I am prudent yet, no lover of such plots,
Nor would I ever endure others' treason.
And first as proof of this go on to Pytho;

See if I told you truly the oracle.
Next proof: see if I plotted with the seer;   580
If you find so at all, put me to death
With my vote for my guilt as well as yours.
Do not convict me just on unclear conjecture.
It is not right to think capriciously
The good are bad, nor that the bad are good.
It is the same to cast out a noble friend,
I say, as one's own life, which best he loves.
The facts, though, you will safely know in time,
Since time alone can show the just man just,
But you can know a criminal in one day.   590

Chorus
A cautious man would say he has spoken well.
O king, the quick to think are never sure.

Oedipus
When the plotter, swift, approaches me in stealth
I too in counterplot must be as swift.
If I wait in repose, the plotter's ends
Are brought to pass and mine will then have erred.

Creon
What do you want then? To cast me from the land?

Oedipus
Least of all that. My wish is you should die,
Not flee to exemplify what envy is.

Creon
Do you say this? Will you neither trust nor yield?   600

Oedipus
[No, for I think that you deserve no trust.]

Creon
You seem not wise to me

Oedipus
                    I am for me.

Creon
You should be for me too.

Oedipus
                    No, you are evil.

Creon
Yes, if you understand nothing.

Oedipus

Yet I must rule.

Creon

Not when you rule badly.

Oedipus

O city, city!

Creon

It is my city too, not yours alone.   610

Chorus

Stop, princes. I see Jocasta coming
Out of the house at the right time for you.
With her you must settle the dispute at hand.

Jocasta

O wretched men, what unconsidered feud
Of tongues have you aroused? Are you not ashamed,
The state so sick, to stir up private ills?
Are you not going home? And you as well?
Will you turn a small pain into a great?

Creon

My blood sister, Oedipus your husband
Claims he will judge against me two dread ills: 620
Thrust me from the fatherland or take and kill me.

Oedipus

I will, my wife; I caught him in the act
Doing evil to my person with evil skill.

Creon

Now may I not rejoice but die accursed
If ever I did any of what you accuse me.

Jocasta

O, by the gods, believe him, Oedipus.
First, in reverence for his oath to the gods,
Next, for my sake and theirs who stand before you.

Chorus

Hear my entreaty, lord. Consider and consent.

Oedipus

What wish should I then grant?   630

Chorus

Respect the man, no fool before, who now in oath is strong.

Oedipus
You know what you desire?

Chorus
                    I know.

Oedipus
                         Say what you mean.

Chorus
Your friend who has sworn do not dishonour
By casting guilt for dark report.

Oedipus
Know well that when you ask this grant from me,
You ask my death or exile from the land.

Chorus
No, by the god foremost among the gods,
The Sun, may I perish by the utmost doom   640
Godless and friendless, if I have this in mind.
But ah, the withering earth wears down
My wretched soul, if to these ills
Of old are added ills from both of you.

Oedipus
Then let him go, though surely I must die
Or be thrust dishonoured from this land by force.
Your grievous voice I pity, not that man's;
Wherever he may be, he will be hated.

Creon
Sullen you are to yield, as you are heavy
When you exceed in wrath. Natures like these   650
Are justly sorest for themselves to bear.

Oedipus
Will you not go and leave me?

Creon
                         I am on my way.
You know me not, but these men see me just.

Chorus
O queen, why do you delay to bring this man indoors?

Jocasta
I want to learn what happened here.

Chorus
Unknown suspicion rose from talk, and the unjust devours.

Jocasta
In both of them?

Chorus
       Just so.

Jocasta
              What was the talk?   660

Chorus
Enough, enough! When the land is pained
It seems to me at this point we should stop.

Oedipus
Do you see where you have come? Though your intent
Is good, you slacken off and blunt my heart.

Chorus
O lord, I have said not once alone,
Know that I clearly would be mad
And wandering in mind, to turn away
You who steered along the right,
When she was torn with trouble, our beloved state.
O may you now become in health her guide.   670

Jocasta
By the gods, lord, tell me on what account
You have set yourself in so great an anger.

Oedipus
I shall tell you, wife; I respect you more than these men.
Because of Creon, since he has plotted against me.

Jocasta
Say clearly, if you can; how started the quarrel?

Oedipus
He says that I stand as the murderer of Laius.

Jocasta
He knows himself, or learned from someone else?

Oedipus
No, but he sent a rascal prophet here.
He keeps his own mouth clean in what concerns him.

Jocasta
Now free yourself of what you said, and listen.   680
Learn from me, no mortal man exists
Who knows prophetic art for your affairs,
And I shall briefly show you proof of this:

An oracle came once to Laius. I do not say
From Phoebus himself, but from his ministers
That his fate would be at his son's hand to die—
A child, who would be born from him and me.
And yet, as the rumor says, they were strangers,
Robbers who killed him where three highways meet.
But three days had not passed from the child's birth   690
When Laius pierced and tied together his ankles,
And cast him by others' hands on a pathless mountain.
Therein Apollo did not bring to pass
That the child murder his father, nor for Laius
The dread he feared, to die at his son's hand.
Such did prophetic oracles determine.
Pay no attention to them. For the god
Will easily make clear the need he seeks.

Oedipus
What wandering of soul, what stirring of mind
Holds me, my wife, in what I have just heard!   700

Jocasta
What care has turned you back that you say this?

Oedipus
I thought I heard you mention this, that Laius
Was slaughtered at the place where three highways meet.

Jocasta
That was the talk. The rumour has not ceased.

Oedipus
Where is this place where such a sorrow was?

Jocasta
The country's name is Phocis. A split road
Leads to one place from Delphi and Daulia.

Oedipus
And how much time has passed since these events?

Jocasta
The news was heralded in the city scarcely
A little while before you came to rule.   710

Oedipus
O Zeus, what have you planned to do to me?

Jocasta
What passion is this in you, Oedipus?

Oedipus
Don't ask me that yet. Tell me about Laius.
What did he look like? How old was he when murdered?

Jocasta
A tall man, with his hair just brushed with white.
His shape and form differed not far from yours.

Oedipus
Alas! Alas! I think unwittingly
I have just laid dread curses on my head.

Jocasta
What are you saying? I shrink to behold you, lord.

Oedipus
I am terribly afraid the seer can see.   720
That will be clearer if you say one thing more.

Jocasta
Though I shrink, if I know what you ask, I will answer.

Oedipus
Did he set forth with few attendants then,
Or many soldiers, since he was a king?

Jocasta
They were five altogether among them.
One was a herald. One chariot bore Laius.

Oedipus
Alas! All this is clear now. Tell me, my wife,
Who was the man who told these stories to you?

Jocasta
One servant, who alone escaped, returned.

Oedipus
Is he by chance now present in our house?   730

Jocasta
Not now. Right from the time when he returned
To see you ruling and Laius dead,
Touching my hand in suppliance, he implored me
To send him to fields and to pastures of sheep
That he might be farthest from the sight of this city.
So I sent him away, since he was worthy
For a slave, to bear a greater grant than this.

Oedipus
How then could he return to us with speed?

Jocasta

It can be done. But why would you order this?

Oedipus

O lady, I fear I have said too much.   740
On this account I now desire to see him.

Jocasta

Then he shall come. But I myself deserve
To learn what it is that troubles you, my lord.

Oedipus

And you shall not be prevented, since my fears
Have come to such a point. For who is closer
That I may speak to in this fate than you?
Polybus of Corinth was my father,
My mother, Dorian Merope. I was held there
Chief citizen of all, till such a fate
Befell me—as it is, worthy of wonder,   750
But surely not deserving my excitement.
A man at a banquet overdrunk with wine
Said in drink I was a false son to my father.
The weight I held that day I scarcely bore,
But on the next day I went home and asked
My father and mother of it. In bitter anger
They took the reproach from him who had let it fly.
I was pleased at their actions; nevertheless
The rumour always rankled; and spread abroad.
In secret from mother and father I set out   760
Toward Delphi. Phoebus sent me away ungraced
In what I came for, but other wretched things
Terrible and grievous, he revealed in answer;
That I must wed my mother and produce
An unendurable race for men to see,
That I should kill the father who begot me.
When I heard this response, Corinth I fled
Henceforth to measure her land by stars alone.
I went where I should never see the disgrace
Of my evil oracles be brought to pass,   770
And on my journey to that place I came
At which you say this king had met his death.
My wife, I shall speak the truth to you. My way
Led to a place close by the triple road.
There a herald met me, and a man
Seated on colt-drawn chariot, as you said.
There both the guide and the old man himself
Thrust me with driving force out of the path.
And I in anger struck the one who pushed me,
The driver. Then the old man, when he saw me,   780

Watched when I passed, and from his chariot
Struck me full on the head with double goad.
I paid him back and more. From this very hand
A swift blow of my staff rolled him right out
Of the middle of his seat onto his back.
I killed them all. But if relationship
Existed between this stranger and Laius,
What man now is wretcheder than I?
What man is cursed by a more evil fate?
No stranger or citizen could now receive me   790
Within his home, or even speak to me,
But thrust me out; and no one but myself
Brought down these curses on my head.
The bed of the slain man I now defile
With hands that killed him. Am I evil by birth?
Am I not utterly vile if I must flee
And cannot see my family in my flight
Nor tread my homeland soil, or else be joined
In marriage to my mother, kill my father,
Polybus, who sired me and brought me up?   800
Would not a man judge right to say of me
That this was sent on me by some cruel spirit?
O never, holy reverence of the gods,
May I behold that day, but may I go
Away from mortal men, before I see
Such a stain of circumstance come to me.

Chorus
My lord, for us these facts are full of dread.
Until you hear the witness, stay in hope.

Oedipus
And just so much is all I have of hope,
Only to wait until the shepherd comes.   810

Jocasta
What, then, do you desire to hear him speak?

Oedipus
I will tell you, if his story is found to be
The same as yours, I would escape the sorrow.

Jocasta
What unusual word did you hear from me?

Oedipus
You said he said that they were highway robbers
Who murdered him. Now, if he still says
The selfsame number, I could not have killed him,
Since one man does not equal many men.

But if he speaks of a single lonely traveller,
The scale of guilt now clearly falls to me.   820

Jocasta
However, know the word was set forth thus
And it is not in him now to take it back;
This tale the city heard, not I alone.
But if he diverges from his previous story,
Even then, my lord, he could not show Laius' murder
To have been fulfilled properly. Apollo
Said he would die at the hands of my own son.
Surely that wretched child could not have killed him,
But he himself met death some time before.
Therefore, in any prophecy henceforth   830
I would not look to this side or to that.

Oedipus
Your thoughts ring true, but still let someone go
To summon the peasant. Do not neglect this.

Jocasta
I shall send without delay. But let us enter.
I would do nothing that did not please you.

Chorus

Strophe A
May fate come on me as I bear
Holy pureness in all word and deed,
For which the lofty striding laws were set down,
Born through the heavenly air
Whereof the Olympian sky alone the father was;   840
No mortal spawn of mankind gave them birth,
Nor may oblivion ever lull them down;
Mighty in them the god is, and he does not age.

Antistrophe A
Pride breeds the tyrant.
Pride, once overfilled with many things in vain,
Neither in season nor fit for man,
Scaling the sheerest height
Hurls to a dire fate
Where no foothold is found.
I pray the god may never stop the rivalry   850
That works well for the state.
The god as my protector I shall never cease to hold.

Strophe B
But if a man goes forth haughty in word or deed
With no fear of the Right

Nor pious to the spirits' shrines,
May evil doom seize him
For his ill-fated pride,
If he does not fairly win his gain
Or works unholy deeds,
Or, in bold folly lays on the sacred profane hands.   860
For when such acts occur, what man may boast
Ever to ward off from his life darts of the gods?
If practices like these are in respect,
Why then must I dance the sacred dance?

Antistrophe B
Never again in worship shall I go
To Delphi, holy navel of the earth,
Nor to the temple at Abae,
Nor to Olympia,
If these prophecies do not become
Examples for all men.   870
O Zeus, our king, if so you are rightly called,
Ruler of all things, may they not escape
You and your forever deathless power.
Men now hold light the fading oracles
Told about Laius long ago
And nowhere is Apollo clearly honored;
Things divine are going down to ruin.

Jocasta
Lords of this land, the thought has come to me
To visit the spirits' shrines, bearing in hand
These suppliant boughs and offerings of incense.   880
For Oedipus raises his soul too high
With all distresses; nor, as a sane man should,
Does he confirm the new by things of old,
But stands at the speaker's will if he speaks terrors.
And so, because my advice can do no more,
To you, Lycian Apollo—for you are nearest—
A suppliant, I have come here with these prayers,
That you may find some pure deliverance for us:
We all now shrink to see him struck in fear,
That man who is the pilot of our ship.   890

Messenger
Strangers, could I learn from one of you
Where is the house of Oedipus the king?
Or best, if you know, say where he is himself.

Chorus
This is his house, stranger; he dwells inside;
This woman is the mother of his children.

Messenger
May she be always blessed among the blest,
Since she is the fruitful wife of Oedipus.

Jocasta
So may you, stranger, also be. You deserve
As much for your graceful greeting. But tell me
What you have come to search for or to show.   900

Messenger
Good news for your house and your husband, lady.

Jocasta
What is it then? And from whom have you come?

Messenger
From Corinth. And the message I will tell
Will surely gladden you—and vex you, perhaps.

Jocasta
What is it? What is this double force it holds?

Messenger
The men who dwell in the Isthmian country
Have spoken to establish him their king.

Jocasta
What is that? Is not old Polybus still ruling?

Messenger
Not he. For death now holds him in the tomb.

Jocasta
What do you say, old man? Is Polybus dead?   910

Messenger
If I speak not the truth, I am ready to die.

Jocasta
O handmaid, go right away and tell your master
The news. Where are you, prophecies of the gods?
For this man Oedipus has trembled long,
And shunned him lest he kill him. Now the man
Is killed by fate and not by Oedipus.

Oedipus
O Jocasta, my most beloved wife,
Why have you sent for me within the house?

Jocasta
Listen to this man, and while you hear him, think
To what have come Apollo's holy prophecies.   920

Oedipus
Who is this man? Why would he speak to me?

Jocasta
From Corinth he has come, to announce that your father
Polybus no longer lives, but is dead.

Oedipus
What do you say, stranger? Tell me this yourself.

Messenger
If I must first announce my message clearly,
Know surely that the man is dead and gone.

Oedipus
Did he die by treachery or chance disease?

Messenger
A slight scale tilt can lull the old to rest.

Oedipus
The poor man, it seems, died by disease.

Messenger
And by the full measure of lengthy time.   930

Oedipus
Alas, alas! Why then do any seek
Pytho's prophetic art, my wife, or hear
The shrieking birds on high, by whose report
I was to slay my father? Now he lies
Dead beneath the earth, and here am I
Who have not touched the blade. Unless in longing
For me he died, and in this sense was killed by me.
Polybus has packed away these oracles
In his rest in Hades. They are now worth nothing.

Jocasta
Did I not tell you that some time ago?   940

Oedipus
You did, but I was led astray by fear.

Jocasta
Henceforth put nothing of this on your heart.

Oedipus
Why must I not still shrink from my mother's bed?

Jocasta
What should man fear, whose life is ruled by fate,
For whom there is clear foreknowledge of nothing?

It is best to live by chance, however you can.
Be not afraid of marriage with your mother;
Already many mortals in their dreams
Have shared their mother's bed. But he who counts
This dream as nothing, easiest bears his life.   950

Oedipus
All that you say would be indeed propitious,
If my mother were not alive. But since she is,
I still must shrink, however well you speak.

Jocasta
And yet your father's tomb is a great eye.[2]

Oedipus
A great eye indeed. But I fear her who lives.

Messenger
Who is this woman that you are afraid of?

Oedipus
Merope, old man, with whom Polybus lived.

Messenger
What is it in her that moves you to fear?

Oedipus
A dread oracle, stranger, sent by the god.

Messenger
Can it be told, or must no other know?   960

Oedipus
It surely can. Apollo told me once
That I must join in intercourse with my mother
And shed with my own hands my father's blood.
Because of this, long since I have kept far
Away from Corinth—and happily—but yet
It would be most sweet to see my parents' faces.

Messenger
Was this your fear in shunning your own city?

Oedipus
I wished, too, old man, not to slay my father.

Messenger
Why then have I not freed you from this fear,
Since I have come with friendly mind, my lord?   970

2. That is, a bright comfort.

Oedipus
Yes, and take thanks from me, which you deserve.

Messenger
And this is just the thing for which I came,
That when you got back home I might fare well.

Oedipus
Never shall I go where my parents are.

Messenger
My son, you clearly know not what you do.

Oedipus
How is that, old man? By the gods, let me know.

Messenger
If for these tales you shrink from going home.

Oedipus
I tremble lest what Phoebus said comes true.

Messenger
Lest you incur pollution from your parents?

Oedipus
That is the thing, old man, that always haunts me.   980

Messenger
Well, do you know that surely you fear nothing?

Oedipus
How so? If I am the son of those who bore me.

Messenger
Since Polybus was no relation to you.

Oedipus
What do you say? Was Polybus not my father?

Messenger
No more than this man here but just so much.

Oedipus
How does he who begot me equal nothing?

Messenger
That man was not your father, any more than I am.

Oedipus
Well then, why was it he called me his son?

Messenger
Long ago he got you as a gift from me.

Oedipus
Though from another's hand, yet so much he loved me!   990

Messenger
His previous childlessness led him to that.

Oedipus
Had you bought or found me when you gave me to him?

Messenger
I found you in Cithaeron's folds and glens.

Oedipus
Why were you travelling in those regions?

Messenger
I guarded there a flock of mountain sheep.

Oedipus
Were you a shepherd, wandering for pay?

Messenger
Yes, and your saviour too, child, at that time.

Oedipus
What pain gripped me, that you took me in your arms?

Messenger
The ankles of your feet will tell you that.

Oedipus
Alas, why do you mention that old trouble?   1000

Messenger
I freed you when your ankles were pierced together.

Oedipus
A terrible shame from my swaddling clothes I got.

Messenger
Your very name you got from this misfortune.

Oedipus
By the gods, did my mother or father do it? Speak.

Messenger
I know not. He who gave you knows better than I.

Oedipus
You didn't find me, but took me from another?

Messenger
That's right. Another shepherd gave you to me.

Oedipus
Who was he? Can you tell me who he was?

Messenger
Surely. He belonged to the household of Laius.

Oedipus
The man who ruled this land once long ago?   1010

Messenger
Just so. He was a herd in that man's service.

Oedipus
Is this man still alive, so I could see him?

Messenger
You dwellers in this country should know best.

Oedipus
Is there any one of you who stand before me
Who knows the shepherd of whom this man speaks?
If you have seen him in the fields or here,
Speak forth; the time has come to find this out.

Chorus
I think the man you seek is no one else
Than the shepherd you were so eager to see before.
Jocasta here might best inform us that.   1020

Oedipus
My wife, do you know the man we just ordered
To come here? Is it of him that this man speaks?

Jocasta
Why ask of whom he spoke? Think nothing of it.
Brood not in vain on what has just been said.

Oedipus
It could not be that when I have got such clues,
I should not shed clear light upon my birth.

Jocasta
Don't, by the gods, investigate this more
If you care for your own life. I am sick enough.

Oedipus
Take courage. Even if I am found a slave
For three generations, your birth will not be base.   1030

Jocasta
Still, I beseech you, hear me. Don't do this.

Oedipus

I will hear of nothing but finding out the truth.

Jocasta

I know full well and tell you what is best.

Oedipus

Well, then, this best, for some time now, has given me pain.

Jocasta

O ill-fated man, may you never know who you are.

Oedipus

Will someone bring the shepherd to me here?
And let this lady rejoice in her opulent birth.

Jocasta

Alas, alas, hapless man. I have this alone
To tell you, and nothing else forevermore.

Chorus

O Oedipus, where has the woman gone   1040
In the rush of her wild grief? I am afraid
Evil will break forth out of this silence.

Oedipus

Let whatever will break forth. I plan to see
The seed of my descent, however small.
My wife, perhaps, because a noblewoman
Looks down with shame upon my lowly birth.
I would not be dishonoured to call myself
The son of Fortune, giver of the good.
She is my mother. The years, her other children,
Have marked me sometimes small and sometimes great.   1050
Such was I born! I shall prove no other man,
Nor shall I cease to search out my descent.

Chorus

Strophe

If I am prophet and can know in mind,
Cithaeron, by tomorrow's full moon
You shall not fail, by mount Olympus,
To find that Oedipus, as a native of your land,
Shall honour you for nurse and mother.
And to you we dance in choral song because you bring
Fair gifts to him our king.
Hail, Phoebus, may all this please you.   1060

Antistrophe

Who, child, who bore you in the lengthy span of years?
One close to Pan who roams the mountain woods,

One of Apollo's bedfellows?
For all wild pastures in mountain glens to him are dear.
Was Hermes your father, who Cyllene sways,
Or did Bacchus, dwelling on the mountain peaks,
Take you a foundling from some nymph
Of those by springs of Helicon, with whom he sports the most?

Oedipus
If I may guess, although I never met him,
I think, elders, I see that shepherd coming   1070
Whom we have long sought, as in the measure
Of lengthy age he accords with him we wait for.
Besides, the men who lead him I recognize
As servants of my house. You may perhaps
Know better than I if you have seen him before.

Chorus
Be assured, I know him as a shepherd
As trusted as any other in Laius's service.

Oedipus
Stranger from Corinth, I will ask you first,
Is this the man you said?

Messenger
                                            You are looking at him.   1080

Oedipus
You there, old man, look here and answer me
What I shall ask you. Were you ever with Laius?

Servant
I was a slave, not bought but reared at home.

Oedipus
What work concerned you? What was your way of life?

Servant
Most of my life I spent among the flocks.

Oedipus
In what place most of all was your usual pasture?

Servant
Sometimes Cithaeron, or the ground nearby.

Oedipus
Do you know this man before you here at all?

Servant
Doing what? And of what man do you speak?

Oedipus
The one before you. Have you ever had congress with him?   1090

Servant
Not to say so at once from memory.

Messenger
That is no wonder, master, but I shall remind him,
Clearly, who knows me not; yet well I know
That he knew once the region of Cithaeron.
He with a double flock and I with one
Dwelt there in company for three whole years
During the six months' time from spring to fall.
When winter came, I drove into my fold
My flock, and he drove his to Laius' pens.
Do I speak right, or did it not happen so?   1100

Servant
You speak the truth, though it was long ago.

Messenger
Come now, do you recall you gave me then
A child for me to rear as my own son?

Servant
What is that? Why do you ask me this?

Messenger
This is the man, my friend, who then was young.

Servant
Go to destruction! Will you not be quiet?

Oedipus
Come, scold him not, old man. These words of yours
Deserve a scolding more than this man's do.

Servant
In what, most noble master, do I wrong?

Oedipus
Not to tell of the child he asks about.   1110

Servant
He speaks in ignorance, he toils in vain.

Oedipus
If you will not speak freely, you will under torture.

Servant
Don't, by the gods, outrage an old man like me.

Oedipus
Will someone quickly twist back this fellow's arms?

Servant
Alas, what for? What do you want to know?

Oedipus
Did you give this man the child of whom he asks?

Servant
I did. Would I had perished on that day!

Oedipus
You will come to that unless you tell the truth.

Servant
I come to far greater ruin if I speak.

Oedipus
This man, it seems, is trying to delay.   1120

Servant
Not I. I said before I gave it to him.

Oedipus
Where did you get it? At home or from someone else?

Servant
It was not mine. I got him from a man.

Oedipus
Which of these citizens? Where did he live?

Servant
O master, by the gods, ask me no more.

Oedipus
You are done for if I ask you this again.

Servant
Well then, he was born of the house of Laius.

Oedipus
One of his slaves, or born of his own race?

Servant
Alas, to speak I am on the brink of horror.

Oedipus
And I to hear. But still it must be heard.   1130

Servant
Well, then, they say it was his child. Your wife
Who dwells within could best say how this stands.

Oedipus
Was it she who gave him to you?

Servant
                    Yes, my lord.

Oedipus
For what intent?

Servant
                So I could put it away.

Oedipus
When she bore him, the wretch.

Servant
                        She feared bad oracles.

Oedipus
What were they?

Servant
                They said he should kill his father.

Oedipus
Why did you give him up to this old man?   1140

Servant
I pitied him, master, and thought he would take him away
To another land, the one from which he came.
But he saved him for greatest woe. If you are he
Whom this man speaks of, you were born curst by fate.

Oedipus
Alas, alas! All things are now come true.
O light, for the last time now I look upon you;
I am shown to be born from those I ought not to have been.
I married the woman I should not have married,
I killed the man whom I should not have killed.

Chorus

Strophe A
Alas, generations of mortal men!   1150
How equal to nothing do I number you in life!
Who, O who, is the man
Who bears more of bliss
Than just the seeming so,
And then, like a waning sun, to fall away?
When I know your example,
Your guiding spirit, yours, wretched Oedipus.
I call no mortal blest.

Antistrophe A

He is the one, O Zeus,
Who peerless shot his bow and won well-fated bliss,   1160
Who destroyed the hook-clawed maiden,
The oracle-singing Sphinx,
And stood a tower for our land from death;
For this you are called our king,
Oedipus, are highest-honoured here,
And over great Thebes hold sway.

Strophe B

And now who is more wretched for men to hear,
Who so lives in wild plagues, who dwells in pains,
In utter change of life?
Alas for glorious Oedipus!   1170
The selfsame port of rest
Was gained by bridegroom father and his son,
How, O how did your father's furrows ever bear you, suffering man?
How have they endured silence for so long?

Antistrophe B

You are found out, unwilling, by all seeing Time.
It judges your unmarried marriage where for long
Begetter and begot have been the same.
Alas, child of Laius,
Would I had never seen you.
As one who pours from his mouth a dirge I wail,   1180
To speak the truth, through you I breathed new life,
And now through you I lulled my eye to sleep.

Second Messenger

O men most honoured always of this land
What deeds you shall hear, what shall you behold!
What grief shall stir you up, if by your kinship
You are still concerned for the house of Labdacus!
I think neither Danube nor any other river
Could wash this palace clean, so many ills
Lie hidden there which now will come to light.
They were done by will, not fate; and sorrows hurt   1190
The most when we ourselves appear to choose them.

Chorus

What we heard before causes no little sorrow.
What can you say which adds to that a burden?

Second Messenger

This is the fastest way to tell the tale;
Hear it: Jocasta, your divine queen, is dead.

Chorus
O sorrowful woman! From what cause did she die?

Second Messenger
By her own hand. The most painful of the action
Occurred away, not for your eyes to see.
But still, so far as I have memory
You shall learn the sufferings of that wretched woman: 1200
How she passed on through the door enraged
And rushed straight forward to her nuptial bed,
Clutching her hair's ends with both her hands.
Once inside the doors she shut herself in
And called on Laius, who has long been dead,
Having remembrance of their seed of old
By which he died himself and left her a mother
To bear an evil brood to his own son.
She moaned the bed on which by double curse
She bore husband to husband, children to child. 1210
How thereafter she perished I do not know,
For Oedipus burst in on her with a shriek,
And because of him we could not see her woe.
We looked on him alone as he rushed around.
Pacing about, he asked us to give him a sword,
Asked where he might find the wife no wife,
A mother whose plowfield bore him and his children.
Some spirit was guiding him in his frenzy,
For none of the men who are close at hand did so.
With a horrible shout, as if led on by someone, 1220
He leapt on the double doors, from their sockets
Broke hollow bolts aside, and dashed within.
There we beheld his wife hung by her neck
From twisted cords, swinging to and fro.
When he saw her, wretched man, he terribly groaned
And slackened the hanging noose. When the poor woman
Lay on the ground, what happened was dread to see.
He tore the golden brooch pins from her clothes,
And raised them up, and struck his own eyeballs,
Shouting such words as these "No more shall you 1230
Behold the evils I have suffered and done.
Be dark from now on, since you saw before
What you should not, and knew not what you should."
Moaning such cries, not once but many times
He raised and struck his eyes. The bloody pupils
Bedewed his beard. The gore oozed not in drops,
But poured in a black shower, a hail of blood.
From both of them these woes have broken out,
Not for just one, but man and wife together.
The bliss of old that formerly prevailed 1240

Was indeed, but now upon this day
Lamentation, madness, death, and shame—
No evil that can be named is not at hand.

Chorus
Is the wretched man in any rest now from pain?

Second Messenger
He shouts for someone to open up the doors
And show to all Cadmeans his father's slayer,
His mother's—I should not speak the unholy word.
He says he will hurl himself from the land, no more
To dwell cursed in the house by his own curse.
Yet he needs strength and someone who will guide him.   1250
His sickness is too great to bear. He will show it to you
For the fastenings of the doors are opening up,
And such a spectacle you will soon behold
As would make even one who abhors it take pity.

Chorus
O terrible suffering for men to see,
Most terrible of all that I
Have ever come upon. O wretched man,
What madness overcame you, what springing daimon
Greater than the greatest for men
Has caused your evil-daimoned fate?   1260
Alas, alas, grievous one,
But I cannot bear to behold you, though I desire
To ask you much, much to find out,
Much to see,
You make me shudder so!

Oedipus
Alas, alas, I am grieved!
Where on earth, so wretched, shall I go?
Where does my voice fly through the air,
O Fate, where have you bounded?

Chorus
To dreadful end, not to be heard or seen.   1270

Strophe A

Oedipus
O cloud of dark
That shrouds me off, has come to pass, unspeakable,
Invincible, that blows no favoring blast.
Woe,
O woe again, the goad that pierces me,
Of the sting of evil now, and memory of before.

Chorus
No wonder it is that among so many pains
You should both mourn and bear a double evil.

Antistrophe A

Oedipus
Ah, friend,
You are my steadfast servant still,   1280
You still remain to care for me, blind.
Alas! Alas!
You are not hid from me; I know you clearly,
And though in darkness, still I hear your voice.

Chorus
O dreadful doer, how did you so endure
To quench your eyes? What daimon drove you on?

Strophe B

Oedipus
Apollo it was, Apollo, friends
Who brought to pass these evil, evil woes of mine.
The hand of no one struck my eyes but wretched me.
For why should I see,   1290
When nothing sweet there is to see with sight?

Chorus
This is just as you say.

Oedipus
What more is there for me to see,
My friends, what to love,
What joy to hear a greeting?
Lead me at once away from here,
Lead me away, friends, wretched as I am,
Accursed, and hated most
Of mortals to the gods.

Chorus
Wretched alike in mind and in your fortune,   1300
How I wish that I had never known you.

Antistrophe B

Oedipus
May he perish, whoever freed me
From fierce bonds on my feet,
Snatched me from death and saved me, doing me no joy.
For if then I had died, I should not be
So great a grief to friends and to myself.

Chorus
This also is my wish.

Oedipus

I would not have come to murder my father,
Nor have been called among men
The bridegroom of her from whom I was born. 1310
But as it is I am godless, child of unholiness,
Wretched sire in common with my father.
And if there is any evil older than evil left,
It is the lot of Oedipus.

Chorus

I know not how I could give you good advice,
For you would be better dead than living blind.

Oedipus

That how things are was not done for the best—
Teach me not this, or give me more advice.
If I had sight, I know not with what eyes
I could ever face my father among the dead, 1320
Or my wretched mother. What I have done to them
Is too great for a noose to expiate.
Do you think the sight of my children would be a joy
For me to see, born as they were to me?
No, never for these eyes of mine to see.
Nor the city, nor the tower, nor the sacred
Statues of gods; of these I deprive myself,
Noblest among the Thebans, born and bred,
Now suffering everything. I tell you all
To exile me as impious, shown by the gods 1330
Untouchable and of the race of Laius.
When I uncovered such a stain on me,
Could I look with steady eyes upon the people?
No, No! And if there were a way to block
The spring of hearing, I would not forbear
To lock up wholly this my wretched body.
I should be blind and deaf.—For it is sweet
When thought can dwell outside our evils.
Alas, Cithaeron, why did you shelter me?
Why did you not take and kill me at once, so I 1340
Might never reveal to men whence I was born?
O Polybus, O Corinth, O my father's halls,
Ancient in fable, what an outer fairness,
A festering of evils, you raised in me.
For now I am evil found, and born of evil.
O the three paths! Alas the hidden glen,
The grove of oak, the narrow triple roads
That drank from my own hands my father's blood.
Do you remember any of the deeds
I did before you then on my way here 1350
And what I after did? O wedlock, wedlock!

You gave me birth, and then spawned in return
Issue from the selfsame seed; you revealed
Father, brother, children, in blood relation,
The bride both wife and mother, and whatever
Actions are done most shameful among men.
But it is wrong to speak what is not good to do.
By the gods, hide me at once outside our land,
Or murder me, or hurl me in the sea
Where you shall never look on me again.   1360
Come, venture to lay your hands on this wretched man.
Do it. Be not afraid. No mortal man
There is, except myself, to bear my evils.

Chorus
Here is Creon, just in time for what you ask
To work and to advise, for he alone
Is left in place of you to guard the land.

Oedipus
Alas, what word, then, shall I tell this man?
What righteous ground of trust is clear in me,
As in the past in all I have done him evil?

Creon
Oedipus, I have not come to laugh at you,   1370
Nor to reproach you for your former wrongs.
[To the attendants]
If you defer no longer to mortal offspring,
Respect at least the all-nourishing flame
Of Apollo, lord of the sun. Fear to display
So great a pestilence, which neither earth
Nor holy rain nor light will well receive.
But you, conduct him to the house at once.
It is most pious for the kin alone
To hear and to behold the family sins.

Oedipus
By the gods, since you have plucked me from my fear,   1380
Most noble, facing this most vile man,
Hear me one word—I will speak for you, not me.

Creon
What desire do you so persist to get?

Oedipus
As soon as you can, hurl me from this land
To where no mortal man will ever greet me.

Creon
I would do all this, be sure. But I want first
To find out from the god what must be done.

Oedipus
His oracle, at least, is wholly clear;
Leave me to ruin, an impious parricide.

Creon
Thus spake the oracle. Still, as we stand   1390
It is better to find out sure what we should do.

Oedipus
Will you inquire about so wretched a man?

Creon
Yes. You will surely put trust in the god.

Oedipus
I order you and beg you, give the woman
Now in the house such burial as you yourself
Would want. Do last rites justly for your kin.
But may this city never be condemned—
My father's realm—because I live within.
Let me live in the mountains where Cithaeron
Yonder has fame of me, which father and mother   1400
When they were alive established as my tomb.
There I may die by those who sought to kill me.
And yet this much I know, neither a sickness
Nor anything else can kill me. I would not
Be saved from death, except for some dread evil.
Well, let my fate go wherever it may.
As for my sons, Creon, assume no trouble;
They are men and will have no difficulty
Of living wherever they may be.
O my poor grievous daughters, who never knew   1410
Their dinner table set apart from me,
But always shared in everything I touched—
Take care of them for me, and first of all
Allow me to touch them and bemoan our ills.
Grant it, lord,
Grant it, noble. If with my hand I touch them
I would think I had them just as when I could see.
[Creon's attendants bring in ANTIGONE *and* ISMENE.*]*
What's that?
By the gods, can it be I hear my dear ones weeping?   1420
And have you taken pity on me, Creon?
Have you had my darling children sent to me?
Do I speak right?

Creon
You do. For it was I who brought them here,
Knowing this present joy your joy of old.

Oedipus
May you fare well. For their coming may the spirit
That watches over you be better than mine.
My children, where are you? Come to me, come
Into your brother's hands, that brought about
Your father's eyes, once bright, to see like this. 1430
Your father, children, who, seeing and knowing nothing,
Became a father whence he was got himself.
I weep also for you—I cannot see you—
To think of the bitter life in days to come
Which you will have to lead among mankind.
What citizens' gatherings will you approach?
What festivals attend, where you will not cry
When you go home, instead of gay rejoicing?
And when you arrive at marriageable age,
What man, my daughters, will there be to chance you,
Incurring such reproaches on his head, 1440
Disgraceful to my children and to yours?
What evil will be absent, when your father
Killed his own father, sowed seed in her who bore him,
From whom he was born himself, and equally
Has fathered you whence he himself was born.
Such will be the reproaches. Who then will wed you?
My children, there is no one for you. Clearly
You must decay in barrenness, unwed.
Son of Menoeceus—since you are alone
Left as a father to them, for we who produced them 1450
Are both in ruin—see that you never let
These girls wander as beggars without husbands,
Let them not fall into such woes as mine.
But pity them, seeing how young they are
To be bereft of all except your aid.
Grant this, my noble friend, with a touch of your hand.
My children, if your minds were now mature,
I would give you much advice. But, pray this for me,
To live as the time allows, to find a life
Better than that your siring father had. 1460

Creon
You have wept enough here, come, and go inside the house.

Oedipus
I must obey, though nothing sweet.

Creon
                              All things are good in their time.

Oedipus
Do you know in what way I go?

Creon

                         Tell me, I'll know when I hear.

Oedipus

Send me outside the land.

Creon

                   You ask what the god will do.

Oedipus

But to the gods I am hated.

Creon

                    Still, it will soon be done.

Oedipus

Then you agree?   1470

Creon

            What I think not I would not say in vain.

Oedipus

Now lead me away.

Creon

                Come then, but let the children go.

Oedipus

Do not take them from me.

Creon

Wish not to govern all,
For what you ruled will not follow you through life.

Chorus

Dwellers in native Thebes, behold this Oedipus
Who solved the famous riddle, was your mightiest man.
What citizen on his lot did not with envy gaze?
See to how great a surge of dread fate he has come!   1480
So I would say a mortal man, while he is watching
To see the final day, can have no happiness
Till he pass the bound of life, nor be relieved of pain.

OEDIPUS AT COLONUS[1]

Sophocles

CHARACTERS

OEDIPUS, *former king of Thebes*

ANTIGONE, *his daughter*

A COUNTRYMAN *of Colonus*

CHORUS *of Elders of Colonus*

ISMENE, *sister of Antigone and daughter of Oedipus*

THESEUS, *king of Athens*

CREON, *brother-in-law of Oedipus and present ruler of Thebes*

Bodyguard of Creon

POLYNEICES, *son of Oedipus*

A MESSENGER

Soldiers and Attendants of Theseus

Servant to Ismene

TIME AND SETTING

Some twenty years have passed since OEDIPUS *blinded himself after discovering that he had murdered his father and married his mother. During much of that time he has been wandering from town to town accompanied by his daughter,* ANTIGONE. CREON, *the regent of Thebes, has turned against him, as also have his two sons, who are now contending for the throne.*

    OEDIPUS *is about sixty-five but looks much older. Gaunt, white-haired, dressed in rags (with a beggar's wallet) and leaning on* ANTIGONE, *he slowly climbs the rocky path that leads to the edge of a wood, where the statue of a hero on a horse can be discerned among the trees. It is early afternoon in April.*

Prologue

Oedipus

So where have we come to now, Antigone, my child,
    this blind old man and you—
    what people and what town?
And who today will dole out charity
    to Oedipus the vagabond?
It's little that I ask, and I make do with less.
Patience is what I've learned from pain;
    from pain and time and my own past royalty.

---

1. A newly revised and updated translation by Paul Roche.

But, do you see any place, dear girl, where I may sit:
    whether in public ground or sacred grove—   10
There sit me down
    Just until we've found out where we are.
For we are only wanderers
    and must ask advice of citizens
    and do as they direct.

Antigone
[looking at her father with concern, and then gazing across the plain toward Athens]
Poor father! Poor wayworn Oedipus! . . .
I can see the walls and turrets of a town,
    a long way off,
And where we stand is clearly consecrated ground
    luxuriant in laurel, olive, vine,   20
and deep in the song of nightingales.
*[*ANTIGONE *peers into the grove]*
So rest yourself upon this boulder here:
    a rough seat, I know.
But you've come too long a way for an old man.

Oedipus
A blind one too! So watch him well and help him down.

Antigone
After all this time, I need no lessons there.
[She leads him to the rock seat inside the grove and settles him there]

Oedipus
Now tell me: have you the slightest inkling where we are?

Antigone
Well, I know it's Athens, but this spot . . . I've no idea.

Oedipus
Of course it's Athens. That much we know from everyone we've passed.

Antigone
Then shall I go and ask what this place is called?   30

Oedipus
Do child, if there's any sign of life.

Antigone
Oh, but there must be!
In fact I don't even have to go. I see a man approaching.

Oedipus
What! Coming our way? Coming here?

Antigone

He's almost on us . . . Quick, you speak, Father—
>here he is.

[*Enter a* COUNTRYMAN *of Colonus*]

Oedipus

Excuse me, good sir, my daughter here
>whose eyes are mine as they are hers,
>tells me you are passing by,

Just in time, I'm sure, to solve our doubts and let us know . . .   40

Countryman

Before you start your questioning
>come off that seat:

You're tresspassing on holy ground.

Oedipus

Holy ground? What god is sacred here?

Countryman

It's untouchable—not to be inhabited—
>abode of most stern goddesses:
>daughters of Earth and Darkness.

Oedipus

Then let me pray to them. What are their holy names?

Countryman

The All-seeing Eumenides or Kindly Ones, we call them here.
>In other places graced no doubt by other names.   50

Oedipus

Then let them welcome me, their suppliant,
>for I shall never set my foot outside this haven here.

Countryman

What do you mean?

Oedipus

I recognize the signs—my journey's end.

Countryman

Well, I've no power to shift you without a warrant.
I must go and let the city know.

Oedipus

Meanwhile, my friend, for the love of all the gods,
>don't disappoint a homeless wanderer, but tell me . . .

Countryman

Ask. I have no call to disappoint.

Oedipus
Then where have we come to? Does this place have a name? 60

Countryman
I'll tell you everything I know.
This whole ground is sacred. Great Poseidon holds it.
Prometheus the Titan who bore fire is present here.
The very spot you occupy is called "The Brazen Threshold,"
    the cornerstone of Athens.
That statue there, that horseman who rides above the fields,
    is Colonus himself, origin and Lord of all this clan,
    who gave the place its name:
Perhaps not much to sing about but, believe me Stranger,
    living music to all who inhabit here. 70

Oedipus
So there are inhabitants in these parts?

Countryman
Certainly, and called after their horseman hero there.

Oedipus
But who governs them? Or do they rule themselves?

Countryman
A king in Athens rules over them.

Oedipus
A respected monarch whose word is law? Who is he?

Countryman
His name is Theseus, son of King Aegeus before him.

Oedipus
Then could I send a message by one of you to him?

Countryman
A message, what? Asking him to come?

Oedipus
To say, "a little favor wins a great reward."

Countryman
Great reward? What can a blind man give? 80

Oedipus
You shall *see*—there's vision in every syllable I say.

Countryman
Listen, stranger, I am out to help.
You are obviously well-born, though down in luck.

Stay where you are, exactly where I found you,
  while I go and tell the local people here.
Let *them* decide whether you are to stay or go.
[*The* COUNTRYMAN *hurries off*]

Oedipus
Daughter, has that person gone?

Antigone
Gone, Father. Be at ease. Say anything you like.
There's no one here but me.
[OEDIPUS *staggers to his knees in an attitude of prayer.* ANTIGONE *stands watching a few paces away*]

Oedipus
Great mistresses of terrifying mien,   90
I salute you first on bended knee
  in this your sanctuary.
Harden not your hearts against me or Apollo,
  for even when he told my doom
  he foretold me too
  that after long journeys I should come
  to my journey's end
  at a faraway place of rest, a shelter
  at the seat of you the dreaded Holy Ones.
"There," he said,   100
"you will close your life of sorrows,
With blessings on the land that harbors you
  and curses on the people who cast you out."
Certain signs, he said, would warn me of these things:
  earthquakes, thunder, lightnings from Zeus.
I realize now
  some gentle spell from you
  has pulled my steps toward this grove.
How else could I have found you first
  and wandered here—   110
I the sober and you the wineless ones—
To sit upon this holy seat not made with human hands?
Therefore, you kind divinities,
  in fulfillment of Apollo's prophecies,
  grant me here to reach my term at last,
  my rounding off of life;
Unless you think me far too vile for that—
  I a slave to sorrow far worse than any slave's.
So, hear me, good daughters of primeval Night.
And Athens, you first of cities, namesake of great Pallas,   120
pity this poor remnant, Oedipus,
  this ghost, this carcass of what he was—a man.

Antigone

Quiet, Father! Some elderly men are coming our way,
    spying out your resting place.

Oedipus

Then quiet I'll be,
    while you hurry me off this path into the grove,
    until I hear just what it is they have to say.
It's always wise to be informed before we act.
[OEDIPUS and ANTIGONE hustle into the trees]

First Choral Dialogue

[Enter the CHORUS of Elders of Colonus. They scurry about, searching among the bushes and behind the rocks, meanwhile uttering severally:]

Strophe I

Look for him?
           Who is it?
                  Where can he lurk?   130
Where has he bolted?
                Oh what a sacrilege!
Comb the ground.
    Strain your eyes.
        Search him out everywhere.
A vagabond, surely,
    some aged vagabond.
No one from here,
    would ever have pushed   140
Into this virgin plot of the unaffrontable maidens,
Whose very name sends shivers,
    whom we pass with averted eyes,
Whom we pray to with quavering lips.
But now a blasphemous rogue
    is hidden somewhere they say,
And I've covered the ground on every side
But still I cannot uncover
    the cranny in which he hides.
[OEDIPUS and ANTIGONE step from the trees]

Oedipus

I am the man and my ears are my eyes,   150
as they say of the blind.

Chorus

Ah! Horrible to see, and horrible to hear!

Oedipus

Listen, please! I am no criminal.

Chorus
Zeus, defend us! Who could this old man be?

Oedipus
No favorite of fate—I can tell you that—
    good guardians of this grove.
For who would borrow eyes to walk,
    or lean his weight on frail support?

Antistrophe I
Look at his eyes!
    Great gods!   160
    He's blind!
Eyeless from birth?
    What a lifetime of horror!
Far be it
    from us, sir,
        to add to your sorrows,
But you trespass, you trespass;
    step no further
Into the still   170
of the grassy dell
Where chaliced water from the spring, blended with honey,
Is poured in a stream of the purest offering. Go
Away from there, you woebegone stranger.
Turn back, come away,
    no matter how far you have wandered.
Can you hear us from there, you derelict outcast?
Speak if you want, and we'll listen, but not
    till you've moved from the sacred close.
[OEDIPUS and ANTIGONE stand motionless]

Oedipus
My daughter, what are we to do?

Antigone
Do as they say, Father. We must yield and listen.   180

Oedipus
Your hand then, come.

Antigone
There, you have it.

Oedipus
Sirs, I am breaking cover.
You must not violate my trust.

Chorus
Never fear, old man!
No one will drag you off from here against your will.

[OEDIPUS *takes a step forward out of the grove. End of strophic pattern but not of* Choral Dialogue]

Oedipus
Further?

Chorus
Come still further.
[He takes another step]

Oedipus
Enough?

Chorus
Lead him, girl, you understand.   190

Antigone
I do indeed—these many years . . . Careful now!

Oedipus
Oh, what it is to walk in the dark!

Antigone
Come, Father, come! Let your blind steps follow.

Chorus
Poor harassed stranger on strange soil!
Learn to loathe what we find loathing.
Learn respect for what we reverence.

Oedipus
Then guide my walking, you my daughter,
Down the path of pious bidding
Where we can talk without offending.
Let's not fight with what is fated.   200
[He advances onto a platform of rock at the edge of the grove]

Chorus
There.
You need not go beyond that ledge of rock.

Oedipus
This far?

Chorus
That is far enough. Do you hear us?

Oedipus
May I sit?

Chorus
Yes, sit to the side of that slab of rock.

Antigone
I have you, Father. Lean on me.

Oedipus
Oh, what a wretched thing it is! . . .

Antigone
Step by step, we together,
Old and young, weak and strong;   210
Lean your loving weight on mine.

Oedipus
Oh, how pitiable my wretchedness!
[ANTIGONE *finally settles him on the rock*]

Chorus
You sad old man, relax at last
And tell us of your birth and home.
What prompts this weary pilgrimage?
What country are you from?

Oedipus
[*alarmed*]
Country? None. . . . Oh please, good friends, do not . . .

Chorus
Do not what, old man? What are you avoiding?

Oedipus
Do not . . . Oh please—
    not ask me who I am!   220

Chorus
Why? What is it?

Oedipus
My frightening origin.

Chorus
Tell it.

Oedipus
[*turning to* ANTIGONE]
Dear child, must I out with it?

Chorus
Sir, your ancestry? Your father's name?

Oedipus
No no, not that! Child, what shall I do?

Antigone
Tell them, since you've gone so far already.

Oedipus
Then I'll say it. There's no way to cover up.

Chorus
Both of you—you're wasting time—get on with it.

Oedipus
Laius . . . Have you heard the name?   230

Chorus
Dear gods! We have.

Oedipus
Of the line of Labdacus?

Chorus
Great Zeus!

Oedipus
And Oedipus the stricken one?

Chorus
What! That man is you?

Oedipus
Wait, listen—do not recoil.

Chorus
Oh monstrous! Monstrous!

Oedipus
It's hopeless now.

Chorus
Intolerable!

Oedipus
Daughter, what will happen now?   240

Chorus
Away with both of you! Leave our land!

Oedipus
But you promised! You will keep your word?

Chorus
There is no blame attached to any
Who hits back where first he's wronged.
You deceived us, so we're playing
Trick for tricking, paying back
Treachery with trouble. Go!
Quit these precincts, quit our country,
Do not pollute our city with your tainted air.

Antigone

You gentle sirs of pious intent,   250
If unmoved by my father's plight
And all those horrors not his fault,
To me at least be kind, who beg you.
He is my father, all I have.
I'm pleading with my eyes to yours:
Eyes not blind, but eye to eye,
Almost as if I were your daughter,
Beseeching you for a beaten man
Needing mercy. Like a god
You have us wholly in your hands.   260
Come, be clement past our hoping.
By all your dearest roots to life,
I implore you: child and wife,
Hearth and godhead. Bear in mind
There never was a human being
Who, god-impelled, had hope in fleeing.
[End of Choral Dialogue]

First Episode

Chorus

Daughter of Oedipus, of course we pity you,
    just as we pity him for what he suffers;
But we dare not risk divine displeasure
    and go beyond what we've said already.   270

Oedipus

Then where has fame and where has reputation gone
    if this be Athens that most pious city?
Sanctuary of the lost, savior of the needy,
    unique in both! What good are they
When you tear me from my seat of stone
    and cast me headlong from the land?
And all because you've merely heard my name!
Me, this carcass, this right hand of mine,
    you can't fear that; for what I've done is simply suffer:
Yes, suffer much more than anything I've done.   280
As I could prove if I but touched upon the story
    of my mother and my father.
It's this that frightens you, as well I know.
Am I then a sinner born?
I, provoked to strike in self-defense?
Why, even if I'd acted with full knowledge,
    it still would not have been a crime.
As it was, where I went I went
All ignorant toward a doom too known
    to those who planned it.   290

Therefore, good sirs,
    since you have moved me from my seat,
    you must—by all the gods—protect me now.
Do not say you reverence heaven,
    then do nothing but ignore what heaven says.
Make no mistake,
    the gods' eyes see the just
    and the gods' eyes see the unjust too,
    and from that blazing gaze,
    never on this earth,   300
will the wicked man escape by flight.
By heaven's grace then,
    let no dishonor blot the name of Athens by abetting wrong.
You accepted me as suppliant and gave a pledge,
    now guard me to the end.
And when you look into my ruined eyes,
    do not look with scorn.

I am a priestly and a holy man,
    and come with blessings for your people in my hands.
And when your prince shall come,   310
whoever be your prince,
Then shall everything be told and all made plain.
But in that space between do nothing mean.

Chorus
Your words, old man, must make us think.
These solemn arguments have weight.
Let authority decide. We are content.

Oedipus
And where is he who wields authority?

Chorus
In Athens, our ancestral city.
The scout who sent us here has gone for him.

Oedipus
What hope is there that he will come?   320
Why should he trouble with a blind old man?

Chorus
Certainly he will come—once he hears your name.

Oedipus
But who will tell him that?

Chorus
The road is long but travelers talk.
He will hear your name and he will come.

For every region of the earth has heard your name, old man.
The instant that it hits his ears
> he will leap up from his recreation and his ease
> and hurry here.

Oedipus
Then may his coming bring rewards   330
for myself and for his city.
Ah! Is not nobility its own reward?

Antigone
Great heavens, I am speechless!
Father, I can't imagine it.

Oedipus
What's happening, Antigone, my child?

Antigone
I see a woman coming straight toward us on a colt,
> an Etnan thoroughbred.
She wears a broad Thessalian hat
> to shade her from the sun.
I can't be sure. Is it she or isn't it?   340
Is my mind wandering? It can't be her . . . surely can it?
But it must be . . . It is.
Her eyes are flashing welcomes.
She's almost on us. She's waving now.
Of course . . . it's no one but our own Ismene.

Oedipus
What are you saying, child?

Antigone
That your daughter—and my sister—is right in front of me.
Wait till you hear her voice.
[ISMENE, *attended by a single servant, advances toward* OEDIPUS *and* ANTIGONE]

Ismene
Dearest Father! Sister!
The sweetest names in the world to me.   350
It was difficult to find you, and now
> it's difficult to see you through my tears.

Oedipus
Darling daughter—you?

Ismene
Poor dear Father!

Oedipus
But, child, you're really here?

Ismene
It was not easy.

Oedipus
Dear girl—let me feel you.

Ismene
Let me hug you both.
[They all embrace]

Oedipus
My children! . . . My sisters!

Ismene
The stricken ones.   360

Oedipus
Yes, she and I.

Ismene
With me the third.

Oedipus
But, Daughter, what has brought you?

Ismene
Concern for you, Father.

Oedipus
You mean, you missed me?

Ismene
Yes. And I've come with news,
    trusting myself to this last loyal servant here.

Oedipus
But those young men your brothers, where are they?

Ismene
Just where they are—in the thick of trouble.

Oedipus
Oh, what miserable and perfect copies   370
have they grown to be of Egyptian ways!
For there the men sit at home and weave
    while their wives go out to win the daily bread,
    as you do, my daughters.
Just so your brothers, who should be
    the very ones to take this load upon them.
Instead they sit at home like girls
    and keep the house,
    leaving the two of you to face my troubles
    and make life a little easier for me.   380

Antigone here,
   ever since she left the nursery
   and became a woman,
   has been with me as guide and old man's nurse,
   steering me through my dreary wanderings;
   often roaming through the tangled forests,
   barefoot and hungry,
   often soaked by rain and scorched by sun,
   never regretting all she'd missed at home,
   so long as her father was provided for. 390

And you, my daughter
   more than once you've sallied forth
   slipping past the Theban sentinels
   to bring your father news of all the latest oracles.
You were my faithful spy
   when I was driven from the land.
But, Ismene, what new tidings do you bring your father?
What mission has summoned you from home?
You don't come empty-handed, that I know.
You've brought me something— 400
something I can fear.

Ismene
I went through fire and water, Father,
   to find out where you were and how you were surviving,
   but let that pass;
I have no desire to live it all again
   by telling you.

The trouble now is those two sons of yours
   that's what I've come to tell you.
They were content at first to leave the throne to Creon,
   and rid the city of the ancient family curse 410
that has dogged our line.
But now they are possessed.
Some demon of pride, some jealousy,
   has gripped their souls
   with a manic lust for royal power.
They want to seize the reins of government.
Eteocles, our hot-brained stripling younger brother,
   has snatched the throne from his elder, Polyneices,
   and driven him from Thebes.
While Polyneices, we hear from every source, 420
has fled to the vale of Argos,
   adds marriage to diplomacy and military alliances,
And swears that Argos will either
   acquit herself with triumph on the Theban plain
   or be lifted to the skies in glorious attempt.

This is no fiction but the agonizing truth.
How far the gods will go before they let some mercy fall—
Oh, Father, fall on you!—it's impossible to tell.

Oedipus
Ah! Did you think that any glances of the gods
    could ever be a glance to save me?   430

Ismene
Yes, Father, that I hoped, exactly that.
There've been new oracles.

Oedipus
My child, what oracles? What have they said?

Ismene
That soon the men of Thebes will seek you out,
    dead or alive: a talisman for their salvation.

Oedipus
Ha! a talisman for what—one such as I?

Ismene
In you, they say, there is a power born—a power for them.

Oedipus
So, when I am a nothing, then am I a man?

Ismene
The gods now bear you up; before they cast you down.

Oedipus
An old man on a pedestal, his youth in ruins!   440

Ismene
Nevertheless, this you ought to know.
Creon is on his way to use you, and sooner now than later.

Oedipus
To use me, Daughter? How?

Ismene
He wants to plant you on the frontiers of Thebes;
    within their reach, of course, but not within their sight.

Oedipus
On the threshold, then? What use is that?

Ismene
It saves them from a curse if your tomb be wronged.

Oedipus
But bestows a blessing if it is honored.
They needed neither god nor oracle to tell them that.

Ismene
And so they want to keep you somewhere near,   450
    but not where you can set up as master of yourself.

Oedipus
And when I die, to bury me in Theban dust at least?

Ismene
No, dear Father, no; you spilled your father's blood.

Oedipus
Then I'll not fall into their hands—no, never!

Ismene
And *that,* one day, will spell the ruin of Thebes.

Oedipus
How so, my child? What way will they be hurt?

Ismene
Scorched by the anger blazing from your tomb.[2]

Oedipus
Who told you, child, all this you're telling me?

Ismene
Pilgrims from the very hearth of Delphi.

Oedipus
And Apollo really said these things of me?   460

Ismene
So those men avowed on their return to Thebes.

Oedipus
Has either of my sons heard this?

Ismene
Both of them alike; each taking it to heart.

Oedipus
Scoundrels! So they knew it! Coveted my presence less
    than they coveted a crown.

Ismene
It hurts to hear you say it, but it's true.

Oedipus
Oh you gods! Tread not down
    the blaze of coming battle between these two.

---

2. This refers to the day when the Theban invaders of Athens will be routed in battle near the tomb of Oedipus.

And give me power to prophesy the end
    for which they now match spear with clash on spear.   470

Then shall the one who now
    enjoys the scepter and the throne
    no more remain,
And he who fled the realm, not return.
I was their father,
    thrust out from fatherland in full disgrace.
They did not rescue or defend me.
No, they cared nothing:
    but watched me harried from my home,
    my banishment proclaimed.   480
And if you say that such was then my wish,
    a mercy granted by the city—apt and opportune—
I answer, "No!"
On that first day I wished it, yes,
    death was sweet—my soul on fire—
    even death by stoning,
    but no man was found to further that desire.
In time my madness mellowed.
I began to think my rage had plunged too far,
    my chastisement excessive for my sins.   490
And then the city—city, mark you, after all that time—
    had me thrust and hurtled out of Thebes.
Then they could have helped,
    my two boys, their father's sons—
    then they could have stirred themselves.
They could. They did not do a thing.
For lack of a little word from them
    I was cast out
    to drag away my life in wandering beggary.
Shelter, devoted care, my daily bread,   500
everything within a woman's power to give,
    these I owe to my two daughters here.
Their brothers sold their father for a throne,
    exchanged him for a scepter and a realm.

No, I'll not help them win a war,
And the crown of Thebes will prove to be their bane.
That much Ismene's oracles make clear
    now that I match them with those others,
    those olden oracles Apollo made me once
    and now at last fulfills.   510
So let them send a Creon to search me out;
    or any other potentate from Thebes.
I shall be your city's champion and the scourge
    of all my enemies,

With you, good people, on my side,
And by the grace of the Holy Ones who here abide.

Chorus
Certainly, Oedipus, you impel our sympathies,
    you and your two daughters here.
And now that you add the sovereign weight
    of your great name to make our city triumph   520
we are more than ready to help you with advice.

Oedipus
Good friends, I'll carry out whatever you suggest.

Chorus
Then expiate at once those goddesses
    whose holy precincts you profaned.

Oedipus
By what ritual, friends? Tell me that.

Chorus
First, from the spring of living waters fetch
    in pure washed hands the ceremonial draught.

Oedipus
And when I've fetched this fresh unsullied cup?

Chorus
You'll find some chalices of delicate design.
Crown with wreaths their double handles and their brims.   530

Oedipus
What kind of wreaths? Olive sprigs or flocks of wool?

Chorus
A eye-lamb's fleece all freshly shorn.

Oedipus
Good. And then, . . . How do I complete the rite?

Chorus
Pour out your offering, with your face towards the dawn.

Oedipus
Pouring from those chalices you spoke of?

Chorus
Yes, in three libations, emptying the last.

Oedipus
And this last, please tell me clearly:
    what should it contain?

Chorus
Water mixed with honey. Add no wine.

Oedipus
And when the green-shadowed ground has drunk this cup? 540

Chorus
Lay thrice nine sprigs of olive on it
    and with both hands offer up a prayer.

Oedipus
The Prayer? That's most important. Tell me that.

Chorus
That these goddesses we call the Kindly Ones, or Eumenides,
    be saving kind to you, who pray to them.
Make that your prayer, or someone make it for you.
Whisper it and do not cry it out.
Then come away. Do not turn back.
This accomplished, we shall gladly stand by you;
    otherwise, my friend, we are afraid. 550

Oedipus
My daughters, did you hear what these locals said?

Antigone
Father, we heard. Tell us what you want.

Oedipus
I cannot go. I am too weak and blind—
    my double disability.
Will one of you two do it for me?
A single person pure of heart, I think,
    can make atonement for a thousand sinners.
So do it now, but do not leave me all alone.
I am not strong enough to get along without a helping hand.

Ismene
Then I shall carry out the rite, 560
    if somebody will point the way.

Chorus
Beyond that clump of trees, young woman.
The guardian of the grove will tell you
    everything you want to know.

Ismene
To my task, then.
Antigone, you watch over Father here.
No trouble is too much for a parent anywhere.
[ISMENE *goes into the grove. The* CHORUS *turns to* OEDIPUS]

Second Choral Dialogue

Strophe I

Chorus
Stranger it hurts
   to stir up the memory
      time has let slumber,   570
      but we must know . . .

Oedipus
What now?

Chorus
The story of suffering
   you have been chained to:
      the fatal ordeal without a cure.

Oedipus
For hospitality's sake, my friends,
   do not uncover my shame.

Chorus
The tale of it echoes
   all over the universe.
      But the truth of it, tell us,   580
      how much is true?

Oedipus
No! No!

Chorus
We beg you tell.

Oedipus
Ah, the shame of it!

Chorus
Grant us this favor
   as *we* favored *you.*

Antistrophe I

Oedipus
Friends, so many sufferings
   suffered unwittingly!
      God is my witness,
         none of it guiltily.   590

Chorus
How did it happen?

Oedipus
An innocent bridegroom,
   a twisted wedding
      yoking Thebes to disaster.

Chorus
Is there truth in the word that you shared
   the incestuous bed of a mother?

Oedipus
Must you, good people?
   It's death to hear it.
      Ah, these maidens are mine,
         but more than that . . .   600

Chorus
Go on! Go on!

Oedipus
Two daughters, two curses . . .

Chorus
Zeus, oh no!

Oedipus
Two shoots from the birthpangs
   of a wife-mother's tree.

Strophe II

Chorus
What! Are you saying, your children are both . . .

Oedipus
Their father's offspring and his sisters.

Chorus
Horrible!

Oedipus
Horror, yes horror. Wave upon wave.

Chorus
Victim!   610

Oedipus
Yes, endlessly victim.

Chorus
Sinner, too!

Oedipus
No sinner.

Chorus
How?

Oedipus
I saved
The city—I wish I had not—
And the prize for this has broken my heart.

Antistrophe II

Chorus
Broken your heart with shedding the blood of . . . ?

Oedipus
What is it now? What more are you after?

Chorus
A father . . .   620

Oedipus
Stab upon stab!
    wound upon wounding!

Chorus
Killer!

Oedipus
I killed him, yes, but can plead . . .

Chorus
What can you . . . ?

Oedipus
Justice.

Chorus
How?

Oedipus
Let me tell you:
    The man that I murdered would have killed *me.*
By law I am innocent, void of all malice.   630
[End of Choral Dialogue. THESEUS *and his retinue are seen approaching. The* CHO-
RUS *turns in his direction]*

Chorus
But here comes our king, Theseus son of Aegeus,
    bent upon your bidding.
[Enter THESEUS *with soldiers and attendants. He stands gazing at* OEDIPUS]

Theseus
That story noised abroad so often in the past,
    the bloody butchering of your sight,

warned me it was you, Son of Laius,
And now, hastened here by rumors,
   I can see it is.
Your clothes, your mutilated face,
   assure me of your name.
And I would gently ask you, tortured Oedipus,   640
what favor you would have of me or Athens:
You and that sad companion by your side?
Tell me.
For no tale of yours however shocking
   could make me turn away.
I was a child of exile too,
   fighting for my life in foreign lands—
   and none so dangerously.
So never could I turn my back on some poor exile
   such as you are now   650
and leave him to his fate.
For I know too well that I am only man.
The portion of your days today
   could be no less than mine tomorrow.

Oedipus

Theseus, in so short a speech
   all your birth's declared,
   and my reply can be as brief.
My name, my father and my country,
   you've touched on all correctly.
There's nothing left for me to say   660
but tell you my desire,
   and all my tale is told.

Theseus

I wait to hear it. Please proceed to tell.

Oedipus

I come with a gift: this my battered body.
No priceless vision, no,
But the price of it is better than of beauty.

Theseus

What makes it precious, this gift you bring?

Oedipus

In time you'll know. Not now perhaps.

Theseus

And when will that time of grace be known?

Oedipus

When I am dead and you have raised my tomb.   670

Theseus
Life's last rites, you ask for that,
  with all before made nothing of, forgotten!

Oedipus
Yes, for in that wish the rest is harvested.

Theseus
You ask a little favor, then, compressing everything?

Oedipus
Perhaps, but not so little—believe me—not so little.

Theseus
Does it, then, concern your sons and me?

Oedipus
It does, my king, they are intent to carry me off to Thebes.

Theseus
Which ought to please you, surely, more than banishment?

Oedipus
No. For when I wanted that they would not have it.

Theseus
This is foolishness to sulk in time of trouble.   680

Oedipus
Wait till you've heard me out before you scold.

Theseus
Proceed. I have no right to judge before I know.

Oedipus
I am the victim, Theseus; of repeated and appalling wrong.

Theseus
You mean the family curse that haunts your line?

Oedipus
No. *That* already rings in Greece's ears.

Theseus
But what could be worse than that—
  the worst wretchedness of all?

Oedipus
Just this:
  I am driven from my native land by my own flesh and blood.
  I can return no more. I am a parricide.   690

Theseus
What, ostracized and summoned home in one?

Oedipus
The god has spoken. His warning makes them want me there.

Theseus
And what is the warning threatened by the oracle?

Oedipus
A mortal wound dealt on this very field of battle.

Theseus
This field of battle? But Athens and Thebes are not at war.

Oedipus
Good son of Aegeus, gentle son,
    only to the gods is given not to age or die,
All else disrupts through all disposing time.
Earth ebbs in strength, the body ebbs in power.
Faith dies and faithlessness is born.   700
No constant friendship breathes
    between man and man, or city and a city.
Soon or late, the sweet will sour,
    the sour will sweet to love again.
Does fair weather hold between this Thebes and you?
Then one day shall ever teeming time
    hatch nights on teeming days,
Wherein this pledge, this harmony, this hour
    will break upon a spear,
    slashed down for a useless word.   710
Then shall my sleeping corpse,
    cold in sepulcher,
    warm itself with draughts of their perfervid blood,
If Zeus is Zeus and truth be truth
    from Zeus's son Apollo.
But I'm not one to bawl away a mystery,
    so let me stop where I began:
Take care to keep your word with me,
    then never shall you say of Oedipus
    you gave him sanctuary without reward;   720
Or, if you do, all heaven is a fraud.

Chorus
Sire, from the first this man has sworn
    he had the power to benefact our land.

Theseus
How could we spurn the overtures of such a friend,
    who not only rightly claims the hospitality
    of Thebes an allied city,
But comes appealing to our goddesses
    and pays no little tribute to our State and me?

I shall reverence and not repudiate his gift
    and grant him all the rights of citizen.   730
But more: if it please our guest to sojourn here,
    I place him in your care.
    yes Oedipus—unless you'd rather come with me—
    the choice is yours,
    your every wish is mine.

Oedipus
Great Zeus, be gentle to such gentleness!

Theseus
Well, what is your wish? Will you come with me?

Oedipus
If only that were fitting, but this very place is where I must . . .

Theseus
Must what? I shall not hinder you.

Oedipus
. . . triumph over those who banished me.   740

Theseus
And as you promised, shower blessings on us with your presence?

Oedipus
Only if you keep your word to me.

Theseus
Never doubt it. I am not one to play you false.

Oedipus
And I'll not make you swear it like a criminal.

Theseus
An oath would be no surer than my word.

Oedipus
But how will you proceed if . . .

Theseus
What now disturbs you?

Oedipus
Men will come.

Theseus
And mine will see to them.

Oedipus
But if you leave me . . .   750

Theseus
You need not tell me what to do.

Oedipus
The fear in my heart compels me.

Theseus
And there is no fear in mine.

Oedipus
But the threats . . . you do not know . . .

Theseus
I know only this:
That no one is going to kidnap you against my will.
Often bluff and bluster, threat and counterthreat
    can bully reason for a time,
But when the mind reseats itself
    disquiet vanishes.   760
These people who have shouted lustily
    for your abduction,
Will, I trust, run into a long and ruffled passage here.
Have confidence!
Apart from all my promises, has not Apollo
    charge of you within this hallowed ground?
And when I'm gone,
    my name's enough to keep you sound.
[THESEUS *leaves with his retinue. The* CHORUS *regroups and faces the audience to
deliver a eulogy on Colonus and Athens*]

Choral Ode

Strophe I
Stranger, here
Is the land of the horse   770
Earth's fairest home
This silver hill Colonus.

Here the nightingale
Spills perennial sound
Lucent through the evergreen.

Here the wine-deep ivies creep
Through the god's untrodden bower
Heavy with the laurel berry.

Here there is a sunless quiet
Riven by no storm.   780
Here the corybantic foot

Of Bacchus beats
Tossing with the nymphs who nursed him.

Antistrophe I
The narcissus
That drinks sky's dew
Here lifts its day
By-day-born eye:

The diadem that crowns
The curls of ancient goddesses.
The crocus casts his saffron glance   790

And unparched Cephisus all day
Wanders out from sleepless springs
Fingering his crystal way

Out among the gentle breasts
Of hills and dales
Swelling with fecundity.
Not seldom here the Muses sing
And Aphrodite rides with golden rein.

Strophe II
Not in Asia
Never in Pelops   800
(Great Dorian island)
Was heard the like of what I sing:
A tree indomitable, self-engendered,
Challenge to the spears of armies
Lush in Athens
Sap of striplings—
Olive, the moon-green olive.
No youth in lustihood
Shall ravish her
Nor calculating age.   810
The sleepless eye of Zeus is on her
Athena's gaze cerulean.

Antistrophe II
Add praise on praise:
Our mother city's
Prize and god-gift:
Prowess in horses, prowess in stallions
Prowess at sea. You Poseidon
Son of Cronus, sat her high,
Rode her down
These roads displaying   820
How the bit and bridle

Breaks the stamping charger
How the oarblade
Sleekly stroking
Cuts the brine behind
The hundred-footed Nereids.

Second Episode

[ANTIGONE's attention is riveted by the approach of an old man hurrying toward them with a squad of soldiers]

Antigone
Look! You much praised land, the hour has come
    for you to make your words shine forth with deeds.

Oedipus
[alarmed]
Child, what now?

Antigone
Creon is coming . . . And, Father, not alone.   830

Oedipus
You generous counselors, now is the time
    to prove the limits of your sanctuary.

Chorus
Take heart! Proof you'll have.
Though we be old, our country's strength is young.
[CREON arrives at the head of his escort of guards]

Creon
Sirs, you worthy men of Attica,
I see some apprehension in your eyes at my approach.
Do not recoil. Do not be ready with abuse.
I have not come to do you harm—
    an old man against a mighty state,
    mighty as ever there was in Greece.   840
My mission is to plead with that old man
    to return with me to Theban territory.
I am no private emissary—ah no!—
    but a nation's full ambassador.
It was my lot as this man's relative
    to bear the crushing load of his estate
    as no man else in Thebes.
[He turns toward OEDIPUS]
Do you hear me, Oedipus?
Come home you woebegotten man!
Everyone in Thebes is rightly calling for you;   850
I most of all, yes, I,
    who'd be a brute indeed

not to weep to see an old man suffer so:
drifting endlessly, unknown, a vagabond,
a girl his single prop—and she poor thwarted creature
Fallen lower than I'd ever dream she'd fall,
dragging out her gloomy squalid life of caring for you:
well ripe for weddings but unwed and waiting,
ah! for some thick-fisted yokel's snatch.
A disgrace? Indeed, we are all disgraced. 860
I point at you and me and all of Thebes.
Who can cover up what so emblazons forth?
You can at last. Yes, Oedipus, you can hide it now.
By all our fathers' gods, consent to come back home,
your own ancestral city.
Say farewell to Athens, kind as she has been.
Home comes first,
the place of your long-gone cradlehood.

Oedipus

You brazen hypocrite! You'd stop at nothing.
Twisting every righteous motive to your ends! 870
You'd trap me, would you, in your cruel coils a second time?
Once in agony I turned against myself
and cried aloud for banishment.
Then it did not fit your pleasure, did it,
to fit yourself to mine?
But when my overbrimming passion had gone down
and home's four walls were sweet,
Then you had me routed out and cast away.
Fine affection *that* for family ties!

And now again, the moment you perceive 880
me being welcomed by this kindly city and her sons,
you want to wrench me away,
your barbed designs wrapped up in words of wool.
Who ever heard of friendliness by force?
You're like a man who spurns to grant a favor when he's asked,
gives nothing, will not lift a finger for you,
Then when your heart's desire has passed,
wants to push that very grace upon you,
now a grace no longer.
Rather barren of delight that gift, do you not think? 890
Yet that precisely is the gift you proffer me,
so fair in form, so hollow in reality.
Therefore, let me shout your falsehood out to these
and let them gaze at your duplicity.
You come to fetch me—home? Ah no!
You come to plant me on your doorstep,
A talisman to ward away the onslaughts Attica will launch.

That wish you'll never have, but this you will:
    my curse forever on your land,
And for my sons this sole realm and heritage—   900
the right, and room enough, to die.
Ha! I'd say my forecast for the fate of Thebes
    was more informed than yours. Oh much!
    So much the more reliable!
It stems from Zeus and from Apollo.
Yours is from a counterfeiting tongue,
    double-edged and whetted to deceit.
But yours, you'll find, will reap more suffering than success.
However, since I cannot make you see this—go!
And leave us here to lead a life of hardship as we may.   910
Hardship to those resigned is no dismay.

Creon
A splendid tirade!
But whom do you think it hurts, you or me?

Oedipus
What care I? So long as you fail as thoroughly
    to dupe these people here as you've duped me.

Creon
Silly obdurate man, whom time has not made wise!
Must you bring even dotage to disgrace?

Oedipus
Such a tricky tongue! I never knew an honest man
    who could dissertate and twist speech so.

Creon
Dissertation is quite different from frothing at the mouth.   920

Oedipus
You, of course, can dissertate and hit the bull's-eye straight.

Creon
Not exactly straight—with such a crooked target.

Oedipus
Be off with you! I speak for all these people here.
I do not want you prowling round my haven.

Creon
Then I appeal to them, these people, not to you.
You I'll deal with once I've got you in my clutches.

Oedipus
Got me in your clutches, eh?
With these my friends all looking on?

Creon
Just wait! I know another way to make you wince.

Oedipus
Another way? I'd like to see exactly how.   930

Creon
Certainly! You have two daughters.
One I've already seized. The other will quickly follow.

Oedipus
Oh no!

Creon
Oh yes! And you'll soon have more to groan about.

Oedipus
You've got my child?

Creon
And soon will have the other.

Oedipus
Friends, my friends, is there nothing you can do?
You must not fail me now. Hound this horrible man away.

Chorus
Sir, be off with you! What you have done
     and what you mean to do is criminal.   940

Creon
[to his guards]
Grab the girl. It's time to act.
Drag her off by force if she won't come.
[The guards advance on ANTIGONE*]*

Antigone
Help! Is there no escape?
You gods! You men!

Chorus
What are you doing, sirrah?

Creon
I shan't touch your man, but *she* is mine.

Oedipus
Elders, help!

Chorus
Sir, you have no right.

Creon
I have indeed a right.

Chorus
What right? 950

Creon
To take what's mine.

Oedipus
Men of Athens, help!
[CREON *lays hands on* ANTIGONE]

Third Choral Dialogue

[*The following lines form a strophe in the Greek which is answered later by an antistrophe when* CREON *attacks* OEDIPUS *himself. This short choral interlude serves both to sustain the excitement and yet to relieve the tension.*]

Strophe

Chorus
[*approaching menacingly*]
How dare you, Stranger!
    Unhand her or you run the danger
    of our attack.

Creon
Stand back!

Chorus
Not until you yield.

Creon
Then it's Thebes and Athens
    on the battlefield.

Oedipus
Ah! My prophecy come true! 960

Chorus
Let loose the girl, or you . . .

Creon
Mind your own authority.

Chorus
I'm telling you to set her free.

Creon
And I'm telling you to unbar my way.

Chorus
Colonians, to the rescue! Help!
The State manhandled, the State itself at bay.

Antigone
Friends! Friends! They're dragging me away.
[End of strophe and of first part of Third Choral Dialogue]

Oedipus
Antigone, where are you?

Antigone
They're dragging me away.

Oedipus
Hold on to my hand, child!   970

Antigone
I haven't the strength.

Creon
[to his guards]
Get on with her!

Oedipus
This is the end of me.
[The guards hustle ANTIGONE *away.* CREON *pauses, then turns to* OEDIPUS *with a sneer]*

Creon
At least you won't go hobbling through your life
    with those two little crutches any more!
If that's the kind of triumph you want,
    trampling over friends and fatherland—
    those whose mandate I, as king,
    am trying to carry out—
Then *have* that triumph.   980
In time I think you'll learn
    you are your own worst enemy, before and now:
    flying into tantrums with your friends—
    those damnable tempers that have ruined you.
*[*CREON *begins to walk away, but realizes his men have gone off with* ANTIGONE *and he is now on his own, with his way blocked by the Athenian Elders]*

Chorus
Hold there, Stranger!

Creon
Don't dare touch me!

Chorus
Stay where you are till you restore those girls.

Creon
[looking around and catching sight of OEDIPUS, *who is backing into the grove]*

In that case I'll present my city with an even greater prize
   worth more than those two women.
[He rounds on the retreating OEDIPUS*]*

Chorus
Whatever next?   990

Creon
Him. He's mine.

Chorus
Braggart! You wouldn't dare.

Creon
Watch me do it!

Chorus
Not if our sovereign king can stop you.

Oedipus
Villain, are you so far gone you'd even lay a hand on *me?*

Creon
Hold your tongue!

Oedipus
That I will not.
If the hallowed spirits of this place allow,
   let me give vent to one more curse.
You scum! My devastated eyes, blank so long,   1000
saw through the eyes of this helpless girl
   and now you've plucked her from me.
So, may Helios, all-seeing god of sun,
   visit you and all your race
   with such dotage and decay as matches mine.

Creon
Do you hear him, men of Athens?

Oedipus
They hear all right. They mark you and me:
You the bully who use sheer force,
And I who can only counter with a curse.

Creon
[advancing on OEDIPUS*]*
I'll stand no more of this.   1010
Old and single-handed though I am,
I'll take this man by the strength of my right arm.
*[*CREON *lays hands on* OEDIPUS *and attempts to drag him away]*

Antistrophe
[matching the Strophe on p. 703 and completing the Third Choral Dialogue]

Oedipus
You'll rue it.

Chorus
Rash man!
What makes you think that you can do it?

Creon
I can.

Chorus
Then is Athens city most degenerate.

Creon
Where right is might the little beat the great.

Oedipus
Hear him?

Chorus
Rant—Zeus knows!   1020

Creon
Perhaps Zeus knows.
                           You don't and can't.

Chorus
Unbridled insolence!

Creon
Then you'll have to bear unbridled insolence.

Chorus
Rally, people! Rulers, rally!
To the rescue—hurry,
Before these ruffians cross our boundary.
[THESEUS arrives at the head of a troop of men. End of Antistrophe and of Third Choral Dialogue]

Theseus
What's all this clamor? What's going on?
Why was I called away by panic cries
   from Poseidon's altar, great sea-god of Colonus?   1030
Explain it all,
   for I've hurried here much too quick for comfort.

Oedipus
Ah! welcome, gentle voice!
I am worsted by a brigand.

Theseus
Worsted? How? Please tell me.

Oedipus
Creon here, this creature that you see,
    has kidnapped my two children,
    my last and darling pair.

Theseus
Is this true?

Oedipus
As I tell it: the most foul truth.   1040

Theseus
[to his men]
Quick, one of you to the altar place.
Break up the concourse at the sacrifice
    and have the people gallop foot and horse
    to the meeting of the roads
    before the women pass:
Quick, off with you!
Before this foreign bully makes a fool of me by force.
[A soldier is dispatched. THESEUS *turns to* CREON*]*
As for him,
    if I should let my anger have full sway
    to deal with him as he deserves,   1050
he'd not leave my hands without a smart.
We will, however, judge him by the very laws
    to which he himself appeals.
[Pointing at CREON*]*
You, you shall not leave this country, sir,
    until those girls are back and stand before my eyes.
You insult us;
    you insult your very race and native land.
You push your way within this realm
    where right is loved and law is paramount,   1060
and then proceed to sweep aside authority,
pillaging and taking prisoners at your will
    as if you thought my city was bereft of men
    or manned by slaves
    and I a nobody.
Well, it was not Thebes that brought you up to steal.
She has no predilection for a rascal brood.
Scant praise you'd have from her
    if she found you plundering me,
    plundering the gods,   1070
carrying off by force
    poor wretched victims come to plead.

Never could I see seize and snatch,
    entering territory of yours—
    not even if I had a more than royal right—
    unless whoever governed gave me leave for it.
I should know how a guest behaves on foreign soil.
But you, you dishonor your own city,
    so undeserving of disgrace.
Length of days has made you ripe in age   1080
but far from ripe in reason.
I have said it once, and I say it once again:
    restore those girls forthwith
    or you'll find your visit here prolonged by force—
    not quite according to your will.
    This is no idle talk. I mean it every syllable.

Chorus
Stranger, see what you've brought upon yourself!
By birth and race you ought to know much better.

Creon
Theseus son of Aegeus,
    I never thought your city was unmanned by men   1090
or drifting rudderless, as you suggest.
That never prompted what I did.
No, I merely took for granted
    that your people here
    were never so devoted to my family
    as to harbor one of them against my will
    and welcome here
    a parricide,
    a tainted man,
    a man discovered—oh the filth of it!—   1100
both bridegroom and his own bride's son.
I took for granted that your famous Council
    on Ares' hill where Justice sits,
    would never in its wisdom let such reprobates
    roam at large within your land.
Convinced of this, I hunted down my prize.
And even then I might have let him go
    had he not heaped on me and all my clan
    the foulest imprecations.
I've stomached quite enough, I think,   1110
to justify reprisals.
Rage, remember, knows no age till death.
Nothing hurts the dead.
Well, do what you will.
Though right is on my side,
    what headway can I make alone?

I may be old but I shall strain
    to counter every plan with counterplan.

Oedipus
Arrant monster!
On whom do you think these insults fall—   1120
on my old head or yours?
Murder, incest, deeds of horror,
    you spew the lot at me:
    and all the lot I bore in misery,
    not through any choice of mine
    but through some scheme of heaven,
    long incensed, it seems,
    against some misdeed of our line.
Examine me apart from this
    and you will find no flaw to cavil at   1130
    that might have drawn me so to floor
    my family and myself.

For tell me this:
    Suppose my father by some oracle was doomed to die
    by his own son's hand,
    could you justly put the blame on me—
    a babe unborn,
    not yet begotten by a father,
    not yet engendered in a mother's womb?
And if when born—as born I was to tragedy—   1140
I met my father in a fight and killed him,
    ignorant of what I did, to whom I did it,
    can you still condemn an unwilled act?

And my mother, your own sister, wretched man . . .
    since you're low enough to drag her in
    and force me to allude to it, I shall.
I'll not keep silent when your own lewd mouth
has broken all the bonds of reticence. . . .
My mother, yes she was my mother—what a fate!
I did not know. She did not know.   1150
And to her shame she gave me children,
    children to the son whom she herself had given.

One thing I know:
    you vituperate by choice, both her and me,
    when not by choice I wedded her,
    and not by choice am speaking now.
Neither in this marriage then
    shall I be called to blame,
    nor in the way my father died—
    which you keep casting in my teeth.   1160

Let me ask you this, one simple question:
If at this moment someone
   should step up to murder you,
   would you, godly creature that you are,
   stop and say, "Excuse me, sir, are you my father?"
Or would you deal with him there and then?
Ah! You love your life enough, I think,
   to turn on him,
   not look around to find a warrant first.

That precisely was the plight that heaven put me in.   1170
My father's very soul, come back, would not say no.
But you, the unscrupulous wretch you are,
A man convinced that everything he says is fit to hear,
   who bawls out every secret thing,
You heap your slanders on me publicly,
   meanwhile making sure to bow and scrape
   before the name of Theseus, with flattery
   and compliments on how the state of Athens runs.
Very well, extoll them to the skies but don't forget,
   if there's any state that knows what true religion is,   1180
that state is this.
And yet it was here you tried to wrest
   a pleading worshipper away, an old man too,
   and have taken captive both my daughters.
Therefore I rest my case before these goddesses,
   lay siege to them in prayer,
   assail them for their help
   to fight for me, and manifest to you
   the caliber of men that guard this realm.

Chorus
Sire, this stranger is an upright man: 1190
A woefully unlucky man and worthy of our aid.

Theseus
Enough of talk!
The criminals are in full flight
   while we stand still discussing it.

Creon
I am helpless then. What is it I must do?

Theseus
My pleasure is
   that you yourself shall show the way
   and I shall escort you
   to where the two missing girls are hidden.
But if your men have already hustled them away   1200

we shall spare ourselves the trouble
   and others will give chase and hunt your soldiers down,
   and none shall escape to thank their gods at home.

All right, lead off! And bear in mind,
   the looter has been looted,
   the trapper's in the trap,
   and stolen goods soon spoil.
Expect no help from your accomplice either.
Oh yes, I'm well aware
   you did not push yourself   1210
to this pinnacle of daring,
   this reckless outrage,
   without some help or backing.
And I must look to it,
   not jeopardize my city for a single man.
Does this make sense?
Or do my warnings seem to you as vain
   as any scruples when you hatched your plan?

Creon
I shall not argue with you on your own terrain.
But once at home, I'll have my inspirations too.   1220

Theseus
Threaten away, but keep moving please.
Oedipus, stay here in peace.
Rest happy in the pledge I give:
I'll have your daughters back, or I'll not live.

Oedipus
Bless you, Theseus, for your nobility;
   bless you for your loving care of me.
[CREON is marched off by THESEUS and his men]

Second Choral Ode

[In a galloping meter, the Elders excitedly follow the chase in imagination, alluding to some of the most religiously evocative centers dear to Athens, notably Apollo's oracle at Delphi and Demeter's mystery-fraught shrine by the sea at Eleusis. They also appeal to Pallas Athena, patroness of Athens, to Poseidon, patron of horses and ships, to Apollo, the supreme archer, and to his sister Artemis, the supreme huntress.]

Strophe I
Oh to be there
   when the brigands at bay
Turn to the clash
   of bronze on bronze   1230

Down by the Pythian shore
Or the flaring sands
    of Eleusis where
The Queens of the Night
    and their honey-voiced hymners
Solemnly seal
    in tongues of gold
The rites that bring blessings to man.

Ah! I think Theseus
    springs to the fight   1240
With presage of victory
    strong in his shout
Soon to make safe
    two sisterly captives
Still in our land.

Antistrophe I
Or perhaps galloping
    onward they go
To the western plains
    past rocky Oéa's
Glens and snowblanched sides.   1250
Neck and neck in the race
    chariots flying
Till Creon is worsted
    by terrible Ares
And by Theseus'
    stalwart men.
Ah, flash of the harness,
    toss of the reins!
Thunder of chargers,
    body of horsemen   1260
Dear to Athena,
    Queen of the horse,
Dear to Poseidon Ocean embracer
    fond son of Rhea.

Strophe II
The tussle is on
    Or just to begin
A beautiful hope
    tells us that soon
The two young women
    are here returned,   1270
Cornered so cruelly
    by an uncle so cruel.
Victory! Victory!
    Zeus win the day!

Success in the struggle
    is what I foretell.
Oh that my eyes—
    high over the battle—
Were the eyes of a dove
    that sails down the storm   1280
And lifts to the passing cloud.

Antistrophe II
All-seeing Zeus,
    all-ruling all,
Let this country's
    guardians conquer.
Let them capture
    quarry and prize.
Grant, oh grant it!
    Your daughter too,
Pallas Athena,   1290
    Our Lady stern.
Grant it Apollo!
    Hunter who
Beside his sister
    Artemis chases
The light-footed moon-speckled
    deer. Oh come!
Twin allies of this land and people.
[As the strains of the Choral Ode die away, a member of the CHORUS *hurries back with a report]*

Third Episode

Chorus Member
Wanderer, look!
The forecast of our watchers was not false,   1300
for I see the girls returning under escort.

Oedipus
Where, where? What are you saying? . . .
*[*ANTIGONE *and* ISMENE *are led in by* THESEUS *and his soldiers.* ANTIGONE *runs forward]*

Antigone
Father, Father!
I wish some god could give you eyes to see
    this princely man who has brought us back to you.

Oedipus
My child—it's you? Ah, both of you!

Antigone
Both of us, saved by his strong arm:
   by Theseus and his gallant men.

Oedipus
Come to me, dear girls.
Let your father press you to his embrace—   1310
redeemed beyond all hope.

Antigone
Beyond all hope! We could not ask for more.

Oedipus
But where—where are you?

Antigone
Both here—hand in hand.

Oedipus
My own sweet darlings!

Antigone
A father's favorites!

Oedipus
Dear props of my life!

Antigone
And partners in pain.

Oedipus
My precious ones—ah, mine again!
If now I died they would not say   1320
he was altogether damned:
   he had his daughters with him in the end.
Press closer to me, each of you,
   don't let your father go.
Rest there from your late roaming
   so cruel and so forlorn
   and tell me in a word what happened:
   young girls need no speeches.

Antigone
Father, our rescuer is here.
You should learn it all from him.   1330
The credit is his.
There—my speech was short!

Oedipus
[turning to where he thinks THESEUS *is]*
Sir, forgive me!
I cannot welcome them enough.

My children were lost. Now they are found.
And you are the one who brings this joy to me:
You rescued them, no man else besides.
The gods reward you far beyond my dreams:
    reward you and this blessed land
    where more than any other place on earth,   1340
among your people, I have found
Reverence and honesty and lips that cannot lie.
These things I recognize and pay my homage to.
All that I have, I have through you and no man else.
Therefore, my king, give me your hand and let me touch it.
And let me put a kiss upon your cheek.
[He takes a step toward THESEUS, *then checks himself]*
What am I saying?
What is this invitation that I make
    to handle me a man of sorrows, a temple of pollution?
No, no! Never let it be; even if you would!   1350
Let my sufferings lodge with those tried souls
    who have drunk with me the bitter cup.
    I salute you from afar.
Keep me always in your gentle care,
    as until this hour you have.

Theseus
No, Oedipus, this is nothing strange:
Your shower of words, your open heart, your joy.
Of course you had to greet your children first.
How could *that* fill me with dismay?
Besides, I'd rather furbish life with sparkling deeds than words, 1360
as I have proved to you, good reverend sir,
    making perfect everything I pledged:
    presenting you with daughters both redeemed,
    rescued from all menaces.
As to the manner of my victory,
    why should I enlarge on that?
They will tell you everything.
Meanwhile, some late news has come my way
    and I should like your thoughts on it.
It hardly sounds to me important,   1370
and yet it puzzles me.
There's nothing that a wise man should dismiss.

Oedipus
What is it, son of Aegeus?
No news of anything has come to us.

Theseus
They say a man, not from Thebes
    and yet a relative of yours,

has unexpectedly appeared;
   is prone in prayer before Poseidon's altar,
Where I was worshiping before I started here.

Oedipus
A man from where?   1380
And what is his petition?

Theseus
I only know he wants a word with you,
   which will not cost you much.

Oedipus
Only a word, yet prostrate in petition?

Theseus
Yes, he only wants to speak with you, they say,
   then go his way in peace.

Oedipus
Who can this be, praying at the shrine?

Theseus
Think of Argos, have you any kinsman there
   who might ask a like request?

Oedipus
[alarmed]
Dear friend, do not go on!   1390

Theseus
Why? What's the matter now?

Oedipus
Don't ask.

Theseus
Don't ask you what? Explain.

Oedipus
Argos, you said. I know now who it is.

Theseus
Someone I must hold at bay?

Oedipus
Sire, my son, my own detested son.
There's no man's voice I find so poisonous.

Theseus
Give him a hearing at least.
If you don't like what he asks, you needn't grant it.
Where's the pain in that?   1400

Oedipus

Hate, my king! Though he *is* my son.
Do not press me to give way.

Theseus

I think you must. The man has come to plead.
You must not fail in reverence to the god.

Antigone

Father, listen to me, young though I am.
Let the king's desire be honored
    and his conscience satisfied
       to give the gods their due.
And for our sakes too, let our brother come.
After all, whatever pain his words may give,   1410
he cannot wrench your will away.
And the sound of his voice—what damage can that do?
Besides, it's talk that best betrays the foul design.
You are his father,
And even if his conduct plumbed the depths of wickedness,
    that would never make it right for you, dear Father,
       to pay him back in kind.
So let him come!
Many a man is pricked to anger by a renegade son
    but yielding to advice more reasonable and loving,   1420
is coaxed from harshness back to gentleness.

Cast your thoughts on what has been,
    not what is now:
All that your own father and mother caused you to endure.
Ponder this, and the lesson that it teaches:
    catastrophic anger brings catastrophe.
Think no further
    than those two sightless sockets once your eyes.
Come, give way to us!
We should not have to plead for a cause so fair.   1430
Can one who has just felt mercy's touch
Then turn his back, not give as much?

Oedipus

Daughter, a hard-won joy you wring from me.
Well, have it as you wish.
[He turns to THESEUS*]*
But, oh my friend, that man—if he must come—
    never let him put me in his power.

Theseus

Enough! I've told you once, old man,
    no need to ask again;
       nor shall I brag. But be sure of this:

Your life is safe while any god saves mine.   1440

[THESEUS *departs with some of his soldiers, leaving a contingent to guard* OEDIPUS]

Third Choral Ode

[*The Elders, shaken by the wrangling and frustrations of the two old men, dwell on the tragedy of life and the hopelessness of old age. The heavy trochaic and iambic beat measures out the sadness.*]

Strophe I

Where is the man who wants
More length of days?
Oh cry it out.
There is a fool
His dawdling years
Are loaded down
His joys are flown
His extra time but trickles on
He awaits the Comforter
Who comes to all.   1450
No wedding march
No dancing song:
A sudden vista down stark avenues
To Hades realms,
Then death at last.

Antistrophe I

Not to be born has no compare
But if you are
Then hurry hence
For after that there is no better blessing.
When one has watched gay youth   1460
Pack up his gallant gear
Vexations crowd without
And worries crowd within:
Envy, discord, struggles,
Shambles after battles
Till at last he too must have his turn
Of age, discredited and doddering:
Disaffected and deserted age
Confined with crabbedness
And every dismal thing.   1470

Epode

So are we senile—he and I:
Lashed from the north by wintry waves
Like some spume-driven cape on every side
Lashed by our agonies those constant waves
Breaking in from the setting sun
Breaking in from the dawn

Breaking in from the glare of noon
Breaking in from Polar gloom.

Fourth Episode

Antigone
Father, I think I see our visitor approach.
He is alone. Tears are streaming from his eyes.   1480

Oedipus
And who is he?

Antigone
Exactly whom we thought.
It's Polyneices who has come.
[POLYNEICES enters, advances, and stares aghast at his father and sisters]

Polyneices
Oh my sisters, I'm at a loss!
Shall I pour out tears for my own calamities
    or for this sorry sight—my decrepit father?
Just look at him:
    jettisoned with two poor girls
    in an alien land;
    arrayed in such unkempt and antique filth   1490
his own antiquity corrodes with it:
    his hair above his sightless eyes
    straggling out upon the breeze;
    and matching this, his beggars scrip
    with pittance for his wasted belly.

Ah, too late! I see it all too late.
I pronounce that this neglect of you
    brands me as the most delinquent thing on earth.
Yes, let me be the first to say it.
But, Father,   1500
Zeus himself sits mercy by his throne,
    so may you seat her near you too.
We can mend mistakes and not make more.
[He pauses anxiously]
You are silent.
Say something, Father, please.
Don't turn away from me.
Have you no reply?
Will you send me off in mute contempt?
Not even tell me what upsets you so?   1510
[He pauses again]
You his daughters, my own sisters, please,
    try to move him from this dumb rigidity.

I must not be dismissed in shame
　　without a word of hope
　　from this blessed seat of appeal—
　　the god's own sanctuary.
[OEDIPUS *turns his back.* ANTIGONE *steps toward* POLYNEICES *and touches his arm*]

Antigone
Tell him yourself, my stricken brother,
　　why it is you came.
Sometimes as words begin to flow,
　　here they strike a spark of joy,   1520
there they fan up anger or bring a touch of tenderness,
And anyhow, to the tongue-tied somehow give a tongue.

Polyneices
Then I'll speak out, for you advise me well.
But first let me make it plain,
　　the god I've called on for his help
　　is that very ocean god, Poseidon,
　　from whose suppliant shrine this country's king
　　has just now raised me up and let me come
　　with safe conduct to confer with you.   1530
Therefore I would ask you gentlemen,
　　my sisters here, and you my father,
　　to respect my rights in this.

And now I'll tell you, Father, why I came.
I am driven out, banished from my native land
　　because as eldest son
　　I claimed my sovereign birthright to your throne.
But Eteocles my younger brother has cast me out:
　　not by making good his claims,
　　not by proof of excellence,   1540
but by cajoling the city to his side.
It all seems part of the curse that dogs your line,
　　and this the various oracles confirm.
So I went to Argos in the land of Doria,
There took to wife the daughter of the king, Adrastus,
　　and made a league
　　of all the famous fighters of the Peloponnese
　　to raise a seven-headed army aimed at Thebes
　　and oust those from the realm who ousted me,
　　or die in the attempt—die gloriously.   1550

Well then, what is my point in coming here?
To petition, Father:
　　to lay our supplications at your feet,
　　mine and all my allies,

Who at this moment raise the standard of their seven spears
    and ring their seven armies round the plain of Thebes.
There's Amphiaraus, the hurricane spearsman,
    first at the spear, first at the reading of riddles.
Then the son of Oeneus: Tydeus of Aetolia.
Third comes Eteoclus, native of Argos.   1560
Fourth, Hippomedon, sent by his father Talaus.
Fifthly Capaneus, swearing to mow down Thebes with fire.
Sixthly Parthenopaeus, born in Arcadia, son of Atalanta,
    that ferocious virgin who finally wedded
    and became the mother of this stalwart boy.
And lastly, I, your son,
    or if not your son
    but the child of some appalling fate,
    then son at least in name.
I am the one who puts this fearless Argos in the field   1570
against the state of Thebes.
Father, will you listen to us, to all of us:
    we beg you for your daughters' and your own life's sake.
Ease the harshness of your rage against me now:
I who sally out to give this wretched brother chastisement,
    the one who thrust me out and robbed me of my home.

If there's any truth in prophecy,
    the oracles have said
    that victory lies with those
    who win you to their side.   1580
So listen, Father,
    if you love our land
    with its springing fountains,
    its Theban deities.
Be persuaded by my prayers.

We are exiles, you and I,
    both of us are beggars.
We have to fawn on others for a home, you and I,
    both share a single destiny.
And all the time   1590
this creature kings it in our house.
Insufferable!
He ridicules us from his cushioned pride.
If you will only bless my scheme,
    I'll make short shrift of him and scatter him.
I'll bring you home again and re-establish you,
    and I shall be established too.
I'll make good this boast, if you make one with me.
I shall not live, if you'll not now agree.

Chorus
Oedipus, for Theseus' sake who sent him here, 1600
you must not let him go without some reasonable reply.

Oedipus
You trustees of this realm,
    since Theseus sent him here
    and asked me to reply, I will.
Nothing less would let him hear my voice.
But now he shall be graced with it
    in accents that will bring him little joy.
[He turns toward POLYNEICES*]*
Liar!
When you held the scepter and the throne
    which your brother at the moment holds in Thebes, 1610
you drove me out,
    drove this your father out,
    displaced me from my city.
You are the reason for these rags—
    rags that make you cry to see,
    now that you have reached rock bottom too.
The season for condolences is past.
What I must bear must last as long as life,
    last in my thoughts of you as my destroyer.
Oh yes, it's you that dragged me down! 1620
You expelled me, you arranged
    that I should beg my daily bread.
But for my two girls
    I should not even be alive if left to you.
It's they who tend me, they preserve me.
They are the ones who play a man's and not a woman's part.
But you, you and your brother—bastards—
    are no sons of mine.

The eye of Fate is on you now.
Her glance is mild to what it soon shall be 1630
if once your armies march on Thebes.
Never shall you topple down that city.
Instead, you'll trip up headlong into blood,
    your brother too,
    spattering each other.
Long ago I cursed you both,
    and now once more I summon up those curses,
    let them battle for me.
Let them teach you reverence
    for those that gave you birth. 1640
Let them teach you what contempt is worth
    of an eyeless Father
    who had such worthless sons.

My daughters did not treat me so.
Therefore, if Justice is still seated
   side by side with Zeus
   in ancient and eternal sway,
I consign to perdition
   your sanctimonious supplications
   and your precious throne.   1650
So, leave my sight. Get gone and die:
   you trash—no son of mine.
Die,
   with these my curses
   ringing in your ears:
Never to flatten your motherland beneath your spear,
Never to set foot again in Argive's vales,
Instead you die,
   die by a brother's blow
   and make him dead by yours   1660
who drove you out.

That's my prayer for you.
I summon the pitchy gloom of Tartarus
   to gulp you down
   to a new paternal home.
I summon the holy spirits of this place.
I summon Ares the Destroyer,
   who whirled you into hatred and collision.
With these imprecations in your ears, get out.
Go publish them in Thebes.   1670
Go tell your bellicose and trusty champions
   the will and testament
That Oedipus bequeaths to his two sons.

Chorus
Polyneices,
   Never have your missions boded peace,
   nor do they now.
Go as quickly as you can.

Polyneices
How pitiful!
My pointless journey here!
My hopes in ruins!   1680
My comrades all betrayed!
What an end
   to our proud marching out from Argos town!
And none of this dare I whisper to my allies
   to try to turn them back.
I cannot halt them in the silent march to doom.
[He turns to ANTIGONE *and* ISMENE*]*

But you, his little ones, my sisters,
   now you've heard our father's prayers,
   his prayers of hate, please,
If ever they should come to bear their mortal fruit,   1690
and you be found in Thebes again,
Then by all the gods,
   on that blessed chance, I beg:
   do not let my shade be damned
   but put me in the tomb with hallowed rites.
So shall you earn more praises from me dead
   than from that living father
   for all you did.

Antigone
Polyneices, wait. One thing I ask.

Polyneices
Antigone, sweet sister, what?   1700

Antigone
Turn your army back to Argos now.
Do not destroy yourself and Thebes.

Polyneices
Impossible! Once seen to flinch
   how could I put an army in the field again?

Antigone
Again, my little brother?
What new madness could ever make you want to?
What can ruin of your native city gain?

Polyneices
Yes, but running from a younger brother,
   a laughingstock . . .

Antigone
Ah, don't you see   1710
you'll make your father's prophecies come true:
   a duel to the death—
   the death of both of you?

Polyneices
That's what he wants. But I'll *not* give way.

Antigone
Oh, I'm sick at heart!
And who will follow you once it's heard
   the future he has threatened?

Polyneices
It shan't be heard. I'll never say.

Good generals do not stress their weakness
    but their strength.   1720

Antigone
Your mind's made up? My poor misguided boy!
[She throws her arms around him]

Polyneices
It is. So do not try to hold me back.
There is an avenue down which I go
    beckoned by my father's prayers
    and dark with Furies answering his call.
May Zeus reward you both
    for the obsequies you do for me
    when I am dead.
In life there's nothing left
    for you to tender me.   1730
Now let me go. Good-bye!
You'll never gaze again into my living eye.
[He gently releases himself from ANTIGONE*]*

Antigone
[breaking down]
It breaks my heart!

Polyneices
Don't cry for me.

Antigone
Oh, Polyneices, who would not cry to see
    you my brother hurrying to die?

Polyneices
If die I must, I'll die.

Antigone
No, hear me—never you!

Polyneices
Don't press me uselessly.

Antigone
Bereft of you, what is left for me?   1740

Polyneices
The future is in Fortune's hands
    whether we live or die.
My prayer for both of you is this:
    Heaven keep you from every harm.
    You deserve none. As all affirm.
[It would be characteristic of ISMENE, *who has remained silent all this time, to have*

been rendered speechless by her tears. She too now advances and clings to her brother in a last farewell. After a moment, POLYNEICES *disengages himself and strides away. The blind* OEDIPUS *has been standing by, mute as a stone.]*

Choral Ode and Dialogue

Strophe I

Chorus

So do we see fresh sorrows strike
Fresh strokes of leaden doom
From the old blind visitor
Or is it Fate unfolding—
Supernal in her workings which   1750
I dare not say can fail—
Watched, yes watched,
By never failing Time
Shuffling fortunes from the top to bottom?
[A clap of thunder]
The sky is rift. Great Zeus defend us!

Oedipus

Quick, children, oh my children,
    send someone to bring Theseus here,
    that princely man.

Antigone

Father, what should make you call him now?

Oedipus

That clap of thunder beating down from Zeus   1760
beckons me to Hades realms.
So hurry, someone, hurry!
[Another peal of thunder, followed by lightning]

Antistrophe I

Chorus

Louder—hear it?—crashing down
Divine report, dumbstriking sound
Pricking up my hair with panic
And shattering my soul.
There again! Light rips the sky
I'm stricken to the core with fear.
Such a pregnant rush of light
Never comes without some meaning   1770
Never not with monstrous issue
Great awful sky! Great Zeus, oh, save us!
[More thunder and lightning]

Oedipus
Dear children, life is closing on me now:
  that predestined end from which there is no turning.

Antigone
What makes you know? What signals do you have?

Oedipus
I am too well aware.
Oh hurry to this country's king
  and fetch him here.
[More thunder]

Strophe II

Chorus
Ha! again, another crack
    shatters the air.   1780
Come gently you powers, oh gently come
    if you must darken
This earth our mother. Show us some pity
    show us some clemency.
Though we have favored a stricken man
    hounded by destiny
  Zeus, our king, be kind!

Oedipus
Daughters, is he here yet?
Shall I be breathing still?
Still master of my mind?   1790

Antigone
What is so urgent on your mind to tell him?

Oedipus
The crowning gift I promised in return.
The blessing to repay him for all he's done.
[More thunder and lightning]

Antistrophe II

Chorus
Hurry, Theseus, my son, step down
    from altar and sacrifice:
Even from worship in the deep of the grove
    at Poseidon's shrine.
Don't tarry, don't linger, oh King, for the stranger
    brings city and people
A grave to reward you, a sovereign blessing   1800
  for all you have done.
    Theseus, Lord, come quickly!
[With another peal of thunder and lightning, THESEUS *bursts in]*

Theseus
What another summons?
Guest and people joined
In general clamor!
Bolts from Zeus
And catapults of hail!
All's possible when God
Hurls down such a storm.
[End of Choral Ode and Dialogue]

Oedipus
King, how glad I am to see you come!   1810
Some god has surely smoothed your way to us.

Theseus
What is it now, son of Laius?

Oedipus
The balance of my life is tilting.
    I must not die a debtor:
    my bargain barren still
    with you and with your city.

Theseus
What signs declare to you the end is near?

Oedipus
This rolling thunder rolled,
    this shuttled light.
The fulminating bolts   1820
of unanswerable artillery.

Theseus
And I believe.
You never did foreshadow falsely.
Declare what we must do.
[With great solemnity, OEDIPUS *draws* THESEUS *aside]*

Oedipus
Come, listen, son of Aegeus.
I lay before you now a city's lasting treasure.
There is a place where I must die.
And I myself unhelped shall walk before you there.
That place you must not tell to any living being:
    not where it lurks, not where the region lies,   1830
if you would have a shield like a thousand shields
    and a more perpetual pact than the spears of allies.

No chart of words shall mark that mystery.
Alone you'll go, alone your memory
    shall frame the spot.

For not to any person here,
    not even to my daughters so beloved,
    am I allowed to utter it.
You yourself must guard it always.
And when your life is drawing to its close,   1840
divulge it to your heir alone
    and he in turn to his, and so forever.

This way you will keep your city safe
    against the Dragon's seed, the men of Thebes,
    though many a state attack a peaceful home,
    though sure be the help from heaven (but exceeding slow)
    against earth's godless men and men gone mad.
Be far from you such fate, good son of Aegeus!
But all this you know without my telling you.
[OEDIPUS's face lights up as if inspired. With slow firm steps he moves forward]
Now to that spot. The god within me calls.   1850
Let us go forward and linger here no more.
Come beloved daughters, follow!
Follow this new leader guiding you:
    the father once you guided.
[ANTIGONE and ISMENE attempt to assist him]
No no, hands off! Let me walk my way
    without a prop toward my holy hidden tomb
    where the promised earth of Attica will cover me.
This way, this way—come!
For this way Hermes beckons me.
    and Persephone, mistress of the dead.   1860
[He turns his blind eyes up toward the sun]
Farewell! Farewell! You blindfold light
    once light of mine,
    last vision felt in darkness.
I walk to Hades now
    to close my life in shade.
[Turning to THESEUS]
Most gentle friend,
    heaven bless you, bless your land and yours.
And in prosperity remember me, the dead,
That every grace abiding be ever on your head.
[OEDIPUS moves slowly into the grove, followed by THESEUS, ANTIGONE, and ISMENE. The CHORUS watches until they are out of sight]

Fourth Choral Ode

[The CHORUS sings a "Requiescat in pace"[3] addressed to Persephone and Hades, the queen and king of the Underworld, and also to the Furies. Even Cerberus, the fierce

---

3. Let him rest in peace (as from the requiem mass).

three-headed hound that guards the portals of the dead, is not left out of their appeal.]

Strophe

Dare we adore the unseen Queen   1870
And you night's children's King?
Then Aidoneus, listen, Aidoneus:
Not in pain and lamentation
May his deathknell ring—
This stranger passing down
Through pallisades of gloom
Toward those prairies of the dead
    His stygian home.
    Much did he suffer
    much beyond deserts   1880
Let the finger of God's fairness
    Raise him now.

Antistrophe

You goddesses or worlds deep down
And you untamed hulk of snarling hound
Watching, they say, the gates of hell
For those arriving at the gaping maw
Of Hades pit . . . Oh let him pass.
And Death you son of Earth and Tartarus
Muzzle the cur, so Cerberus
Shall not molest the lonely path   1890
of Oedipus, who walks
    Toward those sunken
    Meadows of the dead
O Death bestow on him eternally
    Eternal rest.
[After a pause, a MESSENGER *appears at the entrance of the grove]*

Fifth Episode

Exodos

Messenger
Fellow citizens,
I could cut this story short and say:
    "Oedipus is gone,"
But what was done was not done shortly,
    and my story breaks away from brevity.   1900

Chorus
So the man of destiny has gone?

Messenger
Gone. He has left this life behind.

Chorus
But did he have a blest demise all free from pain?

Messenger
It was extraordinary, most marvelous.
You yourselves saw how he went:
    unled by those he loved but walking on
    and showing us the way.
And when he'd reached that yawning orifice
    where steps of brass sink rooting down,
    he halted by the many branching ways   1910
where Theseus is remembered for his famous pact
    with Peiritheus to raid the underworld
    and bring Persephone back. And there,
    he stood at the chasm
Halfway between that basin and the slab of Thoricus,
By the old wild pear tree's hollow trunk and the marble tomb.
Then sitting down he undid his squalid dress,
    and calling for his daughters bade them fetch
    water to wash with from the spring
    and some to pour in ritual for the dead.   1920

So the women went to Demeter's hill in front of them
    (that goddess of unfolding spring),
    and soon had done all their father had enjoined;
Then bathed and tended him and dressed him fittingly.
And when he was content that all was done,
    with nothing further he could wish,
    there came a grumbling sound from Zeus's underworld.
It shook the girls with trembling and they fell
    weeping at their father's knees.
Nor would they stop but beat their breasts and sobbed.   1930
And when he heard this bitter burst of grief,
    he took them in his arms and said:
    "This day, my daughters,
    you shall have no father left to you,
For all my life is done,
    your double burden of me done.
It was not easy, children, *that* I know,
    and yet one little word can change all pain:
That word is LOVE, and love you've had from me
    more than any man can ever give.   1940
But now you must live on, when I am gone."

So did the three of them cling to one another
    calling out and crying
    until at last they came to the end of tears,
    and sobs gave out and all was still.

Then in that stillness suddenly a voice was heard,
    terrifying: their hair stood up with fear.
The voice of the god it was, calling out and calling:
    "Oedipus, Oedipus, why do we delay?
    You stay too long—too long you stay." 1950
And when he knew it was the god that called,
    he craved King Theseus to draw near,
    and when he had he said to him:
    "Dear friend, put out your hand,
    my children, put yours here.
Now swear you never will abandon them
    but wisely further all their needs
    as friendship and the time will tell."
And Theseus, noble that he is, holding back his tears,
    swore to keep his promise to his friend. 1960

As soon as this was done,
    Oedipus, groping for his daughters with blind hands,
    said: "Sweet children, now be brave,
    as you were born to be, and leave this place.
Do not ask to see what you should not see
    or hear what you should not hear.
But go at once.
Only Theseus has the right to stay
    and see what now unfolds."

Such was his converse. We heard it all of us. 1970
So, sobbing with the girls, we left.
But after a little while, some paces off,
    we glanced around
    and Oedipus was nowhere to be seen
    but only the King,
    holding up his hands to screen his eyes
    as if he had beheld a vision—
    one too dazzling for a mortal's sight.
Then presently we saw him hail the earth and sky
    in one great prayer. 1980
[*The* MESSENGER *pauses*]
How Oedipus has passed, no man shall ever tell,
    no man but Theseus.
For in that hour no whitehot thunderbolt from Zeus came down,
    no surge of giant sea to take him.
Some emissary maybe from heaven came;
    or was the adamantine floor of the dead
    gently reft for him with love?
The passing of the man was pangless
    with no trace of pain nor any loud regret.
It was of mortal exits the most marvelous. 1990

But if you think that none of this makes sense,
I am content to go on talking nonsense.

Chorus
Where are the girls and their escort now?

Messenger
Not far away,
    for I hear the sound of sobbing.
[ANTIGONE *and* ISMENE, *escorted by a solemn company of attendants, slowly walk into view*]

Fourth Choral Dialogue

[which lasts until the end of the play]

Strophe I

Antigone
Cry, cry, and cry again!
Our cause is too complete:
Two sisters and their sire
    Stained to the core.
Oh tears for the spellbound blood!   2000
We lived his long-drawn life of pain
Until this dazing hour
    This last suffering
His ineffable demise.

Chorus
What took place?

Antigone
We can only guess.

Chorus
So he is gone?

Antigone
Gone as you would wish.
    No bloody war
No deep sea caught him up   2010
But he was plucked
By some unseen design:
Rapt to the land of blind horizons.
And now a deathlike night
Has blanketed our vision.
In distant lands, over drifting seas,
How shall we live our bitter living?

Ismene
    I know not how.

Come blood-dripping Death
    And carry me down   2020
And lay me by my ancient father's side.
    So should I miss
The unliveable life to come.

Chorus
Dear children, stop your tears,
    You best of daughters.
Such is our end which heaven sends us
    And Fate is our friend.

Antistrophe I

Antigone
Ah! What was pain was joy
What lacked all love was love
When I had him in my arms.   2030
Father, my father,
Wrapped in perpetual gloom
In that territory of shade—
Not even there shall her
    Love and mine
Be barred from you.

Chorus
So his work is done?

Antigone
He had his wish.

Chorus
His wish?

Antigone
He wished to die on foreign soil   2040
He did:
His bed beneath the mantle
    of the gentle dark,
His aftermath of mourning
    Rich in tears.
    Oh Father, yes
I cannot staunch their flow,
It is a flood of sorrow . . .
To die on foreign soil,
You wanted that, but ah,   2050
So far away from me!

Ismene
    Poor dear sister,

With Father gone forever
What fate remains for you and me?

Chorus
Dear children, think of this
He made a blessed end
    So cease your crying.
    There's none alive
    That's free from trial.

Strophe II

Antigone
Dearest, let's go back there.   2060

Ismene
Whatever for?

Antigone
I'm gripped with sudden longing.

Ismene
What?

Antigone
To see his hidden home.

Ismene
Whose home?

Antigone
Our father's.

Ismene
It is forbidden. And also, don't you see . . .

Antigone
Why this reluctance?

Ismene
But don't you see . . .

Antigone
I do not, go on.   2070

Ismene
He has no tomb.
He died away from all of us.

Antigone
Then take me there and kill me too.

Ismene
And leave me helpless and deserted,
    dragging out my hopeless life alone?

Antistrophe II

Chorus
Bear up, dear girls, take heart!

Ismene
But where, oh where
is there left to go?

Chorus
There is a place . . .

Ismene
But where?   2080

Chorus
Here. Nothing shall molest you here.

Ismene
That I know.

Chorus
Then what is on your mind?

Ismene
We can't go home to Thebes.

Chorus
Don't even try.

Ismene
How terrible!

Chorus
It always was.

Ismene
No, worse
than the worst before.

Chorus
I know, a surge of sorrow   2090
sweeps over you.

Ismene
Oh where are we to turn, great Zeus?
What hope, what destiny to drive us on,
    and what the use?
[End of strophic pattern but not of Choral Dialogue. THESEUS *and his escort enter]*

Theseus
Weep no more, sweet women.
Where death has dealt so kindly

There is no room for sorrow
or nemesis will follow.

Antigone
Good son of Aegeus, we beg you . . .

Theseus
Daughters, for what favor?   2100

Antigone
Let these eyes of ours regard
our father's place of resting.

Theseus
That may not be.

Antigone
But you are king of Athens. Why?

Theseus
Because, dear children,
he himself has charged me
not to let a mortal being
approach these hallowed precincts
or invade with prayers and voices
his sanctuary of quiet.   2110
And if I keep this covenant,
he said I keep my country
free from every hurt.
The gods' ears heard these pledges
And Zeus the god of treaties,
the all-seeing god, has sealed it.

Antigone
Then if his wish be this,
enough for us. So be it.
But send us back to Thebes:
Thebes our ancestral city.   2120
There we must try to stem
the bloodbath of our brothers.

Theseus
Why, so I shall,
and spare no pains
to gladden you and grace his tomb:
the dauntless dead so lately swept away.

Chorus
Come then cease your crying
Keep tears from overflowing
All's ordained past all denying.

Questions for Discussion and Review

1. In what ways does Sophocles's portrayal of the chorus reflect the Athenians' attitude toward Thebes? Why are the Theban citizens punished with the plague? Why would Sophocles's Athenian audience consider Thebes to be a city whose citizens were corrupt?

2. Does the chorus's last speech in *Oedipus Rex* adequately explain what has happened to Oedipus? Why or why not? (When they state the "lesson" of Oedipus's story, do they understand his insights into the human psyche or the nature of the gods?)

3. What is the riddle of the Sphinx? What answer does Oedipus give? How is it possible for Oedipus to give the "right" answer without fully understanding what it means? Discuss the aspects of the riddle that Oedipus fails to understand. How does that failure of understanding reflect Oedipus's self-image?

4. Jocasta knows the truth about Oedipus before he himself completes his investigation and wants him to stop asking questions so that their lives can be allowed to continue as before. What does her attitude reveal about her? Contrast her response to Oedipus's.

5. Theseus plays an important role in *Oedipus at Colonus*. In what ways are the early myths about Theseus (see chapter 10) relevant to his portrayal here?

6. Why does Oedipus enter the grove of the Furies? Discuss some of the attributes he shares with the Kindly Ones, and explain how they contribute to the mysterious end of Oedipus.

Works Cited

Rukeyser, Muriel. "Myth." *A Muriel Rukeyser Reader,* ed. Jan Heller Levi. New York: W. W. Norton, 1994.

Recommended Reading

Bloom, Harold, ed. *Sophocles: Modern Critical Views.* NY: Chelsea House, 1990. A well-chosen cross section of contemporary interpretations of the plays.

Knox, Bernard M. W. *The Heroic Temper: Studies in Sophoclean Tragedy.* Berkeley: U of California P, 1964. A solid analysis of the plays, with emphasis on the character of the protagonists.

Euripides's *Medea*: A Different Perspective on Tragedy

KEY THEMES

The Medea *addresses the plight of a strong, intelligent, and articulate woman in a society in which women were supposed to be none of those things. Having few rights, they endured various forms of oppression and exploitation. Medea's common-law husband, Jason, was the leader of the Argonauts and had won the Golden Fleece only because Medea had helped him to do so. But now he has abandoned her for the attractive and wealthy princess of Corinth and soon demands custody of the children as well. Euripides uses Medea's violent response to her predicament as a source of commentary on the condition of women in Athens and on the conventions of tragedy itself.*

Euripides

A younger contemporary of Aeschylus and Sophocles, Euripides (c. 485–406 B.C.) was considered somewhat unconventional, both personally and intellectually. A loner who had his own private library, Euripides took little part in the public affairs that dominated the lives of most of his fellow Athenians.

Euripides wrote eighty-eight plays, of which nineteen survive. But although his fellow playwrights (especially Sophocles) were interested in his work, and although he achieved enormous popularity after his death when revivals began to be performed, he won only four first prizes at the **City Dionysia** in his lifetime. His rather complex plays may have seemed too strange, too repulsive, or possibly even too decadent for the taste of his generally conservative audience. In his last year, he left Athens altogether and went to Macedonia.

The Woman's Perspective

It is easy to see why Euripides's *Medea* (431 B.C.) might have startled an audience expecting plays like those of Aeschylus or Sophocles. The play stresses the female perspective, which was not in itself unusual, but Euripides provides a sympathetic portrayal both of one woman's plight in particular and of all women in general. **Medea,** for example, has done everything for **Jason,** giving up, in exchange for his false promise to marry her later, her home, her family ties, and her reputation. She saved his life by helping him attain the Golden Fleece and by conspiring in the killing of his uncle, **Pelias,** who had usurped the throne of Aeson (Jason's father) and would have killed Jason. Her reward is to have Jason desert her in Corinth for a younger, richer, and prettier (if not very bright) woman, who happens to be the daughter of the king.

Medea had the misfortune of having fallen in love with a hero and having found him to be, after all, just a man—and not a very admirable one at that. Early in the play, Jason denies Medea's part in helping him get the Golden Fleece, insisting that it was Cypris (Aphrodite), not Medea, who saved him. Her unofficial "marriage" in ruins, the only meaningful role Medea has left is that of mother. But Jason, demanding custody of the children, wants to deprive her of that, too. Utterly isolated in the unfamiliar city to which he has brought her, she speaks convincingly both of the woman's role—trapped whether she marries or not—and of society's negative attitude toward strong, intelligent, and highly articulate women.

The Heroic Medea

Medea indeed has all the strengths more typically associated with male tragic protagonists in the heroic mold: the intensity, the sense of total commitment, and the heroic acts. The leader of the chorus of townswomen implies that all mothers are heroic: Medea, she says, has, like the Argonauts, passed between the "grey Clashing Rocks" that guard the navigational route to Colchis, which she also associates with the dangers faced during childbirth.

Words versus Action

Medea believes that, like all heroes, she has the gods on her side—not just **Hecate,** her personal deity, but also **Themis,** Lady of Vows, and Zeus, protector of oaths, whose lightning is identified with Medea's fury. For the Greeks, oaths were not just casually uttered words—they were sacred. Breaking a vow was a major violation that even the gods themselves would hesitate to commit. Yet Jason is a breaker of oaths, specifically the vows he made to Medea when he needed her help. Hence his fate, which Medea foresees, is fully deserved. Some readers thus argue that Medea is acting as an agent of Zeus, carrying out divine retribution against Jason. But it is not Jason who dies—it is the princess, whose only crime is to have been superficial, and the children, whose offenses consist merely of being Jason's sons.

By the time we meet Medea, she has already exhausted all other avenues, and even now, despite her rage, we find her still engaged in last-ditch attempts to use rhetoric, not violence. In fact, many speeches in the play are about rhetoric—about words and the logic of arguments. But words mean nothing to a breaker of vows; once the link between rhetoric and truth is broken, words become mere babble. Jason never listens to Medea's arguments. And while he accuses her of being verbally aggressive (women should presumably be quiet!), she accuses him, quite properly, of using empty words. In language as in life, Jason confuses style with substance, just as he opts for the style of a successful life (a "good" home, adequate income), ignoring the foundation of familial bonds on which a good home must rest.

Jason's actions have not matched his words; Medea's will. She, too, has made a vow—to Queen Hecate. And she openly does what she says: she announces her intentions, carries out the murders, and, just as Clytemnestra had done, acknowledges the deeds afterwards.

Once determined to act, Medea announces, "From now on all words are superfluous." It is from this point in the play that she speaks Jason's language—the language of clichés and lies, weapons in the war between the sexes. Only then does she engage in a bit of playacting, miming the stereotypical "feminine" role—a weak creature given to crying instead of acting—in order to beguile Jason into unwittingly helping her, cooperating with her scheme to send the children with gifts to the princess! Naturally, unable to accept the truth about Medea or his dependence on her, he immediately accepts this lie.

Tragedy and the Irrational

Like most tragic protagonists, Medea is also a very passionate woman, as extreme in her love as she is in her hatred. We watch what happens when the irrational forces that tragedy always confronts (here depicted as almost elemental forces, "like a rock, or a wave of the sea") drive Medea to act out her impulses in a way that is out of control and that ends up hurting those she loves: killing her brother, landing Jason in exile, and, finally, like Agave, murdering her own children. But like Agave, Medea is a woman, for whom all such actions are deemed inexcusable. The gods and the male heroes who follow their divine models may get away with destroying their children, but no expiatory rituals release the woman from that sin.

Another View of Medea

One of the most important characteristics of drama is its capacity to hold up multiple points of view for the audience's inspection. In this play, as in many others, Euripides enhances that multiplicity of perspectives. No sooner do we begin to accept one perspective, than he shifts the angle slightly and a different perspective emerges. Thus, no sooner do we begin to sympathize with Medea's predicament and to see her as a strong, tragic heroine, than we find ourselves confronting another side of Medea. For example, portraying herself as victim, she does not mention that she eloped with Jason willingly; further, although marriage is in some ways always a betrayal of the woman's family, she alienated her father in more than the usual way—she killed her younger brother and scattered the pieces of his corpse over the waves to stop her father's pursuit of Jason and the fleeing Argonauts. Nor does she mention her role as a practitioner of the magical arts of the chthonic goddess, Hecate, whom she reveres above all gods. Although Medea may not literally be a witch, she clearly has a sophisticated knowledge of poisons, as well as of fertility potions, and can command the services of dragons.

Other playwrights had, of course, written plays with strong female protagonists, even protagonists who, like Medea, committed crimes (Clytemnestra, for example). But those women eventually paid the price for their crimes, whereas Medea escapes punishment. In fact, she escapes to Athens, where King Aegeus gives her refuge (Figure 17-1) (a fact that Euripides stresses, taking a jab at the Athenian audience, whose attitudes toward women were much like Jason's, and perhaps warning them of the dangers of their views). Further, heroines like Clytemnestra performed their murders according to convention, decorously offstage, describing the result but not dwelling on the techniques; Medea's poisoning of the princess, however, is described at length, in all its gory detail.

A Proletarian Perspective

Before we can decide whether Medea is a hero or a monster, Euripides shifts the viewpoint yet again, revealing still another unusual perspective. Unlike the essentially aristocratic focus on the noble protagonists in other tragedies of the time, in Euripides's plays, the voice of the common people often stands out as presenting the most legitimate or compelling vision in the play. In the *Medea,* the most sensible voices are those of the tutor, the nurse, and the chorus of Medea's neighbors—ordinary women of Corinth who sympathize with her predicament as a woman (indeed, what woman could fail to identify with such statements as, "I had rather fight three battles than bear one child"?) and who share her hatred of Jason. In fact, they become co-conspirators who, knowing of Medea's plans, neither intervene nor report the danger. But even they, who are willing to go so far as to make themselves accessories to murder, draw the line at attacking the children. They are capable of moral distinctions: Jason deserves punishment; the children do not. Medea is capable only of rage that lashes out, when she is angered, at whatever she sees: "May it be an enemy and not a friend she hurts," says the nurse, implying that either is possible. Once again, such unfocused rage is entirely within the heroic tradition, as when Aias, angered over his failure to win Achilles's armor, tries to kill the Greek soldiers in their sleep; when intercepted by Athene, he vents his rage on the horses and cattle instead!

In explicit statements, as well, the nurse comments on the perversity of a self-indulgent upper class that, like the warrior-heroes who represent its highest aspirations, does not have to be answerable to its neighbors. "Great people," she observes, tend to be excessive, vindictive, and violent tempered, and when they fall, their ruin is that much more complete. "What is moderate is best," she concludes. On the surface, her advocacy of moderation may resemble that of the chorus in Sophocles's *Oedipus Rex,* where it applied to not asking too many questions or to not insisting on pursuing ideas to their last logical conclusions. For Sophocles's chorus, adhering to "what is moderate" is a way of avoiding trouble, of keeping a low profile, suitable to people who lack the courage of heroes. In Euripides's play, the women of the chorus are much more independent and aggressive. And the moderation that the nurse recommends applies not to knowledge but to behavior; what she advocates is not cowardice or passivity but self-control.

FIGURE 17-1 Medea and Aegeus. Medea is shown, in this medallion from an Attic cup, appealing to the elderly figure of Aegeus, King of Athens, promising to make him fertile in exchange for his assurance of safe refuge for her in his city (see Chapter 10). He accepts her offer, thus enabling Medea to proceed with her planned murders. (*Vatican Museums, Rome.*)

The Tragic Hero Revisited

Medea and Jason, of course, are "great people": Medea is the daughter of the king of Colchis, and Jason is the rightful heir to the kingdom of Iolcos and the hero of the Argonauts. The fact that they are without the status that derives from property, a situation referred to frequently in the play, is a reminder of the connection between power and territory. Having no place where they belong, these "important people" still behave as if power is theirs; but it isn't. The fact is that they are both dispossessed—Jason by political usurpation, Medea by marriage and exile. And we see them in action not through the idealized medium of myth—of epic quests and extraordinary feats of courage and skill—but back at home, close up. If we see "heroes" here, we see them as they really are, behind their public masks; and instead of a domestic quarrel presented as high tragedy (as in Aeschylus's *Agamemnon*), we have domestic drama presented on its own terms.

In the fate of these "displaced" persons, we confront the displacement of an entire class structure: the feudal society in which the warrior-hero and the landed aristocrat were interchangeable has long since become, except in the still-revered ancient myths, an anachronism. Agamemnon and Clytemnestra argue about pride and its relationship to human morality and the gods. Oedipus and Jocasta discuss fate and free will. Jason and Medea argue about where the money is coming from, whose fault the divorce is, who started the quarrels, and who gets custody of the kids. When Medea kills their two sons rather than allow Jason to take possession of them, we feel we are on all-too-familiar territory. We see the headlines all the time: "Mother of Two, Distraught Over Divorce and Loss of Custody Battle, Poisons Ex-Husband's New Flame, Kills Children." Seen close up, heroes suddenly look more like ordinary people.

Of the two, it is clearly Medea who comes closest to the conventional tragic protagonist of the Greek dramas: it is she who suffers; she who feels guilt for the death of the children (even as she plans their death); she who is carried away by an irresistible tide of passionate hatred, as she had earlier been by the irrational power of passionate love; she who has the courage to acknowledge her deeds; and she who, in typical heroic fashion, much like Oedipus, refuses to compromise.

Jason

The great Jason, who not only acquired his reputation but, indeed, survived only with Medea's help, will not acknowledge his complicity in the crimes she had committed on his behalf and is revealed before us as a lying coward, using women for his own gain—first Medea and now the princess. He offers to console Medea with the comment that, after all, she's better off now since she lives in Greece instead of among "barbarians" (another of Euripides's sarcastic references to the Athenians' snobbery). Jason's pitiful argument reaches a low point of illogic when he asserts that it would be better if men could have children on their own and women did not exist!

The predicted death of Jason is the final nontragic point in what has been a mockery of the heroic life. He will die not on the battlefield nor in pursuit of some great revelation; rather, he will be struck on the head by a rotten beam as he sleeps under the prow of his ship—a fittingly ignominious death.

Euripides's Indictment of Tragic Violence

In traditional tragedies, like those of Aeschylus and Sophocles, important people commit appalling deeds: they go mad; they kill their husbands, mothers, or children; they commit incest. And because they do so, ostensibly in pursuit of justice or freedom or integrity, their passions—and their violence—are portrayed nobly. "This is my deed, and I claim it," boasts Clytemnestra of her murder of Agamemnon, re-enacting the heroic stand that the heroes of the *Iliad* made over the corpses of their victims. And Orestes, in Aeschylus's *Oresteia,* kills his mother with far less debate or hesitation than Medea in killing her children! But while Aeschylus brings in Pylades to utter his one line, telling Orestes, in effect, "do it," and thus justifying Orestes's act, Euripides has the chorus express their revulsion for Medea's murder of her children, which reinforces our own horror at her deed. Thus, while Aeschylus allows us to see Orestes as a noble individual trapped, through no fault of his own, in an unfortunate predicament, Euripides forces us to confront the inhuman brutality of the act.

Further, in Aeschylus's plays, we do not get to see the vomiting of blood, the guts spilling out on the floor, the writhing of the corpse. And perhaps because we are not forced to watch the violent acts, it is easy for us to go along with the illusion that such deeds can be somehow ennobling. Euripides, however, stops us short. Forbidden to literally enact violence on the stage, he gets around the restriction by a prolonged description of the details of the princess's death, forcing us to see, however much we might sympathize with Medea in her predicament, how truly revolting as well as immoral such behavior really is. If Jason the Argonaut has become Jason the hypocritical coward, so Medea the wronged woman has become Medea the psychotic housewife who enjoys hearing the horror of her deeds described. Violence, far from being ennobling or transforming, far from precipitating some kind of tragic insight into oneself, as was the case with heroes like Oedipus, produces only the sadistic relishing of the deeds.

Heroes are special, convinced by their divine ancestry and their unique drives and accomplishments that they are not bound by the limits that confine the rest of us. It is perfectly logical to assume, as both Jason and Medea do in this play, that somehow their needs reflect the gods' will and that they are free to enact their desires, however extreme. If these people are what heroes are like and these deeds are what heroes do, then perhaps we would do better to reserve our admiration for the tutors, the nurses, the village girls, and the peasants, who are the only rational or moral characters in many of Euripides's plays.

The Tragic Universe Parodied

Tragedies typically take place in an unpredictable universe in which the gods do not inevitably return good for good and evil for evil; hence the suffering of the tragic protagonist is usually disproportionate to whatever sins he might have committed or mistakes he might have made. Euripides turns this universe on its head and explores its underside: if the good can suffer, the converse is that the wicked can prosper. At the end of Euripides's version of *Electra,* for example, Orestes's acquittal is guaranteed in advance, although he stabbed Aegisthus in the back; further, Electra, who in this version slays her mother with her own hand, gets to marry Orestes's friend Pylades and, presumably, live happily ever after, while the self-sacrificing peasant who aided and protected her is bought off with a few coins and dismissed.

The Athenian audience was fond of parody, although it was usually associated with comedy. In fact, Euripides was himself parodied in Aristophanes's comedies the *Frogs* and *Thesmophoriazusae.* To incorporate parody in a tragedy, however, was more unusual. One scene in Euripides's *Electra* makes clear the playwright's intentional parody of his fellow tragic dramatists—in this case, the recognition scene in Aeschylus's the *Libation-Bearers* (see Chapter 15). In Euripides's play, his Electra asks whether a man would still wear the same size shirt he wore as a boy, whether the color of his hair, surely shared by many, is of any use as an identifying clue, and whether a man's footprint is likely to be the same size as his sister's! Poking fun at the absurdities of Aeschylus's version of the story, Euripides reveals the parodic (and more realistic) elements of his own.

The *Medea,* too, though it does not mock any specific play, seems to ask us to reconsider the traditional tragic vision still trailing the glorious heroic values of the ancient myths. In that mockery, the playwright undermines its characters, its actions, and its social, sexual, and moral premises. What seemed decadent to some of Euripides's more conservative contemporaries may in fact be the instrument of a radical revisionist taking a new look at an old story.

The Play's Conclusion

And so it is with Medea. We last see her on the roof of her home, about to fly off with the bodies of her children in a chariot drawn by dragons. Her "punishment" is to escape to Athens, where she will be supported and protected by the king! In the play's final speech—one that was apparently so compelling to Euripides that he used it again in the final passage of the *Bacchants*—the chorus comments on the unpredictable nature (the unreliability) of the gods: what we counted on is not what actually happened; the gods are not answerable to us and do not run the universe according to our needs or expectations.

In the *Odyssey,* when Odysseus prepares to fight the suitors, Zeus gives a sign, a crack of thunder overhead, as a warning to the suitors and as a reminder that his will is being carried out. In the last scene of the *Medea,* Jason calls, as he has before, upon the gods, asking for a sign, but fruitlessly: Medea gloats that no god will respond to him, an oath-breaker. But neither do the gods provide Medea with such symbolic sanctions. Jason lives, and he will die in a humiliating incident, the very sort of unheroic death that Achilles and Odysseus most feared—the very prosaic death of a failure, not a hero. (And why is he sleeping under the prow of his ship? No longer having any women to exploit, is he now homeless?) Nor will even that fate occur just yet. Who is to say whether his fate represents the delayed action of angry gods or a random accident?

The same ambiguity surrounds Medea's fate. Is her escape an act of divine intervention? The chariot and dragons, she claims, were a gift from Helios, her grandfather. Is this vehicle, like Odysseus's bow or Achilles's shield, one of the special attributes of heroes, or did the chariot appear at that moment, a special dispensation to reward her behavior? Either way, Medea has powers beyond the reach of ordinary mortals. She drives the chariot of the Sun and commands its dragons. She has, as well, the power of life (as she gave the old king, Aegeus, the gift of fertility), of death, and possibly even of rebirth, a skill alluded to when, according to some versions of the myth, she instructs the daughters of Jason's wicked uncle Pelias to kill their father. She tells them to place the dismembered pieces of his corpse into a cauldron that supposedly will bring about his regeneration—a mockery of ancient sparagmos rituals. In fact, Medea's powers recall those of the ancient Great Goddess herself. No wonder, in this thoroughly patriarchal society, she is depicted as a witch!

Further, the god Medea has appealed to most frequently is Hecate, the dread triple goddess (sometimes depicted as having three heads) of the Underworld. (Medea invokes Zeus only in his role as oath-keeper, not as guardian of moral values such as family love—how could she, who kills her own children!) And neither Helios nor Hecate, as some scholars have pointed out, had local cults in Athens and thus would have appeared exotic, somewhat "foreign" gods to the Athenian audience, as strange (and "barbaric"?) as Medea herself must have seemed.

Perhaps, when Medea taunted Jason with the notion that he thinks the "old gods" no longer prevail, she meant not "traditional" gods but an older generation of gods, more elemental, more primitive from the Athenian view. If such bizarre and unfamiliar gods indeed now have the upper hand and heroes like Jason, beloved in ancient myth, are denigrated, then truly, as the chorus remarks, "the world's great order is reversed." Not only has a woman, conventionally thought to be too helpless to plot and carry out such deeds, assumed the active, heroic role in this drama, but the usual gods, despite the expectations of both Jason and Medea, seem to have "ceased to rule" as enforcers of moral law. If that is so, then what is to stop Medea, strong, clever, and daring, from escaping divine as well as human retribution?

If strange, even chthonic gods like Hecate are truly supporting Medea (as would be appropriate for a woman who has been driven by the irrational passions of love and hate), then it is the law of vengeance they enforce, along with the implacable inviolability of oaths. We are thrust back into an amoral universe such as the one the Furies tried, unsuccessfully, to maintain in Aeschylus's *Oresteia.* There, they were displaced, for the moment, by a new world order based on compassion and justice. In the *Medea,* we seem to be back in a world where powerful, natural, but irrational forces prevail and human concepts like family love and justice are easily abrogated. And although Medea seems to recapitulate the powers of the primordial goddess, she has clearly perverted them, under the pressures of an oppressive social structure, to unnatural uses.

Athens was a city ostensibly devoted to freedom and equality, but Athens oppressed its women just as Jason did. The city was, further, presently involved in what would end up being a mutually destructive war with the militaristic, old-style heroes of Sparta. Perhaps presenting the Athenian audience with the spectacle of a world gone mad, given over to irrational passions, in which order and justice could no longer be counted on (if they ever could), was not as unrealistic as its fantastic details, taken out of context, might suggest. Perhaps in such a world, a dramatic vision of a world turned upside down was entirely appropriate.

MEDEA[1]

Euripides

CHARACTERS

NURSE

CREON, *King of Corinth*

CHILDREN OF MEDEA

MEDEA

TUTOR

JASON

CHORUS, *Corinthian Women*

AEGEUS, *King of Athens*

MESSENGER

THE SCENE

The home of Medea at Corinth.
Medea *was acted 431* B.C.

[Enter NURSE.*]*

Nurse

How I wish that the ship Argo had never winged its way through the grey Clashing Rocks to the land of the Colchians! How I wish the pines had never been hewn down in the glens of Pelion, to put oars into the hands of the Heroes who went to fetch for Pelias the Golden Fleece! Then Medea my mistress would not have sailed to the towers of Iolcus, her heart pierced through and through with love for Jason, would not have prevailed on the daughters of Pelias to murder their father, would not now be dwelling here in Corinth with her husband and children. When she fled here she found favor with the citizens to whose land she had come and was herself a perfect partner in all things for Jason. (And therein lies a woman's best security, to avoid conflict with her husband.) But now there is nothing but enmity, a blight has come over their great love.

Jason has betrayed his own children and my mistress to sleep beside a royal bride, the daughter of Creon who rules this land, while Medea, luckless Medea, in her desolation invokes the promises he made, appeals to the pledges in which she put her deepest trust, and calls Heaven to witness the sorry recompense she has from Jason. Ever since she realized her husband's perfidy, she has been lying there prostrated, eating no food, her whole frame subdued to sorrow, wasting away with incessant weeping. She has not lifted an eye nor ever turned her face

1. Translation by Moses Hadas.

from the floor. The admonitions of her friends she receives with unhearing ears, like a rock or a wave of the sea. Only now and then she turns her white neck and talks to herself, in sorrow, of her dear father and her country and the home which she betrayed to come here with a husband who now holds her in contempt. Now she knows, from bitter experience, how sad a thing it is to lose one's fatherland. She hates her own children and has no pleasure at the sight of them. I fear she may form some new and horrible resolve. For hers is a dangerous mind, and she will not lie down to injury. I know her and she frightens me [lest she make her way stealthily into the palace where his couch is spread and drive a sharp sword into his vitals or even kill both the King and the bridegroom and then incur some greater misfortune]. She is cunning. Whoever crosses swords with her will not find victory easy, I tell you.

But here come the children, their playtime over. Little thought have they of their mother's troubles. Children do not like sad thoughts.
[Enter TUTOR, *with boys.]*

Tutor
Ancient household chattel of my mistress, why are you standing here all alone at the gates, muttering darkly to yourself? What makes Medea want you to leave her alone?

Nurse
Aged escort of Jason's children, when their master's affairs go ill, good slaves find not only their misfortune but also their heart's grief. My sorrow has now become so great that a longing came over me to come out here and tell to earth and sky the story of my mistress's woes.

Tutor
What? Is the poor lady not yet through with weeping?

Nurse
I wish I had your optimism. Why, her sorrow is only beginning, it's not yet at the turning point.

Tutor
Poor foolish woman!—if one may speak thus of one's masters. Little she knows of the latest ills!

Nurse
What's that, old man? Don't grudge me your news.

Tutor
It's nothing at all. I'm sorry I even said what I said.

Nurse
Please, I beg of you, don't keep it from a fellow slave. I'll keep it dark, if need be.

Tutor
I had drawn near the checkerboards where the old men sit, beside the sacred water of Pirene, and there, when nobody thought I was listening, I heard somebody say that Creon the ruler of this land was planning to expel these children

and their mother from Corinth. Whether the tale is true or not I do not know. I would wish it were not so.

Nurse

But will Jason ever allow his children to be so treated, even if he *is* at variance with their mother?

Tutor

Old loves are weaker than new loves, and that man is no friend to this household.

Nurse

That's the end of us then, if we are to ship a second wave of trouble before we are rid of the first.

Tutor

Meanwhile you keep quiet and don't say a word. This is no time for the mistress to be told.

Nurse

O children, do you hear what love your father bears you? Since he is my master, I do not wish him dead, but he is certainly proving the enemy of those he should love.

Tutor

Like the rest of the world. Are you only now learning that every man loves himself more than his neighbor? [Some justly, others for profit, as] now for a new bride their father hates these children.

Nurse

Inside, children, inside. It will be all right.
[*To the* TUTOR.]
And you keep them alone as much as you can, and don't let them near their mother when she's melancholy. I have already noticed her casting a baleful eye at them as if she would gladly do them mischief. She'll not recover from her rage, I know well, till the lightning of her fury has struck somebody to the ground. May it be enemies, not loved ones, that suffer!

Medea
[*within*]
Oh! my grief! the misery of it all! Why can I not die?

Nurse

What did I tell you, dear children? Your mother's heart is troubled, her anger is roused. Hurry indoors, quick. Keep out of her sight, don't go near her. Beware of her fierce manner, her implacable temper. Hers is a selfwilled nature. Go now, get you inside, be quick. Soon, it is clear, her sorrow like a gathering cloud will burst in a tempest of fury. What deed will she do then, that impetuous, indomitable heart, poisoned by injustice?
[*Exeunt* CHILDREN *with* TUTOR.]

Medea

[within]

O misery! the things I have suffered, cause enough for deep lamentations! O you cursed sons of a hateful mother, a plague on you! And on your father! Ruin seize the whole household!

Nurse

Ah me, unhappy me! Why will you have your sons partake of their father's guilt? Why hate them? Ah children, your danger overwhelms me with anxiety. The souls of royalty are vindictive; they do not easily forget their resentment, possibly because being used to command they are seldom checked. It is better to be used to living among equals. For myself, at any rate, I ask not greatness but a safe old age. Moderation! Firstly, the very name of it is excellent; to practise it is easily the best thing for mortals. Excess avails to no good purpose for men, and if the gods are provoked, brings greater ruin on a house.

[Enter CHORUS.]

Chorus

I heard a voice, I heard a cry. It was the unhappy Colchian woman's. She is not yet calm. Pray tell us, old woman. From the court outside I heard her cries within. I do not rejoice, woman, in the griefs of this house. Dear, dear it is to me.

Nurse

It is a home no more; the life has gone out of it. Its master a princess' bed enthralls, while the mistress in her chamber is pining to death, and her friends have no words to comfort her heart.

Medea

[within]

Oh! Would that a flaming bolt from Heaven might pierce my brain! What is the good of living any longer? O Misery! Let me give up this life I find so hateful. Let me seek lodging in the house of death.

Chorus

O Zeus, O Earth, O Light, hear what a sad lament the hapless wife intones. What is this yearning, rash woman, after that fearful bed? Will you hasten to the end that is Death? Pray not for that. If your husband worships a new bride, it is a common event; be not exasperated. Zeus will support your cause. Do not let grief for a lost husband waste away your life.

Medea

[within]

Great Zeus and Lady Themis, see you how I am treated, for all the strong oaths with which I bound my cursed husband? May I live to see him and his bride, palace and all, in one common destruction, for the wrongs that they inflict, unprovoked, on me! O father, O country, that I forsook so shamefully, killing my brother, my own!

Nurse

Hear what she says, how she cries out to Themis of Prayers and to Zeus whom mortals regard as the steward of oaths. With no small revenge will my mistress bate her rage.

Chorus

I wish she would come into our presence and hear the sound of the words we would speak. Then she might forget the resentment in her heart and change her purpose. May my zeal be ever at the service of my friends. But bring her here, make her come forth from the palace. Tell her that here too are friends. Make haste before she does any harm to those within. Furious is the surge of such a sorrow.

Nurse

I shall do so, though I am not hopeful of persuading the mistress. But I freely present you with the gift of my labor. Yet she throws a baleful glare, like a lioness with cubs, at any servant who approaches her as if to speak. Blunderers and fools! that is the only proper name for the men of old who invented songs to bring the joy of life to feasts and banquets and festive boards, but never discovered a music of song or sounding lyre to dispel the weary sorrows of humanity, that bring death and fell havoc and destruction of homes. Yet what a boon to man, could these ills be cured by some! At sumptuous banquets why raise a useless strain? The food that is served and the satisfaction that comes to full men, that in itself is pleasure enough.
[Exit NURSE.*]*

Chorus

I hear a cry of grief and deep sorrow. In piercing accents of misery she proclaims her woes, her ill-starred marriage and her love betrayed. The victim of grievous wrongs, she calls on the daughter of Zeus, even Themis, Lady of Vows, who led her through the night by difficult straits across the briny sea to Hellas.
[Enter MEDEA.*]*

Medea

Women of Corinth, do not criticize me, I come forth from the palace. Well I know that snobbery is a common charge, that may be levelled against recluse and busy man alike. And the former, by their choice of a quiet life, acquire an extra stigma: they are deficient in energy and spirit. There is no justice in the eyes of men; a man who has never harmed them they may hate at sight, without ever knowing anything about his essential nature. An alien, to be sure, should adapt himself to the citizens with whom he lives. Even the citizen is to be condemned if he is too selfwilled or too uncouth to avoid offending his fellows. So I . . . but this unexpected blow which has befallen me has broken my heart.

It's all over, my friends; I would gladly die. Life has lost its savor. The man who was everything to me, well he knows it, has turned out to be the basest of men. Of all creatures that feel and think, we women are the unhappiest species. In the first place, we must pay a great dowry to a husband who will be the tyrant of our bodies (that's a further aggravation of the evil); and there is another fearful hazard: whether we shall get a good man or a bad. For separations bring disgrace on the woman and it is not possible to renounce one's husband. Then, landed among strange habits and regulations unheard of in her own home, a woman needs second sight to know how best to handle her bedmate. And if we manage this well and have a husband who does not find the yoke of intercourse too galling, ours is a life to be envied. Otherwise, one is better dead. When the man wearies of the company of his wife, he goes outdoors and relieves the disgust of his heart [having recourse to some friend or the companions of his own age], but we women have only one person to turn to.

They say that we have a safe life at home, whereas men must go to war. Nonsense! I had rather fight three battles than bear one child. But be that as it may, you and I are not in the same case. You have your city here, your paternal homes; you know the delights of life and association with your loved ones. But I, homeless and forsaken, carried off from a foreign land, am being wronged by a husband, with neither mother nor brother nor kinsman with whom I might find refuge from the storms of misfortune. One little boon I crave of you, if I discover any ways and means of punishing my husband for these wrongs: your silence. Woman in most respects is a timid creature, with no heart for strife and aghast at the sight of steel; but wronged in love, there is no heart more murderous than hers.

Leader
Do as you say, Medea, for just will be your vengeance. I do not wonder that you bemoan your fate. But I see Creon coming, the ruler of this land, bringing tidings of new plans.
[Enter CREON.]

Creon
You there, Medea, looking black with rage against your husband; I have proclaimed that you are to be driven forth in exile from this land, you and your two sons. Immediately. I am the absolute judge of the case, and I shall not go back to my palace till I have cast you over the frontier of the land.

Medea
Ah! Destruction, double destruction is my unhappy lot. My enemies are letting out every sail and there is no harbor into which I may flee from the menace of their attack. But ill-treated and all, Creon, still I shall put the question to you: Why are you sending me out of the country?

Creon
I am afraid of you—there's no need to hide behind a cloak of words—afraid you will do my child some irreparable injury. There's plenty logic in that fear. You are a wizard possessed of evil knowledge. You are stung by the loss of your husband's love. And I have heard of your threats—they told me of them—to injure bridegroom and bride and father of the bride. Therefore before anything happens to me, I shall take precautions. Better for me now to be hateful in your eyes than to relent and rue it greatly later.

Medea
Alas! Alas! Often ere now—this is not the first time—my reputation has hurt me and done me grievous wrong. If a man's really shrewd, he ought never to have his children taught too much. For over and above a name for uselessness that it will earn them, they incur the hostility and envy of their fellow men. Offer clever reforms to dullards, and you will be thought a useless fool yourself. And the reputed wiseacres, feeling your superiority, will dislike you intensely. I myself have met this fate. Because I have skill, some are jealous of me, others think me unsociable. But my wisdom does not go very far. However, you are

afraid you may suffer something unpleasant at my hands, aren't you? Fear not, Creon; it is not my way to commit my crimes against kings. What wrong have you done me? You have only bestowed your daughter on the suitor of your choice. No, it is my husband I hate. You, I dare say, knew what you were doing in the matter. And now I don't grudge success to your scheme. Make your match, and good luck to you. But allow me to stay in this country. Though foully used, I shall keep my peace, submitting to my masters.

Creon

Your words are comforting to hear, but inside my heart there is a horrible fear that you are plotting some mischief, which makes me trust you even less than before. The hot-tempered woman, like the hot-tempered man, is easier to guard against than the cunning and silent. But off with you at once, make no speeches. My resolve is fixed; for all your skill you will not stay amongst us to hate me.

Medea

Please no, I beseech you, by your knees, by the young bride . . .

Creon

You are wasting your words; you will never convince me.

Medea

Will you drive me out and have no respect for my prayers?

Creon

Yes, for I love you less than I love my own family.

Medea

O fatherland, how strongly do I now remember you!

Creon

Yes, apart from my children, that is *my* dearest love.

Medea

Alas! the loves of men are a mighty evil.

Creon

In my opinion, that depends on the circumstances.

Medea

O Zeus, do not forget the author of this wickedness.

Creon

On your way, vain woman, and end my troubles.

Medea

The troubles are mine; I have no lack of troubles.

Creon

In a moment you will be thrust out by the hands of servants.

Medea

No, no, not that. But Creon I entreat you. . . .

Creon

You seem to be bent on causing trouble, woman.

Medea

I shall go into exile. It is not *that* I beg you to grant me.

Creon

Why then are you clinging so violently to my hand?

Medea

Allow me to stay for this one day to complete my plans for departure and get together provision for my children, since their father prefers not to bother about his own sons. Have pity on them. You too are the father of children. It is natural that you should feel kindly. Stay or go, I care nothing for myself. It's them I weep for in their misfortune.

Creon

My mind is not tyrannical enough; mercy has often been my undoing. So now, though I know that it is a mistake, woman, you will have your request. But I give you warning: if to-morrow's divine sun sees you and your children inside the borders of this country, you die. True is the word I have spoken. [Stay, if you must, this one day. You'll not have time to do what I dread.]
[Exit CREON.]

Chorus

Hapless woman! overwhelmed by sorrow! Where will you turn? What stranger will afford you hospitality? God has steered you, Medea, into an unmanageable surge of troubles.

Medea

Ill fortune's everywhere, who can gainsay it? But it is not yet as bad as that, never think so. There is still heavy weather ahead for the new bride and groom, and no little trouble for the maker of the match. Do you think I would ever have wheedled the king just now except to further my own plans? I would not even have spoken to him, nor touched him either. But he is such a fool that though he might have thwarted my plans by expelling me from the country he has allowed me to stay over for this one day, in which I shall make corpses of three of my enemies, father and daughter and my own husband.

My friends, I know several ways of causing their death, and I cannot decide which I should turn my hand to first. Shall I set fire to the bridal chamber or make my way in stealthily to where their bed is laid and drive a sword through their vitals? But there is one little difficulty. If I am caught entering the palace or devising my bonfire I shall be slain and my enemies shall laugh. Better take the direct way and the one for which I have the natural gift. Poison. Destroy them with poison. So be it.

But suppose them slain. What city will receive me? Whose hospitality will rescue me and afford me a land where I shall be safe from punishment, a home where I can live in security? It cannot be. I shall wait, therefore, a little longer and if any tower of safety shows up I shall carry out the murders in stealth and secrecy. However, if circumstances drive me to my wits' end, I shall take a sword in my own hands and face certain death to slay them. I shall not shirk the diffi-cult adventure. No! by Queen Hecate who has her abode in the recesses of my hearth—her I revere above all gods and have chosen to assist me—never shall any one of them torture my heart with impunity. I shall make their marriage a torment and grief to them. Bitterly shall they rue the match they have made and the exile they inflict on me.

But enough! Medea, use all your wiles; plot and devise. Onward to the dread-ful moment. Now is the test of courage. Do you see how you are being treated? It is not right that the seed of Sisyphus and Aeson should gloat over you, the daughter of a noble sire and descendant of the Sun. But you realize that. More-over by our mere nature we women are helpless for good, but adept at contriving all manner of wickedness.

Chorus

Back to their sources flow the sacred rivers. The world and morality are turned upside-down. The hearts of men are treacherous; the sanctions of Heaven are under-mined. The voice of time will change, and our glory will ring down the ages. Wom-ankind will be honored. No longer will ill-sounding report attach to our sex.

The strains of ancient minstrelsy will cease, that hymned our faithlessness. Would that Phoebus, Lord of Song, had put into woman's heart the inspired song of the lyre. Then I would have sung a song in answer to the tribe of males. History has much to tell of the relations of men with women.

You, Medea, in the mad passion of your heart sailed away from your father's home, threading your way through the twin rocks of the Euxine, to settle in a foreign land. Now, your bed empty, your lover lost, unhappy woman, you are being driven forth in dishonor into exile.

Gone is respect for oaths. Nowhere in all the breadth of Hellas is honor any more to be found; it has vanished into the clouds. Hapless one, you have no father's house to which you might fly for shelter from the gales of misfortune; and another woman, a princess, has charmed your husband away and stepped into your place.
[Enter JASON.*]*

Jason

Often and often ere now I have observed that an intractable nature is a curse almost impossible to deal with. So with you. When you might have stayed on in this land and in this house by submitting quietly to the wishes of your superiors, your forward tongue has got you expelled from the country. Not that your abuse troubles *me* at all. Keep on saying that Jason is a villain of the deepest dye. But for your insolence to royalty consider yourself more than fortunate that you are only being punished by exile. I was constantly mollifying the angry monarch and expressing the wish that you be allowed to stay. But in unabated folly you keep on reviling the king. That is why you are to be expelled.

But still, despite everything, I come here now with unwearied goodwill, to contrive on your behalf, Madam, that you and the children will not leave this country lacking money or anything else. Exile brings many hardships in its wake. And even if you do hate me, I could never think cruelly of you.

Medea

Rotten, heart-rotten, that is the word for you. Words, words, magnificent words. In reality a craven. You come to me, you come, my worst enemy! This isn't bravery, you know, this isn't valor, to come and face your victims. No! its the ugliest sore on the face of humanity, Shamelessness. But I thank you for coming. It will lighten the weight on my heart to tell your wickedness, and it will hurt you to hear it. I shall begin my tale at the very beginning.

I saved your life, as all know who embarked with you on the Argo, when you were sent to master with the yoke the fire-breathing bulls and to sow with dragon's teeth that acre of death. The dragon, too, with wreathed coils, that kept safe watch over the Golden Fleece and never slept—I slew it and raised for you the light of life again. Then, forsaking my father and my own dear ones, I came to Iolcus where Pelias reigned, came with you, more than fond and less than wise. On Pelias too I brought death, the most painful death there is, at the hands of his own children. Thus I have removed every danger from your path.

And after all those benefits at my hands, you basest of men, you have betrayed me and made a new marriage, though I have borne you children. If you were still childless, I could have understood this love of yours for a new wife. Gone now is all reliance on pledges. You puzzle me. Do you believe that the gods of the old days are no longer in office? Do you think that men are now living under a new dispensation? For surely you know that you have broken all your oaths to me. Ah my hand, which you so often grasped, and oh my knees, how all for nothing have we been defiled by this false man, who has disappointed all our hopes.

But come, I shall confide in you as though you were my friend, not that I expect to receive any benefit from you. But let that go. My questions will serve to underline your infamy. As things are now, where am I to turn? Home to my father? But when I came here with you, I betrayed my home and my country. To the wretched daughters of Pelias? They would surely give me a royal welcome to their home; I only murdered their father. For it is how it is. My loved ones at home have learned to hate me; the others, whom I need not have harmed, I have made my enemies to oblige you. And so in return for these services you have made me envied among the women of Hellas! A wonderful, faithful husband I have in you, if I must be expelled from the country into exile, deserted by my friends, alone with my friendless children! A fine story to tell of the new bridegroom, that his children and the woman who saved his life are wandering about in aimless beggary! O Zeus, why O why have you given to mortals sure means of knowing gold from tinsel, yet men's exteriors show no mark by which to descry the rotten heart?

Leader
Horrible and hard to heal is the anger of friend at strife with friend.

Jason
It looks as if I need no small skill in speech if, like a skilful steersman riding the storm with close-reefed sheets, I am to escape the howling gale of your verbosity, woman. Well, since you are making a mountain out of the favors you have done me, I'll tell *you* what *I* think. It was the goddess of Love and none other, mortal or immortal, who delivered me from the dangers of my quest. You have indeed much subtlety of wit, but it would be an invidious story to go into, how the inescapable shafts of Love compelled you to save my life. Still, I shall not put too

fine a point on it. If you helped me in some way or other, good and well. But as I shall demonstrate, in the matter of my rescue you got more than you gave.

In the first place, you have your home in Greece, instead of in a barbarian land. You have learned the blessings of Law and Justice, instead of the Caprice of the Strong. And all the Greeks have realized your wisdom, and you have won great fame. If you had been living on the edges of the earth, nobody would ever have heard of you. May I have neither gold in my house nor skill to sing a sweeter song than Orpheus if my fortune is to be hid from the eyes of men. That, then, is my position in the matter of the fetching of the Fleece. (It was you who proposed the debate.)

There remains my wedding with the Princess, which you have cast in my teeth. In this connection I shall demonstrate, one, my wisdom; two, my rightness; three, my great service of love to you and my children. (Be quiet, please.) When I emigrated here from the land of Iolcus, dragging behind me an unmanageable chain of troubles, what greater windfall could I have hit upon, I an exile, than a marriage with the king's daughter? Not that I was weary of your charms (that's the thought that galls you) or that I was smitten with longing for a fresh bride; still less that I wanted to outdo my neighbors in begetting numerous children. Those I have are enough, there I have no criticism to make. No! what I wanted, first and foremost, was a good home where we would lack for nothing (well I knew that the poor man is shunned and avoided by all his friends); and secondly, I wanted to bring up the children in a style worthy of my house, and, begetting other children to be brothers to the children born of you, to bring them all together and unite the families. Then my happiness would be complete. What do *you* want with more children? As for me, it will pay me to advance the children I have by means of those I intend to beget. Surely that is no bad plan? You yourself would admit it, if jealousy were not pricking you.

You women have actually come to believe that, lucky in love, you are lucky in all things, but let some mischance befall that love, and you will think the best of all possible worlds a most loathsome place. There ought to have been some other way for men to beget their children, dispensing with the assistance of women. Then there would be no trouble in the world.

Leader
Jason, you arrange your arguments very skillfully. And yet in my opinion, like it or not, you have acted unjustly in betraying your wife.

Medea
Yes! I do hold many opinions that are not shared by the majority of people. In my opinion, for example, the plausible scoundrel is the worst type of scoundrel. Confident in his ability to trick out his wickedness with fair phrases he shrinks from no depth of villainy. But there is a limit to his cleverness. As there is also to yours. You may as well drop that fine front with me, and all that rhetoric. One word will floor you. If you had been an honorable man, you would have sought my consent to the new match and not kept your plans secret from your own family.

Jason
And if I had announced to you my intention to marry, I am sure I would have

found you a most enthusiastic accomplice. Why! even now you cannot bring yourself to master your heart's deep resentment.

Medea

That's not what griped you. No! your foreign wife was passing into an old age that did you little credit.

Jason

Accept my assurance, it was not for the sake of a woman that I made the match I have made. As I told you once already, I wanted to save you and to beget princes to be brothers to my own sons, thereby establishing our family.

Medea

May it never be mine . . . a happiness that hurts, a blessedness that frets my soul.

Jason

Do you know how to change your prayer to show better sense? "May I regard nothing useful as grievous, no good fortune as ill."

Medea

Insult me. *You* have a refuge, but I am helpless, faced with exile.

Jason

It was your own choice. Don't blame anyone else.

Medea

What did I do? Did I betray you and marry somebody else?

Jason

You heaped foul curses on the king.

Medea

And to your house also I shall prove a curse.

Jason

Look here, I do not intend to continue this discussion any further. If you want anything of mine to assist you or the children in your exile, just tell me. I am ready to give it with an ungrudging hand and to send letters of introduction to my foreign friends who will treat you well. If you reject this offer, woman, you will be a great fool. Forget your anger, and you will find it greatly to your advantage.

Medea

I would not use your friends on any terms or accept anything of yours. Do not offer it. The gifts of the wicked bring no profit.

Jason

At any rate, heaven be my witness that I am willing to render every assistance to you and the children. But you do not like what is good for you. Your obstinacy repulses your friends; it will only aggravate your suffering.

Medea

Be off with you. As you loiter outside here, you are burning with longing for the girl who has just been made your wife. Make the most of the union. Perhaps, god willing, you are making the kind of marriage you will some day wish unmade.

[Exit JASON.*]*

Chorus

Love may go too far and involve men in dishonor and disgrace. But if the goddess comes in just measure, there is none so rich in blessing. May you never launch at me, O Lady of Cyprus, your golden bow's passion-poisoned arrows, which no man can avoid.

May Moderation content me, the fairest gift of Heaven. Never may the Cyprian pierce my heart with longing for another's love and bring on me angry quarrelings and never-ending recriminations. May she have respect for harmonious unions and with discernment assort the matings of women.

O Home and Fatherland, never, never, I pray, may I be cityless. It is an intolerable existence, hopeless, piteous, grievous. Let me die first, die and bring this life to a close. There is no sorrow that surpasses the loss of country.

My eyes have seen it; not from hearsay do I speak. You have neither city nor friend to pity you in your most terrible trials. Perish, abhorred, the man who never brings himself to unbolt his heart in frankness to some honored friends! Never shall such a man be a friend of mine.

[Enter AEGEUS, *in traveler's dress.]*

Aegeus

Medea, good health to you. A better prelude than that in addressing one's friends, no man knows.

Medea

Good health be yours also, wise Pandion's son, Aegeus. Where do you come from to visit this land?

Aegeus

I have just left the ancient oracle of Phoebus.

Medea

What sent you to the earth's oracular hub?

Aegeus

I was enquiring how I might get children.

Medea

In the name of Heaven, have you come thus far in life still childless?

Aegeus

By some supernatural influence I am still without children.

Medea

Have you a wife or are you still unmarried?

Aegeus
I have a wedded wife to share my bed.

Medea
Tell me, what did Phoebus tell you about offspring?

Aegeus
His words were too cunning for a mere man to interpret.

Medea
Is it lawful to tell me the answer of the god?

Aegeus
Surely. For, believe me, it requires a cunning mind to understand.

Medea
What then was the oracle? Tell me, if I may hear it.

Aegeus
I am not to open the cock that projects from the skin. . . .

Medea
Till you do what? Till you reach what land?

Aegeus
Till I return to my ancestral hearth.

Medea
Then what errand brings your ship to this land?

Aegeus
There is one Pittheus, king of Troezen. . . .

Medea
The child of Pelops, as they say, and a most pious man.

Aegeus
To him I will communicate the oracle of the god.

Medea
Yes, he is a cunning man and well-versed in such matters.

Aegeus
Yes, and of all my comrades in arms the one I love most.

Medea
Well, good luck to you, and may you win your heart's desire.

Aegeus
Why, what's the reason for those sad eyes, that wasted complexion?

Medea
Aegeus, I've got the basest husband in all the world.

Aegeus
What do you mean? Tell me the reason of your despondency, tell me plainly.

Medea
Jason is wronging me; I never did him wrong.

Aegeus
What has he done? Speak more bluntly.

Medea
He has another wife, to lord it over me in our home.

Aegeus
You don't mean that he has done so callous, so shameful a deed!

Medea
Indeed he did. Me that used to be his darling he now despises.

Aegeus
Has he fallen in love? Does he hate your embraces?

Medea
Yes, it's a grand passion! He was born to betray his loved ones.

Aegeus
Let him go, then, since he is so base, as you say.

Medea
He became enamored of getting a king for a father-in-law.

Aegeus
Who gave him the bride? Please finish your story.

Medea
Creon, the ruler of this Corinth.

Aegeus
In that case, Madam, I can sympathize with your resentment.

Medea
My life is ruined. What is more, I am being expelled from the land.

Aegeus
By whom? This new trouble is hard.

Medea
Creon is driving me out of Corinth into exile.

Aegeus
And does Jason allow this? I don't like that either.

Medea
He says he does not, but he'll stand it. Oh! I beseech you by this beard, by these knees, a suppliant I entreat you, show pity, show pity for my misery. Do not

stand by and see me driven forth to a lonely exile. Receive me into your land, into your home and the shelter of your hearth. So may the gods grant you the children you desire, to throw joy round your deathbed. You do not know what a lucky path you have taken to me. I shall put an end to your childlessness. I shall make you beget heirs of your blood. I know the magic potions that will do it.

Aegeus

Many things make me eager to do this favor for you, Madam. Firstly, the gods, and secondly, the children that you promise will be born to me. In that matter I am quite at my wits' end. But here is how I stand. If you yourself come to Athens, I shall try to be your champion, as in duty bound. This warning, however, I must give you! I shall not consent to take you with me out of Corinth. If you yourself come to my palace, you will find a home and a sanctuary. Never will I surrender you to anybody. But your own efforts must get you away from this place. I wish to be free from blame in the eyes of my hosts also.

Medea

And so you shall. But just let me have a pledge for these services, and I shall have all I could desire of you.

Aegeus

Do you not trust me? What is your difficulty?

Medea

I do trust you. But both the house of Pelias and Creon are my enemies. Bound by oaths, you would never hand me over to them if they tried to extradite me. But with an agreement of mere words, unfettered by any sacred pledge, you might be won over by their diplomatic advances to become *their* friend. For I have no influence or power, whereas they have the wealth of a royal palace.

Aegeus

You take great precautions, Madam. Still, if you wish, I will not refuse to do your bidding. For me too it will be safer that way, if I have some excuse to offer to your enemies, and *you* will have more security. Dictate the oath.

Medea

Swear by the Floor of Earth, by the Sun my father's father, by the whole family of the gods, one and all———

Aegeus

To do or not do what? Say on.

Medea

Never yourself to cast me out of your country and never, willingly, during your lifetime, to surrender me to any of my foes that desire to seize me.

Aegeus

I swear by the Earth, by the holy majesty of the Sun, and by all the gods, to abide by the terms you propose.

Medea

Enough! And if you abide not by your oath, what punishment do you pray to receive?

Aegeus

The doom of sacrilegious mortals.

Medea

Go and fare well. All is well. I shall arrive at your city as soon as possible, when I have done what I intend to do, and obtained my desire.

Leader

[as AEGEUS *departs*]

May Maia's son, the Lord of Journeys, bring you safe to Athens, and may you achieve the desire that hurries you homeward; for you are a generous man in my esteem.

Medea

O Zeus and his Justice, O Light of the Sun! The time has come, my friends, when I shall sing songs of triumph over my enemies. I am on my way. Now I can hope that my foes will pay the penalty. Just as my plans were most storm-tossed at sea, this man has appeared, a veritable harbor, where I shall fix my moorings, when I get to the town and citadel of Pallas.

Now I shall tell you all my plans; what you hear will not be said in fun. I shall send one of my servants to ask Jason to come and see me. When he comes, I shall make my language submissive, tell him I approve of everything else and am quite contented [with his royal marriage and his betrayal of me, that I agree it is all for the best]; I shall only ask him to allow my children to remain. Not that I wish to leave them in a hostile land [for my enemies to insult]. No! I have a cunning plan to kill the princess. I shall send them with gifts to offer to the bride, to allow them to stay in the land—a dainty robe and a headdress of beaten gold. If she takes the finery and puts it on her, she will die in agony. She and anyone who touches her. So deadly are the poisons in which I shall steep my gifts.

But now I change my tone. It grieves me sorely, the horrible deed I must do next. I shall murder my children, these children of mine. No man shall take them away from me. Then when I have accomplished the utter overthrow of the house of Jason, I shall flee from the land, to escape the consequences of my own dear children's murder and my other accursed crimes. My friends, I cannot bear being laughed at by my enemies.

So be it. Tell me, what has life to offer them. They have no father, no home, no refuge from danger.

My mistake was in leaving my father's house, won over by the words of a Greek. But, as god is my ally, he shall pay for his crime. Never, if I can help it, shall he behold his sons again in this life. Never shall he beget children by his new bride. She must die by my poisons, die the death she deserves. Nobody shall despise *me* or think me weak or passive. Quite the contrary. I am a good friend, but a dangerous enemy. For that is the type the world delights to honor.

Leader
You have confided your plan in me, and I should like to help you, but since I also would support the laws of mankind, I entreat you not to do this deed.

Medea
It is the only way. But I can sympathize with your sentiments. You have not been wronged like me.

Leader
Surely you will not have the heart to destroy your own flesh and blood?

Medea
I shall. It will hurt my husband most that way.

Leader
But it will make you the unhappiest woman in the world.

Medea
Let it. From now on all words are superfluous.
[To the NURSE.*]*
Go now, please, and fetch Jason. Whenever loyalty is wanted, I turn to you. Tell him nothing of my intentions, as you are a woman and a loyal servant of your mistress.
[Exit NURSE.*]*

Chorus
The people of Erechtheus have been favored of Heaven from the beginning. Children of the blessed gods are they, sprung from a hallowed land that no foeman's foot has trodden. Their food is glorious Wisdom. There the skies are always clear, and lightly do they walk in that land where once on a time blonde Harmony bore nine chaste daughters, the Muses of Pieria.

Such is the tale, which tells also how Aphrodite sprinkled the land with water from the fair streams of Cephissus and breathed over it breezes soft and fragrant. Ever on her hair she wears a garland of sweet-smelling roses, and ever she sends the Loves to assist in the court of Wisdom. No good thing is wrought without their help.

How then shall that land of sacred rivers, that hospitable land receive you the slayer of your children? It would be sacrilege for you to live with them. Think. You are stabbing your children. Think. You are earning the name of murderess. By your knees we entreat you, by all the world holds sacred, do not murder your children.

Whence got you the hardihood to conceive such a plan? And in the horrible act, as you bring death on your own children, how will you steel your heart and hand? When you cast your eyes on them, your own children, will you not weep that you should be their murderess? When your own children fall at your feet and beg for mercy, you will never be able to dye your hands with their blood. Your heart will not stand it.
[Enter JASON, *followed by the* NURSE.*]*

Jason
I come at your bidding. Though you hate me, I shall not refuse you an audience. What new favor have you to ask of me, woman?

Medea

Jason, please forgive me for all I said. After all the services of love you have rendered me before, I can count on you to put up with my fits of temper. I have been arguing the matter out with myself. Wretched woman (thus I scolded myself), why am I so mad as to hate those that mean me well, to treat as enemies the rulers of this land and my husband who, in marrying a princess and getting brothers for my children, is only doing what is best for us all? What is the matter with me? Why am I still furious, when the gods are showering their blessings on me? Have I not children of my own? Am I forgetting that I am an exile from my native land, in sore need of friends? These reflections let me see how very foolish I have been and how groundless is my resentment. Now, I want to thank you. I think you are only doing the right thing in making this new match. I have been the fool. I ought to have entered into your designs, helped you to accomplish them, even stood by your nuptial couch and been glad to be of service to the new bride. But I am what I am . . . to say no worse, a woman. You ought not therefore to imitate me in my error or to compete with me in childishness. I beg your pardon, and confess that I was wrong then. But now I have taken better counsel, as you see.

Children, children, come here, leave the house, come out and greet your father as I do. Speak to him. Join your mother in making friends with him, forgetting our former hate. It's a truce; the quarrel is over. Take his right hand. Alas! my imagination sickens strangely. My children, will you stretch out loving arms like that in the long hereafter? My grief! How quick my tears are! My fears brim over. It is that long quarrel with your father, now done with, that fills my tender eyes with tears.

Leader

From my eyes, too, the burning tears gush forth. May Sorrow's advance proceed no further.

Jason

That is the talk I like to hear, woman. The past I can forgive. It is only natural for your sex to show resentment when their husbands contract another marriage. But your heart has now changed for the better. It took time, to be sure, but you have now seen the light of reason. That's the action of a wise woman. As for you, my children, your father has not forgotten you. God willing, he has secured your perfect safety. I feel sure that you will yet occupy the first place here in Corinth, with your brothers. Merely grow up. Your father, and any friends he has in heaven, will see to the rest. May I see you, sturdy and strong, in the flower of your youth, triumphant over my enemies.

You there, why wet your eyes with hot tears, and avert your pale cheek? Why are you not happy to hear me speak thus?

Medea

It's nothing. Just a thought about the children here.

Jason

Why all this weeping over the children? It's too much.

Medea

I am their mother. Just now when you were wishing them long life, a pang of sorrow came over me, in case things would not work out that way.

Jason

Cheer up, then. I shall see that they are all right.

Medea

Very well, I shall not doubt your word. Women are frail things and naturally apt to cry.

But to return to the object of this conference, something has been said, something remains to be mentioned. Since it is their royal pleasure to expel me from the country—oh yes! it's the best thing for me too, I know well, not to stay on here in the way of you and the king; I am supposed to be their bitter enemy—*I* then shall go off into exile. But see that the children are reared by your own hand, ask Creon to let *them* stay.

Jason

I don't know if he will listen to me, but I shall try, as I ought.

Medea

At least you can get your wife to intercede with her father on their behalf!

Jason

Certainly, and I imagine I shall persuade her.

Medea

If she is a woman like the rest of us. In this task, I too shall play my part. I shall send the children with gifts for her, gifts far surpassing the things men make today [a fine robe, and a head-dress of beaten gold]. Be quick there. Let one of my maids bring the finery here. What joy will be hers, joys rather, joys innumerable, getting not only a hero like you for a husband, but also raiment which the Sun, my father's father, gave to his children.
[MEDEA *takes the casket from a maid who has brought it, and hands it to the* CHILDREN.]
Here, my children, take these wedding gifts in your hands. Carry them to the princess, the happy bride, and give them to her. They are not the kind of gifts she will despise.

Jason

Impetuous woman! Why leave yourself thus empty-handed? Do you think a royal palace lacks for raiment and gold? Keep these things for yourself, don't give them away. If my wife has any regard for me at all, she will prefer me to wealth, I'm sure.

Medea

Please let me. They say that gifts persuade even the gods, and gold is stronger than ten thousand words. Hers is the fortune of the hour; her now is god exalting. She has youth, and a king for a father. And to save my children from exile, I would give my very life, let alone gold.

Away, my children, enter the rich palace and entreat your father's young wife, my mistress, to let you stay in Corinth. Give her the finery. That is most important. She must take these gifts in her hands. Go as fast as you can. Success attend your mission, and may you bring back to your mother the tidings she longs to hear.

[*Exeunt* CHILDREN *with* TUTOR, *and* JASON.]

Chorus

Now are my hopes dead. The children are doomed. Already they are on the road to death. She will take it, the bride will take the golden diadem, and with it will take her ruin, luckless girl. With her own hands she will put the precious circlet of death on her blonde hair.

The beauty of it, the heavenly sheen, will persuade her to put on the robe and the golden crown. It is in the halls of death that she will put on her bridal dress forthwith. Into that fearful trap she will fall. Death will be her portion, hapless girl. She cannot overleap her doom.

And you, poor man. Little luck your royal father-in-law is bringing you. Unwittingly, you are bringing death on your children, and on your wife an awful end. Ill-starred man, what a way you are from happiness.

And now I weep for your sorrow, hapless mother of these children. You will slaughter them to avenge the dishonor of your bed betrayed, criminally betrayed by your husband who now sleeps beside another bride.

[*Enter* CHILDREN *with their* TUTOR.]

Tutor

Mistress, here are your children, reprieved from exile. Your gifts the royal bride took gladly in her hands. The children have made their peace with *her*. What's the matter? Why stand in such confusion, when fortune is smiling? [Why do you turn away your cheek? Why are you not glad to hear my message?]

Medea

Misery!

Tutor

That note does not harmonize with the news I have brought.

Medea

Misery, and again Misery!

Tutor

Have I unwittingly brought you bad news? I thought it was good. Was I mistaken?

Medea

Your message was . . . your message. It is not you I blame.

Tutor

Why then are your eyes downcast and your tears flowing?

Medea

Of necessity, old man, of strong necessity. This is the gods' doing, and mine, in my folly.

Tutor

Have courage. Some day your children will bring you too back home.

Medea

Ah me! Before that day I shall bring others to another home.

Tutor

You are not the first woman to be separated from her children. We are mortals and must endure calamity with patience.

Medea

That I shall do. Now go inside and prepare their usual food for the children.
[Exit TUTOR.*]*

O my children, my children. For you indeed a city is assured, and a home in which, leaving me to my misery, you will dwell for ever, motherless. But I must go forth to exile in a strange land, before I have ever tasted the joy of seeing *your* happiness, before I have got you brides and bedecked your marriage beds and held aloft the bridal torches. Alas! my own self-will has brought me to misery. Was it all for nothing, my children, the rearing of you, and all the agonizing labor, all the fierce pangs I endured at your birth? Ah me, there was a time when I had strong hopes, fool as I was, that you would tend my old age and with your own hands dress my body for the grave, a fate that the world might envy. Now the sweet dream is gone. Deprived of you, I shall live a life of pain and sorrow. And you, in another world altogether will never again see your mother with your dear, dear eyes.

O the pain of it! Why do your eyes look at me, my children? Why smile at me that last smile? Ah! What can I do? My heart is water, women, at the sight of my children's bright faces. I could never do it. Goodbye to my former plans. I shall take my children away with me. Why should I hurt their father by *their* misfortunes, only to reap a double harvest of sorrow myself? No! I cannot do it. Goodbye to my plans.

And yet . . . what is the matter with me? Do I want to make myself a laughing-stock by letting my enemies off scot-free? I must go through with it. What a coward heart is mine, to admit those soft pleas. Come, my children, into the palace. Those that may not attend my sacrifices can see to it that they are absent. I shall not let my hand be unnerved.

Ah! Ah! Stop, my heart. Do not you commit this crime. Leave them alone, unhappy one, spare the children. Even if they live far from us, they will bring you joy. No! by the unforgetting dead in hell, it cannot be! I shall not leave my children for my enemies to insult. [In any case they must die. And if die they must, *I* shall slay them, who gave them birth.] My schemes are crowned with success. She shall not escape. Already the diadem is on her head; wrapped in the robe the royal bride is dying. I know it well. And now I am setting out on a most sorrowful road [and shall send these on one still more sorrowful]. I wish to speak to my children. Give your mother your hands, my children, give her your hands to kiss.

O dear, dear hand. O dear, dear mouth, dear shapes, dear noble faces, happiness be yours, but not here. Your father has stolen this world from you. How sweet to touch! The softness of their skin, the sweetness of their breath, my babies! Away, away, I cannot bear to see you any longer.

[CHILDREN retire within.]

My misery overwhelms me. O I *do* realize how terrible is the crime I am about, but passion overrules my resolutions, passion that causes most of the misery in the world.

Chorus

Often ere now I have grappled with subtle subjects and sounded depths of argument deeper than woman may plumb. But, you see, we also have a Muse who teaches us philosophy. It is a small class—perhaps you might find one in a thousand—the women that love the Muse.

And I declare that in this world those who have had no experience of paternity are happier than the fathers of children. Without children a man does not know whether they are a blessing or a curse, and so he does not miss a joy he has never had and he escapes a multitude of sorrows. But them that have in their home young, growing children that they love, I see them consumed with anxiety, day in day out, how they are to rear them properly, how they are to get a livelihood to leave to them. And, after all that, whether the children for whom they toil are worth it or not, who can tell?

And now I shall tell you the last and crowning sorrow for all mortals. Suppose they have found livelihood enough, their children have grown up, and turned out honest. Then, if it is fated that way, death carries their bodies away beneath the earth. What then is the use, when the love of children brings from the gods this crowning sorrow to top the rest?

Medea

My friends, all this time I have been waiting for something to happen, watching to see what they will do in the royal palace. Now I see one of Jason's attendants coming this way. His excited breathing shows that he has a tale of strange evils to tell.

[Enter MESSENGER.]

Messenger

What a horrible deed of crime you have done, Medea. Flee, flee. Take anything you can find, sea vessel or land carriage.

Medea

Tell me, what has happened that I should flee.

Messenger

The princess has just died. Her father Creon, too, killed by your poisons.

Medea

Best of news! From this moment and for ever you are one of my friends and benefactors.

Messenger

What's that? Are you sane and of sound mind, woman? You have inflicted a foul outrage on a king's home, yet you rejoice at the word of it and are not afraid.

Medea

I too have a reply that I might make to you. But take your time, my friend.

Speak on. How did they die? You would double my delight, if they died in agony.

Messenger

When your children, both your offspring, arrived with their father and entered the bride's house, we rejoiced, we servants who had been grieved by your troubles. Immediately a whisper ran from ear to ear that you and your husband had patched up your earlier quarrel. And one kisses your children's hands, another their yellow hair. I myself, in my delight, accompanied the children to the women's rooms. The mistress, whom we now respect in your place, did not see the two boys at first, but cast a longing look at Jason. Then, however, resenting the entrance of the children, she covered her eyes with a veil and averted her white cheek.

Your husband tried to allay the maiden's angry resentment, saying, "You must not hate your friends. Won't you calm your temper, and turn your head this way? You must consider your husband's friends your own. Won't you accept the gifts and ask your father to recall their sentence of exile, for my sake?" Well, when she saw the finery, she could not refrain, but promised her husband everything, and before Jason and your children were far away from the house she took the elaborate robes and put them on her. She placed the golden diadem on her clustering locks and began to arrange her coiffure before a shining mirror, smiling at her body's lifeless reflection. Then she arose from her seat and walked through the rooms, stepping delicately with her fair white feet, overjoyed with the gifts. Time and time again, standing erect, she gazes with all her eyes at her ankles.

But then ensued a fearful sight to her. Her color changed, she staggered, and ran back, her limbs all atremble, and only escaped falling by sinking upon her chair. An old attendant, thinking, I suppose, it was a panic fit, or something else of divine sending, raised a cry of prayer, until she sees a white froth drooling from her mouth, sees her rolling up the pupils of her eyes, and all the blood leaving her skin. Then, instead of a cry of prayer, she let out a scream of lamentation. Immediately one maid rushed to Creon's palace, another to the new bridegroom, to tell of the bride's misfortune. From end to end, the house echoed to hurrying steps. A quick walker, stepping out well, would have reached the end of the two hundred yard track, when the poor girl, lying there quiet, with closed eyes, gave a fearful groan, and began to come to. A double plague assailed her. The golden diadem on her head emitted a strange flow of devouring fire, while the fine robes, the gifts of your children, were eating up the poor girl's white flesh. All aflame, she jumps from her seat and flees, shaking her head and hair this way and that, trying to throw off the crown. But the golden band held firmly, and after she had shaken her hair more violently, the fire began to blaze twice as fiercely. Overcome by the agony she falls on the ground, and none but her father could have recognized her. The position of her eyes could not be distinguished, nor the beauty of her face. The blood, clotted with fire, dripped from the crown of her head, and the flesh melted from her bones, like resin from a pine tree, as the poisons ate their unseen way. It was a fearful sight. All were afraid to touch the corpse, taught by what had happened to her.

But her father, unlucky man, rushed suddenly into the room, not knowing what had happened, and threw himself on the body. At once he groaned, and embracing his daughter's form he kissed it and cried, "My poor, poor child, what god has destroyed you so shamefully? Who is it deprives this aged tomb of his only child? Ah! let me join you in death, my child." Then, when he ceased his weeping and lamentation and sought to lift his aged frame upright, he stuck to the fine robes, like ivy to a laurel bush. His struggles were horrible. He would try to free a leg, but the girl's body stuck to his. And if he pulled violently, he tore his shrunken flesh off his bones. At last his life went out; doomed, he gave up the ghost. Side by side lie the two bodies, daughter and old father. Who would not weep at such a calamity?

It seems to me . . . I need not speak of what's in store for you; you yourself will see how well the punishment fits the crime . . . it's not the first time the thought has come, that the life of man is a shadow. [I might assert with confidence that the mortals who pass for philosophers and subtle reasoners are most to be condemned.] No mortal man has lasting happiness. When the tide of fortune flows his way, one man may have more prosperity than another, but happiness never.

[Exit MESSENGER.*]*

Leader

It seems that this day Fate is visiting his sins on Jason. Unfortunate daughter of Creon, we pity your calamity. The love of Jason has carried you through the gates of death.

Medea

My friends, I am resolved to act, and act quickly [to slay the children and depart from the land]. I can delay no longer, or my children will fall into the murderous hands of those that love them less than I do. In any case they must die. And if they must, I shall slay them, who gave them birth. Now, my heart, steel yourself. Why do we still hold back? The deed is terrible, but necessary. Come, my unhappy hand, seize the sword, seize it. Before you is a course of misery, lifelong misery; on now to the starting post. No flinching now, no thinking of the children, the darling children, that call you mother. This day, this one short day, forget your children. You have all the future to mourn for them. Aye, to mourn. Though you mean to kill them, at least you loved them. Oh! I am a most unhappy woman.

[Exit MEDEA.*]*

Chorus

O Earth, O glorious radiance of the Sun, look and behold the accursed woman. Stop her before she lays her bloody, murderous hands on her children. Sprung are they from your golden race, O Sun, and it is a fearful thing that the blood of a god should be spilt by mortals. Nay, stop her, skyborn light, prevent her. Deliver the house from the misery of slaughter, and the curse of the unforgetting dead.

Gone, gone for nothing, are your maternal pangs. For nothing did you bear these lovely boys, O woman, who made the inhospitable passage through the grey Clashing Rocks! Why let your spleen poison your heart? Why this murderlust, where love was? On the man that spills the blood of kinsmen the curse of heaven descends. Go where he may, it rings ever in his ears, bringing sorrows and tribulations on his house.

[The CHILDREN are heard within.]
   Listen, listen. It is the cry of the children. O cruel, ill-starred woman.

One of the Children
[within]
Ah me! What am I to do? Where can I escape my mother's murderous hands?

The Other
[within]
I know not, my dear, dear brother. She is killing us.

Chorus
Should we break in? Yes! I will save them from death.

One of the Children
[within]
Do, for god's sake. Save us. We need your help.

The Other
[within]
Yes, we are already in the toils of the sword.

Chorus
Heartless woman! Are you made of stone or steel? Will you slaughter the children, your own seed, slaughter them with your own hands?
   Only one woman, only one in the history of the world, laid murderous hands on her children, Ino whom the gods made mad, driven from home to a life of wandering by the wife of Zeus. Hapless girl, bent on that foul slaughter, she stepped over a precipice by the shore and fell headlong into the sea, killing herself and her two children together. What crime, more horrible still, may yet come to pass? O the loves of women, fraught with sorrow, how many ills ere now have you brought on mortals!
[Enter JASON, attended.]

Jason
You women there, standing in front of this house, is Medea still within, who wrought these dreadful deeds? Or has she made her escape? I tell you, she had better hide under the earth or take herself off on wings to the recesses of the sky, unless she wishes to give satisfaction to the family of the king. Does she think she can slay the rulers of the land and get safely away from this house? But I am not so anxious about her as I am about the children. The victims of her crimes will attend to her. It's my own children I am here to save, in case the relatives of the king do them some injury, in revenge for the foul murders their mother has committed.

Leader
Jason, poor Jason, you do not know the sum of your sorrows, or you would not have said these words.

Jason
What is it? She does not want to kill me too, does she?

Leader

Your children are dead, slain by their mother's hand.

Jason

For pity's sake, what do you mean? You have slain me, woman.

Leader

Your children are dead, make no mistake.

Jason

Why, where did she slay them? Indoors or out here?

Leader

Open the doors and you will see their bodies.

Jason

Quick, servants, loosen the bolts, undo the fastenings. Let me see the double horror, the dead bodies of my children, and the woman who . . . oh! let me punish her.

[MEDEA appears aloft in a chariot drawn by winged dragons. She has the bodies of the CHILDREN.]

Medea

What's all this talk of battering and unbarring? Are you searching for the bodies and me who did the deed? Spare yourself the trouble. If you have anything to ask of me, speak if you will, but never shall you lay a hand on me. I have a magic chariot, given me by the Sun, my father's father, to protect me against my enemies.

Jason

You abominable thing! You most loathsomest woman, to the gods and me and all mankind. You had the heart to take the sword to your children, you their mother, leaving me childless. And you still behold the earth and the sun, you who have done this deed, you who have perpetrated this abominable outrage. My curses on you! At last I have come to my senses, the senses I lost when I brought you from your barbarian home and country to a home in Greece, an evil plague, treacherous alike to your father and the land that reared you. There is a fiend in you, whom the gods have launched against me. In your own home you had already slain your brother when you came aboard the Argo, that lovely ship. Such was your beginning. Then you married me and bore me children, whom you have now destroyed because I left your bed. No Greek woman would ever have done such a deed. Yet I saw fit to marry you, rather than any woman of Greece, a wife to hate me and destroy me, not a woman at all, but a tigress, with a disposition more savage than Tuscan Scylla. But why all this? Ten thousand reproaches could not sting you; your impudence is too engrained. The devil take you, shameless, abominable murderess of your children. I must bemoan my fate; no joy shall I have of my new marriage, and I shall never see alive the children I begot and reared and lost.

Medea

I might have made an elaborate rebuttal of the speech you have made, but Zeus the Father knows what you received at my hands and what you have done. You could not hope, nor your princess either, to scorn my love, make a fool of me, and live happily ever after. Nor was Creon, the matchmaker, to drive me out of the country with impunity. Go ahead, then. Call me tigress if you like, or Scylla that haunts the Tuscan coast. I don't mind, now I have got properly under your skin.

Jason
You too are suffering. You have your share of the sorrow.

Medea
True, but it's worth the grief, since you cannot scoff.

Jason
O children, what a wicked mother you got!

Medea
O children, your father's sins have caused your death.

Jason
Yet it was not *my* hand that slew them.

Medea
No, it was your lust, and your new marriage.

Jason
Because your love was scorned you actually thought it right to murder.

Medea
Do you think a woman considers that a small injury?

Jason
Good women do. But you are wholly vicious.

Medea
The children here are dead. That will sting you.

Jason
No! they live to bring fierce curses on your head.

Medea
The gods know who began it all.

Jason
They know, indeed, they know the abominable wickedness of your heart.

Medea
Hate me then. I despise your bitter words.

Jason
And I yours. But it is easy for us to be quit of each other.

Medea
How, pray? Certainly I am willing.

Jason

Allow me to bury these bodies and lament them.

Medea

Certainly not. I shall bury them with my own hands, taking them to the sanctuary of Hera of the Cape, where no enemy may violate their tombs and do them insult. Here in the land of Sisyphus we shall establish a solemn festival, and appoint rites for the future to expiate their impious murder. I myself shall go to the land of Erechtheus, to live with Aegeus, the son of Pandion. You, as is proper, will die the death you deserve, [struck on the head by a fragment of the Argo,] now you have seen the bitter fruits of your new marriage.

Jason

May you be slain by the Curse of your children, and Justice that avenges murder!

Medea

What god or power above will listen to you, the breaker of oaths, the treacherous guest?

Jason

Oh! abominable slayer of children.

Medea

Get along to the palace and bury your wife.

Jason

I go, bereft of my two sons.

Medea

You have nothing yet to bemoan. Wait till you are old.

Jason

My dear, dear children!

Medea

Yes, dear to their mother, not to you.

Jason

And yet you slew them.

Medea

I did, to hurt you.

Jason

Alas! my grief! I long to kiss their dear mouths.

Medea

Now you speak to them, now you greet them, but in the past you spurned them.

Jason

For god's sake, let me touch my children's soft skin.

Medea

No! You have gambled and lost.

Jason
O Zeus, do you hear how I am repelled, how I am wronged by this foul tigress, that slew her own children? But such lament as I may and can make, I hereby make. I call upon the gods. I invoke the powers above to bear me witness that you slew my children and now prevent me from embracing their bodies and giving them burial. Would that I had never begotten them, to live to see them slain at your hands.

Chorus
Zeus on Olympus hath a wide stewardship. Many things beyond expectation do the gods fulfil. That which was expected has not been accomplished; for that which was unexpected has god found the way. Such was the end of this story.
[Exeunt.]

Questions for Discussion and Review

1. Medea has been variously described as a strong, independent woman, as a woman mad with passion, and as a witch. Using specific examples from the *Medea,* discuss what view finally is conveyed by the play.

2. Medea is granted refuge by King Aegeus of Athens in return for a potion that will restore his fertility. As a result, the child Aegeus will father will turn out to be the Athenian hero Theseus. How does this relationship affect our view of Medea?

3. Compare Medea and Clytemnestra as heroines. What strengths do they have in common? How do they feel about being confined to the conventional role of women? Although they both murder members of their own families, what do their different fates reveal about moral responsibility in these two plays?

4. Compare Euripides's portrayal of Jason with the myths that present Jason as the leader of the Argonauts. Explain what typically heroic characteristics reappear in Euripides's Jason and which do not.

Recommended Reading

Conacher, D. J. *Euripidean Drama: Myth, Theme and Structure.* Toronto: U of Toronto P, 1967. Discusses the innovative ways in which Euripides used mythic material and includes a discussion of the relationship of the *Medea* with traditional folktales.

Meagher, Robert. *Mortal Vision: The Wisdom of Euripides.* New York: St. Martin's, 1989. An overview of Euripides, sounding the playwright's complex views of such issues as the divine, the human realm, politics, and the roles of women.

PART FOUR

The World of Roman Myth

CHAPTER 18

The Roman Vision: Greek Myths and Roman Realities

KEY THEMES

The Romans borrowed freely from other neighboring cultures, including the Etruscans and the Greeks. They especially admired Greek mythology, adding it to their own myths, such as the myth of the founding of Rome. They changed the Greek names and adapted the stories to fit their own concepts and values in four major ways: shifting their emphasis to reflect Roman views on what was important; attaching the stories to historical events and individuals; orienting them toward their overriding concern with the state of Rome; and reinterpreting them to reflect Roman ideas.

The Connection between Greek and Roman Myths

Like much of Roman culture, Roman mythology is eclectic, including both indigenous material and myths and symbols borrowed from neighboring peoples, especially from the Etruscans, who had ruled the region before the Romans rebelled and founded their own republic (509 B.C.), and, of course, from the Greeks. From the Etruscans they borrowed the names of several of their gods (such as Minerva), animal symbols (such as the she-wolf; Figure 18-1), and many rituals and superstitions.

They particularly admired the Greeks, borrowing their myths and incorporating many other aspects of Greek culture into their own. "I found Rome a city of brick," the first Roman emperor, **Augustus,** is said to have boasted, "but I left it a city of marble." Augustus's statement reflects the Roman perception of the cultural status as well as the beauty of Greek public architecture, with its elegant marble temples and harmonious design, as contrasted with the solid, practical brick of Roman buildings. Despite his boast, however, Augustus did not order that Rome be demolished and reconstructed in solid marble; nor could the large buildings required for a city the size of Rome have been safely constructed on the post-and-lintel system preferred by the Greeks. Rather, to make Rome resemble a Greek city without sacrificing practical

FIGURE 18-1   The She-Wolf of Rome. To this late-sixth or early-fifth-century Etruscan bronze, the Roman sculptor added the twins Romulus and Remus, legendary founders of Rome. (The twins here are Renaissance reconstructions of the Roman originals, which were destroyed.) The Romans not only took the sculpture and brought it to Rome but added to it representations of the myth of the founding of their state, thus making it figuratively as well as literally their own. This sculpture thus provides a visual image of the eclectic nature of Roman culture. (*Conservatori Museum, Rome.*)

needs, Roman architects continued designing brick buildings supported by sturdy Roman arches that they overlaid with a veneer of marble tiles and decorated with marble "columns" (which supported nothing), sculpted onto the exterior walls, often adding a mock Greek portico (porch) at the entrance (Figure 18-2).

Beneath the facade of Augustus's "city of marble," of course, Rome was still Rome. His metaphor, however, might equally serve to describe the relationship between Greek and Roman mythology. Although justifiably proud of their own skills at organization, engineering, and government, the Romans imagined themselves inferior to the Greeks in terms of literary and artistic achievements. Long before they conquered Greece in 146 B.C., bringing back Greek statues to set up in their gardens, the Romans were familiar with Greek culture. Greek city-states had long ago established colonies in Sicily and southern Italy. And the Romans had adopted Greek literature (educating their children for example, on Homer's works) and Greek mythology, keeping the stories intact to maintain the veneer of Greek culture but changing the names and adapting the concepts to fit their own solid core of Roman ideas and values. They also created links between the Greek myths they borrowed and existing Roman myths. It is largely through the works of Roman writers such as Virgil and Ovid (see chapters 19 and 20) that the cumulative body of classical mythology—reinterpreted in characteristically Roman ways—was in turn transmitted to later periods of Western culture (see Chapter 21).

FIGURE 18-2   The Pantheon. A feat of engineering unprecedented in its time, the Pantheon, a temple to all the Roman gods (Rome, c. A.D. 120), enclosed a huge interior space spanned by an enormous dome. The central structure, however, was not permitted to stand on its own merits: rather, the architect added a "Greek" facade—a portico (porch) that creates the illusion of a classical Greek temple, complete with pillars that support only the roof of the porch itself.

A Roman Myth: Romulus and Remus

The most important Roman myth was probably the story of **Romulus** and **Remus** and the founding of Rome. According to this myth, **Rhea Silvia** [REE-a SIL-vih-a] (or, in some variants, **Ilia**) was assigned to the office of Vestal Virgin by her wicked uncle Amulius, who had usurped the throne of her father, Numitor; Amulius hoped to prevent his niece from producing heirs, who would contest his claim to the throne. But, seduced by the god **Mars,** she bore twin sons, Romulus and Remus. Determined to exterminate the line, Amulius exposed the infants to die in a basket on the river Tiber. Washed up safely on shore, of course, the twins survived, and were nursed by a she-wolf (originally an Etruscan symbol) and fed bits of food by a bird until they were found and raised by a shepherd. Growing to manhood, they discovered their real identities and, aided by loyal shepherds who followed them, they restored their grandfather Numitor to the throne of his city, **Alba Longa.**

The brothers, however, wanted a city of their own and argued over which one of them to name the city after. To settle the quarrel, they agreed to a contest: the winner would be the first one to see a sign from the gods—a flock of vultures. Remus first saw six, but Romulus, immediately afterward, saw twelve, which he claimed was a more powerful sign, albeit a later one. Supported by their respective followers, they fought, and Remus was killed. (Or perhaps, as another variant suggests, Romulus killed him for defiantly jumping over a wall Romulus had built around the perimeter of his new city, marked out with a plow.) The city thus founded was named *Rome*— conceived in the policy of aggressive expansion enforced by violence and all part of a divine plan for the establishment of Rome.

The Rape of the Sabine Women

The city prospered, but the shepherds-turned-warriors and the other men (often escaped slaves and other fugitives) who joined them lacked marriageable women, people in the surrounding towns being understandably unwilling to marry their daughters to such aggressive intruders. (Or perhaps the Romans wanted to form a link with the **Sabines** [SAY-binz] in order to annex their territory and secure it permanently.) Romulus prepared a festival and invited the residents of neighboring cities, including the Sabines. When the guests were assembled, the Romans forcibly abducted and raped the daughters of the Sabines and, refusing to return their captives, married them.

For several years the Sabines warred against the Romans, until the Romans' wives themselves interfered to assure their families that they were happy to be Roman wives! The Roman and Sabine territories were then combined under a single (and ultimately Roman) government. Romulus ruled, with support from commoners and soldiers, for thirty-eight years. Then, during a storm, he suddenly vanished in a dark cloud. Some suspected that resentful patrician senators had killed and dismembered him, but he was officially said, by the senators who witnessed the incident, to have been taken up to the heavens to be henceforth worshiped as the warrior god Quirinus.

The Characteristics of Roman Myth

The Focus on the City and Its History

The myth of Romulus and Remus and the founding of Rome reveals quintessentially Roman elements. First, it is focused on the city and its process of expansion from a mere plot of ground to an empire in progress, beginning with the Sabine territories, while nostalgically attesting to its roots among simple shepherds. Second, although the myth begins with strong mythic components (Mars and the she-wolf), it swiftly moves into the actual history of Roman expansion into the rest of Italy.

The Patriarchal Perspective

Third, the myth's perspective is intensely patriarchal: determined to father children, the original inhabitants of Rome have no qualms about raping the Sabine women, thereby reenacting the original rape of Rhea Silvia by Mars. Greek myths, of course, are also largely patriarchal. But we can usually perceive in them some vestige of ambivalence, some trace of the feminine powers in the symbols whose meanings lurk beneath the surface or literally lie in wait behind it. That the rape of the Sabine women is approved by the gods and, more revealingly, by the women themselves demonstrates both the total subservience of women in this myth and the myth's complete obliteration of the female perspective.

There are, of course, many instances of rape in Greek myths as well. And in the Roman poet Ovid's *Metamorphoses* (see Chapter 20), as in the Greek myths on which they are based, rapes are not portrayed approvingly. Nevertheless, it is instructive to contrast the myth of the Sabine women with a depiction of rape in Greek mythology. The abduction of Helen—along with Paris's violation of the guest-host relationship and the laws of marriage that preceded it—is treated as a violation of principles sacred to the gods, and the war that follows causes the destruction, not the expansion, of Troy. Even more revealing is the contrast with the Greek myth of the centaurs' attempted rape of the Lapith women at the wedding of the Lapith princess: whereas the centaurs are reviled and driven off by the Greeks for their savage, irrational behavior, the Romans are rewarded for the same behavior with wives, land, and divine approval.

The Demythologizing Tendency

Finally, we can see in the Romulus and Remus story the strong resistance to its more fantastic components by contrasting the story of this city founded in violence with the Greek myth of the founding of Thebes. In the Greek myth, Cadmus sows dragon's teeth, which magically grow into a race of armed men. The armed men of Rome, however, arrive in a more pedestrian fashion—as disgruntled farmers and shepherds, runaway slaves, and fugitives from justice. And to propagate their race, they require the services of women. The Greek writer Plutarch (A.D. 46–120), whose *Lives* compared figures from Greek and Roman myth and history, would surely have felt compelled, in his role as a biographer and historian, to offer an alternative (and more realistic) explanation of the "divine conception" of the twins; nevertheless, his work serves to illustrate the demythologizing impulse frequently at work in Roman myths. According to Plutarch, the story of the rape of Rhea Silvia by the war god, he suggested, was probably planted as a cover-up to a more likely scenario—a rape by her uncle Amulius. Plutarch's demythologizing tendency is likewise illustrated in his version of the myth of Theseus and the Minotaur: **Pasiphae,** he asserted, was in love not with a bull (*taurus,* in Greek) but with a captain of the king's guard named Taurus, who lost an athletic contest to Theseus. Similarly, he stated that Taurus went not to the Underworld, but to a land governed by a king who happened to be named Pluto, who had a wife called Persephone and a dog named **Cerberus.** Heracles, according to Plutarch, rescued Theseus from the dog! In a similar vein, the poet Horace, in one of his odes (Book 3, Number 16), described Zeus as coming to Perseus's mother, **Danae,** safely locked in her tower, in a shower of gold, but equated the gold with bribery—which can always break down barriers!

While such "realistic" explanations of mythic materials were not unknown in the work of earlier writers about Greek myth, they are for the Romans consistent with a widespread sense of pride in their own practical nature. The Romans wanted their myths, but without having to relinquish their sense of themselves as realistic, practical men of the world.

The Links between Greek and Roman Mythology

The myth of the founding of Rome, however, would not have been as satisfying had the Romans not been able to forge, in both senses of the word, a link between it and Greek mythology. Thus, not only is Romulus a son of Mars (the Roman name for the Greek god Ares), but his mother is descended from **Ascanius** [as-KAY-nih-uhs], son of **Aeneas** [ee-NEE-as], the only Trojan hero to escape the destruction of Troy. Thus the "missing" descendants of Troy are thereby accounted for—they are Romans! And although the Trojans were not exactly Greek, they were, in effect, honorary Greeks by virtue of being the subject of Homer's *Iliad.* Moreover, because Aeneas is the son of the goddess Aphrodite (whom the Romans renamed **Venus**), he is in any case half-"Greek." Like Augustus's "marble city," these links between Greek and Roman myths satisfied the Romans' desire to be "Greek" without having to give up being Roman.

Roman Transformations of Greek Myths

The Romans went beyond merely creating a Greek connection to their own myths. In fact, they adopted the entire body of Greek mythology. But they changed as they borrowed, transforming Greek mythology in four characteristic ways: (1) they refocused the myths, redefining the characters of the gods and shifting the emphasis to those they considered especially important; (2) they historicized the myths, attaching them to real events and individuals in Roman history; (3) they politicized the myths, making them serve the needs of the Roman state; and (4) they reinterpreted the myths to reflect Roman ideas and values.

The Refocusing of Myth: Greek versus Roman Gods

The Greek pantheon is dominated by the figures of Zeus and Hera, along with Athene—the wisdom of Zeus—and Apollo, who likewise comes to embody enlightenment and the wisdom of self-knowledge and self-control. For the Romans, however, abstractions like Wisdom and introspective pursuits of self-awareness were, though certainly important, clearly less pressing concerns than were practical problems like managing the grain supply to feed an enormous and growing population. Thus, in the Roman pantheon, although the main figures are still **Jupiter** and **Juno** (figures 18-3 and 18-4—Roman equivalents of Zeus and Hera), Apollo and **Minerva** (the Roman counterpart of Athene) occupy a less central position, while **Ceres** [SEE-reez] (from whose name we derive the word *cereal* and who is the Roman version of Demeter, goddess of grain) becomes correspondingly more important. Similarly, Hestia, the Greek goddess of the hearth (the cooking fire), was mentioned only infrequently in Greek myths. Hestia's Roman counterpart, **Vesta,** however, was worshiped not only in every Roman home, but in a public temple served by Vestal Virgins, where a sacred fire that they kept always burning became the central symbol of Eternal Rome.

A similar shift of emphasis is illustrated in the changing attitude toward the war god. Although they admired their warrior heroes, sometimes even making gods of them, the Greeks exalted Athene as goddess of the defensive war that saved the city

FIGURE 18-3   Jupiter. Jupiter, the Roman version of the Greek god Zeus, adds a political dimension to the gods' domain. Bearing the Roman eagle at the end of his scepter, Jupiter is presented in this sculpture as a divine emblem of imperial power and a guarantor of its eternal dominion. (*Vatican Museums, Rome.*)

FIGURE 18-4   Juno, Queen of Heaven (also known as *Hera Barberini*). In this fifth-century-B.C. sculpture, Juno (the Roman equivalent of the Greek goddess Hera) is portrayed as a figure of royal bearing, reflecting the dignity of her position as the most powerful goddess in Rome. Like Jupiter, she is associated with the stability of the Roman state. (*Vatican Museums, Rome.*)

but were somewhat ambivalent about Ares, the god of offensive war, whom they sometimes portrayed as two-faced and violent and not very bright. Clearly, for a nation with imperial ambitions, such a portrayal would not do: in fact, the Romans, although seeing themselves as bringers of peace, proudly traced their ancestry to the war god Mars (Figure 18-5). Possibly originating as an agricultural deity, Mars was portrayed as an implacable god whose purpose was to inspire the Roman legions and bring them victory.

FIGURE 18-5   Mars. Whereas respect for their war god, Ares, was somewhat ambiguous
among the Greeks, the Roman war god, Mars, was proudly claimed as the ancestor of the
Romans. Depicted in this bronze statue as a Roman soldier, the war god Mars personifies the
military strength on which Rome relied. (*Capitolino Museum, Rome.*)

The Historicizing of Myth

In addition to shifting the focus of the myths and redefining the gods accordingly, the Romans, intensely proud of their own history, insisted on historicizing the myths. Greek myths, too, are often loosely based on historical events: the Troy saga, for instance, undoubtedly has some basis in a war or series of wars between the Greeks and Trojans, whose city was strategically located at the entrance to the Dardanelles, and the myth of Theseus and the Minotaur may reflect in a general way the shift of power from Crete to the mainland and the end of the colonial status of the Greek city-states. But the Romans were more precise and insistent about the historicizing process, tying the myths whenever possible to real names, dates, places, and events. Plutarch, for example, treated Romulus and Remus as historical, not mythical, figures.

Unlike the relatively timeless world of Greek myths, Roman myths are often precisely located in time and space and explained as realistically as possible. Whereas Heracles may have explored the unknown regions of the mythical North and West, Romulus is much more interested in expanding Roman territory into adjacent Italian lands. Descended from the gods and Homeric heroes on the mythical side, Romulus is also linked to history as the ancestor of Julius Caesar and his great-nephew, the emperor Augustus. Virgil explained the link: Ascanius, Aeneas's son, was nicknamed *Ilus,* and by the simple addition of another vowel picked up along their journey, he became *Iulus;* thus he was deemed the progenitor of the family of Julii—as the family had indeed claimed since the third century B.C.—and hence of Julius Caesar! The family tree of flesh-and-blood contemporary Romans, rooted in the soil of mythology, sprouts real fruit. To the down-to-earth Roman sensibility, these historical links justified the myths, even as the myths chartered real political claims.

Trajan's column (Figure 18-6) is a visual illustration of the Roman fascination with the points of intersection of myth and history. The bas-reliefs winding around this column in scroll-like fashion narrate the story of the Roman defeat of the Dacians (in what is now, as a result of that conquest, called Romania) under the Emperor Trajan. In a scene at the base describing the beginning of the campaign, the river god of the Danube supports the bridge over which the Roman legions pass. Amid realistic scenes of contemporary events of that war, in which the emperor figures prominently, Jupiter and the goddess Victory also appear. Such works, like the myths, reflect the Roman belief that art, to be useful, should instruct as well as delight. The more grounded in reality the myths were, the more they could perform their didactic function, illuminating both historical and contemporary events.

The Politicizing of Myth

A famous Roman statue features an Apollo-like portrait of the emperor Augustus with a small **Cupid**—an agent of the goddess Venus—at his feet (Figure 18-7). If history justified the myths, the myths in turn were used to justify political realities—in this case, the imperial regime is granted a divine connection, while private emotions (here, Love) are subordinated to duty to the state.

In Roman religious practices, as in their myths, the same connection between private worship and public rites prevailed. For example, Romans in their homes typically worshiped three kinds of gods: the **Lares** [LAR-eez], who were (possibly ances-

FIGURE 18-6   Detail from Trajan's Column. In a typical Roman combination of mythology and actual history, the 128-foot-high marble column of Trajan (Forum of Trajan,
Rome, A.D. 106–113) depicts, in spiral bands over 4 feet high, the Emperor Trajan's two
campaigns against the Dacians. In this detail near the base, the river god of the Danube supports the bridge—and hence the Roman enterprise—as columns of armored imperial troops
cross safely over the Danube River. Portraits of Emperor Trajan occur frequently in the unfolding story told in the bas-reliefs. The figure of Jupiter also appears, supporting the Roman
cause. The narrative culminates in the Romans' victory, attended by the winged goddess of
Victory herself.

tral) spirits who guarded the family; the **Penates** [pe-NAY-teez], spirits of the pantry,
who also protected the house and especially its food supply; and the Vesta, goddess
of the blazing hearth, where the meals were cooked. These domestic gods had their
public counterparts in the state gods Jupiter, Juno, and Ceres, who performed the
same protective functions for the nation as the domestic gods did for the home. Thus,
even in the domestic rituals of daily life, Romans ended up paying service to the gods
of state and hence to the state itself. This link was further tied to political life when
deceased emperors were deified and their spirits were said to have joined the other
guardians of Rome.

For the Romans, in myths as in all aspects of their lives, all roads led to Rome. It
is true, of course, that Greek myths were often used to express political ideas: Aeschylus's *Eumenides,* for example, underwrites the Athenian court system; the *Iliad* surely
comments on political values; and the spirit of Theseus was said to protect Athens.
Nevertheless, the gods of the Greeks were not typically nationalistic in their political aims. Although individual Greek localities had their resident deities (indeed,

FIGURE 18-7   Augustus of Prima Porta. In this marble statue (c. 20 B.C.), the Emperor Augustus is portrayed as a Roman soldier directing his troops. The portrait is recognizably Augustus himself, but idealized and slightly larger than life (6′ 8″), and is reminiscent of Greek sculptures of the god Apollo. The facial expression, however, is unlike those calm, detached Greek images. In characteristic Roman fashion, Augustus's expression is serious and clearly intent on the business at hand. He is accompanied by a small Cupid at his feet, the real and the mythic thus intersecting. The relative proportions and positions of the two figures seem to suggest that the real world in which Augustus actually ruled predominates, while the subordinate mythic material provides a support system: the gods are on the side of Rome. (*Vatican Museums, Rome.*)

every stream or grove seems to have had its local nymph or god), the major gods, the Olympians, were not gods of specific places—of Argos, say, or Mycenae or Troy. Rather, they were *the* gods—of Trojans and of Greeks. Roman gods, on the other hand, were emphatically Roman. And although conquest spread their worship through many lands, the gods themselves remained identified as gods of Rome, as gods who had a vested interest in Roman destiny. Thus, even Ovid, telling myths of adventure and love in the *Metamorphoses,* set the tales within the framework of Roman ambitions. Roman destiny, further, was divinely predetermined: the establishment and maintenance of Eternal Rome and the incorporation of all the earth within its borders. This obsession with Rome was so pervasive that even writers who were skeptical of the "official" view of the state, its destiny, or its gods felt compelled nevertheless to discuss it or at least include it in their works. Rome was not a topic a Roman could simply ignore.

The Myths Reinterpreted

The use of myths to support these political aims required a major reinterpretation of the material inherited from the Greeks. Thus, the dynamic, open-ended, ambiguous, and often contradictory universe of the Greek myths gave way to a universe that was teleological—that is, directed in linear fashion toward a single, inevitable goal: the subjection of all the world to the rule of Roman gods and Roman law. Consequently, all acts that furthered that goal were deemed good; all that hindered it were necessarily evil. In Roman myth as in Roman culture, piety (*pietas*) and patriotism were inseparably linked.

The Romans had witnessed, both in their history and in their immediate experience, what happens when governments are unprepared for external threats or vulnerable to the outbreak of civil wars. If they were to be truly bringers of peace (an aim that, to their credit, they more or less accomplished during the long period of the **Pax Romana**), they would need to be able to count on the commitment to duty and loyalty on the part of the citizens of their empire. Patriotism was thus neither abstract nor sentimental—it was a survival tool. To worship and obey the gods, then, became an act of patriotism; conversely, defiance of the gods of Rome constituted both impiety and treason. (Historically, this attitude was reflected in the otherwise tolerant Romans' antagonism toward groups like the Christians and Jews, who would accept Roman governors but refuse to worship their gods.) Further, events that seemed to have human causes were, when seen from the gods' perspective (the big picture), revealed to be part of a divine plan. If for the Greeks the fall of Troy was the consequence of choices made by a Paris, a Priam, or a Hector, for the Romans, Troy fell so that Rome could arise, and Aeneas had to go into exile so that the Romans could claim Trojan as well as Latin ancestry. In such a universe, there can ultimately be no tragedy—only history incompletely understood.

The Roman Hero

The ego-driven hero of Greek myth typically sets his ambiguous, divided nature against a confusing and contradictory world and succeeds by acquiring self-knowledge while maintaining his integrity. Such a hero, however, is far too concerned with his own needs and goals and far too prone, in his reckless pursuit of immortality, to commit antisocial acts to constitute a proper role model for Romans. Along with the powers of Mars and the territorial ambitions of Romulus, the Romans wanted their heroes to exemplify the ideal Roman soldier and citizen, adamant and unswerving in championing the Roman way.

Three qualities nostalgically associated with the early republic are essential for the Roman hero: *gravitas,* or seriousness of purpose and devotion to duty (especially duty to the state); *pietas,* or devotion to the gods of Rome; *frugalitas,* or the idealizing of the simple life, free from the distractions of vanity and self-indulgence. The proper Roman hero subordinates his own needs to those of the state he serves, accepts whatever burdens and sacrifices patriotic duty imposes on him, and does not ask to be rewarded: it is enough that Rome be immortal—sharing in the immortality of the state, he finds all the fulfillment he needs.

Nor should the Roman hero indulge in the emotional excesses of his Greek counterparts—duty requires that he avoid giving way to passionate excesses of grief, anger, or rage. While the Romans admired and perpetuated the Greek hero myths, a Hercules (the Latin name for Heracles) or an Achilles, behaving as these heroes did in Rome itself would be considered outrageous. Further, the Roman hero is not to invest such emotional energy in his own life that the prospect of his death becomes the one overwhelming fact determining his choices. Rather, he must recognize that his individual life occupies one brief instant in a long span of history. To become obsessed with his personal needs or private sufferings would perpetuate the illusion of egocentrism: in fact, neither his triumphs nor his tragedies matter, except insofar as they contribute to the ultimate goal—the triumph of Eternal Rome.

Such heroes will, of course, be rewarded—but not in this life: for true patriots, Elysium awaits, in the Underworld, where worthy souls can sing, curry their horses, polish their chariots, and, of course (this being a Roman version of paradise), partake in the inevitable feast.

Questions for Discussion and Review

1. The Romans, who were great admirers of Greek culture, borrowed Greek myths but changed the myths they borrowed to reflect their own values and ideas. Describe at least two ways in which the Romans transformed Greek myths.

2. Contrast the rape of the Sabine women with the Greek myth in which the centaurs attempt to rape the Lapith women. What do these two myths suggest about the female perspective in the Roman and Greek culture, respectively? How do Greek and Roman myths differ in their response to rape?

3. In what ways does Romulus reflect a specifically Roman concept of the hero? Consider his ancestry, his attitude toward the city and its role, and his self-image.

4. Explain how the Roman hero differs from his Greek counterparts. What qualities of a Hercules or an Achilles would a Roman admire? What aspects of their behavior might a Roman hero disapprove of?

Recommended Reading

Cairns, Francis. *Virgil's Augustan Epic.* Cambridge: Cambridge UP, 1989. Grounding his discussion of the *Aeneid* in the attitudes and values of its time, Cairns provides a detailed discussion of Augustan views of political and literary issues.

Ogilvie, R. M. *Roman Literature and Society.* London: Penguin, 1980. A study of the political and cultural world of Rome from the early republic to the empire as reflected in its literature.

The *Aeneid*: Virgil's Roman Epic

KEY THEMES

Virgil's Aeneid, *the great Roman "sequel" to the Homeric epics, describes the wanderings of Aeneas, the only Trojan hero to escape from the destruction of Troy, along with his father, his son, and a band of retainers. After a series of adventures, including a year spent in Carthage as the consort of Queen Dido, he makes his way, commanded by Jupiter, to Italy. After a prolonged war there, he will marry the Latin princess and become the progenitor of the Romans. Although paying tribute to both the* Odyssey *and the* Iliad, *Virgil transforms Greek myths and heroes and presents a uniquely Roman epic with a uniquely Roman hero.*

Virgil

Publius Virgilius Maro, known in English as Virgil (70–19 B.C.), was raised in Mantua on his father's successful farm. Sent to Rome to complete his education, he watched in dismay the civil wars that began in 48 B.C., marking Rome's painful transition from republic to empire. His own family farm was confiscated during that chaotic time. Determined that such disorder should not recur, Virgil supported the empire, seeing the Emperor Augustus, its most visible symbol, as a restorer of peace and civil order.

A careful poet, Virgil wrote slowly and revised his poems extensively. His work includes two groups of pastoral poems (the *Eclogues* and the *Georgics*) that nostalgically idealize the peaceful simplicity of the rural life of farmers and shepherds. These works, highly appealing to the residents of a city characterized by the noise, the crowds, the traffic, and all the tensions of urban life as we still know them, made Virgil the most popular poet of his time.

Emperor Augustus himself encouraged and funded Virgil's work on his epic poem, the *Aeneid* [ee-NEE-id], which he worked on for the last eleven years of his

The World of Roman Mythology	
753 B.C.	Traditional date of Rome's founding by Romulus and Remus
510	Expulsion of Tarquin; traditional date of establishment of Roman Republic
264–241	First Punic War; Roman army enters Sicily
218–201	Second Punic War; Hannibal invades Italy and is defeated by Scipio Africanus at battle of Zama (202)
149–146	Third Punic War; Carthage destroyed (146)
60	First Triumvirate formed by Pompey, Crassus, and Julius Caesar
47–44	Dictatorship of Caesar; assassinated in 44
43	Second Triumvirate formed by Antony, Octavian, and Lepidus; defeats opposition at Battle of Philippi (42)
41–32	Marc Antony rules eastern empire
31	Octavian defeats Antony at battle of Actium
27 B.C.–A.D. 14	Reign of Augustus (Octavian)
c. 4 B.C.–A.D. 33	Life of Jesus of Nazareth; 1st Gospel (c. A.D. 70)
313	Constantine issues the Edict of Milan, making Christianity the empire's favored religion

life. Not yet finished with his revisions, Virgil ordered the manuscript to be burned at his death, but Augustus prevented its destruction—and no wonder! Apart from his personal admiration for the poem, what better public-relations device could an emperor imagine than to have the nation's most honored poet describe the empire and its current ruler as divinely inspired? Whatever interpretations later readers might develop, it is clear that the emperor and his court found this work a most flattering tribute to both emperor and empire.

The *Aeneid:* Significant Themes and Characters

The Greek Connection

The characteristic Augustan desire to envelop a Roman work in an aura of classical Greece is manifested in the *Aeneid* in several ways. Determined to be the Roman Homer, Virgil set out to write in an elegant style, calculated to lift the Latin tongue from the prosaic language of everyday affairs to a self-consciously poetic vehicle with a cultural status equal to that of Greek—a foreign language that educated Romans would have learned as part of their formal schooling.

In addition to asserting the genealogical link that makes Augustus into a descendant of the mythical Trojan **Aeneas,** Virgil frequently reminds his readers of the similarities between his epic and Homer's. Not only does he adopt all the standard features of the Homeric epic, beginning with the invocation of the Muse, but he also draws explicit parallels between his work and Homer's. The first six books of the *Aeneid* are carefully modeled on the *Odyssey*. The wanderings of a hero trying to get home, the search for a bride, the devotion of Aeneas to his son, the following of Odysseus's route from Troy (so that Aeneas lands, for example, at the Cyclops's cave just as Odysseus did), the danger of temptation by a woman who would keep him from his journey if she could, as well as other features, point to the similarities between the two works.

In Book 7, with a second invocation, Virgil shifts gears and, to describe his battle scenes, models the rest of the work on the *Iliad*. The parallels include the councils of the gods, their rivalries and interventions, the relationship between the hero and his divine mother, the gathering of the troops (including one army led by a woman), the death of the hero's best friend at the hands of his rival, and other similar details.

The Historicizing of Myth

Despite the Greek veneer, however, the *Aeneid* is a thoroughly Roman poem. Like his contemporaries, Virgil was concerned with the historicizing of myth, linking the characters of the story with individual events and persons in Roman history. At several crucial points in the poem, the poet has reliable characters (the god Jupiter, the hero's father Anchises) narrate the "history" of Rome, giving dates even to mythological events: Aeneas will rule **Latium** [LAY-shee-uhm] for three years; his son will rule for thirty years and build a new city at Alba Longa, which will be the capital for 300 years until Romulus builds Rome itself. The narration includes the conquest of Greece—delayed vengeance for the destruction of Troy—as well as the expansion of Rome, and culminates in the reigns of Julius and his grandnephew Augustus Caesar, who will renew a Golden Age in Latium. Similarly, Aeneas's shield, forged for him by **Vulcan** (the Latin name for Hephaestus) as Achilles's was, depicts contemporary Roman events, including the Battle of Actium (31 B.C.) between Marc Antony and Octavian (who shortly thereafter became Emperor Augustus).

Another example of the linkage of myth and history occurs in the curse that **Dido** [DYE-doh] calls down upon Aeneas when he abandons her. She calls for an "avenger" from **Carthage** who will make endless war on Rome, thus predicting both the series of the Punic Wars that Rome fought with Carthage and the invasion of Rome during the second of those wars (218–201 B.C.) by the Carthaginian general Hannibal, who wreaked devastation from which the nation never fully recovered.

The Role of the City   The first role of the city is to create the conditions under which civilized life can flourish: to establish laws and good government (the prerequisites for civic order and justice); to erect buildings and monuments; to encourage the arts, theater, trade, and commerce; and to enclose them all within walls which serve to mark off the city's legal boundaries as well as to protect its inhabitants. The Romans' concern with boundaries and barriers such as borders, ramparts, or walls, which was reflected in the earlier myth that describes Romulus marking off his territory with a plow, is evident throughout the *Aeneid*. Jupiter, for example promises Venus that the walls of Rome will surely rise. When Aeneas first enters Carthage, he comments enviously on the happiness of those "whose walls already rise." In fact, almost every mention of a city in the epic includes a reference to its walls so that the walls come to stand for the entire city and the way of life and the people it contains.

Although we don't get to see Rome itself in the *Aeneid,* we do get to watch Carthage under construction, a model for Aeneas to admire, until Dido (queen of Carthage), caught up in her love affair with Aeneas, forgets her responsibilities; her neglect of duty is thus a warning to the would-be Roman. In this process, the appointed leader is in charge. If he or she neglects the task, the city will suffer: Carthage, as every Roman knew, was ultimately destroyed by Rome (146 B.C.). Troy, defending the self-indulgent Paris, was also destroyed.

But it is not enough to create peace and order within one city's borders and walls if there are enemies outside. Thus the second role of the city is to spread its civilization, to "curb haughty nations by justice," to "teach the ways of peace to those they conquer," even if it must fight endless wars to do so. Like many well-intentioned modern nations, the peace-loving Romans apparently fought wars, which they hated, in order to create the conditions that would end the necessity for war! Although in the late twentieth century we have come to consider such acts and intentions as imperialist aggression, in their own time, the Romans' vision of one world united under Roman auspices was not always considered undesirable.

Many lands actually welcomed the Romans who, along with their governors and their gods, brought the blessings of security, advanced technology (as they constructed water and sanitation systems and built roads that still function today), an improved economy (as goods and services were traded), education (as young people from the colonies came to Roman universities to study), and opportunities both for Roman citizenship and for advancement in the vast Roman bureaucracy. Further, whenever possible, the Romans respected the cultures they absorbed, usually allowing the colonial peoples to maintain their own language, culture, and religion.

The Roman Hero

In the *Iliad*—the story of Troy—we met the hero Achilles in the opening lines of the poem; in the *Odyssey,* although we didn't actually meet Odysseus until book 5, we heard of him (and of the poet's judgment of him) in the poem that opens the work. Not so in the Roman epic: the subject of the *Aeneid*—its real hero—is not a man but a city and the nation that shares its name. In the opening line, the poet announces his subject: "arms" and "a man." Clearly, the "arms"—warfare—comes first, whereas the "man" remains anonymous for the first 130 lines of the poem.

The focus on the city skews the portrayal of the human contenders in one very specific and exclusively Roman direction. In the *Iliad,* Hector and Achilles faced each other as equals, respecting each other's worth and honor. But though **Turnus** is portrayed with considerable sympathy, and though he and Aeneas are equally skilled and courageous, they are seen from the Roman perspective: Aeneas is a patriot, but Turnus, who does what Aeneas does but on the wrong side, is repeatedly described as "mad" and "fanatical"—an enemy to Rome and, as he explicitly states, to Jupiter. He is thus a foil to Aeneas in war, as Dido was in love. In the *Iliad,* Zeus respected and sympathized with both sides. In the *Aeneid,* there is no question about which is the good side: Turnus fights for personal glory, whereas Aeneas fights for gods and country—for Rome. An exchange such as that between Hector and Ajax in the *Iliad*—Trojan and Greek fighting to a draw, proving their prowess, and exchanging gifts—is no longer possible. War is no longer a game fought for the glory of the players; war is now grim—and avoidable. If only Rome's opponents would do the sensible thing and yield peacefully to the inevitable, the "iron gates of war" would close forever. Until then, the kind of peace found in the image of **Arcadia** will remain a dream of the Golden Age long past (associated by the Romans with the good old days of the early republic) or of the life in Elysium to come. The persistence in Roman culture of nostalgia for the imagined simplicity of the past and the fondness of well-to-do Romans for keeping country houses for pastoral weekend retreats are expressed in these mythic images, perhaps representing an undercurrent of suspicion that the price paid for civilization—even (or perhaps especially) one as glorious as Rome's—was too high.

In return for their troubles, the Greek heroes received some kind of reward: Achilles got his glory and Odysseus his family and home. Meanwhile, the hero of the *Aeneid* will not even get to see the promised land for which he risks his life and sacrifices everything—his comfort, his home, his wife, his lover, his friends (including Palinarus, the helmsman, and the Arcadian Prince **Pallas** himself), along with his freedom and his fortune. What kind of hero would sacrifice so much to gain so little?

Aeneas: An Exemplary Roman

Aeneas is presented from the beginning of the epic as a man "remarkable for goodness," who is nevertheless forced by the gods to bear the burden of being the founder of Rome. Achilles was offered two fates and chose to fight (and die) at Troy; Odysseus, despite many tempting alternatives offered to him, chose to go home to Ithaca, whatever the risks. Aeneas, however, has no such choices. From the beginning, he is the victim of divine politics. So that Rome may come into being, Troy falls, and he is ordered by his mother, the goddess Venus, to flee to "Italy," a destination he's never seen or heard of. When he falls in love with Dido, he stays with her until **Mercury** orders him to leave: "You must set sail" is the message Mercury brings from Jupiter. For the Roman hero, unlike his Greek counterpart, his only choice is in the way he accepts his destiny.

Why, the poet asks, would the gods impose such suffering on such a good man? Can the gods be malevolent? The answer, not stated explicitly until Aeneas's visit to the Underworld in Book 6, is already implied in the opening dozen lines of the poem: it is for the good of Rome. Conscious of his responsibility to the gods, to his son, and to the future of Rome (if you won't do it for yourself, his mother and Jupiter both ask him, would you deny your son the walls of Rome?), Aeneas accepts his burdens—despite his sorrow at the losses he has experienced—not only with the tranquillity that the Roman philosophers urged but with the kind of zeal, once he is committed, that characterized the Greek heroes' pursuit of their own more personal goals. This contrast in the Greek and Roman heroes' sense of their own identities is revealed even in the epithets attached to their names. For the Greek heroes, the epithets described personal skills or qualities—"wily Odysseus," "swift-footed Achilles." For Aeneas, however, the epithets describe moral commitments and responsibilities—"pious Aeneas," "father Aeneas"—qualities so utterly given in his character that he can use them to describe himself: "I am pious Aeneas," he says, introducing himself to Dido. As such, one of his burdens is quite literal: he is responsible for carrying the household gods of Troy—the Lares, the Penates, and the Vesta—to Rome, where they eventually will be established as the gods of Rome and (in the Temple of the Vesta, the hearth fire of the state) the Eternal Flame of Rome will be kept burning.

Aeneas's Discipline   Another difference between Aeneas and the Greek heroes is his self-control. Achilles was naturally excessive; Odysseus was typically impulsive, giving in to curiosity or egotism until he acquired self-control and responsibility the hard way, through painful experience. Aeneas, however, seems to come already equipped with the Roman virtues of responsibility and firm self-control. An instructive instance is the landing of the two heroes Aeneas and Odysseus at the land of the Cyclops. There, in the place where Odysseus's impulsive egotism got him into trouble with Poseidon, Aeneas exhibits both self-control and compassion: he takes aboard an enemy sailor, Achaemenides, supposedly "left behind" by the irresponsible Odysseus (an incident that appears nowhere in Homer but which clearly illustrates the virtues that Virgil attributed to his more proper Roman hero). In another ironic comment on Homer's Odysseus, Aeneas insists that the Trojans do not land at Carthage to raid the city—"to loot the household gods of Libya, or to drive down stolen booty toward the beaches."

The difference between Greek and Roman heroes is most blatantly seen in a pair of parallel incidents in Book 10, in which Virgil contrasts the behavior of the Greek-style hero Turnus (explicitly compared to "a new Achilles") with that of the Roman hero Aeneas. Turnus, an experienced general, comes upon the young prince Pallas, in his first battle, on the battlefield. He not only kills the young man but strips him of his gold belt and wears it to boast of his victory. For Turnus, the glory is in the body count, and the belt is his trophy. In a similar incident, Aeneas comes upon a young Latin soldier, Lausus, who is taking incredible risks to defend his father, a notorious tyrant. So struck is Aeneas by the young man's pious devotion to the idea of father-hood that, remembering his own father, Aeneas treats Lausus respectfully, offering him the opportunity to avoid the encounter. When Lausus insists on fighting and is killed, Aeneas makes a point of refusing to strip the armor, and he returns the corpse with honor to the youth's companions.

Aeneas's Rage   Despite his courtesy and stated preference for treaties rather than battles, Aeneas is not passive. Not only does he fight like a demon when necessary, but when his anger is aroused, "his wrath is terrible." Unlike Achilles's, though, Aeneas's anger is not aroused by slights to his ego. It is only when he experiences a deep sense of moral outrage that he allows his anger to express itself in the service of a higher goal: when he comes upon Helen in the ruins of Troy; when Turnus kills Pallas and strips his armor; when the Latins violate treaties time after time; and, of course, after their last battle, when Aeneas sees Pallas's belt on Turnus's shoulder.

Women in the *Aeneid*

Like the heroes, the women, both divine and human, in the *Aeneid* are divided into those who are on the Roman side and those who are Rome's enemies. On the pro-Roman side are Aeneas's wife, **Creusa** [kree-OO-sa], and his mother, Venus.

Creusa   In an image that emphasizes the epic's patriarchal focus, Aeneas escapes from Troy carrying his father (the burden of the past) on his back and leading his son (his duty toward the future) by the hand (Figure 19-1). His wife, Creusa, is left to follow along behind and is killed by Greek soldiers. When Aeneas realizes that she is gone, he goes back to find her and discovers only her shade. In a scene reminiscent of Odysseus's attempt to embrace the shade (or ghost) of his mother in Hades, he

FIGURE 19-1   Aeneas and Anchises. Shown in this Attic vase painting (c. 510 B.C.) carrying his father, Anchises, on his back and leading his son, Ascanius, by the hand, Aeneas is an apt emblem of the duty of a Roman hero—or a Roman citizen: to carry on the ancient traditions, to sustain the Roman state, and to lead it on to an even greater future. But that great responsibility is clearly a heavy burden: Aeneas, his head with its great helmet bowed, droops under the weight. (*Martin von Wagner Museum, Wurzburg.*)

tries three times unsuccessfully to embrace her, only to find nothing there but air, an apt image of her insubstantial value when compared with the larger enterprise of founding Rome.

The behavior of Creusa's shade is nevertheless a model of Roman devotion to duty. Characterizing Aeneas's weeping as "fanatic sorrow," she instructs him to accept the gods' arrangement of their destinies, to go to seek a new kingdom and a new bride, and to stop fretting and get on with his mission. That is the last we hear of her, or of mourning—a revealing contrast to the extended funeral games (exactly like those Achilles held in honor of Patroclus) that Aeneas holds for his dead father. Women in Roman myth are clearly expendable.

Marriage and the Family   Marriage, for the Romans, is a sacred institution. But marriages are made for political or economic reasons—love is not essential. Thus Aeneas will wed the Latin Princess **Lavinia** in order to cement the bond between Latins and Trojans, despite her hostility and his lack of any personal relationship with her. And Dido, whom he loves, he does not marry—an omission he reminds her of

("I have never entered into such agreements," he says) when she, thinking of him as her husband, begs him to stay.

Fatherhood, in this patriarchal world, is essential. Motherhood, however, is subsumed in the larger affairs of state. Lavinia's mother, for example, explaining her disapproval of King **Latinus**'s plan to break their daughter's engagement to Turnus and marry her instead to Aeneas, is simply dismissed.

Two Mothers: Thetis and Venus   It is also instructive to contrast the maternal relationship, outwardly similar, of Thetis and Achilles with that of Venus and Aeneas. They both have similar functions, carrying messages between Zeus/Jupiter and their respective sons or appealing to Hephaestus/Vulcan for new shields when their sons are about to face battle. But their goals for their respective offspring differ radically. Thetis wanted to protect Achilles from harm; of his two fates, she'd clearly prefer the safer choice—long life, even without glory. Not so Venus: committed to her own political agenda, as well as to her son's political responsibilities as future father of his country, she wants him to found Rome, even if it means struggle, sacrifice, and sorrow for him personally. Thus she participates in the plot with Juno to cause him to fall in love with Dido in order to protect his ships—and his mission—knowing that he will have to leave and will suffer emotionally as a result.

Juno and Juturna   On the anti-Roman side are Juno (always described, until she yields to Jupiter, as "savage Juno") and the goddess **Juturna** (the "fanatic" sister of Turnus). Between themselves, these two goddesses encourage Dido's neglect of Carthage, the fury of Amata (queen of Latium), Turnus's rage, the Latins' repeated breaking of treaties, and acts of violence such as the burning of Aeneas's ships. They even interfere, in trying to prevent Aeneas's victory, by preventing Aeneas from finding Turnus on the battlefield, often plucking him up, chariot and all, and depositing him, much to his consternation, on the other side of the river.

Even more revealing of the "savage" goddess's chthonic powers (characterized throughout the epic as violent and irrational), Juno calls up the powers of **Allecto,** one of the Furies, from her home in the Underworld. Associated by Virgil with the poison of the Gorgon, she sends a snake into the breast of Amata and implants a firebrand in the heart of Turnus, driving both mad, so that Amata is driven to Bacchic frenzies and Turnus is driven to equally frenzied violence in war.

Thus, whether they are loved or hated, men are victims of the terrible goddesses. Juno may not have the power to change Jupiter's plan for Rome, but she can delay its implementation as long as possible, as Poseidon had delayed Odysseus. But the difference is revealing. Poseidon's delay was caused by Odysseus's own pride, his vain boasting that revealed his identity to the Cyclops, and its duration (a finite sentence that Zeus insisted must not exceed the crime) coincided with Odysseus's moral development. Juno's delaying the founding of Rome and her persecution of Aeneas is not in proportion to Aeneas's behavior or moral condition. As many scholars have noted, even Turnus, whom Juno ostensibly protects, is destroyed in the process, and Aeneas, despite Venus's assistance, never gets to see the promised city of Rome—nor will anyone for several centuries. Meanwhile, the firebrand of war will keep burning. According to some readers, Juno thus has, in effect, the last word, despite "yielding" to Jupiter. In fact, immediately after Juno and Jupiter settle affairs between themselves, Jupiter himself sends a Fury to paralyze Turnus, setting him up for Aeneas to kill him.

Dido Between these pro- and anti-Roman extremes is the figure of Dido. Like Aeneas, caught up in an affair beyond her control, she is portrayed sympathetically— the victim first of the gods and then of Aeneas, who loves her and then, ordered by the gods, rather unceremoniously dumps her. Aeneas is not gifted, like Odysseus, with "honeyed words" to let her down gently. Virgil grants Dido a long lament in which she expresses her grief and sorrow. Like Cleopatra, to whom she is implicitly compared in the later description of Aeneas's shield, she has abandoned her city, compromised her reputation, all for love—and now she has lost that. In anger and despair, she curses Aeneas, calls for an avenger, and commits suicide. Pitying her in her agony, as she dies an unmerited death brought on by her emotional frenzy, Juno sends **Iris** to free her spirit from her body, ending her misery.

On a personal level, Virgil clearly sympathizes with Dido in her predicament, just as he does with Turnus; neither understands what has gone wrong. Dido has devoted herself to love as Turnus has to honor, and both die bewildered, watching a world they thought they understood crumble about them. In Dido's death (as in that of Turnus, which Virgil likewise presents sympathetically), we see the poet burying with honor a set of values long admired by, but no longer appropriate for, contemporary Romans.

Wrapped up in the pursuit of purely personal satisfactions, Dido has abandoned her responsibility and neglected her city-in-progress. Many modern readers find Aeneas cold, even inhuman, in his response to Dido. However, she has allowed an excess of emotion to break down her self-control. A good Roman would have mourned briefly and then gotten back to work, as Aeneas did on losing Creusa.

It is not Dido's plight itself but her response to the burdens and sorrows of her life that is characterized as understandable but ultimately un-Roman—a foil to Aeneas's proper response. Virgil is sorry for Dido (witness Aeneas's appeal to her shade in the Underworld, which she rejects), but although the worthy Roman sheds "tears for passing things"—for Creusa, for Troy, for Dido, for Pallas, for all the personal betrayals, losses, and sorrows that life entails—and even memorializes them in stone, or in verse, he must not allow sorrow to prevent him from carrying out his duty to Rome or from seeing the historical perspective, from which his personal fate is relatively insignificant.

The Gods and Human Fate

In one of the most revealing scenes in the epic, Venus tears away the "cloud" from Aeneas's eyes so that he can see the destruction of Troy from the gods' viewpoint. In a superficially similar scene in the *Iliad,* Athene removed the cloud from the eyes of Diomedes so that he could distinguish the gods from the humans intermingled on the battlefield. The differences, however, are striking: whereas in the Greek epic the gods and humans were caught up in the same battle, in the Roman version, human action is ultimately an illusion—at best, the humans are agents in a divine plan they cannot see or comprehend. They may think that Greeks fight with Trojans, but it is actually the gods doing battle with gods, Venus reveals. Thus there is no point in Aeneas's killing Helen—she isn't the real cause of the Trojan War. If Troy falls, it falls so that Rome can eventually arise. The most significant things Aeneas can take out of the ruins of Troy, apart from his son (who will be the ancestor of the Romans), are the Vesta (the statue of the hearth goddess) and the Eternal Flame (the divine spirit of Rome), which Aeneas is to keep burning until it can be enshrined anew in the Eternal City itself.

At every level in the *Aeneid,* human destiny is revealed to be a function of divine politics. Even love, that most intimate of emotions, is not exempt: Venus and Juno, each for her own political aims, cause Dido and Aeneas to fall in love—Venus to protect Aeneas's Roman mission by ensuring that Dido won't attack him or burn his ships, Juno to transfer Rome's destiny as Eternal City to Carthage. The goddesses, acting on a script they have prewritten, further cause the two to consummate their love in a carefully prepared setting—a cave in which they take shelter right on cue from a storm arranged by Juno.

Unlike the *Iliad,* where "fates" were always plural, or the *Odyssey,* where one's destiny was determined by one's moral status, in the *Aeneid,* the humans find themselves acting out roles in a scenario the gods have devised. Their only choices lie in how to respond to the burdens the gods dole out. Jupiter assures Venus from the very first that her "children's fate is firm," that Rome will indeed be established, prosper, and endure eternally.

The Underworld

It is in the Underworld that Aeneas, guided by the **Cumaean Sibyl** [koo-MEE-an SIB-il] and instructed by the shade of his father, Anchises, finally learns his ultimate destiny and the meaning of his suffering. It is then that the question—why is a good man compelled by the gods to suffer?—is at last answered.

Borrowing from Homer's description of Odysseus's descent to the Underworld, with additional details extrapolated from Plato's description in his dialogue *Phaedo,* Virgil elaborates on an Underworld divided into nine circles, each administering eternal justice to a different category of human souls. The upper circles include the innocent (such as infants and martyrs), the suicides, and a separate circle for the "Fields of Mourning," those who were "consumed with bitter love." It is here that Aeneas meets the shade of Dido, still unreconciled to her fate, who turns from him as the eternally unforgiving Ajax did from Odysseus.

The road through the Underworld then divides. (Wherever the Romans went, they seem to have built highways, complete with roadsigns!) The highway to the left leads to **Tartarus,** where various kinds of wickedness are punished, and the road to the right leads toward **Elysium,** where the souls of the blessed spend eternity.

It is here that the shade of Anchises, like Tiresias in the *Odyssey,* points his son toward the path that will lead him to his goal. As moral guide to the upper world as well as tour guide of the lower, he explains to Aeneas how the good are eventually rewarded—not in their lives on earth, where sorrow and loss may prevail even for the deserving, but in eternity. In a modification of the doctrine of reincarnation of souls borrowed from Plato, Anchises tells Aeneas that, for most souls, awareness of the "Universal Mind" within them is dulled by the body and that the resulting blindness clings even after death. Consequently, most souls, washed clean of memory by the river **Lethe** [LEE-thee], are recycled every millennium until they can manage to purify themselves sufficiently. A few—pure priests, patriots, and pious poets (Virgil himself undoubtedly one of them)—escape the endless cycle of reincarnations and enter Elysium, where they spend eternity, Roman style, listening to music, feasting, currying their horses, and polishing their chariots and weapons.

This, in the long run, is the eternal reward for service—for those who accept the burdens and losses and serve Rome faithfully. From this perspective, to get overly upset about the pains (or overly committed to the pleasures) of life in the present world is to take only the short view. In the big picture, everyone gets exactly what he or she deserves.

Anchises also gets the opportunity here to explain the future of Rome, as well, from the founding to Augustus, who will renew the Golden Age and extend his empire to the ends of the earth, making war redundant. Rome's unique contribution to the renewal of the Golden Age will be its mastery of the art of government and its ability—through conquest if necessary—to teach peace to all the world. Having seen Elysium, Aeneas is understandably reluctant to leave. Nevertheless, the vision of Rome before him, he accepts the burden of his mission with a new commitment. We never again hear him complaining that his life is not his own. From this point on, he never hesitates. To achieve that grand vision, no suffering, no sacrifice is too great.

An Ironic View   Some contemporary scholars interpret this vision of "Rome triumphant" as ironic. One might ask whether Augustus would have continued to provide government funds to the poet or would have rescued the poem from the flames to which Virgil consigned it in his will if he saw it as condemning himself and his plans or even as presenting them ambivalently. (It is perhaps for just such a suspicion that he may have later forced the poet Ovid into exile!)

Personal political views apart, there is some evidence to support the ironic view. On leaving Elysium, Aeneas is led through the Gate of Ivory, traditionally the source of false dreams (as opposed to the Gates of Horn, that led to true or prophetic dreams). Is Virgil a prophet of Rome's grandeur or of its doom, prefigured here in the gloom of the Underworld? In a complex work such as this, to be sure, many readings are possible. But could Augustus have missed such a broad hint? The image of the two gates through which all dreams pass is hardly an esoteric reference whose meaning might have eluded a mere politician; it was, after all, a commonplace metaphor. It even occurred in the *Iliad,* the common reading of every Roman schoolboy. And although an ironic reading is conceivable, the fact that readers and scholars for almost two millennia thereafter did not note the possibility suggests that, whatever inherent meaning we might now find in the material, the poet and his contemporaries did not find in the image of the Gate of Ivory an implicit rejection of the Augustan vision. Further, even if Anchises's vision is deceptive, Jupiter himself has already made the same statement at the beginning of the epic, reciting the future history of Rome to Venus. And he will repeat it to Juno at the end.

Surely, Virgil never implies that founding or preserving Rome will be quick or easy, or without pain or loss—on the contrary. In fact, Anchises alludes to but denies his son a prevision of the death of Pallas, perhaps fearing that such foreknowledge would keep Aeneas from persevering. But the difficulties entailed do not deny the value of the vision itself. Rome, after all, did come about, and, the hated civil wars over, Virgil and his fellow poets (his friend Horace, for instance, who also wrote poems celebrating Augustus) seemed to share in the sense of relief and the renewed hope for the future. If Eternal Rome, further, was in fact a dream, it may have been a dream worth holding on to.

Finally, we might recall here the Roman preference for demythologizing their mythic material and presenting it more realistically. In the real world, even in a culture given to superstition, people simply don't go to the Underworld! Nevertheless, to share in the tradition of epic heroes before him, Aeneas must go there as well. Presenting the obligatory voyage of the hero to the Underworld as an illusion, a false dream, allows the poet to have it both ways—to present his vision and to explain away its more difficult-to-swallow components. And yet, it would not be altogether inconsistent with this vision of hope for Virgil to have used the Underworld episode as a subtle reminder that around the edges of every dream lurks the possibility of nightmare.

The Last Battle

As in the *Iliad,* the climax of the *Aeneid* is the long-delayed combat between the two opposing warriors, and once again the contrast between the *Iliad* and the *Aeneid* is revealing. In Homer's work, the tension between the possible outcomes was stressed—even if the audience knew the end, the participants (including the gods) did not. Until the last moment, Apollo had hopes for Hector. And when Zeus held up his scales, he did not know in advance which side would sink down. In the *Aeneid,* Jupiter possesses a similar pair of scales, one of many Homeric trappings that Virgil borrows. But it is ultimately a meaningless gesture. Not only does Jupiter himself weight the scales, adding two "different fates," but the gods know in advance the outcome of the battle, as does the shade of Anchises in the Underworld. Before Aeneas and Turnus even meet on the battlefield, Juno yields and asks instead for a union of the two peoples: the Latins will be allowed to keep their name and language; they will become one larger, eclectic culture, Latin and Trojan (Greek) merged; and Juno will be worshiped alongside Jupiter as queen of the Roman gods. Only then does the no-longer-climactic battle take place.

When Aeneas finally encounters Turnus, he defeats the Latin general fairly rapidly, taking advantage of the paralysis wrought by the Fury sent by Jupiter. Turnus is reduced to begging on his knees for mercy, not for his corpse to be respected, as Hector had, but for his life. Achilles, in the parallel Homeric encounter, enraged at Hector for killing Patroclus and wearing his helmet, would not listen to any such pleas. Aeneas, in contrast, is moved to be compassionate and is about to grant Turnus's request when he sees the belt of Pallas that the Latin had boastfully confiscated and worn to display his prowess, as heroes in the *Iliad* regularly did.

Two Views of Aeneas   Some readers argue that this scene, too, is presented ironically, showing an Aeneas corrupted by war and by serving as the agent of an exploitative, imperialist government. Beginning as a model Roman hero, he becomes just like the Greeks—another Achilles, who coldheartedly murders a man begging for mercy. Aeneas's last act, they argue, reveals how service to such a government institution gradually destroys the humanity of those who serve it. Others see the "two Aeneases" as representing the gap between the public figure and the private man that political leaders must experience, requiring a public display of confidence and suppression of private doubts. (One writer asserts that the contradictions in Aeneas's character are the result of Virgil's having changed his mind in the middle of writing but not having finished the necessary revisions.)

Such interpretations would certainly help rescue the work for contemporary readers whose sensibilities are offended by a poet who both supports the Establishment and portrays at least some circumstances in which violence is acceptable. But those interpretations must be argued despite Virgil's repeated presentation of Turnus's fanatic behavior. It is true, of course, that Turnus is a victim, trapped by the gods, as were Aeneas and Dido. But sympathy is not the same as approval. And neither Dido nor Turnus is merely a victim. Turnus is also a cruel, fanatical, ego-driven, and treacherous man.

Another View   One might alternatively argue that Aeneas starts out as a Greek-style hero—witness his Achilles-like rage at Helen, which Venus must interrupt by seizing his hand (just as Athene in the *Iliad* had prevented Achilles from stabbing Agamemnon), and his Odysseus-like lingering on the couch of Dido. But already he is more compassionate (he rescues Achaemenides) and more civilized (he doesn't "raid" Carthage). And instructed (and occasionally scolded) by Venus and Jupiter, he learns to become a complete Roman hero, his outbursts of rage now coming only when the state is at risk or the gods are offended or denied. It is significant that no god intervenes when, following the death of Pallas, Aeneas grows uncharacteristically savage in battle. There is, pointedly, no parallel here to the equivalent scene in the *Iliad* when the river god Scamander attacked Achilles, who had been venting his rage and heaping up corpses into the river. The very same gods who condemned Turnus's behavior apparently approve of Aeneas's.

Further, beneath the momentary surface resemblance between Achilles and Aeneas, important differences emerge. First, whereas Patroclus was an experienced fighter (albeit no Achilles) who took out twenty-seven men with him in his last moments, Pallas is a youth in his first battle, an unfair match to begin with, as Virgil earlier made clear. Thus for Turnus to boast of the kill and wear Pallas's belt is not only a reversion to the other heroic model but also an unwarranted boast—Pallas is a relatively easy mark. Second, Jupiter himself takes pains to comment on the inappropriateness of Turnus's wearing the belt and warns that punishment will inevitably follow.

Moreover, unlike Achilles, who vowed to eat Hector's body raw, Aeneas is tempted to show mercy—an exact inversion of the earlier scene where he is tempted to kill Helen—only to have the moral outrage of that senseless and shameful killing propel him to act *against* instinct and do whatever the gods have already acknowledged must be done. Only then, in an outburst of what the later Roman poet Juvenal (c. A.D. 60–128) called *saeva indignatio* ("righteous indignation"), does the otherwise restrained Aeneas allow himself to vent his rage in violence and kill Turnus. That his rage helps him overcome his initial reluctance, that he kills in anger and precisely *not* with the cool detachment of a state assassin, and that he feels compelled even in the act of killing Turnus to shout that it is Pallas who kills him makes his final act, one might argue, more rather than less human. Like the shades of the suitors in the *Odyssey*, Turnus's shade flees to Hades, unrepentant and angry still.

The *Aeneid*: An Overview

Virgil, then, presents us with a complex work, a character who, for better or worse, grows and changes, and a multiple and often ambivalent perspective on the events portrayed. The world of the *Aeneid* is one in which individuals, burdened by the need to serve, driven and even deceived by gods with political agendas of their own, are bound to suffer "loss on bitter loss." The question is, is the goal worth the sacrifice? Even if the answer turns out to be no, what choice is there? Not only do the gods do what they need to do, regardless of the consequences to individuals, but the humans, to be moral (not merely government) agents, must do what they believe is right, not merely what is comfortable. Finally, what is the alternative? Rome in general and Virgil in particular had already seen the alternative, and nothing in the gloom of the Underworld could match the horrors of real-life series of wars, both foreign and civil, that produced not human freedom but only terror and chaos. Of course Virgil was ambivalent about war—what compassionate human being isn't?

There is certainly a conflict between humanism and war, and there may well be a conflict between humanism and government. But to argue (as Freud did) that war is the price that we pay for civilization and then to argue (as Freud did not) that the price is too high is to condemn humans to live in a psychological Underworld, where the terrible forces of unrestrained libido are unleashed and in control. However imperfect a ruler Augustus might be, the alternative to a world ruled by Augustus, Virgil seems to imply, is a world ruled by Allecto.

AENEID [1]

Virgil

BOOK 1

I sing of arms and of a man: his fate
had made him fugitive; he was the first
to journey from the coasts of Troy as far
as Italy and the Lavinian shores.
Across the lands and waters he was battered
beneath the violence of High Ones, for
the savage Juno's unforgetting anger;
and many sufferings were his in war—
until he brought a city into being
and carried in his gods to Latium;   10
from this have come the Latin race, the lords
of Alba, and the ramparts of high Rome.

Tell me the reason, Muse: what was the wound
to her divinity, so hurting her
that she, the queen of gods, compelled a man
remarkable for goodness to endure
so many crises, meet so many trials?
Can such resentment hold the minds of gods?

There was an ancient city they called Carthage—
a colony of refugees from Tyre—   20
a city facing Italy, but far
away from Tiber's mouth: extremely rich
and, when it came to waging war, most fierce.
This land was Juno's favorite—it is said—
more dear than her own Samos; here she kept
her chariot and armor; even then
the goddess had this hope and tender plan:
for Carthage to become the capital
of nations, if the Fates would just consent.
But she had heard that, from the blood of Troy,   30
a race had come that some day would destroy
the citadels of Tyre; from it, a people
would spring, wide-ruling kings, men proud in battle
and destined to annihilate her Libya.
The Fates had so decreed. And Saturn's daughter—
in fear of this, remembering the old war

1. Translation by Allen Mandelbaum.

that she had long since carried on at Troy
for her beloved Argos (and, indeed,
the causes of her bitterness, her sharp
and savage hurt, had not yet left her spirit;   40
for deep within her mind lie stored the judgment
of Paris and the wrong done to her scorned
beauty, the breed she hated, and the honors
that had been given ravished Ganymede)—
was angered even more; for this, she kept
far off from Latium the Trojan remnant
left by the Greeks and pitiless Achilles.
For long years they were cast across all waters,
fate-driven, wandering from sea to sea.
It was so hard to found the race of Rome.   50

. . . .

**[Juno persuades Aeolus, the wind god, to send a hurricane to damage Aeneas's ships.
Several are lost, but to prevent total destruction, Neptune calms the seas. Aeneas lands
the remainder on Libya's coast:]**

And now Aeneas' weary crewmen hurry
to find the nearest land along their way.
They turn toward Libya's coast. There is a cove
within a long, retiring bay; and there
an island's jutting arms have formed a harbor
where every breaker off the high sea shatters
and parts into the shoreline's winding shelters.
Along this side and that there towers, vast,
a line of cliffs, each ending in like crags;
beneath the ledges tranquil water lies   60
silent and wide; the backdrop—glistening
forests and, beetling from above, a black
grove, thick with bristling shadows. Underneath
the facing brow: a cave with hanging rocks,
sweet waters, seats of living stone, the home
of nymphs. And here no cable holds tired ships,
no anchor grips them fast with curving bit.

Aeneas shelters here with seven ships—
all he can muster, all the storm has left.
The Trojans, longing so to touch the land,   70
now disembark to gain the wished-for sands.

. . . .

[Aeneas sees that his followers are fed and then addresses them:]

"O comrades—surely we're not ignorant
of earlier disasters, we who have suffered
things heavier than this—our god will give
an end to this as well. You have neared the rage
of Scylla and her caves' resounding rocks;

and you have known the Cyclops' crags; call back
your courage, send away your grieving fear.
Perhaps one day you will remember even   80
these our adversities with pleasure. Through
so many crises and calamities
we make for Latium, where fates have promised
a peaceful settlement. It is decreed
that there the realm of Troy will rise again.
Hold out, and save yourself for kinder days."

These are his words; though sick with heavy cares,
he counterfeits hope in his face; his pain
is held within, hidden. His men make ready
the game that is to be their feast; they flay
the deer hide off the ribs; the flesh lies naked.   90
Some slice off quivering strips and pierce them with
sharp spits, while on the beach the others set
caldrons of brass and tend the flame. With food
their strength comes back again. Along the grass
they stretch and fill their bellies full of fat
venison meat and well-aged wine. That done—
their hunger banished by their feasting and
the tables cleared—their talk is long, uncertain
between their hope and fear, as they ask after
their lost companions, wondering if their comrades   100
are still alive or if they have undergone
the final change and can no longer hear
when called upon. Especially the pious
Aeneas moans within himself the loss
now of the vigorous Orontes, now
of Amycus, the cruel end of Lycus,
the doom of brave Cloanthus, of brave Gyas.

Their food and talk were done when Jupiter,
while gazing from the peaks of upper air
across the waters winged with canvas and   110
low-lying lands and shores and widespread peoples,
stood high upon the pinnacle of heaven
until he set his sight on Libya's kingdom.
And as he ponders this, the saddened Venus,
her bright eyes dimmed and tearful, speaks to him:

"O you who, with eternal rule, command
and govern the events of gods and men,
and terrify them with your thunderbolt,
what great offense has my Aeneas given,
what is his crime, what have the Trojans done   120
that, having undergone so many deaths,
the circle of all lands is shut against them—

and just because of Italy? Surely
you have sworn that out of them, in time to come,
with turning years, the Romans will be born
and, from the resurrected blood of Teucer,
rise up as rulers over sea and land?
What motive, Father, made you change? That promise
was solace for Troy's fall and its sad ruin;
I weighed this fate against the adverse fates.   130
But now their former fortune still pursues
the Trojans driven by so many evils.
Great king, is there no end to this ordeal?
Antenor could escape the Argive army,
then make his way through the Illyrian bays,
the inner lands of the Liburnians,
and safely cross the source of the Timavus,
where, with a mighty mountain's roar, it rushes
through nine mouths, till its flood bursts, overwhelming
the fields beneath with its resounding waters.   140
Yet here he planted Padua, a town
and home for Teucrians, and gave his nation
a name and then hung up the arms of Troy;
and now, serene, he tastes tranquillity.
But we, your very children, we whom you
had promised heaven's heights, have lost our ships—
unspeakable! Just for the rage of one
we are betrayed, kept far from Italy.
Is this the way you give us back our scepter?"

But then he smiled upon her—Jupiter,   150
father of men and gods—just as he calms
the heavens and the storms. He lightly kissed
his daughter's lips; these were his words to Venus:
"My Cytherea, that's enough of fear;
your children's fate is firm; you'll surely see
the walls I promised you, Lavinium's city;
and you shall carry your great-hearted son,
Aeneas, high as heaven's stars. My will
is still the same; I have not changed. Your son
(I now speak out—I know this anxiousness   160
is gnawing at you; I unroll the secret
scroll of the Fates, awake its distant pages)
shall wage tremendous war in Italy
and crush ferocious nations and establish
a way of life and walls for his own people—
until the time of his third summer as
the king of Latium, until he has passed
three winters since he overcame the Latins.
But then the boy Ascanius, who now

is carrying Iülus as his surname (while   170
the state of Ilium held fast, he still
was known as Ilus), with his rule shall fill
the wheeling months of thirty mighty years.
He shall remove his kingdom from Lavinium
and, powerful, build Alba Longa's walls.
For full three hundred years, the capital
and rule of Hector's race shall be at Alba,
until a royal priestess, Ilia,
with child by Mars, has brought to birth twin sons.
And then, rejoicing in the tawny hide   180
of his nursemaid, the she-wolf, Romulus
shall take the rulership and build the walls
of Mars' own city. Romulus shall call
that people 'Romans,' after his own name.
I set no limits to their fortunes and
no time; I give them empire without end.
Then even bitter Juno shall be changed;
for she, who now harasses lands and heavens
with terror, then shall hold the Romans dear
together with me, cherishing the masters   190
of all things, and the race that wears the toga.
This is what I decree. An age shall come
along the way of gliding lustra when
the house born of Assaracus shall hold
both Phthia and illustrious Mycenae
and rule defeated Argos. Then a Trojan
Caesar shall rise out of that splendid line.
His empire's boundary shall be the Ocean;
the only border to his fame, the stars.
His name shall be derived from great Iülus,   200
and shall be Julius. In time to come,
no longer troubled, you shall welcome him
to heaven, weighted with the Orient's wealth;
he, too, shall be invoked with prayers. With battle
forgotten, savage generations shall
grow generous. And aged Faith and Vesta,
together with the brothers, Romulus
and Remus, shall make laws. The gruesome gates
of war, with tightly welded iron plates,
shall be shut fast. Within, unholy Rage   210
shall sit on his ferocious weapons, bound
behind his back by a hundred knots of brass;
he shall groan horribly with bloody lips."

The words of Jupiter are done. He sends
the son of Maia down from heaven that
the newfound lands and fortresses of Carthage

be opened wide in welcome to the Trojans;
that Dido, ignorant of destiny,
not drive away Aeneas from her boundaries.
He flies across the great air; using wings   220
as oars, he quickly lands on Libyan shores.
He does as he was told. And the Phoenicians
now set aside their savagery before
the will of god; and Dido, above all,
receives into her spirit kindliness,
a gracious mind to greet the Teucrians.

But, nightlong, many cares have held the pious
Aeneas. And as soon as gracious daylight
is given to him, this is his decision:
to go out and explore this foreign country,   230
to learn what shores the wind has brought him to,
who lives upon this land—it is untilled—
are they wild beasts or men—and then to tell
his comrades what he has found. He hides his fleet
inside the narrows of the wooded cove,
beneath a hollow rock shut in by trees,
with bristling shades around. And he himself,
only Achates at his side, moves on;
he brandishes two shafts tipped with broad iron.

But in the middle of the wood, along   240
the way, his mother showed herself to him.
The face and dress she wore were like a maiden's,
her weapons like a girl's from Sparta or
those carried by Harpalyce of Thrace
when she tires out her horses, speeding faster
even than rapid Hebrus as she races.
For, as a huntress would, across her shoulder,
Venus had slung her bow in readiness;
her hair was free, disheveled by the wind;
her knees were bare; her tunic's flowing folds   250
were gathered in a knot. And she speaks first:
"Young men there! Can you tell me if by chance
you have seen one of my sisters pass—she wore
a quiver and a spotted lynx's hide—
while she was wandering here or, with her shouts,
chasing a foaming boar along its course?"

So Venus. Answering, her son began:
"I have not seen or heard your sister, maiden—
or by what name am I to call you, for
your voice is not like any human voice.   260
O goddess, you must be Apollo's sister
or else are to be numbered with the nymphs!

Whoever you may be, do help us, ease
our trials; do tell us underneath what skies,
upon what coasts of earth we have been cast;
we wander, ignorant of men and places,
and driven by the wind and the vast waves.
Before your altars many victims will
fall at our hands, as offerings to you."

Then Venus: "I can hardly claim such honor.   270
The girls of Tyre are used to wearing quivers
and bind their calves with scarlet hunting boots.
You see a Punic country, men of Tyre,
the city of Agenor; but at the border
the Libyans lie—a tribe that swears by war.
Our ruler here is Dido, she who left
her city when she had to flee her brother.
The tale of wrong is intricate and long,
but I shall trace its chief events in order.

"Her husband was Sychaeus: wealthiest   280
landowner in Phoenicia. For her father
had given her, a virgin, to Sychaeus
and joined them with the omens of first marriage.
Unhappy Dido loved him with much passion.
Pygmalion, her brother, held the kingdom
of Tyre; beyond all men he was a monster
in crime. Between Sychaeus and her brother
dividing fury came. Pygmalion—
unholy, blind with lust for gold—in secret
now catches Dido's husband off his guard   290
and cuts him down by sword before the altars,
heedless of his own sister's love. For long
he kept this hidden and, insidious,
invented many stories to mock Dido—
she is sick and longing—with an empty hope.
But in her sleep, to Dido came the very
image of her unburied husband; he
lifted his pallid face—amazingly—
and laid bare to his wife the cruel altars,
his breast impaled upon the blade, revealing   300
to her the hidden horror of the house.
He urges her to speed her flight, to leave
her homeland; and to help her journey, he
discloses ancient treasure in the earth,
a hoard of gold and silver known to none.
And Dido, moved by this, prepared her flight
and her companions. Now there come together
both those who felt fierce hatred for the tyrant

and those who felt harsh fear. They seize the ships
that happen to be ready, loading them   310
with gold. The wealth of covetous Pygmalion
is carried overseas. A woman leads.
They landed at the place where now you see
the citadel and high walls of new Carthage
rising; and then they bought the land called Byrsa,
'The Hide,' after the name of that transaction
(they got what they were able to enclose
inside a bull's skin). But who, then, are you?
From what coasts have you come? Where are you going?"
To these her questions he replied with sighs;   320
he drew his words from deep within his breast:

"O goddess, if I tracked my story back
until its first beginning, were there time
to hear the annals of our trials, then
the evening would have shut Olympus' gates
and gathered in the day before I ended.
But we were sailing out from ancient Troy—
if Troy means anything to you—across
strange seas when, as it willed, a tempest drove us
upon the coasts of Libya. I am pious   330
Aeneas, and I carry in my ships
my household gods together with me, rescued
from Argive enemies; my fame is known
beyond the sky. I seek out Italy,
my country, my ancestors born of Jove.
When I set out upon the Phrygian sea,
I had twice-ten ships, and my goddess-mother
showed me the way; I followed my firm fates.
Now I am left with scarcely seven galleys,
ships shattered by the waves and the east wind;   340
and I myself, a needy stranger, roam
across the wilderness of Libya; I
am driven out of Europe, out of Asia."
But Venus had enough of his complaints,
and so she interrupted his lament:

"Whoever you may be, I hardly think
the heaven-dwellers hold a grudge against you:
the breath of life is yours, and you are near
a Tyrian city. Only make your way
until you reach the palace of the queen.   350
For I can tell you truthfully: your comrades
are given back to you, your fleet is saved
and driven toward sure waters by the winds
that shifted to the north—unless my parents

have taught me augury to no good end.
Look there, where you can make out twice-six swans
that gladly file along, whom once the bird
of Jupiter had scattered, swooping down
from upper air into the open sky.
And now, in long array, they either seem   360
to settle down or else to hover, waiting
and watching those that have already landed;
and just as they, returning, play with rustling
wings, as they wheel about the sky in crews,
and give themselves to song—not otherwise
your ships and youths are either in the harbor
or near its mouth with swelling sails. Only
move on and follow where this pathway leads."

These were the words of Venus. When she turned,
her neck was glittering with a rose brightness;   370
her hair anointed with ambrosia,
her head gave all a fragrance of the gods;
her gown was long and to the ground; even
her walk was sign enough she was a goddess.
And when Aeneas recognized his mother,
he followed her with these words as she fled:
"Why do you mock your son—so often and
so cruelly—with these lying apparitions?
Why can't I ever join you, hand to hand,
to hear, to answer you with honest words?"   380

So he reproaches her, then takes the road
to Carthage. But as goddess, Venus cloaks
Aeneas and Achates in dark mist;
she wraps them in a cape of cloud so thick
that none can see or touch them or delay
their way or ask why they had come. And she
herself glides through the skies to Paphos, gladly
revisiting her home, her temple and
her hundred altars fragrant with fresh garlands
and warm with their Sabaean frankincense.   390

Meanwhile Aeneas and the true Achates
press forward on their path. They climb a hill
that overhangs the city, looking down
upon the facing towers. Aeneas marvels
at the enormous buildings, once mere huts,
and at the gates and tumult and paved streets.
The eager men of Tyre work steadily:
some build the city walls or citadel—
they roll up stones by hand; and some select

the place for a new dwelling, marking out   400
its limits with a furrow; some make laws,
establish judges and a sacred senate;
some excavate a harbor; others lay
the deep foundations for a theater,
hewing tremendous pillars from the rocks,
high decorations for the stage to come.
Just as the bees in early summer, busy
beneath the sunlight through the flowered meadows,
when some lead on their full-grown young and others
press out the flowing honey, pack the cells   410
with sweet nectar, or gather in the burdens
of those returning; some, in columns, drive
the drones, a lazy herd, out of the hives;
the work is fervent, and the fragrant honey
is sweet with thyme. "How fortunate are those
whose walls already rise!" Aeneas cries
while gazing at the rooftops of the city.
Then, sheltered by a mist, astoundingly,
he enters in among the crowd, mingling
together with the Tyrians. No one sees him.   420

Just at the center of the city stood
a thickly shaded wood; this was the place
where, when they landed, the Phoenicians first—
hurled there by whirlwind and by wave—dug up
an omen that Queen Juno had pointed out:
the head of a fierce stallion. This had meant
the nation's easy wealth and fame in war
throughout the ages. Here Sidonian Dido
was building a stupendous shrine for Juno,
enriched with gifts and with the goddess' statue,   430
where flights of steps led up to brazen thresholds;
the architraves were set on posts of brass;
the grating hinges of the doors were brass.
Within this grove, the sights—so strange to him—
have, for the first time, stilled Aeneas' fear;
here he first dared to hope he had found shelter,
to trust more surely in his shattered fortunes.
For while he waited for the queen, he studied
everything in that huge sanctuary,
marveling at a city rich enough   440
for such a temple, at the handiwork
of rival artists, at their skillful tasks.
He sees the wars of Troy set out in order:
the battles famous now through all the world,
the sons of Atreus and of Priam, and
Achilles, savage enemy to both.

He halted. As he wept, he cried: "Achates,
where on this earth is there a land, a place
that does not know our sorrows? Look! There is Priam!
Here, too, the honorable finds its due   450
and there are tears for passing things; here, too,
things mortal touch the mind. Forget your fears;
this fame will bring you some deliverance."
He speaks. With many tears and sighs he feeds
his soul on what is nothing but a picture.

He watched the warriors circling Pergamus:
here routed Greeks were chased by Trojan fighters
and here the Phrygian troops pursued by plumed
Achilles in his chariot. Nearby,
sobbing, he recognized the snow-white canvas   460
tents of King Rhesus—with his men betrayed,
while still in their first sleep, and then laid waste,
with many dead, by bloody Diomedes,
who carried off their fiery war horses
before they had a chance to taste the pastures
of Troy, or drink the waters of the Xanthus.

Elsewhere Young Troilus, the unhappy boy—
he is matched unequally against Achilles—
runs off, his weapons lost. He is fallen flat;
his horses drag him on as he still clings   470
fast to his empty chariot, clasping
the reins. His neck, his hair trail on the ground,
and his inverted spear inscribes the dust.
Meanwhile the Trojan women near the temple
of Pallas, the unkindly; hair disheveled,
sad, beating at their breasts, as suppliants,
they bear the robe of offering. The goddess
averts her face, her eyes fast to the ground.

Three times Achilles had dragged Hector round
the walls of Troy, selling his lifeless body   480
for gold. And then, indeed, Aeneas groans
within the great pit of his chest, deeply;
for he can see the spoils, the chariot,
the very body of his friend, and Priam
pleading for Hector with defenseless hands.
He also recognized himself in combat
with the Achaean chiefs, then saw the Eastern
battalions and the weapons of black Memnon.
Penthesilea in her fury leads
the ranks of crescent-shielded Amazons.   490
She flashes through her thousands; underneath

her naked breast, a golden girdle; soldier-
virgin and queen, daring to war with men.

But while the Dardan watched these scenes in wonder,
while he was fastened in a stare, astonished,
the lovely-bodied Dido neared the temple,
a crowding company of youths around her.
And just as, on the banks of the Eurotas
or through the heights of Cynthus, when Diana
incites her dancers, and her followers,   500
a thousand mountain-nymphs, press in behind her,
she wears a quiver slung across her shoulder;
and as she makes her way, she towers over
all other goddesses; gladness excites
Latona's silent breast: even so, Dido;
so, in her joy, she moved among the throng
as she urged on the work of her coming kingdom.

And then below the temple's central dome—
facing the doorway of the goddess, guarded
by arms—she took her place on a high throne.   510
Dido was dealing judgments to her people
and giving laws, apportioning the work
of each with fairness or by drawing lots;
when suddenly Aeneas sees, as they
press forward through the mighty multitude,
Sergestus, Antheus, and the brave Cloanthus,
and other Trojans whom the black whirlwind
had scattered on the waters, driven far
to other coasts. Aeneas is astounded;
both joy and fear have overcome Achates.   520
They burned to join right hands with their companions,
but this strange happening confuses them.
They stay in hiding, screened by folds of fog,
and wait to see what fortune found their friends,
on what beach they have left the fleet, and why
they come; for these were men who had been chosen
from all the ships to ask for grace, who now
made for the temple door with loud outcries.

When they had entered and received their leave
to speak in Dido's presence, then the eldest,   530
Ilioneus, calmly began: "O Queen,
whom Jupiter has granted this: to bring
to being a new city, curbing haughty
nations by justice—we, unhappy Trojans,
men carried by the winds across all seas,
beg you to keep the terror of fire from

our fleet, to spare a pious race, to look
on us with kindliness. We do not come
to devastate your homes and with the sword
to loot the household gods of Libya or   540
to drive down stolen booty toward the beaches.
That violence is not within our minds;
such arrogance is not for the defeated.
There is a place the Greeks have named Hesperia,
an ancient land with strong arms and fat soil.
Its colonists were the Oenotrians.
Now rumor runs that their descendants call
that nation 'Italy,' after their leader.
Our prows were pointed there when suddenly,
rising upon the surge, stormy Orion   550
drove us against blind shoals; and insolent
south winds then scattered us, undone by brine,
across the crushing sea, the pathless rocks.
A few of us have drifted to your shores.
What kind of men are these? Or is your country
so barbarous that it permits this custom?
We are denied the shelter of the beach;
they goad us into war; they will not let us
set foot upon the border of their land.
If you despise the human race and mortal   560
weapons, then still consider that the gods
remember right and wrong. We had a king,
Aeneas, none more just, no one more pious,
no man his better in the arts of war.
If fate has saved this man, if he still feeds
upon the upper air, if he is not
laid low to rest among the cruel Shades,
then we are not afraid and you will not
repent if you compete with him in kindness.
Within Sicilian territory, too,   570
are fields and cities and the famed Acestes,
born of the blood of Troy. Let us haul up
our fleet, smashed by the winds, along your beaches
and fit out timber from your forests, trim
our oars; and if we find our king and comrades
and are allowed to turn toward Italy
and Latium, then let us sail out gladly.
But if our shelter there has been denied us,
and you, the finest father of the Trojans,
were swallowed by the sea of Libya, and   580
no hope is left us now for Iülus, then
at least let us seek out again the straits
of Sicily, the land from which we sailed.
There houses wait for us, and King Acestes."

So spoke Ilioneus. The other sons
of Dardanus approved his words with shouts.

Then Dido softly, briefly answers him:
"O Teucrians, enough of fear, cast out
your cares. My kingdom is new; hard circumstances   590
have forced me to such measures for our safety,
to post guards far and wide along our boundaries.
But who is ignorant of Aeneas' men?
Who has not heard of Troy, its acts and heroes,
the flames of that tremendous war? We Tyrians
do not have minds so dull, and we are not
beyond the circuit of the sun's yoked horses.
Whatever you may choose—Hesperia and
the fields of Saturn, or the land of Eryx
and King Acestes—I shall send you safe   600
with escort, I shall help you with my wealth.
And should you want to settle in this kingdom
on equal terms with me, then all the city
I am building now is yours. Draw up your ships.
I shall allow no difference between
the Tyrian and the Trojan. Would your king,
Aeneas, too, were present, driven here
by that same south wind. I, in fact, shall send
my trusted riders out along the shores,
to comb the farthest coasts of Libya and   610
to see if, cast out of the waters, he
is wandering through the forests or the cities."

The words of Dido stir the brave Achates
and father Aeneas; long since, both of them
had burned to break free from their cloud. Achates
speaks first to his companion: "Goddess-born,
what counsel rises in your spirit now?
You see that everything is safe, our ships
and sailors saved. And only one is missing,
whom we ourselves saw sink among the waves.
All else is as your mother said it would be."   620

Yet he was hardly done when suddenly
the cloud that circled them is torn; it clears
away to open air. And there Aeneas
stood, glittering in that bright light, his face
and shoulders like a god's. Indeed, his mother
had breathed upon her son becoming hair,
the glow of a young man, and in his eyes,
glad handsomeness: such grace as art can add
to ivory, or such as Parian marble

or silver shows when set in yellow gold.   630
But then, surprising all, he tells the queen:
"The man you seek is here. I stand before you,
Trojan Aeneas, torn from Libyan waves.
O you who were alone in taking pity
on the unutterable trials of Troy,
who welcome us as allies to your city
and home—a remnant left by Greeks, harassed
by all disasters known on land and sea,
in need of everything—we cannot, Dido,
repay you, then, with gratitude enough   640
to match your merits, neither we nor any
Dardans scattered over this great world.
May gods confer on you your due rewards,
if deities regard the good, if justice
and mind aware of right count anywhere.
What happy centuries gave birth to you?
What splendid parents brought you into being?
While rivers run into the sea and shadows
still sweep the mountain slopes and stars still pasture
upon the sky, your name and praise and honor   650
shall last, whatever be the lands that call me."
This said, he gives his right hand to his friend
Ilioneus; his left he gives Serestus;
then turns to brave Cloanthus and brave Gyas.

First at the very sight of him, and then
at all he had endured, Sidonian Dido
was startled. And she told the Trojan this:
"You, goddess-born, what fortune hunts you down
through such tremendous trials? What violence
has forced you onto these ferocious shores?   660
Are you that same Aeneas, son of Dardan
Anchises, whom the gracious Venus bore
beside the banks of Phrygian Simois?
Indeed, I still remember banished Teucer,
a Greek who came to Sidon from his native
kingdom, when with the help of Belus he
was seeking out new realms (my father Belus
was plundering then, as victor, wealthy Cyprus).
And even then I learned of Troy's disaster,
and of your name and of the kings of Greece.   670
And though he was the Trojans' enemy,
Teucer would often praise the Teucrians
and boast that he was born of their old race.
Thus, young men, you are welcome to our halls.
My destiny, like yours, has willed that I,
a veteran of hardships, halt at last

in this country. Not ignorant of trials,
I now can learn to help the miserable."

So Dido speaks. At once she leads Aeneas
into the royal palace and announces   680
her offerings in the temples of the gods.
But meanwhile she does not neglect his comrades.
She sends down to the beaches twenty bullocks,
a hundred fat lambs with their ewes, and Bacchus'
glad gift of wine. Within the palace gleam
the furnishings of royal luxury;
the feast is readied in the atrium.
And there are draperies of noble purple
woven with art; and plates of massive silver
upon the tables; and, engraved in gold,   690
the sturdy deeds of Dido's ancestors,
a long, long line of happenings and heroes
traced from the first beginnings of her race.

Aeneas (for his father's love could not
permit his mind to rest) now quickly sends
Achates to the Trojan ships, to carry
these tidings to Ascanius, to lead
Aeneas' son up to the walls of Carthage:
all his paternal love and care are for
Ascanius. He also tells Achates   700
to bring back gifts snatched from the wreck of Troy:
a tunic stiff with images of gold,
and then a veil whose fringes were of saffron
acanthus—these once worn by Argive Helen,
who had borne them off to Troy and her unlawful
wedding when she had fled Mycenae—splendid
gifts of her mother Leda; and besides,
the scepter that had once been carried by
Ilione, eldest of Priam's daughters,
a necklace set with pearls, and then a crown   710
that had twin circles set with jewels and gold.
And hurrying to do all he was told,
Achates made his way down to the boats.

But in her breast the Cytherean ponders
new stratagems, new guile: that Cupid, changed
in form and feature, come instead of sweet
Ascanius and, with his gifts, inflame
the queen to madness and insinuate
a fire in Dido's very bones. For Venus
is much afraid of that deceptive house   720
and of the Tyrians with their double tongues.

The thought of savage Juno burns; by night
her care returns. Her words are for winged Love:

"Son, you are my only strength, my only power;
son, you who scorn the shafts of the great Father's
Typhoean thunderbolts, I flee to you
for refuge; suppliant, I call upon
the force within your godhead. For you know
how, through the hatred of resentful Juno,
across the sea and every shore your brother   730
Aeneas has been hunted down; and often
you have sorrowed with my sorrow. Now Phoenician
Dido has hold of him; with sweet words she
would make him stay. The hospitality
of Juno—and where it may lead—makes me
afraid; at such a turn I know she'll not
be idle. So, before she has a chance,
I plan to catch the queen by craftiness,
to girdle Dido with a flame, so that
no god can turn her back; I'll hold her fast   740
with great love for Aeneas. Hear me now;
I need your help to carry out this plot.
Ascanius, my dearest care, is ready
to go along to the Sidonian city,
called by his loving father, carrying
gifts saved from Troy in flames and from the sea.
But I shall lull the royal boy to sleep
on high Cythera or Idalium
and hide him in my holy house, so that
he cannot know—or interrupt—our trap.   750
And you will need—for one night and no more—
to counterfeit his features; as a boy,
to wear that boy's familiar face, and so
when Dido, joyful, draws you close during
the feasting and the flowing wine, when she
embraces you, and kisses tenderly,
your breath can fill her with a hidden flame,
your poison penetrate, deceivingly."

Love does what his dear mother asks. He sheds
his wings and gladly tries the walk of Iülus.   760
But Venus pours upon Ascanius
a gentle rest. She takes him to her breast
caressingly; and as a goddess can,
she carries him to her Idalium
where, in high groves, mild marjoram enfolds him
in flowers and the breath of its sweet shade.

Now Cupid's on his way, as he was told.
Gladly—Achates is his guide—he brings
the Tyrians royal gifts. As he arrives,
he finds the banqueting begun, the queen   770
already settled on her couch of gold
beneath resplendent awnings, at the center.
Father Aeneas and the Trojan warriors
now gather; they recline on purple covers.
The servants pour out water for their hands
and promptly offer bread from baskets and
bring towels smooth in texture for the guests.
Inside are fifty handmaids at their stations—
their care to stock the storerooms and to honor
the household gods with fire—and a hundred   780
more women, and as many male attendants
of equal age with them, to load the tables
with food and place the cups. The Tyrians, too,
have gathered, crowding through the happy halls—
all these invited to brocaded couches.
They marvel at Aeneas' gifts, at Iülus—
the god's bright face and his fictitious words—
and at the cloak, the veil adorned with saffron
acanthus borders. And above all, luckless
Dido—doomed to face catastrophe—   790
can't sate her soul, inflamed by what she sees;
the boy, the gifts excite her equally.
And he pretends to satisfy a father's
great love by hanging on Aeneas' neck
in an embrace. Then he seeks out the queen.
Her eyes cling fast to him, and all her heart;
at times she fondles him upon her lap—
for Dido does not know how great a god
is taking hold of her poor self. But Cupid,
remembering his mother, Venus, slowly   800
begins to mist the memory of Sychaeus
and with a living love tries to surprise
her longings gone to sleep, her unused heart.
And at the first pause in the feast the tables
are cleared away. They fetch enormous bowls
and crown the wine with wreaths. The uproar grows;
it swells through all the palace; voices roll
across the ample halls; the lamps are kindled—
they hang from ceilings rich with golden panels—
and flaming torches overcome the night.   810
And then the queen called for a golden cup,
massive with jewels, that Belus once had used,
Belus and all the Tyrian line; she filled
that golden cup with wine. The hall fell still.

"O Jupiter, for they say you are author
of laws for host and guest, do grant that this
may be a day of happiness for those
who come from Tyre and Troy, and may our sons
remember it. May Bacchus, gladness-giver,
and gracious Juno, too, be present here;   820
and favor, Tyrians, this feast with honor."
Her words were done. She offered her libation,
pouring her wine upon the boards; and then
she was the first to take the cup, but only
touching her lips to it. She passed it next
to Bitias and spurred him to be quick.
He drained the foaming cup with eagerness
and drenched himself in that gold flood; in turn
the other chieftains drank. Long-haired Iopas,
whom mighty Atlas once had taught, lifts up   830
his golden lyre, sounding through the hall.
He sings the wandering moon; the labors of
the sun; the origins of men and beasts,
of water and of fire; and of Arcturus,
the stormy Hyades, and the twin Bears;
and why the winter suns so rush to plunge
in Ocean: what holds back the lingering nights.
The Tyrians applaud again, again.
The Trojans follow. So the luckless Dido
drew out the night with varied talk. She drank   840
long love and asked Aeneas many questions:
of Priam; Hector; how Aurora's son
was armed; and now, how strong were Diomedes'
horses; now, how tremendous was Achilles.

"No, come, my guest," she calls, "and tell us all
things from the first beginning: Grecian guile,
your people's trials, and then your journeyings.
For now the seventh summer carries you,
a wanderer, across the lands and waters."

BOOK 2

[Aeneas tells his story to Dido:]

A sudden silence fell on all of them;
their eyes were turned, intent on him. And father
Aeneas, from his high couch, then began:

"O Queen—too terrible for tongues the pain
you ask me to renew, the tale of how
the Danaans could destroy the wealth of Troy,
that kingdom of lament: for I myself

saw these things; I took large part in them.
What Myrmidon or what Dolopian,
what soldier even of the harsh Ulysses,   10
could keep from tears in telling such a story?
But now the damp night hurries from the sky
into the sea; the falling stars persuade
to sleep. But if you long so much to learn
our suffering, to hear in brief the final
calamity of Troy—although my mind,
remembering, recoils in grief, and trembles,
I shall try.

       "The captains of the Danaans,
now weak with war and beaten back by fate,   20
and with so many gliding years gone by,
are able to construct, through the divine
art of Minerva, a mountainous horse.
They weave its ribs with sawed-off beams of fir,
pretending that it is an offering
for safe return. At least, that is their story.
Then in the dark sides of the horse they hide
men chosen from the sturdiest among them;
they stuff their soldiers in its belly, deep
in that vast cavern: Greeks armed to the teeth.   30

. . . .

[Aeneas describes the Trojan horse and the treachery of Sinon, who lied to the Trojans
in order to persuade them to accept the gift, deceiving them by false tears. As Troy is
falling, the shade of Hector appears to Aeneas, giving him responsibility to carry the
Vesta and other holy objects from Troy to Rome. Watching in horror as the youngest
son of Priam is murdered before his father's eyes, Aeneas is reminded of his own family.
He discovers that all of his troops are gone:]

Before me rose Creüsa, left alone,
my plundered home, the fate of small Iülus.
I look behind and scan the troops around me;
all of my men, worn out, have quit the battle,
have cast their bodies down along the ground
or fallen helplessly into the flames.

"And now that I am left alone, I see
the daughter of Tyndareos clinging
to Vesta's thresholds, crouching silently
within a secret corner of the shrine;
bright conflagrations give me light as I   40
wander and let my eyes read everything.
For she, in terror of the Trojans—set
against her for the fall of Pergamus—
and of the Danaans' vengeance and the anger

of her abandoned husband; she, the common
Fury of Troy and of her homeland, she
had hid herself; she crouched, a hated thing,
beside the altars. In my mind a fire
is burning; anger spurs me to avenge
my falling land, to exact the debt of crime.   50
'Is she to have it so: to leave unharmed,
see Sparta and her home Mycenae, go—
a victor queen in triumph—to look on
her house and husband, parents, children, trailing
a train of Trojan girls and Phrygian slaves?
Shall Troy have been destroyed by fire, Priam
been beaten by the blade, the Dardan shore
so often soaked with blood, to this end? No.
For though there is no memorable name
in punishing a woman and no gain   60
of honor in such victory, yet I
shall have my praise for blotting out a thing
of evil, for my punishing of one
who merits penalties; and it will be
a joy to fill my soul with vengeful fire,
to satisfy the ashes of my people.'

"And carried off by my mad mind, I was
still blurting out these words when, with such brightness
as I had never seen, my gracious mother
stood there before me; and across the night   70
she gleamed with pure light, unmistaken goddess,
as lovely and as tall as she appears
whenever she is seen by heaven's beings.
And while she caught and held my right hand fast,
she spoke these words to me with her rose lips:
'My son, what bitterness has kindled this
fanatic anger? Why this madness? What
of all your care for me—where has it gone?
Should you not first seek out your father, worn
with years, Anchises, where you left him; see   80
if your own wife, Creüsa, and the boy
Ascanius are still alive? The Argive
lines ring them all about; and if my care
had not prevented such an end, by now
flames would have swept them off, the hostile sword
have drunk their blood. And those to blame are not
the hated face of the Laconian woman,
the daughter of Tyndareos, or Paris:
it is the gods' relentlessness, the gods',
that overturns these riches, tumbles Troy   90
from its high pinnacle. Look now—for I

shall tear away each cloud that cloaks your eyes
and clogs your human seeing, darkening
all things with its damp fog: you must not fear
the orders of your mother; do not doubt,
but carry out what she commands. For here,
where you see huge blocks ripped apart and stones
torn free from stones and smoke that joins with dust
in surges, Neptune shakes the walls, his giant
trident is tearing Troy from its foundations;   100
and here the first to hold the Scaean gates
is fiercest Juno; girt with iron, she
calls furiously to the fleet for more
Greek troops. Now turn and look: Tritonian Pallas
is planted there; upon the tallest towers
she glares with her storm cloud and her grim Gorgon.
And he who furnishes the Greeks with force
that favors and with spirit is the Father
himself, for he himself goads on the gods
against the Dardan weapons. Son, be quick   110
to flee, have done with fighting. I shall never
desert your side until I set you safe
upon your father's threshold.' So she spoke,
then hid herself within the night's thick shadows.
Ferocious forms appear—the fearful powers
of gods that are the enemies of Troy.

"At this, indeed, I saw all Ilium
sink down into the fires; Neptune's Troy
is overturned: even as when the woodsmen
along a mountaintop are rivals in   120
their striving to bring down an ancient ash,
hacked at with many blows of iron and ax;
it always threatens falling, nodding with
its trembling leaves and tossing crest until,
slowly, slowly, the wounds have won; it gives
one last great groan, then wrenches from the ridges
and crashes into ruin. I go down
and, guided by a god, move on among
the foes and fires; weapons turn aside,
the flames retire where I make my way.   130

"But now, when I had reached my father's threshold,
Anchises' ancient house, our home—and I
longed so to carry him to the high mountains
and sought him first—he will not let his life
be drawn out after Troy has fallen, he
will not endure exile: 'You whose lifeblood
is fresh, whose force is still intact and tough,

you hurry your escape; if heaven's lords
had wanted longer life for me, they would
have saved my home. It is enough—and more—   140
that I have lived beyond one fall and sack
of Troy. Call out your farewell to my body
as it is now, thus laid out, thus; and then
be gone. I shall find death by my own hand;
the enemy will pity me and seek
my spoils. The loss of burial is easy.
For hated by the gods and useless, I
have lingered out my years too long already,
since that time when the father of the High Ones
and king of men let fly his thunderbolt   150
against me with the winds, touched me with lightning.'

"These were the words he used. He did not move.
We stood in tears—my wife, Creüsa, and
Ascanius and all the household—begging
my father not to bring down everything
along with him and make our fate more heavy.
He will not have it. What he wants is set;
he will not leave his place. Again I take
to arms and, miserable, long for death.
What other stratagem or chance is left?   160
And then I ask: 'My father, had you thought
I could go off and leave you here? Could such
unholiness fall from a father's lips?
For if it please the High Ones that no thing
be left of this great city, if your purpose
must still persist, if you want so to add
yourself and yours to Ilium's destruction—
why then, the door to death is open: Pyrrhus—
who massacres the son before his father's
eyes, and then kills the father at the altars—   170
still hot from Priam's blood, will soon be here.
And was it, then, for this, my gracious mother,
that you have saved me from the blade, the fire—
that I might see the enemy within
the heart of home, my son Ascanius,
my father, and Creüsa at their side,
all butchered in each other's blood? My men,
bring arms; the last light calls upon the beaten.
Let be, and let me at the Greeks again,
to make my way back to new battles. Never   180
shall we all die this day without revenge.'

"At that I girded on my sword again
and fixed it firm, passing my left hand through

my shield strap as I hurried from the house.
But suddenly Creüsa held me fast
beside the threshold; clinging to my feet,
she lifted young Iülus to his father:
'If you go off to die, then take us, too,
to face all things with you; but if your past
still lets you put your hope in arms, which now   190
you have put on, then first protect this house.
To whom is young Iülus left, to whom
your father and myself, once called your wife?'

"So did Creüsa cry; her wailing filled
my father's house. But even then there comes
a sudden omen—wonderful to tell:
between the hands, before the faces of
his grieving parents, over Iülus' head
there leaps a lithe flametip that seems to shed
a radiance; the tongue of fire flickers,   200
harmless, and plays about his soft hair, grazes
his temples. Shuddering in our alarm,
we rush to shake the flames out of his hair
and quench the holy fire with water. But
Anchises raised his glad eyes to the stars
and lifted heavenward his voice and hands:
'O Jupiter, all-able one, if you
are moved by any prayers, look on us.
I only ask you this: if by our goodness
we merit it, then, Father, grant to us   210
your help and let your sign confirm these omens.'

"No sooner had the old man spoken so
than sudden thunder crashed upon the left,
and through the shadows ran a shooting star,
its trail a torch of flooding light. It glides
above the highest housetops as we watch,
until the brightness that has marked its course
is buried in the woods of Ida: far
and wide the long wake of that furrow shines,
and sulphur smokes upon the land. At last,   220
won over by this sign, my father rises,
to greet the gods, to adore the sacred star:
'Now my delay is done; I follow; where
you lead, I am. Gods of my homeland, save
my household, save my grandson. Yours, this omen;
and Troy is in your keeping. Yes, I yield.
My son, I go with you as your companion.'

"These were his words. But now the fire roars
across the walls; the tide of flame flows nearer.
'Come then, dear father, mount upon my neck;   230
I'll bear you on my shoulders. That is not
too much for me. Whatever waits for us,
we both shall share one danger, one salvation.
Let young Iülus come with me, and let
my wife Creüsa follow at a distance.
And servants, listen well to what I say:
along the way, just past the city walls,
in an abandoned spot there is a mound,
an ancient shrine of Ceres; and nearby
an ancient cypress stands, one that our fathers'   240
devotion kept alive for many years.
From different directions, we shall meet
at this one point. My father, you will carry
the holy vessels and our homeland's gods.
Filthy with war, just come from slaughter, I
must never touch these sacred things until
I bathe myself within a running stream.'

"This said, I spread a tawny lion skin
across my bent neck, over my broad shoulders,
and then take up Anchises; small Iülus   250
now clutches my right hand; his steps uneven,
he is following his father; and my wife
moves on behind. We journey through dark places;
and I, who just before could not be stirred
by any weapons cast at me or by
the crowds of Greeks in charging columns, now
am terrified by all the breezes, startled
by every sound, in fear for son and father.

"And now, as I approached the gates and thought
I had found the way of my escape, the sudden   260
and frequent tramp of feet was at my ears;
and peering through the shades, Anchises cries:
'My son, take flight; my son, they are upon us.
I see their gleaming shields, the flashing bronze.'
At this alarm I panicked: some unfriendly
god's power ripped away my tangled mind.
For while I take a trackless path, deserting
the customary roads, fate tears from me
my wife Creüsa in my misery.
I cannot say if she had halted or   270
had wandered off the road or slumped down, weary.
My eyes have never had her back again.
I did not look behind for her, astray,

or think of her before we reached the mound
and ancient, sacred shrine of Ceres; here
at last, when all were gathered, she alone
was missing—gone from husband, son, companions.

"What men, what gods did I in madness not
accuse? Did I see anything more cruel
within the fallen city? I commit   280
Ascanius, Anchises, and the gods
of Troy to my companions, hiding them
inside a winding valley. I myself
again seek out the city, girding on
my gleaming arms. I want to meet all risks
again, return through all of Troy, again
give back my life to danger. First I seek
the city walls, the gateway's shadowed thresholds
through which I had come before. And I retrace
my footsteps; through the night I make them out.   290
My spirit is held by horror everywhere;
even the very silence terrifies.
Then I move homeward—if by chance, by chance,
she may have made her way there. But the Danaans
had flooded in and held the house. At once
the hungry conflagration rolls before
the wind, high as the highest rooftop; flames
are towering overhead, the boiling tide
is raging to the heavens. I go on;
again I see the house of Priam and   300
the fortress. Down the empty porticoes,
in Juno's sanctuary, I can see
both Phoenix and the fierce Ulysses, chosen
as guardians, at watch over the booty.
And here, from every quarter, heaped together,
are Trojan treasures torn from burning altars—
the tables of the gods, and plundered garments,
and bowls of solid gold; and Trojan boys
and trembling women stand in a long line.

"And more, I even dared to cast my cries
across the shadows; in my sorrow, I—   310
again, again, in vain—called for Creüsa;
my shouting filled the streets. But as I rushed
and raged among the houses endlessly,
before my eyes there stood the effigy
and grieving shade of my Creüsa, image
far larger than the real. I was dismayed;
my hair stood stiff, my voice held fast within
my jaws. She spoke; her words undid my cares:

"'O my sweet husband, is there any use   320
in giving way to such fanatic sorrow?
For this could never come to pass without
the gods' decree; and you are not to carry
Creüsa as your comrade, since the king
of high Olympus does not grant you that.
Along your way lie long exile, vast plains
of sea that you must plow; but you will reach
Hesperia, where Lydian Tiber flows,
a tranquil stream, through farmers' fruitful fields.
There days of gladness lie in wait for you: 330
a kingdom and a royal bride. Enough
of tears for loved Creüsa. I am not
to see the haughty homes of Myrmidons
or of Dolopians, or be a slave
to Grecian matrons—I, a Dardan woman
and wife of Venus' son. It is the gods'
great Mother who keeps me upon these shores.
And now farewell, and love the son we share.'

"When she was done with words—I weeping and
wanting to say so many things—she left   340
and vanished in transparent air. Three times
I tried to throw my arms around her neck;
three times the Shade I grasped in vain escaped
my hands—like fleet winds, most like a winged dream.

"And so at last, when night has passed, I go
again to my companions. Here I find,
to my surprise, new comrades come together,
vast numbers, men and women, joined for exile,
a crowd of sorrow. Come from every side,
with courage and with riches, they are ready   350
for any lands across the seas where I
may lead them. Now the star of morning rose
above high Ida's ridges, guiding the day.
The Danaans held the gates' blockaded thresholds.
There was no hope of help. Then I gave way
and, lifting up my father, made for the mountains."

BOOK 3

[Aeneas tells Dido of the divine command to seek out Italy. He describes his wanderings, including his encounters with the Harpies, filthy birds that foul everything they
touch. Helenus, a priest, tells him of the sign by which he will recognize the future site
of Rome when he arrives there—a white sow with thirty suckling pigs under a holly
branch. Arriving at the Cyclops's cave, Aeneas comes upon a sailor, Achaemenides, apparently left behind by Odysseus. Although Achaemenides is a Greek, and therefore an
enemy of Troy, Aeneas rescues him. At last, Aeneas and his men arrive at Libya. Meanwhile, Anchises, Aeneas's father, dies. With this last grief, Aeneas, now "father Aeneas,"
ends his tale.]

BOOK 4

Too late. The queen is caught between love's pain
and press. She feeds the wound within her veins;
she is eaten by a secret flame. Aeneas'
high name, all he has done, again, again
come like a flood. His face, his words hold fast
her breast. Care strips her limbs of calm and rest.

A new dawn lights the earth with Phoebus' lamp
and banishes damp shadows from the sky
when restless Dido turns to her heart's sharer:
"Anna, my sister, what dreams make me shudder?   10
Who is this stranger guest come to our house?
How confident he looks, how strong his chest
and arms! I think—and I have cause—that he
is born of gods. For in the face of fear
the mean must fall. What fates have driven him!
What trying wars he lived to tell! Were it not
my sure, immovable decision not
to marry anyone since my first love
turned traitor, when he cheated me by death,
were I not weary of the couch and torch,   20
I might perhaps give way to this one fault.
For I must tell you, Anna, since the time
Sychaeus, my poor husband, died and my
own brother splashed our household gods with blood,
Aeneas is the only man to move
my feelings, to overturn my shifting heart.
I know too well the signs of the old flame.
But I should call upon the earth to gape
and close above me, or on the almighty
Father to take his thunderbolt, to hurl   30
me down into the shades, the pallid shadows
and deepest night of Erebus, before
I'd violate you, Shame, or break your laws!
For he who first had joined me to himself
has carried off my love, and may he keep it
and be its guardian within the grave."
She spoke. Her breast became a well of tears.

And Anna answers: "Sister, you more dear
to me than light itself, are you to lose
all of your youth in dreary loneliness,   40
and never know sweet children or the soft
rewards of Venus? Do you think that ashes
or buried Shades will care about such matters?
Until Aeneas came, there was no suitor
who moved your sad heart—not in Libya nor,

before, in Tyre: you always scorned Iarbas
and all the other chiefs that Africa,
a region rich in triumphs, had to offer.
How can you struggle now against a love
that is so acceptable? Have you forgotten 50
the land you settled, those who hem you in?
On one side lie the towns of the Gaetulians,
a race invincible, and the unbridled
Numidians and then the barbarous Syrtis.
And on the other lies a barren country,
stripped by the drought and by Barcaean raiders,
raging both far and near. And I need not
remind you of the wars that boil in Tyre
and of your brother's menaces and plots.
For I am sure it was the work of gods 60
and Juno that has held the Trojan galleys
fast to their course and brought them here to Carthage.
If you marry Aeneas, what a city
and what a kingdom, sister, you will see!
With Trojan arms beside us, so much greatness
must lie in wait for Punic glory! Only
pray to the gods for their good will, and having
presented them with proper sacrifices,
be lavish with your Trojan guests and weave
excuses for delay while frenzied winter 70
storms out across the sea and shatters ships,
while wet Orion blows his tempest squalls
beneath a sky that is intractable."

These words of Anna fed the fire in Dido.
Hope burned away her doubt, destroyed her shame.
First they moved on from shrine to shrine, imploring
the favor of the gods at every altar.
They slaughter chosen sheep, as is the custom,
and offer them to Ceres the lawgiver,
to Phoebus, Father Bacchus, and—above all— 80
to Juno, guardian of marriage. Lovely
Dido holds the cup in her right hand;
she pours the offering herself, midway
between a milk-white heifer's horns. She studies
slit breasts of beasts and reads their throbbing guts.
But oh the ignorance of augurs! How
can vows and altars help one wild with love?
Meanwhile the supple flame devours her marrow;
within her breast the silent wound lives on.
Unhappy Dido burns. Across the city 90
she wanders in her frenzy—even as
a heedless hind hit by an arrow when
a shepherd drives for game with darts among

the Cretan woods and, unawares, from far
leaves winging steel inside her flesh; she roams
the forests and the wooded slopes of Dicte,
the shaft of death still clinging to her side.
So Dido leads Aeneas around the ramparts,
displays the wealth of Sidon and the city
ready to hand; she starts to speak, then falters   100
and stops in midspeech. Now day glides away.
Again, insane, she seeks out that same banquet,
again she prays to hear the trials of Troy,
again she hangs upon the teller's lips.

But now the guests are gone. The darkened moon,
in turn, conceals its light, the setting stars
invite to sleep; inside the vacant hall
she grieves alone and falls upon the couch
that he has left. Absent, she sees, she hears
the absent one or draws Ascanius,   110
his son and counterfeit, into her arms,
as if his shape might cheat her untellable love.

Her towers rise no more; the young of Carthage
no longer exercise at arms or build
their harbors or sure battlements for war;
the works are idle, broken off; the massive,
menacing rampart walls, even the crane,
defier of the sky, now lie neglected.

As soon as Jove's dear wife sees that her Dido
is in the grip of such a scourge and that   120
no honor can withstand this madness, then
the daughter of Saturn faces Venus: "How
remarkable indeed: what splendid spoils
you carry off, you and your boy; how grand
and memorable is the glory if
one woman is beaten by the guile of two
gods. I have not been blind. I know you fear
our fortresses, you have been suspicious of
the houses of high Carthage. But what end
will come of all this hate? Let us be done   130
with wrangling. Let us make, instead of war,
an everlasting peace and plighted wedding.
You have what you were bent upon: she burns
with love; the frenzy now is in her bones.
Then let us rule this people—you and I—
with equal auspices; let Dido serve
a Phrygian husband, let her give her Tyrians
and her pledged dowry into your right hand."

But Venus read behind the words of Juno
the motive she had hid: to shunt the kingdom   140
of Italy to Libyan shores. And so
she answered Juno: "Who is mad enough
to shun the terms you offer? Who would prefer
to strive with you in war? If only fortune
favor the course you urge. For I am ruled
by fates and am unsure if Jupiter
would have the Trojans and the men of Tyre
become one city, if he likes the mingling
of peoples and the writing of such treaties.
But you are his wife and it is right for you   150
to try his mind, to entreat him. Go. I'll follow."

Queen Juno answered her: "That task is mine.
But listen now while in few words I try
to tell you how I mean to bring about
this urgent matter. When tomorrow's Titan
first shows his rays of light, reveals the world,
Aeneas and unhappy Dido plan
to hunt together in the forest. Then
while horsemen hurry to surround the glades
with nets, I shall pour down a black raincloud,   160
in which I have mixed hail, to awaken all
the heavens with my thundering. Their comrades
will scatter under cover of thick night.
Both Dido and the Trojan chief will reach
their shelter in the same cave. I shall be there.
And if I can rely on your goodwill,
I shall unite the two in certain marriage
and seal her as Aeneas' very own;
and this shall be their wedding." Cytherea
said nothing to oppose the plan; she granted   170
what Juno wanted, smiling at its cunning.
Meanwhile Aurora rose; she left the Ocean.
And when her brightness fills the air, select
young men move from the gates with wide-meshed nets
and narrow snares and broad-blade hunting spears,
and then Massylian horsemen hurry out
with strong, keen-scented hounds. But while the chieftains
of Carthage wait at Dido's threshold, she
still lingers in her room. Her splendid stallion,
in gold and purple, prances, proudly champing   180
his foaming bit. At last the queen appears
among the mighty crowd; upon her shoulders
she wears a robe of Sidon with embroidered
borders. Her quiver is of gold, her hair
has knots and ties of gold, a golden clasp

holds fast her purple cloak. Her Trojan comrades
and glad Ascanius advance behind her.
Aeneas, who is handsome past all others,
himself approaches now to join her, linking
his hunting band to hers. Just as Apollo,   190
when in the winter he abandoned Lycia
and Xanthus' streams to visit his maternal
Delos, where he renews the dances—Cretans,
Dryopians, and painted Agathyrsi,
mingling around the altars, shout—advances
upon the mountain ridges of high Cynthus
and binds his flowing hair with gentle leaves
and braids its strands with intertwining gold;
his arrows clatter on his shoulder: no
less graceful is Aeneas as he goes;   200
an equal beauty fills his splendid face.
And when they reach the hills and pathless thickets,
the wild she-goats, dislodged from stony summits,
run down the ridges; from another slope
stags fling themselves across the open fields;
they mass their dusty bands in flight, forsaking
the hillsides. But the boy Ascanius
rides happy in the valleys on his fiery
stallion as he passes on his course
now stags, now goats; among the lazy herds   210
his prayer is for a foaming boar or that
a golden lion come down from the mountain.

Meanwhile confusion takes the sky, tremendous
turmoil, and on its heels, rain mixed with hail.
The scattered train of Tyre, the youth of Troy,
and Venus' Dardan grandson in alarm
seek different shelters through the fields; the torrents
roar down the mountains. Dido and the Trojan
chieftain have reached the same cave. Primal Earth
and Juno, queen of marriages, together   220
now give the signal: lightning fires flash,
the upper air is witness to their mating,
and from the highest hilltops shout the nymphs.
That day was her first day of death and ruin.
For neither how things seem nor how they are deemed
moves Dido now, and she no longer thinks
of furtive love. For Dido calls it marriage,
and with this name she covers up her fault.

Then, swiftest of all evils, Rumor runs
straightway through Libya's mighty cities—Rumor,   230
whose life is speed, whose going gives her force.

Timid and small at first, she soon lifts up
her body in the air. She stalks the ground;
her head is hidden in the clouds. Provoked
to anger at the gods, her mother Earth
gave birth to her, last come—they say—as sister
to Coeus and Enceladus; fast-footed
and lithe of wing, she is a terrifying
enormous monster with as many feathers
as she has sleepless eyes beneath each feather   240
(amazingly), as many sounding tongues
and mouths, and raises up as many ears.
Between the earth and skies she flies by night,
screeching across the darkness, and she never
closes her eyes in gentle sleep. By day
she sits as sentinel on some steep roof
or on high towers, frightening vast cities;
for she holds fast to falsehood and distortion
as often as to messages of truth.
Now she was glad. She filled the ears of all   250
with many tales. She sang of what was done
and what was fiction, chanting that Aeneas,
one born of Trojan blood, had come, that lovely
Dido has deigned to join herself to him,
that now, in lust, forgetful of their kingdom,
they take long pleasure, fondling through the winter,
the slaves of squalid craving. Such reports
the filthy goddess scatters everywhere
upon the lips of men. At once she turns
her course to King Iarbas; and his spirit   260
is hot, his anger rages at her words.
Iarbas was the son of Hammon by
a ravished nymph of Garamantia.
In his broad realm he had built a hundred temples,
a hundred handsome shrines for Jupiter.
There he had consecrated sleepless fire,
the everlasting watchman of the gods;
the soil was rich with blood of slaughtered herds,
and varied garlands flowered on the thresholds.
Insane, incited by that bitter rumor,   270
he prayed long—so they say—to Jupiter;
he stood before the altars in the presence
of gods, a suppliant with upraised hands:
"All-able Jove, to whom the Moorish nation,
feasting upon their figured couches, pour
Lenaean sacrifices, do you see
these things? Or, Father, are we only trembling
for nothing when you cast your twisting thunder?
Those fires in the clouds that terrify

our souls—are they but blind and aimless lightning   280
that only stirs our empty mutterings?
A woman, wandering within our borders,
paid for the right to build a tiny city.
We gave her shore to till and terms of tenure.
She has refused to marry me, she has taken
Aeneas as a lord into her lands.
And now this second Paris, with his crew
of half-men, with his chin and greasy hair
bound up beneath a bonnet of Maeonia,
enjoys his prey; while we bring offerings   290
to what we have believed to be your temples,
still cherishing your empty reputation."

And as he prayed and clutched the altar stone,
all-able Jupiter heard him and turned
his eyes upon the royal walls, upon
the lovers who had forgotten their good name.
He speaks to Mercury, commanding him:
"Be on your way, my son, call up the Zephyrs,
glide on your wings, speak to the Dardan chieftain
who lingers now at Tyrian Carthage, paying   300
not one jot of attention to the cities
the Fates have given him. Mercury, carry
across the speeding winds the words I urge:
his lovely mother did not promise such
a son to us; she did not save him twice
from Grecian arms for this—but to be master
of Italy, a land that teems with empire
and seethes with war; to father a race from Teucer's
high blood, to place all earth beneath his laws.
But if the brightness of such deeds is not   310
enough to kindle him, if he cannot
attempt the task for his own fame, does he—
a father—grudge Ascanius the walls
of Rome? What is he pondering, what hope
can hold him here among his enemies,
not caring for his own Ausonian sons
or for Lavinian fields. He must set sail.
And this is all; my message lies in this."

His words were ended. Mercury made ready
to follow his great father's orders. First   320
he laces on his golden sandals: winged
to bear him, swift as whirlwinds, high across
the land and water. Then he takes his wand;
with this he calls pale spirits up from Orcus
and down to dreary Tartarus sends others;

he uses this to give sleep and recall it,
and to unseal the eyes of those who have died.
His trust in this, he spurs the winds and skims
the troubled clouds. And now in flight, he sights
the summit and high sides of hardy Atlas   330
who props up heaven with his crest—Atlas,
whose head is crowned with pines and battered by
the wind and rain and always girdled by
black clouds; his shoulders' cloak is falling snow;
above the old man's chin the rivers rush;
his bristling beard is stiff with ice. Here first
Cyllene's god poised on his even wings
and halted; then he hurled himself headlong
and seaward with his body, like a bird
that, over shores and reefs where fishes throng,   340
swoops low along the surface of the waters.
Not unlike this, Cyllene's god between
the earth and heaven as he flies, cleaving
the sandy shore of Libya from the winds
that sweep from Atlas, father of his mother.

As soon as his winged feet have touched the outskirts,
he sees Aeneas founding fortresses
and fashioning new houses. And his sword
was starred with tawny jasper, and the cloak
that draped his shoulders blazed with Tyrian purple—   350
a gift that wealthy Dido wove for him;
she had run golden thread along the web.
And Mercury attacks at once. "Are you
now laying the foundation of high Carthage,
as servant to a woman, building her
a splendid city here? Are you forgetful
of what is your own kingdom, your own fate?
The very god of gods, whose power sways
both earth and heaven, sends me down to you
from bright Olympus. He himself has asked me   360
to carry these commands through the swift air:
what are you pondering or hoping for
while squandering your ease in Libyan lands?
For if the brightest of such deeds is not
enough to kindle you—if you cannot
attempt the task for your own fame—remember
Ascanius growing up, the hopes you hold
for Iülus, your own heir, to whom are owed
the realm of Italy and land of Rome."
So did Cyllene's god speak out. He left   370
the sight of mortals even as he spoke
and vanished into the transparent air.

This vision stunned Aeneas, struck him dumb;
his terror held his hair erect; his voice
held fast within his jaws. He burns to flee
from Carthage; he would quit these pleasant lands,
astonished by such warnings, the command
of gods. What can he do? With what words dare
he face the frenzied queen? What openings
can he employ? His wits are split, they shift   380
here, there; they race to different places, turning
to everything. But as he hesitated,
this seemed the better plan: he calls Sergestus
and Mnestheus and the strong Serestus, and
he asks them to equip the fleet in silence,
to muster their companions on the shore,
to ready all their arms, but to conceal
the reasons for this change; while he himself—
with gracious Dido still aware of nothing
and never dreaming such a love could ever   390
be broken—would try out approaches, seek
the tenderest, most tactful time for speech,
whatever dexterous way might suit his case.
And all are glad. They race to carry out
the orders of Aeneas, his commands.

But Dido—for who can deceive a lover?—
had caught his craftiness; she quickly sensed
what was to come; however safe they seemed,
she feared all things. That same unholy Rumor
brought her these hectic tidings: that the boats   400
were being armed, made fit for voyaging.
Her mind is helpless; raging frantically,
inflamed, she raves throughout the city—just
as a Bacchante when, each second year,
she is startled by the shaking of the sacred
emblems, the orgies urge her on, the cry
"o Bacchus" calls to her by night; Cithaeron
incites her with its clamor. And at last
Dido attacks Aeneas with these words:

"Deceiver, did you even hope to hide   410
so harsh a crime, to leave this land of mine
without a word? Can nothing hold you back—
neither your love, the hand you pledged, nor even
the cruel death that lies in wait for Dido?
Beneath the winter sky are you preparing
a fleet to rush away across the deep
among the north winds, you who have no feeling?
What! Even if you were not seeking out

strange fields and unknown dwellings, even if
your ancient Troy were still erect, would you   420
return to Troy across such stormy seas?
Do you flee me? By tears, by your right hand—
this sorry self is left with nothing else—
by wedding, by the marriage we began,
if I did anything deserving of you
or anything of mine was sweet to you,
take pity on a fallen house, put off
your plan, I pray—if there is still place for prayers.
Because of you the tribes of Libya, all
the Nomad princes hate me, even my   430
own Tyrians are hostile; and for you
my honor is gone and that good name that once
was mine, my only claim to reach the stars.
My guest, to whom do you consign this dying
woman? I must say 'guest': this name is all
I have of one whom once I called my husband.
Then why do I live on? Until Pygmalion,
my brother, batters down my walls, until
Iarbas the Gaetulian takes me prisoner?
Had I at least before you left conceived   440
a son in me; if there were but a tiny
Aeneas playing by me in the hall,
whose face, in spite of everything, might yet
remind me of you, then indeed I should
not seem so totally abandoned, beaten."
Her words were ended. But Aeneas, warned
by Jove, held still his eyes; he struggled, pressed
care back within his breast. With halting words
he answers her at last: "I never shall
deny what you deserve, the kindnesses   450
that you could tell; I never shall regret
remembering Elissa for as long
as I remember my own self, as long
as breath is king over these limbs. I'll speak
brief words that fit the case. I never hoped
to hide—do not imagine that—my flight;
I am not furtive. I have never held
the wedding torches as a husband; I
have never entered into such agreements.
If fate had granted me to guide my life   460
by my own auspices and to unravel
my troubles with unhampered will, then I
should cherish first the town of Troy, the sweet
remains of my own people and the tall
rooftops of Priam would remain, my hand
would plant again a second Pergamus

for my defeated men. But now Grynean
Apollo's oracles would have me seize
great Italy, the Lycian prophecies
tell me of Italy: there is my love,   470
there is my homeland. If the fortresses
of Carthage and the vision of a city
in Libya can hold you, who are Phoenician,
why, then, begrudge the Trojans' settling on
Ausonian soil? There is no harm: it is
right that we, too, seek out a foreign kingdom.
For often as the night conceals the earth
with dew and shadows, often as the stars
ascend, afire, my father's anxious image
approaches me in dreams. Anchises warns   480
and terrifies. I see the wrong I have done
to one so dear, my boy Ascanius,
whom I am cheating of Hesperia,
the fields assigned by fate. And now the gods'
own messenger, send down by Jove himself—
I call as witness both our lives—has brought
his orders through the swift air. My own eyes
have seen the god as he was entering
our walls—in broad daylight. My ears have drunk
his words. No longer set yourself and me   490
afire. Stop your quarrel. It is not
my own free will that leads to Italy."

But all the while Aeneas spoke, she stared
askance at him, her glance ran this way, that.
She scans his body with her silent eyes.
Then Dido thus, inflamed, denounces him:

"No goddess was your mother, false Aeneas,
and Dardanus no author of your race;
the bristling Caucasus was father to you
on his harsh crags; Hyrcanian tigresses   500
gave you their teats. And why must I dissemble?
Why hold myself in check? For greater wrongs?
For did Aeneas groan when I was weeping?
Did he once turn his eyes, or, overcome,
shed tears or pity me, who was his loved one?
What shall I cry out first? And what shall follow?
No longer now does mighty Juno or
our Father, son of Saturn, watch this earth
with righteous eyes. Nowhere is certain trust.
He was an outcast on the shore, in want.   510
I took him in and madly let him share
my kingdom; his lost fleet and his companions

I saved from death. Oh I am whirled along
in fire by the Furies! First the augur
Apollo, then the Lycian oracles,
and now, sent down by Jove himself, the gods'
own herald, carrying his horrid orders.
This seems indeed to be a work for High Ones,
a care that can disturb their calm. I do not
refute your words. I do not keep you back.   520
Go then, before the winds, to Italy.
Seek out your kingdom overseas; indeed,
if there be pious powers still, I hope
that you will drink your torments to the lees
among sea rocks and, drowning, often cry
the name of Dido. Then, though absent, I
shall hunt you down with blackened firebrands;
and when chill death divides my soul and body,
a Shade, I shall be present everywhere.
Depraved, you then will pay your penalties.   530
And I shall hear of it, and that report
will come to me below, among the Shadows."

Her speech is broken off; heartsick, she shuns
the light of day, deserts his eyes; she turns
away, leaves him in fear and hesitation,
Aeneas longing still to say so much.
As Dido faints, her servants lift her up;
they carry her into her marble chamber;
they lay her body down upon the couch.

But though he longs to soften, soothe her sorrow   540
and turn aside her troubles with sweet words,
though groaning long and shaken in his mind
because of his great love, nevertheless
pious Aeneas carries out the gods'
instructions. Now he turns back to his fleet.

. . . .

[Dido utters a long lament over her fate. Furious at Aeneas, she appeals to Juno, Hecate, and the Furies to punish Aeneas with suffering and calls for an avenger:]

These things I plead; these final words I pour
out of my blood. Then, Tyrians, hunt down
with hatred all his sons and race to come;
send this as offering unto my ashes.
Do not let love or treaty tie our peoples.   550
May an avenger rise up from my bones,
one who will track with firebrand and sword
the Dardan settlers, now and in the future,
at any time that ways present themselves.

I call your shores to war against their shores,
your waves against their waves, arms with their arms.
Let them and their sons' sons learn what is war."

This said, she ran her mind to every side,
for she was seeking ways with which to slice—
as quickly as she can—the hated light;   560
and then, with these brief words, she turned to Barce,
Sychaeus' nurse—for Dido's own was now
black ashes in Phoenicia, her old homeland:
"Dear nurse, call here to me my sister Anna;
and tell her to be quick to bathe her body
with river water; see that she brings cattle
and all that is appointed for atonement.
So must my sister come; while you yourself
bind up your temples with a pious fillet.   570
I mean to offer unto Stygian Jove
the sacrifices that, as is ordained,
I have made ready and begun, to put
an end to my disquiet and commit
to flames the pyre of the Trojan chieftain."
So Dido spoke. And Barce hurried off;
she moved with an old woman's eagerness.

But Dido, desperate, beside herself
with awful undertakings, eyes bloodshot
and rolling, and her quivering cheeks flecked
with stains and pale with coming death, now bursts   580
across the inner courtyards of her palace.
She mounts in madness that high pyre, unsheathes
the Dardan sword, a gift not sought for such
an end. And when she saw the Trojan's clothes
and her familiar bed, she checked her thought
and tears a little, lay upon the couch
and spoke her final words: "O relics, dear
while fate and god allowed, receive my spirit
and free me from these cares; for I have lived
and journeyed through the course assigned by fortune.   590
And now my Shade will pass, illustrious,
beneath the earth; I have built a handsome city,
have seen my walls rise up, avenged a husband,
won satisfaction from a hostile brother:
o fortunate, too fortunate—if only
the ships of Troy had never touched our coasts."
She spoke and pressed her face into the couch.
"I shall die unavenged, but I shall die,"
she says, "Thus, thus, I gladly go below
to shadows. May the savage Dardan drink   600

with his own eyes this fire from the deep
and take with him the omen of my death."

Then Dido's words were done, and her companions
can see her fallen on the sword; the blade
is foaming with her blood, her hands are bloodstained.
Now clamor rises to the high rooftop.
Now rumor riots through the startled city.
The lamentations, keening, shrieks of women
sound through the houses; heavens echo mighty
wailings, even as if an enemy   610
were entering the gates, with all of Carthage
or ancient Tyre in ruins, and angry fires
rolling across the homes of men and gods.

. . . .

BOOK 5

[Having escaped from Carthage, Aeneas holds funeral games to commemorate the death
of his father, Anchises. Neptune casts the helmsman Palinarus into the sea as a sacrifice
to Juno's anger.]

BOOK 6

[Guided by the Cumaean Sibyl, Aeneus enters the Underworld, where he uses the Golden Bough to compel Charon to ferry him across the River Styx:]

. . . .

The journey they began can now continue.
They near the riverbank. Even the boatman,
while floating on the Styx, had seen them coming
across the silent grove and toward the shore.
He does not wait for greeting but attacks,
insulting with these words: "Enough! Stop there!
Whoever you may be who make your way,
so armed, down to our waters, tell me now
why you have come. This is the land of shadows,
of Sleep and drowsy Night; no living bodies   10
can take their passage in the ship of Styx.
Indeed, I was not glad to have Alcides
or Theseus or Pirithoüs cross the lake,
although the three of them were sons of gods
and undefeated in their wars. Alcides
tried to drag off in chains the guardian
of Tartarus; he tore him, trembling, from
the king's own throne. The others tried to carry
the queen away from Pluto's wedding chamber."

Apollo's priestess answered briefly: "We   20
bring no such trickery; no need to be

disturbed; our weapons bear no violence;
for us, the mighty watchman can bark on
forever in his cavern, frightening
the bloodless shades; Proserpina can keep
the threshold of her uncle faithfully.
Trojan Aeneas, famed for piety
and arms, descends to meet his father, down
into the deepest shades of Erebus.
And if the image of such piety   30
is not enough to move you, then"—and here
she shows the branch concealed beneath her robe—
"you may yet recognize this bough." At this
the swollen heart of Charon stills its anger.
He says no more. He wonders at the sacred
gift of the destined wand, so long unseen,
and turns his blue-black keel toward shore. He clears
the other spirits from the gangways and
long benches and, meanwhile, admits the massive
Aeneas to the boat, the vessel's seams   40
groaning beneath the weight as they let in
marsh water through the chinks. At last he sets
the priestess and the soldier safe across
the stream in ugly slime and blue-gray sedge.

These regions echo with the triple-throated
bark of the giant Cerberus, who crouches,
enormous, in a cavern facing them.
The Sibyl, seeing that his neck is bristling
with snakes, throws him a honeyed cake of wheat
with drugs that bring on sleep. His triple mouths   50
yawn wide with rapid hunger as he clutches
the cake she cast. His giant back falls slack
along the ground; his bulk takes all the cave.
And when the beast is buried under sleep,
Aeneas gains the entrance swiftly, leaves
the riverbank from which no one returns.

Here voices and loud lamentations echo:
the souls of infants weeping at the very
first threshold—torn away by the black day,
deprived of their sweet life, ripped from the breast,   60
plunged into bitter death. And next to them
are those condemned to die upon false charges.
These places have not been assigned, indeed,
without a lot, without a judge; for here
Minos is magistrate. He shakes the urn
and calls on the assembly of the silent,
to learn the lives of men and their misdeeds.

The land that lies beyond belongs to those
who, although innocent, took death by their
own hands; hating the light, they threw away   70
their lives. But now they long for the upper air,
and even to bear want and trials there.
But fate refuses them: the melancholy
marshland, its ugly waters, hem them in,
the prisoners of Styx and its nine circles.

Nearby, spread out on every side, there lie
the Fields of Mourning: this, their given name.
And here, concealed by secret paths, are those
whom bitter love consumed with brutal waste;
a myrtle grove encloses them; their pains   80
remain with them in death. Aeneas sees
Phaedra and Procris and sad Eriphyle,
who pointed to the wounds inflicted by
her savage son; he sees Pasiphaë
and then Evadne; and Laodamia
and Caeneus, once a youth and now a woman,
changed back again by fate to her first shape.

Among them, wandering in that great forest,
and with her wound still fresh: Phoenician Dido.
And when the Trojan hero recognized her   90
dim shape among the shadows (just as one
who either sees or thinks he sees among
the cloud banks, when the month is young, the moon
rising), he wept and said with tender love:
"Unhappy Dido, then the word I had
was true? That you were dead? That you pursued
your final moment with the sword? Did I
bring only death to you? Queen, I swear by
the stars, the gods above, and any trust
that may be in this underneath, I was   100
unwilling when I had to leave your shores.
But those same orders of the gods that now
urge on my journey through the shadows, through
abandoned, thorny lands and deepest night,
drove me by their decrees. And I could not
believe that with my going I should bring
so great a grief as this. But stay your steps.
Do not retreat from me. Whom do you flee?
This is the last time fate will let us speak."
These were the words Aeneas, weeping, used,   110
trying to soothe the burning, fierce-eyed Shade.
She turned away, eyes to the ground, her face
no more moved by his speech than if she stood

as stubborn flint or some Marpessan crag.
At last she tore herself away; she fled—
and still his enemy—into the forest
of shadows, where Sychaeus, once her husband,
answers her sorrows, gives her love for love.
Nevertheless, Aeneas, stunned by her
unkindly fate, still follows at a distance   120
with tears and pity for her as she goes.

He struggles on his given way again.
Now they have reached the borderlands of this
first region, the secluded home of those
renowned in war. Here he encounters Tydeus,
Parthenopaeus, famous soldier, and
the pale shade of Adrastus; here are men
mourned in the upper world, the Dardan captains
fallen in battle. And for all of these,
on seeing them in long array, he grieves: 130
for Glaucus, Medon, and Thersilochus,
the three sons of Antenor; Polyboetes,
who was a priest of Ceres; and Idaeus,
still clinging to his chariot, his weapons.
The spirits crowd Aeneas right and left,
and it is not enough to see him once;
they want to linger, to keep step with him,
to learn the reasons for his visit there.
But when the Grecian chieftains and the hosts
of Agamemnon see the hero and   140
his weapons glittering across the shadows,
they tremble with an overwhelming terror;
some turn their backs in flight, as when they once
sought out their ships; some raise a thin war cry;
the voice they now have mocks their straining throats.

And here Aeneas saw the son of Priam,
Deiphobus, all of his body mangled,
his face torn savagely, his face and both
his hands, his ears lopped off his ravaged temples,
his nostrils slashed by a disgraceful wound.   150
How hard it was to recognize the trembling
Shade as he tried to hide his horrid torments.
Aeneas does not wait to hear his greeting
but with familiar accents speaks to him:
"Deiphobus, great warrior, and born
of Teucer's brilliant blood, who made you pay
such brutal penalties? Who was allowed
to do such violence to you? For Rumor
had told me that on that last night, worn out

by your vast slaughter of the Greeks, you sank   160
upon a heap of tangled butchery.
Then I myself raised up an empty tomb
along Rhoeteum's shore; three times I called
loudly upon your Shade. Your name and weapons
now mark the place. I could not find you, friend,
or bury you, before I left, within
your native land." The son of Priam answered:

"My friend, you left no thing undone; you paid
Deiphobus and his dead Shade their due.
But I was cast into these evils by   170
my own fate and the deadly treachery
of the Laconian woman; it was she
who left me these memorials. You know
and must remember all too well how we
spent that last night among deceiving pleasures.
For when across high Pergamus the fatal
horse leaped and, in its pregnant belly, carried
armed infantry, she mimed a choral dance
and, shrieking in a Bacchic orgy, paced
the Phrygian women; it was she herself   180
who held a giant firebrand and, from
the citadel, called in the Danaans.
I lay, sleep-heavy, worn with cares, within
our luckless bridal chamber, taken by
a sweet, deep rest much like the peace of death.
And meanwhile my incomparable wife
has stripped the house of every weapon, even
removing from beneath my head my trusted
sword; and she throws the doorway open, calls
her Menelaeus to my palace, hoping   190
her lover surely will be grateful for
this mighty favor, and her infamy
for old misdeeds will be forgotten. Why
delay? They burst into my room. The son
of Aeolus joins them as a companion,
encourager of outrage. Gods, requite
the Greeks for this if with my pious lips
I ask for satisfaction. But, in turn,
come tell me what misfortunes bring you here
alive? Have you been driven here by sea   200
wanderings or by warnings of the gods?
What fate so wearies you that you would visit
these sad and sunless dwellings, restless lands?"

But as they talked together, through the sky
Aurora with her chariot of rose

had passed her midpoint; and they might have spent
all this allotted time with words had not
the Sibyl, his companion, warned him thus:
"The night is near, Aeneas, and we waste
our time with tears. For here the road divides   210
in two directions: on the right it runs
beneath the ramparts of great Dis, this is
our highway to Elysium; the wicked
are punished on the left—that path leads down
to godless Tartarus." Deiphobus:
"Do not be angry, mighty priestess, I
now leave to fill the count, return to darkness.
Go on, our glory, go; know better fates."
He said no more; his steps turned at these words.

Aeneas suddenly looks back; beneath   220
a rock upon his left he sees a broad
fortress encircled by a triple wall
and girdled by a rapid flood of flames
that rage: Tartarean Phlegethon whirling
resounding rocks. A giant gateway stands
in front, with solid adamantine pillars—
no force of man, not even heaven's sons,
enough to level these in war; a tower
of iron rises in the air; there sits
Tisiphone, who wears a bloody mantle.   230
She guards the entrance, sleepless night and day.
Both groans and savage scourgings echo there,
and then the clang of iron and dragging chains.

Aeneas stopped in terror, and the din
held him. "What kind of crimes are these? Virgin,
o speak! What penalties are paid here? What
loud lamentations fill the air?" The priestess
began: "Great captain of the Teucrians,
no innocent can cross these cursed thresholds;
but when the goddess Hecate made me   240
the guardian of Avernus' groves, then she
revealed the penalties the gods decreed
and guided me through all the halls of hell.
The king of these harsh realms is Rhadamanthus
the Gnosian: he hears men's crimes and then
chastises and compels confession for
those guilts that anyone, rejoicing, hid—
but uselessly—within the world above,
delaying his atonement till too late,
beyond the time of death. Tisiphone   250
at once is the avenger, armed with whips;

she leaps upon the guilty, lashing them;
in her left hand she grips her gruesome vipers
and calls her savage company of sisters.
And now at last the sacred doors are opened,
their hinges grating horribly. You see
what kind of sentry stands before the entrance,
what shape is at the threshold? Fiercer still,
the monstrous Hydra lives inside; her fifty
black mouths are gaping. Tartarus itself   260
then plunges downward, stretching twice as far
as is the view to heaven, high Olympus.
And here the ancient family of Earth,
the sons of Titan who had been cast down
by thunderbolts, writhe in the deepest gulf.
Here, too, I saw the giant bodies of
the twin sons of Aloeus, those who tried
to rip high heaven with their hands, to harry
Jove from his realms above. I saw Salmoneus:
how brutal were the penalties he paid   270
for counterfeiting Jove's own fires and
the thunders of Olympus. For he drove
four horses, brandishing a torch; he rode
triumphant through the tribes of Greece and through
the city in the heart of Elis, asking
for his own self the honor due to gods:
a madman who would mime the tempests and
inimitable thunder with the clang
of bronze and with the tramp of horn-foot horses.
But through the thick cloud banks all-able Jove   280
let fly his shaft—it was no firebrand
or smoky glare of torches: an enormous
blast of the whirlwind drove Salmoneus headlong.
And I saw Tityos, the foster child
of Earth, mother of all, his body stretched
on nine whole acres; and a crooked-beaked
huge vulture feeds upon his deathless liver
and guts that only grow the fruits of grief.
The vulture has his home deep in the breast
of Tityos, and there he tears his banquets   290
and gives no rest even to new-grown flesh.
And must I tell you of Ixion and
Pirithoüs, the Lapithae? Of those
who always stand beneath a hanging black
flint rock that is about to slip, to fall,
forever threatening? And there are those
who sit before high banquet couches, gleaming
upon supports of gold; before their eyes
a feast is spread in royal luxury,

but near at hand reclines the fiercest Fury: 300
they cannot touch the tables lest she leap
with lifted torch and thundering outcries.
And here are those who in their lives had hated
their brothers or had struck their father or
deceived a client or (the thickest swarm)
had brooded all alone on new-won treasure
and set no share apart for kin and friends;
those slain for their adultery; those who followed
rebellious arms or broke their pledge to masters—
imprisoned, all await their punishment.   310
And do not ask of me what penalty,
what shape or fate has overwhelmed their souls.
For some are made to roll a giant boulder,
and some are stretched along the spokes of wheels.
Sad Theseus has to sit and sit forever;
and miserable Phlegyas warns them all—
his roaring voice bears witness through the darkness:
'Be warned, learn justice, do not scorn the gods!'
Here is one who sold his fatherland for gold
and set a tyrant over it; he made   320
and unmade laws for gain. This one assailed
the chamber of his daughter and compelled
forbidden mating. All dared horrid evil
and reached what they had dared. A hundred tongues,
a hundred mouths, an iron voice were not
enough for me to gather all the forms
of crime or tell the names of all the torments."
So did the aged priestess of Apollo
speak, and she adds, "But come now, on your way,
complete the task you chose. Let us be quick.   330
I see the walls the Cyclops forged, the gates
with arching fronts, where we were told to place
our gifts." She has spoken. Side by side they move
along the shaded path; and hurrying
across the space between, they near the doors.
Aeneas gains the entrance, and he sprinkles
his body with fresh water, then he sets
the bough across the threshold facing them.

Their tasks were now completed; they had done
all that the goddess had required of them.   340
They came upon the lands of gladness, glades
of gentleness, the Groves of Blessedness—
a gracious place. The air is generous;
the plains wear dazzling light; they have their very
own sun and their own stars. Some exercise
their limbs along the green gymnasiums

or grapple on the golden sand, compete
in sport, and some keep time with moving feet
to dance and chant. There, too, the Thracian priest,
the long-robed Orpheus, plays, accompanying   350
with seven tones; and now his fingers strike
the strings, and now his quill of ivory.

The ancient race of Teucer, too, is here,
most handsome sons, great-hearted heroes born
in better years: Assaracus and Ilus
and Dardanus, who founded Pergamus.
From far Aeneas wonders at their phantom
armor and chariots; their spears are planted,
fixed in the ground; their horses graze and range
freely across the plain. The very same   360
delight that once was theirs in life—in arms
and chariots and care to pasture their
sleek steeds—has followed to this underearth.

And here to right and left he can see others:
some feasting on the lawns; and some chanting
glad choral paeans in a fragrant laurel
grove. Starting here, Eridanus in flood
flows through a forest to the world above.
Here was the company of those who suffered
wounds, fighting for their homeland; and of those   370
who, while they lived their lives, served as pure priests;
and then the pious poets, those whose songs
were worthy of Apollo; those who had
made life more civilized with newfound arts;
and those whose merits won the memory
of men: all these were crowned with snow-white garlands.
And as they streamed around her there, the Sibyl
addressed them, and Musaeus before all—
he stood, his shoulders towering above
a thronging crowd whose eyes looked up to him: 380
"O happy souls and you the best of poets,
tell us what land, what place it is that holds
Anchises. It is for his sake we have come
across the mighty streams of Erebus."

The hero answered briefly: "None of us
has one fixed home: we live in shady groves
and settle on soft riverbanks and meadows
where fresh streams flow. But if the will within
your heart is bent on this, then climb the hill
and I shall show to you an easy path."   390
He spoke, and led the way, and from the ridge
he pointed out bright fields. Then they descend.

But in the deep of a green valley, father
Anchises, lost in thought, was studying
the souls of all his sons to come—though now
imprisoned, destined for the upper light.
And as it happened, he was telling over
the multitude of all his dear descendants,
his heroes' fates and fortunes, works and ways.
And when he saw Aeneas cross the meadow,   400
he stretched out both hands eagerly, the tears
ran down his cheeks, these words fell from his lips:

"And have you come at last, and has the pious
love that your father waited for defeated
the difficulty of the journey? Son,
can I look at your face, hear and return
familiar accents? So indeed I thought,
imagining this time to come, counting
the moments, and my longing did not cheat me.
What lands and what wide waters have you journeyed   410
to make this meeting possible? My son,
what dangers battered you? I feared the kingdom
of Libya might do so much harm to you."

Then he: "My father, it was your sad image,
so often come, that urged me to these thresholds.
My ships are moored on the Tyrrhenian.
O father, let me hold your right hand fast,
do not withdraw from my embrace." His face
was wet with weeping as he spoke. Three times
he tried to throw his arms around Anchises'   420
neck; and three times the Shade escaped from that
vain clasp—like light winds, or most like swift dreams.

Meanwhile, Aeneas in a secret valley
can see a sheltered grove and sounding forests
and thickets and the stream of Lethe flowing
past tranquil dwellings. Countless tribes and peoples
were hovering there: as in the meadows, when
the summer is serene, the bees will settle
upon the many-colored flowers and crowd
the dazzling lilies—all the plain is murmuring.   430
The sudden sight has startled him. Aeneas,
not knowing, asks for reasons, wondering
about the rivers flowing in the distance,
the heroes swarming toward the riverbanks.
Anchises answers him: "These are the spirits
to whom fate owes a second body, and
they drink the waters of the river Lethe,
the care-less drafts of long forgetfulness.

How much, indeed, I longed to tell you of them,
to show them to you face to face, to number   440
all of my seed and race, that you rejoice
the more with me at finding Italy."

"But, Father, can it be that any souls
would ever leave their dwelling here to go
beneath the sky of earth, and once again
take on their sluggish bodies? Are they madmen?
Why this wild longing for the light of earth?"
"Son, you will have the answer; I shall not
keep you in doubt," Anchises starts and then
reveals to him each single thing in order.   450

"First, know, a soul within sustains the heaven
and earth, the plains of water, and the gleaming
globe of the moon, the Titan sun, the stars;
and mind, that pours through every member, mingles
with that great body. Born of these: the race
of men and cattle, flying things, and all
the monsters that the sea has bred beneath
its glassy surface. Fiery energy
is in these seeds, their source is heavenly;
but they are dulled by harmful bodies, blunted   460
by their own earthly limbs, their mortal members.
Because of these, they fear and long, and sorrow
and joy, they do not see the light of heaven;
they are dungeoned in their darkness and blind prison.
And when the final day of life deserts them,
then, even then, not every ill, not all
the plagues of body quit them utterly;
and this must be, for taints so long congealed
cling fast and deep in extraordinary
ways. Therefore they are schooled by punishment   470
and pay with torments for their old misdeeds:
some there are purified by air, suspended
and stretched before the empty winds; for some
the stain of guilt is washed away beneath
a mighty whirlpool or consumed by fire.
First each of us must suffer his own Shade;
then we are sent through wide Elysium—
a few of us will gain the Fields of Gladness—
until the finished cycle of the ages,
with lapse of days, annuls the ancient stain   480
and leaves the power of ether pure in us, .
the fire of spirit simple and unsoiled.
But all the rest, when they have passed time's circle
for a millennium, are summoned by

the god to Lethe in a great assembly
that, free of memory, they may return
beneath the curve of the upper world, that they
may once again begin to wish for bodies."

Anchises ended, drew the Sibyl and
his son into the crowd, the murmuring throng,   490
then gained a vantage from which he could scan
all of the long array that moved toward them,
to learn their faces as they came along:

"Listen to me: my tongue will now reveal
the fame that is to come from Dardan sons
and what Italian children wait for you—
bright souls that are about to take your name;
in them I shall unfold your fates. The youth
you see there, leaning on his headless spear,
by lot is nearest to the light; and he   500
will be the first to reach the upper air
and mingle with Italian blood; an Alban,
his name is Silvius, your last-born son.
For late in your old age Lavinia,
your wife, will bear him for you in the forest;
and he will be a king and father kings;
through him our race will rule in Alba Longa.
Next Procas stands, pride of the Trojan race;
then Capys, Numitor, and he who will
restore your name as Silvius Aeneas,   510
remarkable for piety and arms
if he can ever gain his Alban kingdom.
What young men you see here, what powers they
display, and how they bear the civic oak
that shades their brows! For you they will construct
Nomentum, Gabii, Fidena's city,
and with the ramparts of Collatia,
Pometia and Castrum Inui,
and Bola, Cora, they will crown the hills.
These will be names that now are nameless lands.   520

"More: Romulus, a son of Mars. He will
join Numitor, his grandfather, on earth
when Ilia, his mother, gives him birth
out of the bloodline of Assaracus.
You see the double plumes upon his crest:
his parent Mars already marks him out
with his own emblem for the upper world.
My son, it is beneath his auspices
that famous Rome will make her boundaries

as broad as earth itself, will make her spirit   530
the equal of Olympus, and enclose
her seven hills within a single wall,
rejoicing in her race of men: just as
the Berecynthian mother, tower-crowned,
when, through the Phrygian cities, she rides on
her chariot, glad her sons are gods, embraces
a hundred sons of sons, and every one
a heaven-dweller with his home on high.

"Now turn your two eyes here, to look upon
your Romans, your own people. Here is Caesar   540
and all the line of Iülus that will come
beneath the mighty curve of heaven. This,
this is the man you heard so often promised—
Augustus Caesar, son of a god, who will
renew a golden age in Latium,
in fields where Saturn once was king, and stretch
his rule beyond the Garamantes and
the Indians—a land beyond the paths
of year and sun, beyond the constellations,
where on his shoulders heaven-holding Atlas   550
revolves the axis set with blazing stars.

.   .   .   .

[The shade of Anchises, telling Aeneas of the wars he must wage, warns him not to let war be "native to his mind" and advises the future Caesar to show tolerance. Aeneas leaves the Underworld through the Gate of Ivory, traditionally the gate of false dreams.]

BOOK 7

[Aeneas and his ships land in Italy. Virgil begins this, his "greater theme," with a second invocation, this time to deal with "arms." Lavinia, daughter of King Latinus, is wooed by many, including Turnus, the Ausonian prince, who is favored by Lavinia's mother. But King Latinus is told by an oracle to marry Lavinia not to a Latin but to a stranger who will raise their name above the stars. Juno renews her threat: Aeneas will be another Paris, to destroy yet another Troy. She persuades Allecto, the spirit of violence and war from the Underworld, to arouse Lavinia's mother and also Turnus, who, thus enraged, calls for war. The series of alliances and a catalogue of the huge armies and their leaders are described.]

BOOK 8

[The river god Tibernius shows Aeneas the sign of the white sow and the thirty suckling pigs and assures him of his fate. He tells Aeneas to seek alliance with Evander, king of Arcadia and father of Prince Pallas, who freely offers to join Aeneas. Arcadia will be the future site of Rome. Venus, Aeneas's mother, persuades Vulcan to aid the Trojans. The god forges a shield for Aeneas decorated with scenes depicting the history of Rome-to-be, including Augustus Caesar, shown leading the Italian Senate and the people, the household gods, and the great gods to battle.]

BOOK 9

[The battle begins. Turnus tries to set the Trojan ships on fire, but they are rescued by Jupiter at the command of Cybele (his mother) herself. On the field, Turnus exhibits "rage and insane desire for slaughter," in contrast to the restraint of Aeneas.]

BOOK 10

[Jupiter requests of the gods in council a league of peace, but Venus and Juno cannot agree. Then Jupiter insists that the gods not intervene in humans' battles. On the field, Turnus kills Pallas, stripping him of the gold belt. The narrator himself steps in here to comment on Turnus's overweening pride and the fact that he will come to regret this act. Pallas's death arouses Aeneas's fury, and he plunges into battle "with hating heart," kicking the bodies of his victims. He searches for Turnus, but Juno tricks Turnus into fleeing the battle, at which Turnus is dismayed. The "pointless anger" and countless deaths are enumerated. Despite his anger, Aeneas sympathizes with the youth Lausus, who piously sacrifices himself to save his father, although his father is the greatest tyrant in Italy. Reminded of his own father, Aeneas offers to let Lausus go, but Lausus insists on fighting. Aeneas kills him but, in contrast to Turnus's treatment of Pallas, does not strip him of his armor.]

BOOK 11

[As the bodies pile up, the Latins ask for a truce to bury the dead. Aeneas insists that he has no quarrel with the Latin people but fights only because the king violated their initial alliance. Turnus, meanwhile, "delerious with courage," objects to the truce. The fighting resumes, but the Latins gradually lose ground in battle.]

BOOK 12

[The battles continue, with both heroes fighting valiantly. King Latinus offers to surrender in order to save Turnus, but "fanatic" Turnus asks only to "barter death for glory." Aeneas and Turnus agree to face each other in single combat. Aeneas vows, if victorious, to build his own city and to name it after Lavinia and not subject Italians to his rule. But Juno incites Juturna (Turnus's sister, a river goddess) to break the treaty and renew general war. She tricks the Latins by showing them a false omen of victory. Aeneas, trying to keep his men from responding to the Latin charge, is wounded by an arrow shot by an unknown hand. In the fray that ensues, Aeneas seeks out Turnus, refusing to fight the others. But Juturna has removed Turnus's chariot from the battle:]

. . . .
        Aeneas' anger seethes;
excited by the treachery of Turnus,
whose chariot and horses have been carried
far off, and having often pleaded with
Jove and the altars of the shattered treaty,
at last Aeneas charges into battle;
and terrible, with Mars behind him, he
awakens brutal, indiscriminate
slaughter, he lets his violence run free.

What god can now unfold for me in song   10
all of the bitterness and butchery
and deaths of chieftains—driven now by Turnus,
now by the Trojan hero, each in turn
throughout that field? O Jupiter, was it
your will that nations destined to eternal
peace should have clashed in such tremendous turmoil?

. . . .

**[Only now does Aeneas feel compelled to attack the city. Meanwhile, Turnus realizes
that his sister has tricked him and that, in her attempt to save him, she has caused the
destruction of both himself and Latium. Turnus is furious and humiliated:]**

Confused by all these shifting images
of ruin, Turnus stood astounded, staring
and silent. In his deepest heart there surge
tremendous shame and madness mixed with sorrow   20
and love whipped on by frenzy and a courage
aware of its own worth. As soon as shadows
were scattered and his mind saw light again,
in turmoil then, he turned his burning eyes
upon the walls and, from his chariot, looked
back to that splendid city. There a whirlwind
of flames was rolling on, storey by storey,
skyward, and gripping fast a tower—one
that he himself had built, of tight-packed timbers;
beneath it wheels were set; above it, tall   30
drawbridges. "Sister, fate has won; do not
delay me; let us follow where both god
and cruel fortune call; I am set to face
Aeneas, set to suffer death in all
its bitterness; sister, no longer will
you see me in disgrace. I beg you, let
me rage this madness out before I die."
So Turnus; then he left his chariot, leaped
down to the field; charging through enemies,
through shafts, he quits his grieving sister; swift,   40
he crashes through the center of the ranks.
Just as a rock when, from a mountaintop,
it hurtles headlong, having been torn up
by wind or washed away by a wheeling storm
or loosened by the long lapse of the years;
the mass, enormous, with a mighty thrust
drives down the slope and bounds upon the earth,
rolls woods and herds and men along its course:
so Turnus rushes through the scattered bands
up to the city walls, there where the ground   50
is soaked in shed blood and the air is shrill
with shafts. He signals with his hand, then shouts

aloud: "Rutulians, stop now; and you,
Italians, stay your steel; whatever chance
is here belongs to me; it is more just
for me alone to pay this covenant,
decide this war by sword." And then they all
drew back and left the center free for combat.

But when he hears the name of Turnus, father
Aeneas leaves the ramparts and tall towers;   60
he casts aside delay, breaks off the siege;
and now, exultant, joyous, and tremendous,
he pounds upon his shield—as huge as Athos,
as Eryx, or as father Apenninus
himself when, roaring, with his trembling oaks
he lifts his snow-topped summit skyward, glad.
Now all—Rutulians, Trojans, and Italians—
turned eagerly to look: both those who manned
high battlements and those below, who ran
a battering ram against the walls; they slung   70
their weapons off their shoulders. King Latinus
himself is wonderstruck to see such giant
men—born within such distant, different lands—
now come together for this trial by steel.
And they, as soon as space was cleared for them
along the open plain, first fling their spears
from far, then swiftly rush to fight; they dash
the brass of clanging shields together. Earth
groans, and their frequent sword blows double; chance
and courage mingle into one. Just as,   80
on giant Sila or on tall Taburnus,
when two bulls charge together into battle
with butting brows, the herdsmen fall back; all
the flock is mute with fear; the heifers wonder
who is to rule the forest, whom the herds
must follow; and the bulls with massive force
trade wounds; they gore with struggling horns; they bathe
their necks and shoulders in a stream of blood;
their groans and bellows echo through the grove:
so did the Daunian hero and the Trojan   90
Aeneas clash their shields; their violence
fills all the air. There Jupiter himself
holds up two scales in equal balance, then
he adds two different fates, one on each hand:
whom this trial dooms, what weight sinks down to death.
Now Turnus, thinking he is safe, springs out:
he rises up to his full height; with sword
upraised, he strikes. The Trojans and the anxious
Italians shout: the tension takes both ranks.

But, treacherous, that blade breaks off, deserts   100
fanatic Turnus at his blow's midstroke
had flight not helped him then. As soon as he
sees that strange hilt in his defenseless hand,
he runs away, swifter than the east wind.
They say that in his first wild dash to battle,
when mounting on his chariot, he had left
his father's sword behind and, rushing, snatched
the weapon of his charioteer. Metiscus,
so long as routed Trojans turned their backs,
that sword had served him well, but when it met   110
the armor that the God of Fire had forged,
the mortal blade, like brittle ice, had splintered;
the fragments glitter on the yellow sand.
So Turnus madly flees across the field;
now here, then there, he wheels in wayward circles.
The Trojans in a dense ring press against him;
to one side lies the vast Laurentian marsh,
and on the other, high walls hem him in.

And though the arrow wound within his knees
stays and delays him, nonetheless Aeneas   120
runs after Turnus. Keen, he presses on
against his trembling enemy, foot to foot:
even as, when a hunting dog has found
a stag hemmed in beside a stream or hedged
by fear before the netting's crimson feathers,
he chases, barking, pressing near; the stag,
in terror of the snare and of the river's
high banks, wheels back and forth a thousand ways;
and yet the lively Umbrian hound hangs close
to him with gaping mouth; at every instant   130
he grasps, he grinds his jaws but, baffled, bites
on nothing. Then indeed the shouting rises;
the shores and lakes resound; confusion takes
the skies. But Turnus, even as he flies
away, rebukes all his Rutulian ranks;
he calls on each by name, he shouts for his
familiar blade. And for his part, Aeneas
now menaces with death and instant ruin
the head of anyone who dares draw near;
he threatens to tear down the city and   140
he terrifies the shuddering Italians;
though wounded, he keeps on. Five times they circle
the field and, just as many times, weave back,
this way and that. They seek no trifling prize:
what they strive for is Turnus' blood and life.

Just here, by chance, had stood a bitter-leaved
wild olive tree, sacred to Faunus; sailors
had long since venerated it; when saved
from waves, they fastened here their offerings
to the Laurentians' god; here they would hang   150
their votive garments. Heedless of this custom,
the Teucrians had carried off the sacred
tree trunk to clear the field, to lay it bare
for battle. Here the shaft Aeneas first
had cast at Turnus stood; its impetus
had carried it and held it fast in that
tenacious root. The Dardan bent, wanting
to wrench his shaft free, then with spear, to catch
the warrior whom he could not overtake
on foot. And Turnus, wild with terror, cries: 160
"I pray you, Faunus, pity me; and you,
most gracious Earth, hold fast that steel if I
have ever kept your rites—those that Aeneas'
men have profaned by war." He spoke, invoked
the help of gods with prayers that were not useless;
for though Aeneas struggled long and lingered
above the gripping root, no force of his
could loose the spearhead from that tough wood's bite.
While, fierce, he wrenches, tugs, the Daunian
goddess, Juturna, once again takes on   170
the form of Turnus' charioteer, Metiscus;
she runs and gives his blade back to her brother.
But Venus, furious that this was granted
the daring nymph, drew near; and then she tore
Aeneas' spearhead free from that deep root.
Both men are high in heart; they face each other,
their arms and courage fresh again—one trusts
his sword; the other, tall and fierce, his shaft—
Aeneas, Turnus, breathless for Mars' contest.

Meanwhile Olympus' king calls out to Juno   180
as from a golden cloud she scans the battle:
"Wife, how can this day end? What is there left
for you to do? You know, and say you know,
that, as a deity, Aeneas is owed
to heaven, that the fates will carry him
high as the stars. What is your plan? What is
the hope that keeps you lingering in these
chill clouds? And was it seemly for a god
to be profaned by a human wound? Or for
a sword that had been lost to be restored   190

to Turnus (without you, Juturna could
do nothing)? Was it right to give fresh force
to those who are defeated? Stop at last;
give way to what I now ask: do not let
so great a sorrow gnaw at you in silence;
do not let your sweet lips so often press
your bitter cares on me. This is the end.
You have harassed the Trojans over land
and wave, have kindled brutal war, outraged
Latinus' home, and mingled grief and marriage: 200
you cannot pass beyond this point." So, Jove;
the goddess, Saturn's daughter, yielding, answered:

"Great Jupiter, it was indeed for this—
my knowing what you wish—that I have left
both Turnus and the earth, unwillingly.
Were it not so, you would not see me now
alone upon my airy throne, enduring
everything; but girt with flames, I should
be standing on the battlefield itself,
to drag the Trojans toward the war they hate.   210
I do confess that I urged on Juturna
to help her luckless brother; I approved
her daring greater things to save his life;
yet not to aim an arrow, not to stretch
her bow. I swear this by the pitiless
high fountainhead of Styx, the only pledge
that fills the upper gods with dread. And now
I yield; detesting wars, I give them up.
And only this—which fates do not forbid—
I beg of you, for Latium, for your   220
own father's greatness, for the race of Saturn:
when with their happy wedding rites they reach
a peace—so be it—when they both unite
in laws and treaties, do not let the native-
born Latins lose their ancient name, become
Trojans, or be called Teucrians; do not
make such men change their language or their dress.
Let Latium still be, let Alban kings
still rule for ages; let the sons of Rome
be powerful in their Italian courage.   230
Troy now is fallen; let her name fall, too."

And Jupiter smiled at her then; the maker
of men and things said: "Surely you are sister
to Jove, a second child of Saturn, for
deep in your breast there surge such tides of anger.
But come, give up this useless madness: I

now grant your wish and willingly, vanquished,
submit. For the Ausonians will keep
their homeland's words and ways; their name will stay;
the body of the Teucrians will merge   240
with Latins, and their name will fall away.
But I shall add their rituals and customs
to the Ausonians', and make them all—
and with one language—Latins. You will see
a race arise from this that, mingled with
the blood of the Ausonians, will be
past men, even past gods, in piety;
no other nation will pay you such honor."
Juno agreed to this; with gladness she
then changed her mind. She quit the skies, her cloud.   250

. . . .

**[Jupiter sends a Fury to terrify Turnus. Juturna recognizes Jupiter's intentions, and,
sorrowing for the impending loss of her brother, she plunges into the river's depths to
spend her immortal life in grief. At last, the combat between Aeneas and Turnus takes
place:]**

And now Aeneas charges straight at Turnus.
He brandishes a shaft huge as a tree,
and from his savage breast he shouts: "Now what
delay is there? Why, Turnus, do you still
draw back from battle? It is not for us
to race against each other, but to meet
with cruel weapons, hand to hand. Go, change
yourself into all shapes; by courage and
by craft collect whatever help you can;
take wing, if you so would, toward the steep stars   260
or hide yourself within the hollow earth."
But Turnus shakes his head: "Your burning words,
ferocious Trojan, do not frighten me;
it is the gods alone who terrify me,
and Jupiter, my enemy." He says
no more, but as he looks about he sees
a giant stone, an ancient giant stone
that lay at hand, by chance, upon the plain,
set there as boundary mark between the fields
to keep the farmers free from border quarrels.   270
And twice-six chosen men with bodies such
as earth produces now could scarcely lift
that stone upon their shoulders. But the hero,
anxious and running headlong, snatched the boulder;
reaching full height, he hurled it at the Trojan.
But Turnus does not know if it is he
himself who runs or goes or lifts or throws
that massive rock; his knees are weak; his blood

congeals with cold. The stone itself whirls through
the empty void but does not cross all of   280
the space between; it does not strike a blow.
Just as in dreams of night, when languid rest
has closed our eyes, we seem in vain to wish
to press on down a path, but as we strain,
we falter, weak; our tongues can say nothing,
the body loses its familiar force,
no voice, no word, can follow: so whatever
courage he calls upon to find a way,
the cursed goddess keeps success from Turnus.
Then shifting feelings overtake his heart;   290
he looks in longing at the Latin ranks
and at the city, and he hesitates,
afraid; he trembles at the coming spear.
He does not know how he can save himself,
what power he has to charge his enemy;
he cannot see his chariot anywhere;
he cannot see the charioteer, his sister.

In Turnus' wavering Aeneas sees
his fortune; he holds high the fatal shaft;
he hurls it far with all his body's force.   300
No boulder ever catapulted from
siege engine sounded so, no thunderbolt
had ever burst with such a roar. The spear
flies on like a black whirlwind, carrying
its dread destruction, ripping through the border
of Turnus' corselet and the outer rim
of Turnus's seven-plated shield; hissing,
it penetrates his thigh. The giant Turnus,
struck, falls to earth; his knees bend under him.
All the Rutulians leap up with a groan,   310
and all the mountain slopes around reecho;
tall forests, far and near, return that voice.
Then humble, suppliant, he lifts his eyes
and, stretching out his hand, entreating, cries:
"I have indeed deserved this; I do not
appeal against it; use your chance. But if
there is a thought of a dear parent's grief
that now can touch you, then I beg you, pity
old Daunus—in Anchises you had such
a father—send me back or, if you wish,   320
send back my lifeless body to my kin.
For you have won, and the Ausonians
have seen me, beaten, stretch my hands; Lavinia
is yours; then do not press your hatred further."

Aeneas stood, ferocious in his armor;
his eyes were restless and he stayed his hand;
and as he hesitated, Turnus' words
began to move him more and more—until
high on the Latin's shoulder he made out
the luckless belt of Pallas, of the boy   330
whom Turnus had defeated, wounded, stretched
upon the battlefield, from whom he took
this fatal sign to wear upon his back,
this girdle glittering with familiar studs.
And when his eyes drank in this plunder, this
memorial of brutal grief, Aeneas,
aflame with rage—his wrath was terrible—
cried: "How can you who wear the spoils of my
dear comrade now escape me? It is Pallas
who strikes, who sacrifices you, who takes   340
this payment from your shameless blood." Relentless,
he sinks his sword into the chest of Turnus.
His limbs fell slack with chill; and with a moan
his life, resentful, fled to Shades below.

Questions for Discussion and Review

1. In what specific ways is the *Aeneid* like the *Iliad* and the *Odyssey?* What themes, plot structures, and even specific episodes in the *Aeneid* resemble those of the Homeric epics? Why does Virgil want to remind us of the similarities between his work and Homer's?

2. In what ways is Aeneas similar to his Homeric counterparts Achilles and Odysseus? In what ways is he different?

3. Why does Aeneas fall in love with Dido? Later, why does he leave her? What part do the gods play in both of those events?

4. What heroic qualities does Aeneas share with Turnus? In what ways are they different in their attitude toward war, in their methods of fighting, and in their moral values?

5. Compare the relationship between Thetis and her son Achilles in the *Iliad* with that between Venus and Aeneas in the *Aeneid.* How does each divine mother help her son? What goal does each goddess have in mind?

6. Why does Aeneas go to the Underworld? What does he learn there? How does his new perspective affect his behavior afterward?

7. Compare the role of Jupiter in the *Aeneid* with that of Zeus in the *Iliad.* How do their powers differ? What goals does each envision? What does each god do to fulfill his plan? How successful is he in bringing it about?

8. Describe some of the ways in which myth and real history intersect in the *Aeneid.* What historical events and figures appear in the poem? How are they related to the mythic events and themes?

9. In their last battle, Aeneas rejects Turnus's plea for mercy and kills him. How should we evaluate this act? Defend your position with specific references to the poem.

Recommended Reading

Bloom, Harold, ed. *Virgil: Modern Critical Views.* New York: Chelsea, 1986. A collection of various contemporary interpretations that address the central critical issues in understanding the *Aeneid.*

Johnson, W. R. *Darkness Visible: A Study of Vergil's* Aeneid. Berkeley: U of California P, 1976. Makes a strong case for an ironic understanding of Virgil's view of Augustus and Roman government.

Wiltshire, Susan Ford. *Public and Private in Vergil's* Aeneid. Amherst: U of Massachusetts P, 1989. Beginning with a survey of the current controversy between realist and idealist interpretations of the poem, the author discusses the ways in which Virgil manages to reconcile the conflicting demands of the public and private spheres, of hope for the future of Rome and the sorrows of immediate experience.

Ovid's *Metamorphoses:* The Retelling of Greek Myths

KEY THEMES

Ovid retells Greek myths in a continuous narrative that focuses on the theme of change. Sometimes comic, sometimes bitter in tone, his tales portray the world of myth (and, some would say, the world of Augustan Rome) as a place where everything—love, the gods, and time itself—changes and thus betrays one's hopes and expectations. The only way to cope with such constant flux is to be transformed into something immobile (like the laurel tree in "Apollo and Daphne" in Book 1) or inanimate (like the human statues in "The Story of Perseus" in Book 5). The tales are framed by a vision of Rome and end with "The Deification of Caesar" (Book 15) and the poet's hope that Rome will endure forever—so that he can have a perpetual audience for his poems!

Ovid

In the case of the poet Ovid (43 B.C.–A.D. 17), the connection between myth and politics turned all too literal. Something in Ovid's elegant and witty writings (which included such works as the *Art of Love* and the collection of tales called *Metamorphoses*—a retelling of many Greek myths) apparently offended Augustus, who banished Ovid from Rome, forcing him to spend his last decade in exile in a little town on the shores of the Black Sea. Perhaps he found that Ovid's worldly, sometimes comic, and sometimes cynical depictions of the lecherous pursuits of gods and humans too obviously undermined the "official" image of sober Roman citizens and their politically correct deities.

The *Metamorphoses*: Significant Themes and Characters

The Story of Creation

Ovid's theme in *Metamorphoses* is "bodies changed." One of the most remarkable aspects of the poem is that, instead of an anthology of separate myths, Ovid created a series of narrative links that allow one tale to flow into another in a continuous stream, thus reflecting his theme of transformations in the structure of the poem itself.

Like Hesiod, he begins with the story of creation—the changes in the body of the cosmos itself. Ovid's universe, like Hesiod's, is in a state of perpetual flux—only more so. He describes a world in which Time dissolves all—even the globe of earth itself—to water, to air, to fire, and back to earth again, just as human figures in the myths change from human to animal and other forms and just as Troy is transformed into Rome. The changes in Ovid's universe, however, move largely in one direction: from chaos to order, from motion to stasis. In Hesiod's description of creation, primal chaos is depicted with a certain exuberance, as Hesiod celebrates, in his catalogues and genealogies, the proliferation of life. For Ovid, in contrast, chaos is an intolerable condition in which the very atoms of the universe war with each other. It is not until god, or nature, separates the warring components of the universe—decreeing a proper place for each in the eternal order, subdividing all creation and, as might be expected from Roman gods, marking out boundaries—that Ovid can celebrate the emergence of the stars. The bureaucratically organized universe thus produced is divided into zones just as Rome was divided into wards. The boundaries between social classes, even among the gods, is as essential to the proper order as are the borders between zones and territories. Even the dwellings of the gods on Olympus are segregated into neighborhoods, with the lesser gods inhabiting a poorer section!

The Comic Tone

As some scholars have noted, in this and other references Ovid is poking fun at Augustus (who, along with other very important Romans, lived on the Palatine Hill), equating him with Jupiter and perhaps satirizing the folly and pretentiousness of the Augustan court. Hoping to add dignity to Roman life and presumably to enhance his own reputation, Augustus had attempted to revive not only neglected Roman religious rites but even the worship of the Greek god Apollo. He also sought to impose moral restraints on a society whose elite patrician class was used to a life-style characterized by various kinds of self-indulgence. In 18 B.C., for example, Augustus made adultery a crime; however, he was subsequently embarrassed by the blatantly licentious behavior of his daughter Julia and, to carry out his own laws, had to banish her from Rome. His granddaughter was likewise banished for the same reason. As several modern readers have pointed out, there is an element of bathos (a sudden dropping off in tone) as Ovid moves from describing Mount Olympus immediately to a reference to the Palatine Hill. Indeed, throughout much of the *Metamorphoses* there is an undercurrent of downsizing the myths, bringing them down to the level of ordinary experience, and an element of parody, mocking the foibles of the gods, the follies and hypocrisies of Augustan society, and perhaps even Augustus himself.

Echo and Narcissus

In the story of Echo and Narcissus, Ovid describes the twin follies of **Echo,** a woman whose discourse was so dependent on others' that she was unable either to begin or to end a conversation on her own initiative, and **Narcissus,** an unusually beautiful young man who was so self-absorbed that he was incapable of relating to any other being, male or female, human or divine.

Ovid tells how Echo served Jove by chattering to distract Juno while Jove made love to nameless nymphs. She thus incurs Juno's anger. The goddess punishes Echo by rendering her capable only of repeating the last statement she has heard, exaggerating the reflective characteristics already present in Echo's speech.

Echo falls in love with Narcissus, an odd pairing of complementary follies: the woman who cannot express what is inside herself paired with the man who cannot respond to anything outside himself. But the slightly comical overtones of that initial ironic juxtaposition soon give way to a far bleaker perspective. Narcissus of course rejects Echo, as he rejects all the women and young men who pursue him, his lack of capacity for love an insult to the powers of Aphrodite and Eros. Persistent but endlessly frustrated in her hopeless pursuit of Narcissus, Echo is gradually reduced to the condition of a disembodied voice.

Meanwhile, one of the young men Narcissus has rejected prays that Narcissus himself will come to feel tormented by the pains of unrequited love he has caused in so many others. Carrying to its most extreme form the self-infatuation of Narcissus, the goddess of vengeance, Nemesis, causes Narcissus to fall in love with his own reflection on the surface of a pond, as if Eros, denied an external object, turns inward, with deadly results. Like Echo, Narcissus is disembodied, dissolving into the watery image of himself visible on the pond's surface, until nothing is left of him but the flower that still bears his name.

The Golden Age

As is often the case in satire, beneath the witty, comic surface lurks a more serious, even bitter indictment, as Ovid moves beyond folly to vice, from the ludicrous to the downright vicious, resulting in a dual vision between whose perspectives the poet can range at will. Like Hesiod, Ovid tells the myth of the Ages of Man (Book 1). But Ovid gives equal attention to those aspects of Roman life for which the Golden Age had no need: judges, laws, and punishments; ships, soldiers, and weapons; aggression and anxiety. In contrast, Ovid somewhat bitterly presents the Iron Age of contemporary Rome, characterized by greed, war, violence, and those very important Roman figures—surveyors—who marked off the boundaries of private property. Caught between the terror of anarchy and the almost equally fearful "threat" of law, the Romans—even a poet who had experienced personally just how fearful the law can be—dreaded disorder more. The role of government, then, in this fallen world of the Iron Age, is to use the force of law and of arms to impose order on an anarchic world. The subtle tension exhibited in Virgil's *Aeneid* between the fear of chaos and the fear of law—the moments of fleeting suspicion that perhaps the price paid for the benefits of Roman civilization might have been too high—becomes even more explicit in Ovid's works and is reflected in the characteristic Roman nostalgia for the Golden Age, or the early republic.

The Nightmare World

In Ovid's poem, however, the nostalgic impulse is short-lived. In a more sinister vein, many of Ovid's tales move beyond follies to vices, portraying a nightmarish world characterized by lust, rape, betrayal, and revenge. Several scholars, having made the link between Jupiter and Augustus in the earlier sections of the poem, now see these more appalling stories as comments on the cruelty of those in power—of the Augustan state and the emperor himself. It is difficult to say, in these cases where the poet himself omits the obvious hints of the comic tales, whether or not he intended such a comment. It is clear, however, in this world in which gods turn on humans, that cruelty and violence are so pervasive that the only escape possible is through transformation into less-than-human or even inanimate states beyond the reach of pain. If Aeneas can be said to have been emotionally dehumanized by his experience, Ovid's mythic characters are literally so. Men and women, driven by uncontrollable inner urges or pursued by those—or by gods—who are thus driven, are saved only by being changed into trees, rocks, or even constellations.

Perseus

In "The Story of Perseus" (books 4–5), we can see most blatantly this compulsion toward immobility. Whereas Odysseus was content to fight one hundred suitors one at a time, **Perseus,** in Ovid's retelling, finds that method too exhausting and thus inefficient. Instead, he whips out the Gorgon's head and transforms all of Andromeda's former suitors to stone. Although that mass transformation is of course part of the ancient Greek Perseus myth, Ovid goes on to describe, in stark detail, the suitors' tears frozen on their faces for all eternity. And Perseus, in a marvelous comic touch, offers the marble "statue" of her former fiancé to **Andromeda,** to set up in her new home! But the image also conveys the more serious theme of the desperate striving for permanence. In these men-turned-statues we can see in its most literal form the Roman petrification of Greek myth. And, of course, Perseus and Andromeda are themselves eventually honored by becoming constellations.

Apollo and Daphne

Traditional Roman heroes like Romulus and Aeneas are, in Ovid's version, transformed into gods. But not even the gods themselves are exempt from the inevitable failures of sensual love. The gods' desires, like those of the humans, remain unfulfilled, as their objects turn to beasts, trees, or flowers before their outstretched hands. Apollo, for instance, may be the god of archery, but he is himself subject to the darts of Cupid (Book 1). "Burning" with futile love for **Daphne,** who rejects both men and marriage (see Chapter 7), he pursues her until she is turned by her father, a river god, into a laurel tree, an etiological tale explaining why the laurel leaves thereafter remain sacred to Apollo. But that provides small consolation to the god, who, instead of erotic bliss, finds himself rather foolishly embracing the trunk of a tree (Figure 20-1). Because of Augustus's particular interest in reviving the worship of Apollo along with other elements of Greek culture, some scholars see in this tale an attempt to ridicule Augustus's plans by revealing the god that he admires to be ridiculous. But to Daphne, who, to escape a "fate worse than death," must be dehumanized, the consequences are anything but comic.

FIGURE 20-1   Apollo and Daphne. In this marble statue (1622–1625), the Italian sculptor Gianlorenzo Bernini depicts the erotic pursuit of Daphne by the god Apollo. Responding to his daughter's plea to be rescued from the impending rape, Daphne's father, a river god, turns her into a laurel tree. Bernini's sculpture captures the moment of transformation of Daphne into the laurel tree: just as Apollo's hand arrests her flight, her forward motion is thrust upward. Her hair, still flowing as she twists to avoid him, sprouts leaves, and the bark begins enclosing her legs and trunk, protecting her as it immobilizes her. (*Galleria Borghese, Rome.*)

Orpheus and Eurydice

Unlike Echo and Narcissus, who are incapable of love, **Orpheus** and **Eurydice** fail to fulfill their love because of forces beyond their, or anyone's, control. At the very moment of their marriage, Eurydice is bitten by a serpent, associated with the chthonic figure of Medusa, "rough with snakes." The "poison of the serpent," death itself, takes Eurydice, and she dies. Her distraught husband/lover, the musician Orpheus, does what the warrior-heroes used to do: he descends to the Underworld. But whereas those heroes typically made such quests to escape domesticity, Orpheus, inverting the usual heroic mode, makes the journey to retrieve his wife. Indeed, more like Demeter seeking reunion with Persephone than like a Heracles or a Theseus seeking his own immortality, Orpheus even offers to die himself if Eurydice cannot be released from the Underworld. Thus he refuses the warrior's defiant stance: he does not come, he insists, to bind the "triple-throated" hound, Cerberus. Trusting that because love is "famous" in the upper world, it will be similarly honored in the lower, Orpheus appeals to Hades and Persephone to release Eurydice, on the grounds of their love for each other.

Attempting to pursue love beyond the grave, Orpheus brings together the forces of Eros (love) and Thanatos (death). But Orpheus is not in love with death; rather, his descent to the Underworld is a variant of the mythic tradition that embraces such couples as Venus and Adonis, the Egyptian lovers Isis and Osiris, or the Babylonian Ishtar and Tammuz. In those stories it is usually the goddess who reaches beyond death to bring her consort back from the Underworld to some form of rebirth.

All people, Orpheus argues, belong to the Underworld eventually: he just wants Eurydice's death to happen later, "in the ripeness of years." What has betrayed these lovers is change, time itself. For a brief interval, as Orpheus charms the inhabitants of the Underworld with his music, time does seem to stop: the Furies themselves weep, the punishments of sinners in Tartarus cease. For a moment, Orpheus's request to stop time, or to run it backward—to undo death—is granted, on one condition: he must not look back as he leads Eurydice up again to the world of light. But it is impossible for Orpheus not to look back. Indeed, he already has done so: the descent into the Underworld, an attempt to reverse time, itself constitutes a looking back. And whereas the traditional warrior-hero achieves a form of rebirth as a result of his trip to the Underworld, no such results occur during the hero's life in this tale.

Unlike many of the later versions of the story of Orpheus and Eurydice, in which Orpheus turns back because he distrusts either the gods or Eurydice herself, Ovid's Orpheus explicitly turns back "in love." Nor does Eurydice reproach her husband for doing so. Nevertheless, "in a moment," the poet tells us, Eurydice is gone. Even when it is mutual and seemingly perfect, love is not eternal. The ultimate dissolution of the self in death is the final metamorphosis: death is the ultimate betrayal.

Having lost Eurydice, Orpheus rejects the love of women and turns to young men instead. As he wanders the hills, playing his lyre Orpheus appears to have acquired a function akin to a fertility god: trees appear in his wake, reminding us of Orpheus's similarities to Demeter and Dionysus. Thus Orpheus incorporates qualities of both Apollo, god of music, and Dionysus, the "twice-born" agricultural god.

In the story that follows Orpheus's in Ovid's poem, Apollo also pursues a youth, Cyparissus, who in turn loves a pet deer, but changing from one kind of love object to another, regardless of gender or species, does not mitigate the ineluctable powers of time and change. Lamenting the loss of his beloved deer, Cyparissus is turned into a cypress tree, associated with mourning. The juxtaposition in the poem of the trees into which Apollo's lovers are transformed, and the trees that spring up on the hills where Orpheus wanders, suggests that the hills are littered with the transformed remnants of Orpheus's male lovers as well.

The Death of Orpheus

Delaying the story of the death of Orpheus and returning to it later, immediately after the story of Venus and Adonis, Ovid implies a link between the two stories of

Underworld experiences. According to the tradition that Ovid describes, Orpheus is killed and mutilated by Maenads, women who followed Orpheus as they did Dionysus. Angered by his rejection of women, they silence his lyre—his Apollonian voice—which is rendered, for the first time, useless. The women then perform a sparagmos ritual in which Orpheus, like Dionysus, is torn limb from limb; he is also compared to Actaeon, the "doomed stag" destroyed by the women as hounds.

Orpheus's head, along with his lyre, is flung into a river, from which it is rescued by Apollo himself, who "freezes" it, performing the only form of metamorphosis still possible: he turns it, gaping jaws and all, to stone. Ovid's description of that transformation to a condition of stillness, beyond the reach of change, is reminiscent of his treatment of the story of Perseus, whose rivals were similarly petrified.

Throughout Ovid's version of the Orpheus myth, some sort of rivalry is suggested between Apollo, who communicates in mediated form through the voice of another (the Oracle at Delphi, the lyre), and Dionysus (**Bacchus**) whose unmediated epiphanies the Maenads have experienced, but which Orpheus has denied them. In Ovid's tale, however, the two gods—dual aspects of Orpheus himself—are reconciled. Bacchus, mourning Orpheus's death, punishes the women who rejected Orpheus and turns them, like Daphne, into trees. Orpheus himself, meanwhile, rejoins Eurydice in the Underworld where he can, the poet assures us, look back without loss: in this world, Ovid seems to imply, betrayal is a universal condition—only sorrow lasts. But in the same sort of consolation that Virgil held out for the Roman hero Aeneas, only in the afterlife, at last, can pious poets sing their songs forever.

The Apotheosis of Caesar

Despite (or rather as a result of) all the changes he describes, the spirit of Rome, in Ovid's work, emerges triumphant, and the *Metamorphoses* ends with "The Deification of Caesar" (Book 15) and his transformation from mortal to star to preside henceforth over the divine destiny of Rome. This section of the work, tracing Roman history from the fall of Troy to Ovid's own time, is fairly serious in tone, its occasional comic touches muted. For all the problems of the Augustan Age, Ovid did not confuse the present actors with the script or reject its larger vision.

In one last, subtle irony, Ovid implies in the "Epilogue" (Book 15) that his own fame will be carried above the stars—that is, above Caesar's! Nevertheless, Ovid is aware of how dependent even the most critical poet is on the stability of a society in which his poems can be transmitted. Like Shakespeare's magician Prospero in *The Tempest*, Ovid has woven an "insubstantial pageant" of shapes that shift before our eyes. And however much he might criticize Roman government, it is only when Rome is at last stabilized that the poet can be confident the work that summons those airy shapes into our presence will endure beyond the reach of Time. Only then, when the history of Rome becomes its own glorious monument, can the omnipresent threat of perpetual change—the fear that, should Roman vigilance ever slip, the world would revert to the chaos from which it came—at last cease.

Fortunately for modern readers, although Rome fell, Ovid, despite his fears, endured to become not only one of our most important sources of information about Greek mythology but also one of the most important influences on Western culture (see Chapter 21).

Excerpts from the
METAMORPHOSES[1]
Ovid

BOOK 1

My intention is to tell of bodies changed
To different forms; the gods, who made the changes,
Will help me—or I hope so—with a poem
That runs from the world's beginning to our own days.

The Creation

Before the ocean was, or earth, or heaven,
Nature was all alike, a shapelessness,
Chaos, so-called, all rude and lumpy matter,
Nothing but bulk, inert, in whose confusion
Discordant atoms warred: there was no sun
To light the universe; there was no moon   10
With slender silver crescents filling slowly;
No earth hung balanced in surrounding air;
No sea reached far long the fringe of shore.
Land, to be sure, there was, and air, and ocean,
But land on which no man could stand, and water
No man could swim in, air no man could breathe,
Air without light, substance forever changing,
Forever at war: within a single body
Heat fought with cold, wet fought with dry, the hard
Fought with the soft, things having weight contended   20
With weightless things.
                Till God, or kindlier Nature,
Settled all argument, and separated
Heaven from earth, water from land, our air
From the high stratosphere, a liberation
So things evolved, and out of blind confusion
Found each its place, bound in eternal order.
The force of fire, that weightless element,
Leaped up and claimed the highest place in heaven;
Below it, air; and under them the earth   30
Sank with its grosser portions; and the water,
Lowest of all, held up, held in, the land.

---

1. Translation by Rolfe Humphries.

Whatever god it was, who out of chaos
Brought order to the universe, and gave it
Division, subdivision, he molded earth,
In the beginning, into a great globe,
Even on every side, and bade the waters
To spread and rise, under the rushing winds,
Surrounding earth; he added ponds and marshes,
He banked the river-channels, and the waters   40
Feed earth or run to sea, and that great flood
Washes on shores, not banks. He made the plains
Spread wide, the valleys settle, and the forest
Be dressed in leaves; he made the rocky mountains
Rise to full height, and as the vault of Heaven
Has two zones, left and right, and one between them
Hotter than these, the Lord of all Creation
Marked on the earth the same design and pattern.
The torrid zone too hot for men to live in,
The north and south too cold, but in the middle   50
Varying climate, temperature and season.
Above all things the air, lighter than earth,
Lighter than water, heavier than fire,
Towers and spreads; there mist and cloud assemble,
And fearful thunder and lightning and cold winds,
But these, by the Creator's order, held
No general dominion; even as it is,
These brothers brawl and quarrel; though each one
Has his own quarter, still, they come near tearing
The universe apart. Eurus is monarch   60
Of the lands of dawn, the realms of Araby,
The Persian ridges under the rays of morning.
Zephyrus holds the west that glows at sunset,
Boreas, who makes men shiver, holds the north,
Warm Auster governs in the misty southland,
And over them all presides the weightless ether,
Pure without taint of earth.
                        These boundaries given,
Behold, the stars, long hidden under darkness,
Broke through and shone, all over the spangled heaven,   70
Their home forever, and the gods lived there,
And shining fish were given the waves for dwelling
And beasts the earth, and birds the moving air.

But something else was needed, a finer being,
More capable of mind, a sage, a ruler,
So Man was born, it may be, in God's image,
Or Earth, perhaps, so newly separated
From the old fire of Heaven, still retained

Some seed of the celestial force which fashioned
Gods out of living clay and running water. 80
All other animals look downward; Man,
Alone, erect, can raise his face toward Heaven.

The Four Ages

The Golden Age was first, a time that cherished
Of its own will, justice and right; no law.
No punishment, was called for; fearfulness
Was quite unknown, and the bronze tablets held
No legal threatening; no suppliant throng
Studied a judge's face; there were no judges,
There did not need to be. Trees had not yet
Been cut and hollowed, to visit other shores. 90
Men were content at home, and had no towns
With moats and walls around them; and no trumpets
Blared out alarums; things like swords and helmets
Had not been heard of. No one needed soldiers.
People were unaggressive, and unanxious;
The years went by in peace. And Earth, untroubled,
Unharried by hoe or plowshare, brought forth all
That men had need for, and those men were happy,
Gathering berries from the mountain sides,
Cherries, or blackcaps, and the edible acorns. 100
Spring was forever, with a west wind blowing
Softly across the flowers no man had planted,
And Earth, unplowed, brought forth rich grain; the field,
Unfallowed, whitened with wheat, and there were rivers
Of milk, and rivers of honey, and golden nectar
Dripped from the dark-green oak-trees.
                                        After Saturn
Was driven to the shadowy land of death,
And the world was under Jove, the Age of Silver
Came in, lower than gold, better than bronze.
Jove made the springtime shorter, added winter, 110
Summer, and autumn, the seasons as we know them.
That was the first time when the burnt air glowed
White-hot, or icicles hung down in winter.
And men built houses for themselves; the caverns,
The woodland thickets, and the bark-bound shelters
No longer served; and the seeds of grain were planted
In the long furrows, and the oxen struggled
Groaning and laboring under the heavy yoke.

Then came the Age of Bronze, and dispositions 120
Took on aggressive instincts, quick to arm,
Yet not entirely evil. And last of all

The Iron Age succeeded, whose base vein
Let loose all evil: modesty and truth
And righteousness fled earth, and in their place
Came trickery and slyness, plotting, swindling,
Violence and the damned desire of having.
Men spread their sails to winds unknown to sailors,
The pines came down their mountain-sides, to revel
And leap in the deep waters, and the ground,   130
Free, once, to everyone, like air and sunshine,
Was stepped off by surveyors. The rich earth,
Good giver of all the bounty of the harvest,
Was asked for more; they dug into her vitals,
Pried out the wealth a kinder lord had hidden
In Stygian shadow, all that precious metal,
The root of evil. They found the guilt of iron,
And gold, more guilty still. And War came forth
That uses both to fight with; bloody hands
Brandished the clashing weapons. Men lived on plunder.   140
Guest was not safe from host, nor brother from brother,
A man would kill his wife, a wife her husband,
Stepmothers, dire and dreadful, stirred their brews
With poisonous aconite, and sons would hustle
Fathers to death, and Piety lay vanquished,
And the maiden Justice, last of all immortals,
Fled from the bloody earth.
                              Heaven was no safer.
Giants attacked the very throne of Heaven,
Piled Pelion on Ossa, mountain on mountain   150
Up to the very stars. Jove struck them down
With thunderbolts, and the bulk of those huge bodies
Lay on the earth, and bled, and Mother Earth,
Made pregnant by that blood, brought forth new bodies,
And gave them, to recall her older offspring,
The forms of men. And this new stock was also
Contemptuous of gods, and murder-hungry
And violent. You would know they were sons of blood.

Jove's Intervention

And Jove was witness from his lofty throne
Of all this evil, and groaned as he remembered   160
The wicked revels of Lycaon's table,
The latest guilt, a story still unknown
To the high gods. In awful indignation
He summoned them to council. No one dawdled.
Easily seen when the night skies are clear,
The Milky Way shines white. Along this road
The gods move toward the palace of the Thunderer,

His royal halls, and, right and left, the dwellings
Of other gods are open, and guests come thronging.
The lesser gods live in a meaner section,   170
An area not reserved, as this one is,
For the illustrious Great Wheels of Heaven.
(Their Palatine Hill, if I might call it so.)

They took their places in the marble chamber
Where high above them all their king was seated,
Holding his ivory scepter, shaking out
Thrice, and again, his awful locks, the sign
That made the earth and stars and ocean tremble,
And then he spoke, in outrage: "I was troubled
Less for the sovereignty of all the world   180
In that old time when the snake-footed giants
Laid each his hundred hands on captive Heaven.
Monstrous they were, and hostile, but their warfare
Sprung from one source, one body. Now, wherever
The sea-gods roar around the earth, a race
Must be destroyed, the race of men. I swear it!
I swear by all the Stygian rivers gliding
Under the world, I have tried all other measures.
The knife must cut the cancer out, infection
Averted while it can be, from our numbers.   190
Those demigods, those rustic presences,
Nymphs, fauns, and satyrs, wood and mountain dwellers,
We have not yet honored with a place in Heaven,
But they should have some decent place to dwell in,
In peace and safety. Safety? Do you reckon
They will be safe, when I, who wield the thunder,
Who rule you all as subjects, am subjected
To the plottings of the barbarous Lycaon?"

They burned, they trembled. Who was this Lycaon,
Guilty of such rank infamy? They shuddered   200
In horror, with a fear of sudden ruin,
As the whole world did later, when assassins
Struck Julius Caesar down, and Prince Augustus
Found satisfaction in the great devotion
That cried for vengeance, even as Jove took pleasure,
Then, in the gods' response. By word and gesture
He calmed them down, awed them again to silence,
And spoke once more:

The Story of Lycaon

          "He has indeed been punished.
On that score have no worry. But what he did,   210

And how he paid, are things that I must tell you.
I had heard the age was desperately wicked,
I had heard, or so I hoped, a lie, a falsehood,
So I came down, as man, from high Olympus,
Wandered about the world. It would take too long
To tell you how widespread was all that evil.
All I had heard was grievous understatement!
I had crossed Maenala, a country bristling
With dens of animals, and crossed Cyllene,
And cold Lycaeus' pine woods. Then I came   220
At evening, with the shadows growing longer,
To an Arcadian palace, where the tyrant
Was anything but royal in his welcome.
I gave a sign that a god had come, and people
Began to worship, and Lycaon mocked them,
Laughed at their prayers, and said: 'Watch me find out
Whether this fellow is a god or mortal,
I can't tell quickly, and no doubt about it.'
He planned, that night, to kill me while I slumbered;
That was his way to test the truth. Moreover,   230
And not content with that, he took a hostage,
One sent by the Molossians, cut his throat,
Boiled pieces of his flesh, still warm with life,
Broiled others, and set them before me on the table.
That was enough. I struck, and the bolt of lightning
Blasted the household of that guilty monarch.
He fled in terror, reached the silent fields,
And howled, and tried to speak. No use at all!
Foam dripped from his mouth; bloodthirsty still, he turned
Against the sheep, delighting still in slaughter,   240
And his arms were legs, and his robes were shaggy hair,
Yet he is still Lycaon, the same grayness,
The same fierce face, the same red eyes, a picture
Of bestial savagery. One house has fallen,
But more than one deserves to. Fury reigns
Over all the fields of Earth. They are sworn to evil,
Believe it. Let them pay for it, and quickly!
So stands my purpose."
                         Part of them approved
With words and added fuel to his anger,   250
And part approved with silence, and yet all
Were grieving at the loss of humankind,
Were asking what the world would be, bereft
Of mortals: who would bring their altars incense?
Would earth be given the beasts, to spoil and ravage?
Jove told them not to worry; he would give them
Another race, unlike the first, created
Out of a miracle; he would see to it.

He was about to hurl his thunderbolts
At the whole world, but halted, fearing Heaven   260
Would burn from fire so vast, and pole to pole
Break out in flame and smoke, and he remembered
The fates had said that some day land and ocean,
The vault of Heaven, the whole world's mighty fortress,
Besieged by fire, would perish. He put aside
The bolts made in Cyclopean workshops; better,
He thought, to drown the world by flooding water.

The Flood

So, in the cave of Aeolus, he prisoned
The North-wind, and the West-wind, and such others
As ever banish cloud, and he turned loose   270
The South-wind, and the South-wind came out streaming
With dripping wings, and pitch-black darkness veiling
His terrible countenance. His beard is heavy
With rain-cloud, and his hoary locks a torrent,
Mists are his chaplet, and his wings and garments
Run with the rain. His broad hands squeeze together
Low-hanging clouds, and crash and rumble follow
Before the cloudburst, and the rainbow, Iris,
Draws water from the teeming earth, and feeds it
Into the clouds again. The crops are ruined,   280
The farmers' prayers all wasted, all the labor
Of a long year, comes to nothing.
                                     And Jove's anger,
Unbounded by his own domain, was given
Help by his dark-blue brother. Neptune called
His rivers all, and told them, very briefly,
To loose their violence, open their houses,
Pour over embankments, let the river horses
Run wild as ever they would. And they obeyed him.
His trident struck the shuddering earth; it opened   290
Way for the rush of waters. The leaping rivers
Flood over the great plains. Not only orchards
Are swept away, not only grain and cattle,
Not only men and houses, but altars, temples,
And shrines with holy fires. If any building
Stands firm, the waves keep rising over its roof-top,
Its towers are under water, and land and ocean
Are all alike, and everything is ocean,
An ocean with no shore-line.
                                     Some poor fellow   300
Seizes a hill-top; another, in a dinghy,
Rows where he used to plough, and one goes sailing
Over his fields of grain or over the chimney

Of what was once his cottage. Someone catches
Fish in the top of an elm-tree, or an anchor
Drags in green meadow-land, or the curved keel brushes
Grape-arbors under water. Ugly sea-cows
Float where the slender she-goats used to nibble
The tender grass, and the Nereids come swimming
With curious wonder, looking, under water,   310
At houses, cities, parks, and groves. The dolphins
Invade the woods and brush against the oak-trees;
The wolf swims with the lamb; lion and tiger
Are borne along together; the wild boar
Finds all his strength is useless, and the deer
Cannot outspeed that torrent; wandering birds
Look long, in vain, for landing-place, and tumble,
Exhausted, into the sea. The deep's great license
Has buried all the hills, and new waves thunder
Against the mountain-tops. The flood has taken   320
All things, or nearly all, and those whom water,
By chance, has spared, starvation slowly conquers.

Deucalion and Pyrrha

Phocis, a fertile land, while there was land,
Marked for Oetean from Boeotian fields.
It was ocean now, a plain of sudden waters.
There Mount Parnassus lifts its twin peaks skyward,
High, steep, cloud-piercing. And Deucalion came there
Rowing his wife. There was no other land,
The sea had drowned it all. And here they worshipped
First the Corycian nymphs and native powers,   330
Then Themis, oracle and fate-revealer.
There was no better man than this Deucalion,
No one more fond of right; there was no woman
More scrupulously reverent than Pyrrha.
So, when Jove saw the world was one great ocean,
Only one woman left of all those thousands,
And only one man left of all those thousands,
Both innocent and worshipful, he parted
The clouds, turned loose the North-wind, swept them off,
Showed earth to heaven again, and sky to land,   340
And the sea's anger dwindled, and King Neptune
Put down his trident, calmed the waves, and Triton,
Summoned from far down under, with his shoulders
Barnacle-strewn, loomed up above the waters,
The blue-green sea-god, whose resounding horn
Is heard from shore to shore. Wet-bearded, Triton
Set lip to that great shell, as Neptune ordered,
Sounding retreat, and all the lands and waters

Heard and obeyed. The sea has shores; the rivers,
Still running high, have channels; the floods dwindle,   350
Hill-tops are seen again; the trees, long buried,
Rise with their leaves still muddy. The world returns.

Deucalion saw that world, all desolation,
All emptiness, all silence, and his tears
Rose as he spoke to Pyrrha: "O my wife,
The only woman, now, on all this earth
My consort and my cousin and my partner
In these immediate dangers, look! Of all the lands
To East or West, we two, we two alone,
Are all the population. Ocean holds   360
Everything else; our foothold, our assurance,
Are small as they can be, the clouds still frightful.
Poor woman—well, we are not all alone—
Suppose you had been, how would you bear your fear?
Who would console your grief? My wife, believe me,
Had the sea taken you, I would have followed.
If only I had the power, I would restore
The nations as my father did, bring clay
To life with breathing. As it is, we two
Are all the human race, so Heaven has willed it,   370
Samples of men, mere specimens."
                              They wept,
And prayed together, and having wept and prayed,
Resolved to make petition to the goddess
To seek her aid through oracles. Together
They went to the river-water, the stream Cephisus,
Still far from clear, but flowing down its channel,
And they took river-water, sprinkled foreheads,
Sprinkled their garments, and they turned their steps
To the temple of the goddess, where the altars   380
Stood with the fires gone dead, and ugly moss
Stained pediment and column. At the stairs
They both fell prone, kissed the chill stone in prayer:
"If the gods' anger ever listens
To righteous prayers, O Themis, we implore you,
Tell us by what device our wreck and ruin
May be repaired. Bring aid, most gentle goddess,
To sunken circumstance."
                              And Themis heard them,
And gave this oracle: "Go from the temple,   390
Cover your heads, loosen your robes, and throw
Your mother's bones behind you!" Dumb, they stood
In blank amazement, a long silence, broken
By Pyrrha finally: she would not do it!
With trembling lips she prays whatever pardon

Her disobedience might merit, but this outrage
She dare not risk, insult her mother's spirit
By throwing her bones around. In utter darkness
They voice the cryptic saying over and over,
What can it mean? They wonder. At last Deucalion   400
Finds the way out: "I might be wrong, but surely
The holy oracles would never counsel
A guilty act. The earth is our great mother,
And I suppose those bones the goddess mentions
Are the stones of earth; the order means to throw them,
The stones, behind us."
                       She was still uncertain,
And he by no means sure, and both distrustful
Of that command from Heaven; but what damage,
What harm, would there be in trying? They descended,   410
Covered their heads, loosened their garments, threw
The stones behind them as the goddess ordered.
The stones—who would believe it, had we not
The unimpeachable witness of Tradition?—
Began to lose their hardness, to soften, slowly,
To take on form, to grow in size, a little,
Become less rough, to look like human beings,
Or anyway as much like human beings
As statues do, when the sculptor is only starting,
Images half blocked out. The earthy portion,   420
Damp with some moisture, turned to flesh, the solid
Was bone, the veins were as they always had been.
The stones the man had thrown turned into men,
The stones the woman threw turned into women,
Such being the will of God. Hence we derive
The hardness that we have, and our endurance
Gives proof of what we have come from.
                              Other forms
Of life came into being, generated
Out of the earth: the sun burnt off the dampness,   430
Heat made the slimy marshes swell; as seed
Swells in a mother's womb to shape and substance,
So new forms came to life. When the Nile river
Floods and recedes and the mud is warmed by sunshine,
Men, turning over the earth, find living things,
And some not living, but nearly so, imperfect,
On the verge of life, and often the same substance
Is part alive, part only clay. When moisture
Unites with heat, life is conceived; all things
Come from this union. Fire may fight with water,   440
But heat and moisture generate all things,
Their discord being productive. So when earth,
After that flood, still muddy, took the heat,

Felt the warm fire of sunlight, she conceived,
Brought forth, after their fashion, all the creatures,
Some old, some strange and monstrous.
                                        One, for instance,
She bore unwanted, a gigantic serpent,
Python by name, whom the new people dreaded,
A huge bulk on the mountain-side. Apollo,   450
God of the glittering bow, took a long time
To bring him down, with arrow after arrow
He had never used before except in hunting
Deer and the skipping goats. Out of the quiver
Sped arrows by the thousand, till the monster,
Dying, poured poisonous blood on those black wounds.
In memory of this, the sacred games,
Called Pythian, were established, and Apollo
Ordained for all young winners in the races,
On foot or chariot, for victorious fighters,   460
The crown of oak. That was before the laurel,
That was before Apollo wreathed his forehead
With garlands from that tree, or any other.

Apollo and Daphne

Now the first girl Apollo loved was Daphne,
Whose father was the river-god Peneus,
And this was no blind chance, but Cupid's malice.
Apollo, with pride and glory still upon him
Over the Python slain, saw Cupid bending
His tight-strung little bow. "O silly youngster,"
He said, "What are you doing with such weapons?   470
Those are for grown-ups! The bow is for my shoulders;
I never fail in wounding beast or mortal,
And not so long ago I slew the Python
With countless darts; his bloated body covered
Acre on endless acre, and I slew him!
The torch, my boy, is enough for you to play with,
To get the love-fires burning. Do not meddle
With honors that are mine!" And Cupid answered:
"Your bow shoots everything, Apollo—maybe—
But mine will fix you! You are far above   480
All creatures living, and by just that distance
Your glory less than mine." He shook his wings,
Soared high, came down to the shadows of Parnassus,
Drew from his quiver different kinds of arrows,
One causing love, golden and sharp and gleaming,
The other blunt, and tipped with lead, and serving
To drive all love away, and this blunt arrow
He used on Daphne, but he fired the other,
The sharp and golden shaft, piercing Apollo

Through bones, through marrow, and at once he loved   490
And she at once fled from the name of lover,
Rejoicing in the woodland hiding places
And spoils of beasts which she had taken captive,
A rival of Diana, virgin goddess.
She had many suitors, but she scorned them all;
Wanting no part of any man, she travelled
The pathless groves, and had no care whatever
For husband, love, or marriage. Her father often
Said, "Daughter, give me a son-in-law!" and "Daughter,
Give me some grandsons!" But the marriage torches   500
Were something hateful, criminal, to Daphne,
So she would blush, and put her arms around him,
And coax him: "Let me be a virgin always;
Diana's father said she might. Dear father!
Dear father—please!" He yielded, but her beauty
Kept arguing against her prayer. Apollo
Loves at first sight; he wants to marry Daphne,
He hopes for what he wants—all wishful thinking!—
Is fooled by his own oracles. As stubble
Burns when the grain is harvested, as hedges   510
Catch fire from torches that a passer-by
Has brought too near, or left behind in the morning,
So the god burned, with all his heart, and burning
Nourished that futile love of his by hoping.
He sees the long hair hanging down her neck
Uncared for, says, "But what if it were combed?"
He gazes at her eyes—they shine like stars!
He gazes at her lips, and knows that gazing
Is not enough. He marvels at her fingers,
Her hands, her wrists, her arms, bare to the shoulder,   520
And what he does not see he thinks is better.
But still she flees him, swifter than the wind,
And when he calls she does not even listen:
"Don't run away, dear nymph! Daughter of Peneus,
Don't run away! I am no enemy,
Only your follower: don't run away!
The lamb flees from the wolf, the deer the lion,
The dove, on trembling wing, flees from the eagle.
All creatures flee their foes. But I, who follow,
Am not a foe at all. Love makes me follow,   530
Unhappy fellow that I am, and fearful
You may fall down, perhaps, or have the briars
Make scratches on those lovely legs, unworthy
To be hurt so, and I would be the reason.
The ground is rough here. Run a little slower,
And I will run, I promise, a little slower.
Or wait a minute: be a little curious

Just who it is you charm. I am no shepherd,
No mountain-dweller, I am not a ploughboy,
Uncouth and stinking of cattle. You foolish girl,   540
You don't know who it is you run away from,
That must be why you run. I am lord of Delphi
And Tenedos and Claros and Patara.
Jove is my father. I am the revealer
Of present, past and future; through my power
The lyre and song make harmony; my arrow
Is sure in aim—there is only one arrow surer,
The one that wounds my heart. The power of healing
Is my discovery; I am called the Healer
Through all the world: all herbs are subject to me.   550
Alas for me, love is incurable
With any herb; the arts which cure the others
Do me, their lord, no good!"
                              He would have said
Much more than this, but Daphne, frightened, left him
With many words unsaid, and she was lovely
Even in flight, her limbs bare in the wind,
Her garments fluttering, and her soft hair streaming,
More beautiful than ever. But Apollo,
Too young a god to waste his time in coaxing,   560
Came following fast. When a hound starts a rabbit
In an open field, one runs for game, one safety,
He has her, or thinks he has, and she is doubtful
Whether she's caught or not, so close the margin,
So ran the god and girl, one swift in hope,
The other in terror, but he ran more swiftly,
Borne on the wings of love, gave her no rest,
Shadowed her shoulder, breathed on her streaming hair.
Her strength was gone, worn out by the long effort
Of the long flight; she was deathly pale, and seeing   570
The river of her father, cried "O help me,
If there is any power in the rivers,
Change and destroy the body which has given
Too much delight!" And hardly had she finished,
When her limbs grew numb and heavy, her soft breasts
Were closed with delicate bark, her hair was leaves,
Her arms were branches, and her speedy feet
Rooted and held, and her head became a tree top,
Everything gone except her grace, her shining.
Apollo loved her still. He placed his hand   580
Where he had hoped and felt the heart still beating
Under the bark; and he embraced the branches
As if they still were limbs, and kissed the wood,
And the wood shrank from his kisses, and the god
Exclaimed: "Since you can never be my bride,

My tree at least you shall be! Let the laurel
Adorn, henceforth, my hair, my lyre, my quiver:
Let Roman victors, in the long procession,
Wear laurel wreaths for triumph and ovation.
Beside Augustus' portals let the laurel   590
Guard and watch over the oak, and as my head
Is always youthful, let the laurel always
Be green and shining!" He said no more. The laurel,
Stirring, seemed to consent, to be saying *Yes*.

There is a grove in Thessaly, surrounded
By woodlands with steep slopes; men call it Tempe.
Through this the Peneus River's foamy waters
Rise below Pindus mountain. The cascades
Drive a fine smoky mist along the tree tops,
Frail clouds, or so it seems, and the roar of the water   600
Carries beyond the neighborhood. Here dwells
The mighty god himself, his holy of holies
Is under a hanging rock; it is here he gives
Laws to the nymphs, laws to the very water.
And here came first the streams of his own country
Not knowing what to offer, consolation
Or something like rejoicing: crowned with poplars
Sperchios came, and restless Enipeus,
Old Apidanus, Aeas, and Amphrysos
The easy-going. And all the other rivers   610
That take their weary waters into oceans
All over the world, came there, and only one
Was absent, Inachus, hiding in his cavern,
Salting his stream with tears, oh, most unhappy,
Mourning a daughter lost. Her name was Io,
Who might, for all he knew, be dead or living,
But since he can not find her anywhere
He thinks she must be nowhere, and his sorrow
Fears for the worst.

BOOK 3
Echo and Narcissus

                    And so Tiresias,
Famous through all Aonian towns and cities,
Gave irreproachable answers to all comers
Who sought his guidance. One of the first who tested
The truths he told was a naiad of the river,
Liriope, whom the river-god, Cephisus
Embraced and ravished in his watery dwelling.
In time she bore a child, most beautiful
Even as child, gave him the name Narcissus,

And asked Tiresias if the boy would ever   10
Live to a ripe old age. Tiresias answered:
"Yes, if he never knows himself." How silly
Those words seemed, for how long! But as it happened,
Time proved them true—the way he died, the strangeness
Of his infatuation.
                        Now Narcissus
Was sixteen years of age, and could be taken
Either for boy or man; and boys and girls
Both sought his love, but in that slender stripling
Was pride so fierce no boy, no girl, could touch him.   20
He was out hunting one day, driving deer
Into the nets, when a nymph named Echo saw him,
A nymph whose way of talking was peculiar
In that she could not start a conversation
Nor fail to answer other people talking.
Up to this time Echo still had a body,
She was not merely voice. She liked to chatter,
But had no power of speech except the power
To answer in the words she last had heard.
Juno had done this: when she went out looking   30
For Jove on top of some nymph among the mountains,
Echo would stall the goddess off by talking
Until the nymphs had fled. Sooner or later
Juno discovered this and said to Echo:
"The tongue that made a fool of me will shortly
Have shorter use, the voice be brief hereafter."
Those were not idle words; now Echo always
Says the last thing she hears, and nothing further.
She saw Narcissus roaming through the country,
Saw him, and burned, and followed him in secret,   40
Burning the more she followed, as when sulphur
Smeared on the rim of torches, catches fire
When other fire comes near it. Oh, how often
She wanted to come near with coaxing speeches,
Make soft entreaties to him! But her nature
Sternly forbids; the one thing not forbidden
Is to make answers. She is more than ready
For words she can give back. By chance Narcissus
Lost track of his companions, started calling
"Is anybody here?" and "Here!" said Echo.   50
He looked around in wonderment, called louder
"Come to me!" "Come to me!" came back the answer.
He looked behind him, and saw no one coming;
"Why do you run from me?" and heard his question
Repeated in the woods. "Let us get together!"
There was nothing Echo would ever say more gladly,
"Let us get together!" And, to help her words,

Out of the woods she came, with arms all ready
To fling around his neck. But he retreated:
"Keep your hands off," he cried, "and do not touch me!   60
I would die before I give you a chance at me."
"I give you a chance at me," and that was all
She ever said thereafter, spurned and hiding,
Ashamed, in the leafy forests, in lonely caverns.
But still her love clings to her and increases
And grows on suffering; she cannot sleep,
She frets and pines, becomes all gaunt and haggard,
Her body dries and shrivels till voice only
And bones remain, and then she is voice only
For the bones are turned to stone. She hides in woods   70
And no one sees her now along the mountains,
But all may hear her, for her voice is living.

She was not the only one on whom Narcissus
Had visited frustration; there were others,
Naiads or Oreads, and young men also
Till finally one rejected youth, in prayer,
Raised up his hands to Heaven: "May Narcissus
Love one day, so, himself, and not win over
The creature whom he loves!" Nemesis heard him,
Goddess of Vengeance, and judged the plea was righteous.   80
There was a pool, silver with shining water,
To which no shepherds came, no goats, no cattle,
Whose glass no bird, no beast, no falling leaf
Had ever troubled. Grass grew all around it,
Green from the nearby water, and with shadow
No sun burned hotly down on. Here Narcissus,
Worn from the heat of hunting, came to rest
Finding the place delightful, and the spring
Refreshing for the thirsty. As he tried
To quench his thirst, inside him, deep within him,   90
Another thirst was growing, for he saw
An image in the pool, and fell in love
With that unbodied hope, and found a substance
In what was only shadow. He looks in wonder,
Charmed by himself, spell-bound, and no more moving
Than any marble statue. Lying prone
He sees his eyes, twin stars, and locks as comely
As those of Bacchus or the god Apollo,
Smooth cheeks, and ivory neck, and the bright beauty
Of countenance, and a flush of color rising   100
In the fair whiteness. Everything attracts him
That makes him so attractive. Foolish boy,
He wants himself; the loved becomes the lover,
The seeker sought, the kindler burns. How often

He tries to kiss the image in the water,
Dips in his arms to embrace the boy he sees there,
And finds the boy, himself, elusive always,
Not knowing what he sees, but burning for it,
The same delusion mocking his eyes and teasing.
Why try to catch an always fleeing image, 110
Poor credulous youngster? What you seek is nowhere,
And if you turn away, you will take with you
The boy you love. The vision is only shadow,
Only reflection, lacking any substance.
It comes with you, it stays with you, it goes
Away with you, if you can go away.
No thought of food, no thought of rest, can make him
Forsake the place. Stretched on the grass, in shadow,
He watches, all unsatisfied, that image
Vain and illusive, and he almost drowns 120
In his own watching eyes. He rises, just a little,
Enough to lift his arms in supplication
To the trees around him, crying to the forest:
"What love, whose love, has ever been more cruel?
You woods should know: you have given many lovers
Places to meet and hide in; has there ever,
Through the long centuries, been anyone
Who has pined away as I do? He is charming,
I see him, but the charm and sight escape me.
I love him and I cannot seem to find him! 130
To make it worse, no sea, no road, no mountain,
No city-wall, no gate, no barrier, parts us
But a thin film of water. He is eager
For me to hold him. When my lips go down
To kiss the pool, his rise, he reaches toward me.
You would think that I could touch him—almost nothing
Keeps us apart. Come out, whoever you are!
Why do you tease me so? Where do you go
When I am reaching for you? I am surely
Neither so old or ugly as to scare you, 140
And nymphs have been in love with me. You promise,
I think, some hope with a look of more than friendship.
You reach out arms when I do, and your smile
Follows my smiling; I have seen your tears
When I was tearful; you nod and beckon when I do;
Your lips, it seems, answer when I am talking
Though what you say I cannot hear. I know
The truth at last. He is myself! I feel it,
I know my image now. I burn with love
Of my own self; I start the fire I suffer. 150
What shall I do? Shall I give or take the asking?

What shall I ask for? What I want is with me,
My riches make me poor. If I could only
Escape from my own body! if I could only—
How curious a prayer from any lover—
Be parted from my love! And now my sorrow
Is taking all my strength away; I know
I have not long to live, I shall die early,
And death is not so terrible, since it takes
My trouble from me; I am sorry only   160
The boy I love must die: we die together."
He turned again to the image in the water,
Seeing it blur through tears, and the vision fading,
And as he saw it vanish, he called after:
"Where are you going? Stay: do not desert me,
I love you so. I cannot touch you; let me
Keep looking at you always, and in looking
Nourish my wretched passion!" In his grief
He tore his garment from the upper margin,
Beat his bare breast with hands as pale as marble,   170
And the breast took on a glow, a rosy color,
As apples are white and red, sometimes, or grapes
Can be both green and purple. The water clears,
He sees it all once more, and cannot bear it.
As yellow wax dissolves with warmth around it,
As the white frost is gone in morning sunshine,
Narcissus, in the hidden fire of passion,
Wanes slowly, with the ruddy color going,
The strength and hardihood and comeliness,
Fading away, and even the very body   180
Echo had loved. She was sorry for him now,
Though angry still, remembering; you could hear her
Answer "Alas!" in pity, when Narcissus
Cried out "Alas!" You could hear her own hands beating
Her breast when he beat his. "Farewell, dear boy,
Beloved in vain!" were his last words, and Echo
Called the same words to him. His weary head
Sank to the greensward, and death closed the eyes
That once had marveled at their owner's beauty.
And even in Hell, he found a pool to gaze in,   190
Watching his image in the Stygian water.
While in the world above, his naiad sisters
Mourned him, and dryads wept for him, and Echo
Mourned as they did, and wept with them, preparing
The funeral pile, the bier, the brandished torches,
But when they sought his body, they found nothing,
Only a flower with a yellow center
Surrounded with white petals.

BOOK 4

Perseus

**[Cadmus and Harmonia, rulers of Thebes who had refused to worship Bacchus, were
changed into serpents.]**

They had one comfort in their changed condition:
India, conquered, worshipped Bacchus; Greece
Thronged to his temples. King Acrisius only,
Of the same stock, still kept him out of Argos,
Took arms against the god, would not admit him
The son of Jove. Nor would he grant that Perseus
Was also son of Jove, the child begotten
On Danae in the golden rain. But truth
Is powerful: Acrisius learned repentance
For his attack on the god, and his denial   10
Of his own grandson. Bacchus was in Heaven,
But Perseus, bringing back the wondrous trophy
Of the snake-haired monster, through the thin air was cleaving
His way on whirring wings. As he flew over
The Libyan sands, drops from the Gorgon's head
Fell bloody on the ground, and earth received them
Turning them into vipers. For this reason
Libya, today, is full of deadly serpents.

From there he drove through space, the warring winds
Bearing him every way, as a squall is driven.   20
From his great height he looked on lands outspread
Far, far below; he flew the whole world over,
Saw the cold Bears, three times, and saw the Crab
With curving claws, three times, whirled often eastward,
Whirled often to the west. As the day ended,
Fearful of night, he came down for a landing
On the West's edge, the realm of Atlas, seeking
A little rest, till the Morning-star should waken
The fires of dawn, and Dawn lead out the chariot
Of the new day. Atlas, Iapetus' offspring,   30
Loomed over all men in his great bulk of body.
He ruled this land and the sea whose waters take
The Sun's tired horses and the weary wheels
At the long day's end. He had a thousand herds,
No neighbors, and he had a tree, all shining
With gold, whose golden leaves hid golden branches,
Whose golden branches hung with golden apples.
Perseus greeted Atlas: "If the glory
Of lofty birth has any meaning for you,
I am the son of Jove; if you prefer   40
To wonder at great deeds, you will find that mine
Are very wonderful. I ask for rest,

For friendly shelter." But Atlas, doubtful,
Thought of an ancient oracle of Themis:
Atlas, the time will come when your tree loses
Its gold, and the marauder is Jove's son.
Fearful of this, Atlas had walled his orchard,
Given its keeping to a monstrous dragon,
And kept all strangers off. He answered Perseus:
"Get out of here, you liar! Neither Jove   50
Nor glory gets you entrance here." He added
A lusty shove, though Perseus resisted,
Argued, and tried appeasement. But at last,
Inferior in strength (for who could equal
The strength of Atlas?), he told the giant:
"Well, anyway, since you will give me nothing,
I have something here for you!" He turned his back,
Held up, with his left hand behind his body,
Medusa's terrible head, and big, as he was,
Atlas was all at once a mountain: beard   60
And hair were forests, and his arms and shoulders
Were mountain-ridges; what had been his head
Was the peak of the mountain, and his bones were boulders.
But still he grew, for so the gods had willed it,
And his great bulk upheld the starry Heaven.

And Aeolus by now had closed the winds
In their eternal prison; the bright star
That wakes men to their toil, had risen brightly
In the clear morning air, and Perseus fastened
His winged sandals to his feet, took up   70
The scimitar, and soared aloft. Below him
Lay many lands, and finally he saw
The Ethiopians, King Cepheus' people.
There the god Ammon, not without injustice,
Ordered a daughter, who had not deserved it,
To pay the penalty for her mother's talking,
And Perseus saw her there, Andromeda,
Bound by the arms to the rough rocks; her hair,
Stirred in a gentle breeze, and her warm tears flowing
Proved her not marble, as he thought, but woman.   80
She was beautiful, so much so that he almost
Forgot to move his wings. He came down to her
Saying: "My dear, the chains that ought to bind you
Are love-knots rather than shackles. May I ask you
Your name, your country, the reason for this bondage?"
At first she made no answer, too much the virgin
To speak to any man; she would have hidden
Her modest features with her hands, but could not
Since they were bound. Her eyes were free, and filling
With rising tears. And Perseus urged her, gently, 90

Not to seem too unwilling, but to tell him
What wrong she had done, if any; so, at last,
She gave her name, her country, adding further
How her mother had bragged too much about her beauty.
She had not told it all, when the sea roared
And over the sea a monster loomed and towered
Above the wave. She cried aloud. Her parents
Were near at hand, both grieving, but the mother
More justly so, and they brought no help with them,
Only the kind of tears and vain embraces   100
Proper on such occasions. This struck Perseus
As pretty futile. "There is time, and plenty,
For weeping, later," he told them, "but the moment
For help is very short. If I were here as suitor,
I, Perseus, son, of Jove and Danae,
Conqueror of the snaky-headed Gorgon,
The daring flier through the winds of Heaven,
You would accept me, I think, before all others.
But to such great endowments I am trying
To add, with the gods' blessing, a greater service.   110
If I save her by my valor, do I have her?"
What could they say but Yes? They promised also
A kingdom as her dowry.
                              As a galley
Bears down, with all the sturdy sweating rowers
Driving it hard, so came the monster, thrusting
The water on both sides in a long billow.
A slinger from the cliff could almost hit him
When Perseus rose cloudward, and his shadow
Fell on the surface, and the monster, seeing   120
That shadow, raged against it. As an eagle
Sees, in open field, a serpent sunning
Its mottled back, comes swooping down upon it,
Grasps it behind its head, to miss the poison
Sent through the deadly fangs, and buries talons
In scaly neck, so Perseus came plunging
In his steep dive down air, attacked the monster
That roared as the right shoulder took the sword-blade
Up to the hilt. The wound hurt deep, the sea-beast
Reared, lashed, and dived, and thrashed, as a wild-boar does   130
When the hounds bay around him. Perseus rose
When the fangs struck, he poised, he sought for openings
Along the barnacled back, along the sides,
At tapering fishy tail; the monster's vomit
Was blood and salty water. The winged sandals
Grew heavy from that spew, and Perseus dared not
Depend upon them further. He found a rock
Projecting out of the sea when the waves were still,

Hidden in storm. There he hung on, from there
He struck, again, again, and the sword went deep   140
Into the vitals, and the shores re-echoed
To Heaven with applause. Father and mother,
Rejoicing, hail their son-in-law, the savior
Of all the house. The chains are loosened
From the girl's arms, and she comes slowly forward,
The cause, and the reward, of all that labor.
Water is brought so that the victor may
Wash his hands clean of blood; before he washes,
Lest the hard sand injure the Gorgon's head,
He makes it soft with leaves, and over them   150
Strews sea-weed for a cover, and puts down
Medusa's head. And the twigs, all fresh and pliant,
Absorb another force, harden and stiffen
In branch and leaves. The sea-nymphs test the wonder
With other boughs, and the same wonder happens
To their delight, and they use the twigs as seedlings,
Strewing them over the water, and even now
Such is the nature of coral, that it hardens,
Exposed to air, a vine below the surface.

Now Perseus built three altars to three gods,   160
The left for Mercury, the right for Pallas,
The central one for Jove, and sacrificed
Heifer and bull and yearling steer. He wanted
No dowry save Andromeda in payment
Of his reward. And Love and Hymen shook
The marriage-torches, fires fed fat on incense,
Glowing and fragrant, and the garlands hung
Down from the timbers, and the lyre and flute
And song made music, proof of happy spirits.
Great doors swung open, and the golden halls   170
Were set for splendid banqueting, and courtiers
Came thronging to the tables.
                              So they feasted
And took their fill of wine, and all were happy,
And Perseus asked them questions about the region,
People and customs and the native spirit.
They told him, and they asked in turn: "Now tell us,
Heroic Perseus, how you slew the Gorgon."
He told them how there lay, beneath cold Atlas,
A place protected by the bulk of the mountain   180
Where dwelt twin sisters, daughters, both, of Phorcys.
They had one eye between them, and they shared it,
Passing it from one sister to the other,
And he contrived to steal it, being so handed,
And slipped away, going by trackless country,

Rough woods and jagged rocks, to the Gorgons' home.
On all sides, through the fields, along the highways,
He saw the forms of men and beasts, made stone
By one look at Medusa's face. He also
Had seen that face, but only in reflection   190
From the bronze shield his left hand bore; he struck
While snakes and Gorgon both lay sunk in slumber,
Severed the head, and from that mother's bleeding
Were born the swift-winged Pegasus and his brother.

And he went on to tell them of his journeys,
His perils over land and sea, the stars
He had brushed on flying pinions. And they wanted
Still more, and someone asked him why Medusa,
Alone of all the sisters, was snaky-haired.
Their guest replied: "That, too, is a tale worth telling.   200
She was very lovely once, the hope of many
An envious suitor, and of all her beauties
Her hair most beautiful—at least I heard so
From one who claimed he had seen her. One day Neptune
Found her and raped her, in Minerva's temple,
And the goddess turned away, and hid her eyes
Behind her shield, and, punishing the outrage
As it deserved, she changed her hair to serpents,
And even now, to frighten evil doers,
She carries on her breastplate metal vipers   210
To serve as awful warning of her vengeance."

[As the story continues in book 5, Phineus, Andromeda's previous fiancé, accuses Perseus of stealing his promised bride and attacks the hero. A huge fight breaks out and Perseus, seriously outnumbered, raises the Gorgon's head, turning his enemies to stone. He petrifies Phineus as he pleads for mercy, promising the statue to Andromeda!]

BOOK 10

Orpheus and Eurydice

So Hymen left there, clad in saffron robe,
Through the great reach of air, and took his way
To the Ciconian country, where the voice
Of Orpheus called him, all in vain. He came there,
True, but brought with him no auspicious words,
No joyful faces, lucky omens. The torch
Sputtered and filled the eyes with smoke; when swung,
It would not blaze: bad as the omens were,
The end was worse, for as the bride went walking
Across the lawn, attended by her naiads,   10
A serpent bit her ankle, and she was gone.

Orpheus mourned her to the upper world,
And then, lest he should leave the shades untried,
Dared to descend to Styx, passing the portal
Men call Taenarian. Through the phantom dwellers,
The buried ghosts, he passed, came to the king
Of that sad realm, and to Persephone,
His consort, and he swept the strings, and chanted:
"Gods of the world below the world, to whom
All of us mortals come, if I may speak   20
Without deceit, the simple truth is this:
I came here, not to see dark Tartarus,
Nor yet to bind the triple-throated monster
Medusa's offspring, rough with snakes. I came
For my wife's sake, whose growing years were taken
By a snake's venom. I wanted to be able
To bear this; I have tried to. Love has conquered.
This god is famous in the world above,
But here, I do not know. I think he may be
Or is it all a lie, that ancient story   30
Of an old ravishment, and how he brought
The two of you together? By these places
All full of fear, by this immense confusion,
By this vast kingdom's silences, I beg you,
Weave over Eurydice's life, run through too soon.
To you we all, people and things, belong,
Sooner or later, to this single dwelling
All of us come, to our last home; you hold
Longest dominion over humankind.
She will come back again, to be your subject,   40
After the ripeness of her years; I am asking
A loan and not a gift. If fate denies us
This privilege for my wife, one thing is certain:
I do not want to go back either; triumph
In the death of two."
                              And with his words, the music
Made the pale phantoms weep: Ixion's wheel
Was still, Tityos' vultures left the liver,
Tantalus tried no more to reach for the water,
And Belus' daughters rested from their urns,   50
And Sisyphus climbed on his rock to listen.
That was the first time ever in all the world
The Furies wept. Neither the king nor consort
Had harshness to refuse him, and they called her,
Eurydice. She was there, limping a little
From her late wound, with the new shades of Hell.
And Orpheus received her, but one term
Was set: he must not, till he passed Avernus,
Turn back his gaze, or the gift would be in vain.

They climbed the upward path, through absolute silence,   60
Up the steep murk, clouded in pitchy darkness,
They were near the margin, near the upper land,
When he, afraid that she might falter, eager to see her,
Looked back in love, and she was gone, in a moment.
Was it he, or she, reaching out arms and trying
To hold or to be held, and clasping nothing
But empty air? Dying the second time,
She had no reproach to bring against her husband,
What was there to complain of? One thing, only:
He loved her. He could hardly hear her calling   70
Farewell! when she was gone.
                              The double death
Stunned Orpheus, like the man who turned to stone
At sight of Cerberus, or the couple of rock,
Olenos and Lethaea, hearts so joined
One shared the other's guilt, and Ida's mountain,
Where rivers run, still holds them, both together.
In vain the prayers of Orpheus and his longing
To cross the river once more; the boatman Charon
Drove him away. For seven days he sat there   80
Beside the bank, in filthy garments, and tasting
No food whatever. Trouble, grief, and tears
Were all his sustenance. At last, complaining
The gods of Hell were cruel, he wandered on
To Rhodope and Haemus, swept by the north winds,
Where, for three years, he lived without a woman
Either because marriage had meant misfortune
Or he had made a promise. But many women
Wanted this poet for their own, and many
Grieved over their rejection. His love was given   90
To young boys only, and he told the Thracians
That was the better way: *enjoy that springtime,*
Take those first flowers!
                        There was a hill, and on it
A wide-extending plain, all green, but lacking
The darker green of shade, and when the singer
Came there and ran his fingers over the strings,
The shade came there to listen. The oak-tree came,
And many poplars, and the gentle lindens,
The beech, the virgin laurel, and the hazel   100
Easily broken, the ash men use for spears,
The shining silver-fir, the ilex bending
Under its acorns, the friendly sycamore,
The changing-colored maple, and the willows
That love the river-waters, and the lotus
Favoring pools, and the green boxwood came,
Slim tamarisks, and myrtle, and viburnum

With dark-blue berries, and the pliant ivy,
The tendrilled grape, the elms, all dressed with vines,
The rowan-trees, the pitch-pines, and the arbute   110
With the red fruit, the palm, the victor's triumph,
The bare-trunked pine with spreading leafy crest,
Dear to the mother of the gods since Attis
Put off his human form, took on that likeness,
And the cone-shaped cypress joined them, now a tree,
But once a boy, loved by the god Apollo
Master of lyre and bow-string, both together.

BOOK 11

The Death of Orpheus

So with his singing Orpheus drew the trees,
The beasts, the stones, to follow, when, behold!
The mad Ciconian women, fleeces flung
Across their maddened breasts, caught sight of him
From a near hill-top, as he joined his song
To the lyre's music. One of them, her tresses
Streaming in the light air, cried out: "Look there!
There is our despiser!" and she flung a spear
Straight at the singing mouth, but the leafy wand
Made only a mark and did no harm. Another   10
Let fly a stone, which, even as it flew,
Was conquered by the sweet harmonious music,
Fell at his feet, as if to ask for pardon.
But still the warfare raged, there was no limit,
Mad fury reigned, and even so, all weapons
Would have been softened by the singer's music,
But there was other orchestration: flutes
Shrilling, and trumpets braying loud, and drums,
Beating of breasts, and howling, so the lyre
Was overcome, and then at last the stones   20
Reddened with blood, the blood of the singer, heard
No more through all that outcry. All the birds
Innumerable, fled, and the charmed snakes,
The train of beasts, Orpheus' glory, followed.
The Maenads stole the show. Their bloody hands
Were turned against the poet; they came thronging
Like birds who see an owl, wandering in daylight;
They bayed him down, as in the early morning,
Hounds circle the doomed stag beside the game-pits.
They rushed him, threw the wands, wreathed with green leaves,   30
Not meant for such a purpose; some threw clods,
Some branches torn from the tree, and some threw stones,
And they found fitter weapons for their madness.
Not far away there was a team of oxen

Plowing the field, and near them farmers, digging
Reluctant earth, and sweating over their labor,
Who fled before the onrush of this army
Leaving behind them hoe and rake and mattock
And these the women grabbed, and slew the oxen
Who lowered horns at them in brief defiance   40
And were torn limb from limb, and then the women
Rushed back to murder Orpheus, who stretched out
His hands in supplication, and whose voice,
For the first time, moved no one. They struck him down,
And through those lips to which the rocks had listened,
To which the hearts of savage beasts responded,
His spirit found its way to winds and air.

The birds wept for him, and the throng of beasts,
The flinty rocks, the trees which came so often
To hear his song, all mourned. The trees, it seemed,   50
Shook down their leaves, as if they might be women
Tearing their hair, and rivers, with their tears,
Were swollen, and their naiads and their dryads
Mourned in black robes. The poet's limbs lay scattered
Where they were flung in cruelty or madness,
But Hebrus River took the head and lyre
And as they floated down the gentle current
The lyre made mournful sounds, and the tongue murmured
In mournful harmony, and the banks echoed
The strains of mourning. On the sea, beyond   60
Their native stream, they came at last to Lesbos
And grounded near the city of Methymna.
And here a serpent struck at the head, still dripping
With sea-spray, but Apollo came and stopped it,
Freezing the open jaws to stone, still gaping.
And Orpheus' ghost fled under the earth, and knew
The places he had known before, and, haunting
The fields of the blessed, found Eurydice
And took her in his arms, and now together
And side by side they wander, or Orpheus follows   70
Or goes ahead, and may, with perfect safety,
Look back for his Eurydice.
                              But Bacchus
Demanded punishment for so much evil.
Mourning his singer's loss, he bound those women,
All those who saw the murder, in a forest,
Twisted their feet to roots, and thrust them deep
Into unyielding earth. As a bird struggles
Caught in a fowler's snare, and flaps and flutters
And draws its bonds the tighter by its struggling,   80
Even so the Thracian women, gripped by the soil,

Fastened in desperate terror, writhed and struggled,
But the roots held. They looked to see their fingers,
Their toes, their nails, and saw the bark come creeping
Up the smooth legs; they tried to smite their thighs
With grieving hands, and struck on oak; their breasts
Were oak, and oak their shoulders, and their arms
You well might call long branches and be truthful.

BOOK 15

The Deification of Caesar

[After summarizing the early history of Rome, Ovid ends on the story of Asclepius (Aesculapius), god of medicine, who arrives in Rome in the form of a serpent to cure a deadly plague.]

                    The old god
Came to our shrines from foreign lands, but Caesar
Is god in his own city. First in war,
And first in peace, victorious, triumphant,
Planner and governor, quick-risen to glory,
The newest star in Heaven, and more than this,
And above all, immortal through his son.
No work, in all of Caesar's great achievement,
Surpassed this greatness, to have been the father
Of our own Emperor. To have tamed the Britons,   10
Surrounded by the fortress of their ocean,
To have led a proud victorious armada
Up seven-mouthed Nile, to have added to the empire
Rebel Numidia, Libya, and Pontus
Arrogant with the name of Mithridates,
To have had many triumphs, and deserved
Many more triumphs: this was truly greatness,
Greatness surpassed only by being father
Of one yet greater, one who rules the world
As proof that the immortal gods have given   20
Rich blessing to the human race, so much so
We cannot think him mortal, our Augustus,
Therefore our Julius must be made a god
To justify his son.
                    And golden Venus
Saw this, and saw, as well, the murder plotted
Against her priest, the assassins in their armor,
And she grew pale with fear. "Behold," she cried
To all the gods in turn, "Behold, what treason
Threatens me with its heavy weight, what ambush   30
Is set to take Iulus' last descendant!
Must this go on forever? Once again
The spear of Diomedes strikes to wound me,

The walls of Troy fall over me in ruins,
Once more I see my son, long-wandering,
Storm-tossed, go down to the shades, and rise again
To war with Turnus, or to speak more truly,
With Juno. It is very foolish of me
To dwell on those old sufferings, for my fear,
My present fear, has driven them from my mind.   40
Look: Do you see them whetting their evil daggers?
Avert this crime, before the fires of Vesta
Drown in their high-priest's blood!"
                              The anxious goddess
Cried these complaints through Heaven, and no one listened.
The gods were moved, and though they could not shatter
The iron mandates of the ancient sisters,
They still gave certain portents of the evil
To come upon the world. In the dark storm-clouds
Arms clashed and trumpets blared, most terrible,   50
And horns heard in the sky warned men of crime,
And the sun's visage shone with lurid light
On anxious lands. Firebrands were seen to flash
Among the stars, the clouds dripped blood, rust-color
Blighted the azure Morning-Star, and the Moon
Rode in a blood-red car. The Stygian owl
Wailed in a thousand places; ivory statues
Dripped tears in a thousand places, and wailing traveled
The holy groves, and threats were heard. No victim
Paid expiation, and the liver warned   60
Of desperate strife to come, the lobe found cloven
Among the entrails. In the market place,
Around the homes of men and the gods' temples
Dogs howled by night, and the shadows of the silent
Went roaming, and great earthquakes shook the city.
No warning of the gods could check the plotting
Of men, avert the doom of fate. Drawn swords
Were borne into a temple; nowhere else
In the whole city was suitable for murder
Save where the senate met.   70
                         Then Venus beat
Her breast with both her hands, and tried to hide him,
Her Caesar, in a cloud, as she had rescued
Paris from Menelaus, as Aeneas
Fled Diomedes' sword. And Jove spoke to her:
"My daughter, do you think your power alone
Can move the fates no power can ever conquer?
Enter the home of the Three Sisters: there
You will see the records, on bronze and solid iron,
Wrought with tremendous effort, and no crashing   80
Of sky, no wrath of lightning, no destruction

Shall make them crumble. They are safe, forever.
There you will find engraved on adamant
The destinies of the race, unchangeable.
I have read them, and remembered; I will tell you
So you may know the future. He has finished
The time allotted him, this son you grieve for;
His debt to earth is paid. But he will enter
The Heaven as a god, and have his temples
On earth as well: this you will see fulfilled,   90
Will bring about, you and his son together.
He shall inherit both the name of Caesar
And the great burden, and we both shall help him
Avenge his father's murder. Under him
Mutina's conquered walls will sue for mercy,
Pharsalia know his power, and Philippi
Run red with blood again, and one more Pompey
Go down to death in the Sicilian waters.
A Roman general's Egyptian woman,
Foolish to trust that liaison, will perish   100
For all her threats that our own capitol
Would serve Canopus. Need I bring to mind
Barbarian lands that border either ocean?
Whatever lands men live on, the world over,
Shall all be his to rule, and the seas also.
And when peace comes to all the world, his mind
Will turn to law and order, civil justice,
And men will learn from his sublime example,
And he, still looking forward toward the future,
The coming generations, will give order   110
That his good wife's young son should take his name,
His duty when he lays the burden down,
Though he will live as long as ancient Nestor
Before he comes to heaven to greet his kinsmen.
Now, in the meantime, from the murdered body
Raise up the spirit, set the soul of Julius
As a new star in Heaven, to watch over
Our market place, our Capitol."
                                  He ended,
And Venus, all unseen, came to the temple,   120
Raised from the body of Caesar the fleeting spirit,
Not to be lost in air, but borne aloft
To the bright stars of Heaven. As she bore it,
She felt it burn, released it from her bosom,
And saw it rise, beyond the moon, a comet
Rising, not falling, leaving the long fire
Behind its wake, and gleaming as a star.
And now he sees his son's good acts, confessing
They are greater than his own, for once rejoicing

In being conquered. But the son refuses 130
To have his glories set above his father's;
Fame will not heed him, for she heeds no mortal,
Exalts him, much against his will, resists him
In this one instance only. So must Atreus
Defer to Agamemnon; so does Theseus
Surpass Aegeus, and Achilles Peleus,
And—(one more instance where the father's glory
Yields to the son's)—Saturn is less than Jove.
Jove rules the lofty citadels of Heaven,
The kingdoms of the triple world, but Earth 140
Acknowledges Augustus. Each is father
As each is lord. O gods, Aeneas' comrades,
To whom the fire and sword gave way, I pray you,
And you, O native gods of Italy,
Quirinus, father of Rome, and Mars, the father
Of Rome's unconquered sire, and Vesta, honored
With Caesar's household gods, and Apollo, tended
With reverence as Vesta is, and Jove,
Whose temple crowns Tarpeia's rock, O gods,
However many, whom the poet's longing 150
May properly invoke, far be the day,
Later than our own era, when Augustus
Shall leave the world he rules, ascend to Heaven,
And there, beyond our presence, hear our prayers!

The Epilogue

Now I have done my work. It will endure,
I trust, beyond Jove's anger, fire and sword,
Beyond Time's hunger. The day will come, I know,
So let it come, that day which has no power
Save over my body, to end my span of life
Whatever it may be. Still, part of me, 160
The better part, immortal, will be borne
Above the stars; my name will be remembered
Wherever Roman power rules conquered lands,
I shall be read, and through all centuries,
If prophecies of bards are ever truthful,
I shall be living, always.

Questions for Discussion and Review

1. What are the "Ages of Man" according to Ovid? Compare Ovid's description of the Ages of Man with that of the Greek poet Hesiod (Chapter 6). What characteristically Roman views and ideas does Ovid incorporate in his version of the myth?

2. How does Ovid characterize his own time? What does he value about Roman life? What does he fear? What does he criticize?

3. What does Apollo want from Daphne? Why does she refuse him? What does Apollo's attempted rape suggest about the relationship between humans and gods?

4. How would you describe Perseus's character as portrayed by Ovid? How does he differ from the hero of the Greek Perseus myths (Chapter 10)? How does Perseus's attitude toward Andromeda in Ovid's poem differ from that in the Greek myth?

5. Both Ovid and Virgil raise the issue of "Eternal Rome" in their poems. Compare and contrast their views. Does each poet value the concept that his nation is destined to last forever or subject that idea to an ironic critique? How does each see Caesar's role? Defend your views with specific references to each work.

6. How does the story of Orpheus and Eurydice compare or contrast with descents into the Underworld, such as those of Heracles, Persephone, or Adonis?

Recommended Reading

Barnard, Mary E. *The Myth of Apollo and Daphne from Ovid to Quevedo: Love, Agon and the Grotesque.* Durham: Duke UP, 1987. In her section on Ovid, the author argues for an ironic view of Ovid's attitude toward Augustus.

Brooks, Otis. *Ovid as an Epic Poet.* 2nd ed. Cambridge: Cambridge UP, 1970. A classic study for modern students of Ovid, with a thoughtful analysis of the *Metamorphoses* as a unified and carefully structured work.

PART FIVE

❦

The Western World's
Transformations of Myth

21

The Persistence of Myth

KEY THEMES

Despite a period of relative decline between the fall of Rome and the late Middle Ages, classical mythology endures throughout the history of Western culture—through translations and revivals, through adaptations and re-interpretations, through the borrowing of themes and images, and through the use of key figures and symbols. During some periods of history, certain mythic figures (such as Icarus during the Renaissance or Prometheus during the Romantic period) have become symbols of the central ideas or concerns of the age.

The Decline and Revival of Classical Mythology

Perhaps the most remarkable attribute of classical mythology is its persistence. Long after ceasing to have even the remotest connections to belief systems, these myths have continued to resonate, reflecting continuing human concerns and providing an enduring cultural resource shared across the boundaries created by politics, language, religion, and time itself.

Classical mythology has not, of course, retained a constant level of popular appeal. In fact, its survival has not been at all a foregone conclusion. During the period historians call the *Dark Ages,* the rise and spread of Christianity, along with the collapse of the Roman Empire and the ensuing economic and political disorders in Europe, contributed to the general disappearance of literacy as well as to a radical change in perspective. Among the effects was a loss of knowledge of or interest in classical learning of all kinds. Although it never entirely disappeared, classical mythology was considered particularly inappropriate for a Christian audience, primarily because of its "pagan" deities. Further, the new guide for human behavior—the imitation of Christ, with its focus on humility and otherworldliness—theoretically negated the mythic hero as an appropriate role model (though that concept, too, survived by being transposed into an acceptably Christian context in such heroes as Roland and the ostensibly Christian Beowulf).

As literacy gradually became more widespread again in the late Middle Ages, it was in the works of writers like Virgil and Ovid that growing numbers of readers rediscovered classical mythology and quickly proceeded to reclaim large territories of the mythological landscape, despite its pagan character. The example of Virgil, in fact, eased the process of assimilating the mythic material into the Christian world-view. In the fourth of a series of poems called *Eclogues,* Virgil had referred to a child who would come to redeem Rome. Claiming this allusion as Virgil's "prediction" of the Coming of Christ allowed medieval Christian readers to justify their attention to a pagan poet. In his three-part poem the *Commedia* (later known as the *Divine Comedy*), the Italian poet Dante expanded the trip to the Underworld from Book 6 of Virgil's *Aeneid* into the subject of the entire first book (the *Inferno*) of his poem, transforming Aeneas's voyage into a spiritual journey of the soul. He also made Virgil himself into a literary character, portraying the Roman poet as his guide through both Hell and Purgatory. While Dante placed the pagan **Ulysses** [oo-LIS-seez] (Odysseus) in Hell for daring to sail beyond the world's limits to Mt. Purgatory, he also borrowed many mythological details of Virgil's Underworld, from the River Styx to figures such as **Charon, Cerberus,** and **Minos.** Virgil's *Aeneid* remained, through the eighteenth century and beyond, the staple of European education, providing an introduction to the larger body of classical mythology that artists, composers, and writers could draw on for centuries to come.

Meanwhile, the Courtly Love tradition, beginning in the twelfth century, sparked a revived interest in Ovid's *Art of Love.* Ovid's metaphor of service to Eros—or Cupid, the god of love whose flames, darts, and arrows wounded lovers—pervades love poems from Dante's own love sonnets, *La Vita Nuova* (*The New Life*), to Petrarch's cycle of sonnets *To Laura,* which in turn became the model for secular love poems from the early Renaissance to the present day.

The Later Uses of Classical Mythology

The popular uses of images from classical mythology in the modern world include fields as diverse as psychology, sociology, television, and advertising, to name a few. Indeed, mythic materials are so common that we are often scarcely aware of the mythic components of advertisements such as the logos of tire companies (Atlas, the Titan who held the sky on his shoulders) or of floral delivery services (Hermes with winged sandals) or the "cupids" whose hearts and arrows adorn Valentine's Day cards. There are mythological references even in apparently abstract phrases like "the culture of narcissism" (a description of an era when people seem obsessed with gratification of their personal needs), which alludes to the myth of **Narcissus,** a young man who fell in love with his own image.

Methods of Transmission

Even if we turn specifically to literature and the arts, a complete list of works that use classical mythology would require hundreds of pages. But despite this scope and diversity, mythic material is most frequently transmitted in four basic ways: (1) rendering ancient plays or poems accessible to modern readers by translating them into modern languages or by reviving them in contemporary performances; (2) updating (by reinterpreting or adapting) ancient stories, plays, or poems to make them relevant to contemporary audiences; (3) taking advantage of an audience's continued familiarity with mythic materials by borrowing their themes and images to create a double vision, ancient and modern, either to reinforce or to contrast each other in thematic counterpoint; (4) using a specific mythic figure as an emblem or a symbol of an idea that an artist, writer, composer, or director wishes to expound or explore.

Translations and Revivals

In ancient Greece itself, of course, as in Rome (as long as educated Romans learned Greek), translations weren't necessary. But by the Middle Ages, the vernacular European languages had replaced Latin as the language of everyday speech, though it was retained as a religious and literary language; meanwhile, the study of Greek dwindled. When interest in classical writers was revived in the Renaissance, the study of Greek once again became popular with humanist scholars, who set about searching for Greek and Roman manuscripts. After the fall of Constantinople to the Turks in 1453, many Greek scholars escaped to Italy, often bringing their prized ancient manuscripts with them and thus fueling the ongoing classical revival. As learning and the taste for classical works spread beyond the elite circles of humanist scholars, translations became necessary. One influential Renaissance translator was the English poet and playwright George Chapman, who was the first to translate Homer's work into English (1616). Later, Alexander Pope did his own translation, rendering the *Iliad* in rhymed couplets, reflecting the eighteenth-century perception of a harmonious and meticulously organized universe where common sense reigned:

> The King of men, on public counsels bent,
> Convened the princes in his ample tent;
> Each seized a portion of the kingly feast,
> But stayed his hand when thirst and hunger ceased.
> Then Nestor spoke, for wisdom long approved,
> And, slowly rising, thus the council moved:
> "Monarch of nations! whose superior sway
> Assembled states and lords of earth obey,
> The laws and sceptres to thy hand are given,
> And millions own the care of thee and heaven.
>
> . . . .
>
> Thee, prince! it fits alike to speak and hear,
> Pronounce with judgment, with regard give ear,
> To see no wholesome motion be withstood,
> And ratify the best for public good. (9.121–135)

Each era since has produced its own crop of translations, each reflective of its own taste. As scholars learned more about the ancient world and its languages, the accuracy as well as the readability of the texts improved, and many fine modern translations became available to everyone.

Adaptations, Revisions, and "Updatings"

The practice of writing "revisionist" versions of extant works began as early as the classical playwrights themselves: Aeschylus, Sophocles, and Euripides wrote plays dramatizing their versions of the same myths as did their fellow playwrights and competitors. Each of the three, for instance, had his own version of the story of the revenge of Orestes and Electra. And although the basic plot outlines remained unchanged, their interpretations and judgments of the action differed radically. For example, whereas Aeschylus's Oresteian trilogy praises the Athenian jury system as superior to a system of justice administered either by individual humans or by gods who have agendas of their own, Euripides's *Electra* comments on the ability of important, well-connected people like Orestes and Electra to get off lightly even after committing the most appalling crimes while peasants and villagers, who are portrayed as comparatively noble and generous, go unrewarded. Ovid, too, rewrote Greek myths in terms that reflected the sensibilities of his Roman audience.

The Revival of Drama   When, after a prolonged interruption during the Dark and Middle Ages, classical drama was revived in the Renaissance, playwrights began immediately revising plays to fit their own conceptions. Some of the earliest plays, such as *Hercules Furens* (1561), were composed and performed in London at the Inns of Court by university students who showed great fondness for the plays of the Roman playwright Seneca, as did William Shakespeare (*Titus Andronicus,* 1594). Later examples include the grand Baroque moral tragedies of the seventeenth-century French playwright Jean Racine (*Phaedre,* 1677, and *Andromache,* 1667, for example) and the twentieth-century rewrites of the American playwright Eugene O'Neill (for example, his trilogy *Mourning Becomes Electra,* 1931, a version of Aeschylus's *Oresteia*). And the French existentialist dramatists Andre Gide (*Oedipus,* 1931), Jean Giraudoux (*Electra,* 1937), Jean-Paul Sartre (*The Flies,* 1943, also a version of the Orestes myth), and Jean Anouilh collectively made a kind of mini-industry of mythological dramas.

Anouilh, for example, wrote a version of *Antigone* (1944) that would have been especially meaningful to a French audience during World War II. In Sophocles's version, the heroine's determination to bury her brother's body in defiance of the law decreed by her uncle Creon is portrayed as a courageous upholding of the gods' moral law against the decrees of a tyrant; in Anouilh's hands, her defiant self-sacrifice is recreated as an example of an existential act of commitment—of asserting one's freedom to define oneself morally in a universe whose absurdity is underlined by the author's portrayal of Creon and his henchmen as members of the Vichy government (French collaborators with the Nazis who were at that moment occupying France).

Musical and Literary Adaptations   Nor are the adaptations confined to plays. In fact, the invention of opera itself may be traced to a desire to revive Greek drama in its "original" form. The Florentine Camarata, a group of Italian humanists devoted to literature and the arts, believed that the Greeks and Romans sang rather than spoke their tragedies in stage performance. They were determined to revive the ancient practice, which they believed to be a perfect marriage of poetry and music. To fulfill that aim, Ottavio Rinuccini, a court poet of the Medici family, wrote *Daphne* (c. 1594), a text based on Greek myth set to music, which is generally taken to be the first opera in European history. Its music has been lost, and thus Rinuccini's second such work, *Eurydice* (1600), also based on a Greek myth, is considered the first complete opera.

It is the Baroque composer Claudio Monteverdi, however, who is credited with creating modern opera as we know it, unifying all the vocal, instrumental, and dra-

FIGURE 21-1   Philip Trager, *The Abduction,* 1996. This striking photo of a performance of *Persephone,* choreographed by Ralph Lemon, was commissioned by the Jacob's Pillow Dance Festival, Dance Anthology Project as part of a collaborative effort by photographer, choreographer, and dancers. The photo shows Persephone being pursued by Hades. (Photo © Philip Trager, 1996.)

matic elements. When he wrote his first opera (*Orpheus,* 1607), he too turned to Greek mythology and, like Rinuccini, chose to retell the story of **Orpheus** and **Eurydice.** Many opera composers since—from Henry Purcell (*Dido and Aeneas,* 1689) to Richard Strauss (*Electra,* 1909) to Igor Stravinsky (*Oedipus Rex,* 1927)—have continued to use adaptations of works based on classical myths as the sources of their libretti. Further continuing the adaptation of mythology were poets such as William Shakespeare ("Venus and Adonis," 1593) and writers of fiction such as John Barth (whose *Chimera,* 1972, tells the stories of three heroes including Perseus and Bellerophon) and James Joyce (whose novel *Ulysses,* 1914, updates the *Odyssey,* setting it in early-twentieth-century Dublin). More recently, the Caribbean poet Derek Walcott also dramatized the Homeric epic in *The Odyssey: A Stage Version* (1992).

The Use of Mythic Themes and Images

Even more frequently than adapting entire myths, plays, or epics, countless artists, writers, and composers have based their work more loosely on mythic themes or have employed mythic images, whether for a brief allusion made in a single line of poetry or prose, for the inspiration of the spirit of a musical composition, or for a concrete embodiment of a feeling or idea or point of view in a novel, poem, painting, film, or even photography or dance (Figure 21-1).

FIGURE 21-2   Claude Lorrain, *Coast View of Delos with Aeneas,* 1672. In this pastoral scene in Lorrain's painting that typically anticipates the neoclassical style, the landscape has become the real subject, a peaceful, bucolic scene tastefully dotted with small structures in imitation of Greek architecture to lend a "classical" flavor. The human figures who occupied most of the space in paintings from the Renaissance through the middle of the seventeenth century have been reduced to the point that they are absorbed into the landscape and are almost incidental—a fitting reflection of an age that saw itself as made up of "pygmies" whose achievements could never surpass those of the "giants," such as Homer and Virgil, of ancient Greece and Rome. (*National Gallery, London.*)

Thus, to cite a mere handful of examples, the Renaissance painter Sandro Botticelli depicted the birth of Venus (see Color Plate 1), revealing the grace, beauty, and harmonious nature of Love; half a century later, in the Mannerist style, Jean Cousin the Elder placed Eve, the "first Pandora" (see Color Plate 2), in the traditional pose of the reclining Venus, depicting her with one hand on her jar and the other resting on a skull, suggesting a more ambivalent response. The painter Claude Lorrain recreated a scene from the *Aeneid* (Figure 21-2)—a vision of a "Golden Age" that reflected the order, balance, and symmetry of neoclassical ideals. Many of Lorrain's paintings depicted similar scenes, and portrayals of the Golden Age remained popular throughout the period.

The Victorian poet Alfred, Lord Tennyson ("Ulysses," 1842) picked up where Homer left off, imagining the frustrations of an aged and enervated Odysseus longing for the thrill of one last voyage, while more recently Constantine Cavafy's poem "Ithaca" (1911) imagines the adventurous journey we all embark on to our own private Ithaca, relishing the voyage itself rather than its destination:

FIGURE 21-3 Salvador Dali, *Leda Atomica*, 1948. In this surrealist painting, Leda (actually a portrait of the artist's wife, Gala) sits on a "throne" floating in space, as the swan floats beside her. In the original myth, the swan is Zeus in disguise, who would make love to Leda, thereby conceiving Helen and setting in motion the destruction of Troy; here the swan looks like nothing more than a realistic domestic fowl. The juxtaposition, as in a dream, of the literal and the symbolic, of the real and the imaginary, of solid objects suspended in unreal space, renders in visual terms the nature of mythology itself. (*Collection of the artist.*)

> Ithaca gave you the marvelous journey.
> Without her you wouldn't have set out.
> She hasn't anything else to give.

Similarly, in the early twentieth century, the poet William Butler Yeats ("Leda and the Swan," 1923) used the myth of the conception of Helen of Troy to consider the irony of seemingly transient moments causing enormously destructive consequences, whereas the modern surrealist painter Salvador Dali rendered the same myth in a much more cerebral and nonthreatening fashion (Figure 21-3).

W. H. Auden ("The Shield of Achilles," 1952) rewrote Homer's description of the two sides of Achilles's shield, with its contrasting scenes of peace and war, in the *Iliad* to comment on the illusions of heroism and the stupidity of power enforced by violence. A similar use of mythic images can be found in the work of Pablo Picasso, who did a series of etchings illustrating Ovid's *Metamorphoses*. The images he employed in the *Minotauromachia* (Figure 21-4) reappeared two years later in *Guernica* (Figure 21-5), a stark black-and-white painting depicting the horrors of the Spanish Civil War. Salvador Dali, on the other hand, used the Ovidian tale of Narcissus to explore the unconscious images generated by a personality undergoing transformation in *The Metamorphosis of Narcissus* (see Color Plate 16).

Extended Uses of Mythic Themes Some examples of more extended uses of mythic themes and images include such diverse works as John Updike's novel *The Centaur* (1962), in which the divided creature of myth is identified with the conflicting impulses and needs of a Pennsylvania high school student, and James Joyce's *Portrait of the Artist as a Young Man* (1916), whose hero, a young poet, is compared with Daedalus, King Minos's "artificer" who designed both the Labyrinth at Knossos

FIGURE 21-4   Pablo Picasso, *Minotauromachia,* 1935. Picasso, who at the time of this painting had recently done a series of etchings illustrating Ovid's *Metamorphoses,* often turned to classical themes. The figure of the Minotaur reappears frequently in his paintings and etchings. In this etching, "The Battle of the Minotaur," the half-human beast creates terror and chaos. Amid the carnage, he points the sword toward a little girl holding a candle and a bouquet of flowers—a peace offering? Has she, like Ariadne, let Theseus (the man on the ladder?) into the labyrinth, naively trusting that he would destroy the monster within with no consequences? This Minotaur has taken the sword of the female matador sent to kill him; her body lies dead across the back of the horse, whose guts pour out on the ground. While the man hurries to escape up the ladder, the two women in the window regard the doves on the windowsill. Are they indifferent, thinking themselves safe up there, or unaware of the threat of war? (*Museum of Modern Art, New York.*)

(the institution of the Catholic Church in Joyce's version) and the waxen wings (now equated with the powers of poetry) with which to escape its confines. Bernard Malamud's novel *The Natural* (1952)—like the film based on it (1984, directed by Barry Levinson)—has a baseball-player hero who undergoes experiences similar to those of both Achilles and Odysseus.

In these and other works based on mythic themes or images, the mythic material provides a way of understanding in greater depth the individual experiences depicted. These authors take advantage of the continuing relevance of the myths to the unchanging conditions of human experience while using the same myths to comment, sometimes ironically, on the experiences they describe.

FIGURE 21-5 Pablo Picasso, *Guernica,* 1937. In this enormous painting (11′6″ × 25′8″), Picasso uses many of the images from the *Minotauromachia* (Figure 21-4)—the disjointed bodies, the scream of the horse, the girl holding the lamp, and even the bull—to depict the horrors of the saturation-bombing of the town of Guernica by Franco's forces during the Spanish Civil War. In this painting, however, no one, not even the bull, escapes the agony, and the flowers lie trampled near the now-broken blade. The artist's exclusion of color and combining of cubist and expressionist techniques—the refusal of three-dimensional forms, the suggestion of "collage" in the newsprint-like sections of the horse's body, the distortion of eyes that reveal inner and outer perspectives simultaneously—allow him to depict raw, unmediated emotions. Instead of the conventional view through the frame of a "window" that gives viewers a glimpse of events happening to others, this painting is a nightmare that envelops the viewers and traps them inside the horror, recreating the experience of the original victims: the only rational response to this painting is a scream. (*Prado, Madrid.*)

Myth as Emblem

Some writers, in the sciences and social sciences as well as in the arts, have seized upon a specific mythic figure to function as an emblem or a symbol of an idea they wished to explain. Thus, the psychoanalyst Sigmund Freud used the figure of Oedipus (*The Interpretation of Dreams,* 1900) to embody the unconscious, infantile erotic drives to which, he argued, all humans are subject; Albert Camus, an existentialist writer, chose **Sisyphus** (who was condemned to push an enormous stone repeatedly up a mountain, only to have it roll down the other side) as a concrete embodiment of the choice an individual makes to define himself in an absurd world in that moment when he decides, each time, to push the stone up the mountain once more (*The Myth of Sisyphus,* 1942). Similarly, contemporary ecologists have singled out the figure of Gaea, the ancient earth goddess, to signify the essential interrelationship of all components of earth's biosphere, and feminist psychologists employ the same goddess—both in her own right and as divided into separate functions in such goddesses as Hera, Athene, Artemis, and Aphrodite—as emblems of various components of the female psyche (Jean Shinoda Bolen, *Goddesses in Everywoman,* 1984).

More recently, John Gray (*Men Are From Mars, Women Are From Venus,* 1992) uses the mythic lovers in his title as emblems of the problems of communication between the genders in modern relationships. John Shay (*Achilles in Vietnam: Combat Trauma and the Undoing of Character,* 1994), a psychiatrist treating Vietnam War veterans suffering from post-traumatic stress disorder, uses Homer's Achilles to illuminate the afflictions of modern combat veterans, while using the modern soldiers' experience to clarify what also happens to Achilles: the sense of betrayal, the withdrawal from one's society, and the "berserk state" that is the climax of extreme combat trauma, apparently, whether in ancient battles or in those of our own era.

Myth and Cultural History

Precisely because they have lasted so long, myths, in whatever form they have been transmitted, can be extremely useful tools for students of cultural history. For example, because so many myths continue to be adapted and reinterpreted, historians can study the various revisions as barometers of cultural change. The story of the musician Orpheus and his ill-fated descent into the Underworld to rescue his beloved Eurydice, for example, can be variously portrayed as a grand but tragic passion or as a descent into the depths of the human psyche or into the abyss of existential despair, or even as a comment on the destructive effect of patriarchal male-female relationships, as H. D. (Hilda Doolittle) does, lamenting in her poem "Eurydice," the "arrogance" and self-sufficiency of Orpheus, who can neither leave Eurydice at peace in the Underworld nor allow her to emerge on her own terms (1917, 1925).

Indeed, the story of Orpheus and Eurydice has been interpreted in these and many other ways in such works as the operas of Monteverdi (*Orpheus,* 1607), Christoph Willibald Gluck (*Orpheus and Eurydice,* 1762), and Franz Joseph Haydn (*Orpheus and Eurydice,* 1791) and a play by Anouilh (*Eurydice,* 1941), among many others. The story has likewise been retold in film, such as *Orpheus* (1949, directed by Jean Cocteau) and *The Fugitive Kind* (1960, directed by Sidney Lumet), itself a version of Tennessee Williams's 1957 play *Orpheus Descending.* In the Brazilian film *Black Orpheus* (1958, directed by Marcel Camus), the Underworld is the Brazilian Carnival when, with normal constraints and inhibitions lifted, the demonic forces of violence and unreason are unleashed. More recently, in *The Hip-Hop Waltz of Eurydice* by Iranian-born playwright Reza Abdoh (an example of performance art staged at the Los Angeles Theatre Center in 1991), the Underworld is portrayed as one segment of the contemporary gay-lesbian subculture, complete with punk costumes and gender reversal (Orpheus is played by a woman, Eurydice by a man)—a nightmare vision of a world living under the threat of AIDS, in which Hades is a fascist police captain and Orpheus goes to hell on a motorcycle.

In the fine arts, similar series of transformations can be traced. For example, in two seventeenth-century paintings done only eighteen years apart, two artists—Peter Paul Rubens and Nicolas Poussin—depicted the same event, the rape of the Sabine women (Figures 21-6 and 21-7). In these two versions of the same theme, one can almost see the shift from Baroque to neoclassical sensibility occur. Rubens's foreshortened, intensely violent painting, with its naked, contorted bodies and writhing motion, places the viewer menacingly close, almost within the scene itself, whereas in Poussin's painting, the women are more decorously clothed, and the entire action is confined within the triangle whose apex is pointed to by the hand of the woman just

FIGURE 21-6 Peter Paul Rubens, *Rape of the Daughters of Leucippus,* c. 1618. In the contrast between this painting by Rubens and the nearly contemporary one by Nicolas Poussin (Figure 21-7) interpreting the same myth of the founding of the Roman people, the transformation from Baroque to neoclassical sensibility is visibly revealed. In Rubens's intensely Baroque work, the human figures are in the foreground and occupy most of the large canvas (7'3" × 6'10"). The figures are approximately life-size, and the foreshortening of perspective puts the viewer right into the scene, intensifying the dramatic effects and getting the viewer personally involved. The writhing bodies of the victims and the twisted configurations of horses and men form intersecting spirals that create a vortex of movement in the center of the painting. But while the viewer, thus visually threatened, instinctively sympathizes with the victims, the latter are nevertheless portrayed in such sensuous fashion that the painting augments the same erotic appeal the rapists are responding to. Forced in this way to assume the perspectives of both victim and rapist, the viewer is implicated in the very act he or she must deplore. (*Alte Pinakothek, Munich.*)

FIGURE 21-7   Nicolas Poussin, *Rape of the Sabine Women,* 1636–1637. In contrast to
Rubens's painting (Figure 21-6), there are no ambiguities in Poussin's version of the same
event, which clearly moves toward the neoclassical mode. Though there are far more figures
in this almost equally large painting (5′1″ × 6′10″), they are less threatening to the viewer.
Smaller in scale relative to the size of the canvas and further diminished by the backdrop of
buildings and sky, they are also organized into a clear, controlling pattern—a classical equilat-
eral triangle with its apex in the light behind the upraised hand of the woman in the center.
The Roman attackers are portrayed as heroic in appearance, in contrast to Rubens's twisted
bodies juxtaposed against the horses whose animal natures the rapists seem to be acting out.
The event has also been moved from the countryside into an urban setting so that the stable
forms of classical buildings and columns (looking, indeed, as if the Romans had already built
their city there!) help enclose and contain the violence. The women here are clothed so that a
sense of decorum is maintained even in the midst of the abduction. Finally, the figure of
Romulus, mythical founder of Rome, on the podium of the temple (and thus presumably
acting with the approval of the gods), appears to be directing the action, emphasizing the
sense that everything is under control. (*Metropolitan Museum of Art, New York.*)

left of center and the sword of the man standing to the right of center. Poussin moves
the point of view discreetly back, presenting a more detached, more controlled, even
heroic spectacle, all taking place under the watchful eye of the Roman soldier on the
pedestal.

Not only can paintings reinterpret myths, but those paintings themselves can be
used as sources for further commentary. Consider, for example, the way in which
Jean-Auguste-Dominique Ingres's painting the *Apotheosis of Homer* (Figure 21-8)
is dismantled and commented on ironically in Dali's painting of the same name
(Figure 21-9).

FIGURE 21-8   Jean-Auguste-Dominique Ingres, *Apotheosis of Homer,* 1827. In Ingres's tribute to the Greek poet, shown in this painting receiving from the winged figure of Victory the laurel crown as Prince of Poets and being welcomed into the company of the divine, we see, in effect, the "apotheosis" of neoclassical painting at its most extreme—an idealized and essentially fixed, static world realistically portrayed with great precision. The triangle made of actual portraits of artists and writers through the ages and forming an apex at the crown is visually repeated in the two figures personifying the *Iliad* (left) and the *Odyssey* (right) seated on the steps beneath their "father." A third triangle is formed by the entablature of the temple behind. This painting also literally enshrines the neoclassical belief that writers and artists, however "great" they may be in their own time, can at best imitate and pay tribute to, but can never hope to equal or surpass, the "giants" of the past. (*Louvre, Paris.*)

FIGURE 21-9   Salvador Dali, *Apotheosis of Homer,* 1945. In this surrealist version, Dali literally decomposes Ingres's painting (Figure 21-8) and with it the illusions of an "eternal" art whose rules and value are unchanging. Dali reduces "Homer" to a broken bit of statuary, a relic, while the solid temple of the Muse itself melts. An ethereal horse (Pegasus?) tries to throw off riders who are attempting to hitch a ride to the stars by desperately clinging to the back of this ancient myth. On the right, a skeletal wooden figure mourns over an empty sarcophagus, which suggests not resurrection but desecration of the dead: the corpse lies outside, untended, on the cart. (*Private collection.*)

FIGURE 21-10 *Aphrodite of Melos (Venus de Milo),* c. 200–150 B.C. A Hellenistic version of the classical goddess of love, Aphrodite is depicted in this statue as elegant, beautiful, and dignified. (*Louvre, Paris.*)

Versions of Venus

The many interpretations of Venus in painting and sculpture through the ages (Figures 21-10 through 21-19) provide an extended illustration of changes in taste, style, and vision that reveal as much about their own eras as about the goddess herself. The calm depiction of divine beauty in the *Venus de Milo* (Figure 21-10) of the second century B.C. differs from the more human but still idealized beauty of Botticelli's Renaissance painting *Venus and Mars* (see Color Plate 11). In stark contrast, the Mannerist interpretations of Titian reveal the goddess in more blatantly sensuous fashion, while showing her from more than one perspective. His reclining *Venus of Urbino* (Figure 21-11) watches the viewer watching her, while his *Venus with the Mirror* (Figure 21-12) multiplies perspectives still further by having the viewers watch Venus while she watches us in a mirror! Finally, Salvador Dali's surrealist sculpture, *Venus de Milo of the Drawers* (Figure 21-19) parodies the original, reminding us

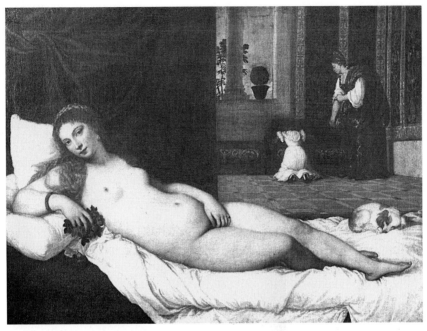

FIGURE 21-11   Titian, *Venus of Urbino,* 1538. The traditional "reclining Venus" in this painting is unbalanced, in characteristic Mannerist fashion, by the extended perspective behind the two figures in the background and the perspective lines on the floor tile that lead the eye toward them. The dog on the bed also distracts our view from the goddess. Her knowing expression and the position of her hand accent the self-conscious sensuality of the portrait. By looking directly at the viewer, the goddess arouses the viewer's equally self-conscious response. (*Uffizi Gallery, Florence.*)

through his hollow plaster figure that "Venus" is an abstract concept into which we must insert, like socks in a drawer, whatever meaning we choose.

Myth as Cultural Icon

Sometimes a whole generation will latch onto a particular mythic figure who will then become a kind of cultural icon to which everyone seems to pay tribute. Notable examples of such occurrences include Icarus in the Renaissance and Prometheus in the Romantic period.

The Renaissance

During the Renaissance (a word first used by the Italian poet Petrarch to describe the rebirth of the cultural achievements of Greece and Rome), the writings of Homer as well as those of Ovid, Plutarch, and the Roman playwright Seneca joined those of Virgil and many others already popularized in the late medieval period as mythology

FIGURE 21-12 Titian, *Venus with the Mirror,* 1555. Perspectives multiply dizzyingly in this theatrically lit painting, as we watch this luxuriously sensual Venus who gazes in the mirror. But the face in the mirror reveals that, while we watch her, she is watching not herself but us! Who is the voyeur, and who is the object? Breaking the one-way mirror that usually allows us to see into a painting, while not being seen ourselves, Titian shatters the barrier that normally separates the "real" world of the viewer from the "unreal" world of "art" and makes the viewer conscious of having been caught intruding on Venus's privacy. (*National Gallery of Art, Mellon Collection, Washington, D.C.*)

FIGURE 21-13 Nicolas Poussin, *Mars and Venus,* c. 1630. In contrast to Botticelli's version of the scene (Color Plate 11), Poussin's painting moves the figures further back and creates further detachment by adding members to the "audience." The landscape becomes correspondingly more significant. (*Augustus Hemenway Fund and Arthur William Wheelwright Fund. Courtesy, Museum of Fine Arts, Boston.*)

FIGURE 21-14 Francois Boucher, *The Toilet of Venus,* 1740. In this delicate painting, a slender, pretty, rather young-looking Venus is attended by cherubic Cupids in a lush, heavily ornate setting. In typical Rococo style, this symmetry of the classical style is overlaid with a profusion of decorative embellishments so that Venus herself takes on the air of another elegant ornament. (*Metropolitan Museum of Art, New York.*)

FIGURE 21-15 Antonio Canova, *Pauline Bonaparte as Venus,* 1808, marble. In this extremely flattering, life-size sculpture, Canova pays tribute to Napoleon's desire to revive the Roman empire by portraying his sister, Pauline Borghese (neé Bonaparte), in the traditional reclining Venus posture. (*Galleria Borghese, Rome.*)

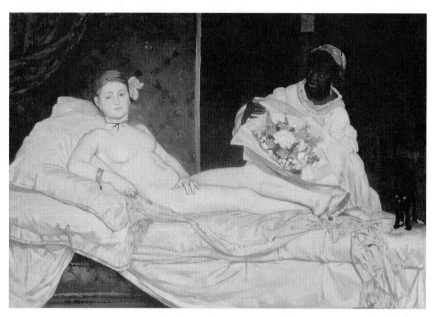

FIGURE 21-16   Edouard Manet, *Olympia,* 1863. Manet's Olympia, portrayed as Venus re-clining, was a famous Parisian prostitute, shown here boldly staring back at the viewer as her maid brings flowers from an admirer. The painting scandalized Manet's contemporaries, which delighted the artist and his friends! The selection of scenes from ordinary and often urban life, as opposed to the "traditional" subjects of academic art, was typical of the Impres-sionists, who found their inspiration in Manet's work. (*Musée de l'Impressionisme, Paris.*)

FIGURE 21-17   Arestide Maillol, *Torso of Venus,* 1925, bronze. Maillol's tribute to classical form, un-like its original predecessors, never had a head or limbs. The sculpture focuses us on the traditional "at ease" posture of the torso, with one hip raised and one knee bent, as an interesting, quasi-abstract solid shape, calling our attention to its weight, vol-ume, and contours, rather than to its representa-tional elements. (*Gallerie Dina Vierny, Paris.*)

FIGURE 21-18   Jules Pascin, *Back View of Venus,* 1924–1925. Like Maillol's sculpture (Figure 21-17), Pascin's painting, with its reversed view, heavy black contours, and almost obliterated head, focuses our attention on line and shape rather than realistic representation. (*Musée d'Art Moderne de la Ville de Paris.*)

FIGURE 21-19   Salvador Dali, *Venus de Milo of the Drawers,* 1936, plaster. Dali's sculpture deconstructs the *Venus de Milo* (Figure 21-10), just as his *Apotheosis of Homer* (Figure 21-9) disintegrates Ingres's painting of the same subject (Figure 21-8). This plaster statue reminds us that sculpture is an artifice—an occupier of volume, a container of space, to be filled (and interpreted) as we choose. One ironic (and typically Daliesque) note: the "brain" drawer is missing! (*Private collection.*)

shared in the general classical revival. The earlier rejection of pagan ideas yielded to the desire of the Christian humanists to unify their religious beliefs with their secular aesthetic and intellectual interests. Thus, service to Eros, the "god of love," is a phrase Renaissance writers often used without the slightest awareness of implicit blasphemy, as in John Lyly's lyric from *Alexander and Campaspe;* or, the poet may have confessed awareness of the contradiction, but he played on the pun, referring to both Christ and Cupid as "god of love," as did John Donne in "Love's Deity." When forced to choose, the Renaissance poet may have even opted for Cupid! For example, in Sir Philip Sidney's sonnet from the series called *Astrophel and Stella,* the poet deals with the conflict between Ovidian images and Christian belief, between the compelling impulses of the heart toward erotic love and the theoretical journey of the soul toward heaven. Maintaining that precarious balance so typical of the paradoxical stance that Renaissance scholars termed *Christian humanism,* Sidney manages to have it both ways, confessing that although Cupid's darts may be dismissed as mere poetic artifice, nevertheless, the erotic drive overwhelms any purely theoretical intention as surely as if there were a god called Cupid who takes unerring aim at human hearts.

During the Renaissance, biblical figures such as David (in Michelangelo's sculpture, Figure 21-20) and Adam and Eve (in his painting on the Sistine Chapel ceiling) are portrayed as Greek gods, whereas mythological stories (as in Lucas Cranach the Elder's *Judgment of Paris,* Figure 21-21) are depicted in Renaissance costumes and settings. Throughout Europe, as artists began to go out of their way to invoke the Muses and recreate the Graces of an earlier age, mythological themes abounded in the paintings, inspired the music, adorned the architecture, and filled the pages of the poems, plays, and stories, providing everything from brief allusions to complete plots, as well as a renewed enthusiasm for the heroic model of experience visible in Benvenuto Cellini's sculpture *Perseus and Medusa* (Figure 21-22).

Icarus

Amid the cornucopia of mythological subjects, one figure seems best to express the fears and aspirations of the time—**Icarus,** the boy who flew too high. For the Greeks, the myth of Icarus was a lesson in the necessity of the Golden Mean of moderation and self-control. The Renaissance Icarus, however, came to be admired for having the audacity to break through the limits of convention and ordinary experience—a tragic figure whose fall into the sea is the price he pays for a glimpse of a higher vision, for a moment of transcendence at the peak of a brief but glorious trajectory.

Dramatized in figures like the conqueror Tamburlaine (in the play by that name by the English Elizabethan playwright Christopher Marlowe, c. 1588) or the seeker of forbidden knowledge Doctor Faustus (Marlowe, c. 1588), Icarus embodied the paradoxical condition of the Renaissance hero—a modern, secular hero in a still-medieval as well as Christian universe. Although doomed to fail, he must literally hit his head against the ceiling of ordained limits—in its most extreme form, the limit is the threat of damnation itself—in order to fulfill the ambition that defines his full humanity. Faustus, for example, sells his soul to the devil (or his servant Mephistophilis) in return for forbidden knowledge, recapitulating the humanistic defiance earlier captured in the myths of Prometheus, Pandora, and Eve.

Perceived as a threat to orthodoxy, Icarus must certainly fall:

His waxen wings did mount above his reach

And melting heavens conspired his overthrow. (Marlowe, Prologue)

FIGURE 21-20 Michelangelo, *David,* 1501–1504, marble. A celebration of the beauty of the human body as well as the potential of the human being, this figure of David, of heroic proportions (18 ft), is portrayed with the same godlike body and air of repose that classical sculptors used in representing the god Apollo. (*Galleria dell'Accademia, Florence.*)

FIGURE 21-21 Lucas Cranach the Elder, *Judgment of Paris,* 1530. In Cranach's painting, Paris is a Renaissance soldier, who looks up at the Cupid aiming arrows from the tree while the three goddesses—Athene at the right, wearing the helmet, Hera at the left, and Aphrodite in the center—calmly, almost indifferently, await the inevitable. The fact that the men are wearing Renaissance battle gear not only updates (and thus universalizes) the myth but also underlines the inevitability of the consequences—the Trojan War for which Paris is already prepared! (*Staatliche Kunsthalle, Karlsruhe.*)

FIGURE 21-22   Benvenuto Cellini, *Perseus and Medusa*, 1545–1554, bronze. Cellini's rather menacing sculpture puts the figure of the hero on an ornate pedestal, as he grips his sword and stands in triumph on the body of Medusa, holding her severed head aloft. (*Loggia dei Lanzi, Florence.*)

But his "aspiring mind" and his quest for "knowledge infinite" (as Marlowe described it in *Tamburlaine,* Part 1) made him one of the most compelling images of the age.

The Fall of Icarus   If images such as Icarus can become cultural symbols, they can also be used to signal changing cultural values. Thus Pieter Breughel the Elder, in his painting *The Fall of Icarus* (see Color Plate 12), shifts the figure of Icarus from center stage off to an insignificant—and almost indistinguishable—spot in a corner of the painting: only the legs, jutting out of the sea, reveal the drowning boy, while the rest of the world, indifferent, goes about its business. In this painting, Breughel signals a shift in values (which occurred somewhat earlier on the Continent than in more remote places like England); instead of the obsessively human-centered world of the Renaissance, we here assume the asymmetrical Baroque perspective of a world adrift in a vast and infinite universe in which individuals have no intrinsic significance and the nobility essential for heroic tragedy is impossible or irrelevant.

The Romantic Age: Prometheus

In the Romantic period, it was Prometheus who seems to have leaped out of the pages of mythology into the consciousness of an entire generation. Identified with the creative energy, the heroic rebellion against oppressive authority, and the sense of being reborn into a new age unleashed by the French Revolution, Prometheus captured the imagination of artists, composers, poets, and novelists alike in works as diverse as Lord Byron's poem "Prometheus" (1801) and Percy Bysshe Shelley's *Prometheus Unbound* (1818), a lyric drama offered in answer to Aeschylus's *Prometheus Bound*.

In the preface to his play, Shelley speaks for his contemporaries as he explains,

> I was averse from a catastrophe so feeble as that of reconciling the Champion with the Oppressor of mankind [the presumed ending of Aeschylus's trilogy]. The moral interest of the fable, which is so powerfully sustained by the sufferings and endurance of Prometheus, would be annihilated if we could conceive him as unsaying his high language and quailing before his . . . perfidious adversary.

Shelley goes on to compare Prometheus to Satan (as depicted in John Milton's Christian epic *Paradise Lost,* 1674), who also defied divine authority. But Shelley finds Prometheus preferable because,

> in addition to courage, and majesty, and firm and patient opposition to omnipotent force, he is susceptible of being described as exempt from the taints of ambition, envy, revenge, and a desire for personal aggrandisement. . . .

Prometheus, Shelley concludes, is the "type of the highest perfection of moral and intellectual nature, impelled by the purest and truest motives to the best and noblest ends." In the last speech of the play, Demagorgon celebrates the Titan's triumph over tyranny:

> This is the day, which down the void abysm
> At the Earth-born's spell yawns for Heaven's despotism,
> > And Conquest is dragged captive through the deep:
> Love, from its awful throne of patient power
> In the wise heart, from the last giddy hour
> > Of dread endurance, from the slippery, steep,
> And narrow verge of crag-like agony, springs
> And folds over the world its healing wings.
>
> .   .   .   .
>
> To suffer woes which Hope thinks infinite;
> To forgive wrongs darker than death or night;
> > To defy Power, which seems omnipotent;
> To live, and bear; to hope till Hope creates
> From its own wreck the thing it contemplates;
> > Neither to change, nor falter, nor repent;
>
> This, like thy glory, Titan, is to be
> Good, great and joyous, beautiful and free;
> This alone is Life, Joy, Empire, and Victory. (4.554–578)

Prometheus and Napoleon   The myth created an aura around historical events and powerful personalities as well. Napoleon, for example, who rather enjoyed having

FIGURE 21-23 Antonio Canova, *Napoleon,* 1802–1810, marble. In this larger-than-life sculpture (11'8"), Canova rather unrealistically portrays Napoleon as having the beauty of a Greek god (compare with Figure 7-1) combined with the power of Jupiter, whose imperial staff he bears. (The fig leaf over the genitals is a concession to the sensibility of the time.) Canova, who was, in fact, not an enthusiast for the Napoleonic regime, was more or less forced to do this sculpture, an offer from the emperor that he couldn't refuse! (*Wellington Museum, London.*)

himself portrayed as a Greek god (Figure 21-23), was imaginatively linked with Prometheus until he "betrayed" the Revolution by declaring himself emperor. Beethoven's Third Symphony (the *Eroica,* 1804), for example, which incorporates musical material from his earlier composition *The Creatures of Prometheus,* was originally dedicated to Napoleon, but Beethoven angrily removed the dedication in response to that betrayal. Napoleon thus revealed exactly those traits that Shelley had identified with Satan. The exhilarating spirit of freedom, released from all restraints, can also be a source of terror.

Prometheus and Satan The convergence of the redemptive and the demonic in Shelley's juxtaposition of Prometheus and Satan was not coincidental. The image of Satan-as-hero prompted a revival of interest in the poetry of Milton, whose *Paradise Lost,* itself based on classical models, had portrayed the Archenemy in terms that the

Romantics found intensely appealing: the poet William Blake even asserted that Milton was "of the Devil's party without knowing it." In a similar juxtaposition, Percy Bysshe Shelley's wife, Mary Wollstonecraft Shelley, titled her novel *Frankenstein, or the Modern Prometheus* (1818). Her protagonist, defying conventional moral limits in order to release the human spirit from "lifeless clay" into a more sublime state, comments on his intention to "explore unknown powers" and to reveal the secrets of creation:

> Life and death appeared to me ideal bounds, which I should first break through, and pour a torrent of light into our dark world. A new species would bless me as its creator and source. . . .

What this "god" creates, however, turns out to be monstrous.

During the Renaissance, such pursuit of forbidden knowledge was identified with Faustus, who was in turn compared with Icarus, the daring boy. Then after a long hiatus during the seventeenth and eighteenth centuries, when acts of individual transcendence were not sought after or admired, Faustus himself was revived in the Romantic period, as in the German poet Johann Wolfgang von Goethe's version (*Faust,* Part 1, 1801). Goethe's poetic drama in turn inspired a series of lithographs (1828) illustrating scenes from Goethe's novel by the French artist Eugene Delacroix, as well as operas by Charles-Francois Gounod (*Faust,* 1859) and Hector Berlioz (*The Damnation of Faust,* 1846). However, this Romantic Faust is compared not with Icarus but instead with the rebel Prometheus.

The Future of Myth

In all the varied forms in which classical myths have been passed on to us through the millennia, they have retained their power to compel our attention and to reveal to us, in myriad ways, their complex capacity for conveying meaning. They will undoubtedly continue to move us for a long time to come, expressing the continuity of the human spirit as well as its infinite variety in as yet unimagined ways.

Excerpt from the
INFERNO [1]
Dante

BOOK 1 (CANTO 26, CIRCLE 8, BOLGIA 8) [2]

[Guided by the shade of Virgil, the poet visits the section of Hell where Ulysses and other Greek heroes are confined.]

. . . .

I stood on the bridge, and leaned out from the edge;
    so far, that but for a jut of rock I held to
    I should have been sent hurtling from the ledge

without being pushed. And seeing me so intent,
    my Guide said: "There are souls within those flames;
    each sinner swathes himself in his own torment."

"Master," I said, "your words make me more sure,
    but I had seen already that it was so
    and meant to ask what spirit must endure

the pains of that great flame which splits away   10
in two great horns, as if it rose from the pyre
    where Eteocles and Polynices lay?"

He answered me: "Forever round this path
    Ulysses and Diomede move in such dress,
    united in pain as once they were in wrath;

there they lament the ambush of the Horse
    which was the door through which the noble seed
    of the Romans issued from its holy source;

there they mourn that for Achilles slain
    sweet Deidamia weeps even in death;   20
there they recall the Palladium in their pain."

"Master," I cried, "I pray you and repray
    till my prayer becomes a thousand—if these souls
    can still speak from the fire, oh let me stay

1. Translation by John Ciardi.

2. Circle 8 spreads out over several cantos. The separate subdivisions are called *bolgias,* or "ditches in the Underworld, in which different categories of sinners are contained."

until the flame draws near! Do not deny me:
    You see how fervently I long for it!"
    And he to me: "Since what you ask is worthy,

it shall be. But be still and let me speak;
    for I know your mind already, and they perhaps
    might scorn your manner of speaking, since they were   30
    Greek."

And when the flame had come where time and place
    seemed fitting to my Guide, I heard him say
    these words to it: "O you two souls who pace

together in one flame!—if my days above
    won favor in your eyes, if I have earned
    however much or little of your love

in writing my High Verses, do not pass by,
    but let one of you be pleased to tell where he,
    having disappeared from the known world, went to   40
    die."

As if it fought the wind, the greater prong
    of the ancient flame began to quiver and hum;
    then moving its tip as if it were the tongue

that spoke, gave out a voice above the roar.
    "When I left Circe," it said, "who more than a year
    detained me near Gaëta long before

Aeneas came and gave the place that name,
    not fondness for my son, nor reverence
    for my aged father, nor Penelope's claim   50

to the joys of love, could drive out of my mind
    the lust to experience the far-flung world
    and the failings and felicities of mankind.

I put out on the high and open sea,
    with a single ship and only those few souls
    who stayed true when the rest deserted me.

As far as Morocco and as far as Spain
    I saw both shores; and I saw Sardinia
    and the other islands of the open main.

I and my men were stiff and slow with age   60
when we sailed at last into the narrow pass
    where, warning all men back from further voyage,

Hercules' Pillars rose upon our sight.
   Already I had left Ceuta on the left;
   Seville now sank behind me on the right.

'Shipmates,' I said, 'who through a hundred thousand
   perils have reached the West, do not deny
   to the brief remaining watch our senses stand

experience of the world beyond the sun.
   Greeks! You were not born to live like brutes,   70
but to press on toward manhood and recognition!'

With this brief exhortation I made my crew
   so eager for the voyage I could hardly
   have held them back from it when I was through;

and turning our stern toward morning, our bow toward night,
   we bore southwest out of the world of man;
   we made wings of our oars for our fool's flight.

That night we raised the other pole ahead
   with all its stars, and ours had so declined
   it did not rise out of its ocean bed.   80

Five times since we had dipped our bending oars
   beyond the world, the light beneath the moon
   had waxed and waned, when dead upon our course

we sighted, dark in space, a peak[3] so tall
   I doubted any man had seen the like.
   Our cheers were hardly sounded, when a squall

broke hard upon our bow from the new land:
   three times it sucked the ship and the sea about
   as it pleased Another to order and command.

At the fourth, the poop rose and the bow went down   90
till the sea closed over us and the light was gone."

3. Mount Purgatory.

SONNET 5 from *Astrophel and Stella*

Sir Philip Sidney

It is most true that eyes are formed to serve
   The inward light, and that the heavenly part
   Ought to be king, from whose rules who do swerve,
   Rebels to nature, strive for their own smart.
It is most true what we call Cupid's dart
   An image is which for ourselves we carve,
   And, fools, adore in temple of our heart
   Till that good god make church and churchman starve.
True, that true beauty virtue is indeed,
   Whereof this beauty can be but a shade,   10
Which elements with mortal mixture breed.
True, that on earth we are but pilgrims made,
   And should in soul up to our country move;
   True, and yet true that I must Stella love.

SONG[1] from *Cupid and My Campaspe*

John Lyly

Cupid and my Campaspe played
At cards for kisses; Cupid paid.
He stakes his quiver, bow, and arrows,
His mother's doves and team of sparrows,
Loses them too; then down he throws
The coral of his lip, the rose
Growing on's cheek (but none knows how),
With these the crystal of his brow,
And then the dimple of his chin:
All these did my Campaspe win.   10
At last he set her both his eyes;
She won, and Cupid blind did rise.
    O Love! has she done this to thee?
    What shall, alas, become of me?

---

1. Attributed to the author in the posthumous collection of his plays, *Six Court Comedies,* printed in 1632.

LOVE'S DEITY

John Donne

I long to talk with some old lover's ghost,
   Who died before the god of love was born:
I cannot think that he, who then loved most,
   Sunk so low as to love one which did scorn.
But since this god produced a destiny,
And that vice-nature, custom, lets it be,
   I must love her that loves not me.

Sure, they which made him god meant not so much,
   Nor he in his young godhead practised it;
But when an even flame two hearts did touch,   10
His office was indulgently to fit
Actives to passives. Correspondency
Only his subject was; it cannot be
   Love, till I love her that loves me.

But every modern god will now extend
   His vast prerogative as far as Jove.
To rage, to lust, to write to, to commend,
   All is the purlieu of the god of love.
Oh, were we wakened by this tyranny
To ungod this child again, it could not be   20
I should love her, who loves not me.

Rebel and atheist too, why murmur I,
   As though I felt the worst that love could do?
Love may make me leave loving, or might try
   A deeper plague, to make her love me too,
Which, since she loves before, I am loath to see;
Falsehood is worse than hate; and that must be,
   If she whom I love, should love me.

Excerpt from PARADISE LOST

John Milton

BOOK 1

. . . .
                            Satan, with bold words
Breaking the horrid silence thus began.
    If thou beest hee; But O how fall'n! how chang'd
From him, who in the happy Realms of Light
Cloth'd with transcendent brightness didst outshine
Myriads though bright: If he whom mutual league,
United thoughts and counsels, equal hope,
And hazard in the Glorious Enterprise,
Join'd with me once, now misery hath join'd
In equal ruin: into what Pit thou seest   10
From what highth fall'n, so much the stronger prov'd
He with his Thunder: and till then who knew
The force of those dire Arms? yet not for those,
Nor what the Potent Victor in his rage
Can else inflict, do I repent or change,
Though chang'd in outward luster; that fixt mind
And high disdain, from sense of injur'd merit,
That with the mightiest rais'd me to contend,
And to the fierce contention brought along
Innumerable force of Spirits arm'd   20
That durst dislike his reign, and mee preferring,
His utmost power with adverse power oppos'd
In dubious Battle on the Plains of Heav'n,
And shook his throne. What though the field be lost?
All is not lost; the unconquerable Will,
And study of revenge, immortal hate,
And courage never to submit or yield:
And what is else not to be overcome?
That Glory never shall his wrath or might
Extort from me. To bow and sue for grace   30
With suppliant knee, and deify his power
Who from the terror of this Arm so late
Doubted his Empire, that were low indeed,
That were an ignominy and shame beneath
This downfall; since by Fate the strength of Gods
And this Empyreal substance cannot fail,
Since through experience of this great event
In Arms not worse, in foresight much advanc't,
We may with more successful hope resolve
To wage by force or guile eternal War   40
Irreconcilable to our grand Foe,
Who now triumphs, and in th' excess of joy
Sole reigning holds the Tyranny of Heav'n.

PROMETHEUS[1]

George Gordon, Lord Byron

1

Titan! to whose immortal eyes
   The sufferings of mortality,
   Seen in their sad reality,
Were not as things that gods despise;
What was thy pity's recompense?
A silent suffering, and intense;
The rock, the vulture, and the chain,
All that the proud can feel of pain,
The agony they do not show,
The suffocating sense of woe,   10
Which speaks but in its loneliness,
And then is jealous lest the sky
Should have a listener, nor will sigh
   Until its voice is echoless.

2

Titan! to thee the strife was given
   Between the suffering and the will,
   Which torture where they cannot kill;
And the inexorable Heaven,
And the deaf tyranny of Fate,
The ruling principle of Hate,   20
Which for its pleasure doth create
The things it may annihilate,
Refused thee even the boon to die:
The wretched gift Eternity
Was thine—and thou hast borne it well.
All that the Thunderer wrung from thee
Was but the menace which flung back
On him the torments of thy rack;
The fate thou didst so well foresee,
But would not to appease him tell;   30
And in thy Silence was his Sentence,
And in his Soul a vain repentance,
And evil dread so ill dissembled,
That in his hand the lightnings trembled.

3

Thy Godlike crime was to be kind,
   To render with thy precepts less

---

1. Diodati, July 1816.

The sum of human wretchedness,
And strengthen Man with his own mind;
And baffled as thou wert from high,
Still in thy patient energy,   40
In the endurance, and repulse
     Of thine impenetrable Spirit,
Which Earth and Heaven could not convulse,
     A mighty lesson we inherit:
Thou art a symbol and a sign
     To Mortals of their fate and force;
Like thee, Man is in part divine,
     A troubled stream from a pure source;
And Man in portions can foresee
His own funereal destiny;   50
His wretchedness, and his resistance,
And his sad unallied existence:
To which his Spirit may oppose
Itself—and equal to all woes,
     And a firm will, and a deep sense,
     Which even in torture can descry
          Its own concenter'd recompense,
     Triumphant where it dares defy,
     And making Death a Victory.

ULYSSES[1]

Alfred, Lord Tennyson

It little profits that an idle king,
By this still hearth, among these barren crags,
Match'd with an aged wife, I mete and dole
Unequal laws unto a savage race,
That hoard, and sleep, and feed, and know not me.
I cannot rest from travel; I will drink
Life to the lees. All times I have enjoy'd
Greatly, have suffer'd greatly, both with those
That loved me, and alone; on shore, and when
Thro' scudding drifts the rainy Hyades   10
Vext the dim sea. I am become a name;
For always roaming with a hungry heart
Much have I seen and known,—cities of men
And manners, climates, councils, governments,
Myself not least, but honor'd of them all,—
And drunk delight of battle with my peers,
Far on the ringing plains of windy Troy.
I am a part of all that I have met;
Yet all experience is an arch wherethro'
Gleams that untravell'd world whose margin fades   20
For ever and for ever when I move.
How dull it is to pause, to make an end,
To rust unburnish'd, not to shine in use!
As tho' to breathe were life! Life piled on life
Were all too little, and of one to me
Little remains; but every hour is saved
From that eternal silence, something more,
A bringer of new things; and vile it were
For some three suns to store and hoard myself,
And this gray spirit yearning in desire   30
To follow knowledge like a sinking star,
Beyond the utmost bound of human thought.
    This is my son, mine own Telemachus,
To whom I leave the sceptre and the isle,—
Well-loved of me, discerning to fulfil
This labor, by slow prudence to make mild
A rugged people, and thro' soft degrees
Subdue them to the useful and the good.
Most blameless is he, centred in the sphere
Of common duties, decent not to fail   40

1. First printed in 1842, and unaltered.

In offices of tenderness, and pay
Meet adoration to my household gods,
When I am gone. He works his work, I mine.
 There lies the port; the vessel puffs her sail;
There gloom the dark, broad seas. My mariners,
Souls that have toil'd, and wrought, and thought with me,—
That ever with a frolic welcome took
The thunder and the sunshine, and opposed
Free hearts, free foreheads,—you and I are old;
Old age hath yet his honor and his toil. 50
Death closes all; but something ere the end,
Some work of noble note, may yet be done,
Not unbecoming men that strove with Gods.
The lights begin to twinkle from the rocks;
The long day wanes; the slow moon climbs; the deep
Moans round with many voices. Come, my friends.
'Tis not too late to seek a newer world.
Push off, and sitting well in order smite
The sounding furrows; for my purpose holds
To sail beyond the sunset, and the baths 60
Of all the western stars, until I die.
It may be that the gulfs will wash us down;
It may be we shall touch the Happy Isles,
And see the great Achilles, whom we knew.
Tho' much is taken, much abides; and tho'
We are not now that strength which in old days
Moved earth and heaven, that which we are, we are,—
One equal temper of heroic hearts,
Made weak by time and fate, but strong in will
To strive, to seek, to find, and not to yield. 70

LEDA AND THE SWAN

William Butler Yeats

A sudden blow: the great wings beating still
Above the staggering girl, her thighs caressed
By the dark webs, her nape caught in his bill,
He holds her helpless breast upon his breast.

How can those terrified vague fingers push
The feathered glory from her loosening thighs?
And how can body, laid in that white rush,
But feel the strange heart beating where it lies?

A shudder in the loins engenders there
The broken wall, the burning roof and tower 10
And Agamemnon dead.
                    Being so caught up,
So mastered by the brute blood of the air,
Did she put on his knowledge with his power
Before the indifferent beak could let her drop?

THE SHIELD OF ACHILLES

W. H. Auden

> She looked over his shoulder
> For vines and olive trees,
> Marble well-governed cities
> And ships upon untamed seas,
> But there on the shining metal
> His hands had put instead
> An artificial wilderness
> And a sky like lead.

A plain without a feature, bare and brown,
 No blade of grass, no sign of neighborhood,   10
Nothing to eat and nowhere to sit down,
 Yet, congregated on its blankness, stood
 An unintelligible multitude,
A million eyes, a million boots in line,
Without expression, waiting for a sign.

Out of the air a voice without a face
 Proved by statistics that some cause was just
In tones as dry and level as the place:
 No one was cheered and nothing was discussed:
 Column by column in a cloud of dust   20
They marched away enduring a belief
Whose logic brought them, somewhere else, to grief.

> She looked over her shoulder
> For ritual pieties,
> White flower-garlanded heifers,
> Libation and sacrifice,
> But there on the shining metal
> Where the altar should have been,
> She saw by his flickering forge-light
> Quite another scene.   30

Barbed wire enclosed an arbitrary spot
 Where bored officials lounged (one cracked a joke)
And sentries sweated for the day was hot:
 A crowd of ordinary decent folk
 Watched from without and neither moved nor spoke
As three pale figures were led forth and bound
To three posts driven upright in the ground.

The mass and majesty of this world, all
    That carries weight and always weighs the same
Lay in the hands of others; they were small   40
And could not hope for help and no help came:
    What their foes liked to do was done, their shame
Was all the worst could wish; they lost their pride
And died as men before their bodies died.

      She looked over his shoulder
        For athletes at their games,
      Men and women in a dance
        Moving their sweet limbs
      Quick, quick, to music,
        But there on the shining shield   50
      His hands had set no dancing-floor
        But a weed-choked field.

A ragged urchin, aimless and alone,
    Loitered about that vacancy; a bird
Flew up to safety from his well-aimed stone:
    That girls are raped, that two boys knife a third,
    Were axioms to him, who'd never heard
Of any world where promises were kept,
Or one could weep because another wept.

        The thin-lipped armorer,   60
        Hephaestos, hobbled away,
        Thetis of the shining breasts
          Cried out in dismay
        At what the god had wrought
          To please her son, the strong
        Iron-hearted man-slaying Achilles
          Who would not live long.

MUSÉE DES BEAUX ARTS

W. H. Auden

About suffering they were never wrong,
The Old Masters: how well they understood
Its human position; how it takes place
While someone else is eating or opening a window or just walking dully along;
How, when the aged are reverently, passionately waiting
For the miraculous birth, there always must be
Children who did not specially want it to happen, skating
On a pond at the edge of the wood:
They never forgot
That even the dreadful martyrdom must run its course   10
Anyhow in a corner, some untidy spot
Where the dogs go on with their doggy life and the torturer's horse
Scratches its innocent behind on a tree.

In Breughel's *Icarus,* for instance: how everything turns away
Quite leisurely from the disaster; the ploughman may
Have heard the splash, the forsaken cry,
But for him it was not an important failure; the sun shone
As it had to on the white legs disappearing into the green
Water; and the expensive delicate ship that must have seen
Something amazing, a boy falling out of the sky,   20
Had somewhere to get to and sailed calmly on.

THE POMEGRANATE

Eavan Boland

The only legend I have ever loved is
The story of a daughter lost in hell.
And found and rescued there.
Love and blackmail are the gist of it.
Ceres and Persephone the names.
And the best thing about the legend is
I can enter it anywhere. And have.
As a child in exile in
A city of fogs and strange consonants,
I read it first and at first I was   10
An exiled child in the crackling dusk of
The underworld, the stars blighted. Later
I walked out in a summer twilight
Searching for my daughter at bedtime.
When she came running I was ready
To make any bargain to keep her.
I carried her back past whitebeams.
And wasps and honey-scented buddleias.
But I was Ceres then and I knew
Winter was in store for every leaf   20
On every tree on that road.
Was inescapable for each one we passed.
And for me.
It is winter
And the stars are hidden.
I climb the stairs and stand where I can see
My child asleep beside her teen magazines,
Her can of Coke, her plate of uncut fruit.
The pomegranate! How did I forget it?
She could have come home and been safe   30
And ended the story and all
Our heartbroken searching but she reached
Out a hand and plucked a pomegranate.
She put out her hand and pulled down
The French sound for apple and
The noise of stone and the proof
That even in the place of death,
At the heart of legend, in the midst
Of rocks full of unshed tears
Ready to be diamonds by the time   40
The story was told, a child can be
Hungry. I could warn her. There is still a chance.

The rain is cold. The road is flint-coloured.
The suburb has cars and cable television.
The veiled stars are above ground.
It is another world. But what else
Can a mother give her daughter but such
Beautiful rifts in time?
If I defer the grief I will diminish the gift.
The legend must be hers as well as mine.   50
She will enter it. As I have.
She will wake up. She will hold
The papery, flushed skin in her hand.
And to her lips. I will say nothing.

Questions for Discussion and Review

1. How does Dante portray Ulysses's motives and goals? How is his portrayal in the *Inferno* different from Homer's portrayal in the *Odyssey?* Where does Dante's Ulysses sail to on his last voyage? Why is he punished for it? How does Dante's version of Ulysses's last voyage differ from Tennyson's?

2. (a) Explain Yeats's interpretation of the tragedy of Troy in his poem "Leda and the Swan." (b) Contrast Yeats's poem with Dali's Painting *Leda Atomica* (Figure 21-5). Explain Leda's role in bringing about the war in the painting and in the poem, and compare it with Zeus's role. Why is Zeus not named in the poem or pictured in the painting?

3. Compare W. H. Auden's "The Shield of Achilles" with Homer's description of the shield in the *Iliad*. How do the differences reflect ancient versus modern beliefs or values? How does each portray war?

4. Compare Salvador Dali's *Venus de Milo of the Drawers* (Figure 21-23), with the original *Venus de Milo* (Figure 21-12). What does Dali's version suggest about the goddess of love? Why did the modern artist depict the figure with drawers? What does the sculpture suggest those drawers might contain?

5. (a) How does the Breughel painting *The Fall of Icarus* (Color Plate 12) comment on the Renaissance interpretation of Icarus as a tragic hero? (b) How does W. H. Auden's sonnet "Musée des Beaux Arts" comment on Breughel's painting? Is Auden's view more like the Renaissance view or more like Breughel's?

6. In a detailed analysis of Rubens's *Rape of the Daughters of Leucippus* and Poussin's *Rape of the Sabine Women* (Figures 21-8 and 21-9), explain how the two paintings present different interpretations of this event from Roman mythology. How do the choices of a close-up view versus greater distance, of few versus many figures, and of a country versus town setting affect the interpretation portrayed in each painting?

7. Choose two illustrations from the section "Versions of Venus" (Figures 21-12 through 21-23), and compare and contrast the two artists' views of the goddess. If possible, relate the differences to the times in which each artist lived.

8. Compare the figure of Prometheus in Byron's poem with either that of Aeschylus's *Prometheus Bound* or with the figure of Satan in the excerpt from Milton's *Paradise Lost*. What political and moral values are associated with each figure?

9. Discuss the metaphor of Cupid, the "god of love," in either Donne's "Love's Deity" or Lyly's "Cupid and My Campaspe." Compare the poem you have selected with Sidney's sonnet from *Astrophel and Stella*. What attitude toward Cupid is present in each poem? How does each poet's use of Cupid reflect his attitude toward the woman he loves? Where relevant, explain how the image of Cupid is related to the poet's own religious beliefs.

(The following questions require outside sources.)

10. Read either Sophocles's or Euripides's version of *Electra*, and compare it to Aeschylus's Oresteian trilogy. How do the playwrights' interpretations of the major characters and of the roles of the gods differ? What purpose do the minor characters each author introduces serve in reinforcing the particular play's perspective?

11. Read Jean Anouilh's play *Antigone*, and compare it to Sophocles's version. How does each playwright portray the protagonist (Antigone) and the antagonist (Creon)? How do their personal and political motives differ? How does each play reflect contemporary problems or concerns in the world of the author?

12. Choose one chapter from Joyce's novel *Ulysses* or one scene from Derek Walcott's *The Odyssey: A Stage Version*, and compare it with the corresponding book in Homer's *Iliad*. What do they have in common? What did the modern author do to make the Homeric poem relevant to the twentieth-century reader?

13. Watch the film *The Natural* (1984, directed by Barry Levinson). In what specific ways are the film and its hero like the *Iliad*? In what specific ways do they resemble the *Odyssey*? How is the modern sports hero similar to or different from the ancient epic hero in his inner nature, his relationship with his peers, and the problems he encounters?

14. Read Cavafy's poem "Ithaca," and compare his portrayal of Odysseus's journey with that of either Tennyson or Homer. What remains constant in the two versions? What changes?

Works Cited

Cavafy, Constantine. *The Complete Poems of Constantine Cafavy*. Trans. Rae Dalven. New York: Harcourt Brace Jovanovich, 1976.

Marlowe, Christopher. *The Tragic History of Doctor Faustus*. New York: Appleton, 1950.

Pope, Alexander. *The Best of Pope*. Ed. George Sherburn. 1929. New York: Ronald, 1940.

Shelley, Mary Wollstonecraft. *Frankenstein, or the Modern Prometheus*. New York: New American, 1965.

Shelley, Percy Bysshe. *Poetical Works*. Ed. Thomas Hutchinson and G. M. Matthews. Oxford: Oxford UP, 1970.

Recommended Reading

Bush, Douglas. *Mythology and the Renaissance Tradition in English Poetry*. 1932. New York: Norton, 1963. An example of how classical mythology endures and continues to influence the works of ages and cultures far removed from ancient Greece and Rome.

Reid, Jane Davidson, with Chris Rohmann. *The Oxford Guide to Classical Mythology in the Arts, 1300–1990s.* 2 vols. Oxford: Oxford UP, 1993. Contains summaries, listed by subject, of the major stories and characters of classical myths, with entries, arranged chronologically, of their treatment in literature, music, dance, and the fine arts.

A Selected List of Primary Works That Reinterpret Classical Myths

Fiction

Barth, John. *Chimera* (1972).

Joyce, James. *Portrait of the Artist as a Young Man* (1916).

——. *Ulysses* (1914).

Malamud, Bernard. *The Natural* (1952).

Shelley, Mary Wollstonecraft. *Frankenstein, or the Modern Prometheus* (1818).

Updike, John. *The Centaur* (1962).

Poetry

Auden, W. H. "Musée des Beaux Arts" (1938).

——. "The Shield of Achilles" (1952).

Boland, Eavan. "The Pomegranate" (1994).

Byron, George Gordon, Lord. "Prometheus" (1816).

Cavafy, Constantine. "Ithaca" (1911).

Dante. *Divine Comedy* (1314–1321).

H. D. (Hilda Doolittle). "Eurydice" (1917, 1925).

Jarrell, Randall, "The Birth of Venus" (1952).

——. "Orestes at Tauris" (1948).

——. "The Sphinx's Riddle to Oedipus" (1960).

Lawrence, D. H. "The Argonauts" (1933).

Lowell, Robert. "Falling Asleep Over the *Aeneid*" (1950).

Plath, Sylvia. "Two Sisters of Persephone" (1951).

Rukeyser, Muriel. "Myth" (1973).

Shakespeare, William. "Venus and Adonis" (1593).

Tennyson, Alfred, Lord. "Ulysses" (1842).

Yeats, William Butler. "Colonus' Praise" (1928).

——. "Leda and the Swan" (1923).

Drama

Abdoh, Reza. *The Hip-Hop Waltz of Eurydice* (1991).

Anouilh, Jean. *Antigone* (1944).

————. *Eurydice* (1941).

————. *Medea* (1946).

Cocteau, Jean. *La Machine Infernale* (1934).

————. *Orpheus* (1927).

Eliot, T. S. *Family Reunion* (1935).

Gide, Andre. *Oedipus* (1931).

————. *Theseus* (1946).

Giraudoux, Jean. *Amphitryon 38* (1938).

————. *Electra* (1937).

O'Neill, Eugene. *Desire Under the Elms* (1924).

————. *Mourning Becomes Electra* (1931).

Racine, Jean. *Andromache* (1667).

————. *Iphigenia at Aulis* (1674).

————. *Phaedre* (1677).

Sartre, Jean-Paul. *The Flies* (1943).

Shelley, Percy Bysshe. *Prometheus Unbound* (1811).

Walcott, Derek. *The Odyssey: A Stage Version* (1992).

Williams, Tennessee. *Orpheus Descending* (1957).

Painting

Botticelli, Sandro. *Birth of Venus* (1480).

————. *Venus and Mars* (1485).

Boucher, Francois. *The Toilet of Venus* (1740).

Breughel, Pieter, the Elder. *The Fall of Icarus* (1555–1556).

Bronzino, Agnolo. *Allegory of Venus* (1550).

Cousin, Jean, the Elder. *Eva Prima Pandora* (1538).

Cranach, Lucas, the Elder. *Judgment of Paris* (1530).

————. *Venus* (1532).

Dali, Salvador. *Apotheosis of Homer* (1945).

————. *Leda Atomica.* (1948).

————. *The Metamorphosis of Narcissus* (1936–1937).

Delacroix, Eugene. *Dante and Vergil in Hell* (1822).

El Greco. *Laocoon* (1610).

Ingres, Jean-Auguste-Dominique. *Apotheosis of Homer* (1827).

————. *Oedipus and the Sphinx* (1808).

Lorrain, Claude. *Coast View of Delos with Aeneas* (1672).

Pascin, Jules. *Back View of Venus* (1924–1925).

Picasso, Pablo. *Minotauromachia* (1935).

————. *Ovid's Metamorphoses* [etchings] (1931).

Poussin, Nicolas. *Mars and Venus* (1630).

————. *Rape of the Sabine Women* (1636–1637).

Rubens, Peter Paul. *Rape of the Daughters of Leucippus* (1618).

————. *The Toilet of Venus* (1613).

Tintoretto. *The Marriage of Bacchus and Ariadne* (c. 1577–1588).

Titian. *Bacchus and Ariadne* (1520).

————. *Venus and Adonis* (1562).

————. *Venus of Urbino* (1538).

————. *Venus with the Mirror* (1555).

Sculpture

Bernini, Gianlorenzo. *Apollo and Daphne* (1622–1625).

Canova, Antonio. *Napoleon* (1802–1810).

————. *Pauline Bonaparte as Venus* (1808).

Cellini, Benvenuto. *Perseus and Medusa* (1545–1554).

Dali, Salvador. *Venus de Milo of the Drawers* (1936).

Girardon, Francois. *Apollo Attended by the Nymphs* (c. 1666–1672).

Maillol, Arestide. *Torso of Venus* (1925).

Pollaiuolo, Antonio. *Hercules Strangling Antaeus* (c. 1475).

Music

Beethoven, Ludwig von. *The Creatures of Prometheus* (1801).

Berlioz, Hector. *The Trojans* (1856–1858).

Britten, Benjamin. *Phaedra* (1975).

Gabrieli, Giovanni. *Oedipus Tyrannus* (1585).

Gluck, Christoph Willibald. *Echo and Narcissus* (1779).

————. *Iphigenia among the Taurians* (1779).

————. *Iphigenia at Aulis* (1774).

————. *Orpheus and Eurydice* (1762).

Handel, George Frideric. *Hercules* (1745).

————. *Semele* (1743).

Haydn, Franz Joseph. *Orpheus and Eurydice* (1791).

Monteverdi, Claudio. *Orpheus* (1607).

————. *The Return of Ulysses* (1637).

Offenbach, Jacques. *Orpheus in the Underworld* (1858).

Parry, Sir Charles Hasting Hubert. *Prometheus Unbound* (1880).

Purcell, Henry. *Dido and Aeneas* (1689).

Rinuccini, Ottavio. *Eurydice* (1600).

Strauss, Richard. *Ariadne on Naxos* (1916).

———. *Electra* (1909).

Stravinsky, Igor. *Oedipus Rex* (1927).

———. *Persephone* (1934).

Film

Black Orpheus. Directed by Marcel Camus (1958).

Clash of the Titans. Directed by Desmond Davis (1981).

The Fugitive Kind. Directed by Sidney Lumet (1960).

The Natural. Directed by Barry Levinson (1984).

Orpheus. Directed by Jean Cocteau (1949).

Medea. Directed by Pier Pasolini (1970).

Mixed Media (Photography, Dance, Poetry)

Trager, Philip, and Ralph Lemon. *Persephone* (1996).

Glossary

Achaeans   Homer's most common term for the Greeks who besieged Troy; he also called them *Argives* or *Danaans*.

Achates   In Virgil's *Aeneid*, the faithful friend and companion of Aeneas.

Acheron [AK-e-rahn]   One of the main rivers of Hades.

Achilles [a-KIL-leez]   Son of the sea nymph Thetis and the mortal Peleus; in Homer's *Iliad*, the most formidable Greek warrior at Troy.

Acropolis   In Athens, the steep fortified hill atop which stood the Parthenon and other temples dedicated to Athene.

Actaeon [ak-TEE-ahn]   The son of Aristaeus and Autonoe, daughter of Cadmus. When he offended Artemis, either by boasting of his superior hunting abilities or by inadvertently seeing her bathe, the goddess changed him into a stag, and he was torn apart by his hounds.

Adam   According to the Book of Genesis, the first human being, whom Yahweh eventually divided into male and female; his name means "humankind."

Admetus   The king of Pherae in Thessaly whom Apollo served as shepherd in penance for having slain the Python at Delphi. According to a variant of the myth, Zeus forced Apollo to serve Admetus after the god had killed the Cyclops, who had created the thunderbolt Zeus used in slaying Apollo's son Asclepius.

Adonis   The youth whom Aphrodite (Venus) loved and who was slain by a wild boar. He resembles certain aspects of Dionysus in that he is a male fertility figure symbolizing the natural cycle of vegetative growth, death, and regeneration.

Aegeus [EE-jee-uhs]   King of Athens, father of the hero Theseus, he gave refuge to Medea after she escaped from Corinth. When he thought Theseus had been killed by the Minotaur, he committed suicide by leaping into the sea named after him.

aegis [EE-jis]   The breastplate of Zeus—a protective garment decorated with a Gorgon's head and surrounded by a fringe of snakes—commonly worn by Athene in her role as goddess of victory.

Aegisthus [ee-JIS-thuhs]   Son of Thyestes and his daughter Pelopia; he became Clytemnestra's lover and was slain by Orestes.

Aeneas [ee-NEE-as]   Son of Aphrodite (Venus) and Anchises, a mortal Trojan prince, the hero of Virgil's *Aeneid*. After Troy's fall, he journeyed to Italy, where he founded a dynasty that eventually produced Romulus and Remus, the legendary founders of Rome.

Aeolus   Greek god of the winds.

Aesculapius   Latin name for Asclepius.

Agamemnon   Son of Atreus and brother of Menelaus, he was commander in chief of the Greek expedition against Troy. Murdered by his wife Clytemnestra, he was avenged by his children Orestes and Electra.

Agave [a-GAY-vee]   Daughter of Harmonia and King Cadmus (founder of Thebes), she was the sister of Semele, Ino, and Autonoe and the mother of Pentheus.

agon   In Greek drama, the term denoting the contest, struggle, or conflict between the principal characters.

Ajax   A leading Greek warrior in the Trojan War who went mad after losing a contest to Odysseus for Achilles's armor. His name is also spelled *Aias*.

Alba Longa   In the *Aeneid,* an Italian city founded by Aeneas's son Ascanius.

Alcestis   Title character of Euripides's tragedy about a wife who volunteered to die in place of her husband, Admetus.

Alcinous [al-SIN-oh-uhs]   King of the Phaeacians, husband of Arete, and father of Nausicaa, he received Odysseus hospitably on his island of Scheria (traditionally identified as Corfu).

Alcmene   The wife of Amphitryon and mother of Heracles, she was said to be the last of mortal women seduced by Zeus.

Alexandros   Another name for Paris, the Trojan prince who abducted Helen.

Allecto   One of the Furies called up from the Underworld in the *Aeneid.*

allegory   A literary narrative in which persons, places, and events are given a symbolic meaning.

Amata   Queen of Latium and mother of Lavinia, whom Aeneas married.

ambrosia   Food of the Olympian gods.

amor [ah-MOHR]   In Roman myth, a personification of love.

Amphitryon   Son of Alceus (son of Perseus), he married Alcmene and became the father of Iphicles, Heracles's half-brother.

anagnorisis   In tragedy, the recognition scene in which a character discovers a previously unknown fact or relationship.

Anchises   Trojan prince, father of the hero Aeneas by Aphrodite.

Andromache [an-DROM-a-kee]   Wife of Hector, Troy's leading defender, and mother of Astyanax.

Andromeda   A maiden chained to a rock as prey for a sea monster. She was rescued by Perseus, who then turned her uncle Phineus to stone by showing him the head of Medusa.

anima   Jungian term for the feminine principle residing in the male psyche.

animus   Jungian term for the male principle residing in the female psyche.

Antenor   A wise Trojan counselor, he advocated Helen's return to the Greeks.

anthropomorphism   The practice of attributing human characteristics to something not human; particularly, ascribing human form to a deity.

Anticleia [an-tih-KLEE-a]   Daughter of Autolycus, wife of Laertes, and mother of Odysseus, she died mourning for her son during his long absence from Ithaca. Her ghost appeared to Odysseus in the Underworld.

Antigone [an-TIG-oh-nee]   Daughter of Oedipus and Jocasta, she was her blinded father's guide in Sophocles's *Oedipus at Colonus* and the heroine of *Antigone.*

Aphrodite [af-roh-DYE-tee] **(Venus)**   Goddess of love and beauty; in Hesiod, she was born from the castration of Uranus; in Homer, she was the daughter of Zeus and Dione.

Apollo   Son of Zeus and Leto, he is also called *Phoebus,* the radiant god of light, music, prophecy, and the arts. His most famous shrine was at Delphi, where his priestess, the Pythia, proclaimed the divine will. His son, Asclepius, the first physician, was patron of the healing arts.

Arcadia   A mountainous region in the south of Greece, sacred to Pan, Hermes, and Apollo, and associated with shepherds.

archetype   The primal form or original pattern from which all other things of a like nature are descended. In myth, the term refers to characters, ideas, or actions that represent the supreme and/or essential examples of a universal type, components of the "collective unconscious."

Areopagus   The "hill of Ares (Mars)," a spur of the Athenian Acropolis, where Athene established a court for homicides, the site of Orestes's trial in the *Eumenides.*

Ares [AR-eez] (Mars)   Son of Zeus and Hera, he is the personification of male aggression and the fighting spirit, an unpopular god in Greece but highly respected in Rome, where he was identified with Mars, an Italian god of agriculture and war.

Arete [a-REE-tee]   The wife of Alcinous, king of the Phaeacians, she was noted for her wisdom and hospitality.

Argives   Homeric term for the Greeks who fought at Troy; virtually interchangeable with *Achaeans* or *Danaans.*

Argonauts   Fifty Greek heroes who sailed with Jason aboard the *Argo* to obtain the Golden Fleece.

Argos   The region ruled by Agamemnon, whose capital was Mycenae.

Argus   (1) The hundred-eyed herdsman whom Hera appointed to spy on Zeus; when Hermes killed him, Hera placed his eyes in the peacock's tail. (2) The faithful dog of Odysseus who died immediately after recognizing that his master had returned to Ithaca.

Ariadne [ar-ih-AD-nee]   The daughter of Minos and Pasiphae who fell in love with Theseus and gave him a thread by which he found his way out of the labyrinth after killing the Minotaur. After Theseus abandoned her on the island of Naxos, she was courted by Dionysus, who made her immortal.

Aristotle   Greek philosopher (384–322 B.C.), a disciple of Plato, and tutor of Alexander of Macedonia. A scientist and logician, he also wrote the *Poetics,* a work of literary criticism.

Artemis [AR-te-mis] (Diana)   Daughter of Zeus and Leto and twin sister of Apollo, she is virgin goddess of wildlife and the hunt. Although her arrows can inflict pains of childbirth, she champions women's societies, such as that formed by the Amazons.

Ascanius [as-KAY-nih-uhs]   Son of Aeneas by the Trojan Princess Creusa. He is also called *Iulus.*

Asclepius [as-KLEE-pee-uhs] (Aesculapius)   Son of Apollo and Coronis, the Greek founder and patron of medicine. When his skills brought the dead back to life, Zeus killed him with a thunderbolt.

Ate   Minor goddess personifying moral blindness.

Athene [uh-THEE-nuh] (Minerva)   Virgin daughter of Zeus born from her father's brain, she was goddess of wisdom, women's handicrafts, and victory in war.

Athens   Dominant Greek city-state during the fifth century B.C., center of the intellectual and artistic developments that created the historical Golden Age.

Atlantis   According to Plato's *Timaeus* and *Critias,* a legendary civilization that sank beneath the sea, perhaps a Minoan city on the volcanic island of Thera (Santorini) that was obliterated by an eruption in 1628 B.C.

Atlas   Titan brother of Prometheus whom Zeus ordered to hold up the broad vault of the sky.

Atreides   Homeric term meaning "son of Atreus," referring to Agamemnon or Menelaus. (The plural is *Atreidae.*)

Atreus [AY-tre-uhs]   A son of Pelops and king of Mycenae, he was the father of Agamemnon and Menelaus.

Atropos   One of the three Fates, she blindly cut the thread of life spun and measured by her sisters Clotho and Lachesis.

Attica   Province in east-central Greece ruled by Athens.

Attis   Young male consort of the Phrygian goddess Cybele, who drove him mad so that he castrated himself.

Augustus   First Roman emperor (30 B.C.–A.D. 14), indirect sponsor of Virgil's *Aeneid.*

Aulis   Seaport at which Greek troops assembled before sailing to Troy; site of Iphigenia's sacrifice.

Aurora [ah-ROR-uh]   The Roman goddess of dawn, a counterpart of the Greek Eos, daughter of Hyperion and Theia.

autochthon   One supposedly sprung from the ground he inhabits, a person derived from earth.

Autolycus [ah-TUHL-ih-kuhs]   A son of Hermes noted for his thievery and trickery; he was the father of Anticleia, mother of Odysseus.

bacchae   Female worshipers of Dionysus (Bacchus). (See **bacchants.**)

bacchants   Ecstatic worshipers of Dionysus (Bacchus).

Bacchus [BAKH-kuhs]   Another name for Dionysus.

Baucis   The aged wife of Philemon, rewarded for her hospitality.

Bellerophon [bel-LER-oh-fahn]   Son of Glaucus (son of Sisyphus) who killed the Chimaera and defeated the Amazons; he tried to ride to heaven on the winged horse Pegasus. He is also called *Bellerophontes.*

Boeotia   A fertile province bordering Attica in central Greece, the principal city of which was Thebes.

Boreas   Personification of the North Wind.

Briseis   Daughter of Brises (ally of the Trojans) and the captive of Achilles whom Agamemnon confiscated, provoking the wrath that ignited the *Iliad*'s action.

Bromius   Another name for Dionysus.

Cadmus   Founder and king of Thebes, husband of Harmonia, and father of Agave, Autonoe, Ino, and Semele. As a young man, he slew a dragon and (by Athene's direction) planted its teeth from which warriors sprang up. These fought among themselves until only five remained alive; the surviving five built Thebes and were the ancestors of the Theban aristocracy.

Calchas   Prophet who accompanied the Achaeans to Troy.

Calliope   Muse of epic poetry invoked by Homer and Hesiod.

Calypso   Minor goddess embodying female sexuality who held Odysseus captive for seven years on the island of Ogygia.

Carthage   Powerful colony of Tyre on the north coast of Africa, directly south of Rome. The chief threat to Roman imperialism, it was destroyed by Scipio Africanus in 146 B.C.

Cassandra   Daughter of Priam and Hecuba, she was Apollo's virgin prophet; part of Agamemnon's booty from Troy, she was brought to Argos (Mycenae), where Clytemnestra murdered her.

Castor and Pollux (Polydeuces)   Twin brothers celebrated for their devotion to each other, they were born from the same union of Zeus and Leda that produced Helen and Clytemnestra.

catharsis   Aristotle's term for the emotional effect of tragedy, the purging or cleansing of the emotions of pity and fear.

centaur   A creature half-man, half-horse; symbol of humanity's divided nature.

Cerberus [SER-ber-uhs]   The three-headed watchdog of Hades.

Ceres [SEE-reez]   Roman equivalent of Demeter, goddess of grain and earth's fertility.

chaos   In Hesiod, a yawning chasm or Void, one of four primal entities from which the universe evolved. In Ovid, it was the primal disorder or dark confusion of matter that was later shaped into an ordered system (cosmos).

Charon [KA-rohn]   Ancient boatman of the Underworld who ferried souls across the River Styx, the symbolic boundary between life and death.

charter myths   Traditional tales that serve to justify or validate some custom or practice, such as Hesiod's story about Prometheus's tricking Zeus into accepting an inferior sacrifice.

Charybdis [ka-RIB-dis]   Female monster who, with Scylla, guarded the Straits of Messina between Italy and Sicily; a whirlpool that sucked ships underwater.

chimaera   A fire-breathing monster with a lion's head, goat's body, and dragon's tail, traditionally an inhabitant of Hades's realm.

Chiron [KYE-rahn]   A wise old centaur who tutored several famous heroes, including Jason and Achilles.

chorus   The band of dancers and singers that performs in a Greek play, sometimes participating in the action but more commonly commenting on and interpreting the principal characters' actions.

Chryseis   In the *Iliad,* daughter of Chryses (priest of Apollo) whom Agamemnon was forced to return to her father after the god sent a plague upon the Greek army.

Chrysothemis   Daughter of Agamemnon and Clytemnestra, a sister of Electra and Orestes.

chthonic [THOH-nik]   Term relating to earth or the infernal regions, commonly associated with goddesses of fertility and/or death and regeneration.

Circe [SIR-see]   In the *Odyssey,* the enchantress who turned the hero's men into swine; she instructed Odysseus on the way to Hades's kingdom and warned him of Scylla and Charybdis. According to some myths, Odysseus fathered a son, Telegonus, by her.

City Dionysia   An annual festival in Athens honoring Dionysus during which tragedies, comedies, and other dramatic and musical performances were staged.

Clio   The Muse of history.

Clotho   One of the three fates. (See **Atropos.**)

Clytemnestra [klye-tem-NES-tra]   The leading female character in the *Oresteia,* she was the daughter of Tyndareus (or Zeus) and Leda, sister of Helen, wife of Agamemnon, mistress of Aegisthus, and mother of Iphigenia, Electra, Chrysothemis, and Orestes. After murdering Agamemnon, she was slain by Orestes.

Cocytus [koh-SYE-tuhs]   One of the four main rivers of the Underworld, it is the River of Lamentation (Wailing).

Colchis   Home of Medea, on the remote shores of the Black Sea.

Colonus   Suburb of Athens, birthplace of Sophocles, and site of Oedipus's death.

cosmogony   The origin or birth of the universe (cosmos).

cosmology   A theory or belief describing the natural order or structure of the universe.

cosmos   Greek term for the orderly structure of the universe.

Creon [KREE-ahn]   (1) Greek word for ruler. (2) In Sophocles's Theban plays, Jocasta's brother. (3) In Euripides's *Medea,* King of Corinth.

Creusa [kree-OH-sa]   (1) In the *Aeneid,* daughter of Priam, first wife of Aeneas, and mother of Ascanius (Iulus); she was killed in the fall of Troy. (2) In the *Medea,* the daughter of Corinth's king, Jason's intended bride.

Croesus   King of Lydia (560–546 b.c.), famous for his great wealth. His kingdom was captured by Cyrus, founder of the Persian Empire.

Cronus [KROH-nuhs]   Titan son of Gaea (Gaia) and Uranus who deposed his father and ruled the cosmos until overthrown by his youngest son, Zeus. The Romans later identified him with Saturn.

Cumaean Sibyl [koo-MEE-an SIB-il]   Italian counterpart of the Delphic Oracle, her shrine was located at Cumae, the oldest Greek colony in the Bay of Naples region. In the *Aeneid,* she acted as Aeneas's guide through the Underworld.

cuneiform [kue-NEE-uh-form]   The wedge-shaped script invented by the ancient Sumerians about 3200 B.C. and later adopted by the Akkadians and other Mesopotamian peoples; the earliest form of writing.

Cupid   The Latin name for Eros, god of love.

Cybele [SIB-e-lee]   Asiatic mother goddess whom the Greeks identified with Rhea. Many of her priests were eunuchs, supposedly imitating the self-castration of Cybele's lover Attis.

cyclopes   (1) The three sons of Gaea and Uranus: Brontes (Thunder), Steropes (Lightning), and Arges (Thunderbolt). Zeus released them from Tartarus, where Cronus had confined them, and enlisted their help in overthrowing the Titans. (2) In the *Odyssey,* a race of savage, one-eyed giants who lived in caves on Sicily. (See **Polyphemus.**) (The singular is *cyclops.*)

cynthia   Another name for the moon.

Cyparissus   A son of Telephus who, for his unusual good looks, was beloved by several gods, including Zephyrus and Apollo. When Cyparissus accidentally killed the stag that was his favorite companion, he asked heaven to let him grieve forever. As a result, he was changed into a cypress, the tree of sadness.

Cypris   Epithet for Aphrodite, who was supposed to have emerged from the sea on the shores of Cyprus.

Daedalus [DEE-duh-luhs]   Master architect who designed the Labyrinth at Knossos for King Minos. When Minos tried to keep him and his son Icarus prisoner on Crete, Daedalus fashioned wings for their escape. (See **Icarus.**)

Danaans   Another term for Achaeans.

Danae [DA-na-ee]   Mother of the hero Perseus, who was sired by Zeus in a shower of gold. Cast into the sea in a chest with her son, Danae was unexpectedly rescued. (See **Perseus.**)

Daphne   A nymph beloved of Apollo, she was changed into a laurel tree, the leaves of which were thereafter sacred to the god.

Dardanus   Legendary founder of Troy, he and his descendants were persecuted by Hera because Zeus had been the lover of his mother, Electra, a daughter of the Titan Atlas whom Zeus changed into a star, one of the Pleiades; when Troy fell, Electra left the constellation and became a comet.

Dark Ages (Greek)   The obscure period of Greek history following the Dorian Invasion of about 1100 B.C. It ended with the Greek renaissance in Ionia during the seventh century B.C.

Deianeira [dee-ya-NYE-ra]   Second wife of Heracles.

Deiphobus   Son of Priam and Hecuba, he was the prince of Troy who married Helen after Paris's death.

Delos   Aegean island sacred to Apollo and Artemis, the site of their birth.

Delphi [DEL-phee]   Ancient shrine of prophecy on the slopes of Mount Parnassus, site of Apollo's Oracle. Formerly a sanctuary of Themis and other chthonic goddesses, its name means "womb."

Delphic Oracle   The priestess (Pythia) who acted as Apollo's mouthpiece or prophet at Delphi, the most sacred prophetic institution in Greece.

Demeter [de-MEE-ter] (Ceres)   Daughter of Cronus and Rhea, she was the Olympian goddess of agricultural fertility. Her myth is closely related to that of her daughter Persephone. (See **Persephone.**)

Demodocus [de-MAH-dah-kuhs]   In the *Odyssey,* the Phaeacian bard or minstrel who sang of the Trojan War at King Alcinous's court.

Demophon (1) Son of Celeus and Metanira and the younger brother of Triptolemus. When searching for Persephone, Demeter became Demophon's nursemaid and tried to make him immortal by holding him in the fire, until the process was interrupted by the child's mother. (2) The son of Theseus and Phaedra (or Ariadne) who fought in the Trojan War.

deus ex machina The "god from the machine," a mechanical device used in Greek theater production to lift an actor impersonating a god onto the stage. The term refers to the practice of introducing a divine being to resolve problems that human characters cannot untangle.

Diana The Latin name for Artemis, goddess of the hunt and commonly identified with the moon.

Dido [DYE-doh] Queen and founder of Carthage who befriended the shipwrecked Aeneas and was later deserted by him at Jupiter's command.

Diomede(s) [dye-oh-MEE-deez] Youngest and one of the most effective Greek fighters in the Trojan War, he even battled against Ares and Aphrodite.

Dione According to some traditions, Titan mother of Aphrodite.

Dionysus [dye-oh-NYE-suhs] Son of Zeus and Semele and god of the vine that produces wine, he was a male fertility figure who represented a great variety of natural forces, including the vegetative cycle of life, growth, death, and rebirth, and the conflicting power of human instinctual passions. He is also called *Bacchus, Bromius,* and *Liber.*

Dionysus Zagreus [dye-oh-NYE-suhs ZAG-re-uhs] In the Orphic version of the Dionysus myth, a son of Zeus and Persephone swallowed by Zeus and reborn as the son of Zeus and Semele.

dioscuri Term meaning "youths of god (Zeus)," refers to Castor and Pollux (Polydeuces, Greek form of Latinized name), twin sons of Zeus and Leda.

Dirae Roman name for the Furies.

Dis Latin name for Hades or Pluto, god of the Underworld.

dithyramb [DITH-ram] Ecstatic dance or choral song performed in honor of Dionysus, out of which tragedy is said to have evolved.

divination Ancient practice of trying to foretell the future from such phenomena as the flight of birds or the condition of internal organs in sacrificial animals.

Dorians A primitive Greek-speaking people who invaded Greece from the north about 1100 B.C., precipitating the Dark Ages.

dragon A monstrous serpent or other reptile, commonly with wings, that typically represented chaotic or evil forces.

Echo Wood nymph cursed by Hera and who wasted away to a mere voice for the unrequited love of Narcissus.

Eden In biblical tradition, a primordial garden from which the first human couple was banished; it represents one version of humanity's lost Golden Age, a theme also found in Hesiod.

ego Latin first-person pronoun, the "I" that Freud's translators use to designate the center of individual consciousness.

Eileithyia(e) [ye-lye-THYE-ya] Daughter of Hera, a minor goddess of childbirth.

Electra Daughter of Agamemnon and Clytemnestra and sister of Orestes, she conspired with her brother to avenge their murdered father.

Eleusinian [el-oo-SIN-ee-uhn] **Mysteries** A cult at the town of Eleusis involving the worship of Demeter, Persephone, and Triptolemus. Initiates were sworn to secrecy.

Elysium [e-LIZ-ih-uhm], **Elysian fields** A posthumous realm of earthly delights reserved for those especially favored by the gods.

Endymion   A handsome shepherd boy with whom the moon goddess Selene fell in love; he sleeps eternally.

Enuma Elish   Ancient Babylonian creation epic celebrating Marduk's victory over an older generation of gods, a Near Eastern counterpart to Hesiod's *Theogony*.

Eos [EE-ohs]   A personification of the dawn, she was the sister of Selene and Helios. She was identified by the Romans with Aurora.

epic   A long narrative poem, in exalted and sometimes deliberately archaic style, that recounts the adventures, in war or travel, of a national hero whose qualities represent the essential values of his society. The Homeric epic typically employs a number of standard poetic devices, such as invoking the Muse, posing an "epic question," and announcing an "epic theme," such as the wrath of Achilles.

Epic of Gilgamesh   An ancient Mesopotamian narrative celebrating the heroic exploits of a legendary king of Uruk famous for slaying monsters and journeying to a mythical paradise, where his ancestor Utnapishtim told him of a prehistoric deluge.

epilogue   In a Greek play, whatever is spoken after the chorus's final exit.

Epimetheus [ep-ih-MEE-thee-uhs]   A brother of Prometheus who, on man's behalf, accepted the Olympian gods' gift of Pandora; his name means "Afterthought."

epiphany   The appearance or manifestation of a divine being; a revelatory perception of almost supernatural intensity.

episode   In Greek drama, the scene occurring between two choral odes, an act.

epode   In Greek drama, the part of a choral song that follows the strophe and antistrophe; it is sung while the chorus stands still.

Erebus   Personification of primal darkness, the offspring of Chaos, it came to represent the intense gloom of Hades.

Erechtheus [e-REK-thee-uhs]   Legendary early king or founder of Athens, to whom a temple on the Acropolis was dedicated.

Erinyes [e-RIN-ih-eez]   Greek term for the Furies.

Eris   Personification of strife or discord. The term can also mean the spirit of competition for excellence.

Eros [ER-ohs] (Cupid)   God of love and sexual desire, he was represented as an unbegotten primal force (Hesiod) or as the son of Ares and Aphrodite (Homer).

Eteocles [e-TEE-oh-kleez]   Son of Oedipus and Jocasta, he was killed in a duel with his brother Polynices.

etiology   A branch of knowledge dealing with causes, it refers to the proposition that all myths represent attempts to explain the origins of natural, social, or psychological phenomena.

Eumenides [oo-MEN-ih-deez]   Greek name for the Kindly Ones, formerly the Furies.

Europa   A princess of Tyre whom Zeus, in the form of a bull, kidnapped and took to Crete, where she became the mother of Minos and Rhadamanthus.

Eurydice [oo-RIH-dih-see]   Wife of Orpheus, whom he tried to retrieve from Hades.

Eurynomos [oo-RIH-noh-mohs]   An underworld demon who devoured the flesh of dead bodies, leaving only the bones.

exodos   In Greek drama, the final speech sung by the chorus as it leaves the stage.

fate   The mysterious power of destiny that shapes human lives and history. (See **Moirae**.)

Fauna   Roman woodland goddess.

Faunus   Minor Roman woodland deity who presided over crops, herds, and fields and who had the ability to foresee the future. He is commonly identified with Pan.

Flora   Roman goddess of fertility, associated with spring and flowers.

folklore Traditional customs, tales, and beliefs of a people.

folktales Anonymous stories that originate and circulate orally among a people.

Fortuna Roman goddess, the "first-born daughter" of Jupiter, a personification of fate. She was associated with Fors, a divinity of chance, in the phrase *Fors Fortuna*. She is also identified with Tyche, the Greek goddess of chance and luck.

Furies (Dirae) Born from Uranus's blood, they were goddesses of blood vengeance; in Aeschylus, they were daughters of Night. They are also called the *Erinyes.*

Gaea [JEE-uh] (Gaia) The Greeks' original Earth Mother, a primal divine power coeval with Chaos. After producing Uranus (Sky), she mated with him to produce the Titans.

Ganymede Trojan shepherd boy with whom Zeus fell in love and, in the shape of an eagle, carried off to heaven, where he became cupbearer to the gods.

Gemini The divine twins, Castor and Pollux, whom Zeus changed into a starry constellation, giving a part of the zodiac its name.

genius In Roman religion, the indwelling procreative spirit of a man or place that imparts distinction or power.

Geryon A three-headed giant whom Heracles killed.

Gilgamesh Legendary ruler of Uruk, a city-state in ancient Sumer, the hero of the world's oldest narrative poem.

Glaucus In the *Iliad,* a grandson of Bellerophon, co-leader of the Lycian allies of the Trojans who foolishly exchanged his gold armor for the bronze armor of Diomede(s).

Golden Age (1) The mythic period of primal innocence described in Hesiod's poems. (2) The historical period of Athenian political and cultural supremacy (c. 480–404 B.C.) that produced enduring models of excellence in art, literature, drama, architecture, and philosophy.

Golden Fleece The wool of a golden ram given to the king of Colchis and, with Medea's help, stolen by Jason.

Gorgons Three hideous sisters with snakes for hair and hypnotic eyes. Medusa, the only mortal Gorgon, had a gaze so terrifying that she could turn men to stone. With Athene's help, Perseus beheaded her.

Graces, the Three goddesses personifying beauty and charm, inspirers of artistic creation.

Graiae [GRYE-eye] Three ancient women who had been born old, they had only one eye and one tooth among them, which they shared in rotation. They were named Enyo, Pephredo, and Dino and lived in the far West, where the sun never shone. Sisters of the Gorgons, they were tricked by Perseus into revealing the three objects he needed to kill Medusa.

Great Goddess, the Ancient parthenogenetic goddess (worshiped in Old Europe and many other cultures) whose functions included overseeing the cycle of life, death, and regeneration. Originally a creator deity, she eventually acquired association with agriculture and was worshiped as an earth goddess. Gaea is the oldest form of the Great Goddess specific to Greek mythology.

Hades [HAY-deez] (Dis) (1) Son of Cronus and Rhea and brother of Zeus, he was given dominion over the Underworld; he is also called *Pluto.* (2) The subterranean realm of the dead, which is named after its gloomy ruler.

hamartia In Greek tragedy, a term derived from the verb "to miss the mark," to fall short in judgment, understanding, or action; the term Aristotle used to denote a serious error in judgment of the tragic hero.

Hannibal General of the Carthaginians who led the invasion of Italy in the Second Punic War.

Harmonia Daughter of Ares and Aphrodite and wife of Cadmus, founder and king of Thebes.

Harpies Three vicious winged female demons believed to kidnap human victims.

Hebe [HEE-bee] (Juventas) Daughter of Zeus and Hera and a personification of youth, she was cupbearer of the Olympian gods until displaced by Ganymede. After Heracles's deification, he married Hebe, symbol of the gods' eternal youthfulness.

Hecate [HEK-uh-tee] In Hesiod, a great and gracious goddess; in later myth, a creature of darkness and the Underworld, patron of magic and witchcraft.

hecatomb In Greek ritual, originally the sacrifice of a hundred oxen; in time the term came to mean the sacrifice of any large number of animals.

Hecatoncheires Zeus's allies in the Titanomachy. (See **Hundred-handed.**)

Hector Son of Priam and Hecuba, chief defender of Troy against the invading Achaeans; he was abandoned by his patron Apollo and slain by Achilles. His funeral rites closed the *Iliad*.

Hecuba [HEK-oo-ba] Wife of Priam and Queen of Troy, she was the mother of Hector, Paris, Cassandra, and many other noble children, nearly all of whom were killed as a result of the Trojan War.

Helen Daughter of Zeus and Leda, sister of Clytemnestra, Castor, and Pollux, and wife of Menelaus. Tyndareus, her legal father, made each of her innumerable suitors swear to uphold her marriage to whichever husband she selected, an oath that bound many Greek heroes after Paris took her to Troy.

Helios [HEE-lee-ohs] Son of Hyperion, he was god of the sun.

Hellas [HEL-luhs] The ancient Greeks' name for their country.

Hellenes [HEL-lee-neez] Name the Greeks used in classical times to denote the Greek people, who were reputedly descended from a mythical ancestor, Hellen.

Hephaestus [he-FES-tuhs] (Vulcan) Son of Hera (Hesiod) or of Hera and Zeus (Homer), he was god of fire and the forge, the master of metalcraft who built the Olympians' palace and fashioned armor for Achilles. He was married to Aphrodite, who preferred Ares as her lover.

Hera [HEE-ra] (Juno) Daughter of Cronus and Rhea, sister and wife of Zeus, she was goddess of marriage and domesticity. Her matriarchal spirit ill fit the patriarchal rule of Zeus.

Heracles [HER-a-kleez] (Hercules) Son of Zeus and the mortal Alcmene (who was married to Amphitryon), he was the strongest as well as the most long-suffering of all Greek heroes; best known for the Twelve Labors imposed upon him by King Eurystheus, he was eventually rewarded by immortality on Olympus.

Hermaphroditus Son of Hermes and Aphrodite, he was physically united with the nymph Salmacis, acquiring the characteristics of both sexes.

Hermes [HER-meez] (Mercury) Son of Zeus and Maia, he was primarily his father's messenger and an embodiment of extreme mobility. The guide of dead souls, he was also patron of travelers, merchants, highwaymen, gamblers, and thieves.

Hermione Daughter of Helen and Menelaus, she was first married to Neoptolemus (son of Achilles) and then to Orestes, son of Agamemnon.

Hesiod Greek poet of the late eighth century B.C., author of the *Theogony* and *Works and Days*.

Hesperides [hes-PER-ih-deez] Known as *Nymphs of the Setting Sun* or *Daughters of the Evening*, they lived in the far West and guarded a tree bearing golden apples.

Hestia [HES-tee-uh] (Vesta)   Eldest daughter of Cronus and Rhea and virgin sister of Zeus, she guarded the Olympian hearth.

hieros gamos [HYE-rohs GAHM-ohs]   A sacred marriage in which male and female entities, human or divine, are united in a way that ensures or promotes peace and fecundity.

Hippolytus [hip-PAHL-ih-tuhs]   Son of Theseus and Antiope, queen of the Amazons, he was falsely accused of sexual assault by his stepmother Phaedra and, when his deceived father cursed him, killed by a monster from the sea.

Homer   Name that the ancient Greeks attributed to the (otherwise unknown) poet of the *Iliad* and the *Odyssey,* the father of epic poetry.

Horae   The three daughters of Zeus and Themis who personified justice (Dike), order (Eunomia), and peace (Eirene). Guardians of natural law, they regulated the seasons and the smooth functioning of the cosmos.

hubris [HYOO-bris]   The kind of excessive pride that blinds the tragic hero to his own limitations, offends the gods, and initiates his doom.

humanism   A conviction that individual human beings occupy a central place in society and the cosmos, a belief in the inherent worth and dignity of all humanity.

Hundred-handed   Three giant sons of Gaea and Uranus who fought on Zeus's side when he battled the Titans. Their names were Cottus, Briareus, and Gyges.

Hyacinthus   A youth whom both Apollo and Zephyrus loved; when Apollo and Hyacinthus were throwing the discus, the jealous Zephyrus interfered, striking the boy with the discus and killing him, after which he was changed into the flower bearing his name.

Hydra   A seven-headed monster that ravaged Argos and was slain by Heracles.

Hylas   The boy whom Heracles loved, lost ashore while looking for water during the voyage of the Argonauts.

Hymen   Son of Apollo and one of the Muses, he was the god of marriage.

Hyperion [hye-PEER-ee-uhn]   Titan son of Uranus and Gaea, father of Helios, Selene, and Eos; a personification of the sun.

Hypnos   A personification of sleep, he was the twin brother of Thanatos (Death).

Icarus [IK-uh-ruhs]   Son of Daedalus who flew from Crete on artificial wings his father had constructed. Ignoring Daedalus's warning, he flew too close to the sun, whose rays melted the wax holding the wings together, causing him to fall to his death.

ichor [IH-kohr]   The colorless liquid that flowed instead of blood in the veins of the Greek gods.

id   English translation of the Freudian term for the subconscious welter of amoral appetites and instincts residing in every human psyche.

Ida, Mount   (1) The mountain in Crete on which Zeus was born and hidden from Cronus. (2) A mountain near Troy.

Ilia   Daughter of the Roman king Numitor, a Vestal Virgin who became by Mars the mother of Romulus and Remus. She is also called *Rhea Silvia.*

Ilion (Ilium)   The name of Priam's city, Troy.

image   The mental picture and/or physical sensation evoked by a verbal description, such as Homer's graphic depiction of Odysseus's attempt to embrace the shade of his dead mother Anticleia (*Odyssey,* Book 11).

individualism   A belief that each human being has a unique value that grants one the right to personal freedom and the opportunity to fulfill one's full human potential.

Ino   Daughter of Cadmus and Harmonia who nursed the infant Dionysus after Semele's death. When Hera drove her mad, she threw herself into the sea and was transformed into Leucothea, the white goddess of sea foam, a friend to sailors.

invocation of the Muse A literary convention in which a poet formally asks Calliope, Muse of epic poetry, to inspire his composition.

Io A young priestess of Hera in Argos whom Zeus raped and whom Hera vindictively changed into a heifer and drove mad with a gadfly.

Ion Son of Apollo and Creusa who, according to some traditions, was the ancestor of the Ionian Greeks.

Iphigenia [if-ih-je-NYE-a] Daughter of Agamemnon and Clytemnestra whom her father sacrificed at Aulis to prevent the Greeks' expedition against Troy from being disbanded.

Iris A personification of the rainbow and Hera's special messenger. She was married to Zephyrus, the West Wind.

irony A literary term based on the Greek word *eironeia,* meaning a "pretense" or "simulation in speech." Dramatic irony occurs when a character acts inappropriately because he or she is ignorant of facts of which the audience is aware, as when Oedipus rashly condemned the man guilty of Laius's murder.

Iulus Another name for Ascanius, son of Aeneas and Creusa.

Ithaca Island kingdom of Odysseus, the rulership of which was bestowed upon him by his parents, Laertes and Anticleia.

ithyphallic A term denoting figures displaying an erect penis, such as satyrs.

Ixion After Zeus had mercifully pardoned him for murder, Ixion treacherously tried to seduce Hera, for which Zeus bound him on an eternally revolving wheel in Tartarus.

Janus Roman god of doorways, beginnings and endings, he is pictured having two faces looking in two different directions. The month of January is named after him.

Jason Greek adventurer who led fifty Argonauts on a quest across the Black Sea for the Golden Fleece. After marrying Medea, who had helped him steal the fleece from her father, Jason divorced her. Her reaction is dramatized in Euripides's *Medea.*

Jocasta [joh-KAS-ta] Widow of Laius, mother and wife of Oedipus, sister of Creon, and mother of Ismene, Antigone, Eteocles, and Polynices.

Jove Abbreviated Roman name for Zeus, king of the gods.

judgment of Paris The decision that Paris, a Trojan prince, made in selecting Aphrodite as the most beautiful goddess, thereby earning the wrath of Hera and Athene and ensuring the destruction of Troy.

Juno Roman name for Hera, queen of the gods.

Jupiter The Roman equivalent of Zeus, king of the Olympian gods.

Juturna Italian goddess of fountains; in the *Aeneid* she was the devoted sister of Turnus.

Juventas Latin equivalent of Hebe, Greek personification of divine youthfulness.

Keres Hideous winged demons who, like the Fates (Moirae), were daughters of Night. Associated with personifications of death and doom, they may represent the destinies assigned persons at birth.

kore [KOHR-ee] A Greek term meaning "maid," commonly applied to Persephone, daughter of Demeter.

labyrinth The maze that Daedalus built for King Minos to house the Minotaur.

Lacedemonia Region in southeast Greece, the political center of which was Sparta.

Lachesis One of the three Fates. (See **Atropos.**)

Laertes [lay-ER-teez] Son of Arcesius and Chalcomedusa, he married Anticleia, by whom he fathered Odysseus.

Laius [LAY-uhs]   Father of Oedipus and first husband of Jocasta, he brought a curse on his family by eloping with Chrysippus, the son of his host, Pelops.

Lamia   A reptilian female who stole unwary children.

Laocoon [lay-AHK-oh-ahn]   Trojan priest who warned against taking the Wooden Horse into Troy and who was crushed by giant sea serpents.

Lares [LAR-eez]   In Roman religion, the deified spirits of family ancestors.

Latinus   King of Latium and father of Lavinia, whom Aeneas married.

Latium [LAY-shee-uhm]   Region on the Tiber River in western Italy where the Latins lived. Rome was founded near its northern border.

Lausus   A young soldier killed by Aeneas in battle but honored for bravely defending his father.

Lavinia   Daughter of King Latinus and Queen Amata, she became Aeneas's second wife.

Leda   Wife of Tyndareus (king of Sparta) by whom Zeus fathered Helen, Clytemnestra, Castor, and Pollux (Polydeuces).

legend   A story transmitted from the distant past, especially one based at least in part on some historical event.

Lemnos   Volcanic island in the Aegean Sea on which Philoctetes was abandoned by the Achaeans.

Lenaea   Athenian drama festival held annually in January at which comedies were performed.

Lethe [LEE-thee]   In Hades, the River of Forgetfulness.

Leto [LEE-toh]   Titan goddess by whom Zeus fathered Artemis and Apollo.

libido   In Freudian psychoanalysis, the term for instinctual desire that drives all human activities, especially the psychic energy embodied in sexual impulses.

lot   In the Greek concept of Fate, the peculiar mixture of good and evil that each person is assigned in life.

lyre   A small, hand-held stringed musical instrument used to accompany songs or recitations of poetry.

maenads [MEE-nadz]   Female worshipers of Dionysus, commonly called *Bacchae* or *Bacchants,* who dressed in fawnskins and carried a thyrsus while performing ecstatic dances.

Manes   In Roman religion, the spirits of the dead, thought to be hostile to the living and euphemistically called the *Kindly Ones.*

Marduk   Chief god of the Babylonian pantheon, the son of Ea (god of wisdom), and creator-hero of the *Enuma Elish.*

Mars   Roman god of agriculture and war identified with the Greek Ares.

Medea [me-DEE-a]   Sorceress daughter of Aeetes (king of Colchis) and wife of Jason, whom she enabled to obtain the Golden Fleece. When he abandoned her for a Greek wife, she killed their children.

Medusa   The only mortal Gorgon, whose terrifying gaze turned men to stone. With Athene's help, Perseus beheaded her.

Megara [ME-ga-ra]   The first wife of Heracles.

Melpomone   Muse of tragedy, commonly represented in a tragic mask.

Menelaus [men-e-LAY-uhs]   Son of Atreus, younger brother of Agamemnon, husband of Helen, and king of Sparta.

Mercury   Roman name for Hermes, messenger of the Olympian gods.

metaphor   A figure of speech in which one object is used to describe the quality of another, an implied comparison of one thing to another, inferring that the first has a hitherto unrecognized likeness to the second (for example, Achilles is a *lion*—meaning that he has the courage, strength, and savagery of the king of beasts).

Metis [MEE-tis]   Personification of wise advice, Zeus's first wife, whom he swallowed to produce Athene.

Midas   A legendary king of Phrygia who got his wish that everything he touched would turn to gold.

mimesis   Aristotle's term for imitation, the mother of all art.

Minerva   Italian goddess of crafts and trade guilds, later identified with Athene as martial defender of the state. With Jupiter and Juno she was a member of the chief Roman triad of divinities.

Minoan [mih-NOH-an]   Term describing the earliest European civilization (c. 2500–1400 B.C.), which was centered on Crete and other Aegean islands and was characterized by elaborate palace complexes, such as that of King Minos at Knossos.

Minos [MYE-nohs]   Name of a king—or line of kings—that ruled at Knossos on Crete. The son of Zeus and Europa, Minos married Pasiphae, whose unnatural union with a bull produced the Minotaur.

Minotaur [MIN-oh-tahr]   A monster half-human, half-bull produced from Pasiphae's union with the sacred bull of Poseidon, it was confined in the Labyrinth of Knossos and slain by Theseus.

Mnemosyne [nee-MAHS-ih-nee]   Personification of memory, daughter of Uranus and Gaea, and, by Zeus, the mother of the Muses.

Moirae   The three Fates, pictured as ancient women who spun, wove, and cut off the individual threads signifying human lives. Named Atropos, Clotho, and Lachesis, they were the daughters of Zeus and Themis.

Morpheus   God of dreams, the son of Hypnos (Sleep).

Museaus   A legendary pre-Homeric poet said to have been either the teacher or pupil of Orpheus.

Muses, the   The nine daughters of Zeus and Mnemosyne, patrons of literature and the fine arts.

Mycenae [mye-SEE-nee]   Ancient Greek city, capital of Agamemnon, after which the Mycenaean civilization is named.

Mycenaean [mye-see-NEE-uhn]   Term describing the first mainland Greek civilization (c. 1600–1100 B.C.); deeply influenced by the older Minoan culture, Mycenaean society produced the large majority of Greek myths, including the Trojan War saga.

Myrmidons   Achilles's faithful troops who accompanied him to Troy.

mysteries   Secret cults typically involving chthonic or fertility deities, such as Demeter and Persephone or Dionysus and Orpheus, that promised their initiates the gods' protection and a joyous afterlife.

myth   From the Greek word *mythos,* a story typically involving gods and/or heroes whose adventures represent significant aspects of human experience.

mythology   (1) The systematic study of myth. (2) A set or collection of myths, such as classical mythology.

Naiads   Nymphs who dwelled in rivers, springs, or lakes.

Narcissus   A beautiful youth beloved by Echo but who, refusing to love anyone else, fell in love with his own image.

narratology   The critical study of structure in narratives.

nature myth   A theory of myth that sees all myths as disguised representations of natural phenomena, such as the cycle of the seasons or the alternation of sun and storm.

Nausicaa [nah-SIK-ay-a]   Daughter of King Alcinous and Queen Arete who found the shipwrecked Odysseus and befriended him at the Phaeacian court.

necessity   The power of Fate or Destiny that determined how all things must be, it was generally conceived of as a force superior to gods as well as human beings.

nectar   The drink of the Olympian gods that sustained their eternal youthfulness.

nemesis   (1) In Homer, the power of retributive justice, the punishment that overtook wrongdoers. (2) In Aristotle, the term describing the fall of the tragic hero.

Neoptolemus   Son of Achilles and Deidamia, known as *Pyrrhus* ("yellow haired"). When Troy fell, he murdered Priam and took Andromache captive but later married Hermione and was killed by Orestes.

Neptune   Roman name for Poseidon, god of the sea and earthquakes.

Nereus   In Homer, the old man of the sea, father of the nereids, or sea nymphs, the most famous of which was Thetis, mother of Achilles.

Nestor   Aged king of Pylos, famous for his sagacity, who advised the Greek expedition to Troy.

Nessus   A centaur whom Heracles killed for attempting to rape Deianeira (Heracles's wife). Nessus gave Deianeira his garment steeped in the poison of the Hydra, a gift that later caused Heracles's painful death.

Nike   Personification of victory, to whom a temple was dedicated on the Athenian Acropolis.

Niobe   Daughter of Tantalus, sister of Pelops, and wife of Amphion, king of Thebes, she foolishly boasted that, because she had twelve (or fourteen) children, she was the superior of Leto, who had only two. Leto's twins, Artemis and Apollo, shot all but two of her children. Eternally weeping, Niobe was changed into stone.

numen   In Roman religion, the force of spirit inhabiting each earthly place or object—a cave, tree, or spring—as well as each person. Certain places or objects were felt to be *numinous*, or filled with the sense or presence of divinity.

nymphs   Female spirits that dwelled in natural formations, such as rivers, forests, mountains, or fields. Although long-lived, they were not necessarily immortal.

Ocean (Oceanus)   (1) In primitive Greek geography, a gigantic river that encircled the earth. (2) A Titan son of Gaea and Uranus, he was the father of all rivers.

ode   From the Greek word *oide,* meaning "song." (1) The lyrics that the chorus sings in Greek drama. (2) A stately, dignified song performed in honor of gods, legendary heroes, or prize-winning athletes, such as the odes of Pindar (c. 522–443 B.C.).

Odysseus [oh-DIS-see-uhs] (Ulysses)   Son of Laertes and Anticleia, husband of Penelope, father of Telemachus, king of Ithaca, and favorite of Athene, he was celebrated for his prudence, ingenuity, and resourcefulness among the Greek forces at Troy, the fall of which he engineered. Hero of the *Odyssey,* he demonstrated an endurance and adaptability that determined his successful return to Ithaca.

Oedipus [E-dih-puhs]   Son of Laius and Jocasta, father (by Jocasta) of Ismene, Antigone, Eteocles, and Polynices, and king of Thebes, his myth demonstrates human inability to circumvent the gods' will.

Ogygia [oh-JIJ-ih-a]   Island home of the nymph Calypso, location unknown.

Olympia   Religious center on the Peloponnesian Peninsula where, every four years (beginning in 776 B.C.), the most famous Greek athletic contests were held.

Olympus, Mount (1) A high mountain along the northern border between Thessaly and Greece proper, near the valley of Tempe, sacred to Apollo. (2) The mythical dwelling place of the Olympian gods, located somewhere in the sky.

oracle (1) The word or utterance of a god, usually a command or prophecy about the future. (2) The person inspired to deliver a divine proclamation, such as the Delphic Oracle.

orchestra In a Greek theater, the circular arena, lower than the main stage, where the chorus danced and sang.

Orestes [ah-RES-teez] Son of Agamemnon and Clytemnestra, brother of Iphigenia and Electra, and husband of Hermione (daughter of Helen).

Orion A giant hunter who was transformed into a major constellation.

Orpheus [OR-fee-uhs] The archetypal poet and singer who descended into Hades to rescue his wife Eurydice, he later suffered *sparagmos,* after which his lyre, symbol of divine harmony, was transformed into a constellation.

Orphism A particularly obscure mystery cult in which devotees were initiated into the secrets of moral transfiguration and future immortality.

Osiris Egyptian guide and judge of the dead, brother and husband of Isis, and (posthumously) father of Horus. He underwent sparagmos, resurrection, and deification, which suggested to the Greeks that he was an African manifestation of Dionysus.

paean (1) A song of thanksgiving or triumph, a hymn of praise. (2) A choral ode invoking the healing power of Apollo. (3) In later times, a song chanted to Ares before marching to war.

palladium A small wooden statue of Pallas Athene, the possession of which the Trojans believed would protect their city. After Odysseus stole it, Troy fell.

Pallas (1) A title of Athene, meaning unknown. (2) A Titan who, by Styx, fathered Nike (Victory). (3) In the *Aeneid,* a son of Evander whom Turnus kills.

Pan A son of Hermes and a daughter of Dryops (leader of an ancient pre-Greek people), he was the quintessential nature deity, usually pictured as a goat from the waist down, with a human torso, a goat's horns, and pointed ears. Patron of goatherds and flocks, he roamed the wilderness playing the panpipes and pursuing nymphs.

Panathenaea [pan-ath-e-NEE-a] Athens's major annual festival honoring its patron, Athene. It included athletic, poetry, and musical contests and culminated in a great procession to the Acropolis.

Pandarus A Trojan commander who broke the armistice with the Greeks, treacherously wounding Menelaus. He was then killed by Diomede(s).

Pandora In Hesiod, the first woman, created by Hephaestus from clay and adorned by Athene with every attraction. She was designed by Zeus to weaken humankind.

Pantheon (1) Term meaning "all the gods." (2) A circular temple built by Hadrian in Rome.

parados The ode sung by a Greek chorus during its first appearance on stage.

paradox A statement or condition in which two or more apparently contradictory elements are in some sense true or valid. An *oxymoron* such as Hesiod's description of Pandora as a "lovely evil" is one type of paradox.

Paris Trojan prince, son of Priam and Hecuba, younger brother of Hector, who selected Aphrodite as the most beautiful goddess, abducted Helen as his prize, and thereby sealed Troy's doom. He is also called *Alexandros.*

Parnassus, Mount A rugged mountain on whose slopes Delphi is located, a landform sacred to Apollo and the Muses.

parody   An imitation of a literary work that deliberately distorts or exaggerates its style or content, thereby opening it to ridicule.

parthenogenesis   The phenomenon by which a female was able to reproduce without being fertilized by a male.

Parthenon   The Doric temple to *Athene Parthenos* (Athene the Virgin) that was built atop the Athenian Acropolis in the fifth century B.C.

Pasiphae [pah-SIF-a-ee]   Daughter of Helios, sister of Circe, wife of King Minos of Crete, and mother of Ariadne, Phaedra, and (by a bull) the Minotaur.

pathos   That part of a Greek tragedy that depicts the suffering and/or death of the hero.

patriarch   A father, founder, or venerable leader of a family, clan, or group.

Patroclus [pa-TROH-kluhs]   Son of Menoetius (one of Helen's former suitors) and beloved friend of Achilles, whom he accompanied to Troy. His death galvanized Achilles to return to the war.

Pax Romana   The "Roman Peace," the political stability that Roman imperial efficiency imposed on the Mediterranean world from the reign of Augustus (30 B.C.–A.D. 14) until the death of Marcus Aurelius in A.D. 180.

Pegasus   A winged horse that sprang from the blood of Medusa after Perseus beheaded her.

Peleus   The mortal to whom the gods married Thetis after Zeus learned that if he had a son by Thetis the boy would be stronger than his father. After Achilles's birth—when Peleus showed the first sign of aging—Thetis deserted him.

Pelias [PEE-lih-uhs]   A son of Poseidon and Tyro who usurped the kingdom of his brother Aeson, father of Jason.

Peloponnesian War   The series of wars (431–404 B.C.) between Athens and Sparta, the dominant power of the Peloponnesus.

Peloponnesus   The southern peninsula of Greece, where Argos, Mycenae, Sparta, and Pylos were located.

Pelops [PEE-lahps]   Son of Tantalus (king of Phrygia), he was served by his father to the gods at a banquet. After Demeter—absorbed in her grief for Persephone—took a bite from his shoulder, the gods restored it with an ivory replacement. The Peloponnesian Peninsula is named after him; his sons included Atreus and Thyestes.

Penates [pe-NAY-teez]   Roman deities of hearth and home, their images were kept in each Roman house and in a temple of the state.

Penelope   Daughter of Icarius of Sparta and Periboea, a naiad, and wife of Odysseus and mother of Telemachus, she was a model of the loyal and prudent wife.

Pentheus [PEN-thee-uhs]   Son of Agave and Echion (one of the men born when Cadmus sowed the dragon's teeth), he was the young king of Thebes who opposed the introduction of Dionysus's cult into his realm, for which the god destroyed him.

Pericles [PER-ik-leez]   Leader of the Athenian democracy (c. 460–429 B.C.) and sponsor of the rebuilding of the Acropolis, whose temples included the Parthenon.

peripeteia [per-ih-pe-TEE-uh]   In tragedy, the sudden reversal or unexpected change of the hero's fortunes, as when the conquering hero Agamemnon was brought down by his wife.

Persephone [per-SEF-oh-nee]   Daughter of Zeus and his sister Demeter, she personified the grain harvest. When Hades took her to the Underworld, her mother (symbolizing the fertility of the soil) fell into such extreme grief that the gods ordered Persephone's return to the daylight world for most of the year. She is also called *Proserpina* and *Kore* (*Core*), the Maiden.

Perseus   Son of Zeus and Danae, he beheaded Medusa, wed Andromeda, and (in some myths) founded Mycenae.

Persian Wars   A series of three Persian invasions into Greece that continued the westward expansion of Persia begun by Cyrus the Great, conqueror of Babylon (539 B.C.). The Greeks repelled the Persians and their allies at Marathon (490 B.C.), but not until after the sea battles at Salamis (480) and Mycale (479) did the Persians permanently retreat into Asia. Herodotus (c. 450 B.C.) left a detailed account of these events.

personification   A literary device by which an abstract quality is given human or divine form, as when Homer made Panic (the sudden fear that seizes a crowd) and Rout (the impulse to flee the battlefield) actual personages. Eros personifies human sexual desire as Eos signifies the dawn.

Phaedra [FE-drah]   Daughter of King Minos and Pasiphae, wife of Theseus (king of Athens), and stepmother of Thesseus's son Hippolytus, with whom she fell in love and later denounced to his father after he rejected her advances.

Phaethon [FEE-e-thahn]   Son of Helios (or Apollo) and Clymene who convinced his father to let him drive the chariot of the sun across heaven, with catastrophic results.

Philemon and Baucis   In Ovid, an aged couple who hospitably received Zeus and Hermes (Jupiter and Mercury) when they posed as poor travelers.

Philoctetes   Greek hero to whom Heracles bequeathed a magic bow and arrow that never failed to hit its target. In Sophocles's *Philoctetes,* Odysseus visited Lemnos, where Philoctetes had been abandoned because he suffered from a stinking wound that did not heal. Using the trusting young Neoptolemus as his foil, Odysseus plotted to steal the bow after a prophet announced that Troy could not be taken without it.

Phlegethon   The fiery river of the Underworld that, in a huge waterfall, joined the Cocytus to form the Acheron.

Phoebus   An epithet of Apollo, meaning the "shining one." (See **Apollo.**)

Phoenix   (1) Mythological Egyptian bird that lived for five hundred years and then consumed itself in flames; from its ashes a new bird arose. (2) In the *Iliad,* Achilles's old teacher who tried to persuade the hero to rejoin his comrades at Troy.

Phrynichus   An early tragedian, the first to produce plays about contemporary history, such as the *Capture of Miletus.*

pietas   The supreme Roman virtue of duty toward the family, state, and gods, expressed in action rather than thought.

Pillars of Heracles   The massive rock formations guarding the narrow passage of Gibraltar linking the Mediterranean Sea and the Atlantic Ocean.

Pirithous [pye-RITH-oh-uhs]   King of the Lapiths who accompanied his friend Theseus into the Underworld to abduct Persephone, for which sacrilege he was condemned to being bound forever in an iron chair.

Pisistratus   The Athenian tyrant during whose administration (560–527 B.C.) were instituted the public recitations of Homer at the Panathenaea and the tragic competitions at the City Dionysia.

Pleiades   A constellation of seven stars, supposedly the daughters of Atlas who were pursued by Orion and changed into heavenly bodies.

plot   The structure or arrangement of incidents in a play or other literary work so that they form a coherent design, typically involving elements of conflict, crisis, and resolution.

Plutarch   A Greek biographer who wrote "parallel" lives of famous Romans and Greeks.

Pluto [PLOO-toh]   The "wealth giver," an epithet of Hades, whose subterranean realm contained precious minerals and other treasures. (See **Hades.**)

Plutus [PLOO-tuhs]   A son of Demeter and Iasion and the personification of wealth.

polis   Greek term for the "city-state," such as Athens or Sparta.

pollution   A state of ritual or moral impurity incurred by the committing of a crime such as homicide. Until a polluted person had expiated his guilt, he was driven from his homeland as unclean and likely to bring on the gods' wrath.

Polynices [pol-ih-NYE-seez]   Son of Oedipus and Jocasta, he was killed in a battle for the throne of Thebes by his brother Eteocles.

Polyphemus   A cyclops, a one-eyed cannibalistic giant whom Odysseus blinded and who retaliated with a curse enforced by his father Poseidon.

Poseidon [poh-SYE-duhn] (Neptune)   Son of Cronus and Rhea, brother of Zeus, and husband of Amphitrite (a nereid); god of the sea and earthquakes, he used his three-pronged trident to raise storms and swamp ships.

Priam   King of Troy, husband of Hecuba, father of Hector, Paris, Cassandra, and (by various concubines) fifty sons.

Procrustes   A brigand (said to be a son of Poseidon) who kidnapped and murdered travelers on the road between Athens and Eleusis. He laid his victims on an iron bed: if they were too short he stretched them out to fit the bed frame; if too tall, he cut off their extremities. Theseus beheaded him.

prologue   In Greek drama, whatever is spoken before the entrance of the chorus.

Prometheus [proh-MEE-thee-uhs]   A Titan cousin of Zeus and son of Iapetus and Clemene, he was punished by Zeus for befriending humanity. Prometheus's theft of fire signified his enlightenment of primitive men, rescuing them from the mental darkness of ignorance and savagery. After suffering for millennia the daily tearing out of his liver by Zeus's fierce eagle, Prometheus was eventually reconciled to his enemy and ascended to Olympus, where he was honored as the divine fire-bearer.

Proserpina   The Latin name of Persephone, daughter of Demeter and Zeus.

protagonist   In Greek drama, the "first actor," the major character.

Proteus   A son of Poseidon or Ocean (Oceanus), he had to tell the future of anyone who held him down. He tried to elude capture by changing his form into that of an animal, plant, or element, such as fire, water, or wind.

Psyche   (1) The Greek word for "soul," it refers to the mental, emotional, and psychological makeup of a human being. (2) Perhaps the last major myth created in classical antiquity: the story of a beautiful young woman named Psyche who, after many hardships and ordeals, at last married Love (Eros or Cupid) and ascended to join the gods on Olympus, a tale representing the human soul as being destined to achieve divine immortality. The myth is contained in the Roman writer Apuleius's novel the *Golden Ass.*

psychology   A science that investigates the human mind and behavior.

Punic Wars   A series of three wars between Rome and Carthage that ended with the latter's total destruction (146 B.C.), foreshadowed in the *Aeneid* by Dido's fatal affair with Aeneas.

Pylades [PYE-la-deez]   Loyal friend of Orestes who accompanied him to Mycenae.

Pylos   Kingdom of old Nestor, which Telemachus visited while searching for his father.

Pyrrhus   A name of Neoptolemus, son of Achilles.

Pythia [PITH-ee-uh]   Title of Apollo's virgin priestess at Delphi, a name commemorating the god's victory over Python.

Pytho [PYE-thoh]   An ancient name of Delphi, where Apollo dispensed his oracles.

Python [PYE-thuhn]   The serpent that guarded the ancient Delphic shrine of Themis and which Apollo killed with his arrow.

Quirinus   A Roman warrior god identified with Romulus after the latter's death.

recognition   From the Greek *anagnorisis,* in Greek drama it refers to the scene in which a character becomes aware of some previously unknown but highly significant fact, such as Electra's recognition of her long-lost brother Orestes or Oedipus's fatal discovery of his true identity.

Remus   Son of Mars and a Vestal Virgin, he was the twin brother of Romulus.

reversal   In Greek tragedy, the point at which the hero's fortunes suddenly change (usually for the worse) or an action that produces the opposite of what was expected.

Rhadamanthus   Son of Zeus and Europa, who, with his brother Minos, became a judge of the dead and ruler of Elysium.

Rhapsode, Rhapsodist   Originally a poet who recited his own works; later, a professional singer of Homeric poems, such as those who performed at the Panathenaea.

Rhea [REE-a]   Titan wife of Cronus, mother of Zeus, Poseidon, Hades, Hera, and Hestia; she was sometimes identified with the Asiatic goddess Cybele.

Rhea Silvia [REE-a SIL-vih-a]   In some myths, the Vestal Virgin mother of Romulus and Remus. She is also known as *Ilia.*

ritual   The established form for a ceremony, a formalized set of words, gestures, or actions assiduously repeated in customary order, especially the prescribed order of a religious rite. According to some mythographers, all myths are related to ritual observances.

Romulus   Son of Mars and Rhea Silvia (a Vestal Virgin) and founder of Rome (traditionally 753 B.C.), he killed his twin brother Remus for criticizing the inadequacy of the walls he had built around Rome.

saga   A series or extensive collection of traditional tales about a person, place, or events, such as those concerning Thebes or the Trojan War.

Saturn   An Italian god whom the Romans identified with Cronus.

Saturnalia   An annual Roman festival held from December 17 to 19 in honor of Saturn, the rebirth of the sun after the winter solstice, and the sowing of crops—a forerunner of Christmas.

satyr [SAY-ter]   Generally human in appearance, but with a horse's tail and ears, half-human, the satyr was characterized by lust and cowardice, a symbol of the amoral and animalistic aspects of human nature.

satyr play   The ribald farce that followed the presentation of a tragic trilogy at the City Dionysia, it reaffirmed the comic and sexual aspects of human life.

Scylla [SIL-la]   In the *Odyssey,* a female monster who, with Charybdis, guarded the Straits of Messina between Italy and Sicily. A whirlpool, Charybdis sucked ships down to their doom, while multiarmed Scylla seized and ate any who came within her reach.

Selene [se-LEE-nee]   A Titan daughter of Hyperion (or Helios), she personified the moon.

Semele [SEM-uh-lee]   Daughter of Cadmus and Harmonia, sister of Agave, and mother (by Zeus) of Dionysus, she was consumed in Zeus's lightning when she demanded to see him in his true form. Dionysus later rescued her from Hades and escorted her to heaven.

serpent   A reptile that can represent evil, such as Typhoeus or the dragon of chaos; alternatively, it can also signify the beneficent or healing powers of nature, such as the snakes associated with Apollo's son Asclepius. The ancient Goddess of Crete was also depicted with serpents, as were classical representations of Athene.

shadow   A term used in Jungian psychology to denote the unconscious part of the personality consisting of emotions or qualities that were repressed as the psyche developed. Although the shadow contains many negative or potentially destructive drives that can motivate antisocial or self-defeating behavior—greed, shame, lust, envy, hatred, selfishness—it also harbors abilities and talents that were never cultivated because they were not encouraged and is thus a source of positive psychic energy.

Sheol   The biblical Underworld, counterpart of Hades.

Sibyl   Title of Apollo's virgin prophetess at Cumae who guided Aeneas through the subterranean kingdom of Hades.

Silenus [sye-LEE-nuhs]   A mythic creature of wild nature, half-man, half-animal in form, typically depicted with a horse's ears and tail. Despite his partly bestial appearance and association with Bacchic revels, Silenus was known for his great wisdom and tutored the young Dionysus. Similarly hybrid figures, the silens (sileni) were depicted on Greek vases as drunken old men with equine features.

simile   An explicit comparison between two unlike objects, using *as* or *like.* In an "epic simile," the poet typically creates an extended comparison that likens two objects or classes of objects at such length that the subject is temporarily forgotten, as when Homer compares soldiers slain in battle to falling autumn leaves.

Sinon   In the *Aeneid,* a Greek spy who persuaded the Trojans to take the Wooden Horse into their city.

sirens   Female creatures, half-bird, half-woman, whose songs lured passing sailors to shipwreck and death.

Sisyphus [SIS-ih-fuhs]   Founder of Corinth who, for his greed and deceit, was condemned in Tartarus forever to roll a huge stone uphill, from whence it always rolled down again.

skene   In Greek drama, the small building at the back of the stage that the actors used as a dressing room, the source of the word *scenery.*

Socrates   Athenian philosopher (c. 469–399 B.C.) and friend and teacher of Plato, he was condemned to death for questioning assumptions deemed essential to maintain civic order and security.

sparagmos [spuh-RAHG-mohs]   The ritual tearing asunder of a young male sacrificial victim, a dismemberment associated with Osiris, Dionysus, Pentheus, and Orpheus, as well as numerous Near Eastern dying and rising gods, such as Attis, Tammuz, and Adonis.

Sparta   (1) In Mycenaean times, the luxurious capital of Helen and Menelaus. (2) In classical times, the austere city-state that was run like a totalitarian military camp.

Sphinx   Enigmatic creature with the head of a woman, body of a lion, and wings of an eagle, infamous for killing anyone who tried but failed to solve its riddles.

strophe   In Greek drama, the choral ode sung while the chorus moved from one side of the orchestra to the other; the antistrophe was the part sung while the chorus rotated in another direction.

structuralism   A method of critical analysis postulating that the human mind has an innate tendency to impose patterns or structured systems on experience, such as the tendency to perceive the world as a duality of opposites. The function of myth is to mediate or reconcile these polarities.

Styx   (1) The oldest child of Oceanus and Tethys, she aided Zeus in his battle with the Titans, for which Zeus honored her by making vows made in Styx's name irrevocable even for gods. (2) River in the Underworld marking the boundary between life and death.

superego   A Freudian term denoting a major component of the psyche that reflects parental and societal restraints imposed on the individual.

symbol   In literary criticism, it is anything—person, place, or object—that stands for something else, typically suggesting a higher or more abstract meaning than the literal entity itself. The fire that Prometheus stole from heaven symbolized all the civilized arts and skills associated with light and dominion over nature.

syncretism   The practice of combining two or more originally distinct ideas or religious traditions together to create a new composite religion or set of beliefs.

Tantalus   Son of Zeus and father of Pelops, whose flesh he served to the Olympians, an act for which he was condemned to eternal torment in Tartarus.

Tarquin   Name of two Etruscan kings of ancient Rome.

Tartarus [TAHR-tahr-uhs]   The dark abyss beneath Hades's realm where Zeus chained the fallen Titans and where the wicked suffered torment.

Telemachus [tee-LEM-a-kuhs]   Son of Penelope and Odysseus who helped his father destroy his mother's hundred suitors.

Teucer   Son of Telamon, the most skilled Greek archer in the war against Troy.

Thanatos [THAN-a-TOHS]   The personification of death, he was the twin brother of Hypnos (Sleep).

Thebes   Leading city of Boeotia, founded by Cadmus and home of Oedipus and his family.

Themis [THEE-mis]   A Titan goddess, daughter of Gaea and Uranus, who personified justice and law; in some myths, she was the mother of Prometheus. Even after Apollo's cult was established there, she had a prophetic shrine at Delphi.

theriomorphism   The practice of depicting divine beings in animal form.

Thersites   In the *Iliad,* a mean-spirited common soldier whom Odysseus beat for daring to argue with his superiors.

Theseus [THEE-see-uhs]   Son of Aegeus and legendary king of Athens, he won fame by slaying the Minotaur at Minos's palace on Crete. He fathered Hippolytus by the Amazon Antiope and later married Phaedra, daughter of Minos.

Thesmophoria [thes-moh-FOHR-ee-uh]   A festival honoring Demeter in which only women (excluding virgins) participated.

Thespis   Although some scholars doubt his historicity, he was probably an Athenian playwright (c. 534 B.C.), known as the father of drama for having created the first role for an actor.

Thetis   A sea nymph married to Peleus, by whom she had Achilles.

Thyestes   Brother of Atreus and father of Aegisthus.

Tiresias [tih-REE-sih-as]   Blind Theban prophet who had temporarily been changed into a woman, giving him the experience to settle a quarrel between Hera and Zeus over which sex has the greater capacity for sexual pleasure. Hera blinded him for his candid answer, while Zeus gave him long life and insight.

Titans   Race of giant gods that Gaea and Uranus begot and which Zeus overthrew and imprisoned in Tartarus.

tragedy   In Greek literature, a serious play containing a pathos or scene of suffering, that was performed at the City Dionysia.

trilogy   In Greek tragedy, a series of three plays dealing with a common subject or theme, of which the *Oresteia* is the only surviving example.

Triptolemus [trip-TOHL-e-muhs]   The young man whom Demeter chose to travel the world teaching the skills of agriculture, in some accounts identified with the child whom Demeter tried to make immortal. He was associated with Demeter and Persephone in the Eleusinian Mysteries.

Trojan Horse   The hollow wooden horse that concealed Odysseus and other Achaeans and was left as a parting gift when the Greeks pretended to leave Troy. It was so large that the Trojans had to tear down part of their protective walls to take it into their city.

Trojan War   The ten-year siege of Troy led by Agamemnon to retrieve Helen, who had eloped with Paris, a Trojan prince.

Troy (Ilium)   The city of Priam and Hecuba that the Greeks, under Agamemnon, destroyed (about 1200 B.C.). Guarding the trade routes between the Mediterranean and the Black Sea, its site is occupied by modern Hissarlik, Turkey.

Turnus   In the *Aeneid,* the Italian king of the Rutulians and suitor of Lavinia. After killing Pallas, he was slain by Aeneas.

Tyndareus   King of Sparta and reputed father of Helen (whom most traditions say is the daughter of Zeus).

Typhoeus [tye-FEE-uhs]   A monstrous giant, in appearance half-human and half-reptile, with one hundred dragon heads; the child of Gaea and Tartarus, a manifestation of the dragon of chaos that Zeus had to defeat before assuming control of the cosmos.

Typhon   A reptilian child of Hera, an incarnation of storm winds.

tyrant   The ruler of a Greek city-state who had neither inherited nor been elected to his position, although he could be appointed to assume governmental control, as was the Athenian Solon. Commonly used to denote a usurper who seized control through a military coup d'etat, the term was eventually applied to a political despot.

Ulysses [oo-LIS-seez]   The Latin name for Odysseus, king of Ithaca.

Uranus [OOR-a-nuhs]   The original sky god and son-husband of Gaea, he was castrated and deposed by his "crafty" son Cronus.

Venus   Italian goddess of gardens and flowers identified with Aphrodite.

Vesta [VES-tuh]   Roman name for Hestia, goddess of the hearth. In Rome, the Vestal Virgins were charged with the sacred duty of keeping alight the Eternal Flame signifying the Roman state.

Vulcan   Roman name for Hephaestus, god of fire and the forge.

Xanthus   Achilles's horse, which prophesied his master's death.

Yahweh   Personal name of Israel's God, commonly misrendered in English as "the Lord."

Zephyrus   Personification of the West Wind.

Zeus (Jove, Jupiter)   The youngest son of Cronus and Rhea, king of the Olympian gods, a personification of atmospheric phenomena—particularly storms and lightning—and the cosmic guarantor of justice, oath-keeping, civic order, and kingship. As head of the Greek pantheon, he was the ultimate court of appeal for both humans and gods. All other Olympians were either his siblings or children, including his sister-wife Hera.

ziggurat [ZIG-oo-rat]   An ancient Mesopotamian temple tower built of successively recessed levels topped by a shrine to the god it commemorated.

Selected Bibliography

Chapter 1   Introduction to the Nature of Myth

Apollodorus (of Athens). *The Library of Greek Mythology.* Trans. Keith Aldrich. Lawrence, KS: Coronado, 1975.

Boardman, John, Jasper Griffin, and Oswyn Murray, eds. *Greece and the Hellenistic World.* Oxford: Oxford UP, 1988.

Bruno, Vincent J., ed. *The Parthenon.* New York: Norton, 1974.

Burkert, Walter. *Greek Religion.* Trans. John Raffan. Cambridge: Harvard UP, 1985.

Calasso, Roberto. *The Marriage of Cadmus and Harmony.* Trans. Tim Parks. New York: Knopf, 1993.

Carpenter, T. H. *Art and Myth in Ancient Greece.* London: Thames and Hudson, 1991.

Cottrell, Arthur, ed. *The Penguin Encyclopedia of Ancient Civilizations.* New York: Penguin, 1980.

Dalley, Stephanie. *Myths from Mesopotamia: Creation, the Flood, Gilgamesh and Others.* New York: Oxford UP, 1989.

Dietrich, B. C. *Death, Fate and the Gods: The Development of a Religious Idea in Greek Popular Belief and in Homer.* London: Athlone, 1965.

Gantz, Timothy. *Early Greek Myth.* Baltimore: Johns Hopkins UP, 1993.

Guthrie, W. K. C. *The Greeks and Their Gods.* Boston: Beacon, 1955.

Hyginus. *Astronomica.* Ed. Paul Chatelain and P. Legendre. Paris: Libraire Honore Champion, 1909.

———. *Fabulae.* Ed. H. J. Rose. Leyden: Sythoff, 1933.

Nilsson, Martin P. *The Mycenaean Origin of Greek Mythology.* New York: Norton, n.d.

Pausanias. *Guide to Greece.* Trans. Peter Levi. New York: Penguin, 1971. Vol. 1 of *Central Greece.*

Plutarch. *The Rise and Fall of Athens: Nine Greek Lives by Plutarch.* Trans. Ian Scott-Kilvert. Baltimore: Penguin, 1960.

Sandars, N. K. *The Epic of Gilgamesh.* Rev. ed. New York: Penguin, 1972.

———. *Poems of Heaven and Hell from Ancient Mesopotamia.* Baltimore: Penguin, 1971.

Handbooks and General References

Grimal, Pierre. *The Dictionary of Classical Mythology.* Trans. A. R. Maxwell-Hyslop. Oxford: Blackwell, 1986.

Hornblower, Simon, and Antony Spawforth, eds. *The Oxford Classical Dictionary.* 3rd ed. New York: Oxford UP, 1996.

Howatson, M. C., ed. *The Oxford Companion to Classical Literature.* 2nd ed. New York: Oxford UP, 1989.

New Larousse Encyclopedia of Mythology. London: Paul Hamlyn, 1968.

Rose, H. J. *Gods and Heroes of the Greeks: An Introduction to Greek Mythology.* Cleveland: Meridian, 1958.

———. *A Handbook of Greek Mythology.* New York: Dutton, 1959.

Chapter 2   Ways of Interpreting Myth

Birenbaum, Harvey. *Myth and Mind.* UP of America, 1988.

Burkert, Walter. *Greek Religion.* Trans. John Raffan. Cambridge: Harvard UP, 1985.

——. *Structure and History in Greek Mythology.* Berkeley, CA: U of California P, 1979.

——. *Homo Necans: The Anthropology of Ancient Greek Sacrificial Ritual and Myth.* Trans. Peter Bing. Berkeley, CA: U of California P, 1983.

Campbell, Joseph. *The Hero with a Thousand Faces.* 2nd ed. Princeton: Princeton UP, 1968.

——. *The Masks of God: Occidental Mythology.* New York: Penguin, 1964.

Dowden, Ken. *The Uses of Greek Mythology.* London: Routledge, 1992.

Edmunds, Lowell, ed. *Approaches to Greek Myth.* Baltimore: Johns Hopkins UP, 1990.

Eisner, Robert. *The Road to Daulis: Psychoanalysis, Psychology, and Classical Mythology.* Syracuse: Syracuse UP, 1987.

Frazer, Sir James G. *The New Golden Bough.* Ed. T. H. Gaster. New York: Criterion, 1959.

Freud, Sigmund. *The Interpretation of Dreams.* 1900. New York: Basic, 1955.

——. *Totem and Taboo.* 1913. New York: Norton, 1962.

Grant, Michael. *The Myths of the Greeks and the Romans.* New York: Mentor, 1964.

Harrison, Jane E. *Mythology.* New York: Harcourt, 1963.

——. *Themis.* Cleveland: Meridian, 1962.

Jung, Carl G. *Man and His Symbols.* New York: Dell, 1964.

——. *Modern Man in Search of a Soul.* Trans. W. S. Dell and Cary Banes. New York: Harcourt, n.d.

——. *Psychology of the Unconscious.* New York: Dodd, 1957.

Kirk, G. S. *The Nature of Greek Myths.* New York: Penguin, 1974.

Malinowski, Bronislaw. *Crime and Custom in Savage Society.* Patterson, NJ: Littlefield, 1959.

——. *The Sexual Life of Savages.* New York: Harcourt, 1929.

Murray, Gilbert. *Five Stages of Greek Religion.* Garden City: Doubleday, 1992.

Schneiderman, Leo. *The Psychology of Myth, Folklore, and Religion.* Chicago: Nelson-Hall, 1981.

Segal, Robert A., ed. *Literary Criticism and Myth.* 6 vols. New York: Garland, 1996.

Slater, Philip E. *The Glory of Hera: Greek Mythology and the Greek Family.* Princeton: Princeton UP, 1968.

Vernant, Jean-Pierre. *Myth and Society in Ancient Greece.* New York: Zone, 1990.

Vernant, Jean-Pierre, and Pierre Vidal-Naquet. *Myth and Tragedy in Ancient Greece.* New York: Zone, 1990.

Chapter 3   In the Beginning: Hesiod's *Theogony*

Athanassakis, Apostolos N., ed. and trans. *Hesiod: Theogony, Works and Days, Shield.* Baltimore: Johns Hopkins UP, 1983.

Burn, Andrew R. *The World of Hesiod: A Study of the Greek Middle Ages ca. 900–700 BC.* New York: Blom, 1936.

Caldwell, Richard S., ed. and trans. *Hesiod's Theogony.* Cambridge, MA: Focus Classical Library, 1987.

Frankel, H. *Early Greek Poetry and Philosophy.* Trans. Moses Hadas and James Willis. Oxford: Irvington, 1975. See ch. 3, 94–131.

Friedrich, Paul. *The Meaning of Aphrodite.* Chicago: U of Chicago P, 1978.

Greene, Mott T. *Natural Knowledge in Preclassical Antiquity.* Baltimore: Johns Hopkins UP, 1992.

Jaeger, Werner. *Paideia: The Ideals of Greek Culture.* Vol. 1. New York: Oxford UP, 1945.

————. *The Theology of the Early Greek Philosophers.* Oxford: n.p., 1936.

Nilsson, Martin P. *Greek Popular Religion.* 1940. Rpt. as *Greek Folk Religion.* New York: n.p., 1961.

Penglase, Charles. *Greek Myths and Mesopotamia: Parallels and Influence in the Homeric Hymns and Hesiod.* New York: Routledge, 1994.

Pucci, P. *Hesiod and the Language of Poetry.* Baltimore: n.p., 1977.

Walcot, P. *Envy and the Greeks.* Warminster: n.p., 1978.

————. *Hesiod and the Near East.* Cardiff: U of Wales P, 1964.

West, M. L., ed. and trans. *Theogony and Works and Days.* New York: Oxford UP, 1988.

Chapter 4   The Great Goddess and the Goddesses: The Divine Woman in Greek Mythology

Baring, Anne, and Jules Cashford. *The Myth of The Goddess: Evolution of an Image.* London: Penguin, 1993.

Berger, Pamela. *The Goddess Obscured: Transformations of the Grain Protectress from Goddess to Saint.* Boston: Beacon, 1985.

Eliade, Mircea. *Patterns in Comparative Religion.* Trans. Rosemary Sheed. 1949. Cleveland: World, 1958.

Gadon, Elinor W. *The Once and Future Goddess: A Symbol for Our Times.* San Francisco: Harper and Row, 1989.

Gilligan, Carol. *In a Different Voice: Psychological Theory and Women's Development.* Cambridge: Harvard UP, 1982.

Gimbutas, Marija. *The Language of the Goddess.* New York: Harper, 1989.

Kerenyi, C. *Eleusis: Archetypal Image of Mother and Daughter.* 1967. New York: Schocken, 1977.

McLean, Adam. *The Triple Goddess: An Exploration of the Archetypal Feminine.* Grand Rapids: Phanes, 1989.

Meyer, Marvin W., ed. *The Ancient Mysteries: A Sourcebook. Sacred Texts of the Mystery Religions of the Ancient Mediterranean World.* San Francisco: Harper, 1987.

Mylonas, George E. *Eleusis and the Eleusinian Mysteries.* Princeton UP, 1961.

Neumann, Erich. *The Great Mother: An Analysis of the Archetype.* Trans. Ralph Manheim. 1963. Princeton: Princeton UP, 1991.

Slater, Philip E. *The Glory of Hera: Greek Mythology and the Greek Family.* 1968. Princeton: Princeton UP, 1992.

Chapter 5   The Olympian Family of Zeus

Athanassakis, Apostolos N., trans. *The Homeric Hymns.* Baltimore: Johns Hopkins UP, 1976.

Burkert, Walter. *Greek Religion.* Trans. John Raffan. Cambridge: Harvard UP, 1985.

Grimal, Pierre. *The Dictionary of Classical Mythology.* Trans. A. R. Maxwell-Hyslop. Oxford: Basil Blackwell, 1986.

Guthrie, W. K. C. *The Greeks and Their Gods.* Boston: Beacon, 1950.

Hamilton, Edith. *Greek Mythology.* New York: Mentor, 1953.

Kerenyi, Carl. *The Gods of the Greeks.* London: Thames, 1951.

Kirkwood, G. M. *A Short Guide to Classical Mythology.* New York: Holt, 1959.

Mikalson, Jon D. *Honor Thy Gods: Popular Religion in Greek Tragedy.* Chapel Hill: U of North Carolina P, 1991.

Otto, Walter. *The Homeric Gods.* Boston: Beacon, 1964.

Rose, H. J. *Gods and Heroes of the Greeks.* Cleveland: Meridian; World, 1958.

Sergent, Bernard. *Homosexuality in Greek Myth.* Boston: Beacon, 1986.

Slater, Philip E. *The Glory of Hera: Greek Mythology and the Greek Family.* Princeton: Princeton UP, 1968.

Vernant, Jean-Pierre. *Myth and Society in Ancient Greece.* Trans. Janet Lloyd. New York: Zone, 1990.

Chapter 6   The World in Decline: Alienation of the Human and Divine

Athanassakis, Apostolos N., ed. and trans. *Hesiod: Theogony, Works and Days, Shield.* Baltimore: Johns Hopkins UP, 1983.

Burn, A. R. *The World of Hesiod: A Study of the Greek Middle Ages, c. 900–700 BC.* New York: Blom, 1936.

Solomon, Friedrich. *Hesiod and Aeschylus.* 1949. n.p.: Johnson Reprint, 1967.

West, M. L., ed. and trans. *Theogony and Works and Days.* New York: Oxford UP, 1988.

Chapter 7   In Touch with the Gods: Apollo's Oracle at Delphi

Athanassakis, Apostolos N., trans. *The Homeric Hymns.* Baltimore: Johns Hopkins UP, 1976.

Boer, Charles, trans. *The Homeric Hymns.* Rev. ed. Dallas: Spring, 1979.

Calasso, Roberto. *The Marriage of Cadmus and Harmony.* Trans. Tim Parks. New York: Knopf, 1993.

Downing, Christine. *Myths and Mysteries of Same-Sex Love.* New York: Continuum, 1989.

Eisner, Robert. *The Road to Daulis: Psychoanalysis, Psychology, and Classical Mythology.* Syracuse: Syracuse UP, 1987.

Fontenrose, Joseph. *Python: A Study of Delphic Myth and Its Origins.* Berkeley: U of California P, 1959.

Parker, R. *Miasma: Pollution and Purification in Early Greek Religion.* Oxford UP, 1983.

Petrokos, Basil. *Delphi.* Athens: "Esperos" [English] Edition, 1971.

Chapter 8   Dionysus: Rooted in Earth and Ecstasy

Alderink, Larry J. *Creation and Salvation in Ancient Orphism.* American Classical Studies 8. Chico, CA: Scholars, 1981.

Alviella, G. d'. *The Mysteries of Eleusis: The Secret Rites and Rituals of the Classical Greek Mystery Tradition.* Wellingborough: Aquarian, 1981.

Athanassakis, Apostolos N., trans. *The Orphic Hymns.* Missoula, MT: Scholars, 1977.

Boer, Charles, trans. *The Homeric Hymns.* Rev. ed. Dallas: Spring, 1979.

Burkert, Walter. *Ancient Mystery Cults.* Cambridge: Harvard UP, 1987.

Calasso, Roberto. *The Marriage of Cadmus and Harmony.* Trans. Tim Parks. New York: Knopf, 1993.

Cantarella, Eva. *Bisexuality in the Ancient World.* Trans. Cormac O Cuilleanain. New Haven: Yale UP, 1992.

Dodds, E. R. *The Greeks and the Irrational.* Berkeley: U of California P, 1951.

Guthrie, W. K. C. *Orpheus and Greek Religion: A Study of the Orphic Movement.* New York: Norton, 1966.

Kerenyi, C. *Dionysos: Archetypal Image of Indestructible Life.* Trans. Ralph Manheim. Princeton: Princeton UP, 1976.

Martin, Luther H. *Hellenistic Religions: An Introduction.* Oxford: Oxford UP, 1987.

Nilsson, Martin P. *The Dionysiac Mysteries of the Hellenistic and Roman Age.* Lund, Swed.: Gleerup, 1957.

Otto, Walter F. *Dionysus: Myth and Cult.* Trans. Robert B. Palmer. Bloomington: Indiana UP, 1965.

Vernant, Jean-Pierre, and Pierre Vidal-Naquet. *Myth and Tragedy in Ancient Greece.* Trans. Janet Lloyd. New York: Zone, 1988.

West, M. L. *The Orphic Poems.* Oxford: Clarendon, 1983.

Wili, Walter. "The Orphic Mysteries and the Greek Spirit." *The Mysteries: Papers from the Eranos Yearbooks.* Vol. 2. Ed. Joseph Campbell. Trans. Ralph Manheim and R. F. C. Hull. New York: Pantheon, 1955.

Chapter 9   Land of No Return: The Gloomy Kingdom of Hades

Apollodorus (of Athens). *The Library of Greek Mythology.* Trans. Keith Aldrich. Lawrence, KS: Coronado, 1975.

Bremmer, Jan. *The Early Greek Concept of the Soul.* Princeton: Princeton UP, 1983.

Burkert, Walter. *Greek Religion.* Trans. John Raffan. Cambridge: Harvard UP, 1985.

Calasso, Roberto. *The Marriage of Cadmus and Harmony.* Trans. Tim Parks. New York: Knopf, 1993.

Dietrich, B. C. *Death, Fate and the Gods: The Development of a Religious Idea in Greek Popular Belief and in Homer.* London: Athlone, 1965, 1967.

Eliot, Alexander. *The Universal Myths: Heroes, Gods, Tricksters and Others.* New York: New American Library, 1990.

Garland, Robert. *The Greek Way of Death.* Ithaca: Cornell UP, 1985.

Homer, "Book 11." *Odyssey of Homer.* Trans. Allen Mandelbaum. New York: Bantam, 1990.

Jackson, Danny P., trans. *The Epic of Gilgamesh.* Introduction by Robert D. Biggs. N.p.: Bolchazy-Carducci, 1992.

Jacobsen, Thorkild. *The Treasures of Darkness: A History of Mesopotamian Religion.* New Haven: Yale UP, 1976.

McCall, Henrietta. *Mesopotamian Myths.* Austin: U of Texas P, British Museum, 1990.

Plato, "Phaedo." *The Last Days of Socrates.* Rev. ed. Trans. Hugh Tredennick. New York: Penguin, 1969.

———. *The Republic of Plato.* Trans. F. M. Cornford. Oxford: Oxford UP, 1941.

———. *The Symposium.* Trans. W. Hamilton. New York: Penguin, 1951.

Sandars, N. K., trans. *Poems of Heaven and Hell from Ancient Mesopotamia.* Baltimore: Penguin, 1971.

Vermeule, Emily. *Aspects of Death in Early Greek Art and Poetry.* Berkeley: U of California P, 1979.

West, Martin L. *The Orphic Poems.* New York: Oxford UP, 1983.

Chapter 10   The Hero: Man Divided against Himself

Calasso, Roberto. *The Marriage of Cadmus and Harmony.* Trans. Tim Parks. New York: Knopf, 1993.

Campbell, Joseph. *The Hero with a Thousand Faces.* 1949. Cleveland: World, 1970.

Dumezil, Georges. *The Stakes of the Warrior.* Trans. David Weeks. 1968. Berkeley: U of California P, 1983.

Galinsky, G. Karl. *The Herakles Theme: The Adaptations of the Hero in Literature from Homer to the Twentieth Century.* Oxford: Blackwell, 1972.

Kirk, G. S. *The Nature of Greek Myths.* London: Penguin, 1974.

Segal, Robert A., Introduction. *In Quest of the Hero.* Ed. Robert A. Segal. Princeton: Princeton UP, 1990.

Chapter 11   Heroes at War: The Troy Saga

Beye, Charles Rowan. *Ancient Greek Literature and Society.* New York: Anchor, 1975.

Clarke, Howard W. *The Art of the Odyssey.* Englewood Cliffs: Prentice-Hall, 1967.

Finley, M. I. *The World of Odysseus.* 1959. Cleveland: World, 1963.

Griffin, Jasper. *Homer.* New York: Hill and Wang, 1980.

Kirk, G. S. *Homer and the Epic.* Cambridge: Cambridge UP, 1965.

Luce, J. V. *Homer and the Heroic Age.* San Francisco: Harper, 1975.

Redfield, James M. *Nature and Culture in The Iliad: The Tragedy of Hector.* Chicago: U of Chicago P, 1975.

Schein, Seth L. *The Mortal Hero: An Introduction to Homer's Iliad.* Berkeley: U of California P, 1984.

Stanford, W. B. *The Ulysses Theme.* Ann Arbor: U of Michigan P, 1963.

Whitman, Cedric. *Homer and the Heroic Tradition.* New York: Norton, 1958.

Chapter 12   A Different Kind of Hero: The Quest of Odysseus

Ahl, Frederick. *The Odyssey Re-formed.* Ithaca: Cornell UP, 1996.

Beye, Charles R. *The Iliad, The Odyssey, and The Epic Tradition.* Garden City: Doubleday, 1966.

Bloom, Harold, ed. *Homer's Odyssey.* New York: Chelsea, 1988.

Clay, Jenny Strauss. *The Wrath of Athena.* Princeton: Princeton UP, 1983.

Cook, Erwin F. *The Odyssey in Athens: Myths of Cultural Origins.* Ithaca: Cornell UP, 1995.

Fenik, Bernard. *Homer: Tradition and Inventions.* Leiden: Brill, 1978.

———. *Studies in the Odyssey.* Hermes, 30. Wiesbaden: Steiner, 1974.

Finley, John H., Jr. *Homer's Odyssey.* Cambridge: Harvard UP, 1978.

Hull, Denison Bingham, trans. *Homer's Odyssey.* Greenwich, CT: Ohio UP, 1978.

Page, Denys. *Folktales in Homer's Odyssey.* Cambridge: Harvard UP, 1973.

Thalmann, William G. *The Odyssey: An Epic of Return.* New York: Twayne, 1992.

Toohey, Peter. *Reading Epic: An Introduction to the Ancient Narratives.* New York: Routledge, 1993.

Chapter 13   The Theater of Dionysus and the Tragic Vision

Baldry, H. C. *The Greek Tragic Theatre.* New York: Norton, 1971.

Carpenter, Thomas H., and Christopher A. Farone, eds. *Masks of Dionysus.* Ithaca: Cornell UP, 1993.

Dodds, E. R. *Euripides' Bacchae.* Oxford: Clarendon, 1960.

———. *The Greeks and the Irrational.* Berkeley: U of California P, 1951.

Else, Gerald. *The Origin and Early Form of Greek Tragedy.* New York: Norton, 1972.

Humphreys, S. C. *The Family, Women, and Death.* Boston: Routledge, 1993.

Jones, John. *On Aristotle and Greek Tragedy.* New York: Oxford UP, 1962.

Kitto, H. D. F. *Greek Tragedy.* 3rd ed. New York: Barnes, 1961.

Mikalson, Jon D. *Honor Thy Gods: Popular Religion in Greek Tragedy.* Chapel Hill: U of North Carolina P, 1991.

Oranje, H. *Euripides' Bacchae: The Play and Its Audience.* Leiden: Brill, 1984.

Otto, Walter F. *Dionysus: Myth and Cult.* Translated by Robert B. Palmer. Bloomington: Indiana UP, 1965.

Pickard-Cambridge, Arthur W. *Dithyramb, Tragedy, and Comedy.* Ed. T. B. L. Webster. 2nd ed. Oxford: Clarendon, 1962.

Segal, Charles. *Dionysiac Poetics and Euripides' "Bacchae."* Princeton: Princeton UP, 1982.

Sewall, Richard B. *The Vision of Tragedy.* New Haven: Yale UP, 1965.

Vernant, Jean-Pierre, and Pierre Vidal-Naquet. *Myth and Tragedy in Ancient Greece.* Trans Janet Lloyd. New York: Zone, 1988.

Walton, J. M. *The Greek Sense of Theatre: Tragedy Reviewed.* London: n.p., 1984.

Webster, T. B. L. *The Greek Chorus.* London: Methuen, 1970.

———. *Greek Theatre Production.* London: Methuen, 1956.

Winkler, John J., and Froma I. Zeitlin, eds. *Nothing to Do with Dionysus? Athenian Drama and Its Social Context.* Princeton: Princeton UP, 1990.

Winnington-Ingram, R. P. *Euripides and Dionysus: An Interpretation of the Bacchae.* Cambridge: Cambridge UP, 1948.

Chapter 14   Cosmic Conflict and Evolution: Aeschylus's Transformation of the Prometheus Myth

Aeschylus. *Prometheus Bound.* Ed. Mark Griffith. New York: Cambridge UP, 1983.

Conacher, D. J. *Aeschylus' Prometheus Bound: A Literary Commentary.* Toronto: U of Toronto P, 1980.

Griffith, Mark. *Aeschylus: Prometheus Bound.* New York: Cambridge UP, 1983.

———. *The Authenticity of Prometheus Bound.* New York: Cambridge UP, 1977.

Herington, C. J. *The Author of Prometheus Bound.* Austin: U of Texas P, 1970.

Hogan, James C. *A Commentary on the Complete Greek Tragedies—Aeschylus.* Chicago: U of Chicago P, 1984.

Jones, John. *On Aristotle and Greek Tragedy.* New York: Oxford UP, 1962.

Lynch, William F. *Christ and Prometheus: A New Image of the Secular.* Notre Dame: U of Notre Dame P, 1970.

Murray, Gilbert. *Aeschylus, the Creator of Tragedy.* Oxford: Clarendon, 1940.

Rosenmeyer, Thomas G. *The Art of Aeschylus.* Berkeley: U of California P, 1982.

Solomon, Friedrich. *Hesiod and Aeschylus.* 1949. N.p.: Johnson Reprint, 1967.

Taplin, O. P. *The Stagecraft of Aeschylus.* New York: Oxford UP, 1977.

Thomson, George. *Aeschylus and Athens.* London: Lawrence, 1941.

Winnington-Ingram, R. P. *Studies in Aeschylus.* New York: Cambridge UP, 1983.

Chapter 15   The House of Atreus: Aeschylus's *Oresteia*

Goldhill, Simon. *Aeschylus: The Oresteia.* New York: Cambridge UP, 1992.

———. *Reading Greek Tragedy.* London: Cambridge UP, 1986.

Heringon, C. J. *Aeschylus.* New Haven: Yale UP, 1986.

Kennedy, G. *The Art of Persuasion in Greece.* London: Routledge, 1963.

Kott, Jan. *The Eating of the Gods: An Interpretation of Greek Tragedy.* New York: Vintage, 1970.

Podlecki, A. *The Political Background of Aeschylean Tragedy.* Michigan: U of Michigan P, 1966.

Rosenmeyer, Thomas G. *The Art of Aeschylus.* Berkeley: U of California P, 1982.

Thomson, George. *Aeschylus and Athens.* London: Lawrence, 1941.

———. *Aeschylus: The Oresteia.* 2 vols. Amsterdam: Hakkert, 1966.

Tyrrell, William B., and Frieda S. Brown. *Athenian Myths and Institutions.* New York: Oxford UP, 1991.

Zak, William F. *The Polis and the Divine Order: The Oresteia, Sophocles, and the Defense of Democracy.* Lewisburg: Bucknell UP, 1995.

Chapter 16   The Tragic Hero: Sophocles's *Oedipus*

Bloom, Harold, ed. *Sophocles: Modern Critical Views.* New York: Chelsea, 1990.

Fergusson, Francis. *The Idea of a Theater.* 1949. Garden City: Doubleday, 1953.

Grene, David. *Reality and the Heroic Pattern: Last Plays of Ibsen, Shakespeare and Sophocles.* Chicago: U of Chicago P, 1967.

Knox, Bernard M. W. *The Heroic Temper: Studies in Sophoclean Tragedy.* Berkeley: U of California P, 1964.

Pucci, Pietro. *Oedipus and the Fabrication of the Father: Oedipus Tyrannus in Modern Criticism and Philosophy.* Baltimore: Johns Hopkins UP, 1992.

Vellacott, Philip. *Sophocles and Oedipus: A Study of Oedipus Tyrannus with a New Translation.* Ann Arbor: U of Michigan P, 1971.

Whitman, Cedric H. *Sophocles: A Study of Heroic Humanism.* Cambridge: Harvard UP, 1956.

Chapter 17   Euripides's *Medea*: A Different Perspective on Tragedy

Conacher, D. J. *Euripidean Drama: Myth, Theme and Structure.* Toronto: U of Toronto P, 1967.

Greenwood, Leonard Hugh Graham. *Aspects of Euripidean Tragedy.* 1953. New York: Russell, 1972.

Lucas, D. W. *The Greek Tragic Poets.* 2nd ed. New York: Norton, 1959.

Meagher, Robert. *Mortal Vision: The Wisdom of Euripides.* New York: St. Martin's, 1989.

Powell, Anton. *Euripides, Women, and Sexuality.* London: Routledge, 1990.

Pucci, Pietro. *The Violence of Pity in Euripides' Medea.* Ithaca: Cornell UP, 1980.

Chapter 18   The Roman Vision: Greek Myths and Roman Realities

Cairns, Francis. *Virgil's Augustan Epic.* Cambridge: Cambridge UP, 1989.

Ogilvie, R. M. *Roman Literature and Society.* London: Penguin, 1980.

Woodman, Tony, and David West, eds. *Poetry and Politics in the Age of Augustus.* Cambridge: Cambridge UP, 1984.

Chapter 19   The *Aeneid:* Virgil's Roman Epic

Bloom, Harold, ed. *Virgil: Modern Critical Views.* New York: Chelsea House, 1986.

Johnson, W. R. *Darkness Visible: A Study of Vergil's Aeneid.* Berkeley: U of California P, 1976.

O'Hara, James J. *Death and the Optimistic Prophecy in Vergil's Aeneid.* Princeton: Princeton UP, 1990.

Poschl, Viktor. *The Art of Virgil: Image and Symbol in the Aeneid.* Trans. Gerda Seligson. Ann Arbor: U of Michigan P, 1962.

Williams, R. D. *Virgil.* Greece and Rome: New Surveys in the Classics 1. Oxford: Clarendon, 1967.

Wiltshire, Susan Ford. *Public and Private in Vergil's "Aeneid."* Amherst: U of Massachusetts P, 1989.

Chapter 20   Ovid's *Metamorphoses:* The Retelling of Greek Myths

Barnard, Mary E. *The Myth of Apollo and Daphne from Ovid to Quevedo: Love, Agon and the Grotesque.* Durham: Duke UP, 1987.

Brooks, Otis. *Ovid as an Epic Poet.* 2nd ed. Cambridge: Cambridge UP, 1970.

Wall, Kathleen. *The Callisto Myth from Ovid to Atwood: Initiation and Rape in Literature.* Kingston: McGill-Queen's UP, 1988.

Wilkinson, L. P. *Ovid Surveyed: An Abridgement for the General Reader of "Ovid Recalled."* Cambridge: Cambridge UP, 1962.

Chapter 21   The Persistence of Myth

Bush, Douglas. *Mythology and the Renaissance Tradition in English Poetry.* 1932. New York: Norton, 1963.

———. *Mythology and the Romantic Tradition in English Poetry.* 1937. New York: Norton, 1963.

Brombert, Victor, ed. *The Hero in Literature.* New York: Fawcett, 1969.

Reid, Jane Davidson, with Chris Rohmann. *The Oxford Guide to Classical Mythology in the Arts, 1300–1990s.* 2 vols. Oxford: Oxford UP, 1993.

Stanford, W. B. *The Ulysses Theme: A Study in the Adaptability of a Traditional Hero.* 2nd ed. Ann Arbor: U of Michigan P, 1968.

Chapter 7 159 Courtesy The Vatican Museum. **162** By courtesy of The Allard Pierson Museum, Amsterdam. **163** Archaeological Receipts Fund (TAP), Greece. **165** (left) Archaeological Receipts Fund (TAP), Greece. (right) Archaeological Receipts Fund (TAP), Greece. **166** Courtesy The Vatican Museum. **167** Antikensammlung, Staatliche Museen Zu Berlin, Preussischer Kulturbesitz. **168** © Erich Lessing/Art Resource, NY. **170** Archaeological Receipts Fund (TAP), Greece. **Chapter 8 185** © Alinari/Art Resource, NY. **187** Ecole Française d'Archéologie, Athens. **188** Courtesy of the Staatliche Antikensammlungen und Glyptothek, Munich. **189** Museo Archaeologico Nazionale, Taranto. **190** Museo Archeologico Nazionale, Ferrara. **191** © Alinari/Art Resource, NY. **193** Hirmer Fotoarchiv, Munich. **194** (top) Hirmer Fotoarchiv, Munich. (bottom) Hirmer Fotoarchiv, Munich. **195** (bottom) © Alinari/Art Resource, NY. **196** © Alinari/Art Resource, NY. **197** Archaeological Receipts Fund (TAP), Greece. **198** (top) © Scala/Art Resource, NY. **198** (bottom left) © Scala/Art Resource, NY. **198** (bottom right) © Scala/Art Resource, NY. **199** © Giraudon/Art Resource, NY. **Chapter 9 208** © British Museum. **209** Archaeological Receipts Fund (TAP), Greece. **211** Courtesy of the Staatliche Antikensammlungen und Glyptothek, Munich. **213** © Alinari/Art Resource, NY. **214** © British Museum. **215** © RMN/Louvre/Orsay. **217** Museo Archeologico, Palermo. **218** © RMN/Louvre. **220** © The Granger Collection, New York. **Chapter 10 234** Museo Archeologico, Palermo. **240** The University Museum, University of Pennsylvania (Neg. #S8-26693). **241** Courtesy of the Staatliche Antikensammlungen und Glyptothek, Munich. **242** © The Bettmann Archive. **243** © British Museum. **244** Archaeological Receipts Fund (TAP), Greece. **246** © British Museum. **247** © British Museum. **250** © RMN/Louvre. **Chapter 11 257** Courtesy The Vatican Museum. **264** © British Museum. **265** Kunsthistorisches Museum, Vienna. **Chapter 12 344** Staatliche Museen, Berlin. **347** Archaeological Museum, Sperlonga. **348** © Alinari/Art Resource, NY. **349** (top) Hirmer Fotoarchiv, Munich. **350** © Scala/Art Resource, NY. **351** Archaeological Receipts Fund (TAP), Greece. **355** © British Museum. **356** © British Museum. **358** © Scala/Art Resource, NY. **359** Hirmer Fotoarchiv, Munich. **Part 3 421** National Museum, Ferrara. **Chapter 13 425** Antiken Museum, Basle. **426** Reconstruction by Al N. Oikonomides. **427** © Ancient Art & Architecture Collection. **428** Antikensammlung, Staatliche Museen Zu Berlin, Preussischer Kulturbesitz. **429** Staatliche Museen, Berlin. **433** Staatliche Museen, Berlin. **435** © Alinari/Art Resource, NY. **436** © British Museum. **438** © RMN/Louvre/Orsay. **439** Courtesy The Vatican Museum. **440** National Archeological Museum, Naples. **Chapter 14 482** © Alinari/Art Resource, NY. **483** © Alinari/Art Resource, NY. **485** © Alinari/Art Resource, NY. **486** © Scala/Art Resource, NY. **Chapter 15 525** © Scala/Art Resource, NY. **528** © Scala/Art Resource, NY. **531** National Museum, Ferrara. **534** Kunsthistorisches Museum, Vienna. **535** National Archeological Museum, Naples. **536** Archaeological Receipts Fund (TAP), Greece. **537** © Alinari/Art Resource, NY. **607** (top) © RMN/Louvre/Orsay. **607** (bottom) © Photo RMN/Hervé Lewandowski. **Chapter 16 615** Bibliothèque Nationale, Paris. **616** Courtesy The Vatican Museum. **Chapter 17 743** © Alinari/Art Resource, NY. **Part 4 779** Courtesy The Vatican Museum. **Chapter 18 782** © Alinari/Art Resource, NY. **783** © Alinari/Art Resource, NY. **787** (left) Courtesy The Vatican Museum. (right) Courtesy The Vatican Museum. **788** © Alinari/Art Resource, NY. **790** © Alinari/Art Resource, NY. **791** Courtesy The Vatican Museum. **Chapter 19 800** Martin von Wagner Museum, Universität Würzburg. Photo: K. Oehrlein. **Chapter 20 875** Courtesy of Soprintendenza per i Beni Artistici e Storici di Roma. **Part 5 911** © Foto Marburg/Art Resource. **Chapter 21 917** Photo © Philip Trager. From *Persephone*, published 1996 by Wesleyan University Press with The New England Foundation for the Arts. Distributed by the University Press of New England. **918** © National Gallery, London. **919** © Descharnes & Descharnes Sarl, Paris. **920** The Museum of Modern Art, New York. Abby Aldrich Rockefeller Fund. Photograph © 1997 The Museum of Modern Art, New York. © 1998 Estate of Pablo Picasso/Artists Rights Society (ARS), NY. **921** © 1997 Estate of Pablo Picasso/Artists Rights Society (ARS), New York/Giraudon/Art Resource, NY. **923** Alte Pinakothek München. **925** (top) © RMN/Louvre/Orsay. (bottom) © Descharnes & Descharnes Sarl, Paris. **926** © RMN/Louvre. **927** © Foto Marburg/Art Resource. **928** (top) Andrew W. Mellon Collection, © 1997 Board of Trustees, National Gallery of Art, Washington, D.C., c. 1555, oil on canvas, 1.245 x 1.055 (49 x 41½). **929** (bottom) Courtesy of Soprintendenza per i Beni Artistici e Storici di Roma. **930** (top) © Photo RMN/Gérard Blot. (bottom) © RMN/Maillol/ADAGP. **931** (top) Phototheque des Musées de la Ville de Paris. (bottom) © Descharnes & Descharnes Sarl, Paris. **933** (top) © Scala/Art Resource, NY. (bottom) Staatliche Kunsthalle Karlsruhe. **934** © Alinari/Art Resource. **996** © Victoria & Albert Museum.

COLOR PLATES 1 © Scala/Art Resource, NY. **2** © Photo RMN. **3** © National Gallery, London. **5** © Erich Lessing/Art Resource, NY. **6** © National Gallery, London. **7** © Alinari/Art Resource, NY. **8** © Photo RMN—H. Lewandowski. **10** © National Gallery, London. **11** © National Gallery, London. **12** © Scala/Art Resource, NY. **13** © 1998 Artists Rights Society (ARS), NY. Coll. Chagall, France/ADAGP, Paris, Art Resource, NY. **14** © Scala/Art Resource, NY. **15** © National Gallery, London. **16** © 1998 Demart Pro Arte (R), Geneva/Artists Rights Society (ARS), Tate Gallery, London, Great Britain/Art Resource, NY.

Index

Numbers in boldface italics indicate primary works. Boldface numbers refer to illustrations.